A GAME OF INCHES

A GAME
OF INCHES

The Stories Behind the Innovations
That Shaped Baseball

Peter Morris

Ivan R. Dee
CHICAGO

This book was originally published in two volumes, The Game on the Field and The Game Behind the Scenes. Both these volumes, with substantial additions and minor revisions, are included in this one-volume edition.

ISBN 978-1-56663-853-1

Book Club Edition

To my father, Dr. Raymond Morris, with love and gratitude, and to Kim Schram, who soars

Contents

CHAPTER 2: BATTING

(i) Variations on a Theme: Refinements to Approaches, Swings, and Stances

(ii) Less Is More: The Bunt and Other Novel Approaches to Hitting

(iii) And When All Else Fails: Trying to Be a Successful Hitter Without Hitting

(iv) Preparation

CHAPTER 3: PITCHING

(i) Deliveries

(iii) Teamwork

(iv) Devising Alternate Methods of Retiring Players

CHAPTER 5: BASERUNNING

(i) Stolen Bases

CHAPTER 6: MANAGERIAL STRATEGIES

(i) Who's in Charge Here?

CHAPTER 7: COACHING

CHAPTER 8: UMPIRES

CHAPTER 9: EQUIPMENT

(i) Baseballs

(ii) Bats

(iii) Gloves

(iv) Protective Equipment

(v) Miscellaneous Equipment

CHAPTER 10: UNIFORMS

CHAPTER 11: SKULLDUGGERY

(i) Garden Variety Trickery

(ii) Gardening Variety Trickery

CHAPTER 12: TIMEOUTS

CHAPTER 13: BUILDING A TEAM

(i) Minor Leagues

(ii) Trades and Sales

(iii) Roster Restrictions

(iv) Scouting and Player Development

(v) Items Added for Spectators

CHAPTER 15: FANS

(i) Getting Them in the Door

(ii) Root, Root, Root for the Home Team

(iii) You Can't Beat Fun at the Old Ballpark

CHAPTER 16: MARKETING AND PROMOTIONS

CHAPTER 17: STATISTICS

CHAPTER 18: MONEY

(i) The Transition from Amateurism to Professionalism

(ii) Owners Grab the Reins

(iii) Players Seek a Bigger Share

CHAPTER 20: INCLUSION

(i) African Americans

(ii) Women

(iii) Other Minorities

CHAPTER 21: PARTICIPANTS

CHAPTER 22: COMPETITION

(i) Determining a Champion

(ii) Postseason Championships

(iii) Bling Bling

(iv) Youth

(v) Is Competition Necessary at All?

(vi) Other Modes and Types of Competition

CHAPTER 23: SPREADING THE WORD

(i) The Writer's Game

(ii) Baseball in Other Media

(iii) Broadcasting Refinements

CHAPTER 24: TRAVELING MEN

(i) Getting from Game to Game

CHAPTER 25: AS AMERICAN AS APPLE PIE

(i) Wrapping the Game in the Flag

(ii) Talking the Talk

CHAPTER 26: MISCELLANY

(i) Keeping Up Appearances

(ii) Rituals

(iii) Customs, Traditions, and Taboos

Preface to the Paperback Edition

IN THE THREE YEARS since the release of the two-volume hardcover edition of *A Game of Inches*, its reception has been most gratifying. The honors and awards bestowed upon it have been greatly appreciated, and it has meant just as much to find the book being discussed and cited by so many who share my fascination with baseball history. Whether they have shared my views or not, there is always a special thrill to feeling that one has stimulated a dialogue about a neglected aspect of baseball's development.

Yet these three years have also brought reminders of the possibility for improvement. For one thing, the book's great length made it necessary to publish it in separate volumes, which was not ideal for users. The lack of a topical index also made it harder to use. Finally, there was the inevitable issue that a book of firsts is never done—many important studies have appeared since then, alert readers have pointed out numerous omissions, and my own research while writing three subsequent books has unearthed a great deal of additional information that refines, supplements, or antedates the conclusions set forth in the first edition. Thus it is a great pleasure to be able to present this paperback edition that combines both volumes for the first time while also incorporating a topical index and a thorough update and revision of the entries.

While I hope these new features will increase its value to readers and researchers, at essence *A Game of Inches* remains the same book. As noted in the Introduction, I have construed the story of each item's entry into baseball as being more than just a list of names, dates, and places. Of course nailing down these details is a vital part of the tale, and sometimes it is the whole story. But whenever possible I try to use these as a means of examining essential questions: Why was this innovation introduced when it was? What prevented it from entering earlier? Who felt that it was a valuable addition and why? Who tried to keep it out and why? What underlying values were at stake? How was the battle fought, and how was it won? Those are the questions I find so fascinating, because seeing how people have reacted to the prospect of something new in baseball brings us a little closer to an understanding of why baseball still means so much to Americans.

P. M.

Haslett, Michigan
January 2010

Acknowledgments

A WORK as ambitious as this one relies on the diligent work of many earlier researchers, and the bibliography reflects many of those debts. In addition I am deeply grateful to the many researchers, almost all of them members of the Society for American Baseball Research (SABR), who have graciously permitted me to cite their unpublished research and/or have read preliminary entries and offered perceptive critiques. These include Bruce Allardice, Bill Anderson, David Anderson, David Arcidiacono, Jean Hastings Ardell, Mark Armour, Priscilla Astifan, Bob Bailey, David Ball, Evelyn Begley, Charlie Bevis, Cliff Blau, David Block, Darryl Brock, Bill Carle, Frank Ceresi, Dick Clark, the late Jack Daugherty, Harry Davis, Bill Deane, Paul Dickson, Jane Finnan Dorward, Stefan Fatsis, Jan Finkel, Scott Flatow, John Freyer, Cappy Gagnon, Glenn Guzzo, Ron Haas, Richard Hershberger, Reed Howard, Paul Hunkele, John Husman, the late Fred Ivor-Campbell, the late Bill Kirwin, Jeff Kittel, Jim Lannen, R. J. Lesch, Larry Lester, John Lewis, Richard Malatzky, Skip McAfee, David McCarthy, Bob McConnell, David McDonald, Wayne McElreavy, Brian McKenna, Eric Miklich, Sammy Miller, Andrew Milner, Jim Moyes, Art Neff, Rod Nelson, David Nemec, Gene Newman, Marc Okkonen, Pete Palmer, Greg Rhodes, Kevin Saldana, Jay Sanford, John Schwartz, Joe Simenic, Bob Schaefer, Tom Shieber, David W. Smith, Alan Smitley, Lyle Spatz, Rick Stattler, Steve Steinberg, Dean Thilgen, the late Richard Thompson, John Thorn, Bob Timmermann, Frank Vaccaro, David Vincent, Mike Welsh and Tim Wiles. My apologies to anyone whose name has been omitted.

Ivan Dee has shown enormous faith in this project and contributed meticulous editing while his staff has been unfailingly helpful. I am very appreciative of the many friends, family members, and co-workers who have offered moral support—or at least refrained from laughing at the idea of a work of such specificity and length. A special thanks to all of the members of the Michigan State volleyball community, past and present, for their friendship and support. Go Green!

Naturally, the errors and shortcomings that remain are solely my responsibility.

A GAME OF INCHES

Introduction: What Makes an Innovation Dangerous?

"But the exact year was not given, so it is impossible to say that [Charles] Bennett's contribution was a 'first,' a very dangerous word to employ in writing baseball history."—Lee Allen, *Sporting News*, April 6, 1968

"Many plays . . . have been 'discovered' about once a decade, and then neglected, if not forgotten, until some other genius brought them into action. In the pioneer days of the game, it seemed that if a player invented or evolved a play, the others, instead of seizing upon it to use, gave him a kind of patent-right to it."—John J. Evers and Hugh S. Fullerton, *Touching Second* (1910), 198

"I'm not the first 400-pound player. I'm just the first to admit it."—NFL player Aaron Gibson, quoted in *Sports Illustrated*, July 29, 2002

A BOOK of baseball firsts could of course be endlessly long. A *Sporting News* publication entitled *Baseball: A Doubleheader Collection of Facts, Feats and Firsts* includes such items as Don Drysdale throwing the first pitch in the first indoor All-Star Game, and Jamie Quirk and Dan Quisenberry forming the first battery where the surnames of both players began with a Q. While it undoubtedly tells us something significant about baseball that anyone would keep track of such firsts, it is not the object of this book to capture such minutiae. For the purposes of this book, firsts are defined more narrowly.

Toward that end, I have by and large defined a first as having only one condition. In other words, I'm interested in the origins of the batting crouch, but not in determining the first left-handed batter to crouch. I have made a few exceptions when the category seemed important or interesting enough but have tried to stick to that rule as much as possible. I have also considered statistical accomplishments to be "mosts" rather than "firsts," and omitted them: Babe Ruth was the first player to hit fifty home runs in a major league regular season, but for my purposes, that is a "most." Baseball already has many record books, and this book is not intended to poach on their territory.

As a rule I have avoided firsts that were primarily chance events that could not be intentionally replicated (for example, the first stray dog to run onto a field, the first time a batted ball rolled into a tin can or hit a bird, etc.) in favor of events that became—or at least had the potential to become—a significant part of baseball. I also generally ignore new names for the same old thing, except as a part of their history. Admittedly these can all be somewhat arbitrary distinctions, and I freely admit that I have included some borderline cases simply because there are good stories involved.

Finally, there are no separate entries for the first time that something happened in the twentieth century. I regard with dismay the willingness of many baseball historians to class the nineteenth century as a different sort of animal. The notion that something called "modern baseball" originated in 1900 or 1901 is as untrue as the idea that baseball began in Farmer Phinney's pasture in 1839. There are times when, for the purposes of a record book, important rule changes may make it necessary to treat records in a particular category this way, but there can be no purpose to doing so in a book of firsts, nor indeed in any book of history.

Perhaps there is no baseball subject on which as much nonsense is written as firsts. There has been a tendency to attribute every innovation of the nineteenth century to a few famous players, such as the White Stockings of Cap Anson and Mike "King" Kelly, or the Orioles of John McGraw and Hughey Jennings. And there are countless accounts of firsts that do not pass the most rudimentary scrutiny.

Accordingly, I have tried as far as possible to present documented evidence for all firsts that appear in this book with specific dates and places and, wherever possible, excerpts of contemporary newspaper coverage. I have used exact quotations as much as possible because they tell us so much about how an innovation came about and how it was received. It may appear that I have been inordinately preoccupied with providing contemporary documentation for firsts, but that is made necessary by the distressingly large number of apocryphal stories that are passed off as history.

Of course, a newspaper account does not necessarily mean that something happened exactly as reported. But it is certainly very important evidence that warrants treating an event differently than one for which there is no contemporary testimony. Readers are strongly encouraged to regard all such accounts as evidence rather than as definitive proof, and to render their own judgments as to the credibility of any report.

I have tried to help in this process by providing any evidence that leads me to take a particular account more or less seriously. I try to weigh all evidence in reaching this conclusion, but a few factors are always paramount: (1) whether the writer is a firsthand witness of the events; (2) any other claims made by the writer that either weaken or strengthen that writer's credibility; and (3) whether the account appeared soon enough after the events and in a sufficiently prominent publication that any errors could be pointed out by other witnesses.

In sifting through contradictory claims, I have given much more weight to ones that seem to bear up to such scrutiny but have tried at least to mention any that cannot be definitively discredited. I have not hesitated to point out trends or draw conclusions when I believed the facts clearly warrant them, but I have been equally willing to withhold judgment when the matter is less clear-cut so that readers can decide for themselves. I have tried to make the distinction between my interpretations and the testimony of witnesses as clear as possible, and thus I have generally resisted the urge to put firsthand evidence in my own words. "The document speaks for itself" is a tenet of the legal profession that I have kept in mind. Readers will find that many of these documents speak powerfully.

Many claimed firsts are challenged in this book. This does not necessarily diminish the accomplishments of those who are displaced. Jackie Robinson was not the first African American to play major league baseball, and neither was Fleet Walker, but this surely does not in any way lessen the importance of either man. In many cases the first practitioner of a tactic may not have perfected or really appreciated it, and my intention is not to make value judgments but merely to document as far as possible.

Some erroneously claimed firsts are attempts to deprive the rightful originator, but most simply reflect lack of awareness. Many of the innovations I describe were essayed several times before they caught on, and a later claimant would have no way of knowing of the earlier efforts. If a first immediately caught on, I generally have given an account only of its origination. But if, as often happens, the new creation took a while to become a significant part of baseball, I try to trace its history until it attained permanence.

One point that I have become very aware of while researching this book is that most firsts did not occur because of a "Eureka!" moment. They occurred when they did because conditions had changed—rules, ethics, finances, etc.—and a strategy became practical, not because earlier generations had lacked imagination. For example, in the early 1870s first basemen stayed relatively close to the base and pinch hitters were not used. To a twenty-first-century observer this may seem primitive, and readers may find themselves wishing to be able to go back in time and set the ballplayers right.

As this book will show, such time travelers would usually be met by reasonable objections. Pinch hitters did not exist for two simple reasons: the rules prohibited them, and clubs could not afford to carry extra players (see **6.2.5**). The positioning of first basemen in these years was a recent and logical response to the rules and conditions, as discussed in greater depth under "Guarding the Lines" (**4.2.3**). Whether this positioning is optimal can be debated, but it should at least be apparent that the placement was not due to a lack of imagination.

Even with the restrictions I laid down, the task of determining any first remains a daunting one. No matter how thoroughly a researcher scours the microfilm, there is always the possibility that an earlier occurrence lurks. Moreover, the danger of committing firsts to paper is increased by the reality that innovators have not always been anxious to claim credit for their breakthroughs. There have been two especially good reasons for this reticence.

The first factor is baseball's traditional role as a test of manliness, embodied by the saying, "There's no crying in baseball." Predictably, the acceptance of many forms of protective equipment was slowed by such concerns. But readers may be surprised by some of the other innovations that have been condemned as unmanly.

For example, sportswriter John B. Sheridan in 1924 denounced an element newly introduced to baseball as: "Spoon-feeding baseball players. Giving them setups. Making things soft for them. Coddling them. Softening them morally. . . . Permitting them to become soft of muscle and weak of will, discontented loafers or semi-loafers" (*Sporting News*, August 7, 1924). The object of Sheridan's venom was platooning. Baseball firsts may truly be said to be a dangerous subject not only for the historian but also for the inventor!

The second factor is that someone who believed they had happened upon a competitive advantage wasn't necessarily eager to share it. Johnny Evers and Hugh Fullerton observed, "In the pioneer days of the game, it seemed that if a player invented or evolved a play, the others, instead of seizing upon it to use, gave him a kind of patent-right to it" (John J. Evers and Hugh S. Fullerton, *Touching Second*, 198).

This was particularly true of early pitchers, who justifiably were wary that if they acknowledged having come up with a clever new idea, the game's rule makers would be swift to ban it. One of the many versions of the origins of the curveball (see **3.2.3**) had "Candy" Cummings unveiling the pitch in an 1867 game and then asking mischievously afterward, "Does it curve?" (*Washington Post*, September 8, 1907). Cummings himself acknowledged having been "jealous of his discovery" and he was not alone (*Sporting News*, December 29, 1921). When asked by St. Louis's George Bradley to show him how to throw the curveball, Louisville's Jim Devlin "refused to explain it to him" (*St. Louis Globe-Democrat*, December 13, 1875).

Nor was this proprietary outlook entirely restricted to the early days of baseball. Pitcher Russ Ford gave a fascinating description of his reasoning process after realizing that his 1909 discovery of a new pitch known as the emery ball (see **3.2.13**) could change the game. Upon consideration, he decided that he had a "pig in a poke" and that it would be of no benefit to him or anyone else if he allowed it to escape (Russell Ford [as told to Don E. Basenfelder], "Russell Ford Tells Inside Story of the 'Emery' Ball After Guarding His Secret for Quarter of a Century," *Sporting News*, April 25, 1935, 5). His discretion turned out to be warranted, as in 1915 the emery ball became the first specific pitch ever banned from baseball.

The length and content of the entries in this book vary considerably as I have sought to fit the format to the facts, rather than the other way around. But in general I have tried to answer a few basic questions: When did the tactic originate? Why didn't it emerge earlier? Was the significance of the innovation immediately appreciated or did it take someone later to fully appreciate it? Did the innovation come as a result of a rule change? Was it immediately accepted as a good thing, or were objections raised? If there were objections, what was the nature of the objections and what do they reveal about how the people playing baseball at that period viewed the game? When did it become a permanent part of baseball?

As a result, I hope this study of firsts will accomplish two basic aims. The first is to serve as testimony to the inventiveness, ingenuity, and resourcefulness that ballplayers and managers have always brought to the national pastime. The second is a reminder that the way baseball is played today is not necessarily the way it has to be played. Rather it is the legacy of an enormous number of people who used both words and actions to create the framework for the way baseball is still played.

Baseball was a popular game with a loose and incoherent structure until the mid-1840s, when a New York club called the Knickerbockers imposed a "frame" upon it by writing down standardized rules. This new frame allowed a boy's game to be reinvented as a man's activity.

Beginning in the mid-1850s the newly elevated game was again repackaged and reframed as the "national game." Distinctions between baseball and cricket were emphasized to characterize baseball as quintessentially American. The game associated itself with the traditional institution of social clubs and thereby appeared unthreatening to social order. Early newspaper coverage also helped by stressing the healthful aspects of the game and downplaying its competitive aspects.

By the mid-1860s the journalist Henry Chadwick had emerged as the game's preeminent creator of baseball's traditional outlines. Chadwick covered baseball for some fifty years, right up to his death in 1908, and yet in many ways he seemed like an old man from the outset. He was a rigid fellow whose austere countenance and flowing beard caused him to be referred to as "Father Chadwick." This impression was reinforced by his fussy prose style and his ceaseless repetition of the same basic themes.

Not surprisingly, Chadwick frequently opposed change. Yet he was far from a reactionary. Indeed, he often embraced radical changes to baseball, such as his long-running campaign to change the game to encompass ten players and ten innings. Such inconsistencies are initially baffling, but they make sense when we recognize Chadwick as a builder of a basic framework for baseball, much of which endures to this day.

In Chadwick's view, a particular strategy, club, player, or result was not of much importance in and of itself. These items gained his approval only if they helped demonstrate one of the planks of his conception of baseball's underpinnings. The most prominent of these themes included: baseball is a healthful game; baseball is a test of manliness; fair play is more important than winning; umpires should be treated with courtesy and respect; baseball is a scientific game, in that success is based upon practice, discipline, and what Chadwick called "headwork," rather than raw talent; low-scoring games are better than high-scoring ones; teamwork wins baseball games; games are won by steady contributors rather than flashy ones; individual statistics should be measured and analyzed because they reveal who those steady contributors are; batters should aim for open spaces rather than swinging for the fences; specialization is good up to a point, but only after the basic skills of hitting and fielding have been mastered.

These themes will all seem familiar, but they are that way in large part because of Chadwick's incessant repetition of them. They have taken on still greater significance as they have been passed down by generations of fathers to their sons, making them our just-so stories. And their whole is greater than the sum of their parts because collectively they form a framework that supports one of the game's most enduring themes—that baseball can be viewed as a test of character.

Not all the planks that Chadwick used to build this framework remain intact, but a surprising number of them do. Fathers who teach their sons baseball still often give them simple moral lessons disguised as playing tips. And when one of these basic tenets is attacked, the offender is greeted with resistance that seems wildly disproportionate. Thus the designated-hitter rule still generates passionate opposition because it challenges the principles that every player needs to master all the skills of baseball and that people should complete what they start. Even when one of the elements of Chadwick's framework seems to become obsolete—as with the emphasis on home runs in today's game—we feel a seemingly irrational guilt about it.

When resistance to a new idea is surprisingly strong, it is a sure sign that it has challenged a fundamental element that we use to construct a meaning for baseball. Thus what is most dangerous about introducing an innovation is that it may threaten something that is perceived to be essential to baseball.

When Malcolm McLean wrote in 1913 that it was a historical fact that "every innovation in base ball has been bitterly fought until finally adopted," he was exaggerating—but not all that much (*Collier's*, reprinted in *Sporting News*, October 23, 1913). Labor-saving devices such as tarpaulins and batting cages, which threaten no underlying principles, have generally been accepted without a fuss. But a surprisingly large number of innovations have been deemed to tread on the toes of some tradition.

In sorting though the wildly conflicting claims regarding firsts and the diverse responses to them, a few basic features have recurred so frequently that it may be helpful to introduce them briefly:

(1) Clinging to the Center. As Robin Lakoff has noted, modern politics is often a linguistic

war in which each side tries to gain the center by depicting its own position as "moderate" and "mainstream" and its opponent as "extremist" (Robin Tolmach Lakoff, *The Language War*, 66–67). Baseball firsts have been the subject of similar linguistic wars. While the terms have changed slightly over time, the fight has usually been to associate one's side generally with tests of character and specifically with magic words like "manliness," "science," "American," and "teamwork." For example, in 1887 walks (see **17.10**) were counted as base hits. At season's end, the *New York Times* observed, "It is true that patience and good judgment on [the batter's] part may help to earn a base under such circumstances, but it is mainly due to the pitcher's error, and the phrase 'phantom hits' shows the popular estimation of such additions to batting records" (*New York Times*, October 9, 1887). The demise of this scoring practice was virtually ensured by its opponents' success in popularizing such a negative term.

(2) Glory or Guilt by Association. Similarly, a first is greatly helped when introduced by players who are successful and generally admired. In the early 1880s, pitcher J Lee Richmond, a Brown University graduate who threw the first perfect game in major league history, began keeping a book on the strengths and weaknesses of opposing batters. The tactic received generally favorable press. In the following decade the same tactic was used by an eccentric pitcher known as "Crazy" Schmit and became the subject of ridicule (see **3.3.4**). During the late nineteenth and early twentieth centuries, sportswriters placed a special emphasis on depicting baseball as a thinking man's game, with the result that any tactic introduced by a collegian was likely to be accorded a favorable reception.

(3) The Good (or Bad) Old Days. Disputes about firsts are often part of an underlying hostility between generations. The process is usually along these lines: something unfamiliar is used and described as a first. There seems to be an implication that baseball is improving, and old-timers react by saying that they used the same play/tactic/approach to illustrate that baseball isn't what it once was. The debate escalates and obscures the question of who was actually first.

(4) Competitive Balance. While the initial reception of a first is often determined by the terms and players with which it is associated, its long-term success also depends upon competitive balance. Most obviously, any significant new element will give some advantage to specific clubs and players. Which clubs and players benefit, and by how much, will have an important effect on its long-term survival, as will be illustrated in the next three principles.

(5) Everyone's Contribution Matters. Whenever the role of one kind of player becomes too great, strong pressure will be brought to bear to increase the involvement of others. This has been most apparent when pitchers' strikeouts are on the rise. The legalization of overhand pitching in the mid-1880s led to several pitchers striking out more than five hundred batters in a season. The game's rule makers tried a series of new approaches in succeeding years to remedy such imbalances, but generally satisfied no one. Ned Hanlon complained in 1888 about rules changes favoring the pitcher: "There is one thing I do know, and that is, there will not be so much interest taken in or as much excitement in the games this year as last. There will be little or no betting at all. This year is going to be a pitchers' contest, and the rest of the players will stand there on the field like wooden men. The pitchers will also have the batsmen at their mercy, and you will find that the managers, or rather the club officials, will be the greatest sufferers in the end" (*Grand Rapids* [Mich.] *Daily Democrat*, March 24, 1888). A series of important rules changes were then implemented to favor batters, as baseball desperately sought "the restoration of the proper equilibrium between the two great principles of the game—attack and defense" (*Sporting Life*, November 12, 1892). Yet by 1905 the *New York Times* was complaining, "The pitcher is now too important and the other players too unimportant" (quoted in Roger Kahn, *The Head Game*, 134). Adjustments were again made to the conditions and rules to reemphasize hitters and fielders. The cycle has continued to this day, with tinkering every time it has seemed that the contributions of one group of players are receiving short shrift.

(6) Speed Versus Power. The Knickerbockers brought power to what had primarily been a game of speed by adopting a harder ball and encouraging grown men to participate. The change to a deader ball in 1870 put a renewed emphasis on speed and led to the introduction of the bunt. In the years since then, the pendulum has swung back and forth. There appears to be a fundamental belief that both speed and power should be part of baseball, because this in turn makes the game accessible to men of different sizes and ages. It is equally clear that it

is difficult to make both part of the game at the same time, since speed favors small, young men while power favors larger and older men. As a result, one or the other skill tends to dominate and a balance has proven difficult to attain. Attempts to shift the emphasis of the game have been greeted with stiff resistance because they throw men out of work.

(7) Risk on Both Sides. The principle of competitive balance is especially applicable to individual plays. Plays in which risk is entirely on one side will offend the sense of fair play and create pressure to abolish them. For example, in early baseball, batters often stood at the plate without swinging with runners on base. Eventually a passed ball would occur, and the runner would advance without risk. The unsporting nature of this tactic led to one of baseball's most fundamental rules: called balls and strikes. Similarly, foul strikes were added because of the tedious practice of "blocking a ball off" by "holding the bat slightly behind the home plate, in no case in front of the center of the plate, and allowing the pitched ball to glance off, with no intention of hitting at all" (Doc Bushong, letter to *National Base Ball Gazette*, reprinted in *Cleveland Leader and Herald*, April 24, 1887). A current example of this is the reaction when a pitcher fakes to second or third to drive a runner back but does not make a throw (see **5.3.7**). At least a few fans will always call for a balk, and they are wrong, for the rules allow such fakes at bases other than first. But such fans are articulating a deeper antipathy to any play in which an advantage is gained without any risk.

(8) Majority Rules. If one club—especially the current champion—is particularly well suited to take advantage of a particular innovation, the others may disregard other factors and vote it down out of self-interest. At the rules meeting after the 1878 season, a bloc of National League clubs led by Cincinnati apparently conspired to make things difficult for specific players. One new rule was "a direct slap" at Boston's Harry Wright (the only non-playing manager) by barring nonplayers from the bench; another modified the pitching box to the disadvantage of Boston's Tommy Bond; a third banned Providence pitcher Johnny Ward's tactic of turning his back to the hitter. The intent of hindering individual players was so apparent that "some joker" introduced a motion that pitchers be prohibited from wearing glasses, in reference to Cincinnati's bespectacled pitcher Will White (*New York Clipper*, December 14, 1878). Henry Chadwick

justifiably groused about clubs that voted for rule changes based on the "selfish principle" of "How will this, that or the other new rule or revised section affect the play of our pitcher or our catcher?" (*New York Clipper*, November 29, 1879; also December 14 and 28, 1878). The guilty clubs responded by becoming subtler about enacting such rules, but it would be naive to think that self-interest has ever ceased to be a consideration. In 1939 the American League tried to slow down the Yankees' juggernaut by introducing a bizarre rule that prevented the defending league champion from making trades without obtaining waivers (see **13.3.7**). This principle also applies to pitchers, who were outnumbered eight to one on most early clubs, which resulted in a barrage of rule changes directed at them that will be discussed in Chapter 3. Johnny Evers and Hugh S. Fullerton commented in 1910 that "the batters, being the majority on each team," were able to "override the pitchers" on many crucial points (John J. Evers and Hugh S. Fullerton, *Touching Second*, 117). This tendency gradually diminished over the years as the number of pitchers on a roster has approached and occasionally surpassed the number of hitters.

(9) Jocko's Law. Hall of Fame umpire Jocko Conlan once succinctly observed, "I've never claimed to be a psychic. Fair or foul. Safe or out. Ball or strike. All of that is plenty tough enough" (quoted in Roger Kahn, *The Head Game*, 217). Rule makers have not always taken this into account in their initial formulation of new rules, often expecting umpires to judge the motives of players. Such rules have quickly proven to be unenforceable. As a result, many rules have been fine-tuned by a two-stage process. The first spells out the general principle that is desired, but does so in such broad strokes that the rule cannot be effectively enforced. A revision generally follows a year or two later that allows umpires to make decisions based upon their eyesight rather than their intuition.

(10) Eureka! Stories of firsts are often told as "Eureka!" moments in which a new idea—previously overlooked—suddenly occurred to the storyteller. In fact it is rare for a first to originate in this way. In particular, complex maneuvers such as the wheel play or the various cutoff plays are developed through a give-and-take between offense and defense and cannot be invented in one step.

Similarly the word "invent" always needs to be scrutinized carefully. Sometimes these statements are simply false (e.g., "Abner Doubleday invented baseball"). Far more often they over-simplify by taking a complex development and reducing it to a statement like "Branch Rickey invented the farm system" or "Candy Cummings invented the curveball." Claims such as these are often more dangerous than out-and-out fictions because they contain a grain of truth that makes them more difficult to refute. This tendency stems from the natural impulse "to make a long story short," but in doing so a critical part of that story is omitted.

(11) Good Stories Often Outlive Good History. If we want to learn the truth, we need to be especially suspicious of memorable stories about a new invention. The picturesque image of Candy Cummings discovering the curveball while throwing clamshells, for example, has become part of the lore of the curveball precisely because it is such an appealing tale. But in order to gain a more nuanced understanding of baseball history, it is often necessary to reject such simple and colorful tales in favor of more complex and homelier ones. As we shall see (3.2.3), the clamshell version has survived primarily because it was what Malcolm Gladwell has termed the "stickiest" version—the rendering of events best suited to stick in people's memories (Malcolm Gladwell, *The Tipping Point*, 25). The premise of this work is to present the version of events most consistent with the evidence at hand, whether or not that makes a good story.

(12) It's New to Me. As we shall see, a great many claims of firsts are not really firsts but merely someone saying that something was new to him. Sometimes such claims merely reflect the ignorance of the speaker. If such a contention is extremely ill-informed or comes long after the fact, I have felt free to ignore it. But I have done so only when it is clear that the item in question was firmly established before the date being claimed.

If a claim of a first is made within a reasonable time span or by a credible source, I have made sure to mention it. Even if it is clearly not a genuine first, such a claim usually shows that the item in question was not yet fully accepted or known. On other occasions such claims demonstrate that a once-standard practice had fallen into disuse.

(13) Victors Write History. There has been a strong tendency to credit all firsts to a few champion teams and players, and more generally to the National League rather than its less successful nineteenth-century rivals. In large part this reflects the fact that influential clubs

like the Red Stockings of Cincinnati and charismatic people such as Mike "King" Kelly and Ted Sullivan were able to use their popularity to ensure that someone else's idea caught on. Nonetheless it is important to remember that innovations are not the exclusive province of the victors.

The saga of baseball firsts offers the peculiar corollary that *survivors* often write history. Quite a few players have waited until their contemporaries have died before claiming to have themselves played an important role in a first. In particular, the late 1930s and 1940s saw the *Sporting News* publish interviews with a number of elderly players whose hazy recollections have often been uncritically accepted as firsts. While these players are not to be blamed, their claims must be scrutinized with great care.

(14) Exceptions Prove Rules. The saying "exceptions prove rules" is sometimes met with the retort, "No, exceptions *disprove* rules." In fact, exceptions can prove rules. This is particularly true when history is being viewed through the prism of daily newspapers, as is often the case in this book. The fundamental principle of journalism is that "man bites dog" is news while "dog bites man" is not. This is because news is fundamentally about exceptions. To take a simple example, a 1905 note stated that "Umpire Tom Connolly is wearing shin pads" (*Sporting Life*, June 17, 1905). This does not mean it was the norm in 1905 for umpires to wear shin pads. In fact it strongly implies just the opposite, for there would be no reason to remark on this if umpires were already commonly wearing shin pads. This principle that exceptions prove rules is essential to bear in mind when using newspapers to determine when and how particular items were introduced to baseball.

(15) Outs Were Not Routine. In today's game it is pretty safe to assume that an out will be recorded whenever a ground ball is hit at an infielder or a ball is hit in the air in the direction of any fielder. Once in a long while something surprising happens, but not very often. That simply wasn't the case in the 1860s, when the rules and customs of baseball were being established. Everything favored hitters: fielders didn't wear gloves or sunglasses; playing grounds were uneven and often included obstacles; and balls were lively and rubbery. The easiest way to record an out was to capture a ball on the first hop, but the eccentricities of the playing field rendered even "bound catches" uncertain. Once the bound rule was eliminated

following the 1864 season (see **1.21**), it became even more the case that there was no such thing as a routine out.

It is hard to overstate the effect that this had on the way the game was played. As we shall see, many of baseball's fundamental precepts developed during this era, and in some cases they persisted long after the conditions of the game had changed.

(16) The Enemies of Change. Before new inventions or innovations were accepted into baseball, especially in early baseball, they had to pass two litmus tests: Is this manly? Can we afford this? Both are such deep-rooted issues that any time an invention seems to come about later than might be expected, it is worth examining whether one of these factors was involved. For example, trainers (see **21.10**) were resisted until a *Sporting News* correspondent observed that the cost of having two star players disabled for a month would exceed the annual salary of a trainer who might have prevented those injuries. Clearly it would have been just as much of a competitive advantage to employ a trainer before this time, yet it didn't become part of baseball until player salaries had reached the point where this innovation made economic sense.

(17) I Can Hold My Breath Longer Than You. Once an enterprising player, manager, or owner decided that an innovation passed both of those tests and showed that it could be successfully used to win games, the pressure would shift to those who had not adopted it.

An instinct against rapid change is especially true in the fiercely competitive environment of professional sport. In consequence, once a new concept is finally accepted in baseball, there is often a race to exploit a strategy that had previously been viewed as unmanly or unaffordable. For example, gloves were still viewed as unmanly by many until the late 1880s. But within a few years of catching on, infielders were taking catcher's mitts out to their positions (see **9.3.3** "Snaring Nets").

(18) There's No Place for Condescension. The rules and conditions of baseball in the nineteenth century were constantly changing. The players, out of necessity, were highly adaptable, constantly revisiting and revising their techniques, tactics, and strategies. By contrast, the twentieth century saw great stability, which enabled the development of a basic consensus on the fundamentals of play and a "book" of strategies. Unfortunately, far too many baseball historians have failed to grasp this reality and

have leaped to the conclusion that nineteenth-century players were unimaginative because they did not evolve the tactics now in use.

I hope readers will come away from this work with an appreciation that such condescension is almost always inappropriate. One of the basic premises of this work has been that, whenever early ballplayers did something differently from how it is now done, the first place to look for an explanation is in the rules and conditions of their era. We shall see time and again that just as many nineteenth-century tactics would not work today, so too many of today's strategies would have been ill-suited to early baseball or would have been too costly for a sport that was still struggling to survive.

In old age, turn-of-the-century ballplayer Bobby Lowe discussed the 3-6-3 double play and said, "I believe [Fred] Tenney was the originator, but I know any such observation will be subject to controversy" (*Sporting News*, July 16, 1942). Bobby Lowe was a wise man. I started out thinking it strange that no one had studied this topic before, but I soon came to understand why. Not only was I rehashing old controversies, I was starting new ones. Worse, my research was never done; just when I thought I had traced something back as far as possible, an earlier claimant emerged.

I have done my best to find and document the earliest instance of all the categories that follow, but it goes without saying that this is not always possible, hence this is a work in progress. Nearly a century ago a sportswriter noted that "no 'new play' ever materialized but there were several claimants for the honor accruing from it" (H. G. Merrill, *Sporting News*, December 22, 1906). Even that early, the complexity was enough to deter any writer from attempting systematically to sort these matters out. The passage of a hundred years makes the task infinitely harder and often makes me feel that I have rushed in where angels fear to tread.

Notes on Nineteenth-century Baseball

Several elements of early baseball will come up repeatedly and confuse twenty-first-century readers, so it is important to address them before we proceed.

Until the 1880s the word "base ball" was almost exclusively written as two words. After that the word began sometimes to be hyphenated and other times to be written as one word. By the early twentieth century it had become most common to write it as one word. This change is sometimes described as puzzling or mysterious; in fact it is a common pattern for compound nouns.

The American Association was a major league formed in 1882 as a rival to the National League. The two leagues reached a truce after one year (see **18.2.3** "National Agreement") but continued to operate as separate leagues for nine years, after which they merged. This American Association has no relationship to the minor league of the same name.

The National Association was baseball's first major league, formed in 1871 and after five years succeeded by the National League. A committee created by major league baseball in 1969 decided that the National Association should not be regarded as a major league because of various irregularities. I believe this to have been an extraordinarily wrongheaded decision that somehow considers minor irregularities to be more important criteria than the fact that the National Association (unlike the early National League) included all the best players of the era. The two points that need to be stressed here are: (1) I describe the National Association as a major league throughout the text, and (2) references to the "National Association" are to this league and not to two entities with confusingly similar names. The National Association of Base Ball Players (NABBP) determined the rules of baseball from 1857 to 1870. To avoid confusion, I will refer to the NABBP by this acronym or by its full name. In addition, the International Association (see the next paragraph) became known as the National Association in 1879. That league was fading out by that point and will not be referred to in this text.

The International Association was a rival founded in 1877 to compete with the National League. It bears no relationship to the International League, a minor league formed in 1885 and still in existence.

Until the 1870s, club names almost always took the following form: the Atlantic Base Ball Club of Brooklyn. Because of the length, the name was often abbreviated to the Atlantic Club of Brooklyn, or the Atlantics of Brooklyn. The modern formulation of "the Brooklyn Atlantics" only began to become common in the 1880s, so I have retained the correct version of these names in referring to earlier clubs.

As this discussion suggests, the distinction between major and minor leagues was not clear-cut in the nineteenth century. Indeed, well into the twentieth century, there continued to be players who preferred to play in what are considered minor leagues rather than major leagues. For the purposes of this book, I have described the National League, American League, American Association, Players' League, Union Association, and National Association as the nineteenth-century major leagues.

Another confusing topic is the names by which players were known. To avoid confusion I wanted to use the same name for a player throughout the book, but which name to choose? The various baseball encyclopedias have been forced to choose a single "use name" for players and have generally chosen the most colorful nickname. This has created the erroneous impression that nicknames were more plentiful in those days than they actually were, and that a single name clung to a player throughout his career. I have done my best to use the version most common during the player's career, and thus have referred to "Old Hoss" Radbourn as Charley, and to "King" Kelly as Mike. Adrian "Cap" Anson was a particularly difficult case; "Cap" wasn't predominant during his career, but neither was any other name. In fact, Anson was such a larger-than-life character that he was usually just referred to as Anson. Since that wouldn't do for this book, I reluctantly opted for Cap.

Finally, I have tried hard to document the source of every quotation used in this book. It has not always been possible. Even when I do cite a source, it needs to be emphasized that this is not necessarily the original source. Nineteenth-century newspapers, especially sporting ones, frequently stole one another's material without attribution. The *Chicago Tribune* harrumphed in 1877, "There is an evening paper in Cincinnati which prints accounts of Chicago games under the heading 'Special Dispatch,' when it is beyond question that said scores were nailed out of the *Enquirer* printed the morning before" (*Chicago Tribune*, May 13, 1877). In 1885 the Cleveland correspondent to the *Sporting Life* complained: "The gentleman who is in charge of [the sporting] department of the [Cleveland] *Leader* evidently has a pair of long scissors, with which he completely cuts up the *Sporting Life* and Cincinnati papers, but fails to credit the source for the news stolen. Nothing original in the sporting line emanates from the *Leader*" (*Sporting Life*, May 13, 1885). This state of affairs naturally makes it impossible to be certain that a note originated in the source cited. When a source was acknowledged in the original, a date was never provided, so I cite such articles in this manner: *Cincinnati Enquirer,* reprinted in *Chicago Tribune,* January 1, 1880. If I feel certain that the item first appeared elsewhere but no acknowledgment appeared (or if the source is listed as "Exchange," which meant an early wire service), I note: reprinted in *Chicago Tribune,* January 1, 1880.

A related problem is that bylines were rare in nineteenth-century periodicals, making it necessary to refer vaguely to a correspondent or reporter. In the case of Henry Chadwick, who served as the exclusive baseball correspondent for many periodicals, I have sometimes taken the liberty of attributing an unsigned piece to him. I have done so only when the article was long enough to exhibit both Chadwick's characteristic style and his point of view; in most cases, passages were verbatim from his other works. If I have any doubt about the authorship of a piece, I left it unattributed.

A Note on Ghostwritten Books

It was common for the books of ballplayers of the late nineteenth and early twentieth centuries to be ghostwritten by sportswriters who received no credit. How much of the content originated from the anonymous author and how much from the ballplayer varied considerably, and the precise ratio for any book is unknowable at this point. Obviously some books and newspaper columns were almost entirely the work of ghostwriters, but these were not the ones that are substantive enough to quote in a book like this. Accordingly, in quoting from works that may have been or are generally accepted to have been ghostwritten, I have credited the ballplayer. While this designation may not be entirely accurate, I feel confident that most of the respective ballplayers played major roles in the books that bear their names.

Christy Mathewson's *Pitching in a Pinch,* for example, was ghostwritten by sportswriter John Wheeler, yet I feel certain that Mathewson, who studied at Bucknell, at the very least approved its content. Ty Cobb used Stoney McLinn as a ghostwriter, but it is inconceivable that the strong-willed and highly intelligent Cobb would have allowed someone else's words to appear as his own. Indeed, a 1939 account said that when McLinn told Cobb that he would be ghostwriting his book, Cobb responded: "No, sir, we don't do it that way. Ty Cobb's name won't be over a story he did not write. You sit down to that typewriter and I'll tell you what to write." Cobb then dictated the copy to McLinn and read it and corrected it (*Sporting News,* January 5, 1939).

I have made similar assumptions about the books of John Montgomery Ward (a Columbia Law School graduate), A. G. Spalding, and Adrian "Cap" Anson. John J. Evers and sportswriter Hugh S. Fullerton are jointly credited as authors of *Touching Second,* so that is how I have designated quotations from that work. I feel much less certain about *Babe Ruth's Own Book of Baseball,* but it is such a perceptive work that I have quoted from it on a number of occasions.

Chapter 1

THE THINGS WE
TAKE FOR GRANTED

BASEBALL abounds with the kinds of questions that inquisitive young children love to ask and that their parents dread trying to answer: Why does the home team bat last? Why are the bases run counterclockwise? Why can't a player come back into a game as in other sports?

It is not entirely a cop-out to say, "Because that's the rule." In some cases, the closest we can come to the origins of these underlying rules and customs is that someone (we're not sure who) decided it should be that way (we're not sure why). But this chapter will, at the very least, try to illuminate the historical developments that helped make possible many of the things we take for granted when we watch a baseball game.

1.1 Clubs. Baseball teams are still often referred to as clubs, but the current meaning bears little relationship to the original one. Early baseball matches were contested by clubs, and when the term "team" first appeared in the mid-1860s it was an indication that the way the game was being played had changed for good.

The change in terminology is significant because clubs were such an integral element of nineteenth-century life. A club was a restricted group of people from similar backgrounds and was primarily social in nature. As Americans moved from the farms to the cities and began to lead less active lives, clubs began to experiment with sporting diversions to give their members much-needed exercise.

The Olympic Ball Club of Philadelphia was founded on July 4, 1833, playing what is now generally described as "town ball." The club survived long enough to celebrate its golden anniversary, though by 1860 it had switched to baseball. Rochester, New York, also had a club devoted to bat and ball games in the 1830s (Stephen Fox, *Big Leagues*, 168–172).

But the club that is generally credited with being the first baseball club is the Knickerbocker Base Ball Club of New York City, because this club introduced so many of the elements of today's game. Formally organized on September 23, 1845, the Knickerbockers quickly adopted detailed rules for playing baseball and modified them over the next decade. Many of the rules they developed—two sides, nine players a side, base runners not being retired by being hit by a thrown ball—form the basis of today's game.

Just as important, the Knickerbockers wrote down their rules and arranged for them to be distributed. (The Olympic Ball Club had had a written constitution as early as 1837, which still survives and is reprinted in Dean Sullivan's *Early Innings*, pages 5–8. But the rules were all administrative in nature, so there is no reason to think that other clubs would have requested copies.) As will be explained in the next two entries, the Knickerbockers' rules were a vital step that made it possible for the game to spread.

1.2 Rules. Of course baseball has always had rules, right? Only in a limited sense. In the first half of the nineteenth century, bat and ball games were almost exclusively children's activities. Similar to hopscotch or tag or marbles, a game might be played on a particular day and in a particular place according to specific conventions, but the same rules wouldn't necessarily apply the next day or in the next county. Baseball in those days was truly "just a game."

The Knickerbockers adopted their first rules on September 23, 1845, which represented a significant step toward a more organized and formal game. Their rules were as follows:

1. Members must strictly observe the time agreed upon for exercise, and be punctual in their attendance.

2. When assembled for exercise, the President, or in his absence, the Vice-President, shall appoint an Umpire, who shall keep the game in a book provided for that purpose, and note all violations of the By-Laws and Rules during the time of exercise.

3. The presiding officer shall designate two members as Captains, who shall retire and make the match to be played, observing at the same time that the players opposite to each other should be as nearly equal as possible, the choice of sides to be then tossed for, and the first in hand to be decided in like manner.

4. The bases shall be from "home" to second base, forty-two paces; from first to third bases, forty-two paces, equidistant.

5. No stump match shall be played on a regular day of exercise.

6. If there should not be a sufficient number of members of the Club present at the time agreed upon to commence exercise, gentlemen not members may be chosen in to make up the match, which shall not be broken up to take in members that may afterwards appear; but in all cases, members shall have the preference, when present, at the making of a match.

7. If members appear after the game is commenced, they may be chosen if mutually agreed upon.

8. The game to consist of twenty-one counts, or aces; but at the conclusion an equal number of hands must be played.

9. The ball must be pitched, not thrown, for the bat.

10. A ball knocked out of the field, or outside the range of the first or third base, is foul.

11. Three balls being struck at and missed and the last one caught, is a hand out; if not caught is considered fair, and the striker bound to run.

12. If a ball be struck, or tipped, and caught, either flying or on the first bound, it is a hand out.

13. A player running the bases shall be out, if the ball is in the hands of an adversary on the base, or the runner is touched with it before he makes his base; it being understood, however, that in no instance is a ball to be thrown at him.

14. A player running who shall prevent an adversary from catching or getting the ball before making his base, is a hand out.

15. Three hands out, all out.

16. Players must take their strike in regular turn.

17. All disputes and differences relative to the game, to be decided by the Umpire, from which there is no appeal.

18. No ace or base can be made on a foul strike.

19. A runner cannot be put out in making one base, when a balk is made by the pitcher.

20. But one base allowed when a ball bounds out of the field when struck.

In mentioning the Knickerbockers, historians often stress the rules that are still part of today's game, such as Rule 15's establishment of three outs per inning and Rule 13's prohibition on throwing the ball at a base runner. Some sources even print only Rule 4 and the last thirteen rules, since these are the playing rules (see, for example, George L. Moreland, *Balldom*, 6).

While understandable, this emphasis is unfortunate because it creates a distorted portrait of the club. The Knickerbockers viewed these playing rules as very provisional and changed many of them in the ensuing years. The club's organizational rules were just as important—both to them and to the history of baseball—because they suggested a seriousness of purpose and a permanence that was essential in reinventing a child's game as an acceptable activity for adults.

1.3 Mass-circulated Rules. The Knickerbockers' rules appeared on December 6, 1856, in a publication called *Porter's Spirit of the Times*. This was an important step for a country that was still making the transition from oral communication to print. It enabled baseball to spread rapidly and also helped the game to make a valuable ally in the burgeoning American newspaper industry. Tom Melville has concluded that "baseball was the first game Americans learned principally from print," noting that town ball was "handed down from generation to generation orally" but that baseball was learned by reading "printed regulations" (Tom Melville, *Early Baseball and the Rise of the National League*, 18).

This process was directly responsible for the 1857 founding of the Franklin Base Ball Club of Detroit, which was likely the first club west of New York to use the Knickerbocker Rules. The December 13, 1856, issue of the *New York Clipper* included a copy of the rules. In an 1884 interview, founding club member Henry Starkey explained, "There was an old fiddler here in the city named Page. . . . He used to take the *New York Clipper*, and one day he showed me a copy in which there was quite a lengthy description of the new game of base ball. . . . There was quite a number of us who felt an interest in the game, and we came to the conclusion that the new way must be an improvement over the old. Anyway, we decided to try it, so I wrote to the *Clipper* for a copy of the new rules, and paid $1 for it. After we got the rules we organized a club—the first in Detroit" (*Detroit Free Press*, April 4, 1884).

The custom of publishing soon spread; on pages 223–224 of *Baseball Before We Knew It*, David Block lists some fifteen clubs that published their rules and bylaws before 1860.

1.4 Matches.

Early clubs made a sharp distinction between informal games and matches, which were formal contests between two clubs. It was long believed that the first official match played under the Knickerbockers' rules took place on June 19, 1846, when the Knickerbockers were beaten at their own game by an informal group known as the New York Club, 23-1. But research by Melvin Adelman and Edward L. Widmer has established that two games had been played between the New York Ball Club and nine Brooklyn players the previous fall, on October 21 and 24, 1845 (Melvin L. Adelman, "The First Baseball Game, the First Newspaper References to Baseball, and the New York Club," *Journal of Sport History*, vol. 7, no. 3 [Winter 1980], 132–135). There is no proof that these games were played by the Knickerbockers' rules, but Frederick Ivor-Campbell concluded that "it is reasonable to suppose the games were played wholly under the rules that had been codified and formally adopted by the Knickerbockers just a month earlier" (Frederick Ivor-Campbell, "When Was the First Match Game Played by the Knickerbocker Rules?," *Nineteenth Century Notes* 93:4 [Fall 1993], 1).

Contemporary newspaper accounts of both matches are reprinted in Dean Sullivan's *Early Innings*. Matches remained very rare for the next decade but then grew exponentially between 1855 and 1857.

1.5 Uniforms.

A "pattern uniform" was one of the requirements specified in the 1837 constitution of the townball-playing Olympics of Philadelphia (reprinted in Dean Sullivan, *Early Innings*, 6). On April 24, 1849, the Knickerbockers adopted a uniform of blue woolen pantaloons, a white flannel shirt, and a straw hat. Jimmy Wood said these choices were prompted by a previous game in which the players had found "that trousers impeded their movements and that the wearing of linen shirts was a handicap" (James Wood, as told to Frank G. Menke, "Baseball in By-Gone Days," syndicated column, *Indiana* [Pa.] *Evening Gazette*, August 14, 1916).

1.6 Nine Innings.

The Knickerbockers' rules called for the game to be played until "21 counts, or aces" had been scored by one side. Playing until one side scored a predetermined number of runs continued to be the custom for the next decade. Nine innings was adopted as the length of the game on March 7, 1857, by the rules committee formed at the meeting that led to the creation of the game's first organizing body, the National Association of Base Ball Players. While the exact reasons for the choice of nine innings remain murky, researcher John Thorn believes there was general agreement that the number of players and innings should correspond. Thus the adoption of the nine-player game meant that nine would also become the number of innings.

1.7 Running Counterclockwise.

In many of the forerunners of baseball, the bases were run clockwise. It is not known why the Knickerbockers opted for the opposite direction, but researcher John Schwartz notes that the counterclockwise direction is more convenient for right-handers since it means that the momentum of right-handed batters leads them toward first base, while right-handed fielders have an easier time throwing to first base. Thus he suspects that the counterclockwise orientation that has proven so beneficial to left-handers was actually adopted for the convenience of right-handers (John Schwartz, "Baseball: The Counterclockwise Sport," *Baseball Research Journal* 1978, 69–72).

It's interesting to speculate about a parallel universe in which the bases were run clockwise. With the extra edge in getting to first base, would all the greatest hitters in baseball history be right-handers? Would the left-handed pitcher, accordingly, be a rare bird? Would all the great defensive catchers, middle infielders, and third basemen be left-handers? Would great players like Ozzie Smith and Luis Aparicio even have played in the major leagues?

Incidentally, softball incorporated a peculiar rule in 1908 by which the leadoff hitter could choose to run the bases clockwise *or* counterclockwise. The other base runners were then obliged to follow the leadoff hitter's cue (Lois Browne, *Girls of Summer*, 15).

1.8   Overrunning Bases. The rules of early baseball did not allow base runners to overrun bases, including first base, which had a number of important consequences. For example, the *Brooklyn Eagle* noted in 1865, "It is a noticeable fact this season thus far, that so many of the players overrun their bases and slip away from them. It has been found, upon investigation, to arise from the fact of their playing without spikes. Complaint is also made that shoes with spikes in, cannot be obtained. Every ball player should wear shoes with good spikes, that he can break up at short notice, and stop short, without slipping down" (*Brooklyn Eagle*, June 19, 1865).

Allowing runners to overrun bases was a hot topic for a number of years. Some observers contended that runners should be allowed to overrun any base while others argued for the status quo. Finally, before the 1871 season, a compromise was reached and runners were allowed to overrun first base only.

According to Jimmy Wood, the impetus for the rule change came from a surprising source. Baseball on ice (see **19.6**) was popular in the 1860s, but players on the base paths "found it impossible to stop at bases after skating out a hit. Many of them were injured by skating into bases, their skates tripping them and sending them to the icy surface. To prevent further accidents the captains decided to permit players to overskate the bags without penalty of being touched out if they turned to the right on their way back to base. When summer baseball was resumed it was decided that the rule made for skater-players should be extended to the regular diamond" (James Wood, as told to Frank G. Menke, "Baseball in By-Gone Days," part

2, syndicated column, *Marion* [Ohio] *Star*, August 15, 1916). Although this explanation sounds farfetched, Wood was a star player of the era and was not known for fanciful tales, so his account must at least be considered.

The decision to let runners overrun first but not the other bases was one of those compromises that seem to have satisfied neither side. Supporters of allowing overrunning at all the bases were particularly outspoken, with Henry Chadwick declaring with his customary assurance: "This rule is confined to the first base, but it should have been applied to all, and no doubt the Amateur Convention will amend it to that effect" (*New York Clipper*, March 4, 1871). But that never happened.

Such a rule change was proposed before the 1875 season and rejected (*St. Louis Democrat*, February 28, 1875). By the end of the 1888 season, National League owners had grown sufficiently tired of losing players to sliding injuries to again consider legalizing the overrunning of second base (*Brooklyn Eagle*, November 9, 1888). A proposal was made at that year's annual meeting but was voted down (*Aberdeen* [S.D.] *Daily News*, November 22, 1888). The Lester Plan of 1892 called for runners to be allowed to run past second or third base, which gave Henry Chadwick the opportunity to reiterate his support (*Sporting Life*, November 12, 1892; *Brooklyn Eagle*, November 14, 1892). In 1894, John B. Foster of the *Cleveland Leader* advocated allowing runners to overrun second and third base in order to reduce the amount of spiking (quoted in the *Brooklyn Eagle*, November 7, 1894).

Others, however, preferred things as they were. One scribe complained that such a rule change would "kill some very exciting incidents. What is more interesting than to watch a runner and a fielder both jabbing at the base like a couple of bantams slugging a third party?" (*Brooklyn Eagle*, September 8, 1894). Whether this argument persuaded anyone or not is unclear, but for whatever reason the campaign to legalize the overrunning of second and third base never picked up enough steam to accomplish its aim.

As a result, what appears to have been a compromise when adopted in 1870 has been retained ever since. The need to make sudden stops has had far-reaching consequences, contributing to such developments as slides and baseball footwear and to the baseball player's own distinctive injury, the charley horse.

1.9   Pitchers Trying to Retire Batters. In many of the bat and ball games that were popular in the first half of the nineteenth century, the action was initiated by a "feeder" who tossed the ball to the batter without any thought of making it difficult to hit. Under the Knickerbockers' rules, the pitcher was initially still expected to simply toss hittable balls to the batter, but this soon changed. The identity of the first pitcher to seek a greater role is unknown, and indeed unknowable, but it can be safely said that the innovation occurred no later than the first great spurt of competitive play between 1855 and 1857. An 1856 account remarked that Knickerbockers pitcher Richard F. Stevens "sends the ball with exceeding velocity, and he who strikes it fairly must be a fine batsman. It is questionable, however, whether his style of pitching is most successful, many believing a slow ball curving near the bat, to be the most effective" (*Porter's Spirit of the Times*, December 6, 1856; quoted by William Rankin, *Sporting News*, May 25, 1901). It is worth noting in passing that Stevens was a member of the family that owned the Elysian Fields on which the Knickerbockers played, which may have made batters reluctant to complain about this tactic! As will be noted in the introduction to Chapter 3 on pitching, rule makers tried everything they could think of to reduce the role of the pitcher, but without success.

1.10   Balls and Strikes. As a result of the pitcher's limited role in very early baseball, batsmen accumulated no balls while strikes were recorded only on a swing and a miss. The premise was that each batter got to strike the ball once and that the pitch was the prelude to the fundamental conflict: the batter's effort to make his way home before the fielders could put him out.

This changed forever when pitchers began to enlarge their role. As noted in the preceding entry, pitchers were using speedy pitching and spinning their pitches as early as 1856. Other pitchers hit upon the simpler and maddeningly effective approach of deliberately throwing wide pitches to tempt batters to swing at pitches that were difficult to hit squarely. Not only was no skill required for this tactic, but there was also no penalty in the game's rules.

Batters retaliated by playing what was known as the "waiting game" and not swinging at all. This earned them rebukes from journals like the *New York Clipper*, which wrote in 1861, "Squires was active on the field, but in batting

he has a habit of waiting at the bat which is tedious and useless" (*New York Clipper*, August 24, 1861). Two years later the *Clipper* added, "The Nassaus did not adopt the 'waiting game' style of play in this match as they did in the Excelsior game. We would suggest to them to repudiate it altogether, leaving such style of play to those clubs who prefer 'playing the points,' as it is called, instead of doing 'the fair and square thing' with their opponents" (*New York Clipper*, October 31, 1863).

But these were appeals to the gentlemanly spirit, and that spirit was giving way to competitive fervor. While the rules had allowed umpires to call strikes since 1858, few did so, and players were increasingly taking the view that any tactic they could get away with was acceptable.

The result was gridlock. Bob Ferguson recalled in an 1884 interview that "a pitcher had the prerogative of sending as many balls as he wanted to across the plate until the batsman made up his mind to strike at one. In an ordinary game, forty, fifty and sixty balls were considered nothing for a pitcher before the batsman got suited" (*St. Louis Post-Dispatch*, July 10, 1884). Ferguson wasn't exaggerating.

Writing in 1893, Henry Chadwick described the first game of the Atlantics of Brooklyn in 1855: "It will be seen that it took the players over 2 hours to play three innings [2:45], so great was the number of balls the pitcher had to deliver to the bat before the batsman was suited" (*Sporting Life*, October 28, 1893). Baseball historian William J. Ryczek reported that the third game of an 1860 series between the Atlantics and Excelsiors saw Jim Creighton deliver 331 pitches and Mattie O'Brien throw 334 pitches in three innings. Ryczek also cited a tightly contested game on August 3, 1863, in which Atlantics pitcher Al Smith threw 68 pitches to Billy McKeever of the Mutuals in a single at bat (William J. Ryczek, *When Johnny Came Sliding Home*, 45).

This presented a grave dilemma for the game's rule makers. The pitcher was not supposed to have such a large role, so almost everyone agreed that something must be done to effect "the transfer of the interest of a match from the pitchers to the basemen and outerfielders" (*New York Clipper*, May 7, 1864). Yet any course of action would disrupt the fundamental balance of the game—exactly what they were trying to prevent. So they attempted to address the problem with a series of tweaks.

In 1863 the concept of called balls was added to the rule book to complement the (rarely enforced) called strike, along with a warning system by which the count began only when the umpire decided that either the pitcher or the batter was deliberately stalling. Henry Chadwick offered this advice on enforcement: "The correct thing for the umpire to do is this: When the striker takes his position, ask him where he wants a ball, and see that the pitcher is made aware of the point to which he must deliver the ball; then, if the first ball pitched is out of the legitimate reach . . . call out 'Ball to the bat,' or some similar warning; and after this is done and two unfair balls are delivered, you can legitimately call 'one ball' on the second one so delivered, and 'two' and 'three balls' on the very next unfair balls sent in. The same rule should be observed in regard to strikes—first a *warning*, and then a *repeated* refusal to strike at fair balls" (*The Ball Player's Chronicle*, July 4, 1867).

As a *Sporting News* article explained many years later, "This rule was construed so that very many real 'balls' as they would be called now, could be delivered to the 'striker' before he was allowed to 'walk.'" Accordingly, "not until the third ball was pitched could a real 'ball' be called. If a 'strike' intervened, another 'ball' would go unchallenged until the charge of 'repeatedly' could be brought by another wide one, and so on until the 'striker' had three called" (*Sporting News*, based on information provided by George L. Moreland, November 4, 1909). The umpire thus had a great deal of discretion and, if he believed that the pitcher was trying to pitch fairly, the pitcher could "send a score or more unfair balls over the base before the umpire picked out the three bad ones" (John H. Gruber, "Bases on Balls," *Sporting News*, January 20, 1916).

This was an imaginative approach, similar to a parent threatening a child with punishment while at the same time explaining that it can be averted if the child just goes back to playing appropriately. Unfortunately this carrot-and-stick approach led only to more creative efforts to grab the carrot while avoiding the stick.

The rule change had been intended to restore baseball to a battle between batters and fielders by reducing the pitcher's resources. Instead it had the unintended consequence of elevating a new figure to prominence—the umpire. For it was the umpire who was now charged with determining the players' intentions, and many umpires were reluctant to do

so. Henry Chadwick wrote of an 1867 game: "both nines had played in somewhat too much of the waiting game style at the bat, ball after ball being sent in by both pitchers, but especially by [Charley] Walker, within the legitimate reach of the bat, but because they were either 'too far out,' 'too close in,' 'too low' or 'too high,' in fact, not just within an inch or two of the spot indicated, the batsman would refuse to strike, the Umpire allowing them full liberty to thus delay the game and make it tedious" (*The Ball Player's Chronicle*, June 20, 1867).

Although the wording of the ruling was adjusted to reduce the umpire's "discretionary power" and force him to call balls, resistance continued (*New York Clipper*, December 22, 1866, 290). A typical example took place in a July 20, 1868, match in which the Detroit Base Ball Club hosted the Buckeye Club of Cincinnati. When the umpire did not appear, that role was filled by Bob Anderson, a highly respectable citizen who around 1859 had helped found the Detroit Base Ball Club. Steeped in the gentlemanly tradition, Anderson occasionally called balls but never strikes. The visiting batters took advantage by waiting up to fifteen minutes before swinging at a pitch. As a result, darkness fell with only seven innings having been played. Most of the crowd had departed long before then.

A match in Rochester, New York, on August 9, 1869, saw the umpire similarly allow a tedious number of pitches to pass without issuing a warning. One spectator became so exasperated that he finally read the rules aloud to the umpire (*Rochester Evening Express*, August 10, 1869; cited in Priscilla Astifan, "Baseball in the Nineteenth Century, Part 3," *Rochester History* LXIII, no. 1 [Winter 2001], 8).

William J. Ryczek reported that an umpire once called star player George Wright out on a called strike. The crowd complained vociferously about the ruling because Wright did not have a reputation for stalling. Having to take such factors into account put the umpire in an impossible position (William J. Ryczek, *When Johnny Came Sliding Home*, 46).

It thus became clear that the warning system had failed to accomplish its purpose, and there was a gradual acceptance that the increase in the pitcher's role was permanent. An 1872 account noted: "Harry Wright went to bat and waited, as is his custom, until the umpire, [Leonard C. 'Doc' Hanna], reminded him of his duty by calling a strike" (*Cleveland Plain Dealer*, August 20, 1872). Harry Wright's use of a tactic was important in legitimizing it, since Wright had played with the Knickerbockers on the Elysian Fields and was universally regarded as an exemplar of fair play.

The approach of waiting out the pitcher soon gained another influential supporter in Henry Chadwick, who commented in 1876, "a batsman, when he finds balls sent in so wide of the base as not to yield one fair ball in six should wait for good balls; for it is no discredit to him to take his base on called balls under such circumstances" (*New York Clipper*, November 11, 1876).

The rules were modified several times between 1867 and 1875 in hopes of finding a more satisfactory system. In 1875 the rule was again changed so that "the umpire must call one ball on each third unfair ball delivered. . . . When three balls have been called, the striker shall take his first base." As the *Sporting News* later explained, "This somewhat disguised nine-ball rule held until 1879, when the rule plainly states what it really meant—'when nine balls have been called, the striker shall take first base'" (*Sporting News*, based on information provided by George L. Moreland, November 4, 1909).

There continued to be strong resistance to the concept of every pitch being called either a ball or strike. When the *Cincinnati Commercial* proposed such a rule in 1878, the *Chicago Tribune* dismissed the notion as "too nonsensical to need comment. Ask one of the Bostons or Olympics of 1871 about the only game that ever was played under that rule. The rule was repealed after one game had been played under it" (*Chicago Tribune*, July 28, 1878, 7). Finally, however, in 1879 it was decreed that each pitch had to be declared a ball or a strike with the exception of a two-strike warning pitch. Since 1881 the umpire has been obliged to call every pitch one way or the other.

The number of balls and strikes allowed changed frequently over the next decade as rule makers sought the ideal balance between hitters and pitchers. Further confusing matters was a peculiar rule that the batter could be thrown out after a base on balls if he walked to first base instead of running (John H. Gruber, "Base on Balls," *Sporting News*, January 20, 1916). (This explains why they were not known as walks until later!)

In 1889, three strikes and four balls were finally settled upon as the parameters for an at bat. And it was not until the early twentieth century that fouls began to count as strikes, a

rule change that will be discussed under "Deliberate Fouls" (**2.3.2**).

Although the four-ball, three-strike balance arrived at in 1889 proved an enduring one, relatively little significance was attached to it at the time. The 1888 season, played with five balls and three strikes as benchmarks, had seen offenses struggle. In response, many radical ideas for ending "the growing tendency of ball playing to degenerate into a 'pitchers' battle'" were proposed at that year's postseason meetings (*Philadelphia Inquirer*, November 24, 1888).

Some argued that the number of strikes per at bat should be doubled to six while others advocated reducing the number of balls to three. Another proposal was to move the pitcher back five feet to approximately today's distance, but that idea was nixed by Brooklyn president Charles Byrne, who persuaded his colleagues that having the pitchers in line with first base would make base stealing too difficult. Others believed that the solution was to again allow batters to request high or low pitches (see **2.1.12**) (*Chicago Tribune*, November 21, 1888, 3; *Aberdeen* [S.D.] *Daily News*, November 22, 1888).

Since none of these approaches gained enough support, a much more modest change carried the day: "The committee discussed the suggestions exhaustively, and finally decided to let the matters stand just as they were last season, except to hold the pitcher down to four balls. Three strikes and four balls will, then, be the rule for next season" (*Chicago Tribune*, November 21, 1888, 3). Or as Henry Chadwick put it, "There is no radical change in the pitching rules, the only prominent amendment made being the reduction of the number of called balls giving the batsman his base from five balls to four" (*Evansville Journal*, April 27, 1889, 7).

This historic rule change was thus a compromise and one that appears to have satisfied no one. Even its supporters could hardly have expected four balls and three strikes to endure very long—after all, the number of balls and strikes had been modified almost every year of that decade. Yet that is precisely what happened, as four balls and three strikes has become one of the staples of baseball.

The terms "ball" and "strike" still reflect the original conflict. The word "strike" initially designated a pitch that the batter had unsuccessfully tried to strike, and it remains in use even though the more expansive definition has prevailed since 1858. "Ball" is an abbreviation of "Ball to the bat," which was one of the warnings called out by umpires before the warning system was abandoned.

1.11   Strike Zones. The concept of a strike zone began to develop once called strikes were established in the late 1850s, but it took a roundabout course. As Paul Hunkele has pointed out to me, in the early days of called strikes there was no real "strike zone," since an umpire could call a strike only if a pitcher hit a precise location.

As one early ballplayer described it, "A man would come to bat and say to the umpire: 'I want a ball knee high,' or 'waist high,' or 'shoulder high,' or hold his bat in position and say 'I want a ball right about there'" ("Old Time Base-ball," *Hartford Courant*, September 20, 1889, 6; see also Henry Chadwick, *The American Game of Base Ball*, 15, and Chadwick, *Haney's Base Ball Player's Book of Reference for 1867*, 96).

Henry Chadwick complained on a regular basis about batters who typically asked for high pitches but who switched their request to low balls when runners were on base in hopes that a passed ball would result. "This the rules do not admit of," he chided, "and whenever the umpire sees this trick resorted to, he should consider every ball as a ball 'fairly for the striker,' if it is within his fair reach" (*The National Chronicle*, July 3, 1869; see also Henry Chadwick, *The American Game of Base Ball*, 75). Chadwick also implied that a batter could not change his request even from game to game (Henry Chadwick, *Haney's Base Ball Player's Book of Reference for 1867*, 12, 41). But this seems to have been one of his idiosyncratic interpretations. When he described the latest rule changes after the 1866 season, Chadwick's gloss on the new wording of Section 6 stated that the batter could henceforth "only demand one pitched to the point he has been in the habit of striking from." Yet the reworded rule itself said nothing of the kind (*New York Clipper*, December 22, 1866, 290).

A. G. Spalding later offered this description of the situation: "The pitcher was required not only to deliver the ball over the home base, but at the height called for by the batsman. This, of course, gave the batsman considerable latitude in judging the balls to suit him, and was a handicap on the pitcher. I remember asking the batsman: 'What was the matter with that ball?' referring to a ball over the base and within fair reach of bat, and his reply would be either 'It

was not high enough' or 'It was too low.' It was some years before this old rule was changed" (*Sporting News*, May 23, 1896). As Spalding's comments suggest, even after balls and called strikes were introduced, the batter played at least as great a role as the umpire in determining the strike zone.

Moreover, umpires had different interpretations as to how close the pitch had to be to the location designated by the batter. As noted in the previous entry, some umpires considered a pitch as having to hit "within an inch or two" of an exact spot. Umpires were criticized if they expected too much precision from the pitcher, but overly lenient umpires were also subject to criticism (*New York Clipper*, June 18, 1864).

Some umpires sought the advice of the two clubs as to how strict they should be. The two sides wouldn't necessarily agree; even if they did, it essentially meant a different strike zone for each match. As a result, it was announced before the 1865 season that "the practice of taking the opinion of the two nines or their captains as to the degree of latitude to be observed in making allowance for unfair balls is to be entirely done away with" (*New York Clipper*, March 25, 1865).

Another vexing question was what an umpire was supposed to do if the batter chose to swing at a pitch outside the area he had designated. Henry Chadwick described a play that occurred on June 1, 1867, in a match between the Lowell Club of Boston and the Harvard nine in which a batter called for a knee-high ball but then struck at a shoulder-high ball. Even though the ball was put in play, the umpire had called a "ball" while it was still in flight and accordingly ruled that the play was of "no account" (Henry Chadwick, *The American Game of Base Ball*, 88–89).

With no meaningful strike zone, the calling of balls was just as problematic. Early in the 1864 season the *Brooklyn Eagle* reported that the "new rules were strictly enforced throughout . . . balls being called on [the pitcher] when he pitched the ball either over the head of the batsman or on the ground before reaching the home base" (*Brooklyn Eagle*, May 2, 1864). But even that enormous range did not suit everyone, and at season's end it was acknowledged that "No two umpires last year agreed upon what constitutes a fair ball . . . some almost ignored that part of the rule which required umpires to call balls on a pitcher" (*New York Clipper*, December 17, 1864).

The confusion was finally cleared up in 1871 when the rule makers restricted the batter to calling only for a "high" or "low" pitch. This created two different strike zones—between the waist and shoulder for a batter who requested "high," and between the knee and the waist for one who chose low balls. Since the pitcher could aim for anywhere within the area the batter had selected, the basic concept of a strike zone had been established.

Henry Chadwick explained in 1874 that the strike zone varied in both height and width depending upon the batter's size: "The umpire, whenever the striker takes his position at the home base, should satisfy himself as best he can as to what constitutes the fair reach of the batsman. No regular rule will apply, as a ball which would be within the legitimate reach of a tall, long armed man would be out of the reach of a short armed man, and vice versa. . . . The circle of the striker's legitimate reach being ascertained, the umpire will then find no difficulty in deciding the question of whether the pitcher sends in balls within the striker's reach or not" (Henry Chadwick, *1874 Chadwick's American Base Ball Manual*, 77–78).

Defining what constituted a high or low ball also caused confusion. At the National League meetings after the 1876 season, "The question of defining high and low balls was considered at some length, and settled by making a low ball one from the knee to the belt of the striker, and a high ball one from the belt to the shoulder. The exact waist ball was defined as a low ball" (*Chicago Tribune*, December 10, 1876, 7).

Gradually, however, the idea of doing away with requests and just having a single strike zone that stretched from the shoulder to the knee began to gain currency. In 1876 the *Chicago Tribune* wrote, "Another fruitful source of dispute has been as to the height at which the ball passed the striker, and it would certainly simplify matters very greatly if a good ball were defined to be one which was over the plate, as high as the striker's knee, and no higher than his shoulder. It would give the pitcher a trifle more leeway, and there-be [sic] a benefit" (*Chicago Tribune*, November 19, 1876, 10). Harry Wright became the most prominent advocate of the uniform strike zone, and he invoked the potent argument that it would make the umpire's job easier. In 1882 he explained: "One of the most difficult tasks [the umpire] has is to correctly call balls and strikes. If it is a little below or above the waist, a kick will follow from the batsman or pitcher. I believe that any ball which passes over the plate between the shoulder and knees should be termed fair. If such a scheme is adopted, it will compel the batter to hit" (*Boston Globe*, November 5, 1882, 8).

The request system was finally abolished after the 1886 season as a direct result of "the question of 'high' and 'low' balls" having become "the cause of more disputes at the hands of pitchers and batsmen than any other point of play the umpire was called upon to decide" (Henry Chadwick, "The New Base-Ball Rules," *Lippincott*, May 1887, reprinted in *Louisville Courier-Journal*, April 24, 1887). This meant that for the first time each batter had to defend a standard strike zone that stretched across home plate from the batter's knee to his shoulder (*Aberdeen* [S.D.] *Daily News*, March 16, 1887). The exact parameters have changed only slightly since, but there have been greater changes in how umpires interpret the strike zone. One could, as a result, view today's strike zone as having reverted to that of a batter between 1871 and 1886 who requested a low pitch.

1.12 Umpires. An 1883 description of the early bat-and-ball games that preceded baseball reported, "As there was never any umpire in these games, the field for controversy was unlimited. One way, as we recollect, of settling disputes was as follows: All proceeding to the spot of the doubtful catch, the best player on one side hurled the ball with all his force upwards; if it was caught by the designated player of the other party, the point was given in the latter's favor, and vice versa" (William Wells Newell, *Games and Songs of American Children*, 185). That was not a terribly fair way of settling matters, so baseball has always used umpires, but their responsibilities have changed dramatically over the years.

The Olympic Ball Club of Philadelphia, a club that played a version of baseball now known as town ball, recognized the need for an umpire as early as the 1830s. The Olympics' constitution, published in 1838, specified that one of the duties of the team recorder was to act as "umpire between the captains on Club days, in the event of a disputed point of the game, and from his decision there shall be no appeal, except to the club at its next stated meeting" (reprinted in Dean A. Sullivan, ed., *Early Innings*, 6).

The Knickerbockers' rules outlined a similar role for the umpire. William R. Wheaton officiated during a game of October 6, 1845, that appears in the club's scorebooks.

Researchers Edward L. Widmer and Melvin L. Adelman discovered a box score for an October 23, 1845, game between the New York Ball Club and the Brooklyn Club that stated, "Messrs. Johnson, Wheaton and Von Nostrand were the umpires" (*New York Herald*, October 25, 1845; reprinted in Melvin L. Adelman, "The First Baseball Game, the First Newspaper References to Baseball, and the New York Club," *Journal of Sport History* 7:3 [Winter 1980], 134). In several subsequent matches, an umpire issued a fine to one of the players for swearing.

In all these examples, however, the responsibilities of the umpire were to enforce decorum and club rules. Befitting this role, the umpire of this period was usually a prominent member of the community. Jimmy Wood later recollected: ". . . In the early part of my baseball career—from 1859 to 1869—an umpire was highly honored. After each game the players would give three cheers for each other and then, as a grand finale, they would bellow forth with three more—and sometimes nine—for the umpire.

"Arbitrators in the early days were chosen from among the crowd. In most cases, at least up to 1865, the umpire often was one of the most distinguished men in the city. The clubs vied with each other in trying to secure the most prominent personages.

"The old time umpires were accorded the utmost courtesy by the players. They were given easy chairs, placed near the home plate, provided with fans on hot days and their absolute comfort was uppermost in the minds of the players. After each of our games in the early '60's, sandwiches, beer, cakes and other refreshments were served by the home team. The umpire always received the choicest bits of food and the largest glass of beer—in case he cared for such beverage. If he didn't, he needed but to express his desires in the thirst-quenching line before the game started—and he got it" (James Wood, as told to Frank G. Menke, "Baseball in By-Gone Days," part 2, syndicated column, *Marion* [Ohio] *Star*, August 15, 1916).

Clarence Deming offered this similar description: "The umpire's place was usually a point even with home plate and about twenty feet away. There an armchair was set for him and, on sunny days, he was entitled to an umbrella, either self-provided or a special one of vast circumference, fastened to the chair and with it constituting one of the fixtures of the game. He had freedom of movement, but the prerogative was rarely used. In his pocket was a copy of 'Beadle's Dime Baseball Book,' then the hornbook of the game, and often in requisition. In his airy perch, shielded by his mighty canopy, the umpire of those days made an imposing figure, bearing his honors with Oriental dignity, though hardly with Oriental ease" (Clarence Deming, "Old Days in Baseball," *Outing*, June 1902, 357–358).

By the late 1860s a dramatic change in the umpire's role was under way. Before long, instead of being provided with easy chairs and canopies, umpires found themselves on the figurative hot seat. Rather than receiving such comforts as the largest glass of beer, these poor men all too often had to dodge glasses of beer that were hurled at them (see **8.2.3**). One major component of that transformation was the umpire's assumption of additional responsibilities, a development already touched upon under "Balls and Strikes" (**1.10**). The umpire's new duties will be described more fully in the next entry.

1.13   Judgment Calls. Today's fans assume without question that the umpire's role is to make decisions and to make them immediately. An umpire nowadays is likely to be criticized for a belated call even if the decision is correct. The situation could scarcely be more different from the early days of baseball when, as Clarence Deming observed, the umpire's decisions were always expected to be *ex post facto* (Clarence Deming, "Old Days in Baseball," *Outing*, June 1902, 358). Yet even in today's game a curious remnant of baseball's early days persists in the fact that players must initiate an appeal in certain circumstances.

In the 1850s, matches were officiated by two umpires, representing the two clubs, and an impartial referee. Their roles are nicely illustrated in this 1857 account: "At the desk are the umpires, watching the game, and noting its progress. The referee, solitary and alone, is seated between the batsman and the marquee, taking an impartial survey of the proceedings, and ready to mete out justice to all when appealed to" (*New York Clipper*, September 19, 1857).

This proved a cumbersome system, as this later description shows: ". . . There were a referee and two 'umpires,' so called. The referee was really the only judge. The 'umpires' were simply special advocates of their respective nines. Upon appeal being made, one umpire would invariably shout 'Not out!' while the other would call 'Out!' The question would have to go the referee, the same as if there had been no umpire" (*New York Clipper*, June 21, 1884).

The threesome was thus replaced in 1858 by a single umpire, but it continued to be his function to make few rulings except "when appealed to." A dissatisfied party would call out "judgment" or "how's that?" to invoke the umpire's intervention. But if his opinion was not solicited, he remained silent unless there was a specific need for a ruling. For example, umpires called out fouls so that runners knew to return to their base, but they remained silent on fair balls. (This is still true today, though the reason now is that the words "fair" and "foul" sound similar enough that it is feared that a fielder might mishear a call of "fair" and not play the ball.)

During the Civil War, umpires were still reticent about passing judgment. Henry Chadwick had to explain in 1864, "We were pleased to see [umpire John Grum] refuse to be guided by the statement of the player on the second base in the case of his touching a man. In the excitement of a play of this kind, one party is just as certain he touched his adversary as the latter is certain he did not, although neither the one or the other may be right, and for this reason, if none other, the umpire should be guided by his own impression of the play" (*Brooklyn Eagle*, July 27, 1864).

By the end of the war, the decision-making function was established as the umpire's unpleasant duty. Even then, it applied only to specific plays, as is shown by this 1864 account: "In the instance where Wood and Miller were put out at first base, Wood made a mistake in thinking the ball foul; it was not only fair, but the Umpire was right in not saying anything until appealed to, it being his duty only to call foul balls and not fair ones" (*New York Clipper*, September 3, 1864).

After the war, competitiveness became rampant, and incessant calls for judgment transferred more and more decisions to the umpire. Henry Chadwick complained in 1867, "The constant cry of 'judgment on that,' 'how's that,' & c., in reference to unfair balls by the pitcher, or refusal to strike at fair balls by the batsman, has become almost a nuisance . . . there should be but one spokesman in a nine, and he should be the captain; and no captain, knowing his duties or having any judgment, will make appeals on points of play which it is the duty of the umpire to decide without any appeal whatever,

such as calling baulks, balls and strikes" (*The Ball Player's Chronicle*, July 11, 1867).

The natural result was described by Chadwick in an 1868 game account: "Frequent appeals to umpire for judgment, when nothing necessitated it, became the order of the day, 'How's that,' from the players were quickly caught up by the crowd, and from this the umpire, because he had not four pair of eyes in his head, was insulted and abused by both nines. . . . Who, after this exhibition, wishes to act as umpire?" (*Brooklyn Eagle*, August 15, 1868).

This development could give an advantage to a contentious club that was playing against one that followed more gentlemanly customs. A Detroit reporter complained after an 1866 match: "[C. J.] McNally, the Chicago pitcher, did not pitch his balls but bowled instead. That the Detroit boys did not ask judgment and obtain the ruling out of this pitching, can only be explained on the supposition mentioned that they thought themselves able to beat their opponents against all odds" (*Detroit Advertiser and Tribune*, July 3, 1866).

On the other hand, it could also backfire against a disputatious player or club. Henry Chadwick's account of an 1868 game between the Athletics of Philadelphia and the Atlantics of Brooklyn stated: "in trying to reach second, however, [Dick Pearce of the Atlantics] was captured by [Al] Reach [of the Athletics]. . . . Dick did not think he was out, but as Reach appealed, and the Col. well knew that 'Al.' is too square a man to appeal except he thinks he has put his man out, the Col. promptly decided him out."

The game was umpired by Colonel Thomas Fitzgerald, who had formerly been president of the Athletic club. Instead of condemning his decision as being partisan, Chadwick editorialized, "The tricky men, who are constantly appealing even when they know the player is not out, too frequently over-reach themselves, as Umpires, when appealed to by men of this tricky style of play, pay no regard to their movements, and the result is that men are sometimes given in who are really out" (*New England Base Ballist*, September 10, 1868).

There is a subtle but important change in Chadwick's logic. Instead of advocating that clubs restrict appeals because it is the right thing to do, he is now suggesting that should they do so to avoid hurting their club. A similar shift from moral to pragmatic reasoning was demonstrated in 1871 when he chastised Dick

McBride for having "overdone one thing, and that is in appealing to the umpire. . . . It may lead to a favorable decision in one or two instances, but only at the cost of adverse ruling in a majority of appeals made, as umpires are bound to revenge themselves in nine cases out of ten for the annoyances the pitcher thereby subjects them to" (*New York Clipper*, February 4, 1871).

The reality that Chadwick and his fellow reporters were very busy keeping score during matches undoubtedly influenced his thinking. In 1867 he declared that the umpire was required to "call balls and strikes in a loud voice the moment they occur, and without 'judgment' being called. And he must also, when a player is put out, at once call out, in a loud voice how and in what position he has been put out without being asked. Thus, if a player be put out on the fly by the centre fielder, the umpire must immediately call out, 'striker out on the fly by centre fielder.' By this means the scoring of the fielding play will be greatly facilitated" (Henry Chadwick, *Haney's Base Ball Player's Book of Reference for 1867*, 27).

There is no evidence that umpires complied with Chadwick's demand for these detailed descriptions, but by the early 1870s the sense of having the umpire rule on every play was acknowledged. Of course this didn't satisfy everyone either. The *Chicago Tribune* noted in 1870: "[Charley] Hodes tried to steal second, but was decided out—one of the closest and most unsatisfactory decisions of the game, which the boys took to unkindly, as the second baseman of the [Brooklyn] Atlantics was so well satisfied that Hodes got his base that he did not call for a decision" (*Chicago Tribune*, July 6, 1870).

The idea of an umpire who rules only when appealed to is not merely a quaint part of baseball's ancient past. The practice continued with respect to the legality of pitching deliveries for many years afterward. For example, an 1887 account noted: "[Detroit captain Ned] Hanlon called for judgment on [pitcher John Clarkson's delivery] and [umpire Ed] Hengle ruled that it was a 'balk'" (*Chicago Tribune*, May 13, 1887, 3).

Remnants of this practice still exist in today's game. In 1928 sportswriter Frank H. Young noted, "There are three rule infringements which may happen in a game and which, even if he sees them, the umpire will not pass on unless asked to by an opposing team. They are: (1) A batsman hitting out of turn; (2) a base runner failing to touch a base on a long hit,

and (3) a player leaving a base too soon after the catch of a sacrifice fly."

Young asked several umpires for an explanation and was told, "it's up to the opposing team to ask for our ruling. We can't be expected to play their game for them." He found this reasoning unsatisfying and wrote that he could "not see where it helps the game any to make flesh of one ruling and fowl of another. The umpires are placed on the field to see that games are played according to the rules and no good explanation has ever been made as to why some rules have to be asked for and others are given as fast as the plays are made" (Frank H. Young, "Umpires Work at 'Trick' Plays Despite Rules of Game," *Washington Post*, June 10, 1928).

Young was quite correct. There is no logical reason for these few remnants of the gentlemanly era to persist while all other areas are governed by a more legalistic approach. And yet all three continue to this day, and yet another partial example has been added—the checked swing, on which either the catcher or the plate umpire may initiate the appeal.

Occasionally this quaint custom has significant consequences. A particularly dramatic instance occurred in the fifth game of the 1911 World Series when Larry Doyle of the Giants missed the plate as he came home with the winning run in the tenth inning. Home plate umpire Bill Klem noticed the oversight and was prepared to call Doyle out, but the Athletics did not appeal so the Giants won the game. Fortunately for the Athletics, they rebounded the next day to capture the series.

This state of having vital information but being unable to convey it puts umpires in an awkward position. Umpire Billy Evans conveyed this nicely in describing a 1914 minor league game in which the base runner had missed home plate but not been tagged. After the runner had returned to the dugout, "the catcher asked the umpire what ruling he made on the play. The umpire diplomatically replied that a runner was always safe when not touched with the ball." The significance of this cryptic response gradually dawned on the catcher, and he "asked the umpire what he should do, and the umpire replied that he was there to decide plays, not to make them" (syndicated column, *Boston Globe*, January 23, 1915). In a 2007 game, Detroit Tigers manager Jim Leyland and several players argued with umpire Bruce Froemming that the opposing runner had been tagged out. Froemming maintained that the tag had been missed, but when Leyland also contended that the base runner had missed the base, the umpire had nothing to say but "Time is out. We've got to put the ball back in play." The Tigers soon deduced that Froemming was unable to respond directly because he knew that the runner had indeed missed the bag, but was not allowed to tell them. At that point, they successfully appealed the play (John Lowe, *Detroit Free Press*, July 13, 2007).

Temptation proved too great for one early umpire. In an 1878 game, Syracuse player Michael Mansell hit a home run, but the Auburn club appealed that he had missed second base. The umpire, a Mr. Woodlin, "said, 'Safe on *second*,' placing a suggestive emphasis on the last word. The hint was accepted and the ball was thrown to [Auburn third baseman George] Fair, when the umpire called Mansell out" (*New York Clipper*, May 18, 1878). A heated argument ensued, and the game was eventually forfeited.

1.14   Nine Players.

It was common to leave the number of players unspecified in early bat-and-ball games. As an 1887 article about "the game called baseball by the country boys of twenty years ago" explained, "There were no regular outfielders, and the game could be played by six boys—three on a side. But while half a dozen could play the game, half a dozen rarely did, and the number was often twenty or more. In such a case the field was covered by the superfluous players as they chose" ("Old Baseball," *Indianapolis Sentinel*, April 3, 1887).

Similarly, the Knickerbockers' initial rules said nothing about the number of players. This proved wise, as it was often a struggle to find enough players for an organized game. Daniel Adams later recalled, "I had to employ all my rhetoric to induce attendance." In spite of his efforts, he reported limited success: "I frequently went to Hoboken to find only two or three members present, and we were often obliged to take our exercise in the form of 'old cat,' 'one' or 'two' as the case might be" (*Sporting News*, February 29, 1896). John Thorn notes that between 1845 and 1849 the Knickerbockers played matches with eight, ten, and eleven players a side, before nine gradually became the norm during the 1850s. In 1857 the rules for the first time mandated the use of nine players. Beginning in 1874, Henry Chadwick unsuccessfully campaigned to have a tenth player—a right shortstop—added to the game (see **19.12**).

1.15   Shortstops.

The positions of pitcher, catcher, and basemen were already established by the time the Knickerbockers wrote their rules, with the remaining players—however many—acting as fielders. Accordingly, the only position to have developed since then is the shortstop, which began to evolve around 1849.

In an 1896 interview, Daniel Adams, one of the leading members of the Knickerbockers, claimed that "I used to play shortstop and I believe I was the first one to occupy that place, as it had formerly been left uncovered." Adams made the move because a more resilient ball had begun to be used that could be hit and thrown farther (*Sporting News*, February 29, 1896). This caused the outfielders to play deeper and made relay throws necessary, which was Adams's primary function.

The player-turned-sportswriter Tim Murnane, who was apparently referring to the 1850s, offered this explanation: "As near as one can learn the position of short-stop was the last one to be added to the make-up of a base-ball nine. In the early days the game was played on large open fields, and the out-fielders had some long runs to get a ball hit by them. Sometimes they were obliged to go to the extreme end of the field. Men played but few games and their arms were not in condition to make long throws, and the basemen hugged their bases much closer than at the present time. The short-stop acted as a utility man and would go out in the field to take the ball from the out-fielders and send it to the home plate or to the in-field" (*Cincinnati Enquirer*, April 1, 1888).

As these two accounts suggest, the position appears to have been in a state of flux in the 1850s, with significant variations between clubs. According to Clarence Deming, the shortstop sometimes also acted as a sort of rover: "The short-stop for many years shifted ground to a point between first and second bases if a left-handed striker was at bat" (Clarence Deming, "Old Days in Baseball," *Outing*, June 1902, 358). Meanwhile other clubs seem to have been slow to adapt, with one reporter offering this description of the division of labor in 1859: "At each of the bases is stationed one man to watch the runner, and the fielders, who are outside throw the ball to him in order that he may touch the runner with it before he reaches the bag" (*New York Herald*, October 16, 1859). And a man named Michael F. Lynch, who played shortstop for Pittsburgh's first baseball club in 1857, later recalled "that there was not one-half the work required of him that would be the case in the game of the twentieth century. There were none of the hot grounders to encounter, and the flies were usually of that high order, which made their capture by a man at his position well nigh impossible" (*Pittsburg[h] Post*, April 4, 1904).

Since all the duties of the early shortstops were to some extent afterthoughts, it was not a very glamorous position. That started to change in 1856 when Dickey Pearce joined the Atlantics of Brooklyn. Pearce was probably put at shortstop because he was short and chubby, but he helped to transform the position into a key defensive one. Tim Murnane explained, "Dickey Pearce . . . was the first man to play the position as it is played now. . . . George Wright was the first man to play the position deep and close to second base, so as to give the baseman an opportunity to move away from his position, and in 1869 Wright and Charley Sweasy were the first players to work the two positions as they are worked to-day" (*Cincinnati Enquirer*, April 1, 1888). The later development of the position is discussed in entry 4.2.6.

1.16 Ninety Feet. The Knickerbockers' fourth rule used paces to set the distances between the bases, and there is dispute as to how to convert these. Some experts believe the initial distance was about ninety feet while others think it may have been shorter.

John Thorn, for example, believes that until the mid-1850s the bases were only about seventy-five feet apart. Still others, such as Fred Ivor-Campbell, have suggested that paces were used to produce "scalable" dimensions: adults could use something close to ninety feet while children would use a shorter distance. Support for either of these views may be derived from the *1864 American Boy's Book of Sports and Games*, which reprinted the official rules and observed "that boys should reduce the distances there set down about one-sixth" (*1864 American Boy's Book of Sports and Games*, 83).

The length was finally clarified in 1857 when the rules were codified. In an 1896 interview, Daniel Adams, one of the leading members of the Knickerbockers, explained that he prepared a set of rules for that convention: "The distance between bases I fixed at thirty yards—the only previous determination being 'the bases shall be from home to second base 42 paces equidistant'—which was rather vague" (*Sporting News*, February 29, 1896).

1.17 Sixty Feet, Six Inches. By 1854 the Knickerbockers had established the pitcher's distance at fifteen paces. This was clarified to mean forty-five feet in 1857, with the distance being marked by an iron plate. In 1881 the pitcher was moved back another five feet to fifty feet.

Then the advent of overhand pitching created an abundance of strikeouts and led to serious consideration after the 1888 season to moving the pitcher back another five feet. Star pitcher Tim Keefe was vehemently opposed to the proposal, claiming that the change would "put a premium on brute strength" instead of skilled pitching. Keefe even preferred letting batters again call for high and low pitches rather than having to pitch from five feet farther back (*Kansas City Star*, October 23, 1888). In the end, the proposal was defeated, but apparently the argument that swayed the rule makers was a very different one advanced by Brooklyn president Charles Byrne. Byrne convinced his colleagues that having the pitchers in line with first base would all but eliminate base stealing (*Chicago Tribune*, November 21, 1888, 3).

In its lone year of existence in 1890, the Players' League modified the distance slightly. While explaining that the length of the pitcher's box was to be increased by six inches and the front line was to be moved back a foot to fifty-one feet from the plate, league secretary Frank Brunell downplayed the significance of the adjustment: "All rules changing the distance between the batsman and pitcher in position have of late been looked upon as important and with awe. It is hardly likely that this change will have any marked effect on batting. Yet it is in the nature of an experiment and ought naturally to increase batting all around less than one per cent" (*Chicago Herald*, March 30, 1890).

That distance died with the Players' League, but by then the idea of increasing the pitching distance was a key plank of the Lester Plan, a series of changes proposed by *Philadelphia Record* sportswriter W. R. Lester. Lester's ideas gained a key ally in *Sporting Life* editor Francis Richter, who argued that another five feet between the pitcher and batter would result in "the restoration of the proper equilibrium between the two great principles of the game—attack and defense. With the pitcher reduced to the ranks, nine men instead of two will play the game" (*Sporting Life*, November 12, 1892).

As a result, the current distance of sixty feet, six inches was adopted by the National League on March 7, 1893, in a 9-3 vote. This change from fifty feet to sixty feet, six inches is sometimes depicted as having moved the pitcher ten and a half feet farther from the plate, and the mysterious six inches is sometimes attributed to a surveyor's error. Neither is the case.

The intention of the rule makers was to move the pitcher back about five feet. But the five-and-a-half-foot pitcher's box had required the pitcher to keep his *front* foot fifty feet from home plate while the new rubber effectively determined the location of the pitcher's *rear* foot. This created the historic distance of sixty feet, six inches, but it also changed what that figure represented, with the result that the change was much less than ten feet. Indeed, as Tom Shieber has shown, for several technical reasons the new distance was actually only four feet, three and a half inches farther from the plate (Tom Shieber, "The Evolution of the Baseball Diamond," in *Total Baseball IV*, 118).

Run scoring soared as a result, leading some to contend that the rule change was designed to create more runs and a spike in attendance. In fact the aim was not so much to decrease the frequency of outs as to shift the way in which they were made. After two years, A. J. Flanner of the *St. Louis Post-Dispatch* concluded that the main objective of the change had been accomplished: "The monotonous strike out game has been legislated into a reminiscence" (quoted in the *Brooklyn Eagle*, November 7, 1894).

1.18   Diamonds. The baseball infield isn't really a diamond at all, since a diamond has two acute and two obtuse angles. The inaccurate name dates back to long before the Knickerbockers. David Block reported that the term "diamond" was being used by 1835 and that the corresponding configuration of the infield had emerged by 1834 (David Block, *Baseball Before We Knew It*, 197–198). At that time it would have been silly to call the resulting shape a square, since the use of "convenient trees, posts and pumps" for bases meant that in most instances "the distance [was] not alike between any two" (*New England Base Ballist*, August 6, 1868).

But why was the word "diamond" retained long after changes to the game rendered it inaccurate? While the question cannot be answered with certainty, it appears that the term was retained because it highlighted one of the distinguishing features of the Knickerbockers' game—that the home base was one of the four bases. For example, an 1887 article comparing the Knickerbockers' version to its rivals stated: "The next important difference lay in the placing of the bases, or 'byes,' as they were then often called, and as many a reader of these lines will doubtless remember. The accompanying diagram will make this point clear. 'A' is the position of the striker, or 'batter' as he was then denominated; '1,' '2,' '3' and '4' are byes, '4' being the home 'bye' and the termination of the runner's journey around what was then the square, and not the diamond" ("Old Baseball," *Indianapolis Sentinel*, April 3, 1887). Others seem to have found the term "diamond" a good way to differentiate this layout, and the term stuck.

1.19   Other Dimensions. The most conspicuous changes to the configurations of the baseball diamond after 1857 were the ones noted in the preceding two entries. But there were also a great number of less noticeable changes, which are enumerated in Tom Shieber's outstanding article "The Evolution of the Baseball Diamond." (The article originally appeared in *The National Pastime* but was reprinted in editions of *Total Baseball*.)

1.20   Foul Ground. The concept of foul territory is one of baseball's distinguishing characteristics. David Block pointed out that most previous bat and ball games had no foul territory at all and that in the two exceptions, trapball and rounders, a foul counted as an out (David Block, *Baseball Before We Knew It*, 84–85).

While it is not known why the Knickerbockers made the novel decision to count a foul as no play, I believe the biggest reason was the troubles the club had in finding suitable grounds in the rapidly developing New York City area. Their decision also had several other key benefits that may have been taken into account in devising the rule change. One was that baseballs were rare commodities, and a lost ball often ended play. In addition, many disliked the fact that batters could simply tip baseballs off behind them in versions with no foul territory. James D'Wolf Lovett even claimed that batters deliberately tried to disable catchers by means of such tips, causing understandable controversy (James D'Wolf Lovett, *Old Boston Boys and the Games They Played*, 131). A final advantage—probably not foreseen by the Knickerbockers—was that foul territory made it possible for spectators to watch the action from close proximity.

In the early rules, whether a ball was fair or foul was determined by where it first struck. For how and why this changed, see "Fair-Fouls" (2.2.2) and "Deliberate Fouls" (2.3.2).

1.21   Out on Fly. In early baseball, a batter was out if a fielder caught his hit on the first bounce. By the late 1850s the Knickerbockers and at least one other club, the Excelsiors of Brooklyn, had begun experimenting with allowing only fly catches. They were pleased with the results, and the Knickerbockers led a campaign to permit an out only for catching a ball on the fly. The issue was heatedly debated for the next few years and was brought up at the annual convention of the National Association of Base Ball Players no fewer than six times.

As Warren Goldstein described, advocates of the change used the potent technique of characterizing the bound rule as a childish custom that was unworthy of men (Warren Goldstein, *Playing for Keeps*, 48–53; see also William J. Ryczek, *Baseball's First Inning*, 176). Yet it wasn't really that simple because the rules and conditions made every out a struggle. Hitting was an easy matter due to lively baseballs and underhand pitching, while fielders faced the multiple handicaps of uneven fields, no gloves, and the sun in their eyes. As one account put it: "The ball used at that time was highly elastic, being composed largely of rubber, and was known as a 'live ball'; consequently there were some marvelous exhibitions of batting, home-runs being more common than base hits of today. This situation put the outfielders in the position of star actors in the game and they were depended upon for at least three-fourths of the put-outs. The result was that a game consisted mostly of a display of heavy batting and base running, with the score usually going up to some forty or maybe fifty runs. A game was not considered probably won at any stage, short of a lead of twenty runs. This of course grew tiresome, and prolonged the game unnecessarily" (Harry Slye, "Early Days of Baseball in Baraboo," *Baraboo Daily News*, June 25, 1925). Because the fielders were so helpless, it appears that even catches on two bounds were sometimes considered outs in games between younger players ("Old Baseball," *Indianapolis Sentinel*, April 3, 1887). So the idea of taking away the easiest way to record an out understandably struck many as a terrible idea!

On December 14, 1864, the proponents of the rule change finally carried their point, and fielders were required to catch fair balls on the fly (*New York Clipper*, December 24, 1864). Until the 1880s, however, fouls could still be caught on the first bounce.

1.22   Tagging. Early versions of baseball allowed fielders to retire base runners by throwing the ball at them and hitting them before they could reach a base. This tactic was variously known as "soaking," "patching," and "plugging." The Knickerbockers explicitly prohibited this practice in their thirteenth rule, and replaced it with tagging and force-outs. Historian David Block observed that "Without a doubt, this rule is the Knickerbockers' single greatest contribution to the game of baseball. . . . It was sparklingly original, given that a central feature of every previous description of baseball and related games mandated throwing the ball at base runners to put them out" (David Block, *Baseball Before We Knew It*, 87).

While hindsight now enables us to perceive the Knickerbockers as visionaries for doing away with soaking, many of their contemporaries did not consider this a change for the better. As one observer recalled in 1873: "thirty years ago the now national game of base ball was unknown, except in its old original form, as played by the school boys, when to put a man out all you had to do was to throw the ball at him while he was running from base to base. This was half the fun of the game at that time" (*Brooklyn Eagle*, July 16, 1873).

Many others thought that baseball without soaking was no fun at all. The pioneer Jerome Trowbridge gave this description of how baseball came to Kalamazoo: "John [McCord] used to play the old game of patch ball with us when he was here, but he went down to Poughkeepsie to school and when he came back to Kalamazoo he told us of the other game and prevailed upon us to try it. We tried it and were thoroughly disgusted with the whole thing and wanted to go back to the old game, but John kept at us telling us that this would soon be the only game that would be played and he was right. We kept at it but there were a great many things that we could not get used to. We still wanted to patch a man and some way we could not get used to this new way of putting a man out" (*Kalamazoo Gazette*, February 11, 1906).

A transplanted Brooklynite named Merritt Griswold encountered similar resistance when he tried to convince a town ball club in St. Louis to adopt the Knickerbockers' brand of baseball: ". . . After considerable urging and coaxing on my part they passed a resolution at one of their meetings that they would try the national rules for one morning if I would . . . teach them, which I consented to do if they would agree to stick to it for the full hour without 'kicking,' for as I told them they would not like it until after playing it for a sufficient length of time to be familiar with some of its fine points, all of which they agreed to and kept their words like good fellows as they were, but in ten minutes I could see most of them were disgusted, yet they would not go back on their word and stuck to it for their hour's play. At the breaking up of the game to go home they asked me if I would coach them one more morning as they began to 'kindy like it'" (quoted in A. H. Spink, *The National Game*, 406).

Soaking was retained in the Massachusetts version of baseball, which was popular in New England until the early 1860s, but when it died out so did the custom. As difficult as this change was for some to accept, the elimination of soaking was crucial to baseball being reinvented as an activity for men. As long as the rule was in effect, the game had to be played with a soft ball and bore the stigma of being a child's activity. The removal of this feature enabled baseball to be viewed in a fresh light.

The Knickerbockers did not immediately develop the current system of force-outs at first and tags at other bases unless all the bases behind are occupied. According to their initial rules, a player could be put out at any base, including home, by holding the ball on the base to which he was running, even if the base preceding him was unoccupied. This would have drastically reduced the amount of running and chasing in the game, and it must have seemed very anticlimactic for a base runner's mad dash for a base to end with a fielder stepping on that base. The Knickerbockers must have concluded that things had gone too far in that direction, and by 1848 tags were required at every base except first. Conventions about when a force-out applied developed gradually in the succeeding years, and by 1864 today's compromise was in place.

It has not gone entirely unchallenged. In 1914 concern about the number of violent collisions on the base paths had prompted calls to eliminate tagging from the game. By then, tagging was firmly entrenched, causing one reporter to observe: "The plan is not feasible, and it would rob baseball of many of its most picturesque features. Tagging, or 'putting the ball on a runner,' is really one of the fine points of baseball, and to eliminate it would virtually kill base stealing, which is an art in itself" (*Washington Post*, July 26, 1914).

1.23 Touching Bases. Early base runners were required only to "make" their base—in yet another reflection of an environment in which competitiveness was considered ungentlemanly. This custom was also shaped by a more practical reality: bases were often posts or hard objects, and landing upon them was at best unpleasant and at worst could cause serious injury. Indicative of changes to both baseball's conditions and attitudes, a rule change after the 1863 season required runners to specifically "touch" their base. Base runners apparently were not keen on this change, as Henry Chadwick wrote in 1867 that it was pretty much a dead letter to get runners to actually tag a base (*The Ball Player's Chronicle*, July 25, 1867). But the next few years saw baseball increasingly governed by the letter rather than the spirit of the law, with the result that base runners who adhered to the old custom were both literally and figuratively put out.

1.24 Batting Orders. The Knickerbockers' sixteenth rule dictated that players bat "in regular turn," but early batsmen did not always take their turns in strict rotation as they do now.

Once an inning begins, it has always been required for batters to come to the plate in the designated order. But the early rules were vague about which batter should lead off the next inning if the preceding inning had ended on an out made by a base runner.

According to Henry Chadwick, the generally accepted custom of the era differed from the current practice. He explained in 1876 that if a base runner made the third out of an inning, the next inning would be led off by the batter who followed that base runner in the lineup. Chadwick was adamant that "This has been the rule of play since the National Association of 1857 first adopted a regular code" (*New York Clipper*, January 1, 1876).

After the 1878 season the rule was changed so that a new inning was led off by the batter following the last one to complete his at bat.

Henry Chadwick commented that this would eliminate a lot of confusion: "Under the old rule, [the fourth] batsman might force [the] third man out at second base, and in the next inning take his strike over again. . . . Under the new rules each batsman will have the same number of times at bat in a match so far as the rules can possibly control the matter" (*New York Clipper*, December 28, 1878).

Even this revamped version led to confusion under some circumstances. In an exhibition game between Troy and the Metropolitans on April 19, 1881, "two men were out on the Metropolitan side, [Jerry] Dorgan was at bat and [Ed] Kennedy was on third base. After a strike had been called, Dorgan hit a foul ball along the line towards third base, which was passed in quickly enough to [pitcher Tim] Keefe to throw out Kennedy, returning on the foul hit, thus ending the inning. In the next inning Dorgan claimed his turn at the bat on the basis of the league rule that said term begins when he takes his position at the bat, and continues until he is put out or becomes a base-runner. Captain [Bob] Ferguson, however, claimed that the fact of his foul hit having put the third hand out was equivalent to a turn at the bat, and [Lew] Say was given his place as first striker" (*Boston Globe*, May 1, 1881).

1.25   "Walkoff" Hits. Once it was established that a game was to last nine innings, the requirement was taken literally. If the club batting last was ahead after eight and a half innings, it wouldn't have occurred to early players not to complete the game. After all, a baseball match was a ceremony rather than a competition, and for the losers to walk off the field would be the ultimate act of poor sportsmanship.

This custom of completing the game persisted throughout the increasingly competitive 1870s while many other gentlemanly traditions died out. Before the 1874 season, a proposal was made to end play after eight and a half innings if the outcome was decided, but the idea was "discussed somewhat unfavorably" and voted down (*Boston Globe*, March 3, 1874, 3). Nor was it simply a case of going through the motions in the bottom of the ninth; in many cases a side that had already won piled up many additional runs against demoralized opponents.

In the deciding match of a tournament in Blissfield, Michigan, held on August 22 and 23, 1879, the Nine Spots of Sturgis led the Adrian Club 5-4 in the bottom of the ninth. But a two-

run single won the game and the tournament for Adrian. The Nine Spots glumly walked off the field and the umpire ruled the game a 9-0 forfeit. The newspapers criticized the club for the breach of etiquette (*Adrian* [Mich.] *Weekly Press*, August 29, 1879). More important, their action in walking off the field helped to pave the way for the "walkoff" hit.

This and similar incidents made it obvious that a custom once designed to promote good sportsmanship was instead creating ill will. The rule was finally changed that offseason, so that "if the side at bat in the ninth innings secures the winning run, the game is to be called without putting out three men as heretofore" (*Stevens Point* [Wisc.] *Journal*, December 13, 1879).

The first sudden-death victory in major league history took place on opening day of the National League's 1880 season and, with the visiting team still generally batting last (see **1.31**), the road team was victorious. In Cincinnati, Chicago rallied with two runs in the bottom of the ninth inning to defeat their hosts 4-3. The *Chicago Tribune* triumphantly reported that "It was nobody's victory till the last moment" (*Chicago Tribune*, May 2, 1880). The dramatic circumstances surrounding the National League's first "walkoff" home run are described in the entry "Rotations" (**6.3.13**).

1.26   New Balls. In early baseball it was customary to use a single ball in a match unless it was lost or entirely demolished. This reflected the simple reality that early baseballs were difficult to obtain and costly to replace.

For example, at one of the first matches ever played in San Francisco, a field had been found and teams arranged before it was realized that no suitable ball was available. A committee was formed, and the problem was solved only when one of its members "came across a German immigrant who was the possessor of a pair of rubber overshoes. These he bought, after much dickering, for $10, and with the yarn unraveled from a woolen stocking and a piece of a rubber overshoe the first ball ever used in this city was made" (John Durkee, quoted in the *San Francisco Examiner*, November 19, 1888).

A similar response was elicited in Rochester, New York, when the secretary of the Flour City Club "ordered the first white horsehide ball, just one" from the Atlantic Club of Brooklyn. He later recalled the reverence with which it was treated: "What a host of the boys came to see it and to have a kindly handling" (quoted in Priscilla Astifan, "Baseball in the Nineteenth Century," *Rochester History* LII, no. 3 [Summer 1990], 10–11).

John Gruber noted that the ball's status as a precious commodity was reflected in the syntax of baseball's early rules: "Until 1876, the word 'ball' was never used in the plural number. One ball was expected to be sufficient. In that year, for the first time, a second ball was provided for. The rule said: 'Should the ball be lost during the game, the umpire shall, at the expiration of five minutes, call for a new ball,' and in 1877, 'the player looking for it shall call "lost ball," so that the umpire can note the time and wait five minutes.' The five-minute rule held until 1886, when it was abolished" (*Sporting News*, November 11, 1915).

The practice of looking for the ball for only five minutes was an improvement over the previous custom of having no limit on such searches. This could lead to long delays, especially when the club that was losing thought that darkness might avert a loss (*New York Clipper*, December 11, 1875). Al Pratt later recalled: "We used but one ball then, too, and when some strong batter would lose it, the whole gang, including the spectators, would set out to find it. Occasionally some scamp would run away with it, and then there would be all kinds of trouble" (quoted in *Sporting News*, March 23, 1895).

Only when baseball became more financially stable did this begin to change. Gruber adds, "In the olden days, when the ball was cut or ripped, needle and thread were brought into requisition there and then and the break mended. If the ball became out of shape, it was squeezed into some semblance of its natural form" (*Sporting News*, November 11, 1915).

In 1874 the National Association gave the umpire "the right to demand a new ball from the club furnishing the first one . . . whenever in his opinion said first one has become injured so as to be unfair for use (*Boston Globe*, March 3, 1874, 3). But when the National League came into existence two years later, the new circuit's umpires were instructed to replace a damaged ball only at the end of a complete inning.

Whether this change was intended to promote fairness or savings is not clear, but it meant that a baseball could not be replaced in mid-inning, no matter how bad its condition. Early that season, St. Louis captain Mike McGeary asked for the removal of a ripped ball, only to be reminded by umpire Mike Walsh that the inning would have to be completed first (*St. Louis*

Globe-Democrat, May 9, 1876). Six years later, Billy Purcell became so frustrated at the state of a baseball that he took a knife to it, earning him a hefty fine and the nickname "Cut-the-Ball" Purcell. It was not until 1884 that the umpire was given the authority to immediately replace an unfit baseball.

Even then, misshapen balls were not typically replaced with brand-new ones. Clubs remained highly cost-conscious and would often roll out a baseball only slightly less worn. As late as the 1880s, managers like Harry Wright were keeping logs of the condition of every ball owned by their team.

Sporting Life reported in 1885, "In Chicago the umpire starts into the game with a couple of extra balls in his pocket and when a foul tip sends the sheepskin over the fence he merely rolls one of the 'extras' to the pitcher and goes right on with the game" (*Sporting Life*, July 15, 1885). This account seems to imply that clubs were letting spectators and passersby keep foul balls, but that was not the case. The novelty introduced in Chicago was merely that club employees, rather than the players themselves, were responsible for retrieving foul balls. It was not until well into the twentieth century that clubs began willingly to relinquish game balls, a development that is discussed under "Keeping Balls in Stands" (see **16.2.7**).

The Chicago model appears to have worked well, and in 1887 the rules formally required the home club to provide two balls for each game. At the end of that campaign the *New York Times* hailed the success of "the rule requiring the use of two balls, to avoid awaiting return of a foul ball batted out of the grounds" (*New York Times*, October 9, 1887).

The presence of multiple balls offered clubs an opportunity for subterfuge that often proved irresistible. Sometimes this entailed clearly illegal efforts to replace the game ball with a dead or lively one, as discussed under "Double-ball Rackets" (see **11.1.12**). But other clubs found more subtle ways to use the presence of an extra ball to their advantage.

Late in the 1884 season, a row took place during a game in St. Louis: "[Henry] Boyle, of the St. Louis, knocked a foul ball over the inner fence separating the field seats from the playing grounds. Captain [Phil] Baker, of the Nationals, called for a new ball under the rule allowing a new ball when the old one was knocked over the fence—the rule having been made to save time. [St. Louis] Captain [Fred] Dunlap ran and got the ball, and asked that the game go on, claiming that the rule about the new ball applied only to the outer fence." The visitors, hoping to benefit from a livelier ball, refused to continue play with the old ball and eventually the game was forfeited to St. Louis (*Cincinnati Enquirer*, October 12, 1884).

Tim Murnane later recalled an 1888 game in which Boston hosted Washington with a steady rain falling. Both game balls became sodden, so Boston manager John Morrill craftily ordered the groundskeeper to pretend to lose foul balls when Boston was at bat so that new, livelier balls would have to be introduced. Instead, every time a foul was hit, a ball would immediately be thrown back on the field. Morrill accused the groundskeeper of insubordination but found that he was not at fault. Washington manager Ted Sullivan had anticipated the ploy and "had borrowed all of their old practice balls, gone into the grandstand and as fast as the balls disappeared sent an old one back in its place" (*Sporting News*, November 21, 1907).

Nor were these the only types of shenanigans that took place as a result of having only two baseballs. Another tactic is described in this 1891 account: "After Terre Haute had piled up eight runs and the visitors only one, Manager [Rasty] Wright made a hard kick because there was no new ball in play. One had been fouled over the fence and was not in play. The other one had been lost or hidden. Wright demanded that the game should be forfeited to him, and after a wrangle of about forty minutes, a new ball was brought out from town. All this 'rag chewing' did not change the result of the game" (*Grand Rapids* [Mich.] *Democrat*, May 21, 1891).

This problem arose even in the major leagues from time to time. In an American Association game in Brooklyn on July 27, 1890, the home team led 18-8 in the eighth inning but had to forfeit because the supply of balls had been exhausted. A National League game in Louisville on May 23, 1895, was forfeited for the same reason (Retrosheet Website, Forfeit List).

In 1896 the National League created a requirement that home clubs have at least twelve balls available for each game. An 1893 article suggested a possible explanation for the newfound extravagance: "It is one of the unwritten rules that the professional clubs, whose prowess is the source of such enthusiastic delight to Young America, get their balls for nothing, the advertisement they give to a brand by using it being considered an equivalent. This is an important item, inasmuch as half a

dozen baseballs are often lost in a single game" ("How Base Balls Are Made," *Manufacturer and Builder*, April 1893).

Yet if this claim were true, the giveaways may not have continued for long, since clubs remained very unwilling to part with baseballs. A 1912 article made this rather perplexing claim: "The manufacturers are understood to donate the balls for the privilege of using the National and American League's endorsement; the balls are furnished the leagues by the makers, but the individual clubs pay the regular price for them to the league headquarters" (*Sporting News*, November 28, 1912).

The nineteenth century closed with owners still adamant about using no more baseballs than absolutely necessary. An 1897 *Sporting News* editorial criticized the regular "delay in providing a new ball when one of the two in play is 'batted out of sight of the umpire'" (*Sporting News*, January 9, 1897). Only in the twentieth century did it became customary to replace a baseball that had been damaged. A 1906 article referred to "the rule of furnishing new balls to umpires, instead of throwing out discolored ones from the bench" (*Sporting Life*, March 31, 1906).

In the teens and twenties, as baseball authorities tried to eliminate the emery ball and other trick pitches, balls began to be removed from play at the first sign of damage. Umpire Billy Evans claimed that during the 1915 season "hardly a game passed by in any league without some manager making accusations against the opposing pitcher. In addition, there was the 'mud ball,' the 'fingernail ball,' the 'talcum ball' and a host of others too numerous to mention." As a result, "the moment a pitcher got his fast ball to sailing, the batter would insist on an examination, a rough spot would usually be found," and the ball would be removed from play (*Atlanta Constitution*, January 16, 1916). As a result, between 1909 and 1916 the number of balls used per season in the major leagues nearly quadrupled (Vince Staten, *Why Is the Foul Pole Fair?*, 163).

Pitcher Eddie Cicotte observed in 1918 that the paranoia remained rampant: "Ban Johnson must have a whole truck full of balls that were thrown out of various games and forwarded to him for inspection. I understand that a number of these balls were analyzed by a chemist to determine if any foreign substance were rubbed on the surface. This analysis, so I am informed, showed that the ball had been treated with tobacco juice" (Eddie Cicotte, "The Secrets of

Successful Pitching," *Baseball Magazine*, July 1918, 268).

As will be discussed under "Rabbit Balls" (**9.1.3**), this new attitude toward replacing baseballs was largely responsible for ushering in the home run era. In 1931, with many feeling that home runs had become too commonplace, Lena Blackburne suggested keeping every ball in play until it became lost.

Professional baseball had become too lucrative an industry ever to go back, but the use of a single ball persisted at other levels of play. Early Wynn grew up in depression-era Alabama and recalled playing other towns with a single ball: "So if someone hit the ball into the bushes, it meant the game was over, unless we found it. We always found it. You had the whole population of two towns looking for that one baseball" (quoted in Roger Kahn, *Memories of Summer*, 209).

Nowadays the phrase "taking his ball and going home" is primarily a metaphor, yet like so many elements of baseball's rich language, it evokes an era when such events could bring a ballgame to a premature end.

1.27 Catchers Signaling to Pitchers.

A child learning the game of baseball is likely to wonder why the catcher signals the pitch to the pitcher rather than the other way around. It is a good question that once caused considerable discussion.

As late as 1896 an observer claimed that "all a catcher cares to know is whether his pitcher is about to throw a curve or a straight ball" (*Sporting News*, March 7, 1896). It might reasonably be supposed that signals were not used before the curveball came to prominence in the 1870s, but this is not entirely the case. The innovative Dickey Pearce, while filling in as a catcher, was already signaling locations to the pitcher in the mid-1860s. While catching Tommy Pratt, Pearce "kept his eye on the striker, and let Pratt know just where to deliver the ball" (*National Chronicle*, May 15, 1869).

In the pre-curve era, however, it appears to have been more common for the pitcher to give the signals, when signals were given at all. Henry Chadwick noted in 1871 that pitcher George Zettlein "will send the ball just where the catcher wants him to; and in this respect, perhaps, he is too compliant, for while the catcher should be allowed to have some influence over the pitcher in directing his fire, the pitcher ought to be master of his own actions" (*New York Clipper*, February 11, 1871). By

1874, Chadwick was counseling, "If the pitcher is familiar with a certain habit of the batsman before him of hitting at a favourite ball, he should give the catcher a sign informing him that he is going to send in a slower or swifter ball or a higher or lower one than ordinarily is pitched" (Henry Chadwick, *1874 Chadwick's American Base Ball Manual*, 14–15).

Arthur "Candy" Cummings, who retired in 1878, later reported: ". . . We used to have signals, but our catchers did not take care of them as they do now. I did all this myself, and they were so simple, too, that no opposing batsman got on to them for that reason" (*Sporting News*, February 20, 1897).

John Ward wrote in 1888: "Every battery, by which is meant a pitcher and catcher, must have a perfectly understood private code of signals, so that they may make known their intentions and wishes to another without at the same time apprising the opposing players. . . . Until within a few years this sign was always given by the pitcher, but now it is almost the universal practice for the catcher to give it to the pitcher, and if the latter doesn't want to pitch the ball asked for he changes the sign by a shake of the head" (John Ward, *Base-Ball: How to Become a Player*, 53).

Despite Ward's apparent certainty, the issue is not as clear-cut as he suggested. In 1871 the *New York Clipper* noted that it was common for the catcher to do "the 'headwork' in strategic play by directing—through private signals—the pitcher how to deliver particular balls" (*New York Clipper*, October 28, 1871). In 1883 a sportswriter commented disapprovingly, "In these days it has become almost a fashion for old catchers to give the pitcher signs to pitch. Such is not the catcher's office. A pitcher, to be effective, should deliver his ball as he chooses himself, sizing up his batsman and signing to his catcher what he pitches. Unless such tactics are followed, half the pitcher's effectiveness is destroyed" ("Chicago exchange," *Rocky Mountain News*, November 26, 1883, 2). Another issue was that many catchers saw signals as an insult, suggesting that they could not catch the pitcher's offerings without advanced warning (Peter Morris, *Catcher*, 160–163).

Accordingly it appears that there was no uniformity as to which member of the battery gave the signals until the 1880s, when the catcher took control. That same decade saw the emergence of "sign stealing" (see **6.5.2**), and it seems safe to assume that the primary reason for the change was that the catcher is out of the batter's range of vision and is also in better position to keep his signals hidden from the coaches and the bench.

Even after it became the norm for the catcher to give the signals, there were exceptions. An 1886 article offered only a conditional endorsement, suggesting that allowing the catcher to give the signs "is a better plan when the catcher is a cool and experienced man" (*Boston Globe*, June 26, 1886). Star pitcher Charley Radbourn continued to do "all the signaling himself, and only [use] a sign for his outcurves" (*Williamsport Sunday Grit*, May 24, 1891). Meanwhile Chicago pitcher Bill Hutchison was said to call his own pitches but to shake his "head 'yes' or 'no' pretending the catcher is calling them" (*Milwaukee Daily Journal*, April 25, 1891; Frank Vaccaro).

Christy Mathewson noted that during the 1911 World Series he gave the signs to catcher "Chief" Meyers in order to thwart the Athletics' sign stealers (Christy Mathewson, *Pitching in a Pinch*, 151). Cy Young and Lou Criger went one step further, simply dispensing with signs if they suspected sign stealing (Reed Browning, *Cy Young*, 159).

At least one pitcher felt that catchers took advantage of the prerogative to call pitches by requesting only pitches that were easy to catch. Al Krumm complained in 1889: "At Dayton catchers would catch nothing but a straight ball and out-curve, and when a pitcher shook his head and delivered anything else, they jumped aside and let it pass as a wild pitch" (*Dayton Journal*, August 14, 1889).

1.28 Specialization. Early baseball clubs selected their nine best players and then assigned them to positions without much agonizing. If that combination did not seem to work, a different one was tried. As Henry Chadwick noted in 1867, "Some ten years ago, and even later, it was a rare sight to witness a ball match, played anywhere, or by any parties, which was not marked by changes in the positions of the players in nearly every innings" (*The Ball Player's Chronicle*, June 13, 1867).

The idea that each position required specialized skills developed very quickly and soon became a key part of baseball's ideological underpinnings. Chadwick was its most ardent champion and, typically, he missed no opportunity to condemn "the old-fogy style of making up even sides on practice-days rather than of playing each member of their nine on their regular positions" (*New York Clipper*, June

10, 1865). In an 1867 article he contended that "The change in regard to keeping players in their regular positions was a natural sequence of an improved knowledge of the points of the game" (*The Ball Player's Chronicle*, June 13, 1867). A few weeks later he offered this illustration of his point: "it is injudicious to take an outfielder, accustomed to running catches and long throws, and place him in the in-field, where his business is to stop hot ground balls and to make short and accurate throws" (*The Ball Player's Chronicle*, July 4, 1867).

Other writers picked up on the theme. An 1866 victory was described as "a striking illustration of the advantages arising from playing a nine in their regular positions always and as a whole" (*New York Tribune*, June 11, 1866). An 1874 defeat led the local paper to "suggest to the Modoc club that they practice oftener, and that each man be assigned the position he is best capable of playing, and retain and play in that place in every game" (*Adrian* [Mich.] *Daily Press*, April 27, 1874).

How this general principle manifested itself in specific requirements for the various positions is discussed in Chapter 4 on fielding.

1.29 Competitiveness. Competitiveness became a part of baseball very early, but the willingness to acknowledge this fact came much more gradually. Whatever may have been in the hearts of baseball players of the 1860s, maxims about chivalry were on their tongues. Indeed, in the 1860s many clubs seemed to protest too much that they didn't really want to win.

A perfect example occurred after two Michigan clubs met on Independence Day, 1863. The Monitor Club of Niles lost to the Daybreak Club of Jackson and was dissatisfied with the outcome. Nonetheless, in voicing this sentiment the club was anxious not to be perceived as caring about the result: "we do not claim [the game], nor do we care for it, but we have made these statements for the purpose of showing that if we were beaten, we were not beaten by the Day Breaks [sic] as a club but by a single member of the club and that member the Umpire." The Daybreaks responded in similar fashion: "we cared very little at that time to win the game . . . [and] regret exceedingly that anything occurred to mar the pleasure of the game" (*Niles Republican*, July 25, 1863).

Clubs were chastised if they gave the impression of caring about "vulgar" considerations like winning and losing. Henry Chadwick wrote in 1862 that "There is far too much of this great desire to win matches prevalent for the best interest of the game" (*Brooklyn Eagle*, July 28, 1862). Chadwick frequently denounced clubs that obeyed the letter rather than the spirit of the rules for what he termed "playing the points." One club's song counseled, "And should any club by their cunning and trick / Dishonor the game that it plays / Let them take my advice and go to 'Old Knick' [the Knickerbocker Club] / And there learn to better their ways" (quoted in James DiClerico and Barry Pavelec, *The Jersey Game*, 27).

By the end of the decade, times were changing. Reflecting the changing times, the 1870s saw baseball's rule makers begin the long slow process of converting the game's governing principles into a set of rules that covered every contingency. They had plenty of help in this endeavor, because every loophole they left was quickly exploited.

An 1885 writer noted: "In the 'good old days' it was considered dishonorable for a player to claim he had put a player out when he knew he hadn't. Now every player is expected to make the claim of bluff, as they call it, and if they can work the umpire so much the better. This is certainly a most reprehensible practice, as it has more to do with putting an audience onto an umpire than any other thing. It is a common thing to see a player make a bluff at putting out a man and throw down the ball, and the whole side start in as a matter of course. . . . It is a common occurrence for the captains and members of the different teams to claim men are out or not, as their interests may dictate, and when they fail to get the decision they want they make remarks or motions indicative of disgust, as much as to say 'we are being robbed of the game'" (*Sporting Life*, June 3, 1885).

In 1886, John I. Rogers, co-owner of the Philadelphia club, accused Chicago of embodying the maxim "Anything to Win" by using "questionable tactics and dishonest points of play, which the rules seem powerless to prevent." Rogers cited these examples: "Disconcerting the opposing pitcher, catcher, or fielder by loud yells or irrelevant remarks under pretense of coaching. Knocking or bunting foul balls with the object of wearing out or demoralizing a pitcher. Colliding with or spiking an opponent. Falling upon or tripping an opposing baserunner. When the baserunner is on third for the coacher to run in along the foul line so that the opposing pitcher or catcher may confuse him with the baserunner. When

a baserunner is on second, while the umpire is looking at an 'out on first,' for the former to steal from short field to home plate without crossing third. Constant kicking, bulldozing, and appeals to the umpire on points not at all doubtful with the hope that the subsequent and really close decisions will compensatorily be in their favor. Objecting to the substitution of a new player for one manifestly injured in the game, as in the subject of this inquiry, and the hundreds of other unmanly, unchivalrous, and unsportsmanlike acts and deeds which have so often disgusted the losers of fair play and honorable rivalry in athletic contests" (*Chicago Tribune*, September 22, 1886).

A generation earlier, the mere mention of terms like "unchivalrous" and "unsportsmanlike" would have been enough to ensure an apologetic reply. Instead this was the response of the *Chicago Tribune*: "talk about 'chivalry' is nonsense. The best ball-players are those who, keeping within the rules of the game, resort to all manner of devices to bring them success. Rattling the pitcher by bunting a number of foul balls or in any other way under the rules is proper. It is a point of the game, and the Captain of the nine and his men are not earning their salaries if they fail to do it. There is no chivalry about it. Everything a club can legally get . . . is so much to its credit" (*Chicago Tribune*, September 23, 1886).

This new attitude created a generation of players for whom the letter of the law was all that mattered. The 1890s spawned players like John McGraw, who freely admitted, "I had trained myself . . . to think up little and big things that might be anticipated by the rule changers. . . . With us, only the written rule counted . . . and if you could come up with something not covered by the rules, you were ahead of the slower-thinking opposition by at least a full season" (quoted in David Voigt, *The League That Failed*, 63).

Such sentiments were very upsetting to old-timers like Henry Chadwick. The venerable sportswriter wrote in 1887, "'hustling,' in base ball parlance—as far as my experience in watching the movements of 'hustling' managers goes—is to gain your ends in working up a team without regard to the character of the means to be employed. 'He's a hustler' means, generally, that the club manager in question is unscrupulous in his methods, tricky in his ways, and only kept within the bounds of honesty in his business by the controlling power of the law. I'd have none such in my club if

I was a club president" (*Brooklyn Eagle*, February 6, 1887).

Chadwick continued to denounce "what is called the 'hustling' and aggressive style of play," complaining that "Too many scribes—one in particular—appear to regard 'aggressiveness' and hustling as especially applicable to manly play in the field, whereas both are terms appropriate to the very reverse object. . . . Webster defines 'hustling' as 'shaking together, pushing and crowding.' The base ball definition of the word as illustrated in the professional arena, is simply to endeavor to win a game either by fair means or foul. 'Hustling' is, according to the base ball definition of the word, to yell like a mad bull on the coaching lines; to prevent a batsman or a fielder or base runner from making his point of play by irritating or balking him; by wilfully colliding with him, or tripping him up by striking him on his arm to prevent his throwing accurately, by yelling at him when about to catch a ball; in fact by any one of the means of prevention of playing his point known under the generic term of 'dirty ball playing.' The other favorite term with the scribes in question as well as magnates and team managers is that of having their team made 'aggressive.' Now Webster defines this word as 'the first act of hostility; also of injury and of calling to war,' and the 'aggressor' he defines as he who first begun a quarrel or an assault. Here you have the correct definition of the terms 'aggressive' and 'hustling.' It is simply quarrelling and assaulting, so forcibly illustrated in the hustling game of foot ball of the period." He concluded by comparing "the 'aggressive' 'hustling' method advocated by certain scribes and managers" to "hoodlumism" and contrasting it with "manly, chivalric and honorable" conduct (*Sporting News*, March 23, 1895).

Chadwick was fighting not merely a losing battle but one that had already been lost. The more he railed against "the 'aggressive hustling' method of play," the more obvious it became that no one was listening (*Sporting Life*, June 9, 1894). As described in entry **6.1.3**, a whole school of managers known as "Hustlers" had come to the fore in the 1870s. Terms like "aggressive" and "hustling" may have been restricted to those meanings to men of Chadwick's generation, but a new generation was adopting them as a badge of honor. An 1895 article contained a boast about a club that was "an outfit of hustlers," while a note the following year stated, "Baltimore always appreciates the services of faithful, hustling players like McGraw" (*Sporting Life*, March 30, 1895; *Boston Globe*, July 2, 1896).

By the early twentieth century the term's new connotations were so established that the *Cleveland News* wrote in 1909, "Hustlers are admired the world over. Men who never will admit defeat, but will keep on fighting to the end always make their marks in the world" (reprinted in *Sporting News*, July 1, 1909). Just as the nineteenth century had seen the connotations of terms such as "prejudice" and "discrimination" transformed from positive to negative, so too formerly derogatory terms such as "aggressive" and "hustling" had been reinvented as the property of overachievers.

By the twentieth century, the rulebook had been tightened to virtually eliminate loopholes. As a result, the few remnants of the days when competitiveness had been frowned upon began to seem increasingly anachronistic. Jim Brosnan commented on the injunction against "deception" in the balk rule: "Deceive is a most ponderous choice of words. What in hell do they think a pitcher is doing when he throws a curve ball? If deceit is, in truth, a flagrant violation of baseball morality, then the next logical step is to ban breaking balls, and let the hitter call his pitch" (Jim Brosnan, *The Long Season*, 86).

1.30   Low Scoring. Most knowledgeable baseball fans today have a sense that a low-scoring game is baseball at its finest. For many of us, this is not really our preference. Yet just as we may read best-sellers while thinking that we ought to be reading classics, there is an indefinable sense of guilty pleasure in watching an 11-9 game. Like so many elements of baseball, this guilt is a legacy of the early days of baseball and, in particular, the influence of pioneer sportswriter Henry Chadwick.

Baseball in the 1850s and 1860s was a very high-scoring game. The combination of rubbery baseballs, restrictions on pitchers, and poor field conditions made it very difficult for gloveless fielders to record outs. As a result, a base hit came to be viewed as nothing special while a putout was a sign of great skill. Reporters picked up on this and heaped praise on great fielders and on clubs that played low-scoring games. As early as 1860 it was becoming a byword that "in baseball low figures represent good play" (*Troy Daily Whig*, account of July 3, 1860, match; quoted in Richard A. Puff, ed., *Troy's Baseball Heritage*, 6).

This tendency was so pronounced that it began to exert a powerful influence on how the game was played. Until 1869 most baseballs contained two and a half ounces of rubber, but the next two seasons saw a dramatic reduction in that amount. By the middle of the 1870 season, adoption of a dead ball was a foregone conclusion: "From the many accidents which have lately happened in consequence of using a 'lively' ball, one in which there is a large quantity of rubber, it has been pretty generally determined by the leading clubs of the country to employ what is known as the 'dead' ball in future" (*Chicago Post*, reprinted in the *Detroit Advertiser and Tribune*, August 1, 1870). The dead ball was formally adopted at the convention of the National Association of Base Ball Players on November 30, 1870, with balls being limited to no more than one ounce of rubber.

Scores naturally plunged as a result, and the trend was accelerated by liberalized pitching rules, improved playing fields, and, eventually, fielder's equipment. By the mid-1870s, shutouts had become commonplace and the 46-38 scores of the 1860s had vanished forever.

What is most surprising about this development is the response from sportswriters, with Chadwick at the forefront. Instead of attributing this trend to changed conditions, they extolled lower scores as proof that baseball had become a "scientific" game. A typical 1878 report exclaimed that "Base ball has been reduced to an exact science, and we read of fifteen innings with only one tally" (*Fremont* [Mich.] *Indicator*, May 15, 1878). In contrast, an 1874 game with a 28-14 score was dismissed out of hand as having a "score too large to call it a good game" (*Adrian* [Mich.] *Press*, June 11, 1874).

In addition to trying to convince readers that lower-scoring games were aesthetically superior, sportswriters of the 1870s and 1880s sought to portray such games as more exciting. Part of this view was that low-scoring games tended to be close, but it went well beyond that. For example, a twelve-inning 1-0 game caused a reporter to gush, "Altogether the closest and most exciting game ever played in the city. . . . From the time the game commenced until the close of the long contest the interest was at fever heat" (*Grand Rapids* [Mich.] *Times*, June 17, 1883). Yet after a ten-inning 10-9 thriller, the players were dourly admonished to "bear in mind that such games are calculated to shake the confidence their backers and the public have had in them, and will have a tendency to lessen their receipts at the turnstile" (*Detroit Free Press*, June 15, 1881).

It is harder to determine whether fans actually found low-scoring games more exciting or whether this notion was a creation of the press. There is some evidence of the latter. Despite Henry Chadwick's advocacy of 1-0 games, a reporter observed in 1891 that, "The public's idea of an exciting game is one where the pitchers are not effective and the game see saws first one way and then another" (*Williamsport Sunday Grit*, April 12, 1891). At the same time, however, strikeouts had begun to dominate baseball and, as discussed in entry **1.17** and in the introduction to chapter 3, no one considered strikeouts entertaining or good baseball.

In any case, the press's insistent preference for low-scoring games had an enormous effect on the perception of baseball. Scores have fluctuated in the years since, but there has remained a sense that low-scoring baseball is purer and that a high-scoring game is, at best, a guilty pleasure.

1.31 Home Team Last. It was not until 1950 that the home team was required by rule to bat last. By then, what had once been viewed as a significant strategic decision had become so routine that hardly anyone noticed.

Robin Carver wrote in 1834 that in "base, or goal ball," play began when "chance decides which shall have the first innings" (Robin Carver, *The Boy's and Girl's Book of Sports*, 37). This custom was maintained by the Knickerbockers, whose third rule dictated a coin toss for first ups. This practice continued for many years, though what was tossed might vary. A 1921 article about Candy Cummings noted that in his era, "ball clubs at the start of the game tossed up for their raps" by playing "'hand over hand' on the bat" (*Sporting News*, December 29, 1921). According to an 1887 reminiscence, in "the game called baseball by the country boys of twenty years ago . . . The two best players were selected to 'choose sides,' and they sometimes decided who should have first choice of players by tossing up a stone, upon which one of them had solemnly spat. One called out 'wet' and the other 'dry'; the falling of the stone decided the matter. But the more common method was for one of the two 'choosers' to toss a ball club into the air; the other would catch it and then there was a superimposing of grasped hands. This method was called 'choosing up,' and the one who held the club last had first choice. But he had to have a firm grip, and it was decided whether he had a fair hold by his ability to toss it over his head. If he had hold by but one finger he often failed. Sometimes this important matter was settled by 'driving down.' If the grasp on the club was less than a full hand (no allusion to the great game of poker intended), it was not enough" ("Old Baseball," *Indianapolis Sentinel*, April 3, 1887).

But the contemporary accounts that are specific invariably refer to a coin toss. For example, Henry Chadwick wrote in 1867 that in New York "our players generally take the field when they win the choice, in order to have the last chance at bat" (*The Ball Player's Chronicle*, June 6, 1867). Note how similar this reasoning is to today's philosophy. Nevertheless, little attention was directed to the issue of which club batted first in the 1860s, suggesting that it was not considered particularly important.

The change to less elastic balls in the early 1870s appears to have changed both the thinking about the decision and its perceived significance. Captains increasingly began to choose to bat first in order to have the first crack at the new ball. The 1921 article about Candy Cummings noted that "Both teams wanted to be on the offensive right off the reel." When Cummings earned the right to choose, as he usually did, "his club took the first clouts and proceeded in a lusty endeavor to whale in enough runs to discourage the opposition at the outset and incidentally put the ball in such a delapidated [sic] condition that it could not be batted far when the opposing team arrived at bat" (*Sporting News*, December 29, 1921).

A 1914 article noted: ". . . Many years ago, it was equally the rule for the home team to bat first, and the argument on which the managers maintained the system was the supposed advantage of 'getting the first crack at the new ball!' When the game was played with only one ball, and was held up till that ball came back after every journey, a hard-hitting club could, very often, get a flock of runs by starting right in at the jump, taking first bat and collecting hits before the other team had any chance. By the time that ball was turned over to the other club it was black and hard to hit—hence an actual and indisputable advantage for the team first at bat" (*Detroit News*, September 1, 1914).

Reflecting this apparent consensus, an 1877 rule change dictated that the home team bat first (*Chicago Tribune*, December 10, 1876, 7). After one season the pregame toss was restored, and most sources suggest that it continued to be the norm for the winners to choose to bat first.

Perplexingly, however, Henry Chadwick wrote in 1879: "In the Boston-Syracuse games at Boston, Mass., the home team has almost won the toss, and, instead of sending their opponents to the bat, as is usual, they have taken the bat first themselves, and in such cases invariably started off with too strong a lead to overcome" (*New York Clipper*, August 30, 1879).

On June 5, 1885, the American Association adopted a new rule making it the home captain's choice, and the National League followed suit in 1887 (David Nemec, *The Beer and Whisky League*, 101). In the mid-1880s most captains elected to bat first, with the *Detroit Free Press* offering this explanation in 1886: "Why does the captain who has won [the coin toss] send his team to bat? Simply this, gentle reader: The ball is new and white and the ball-tosser loves a shining mark to bang at with a bat. Again the new ball is so smooth and slippery, the pitcher cannot grasp it firmly, and is unable to impart to the sphere the delusive drops, or the deadly in-shoot, with as much effect as when the ball has become black from the pounding it has received, and from incidental excursions into the mud. Thus it is that Captain [Ned] Hanlon and all other field captains when they win the toss, elect to go to bat" (*Detroit Free Press*, May 17, 1886).

By 1887, however, the question was again being reexamined: "Some managers believe that it is an advantage to go to bat first in a game, because the opposing pitcher has not yet settled down and the batsmen are fresh and eager. Other managers, however, consider it a special advantage to go to bat last, as in event of a close game the pitcher knows that his side has an extra opportunity to overcome any lead of their opponents, and is therefore not as apt to become uneasy and nervous as if his opponents had another inning to play" (*St. Louis Post-Dispatch*, June 25, 1887).

A later article gave this account of the reasons: ". . . When the statute was introduced providing a fresh white ball whenever the original ball vanished, this advantage was destroyed. . . . And yet, though the situation was thus altered, it took seven or eight years to wake up the managers and make them realize that they didn't get anything by taking first bats any more. Now, you couldn't get them to budge from the present custom. [Cap] Anson was the last manager who occasionally changed round. If the Old Man saw a young, green and nervous pitcher getting ready—especially on a cold day—he'd take first bats, and his sluggers would make life a burden for the kid before he got his bearings. Many and many a time Anson's men rolled up 6 or 7 runs on kid pitchers in the first inning—and if the other manager replaced his novice with a veteran, the vet probably had a chilled arm, went in unprepared to pitch, and got his beatings likewise" (*Detroit News*, September 1, 1914).

By 1891 batting last had become the norm, though there were still exceptions. A game account that year observed: "Captain [Johnny] Ward varied his point of going in last at the bat on this occasion for a special reason. In the first place it was a batsman's day in having the wind with him; secondly, it was a good point to play to try and take the wind out of the sails of the enemy by a brilliant onslaught on their works at the outset, and it worked beautifully in yesterday's game" (*Brooklyn Eagle*, June 13, 1891).

A rule change the following year gave managers an added incentive to bat last, as the *Brooklyn Eagle* explained: "There is an important advantage accruing to the position of being last at the bat which the new rule governing the ending of a game after four and a half innings have been played has very plainly developed, and the Philadelphia team was the first to benefit by it. The rule in question provides that, if four and a half innings are played, the side that has not been at bat wins if it was in the lead at the close of the first part of the inning. Suppose that in Monday's game, with the score of 3 to 2 in favor of Cleveland at the end of the fourth inning, Brooklyn had drawn a blank in their fifth inning, and at the close of the first part of the fifth inning a storm of rain had set in and stopped play for the day, Cleveland would have won the incompleted four and a half inning game legally by 3 to 2, owing to their being last at bat. This advantage causes Harry Wright to send his team last to the bat every time they play on home grounds. Captain Ward, apparently, loses sight of this new rule" (*Brooklyn Eagle*, June 8, 1892).

Eventually it became customary for the home captain to choose last ups. A rare but noteworthy exception took place when Frank Chance chose to bat first in a July 16 game against the Giants during the legendary 1908 pennant race; the strategy did not work, however, as Chicago lost the game.

The introduction of the cork-centered ball and the increased use of new baseballs eliminated the one perceived benefit to batting first. By 1914 "all clubs go to the field first when on the home grounds; the custom has become firmly rooted, and no manager ever thinks of changing" (*Detroit News*, September 1, 1914). Nevertheless it was not until 1950, with a general recodification of the rules, that what had become the universal practice of the home team batting last was written into the rules.

1.32   Substitutions. In early baseball the nine players in a club's lineup were usually the only ones who participated in the game. Clubs generally brought no more than ten men to a game, and the substitute was not allowed to enter the game unless one of the starters became ill or injured. This was typical of nineteenth-century team sports; even early hockey did not allow substitutes (Michael McKinley, *Putting a Roof on Winter*, 7).

For many years the opposing team's captain actually had to approve injury substitutions, which could lead to conflict. In an 1867 match between the Mutuals and Irvingtons, a brawl broke out in the stands and Hugh Campbell of the Irvingtons was injured in trying to break it up. The Mutuals at first refused to allow a substitute, but the captain finally relented when the Irvingtons said they would have to play with only eight players. Henry Chadwick wrote that the Mutuals were correct that the substitution did not have to be accepted since it did not occur during the game. But he commended them for their sportsmanship (*The Ball Player's Chronicle*, July 4, 1867).

The lone exception to the prohibition on substitutions was the courtesy runner (see **6.2.6**). But it was other members of the starting lineup who were used in this role, rather than reserve players. The concept of replacing a player during a game for poor performance or for tactical reasons was simply not part of early baseball. Players were expected to finish what they started—a mind-set that continued to be part of baseball for many years and, to some extent, still is.

The rules were modified in the 1870s to allow a substitution in the early innings. The purpose of this rule was not to enable strategic substitutions but instead had a more practical intention. If a game was scheduled to begin and a starter had not made his appearance, that player's club was likely to try to stall until he arrived. The early-inning substitution rule thus served a practical purpose by allowing the game to begin with a backup who could be replaced when the regular arrived (William J. Ryczek, *Baseball's First Inning*, 58).

At first the rule permitted substitutions until the start of the fourth inning, but that was too lax for many. Following the 1876 season, the *Chicago Tribune* grumbled that the rule "as it now stands, is indefinite, and means nothing, or if it has a meaning, it is that either club have a right to change any part, or the whole, of their nine up to the end of the fourth inning—a thing probably never contemplated by the gentlemen who made the rule" (*Chicago Tribune*, November 19, 1876, 10). At the winter meeting the following month, the rule was changed to allow latecomers to be substituted only if they had arrived by the end of the first inning (*Chicago Tribune*, December 10, 1876, 7).

This led to some ticklish situations. Boston's Curry Foley missed the train for an 1880 game in Worcester and, since he was one of the few players who had had success against Worcester pitcher Lee Richmond, Boston sought to prolong the game until he arrived on a later train. As it turned out, the first inning was indeed lengthy enough, and "the wanderer was rushed on the field in a hack before the inning was over." There was, however, no rejoicing by his teammates because the home side had piled up fifteen runs in that extended first inning (*Worcester Gazette*, May 18, 1880).

In 1881 the old rule that replacements were allowed only in the case of injury or illness was restored. One problem that ensued was that there was often no substitute ready when the need arose—with strategic substitutions illegal, clubs usually had only nine or ten players on hand. If there was an extra, he often manned the turnstile or had other duties, with the result that many early diamonds featured only one bench (see 14.4.6). The *Cincinnati Enquirer* suggested in 1878, "The tenth man should be held ready in uniform to take the place of a disabled player at a moment's notice. Then there would be no unpleasant delay" (*Cincinnati Enquirer*, May 3, 1878). But even after an 1887 rule mandated that substitutes be in uniform, few clubs seem to have complied.

A more serious problem was caused by the provision that the opposing captain had to approve these substitutions as the result of "illness or injury." During a game on August 28, 1886, Chicago's "Cap" Anson refused to allow injured Philadelphia catcher Jim McGuire to be replaced, causing Philadelphia co-owner John I. Rogers to denounce Chicago for its "questionable tactics and dishonest points of play, which the rules seem powerless to pre-

vent" (*Chicago Tribune*, September 22, 1886). The matter became so contentious that depositions of the participants were taken. Two years later, New York forfeited a game after Anson refused to allow injured catcher "Buck" Ewing to be replaced, prompting another volley of angry charges and countercharges (*Chicago Tribune*, September 13, 1888, 3; see Peter Morris, *Catcher*, 155–156, for a full discussion of both incidents and their aftermaths). And Anson was not alone. His intransigence on the issue may have been the result of a game on August 5, 1884, in which deaf-mute pitcher Thomas S. Lynch made his only major league appearance for Chicago. Lynch held the lead after seven innings but then claimed to have hurt his arm. When the opposing captain refused to allow a replacement, Lynch and Anson were forced to switch places. Anson then gave up four runs to earn the loss, his only major league decision.

With the Ewing incident in mind, replacing a healthy player was finally made legal after the 1888 season, but only one such move could be made per game, and the substitute had to be specified on the scorecard. Although he recognized this provision as the "most radical change made in the playing rules," Henry Chadwick saw it as a more lenient interpretation of the problematic term "illness or injury." He explained that captains could now make a substitution if "the pitcher is giving out or . . . his catcher's hands are not in good condition, though neither player is disabled to the extent covered by the terms 'illness or injury'" (Henry Chadwick, *Evansville Journal*, April 27, 1889, 7). The number of substitutes was increased to two in 1890, but they still had to be designated beforehand. Unlimited substitutions were finally legalized in 1891, though for cost and philosophical reasons their use remained limited for several years.

This development brought a new degree of complexity to the manager's role, as is discussed in part two of Chapter 6. It also had a pervasive but subtler influence on many other elements of baseball, such as making it feasible for umpires to eject players from games (see 8.3.2) and leading to a change in the numbering system used by scorekeepers (see 26.3.6).

In a 1958 column, Red Smith reported that Lew Fonseca had proposed that players be allowed to return to the game after being substituted for, as happens in most other sports (Red Smith, August 7, 1958, reprinted in *Red Smith on Baseball*). In some ways this notion represented the logical culmination of the direction in which baseball had been heading since its earliest days.

Nonetheless baseball has been reluctant to go too far down the path of specialization, as demonstrated by the strong feelings that are still generated by the designated hitter. The continued emphasis on "finishing what you start" is also reflected in the frequent complaints about "seven-inning pitchers" and the demise of the complete game. Yet this principle is at odds with another important one: the belief that baseball should include and value the participation of as many people as possible. The inevitable clash between these two underlying principles is, I believe, the reason for the passion engendered by debates about the designated hitter.

1.33 Overhand Pitching.

In early baseball the pitcher was restricted to a fully underhand, straight-arm motion. The term "pitching" was thus very apt, because the motion was akin to pitching a horseshoe. But very early on, pitchers began to bend their arm or break their wrist in order to create greater speed or spin.

A series of rules were enacted in the 1860s and 1870s to try to restrict pitchers, but they quickly found ways around them. In 1872 pitchers were allowed to release the ball from the hip, but the liberalized rule only encouraged many of them to try to get away with still higher release points. When the National League legislated in 1878 that pitchers had to release the ball from below the waist, pitchers began wearing their belts deceptively high (A. G. Spalding, *America's National Game*, 484; James Wood, as told to Frank G. Menke, "Baseball in By-Gone Days," part 2, syndicated column, *Marion* [Ohio] *Star*, August 15, 1916). Each new rule change just led to more bickering and more hardships for umpires. The pitcher's motion eventually bore so little resemblance to the original intent that the *New Orleans Times* quipped in 1877, "[Ed "The Only"] Nolan, it may be remarked, is called the pitcher of the Indianapolis club; but why pitcher does not appear upon the surface, for the reason that his delivery of the ball is an underhand throw" (*New Orleans Times*, March 15, 1877; reprinted in *New York Clipper*, March 24, 1877).

Finally, in 1884, "the league gave up trying to fight the pitchers who wanted to deliver the ball with a swift overhand motion, and the pitching rules were so amended that the pitcher could throw or pitch the ball as suited his fancy. It was found useless trying to contend against the advances of the pitcher, and, in order to even matters as much as possible, the number of balls entitling a batter to first base was reduced" (*Detroit Free Press*, March 31, 1895).

Although this change would prove to be of monumental significance, not all saw it that way at the time. Star pitcher Tim Keefe believed that overhand pitching would prove impractical, explaining: "the higher the ball is thrown, the harder it is upon the arm. No pitcher can stand the strain, and the result will be that the arm must be kept down. [Jim] Whitney, Radbourne [Charley Radbourn], and [Jim] Galvin kept their arms up as high as they cared to last season, which is the best reason in the world for the fact that they won't throw any higher this season. They would not be able to stand the strain if they ever tried it. Then a high thrown ball is not so deceptive nor so hard as a ball delivered from below the shoulder. The pitcher delivering the ball high above his shoulder will probably deliver it straight, as the curve entails too much of a strain upon the arm" (*Cleveland Leader*, April 10, 1884). As we know, Keefe's prediction was wrong, but he was correct that baseball as constituted in 1884 could not accommodate overhand pitching. But instead of pitchers abandoning the overhand motion, as Keefe had forecasted, the game was forced to make a volley of changes that included pitching rotations (see 6.3.13), catcher's chest protectors and mitts (see 9.4.5 and 9.3.2), and the sixty feet, six inches pitching distance (see 1.17).

The American Association stuck with the shoulder restriction in 1884, but its umpires were becoming increasingly restless. Longtime umpire Charles Daniels expressed the view "that it will be impossible to enforce the pitching rules of the American Association code, which obliges the pitcher to deliver the ball from below the line of the shoulder. He prefers the League rule, which gives the pitcher perfect freedom to deliver the ball as high as he likes" (*National Police Gazette*, April 26, 1884). The American Association finally followed the lead of the National League on June 7, 1885, in a rare mid-season rule change. Pitchers' deliveries are discussed at much greater length in Chapter 3, part one.

Chapter 2

BATTING

THE ART of hitting has been aptly described as the paradox of swinging a round bat at a round ball and trying to hit it squarely. Lengthy treatises are now written on the proper biomechanical and psychological approaches to hitting. In the early days of baseball, however, hitting didn't seem all that difficult, and with good reason. Pitchers were restricted to underhand tosses to batters, who could request high or low pitches. Fielders wore no gloves and played on wildly uneven surfaces with nothing to shield their eyes from the glare of the afternoon sun. With everything in their favor, batters understandably saw little reason to do anything other than whale away and try to hit the ball out of sight.

Robert Smith captured the spirit when he claimed: "The Knickerbockers had taken it for granted that any red-blooded man would want to take a healthy cut at the ball to see how far he could drive it" (Robert Smith, *Baseball*, 42).

Things began to change when new pitching techniques, new equipment, and better playing fields began to alter the balance of power. The 74-56 scores of the 1860s gave way to 4-2 results in the 1870s. As a result, frustrated hitters began to develop new techniques and tactics and even to define success differently.

These innovations have been divided into four categories: (i) evolutionary attempts that modified the approach but didn't directly challenge the premise that success was a ball well struck; (ii) the revolutionary approach of trying to achieve success without hitting the ball squarely, as represented by the bunt and its offspring; (iii) the openly subversive efforts that could enable the batter to declare success

without hitting the ball at all; (iv) the possibly even more subversive notion that preparation done before the game even started could help the batter in the split-second during which he swung.

(i) Variations on a Theme: Refinements to Approaches, Swings, and Stances

2.1.1 Place Hitting. As long as there has been baseball, hitters have recognized the benefit of a well-placed hit. But a far more contentious issue, then as now, is how much it is within a batter's power to place a ball. Baseball, after all, is not like golf or T-ball, where the ball just sits there waiting to be hit. When thrown by a skillful pitcher, it is a feat to make contact with the ball at all, let alone to determine where it will go. Moreover it is generally necessary to cut down on a swing to gain even a measure of control over the baseball's destination. Thus the perception of place hitting has fluctuated throughout baseball history based on whether conditions favored offense or defense.

The triumph of the New York Game with its rule about "Foul Ground" (**1.20**) meant that batters could not hit the ball in a direction unguarded by fielders. In addition, the lively ball, uneven fields, and gloveless fielders of the early 1860s all favored the hitters and meant that a solidly hit ball was far from a routine out even if it headed straight toward a fielder. Batters of the period consequently concluded that they would be doing fielders a favor if they cut down on their swings in an attempt to place the ball.

The lone advantage that fielders did have was the bound rule, by which a batter was retired if his hit was caught on the first bounce. But this too discouraged place hitting, since a batter who seemed to have found a hole between fielders was liable to see one of them run in and scoop it up on the hop for an out.

After the 1864 season the bound rule was eliminated, offering a little more incentive for place hitting. Henry Chadwick immediately picked up on this and began one of the most doggedly persistent of his many long crusades by observing that "one of the 'beauties' of the 'fly' game" was that hitters "who can send a ball about where they please, need not be put out often by fly catches from fair balls. If the field [i.e., the outfielders] be stationed far out, then by batting ball just beyond [the infield], the bases are certainly secured" (*Brooklyn Eagle*, May 6, 1865).

At the end of the decade, with the introduction of the first dead balls, hitters received another incentive to try to place balls. One of the first players to emphasize place hitting was the five-foot-three Dickey Pearce, whom veteran baseball writer William Rankin later described as "the first to place the ball in any part of the field he desired" (*Sporting News*, March 3, 1910). The *Boston Chronicle* observed in 1869, "Pearce in an important match comes to bat, views the position of the field and finds an open spot or weak point on the field and aims to send the ball there" (quoted in Duane Smith, "Dickey Pearce: Baseball's First Great Shortstop," *National Pastime* 10 [1990], 38–42). In 1870 the *Chicago Tribune* praised Pearce for having "demonstrated the difference between wild hits to the field and scientific batting" (*Chicago Tribune*, July 6, 1870). The *Tribune* pointed out the benefits of this tactic the next day: "The Mutuals [of New York] patiently waited, and, after they got the ball in the desired place, scientifically batted it to where there was nobody. The White Stockings batted more with a desire to knock the ball a great, rather than a safe, distance" (*Chicago Tribune*, July 7, 1870).

Thus encouraged, batters began to experiment with techniques that would make place hitting easier. Henry Chadwick continued to advocate this approach, leading John Thorn and Pete Palmer to suggest that he viewed it as baseball's equivalent to the cricket concept of "good form" (John Thorn and Pete Palmer, *The Hidden Game of Baseball*, 16). Chadwick repeatedly extolled the merits of "facing for position," his fancy term for a batter using the positioning of his feet to influence the direction in which the ball went (e.g., *Spalding's Official*

Base Ball Guide, 1902, 90: "facing for position, that is, standing in such a manner as to ensure the bat's meeting the ball so as to have it go to the right, the centre or the left, just as you stand to ensure such a hit").

Chadwick brought all his rhetorical force to bear on the question. He wrote approvingly, "[Ross] Barnes is not one of the class of chance hitters who, when they go to the bat, simply go in to hit the ball as hard as they can, without the slightest idea as to where it is going; but he studies up the position, and makes his hits according to circumstances. . . . In fact, as 'a scientific batsman'—one who goes in to place a ball advantageously—we never saw his superior" (*New York Clipper*, May 3, 1879). In contrast, he sneered that "going in to hit a ball blindly, as it were, not knowing where it is going, is child's play at the bat" (*Brooklyn Eagle*, April 24, 1876).

In 1890, Chadwick noted that the previous season had seen "increased attention paid to *place hitting* by the more intelligent class of batsmen. Under the rule of the swift pitching which has been in vogue for several years past, there was a general idea prevalent among batsmen that it was next to an impossibility to *place* a ball from the bat in the face of the swift pitching batsmen had to encounter; but this rutty idea has been got rid of by headwork batsmen, and last year saw many very successful attempts made to place balls against the fire of a swift delivery" (*Spalding's Official Base Ball Guide, 1890*, 59).

Thus for Chadwick, place hitters were "scientific" and "intelligent" while hitters who took other approaches were compared to children who relied upon "chance" and clung to "rutty ideas." It seems safe to say that Chadwick was writing less about the mechanics of hitting—something at which he had almost no experience—than about what he had to believe in order to conceptualize baseball as a test of character. Such ideologically charged language had its effect, but it still didn't make it easy for batters actually to hit the ball where they were aiming.

A bat with one flattened side was made legal in 1880 by the body governing amateur play, in the hope it would "give the power to batsmen to 'place' balls better than is possible from the use of round bats" (Henry Chadwick, *New York Clipper*, January 10, 1880). As is discussed under "Shapes" (see **9.2.4**), it was rarely used but was nonetheless legalized by the National League after the 1884 season. Instead of leading to more place hitting, the innovation had the unexpected result of helping to bring back the bunt (see 2.2.1), and it was banned after the 1893 season when many were calling for the bunt to be abolished altogether.

One 1880s batter who seems to have had success with place hitting was Charley Ganzel, whose "style of batting differs materially from that of other members of the team and in fact from any ball player on the diamond. He does the work with the forearm. Gently swinging his bat perpendicularly, he watches the ball like a hawk. When he sees one that suits him, quick as a flash he meets it squarely with a firm but gentle rap and it darts out on a line over the heads of the infield, but usually plows the ground before the outfield can reach it. It is seldom he hits for more than a base, but almost always puts the ball out of everybody's reach. He comes nearer to 'placing' the ball, if such a thing is possible, than any player in the country, his favorite spot being between left and center. With men on bases it is a most satisfactory thing to see him come to the plate because it is almost a certainty he will hit the ball" (*Detroit Free Press*, April 28, 1887).

Other batters also discovered success by cutting down on their swings. Chris Von der Ahe wrote that "The nickname 'Tip' was given to [Tip O'Neill] because he merely seemed to 'tip' the ball when batting. He stood at the plate straight as an arrow, a giant in physique, and it seemed that he would just push out his bat and the ball would shoot like lightning. He seldom drew back and made a 'swipe' at the ball" (*St. Louis Post-Dispatch*, April 17, 1904).

Before long the dominant philosophy of batters was to "hit 'em where they ain't," a phrase that became associated with Wee Willie Keeler. This philosophy became so dominant that many made it sound as though it was the only possible approach to hitting. Bill Carrick said in 1901, "About the only man that I know who can swing hard to good effect is [Buck] Freeman. Lajoie sometimes uses the body swing, but his general action is all in the forearm" (quoted in *Washington Post*, July 1, 1901). Christy Mathewson wrote in 1912: "In the history of baseball there have not been more than fifteen or twenty free swingers altogether, and they are the real natural hitters of the game, the men with eyes nice enough and accurate enough to take a long wallop at the ball." He cited Honus Wagner as an example, noting that the great Pittsburgh shortstop "takes a long bat, stands well back from the plate, and steps into the ball, poling it" (Christy Mathewson, *Pitching in a Pinch*, 7).

It may thus be argued that place hitting was the method of hitting best suited to the 1890s and the first decade of the twentieth century. According to this view, it was the introduction of the cork-center ball (see 9.1.6) in 1909 that swung the pendulum away from place hitting.

There is also, however, the possibility that place hitting was at least in part an illusion supported by rhetoric like Chadwick's. Johnny Evers and Hugh Fullerton, though advocates of place hitting, remarked that many believed it to be "more or less of a myth" (John J. Evers and Hugh S. Fullerton, *Touching Second*, 160). Proponents of the view that place hitting was a myth contended that the shorter swings only ensured more solid contact, not precise placement.

For example, in 1875 a *Hartford Courant* sportswriter denounced place hitting as an "absurd notion." He contended: "More games than a few have been lost by players who have forced themselves to believe that a ball should only be hit at scientifically, and with a view of sending it to some particular point in the field. There probably is not a player in the profession who would not admit that he has driven a ball in a contrary direction to that intended more times than he has where he set his mind upon sending it . . . scientific batting is an absurdity. The only thing to do is to hit the ball, and its course after is as much a matter of luck as science" (*Hartford Courant*, reprinted in the *Chicago Tribune*, October 10, 1875).

In addition, an 1883 article described a heated debate between Cap Anson and Larry Corcoran about place hitting. Anson claimed that he could hit the ball wherever he wanted to; Corcoran offered to bet him that he couldn't. Anson declined the bet but indicated that he would prove his ability to place his hits in that afternoon's game. Instead Anson went hitless in six at bats, and only half the balls he hit went in the intended direction, prompting the author to crow: "Admitting that Anson can probably come nearer to controlling the direction of a batted ball than any other batsman in the league can do, it will be seen that he cannot do it more than half of the time, and even then cannot regulate the hits as between high balls, grounders or fouls. Like every other batsman who faces curve-throwing, Anson will accomplish more for his side and will improve his individual batting record by limiting his efforts to hitting the ball hard and strong" (*American*

Sports; quoted in *Chicago Tribune*, September 9, 1883). Longtime *Chicago Tribune* sports editor T. Z. Cowles vividly recalled this incident many years later, though his colorful version added some impossible details (*Chicago Tribune*, May 26, 1918).

Skeptics about place hitting can gain further support from the highly ambiguous nature of the phrase "Hit 'em where they ain't." Nap Lajoie was quoted in 1904 as saying: "I am heartily in accord with that wise youth—I think it was Schmidt, the old pitcher—who, when asked the best way to bat, replied, 'Hit 'em where they ain't'" (*Washington Post*, July 24, 1904, reprinted from a source identified only as the *Evening Journal*). Lajoie's sincerity must be doubted since he was noted as a free swinger. Moreover, "Schmidt the old pitcher" was none other than "Crazy" Schmit, a pitcher who was notorious for his crackpot theories (see **3.3.5**, **14.3.2**).

Lajoie accordingly seems to be implying that place hitting is an illusion. Is he also suggesting that the phrase "hit 'em where they ain't" was an inside joke by which hitters told reporters what they wanted to hear? Was this a case like the Emperor's New Clothes, in which sportswriters, especially Chadwick, breathlessly informed their readers of the merits of place hitting while the hitters quietly guffawed?

Willie Keeler similarly seems to have regarded his signature phrase as a bit of a joke. When a fan wrote and asked if he had written a hitting instructional, Keeler quipped, "I've already written that treatise and it reads like this: 'Keep your eyes clear and hit 'em where they ain't'" (*Brooklyn Eagle*, August 7, 1901; quoted in Al Kermisch, "From a Researcher's Notebook," *Baseball Research Journal* 28 [1999], 141).

This possibility is lent additional credence by the unidentified reporter who wrote in 1889: "If some of the wild-eyed scribes who have been spoiling good paper with idiotic slush about place batting would get in front of the cyclone pitchers of to-day, they would change their opinion materially. It would take about three hard pitched balls to convince them that the players are unable to hit the ball, much less to place it. 'Place' hitting in the days of straight-arm pitching and slow-coach deliveries was a possibility. Now there is no such feature in base ball" (*Perry* [Iowa] *Chief*, September 6, 1889).

Even more emphatic was Ginger Beaumont who, after leading the National League in batting average in 1903, proclaimed, "There are no place hitters." He maintained, "When a player tells you that he can put a ball where he pleases, he is insinuating that you are weak-minded and woefully gullible. Don't take any stock in such twaddle. When it comes to delivering the goods I have noticed that they are generally short of stock" (quoted in *Oshkosh Northwestern*, July 16, 1904).

The most compelling evidence for this viewpoint comes from none other than Ty Cobb, who condemned "the futility of trying to place hits instead of merely concentrating the mind and muscles on hitting the ball on the nose." Cobb instead advised young hitters: "never try to place a hit. In the first place, you can't do it, and it is not a good idea, anyway. Very few batters ever successfully acquired the art. I never try to place hit. I have tried simply to meet the ball solidly and let the hits find holes for themselves" (Ty Cobb, *Memoirs of Twenty Years in Baseball*, 78–79).

Cobb called Willie Keeler "the best of the so-called place hitters." He explained that Keeler was really a poke or slap hitter rather than a place hitter: "Keeler combined several things to make this possible. He gripped his bat far down toward the middle and poked at the ball, rather than hit at it. His swing was short and naturally more accurate than the longer swings of the average batter. He was able to wait until the ball was almost upon him before poking at it. Many of Keeler's hits were pokey little flies, just past the infield" (Paul Purman, "Place Hitting," syndicated column, *Sheboygan* [Wisc.] *Press*, July 9, 1918).

As Cobb's description suggests, Keeler's ability to find holes was often the result of poking at the ball so that it would go a specific distance and land in the spaces between the infielders and outfielders, rather than of aiming for a particular location such as the gaps between fielders. An 1897 note, for instance, claimed: "There is such a thing as scientific batting. [Fred] Tenney of Boston, [Mike] Griffin of Brooklyn, [Hugh] Jennings, Keeler, and [William] Clarke of Baltimore are extremely successful in 'lifting' flies over the infield, and each man does so with evident intention" (*Chicago Tribune*, May 21, 1897, 6).

It was only with the success of Babe Ruth that swinging hard without regard to placement gained general acceptance. According to Ty Cobb, Ruth was allowed to develop his batting style because he was a pitcher. Cobb explained that "A pitcher is not expected to hit. Therefore, he can follow his own system without managerial interference. Ruth made the most of this opportunity. As a pitcher he took a tremendous cut at the ball. At first he was awkward. . . . Gradually he gained confidence, experience and knowledge of pitchers" (quoted in F. C. Lane, *Batting*, 71).

2.1.2   Swings. Henry Chadwick wrote in 1860, "Players have different modes, and adopt different styles of batting; some take the bat with the left hand on the handle, and slide the right from the large end toward the handle; others grasp it nearly one-third of the distance from the small end, so that both hands appear near the middle of the bat; others again take hold with both hands well down on the handle, and swing the bat with a natural and free stroke, while great force is given to the hit; all give good reasons for their several styles" (*Beadle's Dime Base-Ball Player*, 19). An 1864 book added, "Some give a blow like a woodman, grasping the handle with the left hand, and sliding the right toward it; some take the bat near the middle, with both hands; others seize that handle with both hands, and give a swinging hit" (*1864 American Boy's Book of Sports and Games*, 19).

According to Chadwick, a single basic approach gained approval in the years that followed. In 1867, he criticized a Columbus club whose "players, in batting, held their bats in front of them before they struck, a style of play which necessitates a double swing with the bat, backward and forward, thereby rendering the aim difficult. The proper way is to half shoulder the bat, bringing it down to meet the ball, especially for swift pitching" (*The Ball Player's Chronicle*, July 4, 1867). A few years later he observed that "The batsman is only in proper 'form' for a good hit when he stands squarely on his feet . . . with the point of the bat resting over his shoulder" (*New York Clipper*, April 12, 1873).

One of the difficulties in researching early baseball history is that Chadwick was so prolific and so unwavering in his beliefs that it can be hard to distinguish his views of how things ought to be from what actually occurred. Batters' swings may be an example of this issue. An 1888 article implied that there were more variations when it stated: "In the National League there are about 125 players, and none of them hold a bat or use it in the same manner. . . . The knowledge of their peculiarities, together with knowing that some players can hit only a high ball and others a low ball, enable pitchers to use strategy when facing opposing teams, and the

best pitchers are those that have made a study of them" (*New York World*, reprinted in *Dallas Morning News*, May 20, 1888).

So had things changed that dramatically from the situation described by Chadwick in his 1867 and 1873 comments? Questions like this cannot be definitively resolved, but it seems likely that the truth lies somewhere in between—in particular, that variations were more common in the positioning of the feet and the rest of the body than in how the bat was held. In addition, as described in the entries that follow, since form follows intended function, other elements of the swing have been modified to reflect changes in the approach to hitting.

2.1.3   Follow-throughs. It is not clear that early batters followed through on their swings, but it seems very likely. In the 1870s the follow-through fell victim to new approaches to hitting. An 1875 article noted: "As batters, the Bostons are making a big record this season. Harry [Wright] has trained them to hit to right field, where pretty much all their hitting is now done" (Charles Randolph, *Chicago Tribune*, May 30, 1875, 6).

Boston would compile the most dominant record in major league history that season. How much this hitting approach had to do with their success is debatable, but winners are often imitated uncritically. Before long, the follow-through seems to have passed entirely out of baseball.

In 1906 sportswriter George M. Graham wrote as though the follow-through was unheard of in baseball: "Possibly batters could improve their hitting by learning to 'follow through,' as the golfer and billiardist do, but if batters stopped to follow through their batting swing the chances are they would be thrown out on what would be otherwise base hits" (*Sporting Life*, January 6, 1906). Another article implied the same thing a decade later when it referred to "Chick Evans, the well-known golfing star, who thinks he can improve the batting of the players by teaching them the 'follow through' that is necessary in swinging golf clubs" (*Sporting Life*, January 13, 1917).

By then, however, there are signs that an increasing number of batters had adopted follow-throughs. In 1911 an observer remarked, "The secret of [Nap] Lajoie's successful hitting lies in the fact that he adopts the 'follow-on' style used by golfers. He doesn't swing his bat from his side, but meets the ball squarely when it reaches a point in front of his chest and then puts his strength into a sort of punch which carries the bat well beyond his left side. All first class batsmen do this, for it enables them to keep their eyes on the ball and to put strength into their bats when they hit the leather" (*Kansas City Star*, August 11, 1911).

It was not until Babe Ruth initiated the home run revolution that it became common for batters to follow through on their swings. F. C. Lane referred in 1925 to "the Babe Ruth follow through motion," suggesting that the swing was inextricably linked to the Bambino. Lane cited Walter Johnson's description of Ruth's swing: "He grasps the bat with an iron grip and when he meets the ball he follows it through with his full strength and weight" (F. C. Lane, *Batting*, 29, 66).

Ruth attributed his success with this new technique to the banning of trick pitches. He explained that when he reached the major leagues "a fellow had to choke his bat, take a short swing and be prepared for anything, or else be 'whiffed'" (Babe Ruth, *Babe Ruth's Own Book of Baseball*, 152).

Even the Babe's success did not convince everyone. Bill Jacobson told Lane, "Perhaps with a heavier bat and a follow through motion, I could hit the ball harder, but I wouldn't hit anywhere near so often" (F. C. Lane, *Batting*, 28). Ruth himself noted that Lou Gehrig had a much shorter follow-through (Babe Ruth, *Babe Ruth's Own Book of Baseball*, 153–155).

2.1.4   Choking Up.

The tactic of choking up on the bat was used very early on, as Henry Chadwick noted in 1872: "The batsman is only in proper form for a good hit when he stands squarely on his feet, with the bat grasped firmly about 6 or 8 inches from the end of the handle, and with the point of the bat partly resting over his shoulder. He should never hold it horizontally, and especially should he avoid pointing it toward the pitcher" (*Brooklyn Eagle*, April 20, 1872; almost the exact same words appear in the *New York Clipper*, April 12, 1873).

Its use, however, appears to have been limited because of a stigma that it was unmanly. Cap Anson, for instance, grasped his bat six inches from the handle until 1876. Then his father "advised his boy, as he still calls him, to take his club like a man and get the whole force of it on the ball" (Tim Murnane, *Boston Globe*, June 16, 1889, 17).

After becoming less frequent in the 1880s, choke hitting was revived in the 1890s and became particularly closely associated with five-foot-four Willie Keeler and his catchphrase "Hit 'em where they ain't." John B. Sheridan recalled later, "The 'choke' craze first began about 1894, when [John] McGraw, [Willie] Keeler, [Hughey] Jennings and [Joe] Kelley choked up a bit and did wonderful things. Keeler was the only real 'choke' hitter of the lot. The others did shorten up a bit, but none so far as Keeler" (*Sporting News*, April 21, 1922). A 1904 article referred to the "Willie Keeler method of holding the stick a foot from the end and simply bumping the ball" (*Washington Post*, September 25, 1904). The 1905 comments of Skel Roach, reprinted under "Keeping the Ball Down" (3.3.3), describe how "an army of others" adopted Keeler's approach and the ripple effect this had on other aspects of the game.

Choke hitting remained the dominant approach until around 1910, when the introduction of the cork-centered baseball began to change things. Even afterward, the conventional wisdom seems to have remained that a skilled hitter should choke up in certain situations. Honus Wagner noted: "Often I swing from the handle, but a good deal of the time I choke up. [Napoleon] Lajoie always did the same thing." Ty Cobb added: "My idea of a real batter is a man who can choke up on the bat when he feels like it or slug from the handle when it is necessary" (quoted in F. C. Lane, *Batting*, 44). It is noteworthy that, as is discussed in the next entry, both Cobb and Wagner were known for splitting their hands on the bat.

2.1.5   Split Hands.

As noted in the entry on "Swings," the technique of dividing the hands on the bat was in use as early as 1860. It appears to have remained in use throughout the nineteenth century by batters who were seeking bat control. The *St. Louis Post-Dispatch* explained in 1888, "Nearly all the heavy batters, except Mike Kelly, grasp the bat close to the end with both hands and swing it around from their shoulder. The sacrifice hitters and the ones who seem to rarely strike out hold one hand close to the end of the bat and the other several inches further up on the stick" (*St. Louis Post-Dispatch*, September 6, 1888).

While the split-hands grip had become less common in the twentieth century, that did not stop two of the greatest hitters of all time from adopting it: Ty Cobb and Honus Wagner. Cobb gave this explanation: "I learned [as a teenager] that the way to hit a ball sharply was to meet it in front of the plate just as it broke. That is how I developed the habit of holding the bat with my hands apart, well up on the handle. I have always batted that way. Hans Wagner batted the same way. He tells me that style came to him just as it did to me."

Cobb appreciated the irony of two of the game's greatest hitters using an approach that was deemed unorthodox: "Two or three years ago one of the bat manufacturers got out a little book on how to bat. Pictures were given of all the different styles. It was pointed out that Cobb and Wagner both used the style of keeping their hands apart on the bat handle. A note said, however, that this style wasn't recommended. Wagner and I both had a laugh about that. At the time we were both leading our leagues—in a style not recommended" (Ty Cobb, *Memoirs of Twenty Years in Baseball*, 16).

Grantland Rice attributed the demise of this batting technique to the home run era. He observed in 1923, ". . . In the old days Keeler held his hands well apart; there were six inches separating Lajoie's hands, and fully that much separating Ty Cobb's. But now [Rogers] Hornsby, [George] Sisler, [Babe] Ruth and most of the leading swatsmen of the era keep their hands in close contact upon the bat, where they can feel the weight of the heavier end of the big mace. And in this fashion there is also more leverage for the long and lusty blow" (Grantland Rice, "The Sportlight," syndicated column, April 17, 1923).

2.1.6 Open Stances. As discussed under "Swings" (**2.1.2**), batting stances are too idiosyncratic to be easily categorized, making it extremely difficult to determine firsts. But it can be said that the extreme open stance of recent players like Tony Batista is not new.

Early rules mandated that the batter stand with at least one foot in line with home plate (see **14.3.5**). As a result, researcher Paul Hunkele reported that an illustration in an 1867 guide edited by Henry Chadwick showed a batsman taking his position with his forward foot turned out with his toe pointing toward the pitcher and his rear foot perpendicular to the batsman's line. The result was a sort of a "T" stance, "as a backwoodsman does when using his axe in cutting down a tree" (Henry Chadwick, *Haney's Base Ball Player's Book of Reference for 1867*, 112, 115).

This illustration continued to appear in Chadwick's guides until 1874 when "Batters' Boxes" (**14.3.5**) were introduced. At that point Chadwick's recommendation changed dramatically, though the change may have had more to do with a new emphasis on hitting to right field than on the batter's increased freedom. The *1876 DeWitt's Guide* includes an illustration of "The Correct Position in Batting," in which the batter employs a radically closed stance "so as to face for a right field hit" (Henry Chadwick, *1876 DeWitt's Base Ball Umpire Guide*, 10).

Even after the introduction of the batter's box, many hitters continued with an open stance. Dasher Troy, an infielder of the 1880s, later explained that facing the pitcher was considered the best approach during his playing days. He provided this description of Cap Anson's stance: "he grasped the bludgeon firmly, faced the pitcher, with his feet squarely on the ground, and as the ball whirled from the pitcher's hand he stepped forward to meet it" (F. C. Lane, *Batting*, 32–33). Sportswriters George M. Graham and Hugh S. Fullerton both confirmed that Anson "faced the pitcher squarely" throughout his lengthy career, which extended from 1871 to 1897 (*Sporting Life*, January 6, 1906; *Chicago Tribune*, April 29, 1906).

An 1888 article that included detailed descriptions of the batting stances of a dozen star batters made clear that facing the pitcher was still the preferred approach, though far from the only one. It noted that Scott Stratton, a left-handed hitter, "is said by some to have the best position for hitting the ball of any player in the Association. He gets exactly in the center of the batter's box, on the left hand side, and places the toes of the left foot close against the front line of the box, the right foot being back several inches. When he strikes he steps squarely forward and swings his entire body toward the pitchers" ("How to Hit a Ball," *New York Sun*, reprinted in *Birmingham* [Ala.] *Evening News*, October 2, 1888).

Anson, along with pupils like Jimmy Ryan and Mike Kelly, kept the extremely open stance in use during the 1890s (Tim Murnane, *Boston Globe*, June 16, 1889, 17). As the decade wore on, however, it grew increasingly uncommon. During Anson's final season in 1897 he was said to be "the only one of the old-timers who continues to bat that way, unless Jimmy Ryan's method is to be taken as a copy" (*Chicago Post*, May 19, 1897). Batters of the 1880s instead incorporated Anson's method of striding toward the pitcher into a radically different stance. An 1890 article advised, "position plays a prominent part in a player's batting. To be a good batsman it is necessary to stand erect with feet close together. If a right hand batsman the weight of the body should be on the right foot, with the left foot free to move. Then when a ball comes at the right height, step forward and meet it at the same time the bat is swung. This adds force to the blow and gives the ball additional momentum." The writer contrasted this model stance to that of "batters who spread their feet apart and plant themselves squarely in their tracks," with the result that they "rarely ever hit the ball hard. They cannot add force to their blow, and after they do hit it lose time in reaching the base by reason of the effort it requires to get started" (quoted in *Pittsburg[h] Press*, April 28, 1890).

The once-dominant wide-open stance remained rare after the turn of the century. George M. Graham wrote in 1906, "[Napoleon] Lajoie is what might be described as a three-quarters face hitter. His whole body is turned toward the pitcher. . . . Lajoie is turned toward the pitcher more than most batsmen, but his position in that regard is not as pronounced as was Anson's" (*Sporting Life*, January 6, 1906).

In 1915 an article on this stance declared Cincinnati's Heinie Groh "the sole survivor in the big leagues of an old tradition immortalized by Pop Anson." Groh offered this explanation: "By standing facing the pitcher, you can see both foul lines, watch the pitcher's windup motion better and follow the ball better. . . . You can see the ball better with two eyes than you can with an eye and a half. For that is about all you really use when you twist your neck to get a sight of the ball." Groh added that his stance forced him to step forward to hit the ball, which gave him a running start toward first base. He reported that he had always hit that way though sometimes advised to switch on the ground that his stance cost him power and left him vulnerable to being hit by pitches.

The unnamed author of this article found Groh's description of these benefits quite convincing and surveyed other major leaguers about why they didn't try the wide-open stance. Some of them offered explanations, such as the difficulty of pulling the ball or hitting for power, but many admitted that the idea had never occurred to them. As a result, the writer suggested that this approach might make a comeback ("Four Hundred to One," *Baseball Magazine*, September 1915, 72–74). Nevertheless, in 1925, F. C. Lane (who was probably the author of the 1915 article) reported that Heinie Groh was "the only batter of recent days who won any prominence by following this once approved old style method of facing the pitcher" (F. C. Lane, *Batting*, 33).

2.1.7   Leg Kicks. This device is probably most closely associated with slugger Mel Ott and with Japanese home run king Sadaharu Oh. More recent practitioners, such as Harold Baines and Ruben Sierra, have also generally been sluggers who used it to generate power. But the leg kick dates back to the nineteenth century and seems to have been designed simply as a timing device to help the batter make contact.

An 1884 article noted that when the amateur Empire club of Detroit played the professional Red Stockings of Boston in 1872, future major leaguer Dan O'Leary of the Empires "had the habit of making his right leg go through the swinging motion of the pitcher's arm as the ball was delivered" (*Saginaw Evening Express*, April 24, 1884). An 1891 *Brooklyn Eagle* article remarked that "[Boxer Dick] Connor has a peculiar style of lifting his right leg something after the manner of Jack Nelson, the base ball player, who lifted one of his limbs whenever he got ready to hit a curve" (*Brooklyn Eagle*, December 17, 1891).

Others were even more idiosyncratic. F. C. Lane gave this description of Jack Bentley's approach: "As the pitcher released the ball, Bentley would step back, raise himself slowly on one foot, much the same as a shot putter would do, and lunge forward. When he met the ball he was literally standing on one leg" (F. C. Lane, *Batting*, 36). Hugh S. Fullerton wrote in 1906, ". . . The oddest of all batters was Doggy Miller. He was short and stout with plump little legs. He stood perfectly still at bat until just as the pitcher was winding up to deliver the ball, then he suddenly stuck his left leg out straight in front of it, gave a funny little ballet girl kick, and threw himself forward to meet the ball. His performance caused so much laughter that Doggy tried earnestly to stop kicking—but he couldn't hit unless he did" (*Chicago Tribune*, April 29, 1906).

2.1.8   Foot in the Bucket. The "foot in the bucket" stance was the signature trait of Al Simmons. While he didn't invent it, he did a much more extraordinary thing by bringing it a legitimacy as a batting stance that would have previously been unthinkable.

Before Simmons, the foot-in-the-bucket stance was inextricably associated with cowardice. Its name was a less than subtle suggestion that the batter was so afraid of being hit by the ball that he was preparing to exit the batter's box. Christy Mathewson in 1912 cited a typical catcher talking to an intimidated young batter:

"Yer almost had your foot in the water-pail over by the bench that time" (Christy Mathewson, *Pitching in a Pinch*, 42).

When Al Simmons first joined Connie Mack's Athletics in 1924, a coach reportedly said, "That boy Simmons never will make a hitter. He pulls away from the plate. He has one foot in the water bucket." But Connie Mack replied, "I don't care if he has both feet in the bucket as long as he keeps on hitting the ball" (*Washington Post*, December 2, 1928).

Simmons confirmed that "Connie never once suggested that I change my style. He always claimed that I was a natural hitter, and that he might ruin me if he tried to move my feet. He probably would have. It is the only way I have ever hit" (quoted in Ed Rumill, "Al Simmons a Natural Hitter," *Christian Science Monitor*, March 13, 1939).

Babe Ruth believed that Simmons was able to overcome the inherent disadvantage of his stance by "using an exceptionally long bat—the longest in the league I think. . . . The result is that he can reach the outside corner for a curve if he has to, and at the same time he's far enough away that the inside stuff doesn't bother him" (Babe Ruth, *Babe Ruth's Own Book of Baseball*, 167).

Early in his career, Simmons was rarely referred to without his unorthodox stance being mentioned, and this scrutiny seems to have irritated him. Sportswriter Frank Young reported: "An interesting discussion was had in the Nats' dressing room before the fracas regarding the batting of Al Simmons, flashy Athletic flyhawk. The general opinion was that continued reference to the player as 'Foot in the Bucket Al' was getting on his nerves, and that he is changing his stance. As a result, the 'experts' claim that this season he neither is hitting as often nor as hard as he did last" (Frank H. Young, *Washington Post*, June 29, 1926).

By this time, however, Simmons was so closely associated with the foot-in-the-bucket stance that nothing could rid him of the label. Sportswriter Edward J. Neil claimed that Simmons made some adjustments in 1931: "Now he steps forward more than he steps away, but his reputation still clings to him" (Edward J. Neil, *Washington Post*, September 23, 1931).

Ultimately the attention turned to admiration. In 1947, Specs Toporcer said that Simmons "always had his foot in the 'bucket,' which is decidedly unorthodox, yet he was one of the greatest hitters the game ever produced. You can frown at his style up at the plate, but

you can't laugh off his record. Geniuses have the privileges of being different" (quoted in *Christian Science Monitor*, March 6, 1947).

2.1.9 Batting Left-handed. *Sporting Life* recorded in 1885, "Johnny Ward says he will continue batting left-handed. He does not make a large number of base hits, but he stands a better chance of beating a slow grounder or a fumbled ball to first base. He says that a left-handed man has an advantage of ten feet or more over a right-handed man in reaching first base. There's meat in this" (*Sporting Life*, September 2, 1885). Of course Ward was not the first man to notice such an obvious fact, and there were natural right-handers in the 1870s who batted left-handed.

But a couple of important factors prevented this from becoming a common strategy before the 1880s. First, until the mid-1870s the shorter distance to first base was the only advantage to batting left-handed. This advantage was apparent to anyone, but it was not perceived as being large enough to relinquish the benefit of batting with one's natural hand. Then around 1876, "pitchers first introduced the wide-out curve. [Terry] Larkin had the first one ever seen [in Chicago] and it was thought to be a wonder. In fact, the papers and people generally refused to believe that it was possible to curve a ball. A great many writers insisted that there was some trick about it. [Jimmy] Hallinan was the only batter that could hit him, and he because he was left-handed" (*Chicago Tribune*, April 1, 1894).

The perception that left-handed batters gained a second important advantage thus emerged around 1876, but there was still a lag before a significant number of natural right-handers began to bat left-handed. This makes sense because batting with the nondominant hand is easiest to pick up when young. Thus there had to be a perception of a sizable advantage to batting left-handed for a couple of years before there could be a generation that fully capitalized on this new state of affairs.

One of the first was Hall of Famer Roger Connor, who signed with New Bedford in 1878, only to be "released because he could not bat. Roger batted right-handed in those days. He went home and turned around and practiced batting left-handed, and blossomed out as one of the greatest hitters of the age" (*Sporting News*, January 9, 1897). After the 1879 campaign, Henry Chadwick noted that one of that season's important developments was the "introduction of batting quartets of left-handed hard hitters" (*New York Clipper*, December 20, 1879). The 1880s saw substantial numbers of natural right-handers batting left-handed for the first time, though it soon became clear that this was not a cure-all.

2.1.10   Switch-hitter. Today's switch-hitters do so primarily because of the advantage of never having to flail at curveballs that are breaking away from them. But the first known switch-hitter, Bob Ferguson, began doing so before the curveball was a large part of baseball.

As William J. Ryczek explained, "[Bob] Ferguson was a switch hitter, but batted right- or left-handed according to disposition or situation, not based upon whether the opposing pitcher threw right- or left-handed" (William J. Ryczek, *When Johnny Came Sliding Home*, 212). In the decisive tenth inning of the June 14, 1870, game that ended the Red Stockings' winning streak, Ferguson "took the bat, and with commendable nerve batted left hand, to get the ball out of [Cincinnati shortstop] George Wright's hands" (*Brooklyn Eagle*, June 15, 1870, 2; George Bulkley, in "The Day the Reds Lost," *National Pastime* 2 [Fall 1982], 9, notes that an account in the *New York Clipper* implied that this was not the first time Ferguson batted left-handed). In a National Association game on August 12, 1875, Ferguson came up with two outs in the ninth, a runner on third, and his Hartford team trailing 1-0. After fouling off several pitches left-handed, he turned around to bat right-handed and drove in the tying run "by the safest kind of a hit over the third-baseman's head" (*New York Clipper*, August 21, 1875).

Left-handed pitchers (see **3.3.6**) were scarce in early baseball, while the curveball (see **3.2.3**) did not become a major force in most pitchers' arsenals until the late 1870s. (According to Tim Murnane, John McMullin was the first left-hander to throw a curve [*Boston Globe*, March 7, 1915].) Almost as soon the left-handed curveball pitcher emerged, left-handed batters seized upon switch-hitting as a way to strike back. The *Chicago Tribune* reported in 1878, "[Bob] Ferguson and [Larry] Reis bat about as well one way as the other" (*Chicago Tribune*, March 31, 1878). The *Cleveland Plain Dealer* observed the following year, "[John] O'Rourke tried to hit [southpaw Bobby] Mitchell's pitching right handed and struck out. Then he tried it left handed and struck out twice" (*Cleveland Plain Dealer*, July 21, 1879).

That setback wasn't enough to end the strategy, and it became even more relevant in response to the success of southpaw J Lee Richmond. In a game on June 19, 1880, three left-handed Chicago batters—Abner Dalrymple, George Gore, and Larry Corcoran—batted right-handed against Richmond. In an 1883 game, "[Sam] Trott and [George] Weidman both took a turn at right-handed batting yesterday on account of Richmond's left-handed delivery. The results were very favorable" (*Detroit Post and Tribune*, May 24, 1883).

2.1.11   Changing Batter's Boxes. The *San Francisco Examiner* reported in 1887, "The Metropolitans have introduced a new and clever play in order to get first base on called balls. After a batter has had four balls called on the pitcher and has less than three strikes against himself he changes position to the opposite side of the plate, and the chances are strongly in favor of the next ball being called. Thus far it has worked like a charm" (*San Francisco Examiner*, July 25, 1887). This tactic remains legal, but a few inventive players tried to take it further.

David Fleitz reports that Cap Anson crossed the plate in a game on July 15, 1894, to reach a pitch that was intended as part of a base on balls (David Fleitz, *Cap Anson*, 227). A rule was created to prevent this tactic, but an 1897 analysis noted that its wording mandated vaguely that the batsman be in his box when hitting the ball. Accordingly, in a similar situation in a game in Pittsburgh on September 25, Bill Lange of Chicago jumped from the right-handed batter's box to the left-handed batter's box just as the pitcher was about to throw, and whacked a double. Anson convinced the umpire that Lange was in the batter's box, and the hit stood (*Sporting Life*, December 11, 1897, 5).

For whatever reason, rule makers did not get around to explicitly banning this tactic until 1907, when it was decreed that "the batsman is out if he steps from one batsman's box to the other after the pitcher has taken his position" (John H. Gruber, "Out for Interference," *Sporting News*, February 24, 1916). Even this didn't stop Honus Wagner from stepping from one batter's box to the other to distract Cincinnati pitcher Harry Gaspar in a game on April 23, 1909. Umpire Bill Klem was aware of the rule but allowed Wagner to do this because he felt that Gaspar was trying to intentionally walk Wagner. But Cincinnati successfully appealed the game, and it was replayed on September 10 (with Pittsburgh winning again) (*Sporting Life*,

June 12, 1909; John H. Gruber, "Out for Interference," *Sporting News*, February 24, 1916).

2.1.12 High-low. As discussed under "Strike
Zones" (**1.11**), the rule allowing batters to call
for either high or low pitches was eliminated after the 1886 season. There were widely differing
predictions about how this would affect hitters
in the habit of having one exclusive request.

Not surprisingly, batters maintained unanimously that their own hitting would not suffer.
Sam Wise declared: "I haven't bothered my
head any. . . . A man ought to smash at any
kind of a ball if he thinks he can hit it. That's
the way I do. I don't care whether it is a high
ball or a low ball, so long as I think I can hit
it" (*Boston Globe*, March 13, 1887, 6). After the
exhibition season, Cap Anson added: "I don't
find any trouble with the pitching. So far I have
been successful in hitting high and low balls.
It hasn't made a great deal of difference to me
which way they come" (*Chicago Tribune*, April
16, 1887, 2). Ezra Sutton was also confident that
he would be unaffected, but he forecasted that
it would prove, "no easy thing for men fixed in
their methods. Now, you take a man like [Sam]
Thompson of the Detroits. He can't hit a high
ball any more than Anson can hit a low ball.
The latter, of course, has had more experience
and will be able to accommodate himself better
to a different ball, but it won't be the ball that
he wants" (*St. Louis Globe-Democrat*, April 3,
1887).

Others shared Sutton's view that the impact
would be uneven. One sportswriter argued that
"The left-handed twirlers will prove effective
this year on account of batsmen not being allowed to call for high balls on them. They can
pitch to suit themselves" (*Rocky Mountain
News*, April 13, 1887, 10). Another predicted
that it would alter the approach of certain batters: "The Detroits, in their practice at Macon,
learned a fact about batting under the new
rules. They say that if a player holds his bat in
the usual position to strike at a low ball, he cannot raise it in time to hit a high ball, but if he
holds the bat in the position to hit a high ball,
it is easy enough to come down on a low one"
(*New York Sun*, April 17, 1887). Pitchers were
naturally excited about the change, with John
Clarkson noting that it would put a premium
on a pitcher's ability to study whether a batter's
"tendency is to swing up or down at the sphere.
If their disposition is to hit up at the ball, I
endeavor to keep it pretty well elevated, reversing the delivery if they are disposed to hit low"

(*Base Ball Gazette*, reprinted in the *Louisville
Courier-Journal*, April 26, 1887).

Indeed Connie Mack claimed in 1924 that
many high-ball hitters could not make the adjustment, including himself: "as I had already
tipped off the big league pitchers to my weakness by asking for a high ball every time I went
to the bat, when the season of 1887 opened
I never got a look at a high ball, but was fed
low ones from that time on" (Connie Mack,
"Memories of When the Game Was Young,"
Sporting Life [monthly], June 1924).

Historian David Nemec noted that at least
one player found a clever strategy to prevent a
similar fate. Bob Caruthers was a high-ball hitter, but during the 1886 season "he had craftily
concealed his weakness for low pitches to an
extent by occasionally calling for low ones, especially against hurlers he knew he couldn't hit
anyway. As a result, pitchers did not catch on to
Caruthers' game immediately" (David Nemec,
The Beer and Whisky League, 123).

2.1.13 Peeking. Not surprisingly, trying to
catch a glimpse at the catcher's positioning is
an ancient tactic that appears to have begun
as soon as signals did (see **1.27** and **6.5.1**). It
seems logical to assume that its use increased
as it became less common for batters to face
the pitcher (see **2.1.6**) and again when catchers
began to crouch (see **4.2.2**), thereby becoming
less able to make last-minute shifts. For more
on Peeking, see the entry on the countermoves
used by catchers in entry **6.5.6**.

(ii) Less Is More: The Bunt and Other Novel Approaches to Hitting

2.2.1 Bunts. Today the bunt is regarded as
the epitome of good fundamental baseball.
Any time a player is unable to execute a bunt
successfully, fans and broadcasters tut-tut and
mutter about the "lost art of bunting." This is
ironic, considering the history of the bunt.

Bunts were an important part of other bat-
and-ball games. Irving A. Leitner gave this description of town ball as played in Philadelphia
in 1833: "If the striker used two hands, the bat
was broad and flat, closely resembling a cricket
bat. If he used one hand, the bat was shaped like
a miniature baseball bat and was called a 'delill.' A good player was able to use either type.
However, when 'delilling,' the striker, instead
of swinging at the ball, would simply allow the
ball to be deflected off his bat, directing it to
whatever area of the playing field he chose by

holding the delill at a given angle" (Irving Leitner, *Baseball: Diamond in the Rough*, 32).

David Block has pointed out that as late as 1856 supporters of the Massachusetts version of baseball "considered the art of tipping a ball over the catcher's head to be one of a batsman's greatest skills" (*Porter's Spirit of the Times*, December 27, 1856; quoted in David Block, *Baseball Before We Knew It*, 85). Similarly, in cricket it was and still is considered good technique for a batsman to simply deflect a ball that might strike his wicket. By contrast, one of the distinctive features of early baseball was that it was taken for granted that batsmen would try to hit the ball as hard and as far as possible. This mind-set would result in significant controversy when the tactics of other bat-and-ball games were used in baseball.

Researcher Tom Shieber found what appears to be the earliest instance of a bunt in baseball in an account of a match game played between the Atlantic and Putnam Base Ball Clubs on June 29, 1860. The following description appeared in the *New York Clipper*: "A circumstance occurred in the 2d innings which we deem worthy of notice: Brown was at the bat, and [John G.] Price pitched him a low ball, which, in bringing his bat down, Brown hit with the bat in a similar manner to that in which a cricketer blocks a straight ball; judgment was asked, and as the Umpire deemed it an accident, it was decided 'no hit,' but we think it should have been considered fair, for the reason, that had a player been on the first base at the time, he could easily have made his second base before the pitcher could have fielded it, and the decision may lead to similar accidents on other occasions when such play would have a more important bearing on the game. If, in the act of striking, the ball be hit forward of home base, however light the touch, it ought to be considered a fair ball, otherwise accidents similar to the above will be of frequent occurrence" (*New York Clipper*, July 14, 1860).

In spite of the umpire's ruling that this bunt was "no hit," the tactic soon reemerged. Its development was spurred by the fact that the rules of the day considered any ball fair if it initially struck in fair territory. This made possible the "fair-foul," a ball struck with sufficient English to bounce once in fair territory and then go well into foul territory. Not only was this extremely difficult to defend against, but there was also little penalty for attempting such a hit since foul balls did not count as strikes (though a foul ball caught on the first bounce

was an out). The bunt complemented the fair-foul, either as an accidental consequence of an attempted "fair-foul" or as an intentional means of keeping the fielders from overcommitting to prevent the fair-foul.

There remains some uncertainty as to whether the bunt or the fair-foul came first, but it seems clear that the two are closely linked. Robert H. Schaefer gives a thorough summary of the issue in his article "The Lost Art of Fair-Foul Hitting" (*National Pastime* 20 [2000], 3–9), which in turn relies heavily on sportswriter William M. Rankin's research on the topic in the 1890s.

The two names that surfaced over and over were Dickey Pearce and Tom Barlow, both Brooklyn natives and teammates on the Atlantics of Brooklyn. Pearce was unanimously credited with inventing the fair-foul, but the testimony regarding bunts was divided. Rankin found three players—Billy Barnie, Henry Dollard, and Herbert Worth—who credited Barlow with inventing the bunt. Worth was particularly adamant, stating: "Tommy Barlow was the inventor of the bunt hit, and was famous throughout the country for his skill. He had a short bat, not over two feet long, which when he hit the ball (if it could be called a hit) he imparted a wrist motion which gave the ball, when it came in contact with the bat, a sort of reversed twist and the ball after striking the ground would almost seem to remain where it struck and then dart off at an angle out of reach of the third baseman or the pitcher should they endeavor to field him out at first" (*Sporting News*, January 1, 1898).

Nonetheless Rankin concluded that Dickey Pearce was responsible for both the first bunt and the first fair-foul hit. George Hall, a teammate of Barlow and Pearce, recalled both men bunting but was convinced that Pearce was first. Another teammate of both players, Jack Chapman, confirmed: "It was early in the sixties that he introduced the fair foul hits and a few years later he adopted the bunt. I remember the late Tommy Barlow and how clever he used to make a bunt hit. Barlow always carried a little bat, about two feet long, and made a great reputation for himself in bunting the ball, but that was in 1871, when he was a member of the Star nine. Pearce, however, had made the bunt hit several years prior to that season. It was from Pearce that Barlow got the idea, although the latter had it down to such a science that he could not be beaten in making a bunt hit." In addition, Rankin found descriptions in the *New*

York Clipper of bunts by Pearce in games played on August 17, 1868, and September 10, 1868, before Barlow's professional career had begun (*Sporting News*, January 1, 1898).

Bob Ferguson, another teammate of both players, initially credited Barlow with inventing the bunt but demurred when told that Pearce also claimed the distinction (*Sporting News*, January 13, 1894). These accounts suggest that the bunt was initially used by Dickey Pearce, but as a rare, and possibly accidental, variant to the more lethal fair-foul. Hall was especially explicit that "the bunt sprang from the fair foul hits." Thus when Rankin first researched the subject he concluded that the bunt "is unequivocally the offspring of the 'fair-foul hit'" (*Sporting News*, January 1, 1898). This view was also supported by Henry Chadwick, who claimed that it was his suggestion that spurred Dickey Pearce to invent the fair-foul in 1864, and that the bunt evolved from it (*Sporting Life*, January 27, 1894).

But Rankin later wrote that the order was reversed—that Dickey Pearce "invented the bunt in the early '60's, and some years later in trying to draw a bunt away from the third baseman he discovered the fair-foul hit, which was impossible to field, except from foul ground" (*Sporting News*, March 3, 1910; also, *Sporting News*, July 1, 1905, and A. H. Spink, *The National Game*, 58: "[Pearce] invented the bunt, and some years later when trying to draw a bunt away from the third baseman, he discovered the fair-foul hit"). Presumably his change of heart was the result of becoming aware of Pearce's own point of view—in 1896 Pearce declared: "Everyone gives me credit for being the first player to use the fair foul hit. The facts are that I learned to hit it from the bunt. It was in this way: There was a man on third and I wanted to get him home. The pitcher delivered the ball so low that I could not bunt, which I tried to do. Finally the ball hit the bottom of the bat and went sailing backward, so you will see that if I am entitled to the credit of originating the bunt I must also get that of the other play. Bob Ferguson was the indirect means of suggesting a bunt. He played so far back of [third] base that I told him if he continued to do so I would fool him and make my base every time. He laughed at me, but I showed him what a bunt would accomplish and from that time on I used the bunt in regular games" (*Brooklyn Eagle*, March 21, 1896, 10).

Even if Pearce preceded him in using the bunt, Tommy Barlow added a distinctive twist with his miniature bat. In so doing he caused considerable controversy over whether this was how baseball should really be played. The *Boston Globe* wrote, "Barlow acknowledged his weakness at the bat by attempting the black game, but [A. G.] Spalding got him out twice, and the attempt, which is rather a weak one for a professional club, was a failure" (*Boston Globe*, September 9, 1873).

Others were more indulgent. The *New York Clipper* gave this account: "After the first two strikers had been retired, [Tommy] Barlow, amid much laughter and applause, 'blocked' a ball in front of the home plate and reached first base before the ball did" (*New York Clipper*, June 15, 1872). In another game, Barlow made six of "what Nick Young calls 'baby hits' . . . by the little judgment shown by Radcliffe [John Radcliff] in his position at third base. All Barlow had to do to secure his base safely with Radcliffe playing his position as he did, was to allow the ball to fall dead from the bat to the left of the base, and so as to touch the ground fair. This he did, and as Radcliffe had to run up and field the ball from third base, the result was Barlow reached first base ahead of the ball. This style of hitting annoys a field exceedingly, besides which it corners a pitcher. As for sneering at it and calling it baby hitting, that is absurd. The object of the batsman is to reach first base, and if by any style of hitting he can send the ball fairly to the field, and in such a way that it cannot be caught on the fly or fielded to first base in time to put him out, he earns his base by skilful, scientific batting. The real baby hits are those which give easy chances for fly catches" (*Brooklyn Eagle*, July 23, 1873). Another game account in the *Clipper* illustrated the factors that made the play hard to defend against when it recorded that Barlow, "in his peculiar style, allowed the ball to drop from the bat just in front of him, and in such a way that it was almost impossible for the pitcher—the catcher was way back—to throw the ball to the first baseman without striking the base runner, as he did, Barlow thereby earning his base" (Hall of Fame 1874 Scrapbook, undated clipping).

Whether it was because of the scorn he received or just that it wasn't very effective, Barlow and his little bat had few if any imitators. Henry Chadwick accordingly referred to the bunt as Tommy Barlow's "patent hit." Even the tactic's use by a widely respected player like George Wright was received with condescension; an 1877 account noted that Wright had "made a 'baby-bunting' hit near home plate"

(*Louisville Courier-Journal*, July 12, 1877). The effectiveness of the bunt was further diminished that year by the banning of the fair-foul and the introduction of the catcher's mask, which enabled catchers to play closer to the plate. When Barlow's career ended prematurely, it seemed that the bunt would also be abandoned.

Jim O'Rourke later explained, "There were two other wonderful hitters that I saw when a mere boy. They were Dicky Pierce [sic], shortstop, and Tommy Barlowe [sic], catcher of the Brooklyn Mutuals [sic], back in 1870. I have seen these men with little short bats, which I believe were later ruled out of the game, make the wonderful bunt hit which we have taken to calling a modern institution. Pierce and Barlowe were famous over the country for their little bats and their bunt hits; but as soon as the short bats were ruled out Pierce and Barlowe, not realizing that a bunt could be made with a long bat, gave up the bunt hits and became ordinary players" ("Forty Two Years of Base Ball," *Kalamazoo Evening Telegraph*, March 3, 1910).

After a decade of disuse, the bunt began to reemerge in 1884, with Art Irwin and Cliff Carroll of Providence among the practitioners. It then made a dramatic rise to prominence in 1886, spurred on by the legalization of flattened bats (see **9.2.4**). In 1905 a *New York World* reporter credited Arlie Latham and Johnny Ward with inventing the bunt in 1888 (*New York World*, June 15, 1905; cited and disparaged by William Rankin, *Sporting News*, July 1, 1905). While this attribution is certainly mistaken, it gives an indication of how completely the bunt disappeared between the mid-1870s and 1886.

Not everyone was pleased by the bunt's return, and questions were again raised about the manliness of its practitioners. "The public called it baby play," recalled Detroit catcher Charley Bennett (Bennett Hall of Fame file, unidentified clipping dated February 19, 1905). The *Detroit Free Press* was particularly dismissive: "[Arthur Irwin] is evidently too weak physically to swing a bat and he therefore holds out the willow and 'bunts' the ball. For this babyish performance he was roundly hissed by the spectators, and concluded to abandon it. Base ball is essentially a manly spirit, and its patrons object to such infantile tricks" (*Detroit Free Press*, May 9, 1886).

But the reemergence of the bunt gained momentum from the recognition that the tactic had benefits besides the possibility of a base hit. The primary one was the advancement of base runners. As players and managers realized that bunts were reliable means of moving runners along even when the batter failed to reach safely, they came into much greater favor. *Sporting News* later credited Arlie Latham and the St. Louis Browns with having popularized the sacrifice bunt (*Sporting News*, October 30, 1897).

This association of the bunt with a successful team and a colorful player certainly added to its appeal. The *New York Sun* reported, "[Arlie] Latham has a great way of butting the ball out in front of the plate, and depending upon his running to get to first. He generally does it" (*New York Sun*, May 23, 1886; "butting" was a common variant of "bunting"). A few weeks later it added, "Several of the Metropolitan players are practising Latham's mode of 'bunting' the ball" (*New York Sun*, June 6, 1886).

Another benefit was that, as discussed in the next entry, the fake bunt emerged as an excellent complement to the bunt, just as the fair-foul had been in the previous decade.

Most important, as discussed under "Deliberate Fouls" (**2.3.2**), the bunting technique proved to be an effective way to wear down opposing pitchers by deliberately spoiling their best pitches. Indeed this practice became so widespread in Chicago that observers there came to view bunting as virtually synonymous with deliberate fouls (*Chicago Tribune*, September 22, 1886). Thus the adoption of the new rule after the 1886 season allowing the umpire to call a strike on a deliberate attempt to foul the ball off prompted the *Chicago Tribune* to write, "Bunting will not hereafter be tolerated. Every batsman must attempt to make a fair hit, and any attempt to hit the ball foul will be called a strike" (*Chicago Tribune*, November 17, 1886). Cap Anson commented, "If I was an umpire, I would call strikes on all bunted fouls, whether intentional or unintentional. I would do that to protect myself, and think umpires should be instructed to do it. If they are the question of whether the foul was intentional or not will never arise" (*Chicago Tribune*, April 16, 1887, 2). But, as explained in the entry on "Deliberate Fouls," that wasn't how umpires were instructed to interpret the rule. As a result, while the new rule reduced the transparently deliberate foul bunts, players like Arlie Latham continued to test its grey areas.

The bunt's return to prominence was helped in no small measure by St. Louis and Chicago winning their respective pennants in 1886. By 1891, Jimmy Williams observed, "Bunt hitting has been reduced to a science in all the Western clubs [in the American Association]" and listed many players on St. Louis, Louisville, Cincinnati, and Columbus who were accomplished bunters (*Sporting Times*, May 16, 1891). That did not, however, mean that everyone liked it, and calls to ban the bunt continued. These calls grew louder in the next few years, focusing in particular on the belief that the compromise arrived at after the 1886 season had failed and that only a ban on bunting could eliminate the deliberate foul.

Opponents continued to refer to the bunt as the "baby hit," thereby invoking ridicule, the most powerful tool available. Indeed the term "bunt" itself appears to have derived from the lullaby "Bye, Baby Bunting" in an attempt by its detractors to associate it with childishness (Peter Morris, "Baseball Term 'Bunt' Was Originally Called 'Baby Hit,'" *Comments on Etymology* 34:1 [October 2004], 2–4). When critics also began to insinuate that the bunt was effeminate, innovative manager Gus Schmelz responded by declaring, "that illusion can easily be dispelled if any of the parties who raise that objection will stand up to the plate and try to turn down a fast, high ball. It will only take one carom of the ball from the bat to the face to knock all the effeminate idea out of their heads. And as for action—why if you don't get it when a greyhound like Tom Brown steps to the plate, bunts the ball before anybody knows what he is going to do, and then shows as pretty a streak of running as mortal man ever looked at, where do you get it?" (*Brooklyn Eagle*, January 19, 1893).

The issue gained new traction in 1893 as a result of the decision to move the pitcher to sixty feet, six inches away from the plate (see **1.17**). The gaping space without any fielder again made the bunt seem embarrassingly easy, which brought renewed calls for its abolition. Instead, rule makers addressed the issue by means of another compromise: in 1893 the flat bat was banned, and in 1894 a foul bunt at last became a strike regardless of intent.

This new compromise approach proved remarkably effective. At the start of the 1894 campaign, Cap Anson stated, "I wanted the bunt entirely abolished. Instead it was so penalized that the pitcher will in a measure get what is his due. If the batter hits the ball foul it will be called a strike, which is right and proper. The pitcher puts the ball over the plate and ought to have the credit for it. That is not so good as cutting it out altogether, but it answers the

purpose admirably. . . . The bunt . . . had degenerated into a nuisance and players who were utterly incapable of making it in a hundred years wore out pitchers by fouling the ball so many times in succession that the man in the box was finally tuckered out" (*Philadelphia Inquirer*, April 8, 1894). When the season ended, J. H. Anderson of the *Baltimore Herald* wrote, "With proper restrictions the bunt is a very scientific play and should be kept in the game" (quoted in the *Brooklyn Eagle*, November 7, 1894).

Sacrifice bunts in particular went from being rare to being routine in a strikingly short period of time. William H. Watkins, who managed the hard-hitting Detroit team from 1885 to 1888, later recalled, "I gave only one order for a sacrifice hit while I had charge of the Detroit team. Sacrificing was not popular in those days, and certainly not with that aggregation of great hitters, and I could not see where the play came in" (*Oklahoma City Daily Oklahoman*, February 18, 1898). But, as described in **6.6.1**, "Playing for One Run," by 1897 even the *Chicago Tribune* regarded sacrifice bunts as obligatory in many situations (*Chicago Tribune*, May 21, 1897, 6).

It takes a long time to change a mind-set, however, and critics of the bunt did not disappear altogether. Another Chicago manager, Frank Selee, called for a ban in 1904 (*Sporting Life*, January 9, 1904). In 1909, President William Howard Taft mentioned his dislike of the bunt to reporters. When told that the bunt was considered a key element of scientific baseball, Taft was unimpressed and declared, "I like to see them hit it out for all that is in them" (*New York Times*, May 31, 1909). In a delicious irony, Charley Bennett asserted in 1906 that "bunting has destroyed base-running. There is no necessity for a runner to take chances like they did before the bunt came into general use. As a result one of the finest points of the great game has become almost a lost art" ("Stories of Early Base Ball Days Told by Charlie Bennett, King of the Olden Catchers," *Detroit News Tribune*, March 11, 1906).

2.2.2   Fair-fouls. All the evidence points to Dickey Pearce having invented the fair-foul in the 1860s. In addition to the statements gathered by William Rankin and Robert Schaefer that were cited in the preceding entry, an account of an 1875 game noted, "Bad Dicky hit one of those fair-foul for which he is famous and made first" (*St. Louis Post-Dispatch*, April

20, 1875). An 1888 article added, "It was Dicky Pearce who conceived the idea of touching the top of the ball with his bat and making the famous fair-foul hits, which were practiced by others with such telling effect" (*Sporting News*, March 10, 1888).

The tactic continued to develop in the 1870s, with Ross Barnes becoming the most expert practitioner of the technique. Whereas Pearce's fair-fouls appear to have been closer to bunts, Barnes generally used a full swing. Jim O'Rourke recalled that Barnes's method was "hitting the ball so it would smash on the ground near the plate just inside of the third base line, and would then mow the grass over the line, away out into the field" ("Forty Two Years of Base Ball," *Kalamazoo Evening Telegraph*, March 3, 1910).

As the fair-foul became more lethal, it grew increasingly controversial. Tim Murnane suggested some of the reasons when he penned this description of the fair-foul in 1910: "Early in the history of the game John McMullen [McMullin], Ross Barnes and a few others made remarkable batting records by hitting the ball into the ground in such a way that it caromed off onto foul ground, and at times clean into the bleachers, the baserunner then being allowed all he could make on the hit" ("Murnane's Baseball," *Boston Globe*, February 6, 1910). As implied by Murnane's comments, the tendency of the fair-foul to leave the playing area raised many issues, beginning with the familiar concerns about the scarcity of baseballs (see **1.20**). In addition, allowing batters to hit the ball to places where no fielders could possibly make a play seemed less than fair. Perhaps most important, fair-fouls posed great difficulties for umpires, both in terms of determining whether they were fair and in sorting out the consequences of the fan interference that ensued (see **12.6**, "Blocked Balls").

Spectators perceived the play as unsporting and tedious because a long series of unpenalized attempts often preceded one of Pearce's successful fair-fouls (*St. Louis Democrat*, July 27, 1874). Eventually onlookers became openly hostile, such as at an 1875 game in Chicago where "The derisive cheers, cat calls, hisses and groans that greeted Dicky Pierce's [sic] first attempt at one of his patent tips were repeated throughout the entire game" (*St. Louis Republican*, July 5, 1875). (Obviously there was more of a consensus about Pearce being the inventor of the fair-foul than about the spelling of his name.)

Henry Chadwick continued to defend the fair-foul for "requiring the most skillful handling of the bat, and a quick eye and a steady nerve, besides" (*New York Clipper*, April 12, 1873). This is another revealing example of Chadwick's insistence on viewing baseball as a test of character, but it is beside the point of the criticism. In addition, not everyone agreed with Chadwick's assessment; the *Chicago Tribune* sniffed that the fair-foul, "although requiring a peculiar kind of skill, was far from being an athletic feat" (*Chicago Tribune*, October 26, 1879, 7).

Everyone agreed that something needed to be done about the fair-foul, but there were two different schools of thinking. Many wanted to eliminate it while others like Chadwick sought a way to preserve the play but reduce the problems it caused umpires. At the 1873 annual convention, an unsuccessful proposal was made to designate balls as foul if they hit the ground before the pitcher's area. The advocates of adding a tenth player in 1874 also argued that it would address the indefensibility of the fair-foul (see **19.12**). In 1875, home plate and the batter's boxes were repositioned to make it more difficult to hit fair-fouls, but this was not as successful as hoped (*St. Louis Democrat*, February 28 and March 7, 1875; Tom Shieber, "The Evolution of the Baseball Diamond," *Total Baseball IV*, 116; Robert H. Schaefer, "The Lost Art of Fair-Foul Hitting," *National Pastime* 20 [2000], 5).

After the 1876 season, Harry Wright began to advocate a new approach that would "consider as foul all hit balls that pass outside the foul lines before reaching first base or third base, and as fair all hit balls that strike the ground and pass into the infield and in front of the first base or third base, or that shall be fielded inside of the foul line" (Chadwick Scrapbooks). Wright argued that this redefinition would solve the long-standing problem of determining whether such hits were fair or foul: "This will equalize the batting and fielding, and also tend to lessen the discretionary power of the umpire, and relieve him of responsibilities now resting upon him. In deciding fair or foul, he need watch the course of the ball only, and only where it strikes the ground before passing the bases." Chadwick cited the same concern in endorsing Wright's scheme: "Though the rules are now nearer perfection than they have yet been, it is yet in order to test any improvement by a season's experience; and of all the plans presented to obviate the difficulties which follow in the wake of fair-fouls, this new rule would appear to be the best. . . . It is . . . desirable that the vexatious doubts of the accuracy of the umpire in judging of fair-fouls should be removed in some way or other, and we know of no more feasible rule than this new one" (Henry Chadwick, "Harry Wright at Work," *New York Clipper*, undated clipping in French Scrapbooks).

To showcase the new idea, Harry Wright arranged to have it used during a postseason exhibition series between Boston and Hartford that was billed as being "for the New England championship" (*Providence Journal*, reprinted in *Hartford Courant*, October 28, 1876). The new approach was unveiled on October 28, 1876, and the response was mixed. The *Boston Globe* commented: "The working of the new rules was of interest to many, as the umpire avoided quandaries in his decisions, and the rabble did not 'Hi-yah' when a fair-foul was made, as the change did away with this kind of batting" (*Boston Globe*, October 30, 1876, 8). Chadwick claimed that the experiment proved "satisfactory to the spectators, though somewhat perplexing to the players through their lack of familiarity with its provisions" (*New York Clipper*, undated clipping). But the contrarian *Chicago Tribune* reported that the players in the trial game "didn't see much difference from the old way" (*Chicago Tribune*, November 5, 1876, 10).

Harry Wright's proposal was adopted at that winter's annual meeting, and, in the process, the fair-foul became extinct. The *Chicago Tribune* pointed out that the legislation that abolished the fair-foul had simultaneously created a new breed of hits: "By the rule of this year a ball which strikes foul ground first, and then bounds into fair ground before passing first or third bases, is a fair ball. Inasmuch as it struck foul ground first, it must be called a 'foul-fair,' following the custom of last year" (*Chicago Tribune*, April 29, 1877).

The wording of the new rule did have one minor flaw, leaving the status of a batted ball that hit first or third base ambiguous. According to Henry Chadwick, "such a ball was called foul because it did not pass 'in front of the base.'" At the end of the 1877 season, the rule was amended to specify that such balls were fair (*Brooklyn Eagle*, January 27, 1878, 3).

The definition of a fair ball created to eliminate the fair-foul remains the basis of the current interpretation, but the status of balls hit out of the park was still a problem. Officially, such balls were supposed to be fair or foul based on where they landed, but this was not always easy to determine. In an 1883 game, National League umpire Stewart Decker simply ignored the rule and declared that his "jurisdiction didn't extend over the fence" (William D. Perrin, *Days of Greatness*, 25). Decker's logic is hard to argue with, but it was nearly half a century before the game's rule makers saw it that way. In light of the difficulties that Babe Ruth's monster shots were causing umpires, they decided in 1931 that a ball hit over the outfield fence would be considered fair if it was between the foul poles when it left the playing field. Aptly, the status of such hits is one of the few situations now subject to review by instant replay.

2.2.3 Fake Bunts. One of the reasons for Arlie Latham's success in reviving the bunt in 1886 was his use of the fake bunt as an effective complement. Obviously this tactic had not been available to earlier practitioners like Barlow who had used a miniature bat. Jim Galvin described Latham's technique as "making believe you are about to bunt the ball, and when the infielders have come up close to field such a ball, then just tap a swift-pitched ball with his bat—a wrist-play hit—and it will go safely out of the reach of any infielder and short of those in the outfield" (*Louisville Courier-Journal*, reprinted in *New York Sun*, October 3, 1886). Tommy McCarthy has been credited with helping to popularize the fake bunt (James D. Smith and Robert L. Tiemann, "Thomas Francis Michael McCarthy," in Frederick Ivor-Campbell, Robert L. Tiemann and Mark Rucker, eds., *Baseball's First Stars*, 102).

2.2.4 Bunting Backward. Jake Beckley apparently turned his bat around to bunt and used the handle side. Half a century later, Casey Stengel recalled Beckley's technique and tried to teach it to some of his Yankee players. He reported: "they say it's the silliest thing they ever saw, which it probably is but Beckley done it" (quoted in David Fleitz, "Jacob Peter Beckley," Tom Simon, ed., *Deadball Stars of the National League*, 232).

2.2.5 Baltimore Chop. During the 1896 season a sportswriter for the *Baltimore News* remarked: "The Baltimore Club has already originated several distinctive plays which have

made it famous and which have been copied
with more or less success by others. Foremost
among these are the 'hit and run' tactics. Now a
new style of hitting will be recorded in the base
ball history of '96 and credited to the Orioles.
It is 'chopping' the ball, and a chopped ball
generally goes for a hit. It requires great skill
in placing to work this trick successfully, and it
is done in this fashion: A middle-height ball is
picked out and is attacked with a terrific swing
on the upper side. The ball is made to strike
the ground from five to ten feet away from the
batsman, and, striking the ground with force
bounds high over the head of the third or first
baseman. In nearly every game lately has this
little teaser been successfully employed, and
yesterday two such hits were made" (*Baltimore
News*, reprinted in *Sporting Life*, November
7, 1896, 1). The Orioles' success with this approach was augmented greatly by the skill of
groundskeeper Thomas J. Murphy, who made
sure that the ground in front of home plate was
as hard as possible.

Use of the Baltimore chop declined after
the demise of the Orioles, ensuring that the
play would be forever linked to this team and
its talented groundskeeper. According to Clark
Griffith, "While the 'chop' ball always worked
perfectly on the Baltimore lot, it was not so successful on the road, and when the Orioles were
finally dropped from the National league, the
'chop' ball died with them. The advanced pitching had much to do with putting the 'chop' on
the hummer, but, in the main, the comparative
softness of other playing fields killed it" (*Cincinnati Times-Star*, January 14, 1909; reprinted
in Howard W. Rosenberg, *Cap Anson 3*, 174).

While the joint efforts of the players and
their groundskeeper created a play that was
novel enough to be named in honor of the
Baltimore club, it was not entirely new. At least
in part, the Baltimore chop was an updated and
modified version of the "Fair-Foul" (**2.2.2**)
as executed by masters like Ross Barnes, who
deliberately hit the ball off the cast-iron home
plate. The play, however, became less viable
after a series of rule changes repositioned home
plate and changed its composition (see **14.3.2**)
(Robert H. Schaefer, "The Lost Art of Fair-Foul
Hitting," *National Pastime* 20 [2000], 5).

*Other related hitting tactics, such as the hit-and-
run and the squeeze play, will be discussed under
"Baserunning" (Chapter 5, part four).*

(iii) And When All Else Fails: Trying to Be a Successful Hitter Without Hitting

2.3.1 Waiting Out the Pitcher. As noted under "Balls and Strikes" (**1.10**), the waiting game
was a familiar element of baseball by the early
1860s. But in those years it was a widely reviled
strategy, and many viewed it as scarcely better
than cheating. Henry Chadwick wrote dismis-
sively in 1860, ". . . It is preferable to play the
game manfully and without resorting to any
such trickery—for it is little else—as this, which
not only tires the spectator, but detracts from
the merit of the game itself" (*Beadle's Dime
Base-Ball Player*, 16).

This perception changed dramatically in
the 1870s as the result of the developments
described in that entry and in the introduction
to chapter 3. In 1876, Chadwick wrote, "Some
batsmen, who have not the moral courage to
play their own game without regard to the
comments of the crowd, are very apt to be
intimidated into a reckless style of hitting, for
fear of being considered 'a waiter at the bat.'"
He thus maintained that "it is no discredit to
him to take his base on called balls under such
circumstances" (*New York Clipper*, November
11, 1876).

This represents an extraordinary reversal in
the perception of a base on balls—from a sign
of moral cowardice to the epitome of courage.
Once this new mind-set had taken hold, batters
felt empowered to originate a whole set of new
approaches to getting on base.

2.3.2 Deliberate Fouls. Baseball batting tactics reached a new level of evolution or devo-
lution, depending on your perspective, when
batters began to unashamedly seek ways to
reach base without hitting the ball. These stratagems had begun to emerge by the 1870s and
have since polarized the baseball community.

On the face of it, the tactic of deliberate
foul balls does not seem that different from
the waiting game of the 1860s (see **1.10**). But
the "waiting game" merely provided the batter
with an advantage in his battle with the pitcher,
and in many cases was a response to deliberate
wild pitching.

The deliberate foul was an entirely different
matter, since it seemed to allow the batter to
avoid the conflict altogether and be rewarded
for doing so. This new reality—that a batter
could use the fact that fouls did not count as

strikes to reach base without even giving the fielders a chance to make a play—flew in the face of the accepted wisdom that taking "bases on called balls [is] something no good batsman likes to do" (*Brooklyn Eagle*, May 9, 1871). It was also at odds with the precious status of baseballs, which made it of paramount importance to keep them from getting lost (see **1.20** and **1.32**).

In a way, the conflict dated back to the earlier one between the New York and Massachusetts versions of baseball. An advocate of the New England rules maintained in 1856 that the concept of foul territory "seems hardly fair; for such players, who from some peculiarity, such perhaps as being left-handed, or any other cause, may find it difficult to get a crack at the ball each in his peculiar style. . . . No, sir! I think half the fun of striking is in the striker's being able, by the novelty of his blow, or the unexpected direction in which he forces the ball, in keeping his side in, by preventing his opponents from catching him out" ("Bob Lively," "Base Ball: How They Play the Game in New England," *Porter's Spirit of the Times*, December 27, 1856, 276–277).

The triumph of the New York version brought a temporary end to such approaches, but by the late 1860s some batters were taking advantage of the catcher being far back of the plate by craftily stepping back into foul territory to swing at pitches. By doing so, they took advantage of the rule of the day, which specified that a ball was fair or foul based on where it first struck the ground or a fielder. Thus if the batter took a swing at a ball and dubbed it, it simply counted as a foul ball. It was also easier for batters to wait until the last minute and spoil a good pitch (Tom Shieber, "The Evolution of the Baseball Diamond," in *Total Baseball IV*, 115).

Players today are commended for being able to foul tough pitches off, but that was not the outlook in the 1860s. Henry Chadwick maintained that a player who hit such a foul "thereby escapes the penalty of his poor batting" (Henry Chadwick, *Haney's Base Ball Player's Book of Reference for 1867*, 21). This philosophy had a dramatic effect on the rule book. There were calls throughout the 1870s to eliminate the foul bound rule, by which batters were out if a foul was caught on the first bounce. But defenders of the rule contended that it was necessary to discourage foul-ball hitting, and the antiquated rule was not permanently repealed until the early 1880s.

The controversy and the importance of keeping balls in play also helped to spawn a couple of important rule changes. First, the rule makers endeavored to force the batter to be in line with the plate when he swung. In doing so, they created early versions of the batter's box (see **14.3.5**), but they failed to accomplish their desired goal. As a result, in 1877 they introduced the current definition of foul territory in which a ball is fair or foul depending on its status when it passes first or third base or is touched by a fielder (see **2.2.2** "Fair Fouls").

This latter change seems to have reduced the use of the intentional foul for a few years, but the tactic made a comeback in the 1880s. Johnny Evers and Hugh S. Fullerton later recalled, "Many of the old timers were skilful in 'pulling' the ball foul in order to wear down pitchers, and by hitting late in fouling off" (John J. Evers and Hugh S. Fullerton, *Touching Second*, 161). As long as such hitters used a full swing, there was little resentment of this ploy since it required skill and entailed risk on both sides.

That perception began to change when such hitters as Mike "King" Kelly found different ways to accomplish the same end. As early as 1880, Kelly was reported to have fouled eleven balls out of play in one game (*New York Clipper*, May 29, 1880). The return of the bunt in 1886 (see **2.2.1**) gave him a more effective way of doing so, as is shown by this account: "Kelly maneuvered to get first on balls. When a fair ball was pitched he held up his bat and tipped it, making it foul. [Pitcher Charles] Getzein pitched seven or eight balls right over the plate, and Kelly made fouls of them. This trick of Kelly's is on a par with his cutting home from second when the umpire is not looking. Some means should be found of making him play an honorable game of ball, as he seems to depend chiefly on trickery. He finally got his base" (*Detroit Free Press*, May 10, 1886).

Kelly accomplished this by "poking out his bat," a tactic that "caused laughter from the spectators at first, but by and by it became as fatiguing to them as to the pitcher" (John H. Gruber, "Strikes," *Sporting News*, January 13, 1916). Others indulged in the still more tedious practice that Doc Bushong described as "blocking a ball off" by "holding the bat slightly behind the home plate, in no case in front of the centre of the plate, and allowing the pitched ball to glance off, with no intention of hitting at all" (*Base Ball Gazette*, April 17, 1887).

The need for a solution became readily apparent during the postseason series between the champions of the two leagues. St. Louis's Arlie Latham "started in the first inning with Kelly's trick of bunting fouls. When after knocking ten of these, he struck out, the crowd howled its approval. When the Chicagos went to bat and Kelly's turn came he bunted 4 or 5 fouls and then, when the crowd had begun laughing heartily, he hit the ball hard enough to get his base, and the laugh turned to cheers" (*Chicago Tribune*, October 19, 1886).

As described in the entry on bunts (**2.2.1**), bunting and deliberate fouls had come to be viewed as virtually synonymous, and many wanted to see both banned. In an attempt to again create risk on both sides, a new rule was introduced after the 1886 season that authorized the umpire to call a strike on "any obvious attempt to make a foul hit." This was a big improvement, but it still left plenty of gray area, which Arlie Latham continued to exploit. The next season, he was described as, "attracting no little attention by a habit he has fallen into of late; namely, at peculiar stages of the game when he comes to the bat he hits foul after foul, some of which go over the fence, the grandstand and out into the street. On one occasion he was warned by the umpire" (*St. Louis Post-Dispatch*, August 13, 1887).

The new rule thus cut down on the most blatant attempts to foul pitches off, but with umpires having to determine that the act was deliberate, borderline cases were not usually called. After the 1893 season the rule was reworded with the intent that "the unskilled will be charged with a strike for 'fouling off' whether through intention or inexpertness" (*Sporting News*, December 23, 1893).

National League President Nick Young instructed umpires to call a strike on any foul bunt, defining "a bunt hit as being made when the bat is pushed or held forward so as to allow the ball to rebound from the bat without its being struck at" (*Sporting Life*, April 21, 1894). This was clear enough, and subsequent tinkering made it possible for umpires to assess a strike on a fouled-off bunt attempt without eliciting much of a protest. Another change was made after the season when a caught foul tip—which had been a nonevent since such plays ceased to count as outs six years earlier (see **11.1.11**)—became a strike. This seemed a fairly minor change, but one sportswriter maintained that it caused a significant drop in bat-

ting over the next two seasons (*Sporting News*, October 31, 1896).

But none of these steps eliminated the deliberate foul. After the change that made a foul bunt count as a strike, standout hitter Jesse Burkett pointed out that "by stepping either forward or back in the box the ball can be sent foul, so as to worry the pitcher and the fielders just as much as if there were no new rules" (quoted in *Sporting Life*, April 14, 1894). Moreover this tactic gained favor as it became apparent that it had additional benefits when a teammate was on base. Horace Fogel explained: "Fouling off balls enabled [a batter] to protect his base runners in stealing, when it was pretty certain they would be thrown out, because of a poor start they had made" (Horace S. Fogel, "Foul Strike Rule Spoils Team Work," syndicated column, *Nevada* [Reno] *State Journal*, February 14, 1909).

An 1897 account noted that Dibby Flynn of Indianapolis "is an adept at driving fouls near left field, and will worry the life out of any pitcher. . . . It is not chance with Flynn, but intent, pure and simple. [Detroit pitcher Thomas R.] Thomas played against him in the Western Association and says that he can bat foul balls all day long against any kind of pitching. If he tries it on here the attention of the umpire will be called to it, as foul balls of this sort are strikes under the rule. Flynn is clever in hitting them, but he does not carry it out well, as he fails to move after hitting the ball, when he would naturally run were he trying to hit it out" (*Detroit Free Press*, May 2, 1897).

But in fact calling the attention of umpires to such tactics was becoming futile. As the "skill of batters in that direction increased through steady practice," umpires concluded that it was pointless to try to gauge the intentions of batters who fouled off a pitch with a full swing (John J. Evers and Hugh S. Fullerton, *Touching Second*, 161). As Francis Richter later recalled, "the question of 'intention' raised such incessant argument that umpires permitted the rule to fall into desuetude" (Francis C. Richter, *Richter's History and Records of Base Ball*, 357).

Johnny Evers and Hugh S. Fullerton indicated that this problem was dealt with swiftly: "The rule makers promptly legislated against foul balls" (John J. Evers and Hugh S. Fullerton, *Touching Second*, 161). Actually, the response was anything but prompt. It was not until 1901, when the warning for an intentional foul had essentially become a dead letter, that the rule makers finally took drastic action (*Sporting Life*, August 17, 1901). The National League legislated that year that any foul with less than two strikes would be a strike.

The new rule proved very unpopular. When it began to be used during that year's exhibition games, there were grumbles that it was "not practical" and would create a return to the days of excessive numbers of strikeouts: "The batters have been 'in the hole' almost every time they faced the pitchers on account of fouls being called strikes, and the number of strike-outs on both sides has been remarkable, even considering that the men have not yet got their batting eyes. The rule will cause a howl from the bleacherites many an afternoon this summer, for the bleachers never forgive a man who strikes out in a tight place, and there will be many who will strike out on account of fouls" ("Players Kick on Rules," *Chicago Tribune*, April 7, 1901, 19).

Two years later the American League very reluctantly followed the National League's lead amid claims that it had been tricked and outwitted into doing so (*Washington Post*, March 1, 1903, 32). Opposition mounted in the years to come as offensive production dropped sharply, with *Sporting Life* editor Francis Richter becoming an especially outspoken critic of what he called "that useless and harmful rule" (*Sporting Life*, January 9, 1904, 4).

Nonetheless the foul strike was retained because the alternative was just as unpalatable. Umpire Hank O'Day regarded the rule change as "one of the best things that ever happened" because it "stopped the tireless process of the batter always trying to get his base on balls. People like to see batters hit. They don't want too much waiting out" (quoted in F. C. Lane, *Batting*, 123).

O'Day claimed in 1901 that the foul strike rule was made necessary by a dramatic increase in the prevalence of deliberate fouls: "When players first made a practice of trying to foul off balls there were only 2 or 3 that could do it. The next year there were about a dozen and this year would have seen still more who were adept at the trick, as players were in the habit of practicing such things in the morning" (*Sporting News*, May 4, 1901).

While O'Day did not name names, others were less reticent, and they almost invariably identified Roy Thomas and John McGraw as the originators. According to the baseball scribe John B. Sheridan: "Batters of the '90s, led by John J. McGraw, made a specialty of fouling off good balls. When fellows like McGraw or Roy Thomas, then with Philadelphia, went to bat the pitchers could expect to have anywhere from 10 to 20 good strikes deliberately fouled off. McGraw would run up half way to the pitcher, swing hard, but late, check his swing and cut fouls along the left line for an indefinite period. Roy Thomas was more skillful than McGraw in this line of work. Thomas had the practice of turning good strikes into mere fouls so perfected that he could take his usual cut at the ball and, getting a piece of it, foul it straight over the catcher's shoulders" (*Sporting News*, February 5, 1925). Connie Mack, reminiscing in 1924, cited Thomas, McGraw, and Hughey Jennings as batters who were adept at using this tactic to draw walks (Connie Mack, "Memories of When the Game Was Young," *Sporting Life* [monthly], June 1924). And a contemporary account provided this description of McGraw's method: "Whenever he picks out a ball he thinks will be a strike he brings his bat to meet it at an acute angle to the catcher, and in consequence the ball is fouled off to the left" (*Chicago Inter-Ocean*, August 29, 1897). One Cincinnati pitcher became so annoyed by Thomas's persistence during a game in August 1900 that he sucker-punched him (Jerrold Casway, *Ed Delahanty and the Emerald Age of Baseball*, 189).

Other sources have filled in the names of the less notorious practitioners who began to imitate Thomas and McGraw. Sportswriter John B. Foster wrote that the "rule was made to stop the dilatory work of McGraw, Thomas, Jennings, [Joe] Kelley, [Cupid] Childs, [Jesse] Burkett, [Win] Mercer, [Fielder] Jones, there are half a score more, who could stand at the plate and knock fouls by the hour" (*Sporting Life*, April 6, 1901). Evers and Fullerton listed "McGraw, Keeler, Roy Thomas, [Jimmy] Slagle and others" as batters who "could prolong the games indefinitely and tire out any pitcher" (John J. Evers and Hugh S. Fullerton, *Touching Second*, 161).

Of course the rule that fouls counted as strikes did not entirely end the practice. Batters continued to foul off pitches that they could not hit effectively, as they still do today. And some teams made a deliberate effort to force an opposing pitcher to throw a lot of pitches so that they could get to him late in the game. Evers and Fullerton wrote in 1910: "Frequently a manager, feeling certain the game will be close, orders his men to wait. . . . Each batter then, instead of hitting, tries to make the pitcher throw as many balls as possible. If a batter can get three balls, foul off three, and then strike out, he may have accomplished far more toward the final result than he would have done had he made a base hit off the first ball pitched . . . every additional ball pitched wearies the pitcher." They credited Chicago with using this approach to beat Detroit in the second game of the 1908 World Series (John J. Evers and Hugh S. Fullerton, *Touching Second*, 165, 266–267).

The effectiveness of the tactic was diminished, however, by the increased likelihood that an unsuccessful attempt to foul the ball off could bring an end to the at bat. As with the 1894 legislation that introduced the automatic strike on a foul bunt, there was now risk on both sides, and that proved a satisfactory compromise. While the years following the creation of the foul strike saw offense decline dramatically and prompted frequent calls to repeal the rule change, the rule was retained.

During the so-called deadball era, batters found an entirely different advantage that could be derived from the deliberate foul. Until the twentieth century, umpires rarely put a new ball in play until the old one was unplayable. This changed during the first two decades of the new century, but it was still common until about 1915 for a misshapen or soiled ball to be in play. Accordingly, a later article in *Sporting News* explained that 1910s slugger Gavvy Cravath would deliberately foul an old ball out of play in order to get the opportunity to hit a new one (*Sporting News*, March 20, 1941).

Needless to say, Cravath was not the only player to recognize this benefit. Roger Peckinpaugh later recalled that, when he first came up in 1910, "if you were behind two or three runs and an old ball was in there, a leadoff man's duty was to get up there and try to foul the ball into the stands so they would have a new ball to hit against" (Eugene Murdock, *Baseball Between the Wars*, 19).

By the twentieth century, major league clubs could afford the loss of the occasional ball fouled out of the grounds. But as soon as this happened, fans began trying to keep foul balls. As described in "Keeping Balls in the Stand" (**16.2.7**), the result was that ball clubs had yet another reason to discourage batters from foul balls. This remained a crucial issue in amateur ball, the minor leagues, and the Negro Leagues long after prosperity enabled the American and National leagues to become more tolerant. Abe Manley, owner of the Newark Eagles of the Negro National League, is said to have once sent a note to one of his players in the middle of an at

bat threatening to fine him if he fouled off any more pitches (Brad Snyder, *Beyond the Shadow of the Senators*, 158).

Even in the twenty-first century the mindset that taking a base on balls is "something no good batsman likes to do" continues to exert influence, as is shown by the differing perspectives of the sabermetric community and traditional baseball analysts about the value of bases on balls.

2.3.3 Crouches. The next logical step after batters began to deliberately strive to gain bases on balls was for them to start trying to help their chances by means of batting crouches. Charles "Duke" Farrell was one of the first, if not the actual originator. A reporter observed in 1889, "Charley Farrell gets many a base on balls by a clever trick that fools most umpires, and he worked it today on [umpire John] McQuaid as he has done before. In bracing himself to hit the ball he drops his shoulder a foot or possibly fifteen inches, and a ball which would be perfectly fair with the batsman standing erect is called 'ball'" (*Chicago Tribune*, May 25, 1889, 7).

This sportswriter clearly felt that McQuaid should not have modified the strike zone for a batter who crouched. It would be nice to know how other umpires interpreted this situation, but unfortunately this is the type of question that is difficult to resolve at this late date. What we can say is that many batters of the era perceived the crouch as a means of drawing bases on balls, which strongly suggests that at least some umpires were reducing the strike zone of these batters. In 1903, *Sporting Life* noted, "The 'Elberfeld crouch' is the latest thing in Metropolitan base ball. The kid's position in trying to work the pitcher for a base on balls is what earned him the new name" (*Sporting Life*, August 8, 1903).

Acceptance of the crouch was slowed by the philosophy that "To be a good batsman it is necessary to stand erect" (quoted in *Pittsburgh Press*, April 28, 1890). But by the turn of the century, some batters were coming to see the crouch as an effective hitting posture. As noted by Skel Roach in "Keeping the Ball Down" (**3.3.3**), Willie Keeler made use of a crouch to chop and cut the ball. Another influential practitioner of a pronounced crouch was George Stone, whose peculiar stance prompted Billy Evans to observe, "[George Stone] uses a very heavy bat and assumes a crouching position at the plate, so much so that a spectator not knowing Stone would believe he was hump-backed. Stone stands close to the plate and in reality half of his body is extending over it when he crouches" (*Sporting News*, February 27, 1908).

The unorthodoxy of Stone's positioning caused many to doubt that he could hit effectively. According to a 1906 article, he had been let go by Boston because manager Jimmy Collins "did not like his [crouching] style and considered him a doubtful batter." But Stone refused to abandon the crouch because he believed "that it gets the eyes in a better position to follow the ball, as they are almost on a direct line with any delivery that comes over the plate. Secondly, the crouch sets the muscles so that a quick chop can be taken at the ball instead of the longer swing employed by most players. As a matter of fact, Stone can and does hit the ball with terrific force, when it looks as though he is going to let it pass without attempting to hit it, so close is the leather to him before he starts his stroke" (*Sporting News* article from 1906; quoted in John McMurray, "George Robert Stone," in David Jones, ed., *Deadball Stars of the American League*, 786–787). Stone was vindicated when he led the American League in batting average in 1906 and began to attract imitators. Washington's Bob Ganley observed in 1907 that his rookie teammate Clyde Milan "has the George Stone crouch at the bat" (quoted in *Washington Post*, August 29, 1907). In the years since, many batters have found a slight or pronounced crouch beneficial.

Of course the ultimate example of using a crouch to increase the chances of drawing a free pass was Eddie Gaedel, the three-foot-seven midget hired by Bill Veeck. Gaedel pinch-hit for the St. Louis Browns in the second game of a doubleheader on August 19, 1951. He crouched so as to have virtually no strike zone and drew a four-pitch walk. Since Gaedel had an official contract that had been submitted to the league, he was allowed to appear in that one game. But American League president Will Harridge refused to approve Gaedel's contract, ending his career.

A James Thurber short story, "You Could Look It Up," features a midget who is used in a similar fashion, but Veeck claimed that the story had not been the source of his inspiration. Researcher Joe Overfield, however, discovered that Gaedel was not the first midget to appear in a professional game. In an inconsequential late-season 1905 Eastern League game at Baltimore, Buffalo manager George Stallings sent midget Jerry Sullivan up to pinch-hit. The first pitch was far too high, but the second was in Sullivan's tiny strike zone and he singled over the third baseman's head. Sullivan ended up scoring and ended his professional career with a 1.000 batting average (Joe Overfield, "You Could Look It Up," *National Pastime* 10 [1990], 69–71).

2.3.4 Getting Deliberately Hit by Pitches.
The rule entitling a hit batsman to take first base was introduced in the American Association in 1884 and the National League in 1887. It would accordingly seem reasonable to assume that hitters didn't deliberately allow themselves to be hit by pitches until after this rule was adopted, but that was not the case. In early baseball the ball was not dead upon hitting the batter, so with a teammate on base, batters could allow a pitch to deflect off them to enable the base runner to advance.

The rule makers attempted to address this in 1872 by instructing umpires to call a batter out if he "willfully" stood "in the way of the ball when pitched to the catcher so that it may touch them and glide off." Unfortunately, like so many rules that required the umpire to determine intent, this was doomed only to start arguments. As a result, two years later a new rule made the ball dead when it hit the batter (John H. Gruber, "Out for Interference," *Sporting News*, February 24, 1916).

This approach solved one problem but created another. Pitchers no longer faced any penalty for trying to intimidate batters. Moreover this change came during the years that pitchers' release points were moving steadily upward, allowing pitchers to generate frightening speed. When brushback pitching (see **3.3.2**) became a major part of the game, the rule entitling a hit batsman to take first base became necessary.

The need for the rule didn't make it popular. One sportswriter was so outraged at the sight of uninjured players trotting to first base that he termed the new rule a "farcical innovation" (*Indianapolis Times*, reprinted in *Rocky Mountain News*, May 5, 1884). His objection was understandable, but of course it was not practical for umpires to determine how badly a hitter was hurt. As a result, batters acquired another way to reach base and baseball drifted further from its original intent of being a game of batting, running, and fielding.

There is of course no way to be sure of who first took intentional advantage of the rule, but it seems clear that Curt Welch of St. Louis was one of the leaders. Hughie Jennings reached base a record 287 times as a hit batsman, but when accused in 1907 of being one of the first to do so deliberately, he denied it and declared, "That gag was working before my time. Quirt Welch [sic], I guess, was the first man to ever reduce it to a science" (*Detroit News*, March 18, 1907). Multiple descriptions of Welch's tactics confirm the claim; in 1891, a sportswriter observed, "No player in the country gets to first base by being hit with a pitched ball as often as 'Curt' Welch. . . . His position at the plate is such that it is difficult for the pitcher to work an inshoot without hitting him. He never jumps out of the way, no matter how swift the ball, and always trots to first as though he did not feel the blow. I have seen his side and arm black and blue from where he has been hit, but his bulldog pride and ignorant courage never permit him to give any sign of pain" (*Sporting Times*, May 16, 1891).

During the first two seasons in which the American Association's rules allowed a free base to a hit batsman, no batter took advantage more than fifteen times. But batters were becoming more proficient and more bold by 1886 when umpire Jim Clinton denied Welch first base after he "pretended to be hit by a pitched ball" (*Sporting News*, May 16, 1886). As a result, when Fred Dunlap was asked if the National League should allow hit batsmen to take their base, he replied, "I will not favor that rule. I think, if we had such a rule as that in the League the players would be colliding with the ball early and often, and that a continuous wrangle would follow" (*Sporting News*, June 28, 1886).

His prediction proved accurate as Welch, Jennings, Tommy Tucker, and John McGraw became the most prominent of a host of players who sacrificed their bodies to reach base. John B. Foster wrote in 1901, "There were batters in the National League last year who played regularly to be hit by the pitcher . . . so many of the pitchers have become perfect in the use of a slow ball that the batters have taken advantage of the fact, and have been schooling themselves in methods to get their base without going to the trouble to hit the ball. Hughey Jennings had lots of fun flirting that big glove of his [presumably a batting or protective glove] into the ball, and many and many a time he was made a present to first when he was no more entitled to it than the Kohinoor [a very valuable diamond]" (*Sporting Life*, April 6, 1901).

This came to pass, however, only after a long series of attempts to prevent batters from allowing themselves to be hit by pitches. In 1892 the so-called Welch Amendment was adopted, by which batters hit on the hands or forearms were not entitled to take first base. But this failed to work and was repealed after five years. In 1901 an unsuccessful effort was made to revoke the free-base rule ("Players Kick on Rules," *Chicago Tribune*, April 7, 1901, 19). Three years later, National League president Harry Pulliam instructed his umpires that a batter should be awarded first base only if he had made an effort to avoid being hit, and that "In no case will he be allowed to become a runner as the result of being hit by a slowly delivered ball" (*Pittsburg[h] Post*, April 7, 1904, 8). But imagine being the umpire who had to tell a batter that the pitch that had hit him was too slow to matter.

While the free base on a hit-by-pitch became a permanent feature, the frequency of batters deliberately exploiting it seems to have ebbed and flowed. Johnny Evers and Hugh S. Fullerton observed in 1910, "The practice of getting to first base by allowing the pitched ball to hit them, is more general with batters than usually is supposed. It is not indulged in as extensively as in former years when 'Red' Galvin used to allow the ball to carrom off his head in order to reach first, but it still is used extensively, despite rules forbidding umpires to allow batters to take first when purposely hit. There is scarcely an important game between contenders for pennant honors, in which a dozen batters do not strive to make the ball hit them" (John J. Evers and Hugh S. Fullerton, *Touching Second*, 165–166). F. C. Lane, writing in 1925, described this tactic as being used "occasionally." He recalled that Fred Snodgrass was accused of getting on base in this way several times during World Series games (F. C. Lane, *Batting*, 142).

This tactic of course remains a part of baseball and is now less painful to batters due to the increasing use of bulky padding. College baseball has been plagued in recent years by an epidemic of batsmen who seem to try to be hit by pitches. It is also noteworthy that, while most rules that require umpires to discern intent have been eliminated from the rulebook, umpires can still negate a hit batsman if they believe the batter did not attempt to get out of the way of the pitch. But such rulings elicit controversy, just as how to handle a hit batsman always has done.

2.3.5 **Deliberate Strikeouts.** On at least a couple of occasions, a batter has been heady enough to anticipate that a two-strike wild pitch presented a novel opportunity to reach base. A *Sporting News* correspondent reported in 1894: "One of the smartest schemes that has been worked on a base ball diamond was that of [Abner] Powell's in a Southern League game last week. After two strikes, [Harrison] Pepper pitched a wild ball which went behind Powell's back and he swung his bat as though he expected to drive a home run. He was past first when [August "Duke"] Jantzen got the ball, and beat the throw to second" (*Sporting News*, June 16, 1894).

Sportswriter Paul H. Bruske gave this description of a play that took place in the second game of a doubleheader between Detroit and Cleveland on June 29, 1905: "[Bill] Donovan was pitching, and Detroit was two runs ahead in the last half of the ninth. [Cleveland batter Bill] Bradley missed two of Bill's benders, and then the twirler let the ball off his wrong finger. It came up ten feet wide of the plate, like a cannot [sic] shot. Bradley's mind worked lightning fast. He whipped his bat around like a flash for the third strike and started for first, all in one motion. The ball was clear out of [catcher Lew] Drill's reach, and Bradley got second on the play" (*Sporting Life*, July 8, 1905).

In 1868, Henry Chadwick instructed umpires that should a batsman "willfully strike at balls for the purpose of striking out, then such strikes are not to be called" (Henry Chadwick, *The American Game of Base Ball*, 52). An addition to the 1872 rules, Rule 3, Sections 5 and 6, incorporated Chadwick's advice. But its purpose was to address games that were about to be stopped by darkness (see "Team Stalling," **12.8**) and there no longer appears to be any rule to prevent the deliberate strikeout.

(iv) Preparation

2.4.1 **Muscle Building.** Until very recently, weight training was considered counterproductive for baseball players, because it was believed that the added bulk was offset by lost flexibility. For example, Bob Shaw told a *Sporting News* reporter in 1960 that he worked with five-pound weights to strengthen his wrist and forearm. But he maintained that heavy weight lifting would be injurious to a baseball player: "Some of this weight lifting is done by people just to build up muscles. In the case of ballplayers, that would be harmful because you might get mus-

cle bound. The entire object of the exercising I'm doing is for strengthening and flexibility. I want to build up my stamina, endurance and power in the throwing arm. However, I'm not seeking bulging muscles. An athlete like a ball player wants to retain fast reflexes and speed" (Edgar Munzel, "Daily Workouts Put Shaw in Pink for Comeback Pitch," *Sporting News*, November 16, 1960).

Of course there have always been exceptions. In 1960, Wally Shannon described his weight-lifting regime to Jack Herman of *Sporting News*, and indicated that he was not alone: "Ralph Kiner lifted weights. So did Hank Greenberg. Jackie Jensen still does and, if I'm not mistaken, Ted Williams did too" (*Sporting News*, January 13, 1960). Williams was endorsing a line of barbells for Sears by 1969, which couldn't have hurt their popularity among aspiring players (*Mansfield* [Ohio] *News*, December 17, 1969).

In the early 1960s, Tony Conigliaro ignored the conventional wisdom and had a grueling weight-lifting regimen. Conigliaro, however, believed that his right arm was what generated his batting power, and focused almost exclusively on that arm. Teammate Rico Petrocelli recalled: "The definition in his arm was just incredible; his right arm. His left arm was sort of atrophied" (quoted in David Cataneo, *Tony C.*, 40).

The Cincinnati Reds of the mid-1970s are usually credited with being the first club to make extensive use of weight-training machines. As usual, the success of the Big Red Machine led to imitators. Red Smith reported near the end of the 1979 season that Carl Yastrzemski had decided to purchase Nautilus equipment because it had helped teammate Fred Lynn (Red Smith, September 14, 1979, reprinted in *Red Smith on Baseball*). Robin Yount's MVP season in 1982, after an offseason of weight training, convinced many others and led John Lowenstein to grumble, "They tell you all your life never to lift weights, then you find out it's just what you should have been doing all along" (quoted by Tom Boswell, *Washington Post*, September 5, 1982; reprinted in Paul Dickson, ed., *Baseball's Greatest Quotations*, 257). Positive results by many of the imitators have made the practice generally accepted, though it is sometimes blamed for a greater frequency of muscle pulls and other specific injuries.

The fact that weight lifting is primarily a recent phenomenon does not of course mean that early baseball players did not have serious workout regimens that were designed to develop their muscles. According to Jimmy Wood, young pitcher Jim Creighton approached Joe Leggett of the Excelsiors of Brooklyn for advice after the 1859 season. Leggett suggested that he spend the winter throwing an iron ball that was the same size as a regular baseball. By the spring, Creighton's "speed was blinding," and he established himself as the game's first dominant pitcher (James Wood, as told to Frank G. Menke, "Baseball in By-Gone Days," part 2, syndicated column, Marion [Ohio] Daily Star, August 15, 1916).

A reporter observed before the 1872 season, "I called in at the Gymnasium, on Elliott street, this forenoon, and found the Red Stocking boys in full preparatory career, pending the opening of the base ball season on next Thursday. As I entered, Calvin McVey was throwing [A. G.] Spalding over his head; George Wright was hanging by his little fingers on a trapeze bar, away up close by the ceiling; Charley Gould was holding Schaefer [Harry Schafer] by the ankles, at arms' length, and about four feet off the floor—the two looking as rigid as if they had been hewed out of granite; Harry Wright was swinging a couple of logs about his head with wonderful ease and perseverence [sic]; [Andy] Leonard and [Fraley] Rogers were climbing what looked like greased poles, but which had no tempting leg of mutton on top to excite their aspirations; [John J.] Ryan, the new man . . . was getting off his lazy muscle through the use of all sorts of pulling and haulings of weights and swinging of dumbbells, each weighing thirty pounds, and [Ross] Barnes was diverting himself on the horizontal bar in a way most cruelly suggestive of hard work. All the boys were as full of health as they could look or be, and if they are not the champions of 1872 it will not be for lack of determination" (Boston correspondent, Cleveland Leader, April 5, 1872).

Tim Murnane later recalled: "The spring practice of the Boston team in the early history of the club consisted of several weeks' training in the old Association gym on Elliot street, commencing March 15 and winding up when the grounds became fit to work on." He reported that a Professor Roberts supervised the workouts (Tim Murnane, Boston Globe, February 19, 1900, also April 19, 1896).

The effectiveness of such a regimen in developing muscles was demonstrated when the Red Stockings visited Detroit to play the Empires, an amateur club that held the championship of Michigan. The local paper was struck by the contrast: "the Empire nine is made up of vigorous and rather athletic young men, all of whom are just attaining mature life. The members of the Boston are athletes, brawny men, trained by long practice to immense muscular power and endurance" (Detroit Advertiser and Tribune, August 22, 1872). Another commented that the Empires appeared "ludicrous by comparison" with their muscular opponents (Detroit Daily Post, August 22, 1872).

But the emphasis was on flexibility, and muscle building continued to be discouraged. Henry Chadwick was especially adamant on the subject, writing in 1880: "What is necessary for a baseball player in gymnastic exercise is to take only that exercise which makes him agile and quick of movement, and which trains the eye to judge the ball, the arms and chest to wield the bat, or the legs to run the bases. Lifting heavy weights, or excercise [sic] which is calculated to develop strength for such purposes is useless. Swinging clubs is carried to excess; jumping is unnecessary; work on the parallel bars, the trapeze, etc., is needless" (New York Clipper, December 25, 1880). St. Louis players were described in 1875 as practicing a "health lift" that involved the use of three- and five-pound weights (St. Louis Democrat, February 28, 1875).

Baseball clubs thus stressed general fitness, as this 1883 account suggested: "The Chicago nine are at work practicing general athletics under the orders of Captain Anson, who acts as trainer, overseeing the work of each of his men. He puts them through a course of running, jumping, weight-lifting, walking and general work. He has not put a ball in their hands yet, saying he has not yet reached the proper point for that" (Chicago Inter-Ocean, reprinted in Cleveland Leader, April 13, 1883).

New York captain John M. Ward told the New York Sun in 1887, "Gymnasium apparatus and gymnastic exercise are going out of favor among ball players for several reasons, and very few of them now attempt to keep in condition through the winter. When you hear of a player going into a gymnasium that usually means he goes in there, tries some feat and lames himself, and then drops in two or three times a week to look on. It is not a good thing for a player to fool with the apparatus. He does not want to develop big bunches of muscle. What he needs is agility, suppleness, quickness of eye, hand and foot. If he goes into a gymnasium he exercises muscles that he does not use in the field, and he either develops [sic] them at the expense of his useful muscles, or he puts too much strain upon them . . . [and] injures himself" (*New York Sun*, March 20, 1887).

Walter C. Dohm noted in 1893 that college players were beginning to focus more on muscle building: "while the snow still lies deep on the ground, the collegian who hopes to get a place on the nine commences putting his muscles in shape in the gymnasium. He pulls chest weights, handles dumb-bells and swings light Indian clubs" (Walter C. Dohm, "College Baseball," *Los Angeles Times*, May 21, 1893).

One professional who followed their example was Buck Freeman, who hit twenty-five home runs in 1899 and credited the development of the muscles of the back and arm. He explained, "I am a crank on exercise. The gymnasium is the best sanitarium on earth. . . . The parallel bars, wrist, and weight machine, and the punch bag are the apparatuses used by me in my winter exercises." But even Freeman stressed that muscle alone did not make a good hitter (*Washington Post*, October 15, 1899).

The general disapproval of muscle building was appropriate to baseball as it was played in the late nineteenth and early twentieth centuries. It is harder to explain why it persisted for so much of the twentieth century in the face of a growing emphasis on power. One likely reason for this delay was the belief that bulky athletes are more prone to certain types of injuries. Tim Murnane, for instance, claimed in 1889 that heavy lifting had fallen out of favor because it had been "known to injure the arms of some of the best men in the business and hurt their ball playing for years" (Tim Murnane, "How the Stars Play Combinations," *Boston Globe*, March 10, 1889, 22).

2.4.2   Swing Practice. Deacon White borrowed from boxing when he devised a regimen for maintaining his swing over the winter. An 1887 article noted that he had been showing it to teammate Charlie Bennett: "It consists of a canvas bag of sawdust suspended from a rafter by a single piece of rope. To keep his arms from becoming too soft during the winter months Deacon White exercises quietly by taking a bat and striking the bag in the same manner that he would strike at a ball. It is not intended to give the eye any practice, but it keeps the arms in good shape without giving them too violent exercise" (*Boston Globe*, February 20, 1887).

Walter C. Dohm noted in 1893 that it had been a common preseason drill for any collegian who hoped to make his school's baseball

nine to train "his eye for the elusive curve ball by banging away for twenty minutes a day with his bat at a big knot at the end of a rope" (Walter C. Dohm, "College Baseball," *Los Angeles Times*, May 21, 1893).

2.4.3   Batting Practice. From time immemorial, batters engaged in some form of pregame practice, but its development into a systematic process was slow and uneven.

The largest obstacles seem to have been practical ones. Baseballs represented a major expense for early baseball clubs, and they could ill afford to lose or deface them for the sake of a little practice. Nor did it make much sense to them to spend their time retrieving baseballs. Another factor was that, as discussed in the entry on "Hitting Coaches" (7.2.4), hitting was viewed as an instinctive skill that could not be learned or taught. As a result, a practice that Henry Chadwick called "fungo hitting" was generally used, and its abolition became the subject of one of his many crusades. Chadwick lost no opportunity to denounce "the absurd fungo practice, which only gives the outfielders practice and is death to good batting" (*Brooklyn Eagle*, April 1, 1889).

The invention of batting practice is sometimes credited to Harry Wright. This is probably based on these 1886 comments by Chadwick: "In April, 1884, we saw something better than [fungo hitting] attempted on the Philadelphia Club field under Harry Wright's tuition, when the batsmen were allowed to bat at a dozen balls each pitched to them for hitting purpose" (Henry Chadwick, *The Art of Batting*, 38). But Wright also kept a tight rein on expenses, and it seems unlikely that he would have been willing to sacrifice many balls to pregame hitting.

By the mid-1880s there were other signs that batters' pregame rituals were taking on greater structure and purpose. *Sporting Life* recorded in 1885: "There are well-developed indications that [Bill] Traffley has improved his batting over last season's record. Judicious practice, and not too much 'batting up' before the commencement of a game, may do much to assist him in this regard. It is believed by many practical base ball men that 'batting up' develops a tendency in *some* players to hit under the ball, which they are unable to overcome when at the plate" (*Sporting Life*, April 8, 1885).

The new approach to batting practice was also reflected in batters using the warm-ups to address specific weaknesses. An 1886 account noted, "The left-handed hitters of the Detroit team—and seven of them bat this way—practice batting a 'south paw' pitcher every morning. His name is Howard Lawrence, and the managers hope that he may develop into a valuable man in time" (*Boston Globe*, May 21, 1886).

In 1888 Baltimore manager Billie Barnie tried to address his team's "weak hitting" by insisting that all his players take a turn practicing batting instead of having just a few players hitting while the rest worked on fielding. Before long he refined this to a specific number of pitches per player (*Baltimore Daily News*, April 30 and May 22, 1888; thanks to Marty Payne for passing these along). Henry Chadwick noted approvingly in 1889 that Louisville captain "Dude" Esterbrook was rotating hitters during pregame practice: "his rule is to have the players take their regular positions on the field and one of the batteries officiate in the points. The other pitchers and catchers will take their turn at the bat" (*Brooklyn Eagle*, April 1, 1889).

By 1891 Chadwick was boasting that his long crusade had finally succeeded. He wrote exultantly that Brooklyn player-manager Johnny Ward had begun "having balls pitched to each batsman instead of knocking 'fungos' for the fielding practice. The latter follows when the team takes their turn to practice in position; but before this good batting practice is in order, and that lies in having balls thrown to the bat instead of batting at balls falling perpendicularly to the ground. I have tried to get teams out of the old fungo rut in this respect for years past, but it is only this year that the needed change has been made. I notice that I am being well backed up in my efforts to advance real team work at the bat, and scientific batting, by such noted captains as Harry Wright, [Cap] Anson, Ward, [Buck] Ewing, etc., and a dozen others I might name, who have had the good sense to get out of the old rut of slugging from the shoulder instead of using wrist play in handling the bat" (*Sporting Times*, May 9, 1891).

New inventions also promoted more productive batting practices. Batting cages originated in college baseball in the 1880s (see **14.4.10**), and by 1894 their benefits had become evident to major league clubs. Tim Murnane explained: "Members of the Boston baseball team are badly in need of a little batting practice. All the work they have been able to get in the way of batting is during the games. When they return to the South end grounds next Thursday the mornings will be devoted to practice, and manager [Frank] Selee will sug-

gest to the owners of the club the putting up of nets such as they use at the big colleges for batting practice" (*Boston Globe*, May 7, 1894). Two years later a pitching gun was unveiled at Princeton. As described in "Pitching Machines" (**14.4.11**), a series of attempts were made to use them to improve batting practices, but success was limited.

Early-twentieth-century batting practices still lacked structure (Benton Stark, *The Year They Called Off the World Series*, 102). But by then there were increasing signs that Chadwick's crusade had paid off. In 1907 new Detroit manager Hugh Jennings began making each of his players "bat about forty times in the course of a day's practice. This shows the system. As soon as the ball has been lined out by one, another steps to the plate. It's like standing in line at a barber shop. 'You're next,' cries Jennings, and each man tries to put one over the fence, while Hughie tells the pitcher how to serve the unhittable ones" (*Detroit News*, March 18, 1907).

2.4.4 Swinging Multiple Bats in the On-deck Circle.

Ty Cobb is sometimes credited with being the first to swing two bats while waiting his turn, but this custom predates his career. An 1897 article noted that the Baltimore players were being credited with starting the "racket of swinging two bats in one hand just before going up to bat" in order to make the "regular bat feel light." But the author of the article maintained that in fact the practice went back to Harry Wright (*Chicago Inter-Ocean*, July 12, 1897). In 1904 Nap Lajoie said, "I have been asked why batters just before they go to the plate swing two bats. It is to make the bat you use feel lighter" (quoted in *Washington Post*, July 24, 1904). Cobb in fact claimed to have improved on the idea: "Another idea that I worked out was the carrying of three bats to the plate so that when two were thrown away the remaining one would feel light. I had seen a batter swing two bats in practice, so I tried three" (Ty Cobb, *Memoirs of Twenty Years in Baseball*, 8).

This form of preparation gradually became more common, and a 1915 article reported, "You will often see a player advancing to the plate swinging two or three bats as he walks. Practically all the good batters in both the National and American Leagues are in the habit of going through this performance before they face the pitcher. Watch men like Ty Cobb, Tris Speaker and Hans Wagner, who are famous for their batting ability, and you will conclude that they consider it part of their day's work" ("Superstition in Baseball," *Washington Post,* September 19, 1915; credited to the *New York Times,* but I could not find the original).

It gradually became standard to recommend this tactic to youngsters, as Billy Evans did in 1922: "As you walk to the plate swing two or three bats until you step into the box. That tends to make the regular bat feel much lighter after you discard the others" (Billy Evans, "How to Play Baseball," syndicated column, *Lima* [Ohio] *News,* May 26, 1922). The practice became less common after the invention of "Doughnuts" (**9.5.2**).

2.4.5   Batting Tees. The batting tee was developed by a coach and former player named Bert Dunne and was unveiled by Dunne's 1945 book *Play Ball Son!* Joe Cronin, in the introduction

to the 1951 edition of Dunne's book *Play Ball!,* wrote, "In the summer of 1946 [Dunne] came East with the Tee which he had finally perfected as a device for teaching hitting." Red Sox teammates Cronin and Ted Williams both saw value in the device, and Williams appeared in a movie that helped popularize the batting tee.

2.4.6   Steroids. The first ballplayer to admit to having taken illegal steroids was the late Ken Caminiti, in a *Sports Illustrated* article published in June 2002. Caminiti acknowledged that steroids helped him win the National League MVP award in 1996. Of course Caminiti wasn't the first major leaguer to take illegal steroids, and other players, most notably Mark McGwire, have acknowledged taking products such as androstenedione, which were not prohibited by baseball at the time.

Chapter 3

PITCHING

OF ALL of the things that it is necessary to understand about early pitching, perhaps the most important is this: almost everyone except the pitchers themselves viewed them as intruders in a game that was supposed to pit fielders against hitters. This perception of pitchers as usurpers endured long after they carved out a larger role for themselves.

Whenever rule changes were contemplated, the opinions of the eight hitters on a club counted for more than the lone pitcher. As a result, while the history of hitting is a tale of techniques, the history of early pitching is a saga of legislative attempts to restore baseball to the way it had once been but would never be again—when the pitcher's role was to give the batter something to hit. As Bozeman Bulger observed in 1912, "Practically every important change in the rules has been aimed at the pitcher. The bat, the ball, the distance between the bases and the fundamental rules of the game have stood for half a century, while the pitching has gone through a steady grind of evolution" (Bozeman Bulger, "Pitching, Past and Present," *Baseball Magazine*, February 1912, no. 4, 71–73).

It appears that the intention of the Knickerbockers was for pitchers to be the least important players on the field, their role being simply to lob fat pitches to the batter. As their name implied, they were required to "pitch" the ball in the manner of a horseshoer. Instead pitchers almost immediately began to hew out a larger role in the game. The frustration this caused was expressed by an unidentified old-timer who grumbled in 1884 about "hifalutin' curves" and concluded by declaring that the

"leather twirlers of to-day" ought to "depend a little more on their support, and not attempt to play the whole game themselves" (*Pittsburgh Evening Penny Press*, July 17, 1884).

Rule makers tried in vain to reclaim the lost ground and restore baseball to a game of hitting and fielding. Again and again, baseball legislators wrestled with the issue neatly summarized by the *Brooklyn Eagle* in 1885: "The question now is, therefore, how can the rules be made so as to not interfere with strategic play in the delivery of the ball, and yet be such as to give greater freedom of play to the batsman, with a view to doing away with the style of play known as 'the pitcher's game,' in which the brunt of the work of the attack in a contest falls upon the pitcher and catcher, while the majority of the fielders stand idly by as mere lookers on" (*Brooklyn Eagle*, November 8, 1885). Again and again, they failed to hit upon a workable solution.

The art of pitching can be divided into two stages: the delivery (what the pitcher does while he still holds the ball) and the pitch itself (the trajectory taken by the ball after it is released). Of course the two are directly and intimately related, yet there is a fundamental distinction. Baseball's rule makers have generally concluded that there is no feasible way to pass legislation based directly on what a ball does after its release—how quickly it travels, how sharply it breaks, etc. But until the mid-1880s they showed no qualms about trying to prevent specific pitches by restricting what the pitcher could do while the ball was in his possession.

The Knickerbockers initially thought it was enough to assert that the ball should be "pitched" rather than "thrown." They saw no need to put any other restrictions on the pitcher. But by the mid-1850s pitchers had begun to make incursions upon those rules in ways that forced the creation of additional rules. This would become a vicious cycle, with each new rule leading to inventive ways of flouting at least the spirit of the rule. The details of this struggle are discussed below.

(i) Deliveries

James A. Williams was a top amateur pitcher in Columbus, Ohio, in the late 1860s when pitching still resembled the act of tossing a horseshoe. By 1884, he was manager of the St. Louis Brown Stockings of the American Association and had seen rule makers struggle for nearly two decades to prevent pitching from becoming overhand throwing. He offered his unique perspective on why it was time to wave the white flag and let pitchers do as they chose.

Williams explained: "The history of the past clearly proves that the pitcher has not been restrained by the rules. That he has always encroached upon them. That for the past two seasons, at least, he has delivered the ball as he pleased." With pitchers in both leagues showing rampant disregard for the rules, the American Association had instructed umpires to strictly enforce the written rules. In contrast, the National League, "recognizing the fact that no rules could be framed that would hold the pitchers in check, as was evidenced by the history of the past years and also believing that no style of pitching or throwing could be invented that would be more effective than the present that would not be used by the pitchers, wisely, in my opinion, discarded all restrictions and thus did away with a rule that has always been a dead letter on the book." Williams believed that the National League's course was the right one because "there is no one point in the game so sure to create a wrangle as for the umpire to attempt to interfere with the pitcher's delivery."

He continued, "So much has been said in the papers in the cities where American Association clubs are located about the great mistake made by the League in doing away entirely with all restrictions in regard to the delivery of the ball by the pitcher, thus allowing him to throw overhand, underhand, round-arm, or even jerk the ball, that it may be of some interest to look at the question minutely, to see if the change is such a great and radical one, and also what effect it is likely to have upon the game.

"Those of your readers who are familiar with the history of the game of base-ball will readily remember the old rule that required the pitcher to keep both feet on the ground when delivering the ball and it was delivered with the arm swinging perpendicular and the hand passing below the knee. That is what is known as a square pitch, and there are many old timers who would like to see it brought into vogue again. Those were the days of lively balls and large scores. With this style of delivery, very little latitude was given the pitcher. The only way of outwitting the batsman was by a change of pace. A few pitchers—notably [Dick] McBride of the Athletics, [Asa] Brainard of the Cincinnatis, and [George] Zettlein of the Atlantics—were able to pitch with considerable speed by an imperceptible whip-like motion of the arm. [A. G.] Spalding of Chicago was perhaps the best exponent of this school of pitching, he having so well disguised the change of pace that he was very effective.

"Then came the underhand throw, and with it a change in the rule allowing an outward movement of the arm but still requiring the hand to pass below the hip. This was gradually encroached upon until the curve was introduced, about 1876, when there was hardly a pitcher who pitched strictly under the rules. Arthur Cummings and Bob Matthews [sic] had pitched a small lateral curve as early as 1868, but it was done by a regular pitch and not by a throw, as later. Later, the rule was still further amended, allowing the hand to pass as high as the waist. But, as before, the pitchers paid but little or no heed to it, and almost every pitcher in the profession got his hand above the prescribed line, the fact being that no curve pitcher can pitch a drop ball, which is one of the most effective of all balls pitched, without getting his hand above his waist. So open and flagrantly was the rule violated that in 1883 the rule was changed so as to allow the hand to pass as high as the shoulder. This concession seemed to make no difference to the pitchers, who pursued the even tenor of their way and delivered the ball in the most effective manner they could; if that required the hand at times to pass as high or higher than the head, that is where they put it. The writer does not remember of seeing but three pitchers in the American Association last season, and he saw all of them, who did not deliver some ball in an illegal manner with the hand passing above the shoulder. The three exceptions were [Will] White and [Jim] McCormick of Cincinnati and

[George] Bradley of the Athletics" (*St. Louis Post-Dispatch*, January 2, 1884).

Others echoed Williams's conclusion that the time had come to admit the futility of trying to legislate against specific delivery techniques. Indeed, many considered the question to be already academic. Early in the 1884 campaign, a Boston sportswriter remarked that the National League's new rule "has not made any noticeable change in deliveries, as had been expected, this well showing that the rule was a recognized dead letter in 1883" (*New York Clipper*, May 17, 1884).

By the end of the first month of the 1885 season, both leagues had abandoned for good the effort to place restrictions on how a ball was released, effectively legalizing overhand pitching. Restrictions continued to be placed on the pitcher's location when he released the ball, his application of substances foreign and organic to it, and his making motions that deceived a base runner. But never again would the pitcher be told that he could not pitch the ball as he saw fit.

How baseball came to that juncture is a fascinating story that begins with a jerk. The Knickerbockers' ninth rule had stated, "The ball must be pitched, not thrown, for the bat." By 1854 the pitcher was required to release the ball from behind a line fifteen paces from the batter and, since there were varying interpretations of the length of a pace, it was clarified in 1857 that this meant forty-five feet. This would be the last time for many years that a restriction on pitching would be introduced without creating turmoil.

The trouble began when the game's legislative body, the National Association of Base Ball Players (NABBP), tried to be more specific about how the pitcher should throw. The rules of 1860 included only one small modification to those of the Knickerbockers: "The ball must be pitched, not jerked nor thrown to the bat." Since the addition of the word "jerked" is the only substantive change, it is clearly significant. But while this term had had a clearly understood meaning when used in cricket, its borrowing by baseball only caused confusion.

The NABBP's rules committee attempted to clarify the intended meaning, but without much success. In 1864 the *Brooklyn Eagle* commented on the latest interpretation: "In reference to the jerking of the ball, no movement can be called a jerk in which the arm used does not touch the side of the body while the body is in an upright position. But when a pitcher stoops on one side in order to deliver the ball, thereby getting all the motive power of a jerk without actually touching the body, then the Umpire is empowered to call a baulk for jerking the ball. According to this interpretation, nearly every swift pitcher now in our clubs jerks the ball every time he delivers it" (*Brooklyn Eagle*, March 28, 1864).

In contrast, *The Ball Player's Chronicle* gave this explanation in 1867: "A 'pitched' ball is one that reaches the batsman without touching the ground. If it touches the ground it becomes a 'bowled' ball. A 'jerked' ball is a ball delivered swiftly from the hand by the arm first touching the side of the pitcher; if the arm does not touch his side the ball is not 'jerked'" (*The Ball Player's Chronicle*, July 18, 1867). (While neither piece is bylined, Henry Chadwick wrote for the *Eagle* and was the editor of *The Ball Player's Chronicle*, so he could well have been responsible for both pieces.)

The inevitable result of these differing interpretations was that every time a pitcher experienced some success, questions were raised as to "whether his pitching was a 'jerk,' 'an underhand throw,' or a 'fair square pitch,'" as Chadwick noted in 1860 (*Brooklyn Eagle*, August 6, 1860). All too often, different authorities had different answers.

Pitchers naturally began to work on deliveries of borderline legality, and the NABBP made a renewed effort to define exactly what the pitcher could and could not do. The first step was to dictate that both of the pitcher's feet must be on the ground at the time the ball was released. (In 1865 it was clarified that a step was permissible before the release.) This rule proved very tricky to enforce since the feet were allowed to leave the ground as soon as the ball was released.

At the same time an even thornier problem had begun to surface. "Pitching" the ball was universally understood to mean a straight-arm motion and a release from an underhand position. Unfortunately, enforcing these requirements was no easy task for umpires. Determining whether a pitcher's hand was low enough at the instant of release was an onerous judgment call. Getting pitchers to adhere to the straight-arm requirement proved still more difficult.

A few pitchers were effective by going to the other extreme. Henry Chadwick reported in 1860, "whenever [Jim] Creighton pitched his balls, he delivered them from within a few inches of the ground, and they rose up above the batsman's hip, and when thus delivered, the result of hitting at the ball is either to miss it or to send it high in the air" (*Brooklyn Eagle*, August 6, 1860). Jim "Deacon" White got around the requirement that a pitcher "stand flat-footed in the box and swing his arm perpendicular without bending his wrist" and achieved greater speed by "[getting] my shoulder behind my heave, and my knuckles almost touched the ground" (Martin Quigley, *The Crooked Pitch*, 44–45). The techniques of Creighton and White seemed to comply with the rules, but this didn't stop both from being accused of illegal pitching.

An even more important new rule in 1863 limited the pitcher from running starts by dictating that he begin and end his delivery from within the confines of two parallel chalked lines. This was the first rudimentary version of what eventually became known as the "pitcher's box" (see **14.3.7**). Over the next thirty years, the dimensions and/or location of the box were altered seven times. The one constant was that the pitcher was boxed in while performing— unless he had the misfortune to be knocked out of the box.

Umpires had trouble keeping the pitcher within the exact constraints of the box, but at least the pitchers couldn't stray too far outside of it. In contrast, the other pitching rules created by the NABBP were proving unenforceable and were only creating disputes. As pitchers routinely ignored them, these rules became dead letters and were eventually removed.

In 1868 the NABBP scrapped the rule that the pitcher's feet had to be on the ground when the ball was released. The Red Stockings' pitchers took advantage by "[advancing] the leg, at the same time they brought the arm forward, and thus gave to the ball the impetus of the whole body and leg" (*Daily Alta California*, September 26, 1869; quoted in Stephen Guschov, *The Red Stockings of Cincinnati*, 85).

By the 1870s, arguments of the legality of specific pitching techniques were rampant, and games often ended with one club marching off the field in a huff. Rule makers had little choice but to liberalize the pitching rules. Before the 1872 season, the bent-arm delivery was explicitly permitted, and the release point elevated to the hip, meaning that "the only style of delivery in pitching in base ball that is illegal now is the overhand throw and the round arm delivery as in bowling in cricket" (*Brooklyn Eagle*, August 13, 1872). Legalizing the bent elbow and pitch-

ing from hip height made it much easier to throw curves.

Albert Goodwill Spalding, probably the most effective pitcher under the old restrictions, gave a couple of intriguing accounts of the reasons for the change. In 1879 he cited competitive balance: "it was found a matter of difficulty to secure good pitchers for all the clubs. In order to remedy the evil the bars which had been built by legislation around the pitcher's position were let down, and the first thing the public knew throwing had come into fashion. At the time I thought it would lead to bad results, but Harry Wright said there was no help for it; there were not first-class pitchers enough in the country" (*Detroit Post and Tribune*, May 31, 1879). He later elaborated that the effect of that scarcity "was to put the question up to the umpire, and if he ruled against the pitcher there was a disappointed crowd, no game, or an utterly uninteresting exhibition." Consequently there was "a growing tendency on the part of umpires to be lax in the enforcement of the rule . . . rather than stop the game and disappoint the crowd" (A. G. Spalding, *America's National Game*, 482–483).

Umpires were no more vigilant about enforcing the new rule, but there was a very important practical consideration that kept release points from going much higher. The *Brooklyn Eagle* noted in 1872 that even "if overhand throwing were allowed, it could never be indulged in to the extent of the full power of the thrower to deliver the ball, simply because no man could stop a ball from an overhand throw—like [John] Hatfield we'll say—thrown with all the speed he could deliver it, consequently such throwing would be useless" (*Brooklyn Eagle*, August 13, 1872).

That restraint was removed when catchers began to wear equipment, and pitchers immediately began to push the limits. An attempt was made in 1878 to make things easier for the umpire by specifying that the pitcher's hand be below his waistline when he released the ball. Predictably, pitchers "elevated their trousers to a point where the 'waist line' was on a level with their chests" (James Wood, as told to Frank G. Menke, "Baseball in By-Gone Days," part 2, syndicated column, *Marion* [Ohio] *Star*, August 15, 1916). Efforts by umpires to enforce shoulder-height delivery were met with similar resistance: "Repeatedly, when the umpire issued a warning note to the pitcher, the latter would answer back: 'Where's your tape measure?'" (John B. Foster, "The Evolution of Pitching" (part 4), *Sporting News*, January 7, 1932). This relentless process led to the sense of resignation articulated by James Williams and made the elimination of virtually all restrictions on pitching techniques inevitable. In 1883 pitchers were allowed to throw from shoulder height, and by 1885 straight overhand pitching was legal in both major leagues.

Thus by the 1880s, experienced observers such as Williams realized that restricting the pitcher's motions was futile. But more than a decade of ceding ground to pitchers had drained the game of much of its offense, making some action essential. Accordingly, rule makers sought to restore some balance by using the only tools that had not sparked controversy: modifying the pitcher's distance from home plate and the size of his box.

In 1881 they moved the front line of the pitcher's box back five feet, to fifty feet from the plate. But the ground thus gained by batters was again lost when first shoulder-height deliveries and then overhand pitching were legalized.

To offset these concessions, a volley of rule changes was made in 1887. The size of the box was reduced, the pitcher was restricted to one step during his delivery, and the pitcher had to begin his delivery with a foot on the back line of the box. Between them, the latter two rules created what was essentially the first pitching rubber, though it was merely a chalk line. (As is discussed under "Pitching Rubbers" [14.3.8], slabs had been part of the pitching area earlier, but they were in areas where the pitcher was not supposed to step.)

These changes were aimed at reducing strikeouts by denying the pitcher the source from which "he derives the power to give the lasting impetus to the ball in delivery" (*Sporting News*, January 29, 1887). By this time there was growing sentiment that efforts to restrict the pitcher had gone too far. Jim Hart, who was to become an influential National League executive in the 1890s and craft many key rule changes, suggested that the new restrictions would leave "no further use for high-priced pitchers" since they could henceforth only "toss the ball up and let the batter whack it" (*Sporting Life*, February 23, 1887). Curry Foley spoke for many pitchers when he grumbled, "The pitcher is now at the end of his rope, for he cannot possibly throw any higher. One year a pitcher makes a wonderful record; the next year, some rule maker wants the number of balls lowered

so as to increase the batting (a moss covered chestnut), and the successful pitcher of the year before suffers" (quoted in the *Cleveland Plain Dealer*, April 21, 1889).

Strikeouts did indeed drop dramatically in 1887, but offense remained lethargic. As a sportswriter put it, "the new rules have made the action of the game faster and thus have been beneficial if they have failed to increase the batting to any great extent." This paradox, he explained, was because pitchers adapted by putting a renewed emphasis on the art of changing pace, with the result that the batter was "either breaking his back at a slow one or hitting at a fast one after it is past him. A good pitcher will tell you that he does not allow a batter to hit the ball only when he pleases, but he makes him hit it. Thus the only way the batting can be increased is to lengthen the distance of the box from the plate so that a batter can gauge the curves and shoots and also 'size up' a slow or fast ball before it reaches him" (*St. Louis Globe-Democrat*, reprinted in *Cleveland Plain Dealer*, April 21, 1889).

This assessment proved prescient. In 1893 the pitcher's box was finally scrapped for good and replaced with a rubber, located sixty feet, six inches from the plate. (See **1.17** for the details and for an explanation of why this actually represented a move of less than five feet for the pitcher.) This second move proved to be sufficient, as offensive production soared in 1894 and 1895. In the years since 1893 there have been occasional calls to revisit the restrictions placed on the pitcher. But the compromise finally hit upon in 1893, after thirty years of trial and error, has proved an enduring one.

3.1.1 Windups. As a result of the frequent changes in the rules governing deliveries, pitchers' windups developed in fits and starts. John B. Foster noted that, before 1863, "The pitcher could take a short preliminary run with the ball, which some of them did" (John B. Foster, "The Evolution of Pitching," part 4, *Sporting News*, January 7, 1932). For example, in a game on October 11, 1862, the pitcher for the Stars of New Brunswick "seized the ball and swinging his hand behind him as if in an effort to dislocate his shoulder, put his head between his legs—almost—and running furiously, discharged the ball some yards away from home base." This pitcher understandably had difficulty with his control, as he had to repeat it "an indefinite number of times" before the

Princeton batter got a pitch that "suited him" (James M. DiClerico and Barry J. Pavelec, *The Jersey Game*, 173).

As discussed in the introduction to this chapter, such contortions led to three important rule changes being adopted in the following year: pitchers were required to keep their feet on the ground when releasing the pitch, the prototype of the pitcher's box was introduced, and balls began to be called when they missed their target. As intended, these new restrictions brought a temporary end to elaborate deliveries. It also ended a number of pitching careers prematurely, as many pitchers could not adapt (John H. Gruber, "The Pitcher," *Sporting News*, December 23, 1915).

R. M. Larner claimed that as a result of these new rules, "The pitcher was required to plant both feet firmly in two holes in the pitcher's box, two feet apart. In that rather uncomfortable attitude the 'slab artist' of ye olden times was obliged to deliver the ball to a batsman by a fair, square pitch. No throwing, or side-stepping, or gymnastic contortions to intimidate the batsman were permitted" (R. M. Larner, "Old-Time Baseball in the White Lot," *Washington Post*, June 26, 1904). This did not mean that all pitchers used identical motions. Henry Chadwick noted in 1867, "Every pitcher has a peculiar style of delivering the ball. Some—like [Charles Wesley] Faitoute of Eureka Club, for instance—have a series of movements in delivery; others simply have but a simple swing of the arm in delivery" (Henry Chadwick, *Haney's Base Ball Player's Book of Reference for 1867*, 55). But there was a basic similarity because the essence of the pitcher's job was to keep runners close to their bases. "The importance of having as few motions as possible," Chadwick added, "is shown in the fact that thereby the chances of making balks are decreased, and, also, but a few chances are offered to base runners in stealing bases on the pitcher" (Henry Chadwick, *Haney's Base Ball Player's Book of Reference for 1867*, 100).

The 1870s saw a few pitchers attempt to conceal the ball from the batter, a development that is discussed in the next entry. Among them was Harvard pitcher Harold Ernst, who was later described as "the pioneer contortion pitcher. It was customary in those days for a pitcher to stand erect and deliver the ball with the hand below the shoulder but Ernst had a way of tucking the ball behind his back, looking over his right shoulder and elevating his left leg as he pitched. That seemed to the spectators a

bad case of monkey business and always called forth derisive remarks from the small boys" (James L. Steele, "How the National Game Developed," *Outing*, June 1904, 336). By and large, however, deliveries remained fairly simple.

In the 1880s, as the pitcher's release point was elevated, elaborate motions made their return. The most celebrated delivery was that of a Yale pitcher named Daniel Jones, whose gyrations earned him the nickname "Jumping Jack." Jones pitched in the major leagues only in 1883 and the results were uneven, but he did pitch the American Association pennant-clincher for Philadelphia. Moreover he did so with such an unimpressive repertoire that one of his catchers, Charley Bennett, claimed that Jones had "very little outside of his peculiar delivery" (*Sporting News*, February 20, 1897).

As a result, Jones's "jumping jack" technique attracted imitators. It was said that the delivery of Washington pitcher John Hamill "takes the cake; he turns his back to the umpire with a get-thee-behind-me-Satan sort of an air, dances a double shuffle on the four corners of the box, and for want of something else to do, pitches" (*Toledo Commercial Telegram*, reprinted in *Sporting Life*, July 23, 1884). "Peek-a-Boo" Veach was another pitcher whose "hop-skip-and-jump motion before delivering the ball" was "extremely puzzling" (*Evansville Journal*, July 30, 1884). A description of Frank Hengstebeck, who pitched in the major leagues under the name Frank Beck, noted that he "shuts himself up like a jack knife and pitches" (*Port Huron Daily Times*, September 20, 1882).

Another scribe later claimed that at this time "the twirler was allowed to take a deliberate run of several feet or even yards before delivering the ball to the bat. Some of the big men, Jim Whitney of Boston, for instance, got the method down so fine that they managed to work up speed which not only puzzled the batsman to a ridiculous degree, but also frightened many of them out of their wits. A pitcher weighing 200 pounds had a tremendous advantage for the reason that he was enabled to put just so much more momentum into his delivery" (*Ottumwa* [Iowa] *Courier*, March 16, 1903). Whitney's antics inspired this amusing description: "When straight he is 6 feet 1 inch high. With the batsman in position, Whitney revolves the ball in his hands several times, then suddenly he curls himself up like a boy attacked with the gripes or a dog retiring for the night, whirls his leg, his right arm shoots straight from the shoulder, and the first thing the sorely perplexed striker knows the sphere has been discharged and started on its errand. For a few minutes the batter is uncertain whether or not the man has a fit, and two or three balls pass by before he fully realizes the situation. Out of all this hysterical demonstration, Whitney manages to put a great deal of speed on the ball, and to practice considerable deception. But the batter is always in danger, because he doesn't know, neither does Whitney, but what the sphere may land on his ear instead of in [catcher Charles] Snyder's hands. He struck several of the Buffalos yesterday, and, as he propels the sphere quite swiftly, it did not create the best of feeling within them. Like the unnamed steed of the western wilds, he ought to be subdued, broken or driven with a curb bit" (Chadwick Scrapbooks, circa 1881 article from the *Buffalo Express*). But while Whitney's "hop, step and jump" delivery was amusing to onlookers, it terrified batters and all too often maimed his catchers: "Whitney, with his long legs and preliminary movements, was able to soak the ball to his catcher with frightful power. He used up both Mike Hines and Mertie Hackett, his backstops, that year, but he puzzled the best batters in the National League" (*Washington Post*, February 11, 1906).

To remedy this situation, the National League dictated before the 1885 season that the pitcher would have to keep both feet on the ground during his preliminary movements. The rule change so exasperated pitcher Adonis Terry that more than a decade later he referred to it as "an idiocy" that "was perpetrated" on pitchers, adding: "If you don't think that rule was a strain just take a ball and try to throw it, even with moderate speed, and keep both feet fixed to the ground. It requires a gyration of arm and body that is worse than seven Delsarte lessons" (*Chicago News*, reprinted in *Sporting News*, October 24, 1896, 3).

As Tim Keefe explained, the rule "was brought in only as an experiment and a protest from any one club against it was to be deemed sufficient to bring back the old 'hop and skip' style." That was exactly what happened on June 7, and Keefe believed it was self-interest that led to the return of "contortionist's movements": "During the season of 1885 the New York club was playing in Boston when everything looked favorable for the Giants winning the championship. But here they struck a snag. . . . Mr. [James] Billings, one of the Boston club Directors, came to the rescue. He held a consultation

with the Providence club, and after considerable pleading they joined hands with him and objected to the new rule. It was immediately changed, previous to the New York club going on the grounds that day. . . . The retrogression to the hop, skip and jump pitching again placed a premium on brute strength. All it demanded to be an effective pitcher was plenty of speed and strength and a series of gymnastics to terrify the batter" (*San Francisco Examiner*, November 18, 1888).

Tony Mullane took advantage of the liberalized rules to unveil a "jumping-jack style. He pauses, then throws both arms aloft, and, taking a short run, delivers the ball hot as a cannon shot to the batter" (*Boston Globe*, June 30, 1886). Guy Hecker also developed "a pretty and lively style. He holds the ball idly in his hand for a moment, then suddenly turns around on one heel, and, if a man is on first base, he frightens him back to the bag by several lightning motions, when the ball leaves his hand and speeds over the batter's square. Sometimes Hecker glances significantly at the umpire, then makes a hop, skip and jump, winding his arm beautifully over his head, and throwing the ball swiftly but accurately just where he has signaled to the catcher. His style is a great favorite" (*Louisville Courier-Journal*, June 21, 1886; thanks to Bob Bailey). But as pitchers found new ways to increase the speed of their pitches, it became clear that the equipment of catchers (see **9.3.2**) had not kept up with their new deliveries. A pitcher named Dan Bickham evolved a style that generated great speed but found that such "pace is useless, as no one could stand the punishment involved in facing such a delivery behind the bat" (*Cleveland Leader and Herald*, April 25, 1886). Bickham's major league career lasted only one game, and experiences like his led to significant adjustments.

In 1887 rule makers mandated that a pitcher hold the ball in front of him and then take only one step during his motion. The intention was, as Harry Wright put it, to ensure that the pitcher would no longer "go through a five minutes' exercise in acrobatic feats before delivering the ball" (*St. Louis Globe-Democrat*, March 7, 1887, 10). Henry Chadwick offered this description of the revised requirements: "In the act of delivering the ball to the bat [the pitcher] can only take one step, and, therefore, if he lifts his rear foot from the line of his position before the ball leaves his hand, he necessarily takes two steps and his delivery becomes 'illegal'" (*Evansville Journal*, April 27, 1889, 7). In essence, the pitcher was beginning to have to pivot as a basketball post player does.

Instead of eliminating preliminary movements, the new rule placed a greater emphasis upon arm pumps, which several pitchers were already employing. Pitchers "began to study deliveries more, and with the swing of the arms over the head coupled with a sort of hitch and kick movement with the feet, they were able to get almost as much speed as formerly" (*Ottumwa* [Iowa] *Courier*, March 16, 1903).

Even before the rule change, pitchers began to adjust to the fact that the benefits of great speed were often offset by the toll it took on catchers. Thus some enterprising souls worked on deliveries that sacrificed pace for deceptiveness. Detroit southpaw Lady Baldwin was described as being "as gentle as a lamb when in the box. He pitches steadily and without any delay or waiting. Usually he throws his arm in a circle about his head, then raises one leg, and a moment later comes down hard with both feet on the ground, when the ball leaves his left hand like a flash" (*Boston Globe*, June 30, 1886).

Another left-hander who had a stint with Detroit, Dupee Shaw, was known for a still stranger set of motions: "There have been long fought and dangerous disputes about the exact number of motions through which Shaw puts himself before delivering the ball. One man claimed thirty-two, holding that he had counted them. An attempt to give all of them would be foolish. A few will be enough. When Shaw first lays his hands on the sphere he looks at it. Then he rolls it around a few times. Then he sticks out one leg; pulls it back and shoves the other behind him. Now he makes three or four rapid steps in the box. When he does all this he holds the ball in his left hand. After he has swapped it to the right he wipes his left on his breeches, changes the ball to his left again and pumps the air with both arms. Then he gets down to work and digs up the ground with his right foot. Then you think he is going to pitch. But he isn't. He starts in and reverses the programme and does it over again three or four times, and just as the audience sits back in the seats with a sigh, the ball flies out like a streak. Nobody knows how it left his hand, but it did" (*St. Louis Post-Dispatch*, June 19, 1886). A later account called Shaw "one of the first pitchers to use the 'wind-up' motion of the arm before delivering the ball, and his antics caused much merriment and good-natured joshing wherever

he appeared" (*Washington Post*, February 11, 1906).

The peculiar motions of Washington pitcher Bob Barr inspired one writer to comment that Barr "steps into the box parrot-toed, and, as he unwinds himself to deliver the ball, he looks not unlike the dissolving view in 'The Black Crook.' From the many preparatory motions he goes through, one might suppose that he was trying to mesmerize the batters" (*Philadelphia North American*, June 11, 1886).

Other onlookers noticed that the pitchers who replaced leg movements with arm movements bore a resemblance to clock-winders. The *New York Sun* remarked in 1889: "[Bert] Cunningham, Baltimore's clever little pitcher, still does the 'wind-the-clock act' while delivering the ball when none of the bases are occupied" (*New York Sun*, April 30, 1889). The *Detroit Free Press* noted in 1902: "Al Orth is not very popular with the Washington fans. His slow motion in delivering the ball has caused it all. He takes plenty of time to wind himself up" (*Detroit Free Press*, May 2, 1902). Thus was born the word "windup."

The 1887 rule changes significantly reduced the variety of deliveries and led to much speculation about which pitchers would be able to remain successful. Larry Corcoran predicted that only Phenomenal Smith and Harry Pyle would suffer greatly, claiming that several other jumpers did so only out of habit (*Detroit Free Press*, February 5, 1887). It turned out that pitchers who had relied upon the banned deliveries had mixed success at adapting. Tom Shieber noted that Guy Hecker, who had used a running start, was never the same. Ed Morris, who used a skipping motion, struggled in 1887, then rebounded in 1888 for one last big season (Tom Shieber, "The Evolution of the Baseball Diamond," in *Total Baseball IV*, 117). Tony Mullane, however, never missed a beat, recording his fifth straight thirty-win season.

On the other extreme was Henry Boyle, who declared before the season that "the new rules would perhaps benefit him more than any pitcher in the League. His natural position in the box is the one prescribed by the new rules" (*Louisville Courier-Journal*, April 10, 1887). Boyle saw his earned run average more than double that year.

After the 1887 changes, a few pitchers still essayed elaborate motions. Baseball writer E. K. Rife offered this description of St. Louis's Cy Duryea in 1891: "He poses on one foot, and executing a grand *pas de seul*, like a $4-a-month man opening a keg of nails, casts his mild blue eye toward [St. Louis first baseman Charles] Comiskey with a sort of 'Willie-do-you-miss-me' look, and sends the ball hustling through the air" (*Williamsport Sunday Grit*, August 9, 1891).

During his first two seasons of 1890 and 1891, Cy Young employed an elaborate pitching motion that sportswriters expended considerable ink in trying to describe. One observed that "he winds up his arm, then his body, then his legs, bows profoundly to his great outfield, straightens up again, then lets her go. It is difficult to tell whether the ball comes from his hands or his feet." Other scribes settled for fanciful analogies, comparing Young's delivery to "a man climbing a stake-and-rider fence" and "a corkscrew with an ecru handle" (*Boston Globe*, quoted in *Cleveland Plain Dealer*, June 5, 1891; *Sporting News*, October 10, 1891; *Cleveland Plain Dealer*, May 9, 1891; all quoted in Reed Browning, *Cy Young*, 151).

Ted Breitenstein was reported in 1892 to have a delivery that "beats [Scott] Stratton's all to pieces for contortion business. He shakes the ball behind the back of his neck a couple of times, brings it around in front of him with a double shuffle, draws back his head and body, pirouettes like Carmencita and then lets the ball go across the plate with a speed that is truly wonderful. When men are on the bases he leaves out the funny business, which lessens his speed considerably" (*Brooklyn Eagle*, May 27, 1892).

In 1898, *Sporting News* reported: "Another 'Jumping Jack' is liable to be seen on the diamond again this year. Jerry Nops, of the Baltimores, is said to be developing a new style of pitching which for weird and eccentric movements is said to far exceed anything ever attempted by the famous Jones, and is most startling in its effect. Nops faces the batter, when with a jump, he lands himself in the box facing second base. Pausing a moment his next move is an awe-inspiring jerk of the ball as he twists around, and another kangaroo jump completes the movement. The effectiveness of the delivery depends upon how badly the paralyzed batter is frightened" (*Sporting News*, May 7, 1898).

But such innovators were members of a dying breed. Reed Browning speculated that Cy Young may have scrapped his elaborate windup when he recognized that Kid Nichols was just as successful as Young with no windup at all (Reed

Browning, *Cy Young*, 151–152). Other pitching stars of the era felt the same way. Clark Griffith dismissed the elaborate windmill windups used by some pitchers as "wasted motion" (Gerard S. Petrone, *When Baseball Was Young*, 98). So too, a description of "Three-Finger" Brown's delivery stated, "Like all truly great pitchers, Brown does not wind up like an eight-day clock before pitching. He gets the ball away with the least possible exertion, throwing with an easy over hand motion and putting his whole body into the swing, thus conserving the strength of his arm and developing tremendous speed at the same time" (*Saginaw Evening News*, March 13, 1909; quoted in Cindy Thomson and Scott Brown, *Three Finger*, 87).

As implied by the comments about Brown's motion, recognition was growing that a fluid windup was easier on the pitching arm. John Clarkson had reacted to the 1887 rule changes by expressing concern that reducing the "swing or body motion" would cause the strain on a pitcher's arm to become "more direct and trying" (*Base Ball Gazette*, April 24, 1887). Minor league manager Charles Faatz observed in 1898 that using "the body-motion . . . relieves the strain, and will add, at least, a third to the probable period of the pitcher's professional effectiveness" when compared to a man who "used only his arm in pitching" (*Oklahoma City Daily Oklahoman*, February 18, 1898).

Growing recognition of the wisdom of these observations is one reason why the twentieth century has seen a pronounced tendency toward orthodoxy in delivery techniques. The selection process begins with scouts, who generally presume that a successful pitcher with an awkward delivery will be unable to sustain his performance. Hugh Jennings recalled that the Tigers once turned down an opportunity to acquire a promising young pitcher because a scout was adamant that his sidearm delivery would never succeed in the major leagues: "If he's going to get anywhere in the major leagues with the stuff he's got, he must pitch overhand, and I don't think this fellow will ever learn to pitch overhand. He's one of those that you can't change the style of." The pitcher in question was Grover Cleveland Alexander (Hugh Jennings, *Rounding First*, Chapter 75).

Despite such blunders, scouts have grown increasingly picky in evaluating pitchers' deliveries. Sportswriter David Rawnsley observed: "Scouts are often quick to classify pitchers according to perceived flaws in their mechanics (i.e., arm action and delivery). One pitcher is a 'stabber,' another one 'wraps,' a third pitcher 'pole vaults' over a stiff front leg, a fourth might be a 'slinger.'. . .'Slingers,' for instance, are considered bigger injury risks because they are opening the front of their shoulder early and exposing both their rotator cuff and the inside of their elbow to more pressure" (*Baseball America*, August 9–22, 1999).

The few pitchers with unorthodox deliveries who make it into professional ball are further winnowed down by pitching coaches. Roger Kahn noted that "Most contemporary pitching coaches preach against elaborate windups. They reason that the more motion, the greater the chance for something to go out of whack." He quoted pitching coach Dick Bosman's maxim: "The simpler the mechanics of a delivery, the easier it is for most pitchers to master it" (Roger Kahn, *The Head Game*, 167).

3.1.2   Deception. Few pitchers wore gloves before the 1890s, which of course made it difficult to conceal the ball. Moreover rules in the 1880s often specified that the pitcher face the batter and present the ball. Nonetheless pitchers were trying to hinder the batter from picking up the ball long before Luis Tiant came along.

Speaking of Luis Tiant, by the late 1870s, a few pitchers were experimenting with deliveries in which they turned their backs to the batter. A man named Williams who pitched for the Ludlows of Ludlow, Kentucky, was described in 1875 as customarily "pitching with his back towards the batsman" (Chadwick Scrapbooks). In a game that year for the Missouri state championship, "'Bobb,' the pitcher of the Nationals, turned his back at times to the batsman, a la Williams' style, but it did no good, as when he did that he generally pitched wild" (*St. Louis Globe-Democrat*, August 8, 1875).

Although Williams's first name was not given, he was probably Dale Williams, who joined Cincinnati for the National League's inaugural season in 1876. Also on that team, Dory Dean "brought out a new delivery, which consisted in facing second base with the ball in hand, and then turning quickly, letting it come in the general direction of the stand, without any idea of where it really was going to land" (*Chicago Tribune*, July 28, 1876). The *Chicago Tribune* characterized this as a "foolish boy's trick," and the White Stockings might have questioned its legality if they hadn't been too busy running around the bases during a 17 to 3 win. According to another game account, "After the visitors [St. Louis] had knocked nine

safe hits out of Dean's back-sided delivery, he faced about, and through the rest of the game threw square from the shoulder. The Browns say they only tolerated it because they have such a soft thing. Unless the Reds get a pitcher they will go to pieces. The crowd to-day hooted Dean and filled the air with quacking in the ninth inning" (*St. Louis Globe-Democrat*, August 4, 1876, 8).

Neither Williams nor Dean experienced any success that year, and neither ever again pitched in the major leagues, but they did leave a legacy. By 1878 Harvard pitcher Harold Ernst, whose motion was described in the preceding entry, was using a similar delivery, and in turn he taught it to Johnny Ward of Providence (*New York Clipper*, December 14, 1878, January 25, 1879). Ward's "fore and aft style of delivery" during the 1878 campaign proved very "puzzling" to National League hitters (*Milwaukee Sentinel*, September 13, 1878).

This led to the introduction of a new rule on December 4, 1878, barring pitchers from completely turning their back on the batter during their delivery. Henry Chadwick noted that there had been "but one pitcher of the League who pitched in that way" and therefore "it certainly looked like an instance of special legislation" against a specific player (*New York Clipper*, December 28, 1878). Ward, however, expressed less concern, telling a reporter that it was "not necessary for him to turn his back to the batsman in pitching in order to be effective. It was only a dodge of his—learned from Ernst of the Harvards—to prevent the batsman from judging the ball. He can pitch with more accuracy by facing him" (*New York Clipper*, January 25, 1879).

Indeed Ward unveiled a new wrinkle the next spring: "In facing the striker he completely hides his delivery by seizing the ball in his right hand, carrying it to the small of his back, then by the aid of his left arm carries over to the right in front of his body, he fixes the ball in preparation for a curve-pitch" (*New York Clipper*, April 26, 1879).

The technique of turning the back to the batter seems to have largely disappeared during the 1880s as pitchers adapted to a series of rules changes. One exception was John Clarkson, yet the sportswriter who described his motion clearly did not think that he benefited from it, writing that he "stands with his face to the second baseman and suddenly whirls around and sends the ball to the plate with a rapidity of motion that should be startling to the batter. Of course, on the man that knows Clarkson's style it hasn't the least effect, but Clarkson thinks it has, and that's just as good" (*St. Louis Post-Dispatch*, June 19, 1886). That winter the rule makers specified that the pitcher had to "hold the ball so that it can be seen in his hand by the umpire" (Henry Chadwick, *Aberdeen* [S.D.] *Daily News*, March 16, 1887).

That rule became increasingly unenforceable in the 1890s due to a number of developments, including pitchers beginning to wear gloves. By 1891, Jimmy Williams observed, "The rule requiring the pitcher to face the batter and hold the ball in front of him before delivery, is evaded to such an extent now that the practice is almost as bad as it was before the rule is adopted. There is hardly a pitcher who delivers the ball according to the strict construction of the rule" (*Sporting Times*, May 16, 1891). Pitcher Lester German declared in 1894 that "a pitcher who allows the batsman to see the ball all the time is at a disadvantage. Of course, the rules will not permit one to hold the ball behind the back before delivering it, as was the case years ago, but if one is blessed with large hands, large palms being plentiful in baseball, it is an easy matter to conceal the ball, or practically so" (*Boston Herald*, May 20, 1894).

Cy Young reportedly turned his back to the hitter while winding up (Robert L. Tiemann, "Denton True Young," in Frederick Ivor-Campbell, Robert L. Tiemann, and Mark Rucker, eds., *Baseball's First Stars*, 180; Reed Browning, *Cy Young*, 151). Most pitchers of the 1890s were more subtle, however; according to an insightful 1895 article, "while every pitcher obeys the rule by holding the ball in front while getting ready, he invariably temporarily puts it out of sight behind him just before his arm swings forward, thus succeeding after all in getting it momentarily beyond the line of vision of the batsman." It then offered detailed descriptions of each New York Giants pitcher before concluding, "The greater the radius in which the arm sweeps while delivering the ball, the more deceptive is the delivery to the batsman, and the more difficult it is for the batsman to measure the angle of the approaching sphere" (unidentified clipping from the Amos Rusie Hall of Fame file, hand-dated June 12, 1895). John J. Evers and Hugh S. Fullerton observed in 1910, "Shadowing the ball, which was an art in former days, is almost lost. A few pitchers try it, but without the skill of Bert Cunningham, Mattie Kilroy, Willie McGill and many of the old school. [Clark] Griffith was the last pitcher

to use it steadily. Shadowing consists of the pitcher sidestepping and placing his body on the line of the batter's vision, so that the ball has no background except the pitcher's body and the batter cannot see it plainly until the ball almost is upon him" (John J. Evers and Hugh S. Fullerton, *Touching Second*, 116).

But as implied by these comments, back-to-the-batter motions became uncommon after the turn of the century. The two biggest factors seem to have been the movement toward standard windups described at the end of the preceding entry, and pitchers choosing methods of hiding the ball that did not affect their control. *Sporting Life* reported in 1908, "Jake Stahl says there are only three pitchers who have the out-of-sight delivery, [Fred] Glade, [Addie] Joss and [Jack] Chesbro. 'Glade,' says Stahl, 'faces the second baseman and then wheels around. That sort of a delivery makes any batter pull a little, and that's the reason Glade is so effective'" (*Sporting Life*, April 18, 1908). Joss created additional deception with a high leg kick that hid the ball from the batter (Scott Longert, *Addie Joss*, 18). All three pitchers, however, were out of baseball by 1911, and the back-to-the-batter motion became a rare sight.

3.1.3 Crossfire.

Until 1872, pitchers were required to use an underhand motion. But this was difficult for umpires to enforce, and pitchers like Boston's Tommy Bond "kept inching up on the rules until he was throwing from a point several inches above his waist" (Bozeman Bulger, "Pitching, Past and Present: The Evolution of the Twirler's Art," *Baseball Magazine*, February 1912, 71–73).

In 1872 the sidearm delivery was legalized and many pitchers used it to great effect, with Bond being one of the most successful. Having won this concession, pitchers continued to try to get away with higher and higher release points. Eventually overhand pitching (1.33) was legalized in the early 1880s, and the sidearm delivery seemed to be headed for extinction.

But sidearm pitching motions never died out altogether, and they received a boost in 1896 when Boston signed pitcher Willie Mains, who used a motion that became known as the "crossfire." The crossfire is not synonymous with a sidearm release point. As researcher Wayne McElreavy explained to me, the term crossfire in fact refers to the direction of the arm's motion and that of the pitcher's step leg—in a crossfire delivery, the movements of the leg and arm make an X. In practice, this is most commonly done with a sidearm release, but that is not necessarily the case.

Mains's novel pitching style startled observers and baffled batters. The *Boston Globe* remarked that Mains "was wilder than a stray cat, but was full of interest for the crowd, who enjoyed seeing him cutting semicolons with his left toe just before letting go a fast 'crossfire.' Captain [Hugh] Duffy has impressed the Maine sapling with the importance of throwing a ball from the direction of third base, while Foot No. 1 is attached to the pitcher's rubber plate." Another article the same day observed that Mains "has a peculiar style. As he starts to pitch he steps into the extreme corner of the box towards third base and delivers the ball cat-a-cornered across the plate. On account of this angle, the batsmen seemed to be easily deceived" (*Boston Globe*, April 21, 1896).

The crossfire made a significant comeback in the next few years and through the first decade of the twentieth century. A primary reason for its success was the deceptiveness inherent in the delivery. Ty Cobb noted that one of the factors in Eddie Plank's success was that his "cross-fire was one of the most deceptive deliveries that I have ever seen" (Ty Cobb, *Memoirs of Twenty Years in Baseball,* 112). Other pitchers whom Cobb credited with inspiring the delivery's revival were Billy Donovan, Addie Joss, and Fred Glade (Ty Cobb, *Memoirs of Twenty Years in Baseball,* 119). Note that in the preceding entry, Joss and Glade were singled out by Jake Stahl for their ability to keep the ball out of the batter's sight during their deliveries. Another early-twentieth-century pitching star, Earl Moore, followed Mains's example by standing in the extreme corner of the pitcher's area to accentuate the angle (Tony Bunting, "Earl Alonzo Moore," in David Jones, ed., *Deadball Stars of the American League,* 644).

By 1910, however, Johnny Evers and Hugh Fullerton were reporting that "the deadly cross fire used with wonderful effect fifteen years ago, almost has been abandoned" (John J. Evers and Hugh S. Fullerton, *Touching Second,* 115). Since then, both the sidearm delivery and the crossfire have remained uncommon, with the latter term falling out of use.

3.1.4 Submarine. Pitchers were restricted to underhand deliveries until 1872. Once higher release points were legal, most pitchers felt they had to use them in order to continue to pitch in the major leagues. This perception was reinforced by the simultaneous development of the curveball, which broke much more sharply when thrown with the extra speed enabled by a higher release point.

By the 1890s, however, Billy Rhines established that the underhand delivery made it difficult for batters to pick up the ball and that, while an underhand curve might not break as dramatically as an overhand one, its unfamiliar trajectory could render it just as baffling. In 1896, *Sporting News* reported, "[Al] Orth, of the Philadelphias, is copying the underhanded movement of Billy Rhynes [sic]. This motion, though an old swing, is new to the majority of major league batsmen, and therein lies its effectiveness."

Tim Murnane commented in 1907, "Other pitchers had worked the raise ball, but Rhines was the first man to get the jump on the ball without actually throwing it, as [Joe] McGinnity does at the present time. In fact, McGinnity is a perfect imitation of Rhines in his book work, and the master was fully as invincible as the student when he was in perfect shape for his best work. Rhines will go down in baseball history as the inventor of the natural raise on a pitched ball. Although Robert Mathews was the first to introduce a slow raise, as far back as '72" (*Boston Globe*, June 27, 1907, 30).

When Rhines began the revival of the underhand delivery, pitcher Dave Foutz, whose career had begun when overhand deliveries were still illegal, commented that no pitcher could use the "same curves and speed, both with an underhand and overhand movement. This is an awful strain on the cords and muscles of the arm, as any pitcher will tell you. The underhand pitch pulls the cords one way, and the overhand pitch another, causing a wear and tear, which no arm will stand for any great length of time" (*Sporting Times*, May 16, 1891). Perhaps he was right, as most underhand pitchers since then have used that release point exclusively.

As with the crossfire, the submarine motion enjoyed a vogue of popularity in the early twentieth century, with such pitchers as McGinnity, Bill Phillips, Deacon Phillippe, Jack Warhop, and Carl Mays experiencing success with it. By the 1930s it had receded again, with the notable exception of Elden Auker.

This trend would suggest that the underhand style was most effective when batters were unaccustomed to seeing it, which may account for why its reemergence in the 1970s was largely restricted to relievers. Since then there have always been a few effective submariners manning major league bullpens. Despite the results achieved by such relievers as Ted Abernathy, Kent Tekulve, Dan Quisenberry, Mark Eichhorn, Chad Bradford, and Byung-Hyun Kim, there has been no corresponding success among underhand starters.

3.1.5 Leg Kicks. The development of the leg kick came relatively late because of delivery restrictions and the ease of stealing against it. An 1886 description of Charley Sweeney's motion explained that he used a leg kick but modified it according to the situation: "When men are on bases Sweeney rolls the sphere continuously between both hands, meanwhile watching the bags carefully. Suddenly his right leg comes up, and, as it comes down, the ball speeds away" (*St. Louis Post-Dispatch*, June 19, 1886). Clark Griffith claimed to have scuffed the ball during his delivery, which implies both a high leg kick and impressive balance. Chief Bender was one of the first pitchers who became well known for a high leg kick.

(ii) Pitches

The development of the pitcher's basic weapons—the pitches—is a fascinating saga of ingenuity, resourcefulness, happenstance, and even intrigue. That might not appear to be the case at first pass. Eddie Lopat once described the introduction of new pitches as "sometimes a pitcher falls into something. George Blaeholder fell into the slider. Elmer Stricklett fell into the spitter. Tom Seaton or somebody else fell into the knuckler. Candy Cummings, back there in Civil War times, fell into the curve ball." Lopat, however, added an all-important qualifier: "But all of these men must have had basic assets of more than ordinary value before they tried to hit the moon" (quoted in *Sporting News*, April 6, 1960). In addition, as we shall see in this chapter, new pitches have arisen in clusters when the success of one pitch has inspired others to try new grips and techniques.

The two most fundamental pitches, the fastball and the change of pace, were in place in the 1860s. These were the only two pitches that could be fully mastered while adhering to the delivery restrictions of the day. Both have remained a basic part of the pitcher's repertoire ever since, even while those repertoires have expanded to include many fancier pitches. Both continue to present the batter with the same fundamental challenge—the fastball overpowers him while the change of pace disrupts his timing.

Most of the additions to the two fundamental pitches have taken place during two revolutionary flurries of inventiveness, which occurred a generation apart. The first was the curveball family of pitches, most notably the sinker and the curve, which began in the mid-1870s when liberalized delivery rules made the curveball practical. The second was the spitball family of pitches, including the forkball, the palm ball, the knuckleball, the emery ball, and the screwball. This second revolution was initiated less predictably shortly after the turn of the century.

It may be argued, especially by those who know a great deal more about pitching than I do, that the pitches included in these families are not similar enough to warrant this classification. But my designation of them is not based primarily on mechanical likeness. Rather, my contention is that the curveball and the spitball created climates in which pitchers felt that it was worth putting in the considerable time necessary to master a new pitch.

The second of these revolutions had finished running its course by about 1915. Since then the number of new pitches has been quite limited, which is not to say insignificant. The primary additions to the pitcher's repertoire since then have been hybrids—the slider, the circle change, the split-fingered fastball, and the cutter—and novelty pitches, such as the eephus and the extremely short-lived kimono pitch (see **3.2.17**).

3.2.1 Fastball. The fastball was one of the crucial differences between the version of baseball played by the Knickerbockers and the Massachusetts Game. In New England, "The ball was thrown, not pitched or tossed . . . and with a vigor, too, that made it whistle through the air, and stop with a solid smack in the catcher's hands" ("Bob Lively," "Base Ball: How They Play the Game in New England," *Porter's Spirit of the Times*, December 27, 1856, 276–277). By contrast, those who played the New York Game imposed a long series of restrictions to try to keep fast pitching from overwhelming batters. Since it would have been futile to try to ban the fastball or specify a maximum legal speed, a variety of restrictions was devised.

By 1854, a minimum distance between pitcher and batter had been added to the rules. That was followed by the series of delivery restrictions discussed in the introduction to this chapter. Descriptions of these restrictions often made it explicit that their aim was to limit the speed of fastballs. An 1864 piece counseled: "Umpires must remember, in deciding on this movement of the feet, that no one can lift his foot in delivering a ball until the ball leaves his hand, the lifting of the hind foot being the result of this delivery, as it is from the pressure of the foot on the ground that he derives the power to impel the ball with speed." The same article later noted: "A strict adherence to these new rules must perforce result in there being less speed in pitching, the making of accuracy in aim the great desideratum in effective play, and the transfer of the interest of a match from the pitchers to the basemen and outerfielders" (*New York Clipper*, May 7, 1864).

As discussed throughout the section on "Deliveries" (3.1), that strict adherence did not occur. The result was that fast pitching came to be curbed in two main ways: by the base on balls and by additional relocations of the pitcher's area that created the current distance of "Sixty Feet, Six Inches" (1.17).

3.2.2 Change of Pace. The change of pace, then known as the slow ball, is the only other pitch to have been extensively used before 1870. Its most celebrated early practitioners were Alphonse "Phonney" Martin of the Eckfords of Brooklyn and Harry Wright, who would pitch in relief when opposing batters were teeing off on a fastball pitcher. *Sporting News* noted in 1891, "Martin was celebrated for his slow drop ball up to 1872, depending on his field for outs. Harry Wright was effective with the same ball until the players got more proficient in the use of the bat" (*Sporting News*, December 19, 1891).

A. H. Spink added that Martin was known as "Old Slow Ball," and that his "slow ball came to the plate at such a snail-like pace that it nearly drove the batsman crazy and when he got ready to hit it good and hard it seemed to carrom away from him. Martin pitched the ball with a twist of the fingers and the wrist, manipulating the sphere about as you would a billiard ball when you wanted to put the English on it. His delivery set the spectators as well as the opposing batsmen nearly wild. It was so long and drawn out that it tired the spectators and so slow that it maddened the batsman so that he tried to kill it. Instead of doing that he usually drove the ball high and generally to the left field where Al Gedney, the Eckfords' speediest and best outfielder, generally took good care of it" (A. H. Spink, *The National Game*, 57, 139).

Some have questioned whether Martin or Wright was really throwing a change of pace, since neither had an effective fastball. John Thorn and John Holway suggested that A. G. Spalding was the first to utilize a pitch with the same motion as a fastball but at slower speed (John Thorn and John Holway, *The Pitcher*, 152). A *Sporting Life* correspondent concurred: "Spalding got his first idea of slow pitching from [Harvard catcher] Archie Bush, and is credited with being the first to combine the two styles of slow and swift delivery, or 'change of pace,' without varying the motion of the arm and body" (*Sporting Life*, September 10, 1883). Hugh Fullerton called Charlie Radbourn "the pioneer of the 'slow ball' and the inventor of the change of pace" (*Chicago Tribune*, August 12, 1906).

It seems clear, however, from Henry Chadwick's contemporaneous descriptions that the pitch was being used in the 1860s just as it is today. Chadwick explained in 1867 that Phonney "Martin is not a slow pitcher, his delivery is medium paced, and, what is more, varies in pace as much as any pitcher's delivery we know of, and therein lies much of his success against all but the most experienced batsmen" (*The Ball Player's Chronicle*, June 13, 1867). Two years later he suggested that Rynie Wolters should "try to acquire Harry Wright's strong point of changing his pace in delivery without any change of motion—one of the most effective points there is in pitching" (*National Chronicle*, February 13, 1869). Elsewhere he described Wright as "a great coaxer, the ball coming at one time so slow that the striker will hit too quick, either missing or making a weak blow; or little above medium pace causing them to strike too slow, with the same result" (*National Chronicle*, June 5, 1869).

Chadwick also observed that "J. Williams, the Capital pitcher, would occasionally drop a ball short, but the change from swift to slow was too apparent to be effective. This style to work well must be done on the sly, the change of pace not being perceptible" (*The Ball Player's Chronicle*, July 18, 1867). That same James Williams was the manager of the St. Louis Brown Stockings seventeen years later when he reviewed the history of pitching. Williams observed then that until the 1870s "very little latitude was given the pitcher. The only way of outwitting the batsman was by a change of pace" (*St. Louis Post-Dispatch*, January 2, 1884).

Chadwick summed up in 1871: "Nothing so bothers the general class of batsmen as a sudden change of pace in pitching, but to be effective in deceiving the batsman, it must be disguised. For instance, when taking his position at the bat to face a swift pitcher he sees the balls pass him at great speed and at once settles himself to strike quickly at the ball. Just as he is prepared to do this the ball is 'dropped short,' that is, it is sent in at a pace a third less swift than before—not tossed in, however—and the batsman, not expecting it, strikes too quickly" (*New York Clipper*, February 4, 1871).

3.2.3   Curves.

Few if any origins have been as heatedly disputed as those of the curve-ball. Sometime during the 1870s, Fred Goldsmith gave a demonstration of the curveball at the Capitoline Grounds in Brooklyn. By the time Goldsmith died in 1939, however, Arthur "Candy" Cummings was generally considered to have invented the curveball. The *Detroit News* announced Goldsmith's death with the headline "Goldsmith Dies Insisting He Invented Curve Ball," and this was almost literally true. Goldsmith still had in his possession a newspaper clipping about his demonstration, in which Henry Chadwick wrote, "This feat was successfully accomplished six or eight times and that which had up to this point been considered an optical illusion and against all rules of philosophy was now an established fact." (The event was said to have taken place on August 16, 1870, but there is no contemporary account of it, and Goldsmith's age suggests that it was actually several years later.)

Writer Bob Carroll asked rhetorically, "Who cares? All right, let's say Candy [Cummings] DID invent the curveball; it makes a nice footnote. . . . Some other guys invented the sacrifice, the hit-and-run, the stolen base, and on and on. How come none of those people—and most of them are known—have not been elected to the Hall of Fame? Is the curveball really of such overriding importance in the history of baseball that its inventor alone gets a plaque at Cooperstown?" (Bob Carroll, *Baseball Between the Lies*, 27). Well, yes.

The first known effort to determine the inventor of the curveball was made by the *Philadelphia Press* in 1883, and there were already "a good many claimants." That list has only grown since then, and the entrants range from the sublime to the ridiculous. Let's consider the more serious claims in reverse chronological order.

Yale pitcher Charles Hammond Avery reportedly used the curveball to pitch a celebrated shutout of Harvard in 1874 and another one

against Princeton on May 29, 1875. As a result, the *Philadelphia Press* article observed, "College men, with the exception of those from Harvard, always insist that Avery brought [the curve] to light at Yale, while the Harvard men, who naturally would refuse to see a curve of two feet in a Yale pitcher's delivery, incline to the opinion that [Joseph McElroy] Mann of Princeton was first on the diamond with it. Harvard's men have grounds for their belief, from the fact that the Harvard team first had practical sight of the curve at Princeton in 1874; but, as it did not have the effect of winning the game from them there, they regarded it more as a curiosity than anything of importance in the game. The fact was that Mann was so much excited about his new delivery that he did not know when to quit, and after the Harvard men had noticed that the ball always turned about a foot outward after leaving the pitcher's hand they made their calculations and hammered at it accordingly. Mann had only one curve, and he did not even vary it by straight balls, so it failed of success against the straight pitching and fine headwork of [Harold] Ernst and [James] Tyng. Avery, at Yale, came out with his curve the same year, and the next year, by his effective pitching, helped his team to the championship" (*Philadelphia Press*, reprinted in the *Grand Rapids* [Mich.] *Morning Democrat*, September 2, 1883).

In 1900, Mann wrote to the *New York Times* to give his version of events after twenty-six years during which "I have never written a line to establish my claim to the honor of its introduction." He acknowledged that nobody really invented the curveball: "As long as baseball has been played and baseballs have had seams with which to catch the air curve balls have been thrown, and the curve was especially noticeable in the case of a left-handed thrower, whose curve was in the opposite direction from that of a right-handed thrower."

Mann went on to make the odd claim that even though "curve balls have always been thrown . . . no one thought of using them in the pitching department till 1874" when he conceived of the idea. His inspiration was Cummings, who "came to Princeton, and before the game and between innings he would stand on the home plate and pitch (he did not throw underhand) the ball down to second base, starting it at an angle of about forty-five degrees. I was greatly interested and wondered how he got the ball to curve as it did. It was said by his catcher that sometimes he pitched a ball that curved, but I failed to notice any curve that day."

Mann was further intrigued when the Philadelphia club came to Princeton and, during practice, the left fielder "would throw the ball with force sufficient to carry it all the way to right field, but after going part of the way the ball would suddenly shoot down and fall far short of right field." Mann thought the matter over, practiced a number of approaches, and finally found one that worked. He spent the winter refining his technique while also arriving at an understanding of the aerodynamics of the pitch (which he explained in considerable detail).

Mann concluded, "In the Spring I had the pleasure of seeing many surprised batters, who did not seem to be able to comprehend the situation. Unfortunately I was quite young at the time and did not know how to conceal the manner in which I produced the curve, and it was only a short time before it spread all over the country, which accounts for the confusion as to who introduced it. I was on the Princeton nine in 1873, 1874, 1875, and 1876 and batted against all the then famous pitchers, and I do not recall a single one who could curve a ball prior to 1874, when I, as I said above, accidentally stumbled upon it and then worked it out. . . . I think I have said enough to establish the fact that I was the one who initiated the movement and revolutionized the pitching department of baseball."

Mann believed that Avery didn't use the pitch until 1875, and his teammate W. J. Henderson vouched for this version of events. But a Yale alumnus asserted in the same issue that "Avery certainly pitched with a curve in 1874" (*New York Times*, June 10, 1900). Meanwhile Tim Murnane declared, "In 1872 Avery, the famous Yale pitcher, discovered the 'in-shoot.' I don't think he could curve a ball, at least I never saw him do it, and I hit against his pitching several times. His effectiveness was handicapped by his inability of any catcher to hold him, as without doubt the 'in-shoot' is the most difficult ball to handle, for in those days were not protected with gloves or masks" (*California Spirit of the Times & Underwriter's Journal*, September 17, 1887).

It is beyond question that Mann and Avery played an important role in popularizing the curveball. The comments of Harvard's James Tyng, reprinted later in this entry, attest to the fact that the pitch was new to many observers. But it is hard to make a serious case that either Mann or Avery "initiated the movement." Despite his obvious intelligence, Joseph Mann seems not to have realized how inconceivable it was that Cummings had been practicing throwing a curve but that neither he nor anyone before Mann had thought of using it for pitching. William Rankin responded with a long letter to the *Times* that cited earlier curveball pitchers (*New York Times*, September 29, 1900, 6). Mann's claim was further weakened when he later declared that he had been inspired to develop the curve after facing Cummings, who threw a pitch that caused catcher Doug Allison to say, "'That ball went zig-zag.' He meant, of course, that the curve was too great for him to judge" (J. C. Kofoed, "Early History of Curve Pitching," *Baseball Magazine*, August 1915, 56).

Moreover, as the *Press* pointed out, before either Mann or Avery came along, "curve pitching was practiced in professional games and, though its nature was not much understood, everybody seemed to know that a peculiar kind of ball could be delivered, and that Matthews [Bobby Mathews], the present 'curver' for the Athletics, was the man who was doing it" (*Philadelphia Press*, reprinted in the *Grand Rapids* [Mich.] *Morning Democrat*, September 2, 1883).

Bobby Mathews occupies a unique role in this saga. While everyone agreed that Mathews was one of the earliest pitchers to master the curveball, he himself disavowed any credit for inventing the pitch: "Matthews himself says that Cummings was curving the ball before he knew anything about it, and he gives further credit to Cummings by adding that he got his first lessons in the art by watching the Mutual pitcher's delivery. Cummings' delivery was known to every man in the profession as very peculiar, and Matthews, whose straight work was beginning to give way before it, made up his mind to take advantage of a position near the bat to learn the secret. He watched Cummings' hands carefully, noting how he held the ball and how he let it go, and after a few weeks' careful practice in the same way could see the curve in his own delivery. Then he began to use it in matches, striking men out in a way that no one but Cummings had ever done before, and in a short time he was known as one of the most effective pitchers in the field" (*Philadelphia Press*, reprinted in the *Grand Rapids* [Mich.] *Morning Democrat*, September 2, 1883).

Fred Goldsmith's case rested almost entirely upon his claim of having given the first exhibition of the curveball. But I have found no support for Goldsmith among his contemporaries, and what really militates against him is his year of birth—1856. To give precedence to Goldsmith, all earlier claimants must be refuted. That would be difficult to do if Goldsmith's demonstration actually occurred in 1870 and impossible if, as seems much more likely, it actually happened in the mid-1870s.

Candy Cummings, in contrast, did have support from his peers. In addition to Mathews's previously mentioned statements, Joe Start told *Sporting Life* in 1895 that he had no doubt that Cummings invented the curveball. Start explained that he and Cummings grew up on the same lots and that Cummings was working on the pitch between 1866 and 1870 (*Sporting Life*, November 16, 1895). A. G. Spalding also endorsed Cummings as the first pitcher to throw a curve (*Fort Wayne News*, May 6, 1895; A. G. Spalding, *America's National Game*, 484).

Tim Murnane considered it an open-and-shut case: "There may be some doubt as to who discovered the North Pole, but none whatsoever as to the boy who discovered and first brought into practical use the curving of a base ball. . . . 'Did Shakespeare write Hamlet?' 'Did Edison invent the kinetiscope [sic]?' They surely did. Well, just as certain did Arthur Cummings not only discover but was the first to make use of curved pitching" (*Sporting News*, November 4, 1909).

On another occasion, Murnane noted that George Wright also credited Cummings with throwing the first curve. Wright informed Murnane that forty years after the fact he still remembered the first time he saw Cummings's curve "as if it were only yesterday." The ball "came straight for the center of the plate and then took a wide curve." Wright said that the pitch was quite unlike anything he had previously seen from Bobby Mathews (who he claimed didn't have a true curve until 1879) or Phonney Martin (*Fort Wayne News*, March 28, 1911).

Cummings himself gave several different accounts of how he first came to throw the curveball, and while many of the details remained the same, there was a noticeable shift in emphasis over the years. The first two that I'm aware of appeared in the *Boston Globe* on April 6, 1896, and in the *Sporting News* on February 20, 1897. They have such similar passages that it is quite possible the author of the second piece relied in part on the earlier article.

The latter version began with a very intriguing fact: "Mr. Cummings was born in Ware, Mass., on October 17, 1848, and played the old-fashioned game that prevailed in the Bay State before he moved to Brooklyn with his parents." In the earlier article, much of which was a letter from Cummings to Tim Murnane, Cummings confirmed that he played the "old Massachusetts game" before the family's move.

While neither account elaborated on the significance, this is a potentially crucial detail. In the "Massachusetts game" of the 1850s, pitchers threw overhand, which made the curveball much more viable than under the restrictions imposed by the Knickerbockers. The 1860 census shows the Cummings family already in Brooklyn, and there is contradictory evidence as to exactly when they arrived. In any event, Cummings's exposure to the "Massachusetts game" appears to have been a key factor in his subsequent interest in the curveball.

Cummings did not address this point, but he did make several of the assertions that would later become celebrated: "It was in a game against the collegians that I first used the curve. I got my theory from throwing clam shells in playing with boys. I saw that they curved to the right and left and I conceived the idea of trying to make a base ball do the same thing. After a great deal of constant practice I accomplished the feat. I received no encouragement from base ball experts and was, in fact, laughed at as no one thought it could be done."

He continued to recount how he "went to work secretly" because of the "chaffing" from his friends and "kept on practicing for it was the dream of my boyhood days." Finally he was able to unveil the pitch against the celebrated Harvard catcher Archie Bush and realized with exultance: "I had succeeded at last."

Cummings also included some important details that would be conspicuously absent from later versions. In his letter to Murnane he pointed out that it was "no easy job for a pitcher to deliver a ball in those days, as he had to keep both feet on the ground and not raise either until after the ball left his hand, and had to keep the arm close to his side and deliver the ball with a perpendicular swing." In the version published the following year, Cummings added, "Some of the pitchers who have claimed to be the inventor of curving the ball, but who did not introduce it in their work until several years afterward, had to deliver the ball on a level with their waist to make it curve at all. Keeping both feet on the ground while delivering the ball was a hard strain, as the wrist and second finger did all the work. I snapped the ball like a whip and this caused me to throw my wrist bone out of place quite often. During one season I was compelled to wear a rubber supporter the whole time. I had great speed, however, even if I was of light frame and apparently not powerful" ("Curved Balls," *Sporting News*, February 20, 1897).

These two accounts suggest an explanation of how Cummings learned to throw the curve that to my mind is more plausible than the version that later emerged. He had probably seen rudimentary curves thrown as a youngster in Massachusetts, but when he moved to Brooklyn and began playing the "New York game," the delivery restrictions made the pitch seem impossible. Yet the example of throwing clamshells made him think that it might be possible, and his arm strength and relentless practice enabled him to realize his ambition.

Unfortunately this version is too complex to make for good storytelling, and in later renderings the crucial factor of the delivery restrictions disappeared. In 1900, Tim Murnane presented a simplified version in which Cummings began trying to master the curve around 1866 but did not succeed until facing Archie Bush two years later. He gave the ball an extra twist, and "When Bush struck at the ball it seemed to go about a foot beyond the end of his stick. I tried again with the same result, and then I realized at last that I had succeeded in mastering the curve, something I had been after for two years" (*Boston Globe*, February 20, 1900). While the basic details are similar, the emphasis has begun to shift to the moment of discovery.

A 1902 book by Seymour Church included this account: "Cummings was one day pitching against a picked nine, and noticed the ball curving. He had no difficulty in striking the batsmen out, and went home that night and tried to study the phenomena [sic]. The next day he invited some gentlemen friends out to see him work. They laughed at him, and when he tried to convince them that he could accomplish what he claimed, he failed, as no doubt, in his anxiety, he sent the ball too fast, and very little curve can be gotten out of a speedily pitched ball. The next day he went out with his catcher, and discovered that the curve came from a certain twist he gave his wrist. He worked hard until he secured full control of the new movement, and then astonished the base ball and scientific world" (Seymour Church, *Base Ball*, 33). In this version, not only have important details begun to disappear but also a gradual

process of discovery has begun to give way to a "Eureka" moment.

Cummings also wrote a 1908 article entitled "How I Curved the First Ball," and the account shows that he had begun to emphasize the details that would appeal to an audience too young to remember the delivery restrictions of the 1860s. In it, Cummings recalled that in the summer of 1863 he and some other boys were throwing clamshells when "it came to me that it would be a good joke on the boys if I could make a baseball curve the same way." He experimented with deliveries for a year and a half, receiving "not one single word of encouragement in all that time, while my attempts were a standing joke among my friends." But he persevered and by 1867 was able to use the pitch to great effect (Arthur Cummings, "How I Curved the First Ball," *Baseball Magazine*, September 1908; reprinted in John Thorn and John Holway, *The Pitcher*, 150 and Roger Kahn, *The Head Game*, 18–21).

In 1910, Alfred Spink reported that Cummings had recently said, "I don't think I was the first man to pitch a curved ball. I think that [Alphonse "Phonney"] Martin of the old Eckfords had the curve—not mine but a kind of curve; and I am sure that [George] Zettlein . . . pitched a curved ball, and that [Charley] Pabor . . . pitched a curve when he was playing with the old Unions of Morrisania, New York. . . . But none of these pitchers knew that he had a curve, and I suppose it is fair to say that I was the first to find out what a curve was and how it was done.

"[Nat] Hicks was catcher and I was pitcher of the semi-professional Stars of Brooklyn. I noticed that very few batsmen could hit me, and finally I saw that when I pitched the ball it swerved outward before it reached the batsman. Then, when I had thought about this a little, I said to myself: 'That ball does not go in a straight line until it begins to fall; it curves outside of the horizontal line, and that is the reason why batsmen can not hit it.'

"Well, I studied and experimented until at last I found that if I held the ball between my fingers and thumb in a certain way, and gave it a certain twist of the wrist just as I delivered it, then the resultant motion that the ball took produced a curve. I wondered how that could be, and I made up my mind that the rotary motion of the ball created a vacuum on one side, the outside, and the pressure of the air on the other side caused it to swerve. I had found out the secret of the curved ball. I afterwards taught it to Tommy Bond, and he could make a ball curve either way" (A. H. Spink, *The National Game*, 139–140).

In 1919, Cummings was quoted thus: "I hit upon the curve ball quite accidentally. Just as I was about to deliver the ball in the usual way one day I lost my balance. That threw my arm out of line and when the ball left my hand there was a twist of my wrist. Imagine my surprise when the ball went sailing up to the plate on a direct line only to take a sharp outcurve as the batsman swung for it. Naturally, noticing the effect on the ball with such wrist motion I practiced the next morning with my catcher and very shortly I had perfected an outcurve" ("Sport World with James J. Corbett," syndicated column, *Fort Wayne News and Sentinel*, February 18, 1919).

In 1921, Cummings provided the *Sporting News* with another account that included many of the by now familiar details. He explained that throwing clamshells as a boy "gave me the idea and the inspiration" that a baseball might be made to curve in a similar manner. He continued to try, though his friends told him it couldn't be done, and finally got the motion down. Cummings also mentioned the role of the restrictions on deliveries, claiming that the only others who ever mastered the underhand curve were Mathews, Avery, and Mann. But there was an intriguing new element. Cummings now maintained that he pitched his first curveball in 1864 yet was "jealous of his discovery" and did not tell anyone about it so that he could be the only one to benefit from it (*Sporting News*, December 29, 1921).

Cummings died in 1924, but even this did not staunch the flow of accounts of the origins of the curveball. Five years later sportswriter Bozeman Bulger maintained that he had been told yet another version: "Cummings often said that he got the idea from watching a billiard ball spin and curve when the player applied English—hitting the ball on one side, with the tip of the cue" (Bozeman Bulger, "Curveball Cause [sic] Revolution," *Lincoln* [Nebr.] *Evening Journal*, January 22, 1929).

Finally we come to a ghastly history of the curveball written by a man named Harold C. Burr and published in *Sporting News* in 1942. Burr embellished the story with invented dialogue ("Gee whillikins! Wouldn't it be great if I could make a baseball curve like that?") and colorful details ("One of the other boys overheard young Art Cummings at his day-dreaming.

He nudged those nearest, beckoned to others to come a-running, and they gathered around Cummings in the glee of ghoulish youth . . .") (*Sporting News*, November 19, 1942). It is sad that such obvious fabrications are passed off as baseball history.

Many different interpretations may be placed on this wide variety of accounts. One is to focus on the inconsistencies and simply disregard all the stories, but this seems extreme. Cummings never comes across as a blowhard, and the role he gives himself is no greater than the one with which he is credited by some of the disinterested firsthand observers. His first account was given about thirty years after the events being described, so we may expect him to be hazy about some of the details, yet he was only in his late forties at the time.

The many subsequent versions include some apparent contradictions, but by and large what changes is the emphasis: a complex sequence of events revolving around pitching restrictions was gradually simplified to a "Eureka!" moment. The reporters who recounted these versions were undoubtedly one factor in their variations. In addition, any oft-told story usually starts to take on some of the characteristics that its audience hopes to hear, and Cummings obviously was asked about the curve many times. In his later years his audience was too young to appreciate the pitching restrictions of the 1860s, so they seized instead upon the "clamshells" image and the triumphant moment in which he realized he had mastered the pitch. As researcher Joe Overfield asked rhetorically after analyzing yet another account: "Is this history, or is it a case of history being created simply because a story has been repeated so many times?" (Joseph M. Overfield, "William Arthur Cummings," in Frederick Ivor-Campbell, Robert L. Tiemann and Mark Rucker, eds., *Baseball's First Stars*, 43).

While Cummings unquestionably played a major role in popularizing the curveball, there are many claims for earlier originators. Jimmy Wood, who saw all the great early pitchers, nominated Joe Sprague as the first to throw the curveball: "Sprague threw a curve ball—that was back in 1862—which means that Sprague, not Arthur Cummins [sic], of the Brooklyn Stars of 1863–64, or Bobby Mathews, of the Baltimores of 1866–67 was the original curve ball pitcher. . . . We always noticed that some of Sprague's deliveries took a sharp twist, sometimes turning in and sometimes turning away from the batter. All of us used to remark about the peculiar gyrations of the ball that he threw. It was not until some years later, however, when curved balls became an established fact, that we recognized the delivery, then called a curve as the same kind of ball that Sprague had thrown in 1862 and 1863" (James Wood, as told to Frank G. Menke, "Baseball in By-Gone Days," part 3, syndicated column, *Indiana* [Pa.] *Evening Gazette*, August 17, 1916). Another teammate, Waddy Beach, also maintained that Sprague "could and did curve the ball while pitching for the Eckfords in 1863" (quoted by William Rankin in *Sporting News*, May 25, 1901; he cites it as originating in the *New York Clipper* in the summer of 1883 but does not provide an exact date).

Cummings himself, on a couple of different occasions, allowed that Phonney Martin "was throwing something akin to a curve some years before my time" ("Sport World with James J. Corbett," syndicated column, *Fort Wayne News and Sentinel*, February 18, 1919; also A. H. Spink, *The National Game*, 139–140, as noted earlier). A. H. Spink claimed that Martin's slow ball would reach the plate and take "a sudden swerve away and the batter would miss. Martin pitched the ball with a twist of the fingers and wrist, manipulating it much as does a billiard player when he wants to put English on a billiard ball" (A. H. Spink, *The National Game*, 139). William Rankin cited an 1870 reference to "the Martin style of curved line delivery" (*New York Clipper*, April 2, 1870; quoted in *Sporting News*, May 25, 1901). On the other hand, George Wright maintained that Martin "simply had a slow 'teaser,' as we called it, something after the style of a slow ball tossed up by my brother Harry. The ball Martin tossed up was hard to meet fair, as he sent it in with a spin, but it was a slow ball, usually sent very high, that dropped as it reached the plate without the semblance of a curve" (quoted by Tim Murnane, *Fort Wayne News*, March 28, 1911). And Martin himself, as described under "Drop Ball/Sinker" (**3.2.5**), claimed to have been the first pitcher to throw the drop curve but was adamant that no pitcher was legally throwing an "outcurve" until the delivery rules were liberalized at the end of the decade.

Another celebrated New York pitcher, Rynie Wolters, nominated yet another candidate: a man named McSweeney who was briefly a member of the Mutual Club in 1866. Phonney Martin, who also played for that club, recalled that "when the curve was proved to be possible, [McSweeney's] name often was used in conjunction with its origin." But Martin was dismissive, describing him as "the wildest pitcher that ever pitched a baseball. The ball seldom if ever came over the home plate, and as the catcher, Nat Jewett, could not hold his pitching, he proved a failure and soon was forgotten." In addition, Martin claimed that McSweeney was able to curve the ball only by being an illegal "underhand thrower, and that was sufficient to prevent him from pitching in a regular game" (Phonnie Martin Curve Scrapbook, National Baseball Hall of Fame).

There are still earlier intimations of the pitch beginning to develop. In 1862 a teenager named Frederick P. Henry moved to Baltimore and became "the first to introduce slow-curved balls" (William Ridgely Griffith, *The Early History of Amateur Base Ball in the State of Maryland*, 32). Henry enrolled at Princeton one year later and perplexed the mighty Athletics of Philadelphia by pitching with "a heavy twist that was extremely irregular" (game account from unidentified source, quoted in J. C. Kofoed, "Early History of Curve Pitching," *Baseball Magazine*, August 1915, 56; Kofoed misidentified Henry as "Frank Henry"). Even after a distinguished career as a physician, Henry's obituary in 1919 featured his role as a curveball pioneer (*Philadelphia Inquirer*, May 25, 1919). Jim Creighton is sometimes said to have pitched a curve, though contemporary descriptions of his pitches sound more like fastballs with considerable movement. Henry Chadwick noted in 1860 that it was advantageous to "impart a bias or twist to the ball" (*Beadle's Dime Base-Ball Player*, 22). And Chadwick would later maintain that pitcher Richard B. Willis of the Lone Star Club of Rochester, New York, was throwing a curveball around 1860 (*Appletons' Annual Cyclopaedia and Register of Important Events of the Year 1885*, 82). One of the participants in the first intercollegiate match, played between Amherst and Williams in 1859, later recalled that Amherst's pitcher, Henry D. Hyde, "had a wonderful knack of making the ball curve in to the catcher" (quoted in Joel Zoss and John Bowman, *Diamonds in the Rough*, 72). Melvin Adelman discovered an 1857 article that noted, "many think that a ball that will curve as it approaches the striker is much more difficult to bat than one that takes a straight course" (*Porter's Spirit of the Times*, March 7, 1857; quoted in Melvin Adelman, *A Sporting Time*, 129).

William Rankin cited this description of a Knickerbockers player named Richard Stevens in 1856: "as pitcher [he] sends the ball with exceeding velocity, and he who strikes it fairly must be a fine batsman. It is questionable, however, whether his style of pitching is most successful, many believing a slow ball curving near the bat, to be the most effective" (*Porter's Spirit of the Times*, December 6, 1856; quoted in *Sporting News*, May 25, 1901). The *Detroit Free Press* reported in 1881, "On the last day of June, 1854, the valiant Knickerbockers were humbled. On that day the feeder of the Gothams resorted to what is now known as the 'Chicago snake ball,' and the Knickerbockers could not get a nick of it" (*Detroit Free Press*, August 27, 1881). David Block discovered an 1845 reference to "one who, in playing 'base,' screws his ball, as the expression is among boys" (*The Knickerbocker*, vol. 26, November 1845, 426–427; quoted in David Block, *Baseball Before We Knew It*, 207–208).

In 1923, Grantland Rice used his syndicated column to revisit the question of who pitched the first curveball and got an unexpected response. A man named William H. Allison wrote, "In July, 1897, I sat at table in a boarding house in London, by the side of a Dartmouth graduate of the class of 1844. He told me one day that when he was in college he discovered that he could throw a ball so that it would curve. As a result, in the crude game which preceded baseball the boys would not allow him to pitch. This man, who for years was president of the Newton Theological Institution and had been my own teacher of systematic theology, was Dr. Allan [sic] Hovey, whose youngest son made a reputation in baseball at both Brown and Harvard and won the tennis championship at Newport in 1895" (Grantland Rice, "The Sportlight," syndicated column, April 13, 1923).

A second letter writer, W. D. Q., Dartmouth, '87, added: "My father was of the class of 1846 at Dartmouth, and he told me of the peculiar ability of Hovey, '44, to throw a ball with a strange curve, 'benders,' they called it then. Everyone was puzzled to know how such a ball was thrown. But it seems to me, looking back upon the feat, that it must have been the original curve. I don't believe anyone can go back of 1844 and it is now perfectly established that Hovey, Dartmouth '44, was curving the ball" (Grantland Rice, "The Sportlight," syndicated column, April 24, 1923).

Finally, a letter from one of Dr. Alvah Hovey's sons read: "I had no idea any one outside of the family had ever heard him speak of it. Not until many years later, when the curve ball had become common, did he recognize just what he had been doing with the ball in the old days. He merely remembered that the ball seemed to jump away from the bat at the critical moment. How he did it he said he never knew.

"It was a fact, however, that his opponents in the informal games then played refused to play if he was put in to pitch. Perhaps that entitles him to another record—that of being the first pitcher too good to be allowed to play. I can picture him saying in his quiet vein of humor: 'I have not noticed Yale refusing to play Harvard because you are on the team'" (Grantland Rice, "The Sportlight," syndicated column, April 28, 1923).

How do we make sense of these wildly divergent claims? It's actually not as difficult as it may appear, for three reasons. First, the curveball occupies a singular place among baseball firsts since it is difficult to identify (unlike, say, a shin guard). Many have assumed that the first to demonstrate a curveball *to them* must have invented it.

Second, once its existence is conceded, a true curveball can be difficult to distinguish from a pitch with a slightly different break. Even today, differences in trajectory, direction of break, and the natural movement produced by a pitcher's arm action combine to make the distinctions between pitches less than crystal clear. The difficulty of distinguishing one breaking pitch from another was even more pronounced in the days when the whole idea of a curve was still a novelty. While it is safe to assume that very early descriptions of pitches with a "twist" or "bias" are not referring to a true curveball, it is significant that the idea of such trajectories was in currency that early.

Third, and most important, the curveball was difficult if not impossible to pitch in games played by the Knickerbockers' rules before restrictions on deliveries began to be relaxed in 1872. Yet the "Massachusetts" version of baseball played in New England in the 1840s and 1850s allowed overhand deliveries, which makes the claims on behalf of Henry Hyde and Alvah Hovey very plausible and potentially puts the origins of "Candy" Cummings's curve in a very different light.

Under the New York rules, only a few pitchers were able to throw curves before the 1870s, and even they probably had to bend the rules to do so. Deacon White later claimed that Candy Cummings "used to curve a ball as early as 1868, but not in regulation games. That was impossible, because the rules then prohibited a wrist throw. Pitchers then were forced to throw underhanded with a stiff arm. If a pitcher bent or twisted his wrist, he was disqualified. Cummings curved a ball across the infield by using a wrist snap during practice, but he couldn't use it in a game—that is, until the rules were changed in 1872" (Gene Kessler, "Deacon White, Oldest Living Player, at 92 Recalls Highlights of Historic Career That Started in 1868," *Sporting News*, June 22, 1939, 19).

As Johnny Evers and Hugh Fullerton explained in 1910: "The first curves pitched were of the variety now known as the 'barrel hoop.' It was a slow curve, pitched underhand, with the hand swung nearly to the level of the knee, fingers downward and hand held almost at right angles with the wrist. As the hand was swung the wrist was jerked sharply and the ball, sliding off the first finger, revolved rapidly and the air pressure on one side of the sphere and the partial vacuum on the other caused by the rotation, forced the ball to move in a slow wide arc. All curves are developments of the 'barrel hoop,' the same principle entering into each" (John J. Evers and Hugh S. Fullerton, *Touching Second*, 103–104).

Note, however, that even the barrel hoop curve was not being pitched with a straight arm. Sportswriter J. C. Kofoed similarly offered a detailed description of the efforts of an early Princeton pitcher named Ed Davis to make the ball swerve but stressed that Davis did so only by breaking the rule that "called for a straight arm delivery" (J. C. Kofoed, "Early History of Curve Pitching," *Baseball Magazine*, August 1915, 56).

This distinction makes it possible to make sense of the baffling number of claimants to having introduced the curveball. As long as the pitch remained tantalizingly just outside the reach of being delivered legally, it was inevitable that a series of pitchers would discover it, experiment with it, find it impossible to pitch legally, and concentrate on other aspects of the art of pitching.

Perhaps the best concise summary of the origins of the curveball is to say that the idea is an old one, predating even the Knickerbocker rules in areas where overhand deliveries were allowed. But the idea was not truly a practical one for the New York version of baseball as long as the rules mandated a straight-arm delivery and a release point below the knee.

According to Cummings, the only pitchers who threw a true underhanded curve were him-

self, Mathews, Mann, and Avery (*Sporting News*, December 29, 1921). Even though the hip-level release was legalized in 1872, Tim Murnane claimed that Cummings and Mathews were still the only pitchers throwing curves in 1873 (*Boston Globe*, January 31, 1915). The situation began to change in 1874, with Chadwick writing at the season's end: "There is a peculiarity of delivery which Creighton had not, and which some of our pitchers now possess, which is worth mentioning, and that is the power to deliver the ball with that puzzling *horizontal curve* which marks the delivery of Mathews and Cummings" (undated review of 1874 season, Chadwick Scrapbooks).

This delay does not mean that pitchers were not experimenting with the pitch before the rule change of 1872. Deacon White later recalled that pitchers were practicing curves seriously as early as 1870, in anticipation that the delivery rules would be relaxed (Gene Kessler, "Deacon White, Oldest Living Player, at 92 Recalls Highlights of Historic Career That Started in 1868," *Sporting News*, June 22, 1939, 19). Yet the curve is not an easy pitch to master, especially with no one willing to act as tutor, and it took a couple of years for the pitch to spread.

This version of events may be much less appealing than the story about clamshells, but it seems to me to be more satisfactory. William Rankin considered the matter in 1901, after Cummings had first claimed credit and when many eyewitnesses were still alive, and reached a similar conclusion: "It is no unusual thing to hear one or more persons coming to the front and posing as the inventor of some important discovery, especially if the real inventor has been unknown to fame. The curve in pitching seems to belong to this class of invention. Many persons have gained renown on the ball field by their cleverness in pitching curves, drops, etc., and may have added to the effectiveness and general conduciveness of that style of delivery, but that does not entitle any of them to the honor of having discovered the curve" (*Sporting News*, May 25, 1901).

An especially authoritative spokesman for this viewpoint was "Phonney" Martin, the man credited by Cummings with "throwing something akin to a curve some years before my time." Martin declared, "The curve in baseball was not born at one time, 'it growed.'" He explained that the pitches he began throwing around 1862 were a "drop" (see **3.2.5**) and a "slight incurve," both of which he could deliver while adhering to the straight-arm requirement. Martin maintained that he threw these pitches throughout his thirteen-year career but insisted that the outcurve was a different matter. Whoever threw the first true outcurve, Martin maintained, "accomplished it by twisting the wrist outward, and consequently the delivery was not within the rules, and could not be used legally until the rules were changed in 1870–71. That was the reason the rules were changed, allowing the pitchers to swing their arms out from the body, using what was called the under arm throw. I do not claim that Cummings never pitched a curve ball, but I do claim that he did not use a curve ball in the games he pitched previous to 1869" (Phonnie Martin Curve Scrapbook, National Baseball Hall of Fame).

Whether or not anyone deserves credit for inventing the pitch, it is difficult to overstate the extent to which the curveball revolutionized baseball in the years after the breakout year of 1874. Most obviously, it changed pitching so fundamentally that "Other pitchers had to take up the curve or quit playing" (*Philadelphia Press*, reprinted in the *Grand Rapids* [Mich.] *Morning Democrat*, September 2, 1883). The success of a curveball pitcher in a tournament in Atlanta around 1879 "ended the 'tournamena' [sic] and 'straight' pitching in Atlanta. . . . The Cranks began to clamor for 'curved' pitching and never stopped until the Southern League was formed" (*Atlanta Constitution*, February 12, 1893).

Henry Chadwick observed after the 1877 season that club managers "seemed to turn up their nose at any man who 'hadn't got the curve'" (*New York Clipper*, December 8, 1877). A year later he added: "during 1878 a pitcher without the 'curve' was nowhere" (*New York Clipper*, January 11, 1879). With their livelihoods at stake, and the ever-present threat that a ban would be placed on any effective technique, pitchers often became secretive or proprietary. An 1875 account noted: "[George] Bradley, of the St. Louis Base Ball Club, has been after Jim Devlin, of the Louisville Nine, and endeavored to learn his 'curve.' But Devlin has refused to explain it to him" (*St. Louis Globe-Democrat*, December 13, 1875). As noted earlier, Candy Cummings became "jealous of his discovery," and he later reported with evident satisfaction that Jim Galvin inspected the delivery "closely and confessed that he could not see what was going on" (*Sporting News*, December 29, 1921). Pitchers kept trying to master the curve even when they had little success, leading to accounts

such as this one from 1879: "One of the pitchers is a splendid 'curve' pitcher, i.e., . . . his balls generally land nearer the first or third baseman than the striker" (*Manistee* [Mich.] *Advocate*, May 31, 1879).

Another example of the ability of the curveball to turn baseball on its head was offered in 1897 by a man named Bennett Wilson. In the 1870s, Wilson had been the pitcher on a club called the Lurlines of Brooklyn that included future major league pitching stars Larry Corcoran, Terry Larkin, and Mickey Welch. Welch was his catcher, but that was to change: "When curve pitching came into vogue, Mr. Wilson says, he and his associates gathered in a big back yard almost every day and used a clothes line horse, which was used by an old widow on which to dry her washing, with which to gain control of the various curves. The horizontal bar across the horse was supposed to represent the height of the batter's knees or waist and the ball was curved around the main sticks. This afforded an effective means of practice and Corcoran and Wilson soon had all the curves at their command" (*Brooklyn Eagle*, April 2, 1897). Before long, Welch was experimenting with the pitch as well, and his days as a catcher were numbered.

The curve also proved to be a litmus test for batters, producing precursors of what Grantland Rice would call the "favorite baseball story . . . about the training camp rookie who wired back to his folks: 'You can expect me any day, now, they're beginning to curve 'em'" (Grantland Rice, "The Sportlight," syndicated column, March 10, 1932).

Harvard's James Tyng later offered a captivating account of how his team responded to Joseph Mann's curveball in 1875: "Out of the first nine men at the bat eight, I think, were unable to hit the ball. We had no idea what was the trouble, except that the bat and ball seemed to have a repulsion for each other which we could not overcome. About the fifth inning one of our men, who had been standing behind the catcher, came back with the announcement that the balls were curving away from the batsman. There was a general exodus on our part to the backstop to watch this unheard of phenomenon. Sure enough, there were the balls coming in for the middle of the plate and curving off beyond the reach of the bat" (*Harper's Weekly*, quoted in Mann's letter to the *New York Times*, June 10, 1900).

When a touring club from San Francisco played a game in Detroit in 1876, they got the surprise of their lives. The Aetnas of Detroit club had acquired a curve pitcher named J. A. Sullivan and a catcher named Edward Brown who knew how to hold him: "Brown would stand away back in the grass to the right of the pitcher, and Sullivan would work the out curve, which was the only one he knew, and man after man was mowed down before him" (*Boston Globe*, October 12, 1887). Eighteen of the visiting batters had the same demoralizing experience: "When the ball starts the striker would wager that it was coming just where he wanted it, but just as he nerves up to bat the ball dodges away and just out of the reach of the bat" (*Detroit Free Press*, July 16, 1876).

The frustration of flailing away at a ball that suddenly veered out of reach was especially palpable for right-handed hitters. Batters in Owosso, Michigan, complained in 1877 about the unfairness of the rule that prohibited them from chasing pitches that curved away from them (*Owosso Weekly Press*, August 8, 1877). A writer later reminisced that in 1876 "pitchers first introduced the wide-out curve. [Terry] Larkin had the first one ever seen [in Chicago] and it was thought to be a wonder. In fact, the papers and people generally refused to believe that it was possible to curve a ball. A great many writers insisted that there was some trick about it. [Jimmy] Hallinan was the only batter that could hit him, and he because he was left-handed" (*Chicago Tribune*, April 1, 1894).

The curve changed not only the lives of batters and pitchers, but also the competitive balance of baseball by renewing the hopes of many clubs. The rise of professionalism in the late 1860s and 1870s had presented a great challenge to the game. Clubs felt pressured to choose between hiring nine professionals and becoming noncompetitive, a dilemma that created a wide talent gap and did great damage to baseball. The curveball revolution changed that by showing that it only took a curve pitcher and a talented catcher to elevate a club's fortunes.

For example, in 1877 a Savannah pitcher named Frank Lincoln was the first Georgian to master the curveball. It soon became obvious that this one pitch more than offset the advantages held by a larger city like Atlanta. Savannah became state champions, but more important was the renewed sense of hope across the state: "The curved pitching, as done by Lincoln, aroused the amateur clubs in Georgia" (*Atlanta Constitution*, February 12, 1893).

For the 1876 season, Chicago had signed A. G. Spalding, the game's premier pitcher.

But Spalding did not throw a curve, and the public fascination with the pitch was so great that Spalding later remembered that the club's supporters became "greatly worried back in 1876 because the White Stockings had no 'curve pitcher'" (*Fort Wayne News*, May 6, 1895). The curveball had emerged as the great equalizer.

This new dynamic dashed any remaining hopes that baseball could return to the days when the pitcher was little more than a bystander in a contest between batters and fielders. But that was a small price to pay for reawakening the sense that a small-town club again had a fighting chance. The curveball had, one might say, introduced to baseball the precept that "good pitching beats good hitting."

As the curveball appeared across the country, awe was mixed with skepticism. A player named James Fitzgibbon of the Charter Oak club of Hartford, Connecticut, traveled to Brooklyn in 1867 to play the Excelsiors and found himself unable to hit Candy Cummings's pitching at all (A. H. Spink, *The National Game*, 41). When a pitcher named George Griffin introduced the curve to Boston around 1874, it was a life-changing event for a veteran named Jack Lanning, who "made thirteen futile attempts to hit the ball and then congratulated the young man on his success" (Jacob Morse, *Sporting Life*, March 5, 1898).

Jimmy Clinton had a different vantage point: "I shall never forget the first curve pitching I ever saw. Tommy Bond did it. It was in a game of the Hartford against St. Louis in '75, and I was umpire. . . . Excitement ran high and all the heelers were on hand, together with an immense crowd. From the first Hartford took a decided lead, and the ill success of the home pets was visited on the umpire, especially as batter after batter of the St. Louis was seen by the audience to jump back from the plate for balls on which I called strikes. The people could not understand it, and hooted and yelled and threatened, and I was beginning to feel rather shaky when I called Pierce [Dickey Pearce] and two or three others of the St. Louis to witness that the balls on which I called strikes cut the plate in two, although they seemed until nearing the plate to be going right for the batter. Pierce confirmed this to the crowd and told them, 'I-hope-I-may-die if it ain't so,' but they wouldn't have it that way. I thanked my lucky stars for a whole hide when the game was over and took the first train for Louisville, without waiting to umpire the other two games for which I had been engaged" (*Sporting Life*, December 3, 1884).

A Kalamazoo paper informed its readers in 1878: "After our boys came back from Ann Arbor they explained the fact of there being such a thing as 'curve pitching,' that being the trick by which the university boys 'foolished' them so badly, and some of our citizens have seemed to doubt it. But WILLIAM L SERGEANT has since got on to the 'curve balls' and has given good practical demonstration of that style of pitching to the entire satisfaction of the incredulous ones. . . . The Sturgis batters would stand up to the home plate grating their teeth and suggestively gazing on the back fence in a manner calculated to impress their many friends and backers that they would make a clean 'three baser,' but to their undisguised astonishment, Sergeant would pitch them one that would make them 'saw the wood'" (*Kalamazoo Daily Telegraph*, May 27, 1878).

Johnny Ward was greeted with similar skepticism when he introduced the curveball in Williamsport, Pennsylvania: "Even after observing the uncanny bends and twists that Ward put on the sphere, many refused to believe their eyes. Among them was Ephraim H. Page. Mr. Page scoffed and said it was nothing more than an optical illusion. As proof of this he offered to stand around a corner and let Ward hit him with the ball if such a thing was possible. Ward accepted the defi. Mr. Page took a position out of sight and serenely awaited the result. Ward cut loose with a 'roundhouse' curve that, to the horrified amazement of Ephraim, described a parabola around that corner and plunked him a sickening thud precisely in the tonneau. No further demonstration was needed to convince Mr. Page" (*Williamsport Sunday Grit*, November 7, 1915).

Charley Lamar gave this description of the reception accorded Frank Lincoln when he introduced the curve to Georgia: "In June, 1877 the 'Dixies' met a picked nine at Macon and beat them by a score of 11 to 0. Tom Clayton, of Atlanta, played short for Macon, and did it well, but 'Old Twist 'Em,' as he called Lincoln, had too much 'curve' for the Macon boys, and they met an inglorious defeat." Two months later the Dixies faced a club from Charleston, South Carolina, for the championship of the two states: "The Carolinas were confident of victory. They were fine amateur ball players and their pitcher was very speedy. When assured by the Savannah cranks that they would be unable to hit Lincoln they readily offered to bet any amount that they could 'kill him.' . . . A large amount of money changed hands and the Carolinas and their friends returned to Charleston minus their enthusiasm and their money. They ran the bases and fielded well. But alas! the 'curved' pitching was a 'Jonah.' It was out of the question to master it, and they went down like chaff before the wind, and Lincoln was a hero" (*Atlanta Constitution*, February 12, 1893).

George Cuyler, the father of Hall of Famer "Kiki" Cuyler, was playing for a town team in Kincardine, Ontario, around this time. He later recollected being scheduled to play a match against the club from the county seat but, "upon learning that the county seat nine had imported a curve-ball pitcher, refused to play as none of the team had ever batted against the then-new curve ball" (R. E. Prescott, *Historical Tales of the Huron Shore Region*, vol. VII, 63).

While Ted Sullivan's tales always need to be taken with at least a grain of salt, there is probably a kernel of truth in a story he told about a game in a small town in Wisconsin around this time. Ted's team was playing a town team in either La Crosse or Prairie-Duchien with Charles Radbourn pitching. Radbourn was throwing curves over the plate, but the home town umpire would not call them strikes. When Radbourn complained, the umpire told him, "I'm agoin' ter give yer snap away! You're a pitchin' with a trick ball! The ball ain't official. Every time it leaves yer hand it ducks in and out so that our boys can't hit it! If yer can't pitch the ball straight or get a new one that ain't a trick ball I'll give the game to our team, b'gosh!" (*Sporting News*, March 19, 1898; A. H. Spink, *The National Game*, 150).

Others sought to use the scientific method to make sense of the mysterious new pitch. In 1876 a student at the Michigan Agricultural College reported: "A considerable discussion is going on among the members of the class in mechanics as to whether it is possible for a pitcher, in playing ball, to give a ball such a combination of forces as to send it for a distance in a straight line and then cause it to make an angle or curve. Those who say it can be done say they have seen it, but do not pretend to explain it, while those opposed think they can prove by the action of forces that it must go in the direction of the resultant, except as it is drawn towards the earth by gravity. If any one . . . can do it, they can get their expenses here paid for and good pay for their time to come and prove it" (*Paw Paw* [Mich.] *True Northerner*, October 13, 1876).

In 1877 the students were taken up on this offer, and team captain William K. Prudden later recalled: ". . . We heard of the 'curve' ball, and made up a purse of $10 to get a player from Detroit to demonstrate it. At the exhibition the Faculty were among the spectators, and we received a demonstration of the curve ball. The $10 was easy to get, as some of the subscribers expected a return of their money, the curver having agreed to perform gratis in case he did not curve the ball" (*M.A.C. Record*, XXI, no. 29, May 2, 1916). The curve pitcher satisfied the skeptics and got his money.

Most of the successful curveball pitchers seem to have had far less curiosity about how the pitch worked: "The reason for the curve is something that professional players have never troubled themselves about, and though Matthews [Bobby Mathews] and [John] Coleman, and, in fact, any of them can tell exactly how a ball will go if it leaves the hand in a certain way, with a certain amount of force, but why or how it does it they decline to explain" (*Philadelphia Press*, reprinted in the *Grand Rapids* [Mich.] *Morning Democrat*, September 2, 1883).

In 1878 righty Tom Bond and left-handed pitcher Bobby Mitchell gave a demonstration of throwing balls that curved around two posts, and according to Spink this settled the question (A. H. Spink, *The National Game*, 124). Nonetheless claims that the curveball was just an optical illusion continued to surface on a regular basis for the next seventy-five years.

3.2.4 The Curve Family.
The awe and astonishment created by the curveball led to a flurry of reports of dazzling new variants. Curves were reported to be breaking in every conceivable direction. But the curveball revolution did not produce as many permanent additions to the pitching repertoire as it might have, at least in part because many of these proved to be exaggerated or entirely fictitious.

The *Philadelphia Press* observed in 1883: "Every pitcher was popularly supposed to have a choice selection of curves which he sent in at pleasure, and his value was usually reckoned on the number of different ones he could use. That idea, by the way, is still prevalent, and there are many people who believe in an 'up' curve and a 'down' curve, an 'in' curve and an 'out' curve, a 'zig zag' and a 'double' curve, and 'shoots' and 'jumps,' and fast and slow balls to match. 'That's all a mistake,' said Matthews [Bobby Mathews], while talking over some of his experiences. 'I never saw but one curve, and never

made any more. Of course, a ball will shoot in a little distance, but you can't call it a curve, because you can't hold that kind of a ball so as to make a curve out of it. The only genuine curve is the one that turns out from the batsmen; but after two or three of that kind a straight ball, if it is properly pitched, looks as if it was turning the other way. 'Drop' balls, or balls which apparently shoot or curve downwards, are all deceptive work, and are thrown from the highest start the rules allow. Rising balls are the same thing, started from as near the ground as possible and pitched upward. 'Slowed' balls are started slow with an apparently fast flourish, for if they were ever started fast I don't know what skill could hold them back, and, as to balls which go both in and out, why that is a manifest impossibility. No, sir. Good, straight pitching, thorough command over the ball, a good 'out-curve' and a good 'in-shoot' are what the great pitchers are working with today, and I, for my part, don't believe in anything else.' Matthews has had enough experience to know all about pitching, but there are other players who disagree with him and believe in balls which change their course downwards or upwards" (*Philadelphia Press*, reprinted in the *Grand Rapids* [Mich.] *Morning Democrat*, September 2, 1883).

Mathews and the author of this article were exaggerating, since many of the pitches being described are legitimate ones. But this response is understandable in light of the proliferation of implausible claims about curves. The mood was summed up in a report that, "[Will] White has got a new curve. It is called the patent-combined-tripartite-quadruplex-quiver" (*Washington Post*, March 16, 1884).

Especially persistent were reports of the "'double shoot,' a ball which so defied the laws of gravitation that it would curve twice in its course, first in and then out, or combining a drop and an up curve" (*Washington Post*, September 4, 1904). The *Chicago Tribune* asked sarcastically in 1877, "A careful scrutiny of the Cincinnati papers fails to show anything about [Bobby] Mitchell, the sensation of the week. It is easy to find out that he is young, an amateur, 'a second Nolan,' left-handed, has 'a double curve,' and is 'the coming pitcher,' but who is he?" (*Chicago Tribune*, April 29, 1877). Another sportswriter sniffed in 1888, "Some men have claimed to have a combination in-and-out curve, but such a ball never existed. Stories have been told of men who could curve a ball in a zig-zag around several posts, but the feat never has and never will be accomplished, simply because a zig-zag curve does not exist" ("How to Curve a Ball," *St. Louis Globe-Democrat*, reprinted in *Cleveland Plain Dealer*, April 29, 1888).

Others, however, took the pitch more seriously. In the early 1880s, Larry Corcoran was said to be pitching the "Chicago snake ball," which writhed its way to the plate. An 1884 article reported that pitcher Al Atkinson had an offering "not unlike the famous 'snake ball' which has made Larry Corcoran the terror of the batters recently" (*Evansville Journal*, July 27, 1884). The *Zanesville Times-Recorder* noted in 1887: "[Frank] Lemons has marvelous speed and [is] the only man except one that has ever pitched on our diamond that could throw the S curve. This difficult ball is produced by firmly grasping the ball and imparting such a twist to it as to cause it to curve to the right until it comes within ten or twelve feet of the batter, when it takes a sudden shoot to the right thus forming a complete S curve" (*Zanesville Times-Recorder*, February 25, 1887). The double shoot later found an enduring home as the core pitch of Frank Merriwell, the fictional hero of a series of baseball tales for juveniles.

A few sources took advantage of the mushrooming of alleged curves to divvy up credit for invention of the pitch. In 1891, *Sporting News* credited Will White with the first sharp curve and "The Only" Nolan with the first outcurve (*Sporting News*, December 19, 1891). A 1903 attempt to sort the matter out credited Fred Goldsmith with having "discovered the 'in shoot,' that is, he was able to deliver a swift ball with a distinct swerve toward a right-handed batter" (*Grand Rapids* [Mich.] *Herald*, May 17, 1903). Charles Francis Carter, who pitched for Yale from 1876 to 1878, claimed later that others beat him to the curve, but "I was one of the early curve pitchers, developing all the variations of the curve and using the inshoot, which I discovered, incidentally, in a Princeton game, earlier than any one else had it, so far as I know" (letter to Grantland Rice, "The Sportlight," syndicated column, April 3, 1923). Tim Murnane also tried to separate the origin of each different curve, and no doubt others did as well (*California Spirit of the Times & Underwriter's Journal*, September 17, 1887).

But by and large the outrageous claims resulted in a jaundiced eye being cast at even the legitimate variants of the curve. After a few years of experimentation, the search for new curves fell into disrepute and faded out. By then, however, it had produced one very successful pitch, along with experimental versions of others that would later reemerge.

3.2.5 Sinker/Drop Ball. The sinker, then known as the drop ball, was the most successful of the pitches associated with the curveball. Its early development was uneven, but many nineteenth-century pitchers used it, and several did so with great effect.

"Phonney" Martin was emphatic: "The first curves in baseball were the 'drop' and 'in' curves, and I am the one responsible for their introduction. In order to do this I made the ball twist toward the batter, and it commenced to drop when about three feet from him, as the drop of the present day does. This was accomplished by the first two fingers and thumb of the hand holding the ball, and by bending the fingers inward and turning the ball around the first two fingers I acquired the twist that made the ball turn towards me. This created the drop curve, and by varying the twist to one side I could get a slight incurve. This style of pitching conformed to the rules, as the arm was straight in delivering the ball, and the hand did not turn outward." Martin said he began using the pitch in 1862 while with the Irvings, a junior club (Phonnie Martin Curve Scrapbook, letter to Sam Crane written after 1910, National Baseball Hall of Fame). Descriptions of the "twist" pitch thrown around the same time by Frederick P. Henry, which is also discussed in the entry on "Curves" (**3.2.5**), suggest that this is probably what he was using.

Stray references appear in the 1870s, including a mention in 1870 that Charles Bierman "pitches a slow drop ball which is very effective" (*New York Clipper*, April 2, 1870; quoted by William Rankin in *Sporting News*, May 25, 1901). Tim Murnane maintained that "Fred Nichols, better known as 'Tricky Nick,' was the first to make good use of the drop ball. He was a great puzzle to the heavy hitters in 1875–6. At Bridgeport and New Haven, Conn., Nichols got a great drop on the ball, when pitchers had to keep their hand below the belt, which would puzzle any of our twirlers of the present day to accomplish" (*California Spirit of the Times & Underwriter's Journal*, September 17, 1887). But few pitchers were using the pitch during the 1870s because the liberalized delivery rules had made the outcurve all the rage.

Pitchers rediscovered the drop ball in the 1880s and found that it had been made lethal by the elimination of the delivery restrictions noted by Martin. Pitcher Mike Sullivan explained in 1897 that the curve "has been improved upon by professionals until we have the inward and outward, drop and raise curve balls, all of which can be thrown by holding the ball the same way, but using a different snap of the wrist. . . . The drop curve is accomplished by snapping the wrist when it is over your head toward the ground, and the ball when leaving the hands slides over the first fingers near the tips" (*Sporting News*, April 17, 1897, 6).

Boston's Charles Buffinton played the greatest role in advancing the pitch's prominence. An unspecified Buffalo paper wrote, "The secret of [Buffinton's] success, the players say, is a peculiar twist that he gives the ball. It comes straight enough to deceive the eye, but shoots downward just before it crosses the plate" (reprinted in *Boston Globe*, July 6, 1884). The *Detroit Free Press* later noted that in 1883, "The fame of Buffington's [sic] drop ball traveled from one end of the country to the other and hundreds of people went miles to see the Bostons play in order that they might see what a 'drop' looked like. It was an innovation in professional pitching" (*Detroit Free Press*, March 31, 1895).

The pitch proved an effective way of negating the batter's advantage of being allowed to call for a high or low pitch (see **1.11** and **2.1.12**). As columnist "Cy" Sherman later explained, Buffinton's delivery "would look like the high ball the batsman called for and its deceptiveness fooled the man at the plate into swinging at it and missing it by a foot or two. Now the batsman who called for a low ball would gaze at the evident high ball sent through by the great Buffinton and settle back with a look of proud disdain, but when the ball took a sudden downward flight and passed the mark at the height called for and a strike call [sic], the look was changed to disgust" ("Hitting the High Spots on the Sporting Pike," *Lincoln* [Nebr.] *Star*, November 6, 1917).

In 1887 batters were deprived of the ability to call for high or low pitches, but by then the drop ball had caught on around the league, with such pitchers as Al Mays, Ed Seward, Nat Hudson, and Charlie Getzein featuring it. Especially adept was Toad Ramsey, who, according to an 1888 account discovered by the researcher David Ball, featured "a combination down and in ball. He brings a ball higher than any pitcher in the profession. When it starts out it seems above the batter's head, but, taking a quick shoot, it passes over the plate waist high, having taken a wonderful drop." But none of

his imitators seem to have surpassed Buffinton, who still had "one of the best drop balls ever seen and when he can command it is almost invulnerable" (*Cincinnati Commercial-Gazette*, January 19, 1888).

Johnny Evers and Hugh S. Fullerton described Charles Radbourn as featuring a pitch in which "he held the ball exactly as if pitching a fast ball, with the thumb on one side and the first two fingers on the other, and at the moment of releasing it from his hand clinched the finger tips tightly into the seams of the ball and jerked backwards with the hand, the ball not only would revolve rapidly but would travel almost on a straight line—yet slowly. The revolution, which was the reverse of the natural twist, helped the ball to hold its straight course, and it lost speed quickly after exhausting the reverse revolution and fell rapidly towards the ground at a point in front of the batter." Evers and Fullerton credited Radbourn with teaching the pitch to Clark Griffith, and suggested that Christy Mathewson's fadeaway was evolved from this pitch (John J. Evers and Hugh S. Fullerton, *Touching Second*, 107–108). Ted Sullivan also attested to Radbourn throwing a drop ball (A. H. Spink, *The National Game*, 152).

Near the end of the decade, the pitch prompted this commentary: "A remarkable ball is the drop ball, now used so much. It comes straight from the pitcher's hand for a short distance, and then falls to the ground. It is produced in several different ways, and by some pitchers is held the same as an out-curve. It must be started at a good hight [sic], most pitchers delivering it from above the shoulder. It is then given a peculiar jerk downward as it leaves the hand. It is a great ball with some of the most effective pitchers in the country, such as [John] Clarkson, Ramsey, Hudson, [Bill (?)] Sowders and others. It is the most fickle of all the curves, and may desert a pitcher for weeks at a time. Thus Clarkson has been known to lose his drop ball entirely for a period, although he delivered the ball the same way all the time. This is probably caused by a stiffening of the muscles brought into play in producing the shoot, and thus preventing the desired effect. A common ball with those pitchers who use the drop ball is the combination down and out shoot, which is very deceptive when coupled with good speed. It is produced by turning the hand in the same manner as to produce an out-curve, and bringing the ball from as high as the shoulder. This is one of the hardest deliveries on a pitcher's arm that is used, and those who continue to use it do not last long as twirlers. Thus after games last year Clarkson's arm would sometimes turn perfectly red and puff up, thus showing the terrible strain upon it" ("How to Curve a Ball," *St. Louis Globe-Democrat*, reprinted in *Cleveland Plain Dealer*, April 29, 1888)."

For reasons explained by Skel Roach in the entry for "Keeping the Ball Down" (**3.3.3**), a combination of factors caused the pitch to fall out of favor in the 1890s and to remain so for two decades. The 1893 decision to move the pitcher farther from the plate seems to have been decisive. Three years earlier, an article written under the mistaken belief that the pitcher was to be moved back three feet that season predicted, "The pitchers whose drop ball has been their main dependence will be more affected by the rule. Speed and control will be the chief requisites, and such pitchers as [Matt] Kilroy and Ramsey will not be the success that they have been in the past" (*Louisville Courier-Journal*, March 23, 1890). When the move did in fact take place, according to Adonis Terry, "Drop curve pitchers had a terrible time the first year, as everything they threw would hit the plate" (*Chicago News*, reprinted in *Sporting News*, October 24, 1896, 3). Ramsey's former catcher, Jack Kerins, considered the new pitching distance such an impediment that in 1896 he declared it "a physical impossibility to pitch the Ramsey drop under the present pitching rules" (*Washington Post*, May 20, 1896, 8).

While the slow-moving "Ramsey drop" vanished from the major leagues, Amos Rusie continued to use a different type of drop ball that derived much of its effectiveness from the way it complemented his legendary fastball. Catcher Malachi Kittridge later observed that the greatest asset a pitcher can possess is "the drop ball that does not break from the right-handed batters. I don't mean one of those outdrops, but a ball that comes up to the plate squarely in the center and falls from one to two feet without changing its lateral direction. Amos Rusie had that ball and he threw it with tremendous speed. Rusie pitched that drop thing and mixed it up with a fast one in close, and the batter who could meet it with any regularity never lived. They tell me that Ramsey and other old-timers depended on it extensively" (quoted in A. H. Spink, *The National Game*, 126).

By 1897 the traditional drop ball had fallen so far out of favor that Al Maul found a young pitcher who had one of the best drop balls he'd ever seen, yet decided not to recommend him to Philadelphia management. Maul was very impressed by the pitch, which "would fall in front of the plate like a needle sprinting after a magnet." But the aspiring pitcher had no other effective pitches and, upon reflection, Maul concluded that "this drop ball would get away from the boy, for under the present rules it is a physical impossibility to pitch that drop, and keep it up without injury to the arm. . . . The drop-ball could be mastered under the old 45-foot rule, but since the pitcher's rubber was removed back, the distance kills this curve. In pitching the drop, the arm is snapped downward, and the strain seems to be confined to the elbow. Tom Ramsey, who had the most puzzling drop ball of any pitcher before or since he was in his prime, had a peculiar experience. He suddenly lost the knack of pitching his favorite downshoot, and try as he would the knack never returned to him, as a man's sight never returns when once it has been destroyed. Ramsey's arm was all right physically, but the cunning had vanished from it." As Maul predicted, the young phenom with the dazzling drop ball soon suffered a career-ending arm injury (*Washington Post*, April 25, 1897, 18). A sportswriter added that the drop "calls for too much exertion on the twirler's part. In pitching the drop the twirler must snap his forearm, and this lodges the strain upon the muscles and tendons of the wrist and forearm. Frank Selee of the Bostons thinks little of pitchers who persist in using the drop ball. He says: "A pitcher who depends on his speed and fast curves is bound to last longer, as a rule, than one who uses a ball that requires so much exertion of the lower arm. . . . In pitching speed the strain is less serious, as it is confined to the shoulder" (*Chicago Times*, August 3, 1897).

Around 1910 the pitch began to return to prominence and received its current name. *Sporting Life* reported during spring training, "A new curve which promises to gain fame equal to that of the spit ball or Christy Mathewson's noted fadeaway, is announced today from the training camp of the New York Giants. The discoverer of the new ball is [Ed] Keiber, one of [manager John] McGraw's new pitchers. The ball has been christened a 'sinker.' With Keiber's delivery the ball starts high, apparently rises a few feet, and then sinks suddenly to about the height of the batter's knee. It can be curved a trifle, either out or in, and though a slow ball, is said to be very effective. McGraw fanned on it Wednesday" (*Sporting Life*, March 12, 1910).

3.2.6 Upshoot or Raise Ball. The "up-shoot" or "raise ball"—a pitch thrown by submarine-style pitchers—is probably not a true member of the curve family. Yet since it is essentially an inverted sinker, this seems the best place to discuss it.

As already noted, Jim Creighton and Deacon White were both throwing pitches in the 1860s that baffled batters by seeming to curve upward. In addition, Henry Chadwick observed after an 1867 game, "The pitching of Hoy [Patrick Hoey of the Excelsiors of Rochester] in this game was very effective. His delivery is from the ground, and the ball comes to the batsman 'on the raise,' so that they are hard to control" (*The Ball Player's Chronicle*, August 29, 1867).

Tim Murnane characterized Bobby Mathews as "undoubtedly the first pitcher to work the raise ball, as far back as 1869. . . . The next ball that seemed to bother the batters was introduced by [Harry] McCormick of the Stars, of Syracuse. This young pitcher had Mike Dorgan, now of the New Yorks, for catcher. They shut out about all the crack clubs of the country that paid them a visit. The ball he deceived the batsmen with was a raise curve, now used by [Charley] Radbourn, of the Bostons. He gave his field easy chances; the out-field had most of the work to do off his pitching. I never saw him pitch a ball below a man's belt. He had perfect control of the ball and a cool head" (*California Spirit of the Times & Underwriter's Journal*, September 17, 1887). On another occasion, however, Murnane described Dick McBride as "the first man to work the raise ball successfully" (*Boston Globe*, February 22, 1900).

A. G. Spalding, the premier pitcher of the early 1870s, later said, "Although I couldn't pitch a curve, I managed to get a 'sail' on a slowly pitched ball that kept it in the air and really did make it rise" (*Fort Wayne News*, May 6, 1895). Spalding was said to have learned the "slow raise" ball from Archie Bush of Harvard (*Oshkosh Northwestern*, December 9, 1905).

Several pitchers experimented with the raise ball in the wake of the curveball revolution. But no one seems to have mastered it, and changing rules and conditions soon deterred the experimenters. An 1888 article declared: "A ball which was formerly used considerably and which yet is seen occasionally in [sic] the raise ball, as it is called. . . . It consists merely in starting the ball from close to the ground and forcing it to rise gradually until after it passes the plate. It is easily produced, but is very hard to command, and hence is not used extensively.

Moreover, it is not particularly effective. It was formerly used with wonderful effect by Tom Bond of the old Boston team. Its chief exponent now is [Jim] McCormick. . . . He has wonderful command of it, and has speed combined, which renders it unusually effective" ("How to Curve a Ball," *St. Louis Globe-Democrat*, reprinted in *Cleveland Plain Dealer*, April 29, 1888).

The introduction of the mound in the 1890s seemed to be the pitch's death knell. But as described in the entry on the "Submarine" delivery (3.1.4), the simultaneous return of underhand pitching motions created new practitioners. In addition, as described by pitcher Mike Sullivan in the preceding entry, the pitch became more effective because the relaxed delivery rules made sharper breaks possible.

The acknowledged master was Joe McGinnity, of whom ballplayer-turned-journalist Sam Crane wrote in 1903: "An effective 'raise' ball very few pitchers have ever had. I remember of only two before McGinnity. They were Jim McCormick and Billy Rhines. It is very difficult to control the ball when the delivery is used, and the majority of twirlers, after trying it once or twice, scratch it off their repertory." McGinnity agreed that unfamiliarity made the pitch more puzzling to batters, adding, "When I have become a 'has been' in the National League that raise ball of mine will carry me along a few years in the minors. There cannot have been many pitchers down here who can work it, for I have 'em all dead to rights, and don't have to use a curve or a drop" (*New York Journal*, reprinted in *Pittsburg[h] Press*, April 22, 1903). Indeed, after completing the major league portion of his Hall of Fame career, McGinnity returned to the minor leagues and won more than two hundred additional games.

It is strangely appropriate to the upshoot's fragmentary history that it was again the featured pitch of a hurler who was active in the major leagues as recently as 2007—Byung-Hyun Kim.

3.2.7 Spitball. The spitball is a pitch of enormous historical significance, and its origins are convoluted. Yet the story of its history is singular, if not unique, because no one ever appears to have claimed more credit for its invention than he deserved.

The spitball came to prominence in 1904, and its impact was extraordinary. The *Washington Post* noted, "This year, however, Jack Chesbro has introduced a novelty into pitching, which, while it is not as wonderful as the visionary double shoot, still is very effective in aiding the possessor to puzzle the opposing batters. This innovation is known as 'the spit ball'" (*Washington Post*, September 4, 1904). Chesbro won forty-one games that season, a total not matched since. His success with the spitball—which he reportedly threw more than 80 percent of the time—naturally attracted attention and imitators (T. H. Murnane, "The 'Spit Ball' Fools 'Em—League Action Needed to Help Batsmen," *Boston Globe*, October 2, 1904, 41).

The copycats had little initial success, and it was reported toward the end of the year that "The so-called 'spit ball' has become famous this season, and but few have been able to master it" (*Washington Post*, September 23, 1904). But by then such pitchers as Jack Powell, "Doc" White, George Mullin, Norwood Gibson, and Bill Dinneen were getting the hang of the spitball, which paved the way for a dramatic breakthrough in 1905 (T. H. Murnane, "The 'Spit Ball' Fools 'Em—League Action Needed to Help Batsmen," *Boston Globe*, October 2, 1904, 41).

Spring training brought reports that "nearly every slabman in both major leagues has been practicing it all winter," along with estimates that three-quarters of them now featured the pitch (*Detroit Times*, reprinted in *Sporting News*, April 22, 1905; *Sporting News*, April 29, 1905). The spitball soon became such a big story that the 1905 season was dubbed "the spit ball year" (Timothy Sharp, *Sporting News*, May 6, 1905). At least with the curveball, batters could anticipate the direction of the break. The spitball presented an entirely new problem, as the sportswriter Bozeman Bulger explained: "The spot on the ball that is usually covered by the tips of the fingers is so moistened with saliva that the fingers slip off without causing any friction. The less friction the greater the break. Therefore, when the ball leaves the hand it is directed by the thumb. This gives it a peculiar wabbling motion and it is liable to 'break' either to the right or to the left" (Bozeman Bulger, "Pitching, Past and Present," *Baseball Magazine*, February 1912, no. 4, 71–73).

The pitch became so popular in the American League that the sportswriter Charles Dryden quipped, "The American League consists of Ban Johnson, the 'spit ball' and the Wabash Railroad" (quoted in John J. Evers and Hugh S. Fullerton, *Touching Second*, 114). But its effects were also felt in the National League, where the Pirates' Fred Clarke observed, "the foul-strike

rule never caused one-half the havoc that this ball is doing with the batting" (*Sporting Life*, May 14, 1905). The sportswriter Timothy Sharp noted succinctly: "You are not in it these days if you are a pitcher without the spit ball" (*Sporting News*, May 6, 1905).

As hitting was virtually submerged by saliva, numerous theories emerged as to how to counteract the spitball. The simplest method was to ban the unhygienic pitch: "The suggestion of Captain [Tommy] Corcoran of the Cincinnati team that the 'nasty' spit ball be referred to the national board of health doubtless will receive the approbation of the White Sox and Cleveland teams" (*Chicago Tribune*, April 30, 1905). This approach received a boost when Dr. Herman C. H. Herold, president of the Newark Board of Health and a baseball fan, called for the abolition of the pitch on sanitary grounds (*Sporting Life*, June 17, 1905).

Others turned to chemistry for relief: "Every city has a scheme to cripple the 'pesky pitch.' In Chicago mustard is the favorite. [Jack] Chesbro awards the palm to Cleveland for originality in that line. The Naps annointed [sic] the sphere with tincture of capsicum, the effects of which remained with him for several days. The capsicum idea is credited to Bradley, who played first base behind a drug store counter in his early days" (*Sporting Life*, August 5, 1905). Cleveland was one of several teams that put licorice on the ball to dissuade the spitball, but resourceful pitchers countered by using benzene to clean off the licorice (*Sporting Life*, May 20, 1905). In a Central League game, members of the Grand Rapids team tried to deter Springfield pitcher Jack Lundbom from throwing his spitball by treating the ball to "a solution of liniment and cayenne pepper" (*Fort Wayne Sentinel*, July 19, 1905).

John Anderson, who was a bit of a wag, claimed that he had invented a technique called the "Tungent," which he described as "a method of putting an 'English' on the ball when he hits it that will cause it to deflect from its true course in a similar manner to a billiard ball that has been 'Englished' by a player." Appropriately enough, Anderson's comments were published in the April Fool's Day issue of *Sporting Life*.

So why wasn't the spitball banned? One obvious reason is that a significant percentage of the players believed they had a vested interest in the spitball. The most conspicuous members of this group were the pitchers who used the new pitch. But they also received support from batters who thought their team's chances might be improved by a pitch which, like the curveball a generation earlier, represented a great equalizer. The sportswriter A. H. C. Mitchell argued: "If the spit ball were eliminated I believe the pennant races would not be so close, especially in the American League" (*Spalding's Guide, 1909*; quoted in David W. Anderson, *More Than Merkle*, 124).

There was even a bit of a public relations campaign mounted to aid the spitball. The *Chicago Tribune* reported that "The players have evolved another name for the spit ball, less offensive than the expressive but inelegant title by which it was christened. They call it the 'eel' ball now, because it has all the characteristics of that aquatic article and is harder to handle generally. They don't expect to hit it any oftener under the new name, but believe it will be more acceptable to the public" (*Chicago Tribune*, April 26, 1905). The *Tribune* made a concerted effort to use the term, but it did not catch on.

A more compelling explanation was given by Ned Hanlon when he grudgingly conceded, "The 'spit ball' is one of the scientific evolutions of the game, and as such I suppose it ought to be encouraged" (*Sporting Life*, June 3, 1905). Equating spitting on a baseball with science seems like twisted logic, but it fits nicely with the spirit of the times.

The efforts of Henry Chadwick and others had succeeded in convincing many that a low-scoring game represented a superior brand of baseball (see **1.30**). One of the basic underpinnings of this contention was the designation of low-scoring baseball as "scientific." In an era where science was making the lives of Americans vastly easier, this was a magic word. An association with science was the equivalent of an endorsement from an unassailable source.

Hanlon's choice of the word "evolution" is also significant. Social Darwinism was at its apex at the turn of the century and exerted a widespread influence. Its emphasis on the "survival of the fittest" lent credence to any advantage gained through innovation and cunning. In contrast, banning such advances seemed to go against the natural order.

A few observers sagely anticipated that the effectiveness of the new pitch would diminish once batters became familiar with its peculiar breaks. Timothy Sharp predicted, "There never was a wrinkle in the pitcher's art that was not solved sooner or later, and I look for the batters to size up this spit ball article before the summer is over" (*Sporting News*, May 6, 1905).

Others argued against outlawing the spitball on practical grounds rather than philosophical ones. The sportswriter I. E. Sanborn believed that a ban would be "difficult to accomplish" while his colleague George M. Graham wrote resignedly, "it would be impossible to formulate a rule which would do away with it" (both in *Spalding's Guide, 1909*; quoted in David W. Anderson, *More Than Merkle*, 124).

For whatever reason, the initial attempt to ban the spitball stalled. Only after the pitch had frustrated batters for more than a decade was the effort successfully renewed. The American Association banned the pitch in 1918, and the circuit's umpires claimed to have "rigidly enforced" the prohibition (Billy Evans, syndicated column, *Atlanta Constitution*, January 5, 1919). The first vote to abolish the spitball was made by the National League on December 10, 1919. On February 9, 1920, the Joint Rules Committee announced that the pitch would be phased out, with a few spitballers being grandfathered.

The timing of the ban is intriguing, because all indications are that by then the spitball was no longer feared in the way it had once been. By 1906 this note appeared: "How the times have changed! A couple of years ago, when Chesbro was mowing down all before him, there was nothing worth mentioning in the line of minor league twirlers, that didn't include a 'baffling spit ball' in his collection. It was the ball of the future and was going to put all the old style twirlers out of business, unless they speedily learned it to keep up with the procession. Most of the veterans did go to work on it and most of them with disastrous results. Arms began to be shatters and, when the batsman began to learn how to master the cuspidor offering, it began to be discarded. The revulsion of feeling has now become nearly complete" (*Detroit Times*, August 20, 1906). While that assessment was overstated, other disadvantages began to emerge. Batters gradually recognized when the pitch was likely to drop out of the strike zone and learned to resist the urge to swing at it. Defensive play behind spitball pitchers also seemed to suffer; fielders complained of being unable to grip the ball cleanly and, according to a 1908 article, "Stealing third base on a spit ball pitcher is easier than when a dry pitcher is in the box. All a runner has to do is to see when the saliva is applied and start for the base. The ball is too wet ordinarily for the pitcher to throw to third and when the catcher gets it he will often grab the wet side and make a bad throw to the base" (*Fort Wayne Journal-Gazette*, June 19, 1908).

By 1920 former pitcher Ralph Works contended that only three pitchers were using the pitch effectively, and he thus applauded the ban for sending pitchers the message "play to win—but lose rather than use discredited pitching" (*Sporting News*, February 19, 1920). Veteran sportswriter Hugh Fullerton maintained that "an examination of the records of the spit ball pitchers over the last eight years shows them losers." He reported that the ban was unpopular only among a few veteran pitchers "who have little else in their repertoire," while the "great majority of pitchers who have used freak deliveries now agree that it is a good thing to get rid of all that kind of stuff" (Hugh S. Fullerton, "On the Screen of Sports," *Atlanta Constitution*, March 21, 1920). Roger Peckinpaugh similarly contended that the spitball was banned only as part of an effort to rid the game of all pitches that relied upon defacing the ball (Eugene Murdock, *Baseball Between the Wars*, 19).

This suggests that ideological concerns, rather than competitive ones, prompted the ban. It seems likely that two factors were of particular importance. First, the esteem in which science was held had been eroded by the devastating uses to which scientific advances had been put during World War I. Second, the popularity of Babe Ruth and his towering home runs demonstrated that the public was not as enamored with low-scoring baseball as had been assumed. These shifts apparently were enough to tip the balance and change the perception of the pitch from "scientific" to "tricky."

The way in which the ban on the spitball was implemented was, to put it mildly, extraordinary. Pittsburgh owner Barney Dreyfuss proposed that a one-year reprieve be granted to recognized spitballers, even though Dreyfuss's Pirates had no pitchers who used the pitch. American League clubs were required to submit the names of two pitchers who would continue to use the pitch, while the National League placed no limit. The Braves and Cardinals accordingly submitted three names apiece (*Sporting News*, February 19, 1920).

At the end of one year it was decided to continue to let acknowledged spitballers throw the pitch, and the names of the seventeen designated pitchers were written into the rulebook. As a result, it was not until Burleigh Grimes was released at the end of the 1934 season that the pitch became entirely illegal. It seems likely that this indulgence was a compromise to gain acceptance for the abolition of the pitch. Another

likely factor was that scoring skyrocketed in the ensuing years, prompting calls again to legalize the spitball (William B. Mead, *Two Spectacular Seasons*, 111–112). In any event, it underscores the fact that the pitch was no longer viewed as the threat it once had been.

Meanwhile, in the Negro Leagues the financial situation was much too shaky for such a ban to be practical. Donn Rogosin explained that the Negro Leagues started with an "inferior 150cc Wilson baseball which cost twenty-three dollars a dozen and saved the league fifty cents over a major league ball," then made matters worse by rarely throwing baseballs out of action. Predictably, spitballs, emery balls, and all sorts of scuff balls remained common in the Negro Leagues long after they had been prohibited in white baseball. In a fabled 1930 showdown that became known as the "Battle of the Butchered Balls," Chet Brewer and Smokey Joe Williams combined for forty-six strikeouts before the game's only run was pushed across in the twelfth inning (Donn Rogosin, *Invisible Men*, 72–73, 56).

The spitball has continued to be used illicitly in the major leagues, and enforcement of the ban has been very sporadic. The first pitcher ejected for throwing a spitball was the Browns' Nelson Potter on July 20, 1944 (William Mead, *Even the Browns*, 157–159). The second such pitcher to be ejected was John Boozer, of the Phillies, who was tossed on May 1, 1968, for throwing spitballs during his warm-up pitches. The Cubs' Phil Regan was ejected for throwing a spitball or doctored ball on August 18, 1968, and Gaylord Perry of Seattle was ejected from a game on August 23, 1982.

But who was responsible for inventing the spitball? Jack Chesbro was most responsible for popularizing the pitch and received some initial credit for its invention. The *Washington Post* reported during the 1904 season, "It was Mr. J. Dwight Chesbro who invented the puzzling delivery to fool batsmen" (*Washington Post*, August 28, 1904). The *Post* corrected its mistake within a month: "The so-called 'spit ball' has become famous this season, and but few have been able to master it. Chesbro, while not the originator of the odd delivery, is superior to all others handling it" (*Washington Post*, September 23, 1904).

Moreover Chesbro made no claim to having invented the pitch, acknowledging that he had learned it from a pitcher named Elmer Stricklett. Stricklett later explained: "After I had got the ball down fine Jack Chesbro saw me pitching it at Columbus, O., and he took it up" (*Sporting News*, January 1, 1920). Reporter Joe S. Jackson similarly concluded that "while no one tried to rob Stricklett of any credit, Jack Chesbro got most of the glory that went with the introduction of the delivery, speedily getting the spit ball down to such a fine point that he made all other users of the delivery look like imitators" (*Detroit Free Press*, March 22, 1908).

Another early master of the pitch, Ed Walsh, also credited Stricklett with having shown him the pitch one spring training when both were with the White Sox: "You hear all kinds of stories about the birth of the spitball, but I believe that Elmer Stricklett was the first pitcher who used it" (quoted in "Walsh Credits Stricklett with Discovery of Spitball," *Washington Post*, March 15, 1914; reprinted in Barry Popik and Gerald Cohen, "Material on the Origin of the Spitball Pitch," *Comments on Etymology* 32:8 [May 2003], 21–28).

So that moves the credit back to Elmer Stricklett, but Stricklett was equally reluctant to accept the mantle of inventor. In 1920 he told a reporter: "The man who discovered the spitball was Frank Corridon. I saw him throwing it in practice and I immediately set about to master it" (*Sporting News*, January 1, 1920). In 1940 he reiterated, "I never discovered the spitball. In countless magazine articles, radio skits and even in some of the baseball records I've been called the originator of the spitter though I never claimed credit for it. A fellow named Frank Corridon really discovered the spitball" (*San Francisco Call-Bulletin*, July 2, 1940; Peter Tamony Collection).

That same year, Edgar Brands of *Sporting News* was producing a radio quiz show when the question arose. A letter was thereupon written to Elmer Stricklett, and this time he tabbed George Hildebrand as the originator, a designation that Hildebrand confirmed (*Sporting News*, June 8, 1960). Hildebrand's role in the saga is especially curious since he was an outfielder and of course did not use the pitch in games.

The two different names cited by Elmer Stricklett reflect not a contradiction but the pitch's convoluted history. Corridon gave this account: "It was back in 1901 that I fell into the knack of throwing it and it was some 'feel' as nobody ever accused me of possessing any inventive genius. I was playing at that time for that famous old manager, Billy Murray, who was then piloting the Providence Grays of the old Eastern League. . . .

"The day in question was one of those where it had rained just enough to make things disagreeable and to make the handling of the ball very uncertain. I was warming up with the catcher, and after throwing five or six balls, I found it impossible to control their course with any degree of accuracy, as the ball was very wet and soggy. I then began fooling and experimenting with the wet ball more in a manner of fun than anything else. To my surprise one ball took a sudden break just before it reached the catcher and landed against his shins. What he said I guess you can figure out for yourself.

"George Hildebrand, now an umpire in the American League, and who was a member of the Providence team at the time, was idly standing by watching the fun. He was much surprised with the way the ball 'broke' and urged me to try again and this time cut out the foolish antics. . . . I took his advice and the next ball acted in the same way as the previous one, except that it didn't get anywhere near the catcher. After a few attempts to control it I gave it up as a hopeless task.

"The thought still stuck with me, though, that perhaps under better conditions and a closer study of it there might be a chance to master it. On the day that followed I practiced it continually, experimenting in every conceivable manner; first, by trying to get the exact amount of moisture on it, and in the right spot on the ball, and also the proper grip. After months of patience and practice success finally crowned my efforts, and I was satisfied that this style of delivery would in future help a pitcher overcome the many handicaps that were being placed in his path to help the batter" (*Sporting News*, January 1, 1920).

George Hildebrand explained how the pitch made its way to Stricklett: "Back in the early part of 1902, Frank Corridon, a young pitcher who was afterward with the Chicago Cubs, was with the Providence Club. He had a habit of spitting on his slow ball, and in fun one day I imitated him in practice, and then said 'Why don't you shoot 'em in faster?' Then I moistened up the ball again and threw a fast one. I noticed it took a peculiar shoot, and I experimented with it a number of times, and even discussed it with Corridon. He used it and in one game I remember he struck out twelve men in six innings, and then wrenched his arm. I doubt if he even realized that it was of much value even then.

"Toward the end of the 1902 season I jumped organized ball to play with Mike Fisher's Sacramento Club. Stricklett was a member of the club. . . . During the warm-up in Los Angeles one day, I said to Stricklett, 'Let me show you something they can't hit,' and I showed him this ball that I had experimented with in the East. He immediately began to experiment with it. That was the beginning of spit ball pitching. Stricklett got so he could control the ball, making it break in any direction he chose" (*Sporting News*, December 11, 1913).

Mike Fisher was present when Hildebrand demonstrated the pitch, and he picked the story up from that point: "Hildebrand saturated the ball and his pitching hand with a generous supply of saliva. 'Now watch me,' he said.

"The ball approached the plate in a manner entirely different from any Stricklett had ever seen. Thereupon followed a long and earnest conversation between the two, Hildebrand agreeing to teach his partner the mystery of the new shoot.

"Some weeks later a company of big leaguers visited the coast and a series of games was arranged in which Stricklett, with a number of others, was to uphold the honor of the west coast pitchers. The big leaguers expected a lot of fun. The day arrived when it came Elmer's turn to assume box duty and, nothing reluctant, he essayed the task.

"When the game was over the visitors were thoroughly subdued. One hit they secured, and they were lucky to get that. Stricklett was besieged by the foreigners to reveal the secret of his craft. A few years previous he had been one of their company and he was never known to be possessed of the effectiveness he displayed that day.

"'What do you call it?' one of them asked.

"Stricklett smiled and replied in a very superior way, 'That's the 'spit ball'" (Francis J. Mannix, "Hildebrand Gave Stricklett First Lessons with 'Spitball,'" *The* [San Francisco] *Bulletin*, September 24, 1913; reprinted in Barry Popik and Gerald Cohen, "Material on the Origin of the Spitball Pitch," *Comments on Etymology* 32:8 [May 2003], 21–28).

Although the story comes to us piecemeal from three different sources, the inconsistencies are minor. Corridon incorrectly gave the year as 1901, but that is the kind of mistake that can be expected after the passage of nearly twenty years. More important, each man was an eyewitness to the events he described, and none claimed a larger role for himself than is justified by the other accounts.

This basic version of events was corroborated by an article that first appeared in the *Washington Post* in 1913 and then in *Sporting News* in 1916. Curiously, when the article appeared in the *Washington Post*, no source or byline was listed, yet when it was reprinted almost verbatim in *Sporting News* three years later, the San Francisco writer Ed Lanhart was cited as its source. Lanhart was in turn said to have been told the story "by a certain party who ought to know." Since George Hildebrand was the only man present at both of the events being described, Gerald Cohen pointed out that he is very likely the unnamed source.

The article presented the same basic facts as the *Bulletin*'s account but added a few new details. For one thing, the Providence catcher who tried to catch Corridon's spitball was identified as Pat McCauley. In addition, it indicated that Elmer Stricklett was on the verge of being released when he mastered the spitball. The later article also claimed that Jack Chesbro toured California after the 1902 season and learned the pitch then (*Washington Post*, April 27, 1913; "History of Two Freak Deliveries," *Sporting News*, May 25, 1916; reprinted in Barry Popik and Gerald Cohen, "Material on the Origin of the Spitball Pitch," *Comments on Etymology* 32:8 [May 2003], 21–28). The researcher Wayne McElreavy discovered that Stricklett beat Chesbro's barnstorming team 13-1 on December 13, 1902, and believes that is when Chesbro first learned of the pitch.

The *Sporting News* version of the article also noted that two other Sacramento pitchers, Win Cutter and Bull Thomas, experimented unsuccessfully with the spitball. Indeed, Elmer Stricklett was not the only pitcher to master the spitball in 1903 and bring the pitch back east. *Sporting Life*'s Chicago correspondent reported at the end of the 1903 season: "Local base ball players and incoming professionals have one topic of conversation now, and that is the new ball the California pitchers are bringing back with them. Among this lot is Skel Roach, who has it down to a science. It is said that every pitcher, big and little, is working on it, and before long there will be fifty, at least, who will have mastered the mysterious 'drop.' It is called the 'spit-ball,' from the fact that the pitcher moistens his pitching forefinger just before delivering the ball. This act in some way takes from the ball all the twist which ordinarily gives the ball its curve near the plate. The result is that it comes from the pitcher's hand with all the speed motion, comes up fair and fast and then drops dully, all speed gone from it, all the twist washed out" (*Sporting Life*, November 7, 1903).

The correspondent also made clear that the 1905 efforts to use chemistry to combat the pitch were not the first such endeavors: "Out in California, they say, the wise manager whose pitcher had not yet learned the drop tried to put red pepper in the seams of the playing ball, figuring this would stop it. It did while the red pepper lasted" (*Sporting Life*, November 7, 1903).

And so the spitball would seem to have resulted from a tag-team effort by several men in the first few years of the twentieth century. Frank Corridon had used it but not appreciated it; George Hildebrand realized what it was and showed it to Elmer Stricklett; Stricklett mastered it and shared it with many others, including Jack Chesbro and Ed Walsh; Chesbro and Walsh brought the pitch to its highest level of attainment.

The astonishment with which the pitch was met would seem enough to establish that it was new. And yet, no sooner did the pitch attain popularity than an extraordinary number of earlier claimants emerged.

Billy Hallman maintained in 1907 that Stricklett may have perfected the pitch, "but he never discovered it. Long before Stricklett was heard of in base ball [catcher] Frank Bowerman had it. When he was with Baltimore in the old National League days he used to use this same ball to have fun with the boys. One day he called me up to play throw and catch and commenced smearing the ball with spit. He called my attention to the way it fooled a fellow and we had considerable fun over it. Just ask 'Robby,' [Wilbert Robinson] or any of the boys on the old Baltimore team, and they'll tell you that Bowerman had it in a limited way, and they all recognized the 'freak work' of the ball when delivered in that way" (quoted in H. G. Merrill, "Jogged to Bench," *Sporting News*, February 9, 1907).

Pitcher-turned-umpire Billy Hart also endorsed Bowerman: "I notice they claim Chesbro and Stricklett were the first to discover the 'spit ball.' Well, back in 1896, when I was pitching for St. Louis, I met Catcher Bowerman, who was with Baltimore that year. Calling me aside in St. Louis one day, he took the ball and requested me to get back of the catcher and watch his curves. I did so and was surprised to see how the ball acted as it neared the catcher. I

asked Bowerman what made the ball act so. He explained that he simply spat on the ball, held onto it with his thumb at the seam and let it go. The odd part of it was that there was no speed to the ball that Bowerman pitched, whereas today they claim that the 'spit ball' can only be delivered with speed. I mastered it after a while, but found that it injured my arm, as it brought into play muscles not generally used. I advise any pitcher with good speed and curves to let the 'spit ball' severely alone. It will ruin an arm of steel in due time" (quoted in the *New York Sun*, February 10, 1908).

Christy Mathewson added, "Bowerman, the old Giant catcher, was throwing the spit ball for two or three years before it was discovered to be a pitching asset. He used to wet his fingers when catching, and as he threw to second base the ball would take all sorts of eccentric breaks which fooled the baseman, and could explain why it did it until Stricklett came through with the spit ball" (Christy Mathewson, *Pitching in a Pinch*, 223).

In 1904, *Sporting Life* unearthed another candidate: "Pitcher George Cuppy, of the Clevelands, had the 'spit ball' seven or eight years ago, and he didn't know it. He had it on the Baltimores all the time and that was why they couldn't hit him" (*Sporting Life*, December 31, 1904).

An 1880 account of James "Pud" Galvin's delivery noted that he "licks the end of his fingers" (*New York Clipper*, January 17, 1880). In 1887 the *Chicago Herald* similarly described Galvin as "a fat, good-natured little fellow who used to go through the business-like performance of expectorating on his fingers before delivering the ball" (*Chicago Herald*, reprinted in the *Detroit Free Press*, May 4, 1887).

Galvin was far from alone in this practice. Sportswriter Walter Barnes wrote in 1905 that Tim Keefe "wet his thumb before delivering the ball" (*Boston Journal*, reprinted in *Sporting Life*, January 21, 1905). William Rankin also came to believe "that Tim Keefe's old slow ball was nothing more or less than the modern 'spit,'" and added, "Tim was a quiet fellow and any discoveries that he ever made in the pitching line he kept to himself. He never talked about them" (*Sporting Life*, May 27, 1905). Charley Snyder told an interviewer in 1907, "They tell us of the new ball this or that pitcher has discovered, but they are not new. I caught the spit ball 25 or more years ago, but we did not call it the spit ball then. Tommy Bond used to wet his fingers and produce a peculiar shoot on his ball, yet he was never given much credit for it, nor was he advertised all over the country as a spit-ball pitcher" (*Cleveland Press*, reprinted in *Sporting News*, December 26, 1907). An 1886 description noted that Mickey Welch "expectorates on either hand" during his preliminary motions (*St. Louis Post-Dispatch*, June 19, 1886). Jim McGuire claimed that Charley Buffinton was the first spitballer while the two were teammates in Philadelphia in 1887 (*Washington Post*, December 26, 1907). And Ted Sullivan made this confusing claim about Charley Radbourn: "He had a drop ball that he did not have to spit on, and called it a 'spit ball'" (A. H. Spink, *The National Game*, 152).

The cases for Galvin, Keefe, Bond, Welch, Buffinton, and Radbourn are weakened by the limited number of attestations for each. On the other hand, none of the claims was made by the men themselves. And while only the descriptions of Galvin and Welch are contemporaneous, the others emerged soon after the spitball became prominent.

Bobby Mathews has far and away the best-documented case of any nineteenth-century spitballer. The *Washington Post* reported in 1904, "Umpire Billy Hart says he use [sic] the 'spit ball' when he pitched in the Union Association back in 1884, and that it was one of Bobby Mathews' best 'foolers,' and yet some say that it is new. The oldest inhabitants are still claiming credit for unearthing all new wrinkles in baseball" (*Washington Post*, September 15, 1904). Note, however, that Hart later was quoted as saying he had been introduced to the pitch in 1896 by Frank Bowerman.

Many other sources gave the credit to Mathews. Ted Kennedy, a pitcher of the 1880s, wrote to Cap Anson in 1905: "What they call the 'spit' ball has moss four ft. thick on it [i.e., is not new]. The old thumb drop ball has found a new name. Bobby Mathews, the grandest little man of the box, used it" (letter to Cap Anson dated May 3, 1905, printed in *Chicago Tribune*, May 5, 1905). Anson later echoed Kennedy: "The spitball. Yes, that may be a new wrinkle, and it may not. I remember how Bobby Matthews [sic] used to pitch. He used to keep wetting the ball, and when he was pitching there was always a nice clean spot on the pill about the size of a half a dollar. Now, that spot was the result of Matthews' wetting the ball, and I believe he was a 'spit ball' pitcher" (quoted in *The* [San Francisco] *Bulletin*, March 6, 1913; reprinted in Barry Popik and Gerald Cohen, "Material on

the Origin of the Spitball Pitch," *Comments on Etymology* 32:8 [May 2003], 21–28).

Phonney Martin recalled many years later that as early as 1868, Mathews "rubbed the balls with his hand and kept one side perfectly white, then he would moisten it with his fingers and let it go. The ball would not only take a decided curve at times, but at other times would drop and curve in" (Francis C. Richter, *Richter's History and Records of Base Ball*, 270). Pitcher-turned-umpire Hank O'Day added that "Mathews used to cover the palm of his left hand with saliva and rub the ball in it" (quoted in John Thorn and John Holway, *The Pitcher*, 164). According to one contemporary account, it was actually tobacco spit that Mathews rubbed on most of the baseball, thereby leaving a white spot that distracted the batter as the pitch approached home plate (*Columbus Times*, July 9, 1884; reprinted in Howard W. Rosenberg, *Cap Anson 3*, 354).

Columnist James J. Corbett wrote in 1919: "Mathews threw a wider and more vicious breaking curve than any other moundsman of his time. And always as a preliminary to throwing such a ball, he would spit on it and then, without rubbing it on his glove, would pitch to the plate. The resultant twister baffled batsmen such as did no other delivery in the days before the National League began" ("Sport World with James J. Corbett," syndicated column, *Fort Wayne News and Sentinel*, February 18, 1919).

Sportswriter Tim Murnane, who played against Mathews, also attested to his having used "what is now known as the spit ball" (*Sporting News*, November 4, 1909). William Rankin similarly concluded, "There is no doubt that [Bobby] Mathews was the originator of the 'spit ball.' He used to rub the ball on the breeches until there was a white spot or one much lighter than the rest of the ball, and then wet his finger. He used to say the grass made the ball slippery, that was why he rubbed it on his breeches, and then he wet his fingers to get a good hold on the ball" (*Sporting News*, February 13, 1908).

The great catcher Charley Bennett was another who believed that Mathews "was using the spit ball before Jack Chesbro was ever heard of." Bennett also implied that the pitcher had made a conscious effort to maintain its secrecy by adding that Mathews "had a big drop and a curve which broke sharply. He never told how it was done, but I noticed that when he pitched, a little white streak appeared on a dirty ball"

(Unidentified clipping, Charley Bennett Hall of Fame file, apparently from February 19, 1905).

A. H. Spink came to a different conclusion: "Some of the players of the present day claim that the ball which Matthews [sic] was pitching then was nothing more nor less than the 'spit' ball now used by many of the best pitchers. But this is hardly possible for the 'spit' ball is fearfully wearing on the pitcher and soon retires him from service" (A. H. Spink, *The National Game*, 140).

Spink is, however, basing his conclusion on an assumption that is dubious at best. Many of the early spitballers had abbreviated careers, but it is more reasonable to attribute this to the extraordinary workloads they handled. Ed Walsh and Jack Chesbro both exceeded 450 innings in their best season—more than "Iron Man" McGinnity ever worked—and both had arm problems soon thereafter. Later spitballers, when assigned more reasonable workloads, proved much more durable. "When the spitball first came out," a sportswriter explained in 1922, "it was popular theory that it was a killing delivery and that no pitcher using it could hope to last long. That fallacy has long been exploded. The spitter is no harder on the arm than any other delivery, and not half as hard as throwing curves" (L. H. Gregory, "Spitball Pitchers One by One Fading into Memory," *Morning Oregonian*, September 2, 1922).

It is an unfortunate fact that, by the time the spitball made its extraordinary rise to prominence in 1905, Bobby Mathews had been dead for eight years. (Galvin and Radbourn were also dead by then.) Given that Mathews declined to take credit for the curveball, it would have been fascinating to have the benefit of his comments on the spitball.

While the history of the spitball is thus a very complex one, a few conclusions seem warranted. One reason for the extraordinary number of claims for nineteenth-century spitballers is apparent from this 1893 account: "Most pitchers when they want to moisten the tips of their fingers expectorate freely on the ball, rub it briskly with both hands and then wipe the aforesaid hands along the front of their curtailed pantaloons, leaving the brand of their tintag tobacco on the surface of their clothing. Mr. [George] Nicol does not do this. He fastens a dampened handkerchief to the surcingle of his uniform, with which he moistens the ball, thus doing away with the time-honored tobacco-juice bath. This act of true gentility on his part was freely and favorably commented on, and it

is said the Colonel's pitchers have been ordered to follow his example" (*San Francisco Examiner*, April 15, 1893).

Baseball historian John B. Foster offered support for this contention: "[Fred] Goldsmith has been quoted as saying that he knew of the spitball and if he is quoted rightly, perhaps he did, because the spitter was known in those early days, although it was not generally used, or called such, and it was not pitched after expectorating on the ball, as became the custom. It was more due to occasional wetting of the fingers of the pitching hand" (John B. Foster, "The Evolution of Pitching," part 3, *Sporting News*, December 24, 1931).

Many contemporaries were aware that this spitting affected a pitcher's control of the ball. In 1886, Pittsburgh manager Horace Phillips blamed a bad outing by pitcher Frank Mountain on the fact that catcher George Miller "is an incessant chewer of tobacco and is ever spitting on his gloves to keep them moist. That makes the ball slippery, and Mountain couldn't grip it firmly at all. However, Miller will chew something else than tobacco henceforth, and that may mend matters" (*Cleveland Leader and Herald*, April 19, 1886).

Indeed, a rule was implemented in 1890 that "Players will not be allowed to spit and rub dirt on the ball this year when a new sphere is thrown upon the diamond" (*Columbus* [Ohio] *Press*, March 16, 1890). It does not appear to have been very strictly enforced. So this raises yet another question: how well the nineteenth-century pitchers who ostensibly used saliva to improve their grip understood and could control its effect upon the pitch's trajectory.

With so many different issues to consider, there are a wide variety of perspectives as to whether the spitball was being thrown in the nineteenth century. Candy Cummings's view was that "when he was pitching they had no spitter but had something like it. He used a similar delivery by gripping the ball on the seams and shooting it over much the same as the spitter does now. He claims, however, that the delivery was dangerous because of the impossibility to control it and as a result it was much like the dreaded 'beaner'" (*Sandusky* [Ohio] *Star-Journal*, May 13, 1921). The *New York Times* rendered this verdict: "Old timers contend that they got peculiar breaks in pitching by wetting the ball, but none specialized in this peculiar delivery up to the time of Stricklett" (*New York Times*, October 31, 1919). Note that both of these viewpoints suggest an awareness of the possibility of producing "peculiar breaks" but question whether it was possible to control the resulting pitch.

Frank Corridon was thus skeptical about claims that any early pitchers had mastered the spitball: "at various times old-time pitchers—twirlers of the 80's and 90's—have declared they used to moisten the ball before delivering it to the batsmen. That may be so, but it is doubtful if they did it with a definite purpose. They may have done so without method or system of distinctive feature. If they used a wet ball, maybe it was not with the knowledge that they were using something they considered better than the dry ball and perhaps they did not use the wet ball twice in the same fashion. Anyway, the peculiar breaks generally attributed to the spitball were not gained by the old-timers, who were not conscious of the possibilities of the ball they claimed to have thrown. They may have used moisture but they did not gain from nor recognize peculiarly definite results therein" (*Sporting News*, January 1, 1920). Connie Mack went further, contending that nineteenth-century pitchers "never heard of the spit ball and don't let anybody try to tell you that they did" (*Sporting Life*, July 18, 1908; quoted in David W. Anderson, *More Than Merkle*, 126).

Still, it is one thing to presume that many nineteenth-century pitchers were inadvertently throwing spitballs and quite another to take it for granted that none of them were aware of what they were doing. It is hard to escape noticing that Keefe, Welch, Galvin, Bond, Radbourn, and Mathews averaged well over three hundred wins apiece. Johnny Evers and Hugh Fullerton later observed that "In the pioneer days of the game, it seemed that if a player invented or evolved a play, the others, instead of seizing upon it to use, gave him a kind of patent-right to it" (John J. Evers and Hugh S. Fullerton, *Touching Second*, 198). The fact that these pitchers performed in an era when effective pitching tactics were often banned would have given them another good reason to be secretive. It seems reasonable to conjecture that at least one of these six greats—especially Mathews—was aware of both the pitch and how to control it, but chose not to publicize the fact.

3.2.8 "Dry Spitters." By the time the spitball came along, the search for new curves had ceased to be taken seriously. Indeed, Christy Mathewson claimed that one reporter who filed a story about the spitball received a telegram from his skeptical editor that read: "It's all right to 'fake' about new curves, but when it comes to being vulgar about it, that's going too far. Either drop that spit ball or mail us your resignation" (Christy Mathewson, *Pitching in a Pinch*, 223).

The remarkable success of the spitball changed everyone's perspective and started the cycle all over again. Innumerable new pitches were soon being invented, and the common aim of most of these efforts was to replicate the break of the spitball without using saliva. As a result, these pitches were often collectively referred to as "dry spitters." A few of these were successful enough to contribute to the actual pitches described in the entries that follow, but most never made it off the drawing board.

Mathewson, who disliked the spitball because he couldn't control it, was one of the experimenters (Christy Mathewson, *Pitching in a Pinch*, 222). *Sporting Life* reported in 1908: "A topic of much discussion among the Giants this morning is the 'dry spitter,' a new pitching delivery of which Chris Mathewson claims to be the originator. Matty calls his freak ball the 'spitless spitter,' for he does not moisten the ball, yet it breaks like a spitter. . . . The 'dry spitter' differs radically from the common spitball not only because the ball is not moistened, but because it is a slow instead of a fast ball. Speed and a quick break have been the essential qualities heretofore, of the 'spit ball' delivery, but Matty throws his deceiver without any effort. In yesterday's game the ball floated up to the plate without any force behind it, and just as the batter would take a healthy swing at it the sphere would suddenly waver and drop dead into [catcher Tom] Needham's mitt. It was like a piece of paper fluttering along and encountering a puff of wind from the opposite direction" (*Sporting Life*, April 18, 1908).

Minor league pitcher Evan "Rube" Evans developed a similar pitch four years later: "The ball is delivered in exactly the same manner as the spitball, but he does not moisten it. Instead of using moisture to slip his first two fingers from the ball he lets them drag off. The ball then takes a peculiar wabbling motion and then jumps as it gets to the batter. The ordinary spitter usually breaks into a right-handed batter, but this one takes an outward and upward jump that is very puzzling" (*Sporting Life*, March 9, 1912).

Sportswriter J. W. Foley wrote in 1915, "[Pete] Standridge was secured from Frisco and is a right-hander. He has a delivery called the 'fork ball' in addition to the regular assortment of twisters. This freak ball is held between the middle and index fingers and is what is sometimes called a 'dry spitter'" (syndicated column, *St. Louis Post-Dispatch*, April 2, 1915).

The constant experimentation during spring training amused veterans like Cy Young, who said in 1905: "This talk about the bewildering shoots that are expected to make the batsmen hammer the atmosphere until they are blue in the face is enough to make one smile. When the season opens such twists as the 'spit ball,' 'snake twist,' and the 'grasshopper shoot' will be relegated to the icebox, and it will be a case of play ball" (*Chicago Tribune*, April 16, 1905).

Christy Mathewson was also struck by the number of pitchers working on new curves in spring training. He commented, "Pitchers, old and young, are always trying for new curves in the spring practice, and out of the South, wafted over the wires by the fertile imaginations of the flotilla of correspondents, drift tales each spring of the 'fish' ball and the new 'hook' jump and the 'stop' ball and many more eccentric curves which usually boil down to modifications of the old ones" (Christy Mathewson, *Pitching in a Pinch*, 222).

Pitchers as successful as Young and Mathewson could afford to poke fun at such extravagant claims. Yet the relentless experimentation by those seeking the "dry spitter" did uncover enough gems that Ty Cobb would later write that the result of "the hullabaloo over the spitball" was that "every pitcher in the land was sitting up at night thinking up ways of doing tricky things to the ball. . . . Most of these pitchers, too, were really clever inventors. They got away with the most astonishing tricks, some of which have not been solved or exposed to this day" (Ty Cobb, *Memoirs of Twenty Years in Baseball*, 65). The next entries will describe a few of those success stories.

3.2.9 Forkball.

John Thorn and John Holway traced the origins of the forkball back to Chattanooga around 1905, when former major league outfielder Mike Lynch experimented with the pitch and found he could get 'astonishing' breaks. But the style tired his fingers, and he could not control it. Three years later, playing with the Tacoma Tigers, he taught it to pitcher Bert Hall, who experimented with it in secret for about three weeks, learning to control it." Hall unveiled the pitch against an "unsuspecting Seattle club and shut them out on four hits. BERT HALL HAS NEW FANGLED BALL WORSE

THAN SPITTER, the local paper headlined. That day the pitch—and the name forkball—were both born" (John Thorn and John Holway, *The Pitcher*, 158).

Rob Neyer discovered that the game in question took place on September 18, 1908. An account the following day observed that Hall "simply put the ball between his first two fingers, drew back his arm and let fly. The result was a lot of wiggles on the ball that had the local help completely mystified, and when they hit the ball at all they were so surprised that they sometimes forgot to run. Hall's assortment yesterday beats all the spit-ball and knuckle ball combinations to death, for he used it overhand, side arm and any old way and kept the ball breaking over the plate" (*Seattle Times*, September 19, 1908; quoted in Bill James and Rob Neyer, *The Neyer/James Guide to Pitchers*, 47).

Hall credited his apprenticeship as a plumber with giving him the wrist strength necessary for the pitch. He explained, "I hold the ball between the first and second fingers, jammed back as far as possible. The ball sort of floats up to the batter with almost no whirling at all, and then, just as the batter is ready to strike, down it shoots to one side or the other, whichever way I let it go from the hand" (quoted in Gerard S. Petrone, *When Baseball Was Young*, 94).

The pitch attracted occasional practitioners in the years that followed, including Pete Standridge, Dave Keefe, and Joe Bush. But it remained enough of a novelty that when Tiny Bonham had success with the forkball in the 1940s, some sources credited him with inventing the pitch.

As has been discussed at some length by Rob Neyer, the distinction between the forkball and the modern splitter is far from clear-cut (Rob Neyer, "The Forkball Fast and Slow," Bill James and Rob Neyer, *The Neyer/James Guide to Pitchers*, 45–51).

3.2.10 Knuckleball.

The knuckleball is one pitch that has had no strong claimants for nineteenth-century origination. The drop curve thrown by 1880s pitcher Toad Ramsey is sometimes said to have been a knuckleball. Ramsey had suffered an injury to his pitching hand that necessitated an unusual grip. But the name of his pitch alone would seem to suggest that it did not have the unpredictable movement that characterizes the knuckleball.

Longtime umpire Bob Emslie stated in 1897 that he had "witnessed many a slow ball float over the home plate, but the slowest one that ever gave a batsman a pain in the back reaching for it was a slow, puzzling ball used by Tim Keefe. Tim's ball fooled any one that ever went against it. It is hard to describe this favorite ball of Tim's. You couldn't call it a drop curve, yet it broke and fell of a sudden in front of the plate. Tim had the distance to the plate well gauged and knew how much force to put behind his ball to barely carry it over the plate. But the motion he used in delivering this slow floater was the same as the maneuvers his arms described in pitching a speedy ball, and when the batsmen were expecting a fast one Tim would hand up one of his slow, lazy, tantalizing floaters. He had wonderful command of his slow ball, which was, in my opinion, as effective as Tom Ramsey's drop" (*Chicago Inter-Ocean,* August 15, 1897). So what was this pitch? Various observers have suggested that Keefe threw a "Screwball" (**3.2.12**) or a "Spitball" (**3.2.7**), and perhaps one of those is the pitch being described. But Emslie had been a successful major league pitcher before turning to umpiring, and his conviction that Keefe's offering was unique makes this seem less likely. So his description of the "lazy, tantalizing" trajectory of the pitch makes one wonder if it could have been a knuckleball.

Ed Cicotte and Nap Rucker are usually credited with inventing the pitch in 1905 while teammates with Augusta of the Sally League. Unlike later practitioners, both Cicotte and Rucker used their knuckles in throwing the pitch. Rucker gave this description: "The knuckleball is held tightly by the thumb and little finger and the knuckles of the other fingers are closed, the ball resting against it. When the ball is pitched it is sent spinning on a horizontal axis. The downward thrust of the hand as the ball leaves, causes the ball to make a spin toward the box artist instead of against him. If this ball could be thrown fast enough, pitchers who have used it say, it would curve upward—something, however, impossible. In its efforts to climb, however, it slows up as it reaches the plate and then shoots quickly as the spinning motion dies, to one side or the other" (quoted in John Thorn and John Holway, *The Pitcher,* 156). Cicotte, by contrast, was far more circumspect about the pitch, even declining in 1910 to explain to President Taft how he threw it (*Boston Globe,* April 29, 1910).

Neither man mastered the pitch immediately, but by the 1908 season it was emerging as a potent weapon. The sportswriter Joe S.

Jackson wrote during spring training that "the 'knuckle ball,' so called . . . which Cicotte is credited with inventing" was the talk of the camps: "Following the stories of this delivery that went out of Little Rock come tales from the training camp of the Brooklyn club, in which the credit for discovery of the 'knuckle ball' is given to Nap Rucker, the big left-hander whom the Superbas got from Augusta. Rucker is using the delivery in the spring games, and is doing wonders with it. His team mates say that he used the ball in games last fall. However, minor leaguers here in the south who came from the American association discount this by claiming that they saw Cicotte use the ball when he was pitching for the Indianapolis club.

"The knuckler is pitched by pressing the knuckles against the seams, instead of folding the fingers over it. It is a medium-paced delivery. In throwing the spit ball there is very little rotary motion. In the 'knuckle ball' those who have watched it, or who have batted against it, say that there is no rotary motion at all. It goes to the batter like an ordinary slow ball, but has a break like a spitter, shooting down, and apparently breaking either to the right or the left of the plate.

"Cicotte used it in games at Little Rock. He had good control of it, and hitting it was about as difficult as hitting the spit ball when the latter is used by a man like [Jack] Chesbro or [Harry] Howell.

"'The way Cicotte used it,' said Lou Criger, 'it's the best slow ball I ever caught. And it's also the hardest slow ball to handle that was ever sent up to me'" (*Detroit Free Press,* March 22, 1908).

Another candidate for having invented the pitch is Lew Moren, who pitched briefly in the major leagues in 1903 and 1904. When he was returned to the minor leagues in 1905, it is said that he recognized the need for another pitch and came up with the knuckleball. It proved his ticket back to the big leagues, where he was hailed as the "inventor" of the knuckleball (*New York Daily Press,* April 17, 1908; quoted in Craig R. Wright and Tom House, *The Diamond Appraised,* 107).

Early in the 1908 season, Clark Griffith predicted that "The knuckle ball will ultimately replace the spit ball and be even more effective than that famous twist" (*Sporting News,* May 7, 1908). Instead a curious thing happened.

That same spring Ed Summers of Detroit unveiled a variant of the pitch. Paul H. Bruske reported that Summers's "slow ball which he pitches from his finger-tip . . . is his adaptation of the knuckle-ball which Eddie Cicotte used last year in the Western League. Cicotte and Summers worked out the thing together with Indianapolis in the spring of 1906, and each did well with it last season. [Detroit catcher] Freddie Payne, who has caught Summers in most of his work down here, says that Summers' particular pet delivery is certainly unique and thinks it should be baffling. The pitcher throws it overhand, underhand or sidearm and gets a different break on every delivery" (*Sporting Life*, March 28, 1908).

Bruske added that Summers "throws the new contrivance in a manner which would better qualify it for the name of 'finger-tip' or 'finger-nail' ball. He clutches it away from the palm of his hands, his finger nails gripping it at the seams. The ball comes up something like a spitter, though with less speed. It actually 'shimmers' before taking the final dive." Grand Rapids manager Bobby Lowe tried to catch "five or six of the finger-tip balls and failed to catch a single one, being hit on the back of the hand with one and missing one other completely, though it lodged in the pit of his stomach" (*Sporting Life*, March 28, 1908).

Sportswriter W. W. Bingay gave a thorough explanation of the difference between the two methods of throwing the pitch: "Baseball's new delivery requires strong, wiry fingers, and these Summers possesses. His fingers are well shaped but long, remarkably long, and he has a grip like that of a vise. The finger nails must be kept down or they will turn in delivering the ball. . . . Summer's [sic] finger nail ball and the knuckle ball are entirely different. As used by Cicotte, Moren, Rucker and others who have mastered it, the knuckle ball is held tightly by the thumb and little finger, and the knuckles of the other fingers are closed, the ball resting against it. When the ball is pitched it is sent spinning on a perfectly horizontal axis." He quoted Summers's explanation that Cicotte rested the ball against his knuckles, but "I found by holding the ball with my finger tips and steadying it with my thumb alone I could get a peculiar break to it, and send it to the batters with considerable speed and good control" (*Sporting Life*, May 16, 1908).

Detroit catcher Charles Schmidt believed that the new method of throwing the pitch had an important advantage, noting that Summers "has as much control of it as any ordinary pitcher has of any ball he uses. The knuckle ball you hear about hasn't this virtue. The pitcher

hardly knows where it is going when it starts. It is hard to handle and hard to get over the plate. Summers uses this finger nail ball, or reverse curve, or whatever you want to call it, any old time, and can almost always get it over" (*Sporting Life*, May 16, 1908). But the pitch also featured the unpredictability that still confounds batters. Summers perhaps said it best when he observed, "You can't describe the darn thing. The nearest I can come to it is a staggering jag coming home" (*Sporting News*, May 12, 1910).

According to teammate Wild Bill Donovan, Summers threw the ball "from below the top knuckles, tearing away the skin down to the finger nails." The resulting pitch was "not only impossible to hit, but almost as hard to catch. I have seen him warming up with Ira Thomas, who was then with Detroit, and almost every other ball would land in the pit of Ira's stomach or break his glove and strike his knee or shin. The ball would frequently come up to the plate, break first to the right, then to the left, and then suddenly duck downward. When the batter hit it, an accident had happened. . . . I was telling Clark Griffith about it and he gave me the hoarse huzza. So one day I got Griff to put on a big mitt and warm up with Summers. He tried and finally succeeded in catching one ball out of four. The others either landed on his shin or up around his chest. When he finally quit he had this to say: 'No batter can hit him, but neither can his catcher catch him if he uses that ball. I could almost swear it broke two ways at the same time.'"

The pitch made Summers virtually invincible, and he won twenty-four games in 1908. Donovan recalled that even the mighty Philadelphia Athletics "quit cold when they saw him warming up. He beat them ten straight games, and he had both [Frank] Baker and [Eddie] Collins throwing their bats away." Summers's use of the lethal offering in that year's World Series added to its mystique and helped the fingernail ball gain popularity at the expense of the pitch originally known as the knuckleball (*Boston Globe*, March 5, 1915).

Another prominent user of the fingernail ball was Ralph Savidge, who apparently developed the pitch independently at about the same time as Summers, and may have preceded him in using it. A *Sporting Life* correspondent filed this report before the 1908 season: "Ralph Savidge, the promising young pitcher purchased from the 1907 Jacksonville South Atlantic League Club by the Memphis club, believes he has invented a new wrinkle in curves. Savidge has mastered the 'finger nail curve.' He believes it is an improvement of the 'fadeaway,' the 'boomerang,' the 'spitter,' or 'knuckle curve.' . . . The 'finger nail' curve is pitched with thumb nail and as many other nails as possible penetrating the covering. The fingers are kept rigid and the ball is thrown with full force. In practice Savidge has baffled the efforts of the best batters. The ball floats lazily toward the batter. There is no revolution at all, but just before the ball passes the plate it takes a quick dart in one of three directions, as desired by the pitcher, certain movement being used to cause the 'finger nail' curve to dart out or in toward the batter" (*Sporting Life*, May 9, 1908).

The following year Savidge gave this description of the pitch and its origins: "All I know about it is that I hold the ball with the tips of all my fingers and there is a sort of a reverse English on it when it leaves my hand. It floats up to the plate very slowly and does not revolve at all until it gets close to the rubber; then it darts suddenly up or down or to one side. It really is not a 'fingernail' ball, for it never comes in contact with my fingernails. Some one just got the idea that it did and gave it that name. I discovered the 'fingernail' by accident while fooling around trying to learn something new. Like Topsy [a character in *Uncle Tom's Cabin*], the 'fingernail' ball wasn't born: 'it just growed.' I never know which way the ball is going to break when I start it toward the plate. If the wind is blowing against the ball it causes it to break sharply and wickedly, but when there is not a breath of air stirring, the break is not so pronounced. The spitball pitcher generally has a faint idea of the direction the ball will take when it breaks, but I never know what's going to happen after the ball leaves my hand. Sometimes it breaks upward and sometimes it drops and it is just as liable to break to either the right or left" (*Sporting Life*, March 20, 1909).

It is not surprising that the fingernail grip became dominant, since most pitchers found it to be easier to control. What is intriguing and rather perplexing is the fact that the fingernail pitch assumed the name of the knuckleball, even though the pitch does not use the knuckles at all.

In 1912 the *Chicago Tribune* reported: "The knuckle ball is thrown by pitcher [Flame] Delhi by pressing the fingernails against the surface of the ball instead of grasping it in his hand. When it travels to the catcher it doesn't even make one revolution. One can see the seam of the ball throughout the entire distance. With sufficient speed back of it it takes a quick break downward or either in or out, just before reaching the batter" (*Chicago Tribune*, March 6, 1912). Delhi pitched only one major league game yet is still remembered for another distinction. He was the first major leaguer to hail from Arizona, and a regional chapter of the Society for American Baseball Research is named in his honor.

Tom Seaton was also successful with the pitch, but it seemed to be dying out by the end of the decade. Then it got a new lease on life when the spitball was banned. Ed Rommel, a minor league spitballer, was one of those for whom the prohibition on his specialty pitch was a major crisis. But a plumber named Cutter Dreuery offered to show him an even better pitch. Rommel soon reached the majors, where he claimed to have been "the first pitcher to make the knuckleball his standby" (Dan Daniel, "Batters Going Batty from Butterflies," *Sporting News*, June 12, 1946).

By this time the distinction between the fingernail ball and the knuckleball was beginning to disappear. The sportswriter Rodger Pippen wrote indignantly in 1923 that Ed Rommel's knuckleball was a myth. He explained: "Rommel's famous ball is a fingernail ball. His knuckles never touch the cover. . . . [Wayne 'Rasty'] Wright of the St. Louis Club is said to employ a real knuckle ball." Pippen blamed the confusion on an ill-informed reporter from a Newark newspaper and noted that Rommel himself "had been under the delusion for five years that he was a knuckle-ball artist" (*Sporting News*, February 1, 1923). As unassailable as Pippen's logic is, by then he was fighting a losing battle. That battle was clearly over by 1953 when Johnny Lindell said, "As a youngster, I had fooled around with what is known as a knuckleball. Actually, mine is a fingertip ball because I hold it with the tips of the three fingers" (*Sporting News*, April 15, 1953).

Bill James and Rob Neyer have noted that when Rommel retired in 1932, the knuckleball again appeared to be on the verge of dying out. At that point there were only two pitchers who relied on the pitch: Jesse Haines and Fred Fitzsimmons (both of whom threw the pitch with their knuckles) (Bill James and Rob Neyer, *The Neyer/James Guide to Pitchers*, 42–43). Nonetheless they were succeeded by a new generation of knuckleballers who threw the pitch with their fingertips, and since then the pitch has almost exclusively been thrown that way.

The resurgence of popularity reached its peak in the mid-1940s when the Washington

Senators featured four knuckleball pitchers—Roger Wolff, Emil "Dutch" Leonard, Johnny Niggeling, and Mickey Haefner. Dan Daniel observed in 1946, "Freakish pitching deliveries run in cycles. The current sensation in the major leagues is the knuckleball. There is scarcely a pitcher in the Big Time who is not either using the butterfly, or fooling around with it in his on-the-field off-time. Infielders and outfielders knuckle the ball to each other in warm-ups" (Dan Daniel, "Batters Going Batty from Butterflies," *Sporting News*, June 12, 1946).

Most of these experimenters found it impossible to control the knuckleball and quickly abandoned it. The extraordinary difficulty the pitch poses to catchers has also limited its spread. But the knuckler has remained a lethal weapon for the select few who master it, and such pitchers as Hoyt Wilhelm, Joe and Phil Niekro, Wilbur Wood, Charlie Hough, Tom Candiotti, and Tim Wakefield have parlayed it into long careers.

Since World War II the pitch's usage has had several elements that distinguish it from other pitches. First, the knuckleball is either a featured pitch or is not used at all. Bill James has observed that this was not the case before World War II, with many pitchers using it as part of their arsenal (Bill James, *The New Bill James Historical Baseball Abstract*, 864; see also Rob Neyer, "The Dancing Knuckleball," Bill James and Rob Neyer, *The Neyer/James Guide to Pitchers*, 40–44).

Pitcher Dick Hall reported that Branch Rickey wanted all the pitchers on the Pittsburgh staff in the early 1950s at least to experiment with the knuckler (quoted in Marty Appel, *Yesterday's Heroes*, 124). Rob Neyer estimated that half the major league pitchers of the 1940s and early 1950s used the pitch at least occasionally (Bill James and Rob Neyer, *The Neyer/James Guide to Pitchers*, 438). Since then, however, pitchers have either made it their primary pitch or have not included it in their repertoires.

Another distinguishing characteristic of the knuckleball's usage since the 1950s is that its practitioners have ended up as starters, though many of them began as relievers. Finally, knuckleballers rarely enjoy major league success before age thirty, but they often last well into their forties.

Since the 1930s it has also become almost automatic for the pitch to be gripped with the fingernails, rather than the knuckles. When a recent pitcher named Jared Fernandez threw the pitch with his knuckles, this was considered such a novelty that his pitch was dubbed the "hard knuckleball" to distinguish it from what has come to be viewed as the real knuckleball.

3.2.11   Knuckle Curve. Like most hybrid pitches, the origins of the knuckle curve are extremely difficult to pin down. To make matters worse, the knuckle curve has been plagued by semantic confusion. Dave Clark, for instance, is emphatic that the knuckle curve is not a knuckleball but a curve (Dave Clark, *The Knucklebook*, 33). Yet as Rob Neyer and Bill James point out, the three most prominent pitchers to throw pitches that they called knuckle curves—Dave Stenhouse, Burt Hooton, and Mike Mussina—were in fact each throwing a different pitch (Bill James and Rob Neyer, *The Neyer/James Guide to Pitchers*, 16). That situation obviously makes it difficult to be consistent in talking about the pitch.

What does at least seem clear is that the idea of combining a knuckleball grip with a curveball delivery is as old as the knuckleball itself. For example, the *Lansing Journal* reported in 1907, "Pitcher Morgan of the Philadelphia club has a new curve that he calls a 'knuckle curve'" (*Lansing* [Mich.] *Journal*, June 5, 1907). There was no pitcher named Morgan on either Philadelphia club that season, so the writer almost certainly meant Lew Moren, whose knuckleball was described in the preceding entry. As noted in that same entry, Ralph Savidge called his pitch a "finger nail curve."

The pitch has never been common, but it resurfaces occasionally. Ed Rommel noted that George Earnshaw, a star of the early 1930s, "had a knuckler, but he pitched it with only one finger. It had more curve and spin than the knuckle pitches you see now" (Dan Daniel, "Batters Going Batty from Butterflies," *Sporting News*, June 12, 1946). Bill James and Rob Neyer noted that Stenhouse and Burt Hooton brought the pitch back to some level of prominence in the 1960s and '70s (Bill James and Rob Neyer, *The Neyer/James Guide to Pitchers*, 16).

3.2.12   Screwball. Christy Mathewson, with his legendary fadeaway, was the first pitcher to bring widespread attention to the pitch now known as the screwball. Mathewson disavowed having invented it, claiming that he learned it around 1900 from a man named Dave Williams (Bozeman Bulger, "Pitching, Past and Present," *Baseball Magazine*, February 1912, 71–73; Dick Thompson, "Matty and His Fadeaway," *National Pastime* 17 [1997], 93–96).

It is therefore safe to assume that the pitch is of nineteenth-century origin. The evidence also makes it possible to draw some general conclusions about the screwball's history. Like several other pitches, it first emerged during the curveball revolution but either it was not fully mastered by any pitcher, or those who did master it successfully kept it under wraps. Only the spitball revolution spawned renewed experiments that led to general recognition of the screwball's effectiveness.

It is much more difficult to pinpoint who actually invented the pitch, as the claims are many and varied. Some accounts of Fred Goldsmith's curve-throwing exhibition have him throwing a screwball (William E. McMahon, "Fred Ernest Goldsmith," in Frederick Ivor-Campbell, Robert L. Tiemann, and Mark Rucker, eds., *Baseball's First Stars*, 69). A 1903 account claimed that Goldsmith "discovered the 'in shoot,' that is, he was able to deliver a swift ball with a distinct swerve toward a right-handed batter" (*Grand Rapids* [Mich.] *Herald*, May 17, 1903).

Ted Sullivan said that Charles Radbourn "had a perplexing slow ball that was never duplicated on the ball field. The nearest approach to him in this delivery was by John Clarkson and Tim Keefe of Rad's time. To this slow ball he could give a lot of speed. It would come toward you and then change its route all of a sudden. It was the delivery they call today the 'fadeaway'" (quoted in A. H. Spink, *The National Game*, 152). Clark Griffith, who was a protégé of Radbourn, was also said to have featured a screwball. Shirley Povich maintained that Griffith "rocketed into stardom" in 1894 because of his discovery "that a curve-ball, released between his thumb and index finger, took an eccentric break toward the right-handed hitters and . . . away from left-handed hitters" (*Washington Post*, January 21, 1938, X19).

Mickey Welch later stated: "I had a fadeaway, although I didn't call it that. I didn't call it anything. It was just a slow curveball that broke down and in on a right-handed hitter, and I got a lot of good results with it in the ten years I pitched for the Giants. Not until Matty came along and they began to write about his fadeaway did I realize that I had pitched it for years. Why, I learned it within a couple of years after I started to play ball and I had no copyright on it. There were several other old pitchers who used it" (Frank Graham, *New York Sun*, reprinted in *Sporting News*, March 2, 1933).

Johnny Evers and Hugh S. Fullerton wrote that "before [Christy] Mathewson learned the trick of pitching his 'fader,' there was one who pitched the same ball in even more wonderful style." The pitcher in question was Virgil Garvin, who "pitched it with his middle finger lapped over his index finger and when he released the ball his hand was turned almost upside down," but he "did not understand its use or worth" (John J. Evers and Hugh S. Fullerton, *Touching Second*, 108–109).

Faith has been a recurring theme in the pitch's history. Bobby Mathews indicated in 1883 that he did not believe that such a pitch was possible at all. He acknowledged that there was an "inshoot" but not an "incurve," explaining, "Of course, a ball will shoot in a little distance, but you can't call it a curve, because you can't hold that kind of a ball so as to make a curve out of it. The only genuine curve is the one that turns out from the batsmen; but after two or three of that kind a straight ball, if it is properly pitched, looks as if it was turning the other way" (*Philadelphia Press*, reprinted in *Grand Rapids* [Mich.] *Morning Democrat*, September 2, 1883). In a delicious irony, "Phonney" Martin later maintained that Mathews threw both an outcurve and a pitch that "would drop and curve in, the exact counterpart, in fact, of Christy Mathewson's famous fadeaway of the present day" (Phonnie Martin Curve Scrapbook, National Baseball Hall of Fame).

It would thus appear that the pertinent question is not who invented the fadeaway but who believed in the pitch enough to develop it to its full potential. And that man, unquestionably, was Christy Mathewson. As Shirley Povich put it, "[Clark] Griffith's screwball, in those early days, was the forerunner of Christy Mathewson's famed fade-away. Mathewson, Griffith always conceded, was the first man actually to perfect the pitch and impart to it an emphatic 'break'" (*Washington Post*, January 21, 1938, X19).

The pitch receded into the background after Mathewson's retirement, only to make a dramatic comeback with another Giant great, Carl Hubbell. Hubbell called his pitch a screwball; the reasons for the name change are complex. Rob Neyer has made a persuasive case that "screw ball" was the name of a different pitch in the 1920s, which was closer to a sinker (Rob Neyer, "The Screwball: Fading Away," Bill James and Rob Neyer, *The Neyer/James*

Guide to Pitchers, 52–55). My own findings support Neyer's contention. According to *Babe Ruth's Own Book of Baseball*, the "screw ball" was developed in response to the banning of the spitball (Babe Ruth, *Babe Ruth's Own Book of Baseball*, 78). A 1921 article confirmed this view, noting that "The day of the spitball and other freak deliveries may be over, but [the Browns'] Dixie Davis displayed an entirely new brand of hurling [today] . . . in the shape of a screw ball that enabled him to stand [the Senators] on their heads" (John A. Dugan, "Davis Has Equal of Freak Pitching," *Washington Post*, May 21, 1921).

Such questions can never be definitively resolved, but there seem to be more similarities than differences between the fadeaway and the screwball. Al Lopez believed that Hubbell's effectiveness with the pitch was in part the result of the seams on the ball being raised in 1933: ". . . In '33 they raised. This let Hubbell get a better grip to turn the ball over and get a better snap with that long wrist he had. That's when his screwball faded away into a real butterfly and he became a big winner" (quoted in Walter M. Langford, *Legends of Baseball*, 218).

3.2.13 Emery Ball. While the emery ball is part of the doctored-ball family discussed in the next entry, it warrants its own entry due to its discrete time frame and historical significance. One major part of the emery ball's legacy is that it became the first pitch ever banned when the American League outlawed it on February 3, 1915. Another singular element of the pitch's history is that it was primarily associated with one pitcher, Russell Ford. And while Ford began using the emery ball around 1910 and was highly successful with it, he kept its secret so well that he was its sole practitioner for several years.

This secrecy helped keep the origins of the emery ball shrouded in mystery. Fortunately Ford provided a detailed account in 1935, when he observed, "Many stories have been told and yarns spun by the yard during the years that have passed, relating to the discovery of the emery ball. None of them came from me, because I never talked about that 'delivery'" (Russell Ford as told to Don E. Basenfelder, "Russell Ford Tells Inside Story of the 'Emery' Ball After Guarding His Secret for Quarter of a Century," *Sporting News*, April 25, 1935, 5). In fact, Ford's memory was faulty in this regard, as he had given a similar account to F. C. Lane of *Baseball Magazine* in 1915 (F. C. Lane, "The Emery Ball

Strangest of Freak Deliveries," *Baseball Magazine*, July 1915, 58–72).

According to Ford, the story begins in the spring of 1908. Ford and Ed Sweeney had formed a battery with Atlanta the preceding year, but Sweeney had been sold to New York near the end of the season. Nonetheless the two practiced together in Atlanta to prepare for the 1908 campaign.

One of Ford's pitches got away from Sweeney and struck a wooden upright behind the plate. Ford's next pitch, which was supposed to be a fastball, instead broke viciously and sailed sideways by about five feet. When Sweeney retrieved the pitch, Ford examined the baseball and noticed that the surface had been roughened by the impact of hitting the stands.

Suspecting that the rough surface of the ball may have caused the peculiar break, Ford threw another pitch with a completely different grip. The ball confirmed his hunch by again taking a mysterious sailing dip. But Ford dismissed the pitch to Sweeney as "a funny one I learned how to throw" and did not use it at all that year.

Russell Ford was drafted by New York at season's end and reported to spring training with the major league club. Because his arm was sore, he was shipped to Jersey City. At that point Ford recalled the funny ball of the previous spring and decided to give it another try. Before a batting practice session, he used a broken pop bottle to roughen the surface of the ball.

Several slow tosses produced nothing out of the ordinary. Then Ford threw the ball harder and the miraculous break returned: "A double curve! Could any baseball pitcher dream of a sweeter thing than that?" Three Jersey City teammates, Earl Gardner, Dan Moeller, and Eddie "Kid" Foster, flailed at the pitch throughout the session without success. When it was finished, the befuddled players told Ford that he was either a one-day "flash" or they were losing their eyesight.

Ford now understood that he was on to something and that he faced an important dilemma: "I had come across a new delivery that without doubt would make me the greatest pitcher in big league baseball—if I kept it to myself! But should I conceal my secret or impart it to the rest of the baseball world? If I did the latter I would lose it and others would also benefit from it. What should I do? I realized you couldn't sell a pig in a poke and once the pig is out, it was anybody's pig.

"I didn't want to talk it over with anybody, so I carried the problem to my Jersey City boarding house when practice was over. Going to my room, I sat down on the bed and pondered the situation. Somewhat selfish, perhaps, I felt that the discovery belonged to me and if anything came of it, I should benefit through its use.

"Then again, if I told other baseball pitchers about it and they started to throw the emery ball, it would soon become outlawed because of the advantage it gave the hurler over a batter. Nothing can survive in baseball which impairs the balance of the game."

Thus, according to Ford, before having ever used what would become his signature pitch in a game, he had made a conscious decision to keep it secret. Realizing that he could not bring broken glass out to the mound with him, he experimented until he found that he could create a similar effect with emery paper, a type of sandpaper. So he cut a piece of emery paper into pieces and sewed a three-quarter-inch square of it into his glove.

Ford took several additional precautions to guard against the discovery of his secret. He pointedly carried his glove back to the dugout with him between innings, defying the custom of leaving gloves on the field. He went through an elaborate pretense of wetting the ball to create the impression that he was throwing a spitball. And he took none of his teammates into his confidence regarding the ruse, not even catcher Larry Spahr.

Once the 1909 Eastern League season began, Ford had the emery ball mastered, and he experienced immediate success with it. He continued to modify his technique for roughening the surface of the ball. First, he moved the emery paper from the outside of his glove to the webbing. Then he moved the emery paper to a ring he wore on his finger. Ford then cut a hole in his glove, allowing him to scuff the ball surreptitiously.

Ford characterized these changes as "seeking to improve ways of pitching the emery ball." It seems a safe assumption, though, that their main intent was to ensure the secrecy of the pitch. No doubt Ford was worried that carrying his glove off the field between innings would attract attention and lead to the discovery of the emery paper.

In July, New York manager George Stallings repurchased Ford's contract, but a spike wound sidelined him for the remainder of the season. The following spring he took the

American League by storm, winning his first eight decisions en route to a 26-6 record and a 1.65 earned run average. He followed that up in 1911 with another 22 victories.

Moreover his secret remained safe, as opposing batters seem to have believed it was a spitball that was baffling them. Ed Sweeney was Ford's personal catcher and was in on the secret, as was his roommate Eddie Foster, but otherwise Ford continued to keep even his teammates in the dark about the pitch.

After two spectacular seasons, Ford's bubble burst in 1912. Sweeney was a holdout that spring, and no other catcher was as accomplished at receiving the emery ball. More important, Ford suffered a series of arm problems and posted losing records in both 1912 and 1913.

Insult was added to injury when the secret of the emery ball finally leaked. Early in the 1913 season Ford realized that Cy Falkenberg of Cleveland was pitching the emery ball. Ford confronted Falkenberg, trying to learn who had revealed the secret of the pitch. Falkenberg offered an unconvincing denial, and Ford warned him not to tell anyone else about the pitch.

Ford now mulled over the question of how his secret had gotten out. Eventually he recalled that one teammate on New York, an infielder, "used to pick up the ball I used, every time an opportunity presented itself, and examine it." According to Ford, after this teammate "ferreted" out the secret, he told Cleveland owner Charles Somers that he could teach the pitch to the journeyman Falkenberg.

Ford deliberately withheld the name of this teammate from the account, and added: "He has never told me to this day [that he revealed the secret] and I have made no effort to find out. There was never any question of a violation of confidence in this matter." Nonetheless Ford offers enough clues that it is easy to deduce the player's identity.

Earl Gardner had been one of the three Jersey City players on whom Ford had first sprung the emery ball in batting practice in 1909. He and Ford were reunited in New York the following season, and Gardner remained a semi-regular at second base until 1912. Midway through that season he lost his job with New York and caught on with Toledo, where one of his new teammates was Falkenberg.

The pitch rejuvenated Falkenberg's previously undistinguished career, and he won twenty-three games in his 1913 return to the majors. He also apparently disregarded Ford's advice and took at least one Cleveland teammate, pitcher George Kahler, into his confidence. (Ford also cited Ed Klepfer as having been taught the pitch by Falkenberg, but Klepfer was not with Cleveland that year.)

Both Cy Falkenberg and Russell Ford jumped to the Federal League in 1914, and both were twenty-game winners that season. But Ford's proverbial pig was now out of the poke. The number of players who knew the secret had grown too large.

Ford noted, "It wasn't two months after the opening of the 1914 American League campaign before everybody in the circuit sought to take his turn on the pitching peak and fling the emery ball." The pitch soon made its way to the National League, and Ford suspected that the responsible party was his former manager George Stallings, now with the Boston Braves.

The secret finally came out in September. In a game on September 14, Eddie Collins of Philadelphia accused New York pitcher Ray Keating of illegally defacing the ball. Umpire Tom Connolly checked Keating's glove and found emery paper. Nine days later Jimmy Lavender of the Cubs was caught scratching the ball against a piece of emery paper that he had taped to his uniform.

Grover Cleveland Alexander admitted that winter, "I experimented with that delivery this season, and frankly, I don't think that I would ever lose a game if permitted to use it. This shoot, which is thrown by roughing a spot on the ball with a piece of emery paper, is simply a corker. It will go in or up, down, or out for a yard, the direction of the slant depending on the position in which you hold the rough spot. The theory of this is that the air catches the rough leather, and the friction forces the ball in the opposite direction from which the emery was used. When I was using it—you know they permitted it in the National League for a short time, I would hold the ball with the rough side down and start it for the catcher's toes. Honestly, it would take such an upward shoot before reaching the batter that the backstop would sometimes have to jump into the air and make the catch. Naturally the ball was ruled out of the league. It placed the batter under a hopeless handicap" (Harry A. Williams, *Los Angeles Times*, November 18, 1914).

The rules could not be changed in mid-season, but American League president Ban Johnson made quick and decisive use of the powers he did have. He announced that any pitcher using sandpaper or emery paper to scuff the baseball would face a thirty-game suspension and a $100 fine.

Once Keating and Lavender were caught, it didn't take long to trace the technique back to Russell Ford. The word was soon out that Ford's "freak or double barreled spitball was nothing more than the emery papered style" (*Sporting News*, October 1, 1914). It was also revealed that Keating and several other Yankee pitchers had been taught the pitch by Ford's old batterymate, Ed Sweeney. Frank Chance explained that Sweeney had "kept the secret well. He was the only man in the business outside of Ford who had the faintest idea of Russ' secret up to a few weeks ago." Chance said that Sweeney decided to show the pitch to others only when he saw George Kahler using it (*Sporting News*, October 1, 1914). Roger Peckinpaugh confirmed that it was Sweeney who had taught the emery ball to the Yankee pitchers (Eugene Murdock, *Baseball Between the Wars*, 18).

That offseason, the pitch was banned and Ford realized that his "bubble had burst." Ford also struggled with arm troubles that year and posted a 5-9 mark. When the Federal League folded at the end of 1915, he wrote to New York owner Colonel Jacob Ruppert that he doubted he could win without the emery ball. Ruppert gave him his release and, as Ford poignantly puts it, "wearily I backtracked the paths of my greatest successes to the baseball minors."

The ban on the pitch also brought an end to Cy Falkenberg's success. After two straight twenty-win seasons, he posted a losing mark in 1915. He was back in the minors in 1916, and resurfaced in the American League just long enough to put up a 2-6 mark which confirmed that his magic had deserted him forever.

Ty Cobb acknowledged that American League batters did not recognize the nature of the pitch, noting that Ford "kept his secret a long time by pretending he was pitching a spitter. He would deliberately show his finger to the batter and then wet it with saliva. This covered up his real trick of using the emery finger-ring to rough the ball" (Ty Cobb, *Memoirs of Twenty Years in Baseball*, 70).

Roger Peckinpaugh suggested that another key to Ford's keeping the pitch a secret was his restraint: "He was satisfied that he could sail the ball just a short distance with a small spot on it the size of a dime. He got away with it for so long because he would go to his mouth every time as if he was throwing a spitter. Everyone thought he was throwing a spitter." Once other pitchers learned the pitch, they "weren't satisfied with a little spot the size of a dime, they wanted a bigger spot. They wound up scuffing half the ball, so it wasn't long until the emery ball was outlawed" (Eugene Murdock, *Baseball Between the Wars*, 18).

Russell Ford's account of the history of the emery pitch included one more intriguing element, though he acknowledged it to be only a "strong hunch" on his part. He suggested that Braves manager George Stallings might have taught the emery ball to pitchers Dick Rudolph, Lefty Tyler, and Bill James during the 1914 season.

Something certainly got into these three pitchers. The Braves had posted thirteen consecutive second-division finishes and were in the National League cellar on July 4, 1914. Then they were transformed into the "Miracle Braves" and stormed to the National League pennant and a World Series sweep of the heavily favored Philadelphia Athletics. The key was the trio of starting pitchers; after posting only one shutout before July 4, they posted eighteen afterward.

The record of the Braves' trio of pitchers in 1915 also seems to support Russell Ford's hunch about the secret of their success. After being virtually unbeatable for much of 1914, Tyler, Rudolph, and James were only five games over .500 in 1915.

Of course banning the pitch did not entirely end its use. In 1919 umpire Billy Evans observed, "The emery ball, under various disguises, still flourishes, and I doubt if it ever will be eliminated from a pitcher's stock in trade. Through a roughening of a very small surface on a ball, it is possible to make said ball do all kinds of funny maneuvers. . . . Pitchers have discovered it is easy to create a small rough spot on the ball without resorting to the forbidden emery paper" (*Cleveland Plain Dealer*, January 5, 1919). But as Evans's comments suggest, the ban did make the pitch much less common.

As noted in the entries on the "Spitball" (**3.2.7**) and the "Doctored-ball Family" (**3.2.14**), such bans were not practical in the Negro Leagues. So hurlers in those leagues developed wider repertoires, with Smokey Joe Williams reputedly developing the best emery ball (Donn Rogosin, *Invisible Men*, 73).

Once the emery ball became famous, there were at least a couple of claimants to prior invention. Clark Griffith confessed to having used the emery ball during the 1890s (*Atlanta Constitution*, September 19, 1913). Hugh S. Fullerton wrote that turn-of-the-century

pitcher Bert Briggs carried emery powder in his hip pocket and applied it to the ball, making it take "the most extraordinary 'hops,' some of which fooled his catchers" (Hugh S. Fullerton, syndicated column, *Reno Evening Gazette*, April 29, 1915). But it is clear that even if others experimented with the pitch earlier, Russell Ford was the man who perfected it.

3.2.14 Doctored-ball Family. In early baseball a single ball was usually used for the entire game, which meant that a pitcher who doctored the ball might hinder the opposing batters but would similarly handicap his own team's hitters. This did not, of course, entirely prevent such tactics.

Several clubs attempted the ethically dubious practice of switching balls between half-innings, as is discussed under "Double-ball Rackets" (**11.1.12**). Other pitchers reasoned that, if it helped them get batters out, they didn't much care if it had a similar effect on their team's batsmen. George W. "Grin" Bradley pitched for Chicago in 1877, but the club did not attempt to resign him for the following season. Bradley caught on with New Bedford and eagerly awaited the opportunity to face his old team and exact revenge.

Bradley "took the box containing the ball into the kitchen of the hotel and steamed it so the label would come off. Then he carried it to a carpenter's shop, wrapped it in the heel of a stocking, put it in a vise and pressed it until it was as mellow as a ripe pear. Then he put it back in the box, sealed it up and took it out to the game. The ball was thrown to the umpire, who broke open the box and tossed it to Bradley. The latter grinned in his own original, fiendish style and took his place in the box. Brad could make the soft ball do everything but talk. He sent it in with all kinds of shoots and curves. In consequence we knocked the Windy City team out by a score of 5 to 1" (*Cincinnati Enquirer*, April 17, 1892; see also Tim Murnane, *Boston Globe*, May 14, 1888).

There was a very fine line between rubbing up a ball and defacing one, as is clear from this 1891 description: "On the occasion of a pitcher entering the box in the first inning having a brand new white ball tossed to him, he thereupon goes through a little performance previous to delivering the ball, for the same reason probably that a violinist tunes up before playing. To deliver a new ball to the bat without this bit of preliminary acting would be considered evidence that the pitcher was not in good trim. Upon receiving the ball from the umpire, the pitcher first examines it in a critical manner. Convinced that it is a regulation ball without flaw, he then rolls it around in his hands with great vigor. Formerly he took up a handful of dirt and rubbed it all over the ball, in order to render it a less shining mark for the batsman, but the rules now forbid that. He is, therefore, compelled to do the rubbing with his hands, and this is done in an energetic manner, as though determined to rub the cover off. Having rubbed the ball until all the dirt on the palm of his hands is transferred to the corner of the sphere, the pitcher looks around to see if all his fielders, in and out, big and little, are alive and in good spirits. Satisfied on this point, he gives the ball one parting rub, and with a look which expresses great dissatisfaction with its bright exterior, he finally throws it" (*Sporting Life*, November 7, 1891).

Al Maul, who pitched in the majors from 1884 to 1901, was particularly vigilant in these efforts. An 1896 account reported that Maul "is said to have an invention of his own of breaking in a new ball. When the new white spheroid is passed to him he anoints it with a piece of pumice stone concealed in a handkerchief. This removes the gloss and roughens the smooth surface, thus giving the fingers a firm grip on the ball" (*Brooklyn Eagle*, May 5, 1896).

But Maul was interested in more than just improving his grip. He later explained, "It's impossible to make a ball with a new, shiny cover break right. . . . In my time, we only used two or three balls to a game. If it was fouled off we waited until it was retrieved and put it in play again, and when a new ball was thrown out we were allowed to saturate it with tobacco juice, rub it in the dirt and roughen it up a bit. Then we could put the old stuff on it. Yes, sir, the batters in those days used to see some funny shoots breaking over the corners of the plate" (*Sporting Life* [monthly], December 1922).

Others went further. Candy Cummings, for example, had a way of pinching the ball that elevated the cover temporarily and gave it an erratic motion. At inning's end he could smooth it back to its original form (*Sporting News*, December 29, 1921). An 1894 account noted that Brooklyn pitcher "Sadie" McMahon had been "accused of carrying lamp black in his pocket to use on new balls" (*Brooklyn Eagle*, July 7, 1894). Researcher David Ball directed my attention to an 1891 charge that George Cuppy was "smearing the ball so thickly with licorice, which he carries in his mouth for that purpose, that opposing pitchers cannot control it" (*Sporting Life*, July 11, 1891). As described in the entry on the "Spitball" (3.2.7), one account reported that Bobby Mathews rubbed tobacco spit on the ball.

Hugh S. Fullerton later enumerated others: "The first record we have of the tricky use of outside agents to cause a ball to perform strange antics in the air was when Tom Bond, pitching for New Bedford, used glycerine and delivered a form of what is now known as the spit-ball. Al Orth, who, according to many old-time players, was the only man to pitch an 'up curve,' used slippery elm, which he applied to his fingers and, throwing underhand, caused the ball to seem to curve upward. Clark Griffith . . . used to knock the dirt from his spikes by striking the ball against his shoe. Grif would strike the ball sharply against his spikes, cut two abrasions in the hide, grip his fingers into them and pitch his famous slow ball. He learned the trick from Hoss Radbourn. While trying to 'wing' the ball Griffith discovered by accident that on some diamonds the grit from his heel, adhering to the ball, made the sphere act strangely in the air. He was pitching a 'sail ball' as long ago as 1896. Bert Briggs, now dead, used emery powder, which he carried in his hip pocket, and his fast ball took the most extraordinary 'hops,' some of which fooled his catchers" (syndicated column, *Reno Evening Gazette*, April 29, 1915; the source of Fullerton's information on Bond was a 1911 interview with Mike Scanlon tracked down by researcher Steve Steinberg. Scanlon told Fullerton that "Bond used to carry a small bottle of glycerin in his hip pocket, and when he wanted to pitch a spitball, he smeared the ends of his fingers with the glycerin. The ball broke exactly as the spitball of today does, and perhaps in Bond's hands as sharply as [Ed] Walsh's does. Old-timers who hit against him will recall it" [*Detroit News*, August 21, 1911]).

The most notorious instance of doctoring a baseball came during a game in Providence on June 6, 1882, when William "Blondie" Purcell of Buffalo earned the nickname "Cut-the-ball" (and a hefty fine) by borrowing Jim O'Rourke's corn knife and using it to slice open the game ball. Ironically, Purcell's intention was to force the umpire to remove the sodden ball from the game so that his team's pitcher could throw his curveball properly. His act created such controversy that the ball was put on display in the window of the *Providence Journal* (William D. Perrin, *Days of Greatness*, 17).

Likewise, 1880s player Abner Dalrymple later claimed: "My post in left field gave me somewhat of a strategic advantage. One of the rules in those days was that a new ball would be put into play by the umpires only after the seams had been torn and the yarn was exposed. Of course, to the players in the field a new ball was desirable at all times. I carried in my pocket a small pen-knife, and I never missed an opportunity to expose the yarn if the ball came my way" (*Chicago Tribune*, September 23, 1928, A7).

In 1897 it was made illegal for a player deliberately to deface the baseball. This was followed in the ensuing years by an increased emphasis on discarding frayed baseballs, as discussed under "New Balls" (**1.26**). Instead of eliminating ball scuffing, this had the opposite effect.

For one thing, the rule was extremely difficult for umpires to enforce. A perfect example was the effort to stop Clark Griffith's previously noted "habit of hitting the ball against the heel of one of his shoes." A *New York Times* article later recalled that "opposing batsmen were always calling the umpires' attention to this, claiming that Griffith nicked the cover of the ball, which aided him in using a freak delivery. After a while the umpires came to the conclusion that this was just a nervous habit of Griffith's, and he merely knocked the ball against the heel of his shoe and had no intention of cutting the cover" ("Leagues May Ban Weird Deliveries," *New York Times*, October 19, 1919). But that didn't satisfy opposing batters, and the Detroit Tigers sent him a bill for eleven baseballs after one of his outings (Mike Grahek, "Clark Calvin Griffith," in David Jones, ed., *Deadball Stars of the American League*, 758).

In 1904 Pirates player-manager Fred Clarke said that the rule allowing umpires to fine players who discolored balls had become a dead letter because team captains had mutually agreed to disregard it. He admitted that captains had no such authority, but explained: "they put it up to the umpire, and as an umpire is always in favor of anything that will lessen trouble, he is willing to shut his eyes to a legal offense if the captains are agreeable" (*Pittsburg[h] Press*, March 23, 1904).

In addition, pitchers came to realize that more frequent ball changes meant that they alone would benefit if they doctored the ball. They soon found that with practice such pitches could often be controlled. This led to what Ty Cobb called the "long siege of trick pitching,"

and even he expressed grudging admiration for the inventiveness behind it. After it ended, Cobb commented, "While the development of trick ball pitching was not a good thing for baseball, the inventors of those mysterious devices for fooling batters are really entitled to more credit than they ever received" (Ty Cobb, *Memoirs of Twenty Years in Baseball*, 119, 68).

The spitball's rise to prominence in 1904 accelerated this trend, and both Cobb and Johnny Evers explicitly linked the two developments. Ty Cobb offered this description: "Every pitcher in the land was sitting up at night thinking up ways of doing tricky things to the ball. This came right on the heels of the hullabaloo over the spitball. Most of those pitchers, too, were really clever inventors. They got away with the most astonishing tricks, some of which have not been solved or exposed to this day. A rule was adopted to do away with all freak pitching, but it still crops out in spots" (Ty Cobb, *Memoirs of Twenty Years in Baseball*, 65).

To the extent that the rule makers tried to prohibit pitchers from defacing the ball, the rules proved easy to get around. Fred Snodgrass later recalled that when an umpire would toss a new ball to the mound, the pitcher "would promptly side step it. It would go around the infield once or twice and come back to the pitcher as black as the ace of spades. All the infielders were chewing tobacco or licorice, and spitting into their gloves, and they'd give that ball a good going over before it got to the pitcher. Believe me, that dark ball was hard to see coming out of the shadows of the stands" (Lawrence Ritter, *The Glory of Their Times*, 99).

Johnny Evers and Hugh Fullerton wrote in 1910: "Immediate variations of the [spit] ball were developed. Slippery elm, talcum powder, crude oil, vaseline were used to lessen the friction of the fingers while other pitchers, to get more friction on the thumb, used gum, pumice stone, resin or adhesive tape" (John J. Evers and Hugh S. Fullerton, *Touching Second*, 113).

Dan Daniel later pinpointed the 1914 and 1915 seasons as the height of the "era of screwy slinging." He noted: "Mud ball, talcum ball, shine ball, phonograph needle ball, raised-seams ball, emery ball, tobacco juice ball—all these daffy inventions made life miserable for the hitters—and the catchers, too. Finally, when Joe Tinker came out with a large steel file and rubbed a ball right out in the open, the time had come to put a stop to the extravaganza" (Dan Daniel, "Batters Going Batty from Butterflies," *Sporting News*, June 12, 1946).

But these years also proved to be the swan song for such tactics. Connie Mack spent much of a game on September 14, 1914, arguing that New York pitcher Ray Keating was illegally defacing the ball with emery paper. The emery ball was banned the following year, and pitchers who engaged in "screwy slinging" began to come under intense scrutiny. Billy Evans explained that during the 1915 season "hardly a game passed by in any league without some manager making accusations against the opposing pitcher. In addition, there was the 'mud ball,' the 'fingernail ball,' the 'talcum ball' and a host of others too numerous to mention." As a result, "the moment a pitcher got his fast ball to sailing, the batter would insist on an examination, a rough spot would usually be found," and the ball would be removed from play (Billy Evans, syndicated column, *Atlanta Constitution*, January 16, 1916).

As a result, pitchers who wanted to doctor the ball had to become more and more devious. In 1915 veteran White Sox catcher Billy Sullivan reported that he had "discovered a new method of using the 'emery ball,' the delivery of which has been officially ruled out of the game by the American League. The obnoxious emery which is needed in preparing the ball is not used. The ball will not have to be scratched, he says, and the cover mutilated like it was with emery paper. The substitute can be placed on the smooth surface of the ball without any extra motion that would attract the attention of the batter. It can be wiped off after the ball is pitched without anyone being the wiser" (Unidentified clipping, hand-dated February 20, 1915, Billy Sullivan Hall of Fame file).

Along the same lines, Eddie Cicotte developed a mysterious pitch that Ty Cobb called a "sailor." The ball "would start like an ordinary pitch and then would sail much in the manner of a flat stone thrown by a small boy" (Ty Cobb, *Memoirs of Twenty Years in Baseball*, 68). The *New York Times* observed, "Eddie Cicotte and Hod Eller are supposed to be shine ball experts, but the methods used in doctoring this particular ball never has [sic] been clearly explained" (*New York Times*, October 31, 1919). Cobb was convinced that Cicotte used some illegal tactic to achieve this effect, but even his teammates were in the dark about his method.

As he had been with the "Knuckleball" (**3.2.10**), Cicotte was tight-lipped about the pitch, even among teammates. In this case he had especially good reason to do so because of the ban that had been enacted on Russell Ford's

"Emery Ball" (**3.2.13**). When the secret leaked out, Cobb noted that all Cicotte "asked was for the ball to be rolled to him on the ground. With a brand new ball that had not touched the dirt he couldn't deliver the sailor" (Ty Cobb, *Memoirs of Twenty Years in Baseball*, 69). Cicotte was banned from baseball in 1920 for his role in the Black Sox scandal, and the nature of his "sailor" was one of the many secrets he took with him.

The shine ball became a cause celebre during the 1917 season, but the term was a catchall for any pitch that generated a peculiar movement. Sportswriter Paul Purman noted that the shine ball was also referred to as the licorice ball or the talcum powder ball and was "caused by rubbing talcum powder, licorice or any other smooth, slippery substance on the ball." He explained that the pitch "depends upon air pressure for its peculiar defiance of the laws of the moving bodies and of gravitation. The shineball is only effective when the shiny spot is on one of the poles of rotation" (Paul Purman, syndicated column, *Fort Wayne Sentinel*, July 5, 1917). Longtime umpire Jocko Conlan contended that the shine ball was a more effective pitch than the spitball because the spitball always broke downward while the shine ball might break either upward or downward (Jocko Conlan and Robert Creamer, *Jocko*, 206).

Calls to ban the shine ball and similar pitches grew louder during the 1917 season with Clark Griffith—of all people—leading the chorus (Mike Grahek, "Clark Calvin Griffith," in David Jones, ed., *Deadball Stars of the American League*, 760). Near the end of the season, American League president Ban Johnson responded by ordering the elimination of the shine ball and decreeing that pitchers could henceforth only use dirt or sand to rub the ball (*Sporting Life*, September 8, 1917). Needless to say, this was easier said than enforced.

Umpire Billy Evans wrote that what he termed the loaded ball was popular among pitchers during the 1918 season: "Through the use of paraffine, an oil rubbed into the palm of the glove, or merely through the use of tobacco licorice juice, or plain saliva, the ball was moistened at the seams. Such moistening acted as a base. A pitcher then rubbed the ball into some dirt, which he managed to get on the palm of his glove. In a short while that seam would become thoroughly loaded, making it considerably heavier at a certain spot. Through proper delivery, and the air resistance which the ball encountered, some fancy dips were possible"

(Billy Evans, syndicated column, *Atlanta Constitution*, January 5, 1919).

While it was impossible to eliminate entirely the doctored-ball family of pitches, increased replacement of baseballs and relentless scrutiny by umpires did the next best thing. Suspected shine-ball practitioner Dave Danforth "was subjected to a showdown test of his alleged illegal pitches. With Commissioner Kenesaw M. Landis and American League President Ban Johnson in the stands, Umpire Billy Evans was instructed to hand Danforth a new ball every time one was hit foul or even into the outfield. Moreover, Danforth was forbidden to rub the ball" (Bob Wolf, "Controversy Like Screaming at Danforth 40 Years Ago," *Sporting News*, May 1, 1957). Such tactics ensured that moundsmen could no longer rely upon these pitches.

Sporting News correspondent Francis J. Powers wrote in 1921 that pitcher Eric Erickson of Washington was following Al Maul's lead in using the pitcher's prerogative to rub up the ball to further his own ends: "With a grip that would put many a professional wrestler and strong man to shame, the Jamestown (N.Y.) Swede can twist the cover loose from a ball with a couple of turns. And once the tightly sewed horsehide is loosened from the interior it is an easy matter to knead it so the ball will sail and dip as it leaves the pitcher's hands and darts toward the batter" (*Sporting News*, December 8, 1921). He seems to have had some imitators, as the writer of a 1923 article reported on the practice of pitchers loosening the cover of baseballs by grasping it with both hands and twisting in opposite directions (*The Literary Digest*; quoted in Dan Gutman, *It Ain't Cheatin' If You Don't Get Caught*, 52).

Apparently at least some umpires considered this technique legal, perhaps because it used no foreign substance. But it didn't help Erickson much, as he never posted a winning record in his seven-year major league career.

As discussed in the entries on the "Spitball" (**3.2.7**), the Negro Leagues could not afford the expense of constantly discarding balls, and so these pitches remained in use. The 1930 "Battle of the Butchered Balls" saw Chet Brewer and Smokey Joe Williams stymie batters for twelve innings by means of sandpaper balls, emery balls, and "goo balls"—a pitch that arrived at the plate dripping with a black, tarry substance (Donn Rogosin, *Invisible Men*, 56).

3.2.15 Slider. Despite its relatively recent emergence, the origins of the slider are cloaked in considerable mystery. Sportswriter Joseph Durso aptly observed in 1968, "Nobody knows for sure who invented the slider or whether it was just there all the time waiting to be harnessed" (Joseph Durso, "Slider Is the Pitch That Put Falling Batting Averages on the Skids," *New York Times*, September 22, 1968).

The two names that come up most frequently are George Blaeholder and George Uhle. John Thorn and John Holway observed that Blaeholder is usually credited with discovering the pitch in the late 1920s (John Thorn and John Holway, *The Pitcher*, 154). Others have suggested that Uhle developed the pitch around 1930.

Uhle himself commented: "I think I was the first one to throw the slider. At least I happened to come up with it while I was in Detroit. And I gave it its name because it just slides across. It's just a fastball you turn loose in a different way. When I first started throwing it the batters thought I was putting some kind of stuff on the ball to make it act that way" (Walter M. Langford, *Legends of Baseball*, 128). On another occasion, he added: "Harry Heilmann and I were just working [on the sideline with catcher Eddie] Phillips. It just came to me all of a sudden, letting the ball go along my index finger and using my ring finger and pinky to give it just a little bit of a twist. It was a sailing fastball, and that's how come I named it the slider. The real slider is a sailing fastball. Now they call everything a slider, including a nickel curve" (quoted in John Thorn and John Holway, *The Pitcher*, 154).

For many, the pitch was just a reincarnation of an older pitch. Phil Rizzuto suggested that it evolved from the "slip pitch" taught by Paul Richards (Joseph Durso, "Slider Is the Pitch That Put Falling Batting Averages on the Skids," *New York Times*, September 22, 1968; according to Rob Neyer, the slip pitch is very similar to the palm ball [Bill James and Rob Neyer, *The Neyer/James Guide to Pitchers*, 21]). Frank Frisch was particularly vociferous in denouncing the slider as just a nickel curve or a dinky curve. He considered the success of the pitch to be a prime example of that eternal lament of retired ballplayers—that baseball was not as good as it had been in his day (Frank Frisch and J. Roy Stockton, *Frank Frisch: The Fordham Flash*; quoted in Dan Daniel, "Fordham Flash Casts Vote for Old-Timers," *Sporting News*, August 4, 1962, 5).

Bucky Walters claimed that Chief Bender had taught him the pitch and had used it as early as 1910. The only difference was that Bender didn't call it a slider, nor did he have any name for the pitch. Martin Quigley cited Frank Shellenback and Elmer Stricklett as other early pitchers who may have used sliders (Martin Quigley, *The Crooked Pitch*, 102–103). Additional names that have come up include Cy Young, Clark Griffith, and Grover Cleveland Alexander (John Thorn and John Holway, *The Pitcher*, 153–154; Bill James and Rob Neyer, *The Neyer/James Guide to Pitchers*, 7). The nature of the pitch and the passage of time make such claims impossible to resolve.

What is not in dispute is the extraordinary growth in the slider's popularity during the '40s and '50s. Phil Rizzuto claimed that when he debuted in 1941, only Cleveland's Al Milnar threw the slider regularly (Joseph Durso, "Slider Is the Pitch That Put Falling Batting Averages on the Skids," *New York Times*, September 22, 1968). But within a few years the pitch had begun to catch on.

Larry Jansen reported that he learned the slider from his catcher while pitching in the Pacific Coast League in 1942, when it was still "a pitch that had hardly ever been used." Jansen perfected the pitch during the war years and then used it to become the PCL's last thirty-game winner in 1946: "The slider just chewed everyone up. That's why I was such a good pitcher in the big leagues. The slider was a very, very new pitch. Everyone thought it was a fastball. They hit ground ball after ground ball" (quoted in Larry Stone, "The Most Wonderful Days I Ever Had," in Mark Armour, ed., *Rain Check*, 102).

Other pitchers followed Jansen in using the slider as a ticket to the majors, with the result that Bill James and Rob Neyer called it "the pitch of the 1950s" (Bill James and Rob Neyer, *The Neyer/James Guide to Pitchers*, 7). By 1960 the slider was so firmly established that sportswriter Dan Daniel could claim that there was "a strong coterie of mound coaches which holds that if you cannot throw a slider, you had better open a shoeshine store" (Dan Daniel, "Lopat Using 'Soft Sell' on Yankee Pitchers," *Sporting News*, April 6, 1960). That master of the turn of phrase, Roger Angell, aptly dubbed it "the pitcher's friend" (Roger Angell, "On the Ball," *Once More Around the Park*, 90).

Stan Musial explained that the slider "changed the game" because its very existence altered a batter's approach. An astute batter, according to Musial, could distinguish a curve from a fastball in plenty of time to take a full swing. The late break of the slider forced batters to remain wary of another option and made it more difficult to attack any pitch (Roger Kahn, *The Head Game*, 157).

Ted Williams observed that, just as important, the pitch proved easy for pitchers to learn and master: "The big thing the slider did was give the pitcher a third pitch right away. With two pitches you might guess right half the time. With three your guessing goes down proportionately. . . . It immediately gives a pitcher a better repertoire" (Ted Williams with John Underwood, *My Turn at Bat*, 234).

Musial concurred, observing in 1961: "When I came to the majors in 1941, only a few pitchers had the slider. Now almost all of them can throw it effectively. It breaks in on the thin handle where there is no wood. I'd say the slider increases the hitter's problem 25 per cent" (quoted in *Sporting News*, November 8, 1961).

Musial's comments raise the interesting possibility that the success of the slider can be at least partially attributed to the tapered bat. It also seems logical that the trend toward fuller swings and follow-throughs (see Chapter 2, section 1, especially **2.1.3** and **2.1.1**) would have made the pitch more effective. This would help explain why old-timers like Frisch considered the slider to be a retread of an old pitch that had not been effective. Musial has also suggested that the slider spurred the trend toward lighter bats (Martin Quigley, *The Crooked Pitch*, 103).

3.2.16 Eephus Pitch. After so many years of hurlers spending their spare time trying to evolve new pitches, Rip Sewell tried a deceptively simple idea in a major league game on June 1, 1943. Sewell turned back the clock a century by lobbing a high, slow ball up to the plate and daring batters to hit it. What was so amazing about the pitch, which Sewell initially called his dew-drop ball but which later became known as the blooper or eephus ball, was that it worked—at least until Ted Williams connected with Sewell's novelty pitch for a memorable home run in the 1946 All-Star game.

Given the simplicity of the pitch, it is not surprising that there were earlier pitchers who appear to have experimented with variations of it. In an 1867 match, a pitcher from the Athletic Club of Dansville, New York, arced his pitches as high as twenty feet in the air with great success (*Rochester Evening Express*, August 3, 1867; reprinted in Priscilla Astifan, "Baseball in the Nineteenth Century, Part Two," *Rochester History* LXII, no. 2, Spring 2000, 17). In an 1869 match, Jack Chapman of the Atlantics of Brooklyn pitched "the last five innings in so peculiar a manner that the Stars [of Brooklyn] could not hit him. The ball was delivered very slowly, and tossed high in the air, descending over the plate and the spot which the striker designated as the place where he wanted a ball. The Stars looked upon this style of pitching as little short of robbery, although they acknowledged it was in accordance with the rules" (*New York Clipper*, January 24, 1880). According to Frank Bancroft, Charley Radbourn had such a hard time retiring Roger Connor that finally, in a crucial situation, "Rad simply lobbed the ball over the plate" and the surprised Connor popped out (*Washington Post*, March 1, 1903, 32). John Thorn and John Holway cite Harry Wright and Bill Phillips as pitchers who evolved similar techniques (John Thorn and John Holway, *The Pitcher*, 153). And a subsequent account maintained that turn-of-the-century pitcher James "Slab" Burns "won considerable fame as a pitcher, and is reported to be the first hurler to pitch the 'balloon' ball which Rip Sewell of the Pittsburgh Pirates has made famous" (*Steubenville Herald Star*, June 22, 1945).

After Sewell revived the unique delivery, pitchers who have experimented with it have included Bill Lee, Steve Hamilton, with his folly floater, and Dave LaRoche, who dubbed his pitch LaLob.

3.2.17   Kimono Ball. Baseball historian Martin Quigley called the kimono ball the "only new pitch introduced to baseball during the latter half of [the twentieth] century." It was the brainchild of Yankee southpaw Tommy Byrne, who invented the pitch during a 1955 postseason exhibition tour of Japan. Quigley gave this description: "From a set position, looking in, he would take his arm back normally and, while striding forward, continue a backward swing and deliver the ball from behind his back. He got so he could control it pretty well. While it did not have much velocity and only a slight rainbow drop, its charm was that it came to batters who were expecting to see it coming toward them from one side, the meanwhile it was still revolving around his back."

While the bizarre pitch was originally intended only to entertain Japanese fans, Byrne showed it to Yankee manager Casey Stengel during spring training and received permission to use it in a preseason game. He did so on March 26, 1956, in a game in Miami against the Brooklyn Dodgers. Batter Pee Wee Reese was too surprised to swing, but umpire Larry Napp called it a "discard" pitch and told Byrne not to throw it again (Martin Quigley, *The Crooked Pitch*, 143–144).

A few days later, American League umpire-in-chief Cal Hubbard announced that the kimono pitch would not be permitted. He agreed that there was no specific rule against the pitch but said it fell under the provisions against making a mockery of the game (Ed Nichols, "Shore Sports," *Salisbury* [Md.] *Times*, March 29, 1956). Hubbard authorized umpires to fine or eject pitchers for using the pitch, and the ultimate novelty pitch passed out of baseball. Perhaps the most amazing thing about the pitch is that Byrne, whose control problems were legendary, was somehow able to throw a pitch from behind his back and get it over the plate.

3.2.18   Palm Ball. Early pitchers lumped all changes of pace as slow balls, without making distinctions based on the technique used to throw the pitch. Bill James and Rob Neyer have noted that it is still very difficult to differentiate the palm ball from other pitches that function as changes of pace (Bill James and Rob Neyer, *The Neyer/James Guide to Pitchers*, 17). As a result, it is impossible to determine the originators of pitches like the palm ball and the circle change, and the best we can do is get some sense of when these deliveries began to be viewed as distinct pitches.

Negro Leagues star Chet Brewer claimed that fellow Negro Leaguer Bullet Rogan invented the palm ball (John Holway, *Blackball Stars*; quoted in Bill James and Rob Neyer, *The Neyer/James Guide to Pitchers*, 17). The pitch gained renown in the late 1940s and early 1950s when it was used by such pitchers as Ewell Blackwell and Jim Konstanty, and it has periodically resurfaced with such pitchers as Dave Giusti.

But with almost all organizations teaching the circle change, the pitch remains scarce. For example, when Cleveland prospect Todd Pennington developed a palm ball, farm director John Farrell remarked, "He's the only pitcher in our system that throws one. You don't see it very often because it's a difficult pitch to command" (quoted in *Baseball America*, September 1–14, 2003).

3.2.19   Circle Change. The circle change is really not a new pitch but at most just a new grip for one of the most ancient pitches. Yet it has become such a major part of pitchers' repertoires in recent years that it deserves to be mentioned.

A recurring theme of baseball firsts is that the subtler an innovation is, the harder it will be to identify its origins. The circle change is a classic example of this, since its distinguishing feature is a grip in which the pitcher's index finger and thumb form a circle (Roger Kahn, *The Head Game*, 290–291). As a result, accounts of how it entered baseball are wildly disparate.

Tim McCarver claimed that Johnny Podres threw the pitch, but other sources suggest that Podres used the conventional grip (Tim McCarver with Danny Peary, *Tim McCarver's Baseball for Brain Surgeons and Other Fans*, 54–55; quoted in Bill James and Rob Neyer, *The Neyer/James Guide to Pitchers*, 12). Roger Angell described Warren Spahn teaching a pitch that he called a sinker-screwball, but which was thrown with the grip of the circle change (Roger Angell, "The Arms Talk," *Once More Around the Park*, 292; quoted in Bill James and Rob Neyer, *The Neyer/James Guide to Pitchers*, 12). Still others try to trace the circle change back to Paul Richards's slip pitch.

While at least a few pitchers undoubtedly threw the pitch earlier, it was not until the 1990s that it began to attract much attention.

3.2.20   Splitter. There are two basic schools of thought on the delivery that became known as "the pitch of the '80s." The first contends that the split-fingered fastball is just a new name for the forkball, albeit thrown with greater speed. The second holds that the pitch's speed and precipitous drop are such an unprecedented combination that it must be considered an entirely new pitch.

Whitey Herzog offered support for the latter viewpoint, arguing, "A fork ball is a fork ball. This is a faster pitch." His explanation of the pitch's effectiveness bears some similarities to Stan Musial's comments on the slider. Herzog noted that batters are forced to commit themselves to swing before the pitch drops out of the strike zone: "The speed doesn't give away anything. It's pretty fast. You can't pick up the rotation, so you don't know what the hell it is" (quoted in Roger Kahn, *The Head Game*, 244).

Roger Craig is generally associated with the pitch, but Roger Kahn suggested that the credit should actually go to a more obscure pitcher named Freddie Martin. Martin pitched for the Cardinals in 1946 but jumped to the ill-fated Mexican League. Toward the end of his career he began to experiment with the grip for the splitter, but he made little use of it.

Martin became a minor league pitching coach, and 1973 found him working for the Chicago Cubs' Quincy team in the Midwest League. One of his charges was Bruce Sutter, a not particularly promising or hard-throwing prospect. Martin showed him the split-fingered grip, and Sutter's exceptionally large hands and long fingers made the pitch extraordinarily effective. According to Sutter, "I threw it, and the first time I did it, it broke down" (quoted in Roger Kahn, *The Head Game*, 247–253).

The results were spectacular. Sutter noted that "Before I learned the splitter, the Cubs were ready to release me from a bottom-level minor league team. . . . Two years after I learned the splitter, I was pitching in the major leagues." After another four years, Sutter captured the National League Cy Young Award.

That kind of success automatically attracts imitators, and Sutter helped the process along by demonstrating his grip to anyone who asked. Sutter noted, "I was the guy who showed Roger Craig how to throw the splitter. I was with the Cubs. Craig was pitching coach for San Diego. Fred Martin was there with me on the major league club that day, and on the sideline there I showed Roger how to throw it. Then Fred spent some time talking to him about it. I'm sure Roger came up with some modifications. But it was Fred Martin and I [who] showed him the pitch" (quoted in Roger Kahn, *The Head Game*, 257).

Roger Craig then brought the pitch to a new level of acclaim. In several high-profile stops as pitching coach, he encouraged his entire staff to throw the splitter. It became known as "the pitch of the '80s."

3.2.21   Cutter. Like the splitter, the cutter is a hybrid, but there is more of a consensus that the cutter is just a fastball thrown with a different grip. Bill James and Rob Neyer discussed the subject at some length and concluded that the terms "cutter" and "cut fastball" are only some twenty years old, but "the pitch itself has been around for a long, long time" (Bill James and Rob Neyer, *The Neyer/James Guide to Pitchers*, 12). Nonetheless, when thrown by a master like Mariano Rivera, the pitch's combination of speed and late movement makes it seem like a new pitch to the unhappy batters who must contend with it.

(iii) Pitching Tactics

3.3.1 Getting Batters to Chase. Of all the tactics in a pitcher's arsenal, none is older or more enduring than trying to get batters to go after bad pitches. Indeed, pitchers were trying to get batters to chase pitches outside the strike zone before there even was a strike zone (see **1.11**). During an 1857 game, for example, the members of the Bay State Club had "very low balls given them, while those they gave were swift and of the right height." By the time a rematch occurred, "they had learned their opponent's tricks of low balls, and paid them in their own coin" (*Spirit of the Times*, May 20, 1857). In addition, as described in the entry on that subject, pitches of this sort could function as "pitchouts" (**5.3.11**).

The approach of the early star Jim Creighton was particularly effective, as this 1862 account shows: "Suppose you want a low ball and you ask him to give you one, you prepare yourself to strike, and in comes the ball just the right height, but out of reach for a good hit. You again prepare yourself, and in comes another, just what you want save that it is too close. This goes on, ball after ball, until he sees you unprepared to strike, and then in comes the very ball you want, and perhaps you make a hasty strike and either miss it or tip out. And if you do neither and keep on waiting . . . being tired and impatient you strike without judgment, and 'foul out' or 'three strikes out' is the invariable result" (*New York Clipper*, August 2, 1862, reprinted in James L. Terry, *Long Before the Dodgers*, 31).

The following year rule makers took action by introducing the concepts of balls and bases on balls. The change had a dramatic effect, as the *New York Clipper* noted: "Last season, McKever's [Billy McKeever's] pitching, like several others, was made effective by his skill in what is called 'dodgy delivery,' that is, the balls he pitched, though apparently for the striker, were not such as he would strike at with any chance of hitting fairly. This style of pitching, and likewise the inaccuracy resulting from efforts to excel in speed, it was that led to the introduction of the new rules in reference to pitching, and hence McKever's style is this season deprived of all its effect" (*New York Clipper*, July 9, 1864).

The introduction of these penalties made this style of pitching more potentially costly, but it did not eliminate it. The large number of balls initially needed for a walk (near ten) left the pitcher with considerable leeway to tempt the batter to expand the strike zone. Hugh Fullerton cited 1880s pitcher Tony Mullane as having "had the art of wasting a ball down long before the other pitchers thought of it, and, aside from his speed, Tony's greatest success was in making batters hit bad balls" (*Chicago Tribune*, August 12, 1906).

The number of balls required for a walk continued to be reduced until the current total of four was reached in 1889, which in turn reduced the viability of waste pitches. So pitchers were forced to try to get ahead of batters and earn the luxury of a wasted pitch, an approach that continues to this day (see **6.6.4**).

3.3.2 Brushback Pitching. The Knickerbockers' ninth rule specified that the ball be pitched "for the bat." There is no reason to think that they foresaw that pitchers might choose instead to throw "for the batter," but it was less than a generation before brushback pitching began.

In early baseball there was no penalty for hitting a batter. Pitchers were taking advantage of this loophole by the early 1860s, causing one reporter to observe in 1863, ". . . All the heavy work of the game [lay] between the pitchers and catchers, the efforts of the former apparently being devoted to the intimidation of batsmen by pitching at them instead of for them as the rules require. . . . Every striker who faces such pitchers as the two in this match is as much engaged in efforts to avoid the ball pitched at him as he is to select one suitable for him to hit at" (*New York Clipper*, October 17, 1863). According to the researcher Tom Shieber, the introduction of the base on balls that offseason was intended to eliminate not only wild pitching but also this intimidating style of pitching (Tom Shieber, "The Evolution of the Baseball Diamond," in *Total Baseball IV*, 114).

As discussed in the preceding chapter (see **2.3.4**), brushback pitching was also kept within limits in the 1860s by other considerations. The fact that pitchers released the ball from below their waist conferred two important benefits for batters: it kept the pitchers from generating great speed and meant that a pitch that did hit a batsman would be likely to do so in less vulnerable spots. In addition, the ball was not dead if it hit the batsman and bounded away, which made it easy for base runners to advance.

These restraints were gradually removed, and by the mid-1870s the predictable increase in brushback pitching had begun. Indeed, for a time there was actually a minor benefit to hitting the batter with a pitch since not even a ball was called. This caused the *Chicago Tribune* to complain after the 1876 season: "In the section which treats of dead balls, the rule, as it has been, has strangely omitted to affix any penalty for their delivery, and it was no damage to a pitcher to deliver a wild ball if he could only hit somebody with it" (*Chicago Tribune*, November 19, 1876, 10).

The ascendance of the curveball (see **3.2.3**) in the late 1870s brought the issue to a head. The curve put a batter in an unenviable position: a pitch that appeared to be headed for him might suddenly break back over the plate, while one that he had started to swing at might suddenly veer toward him. Moreover the curve was very difficult for most pitchers to control. Ernest Lanigan later maintained that the hit-batsman rule was necessitated by a pitcher named "Wild Bill" Serad who "couldn't make his curves behave" (*Sporting News*, November 28, 1912). With bases on balls requiring close to ten balls, pitchers had plenty of opportunities to experiment. Unfortunately for batters, this meant that pitchers with good control could afford to waste pitches. It is hard to miss the hint implicit in Henry Chadwick's reference to Bobby Mathews's "habit of throwing away the first ball to each striker by tossing it over the batsman's head" (*New York Clipper*, August 14, 1875).

By the end of the decade, pitchers were throwing from shoulder height or higher, which created an urgent need for "some rule to prevent the injury and intimidation of batsmen by pitchers." But as a Chicago reporter noted in 1878, "Two years in succession the League has tried to draw such a rule, and abandoned it because they could not agree on a penalty. It is a great evil, and must be stopped; it gives the unscrupulous pitchers a great advantage over the fair-minded ones, and places too much power in their hands. [Tommy] Bond is the worst of the intimidating pitchers, and [Ed "The Only"] Nolan is little better. In the last two weeks' play of the Chicagos they have been hit by the ball from the pitcher and temporarily disabled eleven times. Per contra, [Chicago pitcher Terry] Larkin has hit only one of his opponents. Now it cannot be suffered to be in fairness a method of winning games to disable and discourage the batters of either side, and every club is interested in making a law which shall stop the evil. How shall a penalty be inflicted?" (*Chicago Tribune*, May 12, 1878, 7)

The search for a solution led in 1879 to a rule that empowered umpires to impose fines of between ten and fifty dollars against pitchers who deliberately threw at batters. This was a very sizable amount and certainly got the attention of pitchers.

But there was an obvious problem with the rule, as Henry Chadwick noted when he inquired: "How is the umpire to judge whether the pitcher intended to hit the batsman or not?" (*New York Clipper*, December 28, 1878). Or, as umpire Jocko Conlan later observed succinctly, "I've never claimed to be a psychic. Fair or foul. Safe or out. Ball or strike. All of that is plenty tough enough" (quoted in Roger Kahn, *The Head Game*, 217). The new rule indeed proved unenforceable, and the situation continued to deteriorate.

Then as now, knockdown pitches caused accusations to fly. When Boston pitcher Tommy Bond hit two Cleveland batters with pitches in an 1879 game, he was criticized by the *Cleveland Leader*. The *Boston Herald* in turn denounced the *Leader* for having "contemptibly insinuate[d] that it was done on purpose" (all reprinted in the *Chicago Tribune*, May 25, 1879). With no way of knowing what was going on in the heads of pitchers, such disputes were inevitable.

Accusations weren't the only thing to fly. When pitcher John Schappert hit a batter during an 1883 game, the two men began throwing the ball back and forth at each other until cooler heads prevailed (*National Police Gazette*, June 23, 1883). Schappert became so notorious for his approach that the *New York Clipper* scolded in 1883: "Schappert in his delivery of the ball to the bat has adopted a line of conduct which is hardly worthy of a manly player, and one which is in direct violation of the American rules of the game; and that is his intimidation of batsmen by sending the ball to them so as to either hit them or oblige them to look more to avoiding a dangerous blow than to hitting the ball" (*New York Clipper*, August 11, 1883, quoted in James L. Terry, *Long Before the Dodgers*, 129).

Tony Mullane was another pitcher who specialized in intimidation. As early as 1881, he was described as having "pitched wildly at times, landing the ball among batsmen's ribs quite too often to please the victims of his uncertain aim" (*Detroit Free Press*, May 1, 1881). It soon became clear that there was nothing wrong with Mullane's aim.

Chris Von der Ahe recalled in 1904 that Mullane "was a great hand at frightening the batters. 'Watch me polish his buttons,' he would frequently say as a good batter faced him. He would throw the ball right at the batter sometimes, particularly if he was a strong batter" (*St. Louis Post-Dispatch*, April 17, 1904). Hugh Fullerton reported that Mullane "insisted was that no player ever should crowd the plate on him. It interfered with his plans of making them hit bad balls. To keep them a proper distance from the plate Tony tried a system which modern pitchers would do well to follow. When a batter got up on the edge of the plate Tony hit him with the ball. After he had wounded half a dozen there was no more crowding the plate" (*Chicago Tribune*, August 12, 1906).

Another star with a reputation as a brushback pitcher was Tim Keefe. After an inside pitch by Keefe in 1888 injured Boston's Kid Madden, the *New York Sun* wrote, "While Boston people always have recognized the merits of Keefe as a pitcher, nevertheless they have no particular love for him, on account of his peculiar habit, fault, call it what you will, of hitting the batsman. In fact, it used to be said here that half of his skill was due to his intentional delivery of the ball so close to the batter as to intimidate constantly and finally actually frighten him into inability to hit the ball" (*New York Sun*, May 6, 1888).

With more and more pitchers throwing overhand pitches at batters, it became apparent that something stronger than a warning was needed "to punish the pitcher for trying to intimidate a batsman by throwing the ball at his person—the Schappert style of pitching" (*Brooklyn Eagle*, December 2, 1883). A new rule was introduced by the American Association in 1884 allowing a hit batsman first base. Some found the whole concept bizarre, such as the sportswriter who filed this report: "Five of the Quincys were given first base yesterday under the rule awarding the batter a base for being struck by a pitched ball. None of those so struck was injured in the least, and it was noticed that they finally scored without exception. Another such farcical innovation was never introduced into the game" (*Indianapolis Times*, reprinted in the *Rocky Mountain News*, May 5, 1884). At least one umpire appears to have felt that the wrong person was being protected and added a novel twist to the new hit-batsman rule during a preseason game. Indianapolis manager Bill Watkins complained that umpire John

McQuaid "would not permit a batsman to take a base on being hit by a pitched ball; then again he allowed Columbus men to take bases on balls which struck him (the umpire)" (*Sporting Life*, April 30, 1884). A reply from Columbus manager Gus Schmelz the next week acknowledged that to have been the case but claimed that McQuaid was actually following a directive to that effect.

Once the wrinkles had been ironed out, the rule proved effective. One observer remarked: "The new rule punishing a pitcher for hitting a batman with the ball is working admirably. Under the old rule the pitcher could not be punished except for intentional hitting, and this could not be proved. Now he is punished whether it is intentional or not, and justly so; for if not intentional it is from want of proper command of the ball, and if he has not that the rule will teach him to acquire it. The blow must be a solid one, however, and not one in which the ball simply glances from his person" (*Sporting Life*, April 30, 1884). The National League adopted the rule three years later.

As with many other compromises, the new rule didn't eliminate brushback pitching, but it did the next best thing by ensuring that there was again risk on both sides. In the years that followed, there were hopes that reducing the number of balls required for a walk would bring an end to the brushback pitch. As late as 1901, John B. Foster wrote, "This talk about any pitcher deliberately driving a man away from the plate by trying to knock out his brains might have had some weight in the old days, when the pitcher had six and eight times to try that little performance, but it is not likely that it will be attempted very often under present conditions" (*Sporting Life*, April 6, 1901).

Eventually it became clear that no rule would eliminate this style of pitching. Instead, inside pitching has come to be governed by a generally agreed-upon set of principles. Johnny Evers and Hugh Fullerton wrote in 1910, "Spectators are not aware that one of the greatest and most effective balls pitched is the 'bean ball.' 'Bean' is baseball for 'head' and pitching at the batter's head, not to hit it, but to drive him out of position and perhaps cause him to get panic-stricken and swing at the ball in self-defense is an art" (John J. Evers and Hugh S. Fullerton, *Touching Second*, 91–92).

As this suggests, it was acceptable in the early twentieth century intentionally to pitch near the batter's head as long as he was given a chance to get out of the way. Christy Mathewson, for instance, expressed no ethical reservations about the beanball. Instead he presented it as a good way to determine if a batter had a "yellow streak" and was not manly enough to belong in baseball (Christy Mathewson, *Pitching in a Pinch*, 35–36).

As the century wore on, beanballs became increasingly unacceptable. This trend is often attributed to the fatal beaning of Cleveland shortstop Ray Chapman in 1920, and yet this conclusion is difficult to justify. Bill James has noted that hit batsmen declined steadily during the first two decades of the twentieth century, then actually increased briefly after the Chapman tragedy. Totals of hit batsmen again dropped steadily from the mid-1920s until the mid-1940s, then increased dramatically over the next two decades, before beginning to drop in 1968.

The causes for these tendencies are more difficult to determine, because no single reason predominated. Instead a number of factors contributed, including changing interpretations of the strike zone, new approaches by batters, and the introduction of the batting helmet (Bill James, "A History of the Beanball," *The Bill James Baseball Abstract 1985*, 131–140).

Through the ups and downs there developed an unwritten but generally understood code that spells out the circumstances in which it was acceptable for a pitcher to hit a batter. Of course there are always instances where a pitcher goes beyond these constraints or where a batter expresses his displeasure by charging the mound.

Speaking of batters charging the mound, this is primarily a recent trend. But there were isolated incidents in earlier eras. Cap Anson's father Henry claimed to have charged A. G. Spalding when hit by a pitch in the late 1860s (Adrian Anson, *A Ball Player's Career*, 43). An 1884 game account described how Charles Eden of Grand Rapids was hit by a pitched ball and, "refusing to take an apology, he rushed at [Muskegon pitcher William F.] Nelson, bat in hand, to punish him for it." In an incredible instance of *deus ex machina*, it began to rain heavily at that very moment, and tempers were calmed (*Sporting Life*, August 13, 1884).

3.3.3 Keeping the Ball Down. While keeping the ball down has long been a standard precept of pitching, that wasn't always the case.

As discussed under "Strike Zones" (1.11), until 1871 pitchers had to fulfill batter's requests for specific locations, and until 1887 batters requested low or high pitches. In addition, pitchers were not allowed to throw overhand until 1884. Since a pitch that changes planes causes difficulties for batters, many felt that "what is called a 'raise ball' (a ball delivered from below the waist for a batter calling for a high ball) is the most difficult to hit" (*Saginaw Evening Express*, May 24, 1884).

Once the pitcher was given the choice of where to throw the ball and the freedom to throw overhand, low pitching quickly came into favor. According to the pitcher "Skel" Roach, by the start of the 1890s "the man who threw low balls was the master of the situation, and the low drop curve was in great demand. Men like [Toad] Ramsey and [Charley] Buffinton, masters of low drop balls, were kings and every pitcher had a drop in his repertoire. . . . The old-time slugger stood right up to his work, grasping the handle of the stick and swatting with all his might. He could kill a waist ball and could reach up after a high shoot with tremendous effect. A ball coming by his knees or sinking as it reached the plate was his hoodoo, and he would break his bat bending down for them" (*Sporting News*, February 18, 1905).

By the start of the twentieth century, many batters had switched to slap and chop hitting, and this in turn convinced many pitchers that it was wiser to keep the ball up. Pitcher Charley "Deacon" Phillippe surprised some in 1903 when he maintained that "more men were weak on low balls these days than on the high pitch." He attributed this "to the habit of all twirlers for years past in pitching high, so as to force the man to put the ball on the ground or lift it into the air. Phil found out not long since that a swift, waist-high pitch worried some of the best batsmen in the League" (*Sporting Life*, September 26, 1903).

Two years later pitcher Skel Roach observed a perceptive analysis that foreshadowed his later career as a distinguished judge: "A pitcher of the present time must keep the ball up, and must send in high shoots continually. If he puts them down and lets them drop around the batter's knees, he will be getting the release envelope in a hurry."

Roach acknowledged that one reason for this trend was the strain that drop balls put on pitchers' arms, but he cited "the changed condition of the batting" as the primary consideration: "One day Willie Keeler arrived, and after him an army of others who realized that it was time for a new era in batting. Keeler and the other fellows caught the bat halfway up the bat. They cut, chopped and bunted. They found low balls just the thing to be whacked under this new system. At about the same time the pitching distance was increased and the drop ball found its funeral. Not only had it became easy prey for the hitters, but it could not be controlled as formerly and, with the changed distance, was breaking anywhere but the proper place. The pitchers had to begin over again, and devise new means of fooling the hitters. While they were doing so, there was plenty of batting, but it wasn't long until the slabmen had the batters gauged again. They began bringing in the shoots right by the neck, and the crouching batsman, waiting to chop on the low balls were deceived.

"The pitchers, I think, accommodate themselves to changed conditions much faster than the batsmen. It took only a few seasons for the pitchers to master the changed style of batting, but the batters could not work either their brains or minds fast enough to cope with the change in pitching. They didn't even go back to the old style of slugging, but just plugged away as best they could—and got the worst of it. The only low ball that's really effective now is Joe McGinnity's raise, and that works because it is just the reverse of a drop—while it sails low, it comes slowly upward just as it reaches the batter" (*Sporting News*, February 18, 1905). This is very insightful commentary, which shows how a rule change and a new technique can work in tandem to have a ripple effect in many seemingly unrelated areas of the game.

While Roach's dig at slow-witted batters may seem gratuitous, the implication that batters were being foolish by not reverting to slugging tactics is not an unreasonable one. As discussed at some length in the entry on "Place Hitting" (2.1.1), and more briefly under "Choking Up" (2.1.4), many of the greatest hitters in these years were men like Napoleon Lajoie and Honus Wagner who did indeed revert to the slugging tactics of earlier generations.

Hitters were provided with an additional reason for modifying their tactics by the introduction in 1909 of the livelier cork-center ball (see 9.1.6). Many remained unwilling to change, but enough did so that pitchers once again began to alter their tactics. Within a couple of years Ty Cobb noticed another dramatic change in pitching tendencies: "pitchers who are keeping the ball low are those who are getting away best. The ball has much to do with

this, and furthermore there are more high ball hitters now than there used to be. The batters have mastered the high ball, but most of them are weak on the low ball" (quoted in *Sporting News*, June 29, 1911).

The following year Addie Joss remarked, "There was a time when it was the accepted theory that one of the requisites of the first-class pitchers was ability to keep the ball around the batter's neck" (*Washington Post*, September 5, 1912). Joss credited the prevalence of the hit-and-run play with having forced pitchers to again rethink their approach.

Jocko Conlan credited John McGraw with a major role in this shift, explaining that "you had to have a curve ball if you played for Mc-Graw. That's why the National League got the reputation for being a low-ball league, because McGraw's pitchers were trained to throw that curve ball low, right at the knee, so that the batter would hit the ball into the ground and you could turn it into a double play. The American League was a fast-ball league" (Jocko Conlan and Robert Creamer, *Jocko*, 47–48).

Several factors have contributed to the development of a consensus that keeping the ball down is the most effective style of pitching. The first and most obvious is the livelier ball, which transformed fly balls from likely outs into peril. At the same time larger gloves and smoother fields have made ground balls routine outs and thus more desirable than in early baseball. The hinged or one-handed catcher's mitt of the 1960s was another important factor as it reduced the risk of a wild pitch or passed ball on a low pitch.

In addition, some believe that the lights used in night baseball make it easier for batters to pick up high pitches and have therefore increased the emphasis on keeping the ball down. Bob Feller commented in 1962, ". . . To win under the arcs you must keep the ball low. The high, hard one doesn't rate with the sinker for success under the lamps" (*Sporting News*, August 4, 1962).

3.3.4 Keeping a Book on Hitters.

Until the 1887 season, batters could specify that they wanted a high or low pitch (see 1.11 "Strike Zones"). As a result, Connie Mack later claimed that before 1887 "there was no use in [the pitcher] knowing a batter's weakness, because the rules prevented him from pitching to it" (Connie Mack, "Memories of When the Game Was Young," *Sporting Life* [monthly], June 1924).

At least one pitcher disagreed. It was reported in 1880 that Worcester pitcher Lee Richmond, a Brown University student, "has a little book in which he has noted the batting peculiarities of all the League batsmen who played against him last year. This book he has thoroughly studied, and will endeavor to put it to good use the coming season" (*St. Louis Post-Dispatch*, March 27, 1880).

Tracking hitters' weaknesses became more viable when batters were stripped of the right to request pitches. Boston pitcher John Clarkson became so renowned for his knowledge of hitters' weaknesses during the 1887 season that other pitchers came to him for advice on how to pitch to specific batters (*Chicago Herald*, reprinted in *St. Louis Globe-Democrat*, August 17, 1887, 6).

Clarkson explained: "I have made something of a study of the vulnerable points of men who face me with the stick. . . . When new men come before me, I don't pitch at them in a hurry. I study their position, the length of their bat, and see whether they stand well up to or away from the plate and whether they are right or left field hitters. After pitching a ball at them I can generally tell whether their tendency is to swing up or down at the sphere. If their disposition is to hit up at the ball, I endeavor to keep it pretty well elevated, reversing the delivery if they are disposed to hit low. Some batters pull away from the ball, involuntarily stepping backwards or to one side. Such a man cannot hit a ball on the outside corner of the plate and that is where I strive to put it" (*Base Ball Gazette*, April 24, 1887).

The tactic that had gained prestige when used by an Ivy Leaguer suffered when it became associated with an eccentric and not very successful turn-of-the-century pitcher known as "Crazy" Schmit. Schmit caused amusement in 1890 by his reliance on "a book when pitching, which contains the weaknesses of all the League batters. He consults this as he faces each man. He must have had the weaknesses wrong last Saturday, for the New York Club made something like twenty-four hits off him" (*Sporting News*, May 31, 1890). Another skeptical reporter observed that all Schmit "has to do is to ask the umpire the name of the man at bat and in less than five minutes he finds his man's weak points by a reference to his library, and then he has him at his mercy. Just exactly how this German scientist is going to pan out it is difficult to tell, but the chances are that he will go the way of all the other brilliant men and

land deep in the soup" (*Sporting News*, June 7, 1890).

The strategy eventually overcame the stigma of being associated with Schmit, and a 1903 account observed: "Nowadays . . . few pitchers of note go into the box without knowing the weak points of every batsman who may come to the plate. In other words, they know or feel sure that they know just what kind of a pitched ball each batsman cannot hit safely, and as a result they 'feed' each hitter what they believe will retire him" (*Ottumwa* [Iowa] *Courier*, March 16, 1903).

Many pitchers kept this information in their heads, but some literally kept books. Win Mercer maintained "a scrapbook for all comments upon batsmen, and before each game he looks up the foibles and eccentricities of the men who are to face him" (*Chicago Post*, June 21, 1897). White Sox pitcher Doc White was said to be "following in the footsteps of the late Win Mercer, and keeps a 'dope' book on all the men he has to work against. He has a neat little vest pocket book, carefully indexed by clubs, in which he writes the weaknesses and strong points of the batters he faces" (*Sporting Life*, May 2, 1903). White was reportedly so proud of the accuracy of his book that he intended to publish it—but only after he retired (Gerard S. Petrone, *When Baseball Was Young*, 71).

3.3.5 Reading Batters. Some early pitchers found they could enhance their success by studying not only batters' tendencies but their stances. Henry Chadwick explained in 1879, "The moment the pitcher faces the batsman in the first inning of a match he should begin to study his man and endeavor to find out his weak points of play." Chadwick suggested that this could be done by studying "how he holds his bat" and "the speed of his stroke" (*New York Clipper*, March 15, 1879).

After the 1886 season the removal of the rule that allowed batters to call for high or low pitches (see **1.11** "Strike Zones") gave pitchers new incentive to do so. One reporter stated in 1888, "In the National League there are about 125 players, and none of them hold a bat or use it in the same manner. . . . The knowledge of their peculiarities, together with knowing that some players can hit only a high ball and others a low ball, enable pitchers to use strategy when facing opposing teams, and the best pitchers are those that have made a study of them" (*New York World*, reprinted in *Dallas Morning News*, May 20, 1888).

This tactic has remained in use ever since. Clark Griffith explained in 1902: "There is a great deal in understanding a batter's feet. It is by studying them that I am able to tell what kind of a ball the man is expecting, and consequently give him something he doesn't want. Every batter has a different position of the feet when he expects a fast one or a floater, a high or a low ball. They try to fool the pitcher when they are going to bunt, and can, too, in the way they hold the bat, but their feet give it away almost invariably. A batter's feet are better to watch than his head in this respect" (*Sporting Life*, May 31, 1902). Jimmy Callahan, a protégé of Griffith, added, "A man's pose at the plate, if it is pronounced, will lead to giving him the ball he is least fitted to hit" (Chadwick Scrapbooks, circa 1898 clipping).

In the 1920s, Urban Shocker remarked that a pitcher "can often tell what is in the batter's mind by the way he shifts his feet, hitches his belt or wiggles his bat" (quoted in F. C. Lane, *Batting*, 33). Warren Spahn suggested that this tactic can be especially effective when facing a batter for the first time: "A man who drops the front shoulder when he cocks the bat is a high-ball hitter. If he drops the back one, he's a low-ball hitter. After he takes one swing you know whether he has good wrists" (quoted in Roger Kahn, *The Head Game*, 176–177).

Stance-reading became such an established part of the pitcher's arsenal that some batters have devised countermeasures. Mike Flanagan cited Chet Lemon as a hitter who would try to mislead pitchers by moving "way up in the box like he was looking for a curve so that you'll throw him a fastball" (quoted in George F. Will, *Men at Work*, 92). George Kell went even further, shifting "two or three times on a single pitcher, just to keep him off balance" (quoted in William Barry Furlong, "The Unlikely Hitter"; reprinted in Tom Stanton, *The Detroit Tigers Reader*, 85).

3.3.6 Advantage to Pitching Left-handed. As early as 1867 a *Dayton Journal* reporter wrote that the Buckeyes of Cincinnati "had a conspicuous advantage in a left-handed pitcher, which baffled the Daytons" (*Dayton Journal*, reprinted in *The Ball Player's Chronicle*, June 13, 1867).

When the curveball revolutionized the game in the mid-1870s, there was a general belief that it was easier for a southpaw to throw a curve. John B. Foster explained: "The boys of that day and the fathers, too, for that matter, were certain that the lefthanded pitcher could throw a natural curve better than a righthanded pitcher, or, to put it another way, did throw a natural curve, while the righthander had to acquire the skill to curve a ball" (John B. Foster, "The Evolution of Pitching," part 1, *Sporting News*, November 26, 1931).

In addition, clubs responded to the curve by stacking their lineups with left-handed hitters, which increased the advantage of a left-handed pitcher. The result was an awed reaction when the first great post-curve southpaw, J Lee Richmond, burst on the scene in 1880 with a dominant season that included major league baseball's first perfect game (see 3.4.4, 6.3.9). In addition, as discussed under "Pickoff Moves" (5.3.1), the development of windups during the 1880s provided another advantage to left-handers since base runners can break with less risk when a right-hander begins his windup.

As the decade wore on, the novelty gradually faded and teams came to realize that being left-handed might give a pitcher an advantage but was not a cure-all. Richmond and several other southpaws soon lost their effectiveness, leading to speculation that physiological factors might prevent left-handed pitchers from sustained success. The 1887 rule changes discussed in this chapter's introduction seemed to affect southpaws unduly, leading to claims that "The left-handed pitchers are not the terrors they were last year. The new rules place them on nearly the same footing with the right-handed twirlers. ["Lady"] Baldwin, [Ed] Cushman, [Ed] Morris, [Elmer (?)] Smith, [Steve] Toole, ["Toad"] Ramsey are being batted rather hard. [Matt] Kilroy alone seems to possess a big advantage" (*Decatur Review*, May 18, 1887). For whatever reason, sustained success continued to elude left-handers, and in 1910 Eddie Plank finally became the first southpaw to record two hundred career victories—two months after Cy Young won his five hundredth game.

3.3.7 Switch-pitcher. The advent of the curveball gave right-handed pitchers a distinct advantage over right-handed batters, and southpaws the upper hand against left-handed batsmen. Some right-handed batters adjusted to this new state of affairs by learning to hit left-handed or to switch-hit. Pitchers, of course, had no such option open to them. Or did they?

With pitchers not yet wearing gloves, several of them saw no reason not to try using both hands for pitching. On July 18, 1882, in the fourth inning of a game against Baltimore, right-handed pitcher Tony Mullane of

Louisville began to pitch with his left hand to left-handed batters. He continued to alternate for the rest of the game but lost 9-8 in the ninth when left-handed batter Charles Householder hit his only home run of the season off one of Mullane's left-handed offerings. (Mullane gave a very confused account of this game in an interview with the *Washington Post* in 1899. Mullane had himself pitching for Baltimore against Louisville and surrendering the home run to Chicken Wolf) (Lee Allen, *The Hot Stove League*, 35).

The disastrous result deterred Mullane from left-handed pitching for many years, though David Nemec reported that "Mullane would sometimes hide his hands behind his back as he began his delivery, keeping a batter guessing until the last instant as to which arm would launch the ball" (David Nemec, *The Beer and Whisky League*, 130). Researcher Cliff Blau has discovered that Mullane again pitched left-handed in a major league game on July 5, 1892. And the following year, on July 14, 1893, Mullane pitched the ninth inning of a game against Chicago left-handed, surrendering three runs.

Larry Corcoran was experimenting with ambidextrous pitching even earlier than Mullane. When he was signed by Chicago in 1880, a local paper noted that the club "has secured an ambidextrous pitcher—a man who can send them in hot with either hand. He is the equal of any man in the country with his left hand, and has no superior in the League to-day as a right-handed pitcher. He is pronounced by competent authority the superior of any League pitcher during the season of 1879. The immense advantage of a pitcher who can throw with either hand—to say nothing of pitching—in the way of holding base-runners to their bases will be recognized as an item in a close game" (*Chicago Times*, reprinted in the *New York Sunday Mercury*, March 27, 1880). The *Chicago Tribune* added, "Corcoran has developed into a left-handed pitcher, and it is expected that his double method of delivery will prove extremely puzzling to batsmen" (*Chicago Tribune*, April 4, 1880).

The experiment allowed a reporter to get off this zinger: "Some one told one of the Chicago ball club directors that the pitcher of the nine was ambidextrous, and the director replied that it was a blamed lie; that the man was in perfect health" (*Worcester Gazette*, April 30, 1880). Otherwise, however, it was much ado about nothing. Corcoran became one of the league's best right-handed pitchers but is known to have

pitched with both hands in a major league game only once, against Buffalo on June 16, 1884. Even on that occasion, he did so only because of an injury to his right hand (*Buffalo Commercial Advertiser*, July 17, 1884; cited in Al Kermisch, "Corcoran Pitched with Both Hands in Regular Game," *Baseball Research Journal* 1982, 66). After Corcoran's right arm went lame in 1885, he attempted a comeback as a left-hander and one reporter marveled, "Corcoran has the various curves down almost as well with his left hand as he has with his right" (*National Police Gazette*, April 10, 1886). But according to a 1915 article unearthed by researcher Steve Steinberg, Corcoran soon injured his left arm as well (*New York Times*, March 14, 1915).

Right-hander Elton "Icebox" Chamberlain also sought a platoon advantage against major league hitters. On May 9, 1888, with Louisville ahead 18-6, he pitched the final two innings with his left hand, surrendering four hits but no runs (Al Kermisch, "Elton Chamberlain Another in Ambidextrous Class," *Baseball Research Journal* 1983, 48). Cliff Blau discovered that Chamberlain repeated the feat on October 1, 1891. Reportedly Chamberlain often made pickoff attempts with his left hand (*The Official Baseball Record*, September 20, 1886).

A 1936 letter writer to the *New York Times* claimed to have witnessed John Roach pitching with both hands for the Giants in his only major league game on May 14, 1887. The writer correctly recalled that the Giants had lost the game 17-2. But there is no contemporary documentation of Roach using both hands during that game, and no mention of his being ambidextrous has been found during his lengthy minor league career (letter from "D.F.P.," *New York Times*, August 8, 1936). Another player on the 1887 Giants, outfielder and occasional pitcher Mike Tiernan, had been described as "the ambidextrous pitcher" while playing for Trenton two years earlier (*Washington Post*, September 18, 1885).

At least one Hall of Famer also pursued the elusive goal of ambidextrous pitching. An 1883 note observed that "[Charles] Radbourn, of the Providence nine, can pitch either right or left handed" (*Washington Post*, May 6, 1883). Philadelphia experimented with an ambidextrous pitcher named Waring before the 1884 season. Unfortunately, when Waring used both hands alternately in an exhibition game, "the Whites found no difficulty in hitting him either way" (*New York Clipper*, April 12, 1884). Another was John H. Campbell, who pitched for a number of clubs in the mid-1880s (*Evansville Journal*, February 6, 1884). Yank Robinson, who was normally an infielder, also experimented with ambidextrous pitching (*Chicago Inter-Ocean*, February 12, 1888, 12).

According to an article written many years later, a minor leaguer named Owen Keenan accomplished the ultimate in ambidextrous achievement in 1885. While pitching for Youngstown, Ohio, Keenan pitched both ends of an Independence Day doubleheader against New Castle, winning one game with each arm (*New York Times*, March 14, 1915).

By the 1890s this unique period of experimentation was coming to an end. The lack of success of the switch-pitchers was the most obvious reason. Just as important, a left-handed pitcher was no longer regarded as a panacea; managers again realized that effective stuff and good control were more important than the pitching hand. The fact that pitchers were now wearing gloves may also have contributed to the end of this era.

The twentieth century has seen occasional efforts to bring back the ambidextrous pitcher. Harold Friene, who went to spring training with the Athletics in 1910 and 1911 but never pitched in a major league game, was billed as an ambidextrous pitcher (*Washington Post*, February 27, 1910; A. H. Spink, *The National Game*, 132). Cal McLish was billed as a switch-pitcher when he arrived in the majors in the mid-1940s but used only his right hand when facing major league competition. After returning to barnstorming in the 1960s, the Indianapolis Clowns used an ambidextrous pitcher named Ulysses Grant Greene (Alan Pollock, *Barnstorming to Heaven*, 285–287). On July 4, 1952, in a Longhorn League game, right-handed pitcher Rudie Malone pitched left-handed to the left-handed slugger Joe Bauman. Bert Campaneris pitched ambidextrously in a Florida State League game on August 13, 1962.

Most organizations frowned on such experiments, but at one point the Dodgers farm system had three pitchers—Ed Head, Paul Richards, and Clyde Day—who experimented with ambidextrous mound work. Researcher Steve Steinberg found a 1928 account in which Richards, while playing for Muskogee against Topeka, gave a preview of the innovative spirit that would characterize his later work as a major league manager and general manager: "[Richards] went along in fine style as a left handed pitcher, until Wilson, a turn-over hitter came to bat. Wilson went to bat right handed

and Richards asked for a left handed glove and wound up right handed. Wilson jumped to the other side of the plate and Richards decided to throw left handed again. Finally he discarded the glove and pitched alternately with his left and right hand. But Wilson was too smart for him and waited him out for a base on balls" (*New York Evening Journal*, July 24, 1928).

The switch-pitcher finally made its return to the major leagues in 1995 after an absence of more than a century. Greg Harris had long experimented with left-handed pitching, though he used his right hand exclusively when facing major league competition. On September 28, 1995, pitching for the Montreal Expos, Harris used both hands to throw a shutout inning against the Cincinnati Reds. He wore a special six-fingered glove that he could use on either hand.

3.3.8   When All Else Fails/Grooving. Researcher Bill Kirwin reported that former Milwaukee catcher Sammy White told him of an unusual ploy that he and Lew Burdette used against Orlando Cepeda in 1961. Kirwin explained that "they both agreed that whatever they tried was unsuccessful. White came up with the idea that they should tell Cepeda what was coming because 'nothing else worked.' Burdette agreed. White crouched behind the plate and told Cepeda what was coming. Cepeda protested to the umpire that this was illegal and was told it was not. From that point on, in that game, White told Cepeda every pitch that he signaled to Burdette and he was retired easily each time." Kirwin later asked Cepeda about the incident, and Cepeda confirmed White's account.

Birdie Tebbetts similarly claimed that the Tigers once let Ted Williams call his own pitches, and he was so unnerved that he went 0-for-5 (Jonathan Fraser Light, *The Cultural Encyclopedia of Baseball*, 566). There are a few other pieces of anecdotal evidence to support that possibility. Ty Cobb, for example, related a story in which Al Bridwell went 0-for-5 on the last day of the season in spite of being allowed to call the pitches. But the details that Cobb provided do not correspond to the known facts (Ty Cobb, *Memoirs of Twenty Years in Baseball*, 86).

This tactic seems so foolish that it seems safe to assume that it would not work if widely used. But considering the old formulation that hitting is timing and pitching is disrupting timing, perhaps with the right hitter the surprise of being told the pitch might disturb that delicate balance. Pitcher Todd Jones, for example, stated: "Hitters tell me if they know what pitch is coming, they will lose their discipline in the strike zone and swing at anything. But when a hitter knows location, the pitcher basically is screwed" (quoted in Dave Clark, *The Knucklebook*, 58). While such sketchy anecdotal evidence doesn't prove anything, it at least suggests that knowing what pitch is coming is less of an advantage than might be expected.

(iv) Measures of Success

While I have generally deemed statistical accomplishments to be outside the scope of this book, I have made an exception for the basic yardsticks used to measure the success of pitchers because these standards have become such a fundamental part of baseball.

3.4.1   Shutouts. On November 8, 1860, Jim Creighton of the Excelsiors of Brooklyn beat the St. George Cricket Club 25-0 at the Elysian Fields. The game was hailed as "the first match on record that has resulted in nine innings being played without each party making runs. The contest with the Flour City Club, wherein they made one run the [sic] Excelsior's 26, was the nearest to it" (*Brooklyn Eagle*, November 10, 1860).

This does appear to have been the first shutout in baseball history. But it was considered a reflection of the unfamiliarity of the cricket players with baseball rather than an accomplishment by Creighton: ". . . The St. George nine were players selected for their ability as fielders, and the pitcher and catcher were experienced ball players; whereas the Excelsiors had two of their muffin players in their nine. The fact is it was a mere practice game for them. Judging from the result we think we could name two or three of our junior clubs that could easily take down the St. George nine at baseball." The catcher for the St. George club was none other than Harry Wright (*Brooklyn Eagle*, November 10, 1860).

Shutouts remained an extremely rare event during the high-scoring 1860s. According to John H. Gruber, "there were exactly five shutouts prior to 1870" (John H. Gruber, "Scoring Rules," *Sporting News*, November 4, 1915).

That changed in 1870. Inspired by the success of the Red Stockings of Cincinnati, a professional nine was organized in Chicago at great expense. The White Stockings initially struggled, especially at the bat, but received little sympathy from other cities or the hometown press. After one lackluster performance the *Chicago Tribune* wrote: "that 'our terrific batters,' 'our scientific hitters,' 'our heavy strikers' should have failed to make more than four runs against any club on earth, was a circumstance of stupendous unaccountability" (*Chicago Tribune*, July 7, 1870).

That was nothing compared to the reaction a few weeks later when the White Stockings were whitewashed 9-0 by Rynie Wolters of the Mutuals of New York. The baseball world erupted with amazement and more than a bit of *schadenfreude*. Because the name "Chicago" derived from an Indian word for "skunk," the word "Chicago" had begun to appear in game accounts in the late 1860s to refer to a score of zero in an inning or game.

But in the aftermath of Wolters's historic accomplishment, the popularity of the term exploded. Within a week, the sports pages were filled with such passages as: "The first two innings gave two 'Chicagos' for the Forest Citys" (*Cleveland Herald*, July 30, 1870). The word continued to be a major part of the baseball lexicon for the remainder of the nineteenth century.

As noteworthy as this game's impact on baseball vernacular was, it had even more significant consequences for baseball play. Harry Wright's Red Stockings had already helped to popularize a deader ball the preceding season (see **9.1.5**). The shutout of the White Stockings went further—by showing that one good pitcher backed by a solid defense could offset an all-star unit gathered at great expense, it made low-scoring baseball trendy! Clubs across the country jumped on the bandwagon, using increasingly dead balls in hopes of reproducing Wolters's result.

Dead balls did indeed produce the desired effect. Shutouts increased dramatically in the next few years, and the trend accelerated with the introduction of the curveball. By the end of the 1870s, shutouts were so common that Harry Wright, who had helped to start the trend, thought it had gone too far (*Detroit Post and Tribune*, January 4, 1879).

3.4.2   1-0 Games. The first 1-0 game apparently took place on August 12, 1874, when the White Stockings of Burlington, New Jersey, defeated the Haymakers of Philadelphia. The first major league 1-0 game took place in a National Association game on May 11, 1875, with Chicago beating the Reds of St. Louis. For several years after this, a 1-0 game was regarded as the ultimate baseball accomplishment by many observers, led as usual by Henry Chadwick.

As the balls used became less and less lively, and batters puzzled over curveballs, 1-0 games became relatively common. To differentiate them, a consensus emerged that the longest 1-0 game was the best. By this criterion, the greatest game of the 1870s was a twenty-four-inning game on May 11, 1877, between Harvard and the Manchester, New Hampshire, club. It appears that the most remarkable thing about this game was that the condition of the ball and the field made scoring almost impossible. Nonetheless the game was talked about for many years afterward.

The Harvard game was finally surpassed on August 17, 1882, when Detroit and Providence played an eighteen-inning 1-0 game. It was immediately and for many years afterward hailed as the greatest game ever played.

3.4.3 No-hitters.

On May 29, 1875, Joseph McElroy Mann of Princeton threw a no-hitter against Yale. The feat was accorded little attention. A four-sentence account of the game in the *New York Mercury* noted that "Mr. Mann's pitching for the Princeton nine was so effective that the Yales did not make a single base hit." The report gave similar accolades to two Princeton fielders for their defensive play (reprinted in H. Allen Smith and Ira L. Smith, *Low and Inside*, 238).

Joseph Borden pitched the National Association's first no-hitter on July 28, 1875. Borden's feat was also reported in only the most matter-of-fact fashion (William J. Ryczek, *Blackguards and Red Stockings*, 218). When George Bradley pitched the first National League no-hitter the following season, the event was heralded with more enthusiasm, but the accomplishment was portrayed as belonging as much to the fielders as to the pitcher: "Bradley's pitching, and the magnificent backing given it by the fielders, won the day for St. Louis. For the first time in the annals of the League, nine innings were played without a single base hit being placed" (*St. Louis Globe-Democrat*, quoted in David Falkner, *Nine Sides of the Diamond*, 10).

The fact that the response to early no-hitters was so subdued is somewhat puzzling in light of the acclaim being accorded low-scoring games during this period. My belief is that, as implied by the account of Bradley's no-hitter, this was a reflection of the continued percep-

tion that baseball ought to be a battle between hitters and fielders and a resulting resentment of pitchers for having usurped too great a role. Low-scoring games could be viewed as the product of good defense, but the absence of any hits at all evoked suspicion that the pitcher had exerted too great an influence. Another factor that may have made Bradley's feat seem less than legitimate is the extremely dead ball that St. Louis used at its home games in 1876 (see **11.1.12** "Double Ball Rackets").

3.4.4 Perfect Games.

The first major league perfect game was pitched by left-hander J Lee Richmond of Worcester against Cleveland on June 12, 1880. As with the first no-hitters, the fielders received more credit than the pitchers. An account in the *Worcester Gazette* gushed, "The Worcester team, by their faultless play against the Clevelands, Saturday afternoon, placed to their credit the best ball game on record. Their rivals did not secure a run; did not make a hit; did not score a base run." A lengthy recap of the fielding statistics followed with little mention of Richmond. Another curious feature was that the account had nothing specific to say about a notable defensive play that preserved the perfect game—a play on which an apparent clean single was foiled when Worcester right fielder Lon Knight threw the batter out at first base (*Worcester Gazette*, June 14, 1880).

Richmond did receive specific praise for having made it to the ballpark. The young southpaw was still a student at Brown University and for the preceding month had been staying up late to study for examinations before doing morning recitations, then taking the 11:30 train to Worcester for the game (*Worcester Gazette*, May 17, 1880). On the day of the perfect game, Richmond's train was delayed, forcing him to rush to the ball field without grabbing anything to eat. But it obviously didn't hinder him (*Worcester Gazette*, June 14, 1880).

The first perfect game known to have been pitched at any level was tossed by James "Pud" Galvin of the Reds of St. Louis against the Cass Club of Detroit on August 17, 1876, in a tournament in Ionia, Michigan. The feat attracted little notice aside from this comment: "The game was in some respects one of the most remarkable on record. The Cass boys did not make a base hit or reach first base during the game. Each man of the club batted three times and each was put out three times" (*Ionia Sentinel*, August 25, 1876).

More extraordinary was the fact that it was Galvin's second no-hitter of the day. That morning he had blanked the Mutuals of Jackson, allowing only three runners to reach base on errors. Thus only three fielding misplays prevented Galvin from accomplishing twice in one day a feat that had never before been accomplished. Nor was his opposition weak; the Cass and Mutuals were both strong professional nines, stocked with former and future major leaguers.

A related question is how "perfect" came to characterize a game in which nothing happened. Henry Chadwick again appears to have played a role. In the 1870s, Chadwick began using the term "model game" to describe a low-scoring game with few hits or errors. The term became so closely associated with Chadwick that those seeking to take shots at the sportswriter did so by assailing this concept. The *Chicago Tribune*, for instance, referred derisively to "what is absurdly called a 'model' game—that is, a game equally devoid of base hits and errors" (*Chicago Tribune*, June 20, 1880).

It took some time for the current mind-set to become widespread, and only in the early twentieth century did the term "perfect game" come into use. Perhaps this change in outlook reflects the longing of our hectic times for less eventful ones, as was articulated by David Byrne's memorable lyric, "Heaven is a place where nothing ever happens."

Chapter 4

FIELDING

IT MIGHT seem logical to assume that there would be few fielding firsts to record. After all, the fielder's role is not to initiate action but to react to the batter, who is in turn reacting to the pitcher. In addition, the nine fielding positions haven't changed since the 1850s. Neither have the basic ways in which the defensive team can retire their opponents: they can catch a batted ball on the fly, they can touch a base that a runner or batter is forced to run to, they can tag a runner between bases, or they can strike a batter out.

Considering these limitations, the number of new stratagems that have been introduced by fielders is impressive. I've subdivided them into four basic categories: (1) choosing how to fill each position, (2) positioning the nine fielders, (3) combination plays or teamwork, and (4) devising alternate methods of retiring players.

(i) Choosing How to Fill Positions

The most basic element of defensive strategy is deciding which player is best suited for each of the nine positions. As discussed under "Specialization" (1.28), the benefits of specialization were recognized by the 1860s, and clubs tried as much as possible to let a player remain at a single position so that he could master it.

The next question to be resolved was what made a player best suited to a particular position. With any out far from routine in the 1860s, the predominant philosophy was to view the defensive positions hierarchically. Catcher was the most important position, followed by shortstop, and since these players were offered the most chances and the most demanding ones, clubs customarily used their two most agile, sure-handed, and strong-armed players in these roles. The three basemen ranked next in importance, and the next most agile players were assigned to them. The three least defensively skilled regulars generally occupied the outfield.

The ensuing years brought shifts in this hierarchy, as rule changes, the use of gloves, new tactics such as the bunt, and better fields increased the role of positions like shortstop and second base and diminished the importance of the first baseman and catcher. There are still, however, discernable remnants of the original philosophy. The positions at which twenty-first-century managers will sacrifice offense to have a good glove man correspond quite closely to the hierarchy of the 1860s.

The period between the 1860s and the 1890s also brought new ideas about the qualifications for specific positions. The emphasis on a player's basic fielding skills—throwing, catching, and agility—was gradually supplemented by the notion that innate characteristics such as size, dexterity, and left- or right-handedness were assets or liabilities at specific positions. This section will discuss the emergence of those perceptions.

4.1.1 Stretches by First Basemen. The idea that height was an important asset at first base was well established by the 1870s. For example, an 1879 profile noted that Levi Meyerle was "peculiarly adapted to [playing first base] by reason of his height—6 ft. 1 in" (*New York Clipper*, June 21, 1879). This, however, was primarily because height meant greater reach.

The stretches now performed by first basemen are quite another matter.

First of all, what constitutes a stretch is a matter of degree. There are vague claims that Charles Comiskey or Cap Anson may have originated the stretch (William P. Akin, "Bare Hands and Kid Gloves: The Best Fielders 1880–1899," *Baseball Research Journal* 10 [1981], 60–65). Undoubtedly these men and many early first basemen reached far out to stab errant throws. As early as 1860, Henry Chadwick was advising first basemen to practice standing "with one foot on the base, and see how far he can reach and take the ball from the fielder; this practice will prepare him for balls that are thrown short of the base" (*Beadle's Dime Base-Ball Player*, 24). But the more difficult stretches and scoops performed by today's first basemen would be impossible without a large, sophisticated fielding glove. Given the additional complication of uneven grounds, my sense is that a nineteenth-century first baseman would have been expected to vacate the bag on throws that were not within his reach and do his best to stop them.

The stretch seems to have begun to develop in earnest only when first basemen's mitts became larger (see **9.3.3**). William Curran said that the tactic was well established in 1905 and suggested that Fred Tenney may have popularized the technique (William Curran, *Mitts*, 121). Turn-of-the-century first baseman George Carey was known by the suggestive nickname of "Scoops" and was known for his "wonderful pick-ups of balls thrown to him on the bound and his great stops of wide thrown balls" (Henry Chadwick, *Sporting News*, December 21, 1895). And a 1904 article referred to the one-handed stops of badly thrown balls made by Philadelphia's Harry Davis (*Sporting Life*, May 21, 1904).

4.1.2   Left-handers Excluded from Positions.
The poor fields and absence of gloves in early baseball meant that quickness, sure-handedness, and accurate throwing arms were the main qualifications looked for in catchers, second basemen, shortstops, and third basemen.

The disadvantage that left-handers had in making throws from these positions did not go unnoticed. But the slight delay in making a throw was considered a relatively minor factor at a time when conditions made no play routine. Thus left-handedness was viewed as a handicap but not a bar to playing these positions. For example, Henry Chadwick observed in 1863, "[Joe] Start was placed at third base, a position any player of the nine can fill better, because he is a left-handed player, and for that reason just the man for the opposite base" (*New York Clipper*, September 12, 1863).

As playing conditions improved there was a corresponding increase in the perception that right-handers were best suited to these positions. By 1867 Chadwick was insisting: "A left hand player is the man for a first baseman; on any other base such a player is out of place" (Henry Chadwick, *Haney's Base Ball Player's Book of Reference for 1867*, 129). In 1879, with gloves still being used only by catchers and first basemen, Chadwick elaborated: "Another mistake last season in the make-up of base-teams was that of placing left-handed men on any base but the first. A left-handed first-baseman finds the hand he can use with greatest facility ready to pick up balls which come on foul ground to the left of him; while, on the other hand, the third-baseman finds his right hand most available to cover a similar class of balls to his right. At third or second base a left-hand player is unquestionably out of position, as he is also at short-stop, though not to so great an extent" (*New York Clipper*, December 13, 1879).

Once gloves came into wider use in the 1880s, the frequency with which plays were executed increased dramatically. This in turn greatly accentuated the previously small edge held by right-handers. Double plays slowly became more common, which increased the importance of having right-handers in the middle infield. The prevalence of bunts similarly helped to drive out the left-handed third baseman (*Sporting Life*, March 12, 1898). By the 1890s, left-handers had become rare at these positions.

As a result the *Cincinnati Times-Star* observed in 1905 that it was a fairly recent tradition "that an infielder, the first baseman excepted, who would be successful must be a right hand thrower. Since the days when 'Hick' Carpenter, covering third base for the Cincinnati team, was a star at that position [1879–1890], but one man has broken into fast company who played the infield for any length of time and used his left wing wherewith to propel the ball to various parts of the field. That man was Billy Hulen, and with all his cleverness he was unable to hold his place in the big League for the reason that his offside throwing disconcerted the other members of the infield, and incidentally made him a somewhat slower man than was desirable for a first-class team" (*Cincinnati Times-Star*, reprinted in *Sporting Life*, April 22, 1905).

4.1.3 Left-handed Catchers.

After the emergence of the curveball (see 3.2.3), it was considered advantageous to pair a left-handed catcher with a left-handed pitcher. The *Detroit Free Press* explained the reasoning: "[Dupee] Shaw's left-handed out-shoots are responsible for [Walter] Walker's sore hand. With a right-handed pitcher, the catcher can do most of the stopping with his left hand, protected by a thickly padded glove. Such a glove cannot be worn upon the right hand as it renders accurate throwing impossible" (*Detroit Free Press*, May 2, 1884).

As the nineteenth century wore on, left-handed catchers became increasingly rare. By 1895 it was reported that the only ones left were Fred Tenney and Jack Clements, with Clements being the last to have a lengthy major league career (*Dallas Morning News*, November 12, 1895). The primary reasons seem to have been the greater difficulties left-handers faced in throwing to bases and in fielding bunts. Another factor was that catchers' mitts (9.3.2) came into common use in 1889 and were not made for left-handers—when Charles Householder joined Grand Rapids that year, he was unable to catch until the arrival of a special mitt made in Chicago (*Grand Rapids Democrat*, July 27, 1889).

Interestingly, Bugs Baer argued in 1923 that those reasons no longer applied: "In those days a catcher with a left-hand drive-wheel was handicapped in throwing to second and third. Right-handed batters would easily balk him when he attempted to put the subpoena on a baserunner. He had to step out to right-field when throwing to second and also had to do a sun dance when tossing to third. He could whale away at first base all he wanted without competition. That was the reason left-hand catchers faded out like a blue serge coat in the land of eternal sunshine. There were too many right-handed batters encouraging him to throw wild. . . . Traditions croak hard. One old folk fable is that left-handed catchers are taboo. But with every batter transferring his batting affections to the wrong side of the plate, there doesn't seem to be any reason against left-handed catchers" (*Detroit Free Press*, April 17, 1923).

And catching great Billy Sullivan scoffed: "These left-handers are queer birds. When a right-hander makes a mistake he gets called for it good and hard, but when a sidewheeler does anything strange or funny in a game, everyone from the boss down says that it's only a left-hander and lets it go at that. . . . you never see a left-handed catcher. They say a left-handed catcher would have to throw over a batter to bases all of the time. Doesn't a right-handed catcher have to throw over the left-handed batters? Wouldn't a left-handed catcher be able to hold them on first a great deal better than a right-handed one? But, no. The right-hand heavers have to do the work. According to my idea they make too much of the left-handers. They should have to face the music, just like the right-handers do. That is, unless they wish to be regarded as freaks, and they don't want that" (Sullivan Hall of Fame File, clipping that apparently originated in the *Minneapolis Journal* in 1915).

As late as 1951, former catcher Branch Rickey proposed to make the return of the left-handed catcher "another of his famed innovations. . . . The hero—or victim—is Dale Long, a handsome Pittsburgh rookie who throws, bats, eats and combs his hair with his left hand. Coach George Sisler, who endorses the experiment, says it is his belief that a reliable left-hander can be a major league player in any position except shortstop" (*Dallas Morning News*, March 8, 1951).

Nonetheless the left-handed catcher seems to have gone the way of the dodo bird. Today a left-hander youngster with the necessary arm strength would be hard-pressed to find a catcher's mitt for his right hand, and in any case he likely instead would be asked to pitch.

4.1.4 Left-handed Outfielders.

While the custom of not placing left-handers at catcher, second base, shortstop, or third base has become deeply entrenched, a similar practice involving outfielders emerged at about the same time and is now entirely disregarded. In 1905 the *Cincinnati Times-Star* remarked: ". . . There was once a feeling that no left-hand thrower ever should play left field or no man who threw right-handed would make a success playing the long field back of first base, but these traditions have proven fallacies by such clever left-hand throwers as Jimmy Ryan, Jesse Burkett, Topsy Hartsel and others who are or were stars in left field, and by 'Dusty' Miller, Hans Wagner, Jack Barry and others who shone brilliantly in the right garden." The *Times-Star* indicated that it was only recently that this rule of thumb had fallen by the wayside (reprinted in *Sporting Life*, April 22, 1905).

4.1.5   First Base for Left-handers.

When Henry Chadwick observed in 1863 that a left-handed player was "just the man" for first base, he certainly implied an advantage. He was more explicit a decade later: "The first base can be best occupied by a left-handed player, as the hand most at command with such players faces the balls going close to the line of the base; while a left-handed player is decidedly out of place at either of the other infield positions" (*New York Clipper*, March 7, 1874).

When bunting became prevalent in the 1880s, first basemen assumed more responsibility for making throws. This provided more reason for concluding that first base was the one infield position where not only was left-handedness not a handicap but an actual advantage.

Hal Chase, widely acclaimed as the best defensive first baseman in the first decade of the twentieth century, explained: "I believe a left-handed first baseman is better fitted for the position than a right-hander. He uses the left hand for throwing. This makes a snap throw to second or third much easier. He naturally faces these bags. The right-hander has to turn around, losing valuable time. As to throwing to the plate, there is no advantage at either style. I believe the time will come when a right-handed first baseman will be almost as rare as a left-handed third baseman now is. Fred Tenney was the pioneer southpaw first sacker. He originated the sacrifice killing play. That is, on a bunt to him, he tried for the man that was to be advanced. I did the same thing before I heard of Tenney. It was as natural for me to do it as to play for the plate with bases full and none out. For a right-hander, the play is more difficult. He loses too much time in turning after getting the ball" (quoted in A. H. Spink, *The National Game*, 174).

4.1.6   Catcher Size.

Early catchers were often regarded as occupying the most important position on the field. It was no coincidence that in the first known fixed game, in 1865, it was the catcher who was the central figure (see **11.1.1**).

Because catchers of this era stood well behind the batter, the position's two main requirements were a strong arm and the ability to stop wild pitches. The latter requirement meant that a catcher needed either agility or a long reach, so large men were sometimes used behind the plate. In 1868 the six-foot-two Charlie

Mills was said to have "an advantage over all other catchers, in his long reach" (*Brooklyn Eagle*, August 15, 1868). As a rule, however, early clubs put one of their best athletes behind the plate, which more often meant a small, athletic man.

Once catchers began to play directly behind the plate (**4.2.1**), the focus shifted away from agility and toward size. The lanky Connie Mack, who had been a catcher during his playing days in the 1880s, later explained why height was a major advantage for a catcher. He observed that a longer reach cut down on wild pitches and also gave a pitcher "greater confidence, inasmuch as he is given a bigger mark behind the plate to throw at." He added, "Weight is also an important factor in blocking a base runner. In case of a collision, a heavy catcher will have the greater advantage with desperate base runners" (Connie Mack, "How to Play Ball," multi-part series, *Washington Post*, March 20, 1904). The advent of chest protectors (**9.4.5**) led catchers to just block wild pitches with their chests, giving larger men another advantage. John McGraw noted in 1900, "A catcher ought to be a man of considerable weight to hold the heavy and speeding pitches" (*New York World*, reprinted in *Milwaukee Journal*, April 19, 1900).

In the next few years, blocking the plate (**4.4.11**) would become an even more prominent part of the catcher's responsibilities. But this requirement was offset by two other developments that set the stage for the small, agile catcher to return to the fore. By this time mitts (**9.3.2**) were lessening the force that was borne by catchers' hands, and bunts (**2.2.1**) were coming into prominence (Peter Morris, *Catcher*, 266–268). With all these factors to consider, it took some time for the prejudice against small catchers to be overcome, as Red Dooin discovered.

Dooin was born in Cincinnati in 1879 and weighed only 110 pounds when he started college at St. Xavier's (now Xavier University). He went out for the baseball team, but the captain took one look at him and said that he didn't want any "little runts" around. After graduation, Dooin got a trial with St. Paul of the Western League, but Charles Comiskey advised him to stick to his trade of tailoring. He caught on with a low minor league club in 1900 and did well enough that he was drafted, sight unseen, by St. Joseph. When Dooin reported to St. Joseph the following spring, manager Byron McKibbon asked him, "What can I do for you, sonny?" Red replied, "I'm Dooin, your new player." McKibbon sized him up carefully and then said, "Why, my boy, I want a catcher, not a jockey" (*New York World*, September 21, 1913).

Nonetheless Dooin went on to become a star catcher in the National League and eventually player-manager of the Phillies. When a slightly built young catcher named Bill Killefer was having a hard time breaking into the major leagues, Dooin was naturally willing to consider him. He liked what he saw and groomed Killefer to be his successor.

Bill Killefer came to be regarded as the prototype of a new breed of catcher: "The time has gone by when the ideal catcher was considered a mountain of beef and bone, something that could stand any kind of knocks and, as long as he was successful as a battering ram, mattering not what his other qualities might be. The catcher now is more than a mere backstop, inserted to break the impact of pitched balls against the grand stand planks. . . . The St. Louis Browns disposed of him because he was considered too light for catching, but now he is doing the bulk of the work for the Phillies and showing that it does not take beef to make a catcher. The old iron man has given way to the more delicate structure of steel and Killifer [sic] is one of that sort, built on graceful lines, but able to give and take with the best of them" (*Sporting News*, August 14, 1913). According to the 1928 *Babe Ruth's Own Book of Baseball*, "The old idea used to be that a catcher had to be a big, strong oversized fellow in order to stand the gaff of holding up a pitcher and blocking runners. That's bunk" (Babe Ruth, *Babe Ruth's Own Book of Baseball*, 131).

In the years since Red Dooin showed that a small man could be successful behind the plate, the bunt has become less common, and there has been a slight trend back toward catchers being larger men. Nonetheless catchers come in a variety of shapes and sizes, and ability is deemed more important than stature. The requirements of the position are thus now not all that different from what they were in the 1860s, with a strong arm and either agility or reach being necessary.

4.1.7 Outfielders' Roles. The current mantra that the fastest outfielder covers center field and the best thrower goes in right field was not accepted in early baseball. The extent to which gloves have changed baseball will be a recurring theme in this book, but it bears repetition.

Today's enormous gloves make catching a ball a simple feat and enable managers to concentrate on other factors in assigning fields for their outfielders. But until outfielders began using gloves in the mid-1880s, the first and foremost consideration with any outfielder was his reliability at catching fly balls.

As a result, there were a number of theories about where to place one's outfielders, but no clear consensus. Henry Chadwick wrote in 1860 that the left fielder had the most important duties and the right fielder the least (*Beadle's Dime Base-Ball Player*, 25–26). But by 1877 he observed, "In old ball-playing days, the left-fielder was the king-pin of the outfield, but this idea has long since been exploded. In fact, if there be any one of the three positions which requires more skillful play than another, it is that of right-field, for the right-fielder has the most frequent opportunities to throw out men on the bases" (*New York Clipper*, February 10, 1877).

A *Sporting Life* correspondent wrote in 1884: "If there 'happens to be a weak spot' on the nine—well, it is better not to have a weak spot—but if there should be a weak spot centre field or first base—preferably the former—should bear it. Centre field has less work to perform on the average than left field and less responsible work generally than right field" (*Sporting Life*, April 16, 1884).

As noted in "Left-Handed Outfielders" (**4.1.4**), in the 1890s an emphasis was placed on using a right-handed thrower in left field and a left-handed thrower in right field. Henry Chadwick suggested that the "peculiar character of the ground" could be the most important factor. He explained that at the Union Grounds in Brooklyn, "the services of the sharpest outfielder are required at right field" because the hills there were so difficult to negotiate (*New York Clipper*, January 12, 1878). As described under "Level Playing Fields" (**14.2.1**), such impediments were commonplace and forced outfielders to keep their eyes on both the ground and the ball as they pursued fly balls. Will White maintained in 1883 that Jimmy Macullar was one of the best outfielders because he was among the few "players in the country who can take their eyes off the ball, run with it for quite a distance, and know just when and where to capture it" (*Cincinnati Gazette*, January 28, 1883; thanks to David Ball). Others implied that consideration be given to finding the right man to play the demanding sun field. These two issues meant that a club might choose to rearrange its outfielders based upon the ballpark.

It does not appear to have been until well into the twentieth century that it became the conventional wisdom for the fielder who covers the most ground to be placed in center field and the strongest thrower in right field. This arrangement was encouraged by the advent of the home run era in the 1920s, which forced outfielders to position themselves much deeper.

(ii) Positioning of the Fielders

4.2.1 Catchers Playing Close. As simple a question as when catchers began to be positioned directly behind the plate remains a confusing topic. We do know that the earliest catchers stood well back of the batter, except in the Massachusetts Game, where some brave souls stood "as close as possible" and had to dodge the swing of the bat ("Bob Lively," "Base Ball: How They Play the Game in New England," *Porter's Spirit of the Times*, December 27, 1856, 276–277). But the rules of the New York Game encouraged a safer positioning. Strict delivery restrictions made strikeouts rare, and therefore the benefits of being close to the plate were few. By contrast, standing farther back gave a catcher more time to react and prevent wild pitches as well as to snag foul popups on the first bounce (such "bound catches" counted as an out until the 1880s).

Catchers under the New York rules had begun to play closer by 1870, but the originator is more difficult to pin down. Doug Allison of the Red Stockings of Cincinnati is occasionally cited, but this is just another example of the tendency to credit this club with every first. Deacon White's name comes up more frequently, as a result of Al Pratt's statement to that effect in 1895 (*Sporting News*, March 23, 1895). Pratt's testimony has to be taken seriously, but the evidence shows that other catchers were employing this positioning well before White.

The practice can be pushed still earlier, but in doing so we quickly run into the problem that "close" is an imprecise term. Henry Chadwick counseled in 1860, "when a player has made his first base, the Catcher should take a position nearer the striker, in order to take the ball from the pitcher before it bounds" (*Beadle's Dime Base-Ball Player*, 21). But how much nearer?

An 1891 article claimed that early catchers stood twenty to twenty-five feet behind plate, and this seems consistent with other evidence (*Williamsport Sunday Grit*, June 7, 1891). Yet how much closer did the catcher have to move before he would be considered "near"? Two feet? Five feet? Ten feet? Fifteen feet? There is obviously no way to answer this question.

None of the sources that give credit to a particular catcher specify exactly what distance they regard as close, though Chadwick wrote in 1874 that "moving up behind the bat" saved the catcher three to four yards on his throws (Henry Chadwick, *Chadwick's Base Ball Manual*, 14). Yet, as we shall see, Chadwick tried in 1872 to prohibit catchers from standing within six feet of the plate, from which it can be inferred that at least a few catchers were coming that near. Thus it seems likely that much of the confusion results from different understandings of what was meant by "close." Pratt's statement—like many of the others we are forced to rely on—most likely means that White played closer to the plate than any previous catcher *that he had seen.*

The vagueness of terms like "close" and "near" and the imprecision of memory itself have led to a baffling array of claims. The issue is further complicated by the fact that positioning was situational, as T. Z. Cowles, sports editor of the *Chicago Tribune* from 1868 to 1875, explained many years later: "A writer in the *New York Sun* of recent date, in reviewing the baseball of long ago, errs in saying that the catcher always played twenty feet or more behind the home plate, and never came up any closer until the rules were changed. This is a mistake. The star catchers played back until a man was on base, and then they went forward to the plate. Some of them would play back on the third strike, which was out when the ball was caught on the first bound, but always came up close to prevent the stealing of bases" (*Chicago Tribune*, June 2, 1918).

But as best as can be determined within those limitations, here is what happened. The earliest catcher to move close behind the batter was Folkert Rappelje Boerum of the Atlantics of Brooklyn. According to William Rankin, Boerum began playing close to the batter in the summer of 1859 at the suggestion of Atlantics president William V. Babcock. He added that the tactic "proved so great a success that it was adopted by all the leading clubs in the vicinity of New York" (Francis C. Richter, *Richter's His-*

tory and Records of Base Ball, 220). The most prominent catcher to follow Boerum's lead was Joe Leggett of the Excelsiors of Brooklyn, who was described as "the first to ever take fly-tips close behind the bat" when his club visited Baltimore in 1860 (William Ridgely Griffith, *The Early History of Amateur Base Ball in the State of Maryland*, 6).

The 1860s saw many other catchers show similar daring, including John Morey of Rochester, Joe Howard of Brooklyn, Fergy Malone of Philadelphia, and George Dawson of Detroit (Peter Morris, *Catcher*, 305). Yet all indications are that this positioning was losing favor until the start of the 1870s, when a fearless catcher named Nat Hicks sparked a revival (Peter Morris, *Catcher*, 41–49). One game account marveled of Hicks: "Player after player went down before his unfaltering nerve, and although struck four times during the game— once squarely on the mouth by the ball and once on the chest and twice with the bat—he could not be driven away from his position" (*New York Times*, July 5, 1873, 5).

During the 1870s, playing directly behind the plate became common but not invariable, with several factors affecting the decision. With no runners on base, catchers always stood farther back until a strikeout loomed. This greater distance also made it easier to catch foul popups and foul bounds, so in 1875, with most catchers inching closer, "Deacon" White made the opposite decision: "We no longer see him come up close to the bat after two strikes have been called on a batsman, he preferring to stay back and take the chances on a foul, and, not getting one, throwing the man out at first base" (Charles Randolph, *Chicago Tribune*, May 30, 1875, 6).

Another problem that resulted from bringing the catcher up close was that he had to adjust to his dangerous proximity to the batter. Henry Chadwick believed that "catchers who are apparently reckless of injuries . . . really amount to an obstruction to the batsman in striking at the ball" and advocated that catchers be required to remain at least six feet behind the plate (*New York Clipper*, November 25, 1871). He later illustrated the point by describing an "amusing incident" in a September 4, 1877, game in which Cap Anson caught and complained to the umpire that the batter's swing was impeding his play. As Chadwick observed, "It is the catcher the umpire has a right to make stand back, so as not to interfere with the batsman's movements in batting, the catcher

having no right to stand so close to the batsman as to cramp his movements in any way" (*New York Clipper*, September 15, 1877).

Other variables such as the conditions of the grounds could also play a crucial role. Many years after the fact, a player named Jim McTague explained that he began playing close to the plate in 1874 while catching for St. John's College in Minnesota because the area behind the plate was very sandy, making it almost impossible to catch a ball on the bound (*The Campion*, May 1916; reprinted in *Sporting News*, June 1, 1916).

The invention of the catcher's mask (see **9.4.2**) in 1877 eliminated one of the main reasons for catchers to set up well back of the plate. Catchers moved noticeably closer to the action, but their positioning remained situational. Henry Chadwick noted at the season's end that catchers were now playing up close with runners on base, and he endorsed that choice. He observed that they also generally played close with two strikes, but he questioned this strategy, claiming that it often resulted "in the loss of chances for long foul-bound tips and high foul balls." Chadwick was even more dubious about the benefit of playing close at other times, noting that it was handy for catching "waist and shoulder balls" but that "difficult low side balls" all too often turned into passed balls (*New York Clipper*, December 1, 1877).

The next few years saw catchers receive a couple of additional incentives to move closer to the plate. In 1879 the strikeout rule was changed to require the catcher to catch the ball on the fly to complete the out. The foul bound rule was permanently eliminated by the National League in 1883, and in the American Association in 1885. (The National League initially revoked the foul bound in 1879 but restored the old rule a year later.) These rule changes pretty much forced receivers to position themselves behind the plate once a strikeout was possible, and some catchers also moved up when a walk appeared imminent so as to provide a target.

Catchers continued to play back early in the count with no runners on base, but even in that situation they seem to have been moving gradually closer. Researcher Greg Rhodes reviewed the diagrams of the diamond in the annual *Spalding Guide* between 1876 and 1892. He found that "the diagrams change from year to year, but for the most part the players stay in the same positions, with the exception of the catcher. He starts off in 1876 many steps behind home, but by 1892, he is within a couple of steps of home (although not yet in the position we see him today)."

It was several more years before the rules required the catcher to remain directly behind the plate throughout an at bat. Connie Mack later credited Chicago president Jim Hart and explained that the change was "made primarily to prevent the tiresome delays which occurred many times during the progress of a game by reason of having to wait for the catcher to come up and don his mask, and other paraphernalia every time a runner got on base or the batter had two strikes" (Connie Mack, "Memories of When the Game Was Young," *Sporting Life* [monthly], June 1924).

Mack's memory seems to have been a bit off, because he recalled this rule change taking place in 1896 or 1897. In fact it appears to have been introduced in the Western League in 1899 by Charles Comiskey (Jim McTague, writing in *The Campion*, May 1916; reprinted in *Sporting News*, June 1, 1916). That year the National League also required the catcher to "stand within the lines of his position, as defined in Rule 3, whenever the pitcher delivers the ball to the bat." The rule was justified with the explanation that it would "prevent the catcher from playing outside the lines of his position in order to field bunted balls, which action permits the pitched ball to go to the backstop . . . greatly delaying the game" (*Indiana State Journal*, February 22, 1899).

This rule also enabled umpires to move closer to the plate. Hank O'Day believed that this would make for better officiating by enabling an umpire to "tell better when a ball that rolls close along the base line is fair or foul, and on a slow hit he can step out on the diamond and he is in a better position to judge the decision at first base than when he stood back with the catcher" (*Sporting News*, May 4, 1901). This shift also led to the emergence of much of today's umpire's equipment over the next decade, as will be discussed in part six of Chapter 8.

4.2.2 Catching from a Crouch. Early catchers stood upright, although usually with a bit of a stoop. An 1871 article noted of the Red Stockings' Doug Allison: "In standing close to the bat, too, he takes a ball hot from the pitcher, while perfectly upright. Most catchers take a stooping position" (*New York Clipper*, January 21, 1871).

Their stance did not immediately change once catchers began to position themselves closer to the plate. There were a number of good reasons for this. Since the emphasis on pitchers keeping the ball low was not yet in place, the advantage of being better positioned to catch the pitch was not a major factor. An upright posture made it a little easier to adjust to stop wild pitches or dodge hot fouls. In addition, catchers who crouched had to expend valuable time uncoiling in order to make their throws. Perhaps most important, a crouch is uncomfortable.

With so many disadvantages, the crouch was slow to catch on. Descriptions of the pioneers of the crouch make it easy to understand why other catchers were reluctant to follow their lead. In 1888 Johnny Ward described Con Daily of Indianapolis as having a "crouch almost to the ground" but then added, "such a position must be not only more fatiguing, but destroy somewhat the gauging of a high pitch" (John Montgomery Ward, *Base-Ball: How to Become a Player*, 68). An 1886 article noted that Doc Bushong "squats, as it were, on his 'haunches,' bends his body down until it is almost parallel with the ground, places his hands about an inch from his kneecaps and thus leaves his elbows sticking out from the whole make-up in a ridiculous manner. The only thing to which he can be properly compared is the appearance of a large frog sitting on the traditional log and making ready to spring into the depths of his favorite pond. In this ridiculous posture 'the Doctor' waits patiently until the ball is within reach when he makes a sudden snap at it" ("King Catchers," *St. Louis Post-Dispatch*, August 14, 1886, 12).

Not surprisingly, the twentieth century opened with crouches still unpopular. Connie Mack advised in 1904: ". . . When a catcher takes his position he should assume a stooping posture. The body should be well bent forward from the hips, so as to enable the player to handle the ball at any height. Crouching to the ground should not be considered, as a player who insists on so doing will never become a first-class catcher. An easy position should be assumed as far as possible. Where the catcher crouches he is unable to control the erratic flight of the ball" (Connie Mack, "How to Play Ball," multi-part series, *Washington Post*, March 20, 1904).

The stoop advocated by Mack appears to have been more pronounced than those of earlier years because of the increased emphasis on shielding signals from the prying eyes of the opposing players (see **6.5.2**). An 1896 article explained, "In these days the most effective method used by catchers in giving signs is by placing the fingers of the right hand in the centre of the big mitt worn on the left hand. The catcher stoops until one knee rests upon the ground and then turns the middle of the mitt toward the pitcher" (*Sporting News*, March 7, 1896). Yet within a few years it became clear that precautions were essential, with one of the factors being the permanent return of first-base coaches after an absence of several seasons (see **7.1.4**).

In response, catchers concluded that it was no longer sufficient to "work the signals from within the shadow of the knee and the big mitt so that they are exposed for the gaze of the pitcher alone and can not be seen from the coaching boxes" (*Sporting News*, June 24, 1899). The return of the first-base coach was accompanied by a rapid increase in sign-stealing, and the price for these transgressions would be borne—quite literally—on the backs of catchers.

According to a 1909 article, crouching had become a necessity because of the need for catchers to give their signals confidentially (*Sporting News*, April 29, 1909). The *Washington Post* confirmed that same year that catchers "must guard against the batsman peeking back to catch his code. That is why the backstop stoops in calling for balls . . . by crouching he shuts out all possible vision of the batsman" (*Washington Post*, July 18, 1909).

Catchers were forced to crouch still lower a couple of years later when word got out that the Athletics had stolen "the signs of big Ed Sweeney, catcher of the Yankees, by having one of the A's players hide behind the water cooler on his stomach. When the backstop gave his signals, he dropped his fingers to the ground and they were clearly visible from beneath the cooler" (Stan Baumgartner, "Signals," *Baseball Guide and Record Book 1947*, 127).

Thus it seems that sign stealers are primarily responsible for nearly a century of catchers' aching backs and legs, though other factors also contributed. The trend toward lower pitching after 1910 (see **3.3.3**) was undoubtedly one such factor. It is also possible that catchers were trying not to block the umpire's view. The 1960s saw catchers given reason to crouch still lower when the introduction of improved mitt designs made it easier to catch low pitches (see **4.4.1**).

4.2.3 Guarding the Lines. The late 1870s saw a dramatic shift as the infield gradually began to assume its current functions. The key event was the elimination of the fair-foul after the 1876 season. Within weeks of the rule's passage, Henry Chadwick noted perceptively that "the infielders will be able to consolidate their forces so as to secure more ground-balls than they did before" (*New York Clipper*, January 13, 1877).

Many chroniclers of baseball history have appreciated the basic fact that a repositioning of the infield took place at this time. But in doing so they have too often misrepresented or grossly oversimplified the reasons for the change. This regrettable trend began soon after the events themselves.

In 1887, for example, a Detroit sportswriter offered this description of how baseball had been played in 1874: "The basemen played throughout the game with one foot on the base and never thought of trying for a ground ball unless it came straight to them" (*Detroit Free Press*, December 18, 1887). Sportswriter Malcolm McLean went further in 1913, penning this florid account of first-base play in 1876: "Like all first basemen who guarded the position since the game graduated from the 'o'cat' stage, [Cap] Anson kept one foot firmly planted on the sack. This was the custom. If he was so careless as to remove said shoe for an instant he quickly corrected himself. First basemen were hired to act as targets and to slug the ball. It was up to their mates to throw within fairly easy reaching distance. Grounders hit a few feet to the right of them went as singles—that is, if the second baseman couldn't cover that far. First-base tactics were in the cave-dwelling age" (Malcolm McLean, *Collier's*, reprinted in *Sporting News*, October 23, 1913).

Both comments are emblematic of a condescending attitude toward early baseball. While these descriptions of the first baseman's positioning are not pure fiction, these writers are engaging in both exaggeration and oversimplification as well as displaying their ignorance. In fact the positioning of first basemen in relation to their base did not betray a lack of imagination but instead fluctuated in response to the rules and conditions of the day.

Henry Chadwick recommended in 1860 that the first baseman "should play a little below his base and inside the line of the foul ball post, as he will then get to balls that would otherwise pass him" (*Beadle's Dime Base-Ball Player*, 23). While this player was clearly not standing on the bag, his relative proximity to it reflected the unique demands of play at first base. From very early in the game's history, sure-handedness and height were stressed as requirements, while foot speed, mobility, and a strong, accurate throwing arm were not particularly important. Since every other position on the field *did* reward these skills, players who lacked them naturally gravitated to first base.

This began to change when left-handers began to be excluded from the other infield positions, which meant that more agile and proficient fielders started to be stationed at first base. The most notable was southpaw Joe Start, a forgotten superstar who remained the standard for first basemen from the early 1860s until his retirement in 1886. Sportswriter William Rankin noted in 1910: "It was Joe Start who made first base a fielding position. Up to the early sixties the first baseman stood at the base and caught, or tried to do so, all balls thrown there, but made no attempt to leave the base to get batted balls. In the early '60's Start revolutionized the first base system of play. It was easy for him to go after hits in his direction with a man like Freddy Crane playing second, for the latter would cover first when Joe had played deep for the ball" (*Sporting News*, March 3, 1910).

Chadwick was a great admirer of Start, and by 1867 he was advising, "In taking his position in the field, he should stand about twenty or thirty feet from the base towards the right field . . . he will of course be guided by the style of batting opposed to him" (Henry Chadwick, *Haney's Base Ball Player's Book of Reference for 1867*, 128). The following year he instructed first basemen to stand eight to ten yards from the base and four to five yards inside the foul line except when a runner occupied first base (Henry Chadwick, *The American Game of Base Ball*, 30). Of course not every first baseman had the skill to follow Chadwick's counsel, yet it seems safe to assume that most were positioning themselves at least a few feet from their base. So why were later observers convinced that they never left the base?

The answer is quite simple. The fair-foul hit (**2.2.2**), which was still unknown in 1867, emerged in the next few years and remained a major part of batters' arsenals until it was banned in 1877. The fair-foul hit meant that first and third basemen were suddenly responsible for covering the ground both to the left and right of their base.

This new factor combined with an existing one to force first and third basemen to regard their respective bases as the midpoint of the territory they were expected to cover. Foul balls that were caught on the first bounce counted as outs until the mid-1880s, meaning that a corner baseman who guarded the lines would have many extra opportunities to record outs.

Fair-fouls and foul bounds applied to both the first and third basemen, but several additional factors led first basemen to remain close to the bag. The first and most obvious is the large number of outs that are registered at first base. The nonroutine nature of outs in early baseball made it helpful for the first baseman to be stationed on the base to await throws. The bases were not always easily visible from afar, so the first baseman could naturally elicit more accurate throws by providing a stationary target. Being on the base beforehand also made it easier for a first baseman to adjust to wild throws, an important and difficult feat in the days before trapping mitts were introduced.

Place hitting (**2.1.1**), curveballs (**3.2.3**), left-handed hitters (**2.1.9**), and closed batting stances (**2.1.6**) were also uncommon before the mid-1870s. The result was that relatively few balls were hit between first and second base, providing another good reason for first basemen not to stray far from the base.

In consequence, first basemen again positioned themselves close to their base between the late 1860s and the mid-1870s, but this reflected not thoughtlessness but a very reasonable decision. The responsibility for covering foul territory meant that even agile players such as Joe Start moved closer to the base. Moreover this trend reinforced itself because the tendency to assign the position to slow-footed players reemerged.

The pendulum swung back after a couple of rule changes reinvented foul territory. The fair-foul was eliminated in 1877, and the consequences for the first baseman were immediately appreciated by Henry Chadwick, who observed, "Under the new rule, the first and third baseman will not be required to stand as near to the foul-ball line as hitherto" (*New York Clipper*, January 13, 1877). The "foul bound" was permanently removed from the books in the early 1880s. (The foul bound was eliminated in the National League in 1879 but restored a year later. It was permanently abolished in the National League in 1883 and in 1885 in the American Association.)

The first baseman was thus liberated from much of the responsibility of covering foul balls. Holdovers who had been placed at first base because of their lack of mobility were not quick to reposition themselves, but newcomers to the position began to experiment.

Lee Richmond credited Walter Meader, the first baseman on his college championship team at Brown University, with being a pioneer at playing off the base. He claimed that Meader was responsible for assisting on putouts more frequently than any first baseman he saw in professional baseball (Ronald A. Mayer, *Perfect!*, 12).

Charles Comiskey is often referred to as having been the earliest first baseman to play off the base. There are many descriptions of Comiskey and Ted Sullivan developing this new tactic while with Dubuque in 1879. As with so many events in which Ted Sullivan figured, the accounts are rather hyperbolic in presenting it as a "Eureka!" type of idea that the two men then honed in clandestine fashion at a freight yard.

Malcolm McLean gave a particularly far-fetched account: ". . . The base ball world was shaken to its foundation. A tall, slender boy named Charley Comiskey had started in to revolutionize the system of playing the initial station. From the first day he signed with the St. Louis Browns, he sprinted after grounders which had formerly been considered hits—and got them. Fouls caught on the first bound were called outs in those first years of the big leagues. Few made much of an effort to trap them. Not so with Comiskey. He took such long chances it became dangerous to foul within running distance of him. Great ball players shook their heads gravely. Other first basemen were furious. It was plainly up to them to wise up and hustle. Yet they were slow in realizing something new had been added to the sport. This is a historic fact—every innovation in base ball has been bitterly fought until finally adopted" (Malcolm McLean, *Collier's*, reprinted in *Sporting News*, October 23, 1913).

This description reads much more like myth than history, and, as we have already seen, Comiskey was at most bringing back a trend introduced by Joe Start a decade and a half earlier. Moreover the extent to which Comiskey was ahead of his peers is doubtless exaggerated, especially since Start was still considered the master of the position. Indeed, Comiskey himself later wrote that his contribution was to "[play] my position 10 or 15 feet deeper than the other first baseman." He added that although he played deeper, he did not stray

far from the baseline: "I always played the foul lines safe, for a hit along the foul lines is the most dangerous of any" (Charles A. Comiskey, "How to Play the Infield," A. H. Spink, *The National Game*, 394–395). Other evidence seems to confirm that Comiskey played an important role but that the change was evolutionary rather than revolutionary.

Consequently the role of the first baseman began to change dramatically in the early 1880s. A *Sporting Life* correspondent observed in 1883, "The old style first baseman was required to play his base—that is, to hug it closely—attend to throwing, and but that. In the modern game the first baseman is required to play half of the right short field ground, to which the superior batting sends many hot, ugly balls, for the reason that it is regarded as safe ground" (*Sporting Life*, December 12, 1883). As this suggests, the new rules concerning foul territory were combining with new hitting approaches to move the first baseman farther from the bag.

4.2.4 Pitchers Covering First. The most obvious consequence of the first baseman moving farther from the base was that pitchers began to routinely cover first base. As might be guessed from the previous entry, this was not entirely a new phenomenon.

Henry Chadwick remarked in 1860, "The Pitcher will frequently have to occupy the bases on occasions when the proper guardian has left it to field the ball" (*Beadle's Dime Base-Ball Player*, 22). An 1861 account of a game in Hoboken between the Eureka of Newark and the Enterprise of Brooklyn singled out "two or three plays . . . that were so superior in their character that we cannot help noticing them. One was the putting out of Leland, in the third innings, when [first baseman Harry] Northrop fielded the ball to [pitcher James] Linen, who was running to first base to receive it, Linen catching the ball on the run in beautiful style, and touching the base before Leland could reach it" (*New York Clipper*, July 20, 1861). There are also documented examples of the Nationals of Washington and the Red Stockings of Cincinnati turning the play in the 1860s.

The prominence of the fair-foul in the early 1870s kept first basemen very close to the bag, enabling pitchers to conserve their energies. But the changes described in the preceding entry meant that by the early 1880s pitchers were again getting plenty of exercise. *Sporting Life* observed in 1883: "Lately pitchers have added to their play the part of covering first when the baseman has to leave his ground for a safely hit ball" (*Sporting Life*, December 12, 1883).

As captain of St. Louis, Charley Comiskey naturally drilled his pitchers to cover first base when he was drawn away from it. Comiskey found a novel way to impress upon the team's pitchers how important it was "to get over to cover the bag." According to Comiskey, "If I saw the pitcher was loafing on me I fielded the ball and then threw to first whether anyone was there or not. Then the crowd saw who was to blame, and pretty soon the pitchers got in the habit of running over rapidly rather than be roasted" (Charles A. Comiskey, "How to Play the Infield," A. H. Spink, *The National Game*, 394–395; see also Revere Rodgers, *Sporting News*, July 16, 1904, and Malcolm McLean, *Collier's*, reprinted in *Sporting News*, October 23, 1913). Harry Wright had a different method of ensuring compliance: "One of Harry Wright's new rules is that every time a pitcher fails to cover first base when [Sid] Farrar goes for a ball he is fined $1" (*Sporting Life*, May 13, 1885).

In 1889 Tim Murnane declared, "The pitcher should always start for first base when a ball is hit to the left of him" (Tim Murnane, "How the Stars Play Combinations," *Boston Globe*, March 10, 1889, 22). "Should" was the key word, however; as the tactics used by Comiskey and Wright suggest, it was far from easy to convince pitchers to add regular sprints to their duties. Deacon Phillippe reported in 1904 that Comiskey's method was still in use: "Several National and American league first basemen follow Comiskey's advice and throw the ball whether the pitcher covers the bag or not, the idea being to 'show him up' if he is lazy or neglectful" (Deacon Phillippe, "Phillippe of Pittsburg Team Discusses Requirements of Successful Pitchers," *Syracuse Post Standard*, March 27, 1904).

In the next few years this technique grew to become a point of emphasis in spring training drills. A 1905 description noted that Washington manager Jake Stahl "believes in the value of pitchers covering first base while the baseman is fielding the ball, and he firmly impressed it upon the minds of all. Stahl proposes to have his boxmen so well drilled in this point of play that he can play a deep field and feel certain that the pitcher will go over to take his throws. Washington pitchers have been prone to remaining in the box when the ball was batted to the first baseman, and often it was impossible for the baseman to get to the bag ahead of the runner, hence a chance was lost owing to the stupidity or indifference of the pitcher" (*Washington Post*, March 16, 1905).

The increased reliance on "inside ball" left other pitchers with little choice about making a habit of covering first.

4.2.5 Second Basemen Leaving the Bag.
A number of diagrams, drawings, and early photographs show a second baseman standing on second base as a pitch is delivered. Such evidence has led some to conclude that early second basemen invariably stationed themselves on the base.

In fact this was not the case. While early second basemen played closer to the base than is the case today and occasionally even stood on it, they changed their position according to the situation. Henry Chadwick recommended in 1860 that the second baseman "should play a little back of his base, and to the right or left of it, according to the habitual play of the striker, but generally to the left as most balls pass in that direction" (*Beadle's Dime Base-Ball Player*, 24).

An 1864 book advised that this player "should play generally to the left and a little back of his base, though he should be guided in it by the customary play of the striker. When the striker reaches the first base, he should return to his base, prepared to receive the ball from the catcher, and be ready to put out the striker by touching him with the ball" (*The American Boy's Book of Sports and Games*, 87). In 1867, Chadwick counseled captains that with a slow or medium-paced pitcher working, "prepare your field for catches by placing your basemen out further, letting the short stop nearly cover second base, and the second baseman play at right short well out, and extending your out-fielders about ten yards or so" (Henry Chadwick, *Haney's Base Ball Player's Book of Reference for 1867*, 84).

The second baseman was especially likely to move away from the base when there were no runners on base, as is shown by Chadwick's description of an 1867 match in which John Hatfield of the Mutuals "led off with a fine hit to [Atlantics second baseman] Charley Smith, who was playing almost at right short, and though Charley found it a hot one to field, he got it to [first baseman Joe] Start in time to send Hatfield back" (Henry Chadwick, *The American Game of Base Ball*, 126).

Another factor in the placement of the second baseman was the skill of the shortstop. An 1869 article noted that second baseman

Alfred D. Martin and shortstop Albro Akin of the Unions of Morrisania "were extremely active and quick runners, and would support one another effectively, thus allowing Martin to play farther from his base than he could with a less active short" (*National Chronicle*, June 12, 1869).

A similar repositioning occurred when a left-handed batter was at the plate. Chadwick explained in 1871 that the second baseman "is required, also, to cover second base and to play 'right short stop,' but his position in the field must be governed entirely by the character of the batting he is called upon to face. If a hard hitter comes to bat and swift balls are being sent in, he should play well out in the field, between right field and second base, and be on the *qui vive* for long bound balls or high fly balls, which drop between the out-field and the second base line. When the batsman makes his first base the second baseman comes up and gets near the base in readiness to receive the ball from the catcher" (*New York Clipper*, March 11, 1871).

In the ensuing years the second baseman also began to inch farther from the bag against right-handed batters. Chadwick noted before the 1874 season: "Of late seasons it has been the custom to cover the open gap between first and second bases by making the second baseman play at 'right short,' but this has left a safe spot for sharp grounders close to second base, while it has also drawn round the short-stop to second, and the third baseman to short-field to such an extent as to make fair-foul hitting a sure style of play for earned bases" (*New York Clipper*, March 7, 1874).

It is thus simply untrue that early second basemen remained planted in one place. In actuality they took a remarkable number of factors into account and changed their position accordingly.

Unlike the first and third basemen, the second baseman's positioning does not seem to have changed dramatically as a result of the abolition of the fair-foul. Researcher Greg Rhodes reported that the second baseman remained a few steps from the bag in the diagrams that appeared in the annual *Spalding Guide* between 1876 and 1892. But the responsibilities of the position did increase as a result of the "marked increase of right-field hitting" (*New York Clipper*, December 20, 1879).

An 1883 analysis found the "second baseman of to-day" to be "an entirely different unit in the field work of a team" from "his fellow tradesman of ten years ago. There is a wide difference between the play of a [Tommy] Beals, a [Wes] Fisler and a [Jack] Burdock of 1873 and a [Fred] Dunlap, a [Jack] Farrell and a [Jack] Burdock of 1883. Not only has the territory over which the second baseman of the first class does not permit a grounder to pass grown larger, but the work in throwing and attention to fly balls has increased nearly as much. To the short stop and the second baseman has gradually been assigned the work of attending to all fly balls 'between the fields' as the gap between the infielders and outfielders of a team in play is called" (*Sporting Life*, December 12, 1883).

In 1889 Tim Murnane noted that most second basemen stationed themselves about fifteen feet to the left of the bag. The majority stood well back of the baseline, but some, such as Fred Pfeffer, moved up near the line with a runner on first so as to have a better chance of turning a double play. Murnane also recalled that Jack Burdock often covered first base when John Morrill left that base to field a bunt, suggesting that some second basemen positioned themselves very close to first base when a bunt was expected (Tim Murnane, "How the Stars Play Combinations," *Boston Globe*, March 10, 1889, 22).

As will be suggested in the next entry, the current custom of having the second baseman and shortstop roughly equidistant from the base dates from around the beginning of the twentieth century. It is no coincidence that the hit-and-run play became a major offensive weapon at the same time (see **5.4.7**).

4.2.6 Shortstops Become Responsible for Base Play.
As discussed in the first chapter (see **1.15**), the shortstop originated as a fourth outfielder and then during the 1850s gradually evolved into a rover. By the 1860s he was playing much closer to the infield but continued to have much more license to roam about than the basemen. Henry Chadwick wrote in 1867, "In selecting your short-stop, let him be an accurate thrower to begin with, but especially should he be noted for his activity in backing up every player in the in-field as occasion may require. The short-stop should always be on the move and on the lookout, first behind third base, then running home to help the catcher, anon playing second base, and even running out to long field for a high ball" (Henry Chadwick, *Haney's Base Ball Player's Book of Reference for 1867*, 82).

By 1879 the role had changed enough for Chadwick to observe that "short-stops are now required to cover bases so frequently—second base in particular—that they have come to be almost part and parcel of the basemen-team of a nine" (*New York Clipper*, December 20, 1879). An increased emphasis on hitting to right field would promote this trend in the next few years.

In 1883, *Sporting Life* surveyed these burgeoning responsibilities: ". . . A change has come to the short stop of this day, when his work is contrasted with the short stops of ten years ago. The short stop not only plays the ground half way from third base to second, but he attends to the base play when the players leave them for stops, backs up the infield throwing, has rambling orders for pop flies in the space between fields, and is especially useful in the run-outs that are so frequent in these days of fast and daring base running" (*Sporting Life*, December 12, 1883). Other new developments that decade also led shortstops to move closer to the bag in some situations, such as the tendency of second basemen to cover first on a bunt (see preceding entry).

Nevertheless it was not until the 1890s that shortstops began truly to share the responsibility for covering second base. Tim Murnane discussed the subject at length in 1889 and explained that the game situation often altered positioning. The general practice, however, was for the second baseman to stand only fifteen feet or so from the bag while the shortstop was often midway between second and third base (Tim Murnane, "How the Stars Play Combinations," *Boston Globe*, March 10, 1889, 22). That changed forever in the mid-1890s, with the "Hit and Run" (**5.4.7**) the biggest factor. As a result, Honus Wagner remarked in 1904, "The position of shortstop has come to be practically a duplicate of that of second base, except that one man plays to the right of the bag while the other plays to the left. Ten years ago the short fielder had a position all to himself, and one which gave him a full share of the work done at that time. The large increase in the number of left-hand batters has brought about a change, and the shortstop is as much a second baseman as the player so designated" (*Washington Post*, July 3, 1904).

4.2.7 Third Base Becomes a Hitter's Haven.
As discussed in "Guarding the Lines" (see **4.2.3**), a number of factors caused third basemen of the late 1860s and early 1870s to stay close to their bag. The *New York Clipper* observed in 1871: "The third baseman

takes a position closer to his base than either of the other basemen. Sometimes, however, he takes the place of the short stop when the latter covers the second base in cases where the second baseman plays at right short for a right-field hitter, a position frequently taken by a first class nine" (*New York Clipper*, March 4, 1871).

Some batsmen of the early 1870s were so adept at the fair-foul that third basemen must have wished they could stand in foul territory. Jim O'Rourke recalled that Ross Barnes "had a trick of hitting the ball so it would smash on the ground near the plate just inside of the third base line, and would then mow the grass over the line, away out into the field, where, of course, the fielders did not stay. No third baseman could get away from his position quickly enough to stop one of Barnes' hits" ("Forty Two Years of Base Ball," *Kalamazoo Evening Telegraph*, March 3, 1910).

As also noted in "Guarding the Lines," that began to change when the fair-foul was banned in 1877. At season's end, Henry Chadwick remarked that "the cutting off of the fair-foul hitting lessened some of the difficulties of the third baseman's work" (*New York Clipper*, December 29, 1877). The basic duties of the third baseman have not changed much since. What has changed is the desirability of having a skilled gloveman at third base, which has corresponded closely to whether the bunt (see **2.2.1**) was in or out of favor.

Sporting Life noted in 1883: "In old times the third baseman was perhaps the most important man on the nine, as the position was regarded as the key of the infield. Those were the days when fair-foul hitting and blocking the ball [i.e., bunting] flourished. Nowadays the third baseman has much less to do than formerly, the changes in the rules and in styles of pitching being responsible therefor. In fact, the second baseman, of the infielders, exceeds in importance" (*Sporting Life*, December 12, 1883).

Just when it appeared that third base was no longer an important defensive position, the bunt made its comeback in the late 1880s. But playing far enough in to defend against the bunt put the third baseman in great peril from a hot line drive. It was no coincidence that in these years third base began to be referred to as the "difficult corner," a term that eventually evolved into the "hot corner" (*Sporting Life*, December 30, 1885; *Sporting News*, August 17, 1889).

The frequency of bunting continued to increase in the 1890s. In an 1892 editorial, the *New York Times* suggested that due to the requirement of having to guard against bunts as well as field line drives, it might be appropriate for third basemen to wear masks and other equipment reserved for catchers (*New York Times*, June 23, 1892). By 1904, Connie Mack observed that "third base has always been considered as the most difficult position on the diamond to play" (Connie Mack, "How to Play Ball," multi-part series, *Washington Post*, April 3, 1904).

Even after the power explosion of the 1920s, bunting remained a common part of baseball (albeit one that many recent analysts believe is overused). Not until the 1950s did the emphasis on the bunt begin to wane and third base begin to be viewed as a hitter's position.

4.2.8 Outfield Placement.

Some writers believe that outfielders in early baseball stood in the same location for each batter. Some clubs do indeed seem to have been unimaginative in this regard, as the *Boston Globe* wrote in 1889, "The [Harvard] outfield seemed all right, but played their positions as they did twenty-five years ago. They went out and stood in the same spot for every man that came to the bat, without any regard to the way the batsman faced" (*Boston Globe*, April 9, 1889).

That was not generally the case, however. Henry Chadwick instructed captains as early as 1867 that it was worth "extending your outfielders about ten yards or so" when a slow or medium-paced pitcher was working. He added, "Always have an understanding with your two sets of fielders in regard to private signals, so as to be able to call them in closer, or place them out further, or nearer the foul-ball lines, as occasion may require, without giving notice to your adversaries. . . . Warn your out-fielders also to watch well the batsmen, so as to be ready to move in the direction he faces for batting" (*Haney's Base Ball Player's Book of Reference for 1867*, reprinted in *The Ball Player's Chronicle*, August 22, 1867).

By 1881 outfielders were being advised to "strictly obey the signals from the pitcher for all such changes of position. Time and again this past season we have seen a pitcher's strategy entirely nullified by the stupidity or obstinacy of some one or other of the outfielders to quickly obey the pitcher's signal to play deeper, or closer, or to get round more to the right or to the left, when he has been preparing to outwit a batsman by something besides the mere speed of his delivery" (*New York Clipper*, December 31, 1881).

4.2.9 Right Fielders Playing Very Shallow.

Right fielders in the very early days of baseball played so shallow in some circumstances that they became essentially right shortstops. Even when they played at more normal depth, they remained alert for opportunities to throw runners out at first on apparent base hits. A 1915 article observed, "In the bygone days of baseball the speediest outfielders were stationed in right field so that they could come in fast on a bounder hit into right field, scoop it up and throw the batter [sic] at first base. In these days such a trick is a rarity; but twenty and thirty years ago it was common. A right fielder who could not arrange an assist on every three bounders hit out his way was considered too slow to keep" (*Nevada* [Reno] *State Journal*, September 14, 1915).

The piece cited Billy Sunday, Mike Tiernan, Mike Kelly, Jake Evans, Tom McCarthy, and Hugh Nicol as right fielders who were proficient at executing this play. The garrulous George "Orator" Shafer was especially skilled at the tactic. A contemporary report observed, "Without exception he is the best right-fielder in the country today, a position in which he has always played, and which he has down to a very fine point. His record of assist on put-outs at first base beats anything that has ever been heard of" (*Cleveland Leader*, March 23, 1882). In 1925 the sportswriter John B. Sheridan described Shafer as "one of the greatest right fielders that I have ever known in one point, throwing out base runners at first base on apparently safe hits" (*Sporting News*, November 26, 1925).

A. H. Spink claimed that in the 1870s and 1880s this play was "pulled off three or four times in each and every contest" (A. H. Spink, *The National Game*, 270). This is probably a slight exaggeration, but not as much as might be expected, as Shafer had fifty outfield assists in seventy-two games in 1879, a major league record that still stands. A particularly historic instance of this play occurred in an 1880 game when Worcester right fielder Lon Knight threw out a batter at first base on what appeared to be a clean single. The play preserved Lee Richmond's 1880 perfect game—the first in major league history.

Gradually a greater emphasis on left-field hitting forced right fielders to play deeper, and this once-common play began to disappear. A notable exception occurred during the second game of a Decoration Day doubleheader on May 30, 1895, when an overflow crowd forced Cincinnati right fielder "Dusty" Miller to play very shallow. He took advantage by throwing out four Philadelphia batters on apparent singles (Greg Rhodes and John Snyder, *Redleg Journal*, 117).

4.2.10   Infield Depth. We have already seen in the entry for "Catchers Playing Close" (4.2.1) that terms like "close" and "near" are too subjective for exact interpretation. This is even more the case with infield depth, but I will venture a few generalizations.

Early infielders did not play particularly deep, typically no more than a step or two behind the base paths. There were several reasons for this. One was so that they could return to their bases in time to provide a target for other infielders. In addition, with all the obstacles that prevented any out from being routine, it made sense to reduce the length of throws. Connie Mack noted another factor that complicated the positioning of early infielders—the "narrow path running between the bases from which the turf was skinned. If an infielder played in front of this path a hard hit ball was apt to kill him, and if he played back of it the ball often hit the edge of it and bounced over his head to the outfield" (Connie Mack, "Memories of When the Game Was Young," *Sporting Life* [monthly], June 1924).

Clubs certainly did play their infielders deeper or shallower depending on the situation, however. In 1889 Tim Murnane offered many examples of situations that could lead infielders to move in or step back (Tim Murnane, "How the Stars Play Combinations," *Boston Globe*, March 10, 1889, 22). The sportswriter H. G. Merrill wrote in 1905 that "bringing the infield in is an antiquated play" and cited Ted Sullivan as one proponent of this philosophy when he managed the St. Louis Brown Stockings in 1883 (*Sporting News*, April 29, 1905).

Sullivan's protégé, Charlie Comiskey, took over the reins of the Brown Stockings later that season and became noted for playing a deep infield. Johnny Evers and Hugh Fullerton reported that the 1885 and 1886 post-season series between Chicago, champions of the National League, and the American Association pennant winners from St. Louis provided a vivid contrast in defensive philosophies, with the Brown Stockings playing much deeper

(John J. Evers and Hugh S. Fullerton, *Touching Second*, 201).

Once infielders began to play deeper, a manager's decision about whether to move the infielders closer in critical situations became more conspicuous and began to attract more attention. Comiskey commented in 1910 that "unless the score is very close and it is near the end of a game, I never pull in my infielders for a possible play at the plate, but rather play for the base runner" (Charles A. Comiskey. "How to Play the Infield," A. H. Spink, *The National Game*, 395).

4.2.11   Moving In During the Pitch. It has long been common for fielders to move a step or two to the left or right as a pitch is thrown. As Tim Murnane explained in 1889, "The infield should always know just the kind of a ball the pitcher is going to give the batsman. If an out curve the third base and short should move around toward second, and, if an in ball, the second baseman can change his position to correspond with the short and third base. Much care should be taken in making the move as the opposing batsman is likely to take notice and change his style of hitting. The men can remain in their usual positions until the pitcher has his arm on the swing; by that time the batsman has no chance to observe the movements of the fielders" (Tim Murnane, "How the Stars Play Combinations," *Boston Globe*, March 10, 1889, 22).

As the preceding entry shows, since deep positioning for infielders was a relatively late development, it is probably impossible to determine the first club to play their infield in or at double-play depth. There is one variant, however, that has developed much more recently. Tim McCarver reported that in the 1990s the Montreal Expos unveiled the tactic of having their middle infielders move in during the pitcher's windup. McCarver noted that this puts pressure on a base runner on third base, since he has already received his instructions from the third-base coach (Tim McCarver with Danny Peary, *Tim McCarver's Baseball for Brain Surgeons and Other Fans*, 322, 324).

4.2.12   Shifts. On July 14, 1946, Lou Boudreau unveiled the famous Williams Shift against Ted Williams, which featured only one defensive player to the left of second base. But clubs had been using shifts against Williams as early as 1941 (Michael Seidel, *Ted Williams*, 103–104). Moreover David Nemec has pointed out that this was not even the first Williams Shift—shifts were used against left-handed pull hitters Ken Williams and Cy Williams in 1922! (David Nemec, *Great Baseball Facts, Feats and Firsts*, 122). Boudreau's version wasn't remotely a first—it just attracted a lot of attention because it was so dramatic.

As this suggests, shifts are a vexed subject. Since there is no clear-cut distinction between shading and a full-fledged shift, there is no way to determine the first shift. It is worth noting, however, that some extreme positioning was in use in the nineteenth century, with Bob Ferguson at the forefront. By 1877 he was adjusting to right-handed pull hitters by placing the second baseman on the left side of the infield (*Louisville Courier-Journal*, May 19, 1877; quoted in David Arcidiacono, *Grace, Grit and Growling*, 61).

An 1879 game account showed that Ferguson was expanding and refining the shift. When a left-handed batter came up for the Athletics, "it was noteworthy how finely Ferguson placed his field for him. [Third baseman] Smith stood at left-short, [shortstop] Ferguson covered second, [second baseman Sam] Crane was deep right-short, and [first baseman George] Latham covered first well back, while [right fielder John] Cassidy was ready for a right-field assistance, [center fielder Lip] Pike at right-centre, and [left fielder Phil] Powers at left-centre. The moment a right-handed batsman took his place, the field was moved round to the regular positions to suit the probable hitting" (*New York Clipper*, May 24, 1879).

Similarly, an 1895 exhibition game saw Chicago position all three outfielders in left field when John Shearon came to the plate. Shearon tried in vain to hit the ball into the gaping hole in right field (*Sporting News*, December 7, 1895). That same year manager Frank Selee remarked, "Men that continually hit in one direction nowadays are not winners, for they are marked and played for" (*Sporting News*, August 17, 1895).

While shifts are generally used on power hitters, Ed Reulbach claimed that one of the most effective ones was used on turn-of-the-century Philadelphia outfielder Roy Thomas, a singles hitter. Reulbach explained that Thomas "not only hit almost all the time to left field, but he was a short field hitter as well. This tendency handicapped him tremendously. When Thomas was at bat, the left fielder moved close to the foul line and came well in. The center fielder shifted away over toward left and at the same time advanced close up behind short and second. Third baseman moved over nearly to the foul line, and the shortstop followed him to a point at least fifteen feet beyond his natural position. At the same time he fell back and played a rather deep field. With this combination against him, Thomas was like clay in the hands of the pitcher" (F. C. Lane, *Batting*, 50).

(iii) Teamwork

4.3.1 Calling for Fly Balls. Given the danger of collisions, it is not surprising that calling for fly balls developed very early. Researcher Priscilla Astifan discovered an 1860 game account in which catcher Joe Leggett of the touring Excelsiors of Brooklyn was praised "for the manner in which he would telegraph advantages to be gained, or the direction as to which one of the fielders should take a 'fly.' There was no rushing for a ball, but each man of the Excelsiors knew his place and kept it, a point which our ball-players will please make a note of" (*Rochester Evening Express*, July 9, 1860).

Henry Chadwick advised in 1860: "The Catcher, whenever he sees several fielders running to catch a ball, should designate the one he deems most sure of taking it, by name, in which case the others should refrain from the attempt to catch the ball on the fly" (*Beadle's Dime Base-Ball Player*, 21).

Researcher Darryl Brock discovered that the Red Stockings drew praise for the sophistication of their system during their 1869 tour of California: "The Red Stockings have arranged a set of orders so brief that frequently only the name of the player is called and he hastens to do what is requisite: an instance of their alacrity and perfect understanding was given on Saturday—a sky ball was sent between shortstop and right field, for which either might have gone, but the captain called 'McVey,' and right field [Cal McVey] at once put himself in position to catch it, but the captain also called 'Wright' in the same breath, and short-stop [George Wright] ran and dropped on his knee under McVey's hands, so that if missed by the first it could still be caught before reaching the ground" (*Daily Alta California*, September 27, 1869).

The primary responsibility of calling for fly balls initially fell upon the captain. In 1879 the *Cleveland Plain Dealer* scolded: "It seems as if Captain [Tom] Carey was ignorant of the fact that the other fielders depend upon him to *call* one of them to take a fly when three or four are in position to capture it" (*Cleveland Plain Dealer*, August 13, 1879).

Since this made it necessary for the captain to play a central position, clubs began to fine-tune the system. The *Chicago Tribune* suggested in 1880, "The player running at full speed, with a chance of getting under the ball, should sing out as he runs, 'Let me have it!' and, whether he can get the ball or not, he should invariably have the right of way" (*Chicago Tribune*, May 19, 1880). Unfortunately, this advice wouldn't have been of much help if two players were running at full speed and called for the ball.

In 1888, Johnny Ward wrote, "The necessity of 'calling' for a fly hit applies with particular force to the centre fielder. As soon as he has seen that he can get to a hit and has decided to take it, he calls out loudly so that every one must hear, 'I'll take it,' and all other fielders near him respond, 'Go ahead'" (John Montgomery Ward, *Base-Ball: How to Become a Player*, 115).

4.3.2 Backing Up. Instances of one fielder backing up another date back to baseball's earliest days. In 1860, Henry Chadwick noted that the shortstop was expected to "back up the second and third bases when the ball is thrown in from the field" (*Beadle's Dime Base-Ball Player*, 23). His advice was heeded at least occasionally. For example, an 1864 account noted that the shortstop of the Excelsiors of Brooklyn "threw the ball over [second baseman Harry Brainard's] head: fortunately [right fielder George] Fletcher was backing up well, and securing the ball, rapidly returned it to Harry at second base in time to cut [Mutuals base runner Tom] Devyr off" (*Brooklyn Eagle*, August 18, 1864).

What is harder to determine is whether such isolated examples were designed or improvised, and when backing up became commonplace. As early as 1871, fielders were being counseled: "Every player should be active in 'backing up' in the in-field" (*New York Clipper*, March 4, 1871). Nonetheless such tactics were not routine in the 1870s, and this should not simply be attributed to a lack of industriousness.

Any time the ball was put in play, the basemen and catcher were expected to remain close to their respective bases and home plate. This left only the shortstop and pitcher available as convenient backups on plays in the infield.

Pitchers did occasionally fulfill this function, such as in a game on May 30, 1879, when Providence pitcher John Ward backed up the plate on a throw from the outfield. But the

technique was considered unusual and with good reason (Jim Charlton, ed., *The Baseball Chronology*, 38). Running around to back up plays could tire a pitcher and hamper his effectiveness. In addition, the blocked-ball rule (**12.6**) meant that the ball might need to be relayed to the pitcher in his box, which made him unsuitable as a backup.

This left only the shortstop, as Henry Chadwick later noted: "In the old times the only infielder who ever thought of backing up a companion was the short-stop, and then he considered that his chief duty in this respect was to attend to the pitcher only. Base-players of the olden time, with some rare exceptions, never thought of leaving their positions to field a ball, or to assist in fielding it, which went to any position save their own" (*New York Clipper*, January 22, 1881).

In the 1880s the idea of backing up gained greater acceptance. Henry Chadwick, for example, commended the Chicago club at the end of the 1880 season because "the pitcher and catcher ran behind the first base to stop the ball in case of a wide throw" (*New York Clipper*, December 18, 1880). But the following examples suggest that execution of the theory sometimes lagged behind.

A *Sporting Life* correspondent observed in 1885, ". . . Every American Association club, with the possible exception of the Metropolitans [exhibits a] want of proper 'backing up' each other in the field. The Chicago League team gave some exhibitions in this line when here that reflect great credit upon the 'drill work' of their captain. When a ball, for example, is batted to left field, the centre fielder should run at full speed to a position on the line of the hit, back some distance of the left fielder, not with a view to catch the ball, but to stop it in case it passes the left fielder" (*Sporting Life*, June 3, 1885).

The blocked-ball rule was gradually superseded by ground rules, leading pitcher John Clarkson to note in 1888 that pitchers were free to act as backups: "In the event of a ball being thrown wide from the outfield or any other point, as the case may be, it is the pitcher's duty to be behind the player to whom the ball is thrown, backing him up." But, Clarkson added, "I make special mention of this because it is so seldom done, and I think it is more through carelessness than anything else" (*New York Sun*, May 6, 1888). Similarly, Tim Murnane stated in 1889 that one of the duties of the pitcher was to "back up the catcher when a ball is sent to the outfield" (Tim Murnane, "How the Stars Play Combinations," *Boston Globe*, March 10, 1889, 22).

As noted earlier, Chicago catchers were backing up first base as early as 1880, but the practice may have been popularized by Charles Ganzel. Hughey Jennings stated in 1907, "I really believe that Herman Long and Bob Lowe when they were playing with that old Boston team used to throw wild to first purposely so that Ganzel could get the ball. The base runner would see the ball going over the first baseman's head and he'd start turning second or leaving first, forgetting the catcher. Charlie would be there with that wing and throw them out" (*Detroit News*, March 18, 1907).

Sportswriter Harold Burr reported that Philadelphia catcher Red Dooin revived this hustling play around the turn of the century (*Sporting News*, November 10, 1938). Dooin was a natural candidate to reintroduce the tactic, because he was a small, quick player at a time when the catcher's position was dominated by larger men. The much-larger Boss Schmidt was one of the catchers who followed Dooin's lead.

4.3.3   Decoys.

It's especially difficult to pin down the first occurrence of an ad hoc play such as a decoy. A 1901 game account described how Cincinnati infielders Jake Beckley, Harry Steinfeldt, and George Magoon "worked the old trick of getting a man on first to run on a fly ball to the outfield" and thereby turned a double play (*Sporting News*, June 15, 1901). Since the decoy was regarded as an "old trick" in 1901, it can be assumed to date well back into the nineteenth century, and indeed an 1887 article mentioned "[Joe] Hornung's pretense of letting the ball pass him, with a base runner just reaching second" (*Boston Globe*, April 11, 1887).

After the turn of the century, Chicago Cubs second baseman Johnny Evers became particularly associated with the play. A 1905 account noted, "Evers' trick in the seventh was a clever one—and but for fate he would have trapped the cardinals [sic] into a double play. [Jack] Dunleavy was at first when [Jack] Warner poked out a short fly to center. Evers pretended the ball had skipped over second, running over and sliding as if trying to reach the ball. Dunleavy, seeing him, tore down to second and rounded towards third—then saw [Jimmy] Slagle tearing in to catch the fly, and he tried to get back to first. Slagle could not quite reach

or it would have been an easy double" (*Chicago Tribune*, May 28, 1905). Evers frequently collaborated with shortstop Joe Tinker on the play and claimed to have fooled Sherwood Magee with it three times in the same season (John J. Evers and Hugh S. Fullerton, *Touching Second*, 205).

In 1912, Christy Mathewson described such decoys as being "as old as the one in which the second baseman hides the ball under his shirt so as to catch a man asleep off first base, but often the old ones are the more effective" (Christy Mathewson, *Pitching in a Pinch*, 136). Nonetheless he commented on their increasing frequency in recent years: "There is a sub-division of defensive coaching which might be called the illegitimate brand. It is giving 'phoney' advice to a base runner by the fielders of the other side that may lead him, in the excitement of the moment, to make a foolish play. This style has developed largely in the Big Leagues in the last three or four years" (Christy Mathewson, *Pitching in a Pinch*, 125).

This trend undoubtedly helped clubs recognize the value of hiring full-time coaches (see 7.2.1), a development that came into vogue at the same time.

4.3.4   Reverse Decoys.

The other main type of decoy, in which a baseman tries to convince a runner that no throw is on its way, also dates back to the nineteenth century. An 1892 game account described how Cleveland third baseman Patsy Tebeau awaited a throw from the outfield while standing "close to the base line, ready to touch [Brooklyn base runner Mike] Griffin as he was running for third, but Tebeau never moved as if the ball was coming to him, and Griffin, thinking himself safe, slacked up a little, and then it was that Tebeau got the ball and suddenly put it on the runner like a flash. It was a finely played point" (*Brooklyn Eagle*, June 5, 1892).

A similar play was made in 1899 by Brooklyn third baseman Doc Casey, who "hoodwinked [New York base runner Mike] Tiernan in the third inning. The little third baseman apparently paid no attention to Mike as he came up to third on [Parke] Wilson's hit, and the runner slowed up, believing that [outfielder Willie] Keeler was throwing to the plate to catch [Ed] Doheny. It was not until Casey received the ball that he turned in Tiernan's direction and Mike put a move on him when it was too late" (*Brooklyn Eagle*, June 16, 1899).

4.3.5   Cutoff and Relay Plays. The concept of a relay is an ancient one. Tim Murnane was apparently referring to the 1850s when he explained, "In the early days the game was played on large open fields, and the out-fielders had some long runs to get a ball hit by them. Sometimes they were obliged to go to the extreme end of the field. Men played but few games and their arms were not in condition to make long throws, and the basemen hugged their bases much closer than at the present time. The short-stop acted as a utility man and would go out in the field to take the ball from the out-fielders and send it to the home plate or to the in-field" (*Cincinnati Enquirer*, April 1, 1888).

As Murnane explained, the shortstop was responsible for all the relaying (and running) while the other basemen guarded their respective bases. By the 1860s the shortstop was beginning to be regarded more as an infielder than a rover, leaving no obvious candidate to relay throws from the outfield.

Henry Chadwick suggested in 1868 that the right fielder should sometimes fulfill this function: "If he sees a ball going over the centre fielder's head, he should at once run for the centre fielder's position, and be ready to help pass the ball in from the outer field, if necessary" (Henry Chadwick, *The American Game of Base Ball*, 23).

It seems reasonable to assume that the second baseman also inherited some responsibility for relays from right field. In many cases, however, the relay was simply scrapped, and the outfielder was expected to throw the ball into the diamond.

This trend was then furthered by two important changes in the playing conditions. By the end of the 1860s outfield fences (see **14.1.1**) had become almost universal in professional play, and around 1870 the dead ball (see **9.1.5**) came into favor. The combined effect of these two developments was to allow outfielders to play significantly closer to the infield.

Consequently the relay system fell into disuse in the 1870s. When a relay did take place, it was usually the result of spontaneous hustle, as is suggested by an 1878 description of a long drive over left fielder Jimmy Hallinan's head that "would have given a home run had not [center fielder John] Remsen cleverly helped Hally field it in. It was not an unheard of point of play, but it pleased the people as showing the earnestness of the men" (*Chicago Tribune*, April 21, 1878).

By the late 1870s, Henry Chadwick was advocating that outfielders use the same teamwork practiced by infielders: "The idea that a left-fielder has only to attend to left-field balls and a right-fielder to those sent to right-field is an exploded rule of the old amateur days." He stressed the need for "good backing-up" among outfielders, noting that relays replaced or at least complemented the custom of "throwing home to the catcher from the outfield" (*New York Clipper*, December 27, 1879). But Chadwick was uncharacteristically vague in describing exactly how this was to be accomplished, and it does not appear that sophisticated cutoff and relay systems were yet in vogue.

It was not until the mid-1890s that such a systematic approach began to develop. According to *Babe Ruth's Own Book of Baseball*, John McGraw and Hughey Jennings invented the cutoff play "when they were playing with the old Baltimore Orioles, and it came near revolutionizing baseball. The Orioles worked it a hundred times in the course of a season, before the other clubs got wise" (Babe Ruth, *Babe Ruth's Own Book of Baseball*, 143). This account sounds a bit suspicious, and an 1895 article suggests that a different club of the same era may deserve credit: "The Boston outfielders are working together in a way different from the usual method. With men on the bases hits to the outfield are not fielded directly to the plate if a man is rounding third, but the ball is sharply thrown to one of the infielders, who is tipped off where to catch a runner. In this way long distance throws with crooked bounds are generally avoided" (*Atlanta Constitution*, May 3, 1895).

This certainly sounds like the rudiments of today's approach to cutoffs and relays. By 1904 it was becoming more common to use the pitcher as the cutoff man, as Connie Mack counseled pitchers: "Never fail to back up the catcher on all throws from the outfield to the plate. There are times, however, when it might be advisable to get in line in front of the catcher, to handle the ball, making the throw to second" (Connie Mack, "How to Play Ball," multi-part series, *Washington Post*, March 13, 1904).

A 1914 article indicated that Manager Buck Herzog of Cincinnati had recently changed the cutoff responsibility from the pitcher to first baseman Dick Hoblitzell: "Herzog knows that not one pitcher in ten knows whether to let the ball go on to the plate to try to catch the runner or catch the ball and shoot back to second to catch the batter who will attempt to take an extra base on the throw home. Therefore, he makes all of his pitchers go back of the catcher when a hit is made, and Hoblitzell comes to the middle of the diamond and handles all balls or decides to let them go" (*Washington Post*, July 12, 1914).

4.3.6 Catchers Coaching Pitchers.

The value of catchers to early pitchers was recognized as being immense, because only a talented catcher allowed a pitcher to throw his best pitches with confidence. The catcher's primary role, however, was reactive, a function symbolized by the distance he stood behind the plate. That began to change once catchers began to assume responsibility for calling pitches. By the end of the century the importance of this duty was starting to earn recognition, as illustrated by comments like: "Of [Dick] Buckley it was said in the National League that his superior as a coaching catcher for young pitchers did not exist" (*Detroit Free Press*, December 30, 1896).

4.3.7 Wheel Play.

Complex plays like the wheel play almost always develop by fits and starts rather than emerging full-blown. During the 1903 World Series, Pirates third baseman Tommy Leach threw to shortstop Honus Wagner covering third to foil a bunt (*Sporting Life*, October 17, 1903). Some observers considered the play new, but others said it was an element of the "sacrifice killer" play, described in the next entry.

4.3.8 Sacrifice Killer.

The "sacrifice killer" was a play used to defense sacrifice bunts. As the following paragraphs show, there were two major variations of the play.

In 1900, Jimmy Callahan of Chicago explained: "I was caught by the neatest trick in the world in one of the early Brooklyn games. This is the play: Man on first and second and nobody out. Now, everybody knows that it is good sense for the captain to tell the next man up to bunt into a sacrifice and advance the runners. So the Brooklyns all play in close for the bunt and the runners take good leads off their bases, seeing no chance for a throw from the pitcher to catch either of them. Suddenly [Bill] Dahlen, at short, wheels about and makes a dash for second, and the pitcher, turning at the same time, makes a bluff to throw to the base. Instead he turns and pitches one where it is certain to be a nice bunt for the batter. The batter, fulfilling orders, bunts. Either the pitcher or third baseman gets it and the runner at second, who has broken his spine trying to get back to the base to avoid the throw he thinks is coming to Dahlen, is an easy victim, for before he can get started back toward third he is out. . . . The only chance to avoid the play is to have a quick-witted batter up who will smash at the ball instead of bunting it" (*Chicago Chronicle*, reprinted in *Sporting Life*, December 8, 1900).

Around the same time, former Chicago third baseman Tommy Burns told a reporter, "Every now and then I see where some club is inventing new plays; for instance, the so-called 'sacrifice killer,' as used by the Brooklyns this year. Why, that play was used by the Chicagos fifteen years ago" (*Sporting Life*, November 17, 1900). It seems likely, though by no means certain, that he meant the same play described by Callahan.

In 1910, A. H. Spink quoted a recent article by first basemen Hal Chase that claimed: "Fred Tenney was the pioneer southpaw first sacker. He originated the sacrifice killing play. That is, on a bunt to him, he tried for the man that was to be advanced" (A. H. Spink, *The National Game*, 174). But Arthur Irwin maintained that the play had flaws that were soon exposed: "Back in the nineties Boston had [Billy] Nash for captain and third base, and the infield played for a bunt in the same way, [first baseman Fred] Tenney going in, [second baseman Bobby] Lowe going over to cover first, and [shortstop Herman] Long crossing to second base. Ordinarily the play worked well, and was a bunt killer. But for a heady bunch that could lay the ball down right it was soft. All that was necessary was to tap the ball where it would get by the third baseman—and, naturally, there was plenty of room for this, and both runner and batsman were safe. Boston didn't vary its play, and Baltimore took advantage of the knowledge of just how the infield would work. Boston didn't win a game from Baltimore that season" (*Sporting Life*, March 31, 1906).

Sportswriter J. Ed Grillo similarly believed that the play was far from foolproof. He observed in 1908, "One play which the New Yorks pulled off against the Nationals on Monday caused much surprise in the stands, and as it was Hal Chase who played a prominent part in it he was given a lot of credit for having performed a most miraculous feat, in that he threw a man out going from second to third on a bunt down the first base line. Chase really only took part in what is known as the 'sacrifice killer,' a play originated by the famous Baltimore Club of a few years ago. This is how it is done:

"With base runners on first base and second and none out, it is almost a certainty that the next man up will bunt. The shortstop allows the man on second to get a good lead, then suddenly runs for the bag, carrying the base runner back with him. As soon as the runner is headed back for second the pitcher lays the ball right over the plate, so it can easily be bunted. The first baseman runs in with the pitcher's motion, while the second baseman covers first. If the ball is picked up clean by the first baseman, he does not have to hurry to get his man at third coming from second, for he is going the other way when the ball is bunted. If the ball rolls to the right side of the pitcher, he makes the play at third, and if it happens to be fumbled by the first baseman, there is time enough to get the man at first base, which is being covered by the second baseman.

"This play is not tried with all batters up, but if it is a pitcher it is sure to go through, for they seldom know enough to switch the play, but usually carry out the orders as given to them by the manager. A wise player, when he sees the play being worked, does not bunt, but hits, and as he has every man on the infield out of position, he has but to keep the ball on the ground to get a hit; but it is not every player who thinks quick enough to switch the play" (*Sporting Life*, May 16, 1908).

Obviously there were a number of different interpretations of the origins of the "sacrifice killer," its effectiveness, and even what the play was. Nonetheless it seems likely that these preliminary efforts were the basis of the wheel play.

4.3.9 Bunt Defense. In 1892 the *New York Times* described an imaginative way of defending against the bunt: ". . . The science of 'bunting' has been so developed that it puzzles pitchers and the infield to meet it. Since the flat-sided bat has been admitted the most skillful pitcher cannot prevent a cool batsman from dribbling a grounder out toward third at so slow a pace that he can beat the ball to first.

"The fact that the entire team in the field knows just what the batter means to do seems to afford no assistance in the solution of the problem. Thus far in the presence of a good bunter the team in the field seems to be helpless. Few lovers of the game have ever before seen the expedient which the Yale boys tried

in their recent game with Princeton in this city when [Yale catcher Walter] Carter left his place behind the bat, and, wearing his mask and pad, stood about thirty feet from the batsman, just inside the third base line. If the striker had bunted then, he would probably have been thrown out at first by Carter. The wily Princetonian, however, calmly made two strikes, whereupon the Yale catcher was forced to go behind the bat to catch the third. Then the Princeton man bunted and went safely to first" (*New York Times*, June 23, 1892).

At least one note suggests that the tactic may have been used the year before: "[St. Louis player-manager Charlie] Comiskey has another wrinkle this year. When a bunter is at the bat the catcher plays on foul ground toward third base, and the umpire is utilized to return balls the batsman lets go by" (*Williamsport Sunday Grit*, June 7, 1891).

Obviously this rather bizarre approach was only practicable when there were no runners on base. At the turn of the century the catcher's box was introduced, rendering this strategy impossible.

4.3.10 Influencing a Foul Ball. One of the more poignant moments in sports occurs when a supremely talented fielder charges a bunt too late and his only option is to watch helplessly and hope that it will roll foul. At least a few enterprising fielders have not been willing to remain passive spectators in such instances.

In a game on May 27, 1981, Seattle infielder Lenny Randle earned notoriety when umpire Larry McCoy ruled that Randle had blown a fair ball into foul territory. The umpire credited Kansas City's Amos Otis with a hit. Randle was indignant: "I didn't blow it. I used the power of suggestion. I yelled at it, 'Go foul, go foul.' How could they call it a hit? It was a foul ball" (*New York Times*, May 29, 1981).

Sixty years earlier, Eddie Cicotte tried a different method of exerting his will over a bunted ball. A sportswriter filed this account: "This is to notify A. D. B. Van Zant and all the rest of the goodly curling club clan that Eddie Cicotte, the White Sox pitcher, is stealing their stuff.

"In the eighth inning of Wednesday's game, [Detroit's] George Moriarty laid down a bunt which oozed along the foul line toward third base trying to make up its mind whether to roll foul or fair. Mr. Cicotte, knowing that he couldn't possibly make a play if the pill stayed in fair ground, assisted the wavering globule to make up its mind by scratching the dirt away from its path on the foul side and digging a little ditch that led it on to foul ground finally.

"In effect, Cicotte's action was exactly that of a curler in 'Sooping 'er up mon.' Just as the devotees of the indoor Scotch and sometimes Rye game sweep in front of a 'stane' to make it carry further, Eddie was aiding the progress of the ball to where he wanted it to travel. Alas for all his cunning, however, [umpire] 'Silk' O'Loughlin ruled that it didn't go. 'Silk' said that in doing his landscape work, Cicotte had accomplished the same object as though he touched the pill while in fair ground and knocked it outside the line. So it went as a base-hit for Moriarty" (*Detroit Free Press*, April 30, 1914).

Ed Wells reported that Joe Sewell of the Yankees once made handprints in the ground in front of a trickling ball in a game in Chicago. According to Wells, "The next day the American League made a rule and you could not do that anymore" (Eugene Murdock, *Baseball Between the Wars*, 74). Joe Sewell gave this account of the play, which occurred while he was playing for the Yankees against the White Sox: "I knew I had no chance to throw [batter Lew] Fonseca out. [Pitcher Red] Ruffing came over to pick up the ball, but as he bent over I yelled, 'Let it roll!' And he did. I got out in front of that ball with my front spikes and scratched a trench across the foul line at a 45 degree angle. The ball hit that trench and rolled foul, and as soon as it did I grabbed it. Fonseca was already at first base, but old Bill Dinneen [sic], the umpire, yelled 'Foul ball!' Donie Bush was managing the White Sox then, and boy did they charge out at old Bill." Sewell added that Dineen told him the next day that League president Will Harridge had passed a temporary rule against such trench-building (Walter M. Langford, *Legends of Baseball*, 20).

(iv) Devising Alternate Methods of Retiring Players

Early fielders, playing without gloves or sunglasses, on uneven fields, and with stringent limitations on pitching, often found it hard to retire the other side at all. Single innings of twenty or thirty runs were not uncommon. Early reporters had a wonderfully apt word to describe the fielders on such a team: "demoralized." That is an understandable reaction to recognizing that none of the ways of retiring an opponent are easy to execute.

A few fielders, however, have turned that helpless feeling into something constructive by devising new ways to retire opposing batters and base runners. These were not, of course, actual additions to the four basic methods of recording an out. Rather they were new techniques that afforded new possibilities of recording outs, and thereby saved many a fielder from that sinking feeling of demoralization.

4.4.1 One-handed and Diving Catches. Early fielders did not wear gloves, so the two-handed catch was necessary for securing the ball and cushioning the impact. When outfielder Dan Patterson of the Mutuals of New York preserved the historic 1870 shutout of the White Stockings of Chicago with a one-handed catch, one game account raved that "such catches are rare as angels' visits" (*New York Tribune*, July 27, 1870). On an 1869 trip to New York, the aptly named Fielding Lucas of the Marylands of Baltimore was praised as "a very superior first base man," but with the equivocal postscript that "his one hand catching, although more showy than prudent, is very fine" (*New York Tribune*, July 30, 1869).

After gloves were introduced and then made bigger and better, the value of using two hands became debatable. Just what a revolutionary development this was is conveyed in a description of how Lave Cross "raised a laugh at the Polo grounds one day when he reached back with his mitt, caught a high foul and then turned the palm of the glove down without dropping the leather" ("When Ball Players Wore Neither Gloves Nor Mask," *Miami Herald*, June 3, 1912). There is an oft-told story that in 1882 first baseman Henry Luff of Cincinnati was fined for making a one-handed catch and quit the team in protest (William Curran, *Mitts*, 119). In fact, researcher David Ball discovered that the incident in question was a "one-handed fancy muff" by Luff (*Cincinnati Commercial*, August 1 and 3, 1882). But the one-handed catch was indeed viewed with such horror and disdain that the popular version easily could have happened. Accordingly, the shift to one-handed catching was fitful.

Some seemed to consider it preferable for a fielder to miss a ball with two hands than to catch one with one hand. Chicago sportswriter William A. Phelon observed in 1906 that second baseman Johnny Evers of the local National League club "will be doing that one-handed grab act of his again this summer. Some of the scribes got the idea last summer that it was grand stand work and roasted Johnny. They were way off. Evers makes those one-handed plays because he can do the trick and get many a ball he could not reach with both hands" (*Sporting Life*, April 28, 1906).

Such logic gradually began to convince the skeptical that there were times when a one-handed catch was the only option available. This was most evident at first base, where the need to stretch to catch wide balls while remaining on the base showed the value of one-handed catches. As first basemen's gloves grew dramatically in size, one-handed catches made more and more sense.

The catcher, being the other fielder who was early equipped with an oversized glove, was the next battlefront. Many sources suggest that one-handed catching was introduced in the 1960s by Randy Hundley and popularized by Johnny Bench. As we shall see, Hundley and Bench did play an important role, but their contributions were not as dramatic a break with the past as is often imagined.

As is discussed at greater length under "Fielders' Gloves" (9.3.1) and "Catchers' Mitts" (9.3.2), early catchers used both hands to catch the ball. If they wore gloves at all, they sported a pair with very light padding to enable them to throw the ball. The advent of overhand pitching in the early 1880s forced them to rethink their technique, and the catcher's mitt had emerged by the late 1880s, allowing the catcher's non-throwing hand to take more of the impact.

This led to a change in technique. Some sources suggest that backstop "Doc" Bushong pioneered the one-handed catch because he wanted to preserve his hand for dentistry. Bushong and other catchers of the early 1880s were undoubtedly allowing their nonthrowing hand to absorb more of the shock. An 1884 account explained that the catcher was trying to "do most of the stopping with his left hand, protected by a thickly padded glove. Such a glove cannot be worn upon the right hand as it renders accurate throwing impossible" (*Detroit Free Press*, May 2, 1884). Bushong's career ended just as mitts were developing, and the padded gloves worn before then could not firmly secure even a perfect pitch without help from the bare hand. As a result, the throwing hand was absorbing less of the impact in the first half of the 1880s, but catching continued to involve both hands.

Once catchers' mitts became larger and more efficiently designed, catchers began to

take greater advantage of the new possibilities. Mitt pioneer Buck Ewing boasted "that during an entire season he didn't catch more than a dozen pitched balls with his bare hand" ("When Ball Players Wore Neither Gloves Nor Mask," *Miami Herald*, June 3, 1912). Connie Mack maintained that turn-of-the-century backstop Osee Schrecongost "caught 99.99 percent of balls thrown to him with one hand, his glove hand. He used his glove hand like a shortstop" (Dan O'Brien, "F. Osee Schrecongost," in David Jones, ed., *Deadball Stars of the American League*, 786). Carmen Hill claimed that catcher Earl Smith used a one-handed technique in the 1920s and, as a result, "He never had a bad finger on his right hand. His fingers were just as straight as they could be. Every other catcher I ever saw had banged up fingers" (Eugene Murdock, *Baseball Between the Wars*, 179).

Sportswriter H. G. Salsinger reported in 1935 that "the average catcher uses the bare hand simultaneously with the glove in receiving pitched balls and when he reaches for a wide pitch the hand does most of the work and, often, all of it." He noted, however, that catchers such as Mickey Cochrane and Ralph "Cy" Perkins had found a way to reduce the risk of injury to the bare hand. As Cochrane explained, "Most catchers made the mistake of using the bare hand too soon and too much. They do not put enough dependence upon the glove and they do not know how to reverse with the glove and catch wild pitches. Also, they use the wrong kind of gloves."

Cochrane's novel approach was made possible by his use of "a glove that has a funnel-shaped indention [sic]. The padding at the top of the glove is about half as thick as the padding in gloves used by other catchers and there is no padding in the palm of the glove. The light top padding enables Cochrane to hook balls that he has to reach for. He takes more pitched balls with the glove hand than any other catcher. If the top of his glove were heavily padded this one-handed work would be impossible; the ball would glance off. Cochrane takes the pitched ball in the glove and then closes the bare hand over the ball" (*Sporting News*, January 3, 1935).

In his 1939 book, Cochrane credited Perkins with having taught him "to become in effect a one-handed catcher; to stop the pitched ball always with the gloved hand, holding your right hand with the finger tips folded against the heel of the hand and the thumb laid along the side of the hand. After a time it becomes natural not to open the unprotected hand until the ball is in the well padded glove. In that way Cy and I caught 2500 games for Mr. Mack without ever suffering a broken finger" (Mickey Cochrane, *Baseball: The Fans' Game*, 12).

Further tinkering with the design of the mitt enabled catchers to further reduce the use of their bare hands. Dan Gutman credited 1950s catcher Gus Niarhos with cutting an opening in his mitt so that he could squeeze the parts together and trap the ball (Dan Gutman, *Banana Bats and Ding-Dong Balls*, 180). Donn Rogosin, however, maintained that Negro Leagues catcher Pepper Bassett had hit on the innovation earlier by "gradually remov[ing] more and more of the padding, toughening his hand in the process. Unknown to history, he helped create the 'squeezer' style of catcher's mitt" (Donn Rogosin, *Invisible Men*, 73). In any event, glove makers eventually refined the idea and thereby changed the nature of catching.

Roger Angell noted that catchers almost universally referred to the result as the "one-handed glove." He explained: "Thanks to radical excisions of padding around the rim and thumb, it is much smaller than its lumpy, pillowlike progenitor, more resembling a quiche than a deep-dish Brown Betty. The glove comes with a prefab central pocket, but the crucial difference in feel is its amazing flexibility, attributable to a built-in central hinge, which follows the lateral line of one's palm. The glove is still stiffer and more unwieldy than a first baseman's mitt, to be sure, but if you catch a thrown ball in the pocket the glove will try to fold itself around the ball and hold it, thus simply extending the natural catching motion of a man's hand. Catching with the old mitt, by contrast, was more like trying to stop a pitch with a dictionary; it didn't hurt much, but you had to clap your right hand over the pill almost instantly in order to keep possession."

Angell characterized Randy Hundley as the one-handed glove's "first artisan" but contended that "Its first and perhaps still its greatest artist, its Michelangelo, was Johnny Bench" (Roger Angell, "In the Fire," reprinted in *Once More Around the Park*, 209). Bench benefited from further tinkering with the mitt, which included reducing the padding and redesigning the pocket so that "My glove squeezed the ball—you had to squeeze with the old mitt. You became another infielder in the sense that the glove just closed around the ball if it hit in there." Bench attributed his facility for catch-

ing balls backhanded to the new design, saying matter-of-factly: "You couldn't do that before" (quoted in David Falkner, *Nine Sides of the Diamond*, 302).

A similar series of design-based improvements have characterized the history of the fielder's glove. According to Donn Rogosin, Negro Leagues shortstop Willie Wells took Pepper Bassett's innovation further by cutting a hole in the center of his glove in order to get a cushioning effect (Donn Rogosin, *Invisible Men*, 73). But no commercial product offered this feature, with the result that for many years the one-handed catch was stigmatized as a showy, unsound play. A 1930s list of baseball slang, for instance, defined a "Fancy Dan" as "a player who would rather make a one-handed catch than use two hands" (Bill Snypp, *Lima [Ohio] News*, April 27, 1937).

For the same reason, diving catches were extremely rare and required extraordinary concentration and body control. Standout turn-of-the-century outfielder Jimmy McAleer, for example, "had all of them beaten running in on a low liner. When he found he could not get to it on the run, he would take a dive at it, nail it as he fell, slide twenty feet on his head and elbows, but come up with the ball. Very few outfielders, however, could master such a demanding play" (Bill Joyce, quoted in *St. Louis Republic*, April 1, 1903).

As Craig Wright has observed, the stigma against one-handed catches reflected the reality that until the start of the 1960s gloves had to be small to be effective catching devices: "Fielding gloves really began to grow after the introduction of the Edge-U-Cated Heel in 1959. This new design eliminated the old open heel, which caused the glove to sit loosely on the hand. By providing a closing flex at the outer heel of the glove, it allowed the sides of the glove to more closely follow the contours and action of the hand and wrist. The hand could now reasonably control a much larger glove" (Craig R. Wright and Tom House, *The Diamond Appraised*, 259).

Longtime Rawlings glove designer Rollie Latina said the Edge-U-Cated Heel was probably the most important improvement to gloves in the twentieth century: "Before that all the gloves had a big, wide-open heel and there was never any actual snugging action of the glove on the hand. In other words it was more or less loose. The Edge-U-Cated Heel brought the sides of the glove into the contours of the hand

and the wrist and the glove actually stayed on your hand better that way" (William Curran, *Mitts*, 83–84).

This innovation thus made the one-handed catch reliable in a way that it had never been before, while also making the diving catch a regular part of baseball. 1930s star Charley Gehringer later observed, "I can't remember anybody catching one by jumping over the fence and it would stick in the big glove, 'cause it wouldn't. Maybe I dove for a ball once or twice, but you'd only hurt yourself probably and still wouldn't do more than knock it down. Now [the balls] stick and you can get up and throw them out if they're hit hard" (quoted in Jonathan Fraser Light, *The Cultural Encyclopedia of Baseball*, 258). In 1968, Joe DiMaggio noted that when he played, "you had to catch the ball in the pocket or you did not catch it" (*Chicago Tribune*, March 23, 1968). Smoky Joe Wood confirmed: "In my day a pitcher could no more catch a ball in one hand, with the glove on, than he could fly. You very seldom saw a backhand play" (Franz Douskey, "Smoky Joe Wood's Last Interview," *National Pastime* 27 [2007], 71).

Long after the one-handed catch became viable, coaches continued to preach that the two-handed catch was fundamentally correct. John Lowenstein complained in 1982, "They tell you always to catch a fly ball with two hands, but, if you think about it, you should almost always catch it one-handed off to the side so your arms don't block your own vision" (quoted by Tom Boswell, *Washington Post*, September 5, 1982; reprinted in Paul Dickson, ed., *Baseball's Greatest Quotations*, 257). No doubt the reluctance to accept the one-handed catch reflected the stigma that had long been attached to this style, but other factors may also have played a role.

First baseman Vic Power became one of the first fielders to make extensive use of the one-handed catch in the 1950s, because he thought it improved his "flexibility and range." He was almost universally criticized for his technique: ". . . Sportswriters wrote I was a showboat and opposing players and their fans cursed at me. Sometimes it even made my own fans nervous. I still get letters from people in Minnesota who remember how I caught the final pop-up of Jack Kralick's no-hitter: they say they almost had a heart attack because I used only one hand." Power was disturbed by all the uproar and asked his manager, Jimmy Dykes, if he should change. Dykes told him to stick with the technique as long as it worked; Power reported that he did so and never dropped a ball that way (quoted in Danny Peary, *Cult Baseball Players*, 368–369).

Detroit first baseman Norm Cash got a more tolerant reception when he began to use the "one-handed catch introduced by Vic Power" in 1961. His manager, Bob Scheffing, said: "I haven't said a word to Cash about it. And I won't either—until he misses one" (Warner Spoelstra, "Drydocking of Boros Helps Whet Tiger Flag Appetite," *Sporting News*, August 2, 1961). The fact that Cash was in the midst of an extraordinary batting season presumably contributed to his manager's indulgence, and followers are generally treated more leniently than trendsetters. But it's hard not to be troubled by the fact that Power, a man with black skin, was perceived as a showboat while Cash, a white man, escaped a similar label.

4.4.2   Trapped-ball Plays.

Researcher Eric Miklich reported that the infield fly rule was introduced by the Players' League in its lone season of 1890. The rule was adopted by the National League on February 26, 1894, and proved much more controversial. These late dates require some explanation, since clever fielders were trapping catchable balls in order to double up base runners as early as 1864.

The raging debate in baseball circles in the late 1850s and early 1860s was whether a ball caught on the first bounce should be an out (see **1.21**). Advocates of the "fly game" argued that a one-bounce catch took little skill. While they did not gain their point until December 14, 1864, they did get a concession that would change the way the game was played in the nineteenth century.

Until 1859 a caught fly ball was dead, so runners could return to their original bases without peril. A rule change that year allowed runners to be doubled up on a caught fly ball, thereby providing fielders with an incentive to catch such hits on the fly instead of one-hopping them. The rule must have proved popular, as it was retained even after the bound rule was eliminated. But the rule was less enjoyable for base runners, since it meant they could be placed in jeopardy by savvy fielders.

A game account in the *New York Clipper* in 1864 reported a "fine display of the fielding qualities of the Eurekas [of Newark], and a striking illustration of their peculiar strategy in playing the 'points' of the game." With runners on first and second, the batter hit an easy pop fly to pitcher Henry Burroughs. The writer explained that Burroughs "could easily have taken on the fly; had he done so, however, but one player could have been out, viz., the striker, while the others would have been on the third [sic] and second bases; for strategical reasons, therefore, he missed the catch, thereby allowing the striker to make his base, by which the others were forced off theirs, and the ball being passed rapidly to third and second and held well on each base, both the players forced off their bases were put out" (*New York Clipper*, June 25, 1864).

The account had no byline, but it seems to be in the distinctive style of Henry Chadwick, who usually expressed disdain for sneaky play. Considering that Burroughs was doing little more than exploiting a loophole in the rules, the language used in this account is strikingly commendatory. In addition to praising the Eurekas for the "fine display," the piece twice made use of forms of the word "strategy," which had strong positive connotations in light of the ongoing Civil War.

A couple of possibilities present themselves. The first is that the play demonstrated two qualities that Chadwick regularly praised—heady play and knowledge of the rules. In addition, the requirement for base runners to attempt to advance was a characteristic that distinguished baseball from cricket. The *New York Herald*, for example, cited the fact that runners were forced to run in baseball to demonstrate its contention that "the English game is so low and tame, and the American so full of life" (*New York Herald*, October 16, 1859).

There is of course no way to be certain that Burroughs originated the so-called trapped-ball play. But the fact that his play warranted such a detailed description, and the use of the word "peculiar," suggest that this was at the very least one of the earliest instances. The only person for whom I have found a claim of inventing the trapped-ball play is Dickey Pearce, whom A. H. Spink cited as "the first player of his day to drop a fly ball in order to make a double play" (A. H. Spink, *The National Game*, 10). But Spink provided no specific basis for this claim.

In the years after the war, the play had plenty of imitators. Veteran sportswriter William Rankin recalled in 1908: "George Wright did that trick as early as 1870, and probably before that year. Certainly at that time. [Bob] Ferguson, [Ezra] Sutton, [Jack] Burdock and others were expert at that play shortly after-

ward" (*Sporting News*, December 24, 1908). Longtime National League president Nick Young cited Davy Force as another early master of the play (*Toledo Blade*, February 4, 1897).

It was George Wright with whom the play became especially closely associated. Tim Murnane credited Wright with introducing "what was called the trap ball" (*Boston Globe*, April 19, 1896). Nick Young described the play as the "pet trick" of Wright: "His equal trapping the ball was never known on the diamond in his or any other generation. George had something that I have never seen in a player, and that was a deft and delicate style in picking up a grounder. He was almost perfect in plowing into the ground and burrowing for a hot one that hugged the earth. And you must remember that the players were not shielded from cauliflower and pretzel fingers by large gloves in those days. George's skill in picking up grounders made him the past master of the trapped ball. Often I noticed that the latter day fielders could not rid themselves of the slow and clumsy habit of breaking into the orbit of the ball, catching it on the fly and deliberately dropping it whenever they were making a trap play. But George Wright was more accomplished. As the ball approached him he stepped back or forward, according to the distance. Planting himself for a pickup, he generally scooped it up on the first low bound, and turned like a flash for his double play" (quoted in *Toledo Blade*, February 4, 1897).

When executed by an alert and skillful fielder like George Wright, the play left base runners in an impossible situation. If they chose to run, he could catch the ball and double them up. If they held their base, he would drop it and start a double play. In an 1872 game, the Empires of Detroit had runners on first and second with no outs when batter Harry Spence lifted an easy pop fly toward Wright. The other Red Stockings began to yell "drop it," so the Empire base runners began to run. Wright then caught the ball and started an easy triple play (Peter Morris, *Baseball Fever*, 290). A much later account of this same game claimed that while the ball was in the air, Harry Wright yelled, "Drop it," and George replied, "No, I won't." The runners therefore held their bases, and George dropped the ball and started a triple play (*Saginaw Evening Express*, April 24, 1884). While it seems more likely that the contemporaneous accounts are accurate, either version illustrates the hopeless dilemma that the play could present to base runners.

It might be assumed that so lethal a play would become widely used, but that does not appear to be the case. One drawback was that the play relied on the umpire's indulgence. In a May 6, 1874, match against Philadelphia, Ross Barnes of Boston tried the play on two successive pop flies. On the first attempt the umpire ruled that Barnes had held the ball too long and called only the batter out. Barnes executed the play more efficiently the next time, but the umpire pronounced it "too thin" and made the same ruling (Preston D. Orem, *Baseball [1845–1881] from the Newspaper Accounts*, 182).

Another complication was the risk of botching the play, which seems to have led many fielders to settle for one sure out. Indeed, after the infield fly rule was introduced, Nick Young contended that "The trap ball will never again be legalized" because it "would scarcely be fair in the up-to-date game, as there are so *few* players who have mastered it" (quoted in *Toledo Blade*, February 4, 1897, my emphasis).

The latter part of Young's claim seems very surprising, but he knew whereof he spoke. In 1883, as National League secretary, Young had tried to limit the play by instructing umpires to rule a catch if a fielder held the ball even momentarily and then deliberately dropped it. He drew sharp criticism for "restricting clever play in the field" from a writer who added, ". . . Such an instruction as this is a mistake and a detriment, and will lead to mischievous results. A fielder who is clever enough to break the force of the ball and to recover it in time for a double play ought to be allowed to make the play, and to deprive him of that right is to diminish the fielding beauties of the game. . . . An umpire has all he can properly attend to when he undertakes to judge of facts; he should not be permitted, much less required, to rule on the question of intention" (*Sporting Life*, June 3, 1883). Young continued to give these instructions to umpires, but all indications are that automatic outs were rarely if ever called on such plays (*Boston Globe*, May 12, 1885).

In 1897, Young cited Fred Pfeffer of Chicago as the only infielder who was expert at making the play, though the article's unnamed author added another name: Bid McPhee of Cincinnati (*Toledo Blade*, February 4, 1897). The sportswriter E. S. Sheridan similarly contended in 1894 that only McPhee and Pfeffer were using the trapped-ball play, though Cleveland manager Patsy Tebeau disagreed (*Sporting Life*, April 28 and May 5, 1894). After

the infield fly rule was instituted, the *Chicago Tribune* reported: "This new rule effactually wipes out the play of trapping the ball for a double play, which was so successfully worked by McPhee and Pfeffer in particular" (*Chicago Tribune*, February 4, 1894). The sportswriter Ren Mulford later referred to the infield fly rule as "the old legislation passed to bottle up King Bid McPhee's famed trap ball play" (*Sporting Life*, October 1, 1904).

Later, the names of Boston's double-play combination, Herman Long and Bobby Lowe, were also added. In 1903 the *Chicago Tribune* observed: "It was to handicap [the Boston] team that the present rule against 'trapping' an infield fly with a runner on first was adopted" (*Chicago Tribune*, July 12, 1903). The following year the same paper specifically cited Long and Lowe (*Chicago Tribune*, June 26, 1904). The *Washington Post* echoed the claim: "Long and Lowe perfected the famous 'trapped ball' play until the National League was compelled to legislate against it by making a batter out on an infield fly" (*Washington Post*, July 3, 1904).

So it seems clear that Cincinnati was using the play in 1894, and a few other clubs were probably doing so as well. Moreover the rise to prominence of the fielder's glove made it unlikely that the other clubs would narrow the gap. A scoop is easy to accomplish with today's fielders' gloves, but the gloves used by fielders in 1894 consisted primarily of padding. Since these gloves lacked pockets, it probably became harder to scoop a ball instead of easier. It is no coincidence that Bid McPhee, one of the masters of the trapped ball, was one of the few infielders still playing without a glove in 1894. (And perhaps it also accounts for why McPhee finally chose to wear one in 1896.)

This brings us back to the question we began with: why ban a play that had been around for thirty years, had initially been praised, and was not becoming more common? There are at least three reasonable possibilities.

The first is implied in Nick Young's comment that it "would scarcely be fair in the up-to-date game, as there are so few players who have mastered it." In a nutshell, the twelve-team league had two or three clubs that were able to use the tactic while the remaining clubs could not. It is pretty obvious which side would be likely to win a vote as to whether that tactic should remain legal. The majority might call this "preserving competitive balance" while the minority would be likely to describe it as jealousy or something worse.

The second reason is that the new approach made the umpire's onerous job less demanding. Nick Young explained that, "One of the objections to the trap play was the amount of kicking it caused between the players and umpires. The side that was made a victim of the trap play was naturally sore, and a kick generally followed the decision of the umpire" (*Toledo Blade*, February 4, 1897). Similarly, when the Players' League adopted the rule, league secretary Frank Brunell cited the fact that the trapped-ball play "has made trouble for umpires."

Third, the play had lost the novelty and aesthetic appeal that had once helped it gain support. As fielders used their gloves to catch and then deliberately release the ball, the perception of it as a "clever play" changed to "slow and clumsy." According to Brunell, "the 'juggle' double play . . . exasperated audiences" (*Chicago Herald* and *Pittsburgh Press*, March 30, 1890).

Dramatic improvements in the quality of playing fields were also making the play appear tricky rather than clever. As John H. Gruber later explained, the trapped ball had long had "an element of danger connected with it"; if the ball were to "strike a pebble or take a 'funny' bound it was likely to shoot out of reach and result in both runners being safe." But as hillocks and other obstacles were removed from playing fields, the play began to look "so much like cold-blooded murder—the runners clearly having no chance." This in turn began to offend "the American idea of fair play" (John H. Gruber, "You're Out," *Sporting News*, February 17, 1916).

The Players' League's introduction of the infield fly rule in 1890 attracted little comment, though the upstart league's umpires did request clarification about when it applied (*Cranbrook* [N.J.] *Press*, May 9, 1890). By contrast, when the same rule was introduced to the National League four years later, it was met with outrage. Many sportswriters assailed it, with Paul Chamberlin calling it a "libel on common sense" (*Sporting Life*, April 14, 1894). Fans were just as upset, according to a reporter who wrote: "A ball crowd, nor any one else, for that matter, cannot see any justice in such rules. The sooner that splendid monument to ignorance is repealed, the better it will be for the game" (*Cincinnati Commercial Gazette*; reprinted in *Sporting Life*, April 21, 1894). One player was openly disdainful, as Arlie Latham showed his disdain for the new rule by folding his arms on

a pop fly and making "no effort to get the ball, remarking, 'We don't have to catch that kind this year'" (*Sporting Life*, April 21, 1894; *Sporting Life*, April 14, 1894).

Sportswriter John H. Gruber anticipated other consequences: "The new rule provides that the batsman is out on flies whether caught or not which can be handled by an infielder, while first base is occupied, with only one or nobody out. One of these days there will be dull-headed men on first and second bases. A pop fly will be shot up and purposely missed. The dull heads, of course, will at once break for the next bases, giving the cute infielder a chance to begin a successful triple play by touching one of the runners and running down the other, the batter being out on the fly. It took the dull-heads several months to understand the strikeout rule adopted in 1891, which is still in force, declaring the batsman out if while first base is occupied with no one out or only one out three strikes are called on him and the catcher misses the ball. Many times the runner on first, thinking he was forced, made a bee line for second only to be thrown out" (*Pittsburgh Post*, May 6, 1894).

As a side note, the original infield fly rule stated: "The base runner is out if he hits a fly ball that can be handled by an infielder while first base is occupied with only one out" (*Sporting Life*, April 28, 1894). This clumsy wording left it ambiguous as to whether the rule applied with multiple runners on base, and also seemed to imply that it did not apply with none out. The wording was changed the following year to make clear that it applied with multiple runners on base, and in 1901 the rule finally made explicit that it also applied with none out.

Some have understandably concluded that the rule originally did not apply in those circumstances. The confusion was shared by umpires, with Ed Swartwood writing to Nick Young to request clarification. As far as I can determine, umpires were told to interpret the rule as applying with none out and with multiple runners on base, and the subsequent rewordings were clarifications rather than changes.

The *Chicago Tribune* reported in 1905 that National League president Harry Pulliam had instructed the league's umpires to call the infield fly rule if first base alone was occupied with less than two out if the batsman was a slower runner than the base runner (*Chicago Tribune*, August 27, 1905, A3). As with Nick Young's many instructions on the subject, there is no evidence that umpires complied, and if they had there would surely have been some heated arguments.

4.4.3 Catcher's Trapped Ball.

Early catchers had an uncommon but highly lethal version of the trapped-ball play. The early rules specified that when the catcher did not catch or one-hop the final strike of a strikeout, the action proceeded as if the ball had been put in play. The *Brooklyn Eagle* pointed out in 1873 that, with the bases loaded, "it is a point in the game for the catcher to allow the ball, on a third strike, to be missed and not caught, in order that the base runners may be 'forced' to leave their bases" (*Brooklyn Eagle*, June 3, 1873). The catcher could then step on the plate and relay the ball around the bases for a double or triple play. While the play appeared clever at first, the novelty soon wore off since this play too "looked like cold-blooded murder, as it gave the fielder an unfair advantage over the runners." According to John H. Gruber, it was not until 1887 that runners were relieved of the obligation to run on a dropped final strike with less than two out (John H. Gruber, "You're Out," *Sporting News*, February 17, 1916).

This play was almost always used with the bases loaded, since only in that situation was at least one out easy. But at least one catcher was bold enough to use it in other situations, thereby giving up the certainty of one out for the possibility of two. Bill Craver made a specialty of deliberately dropping third strikes in hopes of starting such double plays (*National Chronicle*, May 29, 1869).

4.4.4 Outfield Trapped Ball.

While the catcher's and infielder's versions of this play have not been legal since the nineteenth century, the outfielder's equivalent remains permissible to this day and has had an interesting history.

The *Washington Post* wrote in 1904: "[Herman] Long and [Bobby] Lowe [of Boston] perfected the famous 'trapped ball' play until the National League was compelled to legislate against it by making a batter out on an infield fly. Then these two conspired with [Tommy] McCarthy and [Hugh] Duffy, who were outfielders on that famous team, and they pulled off the 'trapped ball' in the outfield, something no other team has ever been able to work successfully" (*Washington Post*, July 3, 1904). While it seems surprising that the play should have emerged after the National League's 1894

adoption of the infield fly rule, that appears to be the case. Indeed, it followed almost immediately.

In a game on April 24, with runners on first and second and one out in the third inning, Baltimore's Willie Keeler "hit a line fly to McCarthy in left field. Mac dropped the ball intentionally, then lined it to [Boston third baseman Billy] Nash. The ball then went to Lowe, who touched his base, forcing the man who was still at first, and then touching the runner who had held second, completing a double play, the like of which was never accomplished before in a ball game" (*Boston Globe*, April 25, 1894).

McCarthy repeated the trick the following week against Philadelphia: "With no out [in the fourth inning], [Sam] Thompson hit a high fly to left field. Mac got under the ball. The base runners, knowing how quick he is, hung close to the bases. The ball was allowed to hit the palm of his hands with fingers raised, then bounded off several yards, but Mac was after it with a bound, and with an eye on the base runners, he jogged over to second, touched [base runner Charlie] Reilly with the ball, and then touched the base, completing a double play, as both men were forced. Umpire [Tim] Hurst, who had witnessed the same play made by McCarthy in Baltimore, promptly gave both men out" (*Boston Globe*, May 1, 1894). He turned another double play this way against Washington on May 25, perplexing the base runners so much that "it was some time before the visitors realized what had happened" (Timothy H. Murnane, *Boston Globe*, May 26, 1894).

Most journalists treated the play as a new innovation, but Baltimore sportswriter Albert Mott had a different perspective: "McCarthy rehabilitated an exceedingly ancient trick in Baltimore, which Tom Tucker announced to the stands as 'a new Boston thing, see?' It was so very ancient and had not been played in so long a time that the players had forgotten it, and it worked like a charm. Every amateur club in the country once used it—that is, when first and second are occupied, to muff a fly ball in the outfield, thus causing a force and making a double play" (*Sporting Life*, May 5, 1894).

McCarthy's success with the ploy encouraged imitators, but they usually were less proficient. Later in the season, a *Sporting Life* correspondent reported: "In the fifth inning of the New York-Cleveland game of August 30 [Cleveland outfielder Jimmy] McAleer attempted Tommy McCarthy's celebrated 'trapped ball' trick, but made a mess of it.

Clark [Dad Clarke] was on second and [Mike] Tiernan on first, with one man out, when Davis sent a short fly to McAleer. The latter, instead of 'trapping' the ball, held it momentarily and then dropped it. He then threw to [second baseman Cupid] Childs, who touched Clark and the bag and made a claim of two out. [Umpire Tim] Hurst, however, declared Davis out, as McAleer had held the ball momentarily" (*Sporting Life*, September 8, 1894).

An effort the following year backfired more spectacularly: "[Boston right fielder Jimmy] Bannon tried the trapped ball trick in the fifth inning [on August 1], when if he had trapped the ball he could never have made a double play. He failed, and his error gave the Orioles five runs" (*Sporting Life*, August 3, 1895).

According to Hughey Jennings, another bungled attempt to imitate McCarthy led to a historic trade: "It was Tommy McCarthy, a famous outfielder with Boston, who developed the art of trapping a short fly with runners on first and second or with bases filled, and making a double play, instead of catching the ball off the ground and retiring only one man. It is the same play that Ty Cobb and other outfielders have used in modern base ball.

"George Van Haltern [sic], playing center field for Baltimore, tried to imitate McCarthy. Van Haltern tried the play with bases filled and none out. The batter hit the ball to short center and Van Haltern, after faking a catch, got down to take the ball on the short bound, but instead of hopping into his cupped hands the ball shot over his shoulder and before it could be recovered and relayed back to the infield it had become a home run, four men scoring.

"Van Haltern had not taken into consideration the condition of the ground. It was almost as hard as brick, due to a long drought. That attempt cost Van Haltern his job, for soon after Baltimore traded him to Pittsburgh for Joe Kelley, a grand swap for Baltimore as Kelley later proved" (Hugh Jennings, *Rounding Third*, Chapter 75).

Even McCarthy on at least one occasion "made a bad mess" of the play (*Boston Globe*, August 3, 1895). By 1903, Patsy Donovan remarked that "McCarthy's play of trapping the outfield flies isn't done nowadays" (*Washington Post*, August 9, 1903). As the *Chicago Tribune* summarized that same year, "the play never became general in its use, because it required an artist like Duffy or McCarthy to do it and it was disastrous to a bungler" (*Chicago Tribune*, July 12, 1903).

The combination of the inherent risks and deeper play by outfielders made the play increasingly uncommon, though it did not become extinct. After Sandow Mertes pulled the play off and doubled up George Schlei in a 1906 exhibition game, John McGraw recollected: "In my career as a ball player I have seen the 'trapped ball' trick, as Mertes worked it on Sunday, performed perhaps a dozen times. The best man in the business on that trick—although he could not have worked it better than did Mertes in the game on Sunday—was Tommy McCarthy, left fielder of the Boston Nationals. He had the play down pat, and on more than one occasion saved his team by resorting to it. I recall one game in which McCarthy had the opportunity of using the play twice, and on both occasions he made a double play out of it, although working it differently. [Wilbert] Robinson, catcher of the old Baltimore team, was the victim on both occasions. The first occasion for performing the play came up in the early part of the game. Robbie was on second and some other player on first, when a little fly was hit to McCarthy in left. He came in on it, and just before it reached his hands he backed off a step, got the ball on a short bound, and tossed it to Herman Long at second, making the double play just as Mertes and [Bill] Dahlen did on Sunday, Robbie being a victim of the same character as Schlei. Later in the game Robbie was on second again, another runner on first, and only one out. Again the batter hit a short fly to left. 'You don't fool me this time,' yelled Robbie, as he started for third base. However, instead of trapping the ball, McCarthy caught it on the fly, threw to second, and again a double play was completed. Those of us who were on the bench almost rolled off with laughter over Robbie's break, but he was as sore as a man can get" (quoted in *Sporting Life*, April 7, 1906).

The researchers at Retrosheet found an instance in a July 3, 1935, game between Philadelphia and New York. The Giants had Mel Ott on first and Bill Terry on second with one out when Hank Lieber lifted a fly ball to shallow center field. Phillies center fielder Ethan Allen "intentionally dropped the ball, snatched it up and fired to [second baseman Lou] Chiozza, who stepped on second, forcing Ott and then shot the ball to [third baseman Johnny] Vergez, who tagged out Terry for a double play. Terry was in a hopeless situation for had he stayed on second Chiozza would have tagged him before stepping on the bag. Had he moved off the base while the ball was in the air Allen wouldn't have trapped it but would have caught it and doubled him anyway" (Richards Vidmer, *New York Herald Tribune*, July 7, 1935).

In 1938 sportswriter Harold Burr observed that the outfielder's trapped-ball play had come into use again that season, and noted that former Giants outfielder George Burns had been especially well known for the play (*Sporting News*, November 10, 1938).

4.4.5   Basket Catches. While now associated with Willie Mays, the basket catch had been the signature maneuver of Boston Braves shortstop Rabbit Maranville more than forty years earlier. A *Sporting Life* correspondent described Maranville's "copyrighted way of catching a fly ball. He never raises his hands, keeping them at his sides till the falling ball is level with his belt. Then he snaps his hands on the ball and clasps it to his belt with lightning speed, and, it is said, never misses one" (*Sporting Life*, August 30, 1913).

Hugh Jennings related that when Braves manager George Stallings first saw Maranville's basket catch, "he said that Maranville would never be able to make the major league grade if he did not change his style of catching fly balls. Maranville's style of catching was to cup his hands and press them against his chest, much in the manner used by most foot ball players in catching a punted ball. Stallings had never seen a similar style and decided it would not do in base ball, because there was no chance of recovering the ball if it bobbed from the hands. He told Maranville that he would have to change the style. Maranville replied that he had always used that style, had never fumbled fly balls, and if Stallings would permit him to use the system until it failed, he would gladly change, or try to. Nothing could be fairer, and Stallings consented. Maranville became one of the best shortstops in the game and he never changed his style" (Hugh Jennings, *Rounding First*, Chapter 75).

And in the years before gloves, Henry Chadwick reported that most players caught fly balls at breast level and that a player named Fred Calloway of the Eurekas of Newark "takes the ball with a spring-like movement of his hands about waist high" (Henry Chadwick, *The American Game of Base Ball*, 24).

4.4.6   Catchers Framing Pitches and Working Umpires. Once catchers began to play closer to the plate, they began to work on ways to influence umpires in the calling of balls and strikes. Umpire Billy McLean noted in 1884, ". . . Such catchers as [Sandy] Nava and Buck Ewing are in the habit of taking a ball from away out and quickly bringing it down in front of them as though it had come straight over the bag, and kicking when we call a ball on them. I tell you, ball players are up to all sorts of tricks, and nothing but the closest watch will keep us from being beaten by them" (quoted in *Boston Globe*, July 20, 1884).

The practice became even more prevalent once a 1901 rule change created the catcher's box and thereby required catchers to remain behind the plate throughout every at bat. Johnny Evers and Hugh Fullerton described Chicago catcher Johnny Kling in 1910 as "a past master of the art of working umpires on balls and strikes, which is one of the duties of a catcher that is not suspected by the spectators. The importance of 'getting the corners' is realized by all players, and the catcher who gets this advantage is invaluable to his club. Some umpires call strikes on both corners, some the outside, some the inside, and some force the pitcher to put the ball square over the plate. Many and varied are the schemes worked by catchers to 'get the corners.' The best tactics, however, are those employed by the catchers who seldom kick, and who win the friendship and confidence of the officials" (John J. Evers and Hugh S. Fullerton, *Touching Second*, 97).

4.4.7   Juggling Fly Balls. The early rules allowed a runner to tag up and advance only after a fly ball settled in the hands of a fielder. A few outfielders daringly tried to take advantage of this wording by juggling fly balls, as this 1879 account shows: "[Buffalo's Dave] Eggler last week played a neat point on the Bostons. A base runner was on third base, when a high ball was hit to Eggler at centre field. In preparing to catch it he placed his hands in such a way that the ball would rebound from them in the air. The base-runner seeing the ball caught, as he supposed, ran for home. Eggler then took the ball on the fly as it came down, and, passing it to [Hardy] Richardson at third, put the base-runner out, the latter being obliged to return to the base on the fly-catch. [Wes] Fisler once played this point well while at centre field in a match at Brooklyn" (*New York Clipper*, May 17, 1879). Eggler repeated the same play a few weeks later, causing Providence to appeal the game.

At least a couple of other outfielders perfected the play. In an 1884 game Johnny Ward "was 'doubled-up,' being caught by the old 'juggling' act, which [Steve] Brady did cleverly" (*Sporting Life*, April 26, 1884). Baltimore sportswriter Albert Mott later recalled Jimmy Clinton pulling off the play several times for Baltimore, where he played in 1883 and 1884 (*Sporting Life*, May 5, 1894). Tommy McCarthy is sometimes credited with inventing this play, but his career began too late for that to be the case, and the attribution is likely the result of confusion with the outfield trapped ball (see 4.4.4).

I have not been able to find a specific rule change that eliminated this practice, but the researcher Cliff Blau reports that it was removed some time between 1917 and 1922. My inference from this lengthy delay is that the adoption of gloves in the mid-1880s made such juggling too difficult, though Harry Hooper did reportedly use this trick occasionally (Timothy Gay, *Tris Speaker*, 16).

4.4.8 Deliberate Passed Ball. Bill James once wrote that intentional walks make about as much sense as intentional passed balls. He was, of course, being facetious, but there have been at least a few instances of intentional passed balls.

In an 1870 exhibition game, the Atlantic Club of New Orleans had the bases loaded and no outs when catcher Bill Craver of the White Stockings of Chicago devised an imaginative ploy: "The back-stop stood sixty feet behind the plate, and its face was padded, and the ground in front covered with sawdust to prevent the bounding back of passed balls. Craver had shrewdly noticed the precise point at which every passed ball had stopped, and formed a plan to bag the man on third. He contrived to give Myerle [pitcher Levi Meyerle] a hint of his design, and as the striker stood at the bat, Craver being close behind, he gave the required sign to Myerle, who pitched a very low ball, giving it but a moderate rate of speed. Purposely Craver allowed the ball to pass between his legs and go rolling on toward the back-stop. The man on third saw the opening, and stepped into the trap. Quick as a flash, Craver wheeled and ran for the ball, while Myerle, well up to the dodge, ran forward to the home plate, and there received the ball from Craver in ample time." The inning ended without a run being scored (*Chicago Tribune*, May 19, 1870).

Ballplayer-turned-journalist Sam Crane wrote that Buck Ewing "was so confident in his ability to head off base runners that even when the speediest of players were on the bases I have seen him very often have passed balls purposely and throw the balls away from him to entice a runner to try for a base" (Sam Crane, "Buck Ewing" [Fifty greatest series], *New York Journal*, January 20, 1912).

Hugh Jennings reported that he had heard from George Mullin "about an unusual strategic move concocted by Charlie Schmidt, who used to be Detroit's first string catcher. In one game with a runner on third, two out and a dangerous man at bat, Schmidt walked down to the box and engaged Mullin in secret conference. He told Mullin: 'Now you heave the next ball over my head and put everything you got on it. This fellow on third will come dashing in. The ball will hit the stand so hard that it'll bound back and you come up and cover the plate. I'll toss the ball to you and we'll nail him.' The strangest part of it was that Mullin made the wild pitch, the runner tried to score, Schmidt recovered the ball and threw to Mullin who tagged the runner, just as Schmidt had planned it all" (Hugh Jennings, *Rounding Third*, Chapter 73).

Sportswriter Joe Jackson recalled in 1911: "At York, Pa., in the Tristate, they had a stand at one time that was almost on top of the plate. . . . The York catchers studied the angles for a little while and experimented with pitched balls. Then they were ready. With a runner on third they would signal for a wild pitch, and let it go to the stand. The runner would start home, the catcher would get the ball on the rebound, and the man would die at the plate. The trick was checked through adoption by the league of a permanent grounds rule for this park" (*Washington Post*, March 24, 1911).

4.4.9 Bounce Throws. Hall of Fame shortstop Pee Wee Reese remarked in the 1980s that there had only been one significant change in shortstop play in the fifty years since his major league debut (William Curran, *Mitts*, 148–149). That lone exception was the intentional bounce throw to first that was pioneered by Cincinnati shortstop Dave Concepcion.

As with so many firsts, the new technique was made possible by new conditions. In Concepcion's rookie season of 1970, artificial turf was installed at the Reds' home park of Riverfront Stadium on all areas except the mound and the cutoffs around the bases. This was more extensive than at any previous ballpark and it brought a new possibility to the shortstop position (Lonnie Wheeler and John Baskin, *The Cincinnati Game*, 51).

Concepcion found that on long throws, his first baseman had an easier time handling a ball that bounced off the turf than one that had to be scooped out of the dirt around the base. Moreover, the ball actually seemed to pick up speed when it skipped off the turf (David Falkner, *Nine Sides of the Diamond*, 153). This in turn enabled him to play deeper, especially against slow runners, and deliberately bounce throws.

Exactly when Concepcion began doing this is less clear. David Falkner indicated that it was not until after a 1980 elbow injury affected Concepcion's throwing ability (David Falkner, *Nine Sides of the Diamond*, 153). If so, other shortstops may have tried the approach earlier, since a 1976 article observed: "Chris Speier practices one-bounce pegs to first base from short left field so that he can play very deep shortstop on Astro Turf" (Dick Young, *Sporting News*, September 25, 1976).

Yet it was unquestionably Concepcion who ensured that the bounce throw was passed on. Ozzie Guillen recalled, "One day, we saw Davey Concepcion on TV throw the ball on the carpet—you know, one hop to the first baseman. We went out after that and every day [Luis] Aparicio's uncle worked with me on that . . . ever since, I've done that" (quoted in David Falkner, *Nine Sides of the Diamond*, 163).

4.4.10   Hidden-ball Trick. The hidden-ball trick has always evoked a wide range of responses. Some have sought to ban it and others have hoped that enough disdain would cause it to go away, while still others have taken a very different perspective by regarding it as the epitome of heady play.

The one thing that everyone agrees upon is that the play is very old. Depending on the source, the play was "the ancient hidden ball trick" (*Sporting News*, September 11, 1946); "born when the game was played in a cow pasture" (*Sporting Life*, February 3, 1894); "the old trick" (*Boston Journal*, reprinted in *Sporting Life*, May 20, 1905); "the trick of 1776 vintage" (*Indianapolis Star*, March 3, 1912); "such a hoary trick" (*Canton Repository*, April 27, 1888); "the hidden ball trick, so ancient that it is not used by pennant ball clubs" (Stanley T. Milliken, *Washington Post*, August 30, 1915); or "one of those old plays found in oil paintings" (Tim Murnane, *Boston Globe*, May 3, 1902).

No one tried to determine exactly how old it was until the researcher Bill Deane thought it might be fun to try to compile a list of occurrences. Deane has become the Gibbon of the hidden-ball trick, enlisting the help of a slew of baseball researchers to document well over two hundred instances of the play at the major league level. In the process, a picture has emerged of a play that, like Rasputin, has implausibly resisted all efforts to kill it.

The earliest documented instance of the hidden-ball trick was discovered by the researcher Bob Tholkes. In the seventh inning of an October 18, 1859, game between two Brooklyn clubs, George Flanley of the Stars "was put out on the second base by a dodge on the part of [second baseman John] Oliver [of the Atlantics], who made a feint to throw the ball, and had it hid under his arm, by which he caught Flannelly [sic]." Was Oliver lauded as a bold innovator? Nope—the account went on to describe his tactic as "an operation . . . which we do not much admire" (*New York Sunday Mercury*, October 23, 1859, 5).

Similarly, in contrast to the many people who have taken credit for other baseball inventions, there has been a noticeable shortage of claimants to originating the hidden-ball trick. The only one I have unearthed appeared in *Sporting News* in 1888: "It was the late little Tommy Barlow who introduced the trick of hiding the ball under his arm after it was returned from the outfield when the hit had been made and then catch the base runner napping on a neat throw to the baseman, who would be on the lookout" (*Sporting News*, March 10, 1888). Note that even this assertion is made by a third party, who had waited until Barlow was dead and could not deny responsibility.

During Tommy Barlow's playing days in the late 1860s and early 1870s, there were a few documented instances. An 1873 article in the *Brooklyn Eagle* noted two recent examples. In one, Jack Burdock waited "quietly" until base runner Bob Addy stepped off second base, then applied the tag. The other saw Mutuals first baseman Joe Start take a more active role in instigating the action: "He argued with [Lip] Pike that he had been put out, whereupon Pike left his base for the purpose of explaining how he had overrun the base, and no sooner had Pike stepped from the sand bag than the wily Start touched him with the ball, thus putting him out, and it was so declared by the umpire." The *Eagle* commended Start for having "performed as clever a piece of base ball generalship as could be wished for." It even expressed compassion for his victim, noting, "It is not often Lip gets caught napping in this style" (*Brooklyn Eagle*, May 20, 1873).

Before long, however, familiarity with the play had begun to breed contempt. George Wright, after being caught by the play in an 1875 game, said in disgust that "he had been tried a hundred times before but that was the first time he had ever been caught" (*St. Louis Republican*, July 25, 1875). A *New York Clipper* reporter wrote later that year, "Tracy marred his fine play by a trick, in putting out Brasher, unworthy of a fair and manly player, by pretending to have thrown the ball to the pitcher while holding it under his arm. This is not legitimate ball-play" (*New York Clipper*, October 30, 1875). This was followed three years later by the comment, "We regretted to see [Herm Doscher] resort to one of [Jack] Burdock's old tricks of hiding the ball under his arm" (*New York Clipper*, November 2, 1878).

When Dan Brouthers hid the ball under his arm in an 1886 game and fooled base runner Ed Andrews, the *Boston Globe* referred to it as a "schoolboy play" (*Boston Globe*, June 26, 1886). While this may not sound particularly hostile, disapproval can be assumed in any wording that evokes childishness. The reception that greeted base runners who were victimized by the play was anything but subtle. When Brouthers caught Cleveland's Billy Taylor with the same ploy, "Taylor hung his head and walked home, nine Buffalos 'snickered,' and 700 Cleveland people said something which doesn't look well in print" (*Cleveland Voice*, reprinted in the *Chicago Tribune*, September 11, 1881).

Occasionally a new variant of the play would be cooked up, such as this one by Cincinnati in 1877: "[Catcher Nat] Hicks turned about carelessly, and, without calling time, purposely walked toward the Grand Stand. [Base runner Mike] Golden fell into the trap and started for home. [Pitcher Bobby] Mitchell, having the ball in his hand, easily ran in and caught him before he reached the home plate" (*Cincinnati Enquirer*, April 24, 1877). But far more often the play was executed in a much more rudimentary fashion.

The hidden-ball trick thus came to be viewed as a reflection of a base runner's recklessness rather than a fielder's cleverness. This perception was fostered by the advent of base coaches, since a successful play now required failure by two men. And the risk factor in the play was entirely one-sided. It was hard to give

much credit to the defense for headiness when the nature of the play meant that they could tediously repeat the effort and would lose nothing when it failed.

As a result, opposition to the play steadily mounted. Harry Wright typically took the high road and "insisted that the trick was unprofessional and he would not allow his players to attempt it on opponents. Mr. Wright argued that the spectators were entitled to see how each man went out, and could not be expected to follow the ball when it was juggled by the players" (*Boston Journal*, reprinted in *Sporting Life*, May 20, 1905; describing Wright's days with Boston in the 1870s).

Others were less restrained, such as this writer in 1894: "It is noticed that [Brooklyn president] Charley Byrne sets his face against such stupid tricks on the field as hiding the ball under the arm to catch a man off his base. He is a whole heap right about such things. Fine points of play and new, snappy tricks are admired by most all spectators, but the loggy calf play of the ball under the arm was born when the game was played in a cow pasture and is the practice of a country lout and not of an up-to-date brainy ballplayer. Of all the stupid and disgust-breeding things among professional players, this ball-hiding custom is among the worst. The man who does it should be disciplined and the base runner who is caught by it should suffer more of a penalty than the usual disgust of spectators at his stupidity. Why, it is not playing ball. It is simply horse play."

Even those harsh words only scratched the surface of this writer's wrath. He went on to dismiss feints by basemen to draw runners off the base as a play performed by "all the children on the lots." He seemed unable to decide whether the bunt was more worthy of children or women, referring to it first as "infantile" and then as an "old woman's push-pin play." After condemning these examples of "exceedingly amateurish cow-pasture play," he concluded with a predictable paean to manliness: "Give us a rousing, bustling, athletic game and all those drawbacks will disappear and the sport will be far more popular even than it is at present" (*Sporting Life*, February 3, 1894).

While these comments may sound extreme, the underlying antipathy to the hidden-ball trick was a widely shared sentiment. Bill Deane discovered that Tim Murnane pulled it at least once during his playing days, in a September 20, 1875, exhibition game against Cincinnati (Bill Deane, "The Old Hidden Ball

Trick," Mark Kanter, ed., *The Northern Game and Beyond*, 69).

Murnane had changed his tune by the time he became a sportswriter. In 1902 he wrote that the play was "not considered good sport in up-to-date ball" (*Boston Globe*, May 3, 1902). His opposition seems to have continued to deepen, because six years later he referred to it as a "trick as old as the game that should never be allowed to go in baseball.... Hiding the ball is an ancient trick, and long since barred from the game by custom. No Boston player has been allowed to attempt the trick since Harry Wright declared it was unsportsmanlike and an insult to the spectators" (*Boston Globe*, May 14, 1908).

Instead of prohibiting the hidden-ball trick, rule makers settled for discouraging it by passing a new rule in 1911 that the pitcher could not go "into his box" unless he has the ball "to render less easy of operation the hidden ball trick" (Joe S. Jackson, *Washington Post*, February 17, 1911). This did not entirely mollify the play's opponents. A 1913 note reported: "President Ban Johnson, of the American League, will issue an order forbidding the ancient 'hidden ball' trick, according to George Hildebrand, one of his umpires, hailing from the Pacific Coast. The latter says that President Johnson is opposed to it because of a tendency to delay the game" (*Sporting Life*, April 12, 1913). This rumor was widely disseminated, but nothing concrete ever came of it.

Two years later National League president John K. Tener concluded that the play was unsportsmanlike and took a different approach to eliminating it. Tener "told his umpires not only to watch the course of the ball from the time that it leaves the pitcher's hand, but if they suspect that an attempt is going to be made to work the hidden ball trick to look directly at the man who is holding the horsehide. In this way the runner or the coachers will be tipped off to what the opposition is trying to do, and the play may be prevented" (*Sporting Life*, May 20, 1915).

This effort seems to have been similarly short-lived. Even with the opposition of the presidents of both the National League and American League, the hidden-ball trick had again survived.

At the 1920 rules meeting at which the spitball was outlawed, Clark Griffith also proposed doing away with the hidden-ball trick. Griffith suggested rewriting the rule that the pitcher could not take a pitching position *on* the rubber

without having the ball to instead read "*on or near*." But this raised the insurmountable problem of how umpires would define "near."

In addition, the much-maligned hidden-ball trick now finally gained ideological support. The sportswriter John B. Sheridan contended that "The rule designed to curtail the hidden ball trick relieves the players of the responsibility of watching the ball, which is the first principle of baseball." He called it "another step in the direction of making players mere automatons moved by managers and by umpires" (*Sporting News*, February 19, 1920).

These failures seem to have chastened the opponents of the play, and calls to ban the hidden ball gradually subsided. The play's success rate gradually declined as professional base coaches became common, but some new twists were devised when gloves became large enough to conceal the baseball. Harold C. Burr observed in 1938, "Another old favorite brought forth from the mothballs is 'Frisco Frank Crosetti's hidden-ball trick. It is one of the most mortifying of tricks, yet one of the oldest, but Crosetti has smartly added an innovation. He conceals the ball inside the heel of his glove, so that he seems to be standing out there at shortstop innocently empty-handed" (*Sporting News*, November 10, 1938).

4.4.11 Catchers Blocking the Plate. The 1880s and 1890s saw more fielders obstructing base runners, taking advantage of the fact that a lone umpire worked most games (see **11.1.15**). A typical example of the rowdiness of the era occurred in an August 5, 1893, game in which the Detroit Athletic Club hosted the New York Athletic Club. When Detroit catcher Frank Bowerman repeatedly attempted "the old 'block' act" by obstructing the plate, one New York runner responded by punching him in the eye (*Detroit Free Press*, August 6, 1893).

The obstruction seems to have generally been more of a nuisance than anything else. Tim Murnane complained in 1894, "The league rule makers would do the game a big favor by allowing the runner to get home without having to push the catcher out of the way" (*Boston Globe*, January 14, 1894).

Plate blocking became more sophisticated after the turn of the century. The sportswriter Ren Mulford, Jr., offered this account in 1902: "[Cincinnati base runner Harry Steinfeldt] beat Jack Farrell's relay at least a dozen feet, but the Texan found the way to home plate full of knees, legs and shoes. [St. Louis catcher John

O'Neill] was squatted over the plate as if he owned it. Before Steinfeldt could bore through O'Neill got the ball, put it on him, [and umpire] Tom Brown called him out."

Mulford observed, "Under a strict interpretation of Section 6, of Rule 35, Steinfeldt might have been declared safe, but there isn't an umpire in the land who enforces that section if he can dodge it. The section in question says the base runner is entitled to his base, 'if he be prevented from making a base by the obstruction of an adversary, unless the latter be a fielder having the ball in his hand ready to meet the base runner.' In this case Steinfeldt beat the ball a full second, the fielder had his obstruction built and was compelled to wait for the ball to arrive to complete the play. Nice question to chew about" (*Sporting Life*, August 2, 1902).

This commentary is extremely revealing. Based upon Mulford's own description, there is no question that O'Neill's action was illegal. So clearly there was more at work here that caused Mulford to call this a "nice question to chew about."

My belief is that his ambiguous response resulted from a combination of several factors. The underlying one was that the size of the corps of umpires was increasing and a corresponding effort was being undertaken to crack down on obstruction. But with fires to put out all over the place, it was hard to know where to start.

As Mulford implied, the umpires realized that they would have a better chance of success if they did not appear too unreasonable in these efforts. So some form of compromise was advisable. That being the case, the drama inherent in the effort to score made plays at the plate the ideal place to turn a blind eye to obstruction.

What's more, blocking the plate took courage since base runners were already bowling over fielders (see **5.5.1**). The resulting risk on both sides caused it to be viewed differently from efforts to trip and grab runners. *Sporting Life*, for example, noted: "Catcher [Fred] Abbott, of the Phillies, is a good plate blocker. He fears no man" (*Sporting Life*, April 15, 1905). Thus plate blocking began to emerge as a reputable practice even as other forms of obstruction were being weeded out.

Catchers gained a great advantage with the introduction of shin guards (see **9.4.6**), which emboldened them to stand their ground against incoming base runners. Christy Mathewson seems to have had mixed feelings about the practice, writing, "Some catchers block off the plate so that a man has got to shoot his spikes at them to get through, and I'm not saying that it's bad catching, because that is the way to keep a man from scoring" (Christy Mathewson, *Pitching in a Pinch*, 267–268).

By 1914 plate blocking was becoming an art form: "There are no more expert backstops in the country, in the matter of stopping runners from sliding into the rubber than are Ed Ainsmith and John Henry, but the practice has developed in the last couple of years to such an extent that on close plays a catcher who does not plant himself in the lines is not considered as doing his duty" (*Sporting News*, March 5, 1914).

The advantages that shin guards gave caused some vocal protests. Frank Haggerty, a college coach, thundered: "Perhaps one might think that the catcher wears guards to prevent being hit by a speedy ball, but rest assured, the majority that wear them do so to protect the legs from the spikes of such men as [Johnny] Evers and 'Ty' Cobb when sliding home. . . . A man should be competent to touch the runner sliding home as does the second baseman get his man sliding into the keystone sack, and do it gracefully. There is no need of blocking the man and holding him away with your body or shins Mr. Catcher. . . . why not put the ban on whatever tends to pollute the game, no matter in what shape or manner it may be found? The shin guard is an aid to him who tried to block a man from the home plate; one who otherwise would make it before the ball reached the catcher's mit [sic]" ("Shin Guards and Armor of the Modern Catcher," *Duluth News Tribune*, April 9, 1911).

But Clark Griffith addressed Haggerty's rhetorical question by explaining why it was no easy matter to prevent this tactic: "There are two ways to stop blocking, one is to leave it to the judgment of the umpire whether the blocking is intentional and the other is to make the catchers shed their shin guards. . . . All blocking is done on close plays, and if you are going to force the umpire to watch blocking and at the same time judge whether the runner is out or safe, you will get a lot of bad umpiring. As for forcing the catcher to do away with his pads, you are taking an action that would be unfair to the catcher. A man who has to stand for fouls, flying bats, and such things as the catcher is now called upon to do, should be given all the protection possible. These are the reasons I would leave plays at the plate as they are" (quoted by Thomas Kirby of the *Washington*

Times, reprinted in *Sporting News*, March 5, 1914).

As a result, plate blocking remained a part of baseball, despite occasional laments like this one by John Kieran in 1933: "A burly catcher, encased in protective armor, is a common sight blocking the road toward the plate for an incoming runner. But how many fans have seen an umpire pin the proper penalty on the catcher and declare the runner safe after he has been blocked off and tagged? It happens once in a long while, which isn't often enough" (John Kieran, "Collision Damage in Baseball," *New York Times*, May 1, 1933).

Bill James has suggested that plate blocking is a recent phenomenon, but the evidence he offers is largely recent and anecdotal (Bill James, *The New Bill James Historical Baseball Abstract*, 214–216). As the above examples demonstrate, this is simply not the case. James may be correct that blocking the plate is more extensive now than when he was a child, but if so, that is simply an example of the ebb and flow of historical patterns. Plate blocking is not new at all but is in fact the one surviving remnant of an era when obstruction was common.

4.4.12   Basemen Blocking a Base. As discussed in the preceding entry, there was a period when it was just as common for basemen to block their bases as for the catcher to block the plate. Base runners did not routinely slide until the 1880s, but once they began to do so, blocking soon came in its wake. Cap Anson said that Tommy Burns "excelled at the blocking game, which he carried on in a style that was particularly his own and which was calculated to make a base runner considerable trouble" (Adrian C. Anson, *A Ball Player's Career*, 129). Tim Murnane's account of a 1900 game noted that the winning run had scored on a passed ball in spite of the efforts of pitcher Bill Dineen: "Dineen took the throw from [catcher William] Clarke and blocked off his man, but [umpire Hank] O'Day could only see Pittsburg and the run was allowed to count" (*Boston Globe*, September 5, 1900).

Connie Mack recommended feet-first slides in 1904 because "A player is easily blocked off who slides with his head foremost" (Connie Mack, "How to Play Ball," multi-part series, *Washington Post*, April 17, 1904). Ty Cobb learned this the hard way in his first major league game. He had always slid headfirst on his way up through the minors, but when he tried this against New York: "Stepping on the bag to receive the ball from the catcher, [Kid Elberfeld] blocked my slide by coming down on my head with his knee. My forehead and face were shoved into the hard ground and the skin peeled off just above the eyebrows. The clever way in which he did this completely blocked me" (Ty Cobb, *Memoirs of Twenty Years in Baseball*, 42).

To prevent blocking, Cobb became a spikes-first slider, as did many other base runners of the period. He described this as "a case of beating the other fellow to the punch." To prevent fielders like Elberfeld from blocking his path to the base, "Instead of taking the long slide I would run close up to the base and then throw myself forward quickly—a sort of swoop. The force of a quick swoop or dart would swerve my body around more quickly. I would surprise the baseman and get out of his way before he knew it" (Ty Cobb, *Memoirs of Twenty Years in Baseball*, 43).

It appears that Elberfeld attempted to make an adjustment of his own. *Sporting Life* reported in 1908: "Elberfeld and [Harry] Niles, of the Highlanders, wear shin guards to protect their legs from the base runners' spikes" (*Sporting Life*, May 2, 1908). Each player wore only a single shin guard, Elberfeld on the right leg, and Niles on his left. The effort was short-lived, however, and since then blocking bases has been used primarily against headfirst sliders.

4.4.13   Shortstop to Second Baseman to First Baseman (6-4-3) Double Play. The *New York Clipper* recorded a 6-4-3 double play on August 17, 1861, and the play was still considered a novelty at that time. Within two years it was becoming common, as was the case with most of the other standard double-play combinations.

4.4.14   First Baseman to Shortstop to First Baseman (3-6-3) Double Play. The 3-6-3 double play was first brought to prominence by longtime Boston first baseman Fred Tenney. Tenney is believed to have turned his first such double play on June 14, 1897, against Cincinnati. Tim Murnane reported the next day, "[Claude] Ritchey cracked a singing grounder at Fred Tenney. The ball was picked up clean and shot to [shortstop Herman] Long for a forceout, and then returned to Tenney at first for a double play" (*Boston Globe*, June 15, 1897). Tenney recalled later that after the play, "It seemed that you could have heard a pin drop for ten seconds, and then the crowd just let out a roar. It had seen something new" (quoted in Mark Sternman, "Frederick Tenney," Tom Simon, ed., *Deadball Stars of the National League*, 309). Boston second baseman Bobby Lowe discussed the play many years later and commented, "I believe Tenney was the originator, but I know any such observation will be subject to controversy" (*Sporting News*, July 16, 1942).

4.4.15 Triple Play. Jim Creighton of the Excelsiors of Brooklyn turned a triple play in an 1860 game in Baltimore that is often described as the earliest one (James H. Bready, *Baseball in Baltimore*, 7). Henry Chadwick maintained that the first triple play was pulled by the Pastime Club in an unspecified 1859 game at Bedford (Chadwick Scrapbooks). But researcher Craig Waff recently found a still earlier instance in this April 1859 account of a game in Fort Hamilton between the Neosho Club of New Utrecht and the Wyandank Club of Flatbush: "The game was played according to the new Convention rules of 1859, under one of which it was observed that the Neosho put out three hands of their opponents with one ball, by catching the ball 'on the fly' and then passing it to two bases in immediate succession so as at the same time to put out both men who were returning to those bases" (*Brooklyn Eagle*, April 18, 1859, 11). The rule change in question was one that deprived base runners of safe passage back to their bases on caught fly balls. Presumably the Wyandank players either forgot about or were unaware of the rule change, making them easy prey for their alert opponents.

4.4.16 Bluff Tags. Henry Chadwick wrote in 1867, "Umpires, in judging of touching men on bases, have to decide according to the probabilities of the play, and not what in reality does take place, as they have no right to take the testimony of a player, even when, as in this case, the base player has the generosity to acknowledge that he did not touch him" (*The Ball Player's Chronicle*, July 25, 1867). While it undoubtedly wasn't Chadwick's intention, these instructions would seem to encourage fielders to apply phantom tags.

Bluff tags became prevalent in the 1880s as a natural response to increasingly sophisticated sliding tactics. Cub Stricker recalled, "I didn't put the ball on one out of four base stealers when I was playing second, but I almost always got the decision" (quoted in Gerard S. Petrone, *When Baseball Was Young*, 112). By 1898, a

sportswriter claimed, "there are just two men in the National League who, as an almost certainty, touch their men—[Hugh] Jennings and [Kid] Gleason. The rest 'lay away from their heels,' touch at the man and make the bluff good" (*Sporting Life*, May 21, 1898).

Of course, the difficulty of being certain whether a tag was actually made could also work to the runner's advantage. A reporter for the *Newburyport Herald* maintained in 1886 that "it is easy to steal bases on the Haverhill grounds if you know how. Simply make a long slide, and the effect will be to envelop the runner and baseman in such an impenetrable cloud of dust that no umpire can see either one for some seconds and naturally will be cautious about calling a man out" (quoted in *Boston Globe*, May 7, 1886).

While bluff tags remain part of baseball, they became harder to get away with after the introduction of base umpires (see **8.1.3**). For example, "king of second sackers" Fred Dunlap "had a trick of making the umpire believed he touched runners by a lightning swing of his arm. It appeared that way to the one lone umpire on the job in the ordinary game." But when a second umpire was used in the 1887 "World's Series" between Detroit and St. Louis, "Umpire [John] Kelly was giving base decisions, and was watching out for 'Dunny's' famous movement." A couple of runners were thus ruled safe "through the oversight on Dunlap's part in not getting on to the fact that Kelly was right behind him" (Maclean Kennedy, "Greatest Backstop of Them All Was the Detroit Boy, Charley Bennett," *Detroit Free Press*, March 30, 1913).

4.4.17 Scoop Throws. Scoop throws were common in the nineteenth century when most fielders wore gloves that were not much larger than their hands—or no gloves at all. Tim Murnane wrote in 1889, "In throwing to bases for double plays care should be taken to give the ball to the baseman in a way that he can handle it. Third base, short and second base will find it a great help to practice throwing with an underhand snap. Much time is saved when the distance is short, and the ball can be handled much better by the baseman" (Tim Murnane, "How the Stars Play Combinations," *Boston Globe*, March 10, 1889, 22).

When gloves became larger, fielders began transferring such balls to their throwing hands. Hall of Fame shortstop Rabbit Maranville appears to have revived the underhand toss on double plays. A 1914 article noted: "Maranville and [Braves second baseman Johnny] Evers are playing a lot of new stuff around second. The chief improvement is in Maranville's change of style of passing balls in force-outs and in starting double plays. He used to snap the ball at the second baseman, which is risky when the baseman is running at top speed toward him. Now he scoops it, getting a fraction of a second more speed and taking infinitely less risk of causing a muff" (*Washington Post*, July 12, 1914).

4.4.18   Glove Flips. Most fielders wore no gloves at all until the 1880s. When gloves finally came into vogue, they were so thin that it was absolutely necessary to use the throwing hand to secure the ball. It can therefore be safely assumed that the glove flip did not develop until much larger gloves came into use.

One might expect that a recent flashy fielder pioneered the glove flip, but that is not the case. Instead the earliest player whom I have been able to document using this technique was so fundamentally sound that he was nicknamed "The Mechanical Man." A 1932 article described Detroit second baseman Charley Gehringer's approach when he fielded a ground ball up the middle with his momentum carrying him away from the bag. Instead of transferring the ball to his throwing hand, Gehringer had mastered the art of flipping the ball directly from his gloved hand to the shortstop covering second base (*Sporting News*, June 9, 1932).

4.4.19   Glove Throws. Orlando Hernandez fielded a comebacker in a 1999 game and found that the ball had become lodged so securely in his glove that he could not get it out. In desperation, he finally threw the glove to the first baseman to record the out. The play was understandably replayed on highlight shows, since most people had never seen anything like it before.

It turned out, however, that the same play had been made by Terry Mulholland on September 3, 1986, as this account shows: "[Keith] Hernandez slammed the ball back to the mound, and it took one hard hop right into the rookie pitcher's glove. He turned toward first base and reached for the ball, but it was stuck in the webbing. Then he seemed to panic a little as he ran toward the base, yanking at the ball.

"Finally, he did the only sensible thing. He took the glove off his right hand and shoveled it—glove and ball—to [Bob] Brenly, the first baseman. The umpire, Ed Montague, after checking the glove to make sure the ball was still inside, waved his arm and called Hernandez out" (Joseph Durso, *New York Times*, September 4, 1986).

4.4.20   Extra Glove. In 1969 catcher Clay Dalrymple attempted to keep a glove in his pocket that would supplement his mitt. His intention was to switch to the glove if he anticipated a play at the plate, but he was told that he could not use the extra glove. This seemed a unique ploy until I discovered this 1910 note: "Catcher Bill Bergen of the Brooklyn club sprang a new one at Cincinnati. When Bill walked into the catcher's box he carried with him three immense catching gloves. Two were placed on the ground near the plate and the third adorned his left hand. This glove was worn until a Cincinnati player reached first, and then discarded in favor of one of the other gloves. If a pitched ball happened to bounce out of this glove, Bill dropped it and used glove No. 3. Bill explained that gloves Nos. 2 and 3 made it easier for him to start his throws when redlegs tried to steal. He was breaking in glove No. 1" (*Fort Wayne Sentinel*, August 30, 1910).

Chapter 5

BASERUNNING

BASERUNNING is the part of the game that young children most readily appreciate, and in many of the games that preceded baseball, the bat was little more than an excuse to begin a game of tag. A good example is a description, many years after the fact, by a man named Adam Ford of a game he played in Canada in 1838. Ford reported that the first "bye" was located only six yards from the home "bye" in order "to get runners on the base lines so as to have the fun of putting them out or enjoying the mistakes of the fielders when some fleet-footed fellow would dodge the ball and come in home" (*Sporting Life*, May 5, 1886).

A base runner's mad dash for a base remains one of the most thrilling plays for baseball fans. And yet the following entries show that even this simple act has been the subject of considerable forethought, scheming, innovation, and experimentation.

This section will be divided into six segments: (1) stolen bases, (2) slides, (3) pickoffs, pitchouts, and other countermoves by fielders, (4) plays like the squeeze bunt and the hit-and-run, where the batting is a pretext to set up running, (5) turf wars between base runners and fielders, and (6) novelty plays.

(i) Stolen Bases

5.1.1 Stolen Bases. It is often reported, even in usually reliable sources, that Ned Cuthbert stole the first base in 1865. That's a perfect indication of how much we still have to learn about early baseball. While there is some doubt about exactly how common stolen bases were in early

baseball, there is no doubt that they were part of baseball well before 1865.

In some earlier bat-and-ball games, base stealing played a featured role. Under the rules of one game, for example, "When all were out but one, who was on one of the bases, the pitcher and catcher, approaching to within some thirty feet, tossed the ball to and fro, and the runner must 'steal' his next base, while the two former watched his movements, ready to throw to the nearest fielder of their side, who in turn would hurl the ball at the remaining player. If under these circumstances he could reach home untouched, he might 'put in' any player of his side" (William Wells Newell, *Games and Songs of American Children*, 185).

While base stealing is not specifically mentioned in the Knickerbocker rules, there is no reason to believe it wasn't legal. Tom Shieber discovered what seems to be the earliest explicit account of a stolen base, which appeared in 1856: "Mr. Valentine who succeeded Mr. Booth, made a good strike and reached the second base. He was followed by Mr. Abrams, a good and sure batter, and we felt certain that he would terminate the game in favor of the Union. Previous to his striking, however, Mr. Valentine run [sic] from the second to the third base, which he undoubtedly reached before being touched with the ball thrown to the guardian of that base; but the referee decided that he was out, and from that decision there was no appeal" (*New York Clipper*, August 7, 1856, based on an account in the *New York Sunday Mercury* of August 3, 1856; reprinted in Frederick Ivor-Campbell, "When Was the First? (Part

4)," *Nineteenth Century Notes* 95:3,4 [Summer/Fall 1995], 12). This may also be the first instance of an umpire being second-guessed and the first base runner to violate the precept about not making the last out at third base.

It remains unclear exactly how common base stealing was in the late 1850s and early 1860s. Paul Hunkele, a leading authority on the period, believes it was quite common. He cites Henry Chadwick's 1860 description of the catcher's responsibilities with a runner on first: "the moment the ball is delivered by the pitcher, and the player runs from the first to the second base, the Catcher should take the ball before bounding, and send it to the second base as swiftly as possible, in time to cut off the player before he can touch the base" (*Beadle's Dime Base-Ball Player*, 21).

Others are less sure, noting that while taking extra bases was common, it was not always by means of base stealing. Patient base runners realized that a passed ball would occur sooner or later, allowing them to advance without risk of being put out. Indeed it was often alleged that batters would deliberately wait until a passed ball occurred before offering at a pitch. Henry Chadwick, for instance, later complained about "the habit the batsman had, under the old rules, of waiting at the bat until a passed or overthrown ball had enabled the base runner to leave the first base" (Henry Chadwick, *Haney's Base Ball Player's Book of Reference for 1867*, 124).

The introduction of called strikes in 1858 was intended to address this "very tedious and annoying feature," but the rule proved ineffectual because of umpires' reluctance to enforce it. Chadwick asked rhetorically in 1860: "How often do we see the striker—the moment his predecessor has made his first base—stand still at the home base, and await the moment when the player on the first base can avail himself of the first failure of the pitcher and catcher to hold the ball, while tossing it backward and forward to each other." He noted that a batter was thus "frequently allowed to stop the progress and interest of the game, by his refusal to strike at good balls, under the plea that they do not suit him, when it is apparent to all that he simply wants to allow his partner to get to his second base" (*Beadle's Dime Base-Ball Player*, 16).

The situation began to change once the enforcement of the called strike rule improved. With batters no longer allowed to stand at the plate indefinitely, base runners could not simply wait for a passed ball, and stolen bases gradually became more common.

5.1.2 Leadoffs. The rules of baseball have never prevented a runner from leading off a base. It is sometimes suggested that leadoffs were not customary in early baseball, and such an assertion is difficult to disprove positively. But it is hard to reconcile with the fact that the leadoff's nemesis, the pickoff move (see **5.3.1**), was in vogue by 1860.

Pitchers' deliveries were severely constrained by the rules in most years before the 1880s, and this kept base runners close to the base. When windups (see **3.1.1**) became more elaborate, leadoffs developed in response. Tommy McCarthy suggested that Mike Kelly was one of the men responsible: "Kelly was a great base stealer for several reasons. In the first place, he always took plenty of room, more room than the average man of his time did. This counts a great deal in successful base-stealing" (quoted in A. H. Spink, *The National Game*, 103). Hugh Nicol also experimented with larger leads, explaining in 1888: "I play as far off of first as to make it nip and tuck which will get back first, me or the ball" (*Brooklyn Eagle*, March 11, 1888).

But the conventional wisdom continued to be that a large lead represented an unnecessary risk. Connie Mack wrote in 1904 that it was a mistake for a base runner to be far enough from the base to have to slide back on a pickoff attempt (Connie Mack, "How to Play Ball," multi-part series, *Washington Post*, April 10, 1904).

5.1.3 Delayed Double Steals. This is a play still in use by which, with runners on first and third, the offensive team tries to steal a run. The runner on first acts as though he is trying to steal, but his real intention is to draw a throw to second base that will allow the runner on third to score.

The venerable sportswriter William Rankin claimed in 1905 that the play had been around as long as he could remember, and it can be documented as early as 1873 (*Sporting News*, July 1, 1905). In a match that year between the Atlantics of Brooklyn and the Athletics of Philadelphia, Dickey Pearce was on first for the Atlantics and teammate Herman Dehlman on third when Pearce "thought he would insure Dehlman's getting home, and so ran closely down to second. [Athletics catcher John] Clapp at once threw to [second baseman Wes] Fisler and Dehlman started for home. Dick stopped half way between first and second, and Fisler, hesitating between his desire to capture Pearce and to catch Dehlman at third, finally threw the ball to [third baseman Ezra] Sutton, who promptly forwarded it to Clapp, but too late to save the run, Pearce in the interim getting to second." But this was not the first occurrence, since the reporter observed that Pearce had "played the same point on the Philadelphians and it was a surprise to us to see the Athletics caught napping by the very same play" (*Brooklyn Eagle*, May 27, 1873).

By 1875 the play had become sufficiently common for Henry Chadwick to chide Ben Loughlin for not initiating it. In a game between the Confidence and Flyaway clubs of New York, "Quinn was on third and Loughlin at first, with two men out, when Spence came to the bat. Under these circumstances, with the Flyaways in the rear in the score, it was Loughlin's play to have drawn a throw from the catcher to second by an attempt to run down to second base, so as to have given a chance for Quinn to run home. By Loughlin doing this and getting caught between first and second, Quinn could have probably crossed home-plate before Loughlin was put out, in which case the run would have scored" (*New York Clipper*, October 6, 1875).

The play became still more commonplace in the next few years. Henry Chadwick wrote in his summary of the 1878 season that "sacrificing oneself between first and second base in order to get the runner at third home" had been one of "the points of baserunning generally played last year" (*New York Clipper*, January 18, 1879).

Naturally, when a play is common and successful, efforts arise to counteract it. The responses to the delayed double steal are discussed under "Short Throws" (**5.3.13**).

5.1.4 Two Bases on Balls.
George F. Will reported that Detroit Tigers greats Ty Cobb and Sam Crawford used to run a play that operated on the same principle as the one described in the last entry. According to Will, the play was executed "when Cobb was on third and Crawford walked. Crawford would stroll toward first and then suddenly sprint around the base and tear toward second as Cobb was creeping down the line from third. If the startled team in the field threw to second, Cobb scored easily. Otherwise Crawford arrived at second with a two-base walk" (George F. Will, *Men at Work*, 74).

5.1.5 Steals of Home.
In 1860, Henry Chadwick wrote of the pitcher, "when a player attempts to run in to the home base while he is pitching, he should follow the ball to the home base as soon as it leaves his hand, and be ready at the base to take it from the catcher" (*Beadle's Dime Base-Ball Player*, 22). Paul Hunkele reasons from this passage that if defenses were planning strategies to combat steals of home, they must have been relatively common occurrences.

If so, the play seems to have almost entirely disappeared for many years. Johnny Evers and Hugh Fullerton reported: "Ross Barnes, in a game between the Chicago and Rockford teams in 1870, stole home twice while the pitcher was in the act of delivering the ball without finding imitators for many years" (John J. Evers and Hugh S. Fullerton, *Touching Second*, 198).

Their belief that the play was highly unusual is supported by additional evidence. In 1886, Ned Williamson of Chicago stole home and a Chicago writer claimed that this was an unprecedented feat. But *Sporting News* pointed out that Buck Ewing had pulled off a steal of home in 1885, while the *New York World* noted that John Ward had done one in 1884, and the *Philadelphia Item* recalled such a play by Jud Birchall in 1882. Obviously though, a steal of home was still a very rare event in the 1880s (*Sporting News*, August 2, 1886).

5.1.6 Triple Steals.
The triple steal is perhaps the ultimate baserunning feat. It is certainly the play on which the risks are divided most inequitably. The runner on third is naturally the one upon whom a play will always be made. The other runners, provided they are alert enough to follow the lead runner's cue, can advance without peril.

Early in the 1908 season, with the Philadelphia Athletics hosting the Washington Senators, the Athletics pulled off the play. In the second inning, "There were two down, with [Harry] Davis on third, [Jack] Coombs on second, and [Rube] Oldring on first, and two strikes called on [Rube] Vickers. Davis figured it out that [Senators pitcher Tom] Hughes would waste a ball, and as it turned out he figured correctly. As soon as Hughes began to wind up, Davis made a dash for the plate. He did not appear to be fifteen feet from the plate when the ball left Hughes' hands, and he was over the plate when the ball hit [catcher Jack] Warner's mitt" (*Washington Post*, April 28, 1908).

The *Post* described this triple steal as "something never before pulled off" in Philadelphia; others went further and claimed that the play had never before occurred. But Fred Clarke of the Pirates declared that he had combined with Honus Wagner and Tommy Leach to pull the play against both Louisville and Boston.

At least a couple of earlier instances have been uncovered. In the fourth inning of a game on September 14, 1900, with Pink Hawley at bat and Chicago's Virgil Garvin pitching, Jack Doyle, George Davis, and Mike Grady of New York pulled off a triple steal (*Sporting Life*, September 22, 1900). Dick Padden, Joe Sugden, and Jesse Burkett of St. Louis pulled the play against the Athletics on September 26, 1904 (*Sporting Life*, October 8, 1904).

The inherent difficulty of stealing home and the need of having the bases loaded have combined to keep the play uncommon, though not unheard of. Timothy Gay reports that Harry Lord, Harry "Doc" Gessler, and Tris Speaker of the Red Sox combined on a triple steal against the Athletics on April 21, 1909 (Timothy M. Gay, *Tris Speaker*, 81). On April 30, 1914, Cleveland base runners Jack Graney (third), Ivy Olson (second), and Fred Carisch (first) pulled one off. On July 25, 1930, the Athletics executed the play twice in a game against Cleveland. This is undoubtedly an incomplete list.

5.1.7   Delayed Steals. A surprising number of players have been credited with inventing the delayed steal on the throw back from the catcher. Lee Allen tabbed Miller Huggins as the originator in 1903 (Lee Allen, *The Hot Stove League*, 97). In 1906, Kid Elberfeld helped popularize the play again, and some credited him with inventing the play. But the sportswriter H. G. Merrill wrote that Bill O'Hara had pulled off the same play a dozen times while playing for Wilkes-Barre in 1905 (*Sporting News*, December 22, 1906). Otto Jordan, another player of the era, also claimed to have invented the delayed steal (*Sporting News*, January 23, 1908).

Yet it was frequently used before any of these instances. Hugh S. Fullerton wrote in 1906: "Bill Lange used to pull off a trick that set catchers wild, and it was this trick that made him the champion baserunner of the league for two years. He had a habit of starting from first base at a terrific clip just as the pitcher pitched the ball, and then, instead of continuing, he would stop short and grin at the catcher, who was in position to throw. The moment the catcher started to throw the ball back to the pitcher or

to shoot it to first Lange would make a dash for second, and eight out of ten times would land in safety. He always claimed that he could beat the relayed throw much easier than a straight throw from the catcher to second" (*Chicago Tribune*, April 15, 1906). While no year is specified, Lange retired after the 1899 season.

Johnny Evers and Hugh S. Fullerton accordingly categorized the delayed steal among plays that "have been 'discovered' about once a decade, and then neglected, if not forgotten, until some other genius brought them into action. . . . Frank Chance, in 1906, commenced to work the 'delayed steal' persistently and was proclaimed the discoverer of the play. Yet [nineteenth-century players Mike] Kelly, [Billy] Hamilton, [Bill] Lange, ['Tip'] O'Neill, [Charles] Comiskey, [Hugh] Duffy and many others used the play, and 'Sadie' Houck stole in that way with much success" (John J. Evers and Hugh S. Fullerton, *Touching Second*, 198, 203).

(ii) Slides

5.2.1   Slides. It is often reported that Eddie Cuthbert made the first slide. The origin of this story seems to be this passage in A. H. Spink's book: "The first attempt to steal a base by sliding head first for the bag was made on [the Capitoline Grounds in Brooklyn] during the summer of 1865. The honor belongs to Eddie Cuthbert, then a member of the Keystone Club of Philadelphia. It was during the progress of a game between the Keystones and the Atlantics of Brooklyn that Cuthbert surprised the spectators by trying to steal second base by diving headlong for the bag. His first attempt was successful, but on a second trial he was caught in the act and retired" (A. H. Spink, *The National Game*, 10).

The game in question occurred on July 29, 1865, but the *Brooklyn Eagle* had only a brief account and did not mention the play. It is quite possible that Cuthbert's slide was new to onlookers and conceivable that it incorporated elements not previously used by base runners. But he was definitely not the first ballplayer to hit the dirt as he approached the base.

An 1857 game account reported, "one of the Liberty's [sic], running to the first base and falling upon it with his hands, was decided in time" (*New York Clipper*, October 10, 1857). This description leaves the possibility that this player's slide was accidental or spontaneous.

Researcher David Arcidiacono discovered this account in James D'Wolf Lovett's 1908 book about early baseball in New England: "Mr. Chandler [Moses E. Chandler of the Tri-Mountains] also had the distinction of being the first ball player in New England who, when running the bases, made a 'dive' for one of them. This happened in 1859 in Portland, Maine, in a match between the Tri-Mountains and Portlands, and the feat fairly astonished the natives, who at first roared with laughter, *but Chandler scored the run*, and they then woke up to the fact that a large, new and valuable 'wrinkle' had been handed out to them" (James D'Wolf Lovett, *Old Boston Boys and the Games They Played*, 153). A similar description of Chandler's "original feature of diving at a base" appeared in a 1905 article that pinpointed the date as June 28, 1859 (*Boston Journal*, February 20, 1905). And an 1867 article noted that the members of the Tri-Mountains "are nearly all swift-footed, and excel at 'getting down' on the base at narrow chances" (*Boston Daily Advertiser*, September 30, 1867).

Another article pegged early Washington player Seymour Studley as "the originator of the slide," relating that when he unveiled it in an 1870 contest, "the large crowd roared in glee, as seven-eighth of the spectators thought he had slipped and by accident beat out the play. But when Studley later repeated the feat the daring runner was loudly cheered for what they called his bravery. While the honor is claimed by others, Studley was undoubtedly the first to slide from 15 to 20 feet on his stomach to a base. 'Uncle Nick' Young, in talking to me recently, said there was no doubt Studley was the pioneer of the slide and recently that veteran of the game, 'Ox' Bielaski, told me that he copied from Studley in sliding, and it was the study that enabled Bielaski to purloin so many bases while a player on the Nationals. In those days the catchers did not throw low, most of them making the play to keep the ball up, hence Studley and Bielaski had little trouble in sliding behind the base in safety, just as the wonderful Mike Kelly did in later years. Bielaski stated that Charley Snyder was the only catcher who could beat him. In making his slides Studley always slid on his stomach, claiming it would be going against the grain to slide feet foremost. Fred Waterman, the third baseman of the Olympics in 1870, was a clever slider, going in feet foremost, and as there was no padding in the uniforms used in those days his hips were always badly lacerated" (*Buffalo American*, reprinted in *Daily Kennebec Journal*, December 9, 1907).

Sliding does appear to have remained uncommon in the early days of baseball, and generally inadvertent. That is, a runner realized at the last moment that he would be unable to avoid overrunning the base and therefore chose instead to dive. Thus a premeditated slide may have been regarded as a novelty.

Henry Chadwick reported in 1868, "Some base runners have a habit of sliding in to a base when they steal one." He was lukewarm about the practice, commenting that "sliding in is serviceable at times" but suggesting that a better approach was "getting around and back of the base player, and catching hold of the bag as he stoops to touch it" (Henry Chadwick, *The American Game of Base Ball*, 26).

In the 1860s runners could overrun bases only at their peril, and this rule was the primary impetus for sliding. In 1871 there was serious talk of allowing base runners to overrun bases and return at their leisure. Eventually it was decided to make this legal at first base. If overrunning had been allowed at all bases, it seems safe to assume that the uncommon practice of sliding would have pretty much died out, at least for many years.

As it was, it was not until the early 1880s that sliding became at all customary, and this did not happen until after there had been serious talk of a ban. After the 1881 season there was a proposal to prohibit sliding, "as it results in too many accidents. [Arthur] Irwin broke his leg by it, and [Emil] Gross was disabled by sliding in. By requiring a player to touch a base on the run, the trouble would be stopped" (*New York Clipper*, September 3, 1881). But the "long, loud and indignant kick . . . ended in smoke, and the boys kept sliding just the same" (*St. Louis Post-Dispatch*, July 31, 1886).

As this suggests, until the 1880s slides were defensive maneuvers rather than aggressive ones. The base runner's intent was generally to defend himself from going past the base and being tagged out. Since form follows function, his method was similarly defensive: to protect himself from injury as he fell. As a result, early base runners who hit the dirt were often not so much sliding as sitting down on the base.

Harry Wright said in an 1885 interview that John O'Rourke was "the first man that I ever heard of sliding." Wright added, "Only once do I remember his being hurt," showing that fear of injury was still one of the main objections to sliding (*St. Louis Post-Dispatch*, June 27, 1885). It's an intriguing claim because of Wright's lengthy involvement with baseball and because John O'Rourke played for Wright in 1879 and 1880. But by then O'Rourke had been playing for prominent New England clubs for a decade, so it may have been quite a bit earlier when Wright first encountered the slide.

In any event, slides seem to have been very rare during the 1870s. Things had begun to change by 1880 when pitcher Lee Richmond made "an unnecessary slide" in one game because of poor coaching and on another occasion was mildly chastised for not having "made a 'slide' when he was put out at the plate" (*Worcester Gazette*, May 12 and July 17, 1880). Slides remained uncommon until a couple of years into the new decade, when Mike Kelly demonstrated the lethal potential that the hook slide offered for evading tags. Copycats ensured that by the end of the decade slides had become commonplace and had undergone a transformation from defensive maneuvers to aggressive ones.

Before the 1887 season the Cincinnati management made plans "to have one of the best baserunning teams in the profession this season. With this end in view, Manager [Gus] Schmelz has been drilling the men in the Gymnasium in this one specialty more than anything else. It has been his endeavor the past two weeks to train the players in the art of sliding both head and feet first. The first named style is the most effective, but any style that provides for the men going into bases near the ground is preferable to the don't-give-a-damn style of standing up and running into a baseman to be touched" (*Cincinnati Enquirer*, March 27, 1887). The management of the Philadelphia Athletics also "insist[ed] on its men getting their clothes dirty by the sliding process" (*Rocky Mountain News*, April 13, 1887, 10).

There continued to be holdouts, and a reporter observed matter-of-factly in 1884, "Many [base runners] don't care to slide" (*New York Clipper*, October 18, 1884). Their reticence was understandable, as sliding on fields that were often strewn with pebbles could be a painful experience. Johnny Ward noted, "Sliding for bases is one of the most prolific causes of wounds and bruises. The hip generally suffers most in this exercise. Many a player, when he gets to his base, misses a patch of skin as big as the palm of his hand, but he doesn't say anything about it" (*San Francisco Examiner*, November 11, 1888). Another article elaborated: "The players generally complain of the cinder paths upon which they are compelled to run

between bases. Sliding is risky unless runners have more clothes on under their uniform than comfort will allow. [Jerry] Denny and [Patsy] Cahill have hurt themselves quite badly in the past two days by sliding, and [George] Myers succeeded in scraping himself a little yesterday. This has a natural tendency to make the players cautious and they can not run bases with that reckless dash and daring which is necessary to steal runs successfully. Besides, the cinders hurt their feet through the thin soles of the running shoes. Those objections should be sufficient to have the cinders removed. A good yellow clay has always been considered best for the purpose" (*Indianapolis Sentinel*, April 9, 1887, 5). As described under "Slow Base Paths" (**11.2.2**), the presence of pebbles was often no accident. In addition to the pain, another consideration was that sliding created laundry bills that the players had to pay for themselves. As discussed under "Contract Perks" (**18.5.3**), sliding pioneer John O'Rourke had a heated battle with team management over his laundry bills.

But the benefits of sliding were too obvious to ignore. Within a few years it was mostly veteran players who were resisting the change and even some of them were won over. An 1886 article reported that "Deacon White made his first slide since he began to play ball at Detroit Monday" (*Boston Globe*, June 26, 1886). Another old-timer gave in two years later: "Ezra Sutton, who began ball playing when this country was in its swaddling clothes, paralyzed the rest of the Boston team the other day by making a belly-buster slide. In his long career, it was the first time the old man ever soiled his clothes stealing a base" (*Cincinnati Enquirer*, April 22, 1888). The next season it was reported that veteran pitcher Jim "Pud" Galvin hated Pittsburgh's orange uniforms so much that he was threatening to slide for aesthetic reasons, prompting a writer to quip, "Just imagine James sliding into second base" (*Boston Globe*, April 16, 1889).

Arthur Irwin claimed later that Pete Browning had refused to slide when the two were teammates in 1890 because he "was afraid of twisting an ankle or springing a charley-horse" (*Washington Post*, July 26, 1899). But according to Johnny Evers and Hugh Fullerton, many base runners began to slide precisely because they feared getting a charley horse by stopping suddenly at bases (John J. Evers and Hugh S. Fullerton, *Touching Second*, 240–241).

By the 1890s the last holdouts had retired, and sliding had become virtually universal.

Once again an exception helps to prove the rule. Jack Kavanagh noted that when a player named Hi Ladd reported to Pittsburgh in 1898, he informed manager Bill Watkins that he did not believe in sliding. Years later Ladd explained to a reporter: "I would see other players slide into bases and get badly hurt. I could hear their bones crack as they broke their legs. I didn't want it to happen to me." Watkins released him after one game ("Hi Ladd: The Man Who Would Not Slide," in Jack Kavanagh, *The Heights of Ridiculousness*, 145).

5.2.2 Headfirst Slides, Feet-first Slides, and Air Dives.
The evidence as to whether headfirst or feet-first slides came first is confusing and often seems contradictory. One reason was that no form of slide was common before the 1880s, meaning that there was little reason to generalize about slides. As we shall see, it does not appear that either approach was ever used exclusively.

More important, nineteenth-century observers classified slides differently from the way we now do. Today we divide all slides into headfirst and feet-first varieties, but in the nineteenth century the slide on the side was often counted as a third type. In addition, many reporters appear to have differentiated a dive from a slide. This means that even contemporary accounts on the subject have to be read with great care.

For example, a sportswriter explained in 1886 that there were three different slides: feet-first, the side slide, and the new headfirst dive. Diagrams illustrated each slide. The side slide was labeled the "old-fashioned method" and in it the player is on his side but with his feet foremost. In contrast, he made clear that the headfirst dive was new: ". . . The third slide and the most terrible of all is that adopted by the Philadelphia Club and practised by them this year. [Jim] Fogarty and [Ed] Andrews did the most of it in the early part of the season, but they must have noted the extreme danger attendant upon the act, for they have abandoned it of late. Right wisely did they encase their hands in the gloves mentioned before for better protection. This peculiar slide consists in the base-runner making an air dive for the bag head foremost and both arms stretched out to the full extent. In this daring act it is simply a matter of impossibility for a man to control himself and he risks broken arms or a cracked skull every time he makes the slide" (*St. Louis Post-Dispatch*, July 31, 1886). Another reporter

confirmed, "The Philadelphias have entirely given up the headforemost slide, and the use of sliding gloves. That mode of making a base is entirely too dangerous, and it is now only used in desperate extremities" (*Boston Herald*, reprinted in *St. Louis Globe-Democrat*, August 17, 1886).

The fact that only the headfirst slide was labeled new led me at first to assume that feet-first slides preceded headfirst ones. After considering all the evidence, however, I now believe that what was considered new about the Philadelphia players' approach was not the fact that their hands were foremost but that they were diving rather than sliding. Support is lent to this view by Harry Wright's 1885 comment that several of the St. Louis Brown Stockings "have a way of sliding when 15 to 20 feet from a base that is awfully hard to cut off" (*St. Louis Post-Dispatch*, June 27, 1885).

This interpretation helps make sense of an account that otherwise reads like a fairy tale. William Stryker Gummere was born in 1850, attended Princeton in the late 1860s, and later became chief justice of the New Jersey Supreme Court. When he died in 1933, a *Sporting News* obituary described a slide he had made more than sixty years earlier while playing for Princeton in a game against the Athletics of Philadelphia. According to the account, when Athletics second baseman Al Reach went to tag Gummere:

"Gummere threw himself feet first at the bag—the original of the hook slide Ty Cobb was to use later—and buried his face in his right arm for protection.

"Reach turned to tag him and had to look for him.

"'What kind of damned fool trick is that?' he demanded.

"'That,' said Mr. Gummere with a dignity fitting to one destined to grace the Supreme Court, 'is a device to evade being put out when running bases.'

"Reach and his companions were quick to see the value of the play and congratulated the Princeton player and adopted the play for themselves" (*Sporting News*, February 2, 1933).

The authenticity of this story is debatable. The detailed account of such long-ago events is suspect, and it seems very likely that some of these were added or exaggerated after the fact. (Possible dates on which this game could have occurred include April 24, 1869, June 18, 1870, and June 28, 1870.) For one thing, the description does not sound like a hook slide. More important, there is no evidence that the Athletics adopted any kind of slide, so that assertion may just have been another way of claiming greater significance for Gummere's slide.

On the other hand, the questionable elements do not mean that the account was entirely fabricated. While a slide would not necessarily have been regarded as a novelty in 1869 or 1870, an air dive would have been. So the story of Gummere's slide seems to me to illustrate that base runners' slides in the 1860s or 1870s were customarily defensive in nature, and that what was new about his slide was the fact that he was trying to "evade being put out when running bases."

While the slides of Gummere and Waterman were described as being feet first, other specific accounts are of headfirst slides. The slide described in the *New York Clipper* in 1857 is clearly of the headfirst variety, since the runner fell upon the base with his hands. Moses Chandler's 1859 "dive" would also appear to be headfirst. Cuthbert's 1865 slide and Studley's slide were said to have been of the headfirst variety while Harry Wright's account of John O'Rourke's slide makes clear that he too was a headfirst slider (*St. Louis Post-Dispatch*, June 27, 1885).

The fact that early slides seem to have been spontaneous rather than premeditated suggests they were often headfirst lunges. Another important factor is that the sharp spikes worn by many early players (see **9.5.4**) would have made sliding very dangerous. So it appears that headfirst slides were more common than feet-first slides in the 1860s and '70s, but as long as slides were defensive in nature, it was just regarded as a matter of personal preference.

That changed in the 1880s when base runners began sliding to evade tags and began aggressively launching themselves at bases. Fielders countered by trying to block them from the bases, and it suddenly mattered whether the runner led with his feet or head.

The account of the technique used by Ed Andrews and Jim Fogarty made clear that their air dives were headfirst. This undoubtedly made it easier for them to adjust and evade a tag, but it had a critical flaw. As discussed in the preceding chapter, fielders resorted to blocking headfirst sliders from the base (see **4.4.12**). Base runners realized that their spikes were their best response, and feet-first slides gradually gained favor.

Ed Williamson gave this account of the reprehensible origins of the foot-first slide in

1891: ". . . Ball players do not burn with a desire to have colored men on their team. It is, in fact, the deep seated objection that most of them have for an Afro-American professional player that gave rise to the 'feet first' slide. You may have noticed in a close play that the base-runner will launch himself into the air and take chances on landing on the bag. Some go head first, others with the feet in advance. Those who adopt the latter method are principally old-timers and served in the dark days prior to 1880. They learned the trick in the east. The Buffalos—I think it was the Buffalo team—had a negro for second base. He was a few lines blacker than a raven, but he was one of the best players in the old Eastern League. The haughty Caucasians of the association were willing to permit darkies to carry water to them or guard the bat bag, but it made them sore to have the name of one in the batting list. They made a cabal against this man and incidentally introduced a new feature into the game. The players of the opposing teams made it their special business in life to 'spike' this brunette Buffalo. They would tarry at second when they might have easily made third, just to toy with the sensitive shins of this second baseman. The poor man played in two games out of five perhaps; the rest of the time he was on crutches. To give the frequent spiking of the darkey an appearance of accident the 'feet first' slide was practiced. The negro got wooden armor for his legs and went into the field with the appearance of a man wearing nail kegs for stockings. The enthusiasm of opposition players would not let them take a bluff. They filed their spikes and the first man at second generally split the wooden half cylinders. The colored man seldom lasted beyond the fifth inning, as the base runners became more expert. The practice survived long after the second baseman made his last trip to the hospital. And that's how [Mike] Kelly learned to slide" (*Sporting Life*, October 24, 1891; reprinted in Jerry Malloy, ed., *Sol White's History of Colored Base Ball*, 140; this claim was oft repeated, with some articles identifying the second baseman as "Bud" Fowler and others as Frank Grant).

An Ohio paper made a similar point in 1890: "The Toledo men are dirty ball players. They slide feet first. It is contemptible work, and should be called down" (*Columbus* [Ohio] *Post*, April 19, 1890). While intimidation seems to have been one factor, it was not the only one. As is discussed in the next entry, Mike Kelly helped to popularize the foot-first slide by showing its potential to evade a tag.

Another factor was that in the early 1880s home plate was still made of marble or stone. In an 1880 game an African-American player named Howard from Utica, New York, was said not to slide with the customary "care." According to a game account, Howard "strikes every base head first. This is not so dangerous on the bags, but it is a little risky when it comes to the home plate" (*New York Clipper*, March 6, 1880). This remained an issue until the middle of the decade, when the rubber home plate was introduced (see **14.3.2**).

As a result, feet-first slides gradually gained ascendance. Cap Anson later claimed that feet-first slides were more common than headfirst ones during the 1880s (Adrian C. Anson, *A Ball Player's Career*, 113–114). A 1907 article also stated that the majority of major leaguers were sliding feet first (*Chicago Tribune*, March 31, 1907). Christy Mathewson noted five years later, "The feet-first slide is now more in vogue in the Big Leagues than the old head-first coast, and I attribute this to two causes. One is that the show of the spikes is a sort of assurance the base runner is going to have room to come into the bag, and the second is that the great amount of armor which a catcher wears in these latter days makes some such formidable slide necessary when coming into the plate" (Christy Mathewson, *Pitching in a Pinch*, 267).

Another explanation was offered by sportswriter John B. Foster in a 1927 article. He noted that during his playing days in the 1880s, Arlie Latham had always been a headfirst slider because of his belief that "The player who slides head first is seldom injured, while broken limbs often result from the feet first slide." But after the turn of the century, when Latham became the first full-time base coach (see **7.2.6**), he followed the lead of Giants manager John McGraw and taught the feet-first slide. When challenged about the change of philosophy, McGraw quipped, "Latham did slide head foremost—but the old boy's head was harder then than it is now" (John B. Foster, "When Baseball Was Young," *Watertown* [N.Y.] *Times*, January 26, 1927).

5.2.3   Hook Slides. Lee Allen wrote that the hook slide was first used by William Gummere of Princeton in a game in the 1860s (Lee Allen, *The Hot Stove League*, 97). But the description of Gummere's slide in the preceding entry suggests that this was not a hook slide at all.

Mike "King" Kelly is one of the names that come up in conjunction with firsts with im-

plausible frequency, and few of the claims are solidly documented. While it is not clear when Kelly began to use the hook slide or whether he originated it, so many of his contemporaries gave him credit for the spectacular slide that it seems safe to assume that at least he was responsible for popularizing it in the early to the mid-1880s. Indeed the hook slide was sometimes referred to as the "Kelly slide," "Kelly spread," or "Chicago slide" before its current name was coined.

Sportswriter Hugh S. Fullerton explained, "Kelly invented the 'Chicago slide,' which was one of the greatest tricks ever pulled off. It was a combination slide, twist, and dodge. The runner went straight down the line at top speed and when nearing the base threw himself either inside or outside the line, doubled the left leg under him (if sliding inside, or the right, if sliding outside), slid on the doubled up leg and the hip, hooked the foot of the other leg around the base, and pivoted on it, stopping on the opposite side of the base. Every player of the old Chicago team practiced and perfected that slide and got away with hundreds of stolen bases when really they should have been touched out easily" (*Chicago Tribune*, May 20, 1906).

Kelly's teammate, Tommy McCarthy, attested that "No man guarding a bag ever had more of Kelly to touch than his feet. He never came into a bag twice in the same way. He twisted and turned as he made his famous 'Kelly slide,' and seldom was he caught. He was a regular boxer with his feet when sliding into bases" (A. H. Spink, *The National Game*, 103).

Ted Sullivan added: "Many a time have I seen catcher or baseman waiting to touch [Mike Kelly], when with a lightning dart he would get under him by a curved slide and be declared safe by the umpire. I had better explain what a 'curved slide' means, as some people of to-day might think it belongs to the 'old rounder age.' A 'curved slide' is a play made by a runner coming into the home plate or other base, where he throws his body and feet one way and hands and head the other to deceive the man that has the ball as to the direction in which he is going to the plate or bag" (*Sporting News*, January 21, 1895).

Sullivan cited Johnny Ward, Ned Williamson, Jim Fogarty, Curt Welch, Sam Crane, Arlie Latham, Bill Gleason, and Ned Hanlon as other players who mastered the evasive slide in the 1880s. Another was Charlie Comiskey, who earned praise during the 1886 postseason series for "a wonderful slide to second in the seventh inning. A snakelike movement of his body twisted him out of the reach of [second baseman Fred] Pfeffer who had the ball but could not touch him" (*Chicago Tribune*, October 19, 1886).

The hook slide was particularly effective when a base stealer had a variety of slides in his arsenal, as this description of Kelly's technique attests: ". . . No man playing ball can match him in thinking on his feet. He can slide both head and feet first, but nine times out of ten will throw himself out of the reach of the baseman, and catch the base from the outside" (*Boston Globe*, June 8, 1889). Kelly's former teammate Hugh Nicol described his own technique in similar terms in 1888: ". . . Just the instant before making the dip, I look to see how the ball is coming. If it's coming high I take the belly buster in front of the baseman, for nine out of ten of them swing back with the ball, and I ain't there. That fools them. If it's coming low I go behind them and twist out with my right toe and left knee. If it's going to be a pretty close thing and the ground is good and dry, I've got all my legs and arms to kick up a big dust, so the umpire can't see how the thing is, and my story is as good as the second baseman's when the cloud clears away, don't you see?" (*Brooklyn Eagle*, March 11, 1888).

An offshoot of the hook slide was the scissors slide, which had the additional benefit that the runner's flailing legs could dislodge the ball from the fielder. Mickey Cochrane explained in 1939: "A few years ago in Boston Jojo White, a master of the scissors kick, gave a startling demonstration of kicking a ball around. He scored from first base on an attempt to steal second. Jojo was out by five feet at second base, but the infielder dropped his hand on a one-handed tag and White lashed out with his scissors slide and kicked the ball into left field." Cochrane added that White then repeated the play at third base and at home plate (Mickey Cochrane, *Baseball: The Fans' Game*, 41).

5.2.4 Stand-up Slides. The pop-up or stand-up slide seems to be one of those innovations that emerged several times before it caught on permanently. In 1887, with the slide still developing, Roger Connor was praised for the "stunning" way that he "slides to bases, feet first, and rises upright as his feet strike the base" (*New York Sun*, May 20, 1887). Another account that year maintained that Ed Williamson's "slide is different from that of any other ball player in America. He does not slide along the ground,

but when within the proper distance of the base he is trying to make, the big shortstop leaps high in air, straightens out, and before the baseman can locate him he is standing up on the opposite side of the bag, wiping the dust from his uniform" (*San Francisco Examiner*, December 12, 1887).

A. H. Spink indicated that another star of the 1880s, Harry Stovey, used a similar technique: "Standing upward of six feet in his stockings, [Stovey] would slide to a base, feet first, and regain a standing position with less effort and greater speed than any other man who has ever played baseball. . . . Stovey always wore a pad on the left hip to protect the bones, and when some twenty feet from a base he would make a great forward feet-first plunge, plowing along on the side of his feet with his face turned toward the man making the throw intending to catch him. His hip would strike the ground about the time his feet reached the base bag, and, rebounding, he would come to a standing position fully prepared to continue his chase around the bases in case the throw was not right on the mark" (A. H. Spink, *The National Game*, 186).

But the pop-up slide appears to have been viewed still as a bit of a novelty in the early twentieth century. The *Washington Post* reported in 1904 that Billy Gilbert "slides more naturally than any other player on the team, with the possible exception of [Sandow] Mertes, in fact, it isn't a slide with Gilbert. He simply doubles up and then straightens out. When he straightens out he is on his feet" (*Washington Post*, September 25, 1904).

Christy Mathewson observed in 1912 that teammate Red Murray got to about eight feet from the base and then jumped "into the air, giving the fielder a vision of two sets of nicely honed spikes aimed for the base. As Murray hits the bag, he comes up on his feet and is in a position to start for the next station in case of any fumble or slip" (Christy Mathewson, *Pitching in a Pinch*, 265).

James Bready contended that this slide was reintroduced, with a new name, much later: "An example of Negro League style later adopted by the majors was the so-called scuttlefish slide: a runner goes into a base feet first and horizontal, but in the same motion bounces up, to end standing on the bag" (James Bready, *Baseball in Baltimore*, 182).

5.2.5 Sliding Drills. As noted under "Slides" (5.2.1), Gus Schmelz engaged his players in extensive sliding practice before the 1887 season. Over the next few years such drills became more widespread. An 1888 article reported, "Pitcher [Amos Alonzo] Stagg, who is training the Yale College nine, has devised a new scheme for teaching them to slide [into] bases. He has constructed and placed in the gymnasium a pine frame, 14 x 7 feet, covered with canvas drawn tightly, and an overcovering of velvet carpet, and with its surface elevated about four feet above the ground. The candidates run a distance of twenty feet or so and then hurl themselves headlong upon this new machine" (*Indianapolis Sentinel*, March 11, 1888). Walter C. Dohm noted in 1893, ". . . While the snow still lies deep on the ground, the collegian who hopes to get a place on the nine . . . practices base running by running at full speed, taking a dive that betrays a reckless disregard of life and limb, and slides along flat on his stomach on a narrow strip of oilcloth placed for that purpose on a thin gymnasium matting on the floor" (Walter C. Dohm, "College Baseball," *Los Angeles Times*, May 21, 1893).

By the early twentieth century the practice had made its way to the major leagues, as this 1913 account shows: "One feature [Cubs manager Johnny] Evers has insisted upon is a sliding pit. That consists of a pit of sand with a regular base attached to the ground in the middle. The athletes can take a good run and slide into the base with little danger of injury. Manager McGraw of the Giants has had this feature in his camp for a number of years and claims it has helped much in developing the great base running team he has" (*Chicago Tribune*, June 19, 1913).

Branch Rickey began using a sliding pit while coaching at the University of Michigan and he then brought these drills back to the major leagues (Lee Lowenfish, *Branch Rickey*, 51, 69). But he was a popularizer of them rather than their inventor.

(iii) Stop, Thief!: Pickoffs, Pitchouts, and Other Countermoves by the Defense

5.3.1 Pickoff Moves. The development of pickoff moves is nearly as old as pitching itself, as is shown by a provision in the 1858 rules that "whenever the pitcher draws back his hand, or moves with the apparent purpose or pretension to deliver the ball, he shall so deliver it." Early pitchers earned praise for their skill in "watch-ing the bases" and in catching runners "napping" (*Brooklyn Eagle*, October 30, 1860).

Pitchers also began to coordinate their efforts with teammates, as is shown by a report of an 1866 match that gushed: "Never was better work done by the pitcher, catcher, and [first] baseman than by the Detroit nine." When a base runner named C. J. McNally reached first base in the sixth inning, the teamwork of pitcher Henry Burroughs, catcher Frank Phelps, and first baseman John Clark "excited intense interest. McNally endeavored to 'steal,' but he was so closely watched that he dared not move his length from the base. The ball would pass with the rapidity of a cannon shot from the hands of Burroughs to Phelps, who stood close to the batsman and received it firmly in his hands, and if McNally was off the base the ball would fly to Clark so quick that one would think it had actually bounded from Phelps' hands in that direction. Clark caught it with the same precision, and not merely caught it, but with the same motion brought it in contact with McNally. The latter soon learned not to leave his base further than his length, and as soon as he saw Burroughs or Phelps make the least motion towards the base, he would drop flat with his hands on it. This interesting scene was finally brought to a close by Burroughs getting the ball into Clark quicker than McNally could drop, and thus putting him out" (*Detroit Advertiser and Tribune*, July 3, 1866).

Burroughs was a transplanted Easterner, and Midwestern observers were impressed by how he "springs from most perfect repose to lightning like pitching, which makes the bases look sharp" (*Chicago Times*, reprinted in the *Detroit Free Press*, June 30, 1866). Others were soon imitating him, such as a Kalamazoo pitcher named J. Ezra White, whose "pitching excited many comments, as it is different from anything we ever saw in that line. He stands squarely, facing the striker, both feet on a line parallel with the striker's position, and so that he can keep a watchful eye on first base, as many know to their sorrow. Many come to grief in attempting to steal bases, but White makes no preliminary movement in delivery before the ball leaves his hand, and the other players feared a throw from [catcher Jerome] Trowbridge" (*Detroit Advertiser and Tribune*, July 16, 1866).

Pitchers did not always earn such commendation for such attentiveness. Henry Chadwick grumbled in 1867, "The Rose Hill pitcher . . .

has an objectionable habit of throwing to bases, which in this game delayed it nearly an hour. Not one time out of twenty does this style of play succeed, wild throwing generally giving men their bases ten times where one is caught napping; besides which, it ought never to be attempted unless by signal from the catcher" (*The Ball Player's Chronicle*, June 20, 1867).

Although these comments show that the pickoff move was established very early, a distinction must be noted. Since underhand pitching and one-step deliveries were mandated, pickoff moves did not have to simulate the windup, which meant that much of the interplay that now exists between pitchers and base runners did not exist. Most base runners began to take modest leads, and pickoff tosses accordingly became scarce in the 1870s. Chadwick was only overstating the case a little when he wrote in 1881: "Throwing to first base to catch a runner napping was a frequent thing in the old days—now it is justly regarded as a play of only exceptional occurrence" (*New York Clipper*, January 22, 1881).

Then overhand pitching (1.33) and windups (3.1.1) came into vogue. Base runners had a brand-new opportunity and pitchers had a whole new problem. If a base runner broke with the pitcher's first motion, the catcher had very little chance to throw him out. The only way to combat this was with a windup that kept the batter guessing as to where the throw was going. Perhaps the most extreme approach was employed by Philadelphia's Con Murphy. Although Murphy was a right-hander, with a runner on first he stood facing the base runner until he suddenly pivoted and threw to the plate (*St. Louis Post-Dispatch*, September 24, 1884).

While the first truly deceptive pickoff move of the windup era is a subjective issue, there is a surprisingly firm consensus as to the man who deserves credit. The name that invariably is cited is left-hander Matt Kilroy. Ernest Lanigan wrote that "Matt was the best man in the country at picking men off base. It was suicide to take a lead of more than a foot off first" (Ernest Lanigan, *The Baseball Cyclopedia*, 86).

Sportswriter William Rankin noted that Kilroy "made the same step forward as though he was going to pitch, but would shoot the ball underhanded to first base, instead of 'putting it over the plate.' . . . A base runner had no more chance than has one when the baseman hides the ball. . . . Tim Keefe introduced the trick in the National League during the summer of 1886, I think it was, but being right-handed,

he could not do it as cleverly as Kilroy did, but he got away with it for a while, and then there was such a grand howl over it that umpires were instructed to call it a balk. After Kilroy had 'turned his trick' at old Washington Park, I went to [Brooklyn owners Charles Byrne and Joseph Doyle] and showed them how it was done and told them that the base runner had no chance what ever, and they made a fight against it" (*Sporting News*, September 2, 1909).

Kilroy explained to Christy Mathewson how he developed his move: "I practised looking at the home plate stone and throwing at first base with a snap of the wrist and without moving my feet. It was stare steady at the batter, then the arm up to about my ear, and zip, with a twist of the wrist at first base, and you've got him!" (Christy Mathewson, *Pitching in a Pinch*, 224).

Sportswriter J. C. Kofoed claimed that Kilroy and Nick Altrock, another left-hander, were the first pitchers to develop deliveries so deceptive that base runners "had no idea whether the ball was going to home or to the plate" (*Sporting News*, December 8, 1921).

5.3.2   Ambidextrous Pickoffs. This tactic was surprisingly frequent in the days before it was common for pitchers to wear gloves. An 1867 account noted, "Schomp's pitching is worthy of notice, as he pitches with his right hand and throws with his left to second base without moving in his position" (*The Ball Player's Chronicle*, June 20, 1867). It was reported in 1886 that right-hander Icebox Chamberlain threw left-handed to first base on pickoffs (*The Official Baseball Record*, September 20, 1886). Cliff Blau found an 1889 account that claimed that John Sowders had pitched left-handed while in the minors but made pickoff throws to first right-handed (*Sporting Life*, June 19, 1889).

David Nemec claimed that Tony Mullane sometimes carried this tactic still further, by hiding "his hands behind his back as he began his delivery, keeping a batter guessing until the last instant as to which arm would launch the ball" (David Nemec, *The Beer and Whisky League*, 130). In 1887 this tactic was eliminated by a new rule mandating that the pitcher "hold the ball, before the delivery, fairly in front of his body, and in sight of the Umpire."

5.3.3   Pickoffs at Second. The preceding entry included a description of an 1867 pitcher who used his nonthrowing hand to try to nab base runners at second base. Pickoffs were clearly established by that year, as Henry Chadwick observed a couple of weeks later: ". . . Not being aware of a sharp dodge which [Phonney] Martin plays to perfection, [base runner Crawford] was caught napping between second and third. The way of it was this: Martin would take his position facing the striker, as if to pitch, but without making any movement to deliver, would suddenly turn and face the second baseman, and nearly every time would catch the base runner off his base by the rapidity with which he would turn and throw the ball to second" (*The Ball Player's Chronicle*, July 4, 1867).

5.3.4   Seesaw Play. Once the shortstop began to share responsibilities for covering second base (see **4.2.6**), a runner at that bag was placed in a uniquely vulnerable position of being outnumbered by the enemy. His peril was increased by his status as the only base runner without a coach in the immediate vicinity to alert him to danger.

Harvard seems to have been the first club to begin systematically to exploit this weakness with "a trick" designed "to confuse the player who may be stealing from second to third base. . . . The player who has succeeded in reaching second base, on seeing that baseman step back to his usual position, about ten feet back of the base line, steals several feet down the path toward third. When he is about in front of the short stop that player makes a dash toward second base, which causes the runner to dart in that direction also, but the short stop's run is only a feint, and the runner, on seeing the short stop stop, also stops before reaching second, and the pitcher throws the ball to the second baseman, who is on base, and whom the runner has entirely forgotten, and the runner is out" (*New York Sun*, April 26, 1889).

As runners became more alert to this play, defensive players varied the method of attack. Dudley Dean of Harvard explained in 1892: "The see-saw play is sometimes well worked by short and second, the runner being caught by a sharp throw by the pitcher to one of the fielders mentioned when the runner's attention is diverted by the movements of the other" (syndicated article, *Atlanta Constitution*, June 5, 1892). Even when the seesaw play did not result in a pickoff, it could still benefit the defense by keeping a base runner closer to second base.

5.3.5   Pickoffs with Second Baseman Covering First. The seesaw play was effective because

of the vulnerability of the outnumbered runner at second base. It was not long before defenses began to experiment with plays that would extend this principle to other bases.

Sporting Life's Pittsburgh correspondent reported in 1905: ". . . The Boston team worked a pretty fair trick here last season and one that looked to have some earmarks of newness at least. [Ed] Phelps was on first base. [Boston first baseman Fred] Tenney, after a few maneuvers to hold Phelps to the bag, pretended not to pay any attention to him and with the pitch started to 'run in' as if expecting the batsman to bunt the ball. Phelps, thus taken off his guard, began to assume a large lead for second base. Tenney again started to 'run in.' The next pitch was a wide one. Suddenly the catcher shot the ball to first base. [Second baseman Fred] Raymer had run up to the bag without Phelps' knowledge. He caught the ball, blocked Phelps off the base and had him out by two yards" (*Sporting Life*, June 24, 1905).

5.3.6   Pickoffs with an Outfielder Covering Second. Already double-teamed on pickoff plays, runners on second base were occasionally victimized by the appearance of a third fielder. On Decoration Day in 1887, New York outfielder George Gore sneaked in on an unsuspecting runner at second base and Tim Keefe threw to Gore for the pickoff (*Cleveland Leader and Herald*, June 5, 1887). Johnny Evers and Hugh Fullerton reported that Chicago infielders Bill Dahlen and Bill Eagan would sometimes run a variation on the seesaw play in which center fielder Bill Lange would sneak in to apply the coup de grâce (John J. Evers and Hugh S. Fullerton, *Touching Second*, 216–217; Eagan had only a very short career with Chicago, so they may be mistaken about that part of their account).

Brooklyn center fielder Hi Myers provided a spectacular example in a game against the Cardinals on July 24, 1915. The game was tied in the ninth inning, but St. Louis had loaded the bases with only one out. Dodgers pitcher Sherrod Smith was engaged in a mound conference with several teammates when "Hi Myers ambled up from center as if to lend a hand to the discussion. He was within a few feet of second, and [Art] Butler, who held the bag, was paying no attention to him, nor were the coaches more wide awake, when Smith received the signal from Otto Miller to throw. Sherrod threw. He wheeled and let the ball go to second, leaving the rest up to Myers. It was a good heave. Myers grabbed the throw and tagged Butler, the while the other Cardinals were so astounded they never made a move." Smith retired the next batter and Brooklyn won the game in the tenth (*Brooklyn Eagle*, July 25, 1915).

Retrosheet uncovered another instance of this play in a game on September 13, 1949, with the Red Sox hosting the Tigers. Johnny Pesky was on second base with two out in the third inning when Detroit center fielder Hoot Evers sneaked in behind him to begin a 1-8-5 pickoff.

Center fielders also occasionally covered second base on bunt plays. Tris Speaker was renowned for playing a shallow center field and he took advantage of this to record a putout at second base in a game on May 2, 1919. Detroit's Ira Flagstead had advanced from first to second on a bunt and, with the infielders in motion and no one apparently covering second, he rounded the base. But Speaker sneaked in behind him and took a snap throw to record the out (*Detroit Free Press*, May 3, 1919).

5.3.7   Fake to Third, Throw to First Pickoffs.
This pickoff play is used with runners on first and third. It takes advantage of the fact that pitchers cannot fake a throw to first without being called for a balk, but can do so at other bases. Accordingly, the pitcher fakes a throw to third, then wheels and throws to first.

This tactic has become common only in recent years, and 1970s pitcher Steve Busby is credited with inventing or at least popularizing it—Jerry Remy states that Busby used it to pick him off during his major league debut on April 7, 1975 (Jerry Remy, *Watching Baseball*, 173). It is much maligned for the ostensible reason that it rarely appears to work. Tim McCarver, for example, complained that it is successful "as often as the sun rises in the west" (Tim McCarver with Danny Peary, *Tim McCarver's Baseball for Brain Surgeons and Other Fans*, 300).

There are of course exceptions, but there is no disputing that the play rarely yields a pickoff. But critics overlook the main purpose: to keep the runner on first close to the base and prevent him from breaking with the pitcher's first move. Remy attests, "The next time I was on first base with a runner on third, I took a lead of about six inches." The play not only accomplishes that goal, but it does so without the risk of a wild throw that sometimes accompanies a pickoff attempt.

Perhaps that lack of risk explains why this play is so frequently and roundly condemned

by announcers and fans. Their displeasure is likely with the unfairness of the play, since the defense gains an advantage—albeit a small one—without any corresponding risk.

5.3.8   Pickoffs by Relay.
In 1900, Arlie Latham attributed to Mike Kelly another play that used a base runner's aggressiveness against him. With Kelly catching and runners on second and third, "I've seen him whip the ball to third. That baseman would pay no attention to the runner at his bag, but relay the ball to second, and nine times out of ten the fellow at that base would be caught off his balance." Latham claimed that the play "rarely failed to land one man" (*Sporting Life*, December 15, 1900).

5.3.9   Pitching from the Stretch.
Until the late 1880s, pitchers worked under restrictions that precluded elaborate windups. Once windups (see 3.1.1) became legal, pitchers immediately began to use simpler deliveries when there were runners on base.

Pitcher Tim Keefe counseled in 1889, "When the bases are occupied by a base runner, the pitcher should shorten and quicken his delivery, so as to enable the catcher to dispose of the base runner in his attempt to steal a base, in case he should run" (*Sporting Times*, reprinted in the *Cleveland Plain Dealer*, May 19, 1889). A newspaper account that year observed: "[Bert] Cunningham, Baltimore's clever little pitcher, still does the 'wind-the-clock act' while delivering the ball when none of the bases are occupied" (*New York Sun*, April 30, 1889).

5.3.10   Slide Steps.
The slide step became a standard part of the pitcher's repertoire in the 1960s in the wake of the revival of the stolen base. But there were forerunners of the slide step among the first wave of sophisticated pickoff moves that were developed in the late 1880s. In 1891 the *Williamsport Sunday Grit* gave this description of Pud Galvin's move to first: "Galvin is a short and rather fat old fellow, and the balk, or rather half-balk, by which he has caught many a good base-runner napping at first, consists of a jumping-jack movement which seems to be perpetual to the old fellow. The minute he steps in the box the movement commences. He always looks as if he were just ready to deliver the ball. He starts with a half-drop of his legs and forward movement of his body without removing one foot from the box. The runner takes a good lead off first. Then, with a smile that is childlike and bland,

the veteran shoots the ball over to first and catches his man. Captains kick and claim that it is a balk, but Galvin gets right back at them and the best of the argument by claiming and proving that the movement is his natural one in the box" (*Williamsport Sunday Grit*, June 14, 1891). While this is less sophisticated than today's slide step, it does seem to include some of the key elements.

5.3.11   Pitchouts. The tactic of "Getting Batters to Chase" (3.3.1) often functioned as a pitchout. For example, in 1860 Henry Chadwick wrote, "We would suggest to the Catcher the avoidance of the boyish practice [of] passing the ball to and from the pitcher when a player is on the first base . . . a feature of the game that is a tiresome one" (*Beadle's Dime Base Ball Book*, 21). This tactic of throwing wide pitches to deter base stealing became impractical when called balls (1.10) were added to the rule book four years later.

In an 1874 game against the Atlantics of Brooklyn, Mutuals batter Jack Burdock "in the seventh was guilty of a very unfair piece of play in attempting to strike at a ball entirely out of his reach in order to keep [Atlantics catcher Jack] Farrow from throwing out [base runner Candy] Nelson trying to steal. For this he should have been declared out by umpire Allison but the umpire not being conversant with the rules, he wasn't" (reprinted in Preston D. Orem, *Baseball [1845–1881] from the Newspaper Accounts*, 185). But as a sportswriter explained two decades later, in the 1880s "the catchers did not purposely have the pitchers waste the ball to get a clear throw, as they do now" (*Washington Post*, September 19, 1909, S3).

During the 1890s the overt pitchout became more common. Catcher Heinie Peitz explained in 1894: "If I am reasonably sure that an attempt to steal will be made on the next pitched ball, I signal for a high straight ball to the right of the plate if the batter is right-handed, and to the left if he is a south-paw, and if my throw is accurate and my pitcher has not allowed him to get too much of a start, I'll nip my man every time" (*St. Louis Post-Dispatch*, September 23, 1894).

The popularity of this stratagem increased greatly after the turn of the century. *Sporting Life*'s Chicago correspondent reported in 1902: "In the New York games here it got so that after every runner got to first [Giants catcher Frank] Bowerman leaned far out on the next ball thrown, and called for a wide one, so as

to nip the expected steal" (*Sporting Life*, May 17, 1902). When Cy Young coached at Mercer University in Georgia in 1903, he taught the pitchout to the students, which was said to be new to the region (Reed Browning, *Cy Young*, 125).

It took very little time before the strategy spread more widely. Deacon Phillippe explained in 1904 that with the hit-and-run on, "the pitcher's play is to deliver the ball so far from the plate that the batter cannot possibly hit it and at the right height to enable the catcher to make a quick throw to second" (Deacon Phillippe, "Phillippe of Pittsburg Team Discusses Requirements of Successful Pitchers," *Syracuse Post Standard*, March 27, 1904).

Later that season the *Washington Post* observed, "Pitchers are so skillful these days that when a batter reaches first base one or two balls may be thrown wide to the succeeding batsmen at times when the twirler believes the base runner is going to try to steal. Throwing the ball wide gives the catcher the chance to receive the ball and throw it to second base without being compelled to straighten out for the throw or side step the batter, who usually attempts to block a throw through a little trickery" (*Washington Post*, September 10, 1904).

Pitchouts became increasingly commonplace, as is shown by sportswriter J. Ed Grillo's description in 1908: "A good catcher must, of course, be a good receiver and thrower, but it is with men on bases that a catcher is required to display judgment. He must know the game and realize when his opponents are going to do a certain thing and block their play. The hit and run game, for instance, can only be broken up by the catcher. He must know when the base runner is going to steal, and in order to prevent the batsman from helping the runner, he wastes the ball, which means to have the pitcher pitch it out of reach of the batsman, so that he cannot hit and at the same time gives the catcher a clear throw to second or third, as the case may be" (*Washington Post*, April 25, 1908).

Many came to believe that pitchouts (or "waste balls") were being overused. Umpire Billy Evans observed in 1917: "If the opposition is standing flatfooted almost every time the catcher calls for the waste ball, it works to the disadvantage of the team in the field, because it has the pitcher constantly in the hole. There is a major league catcher who is known as the 'waste ball king.' He has a wonderful throwing arm and is proud of it. It gives him pain any time a runner steals a base. With his marvelous whip he really never need call for a waste ball. However, he likes to turn them back a mile, and the players know it. When a runner reaches first all he need do is to take a good lead, and it is a good bet the catcher will call for a waste. The theory on which the opposing players work is that the first two balls are almost certain to be waste balls, if the runner has any reputation for speed. It can easily be seen what a load it makes for the pitcher" (Billy Evans, "Catcher Can Make or Break a Club," *Philadelphia Inquirer*, January 21, 1917).

5.3.12 Spontaneous Pitchouts.

In 2000, *Sports Illustrated* reported on an innovative new version of the pitchout: "Padres catcher Carlos Hernandez has found a way to make up for righthander Stan Spencer's glacial move to the plate, against which the Marlins stole 10 bases on May 18. Hernandez told Spencer about a trick he learned while playing winter ball with former major league pitcher Urbano Lugo five years ago: When the catcher sees the runner take off, he jumps from behind the plate as if expecting a pitchout. Whereupon the pitcher throws a fastball, regardless of what was called. The tactic worked in Spencer's next start, against the Mets, when Hernandez gunned down Edgardo Alfonzo in the first inning. Alfonzo was the last Met to try to steal in that game" (*Sports Illustrated*, June 5, 2000).

5.3.13 Short Throws.

The use of the short throw to defend against delayed double steals (see 5.1.3) was already well known by 1874 when Henry Chadwick reported, "When a player is on the first base and one on the third, and the catcher holds the ball ready to throw to second, the short-stop should get nearly on the line of the pitcher and second baseman, and have an understanding with the catcher to have him throw the ball to short-stop instead of second base, for, seeing the ball leave the catcher's hands apparently for second base, the player on third will be apt to leave for home, in which case the short-stop will have the ball in hand ready to throw to the catcher on third base" (Henry Chadwick, *The American Base Ball Manual*, 28).

In 1879, Chadwick observed that a new wrinkle had been developed: "A point played last season with good effect at times was that of the catcher throwing to short-stop when a runner was on third, and another ran down from first to second to get the man on third home. This was not done in the old style of throwing to

short-stop's position, but in throwing a little to the left of second base, the short-stop jumping forward and taking the ball and promptly returning it to the catcher in time. When the ball [is] swiftly thrown and accurately returned, the play invariably yields an out; but it must [be] understood by signal to be done effectively" (*New York Clipper*, December 20, 1879).

Another instance occurred in an 1886 exhibition game between Boston's National League club and the Haverhills of the New England League. In the third inning the visiting Haverhills "were prevented from scoring by sharp fielding. In this inning [James] McKeever got in a safe hit, stole second and went to third on [John] Irwin's single. With only one out the crowd fully expected a run, but [catcher Pat] Dealey and [second baseman Jack] Burdock rigged an amateur derrick on McKeever, who was swung up on it like a lamb. Irwin made a break for second. Dealey threw the ball in the same direction. McKeever started home only to be met by the ball, which Burdock received just back of [pitcher Charlie] Parsons and returned to Dealey to McKeever's sorrow" (*Boston Globe*, June 10, 1886).

Although that account referred to the short throw rather condescendingly as an "amateur derrick," the play continued to develop in succeeding years and often proved effective. In 1904 the *Washington Post* noted: "Of the various problems that are presented in baseball, the proper time to steal a base and whether or not to try to prevent it is one of the most complicated. A puzzling feature of this important point of the game, and one that invariably causes comment among spectators is the ease with which a runner generally achieves a steal of second base with a team mate on third and none or one out. This play has resulted in the evolution of the 'short throw,' one of the best of baseball tactics, and a play that has been developed to a high state of efficiency by some catchers . . . The idea of a runner stealing from first to second with a man on third is to draw a throw and allow the runner on third base to score during the resultant put-out or attempt to retire. Different managers hold various ideas about the wisdom of taking a certain put-out at the expense of a run. Some instruct their catchers in such cases to be guided by the score and to throw to second if their team is behind on the score board.

"The 'short throw,' however, while it allows the runner to reach second safely, usually results as intended—in catching the runner at third in an attempt to score on the play. It is not a throw to be relayed by the pitcher. Instead, the ball is jerked quickly to a point about ten feet short of second, to be met there by the shortstop, and as the man on third forms the conclusion that the ball was intended to go into play to catch the runner from first, he immediately starts for home, where quick return by the shortstop catches him off the plate. The advantage gained by shortening the throw is just what is required to get the ball back to the plate in time, and, unlike the relay from catcher to pitcher and to second, is quick and deceptive. Few pitchers are quick enough to take a throw and turn in time to get it to second to catch the runner from first. On the other hand, any shortstop can take a 'short throw,' provided he is looking for it, and the return to first or a throw to third involves no particular headwork. A third method of dealing with such a situation is the bluff by a catcher that he is going to throw to second, although the ball is not allowed to leave his hand in the swing around. At times this entices a runner to leave third base for the run home, but as a general thing he is not deceived and the base is stolen without effort" (*Washington Post*, September 18, 1904).

(iv) Plays

As discussed in the chapter on hitting, early batters had all the advantages and therefore had little reason to do anything other than swing from the heels. Only when pitchers began to gain the upper hand in the 1870s did batters begin to work on more innovative ways of getting on base. The origins of the bunt are discussed in the chapter on hitting, but by the 1880s the "baby hit" also had come of age and was spawning new plays, many of which turned back the clock to the pre-Knickerbocker games in which the bat was little more than a mechanism for commencing a lively chase.

5.4.1 Bluff Bunts. Once the bunt had become a major part of the offensive repertoire, players realized that a crafty fake bunt could sometimes accomplish the same end without sacrificing an out.

Johnny Evers and Hugh S. Fullerton explained in 1910, "The 'bluff bunt,' aimed to pull defensive infielders out of position, has resulted in a variety of plays, all based on the same principle. Possibly the cleverest variation is the 'bluff bunt' used as a substitute for the sacrifice hit to advance runners, especially from second

to third base. . . . The batter was ordered to pretend to bunt, miss the ball purposely and shove his body over the plate so as to interfere slightly with the catcher's vision. The third baseman, expecting a bunt, comes forward rapidly, leaving the base unguarded. The runners, who have been signaled, start to run as the pitcher winds up, and the leading runner is expected to slide safe back of third base before the third baseman can get back to the base and catch the throw" (John J. Evers and Hugh S. Fullerton, *Touching Second*, 205–206).

The Detroit Tigers were masters of the play, as is shown by this 1914 account: "[Marty Kavanagh's] steal of third in the opening frame was a pretty play. [Ty] Cobb drew [Boston third baseman Larry] Gardner in with a bluff bunt and Marty beat him in a race to the bag after [catcher Bill] Carrigan had pegged to the baseman. This maneuver has been worked repeatedly since the start of the season and seldom fails to accomplish its purpose" (*Detroit Free Press*, May 17, 1914).

5.4.2 Push or Force Bunts. Johnny Evers and Hugh Fullerton explained in 1910, "The 'force bunt' was brought into prominence by little [Frank] Butler, of Columbus. . . . He pushed the ball slowly down the infield, striving to make it roll fast enough to pass the pitcher either to his right or his left, yet so slowly that the short stop or second baseman, playing deep, would have to take it while sprinting forward at top speed and make a perfect throw" (John J. Evers and Hugh S. Fullerton, *Touching Second*, 161–162).

5.4.3 Drag Bunts. F. C. Lane observed in 1925, "There is a method of diversified attack which has crept into batting which combines some of the peculiarities of the bunt and the hit. Players call it, 'dragging the ball.'" He quoted John Tobin: "Dragging the ball is simple on paper. Before the ball even gets to the plate, you start full speed for first. As the ball crosses the plate, you hook the bat around it and drag it past the pitcher. You hold the bat precisely as if you were going to hit the ball through the infielders. If you execute the play properly, you will have a grand lead to first base" (F. C. Lane, *Batting*, 85). Carson Bigbee added, "I use the drag play perhaps fifty times a year. It's a neat little play when properly executed" (F. C. Lane, *Batting*, 86).

5.4.4 Left-side Hit-and-run. Merwin Jacobson, who starred for the Baltimore Orioles'

International League dynasty of the early 1920s, described a play that the club called the left-side hit-and-run: "[Fritz] Maisel, leading off, would get aboard; [Otis] Lawry would sacrifice; I was up next, the heavy hitter, and I'd bunt, toward third. Maisel, off with the pitch, would round third, never slowing. While the third baseman was running in after the ball and trying to throw me out, Maisel would score, most often standing" (quoted in James Bready, *Baseball in Baltimore*, 142).

5.4.5 Squeeze Play. The squeeze play was popularized and probably named by Clark Griffith's New York Highlanders in 1905.

Early that season the *Chicago Tribune* referred to "the new 'squeeze' play" (*Chicago Tribune*, April 25, 1905). Nine days later the same newspaper described it as "Griffith's famed 'squeeze' play." The most popular version of the play's origins was that pitcher Jack Chesbro, after reaching third base in a 1904 game, broke for home because he mistakenly thought he had been given the steal sign. Batter Wee Willie Keeler alertly bunted, and Chesbro scored easily. Manager Clark Griffith saw promise in the play, practiced it during spring training in 1905, and began to use it.

Joe Yeager's obituary in 1937 credited him with inventing the squeeze play (*Sporting News*, July 15, 1937). The article offered no details, but Yeager was also on the Highlanders in 1905.

Other clubs soon began to imitate the play, though mostly in the American League. In 1907 the play was worked 108 times—87 of them in the American League but only 21 times in the National League (*New York Sun*, March 3, 1918).

As soon as the squeeze play became popular, earlier claimants emerged. Algy McBride said: "I have been reading up a play where a man bunts with a fast runner on third base and the latter starts with the pitch. That isn't new. [Ned] Hanlon and his Baltimores when we faced them were always pulling off something that you wasn't [sic] looking for. This was one of their tricks. Of course they could not work it often, but when they had a rapid runner on third bag and a good bunter up, I tell you an infield had to be up and moving to get the ball home" (quoted in *Sporting Life*, May 20, 1905).

Lee Allen credited Yale's George Case and Dutch Carter with using the play against Princeton in 1894 (Lee Allen, *The Hot Stove League*, 95). Others maintained that it dated back to

Cap Anson, Mike Kelly, and the Chicago White Stockings (Lee Allen, *Cooperstown Corner*, 83).

An alternative view was that it was a play that had been tried previously and found wanting. Longtime player and manager Charley Morton contended, "I recall the squeeze play as early as 1883, but it was not worked extensively. Such plays then were considered 'freaks,' to be used only infrequently" (quoted in *Sporting News*, March 19, 1908).

The outspoken Joe Cantillon went further, contending that the play wasn't worth inventing in the first place. After proclaiming in 1914 that no new plays of merit had been invented in recent years, he added: "I will admit that the new school has brought the squeeze play into the game. I will also admit that it is the rottenest play in base ball when it fails. Furthermore it is an admission from the player who makes it on his own accord that he cannot hit and when the manager asks for it he shows that he has lost confidence in the hitting of the player asked to squeeze" (*Minneapolis Journal*, reprinted in *Sporting News*, May 28, 1914).

One candidate for the earliest squeeze play is one that occurred in 1877, when a game account recorded that Tim Murnane's "bunt near the home-plate allowed [Ezra] Sutton to score while [catcher Charley] Snyder was throwing the striker out" (*Louisville Courier-Journal*, July 13, 1877). But this raises the important and unanswerable issue of Murnane's intentions and the equally irresolvable philosophical question of whether something is really a first if it occurs by accident.

Clark Griffith answered the second query with a resounding no: "I don't doubt that base runners were scored years ago with the aid of bunts, but these plays were of a desultory and accidental nature. The highlanders were the first team to adopt the 'squeeze' as a regular play, as the first team to work it scientifically. The way we came to work the 'squeeze play' was this: We had several men on the team who, while they were good hitters, did not punch the ball any great distance, as a rule—men like Billy Keeler, 'Kid' Elberfeld and one or two others. Whenever we had a man on third and one of those chaps at the bat, we could not depend on them to drive out a long fly. Then the question arose: How could we best turn the batting ability of these men to account under such conditions? Every one of them could bunt, and so the idea of having them bunt at the same time that the man on third dashed for home occurred to us. And that's how the 'squeeze' play originated and was made a scientific adjunct to base ball" (*Sporting News*, March 25, 1909).

Griffith made a valid point, but he over-stated his case in claiming that earlier squeeze plays had been "of a desultory and accidental nature." Doc Bushong of the St. Louis Brown Stockings wrote in 1887: "With a man on third, it is confessedly the play in base ball to bring him in. A man comes to the bat, and to make a successful 'bunt' he must bring the bat in front of the plate, the same as if he were batting, only not with the same force. If he bunts and it goes fair, the run is made" (letter to *Base Ball Gazette*; reprinted in the *Cleveland Leader and Herald*, April 24, 1887). In addition, the next entry suggests that the double squeeze may have been in use as early as 1890.

It seems clear, then, that the squeeze play was far from unknown in the nineteenth century but was raised to a new level of promi-nence in 1905 by Clark Griffith and the New York Highlanders. The play then became enor-mously popular in the low-scoring environ-ment of the next few seasons, but that level of frequency could not be sustained. John McGraw pronounced the play fundamentally unsound and used it rarely. Christy Mathewson explained: "McGraw objects to the squeeze play because he believes that a brainy pitcher ought to break up the play and prevent its success by pitching the ball so wide that the batsman is not able to bunt it" (quoted in A. H. Spink, *The National Game*, 281).

As defenses became more alert to the pos-sibility, the play declined in effectiveness and frequency, leading one 1911 article to refer to the "practical abolishment of the squeeze play by managers" (*Mansfield* [Ohio] *News*, Septem-ber 23, 1911). Of course the squeeze play did not entirely die but instead receded to a level of usage where it could again benefit from the element of surprise.

5.4.6 Double Squeeze Play.

The double squeeze is an electrifying play that had a brief period of prominence but is largely forgotten today. With runners on second and third and less than two out, both runners break with the pitch. The batter then bunts, allowing the run-ner on third to score easily. When the infielder throws to first to retire the batter, the runner on second rounds third and continues home. Thus two runs score on a bunt.

There is at least one claim that the play originated as early as 1890. Sportswriter Stanley T. Milliken recorded in 1913, "As far back as the Brotherhood year, which was 1890, the Boston Players' League team used to use this scheme for acquiring runs. Arthur Irwin, scout of the Highlanders, has in his possession scrapbooks showing that Kelly's Killers frequently made two runs on a bunt to the infield" (Stanley T. Milliken, *Washington Post*, October 31, 1913).

Sportswriter Biddy Bishop wrote in 1911 that Pacific Coast League player Mike Lynch of Tacoma had invented the double squeeze in 1904. During an exhibition game, Lynch was on second when a squeeze was ordered. He broke with the pitch and scored, but captain Charley Graham dismissed the play as a fluke.

So Lynch "put the 'double squeeze' on record" in a game against Portland: "The op-portunity came in the fourth inning. [George] McLaughlin was on third and Lynch on second as in the previous game. 'Happy' Hogan . . . was batting. The signal came on the third ball and McLaughlin took a long lead. As he did so Lynch was almost down to third. McLaughlin tore in and Lynch came on like a deer for third. Rounding the bag he dug his spikes into the dirt and beat it hard. . . . McLaughlin crossed the plate before the ball had hardly left the pitcher and Lynch was right at his heels, scoring stand-ing up."

That still didn't convince Graham, who "declared he was taking a drink of water at the time and didn't see the play. 'Well, I'll show it to you again,' said Mike, and the very next day at Los Angeles he pulled off the same identical thing" (*Sporting News*, March 30, 1911).

The first documented occurrence of the double squeeze in a major league game took place when the Cubs faced Brooklyn on July 15, 1905. With the bases loaded and one out in the fifth, "[Chicago base runner Jimmy] Slagle started for home and [Chicago batter Joe] Tinker bunted, going out on [Brooklyn catcher Bill] Bergen's throw to [Brooklyn first baseman Doc] Gessler, but before Gessler had returned the ball to the plate [Chicago base runner Billy] Maloney was over with the second run, making the record number of runs off the squeeze play" (*Chicago Tribune*, July 16, 1905; *New York Sun*, March 3, 1918).

The play was copied by Detroit a week later during the first game of a July 22 doubleheader against Philadelphia: "With men on second and third, [Herman] Schaefer bunted. [Tom] Doran, on third, had started for the plate with the swing of [pitcher Eddie] Plank's arm and the Athletics' infield dashed to get the bunt. [First baseman] Harry Davis took it almost off the bat, but even then couldn't get Doran. Accordingly, he fired to [second baseman Danny] Murphy at first and retired Schaefer, never thinking of Dick Cooley, who had taken a big lead off second and never stopped, scoring with ease" (Paul Bruske, *Sporting Life*, July 29, 1905). That was likely the first time Athletics manager Connie Mack saw the play, and it may have planted a seed in his mind.

The double squeeze continued to appear from time to time in the next few years but was generally regarded as a novelty. A 1907 article noted: "To add more interest to the uncertainty of the 'squeeze' play's birthplace 'Kid' Elberfeld and 'Hal' Chase have invented the 'double squeeze' and it is even more spectacular than its sensational predecessor. They tried the new play in a game with Boston at Highland Park and but for the fact that Elberfeld stumbled and fell on the base line both men would have scored on the out. Imagine what ball players twenty years ago would have said if such a play had been even suggested! For one runner to score on an infield out is hard enough, but for two to do so seems physically impossible. They are going to do it this summer, just the same" (*Sporting News*, May 4, 1907). Two years later, in the Virginia League, the Norfolk club "made a double squeeze play, which is said to be the first one ever even tried" (*Los Angeles Times*, July 4, 1909). The Giants pulled a double squeeze in a 1910 exhibition game against Jersey City (*New York Times*, April 12, 1910). Sportswriter Abe Kemp must have been referring to some time around 1910 when he wrote in 1943: "Twice in one season, [Los Angeles] manager Frank Dillon successfully pulled off the double squeeze—unheard of today—in which runners score from second and third on a bunt. Each time the play was maneuvered, [Hughie] Smith was the batter" (*San Francisco Examiner*, January 17, 1943; Smith played for Los Angeles from 1909 to 1912).

In 1913 the play suddenly lost its novelty status. Harry Davis became a full-time coach for Connie Mack's Athletics that year, and he was later credited with refining and developing the play (*Sporting Life*, November 1922 [monthly]). The Athletics practiced the play extensively during spring training and unveiled it in an exhibition game in San Antonio (*Sporting Life*, March 22, 1913). Once the regular season began, they worked it successfully on no less than eight occasions. Three of those games—on May 22, June 5, and September 22—were against the same Detroit team that had used the

play against the Mackmen eight years earlier. The Athletics also pulled off the play on August 2 and 26 versus St. Louis; on September 4 and 6 against Boston; and on September 1 versus Washington. Each time, shortstop Jack Barry was at the plate, and he beat out the bunt on three of those occasions (Stanley T. Milliken, *Washington Post*, October 31, 1913).

In the September 22 game the double squeeze brought home the winning runs in the game that clinched the pennant for the Athletics (*New York Times*, September 23, 1913). Philadelphia again tried "their famous double squeeze" in the eighth inning of the opening game of the World Series, but it failed and base runner Stuffy McInnis was picked off second (*New York Times*, October 8, 1913).

The Athletics continued to use the play in 1914 until it backfired spectacularly in a game against Washington on April 29. Jack Barry popped the bunt up and Chick Gandil caught it and started a triple play. Washington then rallied to win the game 6-4 (Stanley T. Milliken, *Washington Post*, April 30, 1914).

After this disaster, Connie Mack seems to have lost confidence in the double squeeze. According to an article tracked down by researcher Steve Steinberg, the play continued to be used in the major leagues at least a few times a year for the next few years, including at least six times in 1917 (*New York Sun*, March 3, 1918). When the home run era began a few years later, the play was almost entirely forgotten.

Retrosheet volunteer Greg Beston did find that Connie Mack brought the play out of mothballs in 1927. In the ninth inning of the nightcap of an August 16, 1927, doubleheader at Cleveland, Zack Wheat and Chick Galloway both scored on a sacrifice by Jack Quinn of the Athletics (David W. Smith, Retrosheet). But by 1933 sportswriter James M. Gould described the double squeeze as "a play which, in these modern days, never is seen and one which the writer saw completed only once" (*Sporting News*, January 19, 1933).

5.4.7   Hit-and-run. In the first series of the 1894 season, the Baltimore Orioles used the hit-and-run play repeatedly against the New York Giants. This brought a new level of prominence to the play and started a long debate about its origins.

Ted Sullivan later said of the hit-and-run, "The renowned Baltimore Club of '94, '95 and '96 was the team that perfected it and made it the dominant feature of their line of strategy"

(*Sporting News*, January 21, 1905). Sportswriter and former player Sam Crane concurred, acknowledging that there were earlier accidental instances of the hit-and-run, but maintaining that it was "inaugurated as a run-making innovation and systematized to a science by the noted Baltimore Orioles in the early 1890s by the shrewdness of John McGraw and Willie Keeler" (Sam Crane, "Hit and Run Play an Oriole Discovery," *Sporting News*, February 10, 1916). But others cited earlier candidates.

Bill James noted that in 1893 John Ward of the New York Giants had credited the Boston club of the early '90s with popularizing the hit-and-run. Boston likely did play an important role in popularizing the play, but James was mistaken to conclude: "It is clear from [Ward's] comments that he had never seen this play before" (Bill James, *The New Bill James Historical Baseball Abstract*, 65).

In fact it can be said with certainty that the hit-and-run was in use before 1893, since the play was described in considerable detail in an 1891 *Sporting Life* article: "There is one point in baserunning which I believe wins many games if systematically carried out. That is the understanding that exists between the base-runner at first and the man at the bat; an understanding the man at bat has that the runner will start to steal on a certain ball pitched—the first, second, third, or whatever it may be. This being communicated to the batter by sign or previous agreement, it becomes his duty to strike at the ball if it be within bounds. Should it be wide the base-runner would probably reach second safely, anyhow.

"But if it be within reach it is the batter's plain duty to hit it or try to hit it. Why? Because the moment the base-runner starts he unsteadies or uncovers one field and sometimes both the second baseman's and short stop's territory. One and sometimes both are sure to start with him toward second base, and if the batter sends a grounder to the man's territory it is turned into a base hit by the tactics instead of a sure out or maybe a double play. This has happened a dozen times in Cleveland during the past season. It is much better to start the base-runner down and let the batsman strike at the ball than keep the runner hugging first and finally get put out in an easy double play" (*Sporting Life*, November 7, 1891).

An article in *Sporting News* confirmed, "The Giants have been practicing all this season at placing the ball with a man on first base, and have been fairly successful. The batter, with a man on first base, can tell pretty well who is going to cover second base, whether the second baseman or short stop, and that leaves him either one loophole or another. More than one game has been won by the big fellows this season by following out this line of tactics" (*Sporting News*, September 5, 1891).

David Ball discovered an 1890 article by one of Ward's teammates that makes it explicit that Ward was familiar with the play before 1893. According to Buck Ewing, "One piece of work that has been very successful with us in 1888 and 1889 was as follows: If [Mike] Tiernan, the batter who preceded me, got first he signaled me when he was ready to start for second, and I would strike at the ball, no matter where it went, endeavoring to put it between the bases toward right, for the second baseman, who was trying to catch Tiernan, would be out of the way. If I hit the ball the speedy Tiernan would surely reach third and Ward, the next batsman would bring in the score" (*Brooklyn Eagle*, November 24, 1890).

It seems just as clear that the play was being used at least occasionally before 1888, but that is where the situation becomes murky. Indeed, there is a baffling array of contradictory statements to sift through.

Longtime sportswriter William Rankin backed up Buck Ewing's claim by crediting Ewing, Ward, Tiernan, and Danny Richardson of Jim Mutrie's Giants with being experts in the play in the late 1880s (*Sporting News*, July 1, 1905; *Sporting News*, March 3, 1910). Meanwhile columnist W. A. Calhoun wrote in 1900: "The 'hit and run' game of the champion Brooklyns is lauded as 'something new!' . . . Was not this very feature the main stay of the old St. Louis Browns and Detroits, both champion teams, and is not this very point a direct legacy to the Brooklyns from Detroit through Ned Hanlon?" (*Sporting Life*, December 15, 1900).

Cap Anson's Chicago squad is the club mentioned most frequently. Anson maintained that "This hit-and-run system, which has been ascribed to the ingenuity of the Baltimores and Bostons, was practiced by the Chicago champions long before the other teams heard of it. The mere fact that the scheme has been divulged and is now widely talked of makes many believe that it is something new" (*New York Sun*, reprinted in *Cleveland Plain Dealer*, June 14, 1897). Ted Sullivan asserted: "The Chicago Club of the early '80's was the team which originated the hit-and-run we hear about so many times of late years" (*Sporting News*, January 21, 1905). A 1905 editorial in *Sporting Life* claimed that the hit-and-run "was in general use in the '80s, and the Providence and Philadelphia teams under Arthur Irwin, and the Chicagos under Anson had it down as fine as any teams in the '90s or the present time" (*Sporting Life*, July 8, 1905). On the other hand, longtime Chicago infielder Tommy Burns said in 1900, "The only thing absolutely new is the hit and run system, and that has only been perfected by a few teams" (*Sporting Life*, November 17, 1900).

The White Stockings of the early 1880s are one of those clubs that has been credited with a suspiciously large number of firsts, but in this case there are a couple of contemporaneous accounts that appear to offer confirmation. On October 7, 1882, in a postseason series against the American Association pennant winners from Cincinnati, Cap Anson's charges pulled a hit-and-run in the first inning. With George Gore running for second, Ned Williamson hit the ball into the hole vacated by second baseman Bid McPhee. The play led to two runs, which held up for a 2-0 Chicago win (Jerry Lansche, *Glory Fades Away*, 30). Researcher David Ball discovered an 1877 account that supports their claim: "Some chap stated the following conundrum, professing not to understand it: 'Why do batsmen strike a ball when a base-runner is half-way to second base on a clever steal?' The answer was found in Thursday's game, when [Cal] McVey started to second base, and [Cap] Anson hit the ball in the exact spot where [St. Louis second baseman Mike] McGeary had been standing before he ran to his base to catch McVey. It is really a clever batting trick to hit to right field when it lies all open" (*Chicago Tribune*, July 1, 1877).

Charley Comiskey also credited the White Stockings with inventing the hit-and-run, but he stated that this occurred in 1876, which was Anson's first year with the club and was before he became captain (*Sporting Life*, November 13, 1897, 12). When Tim Murnane heard of the claims of Anson and Comiskey, he responded that Boston had invented the play in 1875 and that it was the "Big Four" of Al Spalding, Jim "Deacon" White, Cal McVey, and Ross Barnes who brought it to Chicago the next year. Murnane commented: "Other teams have tried it ever since, but usually give it up as a bad job, as it is not always possible to make this play a success" (*Boston Globe*, November 8, 1897, 3). Jim O'Rourke also claimed that Harry Wright was using the play in the 1870s.

There is no way to entirely reconcile such divergent claims from credible firsthand witnesses. Part of the confusion seems to stem from exaggeration about how frequently the play was made. Mickey Welch, for example, commented in 1901, "They played the hit and run game in the eighties; but . . . did not have as many players who could work it as now" (*New York Sun*, reprinted in *Sandusky Daily Star*, July 16, 1901). Another issue is that the play can be executed accidentally. For example, Lave Cross gave this account in 1905: "Pete Browning was the originator of the hit-and-run game. He was hard of hearing, and one day he couldn't hear the coacher after getting to first on a hit, and started for second on the first ball pitched. He ran like a wildcat and got to third on a single. Pete would not have gotten past second had he not misunderstood the signals, or if he could have heard the coacher. As it was, when he started off on his mad run he got to third safely, and would have been on the way home if he hadn't been held by the man coaching third. Hughey Jennings heard of it, and the system was introduced in Baltimore and worked with great success" (*Detroit Tribune*, March 16, 1905). Arlie Latham similarly recounted an incident during the glory days of the St. Louis Browns in which Tip O'Neill inadvertently executed a perfect hit-and-run but was bawled out by captain Charlie Comiskey because the club's system was that whenever a base runner took off, "the batsman was supposed to protect the steal by shoving his anatomy in front of his catcher" (*Washington Post*, March 19, 1899). Note that it is possible to read the two accounts of the White Stockings executing the hit-and-run as happenstance.

As Comiskey's disapproval suggests, yet another wrinkle in the early history of the hit-and-run play is that many viewed it as poor strategy. For example, in an 1872 game Anson swung at a pitch while Athletics teammate Fred Treacey was trying to steal, prompting a local sportswriter to denounce his course as "Not only unfair to the runner, but generally disastrous, as it affords an opportunity for a double play either by foul or by sharp play at second. We thought the Athletics had made a rule against this practice?" (*Philadelphia City Item*, July 15, 1872; reprinted in Howard W. Rosenberg, *Cap Anson 4*, 55). To further complicate matters, the play is not dissimilar to a play that was well known by 1877 when Henry Chadwick observed, "When a base-runner is on first base, not only is the first-baseman kept close to his position, but the second-baseman has to be near his, in readiness for a throw by the catcher. By this a wide, open space is generally left free for a successful hit" (*New York Clipper*, June 23, 1877).

As discussed under "Second Baseman Leaving the Bag" (4.2.5), the 1870s and 1880s saw the second baseman gradually position himself farther from the base. As he did, the hit-and-run saw a corresponding rise to prominence. Perhaps it is thus more accurate to view the hit-and-run as a play that slowly but surely developed in response, rather than one that was invented by anyone.

5.4.8 Steal and Slam.

John McGraw believed that plays like the hit-and-run and the squeeze were fundamentally unsound because an alert pitcher could detect the movement of the runner and pitch out. McGraw accordingly preferred a variant that he called the "steal and slam": "The man on first would take a lead to actually steal the base. In that case, if the ball was a good one, the batter would slam at it. If the pitcher, expecting a hit and run, pitched out, the batter would simply let it go and take a chance on the runner stealing the base. The batter then would be in a better position than ever" (John McGraw, *My Thirty Years of Baseball*, 88).

(v) Turf Wars

5.5.1 Running into Fielders.

In 1878 new rule 5.25 was introduced, which clarified that a fielder had to hold on to the ball after applying a tag. Henry Chadwick noted his concern that the amendment "offers a premium to collide with base players purposely to prevent their holding the ball" (*Brooklyn Eagle*, January 27, 1878). By the following season he was convinced that the rule was a mistake: "This vicious rule simply offers a premium to the runners to collide with the base player every time he can do so when the latter has the ball in hand ready to touch him." He incorrectly predicted that the rule would be repealed at the end of the season (*Brooklyn Eagle*, August 24, 1879).

Instead the rule remained, and contact between fielders and base runners did indeed become more common, spurred by a modest increase in the frequency of infield double plays over the next two seasons. The St. Louis Brown Stockings of the mid-1880s became particularly associated with the technique of bowling over the shortstop or second baseman to prevent a double play. In a game on May 14, 1886,

Charles Comiskey caused a furor by running into Cincinnati second baseman Bid McPhee, but the umpire ruled the play legal. On June 16, 1887, St. Louis's Curt Welch ran over Baltimore second baseman Bill Greenwood to try to break up a double play and was arrested. Team owner Chris Von der Ahe had to bail his center fielder out of jail, and Welch was eventually fined $4.50.

Catchers also became targets for base runners, with Adrian "Cap" Anson being one of the leaders in this regard. An 1886 game account noted: "In Friday's game [against St. Louis] Anson was on third when [Tom] Burns knocked a fly to [John] Cahill at right field; the latter fielded it to catcher [George] Myers, who had Anson ten feet, and instead of stopping or sliding, Anson went up into the air and threw the full force of his 210 pounds against George Myers' 150 pounds. Myers was knocked almost senseless ten feet or more away from the home plate, but pluckily held on to the ball, thus retiring the side. Myers has not yet recovered from the severe shock. The storm of hisses which greeted Anson ought to admonish him that audiences do not consider brutal work of that kind ball playing" (*Sporting Life*, May 12, 1886).

With such tactics being associated with the champions of the respective major leagues, and with the umpires having limited recourse against offenders, they gradually became more common. Needless to say, Henry Chadwick continued to deplore this development, and most sportswriters followed his cue by raising an uproar whenever an especially violent incident occurred.

The early 1880s saw the conditions of playing fields improve and the introduction of fielders' gloves, both of which might have been expected to contribute to an increase in infield double plays. Instead, after increasing in 1880 and 1881, they returned to earlier levels. It seems logical to attribute it to the increased emphasis on attempting to break up double plays.

5.5.2 Low-bridging.

Catchers had little recourse but to steel themselves for the impact of collisions with onrushing base runners. Middle infielders, however, soon found a way to get even with runners who attempted to "balk" them by going into second base standing up on potential double plays. *Sporting News* reported in 1890, "The so-called 'dirty ball' players who delight to prevent double plays by what they look upon as legitimate balking, have doubtless been taught a lesson by the accident that has overtaken [Joe] Mulvey of the Brotherhood. He attempted to balk [New York's] Arthur Whitney, but was hit in the face [with the ball] when not five feet off. He fell like a beef hit with a mallet. He will not try it again for some time" (*Sporting News*, June 28, 1890).

Tim Murnane offered this illuminating 1889 explanation of why he considered Chicago second baseman Fred Pfeffer "without a doubt the best player in the league to make a double play. He seldom looks at the first base, always being prompted by Ed Williamson, the short stop, when to turn and let go of the ball and when to hold it; for there is nothing made by throwing the ball around when there is no chance to get the runner. Pfeffer covers the second base the instant the ball is sent to the right of the pitcher, and makes it a rule to keep well inside the bag, so the runner will not interfere with him. As quick as the ball hits his hands he is on the swing and throws to first without raising his head, judging the direction wholly by the base line. Sometimes he will stop and toss the ball to the pitcher. This is when he has heard Williamson sing out 'No.' That one word is enough. He knows that there is no chance to get his man. Many second basemen are slow in returning the ball to first on a double, fearing they may hit a runner, but the Chicago man never stops to think of this. He swings with the throw and lets her go. If a man is in the way he gets hit, and knowing this they generally duck out of the way" (Tim Murnane, "How the Stars Play Combinations," *Boston Globe*, March 10, 1889, 22).

5.5.3 Nonviolent Ways of Breaking Up a Double Play.
Violent methods of breaking up double plays were eventually supplemented by less brutal tactics. Mike Kelly unveiled this one in 1889: "When he is on first base and the ball is hit to second, and he sees that by running down the line he is likely to be the victim of a double play, he will turn back and run for first. This makes it hard for the second baseman to throw, and the chances are that he will hold the ball, and if he should let it go he is just as likely to hit Kelly as he is to get his man" (*Boston Globe*, June 8, 1889).

Honus Wagner described another approach in 1915: "My namesake, Heine Wagner, of the Boston Red Sox, told me a good one of how he endured the roasts for being a 'bonehead' on a really bright play. Heine was [a base runner] on second base and they had a hit-and-run play

on. He started for third, but instantly saw a soft liner going square into the shortstop's hands. Unable to get back, Heine stopped and let the ball hit him. The crowd hooted and jeered and one Boston paper roasted Wagner and hailed him as 'the worst bit of ivory in the business.' They didn't realize that Heine's quick thinking had averted a double-play. In getting hit he prevented the catch from being made and a double play resulting from a toss to second" (syndicated column, *Detroit Free Press*, August 22, 1915).

Heine Wagner's tactic seems to have been a spontaneous onetime reaction to an unusual situation, but more than forty years later this ploy enjoyed a sudden renaissance. In a game at Boston on April 16, 1957, Baltimore base runner George Kell allowed himself to be hit by a likely double-play ball. Following the game, Kell admitted not only that the tactic was deliberate but that it was one that the Orioles "have talked about and practiced all spring" under innovative manager Paul Richards.

Umpire Joe Paparella said that there was "nothing in the rules" that would permit him to rule the batter out on the play. He added, "I have always been surprised that more base runners don't do the same thing that Kell did. The base-runner can catch the ball, if he wants to be declared out. But once it touches him, the ball is dead. Jackie Robinson got away with the same trick several years ago for Brooklyn in a big game. It raised quite a controversy at the time, but nothing ever has been done by the rules makers to legislate against it. After all, who can assume the double play would have been made?" (*Baltimore Sun*, April 17, 1957).

The following week the Cincinnati Reds pulled this tactic on three successive days. In Milwaukee on April 20, Johnny Temple let a Gus Bell grounder glance off him. The next day Don Hoak was even less subtle, picking up a ground ball hit by Wally Post rather than risk a double play. One day later, this time in St. Louis, Post allowed himself to be hit by a ball off the bat of Ed Bailey (*Sporting News*, May 1, 1957).

The authorities had seen enough. On April 25 the American and National leagues jointly announced that umpires would have the power to call a double play if a base runner allowed himself to be hit by a batted ball.

5.5.4 Another Dimension.
David Falkner suggested that Joe Gordon, second baseman for the Yankees and Indians between 1938

and 1950, popularized the practice of middle infielders leaping in the air on double plays to avoid collisions (David Falkner, *Nine Sides of the Diamond*, 81–82).

(vi) Novelty Plays

5.6.1 Stealing First. In *The Glory of Their Times*, Davy Jones described how Herman "Germany" Schaefer drove an opposing team to distraction with a steal of first. The play has become a part of baseball lore, yet there is no evidence that it happened, at least as described. Schaefer did steal first in a game on August 4, 1911, but the details are very different from those related by Jones. To date, no one has discovered an actual sequence that closely resembles the events recounted many years later by Jones and by Ty Cobb. (Thanks to Brian McKenna for helping to straighten out this part of the entry, which was incorrect in the first edition.)

Moreover, even if the play had occurred, it was neither unique nor new. In a game between Philadelphia and Detroit on August 13, 1902, Harry Davis stole second but did not draw a throw. He then stole first and then again attempted to steal second, this time drawing a throw that allowed the runner on third to score. Bob Davids discovered that Mickey Doolan of the Phillies pulled the play against the Braves on May 7, 1906 (*National Pastime* [2001], 16). The tactic was also employed by Fred Tenney for Boston versus St. Louis on July 31, 1908, but this was a lopsided game that featured considerable clowning. Researcher Norman Macht pointed out that Davis was the only one of these examples actually to accomplish the play's aim—to draw a throw from the catcher and enable the lead runner to score.

Hugh Jennings later claimed: "Although Herman Schaefer caused a new rule to be written into the base ball books by stealing first, he was not the originator of the idea. Dave Fultz used to do it while playing with the Athletics. He first tried it with [Harry] Davis on third and Fultz on first. Fultz stole second, but the catcher did not throw. Fultz ran back to first, hoping to draw a throw and give Davis a chance to score, but the catcher did not bite. He let Fultz run back and forth to his heart's content" (Hugh Jennings, *Rounding Third*, Chapter 72).

The practice was finally banned by a rule change in 1920.

5.6.2 Deliberately Not Advancing. A strategy occasionally used in the nineteenth century that will seem very strange to today's baseball fans was the tactic of intentionally turning down an opportunity to score.

J. P. Caillault, for example, found an account of an 1889 game in which Boston trailed New York by two runs in the ninth inning. With two out, Boston's Hardy Richardson "hit over the left-field fence for a home run, but preferred to remain at third base so as to make Catcher [Bill] Brown get close to the batter. The latter, however, did not bite at his bait. He paid no attention to Richardson, but retired the batsman after the occupant of third base had walked home" (*New York Times*, April 26, 1889; reprinted in J. P. Caillault, *A Tale of Four Cities*, 58).

The *Brooklyn Eagle*, however, placed a wildly different interpretation on the same events: "Richardson made a stupid play for Boston in the ninth inning. He hit the ball over the fence, and could easily have scored a run, but he stopped at third in order to keep the catcher close up behind the bat. This is one of those rutty notions that should be got rid of. It is stupid work to refuse a run when the chance is offered. It lost Boston the chance to tie the score" (*Brooklyn Eagle*, April 26, 1889).

Boston apparently worked this ploy more successfully in a game on May 19, 1893. Billy Nash of Boston hit a home run in the bottom of the ninth but elected to stay on third base to distract the Brooklyn pitcher (*Boston Globe*, May 20, 1893; the *Eagle*'s account, however, implied that Nash could not have advanced home). Boston rallied to tie the game but lost in extra innings.

David Nemec observed that this "was a well-respected tactical move that certain teams (Boston in particular) were not loath to try in the final inning of a tight game in the late 1800s." He explained that its usual intention was to allow the base runner to disrupt the pitcher. Cap Anson's Chicago White Stockings also used this ploy on at least two occasions (David Fleitz, *Cap Anson*, 83, 152). The strategy was no doubt influenced by the fact that one of the main functions of third-base coaches in this era was to annoy the opposing pitcher, as is discussed in the chapter on coaches.

5.6.3 Keep On Running. It seems hard to believe that a play like this was deemed legal as recently as 1926, but entries in the baseball rulebook usually were written in response to an innovation, so if no one had ever thought to try something before, there might not be a rule to prohibit it. On June 17, 1926, the Cubs loaded the bases against the Dodgers in the sixth. With one out, Joe Kelly hit a sharp ground ball to Dodger first baseman Babe Herman, who threw to shortstop Rabbit Maranville to force Johnny Cooney at second. Maranville returned the ball to first to try to complete the inning-ending double play, but his throw went astray—and then the fun began.

Brooklyn pitcher Jess Barnes retrieved the ball, saw a base runner headed for the plate and threw it to catcher Mickey O'Neil. The Chicago runner stopped short before reaching the plate and turned toward the dugout. O'Neil followed the runner into the Cub dugout and tagged him for the apparent third out. The problem was that the runner was none other than Cooney, who had kept running after being put out at second. Meanwhile Kelly had moved up to third.

After some thought, home plate umpire Bill Klem ruled that the inning had to continue. "There ought to be a law against such a thing, but there isn't," was the decision of the celebrated arbitrator. Chicago counted two more runs that inning, but Brooklyn eventually won the game. Columnist Thomas Holmes wrote, "Cooney's little 'joke' was unique. If it ever has been pulled in a ball game before it must have been pulled in China. Nobody ever saw or ever heard of anything quite like it" (*Brooklyn Eagle*, June 18, 1926).

5.6.4   Gag Rundowns. Johnny Evers and Hugh S. Fullerton noted that, when a pitcher was caught in a rundown, it was customary to keep running him back and forth in hopes of tiring him out (John J. Evers and Hugh S.

Fullerton, *Touching Second*, 214–215). The play became prevalent enough that umpire John Gaffney suggested in 1898 that courtesy runners be allowed for pitchers (Gerard S. Petrone, *When Baseball Was Young*, 101).

The "old gag" was also tried on Cap Anson: "If they could get the Chicago man between bases they would run him up and down the lines until the big fellow dropped exhausted. On one occasion 'Buck' Ewing refused to touch Anson and called for a bat that he might warm him up" (*Grand Valley* [Moab, Utah] *Times*, September 1, 1899).

In 1903, Patsy Donovan lamented that fielders no longer tried to "catch the other side's pitcher and run him to death as they used to. Why, if the old boys could get a pitcher between second and third they'd keep him going for five minutes before they touched him, and he couldn't pitch for beans in the next innings" (*Washington Post*, August 9, 1903).

5.6.5   Not Running to First. Researcher Frank Vaccaro brought to my attention a novel ploy that Boston's Joe Hornung tried in a June 30, 1883, game against Providence. In the sixth inning, with no outs and runners on first and second: "Hornung hit to [Providence second baseman Jack] Farrell, and, instead of running and forcing [Ezra] Sutton and [Sam] Wise, he stood on the home plate. Wise started for second, and, not being a forced runner, he had to be touched by the ball before he could be declared out. While Farrell and [first baseman Joe] Start were engaged in doing this Sutton was speeding for the home plate and . . . scored the winning run" (*Sporting Life*, July 8, 1883). The *Boston Globe* confirmed this interpretation, explaining that Hornung was declared "out for not running on the hit" but that this removed the force (*Boston Globe*, July 1, 1883).

Chapter 6

MANAGERIAL STRATEGIES

IN PRECEDING chapters I have tried to discuss strategies that could be implemented by a single player. In this chapter I describe changes made by managers. Of course there is a fine line between the two and plenty of overlap.

The task of drawing that line was made a little easier by the rule changes between 1889 and 1891 that legalized substitutions. These rules made many of today's most prominent strategies—pinch-hitting, relief pitching, platooning, etc.—possible for the first time. From that point on, managers became increasingly responsible for on-the-field decisions. By 1910, thanks to the savvy and forceful personalities of managers such as Ned Hanlon, Frank Selee, John McGraw, Connie Mack, Fred Clarke, and Clark Griffith, the prototype of today's manager was established and the related development of coaching staffs was beginning.

(i) Who's in Charge Here?

6.1.1 Captains. Captains were specified in the Knickerbockers' original rules, but their responsibilities appear to have been limited to choosing sides and determining who batted first. Moreover the position was not a permanent one but changed from match to match. Early clubs generally had few decisions to make, and those were settled democratically.

As the game increased in complexity, clubs began to centralize the decision-making process. In 1852 the Knickerbockers gave captains the authority to assign players to positions. Before the 1864 season the Star Club of Brooklyn voted "to abolish the committee on nines, substituting the conferring of arbitrary power on the captains of the nines, whereby he can dismiss from the nine any unruly or rebellious player. This is a good rule, providing the captain is not one likely to play the tyrant" (*Brooklyn Eagle*, April 2, 1864). By 1865 the rules specified that clubs should have a captain, who assumed many of the functions now handled by managers.

The military connotations of the word "captain" bore special significance for a country that had just completed a long civil war. For example, the members of the Continental Club of Kalamazoo were praised in 1866 for giving "evidence of discipline and drill, the different players yielding implicit obedience to every suggestion of their captain" (*Niles* [Mich.] *Weekly Times*, May 24, 1866).

Baseball clubs were encouraged to adopt the military's hierarchical structure, with a Tecumseh, Michigan, newspaper noting that the local club "needs a smaller corps of Captains" and should "leave the command with Capt. Charles Augustus" (*Tecumseh Herald*, September 20, 1866). In 1887 a rule of the Zanesville, Ohio, club counseled: "Players must not criticize each other during play. The Captain will do that" (*Zanesville Times-Recorder*, May 2, 1887).

The responsibilities of the captain were reflected in a resolution adopted by the Excelsior Club of Chicago: "That a member be appointed Field Captain of this Club to serve during the current year, to have control of the several nines, select the same, and take general charge of the players on all occasions, except while the nine are engaged in a game" (*Chicago*

Tribune, August 16, 1867). As discussed in the next entry, the captain was also responsible for directing base runners.

6.1.2 Managers. Harry Wright of the Red Stockings of Boston and Cincinnati deserves to be recognized as baseball's first manager, since he took charge of the strategy and finances of those clubs. Wright first assumed the dual role while with Cincinnati in 1868 and was acknowledged as the master of both jobs during the 1870s. Nonetheless, until the 1880s he had few counterparts (Henry Chadwick, *New York Clipper*, November 15, 1879).

The reason for this was simple. As Fred Stein noted, Harry Wright's duties with the Cincinnati club included "field manager, center fielder, relief pitcher, team trainer, tracker of team baseballs and field equipment, disciplinarian, schedule of games and travel arrangements, checker of game receipts, and bursar" (Fred Stein, "Managers and Coaches," *Total Baseball*, 2nd edition, 452). When he got to Boston, Wright relinquished the playing duties but continued in the other roles. Understandably, it was believed that no one else could hope to match Wright's versatility, with Henry Chadwick calling it a "blunder" to "give the club manager a double duty to perform, namely, the work of Captaining the nine in the field, as well as managing the business affairs of the team in general" (*New York Clipper*, November 17, 1877).

In 1882 the *Detroit Free Press* noted that future managing great Ned Hanlon, then still a player, "thinks it is a mistake to ask [George] Derby to both manage and captain the club. Derby would make a good manager, but a pitcher should be allowed to rest between innings, instead of being required to direct the running of bases" (*Detroit Free Press*, January 10, 1882). As this suggests, most clubs of this period delegated in-game strategy to the club's captain while letting a manager handle scheduling and finances. Meanwhile managers of the period were generally financial managers who had little or no playing experience.

The next few years would see this begin to change. Sportswriter William Perrin noted later that after the 1881 season the directors of the Providence club realized "the necessity of having a manager at the head of affairs who knew the game" rather than one who was "successful enough in business but innocent of baseball" (William D. Perrin, *Days of Greatness*, 15).

Other clubs began to follow suit. This did not, however, mean that a manager would simply make strategic decisions, as is discussed in the next entry.

The division of responsibilities was nicely summed up in a bylaw adopted by the Aetna Club of Detroit on November 27, 1874: "The captain shall have absolute control of the playing nine while on the field. . . . The manager shall have an absolute control over the financial affairs of the club" (*Aetna Base Ball Association Constitution and By-Laws*, 11).

As managers increasingly took control, the responsibilities of the captain were correspondingly reduced. Charley Snyder reported that in the early 1880s "a captain was often called upon to negotiate with the railroads for rates, look out for the baggage, and do all the business with the hotel people" (*Washington Post*, August 30, 1899). Once others were hired to handle these duties, the importance of the captain was further diminished. In 1899, Washington manager Arthur Irwin remarked, "The only use for a Captain on a ball team, when a manager is on the bench, is to answer all arguments in which any of his players are involved with the umpires" (quoted in the *Washington Post*, March 19, 1899).

Nevertheless it was many years before clubs saw fit to eliminate the role. An initial reason for this reluctance was that owners used bonuses to captains to evade their own salary caps (see **18.5.12**, "Performance Bonuses"). Yet the use of captains persisted even after that practice waned and they had no obvious function. In 1917 Cleveland manager Lee Fohl decided to "dispense with the figure-head" of a captain, commenting, "The idea of a captain is a joke, in my way of thinking" (*Warren Evening Times*, April 12, 1917).

6.1.3 Hustlers. In the 1870s all players were free agents at the completion of their contracts, which meant that one of a manager's most important responsibilities was signing up the best players for the next season. Despite efforts to prevent the inevitable conflicts of interest, this often included negotiating with players while they were playing for rival clubs. "The way to engage a first-class club for next season," noted one sportswriter in 1876, "is not to sit down, fold your hands and wait for the players to come to you and beg to be engaged. The managers who mean 'business' next year, are now buzzing around from city to city among the players like a fly-trap swallows flies" (*Cincinnati Enquirer*, reprinted in *Louisville Courier-Journal*, July 7, 1876).

This spawned a new breed of managers who became known as hustlers. These men were generally ex-players with a flair for salesmanship who could take on the role of finding and recruiting players while also scheduling matches and building up interest around town. For example, the local papers in Grand Rapids, Michigan, criticized player-manager Henry Monroe Jones in 1883 for failing to schedule enough games against attractive opponents. This obviously wouldn't be expected of today's managers, but this was an essential function for clubs being run on razor-thin margins. As a result, the following year Jones was relieved of managing duties and replaced by "Hustling" Horace Phillips.

Phillips was the epitome of this new breed of manager. Tom Brown, who played for Phillips in both Columbus and Pittsburgh, recalled that the manager used "Barnum methods" that he had learned while managing show business acts: "Lithographs of the various players were sent ahead of the various cities on the trip and were billed like a circus. 'Al Maul, king of pitchers,' 'Tom Brown, the young California sprinter,' 'Ed Morris, the wizard of the slab,' and other catchy titles were applied to the players on Phillips' team in the lithos, the three-sheets and strands of bills that were plastered all over. . . . Then Horace used to put a large display ad in the papers and rain thousands of dodgers over the streets. This application of the theatrical idea to baseball proved a profitable investment" (*Chicago Times*, August 18, 1897). Phillips and kindred spirit Dan O'Leary were described as being "about as fine an article in the way of managers as there are in the profession. Either one of the above pair could go to Egypt, Honolulu or some other out of the way post and inside of a week organize a good base ball team and have the populace worked up to a high pitch of excitement over the game" (*Cincinnati Enquirer*, reprinted in the *Grand Rapids* [Mich.] *Daily Democrat*, August 14, 1883).

This could prove a mixed blessing, as the enthusiasm they drummed up was often short-lived. An 1886 article noted, "Mr. Phillips is a 'hustler,' a faculty that Mr. [Harry] Wright does not lay claim to. 'Hustlers' seldom have the faculty of properly handling players after they get them" (*The Official Baseball Record*, May 14, 1886). By then, however, the 1879 adoption of the "Reserve Rule/Clause" (**18.2.1**) and its sub-sequent expansion to include all the players on a major league roster had eliminated one of the main reasons for the rise of the "hustler."

6.1.4 College of Coaches. Does one person have to be in charge? A hierarchical structure with one person overseeing everything entered baseball at the end of the Civil War and has been largely taken for granted ever since. But one notable reexamination of that premise occurred, appropriately enough, during the 1960s.

During the 1961 and 1962 seasons, innovative Chicago Cubs owner Philip K. Wrigley initiated a strange experiment in which the Cubs had no permanent manager. The club instead employed a group of coaches who rotated responsibilities every few weeks. Included in the rotation was the role of "head coach," as the manager was called.

Elvin Tappe, who became one of the rotating coaches, later claimed to have suggested the concept but in a very different form. He approached Wrigley with the idea to "rotate the coaches in the Cubs' minor league system so that all the young players would learn the basics the same way. . . . This would really help if you had a manager who had been a good pitcher in his playing days but didn't know much about hitting, or a guy who was a good hitter." Tappe noted that he "never intended it to be used at the big league level," but "Mr. Wrigley got all carried away and . . . started at the top and worked his way down, instead of the other way around. That was a mistake" (quoted in John Skipper, *Inside Pitch*, 42–44).

It was an imaginative idea in theory but in practice was reportedly a disaster. The Cubs remained near the bottom of the National League for the next two seasons, which was not unexpected. What was worse was that their young players didn't show much improvement. Pitcher Don Elston recalled that players found the lack of continuity "very confusing." Ron Santo believed that the development of Lou Brock in particular was hindered by the College of Coaches. Elston later claimed that, instead of giving the players the benefit of multiple coaches, the opposite happened: ". . . Not one of them helped one of the others. My impression was that whoever was the manager—or the head coach—was pretty much on his own. All they did was wait until it was their turn" (both quoted in Peter Golenbock, *Wrigleyville*, 371, 375).

The experiment apparently ended after two seasons when Bob Kennedy was appointed as permanent "head coach." The *Chicago Tribune* hailed the event with the headline, "CUBS COACHING STAFF STOPS REVOLVING" (*Chicago Tribune*, February 21, 1963). Stuart Shea, however, contends that the rotating system continued even after Kennedy was named head coach and did not end until after the 1965 season (Stuart Shea, "1967: The Rebirth of the Cubs," *Wrigley Season Ticket 2007*, 101).

6.1.5   Managers Are Hired to Be Fired. At least one nineteenth-century manager didn't accept the premise that managers are hired to be fired. Brothers George and J. Earl Wagner, who owned the Athletics in 1891, "called for the resignation of Manager William Sharsig. The latter refuses to step aside, declaring that he has a contract that holds good in law, and he proposes to stick. . . . As he proposes to stick, and the Wagners say he must go, there will be fun" (*Williamsport Sunday Grit*, May 10, 1891). The manager maintained that he had accepted the job and signed a one-year contract only after receiving a "solemn promise that it should be for the full season, and he set aside other engagements to take it" (*Sporting Times*, May 16, 1891). Apparently the Wagners won the power struggle, as Sharsig was replaced soon thereafter.

6.1.6   Firing the Team. While it's a baseball commonplace that you can fire the manager but not the players, at least one minor league team tried the latter strategy. The event took place in 1902 in the Pennsylvania League. *Sporting Life* recorded: "The players of the Lebanon Club on Friday morning [May 23] revolted against Manager [M. F.] Hynes, with the result that all were fined seven days' pay and released. Manager Hynes went to Lancaster Friday after declaring he would return here on May 28 with an entirely new team" (*Sporting Life*, May 25, 1902). Instead the entire league disbanded.

6.1.7   Trading the Manager. Midway through the 1960 season, Cleveland and Detroit pulled the only trade of managers in major league history, with Joe Gordon and Jimmy Dykes changing jobs. The unique transaction cemented Cleveland general manager Frank Lane's reputation as "Trader Lane," but the swap apparently wasn't his idea. Lane later claimed that the deal was initiated by Detroit general manager Bill DeWitt, and Lane expressed his regret for agreeing to the trade. He explained, "There's a certain dignity to a manager and he shouldn't be subjected to a trade" (quoted in *Sporting News*, March 20, 1965).

6.1.8   Firing During Spring Training. The first manager to be fired during spring training was Phil Cavaretta in 1954. He has since been joined by Alvin Dark and Tim Johnson.

(ii) Substitutions

The manager's role became far more complex once substitutions became legal. A wide variety of previously impossible or impractical strategies, including pinch hitting, pinch running, and relief pitching, became viable. Managers became responsible for an increasing number of players and suddenly had the luxury of making in-game adjustments.

6.2.1   Insertion of Substitutes. As discussed under "Substitutions" (1.32), until the 1890s a player could not be replaced except under special circumstances. As a result, clubs tried to ensure that their nine contained several players capable of filling the key positions, especially the battery. By doing so they could move an injured player to the outfield and replace him with a healthy player. In 1873, Henry Chadwick referred to "the rule requiring two pitchers and two catchers in a nine" (*New York Clipper*, April 5, 1873). While this does not appear to have been an explicit rule, it only made sense to have players in the lineup who were able to fill in at these critical positions.

By the early 1870s top clubs generally had a tenth player on hand to play if needed. The *Chicago Tribune* aptly summed up his duties in 1870 when they described Clipper Flynn as "one of those thoroughly useful and sensible ball players who can afford to be the tenth, or general utility man, for the sake of the credit to be derived by doing everything well" (*Chicago Tribune*, June 1, 1870).

By the end of the decade, the role was a staple of professional clubs. Notes such as "The tenth man will be either [Doc] Bushong or [Joe] Roche" and "Mr. Michael Muldoon, the tenth man of the New Bedford club, arrived the first of the week" became commonplace (*Chicago Tribune*, December 15, 1878; *Boston Globe*, April 13, 1879).

Budgets remained very tight, however, and extra players were a luxury that clubs could ill afford. Many tried to justify the expense by assigning the substitute extra responsibilities. Ticket-taking duty was the most common task, with an 1877 note stating: "Finley, Chicago's eleventh man, will play in the ticket office. He was placed under a League contract to keep him in good condition" (*St. Louis Globe-Democrat*, March 25, 1877, 7). In 1876 a St. Louis club engaged a player named Al Turner as an umpire and extra man (*Detroit Free Press*, August 19, 1876). John J. Piggott was hired as a groundskeeper and occasional substitute (*Detroit Post and Tribune*, March 30, 1882; the *Detroit Free Press* of March 26, 1882, listed his duties as janitor and sub).

Clubs that engaged extra players were considered to be setting a bad example. When Chicago began rotating pitchers Larry Corcoran and Fred Goldsmith in 1880, it was said that "there is good ground for believing that certain of the league magnates wrote letters to the Chicago magnates, denouncing them for establishing a bad precedent in the matter of expense" (*Detroit Free Press*, March 31, 1895). In 1881 in-game substitutions were banned, except with the consent of the opposing captain.

Clubs continued to have a tenth man, but often he wasn't even in uniform. Before the 1884 season Washington manager "Holly" Hollingshead told a reporter, "the Washington nine will have one reserve man, who will be in trim and ready to play ball at a moment's notice. His name is 'Holly'" (*Washington Post*, March 16, 1884). But when a substitute was needed a few weeks later, the *Washington Post* chided: "[Bob] Barr was disabled in the fourth inning . . . This necessitated quite a delay while [John Hamill] donned his uniform. It would be a good plan for Manager Hollingshead to have a substitute ready with uniform on, to take the place of any disabled player" (*Washington Post*, April 8, 1884). Similarly, John Coleman of Philadelphia was said to be "Harry Wright's general utility man. He carries the bats to and from the ground, sees that the water-pail is always full and contains plenty of ice and oatmeal, as well as sweeping and dusting the grand stand each morning, and scrubbing out the club-rooms once a week. He is a valuable and useful man as he is a pretty fair pitcher" (*National Police Gazette*, May 10, 1884).

The following year the *Boston Globe* observed: "The plan adopted by the St. Louis of having a tenth player on the grounds in uniform is a good one, and should be followed by all visiting clubs" (*Boston Globe*, August 7, 1885). A few clubs continued to balk at paying someone to do little or nothing, with Detroit manager Charlie Morton keeping in playing condition so

that he could fill in if needed (*Detroit Free Press*, February 8, 1885). Most, however, gave in, and by mid-season it was reported that "Each league club seems to have one or more general utility men" (*Sporting Life*, July 22, 1885).

An 1889 rule change allowed clubs to use one substitute. But his name had to be printed on the score sheet, and he could enter only at the start of an inning (*Aberdeen* [S.D.] *Daily News*, November 22, 1888). The strategy created new opportunities: "Beginning the tenth inning [Cap] Anson relieved [Gus] Krock and put in [Frank] Dwyer, who was on the card as tenth man" (*Chicago Tribune*, April 30, 1889). It also opened managers up to second-guessing: "The tenth man rule should have been taken advantage of in the third inning, when it was seen that [Bob] Caruthers' pitching was being easily punished" (*Brooklyn Eagle*, April 26, 1889).

The next year the number of substitutions was increased to two. Their names still had to appear on the score sheet, but they could enter the game at any time (*Columbus* [Ohio] *Post*, November 13, 1889). Indeed minor league clubs were informed that they had to have two substitutes present for games. This prompted complaints that the extra expense was not feasible given the strict salary limits (*Columbus* [Ohio] *Press*, April 17, 1890).

The introduction of tactical substitutions created a new breed of player, and of course it was no honor to be relegated to the bench. The *Sporting News* noted: "'Bench warmer' is the most opprobrious epithet you can apply to a modern professional ball player" (*Sporting News*, December 24, 1892). Of course it was better than "unemployed."

In a revealing 1909 article, sportswriter Paul H. Bruske presented the contrasting attitudes of Detroit Tiger reserves Davy Jones and Wade Killefer. Jones admitted that the role of sub was an "unwelcome assignment," yet he was philosophical, he said, because team president Frank Navin had assured him his pay would not be cut. But Wade Killefer was frank about his unhappiness: "there I sit, year after year, like a turkey buzzard on a limb, waiting for somebody to get hurt. My soul craves action and I think I'm getting there with the ability to act, if I get the regular chance. No man can duck into a game of ball and play a day or two at the speed which he should be able to show, when given a regular assignment. Philosophy? Well, that's all right for a player like Davy Jones who is drawing the stipend of a regular. I can't philosophize on the wage scale of a Southern Michigan league graduate, though, and that's what I'm regarded in this league. I wasn't in any rush about signing in the winter and I haven't signed yet. After I showed my reluctance, Mr. Navin wrote me, advising me to sign up in a hurry, lest I be sent down to Jersey City. . . . I wrote back, advising him to do his worst. A regular assignment to Jersey City would give me a chance to show whether I'm there or not and would be regarded by me in the nature of an investment. If I made good, I'd be back in the big league somewhere, getting what I could earn. If I'm only a minor leaguer, I can always console myself by the thought that perhaps I can do something else than play ball and make more money at it. But here I am" (*Detroit Times*, March 17, 1909).

6.2.2 Pitchers Being Required to Face One Batter.

This requirement was first introduced in 1909 and has been the subject of considerable shenanigans, which have caused it to be modified several times.

In 1913 umpire Billy Evans explained the impetus for the rule's creation four years earlier, "Every umpire, player and fan can recall what a lot of jockeying a manager used to do when one of his pitchers suddenly showed signs of distress. In such cases, usually no pitcher would be warmed up. Naturally it would then become the purpose of the manager to consume enough time to allow his star twirler to get in proper shape to pitch. In response to a request for the name of a pitcher who would take the place of the man removed, the manager, after carefully looking over the available men on the bench, would inform the umpire that So and So would be the pitcher. The pitcher so announced would slowly remove his sweater, take a drink of water, a chew of tobacco, and then leisurely stroll out to the pitcher's box. In the meantime the twirler the manager really intended to use would be pitching his head off out by the club house in an effort to get in shape to stop the batting rally that had been going on at the expense of the pitcher just removed.

"The rules several years ago gave the new or substitute pitcher the right to throw five balls. The pitcher announced would take his time throwing the regulation number. Then the manager would hasten out to the box, and inform the umpire that he had decided not to use pitcher So and So, but would depend on pitcher Such and Such. Mr. Such and Such would then go through the same routine as did

Mr. So and So, only to be recalled after throwing five balls, to allow the pitcher originally selected to take his place on the rubber. These two players by being so sacrificed enabled the real pitcher to get himself into shape to pitch, without possible injury to himself, or jeopardizing his club's chances by not being ready to give his best efforts.

"This practice was worked so much that it became a great nuisance to the spectators, delayed games 10 or 15 minutes, and was a custom generally obnoxious to the rooters who support the game. The rule makers realized the necessity of a change and incorporated a clause that practically did away with jockeying the pitchers for time. Now, when a twirler is substituted he must pitch until the batter has either been retired or reaches first. This condition made it foolhardy for a manager to substitute a man in whom he had no confidence. Incidentally it was the start of a system of constantly having a pitcher ready to step into the game.

"As a result of the change in the rules nearly every manager these days selects a couple of rescue pitchers at the start of the game. It is the duty of these players to keep limbered, and to start a real warming up at a signal, perhaps to desist when the pitcher in the box appears to have weathered the storm, but to be always at least half ready for a possible call that may be made upon their services" (*Sporting News*, January 9, 1913).

Illustrative of Evans's contention is John McGraw's use of Rube Marquard in 1908, just before the rule change. After he purchased Marquard for a record-breaking $11,000, McGraw twice ushered the rookie out to the mound during a game and had him warm up before he finally faced his first major league batter on September 25 (Larry Mansch, *Rube Marquard*, 43–44).

After the requirement of facing one batter was established, the desire to keep the game moving meant that relief pitchers were expected to be prepared to enter the game at all times. Their readiness was strictly enforced— sometimes more scrupulously than seemed fair. Billy Evans noted after the 1912 season that Clark Griffith had suggested allowing a new pitcher three minutes to warm up if the preceding pitcher had been ejected (*Sporting News*, November 28, 1912). Similarly, in a May 19, 1946, game between the Cubs and Braves, Cubs reliever Ray Prim came into the game but hurt his arm on his second pitch. The Cubs attempted to remove him but Boston manager

Billy Southworth objected, and the umpires ruled that Prim had to face at least one batter (Shirley Povich, *Sporting News*, June 5, 1946).

6.2.3 Interchanging Pitchers.

In a National League game on June 19, 1880, Worcester manager Frank Bancroft tried to take advantage of the spacing of Chicago's left- and right-handed batters by twice switching right-hander Fred Corey and left-hander Lee Richmond between the pitcher's box and the outfield (*Worcester Gazette*, June 21, 1880). The tactic didn't work out that day, but it was tried again with greater success on August 13, 1880, when Corey and Richmond changed positions five times during a 3-1 win over Cleveland. Henry Chadwick stated in 1891 that such ploys had been prohibited, declaring that "the rules admit of a change of pitchers during any part of a contest, but when they are taken out of the box they are not allowed to return again" (*Sporting Times*, July 4, 1891, 6).

This tactic reemerged in the early twentieth century after relief pitchers became common. Washington sportswriter J. B. Abrams gave this description of a seventeen-inning tie game between the Washington Nationals and Chicago White Sox on May 13, 1909: "Though [Chicago pitcher] Doc White held the locals in the hollow of his hand and allowed but six hits and one pass in the full route, [Washington manager Joe] Cantillon kept his crowd abreast even to the finish by as clever a manipulation of his players as was ever seen. He outguessed [White Sox manager] Bill Sullivan, and deserved the victory, even though his pitchers were hit thirteen times and gave nine passes. Twenty White Sox were left on bases, which shows how the National pitchers rose to emergencies. [Walter] Johnson, [Bill] Burns, [Dolly] Gray and [Tom] Hughes were used in the box, the shifts from left to right-handers, and back, being made as occasion seemed to demand of Cantillon. He would pit against a batter of like ilk, and then, when another tight place arose, he would change to a starboard flinger. When he wanted to use Gray, he shunted Hughes to right field so that he could call Tom back to the box later, which he did. While Thomas was in right, though, there was many a prayer offered that no ball would be hit out that way. But for once, luck was with us, and the game was called with honors even" (*Sporting News*, May 20, 1909).

The account of the game in the *Washington Post* explained that Cantillon was allowed to make unlimited switches. Although the rules specified that a pitcher had to face at least one batter, the wording of the rule began, "In the event of a pitcher being taken from the game . . ." Since Cantillon was not taking his pitcher from the game, the umpire decided that the rule did not apply. The *Post* noted: "This perhaps is not the spirit of the rule, but it certainly is the letter of it" (*Washington Post*, May 14, 1909).

Before the next season the wording was changed to read "In the event of the pitcher being taken from his position . . ." That modification seems to have eliminated the practice for many years, but it was brought back in the 1950s by innovative White Sox manager Paul Richards.

In a 1951 game Richards brought in left-handed pitcher Billy Pierce just to face Ted Williams and moved his pitcher, right-hander Harry Dorish, to third base. After Williams's at bat, the original pitcher returned to the mound (Red Smith, January 11, 1952, reprinted in *Red Smith on Baseball*). Richards repeated the ploy in 1953—this time replacing Pierce with Dorish on the mound for two batters and having Pierce play first base—and on two occasions in 1954 (Joseph M. Overfield, "The Richards-Jethroe Caper: Fact or Fiction?," *Baseball Research Journal* 16 [1987], 33; David Nemec, *The Rules of Baseball*, 49–51).

The tactic has occasionally been used since then, though its usefulness was limited by the addition of a clause to rule 3.03 that a pitcher and position player could switch roles only once in an inning.

6.2.4 Double Switches.

Researcher Frank Vaccaro has investigated double switches and has documented at least one occurrence in the 1906 season. In an August 2 game at Detroit, Highlanders manager Clark Griffith put himself in as a relief pitcher in the eighth inning and brought catcher Ira Thomas in at the same time. The previous catcher had batted eighth and the previous pitcher ninth, but Griffith reversed the order by putting himself in the eighth slot and Thomas ninth.

The tactic must have remained rare as it caused great confusion when Detroit manager Hughey Jennings used it in a 1913 game against Cleveland: "There was some confusion among the fans Thursday afternoon over the manner in which Jennings arranged his batting order after putting in substitutes.

"[Henri] Rondeau batted for [Ossie] Vitt and went in to catch in place of [Oscar] Stanage, thus keeping the second position in the swatting list throughout. [William] Louden, who replaced Stanage on the bases, was in turn replaced by Peplowske [Joseph Peploski] in the batting order, while Peplowske assumed [George] Moriarty's fielding position. [Les] Hennessey replaced [Jean] Dubuc, who batted for Moriarty, but went to second base instead of third.

"[Cleveland manager George] Stovall protested when Peplowske went to bat ahead of Hennessey in the ninth, claiming that 'Pep' was Moriarty's substitute. Jennings had explained to the umpire, however, that Hennessey was the man who had taken Moriarty's place and Peplowske was in for Stanage, and that he had changed their fielding positions after putting them in the game.

"A manager can make any shift in position he desires, but it is essential that a man remain in the same place in the batting order throughout the game, so Hughie was within his rights in arranging the two youngsters in the way he saw fit" (*Detroit Free Press*, June 27, 1913).

6.2.5 Pinch Hitters.

The early history of the pinch hitter is confusing. The first issue is the term itself. What we have known since the 1930s as "clutch hitting" was by the early twentieth century called "pinch hitting." Substitute batters were almost always used in situations where a timely hit was needed—in a pinch—so they became known as pinch hitters. One sportswriter even defined "pinch" as "the term applied to a hit which scores runs after two are out in an inning" (*Chicago Tribune*, October 28, 1906).

The second issue is the history of the tactic, which is complicated by rules and customs that made it either illegal or impractical in early baseball. Substitutes were legal only under special circumstances in early baseball, and it was customary to have only nine players in uniform.

Thus there are only a few isolated incidents from the 1870s where an injured player was replaced by a substitute who essentially functioned as a pinch hitter. The first appears to have been Frank Prescott Norton, a star of the 1860s who made his only major league appearance on May 5, 1871, when Doug Allison was hurt. Jim Devlin pinch-hit for Philadelphia in a game played on October 2, 1873 (David Nemec, *Great Baseball Feats, Facts and Firsts*, 228–229). Researcher Al Kermisch found that Bobby Clack batted for Dave Pierson in a game

on May 13, 1876 (*Baseball Research Journal* 19 [1990], 93).

Kermisch also compiled a list of several pinch hitters who were used during the 1880s (*Baseball Research Journal* 21 [1992], 112). The list, however, was a short one because a rule change in 1881 prohibited any substitutions except in case of an injury that was approved by the opposing captain.

Substitutions were again legalized in 1889, but still on a very limited basis. Only one substitute could be used during a game, and his name had to appear on the scorecard before the game. In addition, he had to enter the game at the end of a complete inning. This would seem to make pinch hitting impossible, but researcher Cliff Blau has documented at least twenty-two instances of pinch hitters being used in 1889.

The following year saw two replacements allowed per game, but they still had to be designated on the scorecard. The *Columbus Press* reported before the 1890 season that "a batsman cannot be superceeded [sic] by a player," which would seem to imply that pinch hitters could not be used (*Columbus* [Ohio] *Press*, March 16, 1890). In 1891 unlimited substitutions were finally allowed, but the strategy of pinch hitting remained extremely rare, with only fourteen documented attempts.

One of the reasons for this scarcity was illustrated on July 25, 1891, in a game in which Chicago led Cleveland 11-10 at the start of the ninth inning. Cleveland was the home team but was batting first and had two runners on and one out when the pitcher's turn came up: "Then from the brain of [manager] Patsy Tebeau sprang a brilliant idea. Ralph Johnson had been on the bench and Tebeau resolved to send him to the bat in place of [pitcher Lee] Viau, whose hitting ability has never yet threatened the world with a conflagration. The idea as far as Johnson was concerned was good enough, but Pat seemed to forget that by sending Johnson to bat he put Viau out of the game entirely." Cleveland scored four runs in its half to take a 14-11 lead. Unfortunately they "went out at last, and then Patsy Tebeau was confronted with a conundrum. He had no pitcher, and the best he could do was to send out [George] Davis, his center-fielder" (*Chicago Tribune*, July 26, 1891).

An account in *Sporting Life* three years later pinpointed this game as having "originated the trick of sending a heavy batter up to the plate in the final inning of a game to take the place of a pitcher. . . . Very few people in the stands understood the move, and neither did Anson. Uncle applied to the umpire for protection, but the rules say plainly enough that a captain of a team has the right to substitute one man for another at any time in the course of the game" (*Sporting Life*, October 6, 1894).

Unfortunately for the innovative Tebeau, Chicago scored four runs off Davis in its half to win the game. As this shows, pinch hitting remained a perilous strategy because of two practical considerations. First, clubs were very unlikely to have a healthy and dangerous hitter on their bench, since such a player would naturally be in the starting lineup. Second, even if one assumed that a hit would be delivered, the lack of capable relief pitchers meant that the benefits were unlikely to outweigh the harm done by removing the starting pitcher.

As a result, the use of pinch hitters increased only marginally in 1892, and there remained widespread confusion about the practice. Charles Reilly batted for pitcher Kid Carsey and singled in a game on April 28, 1892, but the *Chicago Tribune* left him out of their box score, explaining, "As he played no part in the game, he is given none in the score" (quoted in Paul Votano, *Stand and Deliver*, 17). Tom Daly hit a dramatic pinch-hit home run on May 14, 1892, to send Brooklyn's game against Boston to extra innings. But he hit not for pitcher Ed Stein but for the next batter, leadoff man Hub Collins, and then went to left field.

As pitching staffs and playing rosters expanded over the next decade, the strategy became more viable. John McGraw was a main proponent, though pinch hitting continued to be regarded with suspicion by many. Sportswriter W. A. Phelon reported that in a game on August 9, 1905, "One of New York's pet tricks went wrong. With the team a little behind, and the bases full of New Yorkers, [John] McGraw decided that the time was ripe for his favorite idea. He yanked [Leon] Ames, warmed up [Joe] McGinnity, and sent [Frank] Bowerman to bat. The trick fell down both ways. Bowerman forced a runner at the plate, and the Cubs knocked the stuffing out of McGinnity" (*Sporting Life*, August 26, 1905). The wisdom of pinch hitting for the pitcher thus continued to appear dubious.

That began to change before the 1905 season when John McGraw purchased the well-traveled Sammy Strang. A major league regular from 1901 through 1903, Strang, like McGraw, was an infielder with an extraordinary ability to draw walks. His defense was shaky, however, and when he had an off year at the plate in 1904, he became available. McGraw realized that Strang could fill a role for his club and made him a utility infielder and pinch hitting specialist.

The *New York Telegram* observed in 1909: "One of the recent developments of base ball has been the 'pinch hitter.' Almost all of the teams in the National and American leagues carry some player these days who is supposed to be able to take his place at bat in an emergency and rap the ball out of the reach of the fielders, thereby restoring his club to good standing and keeping peace in the community. To some extent John J. McGraw of the New York Nationals is responsible for this innovation. He was quick to see the advantages which were likely to be gained when the rule was passed that one player could be substituted for another at any time, and after it was put into effect by the rules committee kept one or two men on his team for not much of any reason than that they could frequently walk to the plate and smash the ball safely to the field when needed. There was 'Sammy' Strang, for instance" (reprinted in *Sporting News*, October 14, 1909).

Other clubs followed McGraw's example. Ham Hyatt was highly successful for the Pittsburgh Pirates. Dode Criss of the St. Louis Browns filled a dual function, as a pinch-hitting specialist who was also used as a relief pitcher. Harry "Moose" McCormick eventually succeeded Sammy Strang as McGraw's primary pinch hitter.

Not everyone welcomed this innovation. One sportswriter sniffed in 1913, "Manager McGraw, of New York, is credited with being the inventor of the pinch-hitter; at least he was the first manager to carry a hard-hitting player at great expense solely for the purpose of inserting him into games at critical stages for the chance of a timely safe hit. Inasmuch as all base ball managers are imitative all clubs now carry at least one pinch-hitter. For this may the Lord forgive McGraw, as there is no doubt that the system has added to the expense of the clubs, the length of the box scores, and the vexation of the scorers; while there is much doubt as to the practical value of the system" (*Sporting Life*, August 30, 1913). Another added, "It has become fashionable within recent years for a big league ball club to carry extra men who might be termed specialists. Washington has two comedy coaches, [Germany] Schaefer and

[Nick] Altrock, the Athletics have their special coach, Harry Davis, and the Giants have their pinch hitter, Harry McCormick" (*Detroit Free Press*, September 30, 1914).

Even the players involved seem to have disliked being used as specialists. Hyatt declared in 1915 that he would rather go back to the minors and play every day than continue to be used as a pinch hitter (*Sporting News*, February 4, 1915, 5). Moose McCormick once said, "I wasn't a ball player, just a batter" (*Sporting News*, July 21, 1962). But it was not long before the pinch hitter began to be accepted as part of the game.

6.2.6   Courtesy Runners. Courtesy runners were an occasional feature of early baseball. When a batter was hurting but not incapacitated, one of his teammates—generally one who was already in the game—would act as a courtesy runner. The courtesy runner stood behind the batter and did his running, but the batter did not have to leave the game. For example, an 1867 article noted, "George [Wright] waited for a good length ball, and away he sent it 'over the hills and far away,' easily securing his second, or rather [Eb] Smith did for him, George being rather too lame for active running" (*The Ball Player's Chronicle*, July 25, 1867).

Like so many of the customs of the gentleman's era of baseball, this practice did not survive the transition to a more competitive environment. The intention of the rule was to make things easier for an ailing player, but clubs began using courtesy runners in order to have a swifter base runner or to get a running start. So the game's rule makers decided to take action, but their efforts were not entirely effective.

In 1873 they decreed that "When a substitute is presented to run a base for another player, the umpire must ask the captain of the field nine if he objects to him; if he does, the umpire must rule him out, as the captain of the fieldside can now select the substitute" (*New York Clipper*, April 5, 1873). Frequent violations of the rule caused Henry Chadwick to comment in 1875, "It has been customary to allow a substitute to run the bases for the pitcher, so as to save him from fatigue. This is unfair, and should be frowned down" (Henry Chadwick, *1875 DeWitt's Base Ball Umpire's Guide*, 83). Following the 1877 season, courtesy runners were prohibited from serving as replacements until after the batter reached base (*Brooklyn Eagle*, January 27, 1878, 3). After 1881 a courtesy runner could not be used at all unless the

opposing captain or manager consented. It was not uncommon for this consent to be granted, and Tip O'Neill is said to have used a courtesy runner frequently in 1885.

When player substitutions were legalized in 1889, the use of pinch runners as we now know them became legal. But it did not become common to make a substitution in order to insert a faster base runner, and courtesy runners continued to be used. For example, the *Chicago Tribune* noted in 1905 that Jack O'Neill had taken the place of Cubs pitcher Ed Reulbach in the ninth "after [Reulbach] made the hit and scored the run for him, as he had a sore foot" (*Chicago Tribune*, May 28, 1905). A list of more than sixty documented instances appears on the Retrosheet website.

The courtesy runner was finally banned in 1950.

6.2.7   Pinch Runners. Pinch runners became legal at the same time that pinch hitters did, but early clubs used them sparingly. In particular, with constraints on budgets and rosters, it would not have been reasonable to make this a primary function of a player.

There were at least a couple of efforts to turn a track star into a well-rounded baseball player. Marty Hogan, an outfielder of the 1890s, once was reported to have tied the world record in the 100-yard dash with a 9.8 time (*Sporting Life*, July 20, 1895). A 1901 article noted: "B. J. Wefers, who is without doubt the greatest sprinter among all the athletes of the last decade, has been signed by the St. Louis National League baseball club as a substitute outfielder" (*Milwaukee Journal*, April 17, 1901). As fast as he was, "the trouble was that he had to get to first before he could give exhibitions of his speed, and the pitchers took care that he did not get there. Wefers could not hit a flock of barns, and he did not last long as a ball player" (*Washington Post*, January 7, 1908). Wefers never appeared in a major league game.

As with pinch hitters, John McGraw was the first manager to experiment with having a player who was primarily used as a pinch runner. In 1914, Sandy Piez filled this role for the Giants. Fifteen years later McGraw tried the concept again, using former pitcher Tony Kaufmann in this way for the 1929 Giants.

The idea was revived nearly forty years later by Charles O. Finley. As Rob Neyer and Eddie Epstein point out, while Herb Washington is better remembered, Allan Lewis was the first Oakland player to be used in that function (Rob

Neyer and Eddie Epstein, *Baseball Dynasties*, 284–286). Lewis occasionally played the outfield or appeared at the plate, but in six seasons he took part in 156 regular season games and batted only 29 times. In his final season in 1973, he appeared in 35 games but only once played defense and never batted.

In 1974, Finley signed sprinter Herb Washington, who had never played professional baseball. He appeared in ninety-two games for Oakland that season as a pinch runner but never once batted or played the field. Washington stole twenty-nine bases but was caught stealing sixteen times. In that year's League Championship Series, Washington was caught stealing twice, and in the World Series he was picked off by Mike Marshall. (Coincidentally, Washington had once been a student in a course taught by Marshall at Michigan State University.)

Washington was released early the next season, but the experiment was not quite over as Oakland used Larry Lintz in the role of designated pinch runner in 1976 and 1977. Cliff Blau has enumerated other major leaguers who primarily saw action as pinch runners (Clifford Blau, "Leg Men," *Baseball Research Journal*, Summer 2009, 70–82).

At the same time Finley was conducting these experiments, the Class A Midwest League adopted a designated-runner rule. In 1975 the Midwest League allowed managers to designate a player in this role on the lineup card. The designated runner could pinch-run no more than three times in the game, and the player he replaced did not have to leave the game. The rule was scrapped after one year (Glen Waggoner, Kathleen Moloney, and Hugh Howard, *Spitters, Beanballs, and the Incredible Shrinking Strike Zone*, 61).

6.2.8   Relief Pitching.

Although substitutions were either impractical or illegal early on, relief pitching is almost as old as competitive baseball. Ineffective pitchers would simply switch positions with another player, and early clubs specifically planned for this contingency. The 1868 Atlantics of Brooklyn, for example, penciled veteran pitcher Tom Pratt into the lineup in the outfield or infield "in matches where it is thought a change pitcher is necessary" (*Brooklyn Eagle*, August 15, 1868).

Henry Chadwick advocated the use of relief pitchers with a different pitching style from the regular pitcher. In one of his early books he counseled, ". . . A first-class team always has two pitchers in it, and it is in your management of these batteries that much of your success will lie. Put your swift pitcher to work first, and keep him in at least three innings, even if he be hit away from the start. . . . Supposing, however, that with good support in the field the swift pitching is being easily punished, and runs are being made too fast, if your pitcher is one who cannot drop his pace well without giving more chances at the bat, you should at once bring in your slow or medium-paced pitcher" (*Haney's Base Ball Player's Book of Reference for 1867*, reprinted in *The Ball Player's Chronicle*, August 22, 1867). He regularly underlined the theme in game accounts, "In the previous innings Blakeslee had been put on to pitch in [C. J.] McNally's place, a change entirely useless, as the delivery of both was about the same, and unless a change of pitchers presents a different style of delivery, no benefit accrues from it" (*The Ball Player's Chronicle*, August 8, 1867).

In the 1870s and 1880s it was common practice for one of the outfield positions to be filled with a "change pitcher" who could be moved to the pitcher's box if necessary. An account of an 1886 game observed: "Pitcher [Ed] Daily was stationed in [the left] garden . . . partly because Harry Wright thought an extra pitcher might come handy" (*Detroit Free Press*, May 19, 1886).

By the 1890s pitching staffs had expanded and substitutions were legal, which enabled relief pitchers to play a somewhat larger role. But the pitchers who were used in relief roles were starting pitchers between turns, and there continued to be resistance to the concept of pitchers not finishing what they started. As Al Pratt put it, "a man hired to pitch was expected to pitch" (*Sporting News*, March 23, 1895).

Before the 1902 season it was reported that White Sox manager Clark Griffith was "planning on using Virgil Garvin scientifically this season, letting the elongated twirler go his distance, and relieving him the moment that he begins to show his weakness, after the sixth inning" (*Mansfield* [Ohio] *News*, February 9, 1902). Traditionalists like Henry Chadwick were appalled by the notion of a starting pitcher who didn't finish what he started. Chadwick fumed, ". . . The argument used by the pitchers in 1901, that the most of them were 'overworked,' was little else than a 'bluff' on their part to avoid their due share of box work during the season. A pitcher occupies the box in a nine-innings games [sic] less than an hour on the average, and it is absurd to claim that an hour's work in the box during each day is either trying to his physique or to his powers of endurance" (*Spalding's Official Base Ball Guide, 1902*, 86). Sound familiar?

The *Washington Post* observed in 1904, "As a general thing managers use their judgment as to when the proper time has arrived to replace a pitcher in a losing game, but some use a system of allowing a certain number of hits on a twirler in one or more innings in a game. Others figure that a pitcher is or is not in form by the number of batsmen he sends to first on balls. Many close observers are of the opinion that a pitcher should be allowed to remain in and 'take his medicine,' if the score is greatly against his team. Pitchers, as a rule, would prefer to remain in and try to turn defeat into victory. . . . The best-minded class of fans do not care to see a twirler replaced, especially if he is at all popular" (*Washington Post*, July 31, 1904).

Obviously no manager would assign an effective pitcher to regular relief duty as long as relievers were used only in lopsided games and the "best-minded class of fans" opposed their use.

6.2.9   Relief Specialists. As noted in the preceding entry, the relief pitchers of the 1890s were simply starting pitchers on their day off—there were no pitchers who worked exclusively in relief. The biggest reason was the mind-set that a relief pitcher should be used only if the situation was hopeless. As long as that was the case, it would make no sense to pay even a struggling pitcher to fill that role, let alone an effective one.

One of the first to challenge that way of thinking was John McGraw, but not in the way that would later become standard. Sam Crane explained in 1903, "Manager McGraw has originated a new plan which he will put into operation when the championship season begins, and will be an entirely new departure in base ball. He intends to work his pitchers throughout the season as he has during the Southern trip, that is, he will use two pitchers in every game, one being in the points five innings and the other four. No manager but one who has originality and nerve would attempt any such innovation, but McGraw has both, and has made up his mind to adopt the plan. There are many things, too, in its favor. The pitchers can surely do more work and go in the box oftener than under the old plan, for a half game will hardly be more than pleasurable exercise for them. Then, again, most games are

lost on one or two innings, and any ball player knows that any change of delivery during a game is more or less puzzling. McGraw says that the only thing to fear in adopting the plan is the 'roasting' he will get if the second pitcher should lose his game after the first pitcher had his opponents tied up. But he will take chances, just the same, and there is not a player among the Giants who does not favor the plan. It will be a radical and sensational plan" (*Sporting Life*, April 18, 1903).

Sporting Life editor Francis Richter commented disapprovingly: "McGraw's idea is by no means new, so far as the suggestion is concerned, although it has never yet been put into practice. No manager has yet had the nerve to try it out, and we have little doubt that McGraw will quietly weaken on it should he be bold enough to try it in championship games. It always was a poor scheme to swap horses crossing a stream, and it would be a still greater mistake to take out a pitcher who happened to be pitching winning ball just because he had completed five innings. The new pitcher would not be warmed up, and the change of style might be just what the batsmen were looking for" (*Sporting Life*, April 18, 1903).

As it turned out, Christy Mathewson pitched a complete game victory for the Giants on opening day, and Iron Man McGinnity followed with another the next day. McGraw essentially abandoned his scheme at that point, yet he does not appear to have entirely forgotten about it. For example, in a 5-2 loss to Chicago on May 23, 1907, he used the unheard of total of six pitchers.

In the ensuing years it became more common for teams to use an ace starter like the Cubs' Mordecai Brown to relieve at critical points in late games. An article after the 1912 season noted the success of pitchers like Walter Johnson, Vean Gregg, and Ed Walsh in relief roles and commented: "The pinch pitcher is becoming a factor in the big league races, and it may be only a short time until teams will have to carry great one and two-inning pitchers—men that hurl shut-out ball for a couple of rounds" (*Sporting News*, January 2, 1913).

Over the next two decades, pitchers like Doc Crandall of the Giants, Firpo Marberry of the Senators, and Wilcy Moore of the Yankees emerged as effective relief specialists. Yet the mind-set that it was wasteful to use a good pitcher in relief must have remained powerful, since none of these pitchers' managers could resist the urge to start them from time to time.

As a result, the first effective pitcher to be used almost exclusively in relief was the Yankees' Johnny Murphy in the late 1930s and early 1940s.

Murphy explained that he was willing to accept this new role because he felt appreciated: "I don't know how I'd feel about it if I had to go to another club. On the Yankees they appreciate the necessity, the value of relief pitching. [Manager Joe] McCarthy repeatedly has told me that he rates me on a par with any of his starting hurlers. I am paid the starters' scale. I am happy" (quoted in John Thorn, *The Relief Pitcher*, 61–62).

6.2.10   Closers.

John Thorn and John Holway characterized John McGraw as "the first genius who suspected the value of the save, although again, even he only dimly grasped the importance of his discovery" (John Thorn and John Holway, *The Pitcher*, 108). McGraw, for example, used Claud Elliott ten times in 1905, and when saves were retroactively calculated in the 1960s it was discovered that Elliott had a then-record six saves in those ten appearances.

Nonetheless, with saves not becoming an official statistic until the 1960s, it was a long time before today's practice of reserving one pitcher for save situations emerged. This trend began in the late 1970s with Bruce Sutter of the Chicago Cubs being one of the first pitchers to be used primarily in save situations.

6.2.11   Designated Hitters.

The American League's adoption of the designated hitter in 1973 was the culmination of a long and circuitous journey.

An 1891 article reported a conversation in which Ted Sullivan said that pitchers should not be allowed to hit, as they are a "lot of whippoorwill stickers." A. G. Spalding's brother J. Walter Spalding suggested that pitchers should just be skipped, leaving eight men in the batting order. Pittsburgh president William Chase Temple instead recommended "the substitution of another man to take the pitcher's place at the bat when it came his turn to go there." It was reported that the idea would be presented to the rules committee, but I found no indication that that happened (*Sporting News*, December 19, 1891).

The idea continued to resurface from time to time, and in 1900 Tim Murnane voiced his support. Connie Mack brought the matter to the rules committee in 1906 (*Sporting Life*, February 3, 1906). John Heydler proposed the designated hitter at the annual National League meeting on December 11, 1928, and John McGraw thought it was a good idea. Ironically it was the American League that opposed the idea. It was probably just the wrong time for the idea, since run scoring was at historically high levels and others were proposing ways to reduce offense (William B. Mead, *Two Spectacular Seasons*, 111–112).

By the 1960s the idea had gained enough support for several minor leagues to express interest. The Pacific Coast League wanted to use the designated hitter in 1961 but was denied permission to do so by the Professional Baseball Rules Committee. During spring training in 1967, the Chicago White Sox experimented with allowing a designated pinch hitter to bat twice in a game.

The experimentation increased greatly in 1969, partly in reaction to the dominance of pitchers during the 1968 season. During spring training the major leagues experimented with a variety of ways of having a "designated pinch hitter." Researcher John Lewis drew my attention to an article about the different rules that appeared in the February 15, 1969, issue of the *Sporting News*. The designated pinch hitter, which was the equivalent of the current designated hitter, was used that year in four minor leagues: the American Association, the International League, the Eastern League, and the Arizona Instructional League. Meanwhile the Texas League used a wild-card pinch hitter who could bat for any player.

Researcher Kevin Saldana reported that Paul Flesner of the Dallas-Fort Worth Spurs became the first wild-card pinch hitter on April 11, 1969, going 2 for 4 with 4 RBIs. According to Lewis, the first true designated hitter in regular season professional baseball was either John Brandt of Oklahoma City, Larry Osborne of Omaha, or Charles Weatherspoon of Denver on April 18.

The American League finally approved the idea as a three-year experiment on December 10, 1972. On March 6, 1973, Larry Hisle became the first designated hitter to appear in an exhibition game and drove in seven runs. On April 6, Ron Blomberg of the Yankees became the first DH in a regular-season game. The AL made the rule permanent in December 1975.

According to sportswriter Red Smith, the National League almost adopted the designated hitter in 1980 (Red Smith, August 18, 1980, reprinted in *Red Smith on Baseball*). Nonetheless more than three decades after the American

League first used the designated hitter this remains a major difference between two leagues
that are otherwise virtually indistinguishable.

(iii) Lineups

Obviously, filling out a lineup card was a
straightforward act in the days when clubs carried nine or at most ten players. But as roster
sizes swelled during the 1880s, lineups increasingly assumed strategic implications.

6.3.1 Submitting Lineups. In early baseball
there were some attempts to require clubs to
submit their lineups before the start of the
game, but they were not very successful. After
the 1877 season the National League decided
that a captain could send his players to bat in
any order he wanted, though he had to continue that order in subsequent trips through the
order (*Chicago Tribune*, December 9, 1877).

An 1880 article complained that the lineups
in the scorecards were too often incorrect because of captains making last-minute changes
to their batting orders. The writer suggested
prohibiting such changes because "The audience has a right to expect that its score-card
should be correct, and, to the many who wish
to keep the score, a lack of correctness is a
serious annoyance. There is little or nothing
in the batting order, anyhow, and it should
not be changed out of a mere freak. The rights
of patrons of the game, who make the game
possible, should be respected, and, in order to
secure accuracy, visiting clubs should always
furnish the home club with their batting order
the evening before the game, sending it by mail,
if necessary, in order to get it there on time. It
might not be a bad idea for the league to inflict
a light penalty for changes, to prevent their
being made without a good cause" (*Chicago
Times*, reprinted in the *New York Sunday Mercury*, May 8, 1880).

Such a policy was indeed adopted in 1881,
in the form of a new rule that "requires the
captain of each nine to furnish the exact batting
order by nine o'clock on the morning of each
game, and prohibits any change in the order
so furnished, except in case of sickness or accident. The requirement was designed to address
declining scorecard sales by ensuring that they
contained accurate lineups (*New York Clipper*,
April 2, 1881).

This was quite a significant change because managers were in the habit of making
adjustments during the first time through the

lineup. One sportswriter predicted that the
new rule "will affect [Cap] Anson very badly.
Last season if [leadoff batter George] Gore and
[second hitter Abner] Dalrymple hit for bases
you might expect to see Anson go to bat third,
but if there was nobody on bases the big captain
would generally be found fourth or fifth in the
list" (reprinted in the *Cleveland Leader*, April 2,
1881). Not everyone seems to have understood
that the manager no longer had this privilege.
In an 1882 game, Buffalo player-manager Jim
O'Rourke "changed the batting order of his
men after the game began, and claimed that
it was not established until all had taken their
turn at the bat." The umpire initially agreed
with O'Rourke, and only changed his interpretation after a protest by opposing manager
Harry Wright (*Chicago Herald*, February 25,
1883).

The "sickness or accident" exception in the
rule also caused difficulty, as umpire Billy Evans
explained in 1913: "Not so many years ago it
was customary for the umpire to get the lineup
some time prior to the start of the game. Often
a manager would say either Jones or Smith
would play left field that day, there being some
doubt because Jones, who is the regular man,
was said to be suffering with a bad ankle.

"The explanation listened swell, but in
reality the manager was waiting to see who
would pitch for the opposition before making
his final selection. Jones, the regular player,
happened to be weak when hitting against
southpaws. Now the manager desired to use
Jones if a right-hander was selected to pitch,
but preferred Smith if a southpaw was selected.
He saw two pitchers, one a right-hander and
the other a left-hander, warming up for his
rivals. That made him undecided. He hears the
announcement that a right-hander will work
for the opposition, whereupon he informs the
umpire that Jones says his ankle is all right, and
that he will play.

"Under the old ruling the fact that the
manager had stated either of the two men
might play did not affect the standing of the
player not selected. He could enter the game
later if the manager desired to use him.

"Under the ruling now in vogue the umpire
accepts only one man for a position. If after the
announcement of pitchers the manager desires
to withdraw a certain player and substitute another, the player withdrawn is through for the
rest of the afternoon, though the game has not
really started. Now, if a manager desires to use
strategy in finding out who is going to pitch, he

must be prepared to sacrifice one of his players to accomplish his end" (*Sporting News*, January 9, 1913).

Enforcement of the revamped rule also seems to have grown lax. For the first few weeks of the 1921 season, Cleveland player-manager Tris Speaker sought to "baffle gamblers" by not announcing his starting pitchers (Timothy Gay, *Tris Speaker*, 216). In 1923 a *Detroit Free Press* article observed: "Manager [Ty] Cobb's refusal to announce his pitchers prior to game time had Lee Fohl guessing. The Browns' pilot nominated both right and lefthand pitchers for his team's batting practice and then watched to see which of the Tiger gunners would participate in the clan's practice. Cobb continued the deception by instructing [right-handed pitcher Rip] Collins and [left-handed pitcher Ray] Francis to hit" (*Detroit Free Press*, April 19, 1923). In 1930 Commissioner Kenesaw Mountain Landis instructed teams not to announce their starting pitchers as a way of hindering gamblers, but he changed his mind when sportswriters suggested "that if the Judge really wanted to keep gamblers in the dark he should keep the schedule a secret, too" (William B. Mead, *Two Spectacular Seasons*, 74).

6.3.2 Batting Orders. Batting orders were fairly malleable in early baseball. A wide variety of theories were employed in devising them, and they tended to be general rather than specific. Henry Chadwick offered this advice in 1867: "In arranging your order of striking, see that strong hitters follow the poor batsmen, and that good base runners precede them. For instance, suppose that your best out-fielder, or your pitcher or catcher, is not as skilful at bat as the others, in placing him on the books as a striker put a good base runner's name down before him; by this means the chances for the first base being vacated by the time he is ready to make it, will be increased, as likewise those for two runs being obtained after he has made his base. Never put three poor hitters together, but support each, if possible, as above recommended" (Henry Chadwick, *Haney's Base Ball Player's Book of Reference for 1867*, 82–83).

Even if a captain chose to follow this advice, it left him quite a bit of flexibility. With no dominant paradigm, it does not appear that captains of the period stayed awake at night worrying about their batting order, which is just as well. Sophisticated modern studies of batting orders show that the difference in runs created does not vary greatly from one lineup to another. Pete Palmer estimated that the worst possible lineup arrangement would score only twenty-five fewer runs per season than the best possible order (John Thorn and Pete Palmer, *The Hidden Game of Baseball*, 162–163).

As described in the preceding entry, batting orders were deemed to mean "little or nothing" at the start of the 1880s and might be changed during the first go-through if desired. But that flexibility ended with the 1881 rule change, forcing captains to plan orders beforehand on the basis of probability. The decision-making responsibility was also beginning to pass to managers, who responded by showing greater uniformity in their lineups. In 1884 Chadwick commented, "The old plan of changing the order of batting every game is not now adopted by the best managed clubs. Experience has shown that better results follow where a regular order of striking is observed throughout the season." After offering the same guidelines as seventeen years earlier, he reiterated that "a regular and sustained order of striking is the only way to promote team work in batting and base running, while the plan of changing the order, with a view of making it a species of reward, is a bad one in every way, it being neither an honor to be at the head of the list, nor any discredit to be the ninth man at the bat" (*Brooklyn Eagle*, August 10, 1884).

Some of the factors that the manager considered in arranging his lineup reflected the conditions of the day, such as the fact that base coaching was still done by players. Researcher David Ball discovered an 1889 account that explained that, as a result, Indianapolis manager Jack Glasscock spaced his three best base coaches in the lineup so that one of them would always be available to coach (*Sporting Life*, August 28, 1889).

By the 1890s managers were putting considerable emphasis on batting orders. *Sporting Life*'s Kansas City correspondent noted in 1892, "The question of the batting order of the team is worrying [Kansas City] Manager [Jimmy] Manning to some extent, as he is not acquainted with the hitting ability of his men" (*Sporting Life*, April 16, 1892). *Sporting Life* editor Francis Richter added in 1903, "A batting order is a serious matter. It can only be well made up on each player's ability in various departments, and once arranged should not be disturbed except when a man's failure to come up to form and expectation is complete and apparently irremediable" (*Sporting Life*, May 2, 1903).

6.3.3 Leadoff Batters.

Today's model for a leadoff hitter developed very gradually. Henry Chadwick advised only: "Let your first striker always be the coolest hand of the nine" (Henry Chadwick, *Haney's Base Ball Player's Book of Reference for 1867*, 83). An 1893 *Atlanta Constitution* article noted that Jimmy Stafford "always leads the batting order for the home team, because he is one of the hardest hitters on the team as well as the surest base getter and runner" (*Atlanta Constitution*, April 23, 1893). Researcher Tom Shieber directed my attention to an 1898 *Sporting Life* article that remarked: "It is customary to have a small, active fellow who can hit, run and steal bases, and also worry a pitcher into a preliminary base on balls, as a leader in the list" (*Sporting Life*, May 28, 1898). A 1906 article reported that Bill O'Neill "looks like a good lead off, being left handed, fast, and a good waiter" (*Chicago Tribune*, March 26, 1906).

6.3.4 Second-place Hitters.

Sporting Life's Kansas City correspondent noted in 1892 that player-manager Jimmy Manning would lead off and "will be followed by [Arthur] Sunday, who is a left-handed hitter. This will give Manning a chance to steal second" (*Sporting Life*, April 16, 1892). The same 1898 *Sporting Life* article that noted the development of customs for leadoff batters added that clubs liked to place a "clever sacrifice hitter" in the second slot (*Sporting Life*, May 28, 1898).

6.3.5 Cleanup Hitters.

Since home runs were rare occurrences between 1870 and 1920, the precept of batting a home run hitter fourth was naturally slow to develop. But the need for a good run producer in that slot was recognized from the early days in baseball history, and Cap Anson generally penciled his own name in there.

As power came to play a larger role in the game, the tendency to bat home run hitters fourth also developed. The 1898 article on batting-order customs gave this job description: "a massive slugger who can drive the ball out of the lot" (*Sporting Life*, May 28, 1898). Tim Murnane noted in 1904: "The heavy hitter of the team is located at the fourth place" (*Washington Post*, July 24, 1904).

The term we now use had come into vogue by 1908 when sportswriter Al Weinfeld wrote:

"That he was the 'cleaner-up' of his team is shown by his being fourth on the batting order for Peoria all season" (*Sporting News*, December 24, 1908).

6.3.6 Spacing Left-handed and Right-handed Batters.

Before the advent of relief pitching there would have been no logical reason to alternate left- and right-handed batters. Indeed, managers generally took the opposite approach.

In 1879 the Holyoke Club used left-handed batters in the first four lineup slots (*St. Louis Globe-Democrat*, July 27, 1879, 3). After the season, Henry Chadwick singled out the "introduction of batting quartets of left-handed hard hitters" as one of the year's most significant developments (*New York Clipper*, December 20, 1879).

As is noted in the entry on "Platooning" (6.3.9), 1883 Grand Rapids player-manager Henry Monroe Jones moved all of the batters with the platoon advantage to the top of his lineup. Evansville manager Charley Lord took this further the following season. When facing a right-handed pitcher, his lineup featured his four left-handed batters in the first four slots. But against a southpaw, "the left-hand batters [were] sandwiched in between the others" (*Evansville Journal*, April 21, 1884). Horace Phillips picked up Jones's approach when he succeeded him as Grand Rapids manager, then brought it along to Pittsburgh in 1888. A reporter explained: "The right and left-handed hitters will be dovetailed together. This is one of Horace Phillips' theories, and it is claimed that it will puzzle a great many pitchers" (*Detroit Free Press*, April 8, 1888).

Before the 1907 season it was reported that Boston manager Chick Stahl had made "a unique change in his batting order by alternating right and left-handed batters through the first seven men" (*Sporting Life*, March 30, 1907). Sadly, Stahl had committed suicide two days before the press date of the issue. Since relief pitchers were still used sparingly, it seems likely that Stahl simply thought that an alternating sequence would keep pitchers off balance.

There were other isolated instances of this approach, but it didn't come to fruition until after the use of relief pitchers became common. (For example, the *Washington Post* of April 15, 1910, reported that Washington manager Jimmy McAleer had separated two left-handed batters against left-handed pitcher Eddie Plank.) Lee Allen credited John McGraw with being the first manager to deliberately space left-handed and right-handed batters in his lineup (Lee Allen, *The Hot Stove League*, 33). Allen did not specify a time frame, but it seems likely that McGraw did this in the late 1910s or 1920s in response to the increased use of relievers.

6.3.7   Shhh! If a batter steps to the plate when it is not his turn, the opposing manager is well advised to keep quiet about it. That enables him to let the result stand if the batter makes an out. But if the batter gets a hit, the manager can have him declared out for batting out of turn. Jim Bouton related in *Ball Four* how Seattle Pilots manager Joe Schultz filled out an incorrect lineup card for a game on May 28, 1969. Schultz's opposite number, Earl Weaver, noticed the error immediately but waited until Seattle had a rally going before pointing it out and nullifying the threat (Jim Bouton, *Ball Four*, 162–163).

6.3.8   Out of a Hat. Occasionally a manager attempts to change the luck of a slumping team by picking his lineup out of a hat. Billy Martin, for example, tried this approach while managing Detroit in 1972 (Red Smith, August 16, 1972, reprinted in *Red Smith on Baseball*). Don Zimmer also resorted to this method of shaking things up while managing the Red Sox. To his chagrin, "seven out of eight came out in the same place they'd batted in the day before. That's how bad I was going" (Roger Angell, *A Pitcher's Story*, 134).

6.3.9   Platooning. As with so many components of baseball, the emergence of platooning was impeded first by practical considerations and later by philosophical ones.

There were few left-handed pitchers in early baseball, and the curveball did not become a major force in most pitchers' arsenals until the late 1870s. Although Bobby Mitchell was briefly effective, the first left-handed pitcher to experience prolonged success was J Lee Richmond.

Richmond won thirty-two games as a rookie with Worcester in 1880, and "columns of room were given to discussion in the newspapers as to why the delivery of a left-hand pitcher should be harder to bat than that of a right-hand pitcher" (*Detroit Free Press*, March 31, 1895). In a game on June 26, 1880, three left-handed Chicago batters, Abner Dalrymple, George Gore, and Larry Corcoran, batted right-handed against Richmond. Even Deacon White, arguably the greatest left-handed bat-

ter of the nineteenth century, was benched for an 1881 game pitched by Richmond (Joseph Overfield, "James 'Deacon' White," *Baseball Research Journal* 1975, 6).

Ned Hanlon, later a legendary manager but then an outfielder with Detroit, was another left-handed batter who was acutely aware of his disadvantage against Richmond. When Detroit and Worcester met for the first time in the 1881 season, it was reported, "for the reason that he had never been able to bat Richmond's left-handed curves, Hanlon was laid off by Manager [Frank] Bancroft and [Charles Reilley] was placed at center field" (*Detroit Free Press*, May 11, 1881). He returned the next day, and the *Free Press* chided: "The placing of Hanlon at center field yesterday proved the error of leaving him out of the nine on Tuesday . . . despite the belief that he cannot hit Richmond, [he] made one of the five base hits credited to Detroit" (*Detroit Free Press*, May 12, 1881). Nonetheless the next series between the clubs again brought word that "Hanlon did not play yesterday for the reason that he, being a left-handed batter, cannot hit Richmond" (*Detroit Free Press*, June 2, 1881).

The following season the *Free Press* reported with obvious pleasure that Ned Hanlon had gotten two hits against Richmond, though he "had solemnly affirmed a score of times that he cannot hit a left-handed pitcher" (*Detroit Free Press*, June 12, 1882). But Hanlon once again was on the bench when the Wolverines faced Richmond on September 12, 1882.

Henry Monroe Jones was player-manager of the Grand Rapids entry in the Northwestern League in 1883. Being a switch-hitter himself, Jones was very aware of the concept now known as the platoon advantage. The limited roster sizes and lack of in-game substitutions limited his flexibility, but he did what he could to give his team the edge. He had a couple of other switch-hitters on the club, and by using his extra players toward this end was able to get mostly right-handed batters in the lineup against lefties, and vice versa. He also moved batters with the platoon advantage to the top of his batting order. As noted in the entry on "Spacing Left-handed and Right-handed Batters" (**6.3.6**), Evansville manager Charlie Lord followed his lead.

By the mid-1880s left-handed pitchers were becoming more common, and an increasing number of clubs were doing what they could to fill their lineups with as many right-handed batters as possible when facing a southpaw.

An 1885 article noted that Sam Wise was not playing shortstop for Boston due to a sore arm, explaining: "Another reason, and a very potent one, for not playing Sam on Thursday was because of his inability to bat [Dupee] Shaw, the latter being a left-handed pitcher and Sam a left-handed batter, consequently for the present [Tom] Poorman and Wise will alternate in right field" (*Sporting Life*, September 9, 1885).

The tactic spread further in 1886 when Detroit southpaw Charles "Lady" Baldwin had an outstanding season. When Harry Wright's Philadelphia charges faced Baldwin, "left field was not occupied by George Wood. Pitcher [Ed] Daily was stationed in that garden. This was partly because Wood is averse to south-paws" (*Detroit Free Press*, May 19, 1886). Chicago's Cap Anson took a similar approach: "Dalrymple and Gore being left-handed batters, and not desiring to face Baldwin, [Jocko] Flynn and [Jimmy] Ryan were substituted" (*Detroit Free Press*, May 7, 1886). Tom Nawrocki has argued that Anson was the first manager to use a platoon system (Tom Nawrocki, "Captain Anson's Platoon," *National Pastime* 15 [1995], 34).

Bill James noted that outfielders Gid Gardner and Tom Brown of Indianapolis were platooned in 1887 (Bill James, *The New Bill James Historical Baseball Abstract*, 117). Pittsburgh's Horace Phillips experimented with a like arrangement in 1888: "[Abner] Dalrymple will lay off in all the games where a left-handed pitcher twirls against the Pittsburg team this season, as he is unable to hit a south paw's delivery" (*San Francisco Examiner*, April 2, 1888).

With so many managers already familiar with the technique, platooning naturally increased in 1891 when unlimited substitutions were legalized. Early in the season, Louisville's Jack Chapman became "the first manager to take advantage of the new rule permitting the use of an unlimited number of substitutions in a game, when he last Saturday took out three left-handed batsmen who could not hit a left-handed pitcher and substituted three right-handed hitters. This was also a new batting wrinkle which is likely to find favor with many managers" (*Sporting Life*, April 18, 1891).

Small roster sizes continued to limit this practice, as did the increasing scarcity of left-handed infielders. But a number of clubs tried platoon arrangements in the outfield. A *Sporting Life* correspondent reported in 1896, "When the Senators face a left-hander Captain [Bill] Joyce rearranges the batting order and sends [Billy] Lush to the field in place of a left-hand hitter" (*Sporting Life*, June 20, 1896).

A 1923 article offered this history of platooning: "Some left-handed hitters are easy picking for a classy southpaw hurler and it is for that reason that a number of managers have devised what is known as the 'reversible outfield,' playing as many left-handers out there as possible when a regular pitcher is in the box and switching to their string of right-handers when the team is called to face a southpaw.

"The famous Buck Ewing, when he was manager of the Reds in the late nineties, was the first manager to make this sort of shift. Buck was a fine leader, a very close student of the game, and a man who played the percentage down to the finest point. On his team he had Dummy Hoy, a great fielder and hardhitter [sic], especially against right-hand pitching. But Hoy was not as strong against the southpaws, so when such men as Frank Killen, Jesse Tannehill or Fred Klobedanz were working against the Reds, Buck would retire Hoy for the day and send in a right-hand hitter" (*Cincinnati Enquirer*, March 4, 1923).

Platooning does not appear to have been common in the first decade of the twentieth century, though it certainly didn't disappear. Detroit manager Bill Armour began using such an arrangement with his catchers in 1906 (Bill James, *The New Bill James Historical Baseball Abstract*, 117). A 1907 article noted that Washington manager Joe Cantillon had "decided that it would be too great a disadvantage to have five left-handed hitters in the game against a left-handed pitcher, and so decided to let [right-handed hitting Charlie] Jones take [left-hander Clyde] Milan's place" (*Washington Post*, September 1, 1907).

George Stallings brought the tactic back to prominence with the Miracle Braves of 1914, and Tris Speaker made use of it in leading the Indians to the 1920 World Series title. The success of platoons on these World Series winners might have been expected to smooth the way for their acceptance, but instead it only increased the vehemence of detractors.

Sportswriter John B. Sheridan inveighed in 1924: "What is the effect of substituting right-handed hitters for left-handers when a left-handed pitcher is on the rubber? Spoon-feeding baseball players. Giving them setups. Making things soft for them. Coddling them. Softening them morally, by keeping them alternately on the bench and sending them in only to pick on crippled birds. Permitting them to become soft of muscle and weak of will, discontented loafers or semi-loafers. . . . Shifting players, in and out, utterly dislocates team work. Oh, yes, I know that George Stallings did win the world's championship in spite of having two sets of duplicate outfielders, but Stallings actually won in 1914 because he had three great pitchers going right, not because he shifted outfields to the opposing pitcher. . . . About the very worst thing that can happen to any young man in any business or profession is to have things 'made easy' for him. Hell's bells, the only way to make a young man worth a cent is to put him out there when things are hard for them" (*Sporting News*, August 7, 1924). Mickey Cochrane more succinctly called platooning "bunk" (Mickey Cochrane, *Baseball: The Fans' Game*, 174).

Platooning finally became established after World War II, thanks in large part to Yankees manager Casey Stengel. Even then, there remained many who were none too keen on the idea. In 1948, Red Smith wrote, ". . . Students interested in trends might find some profit in studying the current passion for 'percentages' among major-league managers. Unless the style changes, we've seen our last Joe DiMaggio or Stan Musial, because today's managers won't let a guy stay in long enough to become an all-around player. They consider it a mortal sin to let a left-handed batter swing against a left-handed pitcher, or a right-hander against a right-hander" (Red Smith, June 15, 1948, reprinted in *Red Smith on Baseball*).

6.3.10   Bait and Switch. An effective way to gain the upper hand on a club that uses platooning is for the opposing team to start one pitcher but soon switch.

Washington manager Bucky Harris started right-hander Curly Ogden in the seventh game of the 1924 World Series with the intention of having him only face one batter. After Ogden fanned leadoff hitter Fred Lindstrom on three pitches, "The crowd, in amazement, saw Ogden roll up his glove, stuff it into his hip pocket and start for the dugout. But [Bucky] Harris, impressed with the hurler's pitching against Lindstrom, sent the righthander back to the mound to pitch to Frankie Frisch" (*Sporting News*, March 14, 1962). Harris had outsmarted himself this time; Ogden walked Frisch, and Harris then made the switch. The Senators ultimately won the game and the Series in the twelfth inning.

San Diego manager Preston Gomez used the same ploy in a May 26, 1971, doubleheader against the Astros. Left-hander Al Santorini started the first game but pitched to only one batter before being relieved by a right-hander. Santorini was again the starter in the second game, and this time he remained in the game. The Padres were swept in the doubleheader.

6.3.11   Lineup Tricks. Managers do have an effective way to counteract an opposing manager who uses the bait-and-switch tactic described in the preceding entry. They can list pitchers whom they don't intend to use in their starting lineup, and this tactic has the additional benefit of allowing them to pinch-hit if a scoring opportunity arises. On September 11, 1958, Baltimore manager Paul Richards handed in a lineup card that included three pitchers. On June 29, 1961, Philadelphia pilot Gene Mauch listed four pitchers in his starting lineup in an attempt to outmaneuver Giants manager Alvin Dark.

6.3.12   Hitter to Be Designated Later. Researcher Wayne McElreavy noted that Baltimore manager Earl Weaver started making use of a similar idea as the result of the events of the first game of a doubleheader on September 8, 1980. The Orioles used a variety of designated hitters that year, with Lee May acting in that capacity in this particular game. May batted in the seventh slot, but Detroit pitcher Milt Wilcox was pulled from the game after facing only four batters. Although the Tigers brought in another right-hander, Weaver realized that he would have ended up wasting May if they had brought in a left-hander.

Accordingly, in twenty-one of the Orioles' remaining twenty-six games that season, Weaver listed a pitcher whom he did not intend to use as his designated hitter. When the player's turn came up, Weaver would insert a pinch hitter depending on which hand the pitcher threw with. Detroit manager Sparky Anderson also used this tactic on two occasions, both of them against Weaver's Orioles. The rule was changed over the offseason to require the starting designated hitter to bat at least once unless the opposing team had made a pitching change.

6.3.13   Rotations. It is sometimes said that early professional baseball clubs had only one pitcher. This is a misconception. In fact, as early as 1867, Henry Chadwick declared that "a first-class team always has two pitchers in it" (*Haney's Base Ball Player's Book of Reference for 1867*, reprinted in *The Ball Player's Chronicle*, August 22, 1867).

These clubs generally had only one primary pitcher, but they always carried a "change pitcher" who would often pitch against the amateur and semipro clubs that made up a significant part of every club's schedule. Al Pratt later explained that in the early 1870s "there was a 'change pitcher,' who played the position when the regular man was sick, but a man hired to pitch was expected to pitch" (quoted in *Sporting News*, March 23, 1895).

As Pratt implied, good pitchers commanded top dollar, so clubs didn't spend comparable money on their "change pitcher." But sometimes they found they had two pitchers of roughly equal skill and tried to make use of both. George Zettlein and Tom Pratt appear to have been used in tandem by the Atlantics of Brooklyn in the late 1860s (William J. Ryczek, "George Zettlein," in Frederick Ivor-Campbell, Robert L. Tiemann, and Mark Rucker, eds., *Baseball's First Stars*, 182). The plans of the Forest Citys of Cleveland in 1872 were that "In some of the games [Rynie] Wolters will pitch, in others [Al] Pratt, according to circumstances" (*Cleveland Plain Dealer*, April 27, 1872). Tommy Bond and Arthur Cummings were hired by Hartford for the 1875 season and told they would both be "regular pitchers," though Cummings ended up getting the lion's share of the work (David Arcidiacono, *Grace, Grit and Growling*, 30).

Yet even on clubs with two strong pitchers, today's idea of a pitching rotation, in which the starting pitchers go out in more or less unvarying order, would have been considered poor strategy. This outlook accounts for the relatively late development of this now-accepted approach. In 1878, for example, it was said of the Utica Club: "We can give visiting clubs just the style of pitching they don't want. If [Nicholas] Alcott's style suits some too well, [Billy] Purcell will oblige with another variety. Both are effective" (*Utica Observer*, May 8, 1878).

It is often contended that Cap Anson used the first rotation in 1880 when he alternated Larry Corcoran and Fred Goldsmith. A December 19, 1891, *Sporting News* article may have originated this claim, and it was expanded upon four years later by the *Detroit Free Press*: "Up to the innovation started by the Chicago club, when Corcoran and Goldsmith were hired by

the Chicago team, and were pitched alternate days, one pitcher was supposed to do all the work. It created an immense amount of gossip among the baseball enthusiasts when the Chicago club adopted the new method, and the baseball cranks of those days, like the baseball cranks of the present, were disposed to be enraged at some of the other teams in the league because they did not engage another pitcher in order to be as well equipped as Chicago" (*Detroit Free Press*, March 31, 1895).

This, however, is a classic case of history being told from the perspective of the victors. Anson's alternate use of Corcoran and Goldsmith in 1880 is the first time that a National League club was very successful in dividing the pitching labors between more than one man, but it is inaccurate to call this a first.

In addition to the earlier examples already cited, Corcoran and Goldsmith had been used in the same manner for part of the preceding season when they were teammates for Springfield, Massachusetts. Goldsmith and Corcoran shared the pitching duties for Springfield until the club disbanded on September 6. While their starts did not follow a strict alternating pattern, neither man had a long skein as the primary starter. Another sportswriter noted that, "The Providence nine has demonstrated the value of having a strong change pitcher. By alternating with [Johnny] Ward and [Bobby] Mathews the club has prevented opposing teams getting the hang of either man's delivery" (*California Spirit of the Times*, October 4, 1879, 17). In fact, Ward and Mathews did not take turns in predictable fashion, but clearly there was a trend in that direction.

Moreover, in pegging Anson's use of Corcoran and Goldsmith as a first, a slightly more complicated but far more interesting story has been overlooked. Here's what actually happened.

With the start of the 1880 season approaching, the National League club in Buffalo was in disarray. Ace pitcher Jim "Pud" Galvin had not signed a contract and was pitching for a club in California. Catcher John Clapp, who had served as captain and de facto manager, had signed with Cincinnati, and no one had been named to replace him, leaving all decisions in the hands of a group of club directors whose knowledge of baseball was inadequate.

At a directors' meeting in March, "The question of hiring a manager for the coming season was deferred until a later date, although letters from two competent gentlemen were received. It was decided to send at once for [catcher Jack] Rowe and [pitcher Tom] Poorman, and they will be telegraphed for this morning. They will reach here by Thursday, when they will at once go into regular practice. The question of hiring another catcher was also debated. It is the present intention to have [pitcher Bill] McGunnigle and Rowe work together, and keep [Bill] Crowley in the centre field. This will necessitate the hiring of a catcher for Poorman. The management have several players in view, and when anything definite is done it will be made public" (*New York Sunday Mercury*, March 13, 1880).

Word followed that the club planned to balance the workloads of its two batteries: new catcher "Dude" Esterbrook paired with Poorman, and Rowe with McGunnigle. The *New York Clipper* noted: "The two batteries will be brought to bear on the teams they are most successful against. Experience has shown that every pitcher in the arena finds one team with which he is invariably more successful than against any other, and the team he is able to pitch against with the most effect should, of course, be that one he selected to play against [sic]. Thus the two batteries will be regular, instead of one being regular and the other the change-battery" (*New York Clipper*, March 20, 1880). Meanwhile Sam Crane was named captain but apparently given no authority over personnel decisions.

A careful look at usage patterns reveals just how ludicrous it is to credit Anson with inventing the rotation. Buffalo started the 1880 campaign with two starts by McGunnigle, one by Poorman, two more by McGunnigle, and one more by Poorman. Chicago, in contrast, began the season with Larry Corcoran starting six straight games. In their seventh outing, Fred Goldsmith was finally given the nod and pitched a shutout.

At this point Chicago hosted Buffalo in a fateful three-game series. Goldsmith did the pitching for the home team in all three games and was outstanding. Buffalo tried both of their starters without success. Thereafter the 8-1 White Stockings and the 2-7 Buffalo squad exchanged tactics. Buffalo re-signed Galvin and made him their primary starter while Anson realized that he had two outstanding pitchers and began to balance their workloads.

For the next eight weeks, Goldsmith and Corcoran more or less alternated with spectacular results. The club ran off six more wins to push their winning streak to a National League

record thirteen games. Chicago then dropped two games—one with each starter—before launching an incredible twenty-one-game winning streak (with one sixteen-inning tie), which has been surpassed only once in the major leagues in the years since.

The streak ended on July 10 when Fred Dunlap of Cleveland broke up a scoreless tie with the first "walkoff" home run in major league history (see **1.25**). Dunlap's blast not only finished the streak but also effectively ended Chicago's pitching rotation. Goldsmith contracted a fever shortly after the game and was sent home to recover. When he finally returned in September, Anson's use of his two ace starters was erratic. So Anson had taken an idea used by others, did so with the same two pitchers who had been used in similar fashion the preceding season, tried it reluctantly for eight weeks and gotten credit for inventing it because his borrowing corresponded with a twenty-one-game winning streak.

What Anson unquestionably did accomplish was to popularize the use of a pitching staff by showing that a rotation could be used successfully in the National League. The *Free Press* article was on much sounder ground when it contended that Chicago's success in 1880 "proved conclusively to many of the base ball managers that it was better to have an alternating pitcher for each series with a club, than to trust to one man to win all the games" (*Detroit Free Press*, March 31, 1895).

At season's end, Henry Chadwick commented that "the plan of having two regular batteries in working order and of working them in alternate games is a new one." He added that because of its success, "no club team of 1881 can be said to be fully organized unless it has two regular batteries, besides a reserve pitcher. A full team for a campaign, run as campaigns are now, must contain a dozen players, and of these there should be two pitchers, with two catchers to suit the pitchers and who are familiar with their peculiarities" (*New York Clipper*, November 20, 1880).

Until this time, roster sizes were generally limited to ten or at most eleven, so the notion of having to pay a twelfth salary was met with resistance by owners. As the *Free Press* later quipped, ". . . There is good ground for believing that certain of the league magnates wrote letters to the Chicago management, denouncing them for establishing a bad precedent in the matter of expense" (*Detroit Free Press*, March 31, 1895).

But competitive factors ultimately trumped financial concerns. That offseason, one of the directors of the Providence Grays expressed the fear that its rivals would become familiar with the delivery of the club's lone pitcher, Johnny Ward. So the directors signed three pitchers for the 1881 season, reasoning that "victories would come oftenest to the club with the heaviest artillery" (William D. Perrin, *Days of Greatness*, 12). Notably, one of the new pitchers was twenty-six-year-old Charley Radbourn, who had played second base and the outfield for Buffalo in 1880 while the club's clueless directors had begun the season with Poorman and McGunnigle pitching.

While Poorman and McGunnigle combined for fourteen career victories, Radbourn went on to win more than three hundred. He also brought back the one-man pitching staff in 1884, posting fifty-nine victories and leading Providence to the National League pennant. A *Sporting Life* correspondent commented that Radbourn's "wonderful success has been achieved at the cost of the complete overthrow of the claim of pitchers being unable to stand the 'great fatigue' incident to continuous work in their positions. What Radbourne [sic] can stand hardier pitchers than he can stand more readily, and he has proved pretty conclusively the absurdity of the claim that consecutive work in the box is too trying an ordeal for pitchers to stand without their breaking down under the pressure" (*Sporting Life*, September 24, 1884).

In fact, however, this was just another example of how perceptions of strategies often bear little relation to their intrinsic merits. In 1883 the constant use of Radbourn when two other pitchers were available "caused a lot of discussion about town" and led Providence stockholders "to wonder why it was necessary to pay salaries to three pitchers when one was doing all the work." And even with the benefit of hindsight, Providence sportswriter William Perrin maintained that the overuse of Radbourn in 1883 was "the rock on which the Grays split" (William D. Perrin, *Days of Greatness*, 24, 35). Yet the same tactic was hailed as a masterstroke one year later, with the only difference being that Radbourn had a better season.

Radbourn never again repeated his Herculean feat, and the advent of overhand pitching ensured that no other pitcher would approach it. The added strain of the overhand motion burned out many pitching arms and caused others to take unprecedented precautions.

The slightly built Billy Mountjoy, for instance, signed a contract with Cincinnati with a clause "that he shall pitch but two games a week" (*Washington Post*, May 18, 1884). Things got worse in 1887 when a rule change (see **3.1.1**, "Windups") made it harder for pitchers to use their legs in their pitching motions, which put even more strain on their arms (*Base Ball Gazette*, April 24, 1887).

Overhand pitching thus led directly to a rapid expansion in the size of pitching staffs. Within a few years most clubs were relying on at least three pitchers, and there was speculation that teams would need "a pitcher for each day in the week" (*Milwaukee Sentinel*, September 20, 1886, 8). Matters didn't get that extreme, but the 1895 *Free Press* article cited earlier did comment: "Nowadays no baseball team considers itself well equipped unless it carries a pitching force of four men." By 1904 a few clubs still relied upon three pitchers, but most were using at least four (*Washington Post*, July 10, 1904).

That season saw Jack Chesbro master the spitball (**3.2.7**), and his dominance prompted new questions about the necessity of large staffs. "If Chesbro can pitch every other day, or every six days in the week if necessary, what need will a club have for carrying along a string of five or six high-priced pitchers?" wondered Tim Murnane. "Three box men will suffice under the new conditions. This will save the clubs about $12,000 a season, or the leagues over $100,000 a year—quite an item and one well worth considering" (T. H. Murnane, "The 'Spit Ball' Fools 'Em—League Action Needed to Help Batsmen," *Boston Globe*, October 2, 1904, 41). Chesbro and fellow spitballer Ed Walsh both endured massive workloads, only to experience predictable arm troubles and prove that expanded pitching staffs had come to stay.

Larger staffs did not necessarily mean pitching rotations, however. As pitching staffs expanded, managers faced growing disparities in the quality of their starters. Thus they pursued all sorts of strategies to try to get more starts from their best pitchers, get those starts in the most critical games, and match specific pitchers against specific clubs. Chicago president Jim Hart explained in 1897, "I am not a believer in the rotation system of pitching men. Why? Because certain men are winners against certain teams and failures against others. . . . A man who is successful in fooling the hard hitters in a team should be used against that team. The very fact that he has puzzled them before takes away the confidence of the batters, and they are half-beaten before the game starts" (*Chicago Tribune*, March 8, 1897, 8).

Gradually, however, increasing credence was attached to the belief that pitchers did their best work when used in predictable sequence. A 1911 article noted that New York Highlanders manager Hal Chase was influenced by this way of thinking: "'Rotation' is the keynote of a new system of handling the pitching staff which has been adopted by the management of the New York Americans for the coming season. Six pitchers, [Russell] Ford, [Jack] Quinn, [Jim] Vaughn, [Ray] Fisher, [Ray] Caldwell and [Jack] Warhop, are relied on to carry the team throughout the summer, and they are to be worked in turn with clock-like regularity. Manager Chase believes that Ford's success last year was wholly due to the fact that he did not pitch out of his regular turn. . . . Ford knew exactly when he was expected to pitch and consequently nerved himself for the task. Chase maintains that if the other pitchers are worked in a similar manner they will prove vastly more effective and in this belief he is supported by many close students of the game. It is urged that a pitcher cannot be expected to do himself justice if he is suddenly called upon to enter the box at a time when he is hardly ready for a grueling test" (*Sporting News*, February 2, 1911).

Other managers seem to have experimented with this approach. Sportswriter James Crusinberry observed in 1916, "The [Cubs] pitchers who seem sure of places and who are likely to be worked in rotation the opening weeks are [Claude] Hendrix, [Jim] Vaughn, [George] McConnell, [Tom] Seaton and [Jimmy] Lavender" (*Boston Globe*, April 6, 1916). But a strict rotation remained uncommon for many years to come.

Johnny Vander Meer, for instance, described the rotation as if it were still a novelty in 1938 when he played for Cincinnati. Reds manager Bill McKechnie, he noted, "would put you on a system of starting every so many days, and we started regardless of who we were playing. He got you on that rotation, he got your system going, and he stayed with it" (Walter M. Langford, *Legends of Baseball*, 192). Similarly Red Barber considered this arrangement unusual enough in 1947 to note that new Brooklyn manager Burt Shotton promised his four starting pitchers that they would work in sequence without variations (*New York Times Magazine*, September 28, 1947; quoted in Lee Lowenfish, *Branch Rickey*, 432).

6.3.14 Weekend Starters. As discussed in the preceding entry, the rapid expansion of pitching staffs in the late nineteenth century led to speculation that teams would need "a pitcher for each day in the week." That specter seemed to have come to pass in 1897 when word came that Pittsburgh manager "Patsy Donovan will work his new left-hander, [Jesse] Tannehill, no oftener than once a week. Tannehill is fragile of physique, weighing but 140 pounds and one game every seven days is enough service for him, especially if he manages to win about fifty per cent of his games" (*Washington Post*, April 25, 1897, 18).

In fact American major league clubs have never made regular use of once-a-week starters, though there was a notable exception. After World War II, managers became increasingly prone to using strict rotations, but there continued to be exceptions when a manager wanted to give more work to one starter or have a pitcher face (or avoid) a particular opponent. One of the more novel consequences was the once-a-week starter, which became a bit of a tradition for the White Sox after Ted Lyons was designated the club's Sunday pitcher. Researcher Thomas Karnes suggests that the strategy was used at least in part because it was good for business—Lyons and the prospect of a likely win was a guarantee of a big Sunday crowd (Thomas L. Karnes, "The Sunday Saga of Ted Lyons," *Baseball Research Journal* 1981, 159–166). When Marty Marion managed the White Sox in 1955 and 1956, he revived the tradition: "I'd only pitch Billy Pierce on Sunday. Billy wasn't a very strong kid, and if you pitched him in rotation every fourth day he'd get murdered. But if you'd give him his rest he'd beat the opposition regularly" (Walter M. Langford, *Legends of Baseball*, 209).

Some Japanese teams use once-a-week starters, and perhaps that trend will yet come to the United States.

6.3.15 No Starters. Are starters who get the lion's share of the work necessary at all? Several years ago Oakland manager Tony LaRussa tried a scheme in which several pitchers would be scheduled to work a few innings apiece in each game. This was not entirely new, however. As discussed in "Relief Specialists" (**6.2.9**), John McGraw had proposed a similar arrangement in 1903.

6.3.16 Personal Catchers. The idea of a personal catcher was revived in the 1970s with such pairings as Tim McCarver and Steve Carlton, and was considered by many to be new. It is more accurate, however, to see it as a throwback to a very common practice in early baseball.

Once sharing the pitching load between two men became popular, many clubs chose to follow the same course with their catchers as well, creating two pairs of batterymates. In 1879 the *Chicago Tribune* noted, "Catchers and pitchers are beginning to make a point of practicing and hiring in teams. This is a good idea, and, if followed up, would produce much more effective catching and pitching" (*Chicago Tribune*, March 16, 1879). One of the more unique teams was the pairing of Frank Hengstebeck and Eugene Vadeboncoeur with the Port Hurons of 1882. When Vadeboncoeur was released, a nearby town's newspaper quipped, "now the Port Huron papers will have space for market reports, as well as base ball" (*Lapeer* [Mich.] *Democrat*, July 25, 1882).

The tactic of revolving batteries continued to be used throughout the 1880s. Catchers understandably thought the extra rest was a great idea, with Doc Bushong commenting, "The 'pairing' of pitchers and catchers so they can work steadily together, is always beneficial" (*New York Sun*, May 6, 1888). Henry Chadwick concurred, writing in 1890: "More than ever before was it plainly manifested last season that without team work together by the two battery players no pitcher, no matter what his individual ability in the position may be, can hope to be successful. 'How can I pitch to-day?' says the rattled star pitcher, 'when I have not got my regular catcher?' And that regular catcher is the player who knows every signal of his pitcher, and who is familiar with all his strategic points of play, and knows how to ably assist him in his work" (*Spalding's Official Base Ball Guide, 1890*, 45).

During the 1890s, however, such arrangements became increasingly rare. The strain of overhand deliveries was causing many clubs to use three or four pitchers. Meanwhile catcher's equipment was improving dramatically, and this enabled a team's best catcher to shoulder more of the load. Personal catchers thus became rare again, though there were occasional exceptions (Peter Morris, *Catcher*, 272–273, 358–359).

(iv) Intentional Walks

6.4.1 Intentional Walks. Bases on balls became part of baseball in the mid-1860s, and it did not take long before the notion of intentional walks arose. The idea was accompanied, however, by doubts about its advisability, since issuing a base on balls was inconsistent with the goal of preventing batters from reaching base.

The intentional base on balls thus was rare in the 1870s and 1880s, but it was not unheard of. Researcher Greg Rhodes found this newspaper account of a June 27, 1870, game between the Red Stockings of Cincinnati and the Olympics of Washington: "The pitcher of the Olympics did his best to let George Wright take his first every time on called balls, as he preferred that to George's style of hitting. George went to first twice on called balls, but on three or four other occasions he managed to strike the ball." Henry Chadwick wrote in 1873, "We have seen a pitcher purposely allow his adversary to take his base on called balls, simply because he knew him to be a skillful hitter, and chose rather to give him a base than let him make two or three by a good hit; and in doing this he purposely tempted the next striker to hit a ball to the shortstop, in order to capture the man on the first at second base" (*New York Clipper*, April 19, 1873).

Researcher David Arcidiacono discovered an account of what appears to have been an intentional walk that pitcher Bobby Mathews of the Mutuals issued to Hartford captain Lip Pike in an 1874 game (*Hartford Post*, September 2, 1874). In 1876 a sportswriter reported having seen "cases where a pitcher would give a heavy batsman his first base, preferring to take the chances of getting him out at second to his making a heavy hit that might let in one or more men" (*New York Sunday Mercury*, August 5, 1876). A *Sporting Life* correspondent noted in 1884 that pitcher Will White had a hard time against left-handed hitters but "understands his weakness in this particular, and we have often seen him give the left-handed batsman a base rather than let him hit the ball when a safe strike would bring in a run" (*Sporting Life*, February 6, 1884). John Clarkson of Chicago twice intentionally walked St. Louis's Tip O'Neill in a postseason game in St. Louis on October 21, 1886, despite manager Cap Anson's apparent efforts to dissuade him (Jerry Lansche, *Glory Fades Away*, 84).

Despite these examples, the intentional walk remained uncommon throughout the 1880s and was met with considerable resistance when it did occur. Clarkson's use of the tactic was denounced by the *St. Louis Globe-Democrat* as "contemptible" (*St. Louis Globe-Democrat*,

October 22, 1886; quoted in Jon David Cash, *Before They Were Cardinals*, 129). Researcher Allan Margulies discovered an account of an 1887 minor league game in which Rochester's [Fred] Lewis, "probably the best batsman in the League," came to the plate with runners on second and third and two out. Syracuse pitcher Dug Crothers "whispered to [catcher Dick] Buckley and then sent in five balls wide of the plate, purposely giving Lewis his base," so as to instead face Doc Kennedy, who had "had little success in hitting him last season." Crothers retired Kennedy, but the reception was anything but warm: "The Rochester contingent in the crowd hissed, and dubbed the play a 'baby act,' and some Syracusans joined in the ungentlemanly demonstration." The *Sporting News* correspondent, however, defended this as a legitimate ploy: "Instead of censure, Crothers is deserving of the highest praise for the act. It proves that he is not a record player [one who thinks only of his own statistics]; but that he plays every point to win the game, and that is all he cares about" (*Sporting News*, May 21, 1887).

As will be discussed under "Playing for One Run" (**6.6.1**), offenses began to feature one-run strategies around 1890. It is thus not surprising that the intentional walk rose to prominence at the same time, since it enables the team in the field to mirror the batting team's strategy by going all out to prevent a single run while risking a big inning.

Patsy Tebeau, manager of the Cleveland Spiders in the 1890s, was one of the men most responsible for popularizing the intentional walk. A later article noted that Tebeau "was a believer in the intentional base on balls if a weak batter were to follow a strong batter whose turn it was at bat. . . . One might go further and say that Tebeau was a near pioneer in the giving of an intentional base on balls. The first few times that he tried it in Cleveland the bleachers jeered. It was a new move to them. It will be found that the bleachers usually are quick to jeer anything out of the ordinary in baseball. . . . The giving of intentional bases on balls went on for a while and then Cleveland discovered that Tebeau was winning games . . . by and by, those who had jeered the Cleveland man began to cheer" (*Sporting News*, December 2, 1920).

The once uncommon strategy had obviously become a familiar one by 1894 when pitcher Ted Breitenstein commented: "I seldom send a man to first on four bad balls purposely and resort to this move only when the game is at a critical stage and I have more confidence in my ability to dispose of the next man up" (*St. Louis Post-Dispatch*, August 12, 1894).

While the 1890s saw the intentional walk become prevalent, opposition continued. Much of it focused on the scoring practice of considering a run to be unearned if a batter drew a walk and subsequently scored (see **17.5**). This prompted objections that "many pitchers save their records by deliberately giving bases on balls, knowing that earned runs cannot be secured, and thus they save their records" (*Sporting Life*, October 24, 1891). Clark Griffith raised a very different concern: "The pitcher who is afraid of any batter ought to quit the business. If he doesn't it will not be long before he is proved a coward, and then he will have to quit. The crowd is not in sympathy with any pitcher who is not game enough to let any batter hit the ball, at the same time depending on his own ability" (*Boston Globe*, July 27, 1896).

In 1900 sportswriter Ren Mulford, Jr., gave this summation: "When the game has reached such a ticklish point that a hit will win it, is it good base ball to give a hard hitter his base on balls and take chances on the man who follows? Al Orth did it once in Cincinnati last May, and held the Reds at bay in the twelfth inning of a tie. Whenever the play succeeds the wise ones chuckle and say 'That was good head-work in sending Sluggers to his base.' On the other hand, if the fellow who is held cheaply cracks out a bingle the same W. M. [wise men] growl about the twirler who 'quit under fire.'" Mulford cited a number of examples of successes and failures of the strategy and concluded: "There will always be two warm sides to the argument, and winners from both ends. It is one of those 'nothing succeeds like success' sort of plays, as uncertain as the national game itself" (*Sporting Life*, September 22, 1900).

The early twentieth century saw regular discussion of banning the intentional walk. In 1913, American League president Ban Johnson came out in favor of a ban, calling the tactic "one of the most, if not the most, unpopular plays in base ball" (*Sporting Life*, December 6, 1913). Hugh Jennings suggested that this could be accomplished by allowing the batter to leave his box to pursue pitches but forcing the catcher to remain in the catcher's box (*Sporting News*, February 12, 1914). Various possible ways to eliminate the intentional base on balls by allowing the batter or runners to advance additional bases were outlined by sportswriter William Peet in 1916 (*Cleveland Leader*,

November 30, 1916). But the lack of consensus on any one plan seems to have killed the idea.

The dislike that Clark Griffith had felt for the intentional walk during his pitching career continued when he became an owner. On February 9, 1920, he presented a proposal to the major leagues' Joint Rule Committee that would allow base runners to advance one base on an intentional walk and two bases for the second offense. But the rule put the onus upon the umpire to determine the pitcher's intentions, and umpires Hank O'Day and Bill Klem successfully contended that this would lead to endless arguments about intentions (John B. Sheridan, *Sporting News*, February 19, 1920).

The issue was again raised at a special meeting of National League owners in 1924, where considerable support was expressed for a ban. Once more, however, no consensus could be reached on a practical scheme for doing away with the intentional walk (*Sporting News*, July 31, 1924).

After the 1933 season the Southern Association announced plans to institute a new rule intended to hinder the intentional walk. If there were two outs and runners on base, four consecutive balls would advance all base runners two bases (with the exception that a runner on second would advance only to third if there was a runner there). The rule change was greeted with excitement but also concern that the national rules committee would disallow the rule (*New York Times*, November 18, 1933). The new rule does not appear to have ever been implemented.

The idea resurfaced in 1937 when Sid Keener of the *St. Louis Star-Times* made an imaginative proposal. He suggested giving a batter who walked on four pitches the option of declining the free pass. If a second four-pitch walk resulted, the batter could choose between a walk to second or again declining the walk. If he declined again and another four-pitch walk ensued, the batter would walk all the way to third base (*Sporting News*, October 28, 1937). Branch Rickey suggested in 1950 that a fair penalty for walking batters intentionally might be to automatically start the next hitter with one or two balls ("World Series 2000 A. D.," *Collier's*, October 7, 1950; quoted in Lee Lowenfish, *Branch Rickey*, 499).

Proposals for eliminating the intentional walk continue to emerge from time to time. But intentional walks—and the ensuing grumbles that they are unsporting—are now such tradi-

tions that it seems unlikely the status quo will ever be changed.

6.4.2 Intentional Walks with the Bases Loaded. Researcher Ev Parker cited two instances of this tactic being employed in the major leagues. The first occurred when Napoleon Lajoie came to the plate for the Athletics in the ninth inning of a game against the White Sox on May 23, 1901, with Chicago leading 11-7. Notwithstanding his dislike for this tactic (see the preceding entry), Clark Griffith deliberately walked Lajoie and then retired the next three batters to complete the victory.

The next bases-loaded intentional walk was ordered by Giants manager Mel Ott in the second game of a doubleheader at the Polo Grounds on July 23, 1944. The free pass was issued to Cubs slugger Bill Nicholson when he strode to the plate in the eighth inning with two out, the bases loaded, and the Cubs behind 10-7. The Giants hung on for a 12-10 victory (Ev Parker, "The Supreme Compliment," *National Pastime* 17 [1997], 138–139).

The year after Parker's article was published, Barry Bonds received a similar token of esteem in a May 28, 1998, game against the Diamondbacks. Arizona manager Buck Showalter ordered pitcher Gregg Olson to walk Bonds with two outs in the bottom of the ninth and a two-run lead. The next batter flied out to seal Arizona's 8-7 victory.

Of course there may have been additional instances in which a pitcher pitched around a dangerous hitter even with the bases loaded. Warren Spahn, for example, claimed that he once intentionally walked Stan Musial in that situation (Roger Kahn, *The Head Game*, 178).

6.4.3 Fake Intentional Walks. There is nothing particularly imaginative about the strategy of pretending to issue an intentional walk and then throwing a pitch across the plate. What is difficult is actually executing it, as the potential of a passed ball seems greater than the likelihood of catching the batter unaware. Nonetheless Oakland manager Dick Williams successfully employed this tactic against Johnny Bench of the Reds in a World Series game on October 18, 1972.

6.4.4 Lip Passes. There is always a risk of a wild pitch or a passed ball in the process of issuing an intentional walk. A few managers have devised imaginative ways to try to eliminate even that small risk.

Researcher Frank Vaccaro reports that a single "illegal" pitch could be used to send a batter to first base in the mid-1880s. He found that Philadelphia manager Harry Wright instructed his pitcher Charlie Buffinton to do that with Jim O'Rourke batting on August 19, 1887, only to have the next batter, Roger Connor, hit a grand slam.

During a July 9, 1924, game between Cincinnati and Philadelphia, Curt Walker came to the plate for the Reds with a runner on third base. On the instructions of Phillies manager Art Fletcher, pitcher Bill Hubbell threw to first baseman Walter Holke four times. According to the umpires' interpretation of a directive from league president John Heydler, each throw was ruled a ball, and Walker was sent to first base. Heydler closed the loophole by issuing a new directive, mandating that such acts be called balks (*Sporting News*, July 31, 1924).

Before the 1968 season, umpires were ordered to be more strict about calling a ball if a pitcher went to his mouth while on the rubber. Cubs manager Leo Durocher spent much of the exhibition season crusading against this directive. Finally, in a spring training game on March 23, Durocher instructed pitcher Jim Ellis to issue two intentional walks by licking his fingers, a tactic that was dubbed the "lip pass." This novel approach was not specifically banned, but a member of the rules committee suggested that Durocher would be fined $1,000 if another "lip pass" occurred. This effectively eliminated the lip pass, but Durocher did get some satisfaction, as umpires were instructed to be less vigilant about enforcing the rule.

6.4.5 Automatic Intentional Walks.

After the 1955 season, American League president Will Harridge announced plans to experiment with automatic intentional walks during the following spring training. A manager wishing to intentionally walk an opposing batter could simply notify the umpire, who would wave the batter down to first base. If the trial proved successful, the rule would be retained for the regular season.

Harridge explained that such drastic measures were necessitated by significant increases in game times. It was "laughable," he said, to look back in his files and read about efforts to speed up the game in 1944, when an average game lasted less than two hours. Harridge noted that the average length of games in 1955 had been two hours and thirty-one minutes. Something had to be done, since "So many times nowadays you hear the comment, 'Oh, Mr. Smith used to be quite a fan but the games are getting far too draggy for him now'" (*Sporting News*, January 18, 1956).

Few, however, agreed that this seemingly minor adjustment was desirable. Sportswriter Dan Daniel observed, "The idea is not exactly new. It has been advocated for some twenty years and, in the past, ridiculed with vehemence by the league which is now going to give it a try" (*New York World-Herald*, quoted in *Sporting News*, February 15, 1956). Yankees general manager George Weiss said, "It is not a good idea because it goes against baseball tradition, tends toward mechanization, and takes away from the suspense of the game" (quoted in *Sporting News*, February 29, 1956). Umpire Cal Hubbard cited the late Clark Griffith's comment that such a rule would "deprive the fans of four chances to boo," while Warren Giles also contended that fans needed the catharsis of booing (*Sporting News*, March 7, 1956).

Sporting News editorialized that the new rule "would remove from the game a small but colorful tradition." One might reasonably wonder how watching four wide ones could be characterized as colorful, so the piece explained: "There's a bit of drama in the picture of a Williams or a Berra or a Mantle standing helplessly in the batter's box, while the opposing manager tells him in actions which speak louder than words: 'You're too tough. In this situation, we can't take a chance on pitching to you.'" The editorial countered Harridge's argument by claiming: "Much of baseball's popularity depends on its allergy to change" (*Sporting News*, March 7, 1956).

Eventually the experiment died, not with a bang but a whimper. Earl Hilligan, chief of the American League's service bureau, explained, ". . . Not one manager experimented with the idea. Our managers were told the thing was strictly voluntary. They didn't have to use it. Evidently none of them wanted to use it" (quoted in *Sporting News*, April 25, 1956).

Similar plans were announced three years later by Texas League president Dick Butler, who explained that it was essential to speed up the game: "This is a different era, and we're competing with entertainment that moves faster and takes less time" (*Sporting News*, February 4, 1959). The automatic intentional walk, however, was immediately vetoed by Commissioner Ford Frick. Frick said the Texas League could experiment with the automatic intentional walk during spring training but would need permission to change the regular-season rules. He cited several reasons, including the importance of "the customer having his chance to boo" (*Sporting News*, February 4, 1959).

(v) Signs

6.5.1 Signs. Signs between ballplayers have been a feature of baseball since at least the 1860s.

Researcher Priscilla Astifan found an article in an 1860 Rochester newspaper describing how catcher Joe Leggett of the visiting Excelsiors of Brooklyn "won encomiums for the manner in which he would telegraph advantages to be gained, or the direction as to which one of the fielders should take a 'fly'" (*Rochester Evening Express*, July 9, 1860). Henry Chadwick added in 1867: "Always have an understanding with your two sets of fielders in regard to private signals, so as to be able to call them in closer, or place them out further, or nearer the foul-ball lines, as occasion may require, without giving notice to your adversaries" (*Haney's Base Ball Player's Book of Reference for 1867*; reprinted in *The Ball Player's Chronicle*, August 22, 1867).

When the Red Stockings of Cincinnati toured California in 1869, the local paper was impressed by the trend-setting Ohio club's use of signs. One article noted that the Red Stockings "have perfected a system of telegraphic signals as easily recognized as if spoken words were used. . . . [They] have really two captains—the ostensible one is in the position of 'centre field' [Harry Wright], and directs the movements of the fielders, and the other is the catcher [Doug Allison], who indicates by signs to the pitcher and base-keepers the proper thing to do at the right moment" (*Daily Alta California*, September 26, 1869; quoted in Paul Dickson, *The Hidden Language of Baseball*, 31).

By the 1870s, Henry Chadwick was advocating a quite sophisticated system of signals. In 1873 he recommended that the catcher "always have a sign ready so as to signalize the pitcher where to send in the ball," while the pitcher "should never commence a match without having an understood arrangement with his catchers and outfielders in regard to their movements by signals" (*New York Clipper*, April 19, 1873). Chadwick elaborated the following year: "The pitcher and catcher should have a code of signals between them, and they should practice these signs until they can read

them as easily as their letters. Thus, when a catcher sees an opportunity to catch a player napping off a base, a certain signal should be given by which the pitcher may understand that he is to throw to the base promptly. Again, if the pitcher is familiar with a certain habit of the batsman before him of hitting at a favourite ball, he should give the catcher a sign informing him that he is going to send in a slower or swifter ball or a higher or lower one than ordinarily is pitched" (Henry Chadwick, *Chadwick's Base Ball Manual*, 14–15).

Over the years, credit for originating signs between the catcher and pitcher has been claimed for many players of the late 1870s. These are obviously not firsts, in light of the examples already presented in this entry and in the earlier entry "Catchers Signaling to Pitchers" (**1.27**), especially the 1871 mention that it was common for the catcher to do "the 'headwork' in strategic play by directing—through private signals—the pitcher how to deliver particular balls" (*New York Clipper*, October 28, 1871).

Nonetheless the various claims are worth briefly reviewing to show how closely the emergence of the practice is tied to the parallel development of the curveball (see **3.2.3**). Tim Murnane gave credit to Charles Snyder when with Louisville in 1877, while H. G. Merrill cited Little Joe Roche of the 1876 Crickets of Binghamton (*Sporting News*, July 16, 1908). A *Boston Globe* writer suggested that pitcher Jim Devlin had been the originator (quoted in *Sporting Life*, July 1, 1893). In 1879 the *Boston Globe* reported that Chicago's Silver Flint used "a system of sign-language, which no one has been able to fathom," to tell pitcher Terry Larkin when a pickoff throw was needed. This prompted the *Chicago Tribune* to retort, "There is nothing at all mysterious about the signal. It consists of Flint turning his cap around on his head. [Boston catcher Charles] Snyder's signal to [pitcher Tommy] Bond is made by putting his hands on his knees" (*Boston Globe*, May 18, 1879; *Chicago Tribune*, May 25, 1879).

As signals between catcher and pitcher became routine, other types of signs also became more common. A Lansing, Michigan, newspaper complained in 1879 that the Lansing captain "had to resort to the questionable method of calling to [the outfielders], when a motion should have been sufficient" (*Lansing Journal*, July 24, 1879). An 1881 article counseled that outfielders "must be required to strictly obey the signals from the pitcher for all such changes of position. Time and again this past season we have seen a pitcher's strategy entirely nullified by the stupidity or obstinacy of some one or other of the outfielders to quickly obey the pitcher's signal to play deeper, or closer, or to get round more to the right or to the left, when he has been preparing to outwit a batsman by something besides the mere speed of his delivery" (*New York Clipper*, December 31, 1881). According to Tim Murnane, after Arthur Irwin joined Providence in 1883 the Grays became "the first team that knew every ball that the pitcher was going to deliver and it won it lots of games" (*Boston Globe*, January 5, 1890, 18).

Researcher David Ball found that signals were being used for base coaching by 1885: "The Baltimores have adopted a system for coaching base-runners a little out of the ordinary. Instead of yelling directions they give signs." But the *Cincinnati Enquirer* reported that spectators disliked this practice because they felt that yelling was a better way of showing spirit (*Cincinnati Enquirer*, May 3, 1885; reprinted in Frederick Ivor-Campbell, "When Was the First? [Part 4]," *Nineteenth Century Notes* 95:3, 4 [Summer/Fall 1995], 12).

It will be noted that most of the signs described in this entry were not given with much emphasis on secrecy. Umpire Tim Hurst claimed in 1894, "I know nearly all the battery signals now, and all signals made by the captain of a team, which is a great advantage for me in my work. . . . I have also to watch for switching of signals by a battery" (*St. Louis Post-Dispatch*, August 11, 1894). The *New York Press* noted in 1904: "For years the signals of professional baseball teams have been easily read by opponents. Their simplicity was readily fathomed, and lack of invention was displayed, which left the only chance of deception in reversing the system by a single sign. It was either a rubbing of the inside or the outside of a knee, the lacing of a glove or shoe, the dropping of a right or left hand to the thigh, the crook of a knee, or some similar expedient" (reprinted in *Washington Post*, July 31, 1904).

As is discussed in the next entry, however, sign stealing was becoming prevalent by the 1880s, which in turn changed the way that signs were given.

6.5.2 Sign Stealing. Sportswriter Dan Daniel claimed that sign stealing was in use by 1876 (Paul Dickson, *The Hidden Language of Baseball*, 33). If so, it cannot have been exten-

sive since signs themselves were still in their infancy.

By the 1880s the curveball (see **3.2.3**) had changed baseball, and one of the ripple effects was that the cat-and-mouse game between sign givers and sign stealers began in earnest. Initially not everyone thought it worth the bother to try to steal signs. An 1888 game saw Detroit captain Ned Hanlon figure out the signs being given by Pittsburgh's Fred Dunlap, but when he relayed the information to teammates Pete Conway and Charley Bennett, "they failed to grasp the idea" (*New York Sun*, April 29, 1888). Over the next few years, however, sign stealing would have an enormous impact.

George Smith claimed in 1891 that the key to his Brooklyn club winning two consecutive pennants was "our studying and learning the signs of the opposing pitchers. There wasn't a club in the League last year that we didn't know the signs of its pitchers. We always had a good deal of trouble with [Cincinnati catcher] Jim Keenan, for he generally made the signs to the pitchers, but we finally got on to him. Jim would crouch down close to the ground in giving the sign, and would use two fingers. The players in the base lines couldn't see him give it, but a man on the base could detect it. He would give the coacher a hand signal, who would in turn 'tip' the batter. . . . The Brooklyns would have beaten the New Yorks for the World's championship if [Buck] Ewing hadn't discovered that we were on to his signs" (*Cincinnati Commercial-Gazette*, reprinted in *Sporting News*, April 25, 1891). That last claim is particularly intriguing because Brooklyn led the Series three games to one before New York swept the last five games.

Another article that same year reported that Oakland captain Norris O'Neill used sign stealing to nose San Francisco out by one game for the 1889 California League championship: "['Pop'] Swett was catching for San Francisco and when 'Pop' wiggled his right hand that meant that he wanted a straight ball. When he moved the left, a curve. O'Neill, who is an observing fellow, 'tumbled' to this sign manual late in the season, and then the Oakland men commenced to fatten up their batting average and make reputations as heavy hitters." The article explained that when a curve was signaled the coach would yell, "Take a good start" to the base runner, tipping the batter off to the pitch. When it was a fastball he would instead holler, "Cover a little ground" (*Williamsport Sunday Grit*, June 14, 1891).

As noted in the preceding entry, early signs were not terribly difficult to steal. That was changed when the emergence of the curveball meant that for the first time there were distinct types of pitches and by claims such as these that pennants could be won by sign stealing. Players naturally began to put an extra effort into encoding their signs. An 1889 account observed, "Arthur Irwin can find out the signs of opposing pitchers quicker than any other man in the League. [Ed] Morris of the Pittsburg team has been inventing signs all winter, and now claims that he will bother the Philadelphian's captain [Irwin] to call the turn" (*St. Louis Post-Dispatch*, April 1, 1889).

Signals now became increasingly complex and experimental. An 1896 article in *Sporting News* explained that catchers were signaling with nearly every part of their body—fingers, arms, mouth, hands, and feet—in hopes of ensuring their confidentiality (*Sporting News*, March 7, 1896). Gus Weyhing complained about the system used by Dallas manager Jack McCloskey during the 1897 season: "McCloskey operated his signals by a series of signs that involved more pantomime than a Mafia meeting. With a man on first Mac would give him the tip to steal by shifting the score card from his right to his left hand. If he scratched his left ear with his right mitt the base runner must anchor himself on the sack till further instructions, no matter if the runner had a 20-foot lead on the pitcher. If he jabbed the toe of his right shoe in the grass the runner on second base must steal third or make the bluff at it. If Mac took a chew of tobacco the batsman and the man on first were given notice that they were to work the hit-and-run scheme."

The obvious danger of an elaborate system was that the signs would be equally impenetrable to the players who were supposed to be receiving them. Weyhing noted that McCloskey confronted Dallas catcher Tub Welch after a game for missing a crucial sign. Welch responded in exasperation, "If you use your pipes so we can hear you and cut out de mitt stuff we can rap to exactly what you want. De reason I got twisted on dat hit-and-run gag is dat you put a chew of gum in your face instead of tobacco" (*St. Louis Post-Dispatch*, April 10, 1898).

Moreover even the most complex system could be breached. Connie Mack was especially renowned for his ability to decipher opponents' signs. Monte Cross noted that "Mack studies the moves of the other side closer than any manager I ever saw. At bat or in the field, he can tell exactly what his opponents are planning, and is often able to block them. Not many men try to figure out the signs of the other team, but an expert with good eyes by close attention can easily detect the hit-and-run, double steal and the many tricks of a crafty club. . . . Nearly all base ball signals are visible movements, such as spitting on the hands, hitching up the trousers, pulling at the cap, etc., and usually they are very simple, even those of the best teams" (quoted in *Sporting News*, April 16, 1908).

6.5.3 Shake Offs. As discussed in the entry "Catchers Signaling to Pitchers" (**1.27**), the first major response to sign stealing seems to have been the assignment to the catcher of pitch-calling responsibilities. Yet almost from the start, pitchers were exercising the veto power inherent in having the ball in their possession. John Ward wrote in 1888: "Until within a few years this sign was always given by the pitcher, but now it is almost the universal practice for the catcher to give it to the pitcher, and if the latter doesn't want to pitch the ball asked for he changes the sign by a shake of the head" (John Ward, *Base-Ball: How to Become a Player*, 53–54). Catcher Doc Bushong explained that "it has always been my practice to give the signs, and if satisfactory, the pitcher would deliver the ball as directed. If not, a shake of the head or a hesitation would lead to a change" (*New York Sun*, May 6, 1888). Pitcher Ted Breitenstein added, "The catcher calls for the kind of ball he thinks I should deliver, but if it is against my judgment, I reverse it by an agreed signal" (*St. Louis Post-Dispatch*, August 12, 1894).

6.5.4 Conferences to Go Over Signs. The earliest such conference that I have found occurred in 1886 and was not a popular success: "Then [catcher James] McKeever held a long discussion with Pitcher [James] Harmon about signs. The crowd got impatient; one man yelled 'Get a telephone!' while the umpire ordered them to 'play ball'" (*Boston Globe*, May 13, 1886).

6.5.5 Signs from the Dugout. Bench managers were rare in early baseball, and signals originated from the field captain or a player in a critical position. An 1886 article noted, "Like Arthur Irwin, Captain [Tom] Burns of Newark, coaches by signals" (*Sporting Life*, May 19, 1886).

Even when bench managers became more common, there was still a widespread belief that signals should remain the responsibility of the players themselves. Catcher Tom Kinslow explained in 1899, "It's impossible for a manager to sit on the bench and direct the playing of his team by a secret service code, by dumb motion or pantomime. It doesn't require a razor-edge think-tank to study out and detect the most intricate of signals. In fact, the more complicated these pantomimics of signs are, the easier they are discovered. . . . The only signals required in the playing of a game are the battery signals, which are, of course, a positive necessity, and the signals for the hit-and-run play, which should be given by the batsman or the baserunner and not the manager on the bench" (quoted in *Sporting Life*, December 23, 1899).

Nonetheless signaling from the bench gradually became more common. Arthur Irwin's playing days essentially ended with the 1890 season, but he continued to direct the action from the bench. In 1895 his method gained another adherent: "Captain-manager [Buck] Ewing has adopted a code of signals by which he directs the movements of his men on the field. It is said that he does not have to get on the coaching lines and shout his commands to the players as [Charlie] Comiskey and [Arlie] Latham have in years gone by" (*Fort Wayne Sentinel*, May 3, 1895). By the early twentieth century it was becoming customary for the manager to signal from the bench.

6.5.6   Peeking.

As noted in entry 2.1.13, batters started trying to sneak a peek at the catcher's signal soon after signs themselves entered the game. An 1889 article observed: "[Bud] Fowler, the colored second baseman of the Greenvilles, is a tricky player. When at the bat he turns his head occasionally and catches the sign made by the catcher to the pitcher and lays his plans accordingly." But countermoves were also already being made. George Meakim, the opposing pitcher, "discovered the act yesterday and fooled him several times" (*Grand Rapids* [Mich.] *Daily Democrat*, June 16, 1889).

In the early twentieth century Connie Mack observed, "Many batters watch the catcher closely to see what position he settles himself in before the ball is delivered" (Connie Mack, "How to Play Ball," multi-part series, *Washington Post*, March 20, 1904). By then, the advent of the catcher's crouch (see 4.2.2) made sign stealing more difficult. One sportswriter counseled that the catcher "must guard against the

batsman peeking back to catch his code. That is why the backstop stoops in calling for balls . . . by crouching he shuts out all possible vision of the batsman" (*Washington Post*, July 18, 1909). But this stance also increased the potential benefits of a glimpse of the catcher's positioning since it was harder for a crouching catcher to shift at the last moment.

As a result, catchers were forced to take additional precautions. A 1913 article explained, "Many catchers, and some of them corkers, too, stick their gloves where they want the ball to be thrown. You've all noticed it. He may hold his hands high and a bit to the outside, right across the heart of the plate, low on the outside and many other ways. A smart batter can notice this out of the corner of his eye and tell in a measure where the ball is coming. Red Dooin, manager of the Phils, is one who has a tendency to do this. The same is true of many others. Johnny Kling probably was the greatest of modern catchers in concealing what he desired. He would move his knee slightly, indicating the spot he wanted the ball to strike. And he did it in so skillful a manner the batter or the coachers couldn't wise up" ("Great Pitchers Twirl Own Game," *Wilkes-Barre Times Leader*, November 8, 1913).

6.5.7   Combination Signs.

As discussed under "Sign Stealing" (6.5.2), by the start of the second decade of the twentieth century sign stealing had reached epidemic proportions. Johnny Evers and Hugh Fullerton reported in 1910 that fielders were becoming increasingly paranoid in response: "The second baseman and short stop have from 20 to 24 signals to keep in mind, most of which are changed every day and sometimes three times during a game. In 1909, when the hint had gone through the American League that the New York team was stealing signals, the Chicago White Sox changed signals nine times in one game, no signal meaning the same thing in any two innings" (John J. Evers and Hugh S. Fullerton, *Touching Second*, 128–129).

According to sportswriter Stan Baumgartner, the solution was combination signs, introduced in 1905. At first catchers combined the pitch signal with a visual signal, such as touching the mask, the knee, or the back of the glove. As explained in 1909, "The usual way [to foil sign stealers] is for the catcher to indicate his signs by his fingers, concealed by his big mitt. It is also done by showing the teeth or shutting the eyes. Sometimes a catcher will use two signs, and one of them will be phony. The runner or catcher cannot tell which is the phony with any degree of accuracy" ("New Method of Signaling Is Disagreeable for the Catcher," *Duluth News Tribune*, July 20, 1909). Sign stealers soon caught on to this new wrinkle, but in 1915 Pat Moran finally gave the upper hand back to the sign givers.

When Moran was hired to manage the Phillies, "The first thing he did in the spring of 1915 was to line up his catchers on the top rail of a fence and teach them combination signs—using fingers exclusively—and giving as many as three or four signs, with only one of them to count. Thus base runners, signal tippers in the clubhouse and coaches were completely stymied. There was only one catch—some pitchers weren't quick enough on the trigger to use the combinations. These hurlers quickly passed out of the majors.

"Moran not only used combinations but he arranged a 'shift' sign by the pitcher so that he could 'rub off' the signal by the catcher and substitute one of his own by pushing his glove across his chest. The only hope left for opposing coaches was to pick what was being pitched by studying the pitcher. Moran made every attempt to thwart this by teaching his pitchers to throw everything with the same delivery" (Stan Baumgartner, "Signals," *Baseball Guide and Record Book 1947*, 133).

The Phillies were the surprise pennant winners in the National League that year. Just as important, their manager had finally ended the dominance of sign stealers.

6.5.8 Reading Pitchers.

Connie Mack's 1911 Philadelphia A's were rumored to be great sign stealers, but several players on that team claimed that the team wasn't stealing signs at all but detecting pitchers who tipped their pitches.

Sportswriter Stan Baumgartner wrote later that Eddie Collins revealed this secret in a postseason article in *American Magazine*. Collins explained that every pitcher in the league had some telltale trait that gave away what he was going to throw. Many of Collins's teammates were angry with him for what they considered a betrayal. Catcher Ira Thomas said, "We felt he had sold us out" (Stan Baumgartner, "Signals," *Baseball Guide and Record Book 1947*, 133).

According to Athletics pitcher Cy Morgan, the leader was Chief Bender, and he was so good at reading pitches that John McGraw

sought to have him banned from the coaching box: "There are lots of little things almost unnoticeable about the motions different pitchers use in their delivery, and most of these motions have a meaning. We sit there in a row on the bench and study the pitcher, and if we detect any difference in his motion we watch to see what kind of a ball it means. Bender gets up on the coaching lines for a while, and if there is anything in it back he comes and tells us what kind of a ball that motion means. . . . Before I joined the Athletics they used to hit me. I did not know why. When I joined them Harry Davis came to me and told me. He said some other team might discover the little thing they had figured out, and then I changed my delivery so as to cut it out. The Athletics had not been able to hit me because they had my catcher's signs, but because they had my spitball figured out. That is all there is to any signal-tipping bureau, as they call it" (*Sporting Life*, April 6, 1912).

Collins's and Morgan's versions of events are confirmed by the Giants' Chief Meyers, who later recalled telling John McGraw during the 1911 World Series, "That coach on third base, Harry Davis, is calling our pitches. When he yells, 'It's all right,' it's a fast ball." McGraw suggested that Davis must have been stealing Meyers's signs, but the catcher responded that he had told the pitchers, "Pitch whatever you want to pitch. I'll catch you without signals" (Lawrence Ritter, *The Glory of Their Times*, 181). Obviously if no signs were being exchanged, the coach indeed must have been picking up clues from the pitchers' movements.

Clever sign stealers also became adept at deciphering signals from the actions of other players. According to sportswriter Stan Baumgartner, catchers were the favorite targets: "Big Frank (Pancho) Snyder, catcher of the New York Giants [in the early twenties], gave away every pitch by the way he held his glove after he got up from giving signals. If he held the glove up, it was a fast ball. If he held the glove pointed down, it was a curve. . . . Such a clever backstop as Roger Bresnahan gave a definite crook of the elbow of his right arm when he called for a fast ball, the batter could see the big muscle in his arm move up and down." The movements of infielders could also sometimes be giveaways. Baumgartner reported that even the savvy Miller Huggins sometimes revealed a pitch by moving to the left or right after receiving a signal (Stan Baumgartner, "Signals," *Baseball Guide and Record Book 1947*, 126–127).

6.5.9 Cover Your Mouth. One innovation that has been introduced to baseball within the memory of most readers of this book is the custom of players covering their mouths with their gloves during mound conferences. It has long been the practice for infielders to do so when giving signals, as middle infielders often use an open or closed mouth—hidden by their glove—to signal which player will cover the base (George F. Will, *Men at Work*, 254–255).

But use of this tactic during mound conferences is a much more recent development, one that went from being unheard of to standard in a very short period of time. Tigers broadcaster Rod Allen said he first saw this while playing in Japan in the late 1980s. When he returned to the States in 1991 the practice had already caught on in the United States (Fox Sports broadcast, August 7, 2004).

One of the impetuses was Will Clark's grand slam off Greg Maddux in the 1989 National League Championship Series and Clark's subsequent claim that he had known what to expect from reading Maddux's lips during a mound conference. Maddux is dubious of this claim, as is Clark's teammate Bob Brenly, who noted that Clark never wanted to know what pitch was coming. But whether true or not, such a charge undoubtedly led many pitchers to cover their mouths (Cubs WGN broadcast, July 31, 2005). The practice has become so customary that in a 2009 game Red Sox pitcher Takashi Saito covered his mouth with his glove during a visit from the trainer.

Like so many strategies, lip-reading can be used by either side. Mel Stottlemyre, Sr., claimed that he took advantage of Carl Yastrzemski's habit of talking to himself between pitches: "If I saw his lips saying 'Be quick, be quick,' I'd throw him a change-up. If he was saying 'Stay back, weight back,' I'd throw him a fastball" (quoted in George F. Will, *Men at Work*, 224).

(vi) Playing by "The Book"

Changes were made so frequently in the early days of baseball that the idea of an unvarying "book" of strategies would have made little sense. What's more, some of the now accepted dos and don'ts of managing would not have made sense given the frequent fluctuations in the era's rules and conditions. As a result, the network of tactics and principles known as "the book" developed in fits and starts.

6.6.1 Playing for One Run. The tactic of playing for one run has been a basic strategy for so many years that one might assume it could not be dated with much precision. The evidence suggests otherwise.

A *Sporting News* correspondent in 1897 quoted Baltimore manager Ned Hanlon as saying "we didn't play ball in 1889 as we play it now." The writer explained that before 1890 "the theory of playing at any and all times for a single run was practically unheard of. . . . The modern principle of baseball is to first make one run, if your opponents have none, and to continue always to try for one run as long as you are in the lead, or not more than a run or two behind. When your opponents have a lead of three or four science can be abandoned and chances taken on 'slugging.' . . . When a player in a team of the present era reaches first base the batsman succeeding him is instructed to go to the plate and advance his comrade, even at the expense of being retired himself. . . . In the old days once a man got to first base the next batter walked to the plate and promptly attempted to knock the cover off the ball" (*Sporting News*, October 30, 1897).

An 1891 article described how Columbus manager Gus Schmelz's "system of playing base ball for games rather than individual records is being adopted more or less by managers everywhere, as experience demonstrates that more games are won than lost by it, especially when the contestants are equally matched or the games are close. When the opposing team is several runs ahead, of course, it is necessary to try to bat it out and sacrificing will do very little good. But when one or two runs only are needed then Schmelz's system comes in play.

"The great object then is to get a man on first base and every scheme possible is used to accomplish that end. With a man on first base a hard hit is more likely not to go safe than to go safe, as the batting averages of the heaviest hitters in the profession will show, and a sharp infield hit is likely to result in a double play, while it is almost impossible with a hard-throwing outfield to make second base on a fly out. A slow hit, bunted, will certainly advance the man to second base, and the batter has a very good chance to beat the hit out himself.

"If the batter is thrown out there is no longer a danger of a double play, and the next man at bat should try to hit the ball hard, for the runner can easily score on a single or go to third on a fly out to the outfield. If the first bunter manages to beat out the ball, then there are two men on bases, with no one out, and in order to prevent a double or possibly a triple play, it is necessary again to bunt the ball or to push a fly into the outfield. In most cases the man would be held on first base in order to draw a throw out of the catcher in a subsequent attempt to steal second, and thus give the third man a chance to score.

"A bunted hit under these circumstances will about certainly score the man on third base, and a long fly out is even better. Of course, the programme is necessarily varied according to the abilities of the player or the weakness or strength of the opposing team. With a sore-arm catcher a double steal would be in order, and other tricks can be introduced as circumstances will permit. It will be seen that in order to carry out this system correctly the manager must have absolute control of his players and his discipline must be perfect" (*Sporting Life*, August 22, 1891).

Another article a few weeks later added, "The Schmelz system of playing ball has been made quite famous by the work of this team this year. With a nine of medium hitters Columbus has managed to play some very creditable games with the strongest teams in the Association, and has won a goodly number of them by clever team work. The men never play for records, and when a sacrifice hit is needed to advance a base-runner or bring him home it is forthcoming in most cases" (*Sporting Life*, September 5, 1891).

By 1897, bunting in situations like this had become so routine that a *Chicago Tribune* columnist responded to a reader's question by stating, "A player should always sacrifice when a runner is at first, no one out, unless the opponents have a lead of more than two runs" (*Chicago Tribune*, May 21, 1897, 6).

Gus Schmelz was a well-known manager of the 1880s and 1890s who is now almost forgotten. He does, however, deserve to be remembered for leaving baseball this important legacy.

6.6.2 Don't Put the Winning Run on Base.
Managers have always avoided this suicidal strategy except in exceptional circumstances. The surprising thing is that such a self-evident principle is considered to be part of the book at all.

6.6.3 Never Make the Third Out at Third Base.
This dictum makes sense today, but that would have been less the case in early baseball,

since passed balls were then a much more common event. There was therefore more benefit to taking a risk to reach third than there is in today's game. For example, in the 1856 account of a steal mentioned in "Stolen Bases" (5.1.1), the runner made the third out of an inning trying to steal third.

Passed balls decreased steadily in the ensuing years, but attitudes were slower to change. As late as 1911 a sportswriter observed that "managers scheme with all their might and main to reach third, which doesn't do them any good after it's attained." He asked rhetorically, "Why is it that all sorts of schemes are worked to get a base runner round to third, but as soon as he reaches that corner all science is thrown to the winds and the issue is left to depend on simple, plain old slug it out?" (*Mansfield* [Ohio] *News*, September 23, 1911).

Nonetheless there were signs by this time that this mind-set was beginning to adapt to changing conditions. Christy Mathewson noted in 1912 that John McGraw "has favorite expressions, such as 'there are stages' and 'that was a two out play,' which mean certain chances are to be taken by a coacher at one point in a contest, while to attempt such a play under other circumstances would be nothing short of foolhardy" (Christy Mathewson, *Pitching in a Pinch*, 118–119). This strongly suggests that the precept of not taking any chance of making the third out at third base had begun to emerge.

6.6.4 Don't Give Him Anything to Hit on 0-2.
This basic principle was being cited even before it took three strikes to retire a batter. For example, in 1880, with the two-strike warning pitch (see 1.10) still in the rulebook, the *New York Clipper* remarked, "The umpiring in Cincinnati, O., on the occasion when Will White pitched out [Cap] Anson on four balls delivered, must have been rather queer. No pitcher would deliver four fair balls in succession to such a batsman as Anson, especially when two men were on the bases" (*New York Clipper*, May 15, 1880). David Ball discovered another illustrative anecdote. In 1898 pitcher Henry Boyle recalled a game on June 7, 1886, in which "I fooled Paul Hines into two strikes at balls close to him, and youngster like, I thought I'd feed him another of the same sort. He didn't do a thing to it but drive out a home run and we were beaten." Player-manager Fred Dunlap called Boyle "a pin-headed chump," and the two men didn't speak for six years (*Sporting News*, February 19, 1898, 4).

6.6.5 Taking 3-0 and 3-1. A walk was not permanently made up of four balls until the late 1880s. Once it was, the idea of taking 3-0 and 3-1 pitches followed almost immediately, and appears to have been adhered to more rigidly than is the case today.

Ned Hanlon credited the Orioles of the mid-1890s with inventing the tactic of "hitting the ball with men on bases with three balls and no strikes on the batters." He cited this as an example of "tactics introduced by the Baltimores [that] were successful because they were unexpected" (*Washington Post*, August 14, 1904). This implies that most batters invariably took pitches in such situations.

Jack Doyle told a similar story, but with a twist. He claimed that pitchers like Clark Griffith took advantage of the fact that hitters wouldn't swing at a 3-0 or 3-1 pitch. So Griffith would deliberately throw three wide ones, and then toss two easy strikes, leaving the hitters with only one swing. Thus Doyle's perspective was that the Baltimore batters began swinging at 3-0 and 3-1 pitches out of "self-defense" (quoted in Ernest J. Lanigan's column, *Sporting News*, July 21, 1932).

Jack Glasscock, who played in the majors from 1879 to 1895, wrote an indignant letter to *Sporting News* in 1938 protesting the tendency of batters to swing at 3-1 pitches. He said that in his day they would have taken such pitches (*Sporting News*, October 20, 1938). Likewise, in 1899 Washington co-owner J. Earl Wagner said disapprovingly of an unnamed National League batter: "I have seen him get three balls on a pitcher with no strikes tabbed against him, and yet he would swipe at the next ball pitched if it was within range of his bat" *(Denver Evening Post*, July 28, 1899).

Just as noteworthy as how early this custom originated is the inflexibility with which it was followed. Cubs manager Bill Killefer reported in 1925, "It is best to ignore the established rules of baseball now and then. For example, in a game at Brooklyn I had [Charley] Hollocher hit with the count three and one. Most people would call this foolish." Even though Hollocher got a hit, Killefer reported that "the fans razzed me unmercifully. Some of them asked me if I didn't know anything about baseball" (quoted in F. C. Lane, *Batting*, 49).

(vii) Miscellaneous Managerial Strategies

6.7.1 Fifth Infielders. Today most managers bring an outfielder into the infield only when the situation is dire. The tactic is usually employed only when the winning run is on third base with less than two out, meaning that even a sacrifice fly would win the game.

George Sisler noted that the circumstances of its origin were different. While he called the play the "six-man infield" in this account, he was counting the pitcher as an infielder and was referring to what is now known as the five-man infield: "The six-man infield was originated and tried out at Vero Beach, Florida, in the spring of 1950 by Branch Rickey, then President of the Brooklyn Dodgers. . . . Here's the theory behind the six-man infield: When a poor-hitting pitcher comes up to the plate with a sacrifice in order, either with one down or no one out, it is wise to bring one of your outfielders from the outfield and place him at a definite place in the infield, making it defense with six rather than the normal five players. The idea, of course, is not to allow a weak-hitting pitcher to sacrifice the runner or runners to the next base or bases, but to put up such a defense that the pitcher will attempt to hit the ball, when he will probably strike out or hit into a double play" (George Sisler, *Sisler on Baseball*, 74).

Rickey's method of implementing the strategy was novel. Rather than keeping his intentions under wrap, Rickey announced plans to use the six-man infield at a banquet, and the scheme was widely publicized (*Sporting News*, February 1, 1950). Rickey contended that it would be very effective against a weak hitter.

The Dodgers tried this tactic during spring training and even used a variant in which two outfielders played the infield (*Sporting News*, April 9, 1952). They do not appear to have used it much if at all once the season began, but a couple of other managers did experiment with it. In the eighth inning of a game on September 30, 1950, Detroit pitcher Hal Newhouser came to the plate with a runner on second and no outs. Knowing that Newhouser would be asked to bunt, Cleveland manager Lou Boudreau "brought Bob Kennedy in from right field and put him midway between home and first on the grass. He put first baseman Luke Easter on third base and brought [third baseman Al] Rosen in close to have a six-man infield" (*Detroit Free Press*, October 1, 1950). All this planning went for naught when Indians pitcher Mike Garcia walked Newhouser on four pitches. Birdie Tebbetts of Cincinnati tried the same strategy against the Giants in a game on July 20, 1954, but infielder Rocky Bridges made an error.

6.7.2   Fourth Outfielders.

An even more uncommon tactic has seen managers temporarily redeploy an infielder in the outfield. This move has been used almost exclusively against sluggers who are so feared that the opposition feels fortunate to hold them to a single. Cincinnati manager Birdie Tebbetts reportedly did this against Stan Musial in 1954, as did the Mets' Gil Hodges versus Willie McCovey in 1969 (Jonathan Fraser Light, *The Cultural Encyclopedia of Baseball*, 697).

Hodges then showed great courage by reprising the fourth outfielder at a critical moment in that year's World Series. Baltimore had won the opening game, and the second contest was tied until New York pushed across a run in the top of the ninth. In Baltimore's half, Mets starter Jerry Koosman got the first two men out, bringing Frank Robinson to the plate with a chance to tie the game with one swing of the bat.

Knowing that Robinson would be aiming for an extra-base hit, "Hodges made a rare strategic move. He shifted [Al] Weis from second base and made a fourth outfielder of him. Thus were the corners guarded as well as both power alleys in right center and left center" (Arthur Daley, *New York Times*, October 14, 1969). Robinson ended up walking, but the Mets hung on to win the game and swept the last three games of the Series.

Five years later another Mets manager revived this unusual defense under similar circumstances. Clinging to a 1-0 lead with two out in the ninth when Atlanta's Hank Aaron came to bat, Yogi Berra called for an "Aaron shift" in which Felix Millan was moved from second base to become a fourth outfielder. The strategy stemmed from Berra's willingness to allow the home-run star to reach first if necessary but to cut down the chances of his getting to second and becoming a possible scorer (Michael Stevens, *New York Times*, August 26, 1974). That script was followed precisely, as Aaron did indeed single—but the next batter whiffed to end the game.

6.7.3   Curfews.

A reporter in Springfield, Massachusetts, hinted in 1878: "attending a dance until 2 o'clock or later is not wise preparation for a game on the day following" (*Springfield Republican*; quoted in *New York Clipper*, May 18, 1878). One in Quincy, Illinois, was much less subtle a few years later: "Last night one of the Quincy players was out on a 'lark' until after 12 o'clock. It is an indisputable fact that a man who is out after midnight 'bumming' around with prostitutes, can not play ball next day. The players of the Quincys should be told in plain words that such conduct will not be tolerated" (*Quincy Whig*, May 8, 1884, 3). That reality was undoubtedly understood by all early captains and managers, but acting upon it was another matter. After all, every employer would like to have their employees come to work well rested, but few would think seriously of trying to enforce such a rule.

Nonetheless clubs did begin to instigate curfews. In 1878 Milwaukee's players were required to be in the hotel no later than 10 p.m. when on the road (*Milwaukee Sentinel*, April 6, 1878; quoted in Dennis Pajot, "1878—Milwaukee a National League City" [unpublished paper]). In 1879 the Albany club was reported to have a 10:30 curfew. In 1883, Fort Wayne manager Jack Remsen devised the first recorded method of enforcement: "Before eleven o'clock every night, players of the Fort Wayne Base Ball Club will be required to register in a book kept for that purpose at the Robinson House. Players retiring after that hour will be fined" (*Fort Wayne Daily News*, April 5, 1883).

6.7.4   Handwriting Analysis.

In 1962, Charlie Metro was a member of the Chicago Cubs' "College of Coaches" (see **6.1.4**). Metro devised an original approach for gaining an advantage: "I had a handwriting expert analyze the signatures of all the National League managers to learn as much about my competition as quick as I could." The graphologist provided Metro with an analysis of each manager's character traits in hopes that Metro could use this information when making decisions. It doesn't seem to have helped much as the Cubs finished ninth, beating out only the expansion Mets. Metro also experimented with the still more novel tactic of using ventriloquism to disrupt opposing base runners, but couldn't master the skill (Tom Altherr, "Know Them by Their Autographs," *National Pastime* 18 [1998], 29–31).

6.7.5   Computers.

The first manager to make extensive use of computers in his decision-making process was Oakland's Steve Boros in 1983 and '84. Boros never brought a computer into the dugout, but his reliance upon computer-generated data was publicized in such periodicals as *Newsweek*, *Sports Illustrated*, and even *Psychology Today*. When the A's struggled, their woes were blamed on the computers, and Boros lost his job (Alan Schwarz, *The Numbers Game*, 145–146).

Chapter 7

COACHING

BASEBALL coaches today have such a staid image that it will come as a surprise to many that the first coaches were so undignified that Christy Mathewson referred to them as the "old school of clowns" (Christy Mathewson, *Pitching in a Pinch*, 118).

The earliest coaching was just advice yelled from teammates on the bench and of course cannot be dated precisely. A reporter wrote sarcastically in 1870, "If a man can shout vociferously, and yell 'Gitty!' with gusto, he is immediately treated with a patronizing air, and is given a place on the 'nine.' There is, however, one man selected on account of his yelling qualities, who seems to be a very important person in the game. When not otherwise engaged, he is yelling, regardless of pitch or stress, such things as 'Downy! Downy!' 'climb' 'leave' 'git' 'hold that!' No one seems to pay attention to him; yet I am told this yelling is necessary" (*Cornell Era*, reprinted in the *Trenton State Gazette*, November 10, 1870).

By 1872, however, the rules specified that a base runner's teammates had to remain at least fifteen feet away from him. Two years later the rules were amended to state that only the captain and one other player could approach that close. These players were known as coachers because, like stagecoach drivers, their job was to direct traffic. Only gradually did the name become shortened to coach.

When American ballplayers made a tour of England in 1874, the use of coaches was remarked upon as a characteristically American concept. One newspaper commented, "The employment of one of the side who are in to watch the movements of the field and advise the runner accordingly is a quaint device which savors of American acuteness" (quoted by William Rankin, *Sporting News*, February 25, 1909). There began to be grumbles about inattentive coaching, with one game account noting, "The patrons of the games begin to ask for a little sharper coaching of the Worcester base runners. [Lee] Richmond hurt his leg by an utterly unnecessary slide yesterday, for want of a warning. It is noticed that the visiting teams put all the men they are allowed on the lines and it looks business-like" (*Worcester Gazette*, May 12, 1880).

This perception that coaching exemplified a peculiarly American approach to sporting activities was strengthened when the American Association was formed in 1882. Coaching became one of the features most closely associated with the upstart league, but there was nothing "business-like" about the loud and annoying style of these coaches. Many of the players who filled this role made little pretense of the fact that they went "in the line to disconcert the opposing players—generally the pitcher—not to 'coach' or assist the base-runner" (*Sporting News*, December 23, 1893).

Leather lungs were the primary requirement, as the *St. Louis Globe-Democrat* observed in 1888: "[Reddy] Mack, [George] Tebeau, and some of the local players' idea of coaching seems to be to stand on the line and yell as loud as they possibly can. It does not seem to matter what they say, just so they make a noise. A ball game at present more resembles a series of Indian war whoops than an exhibition of the national pastime" (*St. Louis Globe-Democrat*, reprinted in the *New York Sun*, May 9, 1888).

But a voice that was both loud and annoying was even more effective, with an 1889 account noting, "Of all base ball coachers' voices that of Bug Holliday is the most excruciating" (*St. Louis Post-Dispatch*, April 26, 1889).

This style of coaching became increasingly associated with the St. Louis Brown Stockings. Arlie Latham had a particularly strong polarizing tendency, which was illustrated during the 1886 postseason series against Chicago. One Chicago reporter wrote that Latham's "insane whooping," "incessant howling," and "meaningless jumble of catch phrases" was "funny for about fifteen minutes. Then it grew tiresome, and before the fourth inning he was universally conceded to be the worst nuisance ever inflicted upon a Chicago audience" (*Chicago Tribune*, October 19, 1886). Another chimed in with complaints about "the disgusting mouthings of the clown Latham." But in St. Louis, Latham drew praise for "his excellent coaching" (both quoted in Jerry Lansche, *Glory Fades Away*, 79–80).

Some went so far as to attribute the club's success to its style of coaching: "It is a well-known fact that St. Louis won the pennant twice through this rowdyism on the field" (*Philadelphia Press*, reprinted in the *St. Louis Post-Dispatch*, July 7, 1887). The claim seems farfetched, but winners always attract imitators and this style of coaching soon spread.

When the Pittsburgh franchise moved from the American Association to the National League in 1887, it brought this approach to coaching along. Its apostle was George Miller, who became known by such appropriate nicknames as "Foghorn" and "Calliope." On his first trip to Detroit, Miller was described as being "a pronounced type of the American Association coacher, and nothing like his bray has ever before been heard at Recreation Park. It is startling to spectators seeing his squatty, Quilp-like form to suddenly hear his foghorn tones exhorting a Pittsburger to 'Getwaygetwayget-way'" (*Detroit Free Press*, May 10, 1887).

By this time there were calls to abolish this style of coaching, or even coaching in general. The American Association held a special meeting on June 9, 1886, and decided, ". . . In order to prevent offensive coaching by captains, the lines being so changed as to keep the captain and his assistants at least 75 feet away from the catcher's lines and on a line 15 feet from and parallel with the four lines. A rule was adopted preventing the captain from addressing remarks to batsmen, except by the way of caution, or to

the pitcher and catcher of the opposing team, and limiting coaching to base-runners under severe penalties" (*Chicago Tribune*, June 14, 1886). Similar restrictions were soon imposed on National League coaches (Henry Chadwick, *Evansville Journal*, April 27, 1889, 7).

The new rule was of some benefit, but the line between a comment directed at a teammate and an opponent was often a thin one, making enforcement difficult. Early in the 1887 season a sportswriter reported that "nearly every coacher [who] has stood upon the lines during games in this vicinity [has] wholly overridden every restraint which the new playing rules impose upon them. One or two captains, while playing in the field, have been incessantly talking to their men in a manner calculated to affect the batting or base running of the opponents. Coachers on the line have kept calling out to the batter, 'Play ball,' 'Make him put it there,' 'Only takes one to hit it.'. . . Others, every time a ball is pitched, yell like a hyena for the evident purpose of disconcerting the pitcher" (*Base Ball Gazette*, April 26, 1887). Still others kept up incessant chatter such as "All right, Billy, play ball. Don't hit it, Billy. That's the way" or "Now play ball there, Larkin. Face the batter. Watch that position. Play ball everybody" (*Base Ball Gazette*, April 22, 1887). Everyone knew that this banter was aimed at distracting the fielding team, but since it was ostensibly aimed at the batter, there was nothing the umpire could do.

In the years to come, coaches continued to find imaginative new ways to raise a ruckus. At an 1894 game in Baltimore, the Orioles' Bill Clarke, "who was coaching from third base, walked out to the bleachers and raised his hands like a 'pop concert' leader, and a volume of sound filled the air, every man, woman and child yelling for all he or she was worth. This was done to rattle the pitcher" (*Boston Globe*, April 25, 1894).

This prompted renewed calls to ban coaching entirely after the 1895 season, but most thought that a prohibition would be going too far. The *New York Advertiser* argued: "To abolish loud coaching entirely would seriously hurt the game in some cities. . . . A game of ball isn't a game of lawn tennis, and one wants it to go through with a certain amount of dash and vigor. Lively coaching has often saved what would otherwise have been a most uninteresting contest. There is a robustness to base ball that will prevent it from becoming a parlor game, and coaching is part of its strength and life" (*New York Advertiser*, quoted in *Sporting*

Life, November 2, 1895). Joe Sugden's reaction was more succinct: "Funeral services are not expected at ball games" (*Pittsburg[h] Post*, May 27, 1894).

There continued to be occasional calls to abolish coaching. Predictably, Henry Chadwick wrote in 1904 that coaching has "degenerated into a dirty-ball method of annoying the pitcher" (*Sporting News*, December 17, 1904). But as signs and strategies increased in complexity, coaches gradually began to acquire prestige. By 1912, Christy Mathewson could look back and summarize: "the old school of clowns passed, coaching developed into a science, and the sentries stationed at first and third bases found themselves occupying important jobs" (Christy Mathewson, *Pitching in a Pinch*, 118).

Even so, there were few full-time coaches in the next decade, and the best-known one literally was a clown. Nick Altrock of the Senators, who was reportedly the only full-time nonplaying major league coach between 1914 and 1920, was known for his shadow-boxing routines and other buffoonery (Fred Stein, "Managers and Coaches," *Total Baseball*, 2nd edition, 461). In 1914 the *Detroit Free Press* observed, "Washington has two comedy coaches, [part-time player Germany] Schaefer and Altrock" (*Detroit Free Press*, September 30, 1914).

Objections to coaches continued to surface from time to time, most notably in 1916 when former President William Howard Taft used the occasion of the National League's fortieth anniversary to denounce noisy coaching (*New York Times*, February 14, 1916). Not until the 1920s did coaching truly become established as a profession.

(i) Directing Traffic

7.1.1 Coaches' Boxes. As noted in the introduction to this chapter, restrictions were placed on coaches as early as 1872, with the 1886 season seeing the creation of the coach's box in an effort to restrain the mayhem that passed for coaching. Boston president Jim Hart blamed two St. Louis players: "[Charles] Comiskey and Bill Gleason used to plant themselves on each side of the visiting catcher and comment on his breeding, personal habits, skill as a receiver, or rather lack of it, until the unlucky backstop was unable to tell whether one or half a dozen balls were coming his way. . . . So for the sake of not unduly increasing the population of the insane asylums or encouraging justifiable homicide,

the coach's box was invented" (quoted in Gustav Axelson, *COMMY*, 74).

7.1.2 Coaching Calls. As discussed in the introduction to this chapter, in early baseball it was not what a coach said but how loudly and gratingly he said it. This led coaches to develop a vivid but largely ad hoc vocabulary.

The coaching of Boston's Joe Hornung inspired this 1886 account: "In the sixth inning [teammate Billy] Nash was on first and Joe rushed down the coacher's line hollering 'Ubbo, Billy, Ubbo.' This was a new thing in coaching for a cowboy crowd, who imagined the mystic words were intended to hoodoo the home players. They were enlightened a moment after, when [Kansas City pitcher George] Weidman drawing back his arm to deliver the ball, Joe sang out to Nash: 'Now you, Ubbo' and Billy 'Ubbod' by sailing toward second bag. He made a fine slide, but the ball beat him there and [umpire Chick] Fulmer called him in [i.e., out]. The word was then caught up by the crowd and the small boy hollered himself hoarse crying 'Ubbo' at the Bostons. Hornung explained afterwards that the word was a tramp's term, which meant to move off" (*Chicago Tribune*, September 12, 1886; according to a version of these events in H. Allen Smith and Ira L. Smith, *Low and Inside*, 122, Hornung thought the term would be unfamiliar, but Weidman was familiar with it and he yelled 'Ubbo' to confuse Nash).

One of the most popular coaching cries was "That's the way," which Arlie Latham was using in 1886 (*Sporting Life*, June 9, 1886). Leather-lunged Detroit manager Hughey Jennings's famous cry of "ee-yah" was a simplified version of this call (*Sporting Life*, April 11, 1908). Sportswriter H. G. Salsinger traced its development: "In his early days of American League leadership he would jump about the coaching box at first or third and yell: 'That's the way.' Later he drew it out into a long 'That's the way-ah.' Then it became 'That's Swaya.' After a time he abbreviated it to 'Swaaa-ah.' And then 'Wee-ah.' But there came still another change. It was slight, but it converted the phrase into 'Eeyah' or 'Ee-yah'" (*Detroit News*, January 10, 1926; Peter Morris, "'Attaboy!' Originated from the Dynamic Managing Style of Hughie Jennings (Detroit Tigers) in 1907," *Comments on Etymology* 33:1 [October 2003], 2–4).

Other early coaches pushed the limits of acceptable language. George Tebeau was chided in 1889, "Such language as 'say, yer rotten, yer stinkin'. . . is rather coarse to be used in the presence of ladies and should not be tolerated on the ball field" (*St. Louis Post-Dispatch*, April 27, 1889). Meanwhile Tommy Tucker pushed the boundaries of language itself and became associated with a "yelping dog style of coaching" (*Galveston News*, January 19, 1890).

Once the rules specified that coaches could not directly address the opposing pitcher, they found clever ways around the restriction. Christy Mathewson noted that Clark Griffith used chants like "watch his foot" and "he's going to waste this one." While these calls were intended to intimidate the pitcher, they were not ostensibly directed toward him. Thus "if a complaint is made, Griffith declares that he was warning the batter that it was to be a pitchout, which is perfectly legitimate. The rules permit the coacher to talk to the batter and the base runners" (Christy Mathewson, *Pitching in a Pinch*, 132–133).

7.1.3 Amplified Coaching. Megaphones were brought to prominence by the U.S. Navy's effective use of them in 1898 during the Spanish-American War. With coaching putting a premium on leather lungs, it occurred to some unknown innovator that megaphones would be a natural. A 1902 article noted, "The megaphone ought to be barred from coaching. It was used on both sides in the great Harvard-Yale game, but there is really no place for it in base ball" (*Sporting Life*, June 28, 1902). That reasoning appears to have been persuasive, as megaphones quietly disappeared from the coaching lines.

7.1.4 First-base Coaches. Another way in which the game's authorities attempted to address the nuisance of noisy coaches was by limiting the number. An 1897 rule change restricted teams to one coach until they had the bases loaded: "This change is recommended because it has been proven in the past that the presence of two coaches allow a 'cross fire' of talk between them foreign to the game and frequently of a character objectionable to spectators" (*Washington Post*, February 8, 1897). The rule was unpopular from the first, with an early-season article reporting: "Trouble is brewing in the National league, and indications point to open rebellion before many days are passed. . . . The rules framed by the magnates have taken all the fun out of the game. They allow only one coacher and make every player sit on the bench. The rule takes all of the life out

of the game. If the rule is not repealed it will kill the game; in fact, it is dead now. No one wants to see the game as now played. Capt. [Hugh] Duffy of the Bostons says: 'Nearly all the players want the single coaching rule abolished. I have heard a good deal of muttering against the magnates'" (*Chicago Tribune*, May 21, 1897, 6). According to Benton Stark, in 1904 clubs were again permitted to use two coaches throughout their at bats (Benton Stark, *The Year They Called Off the World Series*, 102–103). The presence of another base coach made it much more difficult for catchers to shield their signs from being stolen and contributed to the introduction of the catcher's crouch (see **4.2.2**).

7.1.5 It's a Bird, It's a Plane . . . No, It's Only the Third-base Coach. Early coaches made occasional efforts to interfere with or distract opposing fielders. There are instances of this practice as early as 1866, when a club captain had to be "told by the umpire that he must not get on the third base with his men and run in with them, thus hindering the play of their opponents, which latter they attempted to do throughout the game" (*Detroit Advertiser and Tribune*, August 25, 1866). The trick became more common during the "old school of clowns" era. For example, base coach Mike Kelly of Chicago ran all the way out to the shortstop position to provide a distraction during an 1886 series against Detroit. At the end of the first full season of the coach's box, the *New York Times* observed that the new lines had succeeded at discouraging "the trick of personating runners from third base to the home plate" (*New York Times*, October 9, 1887). It doesn't seem to have entirely eliminated the practice. While coaching for Brooklyn in 1890, George Smith got carried away and ran home ahead of the base runner he was coaching. The catcher tagged Smith instead of the runner and, after a long argument, the umpire ruled the runner out (Robert L. Tiemann, "George J. Smith," in Frederick Ivor-Campbell, Robert L. Tiemann, and Mark Rucker, eds., *Baseball's First Stars*, 151). The tactic was explicitly prohibited by a 1904 rule change (*Pittsburg[h] Post*, April 7, 1904, 8).

(ii) Coaching Staffs

7.2.1 Full-time Coaches. Early base coaching was done by teammates and had obvious shortcomings. A Troy sportswriter remarked caustically in 1880, "If a Trojan, by the kindness of

Providence, gets to first base, and [Troy manager Bob] Ferguson orders some other player to coach the man, the fellow selected rises from his seat with about as much alacrity as an indisposed mud-turtle, and having at last reached a commanding location, he becomes dumb at the critical moment" (*Troy Times*, reprinted in the *New York Sunday Mercury*, June 19, 1880). Four years later a Pittsburgh sportswriter contrasted the "judicious, spirited, intelligent, inspiring and effective coaching" of the visiting Athletics to the "listless slouchy way in which the same work was done by the Alleghenys" (*Pittsburgh Post*, May 2, 1884).

While the need for full-time coaches was evident, the cost was prohibitive. A few sources suggest that Bobby Mathews became the first paid major league coach around 1888, but the evidence does not support the claim. Mathews did coach the University of Pennsylvania team during their preparations for the 1888 season, and there was talk he would serve as an adviser to Philadelphia's young pitchers, but the arrangement fell through (*St. Louis Globe-Democrat*, December 9, 1887, 8; research by David Ball). Many other sources tab Arlie Latham with the New York Giants in 1909. That, however, can't be true because Latham had been employed as a full-time coach nine years earlier.

In July 1900, Latham was hired by the Cincinnati Reds as a coach. *Sporting Life*'s correspondent enthused that "Cincinnati critics have it that Latham's coaching has greatly improved the Reds' base running" (*Sporting Life*, September 1, 1900). He later added: "Manager [Bob] Allen says he is delighted with the coaching of Latham. He says the base running of the team has improved fully 100% after the veteran got on the lines" (*Sporting Life*, September 29, 1900).

Sportswriter J. Ed Grillo painted a different picture, reporting that most Cincinnati players suspected that Latham had been hired by owner John T. Brush to spy on the newly formed Professional Ball Players' Protective Association. Others thought that Latham was "simply there to amuse the crowd with his coaching." In response to Brush's claim that Latham would teach the players the finer points of the game, Grillo wrote, "This might be construed as a direct slap at Manager Allen whose duty it was supposed was to give players such instructions" (*Sporting News*, August 4, 1900).

For whatever reason, it was an idea whose time had not yet come. During the first decade of the twentieth century, clubs made do with coaching from players, though the quality was often not high. A 1901 article, for instance, observed that Mike Donlin "likes to 'coach' but he has no conception of the meaning of the word. As he construes it, coaching consists entirely of saying mean and disagreeable things to the pitcher of the other team and showing off his own smartness. He does not aid the base runner at all, and the words of 'advice' that he shouts to the men on the bags are stereotyped and seldom timely" (*Sporting News*, March 16, 1901).

Between 1900 and 1910 the complexity of signals and managerial strategy increased greatly, and the need for full-time coaches became apparent. At least one minor league club had a full-time coach in 1908, with Perry Werden filling that role for Indianapolis (*Sporting Life*, May 1, 1909). In 1909, Duke Farrell was a full-time coach for New York's American League team and Arlie Latham for the cross-town Giants. Not everyone was impressed with Latham's work, and Fred Snodgrass later called him "probably the worst third-base coach that ever lived" (quoted in Lawrence Ritter, *The Glory of Their Times*, 94). Researcher Cliff Blau notes an additional problem: National League president Thomas Lynch ruled that coaches counted against a team's twenty-five-man limit (see **13.3.1**), though managers didn't (*New York Times*, May 10, 1910).

Nonetheless the benefits of Latham's coaching were sufficiently evident to journalist Ren Mulford, Jr., that he suggested in 1912 that Cincinnati follow New York's lead: "New York carries Arlie Latham, and the old boy is quite a card as a coacher and undoubtedly earns his salary. If there is any value at all in coaching surely 'Lath' delivers the goods. He was one of the game's best run-getters and he knows the way around the bases without a guide. Take it for granted that his coaching does get a percentage of runs across—runs that might not otherwise be made—then he is baggage well carried. Heiny Peitz was one of the prize coachers when he wore the red. His cheery voice was an inspiration to the players on base and as a matter of whispered fact there were qualities in that sarcastic little yelp of his that never helped the fellow on the firing line. . . . Cincinnati would have in Peitz a valuable all-season coach on the lines and one of the most valuable aids to good pitching in balldom" (*Sporting Life*, March 9, 1912).

In the next couple of years the benefits of skilled base coaching were attracting more general recognition. A 1913 article reported, "Pitcher Frank Allen cost Brooklyn a chance to tie a recent game with the Phillies in the ninth inning by bad coaching at third base, and yet managers—some of them—persist in sending pitchers to the coaching lines. In fact some managers seem to think that if a player is good for nothing else he is just the man to do the coaching. Such managers, however, never win pennants" (*Sporting News*, September 11, 1913). The growing perception that experienced coaching translated into victories paved the way for full-time coaches to become a permanent part of baseball.

As it grew increasingly common for the coaching lines to be manned by full-timers, the position assumed greater dignity. Nonetheless the men who manned it were veterans of the era when a prime goal was "to disconcert the opposing players," and some remnants of this approach persisted. Christy Mathewson observed in 1912: "There is a sub-division of defensive coaching which might be called the illegitimate brand. It is giving 'phoney' advice to a base runner by the fielders of the other side that may lead him, in the excitement of the moment, to make a foolish play. This style has developed largely in the Big Leagues in the last three or four years" (Christy Mathewson, *Pitching in a Pinch*, 125).

Wartime austerity temporarily reduced the number of full-time paid coaches at the end of the decade. The profession of coaching made great strides toward respectability in the 1920s, only to be threatened again during the Great Depression. Many of the lower minor leagues reacted to the straitened economic climate by eliminating coaches. The International League announced plans to do so on May 5, 1933, but quickly reversed course. The major leagues appear never to have been forced to contemplate such measures (Jonathan Fraser Light, *The Cultural Encyclopedia of Baseball*, 204).

7.2.2   Bench Coaches.

Leigh Montville credited Ted Williams with creating the position of the bench coach—a coach who, instead of being responsible for a specific department or group of players, aids the manager with strategy. When he was hired to manage the Washington Senators in 1969, Williams had no managing experience at any level. Accordingly, he offered the job to Johnny Pesky, who declined, and then hired Joe Camacho (Leigh Montville, *Ted Williams*, 273).

The 1980s saw the position become more common, though some questioned whether it was necessary. Columnist Gerry Fraley observed in 1999: "Twins manager Tom Kelly cannot understand the recent creation of 'bench coach.' Doesn't a bench coach do what a manager should be doing, Kelly has asked" (Gerry Fraley, *Baseball America*, December 27, 1999–January 9, 2000). But by then it had become almost standard for every major league club to employ a bench coach, and the position began to replace third-base coach as a stepping-stone to a managerial position.

Neither the function nor questions about its usefulness are entirely new. In 1877 the *Chicago Tribune* noted, "Joe Simmons is 'assistant manager' [of the Rochester club], whatever that may be" (*Chicago Tribune*, August 12, 1877). Christy Mathewson served as assistant manager of the Giants from 1919 to 1921 (Eddie Frierson, "Christy Mathewson," Tom Simon, ed., *Deadball Stars of the National League*, 36).

7.2.3   Pitching Coaches.

The position of pitching coach took a long time to develop and did not become commonplace until the 1950s. Mel Harder is sometimes credited with being the first pitching coach, and he appears to have believed that to be the case: "During my active career they didn't have pitching coaches. At the end of the '47 season [Bill] Veeck gave me a job as pitching coach for the entire Cleveland organization. I went to the major league camp in spring training and when they broke camp I went to the minor league camp in Florida. I worked with their minor league teams for a while and then went back to the Indians and stayed there" (quoted in Walter M. Langford, *Legends of Baseball*, 72–73). But Harder's claim does not stand up to scrutiny.

A few signs indicate that pitching coaches were beginning to emerge before 1910, but the position was not yet a formal one. The great African-American pitcher Rube Foster is sometimes said to have worked as an informal pitching coach for John McGraw's New York Giants, but the evidence for this claim is weak. Veteran catchers like Deacon McGuire often functioned as pitching coaches; during spring training in 1906 it was noted that "'Deacon' McGuire has charge of the pitchers of the Highlanders who are working at Hot Springs" (*Washington Post*, February 26, 1906).

By the teens there is much clearer evidence that the position had begun to emerge. Wilbert

Robinson annually coached the Giants' pitchers during spring training from 1911 to 1913. One of his special projects was Rube Marquard, and the pitcher formerly dubbed the $11,000 lemon blossomed into a star. (Marquard lost his form when Robinson left the Giants in 1914 to manage the Dodgers, but bounced back when reunited with Robinson in Brooklyn.) At least once, McGraw called on Robinson during the season when he sensed that the team was "about to go to pieces" (Larry Mansch, *Rube Marquard*, 70–71, 82).

In the next few years pitching coaches began to become quite common, though like Robinson, many of these coaches concentrated on the pitchers during spring training and then assumed additional responsibilities once the season began. Others may have served only as instructors during spring training rather than being permanent members of the coaching staff.

In 1911, for example, Detroit owner Frank Navin reportedly offered Newark manager Joe Sugden "the job of teaching the Tiger pitchers and catchers this year and next season. The New York Highlanders have made Sugden a similar offer" (*Detroit News Tribune*, April 2, 1911). Jack Ryan was referred to in 1912 as "the Nationals' crack coach of young pitchers" (*Sporting Life*, December 21, 1912). Pat Moran was said to have functioned as an informal pitching coach in the last few years of his playing career (Dan Levitt, "Patrick Joseph Moran," Tom Simon, ed., *Deadball Stars of the National League*, 207).

In 1915 the *Washington Post* mentioned "Charles 'Duke' Farrell's position as coach for the Yankee pitchers" (*Washington Post*, May 2, 1915). This was followed in 1920 by news that "The Joplin Club also has signed the veteran Jim Drohan to act as a coach of pitchers" (*Sporting News*, March 11, 1920). Two years later *Sporting News* referred to "Dan Howley, for the past four years coach of pitchers of the Detroit Tigers" (*Sporting News*, October 12, 1922). Grover Land was hired before the 1925 season "to coach the kid pitchers of the Reds" (*Zanesville Times Signal*, December 14, 1924). Hook Wiltse served as pitching coach for the Yankees in 1925 (Gabriel Schechter, "George LeRoy 'Hook' Wiltse," Tom Simon, ed., *Deadball Stars of the National League*, 54). The second volume of the "Deadball Stars" books adds the names of Oscar Stanage (in 1914 while still active), Frank Roth (1921 Yankees), and Chief

Bender (1925 White Sox and several subsequent clubs) (profiles by Jim Moyes, Tom Swift, and Dan Holmes in David Jones, ed., *Deadball Stars of the American League*, 567, 689, 609).

Since Mel Harder pitched in the major leagues from 1928 to 1947, it might be theorized from his claim to have been the first pitching coach that the position fell victim to depression-era and World War II cutbacks. But once again the evidence paints a very different picture. AP wire reports listed Ed Walsh as the White Sox' pitching coach in 1928, Tom Clarke filling that role for the Giants in 1933, and Johnny Gooch coaching the Pirates' pitchers in 1938 (*Reno Evening Gazette*, February 28, 1928; *Gettysburg Times*, July 27, 1933; *Wisconsin Rapids Tribune*, August 6, 1938). George Moriarty noted in 1928 that Allan Sothoron had recently been hired as pitching coach of the Braves (George Moriarty, syndicated column, *Lincoln* [Nebr.] *Evening State Journal*, June 26, 1928). Hank Gowdy was occupying that position five years later (Cleon Walfoort, "The Sport Dial," *Sheboygan* [Wisc.] *Press*, April 17, 1933). Roger Bresnahan reportedly served as pitching coach of the Giants at some point (Frank Graham, "No Stranger to the Polo Grounds," *New York Sun*, August 26, 1943). Charlie Berry was described as the pitching coach of the Athletics in 1937 (*Williamsport Gazette-Bulletin*, January 29, 1937). George Uhle claimed: "I was a coach with the Chicago Cubs in 1940. My job was to work with the pitchers" (Walter M. Langford, *Legends of Baseball*, 126). In 1941 the White Sox' and Senators' pitchers were coached by Muddy Ruel and Benny Bengough respectively (INS wire service: *Zanesville Signal*, October 14, 1941). Branch Rickey announced after the 1942 season that veteran pitcher Freddie Fitzsimmons would become an informal pitching coach for the Dodgers (*Coshocton* [Ohio] *Tribune*, December 11, 1942). Red Faber served as pitching coach of the White Sox from 1946 to 1948 (Brian Cooper, "Red Faber," David Jones, ed., *Deadball Stars of the American League*, 519).

While pitching coaches do appear to have become less common during World War II, it is hard to understand how Mel Harder could have thought he was the first pitching coach.

7.2.4   Hitting Coaches. In 1912, Damon Runyon noted that Brooklyn owner Charles Ebbets was about to hire Willie Keeler "to coach the young Brooklyn players in the art of batting next Spring." While it was becoming common for clubs to bring a veteran player to training camp to tutor young players, Ebbets was reputedly "about the first to introduce a batting instructor" (*Sporting Life*, December 14, 1912).

Just as the earliest pitching coaches worked only during spring training, so too Keeler's duties apparently were limited to the preseason. In addition to the usual resistance to adding another salary, the emergence of hitting coaches also was slowed by the belief that hitting was an instinctive skill that could not be taught. A 1907 note, for example, mentioned that Washington manager Joe Cantillon "has been holding little lectures on hitting after the morning practices of the Senators. Many cynical persons were inclined to scoff at this idea, but judging from the stunts that Washington gang have been doing to opposing pitchers, Joe must have something in his talk" (*Washington Herald*, April 19, 1907, 8). But few followed Cantillon's lead; in 1915 Jimmy Archer declared that "the managers never try to teach a player how to hit. They know that every man must hit in his own way if at all" ("Four Hundred to One," *Baseball Magazine*, September 1915, 74).

With this strong consensus that "no one can learn to bat unless he is a natural batter . . . no amount of advice, schooling or practice can make a .300 hitter out of a natural .200 batter," it is not surprising that it was not until the 1950s that the position emerged as full-time ("Catchers Are Scarce," *Dallas Morning News*, December 11, 1904). Jonathan Fraser Light cited Harry Walker and Wally Moses as two of the first full-time hitting coaches (Jonathan Fraser Light, *The Cultural Encyclopedia of Baseball*, 84).

7.2.5   Strength and Conditioning Coaches. The Cincinnati Reds became the first club to have a full-time, season-long strength and conditioning coach in 1961 when they hired Otis Douglas, a former NFL player and Canadian Football League head coach (Greg Rhodes and John Snyder, *Redleg Journal*, 407). It seems to have paid off, as the Reds made it to the World Series that year and the players voted Douglas a full share (*Sporting News*, October 25, 1961).

As with pitching coaches and hitting coaches, however, a number of earlier clubs had engaged strength and conditioning coaches for spring training. Their programs were often quite rigorous, as this 1943 article shows: "Every club in baseball, large or small, has a

trainer, but only the Philadelphia Phillies have a physical director. He is Harold Anson Bruce, internationally known track and field coach, who was appointed by owner Bill Cox to give the faltering Phils a taste of 'commando training' this spring and to keep them in condition after the season gets under way. Commando training is a catchword contributed to baseball terminology by Cox and what the Phillies' physical director really is giving them is an adaptation of the usual program of exercises given runners, jumpers, et al." (Judson Bailey, "Cox Gives Phillies Commando Drill," *Troy* [N.Y.] *Times Record*, March 24, 1943).

Many of these pioneers shared Douglas's football background. In 1948, Branch Rickey hired Brooklyn Dodgers football coach Carl Voyles to help condition his baseball team. In 1957, Gabe Paul brought in former Notre Dame football coach Terry Brennan to help the Reds get into shape during spring training (*Sporting News*, February 11, 1959).

The Yankees hired a new coach named Marty Miller before the 2007 season and gave him the unfortunate title of "Director of Performance Enhancement." When the team got off to a lackluster 10-14 start and suffered a series of hamstring injuries, Miller was fired. It was quite a testimony to the emphasis on strength and conditioning in today's game (Tyler Kepner, "Yankees, Hurting, See Culprit: The Fitness Coach," *New York Times*, May 3, 2007).

7.2.6   Baserunning Coaches. The emergence of coaches whose primary responsibility is baserunning is mostly a recent development. But as discussed under "Full-time Coaches" (**7.2.1**), Arlie Latham was the first to have assumed that function. His main duty with the Reds in 1900 seems to have been baserunning and in 1909 he again served as third base and baserunning coach for the New York Giants.

(iii) Teaching Techniques

7.3.1   Charting Pitches. Longtime International League standout Eddie Onslow recalled that in the mid-1920s Rochester manager George Stallings had pitchers on the bench keep charts of "bases on balls, hits, and errors." Stallings apparently did this to demonstrate his contention that walks led to more runs than hits or errors. While this is not the same as the current practice of charting pitches, it may have helped to influence its development (Eugene Murdock, *Baseball Between the Wars*, 100).

Former pitcher Dave Baldwin reports that the type of pitch charting done today was originated by George Earnshaw when he was pitching coach of the Phillies in 1949, and it became common in the 1950s. He adds that some managers made use of the data thus collected while others just used the practice to ensure that the chart-taker, who was usually the pitcher scheduled to start the next game, paid attention to the game.

7.3.2   Pitch Limits.
During the 1990s pitch counts and pitch limits went from being almost unheard of to becoming common and sometimes controversial. Pitch counts date back to the 1860s, but they were kept by the scorekeeper and no particular significance was attached to them.

The advent of overhand pitching (1.33) in the 1880s led to new attention being paid to pitch counts. In 1886 an observer estimated that pitchers faced 36 batters per game and averaged four pitches per at bat, making a total of "144 in the game for each pitcher, to say nothing of his catches, his throwing to bases and other necessary exertion a pitcher is subjected to. One hundred and forty deliveries require an extraordinary amount of strength" (*Milwaukee Sentinel*, September 20, 1886, 8). But while pitch counts were beginning to be noticed, with relief pitching playing only a limited role in baseball (see 6.2.8), there was no question of instituting pitch limits.

According to Robin Roberts, Paul Richards was recording pitch counts when he managed Baltimore in the 1950s (Hal Bodley, "Teams Obsess Too Much Over Pitch Counts," *USA Today*, September 17, 2004, 4C). The idea of team-enforced pitch limits is a more recent one, but not as new as some assume. In 1971 Roger Angell reported, "One team limits its youngsters to a maximum of a hundred pitches per game" (Roger Angell, *The Summer Game*, 267).

Little League baseball mandated 75-pitch limits in 2007. Reporter Bill Pennington went to a Little League game in Long Island to gauge how young players felt about the rule. Ten-year-old Anthony Service looked a bit disappointed when he reached the quota and was forced to leave the game. But afterward he was philosophical, saying, "I didn't really mind coming out. I don't want to have arm surgery

when I get old, you know, like when I'm 15 or something" (Bill Pennington, "Pitching Change Intended to Save Young Players' Arms," *New York Times*, May 21, 2007).

7.3.3   Batting Dummy.
After abandoning Professor Hinton's pitching gun (see **14.4.11**), the Princeton baseball club tried a new way of facilitating practice: "A 'dummy batter' was set up by the side of the home plate, and the Princeton twirlers took turns at pitching to it. The idea was to give the pitchers practice in accurate throwing without subjecting the batters to the dangers of being hit or having to dodge" (*North Adams* [Mass.] *Transcript*, June 13, 1898).

The concept made it to the major leagues in 1906 when Detroit manager Bill Armour placed a dummy in the batter's box during practice to help pitchers with their control. The players nicknamed the dummy "Hick" (*Sporting Life*, March 24, 1906).

7.3.4   Visual Aids for Coaching Hitting.
Hitting coaches have long sought tools that enable them to *show* batters how they can improve instead of merely telling them.

Some hitters made use of visual aids even before coaches became involved in the process. George S. Davis observed in 1894, "I know a great many clever batsmen who practice daily before a looking glass just as actors and actresses do when they are rehearsing a part. By standing in front of a big glass, bat in hand, one can study his position and remedy any defects he may have" (George S. Davis, "How to Bat," syndicated column, *Warren* [Pa.] *Evening Democrat*, May 26, 1894).

Detroit manager Hughey Jennings appears to have been the first to use technology to improve this process. Jennings started in 1908 by showing his hitters a photograph of Honus Wagner to exemplify an ideal stance. During spring training in 1910 he took photographs of Joe Casey's ungainly stance, causing the rookie to exclaim that it "must be awful to look that way at the plate" (*Detroit News*, March 7, 1910). Jennings then hired a photographer to snap his players so he could discuss their stances with them (H. G. Salsinger, *Detroit News*, April 25, 1910).

Some hitters turned to photographs on their own, as described in a 1921 article: "When [George] Burns was enjoying his greatest batting season in 1918, he was photographed, in action, by a Cleveland camera man. This spring, he felt that something was wrong with his position at the plate and accordingly hunted up the film shooter to get one of his 1918 photos, figuring that would show up any differences in his stance or way of holding his bat" (*Sporting News*, May 19, 1921).

Photographs did not entirely drive out older methods of hitting instruction, as shown by this 1942 account: "[Ted] Williams has stood before a mirror by the hour and practiced his swing. And that is the pet method of old Hugh Duffy for improving the hitting of batting pupils in his care. . . . In his time old Hughey has seen many a great batter come and go. He has helped to make some of them great with his 'looking glass' method of batting instruction" (Dwight Freeburg, "Batter Number One," *Baseball Magazine*, January 1942).

By the 1940s film was being used by innovative football coaches like Paul Brown, but baseball was slow to follow suit. Researcher Dean Sullivan discovered a 1969 article describing how Twins manager Billy Martin videotaped telecasts of his team and replayed them to his players. Martin saw this as a good way of showing players specific strengths and weaknesses, but others remained skeptical. Ted Williams, for example, commented doubtfully, "It may be a good idea. But you know what pitches are being thrown and what ones are being hit without the television" ("Martin Uses TV Tapes in Twins' Move," *Hartford Courant*, May 28, 1969, 47B). Joe Morgan claimed that Ted Kluszewski was the first to make extensive use of videotape while coaching the Reds in 1975 (ESPN broadcast, June 25, 2000). Tony Gwynn helped to popularize videotape instruction in the 1980s and 1990s by making extensive use of it to refine his own technique and study opposing pitchers.

Chapter 8

UMPIRES

"The umpire is the sole judge of play, and is entitled to the respect of the spectators, and any person hissing or hooting at, or offering any insult or indignity to him, must be promptly ejected from the grounds."—(1876 National League Constitution)

THE ROLE of the umpire is to ensure that things are even. But the word "umpire" itself is derived from an Old French word that literally means uneven. That is somehow appropriate, as it has always been the role of the umpire to be alone and friendless. While still true today, imagine how much more evident it was in the early days of baseball, when a lone umpire had to keep track of all of the action on the field.

The evolution of the umpire's general role is discussed in Chapter 1 (see **1.12** and **1.13**). In this chapter, the origins of more specific elements will be examined.

(i) Growth of the Profession

8.1.1 Professionals. In the earliest days of baseball, being chosen to umpire was an honor, and there was no thought of paying for these services. As competitiveness changed the nature of the game, it became increasingly difficult to find qualified men who were willing to volunteer. When an umpire was verbally abused following an 1868 game, a reporter asked rhetorically, "Who, after this exhibition, wishes to act as umpire? . . . If this continues we will loose [sic] all our good umpires" (*Brooklyn Eagle*, August 15, 1868).

The idea of professional umpires was resisted, with Henry Chadwick warning in 1871,

"The fraternity should bear in mind the important fact that the moment they legalize the system of paying umpires impartial umpiring will become a thing of the past" (*New York Clipper*, November 25, 1871). Nonetheless it became increasingly clear that the abuse being heaped upon umpires and the low quality of many volunteers left little alternative. A rule introduced in 1874 permitted payment of an umpire—as long as both clubs paid him equal amounts! (*Boston Advertiser*, March 3, 1874).

The idea of using professional umpires was seriously debated after the 1876 season, with the *Cincinnati Enquirer* predicting a staff of four or five salaried National League umpires in 1877 (quoted in the *New York Sunday Mercury*, September 2, 1876). But the *Chicago Tribune* retorted, "There is no end of talk in some of the papers south of here concerning professional umpires for the League next year, and it is well enough to state that there is not a ghost of a show that the League will pass favorably upon the matter. The managers profess to believe that they can get their work done cheaper under the old system, and they are doubtless right in their assertion. At any rate, not more than two members of the League will be prepared to vote for the idea" (*Chicago Tribune*, November 5, 1876, 10). In a subsequent article the *Tribune* reported that the idea had been "abandoned on a unanimous protest from the managers, to whom the idea was submitted" (*Chicago Tribune*, December 3, 1876, 7).

While there were earlier umpires who received pay, the first man to make umpiring a profession was likely Billy McLean, who was sent on the road by the National League in 1878 and received five dollars per game plus all his expenses. It is apt that McLean was a former boxer, for umpiring had become a very tough profession (Larry R. Gerlach, "William H. McLean," in Frederick Ivor-Campbell, Robert L. Tiemann, and Mark Rucker, eds., *Baseball's First Stars*, 110).

8.1.2 Assignments. The dawn of the professional umpire was accompanied by another development that umpires were less grateful for, but which was just as crucial for maintaining the integrity of the game. This was the transition from the umpire being chosen by one or both of the teams to his being designated by an ostensibly neutral officer of the league.

Until well into the 1870s, games were umpired by locals who were hired by the home team, which led to frequent howls from the visitors. Everyone agreed that this system was less than ideal, but it was not easy to devise a better one within the razor-thin budgets. The result was that arguments about who would umpire were frequent in the ensuing years. In the mid-1870s the rules called for the visitors to submit five names, the home team to winnow the list to two, and the visitors to try to hire one (*St. Louis Globe-Democrat*, April 4, 1875). The complexity of this process led to numerous snags, and more than a few games were never played at all because the issue could not be resolved.

Perhaps the ultimate such instance came during the 1884 best-of-three postseason series between New York and Providence. Providence clinched the series by winning the first two games and didn't want to play the third game, so New York manager Jim Mutrie offered to let Providence choose the umpire. Providence then selected New York's star pitcher Tim Keefe to umpire, and were able easily to beat New York's change pitcher (Jerry Lansche, *Glory Fades Away*, 42–43).

In 1875 the National Association introduced a rule that umpires could not be residents of either of the contesting towns. But with clubs unwilling to pay for traveling expenses, this was a hollow gesture (*Cincinnati Enquirer*, April 25, 1875). In 1879, the National League introduced the prototype of an umpiring staff (James M. Kahn, *The Umpire Story*, 30). The fact that these men had ongoing roles gave the league some much-needed control over quality. But, with the exception of Billy McLean, these umpires did not generally travel, which still left their objectivity open to question.

In addition, traveling umpires created a new potential conflict of interest. In 1880 a sportswriter commented, "The practice of umpires traveling about the country with one club, or associating more with one club than another, is one that should be condemned. Umpires are but human beings, and constant association tends to form strong friendships, and, unintentionally perhaps, an umpire thus situated gives a club with which he is on intimate terms several advantages which tend to win games" (*New York Sunday Mercury*, June 12, 1880).

On July 2, 1882, the American Association held an emergency meeting and replaced the use of locals with the first staff of umpires who traveled to games (David Nemec, *The Beer and Whisky League*, 34). This proved satisfactory enough that at season's end the rules were amended to reflect the fact that umpires were now salaried employees.

Sporting Life gave this summary of the issue in 1885, though it was mistaken about the year in which the change took place: "There was a time when mediocre ability, if supplemented by known fairness on the part of the umpire was acceptable, but that day has gone by, for in these days of great skill and close championship contests the umpiring must be on a par with the other features of the exhibition.

"To make this attainable, all professional associations now have a corps of professional umpires, selected for their abilities and paid by the association, and hence with no incentive for unfairness.

"Up to 1883 [sic] it was customary to appoint a corps of umpires at large in the League, and the different clubs agreed upon which of them should umpire their games, but as there was no steady employment it was hard to get good men to serve. This plan, however, developed some good men, notably [John] Kelly and [Charles] Daniels, neither of whom has a superior in the profession today.

"The American Association depended upon the selection of umpires in each city, but this was soon found to have its objections. The rivalry became so intense that local umpires were compelled to succumb to partisan influence, and it seemed almost impossible for a club to get a square deal in a strange city. This finally culminated in a big squabble in St. Louis in the latter part of June, 1883 [sic], during which the Louisville Club left the field. The result of the trouble was the meeting of the American Association in Cincinnati July 2, 1883 [sic], at which meeting a regular corps of Association umpires were chosen at a fixed salary and expenses. Since that time all the associations have a regular corps of umpires, and the best umpiring ever done in the history of the game was done last year" (*Sporting Life*, June 3, 1885).

Despite the benefits of such a staff, the perennially cash-strapped minor leagues continued to wrestle with the question. When the Southern League began in 1885, it was reported that "games are umpired by local umpires, who, the game being new, are inexperienced and not well posted on the rules, and also lean to their home club. This has threatened serious trouble and Secretary Deadrick proposes to take the bull by the horns and appoint a regular staff, as all the other associations have. He has the legal power to do this and should not hesitate to use it, as good umpiring is essential to the proper conduct and enjoyment of the game. He should appoint a staff of competent men at once" (*Sporting Life*, April 29, 1885).

8.1.3 You've Got a Friend. By the 1880s the need for more than one umpire was very clear. Base runners were increasingly taking advantage of the umpire's helplessness by cutting bases (see 11.1.5). The advent of evasive slides (see 5.2.3) made the inadequacy of long-distance umpiring all the more obvious.

The desirability of at least one additional umpire didn't mean that owners were anxious to assume the added expense. As a result, A. G. Spalding's brother proposed an idea that reprised the much earlier system of two umpires and a referee (see 1.13). In Walter Spalding's scheme, the two umpires would be members of the respective teams while the referee was a neutral party who would only have "a voice when a decision is questioned" (*Chicago Tribune*, October 19, 1886). It was also hoped that this would cut down on arguments: "unless the in umpire's decision is questioned by the out umpire it shall stand . . . on balls, strikes, and base decisions the only man entitled to appeal is the opposing umpire. On a question of rules the captain may appeal. In no case has a player other than the captain a right to protest or appeal to the referee" (*Chicago Tribune*, October 20, 1886).

The idea had the obvious advantage of increasing the number of officials without adding any expense. As a result, it was decided to experiment with it in the 1886 "World's Series" between Chicago and St. Louis, "and upon the result may depend the introduction of some such scheme into the league next year." But one critical change was made for the purposes of the test—all three arbiters were experienced major league umpires. This meant that the most vulnerable part of Walter Spalding's idea would not be tested: "With three experienced men, it should work well; whether it would be satisfactory were the umpires members of the contesting clubs, instead of outsiders, is a question" (*Chicago Tribune*, October 19, 1886).

The concept was first tried in an October 19 game in Chicago, with John Kelly serving as referee and Joe Quest and John McQuaid as umpires. Things ran smoothly for most of the game, with sportswriter O. P. Caylor noting that Kelly was able to correctly reverse four of the decisions of the umpires because he "stood *back* of the basemen and moved around with the base runner, so that it was impossible for him to miss seeing a play, just as it occurred. The baseman in every instance was on the opposite side of the base runner from the referee, whereas the baseman was invariably between the umpire and base runner. Ex-Umpire John Kelly, as well as Captains [Cap] Anson and [Charley] Comiskey, are warm advocates of this plan" (*Base Ball Gazette*, April 19, 1887).

One incident, however, revealed a critical flaw. On a close play, McQuaid's ruling was questioned by the players but not by Quest. Nonetheless Kelly overruled the call, which naturally led to subsequent appeals of all close plays: "Yesterday the players seemed to think that any one of them had a right to appeal to the referee, and there was much needless waste of time" (*Chicago Tribune*, October 20, 1886).

This made it clear that Walter Spalding's system would fail for the same reason that a nearly identical one had been abandoned three decades earlier (see 1.13). The same three men officiated again in the fifth game of the series with no major problems, but the scheme does not appear to have ever been used with club members serving as umpires (*Chicago Tribune*, October 23, 1886).

The following year John Gaffney and John Kelly, both nicknamed "Honest John," teamed to umpire the fifteen-game 1887 World's Series. The benefits became apparent when Detroit second baseman Fred Dunlap tried to use his customary phantom tag. But "Umpire Kelly was giving base decisions, and was watching out for 'Dunny's' famous movement," with the result that a couple of runners were ruled safe before Dunlap caught "on to the fact that Kelly was right behind him" (Maclean Kennedy, "Greatest Backstop of Them All Was the Detroit Boy, Charley Bennett," *Detroit Free Press*, March 30, 1913).

The success of the innovation led to sporadic attempts to introduce an extra official in the years that followed, with even semipro clubs making such trials. Immediately after the 1887 World's Series, it was announced in San Francisco that "The double umpire system will be worked for the remainder of the season at Central Park" (*San Francisco Examiner*, December 19, 1887). In an 1891 game in Henderson, Minnesota, two umpires rotated between the plate and field, but the resulting inconsistency caused the scheme to be termed "a rank failure" (Tom Melchior, *Belle Plaine Baseball, 1884–1960*, 42).

When the Players' League mandated a second umpire in 1890, league secretary Frank Brunell characterized the decision as a response to "the public call for the double umpire system. . . . It will be a costly change, but it is expected to satisfy the public, which pays the bills, and in consequence has a right to demand satisfaction. The majority of the playing rules committee of the new league, practical and experienced players like [Buck] Ewing, [Fred] Pfeffer and [Johnny] Ward, say that their observations have led them to believe that the double umpire system is the only one fit for use in important games, and every game in the championship season is important. The old league's talk about one man being able to do the work and refusal to comply with a public demand are . . . not calculated to please the public" (*Chicago Herald*, March 30, 1890). The league also introduced umpiring crews, with arbiters working "in couples, each pair remaining together throughout the season" (*Chicago Globe*, April 13, 1890). But the change was an expensive one, and may have been a factor in the demise of the Players' League after one season.

The American Association occasionally experimented with a second umpire between 1888 and its demise following the 1891 season, as did the National League from time to time between 1888 and 1897 (John Schwartz, "From One Ump to Two," *Baseball Research Journal* 30 [2001], 85–86). Throughout these years there were periodic proposals to make the extra arbiter a permanent feature. An 1888 article, for instance, stated that Indianapolis owner John T. Brush was trying to convince National League president Nick Young of the need for base umpires (*New York Sun*, February 5, 1888).

During the 1895 season, Young declared that the league would use the double umpire system in 1896, but that didn't come to pass (*St. Louis Post-Dispatch*, August 10, 1895).

Instead, whenever the idea of a second umpire came to a vote, concerns about expense ruled the day. One reporter observed in 1897, "The cost of the experiment, $12,000, will scarcely warrant the engagement of another crew, and on this point the Little Five and the Big Seven heartily concur, as they do on every question where the wallet comes directly into play" (*Washington Post*, February 17, 1897).

Arguments in favor of the lone umpire were occasionally advanced, but they were less than convincing. Henry Chadwick, for example, maintained that "it only requires a little extra activity in running into the field to judge the play close to the locality of the point played, to admit of as correct a judging as a special umpire for the duty would be likely to give it" (Henry Chadwick, "The New Base-Ball Rules," *Lippincott*, May 1887, reprinted in *Louisville Courier-Journal*, April 24, 1887). Following this dubious logic, the National League hired a couple of sprinters to umpire during the 1890s, including Billy Stage, the world record holder in the one-hundred- and two-hundred-yard dashes. Stage had a short umpiring tenure but was long remembered for his ability to outrace batters to first base (Peter Morris, "'A Motion as Near Flying as Any Human Being Could Attain': The 19th Century Umpire as Sprinter," *Base Ball* [2:2], Fall 2008, 18–25).

The National League finally added the second umpire after the 1897 season, explaining that "the game must have this number next year if the rough element is to be eliminated from the field, as players seldom kick when two umpires are in the game" (*Chicago Tribune*, September 28, 1897, 4). The change made it necessary to adapt the game's terminology, and this proved a contentious issue. John T. Brush proposed calling the man behind the plate the "referee umpire" and his partner the "assistant umpire," but objections were raised to the redundancy of "referee umpire." A suggestion to use "referee" and "umpire" was even more unpopular, as "some of the magnates, who are sticklers on tradition, objected to plain referee, because such an official by that title would be new to the League, while others thought referees officiated at prize fights, forgetting that they also officiate at football, field and track sports and other games participated in by gentlemen." Eventually "umpire" and "assistant umpire" were selected over objections that it "takes the dignity from the base umpire's position to call that official an assistant" (*Philadelphia Public Ledger*, March 3, 1898).

Nobody was happier about the change than the beleaguered Nick Young, who commented: "The double system will undoubtedly relieve me of the most excruciating worry that ever brought threads of white to the locks of man, and next season I hope to make up for many an hour of lost sleep. No more wire-burning telegrams from fiery managers and outraged owners. Two umpires to a game will bring about more artistic ball and cut out much of the pyrotechnic elocution that was exchanged by player and umpire in seasons past" (*Oklahoma City Daily Oklahoman*, February 18, 1898). But league owners could not have cared much about Young's slumbers, because after the 1899 season they again shelved the two-umpire system.

Researcher John Schwartz has meticulously examined early-twentieth-century umpiring assignments. He reported that the National League used only 1.13 umpires per game in 1901, and the American League 1.21. By 1908 the figures were 1.39 in the senior circuit and 1.51 in the junior circuit (John Schwartz, "From One Ump to Two," *Baseball Research Journal* 30 [2001], 85–86). While umpire injuries and illnesses kept the increase from being steady, the base umpire was becoming a common sight.

Researcher David W. Anderson analyzed 1908 assignments carefully and found, not surprisingly, that two umpires were generally assigned to games between contenders and to ones where a sizable crowd was expected. What's more surprising is that some veteran umpires, including Tom Connolly and Hank O'Day, expressed a preference for working without a partner (David W. Anderson, *More Than Merkle*, 102–103, 88–89).

Other umpires, however, were vocal supporters of the two-umpire system. Their viewpoint carried the day, as the number of umpires per game rose dramatically to 1.72 (National League) and 1.91 (American League) in 1909 and 1.99 and 1.83 in 1910. It was not until 1911 that the second umpire was required by the rulebook. According to Schwartz, the last major league umpire to work a game entirely by himself was Cy Pfirman, who did so in the second game of a doubleheader in Philadelphia on July 11, 1923, after his partner Ernie Quigley was injured in the opener (John Schwartz, "From One Ump to Two," *Baseball Research Journal* 30 [2001], 85–86).

8.1.4 Three-man Crews. Like the second umpire, the three-man umpiring crew was introduced to regular-season major league baseball in fits and starts. The American League began the 1917 season with nine umpires, so it used an extra umpire on a regular basis until August. In the next few years the league president would occasionally assign a third arbiter to a big game (*Chicago Tribune*, August 9, 1920). The American League returned to nine umpires in 1921, and two years later it went to ten and the National League to nine. By the mid-1920s the major leagues began to hire ten umpires, which meant that three-man crews could be used in half the games if all the umpires were healthy (*New York Times*, April 13, 1925; research by John Schwartz). The number had increased to eleven or twelve umpires in the late 1920s. In 1932 both leagues went back to ten umpires to save money, but the three-man crew was restored at season's end (*Washington Post*, April 12, 1932; *New York Times*, November 5, 1932). John Schwartz reports that the number fluctuated for several years, and it was not until 1944 that both leagues permanently employed enough umpires to ensure three-man crews at each game. As far as he can tell, the last major league game with only two umpires on the field occurred in St. Louis on August 19, 1951—a game better remembered for the pinch-hitting appearance of midget Eddie Gaedel (see **2.3.3**). A few innings later, first-base umpire Art Passarella was injured, and the game was completed with two arbiters.

8.1.5 Four-man Crews. The now-customary practice of using four umpires likewise has a very sporadic history.

The first major league game that appears to have made use of four umpires occurred by accident during the Players' League's sole campaign of 1890. For a July 14 game with Brooklyn hosting Pittsburgh, "There was no room for any kicking, as owing to an error in calculation Secretary [Frank] Brunell had assigned four umpires to the Brooklyn game instead of sending two to New York and two here. It was the first championship contest ever decided with the aid of an umpire at each bag and one behind the catcher. The game began with Mr. [Bob] Ferguson judging balls and strikes, Mr. [Lon] Knight at first base, Mr. [Charles] Jones at second and Mr. [Bill] Holbert at third. They moved round at the conclusion of every inning, each taking his turn at each base" (*Brooklyn Eagle*, July 15, 1890).

The 1909 World Series saw four-umpire crews become a custom for the World Series. The plan was to alternate a pair of two-man crews: Jim Johnstone (NL) and "Silk" O'Loughlin (AL) rotating with Bill Klem (NL) and Billy Evans (AL). But the erection of temporary seating for the overflow crowds made life very difficult for the arbiters.

Evans and Klem officiated the second game on October 9 and were forced to determine whether a ball that bounced into the stands had landed in the permanent seats (making it a home run) or the temporary seats (making it a double). After a long huddle, they eventually ruled it a double but admitted afterward that the decision was little more than a guess, and were fortunate that it did not affect the outcome (James M. Kahn, *The Umpire Story*, 121–125).

The series resumed two days later with Johnstone and O'Loughlin scheduled to umpire. Prior to the game a conference about the ground rules took place with the result that Klem was asked to stand down one of the outfield lines in an "advisory capacity" (*Los Angeles Times*, October 12, 1909).

Before the next game the decision was made to make use of all four umpires for the remainder of the series. All four men took the field for game five on October 12, causing Ring Lardner to chronicle: "Klem was behind the bat and Evans on the bases. Silk O'Loughlin was out in left field to help decide whether balls were fair or foul and Johnstone was in right on the same job. Another reason for using the two extra ones was to avoid disputes over balls hit into the stands. There didn't happen to be any over which any discussion could arise, so Silk and Johnstone almost froze to death standing still" (R. W. Lardner, *Chicago Tribune*, October 13, 1909).

Despite the hardship, frozen umpires seemed preferable to having the outcome of the World Series potentially decided by a guess from a man hundreds of feet away. Thereafter four umpires became a World Series tradition.

A similar reason led to four umpires next being used in a regular-season major league game in Cincinnati on August 3, 1919. With a crowd of some 33,000 necessitating seating in the outfield, National League president John Heydler assigned four umpires to the game. Bill Klem was behind the plate and Bob Emslie covered the bases, with Pete Harrison and Barry McCormick stationed on the foul lines to make rulings on balls hit into the overflow crowd.

It was another three decades before today's system of umpires at each base came into use. According to John Schwartz, the National League went to thirteen umpires in 1945, which meant that—barring injuries—a four-man crew would work in one game out of four. The number rose steadily until 1953 when both leagues engaged sixteen men, and since then four-man crews have been standard except when unusual circumstances arise.

8.1.6 Five-man Crews. Ed Sudol explained to Larry Gerlach how he became part of the first five-man crew. National League umpire Dusty Boggess suffered a heart attack in late June 1957, and Sudol was called up to replace him. When Boggess returned in late August, the league was pleased with Sudol's work and let him remain in the major leagues as a fifth umpire. Sudol recalled, "For the rest of the season I alternated working the foul lines" (Larry R. Gerlach, *The Men in Blue*, 222).

David W. Smith of Retrosheet used the Retrosheet database to corroborate Sudol's account. He found seventeen games in September 1957 where five umpires were used, all of them involving Sudol. Smith also found that Bill Jackowski was used as a fifth umpire for two games in 1959 and John Kibler for three games in 1964. In 1961 the National League made extensive use of five-umpire crews to break in the new umpires who would be necessary in 1962 due to expansion.

8.1.7 Six-man Crews. After Sam Rice's controversial tumbling-into-the-stands catch in the 1925 Fall Classic, umpire Cy Rigler publicly recommended that two extra umpires be used in the World Series. Commissioner Kenesaw Mountain Landis, however, took no action (Dan Krueckeberg, "Take-Charge Cy," *National Pastime*, Spring 1985, 11). Beginning in 1939, six umpires were on hand for all World Series games in case of an injury to any of the four who officiated (James M. Kahn, *The Umpire Story*, 233). There was now every reason to use the two extra umpires in the outfield, but when Joe McCarthy proposed this idea in 1943, Landis again nixed it (Jocko Conlan and Robert Creamer, *Jocko*, 221).

The practice of using all six umpires in the World Series began only after Landis's death. Shortly before the start of the 1947 series, Commissioner Happy Chandler made the decision to use two extra arbiters, reasoning that the "active alternates" who were already on hand might as well be put to use. So the two umpires were assigned to "sit in the park at first and third base to determine if balls are fair or foul, to decide if outfielders trap or actually catch fly balls on shoestring catches, and rule whether or not fans interfere with balls close to the railing" (AP: *Washington Post*, September 30, 1947).

8.1.8 Rotations.

It took some time after it became customary for multiple umpires to work major league games before a rotation became conventional. Bill Klem, most notably, continued to monopolize home-plate assignments for many years.

Sportswriter Herbert Simons noted in 1942 that a rotation had become the norm. He explained: "The stationing of umpires on bases and at the plate is up to the men themselves. It is a tradition, however, that the veteran in point of service opens the season behind the plate, the next oldest umpire at first and the junior member at third. They then rotate clockwise with each game for the rest of the season. . . . Sometimes an umpire may seem more proficient calling 'em on the bases than he is behind the plate, but he rarely is assigned to specialize, barring injury" (Herbert Simons, "Life of an Ump," *Baseball Magazine*, April 1942; reprinted in Sidney Offit, ed., *The Best of Baseball*, 156–162).

8.1.9 Chief of Umpires.

When the legendary Harry Wright was fired as Philadelphia manager after the 1893 season, it caused a public outcry. As a result, the position of chief of umpires was created for him. Some claim this was an honorary position, but that was not the case. While National League president Nick Young continued to be in charge of appointing umpires, Wright took his duties seriously in 1894, visiting ballparks to observe umpires, asking Young for rule clarifications, and lobbying for greater respect for umpires (*Sporting Life*, April 14, 1894).

During the 1895 season, Wright's deteriorating health interfered with his duties. He died on October 3, and the position was not again filled until John B. Day was appointed in 1897. He was given the title "Inspector of Umpires and Players," and his job description suggested that he was to spend much of his time handing out fines to players ("Create a New Office," *Chicago Tribune*, February 28, 1897, 7). Day was a former owner of the New York Giants who had suffered financial reversals, and his appointment was widely viewed as "a sinecure position" or "pension job" (*Chicago Times*, July 19 and August 30, 1897).

Longtime umpire Tommy Connolly was appointed as the first supervisor of American League umpires on June 17, 1931. The National League revived the position for Cy Rigler in 1935, but he died two weeks later (Dan Krueckeberg, "Take-Charge Cy," *National Pastime*, Spring 1985, 11).

8.1.10 Umpire School.

The earliest umpire school may have been one operated by Nick Young in Washington in the late nineteenth century (Richard Puff, "Nicholas Emanuel Young," in Frederick Ivor-Campbell, Robert L. Tiemann, and Mark Rucker, eds., *Baseball's First Stars*, 181). It seems unlikely that the instruction was extensive; most umpires continued to learn on the job. In 1899, Cleveland and St. Louis owner M. Stanley Robison advocated "the establishment of a school for umpires." Robison argued that better officiating was necessary for the sport to continue to advance and that the National League should sponsor the school. His fellow owners apparently did not agree (*Grand Valley* [Utah] *Times*, August 11, 1899). Early-twentieth-century umpire Billy Evans was also outspoken about the need for umpiring schools (David Anderson, "William George Evans," in David Jones, ed., *Deadball Stars of the American League*, 398). It was not until the 1930s that umpire schools with systematic instruction began to appear, with George Barr operating one of the first prominent ones.

8.1.11 Unions.

Negro Leagues umpires had a union by the 1940s, but it took much longer for one to be successfully formed in the white major leagues (Neil Lanctot, *Negro League Baseball*, 181–182). American League umpire Ernie Stewart was forced to resign in 1945 after league president William Harridge accused him of trying to form a union. Stewart maintained that he was merely trying to obtain better working conditions for umpires, and had done so at the suggestion of Commissioner Happy Chandler (Larry R. Gerlach, *The Men in Blue*, 123–126).

In 1963 National League umpires secretly formed a union. According to Tom Gorman, Augie Donatelli was the driving force behind the movement. The umpires hired negotiator Jack Reynolds to represent them, and he won improvements in salaries, benefits, and working conditions (Tom Gorman, *Three and Two!*, 38).

American League umpires had initially declined to join the union, but after five years they changed their minds. An Association of Major League Umpires was formed on September 30, 1968, but it was met with greater resistance. One of the union's first demands was the reinstatement of Al Salerno and Bill Valentine, two American League umpires who had been fired two weeks earlier. The umpires alleged that the pair was fired for their role in helping to start the union.

The umpires' union has attracted less attention than the players' union, but it has had its share of showdowns with the owners. The umpires staged a one-day walkout on October 3, 1970, and there have been several subsequent ones, one of which forced the 1979 season to begin with replacement umpires. A disastrous union tactic in 1999 saw the mass resignation of fifty-seven of the sixty-six major league umpires. Union head Richie Phillips intended to evade a no-strike clause in their contract, but his ploy backfired when major league baseball accepted many of the resignations. Twenty-two umpires lost their jobs, though most of them have since been rehired. A new union now represents the umpires.

(ii) Kill the Ump!

8.2.1 Verbal Abuse. It is hard to imagine any professional more prone to being second-guessed than the baseball umpire. In the early 1950s the wife of Supreme Court Chief Justice Fred Vinson reported that one of her husband's favorite forms of recreation was watching baseball on television and "hollering at the umpire whenever he thinks a poor decision is made" (James M. Kahn, *The Umpire Story*, 4).

Of course the umpires could not hear Vinson's catcalls, but that consideration has not deterred fans since the earliest days of baseball from heaping verbal abuse on umpires. As early as 1861, Henry Chadwick was chiding, "Clubs should remember that the umpire in a match confers a favor by accepting the office, and tries his best to act fairly in every instance; and common courtesy should lead them to act respectfully towards him, no matter how he may err in his decisions. This grumbling at adverse decisions is unworthy of true ball players" (*New York Clipper*, October 19, 1861).

It was not long before spectators were following the players' lead. By 1867 a Boston crowd was being taken to task by Chadwick for having "hissed nearly every decision of the Um-

pire" and an audience in Chicago for "hissing the umpire" (*The Ball Player's Chronicle*, June 6, 1867; *Detroit Post*, October 8, 1867). Chadwick reiterated this theme at every opportunity, but it soon became clear that he was fighting a losing battle. This did not deter him in the least, and the topic would be a recurrent theme of his writing for the next forty years.

8.2.2 Cotton. In 1896 one National League umpire found a unique way to shield himself from verbal abuse: "William Betts puts cotton in his ears and does not hear the players' abusive language" (*Brooklyn Eagle*, July 18, 1896).

8.2.3 Physical Abuse. It would be nice to report that early umpires were subject only to verbal abuse. Direct physical assaults on umpires were rare, though not unheard of, but a far more common menace was objects being thrown from the stands. As noted in an earlier entry (see **1.12**), umpires of the 1860s were customarily offered the largest glass of beer. Before the end of the century, the glasses of beer were instead being thrown at them.

Nor did the defenseless umpires have any recourse, as was shown by a National League game on August 4, 1897. When a fan threw a beer glass at umpire Tim Hurst, Hurst threw it back but hit a different spectator and was arrested for assault and battery.

The autobiography of Harry "Steamboat" Johnson, a prominent minor league umpire from 1909 to 1935, regularly refers to spectators throwing pop bottles at umpires (Harry "Steamboat" Johnson, *Standing the Gaff*, 62, 68–70, 112, etc.). In spite of the obvious dangers, baseball clubs moved very slowly to address the issue.

The 1907 season saw umpire Billy Evans and Cubs player-manager Frank Chance both seriously injured by flying bottles. The possibility of a ban on bottles was raised at the league meetings before the 1908 season, but no action was taken. *Sporting Life* editor Francis Richter felt this was a reasonable course since fans ought to be able to quench their thirst. More cynical was sportswriter I. E. Sanborn, who observed, "Whenever the good of the game conflicts too seriously with the pockets of the club owners, no reform ever has been made until something happens to unite the public in demanding reform" (*Sporting Life*, February 15, 1908; *Chicago Tribune*, March 1, 1908; both quoted in David W. Anderson, *More Than Merkle*, 18).

As a result, this easily preventable hazard continued to menace umpires. Umpire Red Ormsby, who had fought in World War I and escaped unscathed, almost had his career ended by a pop bottle that gave him a severe concussion and caused him to miss nine weeks of action (*Sporting News*, May 12, 1932). Not until the late 1920s and early 1930s did owners begin agreeing to prohibit pop bottles from stadiums (Joe Williams, *New York World Telegram*, July 24, 1930, reprinted in *The Joe Williams Baseball Reader*).

(iii) The Umpire Strikes Back: Discipline

Umpires have never had much recourse against fan abuse unless they chose to emulate umpire William Betts and stick cotton in their ears. But over the years they have been given a number of ways of responding to impertinent players and managers.

8.3.1 Fines. In early baseball the umpire enforced discipline by assessing fines for misbehavior. As noted in Chapter 1, this practice dates back to the Knickerbockers. The most common fine was for swearing, and the scorekeeper would record the fine—and sometimes the offending word—in the club's scorebook. Because club membership was highly valued, there was no difficulty in collecting these fines. The 1860 bylaws of the Excelsior Base Ball Club of Brooklyn, for instance, prescribed, "All fines incurred for violation of Sections 9, 10 and 11 must be paid to the umpire, before leaving the field."

This worked only as long as the umpire and players were members of the same club and collection of the fines was ensured by the value attached to membership. Once the gentlemanly era of baseball began to wane, fines disappeared, and they were not again practical until the dawn of professional leagues with their centralized power.

It is usually reported that professional umpires did not issue fines until 1879, but this is not technically correct. In fact National League umpires could assess fines in 1878, but they did not prove much of a deterrent. In a game in Boston, for example, umpire Dickey Pearce "made several very cross decisions against the Bostons, and thereby drew upon his head the maledictions of the crowd. It seems that [Boston catcher Charles] Snyder had a good deal to say to him by way of assisting him in his duties, for suddenly Pearce turned about and gave

Snyder an emphatic warning, exclaiming that he had heard enough from him. At this time there was a voice from the stockholders' seats, telling Snyder to 'Go for the umpire; I'll pay your fine.' With a few stockholders of this temper, the management of the Boston Club would find it difficult to maintain discipline among the players or decency among the spectators" (*Chicago Tribune*, July 28, 1878). An additional problem was that the umpire had the authority later to cancel a fine. The result was that, "out of all fines imposed, only one was enforced during the year 1878," and even that lone fine was never collected by the league (*New York Clipper*, December 14, 1878, and March 8, 1879).

Consequently the National League created a rule after the 1878 season "to remedy the evil of forgiveness" by making it impossible to revoke a fine (*New York Clipper*, December 14, 1878). Collecting fines still remained problematic, as is demonstrated by an 1889 rule adopted by the Michigan State League: "If [the umpire] fines a player during the game, the contest stops until the fine is paid. If the assessment is not settled within fifteen minutes, the game is awarded to the other club. This . . . may seem severe, but was thought necessary, as of the twenty fines imposed in the league this season, the only one which has been paid was the $5 Keyes assessed [Edward] Phalen for calling him a fool in a recent Grand Rapids game" (*Grand Rapids* [Mich.] *Daily Democrat*, July 3, 1889).

Umpires were understandably reluctant to take money out of the players' pockets. As Billy McLean put it, "Several times I have had to fine players for abusing me in the field. I hate to do it, and find that they generally obey when I speak sharply to them, but once in a while they let their feelings run away with them, and then they suffer" (*Macon Telegraph*, August 17, 1884).

In the early 1890s the National League attempted to deal with player misconduct by encouraging umpires to issue heavy fines, but the principal consequence was ill will between players and umpires. Sportswriter H. G. Merrill asked in 1897, "Can anyone state where anything is gained by the fining system? The umpire in the heat of passion, exasperated as well, imposes a fine—large or small. The player loses a portion of his salary and in his sober moments ruminates over his indiscretion. He realizes he was wrong in abusing the umpire, but there rankles in his breast the thought that the umpire took away his money. . . . The player views the umpire as a highwayman and subsequently this same player and umpire are likely to have another tilt" (*Sporting News*, October 9, 1897). Cleveland's Jack O'Connor even went to court and got an injunction over a fine levied on him by an umpire, though he eventually dropped the lawsuit (*Brooklyn Eagle*, August 16, 1895).

Fines were further undermined by the fact that owners often paid them on the player's behalf. As one unidentified former umpire asked rhetorically, "Of what benefit are the rules when the players are tacitly encouraged to their erasion and infraction by the clubs paying the fines of players imposed by the umpire to enforce discipline?" (*Cincinnati Times-Star*, May 21, 1892).

Former American Association umpire John Dyler added that "all the fines in the world— unless the players themselves are compelled to pay them—will never stop the rowdies." He suggested that umpires needed the power "to fine them good and hard and not only put them out of the game, but stop them from playing for a time, and you'll soon put an end to the fighters and toughs" (*Sporting News*, October 30, 1897).

The 1890s saw the legalization of substitutions and increasing roster sizes, which made it possible for umpires to eject players instead of fining them. This had some advantages, but ejection by itself came to be perceived as too lenient a punishment, so rules were enacted in the early twentieth century that made fines mandatory for ejected players. Yet this still had the disadvantage of creating resentment between players and umpires, and it became increasingly clear that any rule requiring the umpire to fine a player would not be enforced. In 1904, for example, Pirates player-manager Fred Clarke described a rule allowing umpires to fine a player who discolored the ball as a dead letter. He explained that, "as an umpire is always in favor of anything that will lessen trouble, he is willing to shut his eyes to a legal offense if the captains are agreeable" (*Pittsburg[h] Press*, March 23, 1904).

The change to the current practice of assessing fines from the league offices was a gradual one. In 1897 John B. Day was hired as the National League's "Inspector of Umpires and Players," and the description of his duties suggested that among them was recommending fines of players ("Create a New Office," *Chicago Tribune*, February 28, 1897, 7). The trend accelerated when former umpire Tom Lynch became president of the National League

in 1910. Lynch was determined to reduce the amount of umpire-baiting and concluded that "if I could touch the players' pockets I could stop this foolishness. So I notified each of the club owners that hereafter when a player was benched for using profane or indecent language on the field he would be suspended indefinitely. Lo, and behold, I haven't had a complaint from an umpire since!" (*Washington Post*, July 24, 1910). American League president Ban Johnson joined Lynch in imposing more severe penalties, and this course relieved umpires of some of the pressure.

8.3.2 Ejections. In 1867, Henry Chadwick noted that an "umpire has the power to order the dismissal of any player from a nine in a match" if he learned that that player had bet on the outcome (Henry Chadwick, *Haney's Base Ball Player's Book of Reference for 1867*, 58). Other than this, before 1889, the rulebook gave the umpire no authority to remove a player, though it appears there were a few ad hoc ejections. For example, Gerard S. Petrone reported that John Gaffney once ejected Cap Anson from an 1884 game (Gerard S. Petrone, *When Baseball Was Young*, 131).

In 1889, with player substitutions legal, a rule was added that stated: "After a player has been once fined for abusing the umpire, that official shall retire said player from game, and substitute one of the men in uniform" (*Washington Post*, April 7, 1889). The rule did not prove effective, though there were different opinions as to whose fault that was.

Henry Chadwick blamed the umpires, writing in 1890: "Umpires did not enforce the rule last year, of removing an offending player from the field for repeatedly disputing an Umpire's decision, as they should have done" (*Spalding's Official Base Ball Guide*, 1890, 180). The umpires, however, saw the matter in a different light. An unidentified former umpire replied in 1892, "When writers like Chadwick inform umpires that an umpire can only remove a player upon the repetition of his offense, of what use is that rule?" (*Cincinnati Times-Star*, May 21, 1892).

In 1896 the National League made a renewed effort to crack down on troublemakers by emphasizing that umpires were expected to eject unruly players. This reflected a growing perception, mentioned in the preceding entry, that umpires who doled out fines created long-term animosity. Soon fines became the prerogative of the league presidents and ejections became the umpire's primary method of disciplining unruly players and managers. In 1898 umpires were further counseled, "In case of the umpire having removed so many players from the game for 'kicking' that one team has less than nine men left he shall at once declare the game forfeited to the other team" (*Philadelphia Public Ledger*, March 3, 1898).

In 1933 Heinie Manush became the first player to be ejected from the World Series. Commissioner Kenesaw Mountain Landis announced that in the future only he would have the authority to eject players from the World Series. While no such rule was specifically enacted, it appears that umpires adhered to this precept for the remainder of Landis's tenure.

8.3.3   Limiting Arguments. In 1887 Henry Chadwick proclaimed, "No one except the Captains of the teams is allowed to address the umpire in the way of disputing a decision at all unless the question is one affecting an alleged misinterpretation of the rules, disputing a decision involving merely an error of judgment not being allowed, under a penalty of heavy fine for each offence" (Henry Chadwick, "The New Base-Ball Rules," *Lippincott*, May 1887, reprinted in *Louisville Courier-Journal*, April 24, 1887). But with fines proving to be ineffective, compliance could not be enforced.

When umpires were given new and more effective disciplinary tools in the 1890s, with them came a renewed effort to restrict the arguing over calls. For example, the *Brooklyn Eagle* reported in 1892: "Hereafter no player—captain or subordinate—will be allowed to dispute any decision marked by a simple error of judgment, such as that involved in the question as to a base runner being touched or not, or on called balls or strikes. Only in cases where an illegal interpretation of a special rule is involved will any appeal from the umpire's decision be allowed" (*Brooklyn Eagle*, March 3, 1892). Note the similar choice of words—in all likelihood, this was again Chadwick writing.

Needless to say, adherence to such guidelines remained far from universal. But disputes came to be more and more governed by some basic conventions. It became accepted that a team's manager would take the lead in arguments and that umpires had the authority to cut short discussions of judgment calls. Matters were further eased as playing managers gave way to bench managers, since this enabled umpires to eject managers without costing a team the services of a star player.

Once this principle was in place, it led to other forms of détente between umpires and managers, such as the understanding that a manager would be automatically ejected if he came on the field to argue balls and strikes. I have not been able to determine the precise origins of this restriction, but it occurred after World War II (Larry R. Gerlach, *The Men in Blue*, 106).

Nonetheless, among the major professional sports baseball remains the most tolerant of stoppages of action to dispute an official's decision.

8.3.4   Clearing the Bench. In another effort to limit disputes, in 1910 the major leagues gave umpires the authority to clear the bench. *Sporting News* found the new measure effective: "The new rule adopted this year empowering umpires to 'clear the bench' has emphasized the need of regulating the retirement of players. Until this season offending players have been sent to the clubhouse singly, except in a few instances and comparatively few players in any one game" (*Sporting News*, July 28, 1910). When the bench was cleared, those players could still enter the game; they simply could not sit on the bench when not playing.

(iv) Making the Call

8.4.1   Making Up Rules. Like judges, umpires are not supposed to make up rules, just enforce the existing ones. But there have been occasions, especially in the early days of baseball, when they had little choice.

Not only were there major omissions in the scope of the rules, but there was also often ambiguity in the points that were covered. An amusing commentary in 1884 claimed: "Disputes over points of play have been unusually frequent this season, for the reason that many of the rules are ambiguous, improperly worded and capable of widely different constructions. In fact the playing rules are anything but models of pure or ordinary good English. An attempt has been made to clothe them in a sort of legal phrase. Evidently the author has taken a wild delight in seizing as many 'thereafters,' 'suches,' 'saids,' 'provides' and the like as he could lay his hand upon, impressing them into the service of the League to the entire neglect of the usual parts of speech, many of which, in these astounding paragraphs, wander up and down like [Dickens character] Mr. Pickwick trying to find his room in the dark and quite as disconsolate. It wouldn't be a bad idea for a joint committee to revise the entire code" (*Sporting Life*, July 30, 1884).

In 1867 a poorly thought-out rule specified that a batter had to be alongside the plate when he hit the ball, but specified no penalty. Accordingly, the accepted practice became for the umpire to call "no play" if the batter moved forward. In one game, umpire Phonney Martin decided to consider such balls "foul," an imaginative ruling that meant the batter could not profit by breaking the rules, but that he could be put out if his hit was caught. (Not coincidentally, Martin was one of the best pitchers of the day.) This led to one batter being called out on a "foul ball" caught by the center fielder. Henry Chadwick lambasted Martin: "This usurpation of the powers of the National Association by an umpire is something new in the history of the game" (*The Ball Player's Chronicle*, August 29, 1867).

For other instances of umpires becoming legislators, see the entries on "Brushback Pitching" (3.3.2) and the "Kimono Ball" (3.2.17). Umpires also chose to ignore certain rules, as was discussed in the entry on "Fines" (8.3.1).

8.4.2 Positioning. In early baseball the sole umpire stood behind the plate and well off to the side, a placement that was necessary for his protection since the catcher stood well behind the plate (see 4.2.1). His vision of the field was less than ideal, a problem that was exacerbated in the 1880s when base runners developed evasive slides (see 5.2.3).

The difficulty of umpiring from behind the plate was further emphasized by having to enforce restrictions on the pitcher's delivery. It was this requirement that may have first prompted an umpire to experiment with a different positioning. An account of an 1885 game noted that Kansas City pitcher Billy O'Brien "persisted in leaving his box with each pitch, until finally the umpire stationed himself back of the pitcher and closely watched his delivery during three or four pitches" (*Milwaukee Daily Journal*, May 26, 1885).

In an 1888 preseason game, John Gaffney "inaugurated a new style of umpiring . . . When the bases were clear he stood behind the catcher, but as soon as a man reached a base he went behind the pitcher. This is practically the double umpire system. It caused no end of comment among the spectators, who could not understand why he kept changing" (*Detroit Free Press*, April 5, 1888). Gaffney continued to

use it in the regular season, and at least one colleague, Billy McLean, also experimented with standing behind the pitcher and commented favorably (*Detroit Free Press*, June 15, 1888). He was joined in 1889 by George Barnum (*Chicago Tribune*, April 30, 1889).

This positioning had several consequences. Cap Anson remarked in 1894 that there was a general impression that umpires called narrower strike zones when standing behind the pitcher, though he disagreed (*Philadelphia Inquirer*, April 8, 1894). Henry Chadwick noted that the innovation had necessitated several new rules: "When the umpire takes up his potion [sic] on fair ground to judge called balls and strikes, or to judge base running, and a batted ball strikes him, the batsman is entitled to his base. . . . In base running there are several new points evolved under the new rules. For instance, if a runner is on first base and the umpire is judging called balls and strikes from a position back of the pitcher on fair ground, and the catcher, in throwing the ball to second base to cut off the runner trying to steal second, hits either the person of the umpire or his clothing with the thrown ball, the runner must return to the base he left. Of course, the umpire must watch carefully that the throw is not made so as to hit him intentionally, with the object of sending the runner back to his base" (*Evansville Journal*, April 27, 1889, 7).

Umpires who stood behind the pitcher seem to have remained in the minority. Eventually the issue was rendered moot by the two-umpire system (see 8.1.3).

8.4.3 Home Umpire. As discussed under "Assignments" (8.1.2), biased hometown umpiring was one of the vexing problems of early baseball. The hiring of traveling umpires like Billy McLean (see 8.1.1, "Professionals") was part of the response to this issue.

Nonetheless the problem was difficult to eliminate entirely, and many were willing to settle for ridding the game of blatantly biased officiating. The *Buffalo Express*, for example, stated, "It is a rule with [International Association] umpires generally in their decisions to give the home Club the benefit of the doubt when there is one. . . . Mr. Charles S. Taylor, acknowledged the best umpire the Uticas ever had, resigned because the Directors required him to make his decisions in their favor whether right or wrong. Mr. Thomas H. Brunton, of the Tecumseh Association, one of the best of umpires, says it is the rule to decide in favor of the home

Club when there is doubt." The *Chicago Tri-bune* commented that such favoritism was not possible in the National League: "This may be so in International games, but if any such 'rule' should be set up in a League game the umpire would be apt to be pitched over the fence, 'with or without appeal'" (*Chicago Tribune*, August 4, 1878, 7).

Ironically, in 1888 National League president Nick Young specifically instructed umpire John Kelly to give the benefit of the doubt to the home team. He explained: "To carry out this idea it is not necessary to be 'a home umpire,' but where an honest doubt exists the home club should not be the sufferer" (*Detroit Free Press*, July 1, 1888).

8.4.4 Appeals on Checked Swings. The automatic appeal on the checked swing is a fairly recent innovation, and several of the umpires interviewed in Larry Gerlach's *The Men in Blue* had strong opinions about it. Shag Crawford maintained, "It's the plate umpire's call, and he should make it." Ed Sudol concurred that the plate umpire had a better view of the play, and also felt that the appeal put the base umpire on the spot. Lee Ballanfant similarly felt that it was passing the buck. On the other hand, Bill Kinnamon liked the checked-swing appeal because it "takes some of the heat away from the home-plate umpire" (Larry R. Gerlach, *The Men in Blue*, 45, 207, 231–232, 245). None of these umpires specified exactly when this custom originated.

8.4.5 Tie to the Runner. This principle is often mentioned when a bang-bang play occurs at first base. Knowledgeable baseball fans sometimes retort that this precept does not appear in the rulebook. In fact the issue is more complex and the history more convoluted.

In 1860, Henry Chadwick declared that when a call "is a doubtful one, the rule is to give the decision in favor of the ball" (*Beadle's Dime Base-Ball Player*, 29). This would certainly appear to mean that a tie went to the defense, which was confirmed by an 1865 game account that observed, "the rule of 'favoring the ball' was followed" (*Detroit Advertiser and Tribune*, October 19, 1865).

But Chadwick removed this advice from the 1864 edition of *Beadle's* and in 1867 suggested just the opposite by noting that "the umpire—who gave excellent decisions as a general thing, erred in giving men out on the base when the ball was held simultaneously with

the player's putting his foot on the base. Now the rule in each case requires that if the ball be not held *before* the player reaches the bases, the latter is not out" (*The Ball Player's Chronicle*, August 1, 1867). No reason was given for the about-face.

This rule of thumb continued to be affirmed by Chadwick for many years and was reiterated by other sources. In 1886 the *Chicago Tribune* answered a fan's inquiry by stating that on a tie, "the base-runner is given the benefit under the rules" (*Chicago Tribune*, September 12, 1886). And in 1888 the *St. Louis Post-Dispatch* reported that the umpires' instructions included this guideline: "The umpire must call the man running to first base safe, if he gets to the base at the same time the ball is held on the base" (*St. Louis Post-Dispatch*, April 9, 1888).

It is easy to imagine that a fielder who protested on such a play and was told that it was a tie would not find this answer very satisfying. As a result, the precept that "a tie goes to the runner" was gradually de-emphasized in umpire instruction. Early-twentieth-century umpire "Silk" O'Loughlin became famous for saying, "There are no close plays. A man is always out or safe" (quoted in Christy Mathewson, *Pitching in a Pinch*, 168). Since then, umpires have been taught to call bang-bang plays one way or the other and "sell" their conviction.

(v) Communicating

8.5.1 Calling "Play Ball." The early rules required the umpire to call "Play" to commence the proceedings. The word "ball" must have been added before long, as an 1867 account noted, "'Play ball' was the cry of the umpire" (*The Ball Player's Chronicle*, August 8, 1867).

In 1915 the *Detroit Free Press* noted, "According to the rules, the umpire is supposed to call 'play' after every foul that is not caught. If you don't believe it read rule 36 in any guide or rule book. That the umpire doesn't call this after [every] foul is due to habit. That formality has been neglected so long that it has come to be understood that play shall be suspended until the runner gets back. Legitimately, the umpire is required to call 'play' at the start of a game or an inning before the pitcher delivers the ball, but only a few of them do it nowadays. Perhaps this disregard of a minor formality is responsible for growth of the misapprehension that the batsman must get out of position after a foul to keep the ball out of play" (*Detroit Free Press*, September 26, 1915).

A club appealed a 1911 defeat on the grounds that the umpire had neglected to call "play" after every foul. The appeal was understandably dismissed (*Sporting News*, June 29, 1911).

8.5.2 Ball and Strike Signals. It is often written that umpires began to use hand signals for the benefit of William "Dummy" Hoy, a deaf outfielder. This attribution makes a great story because Hoy overcame both his physical handicap and a diminutive stature to become a star major league outfielder—between 1888 and 1902 he collected more than two thousand hits and nearly six hundred stolen bases. Unfortunately the evidence does not support this version of events.

Researcher Bill Deane found that Hoy was indeed informed of the count by means of hand signals but that these cues came from his own third-base coach. Deane cited an article from Hoy's rookie season of 1888 that said of Hoy, "When he bats a man stands in the Captain's box near third base and signals to him decisions of the umpire on balls and strikes by raising his fingers" (*Washington Evening Star*, April 7, 1888). Another article similarly observed: "Hoy is the only deaf and dumb player in the League. When he is at bat a man must be stationed at third base to sign with his fingers the number of balls and strikes that are called on him" (*St. Louis Post-Dispatch*, March 24, 1888; whether Hoy was actually dumb is a matter of definition, as he developed some ability for speech).

In 1900 a Cincinnati fan named Warren Lynch suggested: "If every time an umpire called a ball he would raise his right hand and every time he pronounced a strike he would lift up his left hand there would be no trouble to follow the game." Hoy pronounced this a "splendid" idea and commented, "The act of lifting up the right hand by a coacher while I am at bat to denote that the umpire has called a strike on me and the raising of the left hand to denote that a ball has been called has come to be well understood by all the League players. The reason the right hand was originally chosen to denote a strike was because 'the pitcher was all right' when he got the ball over the plate and because 'he got left' when he sent the ball wide of the plate. I have often been told by frequenters of the game that they take considerable delight in watching the coacher signal balls and strikes to me, as by these signals they can know to a certainty what the umpire with a not too

overstrong voice is saying." The *Sporting News* endorsed this idea in an editorial, but there is no evidence that it was tried at that time (*Sporting News*, January 27, 1900).

Hoy reported the following season that he also received other types of signals in a similar fashion: ". . . My team mates tell me whether a ball or strike is called by using the left fingers for balls and the right fingers for strikes. In base running the signals of the hit and run game and other stratagems are mostly silent, and the same as for the other players. By a further system of sign [sic] my team mates keep me posted on how many are out and what is going on around me. . . . So it may be seen the handicaps of a deaf ball player are minimized" (*Grand Valley* [Moab, Utah] *Times*, July 12, 1901).

Thus there is clear evidence that during his career Hoy received signals about balls and strikes from his teammates rather than from the umpire. The only eyewitness source that linked Hoy to umpire signals is his statement more than fifty years later that "the coacher at third kept me posted by lifting his right hand for strikes and his left for balls. This gave later day umpires an idea and they now raise their right . . . to emphasize an indisputable strike" (*The Silent Worker*, April 1952).

Even here, Hoy suggested only that his deafness had an influence on umpires' hand signals, not that there was a direct connection. Such a claim is conceivable, and it can never be positively refuted. And yet a review of the evidence reveals that umpire signals had occasionally been used before Hoy's career but did not become common until afterward.

In early baseball the ideal umpire was a leather-lunged man whose decisions could be heard all over the field and throughout the stands. This was not merely for the benefit of the audience. An umpire's lung capacity could have a direct impact on the outcome of the game, since base runners could be put out if they did not return promptly to their bases after a foul ball had been called.

The idea of replacing this hollering with signals was raised on several occasions. For example, an 1870 letter writer proposed: "If the umpire would hold a small flag or some other signal in his hand and elevate it above his head when a ball is struck 'foul'; every player in the field could see it, and it would do away with mistakes as regards 'fouls.' The signal might also be used to advantage in calling 'in' players who are 'out' on bases, & c.; but, of course, this could not relieve the umpire from giving his signals orally" (*Chicago Tribune*, June 18, 1870).

Bill Deane noted that Harry Wright wrote in 1870: "There is one thing I would like to see the umpire do at [a] big game, and that is, raise his hand when a man is out. You know what noise there is always when a fine play is made on the bases, and it being impossible to hear the umpire, it is always some little time before the player knows whether he is given out or not. It would very often save a great deal of bother and confusion" (letter to the *New York Sunday Mercury*, March 27, 1870).

At least a few umpires put this idea into practice during the 1880s, though they were prompted to do so by unusual circumstances. Al Kermisch discovered that umpire Robert I. McNichol was hit in the throat with a foul ball in the seventh inning of an American Association game between St. Louis and Columbus on August 11, 1883. Temporarily unable to speak, he used hand signals to communicate his decisions (Al Kermisch, "Umpire Used Hand Signals in 1883," *Baseball Research Journal* 21 [1992], 111).

Several other members of the school where Hoy learned to play baseball, the Ohio School for the Deaf in Columbus (see **20.3.5**), also relied upon signals. When the school team went on a tour in 1879, one account noted that "only one player speaks, he acting as captain, giving them signs for strikes, called balls, etc." (*New York Clipper*, July 19, 1879).

In 1886 another alumnus, former major leaguer Ed Dundon, umpired a minor league game and communicated his decisions by means of signals: "Dundon, the deaf and dumb pitcher of the Acid Iron Earths, umpired a game at Mobile between the Acids and Mobiles, on October 20. . . . He used the fingers of his right hand to indicate strikes, the fingers of the left to call balls, a shake of the head decided a man 'not out,' and a wave of the hand meant out'" (*Sporting News*, November 6, 1886).

Paul Hines, who starred in the major leagues from 1872 to 1891, suffered from a serious loss of hearing. One contemporary claimed many years later that sympathetic umpires such as John Gaffney, Phil Powers, Sandy McDermott, and Tom Lynch held up "their fingers to indicate balls or strikes to [Hines]" (Guy Smith, *Sporting News*, July 25, 1935; quoted in Tony Salin, *Baseball's Forgotten Heroes*, 86).

During the 1880s crowds grew larger and more dispersed, and by the end of the decade it was apparent that many spectators, "in case of unusual noise cannot hear the umpire's decision" (*New York Sun*, May 27, 1888). One Union Association umpire, Mike Hooper, was fired "on account of his weak voice" (*Cleveland Herald*, May 21, 1884). But umpires were hard to come by, so this wasn't a viable solution.

A reader named John J. Rooney wrote to the *New York Sun* in 1889 to complain that the umpire's decisions could not be heard by much of the audience. He suggested hiring a "man or boy with a pleasant-sounding gong" to convey the umpire's rulings to the spectators (*New York Sun*, April 14, 1889). A second reader, James Sullivan of New Haven, Connecticut, suggested that, instead of using a gong, the umpire should "telegraph his decisions." His idea was, "For every strike the umpire shall raise one hand straight over his head; for a ball he shall make no significant motion. Whenever a man is out he shall raise both hands over his head, and if a man is safe, whether at the bat or running bases, he need make no significant motion" (*New York Sun*, April 16, 1889).

Rooney replied that "the umpire has enough to do in watching the game. . . . His attention must be centred on the play, and any distraction or unnecessary increase of duties weakens and burdens him. The umpire would be compelled to shout, throw up his hands and work the hand register at the same time." He contended that the umpire would resemble a "jack-in-the box" and further argued that hand signals were not sufficiently "emphatic." By contrast, he claimed, "A bell demands attention, speaks unmistakably, and at once stamps the decision with authority" (*New York Sun*, April 18, 1889).

The powers-that-be ignored the complaints of fans like Rooney and Sullivan for more than a decade. The press also remained largely unsympathetic to this viewpoint, with one correspondent writing in 1896, "Last season some of the umpires had a habit of indicating their reasons for giving judgment on balls and strikes by a gesture of the hand, indicating too high, too low, too wide, etc. It is not a good plan. When one gives reasons there are thousands to differ as to the facts. . . . An umpire serves best when he confines his work to giving judgment on plays and going no farther until the decision is protested by the captain of the team. . . . Even the old 'what's-the-matter-of that' from the pitcher had best be replied to, if at all, by the quiet rejoinder that 'it is a ball'" (*Sporting Life*, March 7, 1896).

By the turn of the century, growing crowd sizes were making the need for a new means of communicating the umpire's decisions too obvious to ignore. Sportswriter W. A. Phelon wrote in 1901: "Noiseless umpiring is to be attempted at the South Side park Monday afternoon. Impossible as this may seem at first hearing, it is to be attempted, and there are even bets that it will be a go. George W. Hancock, famed in Chicago as the man who invented indoor base ball, will be responsible for the success or failure of the scheme. The umpire is to wear a red sleeve on the right arm and a white one on the left. For a strike he will raise the right arm, for a ball the left; for an out he will hoist the right arm, for a ball [sic] the other. People at the far end of the park, unable to hear even that human buffalo, [Jack] Sheridan, can see the colors, and there seems a good chance for the trick to make a hit" (*Sporting Life*, September 14, 1901).

Coincidentally, "Dummy" Hoy was on that Chicago team, though it is clear from the account that the experiment had nothing to do with him. But I could find no indication that the scheme was actually tested. The White Stockings' last home Monday appearance came with a doubleheader on September 9, and the *Tribune*'s account of the game gave no mention of such an experiment. Game accounts over the next couple of weeks made no other reference to the scheme.

It was not until a few years after Hoy's retirement that the idea of umpires using signals began to gather momentum. Researcher Dan Krueckeberg reported that umpire Cy Rigler introduced the practice in a Central League game in 1905: "One feature of Rigler's work yesterday that was appreciated was his indicating balls by the fingers of his left hand and strikes with the fingers of the right hand so everyone in the park could tell what he had called" (*Evansville Courier*, May 1, 1905). Krueckeberg added that "When Rigler entered the National League a year later, he found that his raised-arm call had preceded him and was in wide use" (Dan Krueckeberg, "Take-Charge Cy," *National Pastime* 1 [Spring 1985], 7–8). This latter assertion is not documented, and the evidence I have found clearly suggests that it was not until 1907 that pressure from fans and reporters led to the change.

New York Highlanders manager Clark Griffith proposed that umpires gesture with their right hand on any called strike (*Chicago Tribune*, February 24, 1907). Umpires continued to resist the idea, and before the season umpire Tom Connolly "presented a strong argument against the proposed rule to have umpires wave their arms to designate balls and strikes" (*Washington Post*, March 1, 1907).

They seemed to have agreed to experiment with signals during spring training, and the *Chicago Tribune* offered this report of the results: "'The *Tribune*'s' agitation for a system of umpire's gestures to indicate decisions seems to be as far reaching as popular. Chief Zimmer has been using signs for balls and strikes and delighting New Orleans patrons. Today Collins, who officiated here [Memphis], adopted the same system and used it successfully, with the result the crowd forgave him for not calling everything the local twirler pitched a 'strike.' To date Hank O'Day appears to be the only opponent of the idea" (*Chicago Tribune*, March 24, 1907; Collins must have been a local umpire as he did not umpire in either major league that season).

The possibility of receiving more sympathetic treatment from the fans must have been alluring to umpires, and by opening day even O'Day had overcome his reservations. Researcher Greg Rhodes noted that an account of the season opener in Cincinnati reported: "Hank O'Day used the arm signals yesterday and they were satisfactory. He raises his left hand for a ball. In case he raises neither hand, it is a strike" (*Cincinnati Commercial-Tribune*, April 12, 1907).

When the opening-day umpire in Chicago didn't follow O'Day's lead, he was lambasted by the *Tribune*: "There is nothing but this habit of looking at baseball matters through the umpire's eyes to explain the failure of the big league presidents to answer the public's demands by instructing their umpires to adopt a simple code of signals to indicate doubtful decisions on pitched balls, the same as on base decisions. The umpires objected to being overworked by the necessity of moving an arm to indicate a 'strike.' Consequently the public must continue to guess, until electric score boards are installed and perfected, and then miss some of the play while studying the score board" (*Chicago Tribune*, April 14, 1907). The following day the *Tribune* reported approvingly that umpire Bill Carpenter had been a big hit with the fans by raising his right hand to indicate a strike.

Obviously umpires still had some work to do to synchronize their signals, but once this had been accomplished umpire signals became a permanent and essential part of baseball. The

1909 Spalding Guide observed: "Two or three years ago Base Ball critics in the East and West began to agitate the question of signaling by the umpires to announce their decisions. At first the judges of play did not want to signal. They thought it detracted from their dignity to go through a dumb show resembling the waving of the arms of a semaphore. . . . It was finally experimented with and has been one of the very best moves in Base Ball as a medium of rendering decisions intelligible, and now there is not an umpire but uses his arms to signal. If he did not, two-thirds of the spectators . . . would be wholly at sea as to what is transpiring on the field, except as they might guess successfully. Even the older umpires, who were more loath to give their consent to the new system on the field, are now frank enough to admit that it has been of invaluable assistance to them in making their decisions understood when the size of the crowd is such that it is impossible to make the human voice carry distinctly to all parts of the field."

8.5.3 Embellished Signals. Bill Klem is sometimes erroneously credited with pioneering umpire signals. It does appear that Klem was among the first to give added emphasis to his signals. His work inspired sportswriter Sid Mercer to file this whimsical report in 1909: "Some of the fans thought that Mr. Klem was picking posies for a while. When the first good one came over he would describe a semi-circle with his right arm somewhat after the manner of a romantic young man blowing a kiss to a fair young maiden. His manner seemed to say: 'There, now, you saucy thing. I'll take you from over there and place you over there, and you've got to be good.' To denote a second strike, Mr. Klem used a sign that is universally recognized as a silent order for two beers. It is also used sometimes by goats butting into the press box" (*New York Globe*; reprinted in *Sporting News*, May 27, 1909).

8.5.4 Safe and Out Signals. Somewhat surprisingly, umpires appear to have been signaling out and safe before it became customary to have signs for balls and strikes. In 1907, when the *Chicago Tribune* was agitating for umpires to have signs for balls and strikes, the newspaper noted, "There is no rule compelling an umpire to motion 'safe' or 'out' on the bases, but nearly all of them do by force of habit on plays which are not at all close" (*Chicago Tribune*, February 24, 1907).

8.5.5 Wired for Sound. Cy Rigler became the first umpire to be wired for sound in a game at the Polo Grounds on August 25, 1929 (see **14.5.13**).

(vi) The Tools of the Trade

8.6.1 Blue. Umpires were wearing blue as early as 1884, when the American Association required its arbiters to wear suits of "blue yacht-cloth" and a black cap (*New York Clipper*, April 12, 1884). Blue had become customary by the early twentieth century and remained so for most of the century (Beth Martin, "Hey, Blue!," *National Pastime* 18 [1998], 36–46).

8.6.2 Masks. Early umpires stood a safe distance from home plate and therefore did not need protective equipment. As catchers moved closer to the action, so did umpires, and they began to adopt similar forms of protection. Larry Gerlach credited Dick Higham, who was banished from the National League in 1882 (see **11.1.3**), with being the first umpire to wear a mask. Ironically Higham was a former catcher who had not used a mask during his playing days (Larry Gerlach, "Richard Higham," in Frederick Ivor-Campbell, Robert L. Tiemann, and Mark Rucker, eds., *Baseball's First Stars*, 77).

It was not long before masks were accepted as a necessity. An 1884 game account noted, "The umpire, Mr. [Arthur] Allison, was struck a terrible blow in the head in the fourth inning, but pluckily continued in his position. He should have followed [Sam] Trott's example on Thursday, and worn a catcher's mask" (*Washington Post*, April 12, 1884).

8.6.3 Chest Protectors. Once umpire's masks were accepted, it was only a matter of time before chest protectors were added. The originator appears to have been John Gaffney, who at the start of the 1888 season was reported to be wearing "an ingenious breast and stomach protector. It is made of pasteboard in sections, joined together with elastic, and made to fit tight around. When Gaffney buttons up his cardigan jacket no one would know that he is provided with a protector. He said he was hit so often in the chest and over his heart that he had to take some means to save his life. The contrivance is Gaff's own make" (*New York Sun*, April 22, 1888).

By the end of the 1891 season, most umpires were following Gaffney's lead by donning cork chest protectors. In the meantime, Gaffney had become convinced that he was catching colds because of the device and was planning to switch to a "wire body protector" (*Sporting Life*, October 17 and 24, 1891).

One minor league umpire was so concerned about his safety that he outfitted himself like a medieval knight. An 1889 account noted that Western Association umpire Thomas "Sandy" McDermott "is bound not to be killed by a pitched ball this season. He has made a helmet and cuirass of stout bull's hide, steel bound and brass riveted, which shields his head and body. The suit is ingeniously constructed to yield with the movements of the wearer, while light but strong steel ribs offer stout resistance from assaults from without. The helmet is lined with a combination of steel bars and springs and cotton wool in such a way that not even the most powerful blow from an irate batsman would be felt on the wearer's head. In fact, the only vulnerable spot in the helmet is the hole necessarily left for the umpire's mouth, and even this is in a measure protected by a wire netting. For his legs he has devised a covering somewhat resembling cricketers' leg pads, but much thicker and stronger, constructed of heavy bull's hide. Cast-iron shoes for his feet and a pair of eight ounce boxing-gloves for his hands complete the costume" (*Chicago Tribune*, March 24, 1889, 6).

In 1891 A. G. Spalding's sporting goods firm marketed an umpire's body protector that "was suggested by Mr. [Charles W.] Jones, the Association umpire, and the first one was made for him. It has proven such a success that they are regularly carried in stock now and sold at the same price as the ordinary 'Gray's protector,' $10 each. It is made same as Gray's catcher's body protector, but of an entirely different shape, which makes it entirely impossible for a foul hit or wild pitch to hit any part of the upper portion of the body, the shoulders being as thoroughly protected as the chest, and it is fastened on in such a way that it does not impede the movement of the body in any way" (*Sporting Times*, May 9, 1891).

A 1913 article credited Bill Klem with having invented the aluminum rib protector, which was worn inside the coat (*Sporting News*, January 30, 1913). For much of the twentieth century, National League umpires followed Klem's lead and wore inside protectors while American League umpires wore outside protectors. In the 1930s and '40s, minor league umpires discovered that their choice of chest protector style

was a factor in which major league was more likely to offer them a promotion (Beth Martin, "Hey, Blue!," *National Pastime* 18 [1998], 36–46). American League umpires finally began to switch in the 1970s.

8.6.4   Headgear. An 1886 article suggested, "Base ball umpires should call at the C. J. Chapin Arms Company's store and see their new sunshade hat for $1. It does away with the nuisance of holding an umbrella in the hand and annoying the catcher. They are lighter than an ordinary hat and much cooler on account having [sic] a space between the head and the inside of the hat, allowing a free circulation of air" (*Sporting News*, June 21, 1886).

8.6.5   Shin Pads. When I was growing up in Canada, an old joke asked: "What was the number one song in Canada when 'Wake Up Little Susie' was number one in the United States?" The answer was, "I don't know, but six months later it was 'Wake Up Little Susie.'" Similarly, the equipment of nineteenth-century umpires generally remained in lockstep but well behind catcher's equipment.

By the twentieth century the gap had pretty much been eliminated and, reflecting their closer proximity to the action, umpires sometimes led the way. Bob Emslie reportedly showed up for a 1900 game wearing cricket pads (Gerard S. Petrone, *When Baseball Was Young*, 143). A 1905 article noted, "Umpire Tom Connolly is wearing shin pads" (*Sporting Life*, June 17, 1905).

At the same time some umpires were going the other direction. Jack Sheridan became known for refusing protective equipment and instead shielding himself by crouching behind the catcher (*Detroit News-Tribune*, September 18, 1904; James M. Kahn, *The Umpire Story*, 41).

8.6.6   Foot Protectors. Toe pads were introduced by Umpire Jim Johnstone in 1912 (*Sporting Life*, June 15, 1912).

8.6.7   Indicators. Not long after the advent of balls and strikes, umpires began using devices to keep track of balls and strikes. Henry Chadwick noted in 1874: "In counting balls unfairly delivered, the umpire should be furnished by the club with a counting tally, consisting of pieces of wood moving on a wire, like a billiard tally. It should be made small, so as to occupy but three or four inches in length" (*New York Clipper*, April 11, 1874).

In 1875, Peck & Snyder's was selling an "Umpire's Assistant" for one dollar. The device was made of black walnut, with "each Ball or Strike . . . registered by turning the thumb-screw," and was endorsed by Chadwick (advertisement in Henry Chadwick, *DeWitt's Base Ball Umpire Guide*). Before long the devices were improved so that they could keep other running tallies as well: "The scoring dial is the latest thing out in the form of a method for keeping the score of runs at a match. It is manufactured by Casseno, May & Shepard, of Glen Allen, Va. It is the handiest thing out for umpires to count balls and strikes" (*Brooklyn Eagle*, August 4, 1885).

8.6.8 Whisk Brooms.

Umpires used large brooms to clean home plate until a game on May 14, 1904, when Cubs outfielder Jack McCarthy stepped on one and sprained his ankle. The injury led National League president Harry Pulliam to mandate the use of whisk brooms, and the American League followed suit.

8.6.9 Glasses.

Eyeglasses are, of course, not standard equipment for an umpire, but a few brave arbiters have donned spectacles. The first to do so may have been Billy McLean, who was also the first major league umpire to be paid to travel: "Some fun is being poked at Umpire McLean for using glasses. Now, why shouldn't McLean wear glasses? Will White has used glasses ever since he has been on the ballfield; and he continues to see a good deal of base ball and know it, too" (*Sporting Life*, July 16, 1884). McLean may have been spared from ridicule due to having formerly been a prizefighter. McLean's eyesight continued to deteriorate and eventually forced him to quit the profession (*Sporting Times*, July 4, 1891; *Williamsport Sunday Grit*, July 19, 1891).

As the vision of umpires became the subject of derision, there arose an increasing unwillingness to acknowledge that the eyesight of the men in blue was imperfect. Minor league umpire Bob O'Regan wore glasses throughout a career that began in 1939, but he never made it to the majors and his eyewear may have been responsible (Gary Waddingham, "Irish Bob O'Regan: A Bespectacled Ump in the Bush Leagues," *Minor League History Journal* 1:1, 33–36).

It was not until 1956 that another major league umpire donned glasses. Frank Umont did so in a game between Detroit and Kansas City on April 24, 1956. Umont was a former NFL tackle, which no doubt limited the abuse he took.

Ed Rommel told sportswriter Paul Menton that he had beaten Umont to the punch, wearing glasses in an April 18 game between the Yankees and Washington. No one noticed Rommel's glasses because he was umpiring on the bases. Rommel indicated that he intended to wear the glasses only when he was a base umpire during a night game (*Lima* [Ohio] *News*, April 27, 1956; attributed to Paul Menton, *Baltimore Sun*, April 26, 1956, though I checked that issue and could not find the article).

The initial reception accorded Umont and Rommel was generally favorable. Columnist Arthur Daley reasoned, "Arbiters in spectacles are operating on firmer ground. Their eyesight has been tested by experts and the specs give 20-20 vision" (Arthur Daley, "Eyes Like Eagles," *New York Times*, May 13, 1956). Organized baseball did not prove to be as receptive. Bespectacled umpires who apply for umpire schools are now told that they may attend the school but will not be considered for positions in professional baseball (Gary Waddingham, "Irish Bob O'Regan: A Bespectacled Ump in the Bush Leagues," *Minor League History Journal* 1:1, 35).

8.6.10 Lena Blackburne's Mud.

When Lena Blackburne, a longtime major league infielder, coach, and manager, was growing up in Clifton Heights, Pennsylvania, he often waded in the Pennsauken Creek, a branch of the Delaware River. He discovered that "the outgoing tides purified the mud at the bottom of the creek, leaving it inky black and sticky. I was a kid pitcher in those days and I often used the mud on a new ball—when we were lucky enough to get one" (quoted in *Sporting News*, March 16, 1968).

After Blackburne reached the majors, he heard umpire Harry Geisel complaining about how difficult it was to get the slickness off of new baseballs. That fall Blackburne dug up a supply from his old location and experimented with it. He discovered a secret ingredient that prevented the mud from staining the balls (*Sporting News*, March 16, 1968). Next spring he presented Geisel with a can of the mud. Geisel found it very effective, and word soon spread.

According to *The Baseball Chronology*, umpires in both leagues began rubbing down balls with Blackburne's clay on June 13, 1921 (Jim Charlton, ed., *The Baseball Chronology*). But Blackburne himself gave the year as 1939, and that date is more consistent with other factors, especially the fact that Geisel did not beginning umpiring in the major leagues until 1925 (Joseph F. Lowry, "Baseball's Magic-Mud Man," *Family Weekly*, September 5, 1965).

At first Blackburne looked at the mud as an amusing way to make a few extra bucks. But as time went by it grew into a lucrative business, and the exact source of the mud and the added ingredient became closely guarded secrets. In 1965 he drove a reporter to Pennsauken Creek but explained, "This isn't the exact spot where I get my goo. Nobody ever will know where that is. But this is close enough. Where I get my mud, two streams come together. That means the mud is filtered twice and is very fine" (Joseph F. Lowry, "Baseball's Magic-Mud Man," *Family Weekly*, September 5, 1965). Blackburne died in 1968, but his family is still supplying mud to the major leagues. As of the mid-1990s they charged $75 for a can of mud; no doubt it has gone up since then (Dan Gutman, *Banana Bats and Ding-Dong Balls*, 161–162).

Chapter 9

EQUIPMENT

(i) Baseballs

An 1884 article gave a fascinating description of the "rude, homemade balls" that were used before 1850. These balls "were made of rubber and were so lively that when dropped to the ground from a height of six or seven feet they would rebound ten or twelve inches. A blow with a bat would not drive them so far as one of the balls now in use can be driven with the same force, but when they struck the ground they were generally much more difficult to stop on account of their bounding propensities. Fifty years ago there were no professional ball players and the demand for manufactured base balls of any description was very small. Many of the balls then in use—in fact nearly all of them—were home made. An old rubber overshoe would be cut into strips a half inch wide and the strips wound together in a ball shape. Over this a covering of woolen yarn would be wound and a rude leather or cloth cover sewn over the yarn. Sometimes the strips of rubber were put in a vessel of hot water and boiled until they became gummy, when they would adhere together and form a solid mass of rubber. This, after being wound with yarn and covered with leather by the local shoemaker, was a fairly good ball and one that would stand considerable batting without bursting. In the lake regions and other sections of the country where sturgeon were plentiful, base balls were commonly made of the eyes of that fish. The eye of a large sturgeon contains a ball nearly as large as a walnut. It is composed of a flexible substance and will rebound if thrown against a hard base. These eyeballs were bound with yarn and afterward covered with leather or cloth.

They made a lively ball, but were more like the dead ball of the present than any ball in use at that time" (*Brooklyn Eagle*, February 3, 1884).

9.1.1 Manufactured Balls. A. J. Reach, one of the first professional players and later a sporting goods magnate, wrote in 1909: "As to the first base balls, my recollection of them dates from about 1855 or '56. The most popular ball in those days was the Ross ball: Harvey Ross, the maker, was a member of the Atlantic Base Ball Club, of Brooklyn, and a sail-maker by trade; his home was on Park Avenue, where he made the balls. John Van Horn was a member of the Union Club, of Morissania [sic], New York; he had a little boot and shoe store on Second Avenue, New York City. These two makers turned out the best base balls for some years, and they were used in nearly all of the match games that were played up to the early '70s" (*Sporting Life*, March 13, 1909).

Henry Chadwick indicated that even with only two ball makers, the demand in the 1850s was so limited that Ross and Van Horn were able to meet "it very readily without entrenching upon the time required for their ordinary avocations." With no need to mechanize, "Van Horn used to cut up old rubber shoes into strips from which he wound a ball of about from two to two and a half ounces of rubber, and then covering this with yarn and the yarn with a sheepskin cover" (*Spalding's Official Base Ball Guide, 1890*, 35).

By the end of the decade baseball had begun to catch on in earnest, and this changed baseball manufacturing. As an 1867 article observed, "Five or six years ago clubs procured the balls they played with from two or three makers, and one bat maker could supply almost the whole demand. Now there is a regular bat and ball manufactory in each city . . . turning bats out by the thousand, and balls by the hundred, where they were previously sold by the dozen and singly" (*The Ball Player's Chronicle*, June 27, 1867). In 1870 a single baseball manufacturer turned out 162,000 new balls. Even this vast quantity did not suffice for the demand, which was estimated at half a million balls per year ("Bats, Balls and Mallets," *New York Times*, May 30, 1871).

This brought many new manufacturers into the business, including "a man named Rice, who commenced business in a small room in a frame building on Nassau street, New York. He continued in the business until about 1870, and became quite an expert base ball maker, although he was never able to make more than a living out of the business. About 1870 he sold out to S. W. Brock, a Brooklyn man who was then doing a small novelty business in the same locality. The new owner soon became convinced that the manufacturing of base balls was likely to become a large and lucrative business. He disposed of his novelty business and invested his entire capital—only about two hundred thousand dollars—in base ball material. From that time the demand for base balls began to increase and the success of the business was assured. It soon became necessary to have more room, and in order to obtain it the business was removed to a large building on Dey street, where it still remains" (*Brooklyn Eagle*, February 3, 1884).

Clubs now had a variety of baseballs to choose from, which created a new problem. An 1870 article reported, "Some dispute has arisen of late in regard to the ball, it being claimed that the Atlantic Club, of Brooklyn, use what has only lately been termed an 'elastic' ball, and which is no more or less than a Ross or Van Horn ball, both being very lively, and made strictly in accordance with the regulations, being 5¼ ounces in weight, 9¼ inches in circumference, and composed of yarn and India rubber covered with sheepskin. These balls sell in this city [Chicago] for $2 and $1.75, respectively. It is optional for nines to use them. They are better for the batters than for fielders. The balls known as Atlantic and Bounding Rock may now be termed dead; that is, they are not so lively—will not bound so high—as the Ross or Van Horn, although they are made according to the requirements of the association. They can be purchased for $1.50 each, and are

the favorites for practice and amateur matches. In addition to these are the Harwood, Peck & Snyder, Junior, Diamond and Practice balls at $1 and 75 cents each. The ball of the New York Rubber Company is a failure for base ball uses, the rubber cores tearing off easily. It is really an 'elastic' dead ball" (Chadwick Scrapbooks, unidentified 1870 clipping). As of 1880, Harrison Harwood's firm in Natick, Massachusetts, was employing 300 people and selling $200,000 worth of balls each year (*New York Sunday Mercury*, March 27, 1880).

The 1870s and 1880s saw numerous attempts to devise a machine to manufacture baseballs, several of which are described in Dan Gutman's *Banana Bats and Ding-Dong Balls*, pages 151–152. The first truly successful machinery for mass-producing standard baseballs was created by Ben Shibe of the A. J. Reach Company. The Reach Company was using hydraulic pressure to mass-produce cheap baseballs by 1883, and as of 1888 was reportedly turning out "the enormous quantity of 1,000 dozen base balls per day in their giant factory, where they employ over 400 hands." Official major league balls still had to be hand-sewn and carried the hefty price tag of 75 cents, but the prices of the cheaper balls dropped rapidly. Machine-made balls composed of leather scraps typically sold for five cents and did much to encourage play at other levels (*Cleveland Plain Dealer*, April 1, 1888).

By 1884 there were major baseball-making factories in Brooklyn, New York City, and Massachusetts, and the manufacturing process was becoming increasingly elaborate: "Over twenty different grades and varieties of base balls are made, and the prices obtained by the manufacturers vary from twenty-eight cents per dozen up to ten dollars per dozen, according to the grade. Those sold at the latter prices are the finest base balls made. Each one of these balls is carefully packed in a paper box by itself and sells at retail at one and a half dollars. The balls being made for next season's use are generally being wound on a small base of rubber, which gives them more elasticity and life than is possessed by the dead balls which have been in use for some time past. The dead balls are said to be going out of favor, because of their liability to burst when struck a hard blow with the bat.

"The first steps to be taken in making base balls is to cut the covers and wind the yarn. The covers are made of sheepskins and are cut into the proper shape by means of a large steel punch. The sheepskins are spread out on large wooden blocks. The operator, with the steel punch in his left hand and a wooden mallet in his right, cuts the covers by placing the sharp edges of the punch on the sheepskin and striking the punch a smart blow with the mallet.

"The covers, when cut, are almost exact imitations of the sole of a shoe. After being cut they are sent into the sewing room, where they are sewn together by girls, one end being left open so that the ball can be placed inside. The balls are wound by men. Each man has a reel in front of him on which a skein of yarn is placed. He also has a block of wood, which stands perpendicularly upon the floor. In the upper end of this block there is a polished indentation somewhat resembling a teacup, though not so deep. When the operator has wound off yarn enough to make a ball as large as a black walnut he stops winding, places the ball in the cup-like form on the block of wood and with a small club which he has close at hand, strikes it several hard blows. He then winds on more yarn and repeats the blows. In this way he proceeds until the ball is large enough to receive the cover. The blows are given for the purpose of hardening the ball. After the covers are put on the balls are rolled, under considerable pressure, in a polished groove. After being rolled they are perfect and present a very smooth and pretty appearance, all the roughness of the seams being completely removed by this operation. They are now thrown into barrels and removed to the packing room, where they are packed into boxes for the trade.

"Base ball makers are paid for their work by the piece. The sewing is all done by girls, and they make as much money as the men. All average from ten dollars to fifteen dollars per week the year round" (*Brooklyn Eagle*, February 3, 1884).

In the ensuing years, more and more of the manual processes were automated. In 1888 a winding machine did away with "the tiresome and tedious process of wrapping the balls by hand." A machine-die was invented in 1890 so that covers no longer had to be cut by hand, followed a few years later by a rolling machine that perfected the shape and smoothness of the finished baseball (William R. Vogel, *The History and Manufacture of the Baseball*, 10-12).

9.1.2 Dimensions.

As early as 1854, there were broad guidelines for the size of baseballs. The 1857 rules specified that the baseball weigh between 6 and 6.25 ounces, with a circumference of not less than 10 and not more than 10.25 inches. But, according to Henry Chadwick, this "ball was too heavy and too cumbersome for really skillful fielding," so the size was gradually reduced (*Appletons' Cyclopedia and Register of Important Events of the Year 1885*, 78). Rules amendments in 1859, 1861, 1868, 1871, and 1872 reduced the size of the ball. By 1872 the weight was between 5 and 5.25 ounces, with the circumference between 9 and 9.25 inches. Those dimensions have not changed since.

Roger Kahn pointed out that these dimensions are very close to the ones that had been established for a cricket ball long before baseball had formal rules (Roger Kahn, *The Head Game*, 34–35). That was not entirely a coincidence. Henry Chadwick maintained that cricketers had arrived at a ball of nine-inch circumference and weighing five and a half ounces through a process of experiments by which that size was determined to be the safest possible for fielders. He crusaded against the tendency of "country clubs" and "clubs who excel in batting powers" to use balls weighing as much as six and a half ounces and measuring up to ten inches in circumference (*The Ball Player's Chronicle*, September 5, 1867, 6).

9.1.3 Covers.

Creating a crude semblance of the innards of a baseball has never been that difficult, but making a cover that fit snugly over it has been another matter. A man named Charles Haswell recalled many years later that around 1816 boys wound yarn over a variety of objects to form the core of the baseball but then "some feminine member of his family covered it with patches from a soiled glove" (Charles Haswell, *Reminiscences of an Octogenarian, 1816 to 1860* (New York, 1896), 77; quoted in Thomas L. Altherr, "A Place Leavel Enough to Play Ball," 245).

Daniel Adams, one of the leading members of the Knickerbockers, originally made the club's baseballs, and he found the covers the most difficult part. He later recalled: "I went all over New York to find someone who would undertake this work, but no one could be induced to try it for love or money. Finally I found a Scotch soldier who was able to show me a good way to cover the balls with horsehide, such as was used for whip lashes." Adams continued to make the covers himself until "some time after 1850," when "a shoemaker was found who was willing to make them for us. This was the beginning of base ball manufacturing" (*Sporting News*, February 29, 1896).

An early Boston ballplayer explained that the baseball of the era was "covered with alum-dressed horse hide, that being the strongest leather known, being very elastic when water soaked, in which way it was used. The body of the horse being smoother, rounder and harder than that of other animals it follows that the skin would be more even throughout. The alum makes the leather white and may add some strength. . . . Sometimes balls would not last through a game and balls were made with two covers, but the Boston manufacturing broke down that business. When leather was not to be had, a cheap and easy way to cover a ball was with twine in a lock stitch, called quilting" (*Boston Journal*, March 6, 1905).

Even after manufacturers became involved, the process remained painstaking and intricate. William Vogel related that during the 1860s covers continued to be "cut by hand in the following manner: They first staked the leather, which consisted of drawing it across the steel tip of a stake with the hands until all the stretch was taken out of it. Then they placed the leather across a block in order to make it smooth, placed the pattern on it and cut it with a knife. In time they came to use a die." This die was then placed on the leather and pounded upon "with a wooden mallet. After the cover was cut the holes had to be made in it by means of an awl, and instead of making them about one-eighth of an inch from the edge, as they do now, they were made as near to it as possible, in order to make the cover smooth when sewed on the ball. It was men they employed for the purpose of stitching the cover over the ball and a blunt needle was used. They used a 'saddler's horse' in sewing the balls and held them in the clamp. This was provided with a row of catches, that it might be used for the various sizes. They just pushed the bar into one of the catches with the foot and thus held the balls in position as long as they desired." During all these operations, the shape of the baseball was often compromised, so the ball was again rolled between wooden blocks. Finally the cover was pounded "with a sort of bat" to remove wrinkles (William R. Vogel, *The History and Manufacture of the Baseball*, 5–7).

John Gruber reported that leather coverings "were used from the very start. Before 1880, any kind of leather was allowed, sheep-skin being mostly preferred, because it was the universal belief that it lasted longer" (*Sporting News*, November 11, 1915). Then the troubles with soft balls described in the entry on "In-

sides" (**9.1.5**) forced a dramatic redesign of the baseball. As a result, "In 1878 the Mahn 'double cover' ball was introduced and was the first ball of its kind ever used. It was made as follows: A ball of molded vulcanized rubber, one ounce in weight, was taken and wrapped with woolen yarn very tightly until it was about two-thirds the size of the ball required, this was then covered with horse hide; this ball was then again wrapped with yarn, but not so tightly until of the requisite size and again covered with horse hide. The 'cushion,' that part of the ball between the inside ball and the outer covering, was not made so hard so as to be more easily handled by catchers and other players; the inside ball being very compact gave enough elasticity to the ball. It was also found out at this time that horse hide was the best covering for base balls and it is still so considered" (*Cleveland Plain Dealer*, April 1, 1888).

To reflect the Mahn baseball, "in 1880 the rule was changed to read that the ball 'must be composed of woolen yarn and two horse-hide covers, inside and outside, with yarn between said covers.' From that year dates the familiar expression of 'hitting the horse-hide.'" But new balls continued to be introduced, and in 1882 "the simple words 'covered with leather' were reinserted" (*Sporting News*, November 11, 1915).

In 1883 the American Association began using the Reach baseball, which, as an 1888 article explained, "is in one sense also a double ball. Its composition is as follows: A round molded ball of pure rubber weighing three-fourths of an ounce. This is wrapped with woolen yarn until about one-half the size of the regular ball, and is then dipped in a composition of rubber. It is again wrapped with woolen yarn until of the proper size and then covered with horse hide. This ball has been found to be the best ball ever used and its success has been a veritable gold mine to Al. J. Reach and his partners, as his ball is in use wherever base ball is known" (*Cleveland Plain Dealer*, April 1, 1888). At the same time, rubber cement was introduced as another means of keeping the cover secure. Rubber cement also helped hold the ball together and prevent the string from unwinding (William R. Vogel, *The History and Manufacture of the Baseball*, 9–10).

By this time the rule makers had recognized that it was silly to spend a lot of time rewording the rulebook every time a new baseball came along. In 1887 they removed the word "leather" altogether and merely specified that the official league ball be used (*Sporting News,* November 11, 1915). Horsehide remained the standard cover until December 2, 1974, when major league baseball announced that cowhide would also be permitted. This followed a similar change of baseball gloves from horsehide to cowhide that took place around 1940 (Dan Gutman, *Banana Bats and Ding-Dong Balls,* 206).

9.1.4 Cover Design. Some sort of stitching was almost always used to secure early baseball covers, but there was no uniformity in the pattern. An 1858 baseball, for example, was later described as having "odd one-piece covers, the leather having been cut in four semi-ovals still in one piece, the ovals, shaped like the petals of a flower, folding over the body of the ball and being sewed in four seams to complete the cover" ("Oldest Baseballs Bear Date of 1858," *New York Times,* January 21, 1909, 7).

There are a number of candidates to have originated the figure-eight design still used today, but not much firsthand evidence. A leather goods worker named Ellis Drake claimed many years later to have developed several designs but found that the corners and joins gave out. After a lot of trial and error, he hit upon the figure-eight design but never patented it (*Boston Globe,* March 28, 1909). Researcher Bob Schaefer, however, noted that Drake makes some implausible claims that weaken his credibility.

A report by the Natick, Massachusetts, Historical Society claimed that a Natick resident named Colonel William Cutler designed the figure-eight cover. Cutler is said to have hit upon the design in the kitchen of his home about 1858 and sold it to early baseball manufacturer Harrison Harwood.

A couple of sources claim the current design was invented by C. H. Jackson in 1860 and subsequently patented (Lee Allen, *Cooperstown Corner,* 84; "Designing a Baseball Cover," by Richard B. Thompson, of the Department of Mathematics, University of Arizona). But Bob Schaefer was unable to locate such a patent in the records of the U.S. Patent Office.

Finally, an 1888 article noted vaguely: "The cover consists of two pieces, each cut in the shape of the figure '8.' By bending one section one way and the other in an opposite direction a complete cover is obtained. That was the discovery of a college boy. For years the balls were covered with four pieces of leather, but the genius of the college chap has proved of great benefit to the manufacturers" (*San Francisco Examiner,* January 8, 1888). William Vogel also credited this mysterious "young college student" (William R. Vogel, *The History and Manufacture of the Baseball,* 9).

9.1.5 Insides. John Gruber noted in 1915 that "India rubber and yarn were from the very first the chief substances of which the ball was made" (*Sporting News,* November 11, 1915). An early ballplayer later recollected the process of scrounging up the innards: ". . . It was not difficult to procure an old rubber shoe for the foundation of a ball. Many a dear old grandma or auntie of today will remember having stockings and mittens being begged of them, which were knit at home by hand, to be unraveled for ball stock" (*Boston Journal,* March 6, 1905).

With availability playing a crucial role, only the weight and the two basic components were initially specified. This meant enormous variations in the liveliness of the balls, and the ideal mixture of rubber and yarn rapidly became a subject of considerable controversy.

The early balls created for the Knickerbockers by Daniel Adams were soft and didn't travel far (*Sporting News,* February 29, 1896). This didn't suit their aims of making the game manlier while also eliminating "soaking" (see **1.22**), so the ball was tinkered with to make it livelier.

Henry Chadwick later reported that, "in the days when the Knickerbocker and Gotham Clubs were the crack organizations of the metropolis," which would be the mid-1850s, "the leading ball maker of New York only used *an ounce and a half* of rubber in the composition of the balls he manufactured" (*New York Clipper,* April 16, 1870).

According to William Vogel, all the major manufacturers used the following basic process to create the core: "The center of the ball consisted of about two ounces of pure rubber, in the form of strips, which were wrapped into a round ball. After the center was formed, they wrapped coarse yarn over it and then fine yarn, all of which was dry. Then they added worsted, the purpose of which was to keep the ball from showing through the cover, which was made of horsehide." Around 1864 the J. D. Shibe Company of Philadelphia made one modification: "The center of the ball was the same, but instead of all dry yarn, they put one-half dry yarn on it and one-half wet. Then they placed it in an oven and baked it until it was dry. This caused the wet yarn to contract, thus drawing tighter around the ball and making it harder. Then they proceeded to put on the other materials in the same manner. This added process made the baseball harder from the center out and made it last almost twice as long as the other balls of this period" (William R. Vogel, *The History and Manufacture of the Baseball*, 4–5, 7).

While the manufacturers brought uniformity to the process, the amount of rubber was not constant, and this created huge variations. For most of the 1860s, clubs chose baseballs with significant amounts of rubber. This produced a great deal of scoring but became tedious to many observers, and a backlash ensued. Harry Wright's Red Stockings popularized a dead ball, and Henry Chadwick began to crusade for less rubber. The result was the 1870 introduction of Peck & Snyder's "Dead Red Ball" featuring a "composition center" that replaced the two ounces of rubber with a mix of "rubber and other materials" (William R. Vogel, *The History and Manufacture of the Baseball*, 8).

Fluctuations in the amount of rubber continued throughout the 1870s. John Gruber explained in 1915: ". . . In the first year of the Professional Association, 1871, the quantity of rubber was limited to one ounce, 'no more, no less,' the rule makers declaring that 'this makes the ball lively enough for the purposes of good batting.' But it seems the manufacturers used strips of rubber which made the ball rather too lively and so the next year, 1872, it was decreed that 'the rubber used shall be vulcanized and in mold form.'"

This was the last time the specifications for the amount of rubber changed, but it was hardly the end of the issue. Some strong-fielding clubs in the mid-1870s disregarded the rule and used baseballs with trace amounts of rubber or none at all, with predictable results (*Cleveland Plain Dealer*, April 1, 1888). In 1876, shortly after the founding of the National League, it was announced that "The regulation ball to be used by the professional clubs this season is the 'all-yarn ball,' without the customary ounce of rubber in it; the rubber making the ball too lively for the players" (*New York Times*, March 12, 1876, 2).

The National League and its rivals finally restored the rubber to the ball, but then, "In 1883, the American Association eliminated the yarn and rubber qualifications and ordained that the ball must be manufactured from the patent plastic composition under the specification and proposition made by A. J. Reach. The National league, however, adhered to the yarn and vulcanized rubber. But, in 1887, when the joint rules committee came into life, the words

'yarn' and 'rubber' disappeared from the rules forever. It was simply stated that the Spalding league ball or the Reach American Association (later the American League) ball 'must be used in all games played under these rules.' Therefore, during the past 29 seasons, from 1887 to date, the manufacturers apparently used any kind of material just so they remained within the limits of weight and measurement. Lately one of the manufacturers sprung a surprise by announcing a 'cork' center for every ball" (*Sporting News*, November 11, 1915; for a description of the 1883 ball, see **9.1.3**, "Covers").

The type of yarn to be used was not specified by the early rules, but in 1874 it was decreed that it had to be woolen. This requirement was never changed, but in 1877 there was a brief and unsatisfactory experiment with cotton yarn. Shortly before the season the National League had informed official ball maker Louis Mahn that his product was too soft. So Mahn attempted to remedy the situation by replacing the woolen yarn with cotton yarn.

The resulting balls were anything but too soft; in fact, they were so hard that fielders feared for their safety. The *Chicago Tribune* explained that with the woolen yarn, "after a few innings' use the outside of the ball becomes 'mellowed,' so that it can be handled without pain. The ball with the cotton outside cannot by any possible amount of use be softened at all." Complaints about the new ball flooded in. Harry Wright and Louisville owner Walter Haldeman registered their objections in a vociferous yet tactful form. Cincinnati owner Si Keck "also expressed a most decided opinion in the same direction, but it was so marked up by dashes as to be necessarily omitted" (*Chicago Tribune*, May 17, 1877). The old baseball was swiftly brought back.

9.1.6 Cork-center Balls. Cricket was using cork-center balls as early as 1863. Baseball, however, stuck primarily with India rubber and yarn, though there were occasional exceptions. Henry Chadwick observed in 1869, ". . . Some base balls are made—illegally—with a small ball of cork in the centre, covered with nearly *three ounces of hard* rubber, and this with about two ounces of yarn and leather. The result is a ball which will rebound on hard ground from 20 to 30 feet, and one which a fielder finds it very difficult to hold" (*National Chronicle*, July 17, 1869).

After the 1880 season Harry Wright staged an exhibition game using a square bat and a ball composed of a "small globe of cork wound round with string, rubber and yarn." Neither innovation was deemed a success. Players complained that the cork-center ball did not "sound natural when hit with the bat and that the infielders had trouble fielding it" (Preston D. Orem, *Baseball [1845–1881] from the Newspaper Accounts*, 335–336). This suggests that the cork center upset the always delicate balance between offense and defense, and it was not until gloves were universally worn that the game would prove to be ready for cork-center baseballs.

By the 1890s the fielder's glove was well established, and in the early twentieth century, as noted in the preceding entry, "one of the manufacturers sprung a surprise." Around 1900, A. G. Spalding & Brothers began experimenting with a cork-center ball.

They met with initial problems because the wool yarn tended to expand after the stitching was in place. But by 1909 this problem had been addressed, and the cork-center ball was tested during the latter part of the season (according to an advertisement in *Sporting News*, March 2, 1911; also Ban Johnson, as told to George Creel, "Slide, Kelly, Slide," *Saturday Evening Post*, April 12, 1930, 17). (Curiously, pitcher George Winter later claimed that when the cork-center baseball was introduced, it became lopsided after being hit a couple of times. Since Winter last pitched in the American League in 1908, this suggests that the cork-center ball may have been experimented with still earlier) (Don Basenfelder, unpublished manuscript in *Sporting News* morgue, cited in Bill James and Rob Neyer, *The Neyer/James Guide to Pitchers*, 430). It must have passed the tests in 1909, as it was unveiled in 1910 by the A. J. Reach Company, which had come under Spalding's control (David Pietrusza, Lloyd Johnson, and Bob Carroll, ed., *Total Baseball Catalog*, 55).

It is frequently claimed that the cork-center ball was secretly introduced during the 1910 season, but nothing could be farther from the truth. The *Los Angeles Times* noted in May, "Manufacturers of the American League official baseball have announced that this year's ball has a cork instead of a rubber center. The cork was dipped in rubber and the rest of the process was the same as usual. The makers say the cork center has resulted in a much livelier baseball" (*Los Angeles Times*, May 8, 1910).

Popular Mechanics explained, "The cork makes possible a more rigid structure and more uniform resiliency. It is said to outlast the rubber center balls many times over, because it will not soften or break in spots under the most severe usage" (*Popular Mechanics*, reprinted in *Washington Post*, July 31, 1910). The manufacturers did their best to herald the new ball, contending "that of 280 clubs over the country using the cork-center ball, not one has been returned from losing its shape" (*Sporting News*, July 28, 1910). The ball was used in that year's World Series, where both managers expressed satisfaction with it.

At the annual meeting in February 1911, the major leagues signed a twenty-year contract to use the cork-center ball. Again, far from being secretive, the manufacturers took an ad in *Sporting News* to publicize the agreement (*Sporting News*, March 2, 1911). Lengthy descriptions and endorsements of the new ball also appeared in *Sporting Life* and in that year's *Reach Baseball Guide* (quoted in William R. Vogel, *The History and Manufacture of the Baseball*, 17–22).

Once the cork-center ball came into general use, it became clear that the "lively ball has brought a lot of hitting" (*Sporting Life*, May 27, 1911). Newspapers published detailed analyses that linked the "much-mooted lively ball" to the surge in offense ("New Lively Ball Places Brain on Par with Muscle," *Fort Wayne Journal-Gazette*, June 8, 1911). The attention led Garry Herrmann of the National Commission to threaten a return to the old ball (*Washington Post*, May 25, 1911).

The outcry prompted A. J. Reach's son George "to give official and emphatic denial to the reports and to add that no change whatever would be made in the ball, as the cork-centre had been designed to make a perfect and durable ball and not solely with an eye to increasing the batting, though that was a satisfactory and popular incident. The dean of the National league umpire staff, Hank O'Day, who usually sizes up a situation shrewdly and correctly, struck the nail on the head when he said last Wednesday: 'Modify the ball to make it deader eh? What do they want? Before the cry was against pitchers' battles; now there is too much hitting'" (*Sporting Life*, May 27, 1911). St. Louis Browns president Robert L. Hedges similarly thought it much ado about nothing: "The fans have been crying for more hitting. They have it now" (*Sporting Life*, June 3, 1911). The controversy quickly simmered down.

Harry Davis showed a more sophisticated understanding of the properties of the new ball when he contended: "The new ball is no livelier than the old one. It retains its resiliency longer than the old ball and that's all there is to it. The rubber-centre began to lose its shape and liveliness after it had been in play a couple of innings, while the cork-centre sphere will stay right much longer" (*Sporting Life*, March 30, 1912). Similarly, an ad in the *Spalding Guide* included a testimonial from Roger Bresnahan that with the new ball, "You can make a home run in the ninth inning just as easily as in the first" (quoted in Dan Gutman, *Banana Bats and Ding-Dong Balls*, 149).

9.1.7 Cushioned Cork Centers.
The baseball's interior was again modified in 1925 with the introduction of the cushioned cork center. Its manufacturers, the A. J. Reach Company, explained the differences: "The old cork center consisted of a live cork core inside a center of pure para rubber. The center of the Reach cushioned cork center ball is made of a lathe-turned perfect sphere of live cork, surrounded by black semi-vulcanized rubber, which is vulcanized by another cover of red rubber" (*Port Arthur* [Tex.] *News*, October 25, 1925).

As with the introduction of the original cork-center ball, there has been confusion about the year of this innovation, with William Curran placing it in 1926 and the *Total Baseball Catalog* listing the year as 1931 (William Curran, *Big Sticks*, 79–80; David Pietrusza, Lloyd Johnson, and Bob Carroll, ed., *Total Baseball Catalog*, 56). Once again, not only was there no secrecy but in fact a press release was issued following the 1925 season that declared: "The new cork center ball, the Reach official American league cushioned cork center ball, patented March 1, 1925, is far superior to its predecessor of fifteen years ago. Use in this year's world's series and other games proved that, while it has better balance, and greater wearing and enduring qualities than the former ball, it is neither less lively nor more lively in play" (*Port Arthur* [Tex.] *News*, October 25, 1925).

9.1.8 Rabbit Balls.
What is more American than a . . . conspiracy theory? It's pretty much a given that if there's even a small increase in home runs, or even just a slow news day, there will be talk about a rabbit ball. Sometimes there is at least some basis for speculation, but often it seems to have been entirely fueled by paranoia.

Such rumors date back to the nineteenth century, with an 1886 note reading: "The Western Association clubs suspect that Al Reach is

quietly supplying a livelier ball in order to give the public what they want—heavy batting" (*Cleveland Leader and Herald*, May 16, 1886).

The term "rabbit ball" had come into use by 1907 when sportswriter Joe S. Jackson wrote, ". . . The Cleveland camp followers, when Macon won on Wednesday, went to the old family chest and brushed the moth powder off the 'rabbit' ball story that was sprung a dozen times during the championship series a year ago" (*Detroit Free Press*, March 31, 1907).

Conspiracy theories escalated after the introduction of the cork-center ball. Dan Gutman reported that the new ball was secretly introduced during the 1910 World Series (Dan Gutman, *Banana Bats and Ding-Dong Balls*, 152). In fact, as noted earlier, (see **9.1.6**), the manufacturers had been advertising their new ball in the sporting press throughout the 1910 season.

The issue was reprised a decade later, and it is often reported today that a livelier ball was introduced to the major leagues in 1920. But William Curran has argued convincingly that no such event transpired (William Curran, *Big Sticks*, 65–85). He noted that the 1922 *Reach Guide* contained a full-page ad stating, "There has been no change in the construction of the CORK CENTER BALL since we introduced it in 1910" (William Curran, *Big Sticks*, 78).

In 1925 the major leagues hired Harold A. Fales, a professor of chemistry at Columbia University, to study the new cushioned-cork-center baseball. Fales tested balls manufactured in 1914, 1923, and 1925 and concluded that the elasticity was "practically the same" (*New York Times*, July 16, 1925). He did acknowledge differences in the cover that might affect the ball's flight. Yet even the *New York Times* reported his findings that there was *no* proof of the existence of a rabbit ball under the headline, "Magnates Approve the 'Rabbit Ball.'"

While denials by manufacturers and other authority figures only fuel such conspiracy theories, Curran noted that a more telling sign is the lack of complaints from pitchers. He cited pitcher Vean Gregg's 1925 assertion that the baseball was no livelier than it had been before the war (William Curran, *Big Sticks*, 81). Curran argued that the increased power of the 1920s can be attributed to more frequent replacement of used balls, banning of trick pitches, and fuller swings by batters.

Nonetheless, the die was cast. The press had figured out that the public gobbled up conspiracy stories about changes inside the baseball and was happy to oblige. When the cushioned-cork-center baseball was introduced in 1925, the para rubber inside might as well have been short for paranoia. While others were suggesting that a rabbit ball had been unleashed, Arthur Mann wrote that the manufacturer had been part of a conspiracy to deaden the ball (Arthur Mann, "The Dead Ball and the New Game," *Baseball Magazine*, August 1926; quoted in William Curran, *Big Sticks*, 80).

In 1929, *Scientific American* compared a 1924 baseball with a 1929 ball and found no difference. It attributed the increase in offense entirely to the greater frequency with which old balls were replaced. Louis S. Treadwell explained that "when a ball is struck a few times it softens up. Its original structural aspect is changed and it becomes slower" (*Scientific American*, quoted in *New York Times*, August 28, 1929). But such sober accounts never had the impact of wild claims about rabbit balls.

A livelier baseball was introduced in 1930 but shelved after one year because of the record levels of scoring that resulted. The following season, longtime Pirates owner Barney Dreyfuss revealed to a reporter a collection of forty years of major league baseballs that he kept in his office safe. He explained that the baseball of 1930 "had an extra rim of rubber around the interior which gave it more resiliency. According to the manufacturer, this was to keep the cork center in shape. The ball now in use has a heavier center, reducing the tendency to hop lightly over the fences and into stands" (*Pittsburgh Press*, July 12, 1931, S2).

Rabbit balls have remained a perpetual topic of speculation among baseball fans ever since. Perhaps the most novel theory to date was described by George F. Will: "In 1987 a sudden increase in home runs produced the 'Happy Haitian' explanation: Baseballs were then manufactured in Haiti and the theory was that the fall of the Duvalier regime so inspirited Haitians that they worked with more pep, pulling the stitching tighter, thereby flattening the seams—and flattening curveballs. The smoother balls had less wind resistance to give them movement when pitched, or to slow their subsequent flight over outfielders" (George F. Will, *Bunts*, 245).

9.1.9 Colorful Baseballs. The baseball has been white throughout most of baseball history, but experiments with other hues have been conducted from time to time.

Early players couldn't be choosers and used whatever color of ball was available. Gradually white became the predominant color. Then, in 1870, Peck & Snyder introduced a "Dead Red Ball," which was dark red in color. The intention, according to an advertisement placed by the company that year, was "getting rid of the objectionable dazzling whiteness of the ball which bothers fielders and batsmen on a Sunny Day" (quoted in Dan Gutman, *Banana Bats and Ding-Dong Balls*, 162).

The Dead Red remained popular for several years. Henry Chadwick liked the ball and recommended "a clause requiring the cover to be of some dark color. The cricketers have found red to be the best color, and this has been the color of cricket balls for fifty years past. White, in the air, is dazzling to the eyes; and when the ball becomes soiled, it is difficult to find it in the grass. There is in fact, nothing to commend the white color, while there is everything in favor of the dark" (*New York Clipper*, December 4, 1875).

The red balls gradually lost favor, though A. G. Spalding & Company continued to sell them into the 1880s. Legendary football coach Amos Alonzo Stagg noted their passing in 1892: "Only a few years ago every boy dreamed of 'red dead' balls, and was discontented until he could have one. Both the 'red' and the 'dead' have since passed away" (Amos Alonzo Stagg, "Ball for the Boys," *Atlanta Constitution*, May 29, 1892).

It was not until 1928 that a colored ball was again seriously considered. A yellow ball was experimented with in the second game of a doubleheader on August 28, 1928, between Milwaukee and Louisville of the American Association. An AP report of the game noted: "The new balls are said to have greater visibility than white ones, particularly with a bleacher background of white shirts. They are not easily discolored and therefore should give longer service. Further experiments will be made and if successful the ball will be officially adopted for 1929" (AP–*New York Times*, August 29, 1928).

Nothing came of that effort, but the idea was revived a decade later. Columnist Irving T. Marsh explained, "In an experiment to eliminate the menace of the 'bean' ball, Columbia and Fordham will play their game next week with a spectrum yellow baseball which, in the opinion of its sponsor, can be more quickly and easily seen than the white ball used now. The originator of the colored ball is Frederic H. Rahr, New York color scientist. He believes that not only will it eliminate 'bean' balls but that better hitting will result, since the sphere can be seen more easily. The yellow ball was given a preliminary test in practice at Columbia a few weeks ago and after that Andy Coakley, coach, suggested that it have a trial in a regular game. He advanced the idea to Jack Coffey, Fordham coach, and Coffey agreed. So it will be tried at Baker Field next Wednesday [April 27th] and the results of the experiment will be watched with interest" (*New York Herald Tribune*, April 21, 1938).

The newspaper gave this account of the actual game: "This was 'the game of the yellow ball,' with the chief interest presumably the debut of the colored missile in actual competition." But the yellow ball was overshadowed by a tight, exciting game, capped by a game-winning triple by future NFL star Sid Luckman. "About the yellow ball, both coaches were agreed that the fancy spheroid had not had exactly a fair test. 'One game isn't enough,' said Andy Coakley, of the Lions, 'but I'm inclined to like it'" (*New York Herald Tribune*, April 28, 1938).

On August 2, 1938, Brooklyn general manager Larry MacPhail introduced yellow baseballs to the major leagues during the first game of a doubleheader against St. Louis. According to Dan Gutman, the balls had the curious side effect of turning the pitchers' fingers yellow (Dan Gutman, *Banana Bats and Ding-Dong Balls*, 163). The Dodgers used them again in games on July 23 and September 17, 1939, and the Cardinals tried them in a game on July 31, 1939.

In 1965, when it was discovered that outfielders could not gauge fly balls at the newly opened Astrodome, the team experimented with yellow, orange, red, and cerise baseballs. Charles Finley's Oakland A's used gold-colored baseballs in a game on April 13, 1970, and attracted considerable publicity. But there was nothing new about the idea.

9.1.10 Clunk Balls. Wartime restrictions threatened the quality of baseballs used by the major leagues in 1943. The horsehide, which had previously been imported from Belgium and France, was replaced with horsehide first from Bolivia and then from the United States. Then cork became scarce and was replaced with balata, a hardened form of gum. When the balata ball was introduced at the start of the 1943 season, it was so dead that it was dubbed the "clunk" ball. Major league baseball and

suppliers A. G. Spalding and Brothers claimed that the problem was with the rubber cement: "The cement used in the 'clunk' ball was made from a poor grade of reclaimed rubber" (AP: *Milwaukee Journal*, May 5, 1943).

An improved version was introduced on May 8: "The new and lively Balata ball made its appearance Saturday. . . . The speedier ball has replaced the dead or 'clunk' ball with which the majors opened the season. The manufacturer discovered that the original ball had hardened when an inferior rubber cement seeped into the wool and dried. The mistake was corrected in the new ball" (AP: *Milwaukee Journal*, May 9, 1943).

The minor leagues had it even worse. According to minor league slugger Howie Moss, a ball with a hard synthetic interior was used in the minors in both 1942 and 1943. The results were both unsatisfactory and unfair: "if you hit the ball squarely, and hard, it would travel about 280 feet and then die like a wounded quail. Thus, it became little more than a pop fly. But, if your timing was off and you would undercut the ball—'pop'—out of the ball park it would go" (David Chrisman, "Howie Moss: Minor League Slugger," *Baseball Research Journal* 1982, 147).

(ii) Bats

9.2.1 Types of Wood. Henry Chadwick reported in 1860, "The description of wood most in use is ash, but maple, white and pitch pine, and also hickory bats are in common use, weight for the size governing the selection. For a bat of medium weight, ash is preferable, as its fiber is tough and elastic. The English willow has recently been used, and is favorably regarded by many. This latter wood is very light and close in fiber, and answers the purpose better than any other wood for a light bat" (*Beadle's Dime Base-Ball Player*, 19).

Batters evidently agreed, as George Wright recalled in a 1915 interview that many types of wood were used in early bats, "but the favorite wood was willow, hence the expression, 'Use the willow'" (*New York Sun*, November 14, 1915). Isaac G. Kimball remembered many years later that during the earliest days of baseball in Fort Wayne the "bats were made of elm at a Fort Wayne spoke factory," but later poplar and basswood were used (E. L. McDonald, "The National Game of Base Ball Was Born in Fort Wayne," *St. Louis Republic*, reprinted in *Fort Wayne Journal Gazette*, January 26, 1902). Chadwick remarked in 1868 that, "Frank Wright, of Auburn, has got up a fine sycamore bat" (Henry Chadwick, *The American Game of Baseball*, 50). Spruce, cherry, and chestnut were also used on occasion (*Colorado Daily Chieftain* [Pueblo], August 18, 1876; A. G. Spalding & Co. advertisement, *New York Clipper*, May 26, 1877; Clarence Deming, "Old Days in Baseball," *Outing*, June 1902, 359). Of course beggars couldn't be choosers, and when nothing else was on hand, "a portion of a stout rake or pitchfork handle was much in demand" ("Bob Lively," "Base Ball: How They Play the Game in New England," *Porter's Spirit of the Times*, December 27, 1856, 276–277).

As baseball grew in popularity, batters were able to become choosier and take more factors into account, as an 1870 article described: "White ash bats are now generally used, weighing from 24 to 48 ounces, and from 34 to 40 inches in length. Michigan furnishes much of the material. Basswood and willow are also used to some extent, and Balm of Gilead wood bats, polished, are very highly recommended; though their cost is [35 cents] more than the ash bats." Basswood and willow were the cheapest varieties (*Chicago Post*, reprinted in *Detroit Advertiser and Tribune*, August 1, 1870). An 1896 article claimed, "Twenty years ago about half the bats were poplar but the style has now changed" (*Sporting News*, March 7, 1896).

After 1870 white ash emerged as the predominant wood for professional bats, with Henry Chadwick recommending "a well-balanced light bat, made of tough and elastic ash" (*New York Clipper*, April 12, 1873). Ash became even more commonplace when soft woods were banned in 1893. A machinist for a leading bat manufacturer said in 1901, "In selecting the bats for the best sticks I am careful to use nothing but second growth white ash. It is the only wood that stands the test and can be made light and still preserve a correct size" (*Grand Rapids* [Mich.] *Evening Press*, April 20, 1901).

Baseball's prosperity led to still more care being given to procuring the best possible timber. A 1908 article reported that the wood of choice for major leaguers now came from Kentucky's hilly regions and was "always grown on the north hillsides, as the atmosphere on that side has a better effect on the trees and enables the grain to be more perfect. The north side of a hill is better for bats, and also the north side of a tree, and in ordering the very finest of bats the players sometimes specify that they want the north side of a tree that was grown on the north

side of a hill" ("Bats Used by Leading Hitters," *New York Herald*, reprinted in the *Washington Post*, September 6, 1908, M3).

Ash was the overwhelming preference of major leaguers for most of the twentieth century but apparently never became their exclusive choice. In recent years a new challenger has emerged. Harmon Killebrew may have been the first to experiment with a maple bat, but he eventually abandoned it (Dan Gutman, *It Ain't Cheatin' If You Don't Get Caught*, 78). In the 1990s a Canadian named Sam Holman revived the idea, and his maple "Sam Bat" became a favorite of many major leaguers, including Barry Bonds. The type of wood that will be used in bats of the future remains in doubt amid concerns that maple bats break far too easily and fears that the emerald ash borer will make the ash tree extinct (Monica Davey, "Balmy Weather May Bench a Baseball Staple," *New York Times*, July 11, 2007).

9.2.2 Dimensions. Early batters "selected the wood and whittled their own bats . . . there are stories told of enthusiasts who faced the pitcher with bats five feet long and nearly as thick as wagon tongues. It was a happy-go-lucky crowd, those pioneers of the national game, and quite as much in earnest as were their fathers who cleared the forests to erect homes, and spoiled many a good bat in doing so" (John H. Gruber, *Sporting News*, November 11, 1915). Henry Chadwick also reported that bats as long as sixty inches were used in the late 1850s (*Appletons' Annual Cyclopaedia and Register of Important Events of the Year 1885*, 78).

In 1857 the rules specified that a bat could not exceed two and a half inches in diameter. The maximum diameter was changed to two and three-quarters inches in 1895 and has never changed since. In 1868 bats were limited to forty inches in length; the next year this was modified to forty-two inches. This rule remains on the book, but it is pretty much moot, as no major leaguer is known ever to have used a bat that long—Shirley Povich reported in 1937 that the longest bat then being used by a major leaguer was Al Simmons's twenty-seven-and-a-half-inch club (*Washington Post*, June 15, 1937, 25).

Minor leaguer Tacks Parrott did, however, use a forty-two-inch bat in 1908. He was playing for Galveston of the Texas League at the time, and that state's wide-open spaces apparently influenced his choice. "There is plenty of room out here to swing a long bat," Parrott explained, "and the only reason I don't have a longer one made is because they wouldn't allow me to use it" ("Bats Used by Leading Hitters," *New York Herald*, reprinted in the *Washington Post*, September 6, 1908, M3).

George Wright explained in 1888 that the curveball (**3.2.3**) was one of the reasons for the change: "Formerly long bats were all the rage, and players, both professional and amateur, held up logs of wood, some of them three and a half feet in length, and fanned the air in a way that would seem perfectly ridiculous for the average player today. . . . The reason for the substitution of the short for the long bat is its lighter weight and the sharp, quick blow one can give with it" (quoted in *Boston Herald*, reprinted in *Cincinnati Enquirer*, April 29, 1888). As we shall see in the next entry, the same issue has been a recurrent theme in the weight of baseball bats.

9.2.3 Weights. There have never been any restrictions placed on the weight of a baseball bat, but there have been a number of changes over the years in the preferences of batters.

As noted in the entry on "Types of Wood" (**9.2.1**), in 1870 bats ranged from twenty-four to forty-eight ounces in weight. Henry Chadwick reported that hollow bats were also experimented with but "have been proven failures" (*New York Clipper*, April 12, 1873). He advised, "The lighter the bat, provided the wood is of a tough kind, the better. It is almost impossible to hit quick enough for swift pitching with a heavy bat, unless the batsman is very strong in the arms. Strength in the wrists is the main thing in batting" (Henry Chadwick, *Haney's Base Ball Player's Book of Reference for 1867*, 10). But whether batters heeded this suggestion is not clear.

By the early twentieth century most batters were swinging significantly heavier bats than the ones favored today. A 1908 article claimed there was a sixty-ounce maximum for bats (an assertion for which I can find no confirmation) and reported that one minor leaguer, William McDonaugh of Denver, was using a sixty-ounce bat ("Bats Used by Leading Hitters," *New York Herald*, reprinted in the *Washington Post*, September 6, 1908, M3). A 1912 article reported that Charlie Hickman's thirty-four-ounce bat was one of the lightest in the majors (*Washington Post*, September 5, 1912). The heaviest bats in that period were often used by singles hitters like Bill Sweeney and Chief Meyers, who took

short, compact swings and tried to drive the ball between the infielders and outfielders.

Babe Ruth's success led to a reexamination of bat weight. Since Ruth was a pitcher, not much was expected of him at the plate, and he was able to disregard the conventional wisdom about hitting (Ty Cobb, quoted in F. C. Lane, *Batting*, 71). The extraordinary results he produced naturally attracted many copycats, and they mimicked what they perceived to be the three keys to Ruth's success: his free swing, his full follow-through, and his heavy bat.

The first two have remained the hallmarks of power hitters ever since. The heavy bat was also obligatory for the generation of power hitters who succeeded Ruth. It was many years before sluggers began to realize that the bat speed that could be generated with a light bat more than offset the extra weight of a heavier bat. So Ruth's influence, such a boon to the home run era in many ways, proved a detriment in this regard.

At least a couple of Ruth's contemporaries figured this out. In 1925, Rogers Hornsby observed, "It doesn't follow, however, that a heavy bat is necessary [for a slugger]. Some sluggers use heavy bats. Chief Meyers did and so does Babe Ruth. Most batters will find that an extra heavy bat cuts down the speed of their swing more than enough to offset what the extra weight of the bat can accomplish. I prefer a rather light bat. . . . There are two things which drive a baseball hard; the weight of the bat and the speed with which it moves. The two are direct opposites. No matter how much strength a batter has, he cannot handle a heavy bat with as much speed as he would a light bat . . . in general the chop hitter would best use a heavy bat and the slugger a light one." And Harry Heilmann added, "I discount weight in a bat almost entirely. In fact, I use a light bat and I think Babe Ruth, with all his success as a slugger, would be a greater hitter if he discarded that wagon tongue of his" (both quoted in F. C. Lane, *Batting*, 67). Even Ruth must have come to realize this. After using a massive fifty-four-ounce club early in his career, he had dropped down to a thirty-six-ouncer by his final season (Shirley Povich, *Washington Post*, June 15, 1937, 25).

Today the advice Henry Chadwick offered in 1867 is followed by all sluggers. It is now rare for any professional to use a bat as heavy as the thirty-four ouncer that in 1912 was described as one of the lightest in the major leagues.

9.2.4 Shapes. There was no requirement that early baseball bats be rounded, yet John Gruber reported that "bats were invariably round and not flat like those used in cricket" (John H. Gruber, "The Ball and the Bat," *Sporting News*, November 11, 1915). This reflects the fact that early hitters generally took lusty swings and tried to hit the ball as far as they could without regard to placement. In 1857 the rules incorporated what was already customary by specifying that bats be round.

By 1870 the dead ball was leading to new approaches to hitting. In a game on May 3, 1875, several Hartford players used a bat that had been whittled down on one side so as to be nearly flat. The Philadelphia captain eventually protested, and the bat was removed from play.

But experiments with square bats continued. Sportswriter W. R. Rose recalled one that occurred in Cleveland in the early 1870s in which Al Pratt pitched and Deacon White was the batter. Although White was one of the game's best hitters, he hit only three of Pratt's twenty offerings squarely, missing three entirely and fouling off the other fourteen. Since the rules of the day meant that either a caught foul tip or a foul caught on the first bounce was an out, the trial was deemed a complete failure (*Cleveland Plain Dealer*, reprinted in the *Salt Lake City Evening Telegram*, June 9, 1914).

In 1880 the body governing amateur baseball legalized square bats. Henry Chadwick reported: "The new bat, in its widest part, viz., from corner to corner at its end, is not wider than the round bat. Its four sides only extend to the handle. It is just as if a round bat had been planed off on four sides. This bat will admit of harder wood for its size than the round bat; that is, two bats of the same size and material, one being made round and the other four-sided, the latter would necessarily be lightest by several ounces. The idea of changing the form from the round to the four-sided is to enable the batsman to 'place' the ball better than is possible with a round bat" (quoted in John H. Gruber, "The Ball and the Bat," *Sporting News*, November 11, 1915; Gruber did not specifically credit Chadwick, but the piece is in his distinctive style and nearly identical portions appeared in a Chadwick article in the *New York Clipper* on January 10, 1880).

There seems to have been little enthusiasm for the square bats. Even Chadwick had to report after an exhibition game at which the new bats were to be tested: "Unluckily, the Park groundkeeper had only provided three of the new four-sided bats and as these were all broken before two-thirds of the game were finished, the contest did not present a fair opportunity for testing the merits of the new sticks" (*New York Clipper*, April 5, 1879).

Following the 1880 season, Harry Wright staged an experimental game that featured cork-center balls and flat bats. Neither innovation was considered a success, with the flat bats being particularly unpopular. Not only did they reduce hitting, they also stung the batters' hands. The bats were abandoned partway through the game (Preston D. Orem, *Baseball [1845–1881] from the Newspaper Accounts*, 335–336). According to John Gruber, the square bat was not popular among amateurs and was soon dropped (John H. Gruber, "The Ball and the Bat," *Sporting News*, November 11, 1915).

Nevertheless after the 1884 season the National League legalized flat bats. While these bats were described as flat, actually they were only flattened. A diagram of the new bat in *Sporting Life* showed that only about one-sixth of it had been shaved off (*Sporting Life*, February 25, 1885).

Several reasons for legalizing the flat bat were offered, yet what ended up being the main function of the flat bat was never mentioned. Harry Wright expressed optimism that, with this new style of bat, "'placing the ball' will be made easier" (*Sporting Life*, December 3, 1884). Researcher Tom Shieber discovered a *New York Times* article that suggested that the aim instead was to "do away with so many foul tips and high fly balls, and in a measure improve batting" (*New York Times*, November 21, 1884). Another article described the rule change as an acknowledgment of the reality that "players have frequently used such bats for a long time without detection" (*Sporting Life*, February 25, 1885).

A few batters experimented with it in 1885, with the *Detroit Post* noting that "Scheffer" of St. Louis—presumably George Shafer—was using a flat bat (*Detroit Post*, May 18, 1885). It was only in 1886, however, that the flat bats seemed to become commonplace, and it was for a purpose no one seems to have anticipated. The bunt (see **2.2.1**) made a dramatic comeback in 1886 after a decade of disuse, and the new flat bats played a major role. An 1892 article observed, "Since the flat-sided bat has been admitted the most skillful pitcher cannot prevent a cool batsman from dribbling a grounder out toward third at so slow a pace that he can beat the ball to first. The fact that the entire team in the field knows just what the batter means to do seems to afford no assistance in the solution of the problem" (*New York Times*, June 23, 1892).

When the sixty-foot, six-inch pitching distance (see **1.17**) was established in 1893, many felt that the bunt would become indefensible and called for it to be banned. Instead a compromise was struck, and flat bats were permanently banned in 1893.

9.2.5 Soft Bats. John Gruber observed that "Scientific batting, especially bunting, was the general craze in the eighties" and led to the use of a "soft" or "sacrifice" bat. He explained, "The bat was made of wood so soft that it was hardly possible for the batter to drive the ball beyond the diamond. The ball became dead after coming in contact with the mush-like bat and dropped to the ground" (John H. Gruber, "The Ball and the Bat," *Sporting News*, November 11, 1915). Connie Mack later remarked: "Remember the bunting bats they had for one season? Soft wood and flattened at the business end" (*Sporting Life*, December 14, 1912). When the rule banning flat bats was adopted in 1893, it was also specified that bats had to be made of hard wood, effectively eliminating the soft bat.

9.2.6 Mass-produced Bats. The *New York Times* reported in 1871 that demand for bats was so great that one firm kept two mills running year round just to turn out baseball bats ("Bats, Balls and Mallets," *New York Times*, May 30, 1871). By 1879 it was becoming evident that "large bat manufacturers have deprived the carpenter, the turner and other hewers of wood of a considerable share of profitable business done on a small scale" (*New York Clipper*, April 26, 1879). That November, A. G. Spalding & Company began mass-producing cheap bats at a factory in Hastings, Michigan. An 1883 article stated that the factory employed 100 men and made 500,000 bats a year, adding, "Ash is the staple bat wood. A proportion of fancy, and necessarily higher priced, bats are made of cherry. Including the different woods and sizes, there are twenty-two styles of bat made for the trade, ranging in price at retail from ten cents for a juvenile article, up to $1.50 for an aesthetic cherry bat. The Hastings factory will use in the neighborhood of 350,000 feet of ash, 250,000 feet of basswood and 50,000 feet of cherry lumber this season, which means about 2,500 gross

or thirty car-loads of bats" (*Cleveland Herald*, reprinted in the *National Police Gazette*, July 7, 1883). Before the factory burned down in December 1887, it reportedly was producing more than a million bats a year (*Sporting News*, April 2, 1887). By 1909 it was claimed that "a kiln-dried bat wouldn't be given honorable mention by the poorest swatter on the Kokomo team. The timber that is to be made into a first-class bat must be seasoned out doors at least four years, and seven is better. Then it is ready to be put into a lathe and turned into a $1.50 club" ("The Great National Game in Dollars and Cents," *Washington Post*, May 9, 1909).

9.2.7 Models. In the early days of baseball, bats were scarce in some areas but easy to come by in mill towns. Thus in Baraboo, Wisconsin: "The bats were all home made, and were mostly turned out at the upper Baraboo mills, either at the Drown factory on the island or at the Thomas & Claude mill just above the upper bridge at Lyons. Usually each individual had his favorite bat, made according to his own specifications, and they all varied considerably in length, diameter, heft and material. The favorite material was willow or ash, but sometimes elm or oak, and various other timber was used and tested out" (Harry Slye, "Early Days of Baseball in Baraboo," *Baraboo Daily News*, June 25, 1925). It seems a safe bet that similar practices occurred in other mill towns as well.

The widespread use of individual models emerged gradually. John Gruber pointed out that, in early baseball, hitters chose any bat they fancied, whether it belonged to a teammate or even an opponent. Batters gradually became more proprietary about their weapons, and disputes ensued. As a result, a rule was passed in 1872 that "The striker shall be privileged to use his own private bat exclusively, and no other player of the contesting nines shall have any claim to the use of such bat, except by the consent of its owner" (John H. Gruber, *Sporting News*, January 27, 1916).

Lee Allen reported that individual bat models came to the major leagues in 1878 when Providence batters began to select their own models (*Sporting News*, April 20, 1968). An 1879 article confirmed, "Each man of the 'Greys' has two bats of his own, marked with his name, and no other man can use them. If by chance he breaks one it has to be replaced at once" (*St. Louis Globe-Democrat*, April 13, 1879, 13). By 1896 it was said that "Some of the crack players will not condescend to use a stock bat, but go to the factory and have bats of the size and weight they desire made for them" (*Sporting News*, March 7, 1896).

9.2.8 Trademarks.
An A. G. Spalding & Brothers ad in 1888 declared that "Spalding's Trade-Marked bats were first introduced in 1877" (advertisement, *Spalding's Official Base Ball Guide, 1888*). The company claimed the trademark "was stamped on each bat to insure its genuineness" (advertisement, *Spalding's Official Base Ball Guide, 1883*). Not everyone accepted that explanation, and slugger Ed Delahanty is said to have told batmaker John "Bud" Hillerich, "You didn't need to put an ad on that bat. If the bat makes good, I'll tell everybody where I bought it—don't you think I'm square enough to give you credit if it's coming to you?" (W. A. Phelon, *Sporting News*, December 19, 1912).

Youngsters today are told not to hit the ball on the trademark, but it is important to note that the opposite advice was given in the nineteenth and early twentieth centuries. An 1885 article reported, "[George] McVey says he hit that first ball on the handle of his bat yesterday. Where would it have gone if he had hit it where it says 'A. J. Reach'?" (*Atlanta Constitution*, May 14, 1885). One of the bats pictured in the 1888 *Spalding's Guide* has the words "Strike This Way Up Grain" on the same side as the trademark. George S. Davis noted in 1894 that "Smacking the ball on the trade mark" had become synonymous with making solid contact (George S. Davis, "How to Bat," syndicated column, *Warren* [Pa.] *Evening Democrat*, May 26, 1894). Cap Anson inscribed copies of his autobiography with the words, "Always hit the ball on the trade-mark" (*Sporting Life*, November 29, 1902).

The difference appears to be mostly one of nomenclature. At some point the trademark seems to have been rotated slightly, so that the batter could easily see it while batting. Thus while the bat's sweet spot continued to line up with the trademark, it became desirable not to hit the ball right on the trademark.

Yogi Berra liked to meet the ball with the trademark, so Hillerich & Bradsby shifted the trademark on his model to accommodate him (Dan Gutman, *Banana Bats and Ding-Dong Balls*, 34).

9.2.9 Louisville Sluggers.
The usual story of the first Louisville Slugger goes something like this: Early in the 1884 season, Louisville's star outfielder Pete Browning broke his favorite bat. A local apprentice woodworker named John "Bud" Hillerich offered to make him a new bat at his father's job-turning shop. Browning was pleased with the result and experienced immediate success. Orders from other players soon followed, and a new business was born.

If this story sounds too good to be true, there's a good reason for that. Researcher Bob Bailey discovered that as late as 1914 Hillerich was saying he had made a bat for himself in 1884 and had given it to weak-hitting pitcher Gus Weyhing (Bruce Dudley, "Every Knock Is a Boost for the Louisville Slugger Bat," *Louisville Herald Magazine*, September 27, 1914). Weyhing began using it, and other local players soon inquired about it and then began requesting their own. The bats became known as Hillerich Bats, then as Falls City Sluggers. They assumed their current name around 1894.

Bailey found that the now familiar story did not begin to emerge until the late 1930s. In 1937, Arlie Latham claimed he triggered the chain of events when he broke his bat while playing in Louisville and happened into the Hillerich shop. Two years later a similar version appeared in *The Sporting Goods Dealer*, a trade publication, but this time Browning had replaced Latham as the central figure.

The author of the article was Sam Severance, head of marketing for Hillerich & Bradsby. Severance didn't even pretend that the story was true; he merely related it as a "legend around the Hillerich & Bradsby factory." It must have struck a chord, however, because it was reprinted in the *Famous Slugger Yearbook* for the next decade and supplemented with new and increasingly melodramatic details. By 1949, Hillerich was "tugging at Browning's sleeve" to offer him the bat.

Such stories, all too often, become accepted as baseball "history" (Bob Bailey, "Hunting for the First Louisville Slugger," *Baseball Research Journal* 30 [2001], 96–98).

9.2.10 Burning Bats.
Many nineteenth-century hitters applied their own treatments to bats after receiving them from the factory. St. Louis Browns secretary George Munson explained in 1894, "The Browns were burning bats when I left the park an hour ago. It was a comical sight to see them in variegated uniforms crowding around a miniature camp fire. 'Burning' a bat properly is considered quite an accomplishment. The 'stick' is first immersed in a preparation of boiled linseed oil and shellac. It is

then held over the flames until it has become perfectly dry. Great care is required to prevent the bat's being scorched during the toasting process. When perfectly dry it is rubbed for an hour or more with a piece of flannel" (*St. Louis Post-Dispatch*, June 28, 1894).

Bat manufacturers soon began to offer this feature. A 1901 article offered this explanation, "There is a superstition widely current among professionals to the effect that a scorched bat is less prone to meet the ball on the top or bottom, but sends out straight line hits. When so ordered a bat is 'burned' by the application of a piece of hard wood to the bat's surface as it turns in the lathe. The result is seen in the series of brown rings which are so common on the bats of the big league players" (*Grand Rapids* [Mich.] *Evening Press*, April 20, 1901). But many batters continued to apply their own treatments. Ty Cobb, for example, would "set" the seams "in neat's-foot oil or chewing tobacco, then clamp them in a vise and rub them with a large hollowed-out steer bone. 'My own favorite prescription was a chewing tobacco called Navy Nerve-Cut,' he recalled, 'the juiciest kind I ever discovered. Using the steer bone, I rubbed in Navy by the hour'" (Richard Bak, *Peach*, 55).

9.2.11 Tapers. Most early baseball bats had a fairly similar diameter from the handle to the barrel. Henry Chadwick observed in 1867, "A well shaped bat tapers gradually from the point to the handle" (Henry Chadwick, *Haney's Base Ball Player's Book of Reference for 1867*, 119). This design reflected, among other things, the reality that bats were expensive; broken bats needed to be avoided if at all possible.

The idea of a more dramatic taper was around as early as 1880, when it was reported that "George Wright is manufacturing bats of regulation length, which, instead of gradually tapering from butt to handle, have long, small, round handles with the full swell at the centre of the bat" (*New York Clipper*, May 1, 1880). The results are unknown, but it seems likely that they broke too frequently to be practical.

By the early twentieth century, handles were becoming slimmer. Dan Gutman noted that "Rogers Hornsby is usually cited as the first player to use a truly tapered bat" (Dan Gutman, *Banana Bats and Ding-Dong Balls*, 9). This appears to be another example of a great player being credited with a first, not because he introduced it but because he was great. Hornsby did not reach the major leagues until 1915,

while a 1910 article indicated that the bat used in the 1870s "was more slender than the one used today, the tapering being more gradual" (*Chicago Tribune*, July 10, 1910). Two years later the *Washington Post* noted that Charlie Hickman used a bat that "loses weight in the handle, which is remarkably slender." The piece described another player's bat as "chopped off about where most bats are beginning to taper." While the most popular model was reported to be the Harry Davis bat, which had no taper, it is clear from this article that a significant number of major leaguers were using tapered bats before Rogers Hornsby (*Washington Post*, September 5, 1912). Hornsby does seem to have played a role in popularizing tapered bats—according to Shirley Povich, his "36-02" bat model became the most frequent choice of major leaguers (Shirley Povich, *Washington Post*, June 15, 1937, 25).

Bill James suggested that Ernie Banks may have started the trend to ultra-thin handles in the 1950s (Bill James, *The New Bill James Historical Baseball Abstract*, 320). Banks, however, gave this version: "When I first came up I used a 35-ounce bat. Late in the season when I got a little tired I switched to a lighter bat after talking to Ralph Kiner. Now I use a 31-ounce all the time" (quoted in AP wire story, *Lima* [Ohio] *News*, July 11, 1956). Whoever was responsible, this was not merely a design innovation but a sign that baseball's growing prosperity was making it possible—even necessary—to trade a lot of broken bats for an improvement in performance.

It seems likely that the increased prominence of narrow handles led pitchers to place a greater emphasis on pitches that moved in on batters.

9.2.12 Bottle Bats. The most novel offspring of the experimentation with tapers was Heinie Groh's bottle bat. Groh explained that in 1913 John McGraw suggested he try a larger-barreled bat. But the five-foot-seven, 160-pound Groh's hands proved too small to grip a large handle. So he went to Spalding headquarters and, in the basement, "we whittled down the handle of a standard bat, and then we built up the barrel, and when we were finished it looked like a crazy sort of milk bottle or a round paddle—real wide at one end and then suddenly tapering real quick to a thin handle" (Lawrence Ritter, *The Glory of Their Times*, 302).

The finished product weighed forty-six ounces, and Groh found that if he held it anywhere near the knob, pitches would knock the bat right out of his hands. By choking up and chopping at the ball, however, Groh became very proficient at driving the ball over the infielders' heads. Occasionally he would also "slide one hand down to the end of the handle and swing more like a slugger" (quoted in F. C. Lane, *Batting*, 30).

As Groh became a star player, it is curious that the bottle bat attracted few imitators. Groh was also puzzled, telling F. C. Lane: "I am convinced that many other chop hitters would find this peculiar bat much better for them than the ordinary club" (quoted in F. C. Lane, *Batting*, 30). As discussed under "Open Stances" (**2.1.6**), Groh's stance was just as unique.

Before Groh debuted, a bat built along somewhat similar principles had been wielded by a minor leaguer named Pete O'Brien. While playing for Minneapolis in 1908, O'Brien used "the 'freakiest' bat ever seen on a baseball field, as his pet stick is twenty-eight inches long and greatly resembles an old-fashioned potato masher. Its handle is so short that it is barely large enough to allow its owner and designer to get his hands on it. The batting end is fat and chubby, and is chopped off about where most bats are beginning to taper. Although small, it is rather a heavy little swatter, as its chubbiness keeps up its weight" ("Bats Used by Leading Hitters," *New York Herald*, reprinted in the *Washington Post*, September 6, 1908, M3).

9.2.13   Extra Knob. Quite a few hitters around the turn of the century batted with their hands apart, most notably Ty Cobb and Honus Wagner (see **2.1.5**). This led to the creation of a bat with two knobs, which became known as the "Lajoie bat" or the "Double Ring Handle." The bat was patented by sportswriter Tim Murnane, and he and several of his colleagues wrote lengthy descriptions of its advantages, but its popularity appears to have been limited (*New York Times*, March 8, 1903, 15; *Boston Globe*, March 9, 1903; "Baseball Inventions," *Boston Globe*, April 24, 1904, 24; Dan Gutman, *Banana Bats and Ding-Dong Balls*, 15).

9.2.14   Cupped Ends. Bats with an indentation scooped out of the end were made legal by the major leagues in 1975, and Lou Brock helped popularize them. The idea, however, was not new. The Hanna Manufacturing Company of Athens, Georgia, began making bats with cupped ends around 1936 (Dan Gutman, *Banana Bats and Ding-Dong Balls*, 26; Dan Gut-

man, *It Ain't Cheatin' If You Don't Get Caught*, 127). Researcher John Schwartz discovered that pitcher Elden Auker used such a bat in an American League game on July 19, 1942. Auker came to the plate with a bat "with a depression in the business end." Plate umpire Ed Rommel scrutinized it and allowed its use (*Washington Post*, July 20, 1942).

9.2.15   Laminated Bats. Among the "Corked Bats" (**11.1.9**) experimented with in the nineteenth century were "spring bats" made of multiple pieces of wood. Researcher Rick Stattler cites one used (illegally) by Paul Hines in 1884 (*Providence Evening Telegram*, August 15, 1884).

Hall of Fame slugger Sam Crawford ended his career in the Pacific Coast League, where he began using a laminated bat that consisted of "three pieces cut wedge shaped and tongue and grooved. Some woodworker in downtown L. A. had a machine that would take the three pieces and push them together after they had been smeared with adhesive. . . . It took over twice the wood to make this lamination as all of the pieces had to be of the right part of the grain." But questions were raised about its legality, and after two years of swinging the same laminated bat, Crawford had to stop using it (February 20, 1957, letter from Jack Corbett, Cap Anson Hall of Fame file). In 1923 Babe Ruth began using a laminated bat given to him by Crawford. The bat was soon ruled illegal by American League president Ban Johnson, who decreed that bats had to be made of a single piece of wood (Al Kermisch, "Ruth's Laminated Bat Banned in 1923," *Baseball Research Journal* 1983, 49).

Laminated bats returned to favor among amateurs and semipros in the early 1950s. Their history had eerie parallels with the later development of aluminum bats. Their use was approved by the American Association of College Baseball Coaches because of their durability (*Syracuse Herald Journal*, April 18, 1954). The laminated bats came to be used extensively by college teams as well as "smaller budgeted school, sand-lot, semi-pro and little league clubs." Professional baseball, however, resisted the innovation on the grounds that the bats were too lively and gave too much advantage to batters (Ed Lukas, *St. Joseph* [Mich.] *Herald Press*, March 30, 1954).

9.2.16   Aluminum Bats. In 1944 plans to manufacture aluminum baseball bats were announced by businessmen in Spokane, Washington (*Spokane Spokesman-Review*, July 20, 1944; *Newark Star-Ledger*, September 19, 1944, both reprinted in Dean Sullivan, *Middle Innings*, 191–192). But nothing came of the idea until the late 1960s when a Pennsylvanian named Anthony Merola, who had been manufacturing aluminum pool cues, turned his attention to baseball and designed an aluminum bat. A bat manufacturer named Worth, Inc., contracted to mass-produce them. The turning point for aluminum bats came in 1971 when Little League baseball adopted them to eliminate the cost of broken bats. High school and colleges began using them in batting practice at about the same time for the same reason. They were approved for play by schools over the next couple of years, and by 1975 sales of aluminum bats topped those of wood bats (Dan Gutman, *Banana Bats and Ding-Dong Balls*, 36; "Aluminum Bats Stand the Test of Time," *Baseball America*, September 1–14, 2003). Professional leagues have been reluctant to adopt them because of fears that the speed of the ball off an aluminum bat poses a hazard to pitchers. In recent years, modifications have been made to aluminum bats and tests conducted to address such concerns.

9.2.17 Pine Tar. George Brett will always be associated with pine tar, because of his July 24, 1983, home run that was disallowed by the game umpires, who in turn were overruled by American League president Lee MacPhail. The issue, however, is of much longer standing. As early as 1886 the rules specified that bat handles could be made of twine or "a granulated substance applied, not to exceed 18 inches from the end." A 1948 article indicated: "Baseball rules prohibit any foreign substance or markings on a bat higher than 18 inches" (*Washington Post*, July 6, 1948).

On July 19, 1975, Thurman Munson of the New York Yankees singled home a run in a game against the Minnesota Twins. The Twins pointed out that Munson's bat "had pine tar rather far up the handle." Umpire Art Frantz declared Munson out and took the run off the board in what turned out to be a one-run loss. Frantz stuck with his ruling even though manager "Bill Virdon and a group of Yankees followed Frantz around shouting." *New York Times* sportswriter Paul L. Montgomery explained to readers that according to Rule 1.10B, "if there is a foreign substance on a bat within 18 inches of the fat end, the bat is illegal and

anyone who uses it at the plate is automatically out" (Paul L. Montgomery, "Yanks Take Suspended Game, Then Lose 2-1," *New York Times*, July 20, 1975).

Just over a month later, new Yankees manager Billy Martin protested that the Angels were using bats with pine tar too far up the handle. Umpire George Maloney denied his protest, saying that he couldn't tell whether the substance was dirt or pine tar. Martin later complained, "The rule says that if a batter gets a hit with an illegal bat, he's automatically out" (*New York Times*, August 23, 1975).

(iii) Gloves

9.3.1 Fielders' Gloves. Gloves are one of a handful of inventions that can be reasonably argued to have had the single most comprehensive effect on every element of the game of baseball. Nonetheless there has been no rush to claim credit for introducing them to the game.

The reason for this is simple: fear of ridicule for violating the ideal of manliness. While many early players must have considered wearing gloves, they were deterred by the possibility of being stigmatized. Those who did wear gloves, rather than advertising the fact, often wore flesh-colored gloves to avoid criticism (A. G. Spalding, *America's National Game*, 476).

Moreover, all indications are that on the rare occasions when gloves were worn in baseball games before the 1870s, those gloves were very thin. One reporter, for example, later claimed: "The greatest helps that any of the old time players could expect were the thin gloves used in cold weather. The protection they afforded was so insignificant as to be hardly worth mention" (Arthur Rockwood, *Idaho Statesman*, August 22, 1914, 6).

Cricket players had been wearing India rubber gloves since the 1830s. They were introduced when bowlers began to throw from shoulder level and were initially "found an impediment and laughed at by older players" (Henry Chadwick, *New York Clipper*, March 20, 1880). Gloves eventually gained acceptance in cricket, but it took much longer in baseball.

An 1855 description of baseball at the Elysian Fields recorded that the players "dress in flannel tights, sandals and gloves, colored all over in harlequin style." But obviously the gloves were a fashion statement, and the players had no idea they would one day be a standard baseball accessory (*Erie Observer*, September 15, 1855, 2).

A 1905 reminiscence described a game played in Boston on May 31, 1858, with a baseball that had a bullet at its center: "Heavy gloves had to be used with such a ball, for bare hands could not hold it and it would twist more fingers and do more injury than the ball of the national game. Gloves had not been seen in play before, neither were gloves used in the national game in old amateur times" (*Boston Journal*, February 22, 1905).

The first baseball player to wear gloves regularly may have been a catcher named Ben Delavergne, around 1860. In 1886, *Sporting News* wrote that "Delavarge [sic], the catcher of the old Knickerbockers, an amateur club of Albany, used gloves when playing behind the bat in the sixties" (*Sporting News*, June 28, 1886; see also *Detroit Free Press*, May 17, 1887).

An 1867 *Detroit Free Press* account of a major tournament being held in Detroit provided an important revelation: "We have noticed in all the matches played thus far that the use of gloves by the players was to some degree a customary practice, which, we think, cannot be too highly condemned, and are of the opinion, that the Custers [of Ionia] would have shown a better score, if there had been less buckskin on their hands" (*Detroit Free Press*, August 15, 1867).

While the *Free Press* seems to imply that players all over the field were wearing gloves, there is little evidence of players other than the catcher and first baseman wearing gloves before the mid-1880s. As had been the case in cricket, there was a close correspondence between the use of gloves and pitchers' release points. As the release points moved higher in the 1870s, the use of gloves gradually caught on among catchers and first basemen. Then when all restrictions were dropped in the 1880s, they quickly became standard at all positions.

As a result, in the early 1870s there are an increasing number of references to catchers and first basemen wearing gloves. Doug Allison, catcher of the Red Stockings of Cincinnati, played in a game on June 28, 1870, with very sore hands. Researcher Darryl Brock alerted me to the note the next day that "Allison caught . . . in a pair of buckskin mittens, to protect his hands" (*Cincinnati Commercial*, June 29, 1870). The following year the *New York Sunday Mercury* replied to a letter writer: "Of course a player may wear gloves if he likes. A half glove covering the palm of the hand and first joints of the fingers is excellent in saving the hand of the catcher and first baseman" (*New York Sunday Mercury*, June 25, 1871; quoted in Jim Charlton, ed., *The Baseball Chronology*).

The stage was set for gloves that not only cushioned the hand but helped make the catch. An 1887 article gave this description: "Al Pratt and Jim White faked up the first pair of catcher's gloves ever worn, and Jim was the first man to wear them. Jim was much younger than he is now, but his hands were sore. He and Pratt dropped into a store on Broadway, New York, and purchased an old-fashioned pair of buckskin gloves. They cut the fingers off the gloves, split them and inserted lacing, until they had a pair of catcher's gloves quite to their liking. If they had had any idea to what extent base ball playing was going to grow, they could have made a ten-strike by getting out a patent on them" (*Pittsburgh Dispatch*; quoted in *Detroit Free Press*, April 28, 1887).

That article did not provide a precise date, but White himself placed these events in 1872, when he was playing for the Forest Citys of Cleveland: "as early as '72, I bought myself a large buckskin glove, put my own padding in it, and stood up behind the batter at the start of an inning as well as when men were on base" (David McCarthy; *Aurora* [Ill.] *Beacon-News*, May 7, 1939). Al Pratt attested that during the 1872 season Deacon White bought a pair of heavy driving gloves and wore one on his left hand (quoted in *Sporting News*, March 23, 1895). While White's glove primarily protected his hand, it paved the way for the revolution that followed, in which the glove actually began to do the catching.

A. G. Spalding claimed that the first player he saw wearing a fielder's glove was Charles Waitt, in 1875. As a result, Waitt is often mistakenly credited with having pioneered the baseball glove. But Spalding's claim is noteworthy because Deacon White was his catcher from 1873 to 1876. It therefore seems reasonable to assume that White had abandoned the glove by the end of the 1872 season and that few others followed his lead.

Another statement by Spalding has attracted far less attention but is probably more important because it suggests that he played a major role in fielder's gloves gaining acceptance. When Spalding switched permanently to first base in 1877, not only did he don a glove but also deliberately chose a black one to make his decision conspicuous. The glove was met with "sympathy" rather than "hilarity," showing that attitudes toward gloves had changed (A. G. Spalding, *America's National*

Game, 476). Probably it is no coincidence that Spalding was starting his sporting goods empire at this time.

9.3.2 Catchers' Mitts.

The catcher's mitt originated in the 1880s, but the particulars are more difficult to disentangle. The biggest complication is that catchers of the 1870s and 1880s were faced with an enormous number of changes in their role. Handling speedier pitching while often standing closer to the plate, catchers were forced to improvise rapidly. As a result, the transition from gloves to mitts was a chaotic one, with the same idea sometimes emerging from independent sources.

As noted in the preceding entry, several players had experimented with gloves in the 1860s, but these gloves offered only minimal cushioning. By the mid-1870s, liberalized delivery rules were leading to much faster pitching and in turn to greater protection for catchers. These comments in the 1876 *DeWitt's Base Ball Guide* also make clear that catchers wore these gloves on both hands: "The catcher will find it advantageous when facing swift pitching to wear tough leather gloves, with the fingers cut off near the joint, as they will prevent him having his hands split and puffed up. If he has the fingers of the glove on he can not retain his hold on the ball so well" (*DeWitt's Base Ball Guide, 1876*, 19).

An 1890 article in the *New York Sun* described how the catcher's mitt gradually began to develop from these early efforts. According to the article, the initial events took place in 1875, but it is more likely that the year was actually 1877. Billy McGunnigle was the catcher for the Fall River Club, and his hands had become very sore. Before a game against Harvard, he went to a glove store and bought a pair of bricklayer's gloves made of thick, hard leather. During preliminary practice he found that he could not throw properly with the gloves on, so he cut off the fingers. It was still awkward to throw the ball with these gloves on, but not impossible. Harvard catcher Jim Tyng borrowed them in the third inning and found them useful. He later bought a pair and increased the protection they afforded by lining them with lead (*New York Sun*, April 27, 1890).

Within the next few years, sporting goods manufacturers began to make gloves specifically designed for catchers, but their efforts were rendered difficult by a fundamental issue: it was necessary to use two hands in order to catch the ball, which meant that equal protection was

needed on both hands. One firm placed an advertisement in 1882 that read: "Our new design, open back, catchers' gloves, made out of very thick buckskin, and padded is the best protection for catchers' hands of anything yet devised. They do not interfere with throwing and no catcher or player subject to sore hands, should be without a pair of these gloves" (quoted in John H. Gruber, "The Gloves," *Sporting News*, December 2, 1915).

Catchers would have been delighted if a glove that could adequately protect the hand without hindering the throwing motion really existed. But the reality was that no glove could do both at once. Chief Zimmer recalled many years later that when he debuted in the majors in 1884, "a mitt similar to the present-day outfielder's glove was in vogue. A hand glove with the fingers cut off was used on the other hand" (Hal Lebovitz, "Zimmer, Oldest Catcher, Leafs Memory Book," *Sporting News*, January 12, 1949). Jim "Deacon" McGuire went further, stating that it was no more than a kid glove and "was really no protection at all" (*Albion Evening Recorder*, August 2, 1932).

And things would get worse before they got better. During the next couple of years, pitchers began to throw overhand with running starts, making the strain on catchers' hands unbearable. Gigantic pitchers like Boston's Jim Whitney threw with such "frightful power" that "he used up both Mike Hines and Mertie Hackett, his backstops," in a single season (*Washington Post*, February 11, 1906). Henry Chadwick later recalled that "the wear and tear upon catchers" became so great that "clubs had to engage a corps of reserve catchers, in order to go through a season's campaign with any degree of success" (*Spalding's Official Base Ball Guide, 1895*, 71).

The beleaguered catchers were willing to try almost anything, with McGuire placing a steak in his glove in 1884 to catch the heavy ball thrown by Toledo pitcher Hank O'Day (Guy M. Smith, "He Could Catch Anything," Typescript in McGuire's Hall of Fame file). Chief Zimmer also claimed to have used beefsteak in his glove (Hal Lebovitz, "Zimmer, Oldest Catcher, Leafs Memory Book," *Sporting News*, January 12, 1949). Others, such as Doc Bushong, padded their gloves with sponges (*San Francisco Examiner*, December 12, 1887). It became "a common thing to see backstops stuffing grass, cotton batting and even strips of meat into the gloves to protect the palms of the hands." While these improvisations eased the pain, they made it harder to snag the ball ("When Ball Players

Wore Neither Gloves Nor Mask," *Miami Herald,* June 3, 1912).

As discussed under "Windups" (**3.1.1**), the situation was so dire by 1886 that it forced two important adjustments. The first was the familiar effort of rule makers to place restrictions on pitchers' deliveries. The more startling development was that some pitchers concluded that too much "pace is useless" and began to put more emphasis on deception than on raw speed.

During these years, however, a new solution emerged as catchers learned to modify their receiving techniques. By 1884 it was recognized that a catcher could "do most of the stopping with his left hand, protected by a thickly padded glove. Such a glove cannot be worn upon the right hand as it renders accurate throwing impossible" (*Detroit Free Press,* May 2, 1884). In response, a Cincinnati firm unveiled "a new catcher's glove that is said to be excellent. The left hand covering is a full one, the right or throwing hand being covered with a half glove to aid throwing. The palm and joint padding is of felt." Another description of what appears to be the same glove reported, "The fingers are stiff cowhide, jointed at the bottom with buckskin. The finger-ends are stout enough to withstand the severest blow, thus preventing the breaking of joints, from which men behind the bat have so long suffered" (*Cleveland Leader,* April 2 and 4, 1884).

As more and more catchers discarded the traditional two-handed catching method for one in which the nonthrowing hand would "bear the brunt of the shock," the search for a way to wear a heavier glove on that hand and a light one on the throwing hand began (*New York Sun,* April 27, 1890). As a result, almost every backstop began to experiment with modifications that would make a padded glove easier to catch with. The sense of urgency helps explain why there are so many nearly simultaneous claimants to having invented the mitt.

It would simplify matters if some of these claims were earlier than others. Indeed, Charley Snyder said he switched from a finger glove to a mitt in 1885, and Connie Mack recalled the big mitt originating in 1885 or 1886 (*Cleveland Press,* reprinted in *Sporting News,* December 26, 1907; Connie Mack, "Memories of When the Game Was Young," *Sporting Life* [monthly], June 1924). Unfortunately both Snyder and Mack gave their accounts many years after the fact, and it seems likely they were mistaken about the exact year. All of the other claims date to 1887 or 1888.

Ted Kennedy's name is cited by several sources. Owney Patton said that the first catcher's mitt was made by Kennedy and worn by Bill Traffley with Des Moines in 1888 (*San Francisco Examiner,* March 28, 1909). Joe Cantillon stated: "All catchers after the '80's had good large catcher's mitts and the first good one was made by Ted Kennedy of Des Moines" (*Minneapolis Journal,* reprinted in *Sporting News,* May 28, 1914; the year cited by Cantillon appears to read 1883 but is difficult to read. Traffley and Kennedy played for Des Moines in 1888).

Jack McCloskey gave this version: "I claim to be the inventor of the original catcher's glove. In 1888, I was catching Red Ehret for the El Paso Club, and used at that time a padded finger glove, called the Sawyer glove, which came from Milwaukee. I improved on that glove, putting a circle of wire around it and filling it with padding. In addition I put a piece of leather on the pocket of the glove.

"In 1887 I met Ted Kennedy, the old pitcher and former glove manufacturer, of St. Louis. I explained the glove to him and he modified it in some respects, which made an improvement, and the glove was afterwards improved by others until the present glove was produced. I think all the credit should go to Kennedy, although the original idea was mine. Of course, many have claimed this honor, but I think that Ted Kennedy and myself were the originators" (*Sporting News,* December 30, 1926).

Another name frequently cited is Joe Gunson. Catcher Sam Trott recalled: "It was Joe Gunson, the catcher of many years ago, who invented the mitt. He made the first one himself and caught with it at Kansas City" (*Sporting Life,* March 26, 1910). Gunson said he first wore one in a Decoration Day doubleheader in 1888 to protect an injured finger. In Gunson's words, fifty years later, "I took the glove I was then wearing—a glove which was something like the kid gloves they wear today—stitched all of the fingers together and made a mitt. Then I fixed up a padding and put it all around the finger ends, sewed a wire in it to help keep its shape, padded the center of the glove with sheepskin and wool and covered the entire mitt with buckskin. The next afternoon I kept my promise to [manager Jimmy] Manning and caught both games" (Charley Scully, "'Father of the Catching Glove' Admits Split Finger Fifty Years Ago, with Twin Bill Ahead, Was 'Mother,'" *Sporting News,* February 23, 1939).

At another point Gunson told a somewhat different version in which he made a few innovations before the doubleheader but then did additional work on the glove afterward: "I stitched together the fingers of my left hand glove, thus practically making a mitt; and then I caught both games. It worked so well that I got to work, took an old paint-pot wire handle, the old flannel belts from our castoff jackets, rolled the cloth around the ends of the finger, and padded the thumb. Then I put sheepskins with the wool on it in the palm and covered it with buckskin, thus completing the mitt" (quoted in Dan Gutman, *Banana Bats and Ding-Dong Balls*, 178).

According to Gunson, the mitt became popular around the league, and he realized that he should patent it. He and Manning decided to produce the mitt jointly, but their plans were delayed when Manning went on a world tour after the 1888 season. By the time Manning returned, Gunson had received a letter from a man in Des Moines—presumably Kennedy—who had designed and patented a mitt identical to Gunson's.

Gunson gave this summary: "I wasn't really interested in making a fortune out of my idea, but I do want the credit for designing and making the original glove. I have in my possession documentary evidence which proves that my glove was made long before any of the gloves designed and patented by others who claimed to have been the original creators of the mitt" (Charley Scully, "'Father of the Catching Glove' Admits Split Finger Fifty Years Ago, with Twin Bill Ahead, Was 'Mother,'" *Sporting News*, February 23, 1939).

This is a strong statement and cannot be entirely reconciled with the other accounts. Gunson did indeed lose the opportunity to profit from his innovation when a patent was awarded on August 8, 1889, to E. Harry Decker. Decker's claims are particularly difficult to assess because he was a habitual thief, forger, and counterfeiter. But he was also a bright and industrious man when he kept to the straight and narrow, and it appears that he came up with the idea for the mitt independently, either before or at about the same time as Kennedy and Gunson (R. M. Larner, "Decker's Glove," *Sporting Life*, May 3, 1890; "Intended for Joke Was Original Mitt," *Fort Wayne Sentinel*, March 2, 1910, 8; Peter Morris, *Catcher*, 189–207).

The use of catcher's mitts had become widespread by the end of the 1888 season, and their impact on the game was immediate. An 1899 article in the *Cincinnati Enquirer* observed that "in the latter part of 1888 came the big glove into use, and from that day began the decline in base running" (*Cincinnati Enquirer*, January 2, 1899).

One of the pioneers was George Myers of Indianapolis, who "caused a general laugh. The fingers were so long and the surface of the glove so broad that Meyers [sic] found it difficult at first to hold a pitched ball." But "after much perseverance he proved that it had merit" ("When Ball Players Wore Neither Gloves Nor Mask," *Miami Herald*, June 3, 1912). Buck Ewing also played an important role in popularizing the mitt. An 1890 article explained: "It is just two years since Buck Ewing created a sensation by wearing an immense glove on his left hand while taking Tim Keefe's hot shot behind the bat at the old Polo grounds. His first appearance with the glove, which looked for all the world like a big boxing glove crushed out flat by a road roller, caused a shout of laughter from the assemblage, but when the game was over Buck declared that his hand was not swollen a particle, and that thereafter nothing could tempt him to relinquish his new guard to his big left hand. All through that season Buck wore the glove, and soon it was recognized as indispensable in the paraphernalia of the big back stop" (*New York Sun*, April 27, 1890).

In addition to its advantages in functionality, Ewing's glove was also visually memorable: "Buck continued to add stuffing to the glove and covering it with patches of new leather. The growth of the glove was closely watched by the fans, who marveled at its expansion. Any rip in it was instantly mended by Buck himself with any kind of leather, so that it sure was one of the most conspicuous things on the ball field, with its patches of all sorts of hide. It really became one of the attractions of the game, and scores of fans, influenced by newspaper comments, went to the game merely to get a look at Buck's glove. Naturally, manufacturers took the hint and began making the big glove" (John H. Gruber, "The Gloves," *Sporting News*, December 2, 1915).

In the next two years, mitts were refined and improved, as is shown by an 1890 article that reported: "One of the best gloves on the market to-day is that called a 'perfect pillow.' It is made of the choicest Plymouth buckskin. A continuous roll or cushion, tightly packed with curled hair, is firmly stitched around the palm, forming a deep hollow, and the thumb of the glove is a sufficient bulwark to make it impossible for a foul tip, fly, or hand-thrown ball to put the human thumb out of joint.

"The 'flexible glove' is made of the choicest buckskin, and is thoroughly padded with chinchilla. The padding extends from the wrist to the finger tips, but there is a break at the roots of the fingers forming a sort of hinge by which the fingers are practically separate from the hand. The right glove is of a lighter grade of buckskin, well padded or not, as the purchaser desires, and fingerless" (*New York Sun*, April 27, 1890). By 1890 the mitt was "worn universally by catchers," with the annual *Spalding's Guide* offering a wide selection of mitts for the catcher's left hand along with throwing gloves for the right hand (R. M. Larner, "Decker's Glove," *Sporting Life*, May 3, 1890).

As noted earlier, a decline in base stealing was attributed to the new mitts, and this was not the only significant change they helped effect. The Knickerbockers' initial rules had specified that a caught foul tip was an out, and the rule had stood ever since, because catching a foul tip with bare hands or kid gloves was a feat that required great skill. That perception changed almost immediately after the introduction of the catcher's mitt. According to John Gruber, "an element of pure luck or ill luck, depending on the viewpoint, guided the whole proceeding," and fans accordingly "growled and grumbled at the injustice of the rule" (John H. Gruber, "Out for Interference," *Sporting News*, February 24, 1916). As a result of this new perspective and the prevalence of fake foul tips (see **11.1.11**), the rule was changed in 1889 and a caught foul tip became simply a strike. Another consequence of the introduction of the mitt was that, as discussed in entry **4.1.3**, the catcher's position came to be almost exclusively played by right-handers.

9.3.3 Snaring Nets.

1920s star Frank Frisch wrote in his 1962 autobiography, "We used to have leather pancakes for gloves. We had to make stops with our hands. Now they have snaring nets they call baseball gloves. The first baseman's glove is like a basketball hoop with a net on it" (Frank Frisch and J. Roy Stockton, *Frank Frisch: The Fordham Flash*; quoted in Dan Daniel, "Fordham Flash Casts Vote for Old-Timers," *Sporting News*, August 4, 1962, 5). Umpire Tim Hurst similarly told the *St. Louis Post-Dispatch*, "It makes me indignant to see a nice, clean grounder smothered by a big glove. Why, it has come to such a pass that the infielder who wears a big glove depends entirely upon his pillow to stop a ball with. None of them ducks do any clean fielding" (*St.*

Louis Post-Dispatch, July 3, 1894). The catch, however, is that Hurst was speaking in 1894. Clearly the history of the glove's evolution from cushion to "snaring net" is a complex and often emotionally charged one.

Until some time in the 1880s, almost all reliable sources agree, most catchers and first basemen were wearing no more than simple finger gloves, and most other fielders were bare-handed. As John Gruber noted, "Before 1880 few fielders even thought of wearing hand-shoes, because nobody could see any advantage in them. On the contrary, there was a prevailing idea that they would prove a handicap, a hindrance to stopping the ball" (John H. Gruber, "The Gloves," *Sporting News*, December 2, 1915). During the next decade, fielders adopted gloves and catchers switched from gloves to mitts. There are different versions of when and how these innovations were introduced and a still wider range of opinion as to whether these changes were improvements or signs of collective madness.

John K. Tener took the latter view, recalling many years later that "in my day they would no more think of wearing a glove than they would of wearing skirts" (*Sporting News*, April 10, 1942). His recollection was that catchers and first basemen wore pads but kept their fingers free, and other fielders remained bare-handed until gloves caught on around 1889. George P. Scannell wrote similarly in 1905 that in the 1870s and 1880s gloves were used mostly by catchers and first basemen. Scannell claimed that it was not until 1889 that Arthur Whitney popularized the use of gloves by other players. He indicated that the practice "jumped into permanent favor" in 1890 (*Sporting Life*, April 1, 1905).

The more common version of events has the padded glove being popularized by Arthur Irwin, who began wearing one after an injury to his hand sidelined him from early July 1885 until August 12. Irwin gave this account: "I started the infielders wearing gloves . . . I reached for a hot one from the bat. Gloves were not known for us in those days. I stopped the ball right, but broke my finger. I had to play later, but my finger was terribly sore. I decided to wear a glove and made one. When I trotted out on the field, I was the object of all sorts of joshing, but it proved a success. I studied the thing out and improved on it. I found even after my finger was better that it helped me. Other players grew curious and I made for them too [sic]. The Spalding and Reach people sent in orders for them too. For four years I made all the gloves they sold. When they started making them I quit" (*Sporting News*, December 9, 1905; see also A. H. Spink, *The National Game*, 228).

An amateur player named C. Wickliffe Throckmorton later recollected, "In the Eighties, when I came north from New Orleans, I thought it was 'sissie' to wear a fielder's glove, but I soon got over that" (letter to the *New York Times*, July 6, 1940). Most other players showed a similar adaptability, though a few holdouts remained.

By the mid-1890s almost all first basemen had switched to "catchers' mitts"—an 1897 article cited Tommy Tucker as the sole one who still wore a "small glove" (*Chicago Inter-Ocean*, July 4, 1897). Other infielders continued to grumble that "gloves made them feel clumsy and foolish," but they had to adapt. As gloves became all but universal, they rapidly increased in size, with the result that they started to make the catch for the fielder ("Modern Ball Hard for Defense," *Bellingham Sunday Herald*, February 27, 1910, 8). The trend climaxed in 1894 when Lave Cross wore a catcher's mitt to play third base. Henry Chadwick denounced this as "making a travesty of skilful infield play" (*Spalding's Official Base Ball Guide, 1895*, 121). Tim Hurst quite accurately predicted, "Why, it will be so after awhile that a player will provide himself with a fan-like contrivance which he will open when he sees a hard grounder coming toward him" (quoted in *St. Louis Post-Dispatch*, July 3, 1894). According to one exaggerated account, his mitt "made it impossible to miss hard brounds [sic] hits or drop a fly ball. Cross raised a laugh at the Polo grounds one day when he reached back with his mitt, caught a high foul and then turned the palm of the glove down without dropping the leather" ("When Ball Players Wore Neither Gloves Nor Mask," *Miami Herald*, June 3, 1912).

This unwelcome development understandably led to a backlash. After the 1894 season several prominent players came out in favor of allowing only catchers and first basemen to wear gloves. The National League enacted a restriction that players at all other positions could not wear gloves that exceeded ten ounces or fourteen inches in circumference. The *St. Louis Post-Dispatch* was pleased that "players can no longer take refuge behind 'pillows,' but are allowed only plain kid or buckskin gloves" (*St. Louis Post-Dispatch*, March 3, 1895). Others felt this was still not enough, and there contin-

ued to be complaints that "One way to bring baseball back to the good old days would be to bar the big mitts from all but the catchers and the first basemen. Outfielders would then have to play the ball properly and not catch flies in a big pillow" (*Boston Globe*, July 5, 1899). But as cynics pointed out, such an action was highly unlikely with highly placed National Leaguers Arthur Irwin, Al Reach, and A. G. Spalding all making healthy profits from the manufacture of mitts (*Milwaukee Journal*, February 13, 1895, 8).

9.3.4   Pitchers Wearing Gloves.

"Last of all to adopt the gloves were the pitchers," remarked a sportswriter in 1910. "It was considered impossible for several years after the gloves came into general use for boxmen to wear them. No one ever thought a pitcher could attend to his duties and at the same time keep a fat mitt upon the other claw" ("Modern Ball Hard for Defense," *Bellingham Sunday Herald*, February 27, 1910, 8). One reason for this was that, as John B. Foster explained, in the early days of baseball, "The pitchers never tried to get the hot ones for fear they would injure their pitching hands" (John B. Foster, "When Baseball Was Young," *Watertown* [N.Y.] *Times*, February 18, 1927).

The identity of the first glove-wearing pitcher is disputed. A 1906 article credited Nig Cuppy, who reached the majors in 1892 (*Sporting News*, November 17, 1906). Cy Young repeated the assertion three years later, adding that "Many base ball critics of the old school rushed into print declaring that the pitcher could not grasp the ball properly because the glove would interfere" (*Cleveland Leader*, quoted in *Sporting Life*, May 15, 1909). But Cuppy wasn't the first. The *New York Sun* remarked in 1888, "[Cannonball] Crane generally has a catcher's glove on his left hand when he pitches" (*New York Sun*, April 14, 1888). And later that year the *St. Louis Post-Dispatch* observed, "[Kid] Gleason, the Philadelphia pitcher, wears a glove on his left hand while pitching" (*St. Louis Post-Dispatch*, September 10, 1888). Meanwhile the 1910 article cited earlier gave the nod to "an almost forgotten minor leaguer" named A. Clyde "Mattie" McVicker.

What is clear is that gloves on pitchers went from being a rare sight to a commonplace one in a short span during the mid-1890s. As late as 1894 it was considered noteworthy that "[Mike] Sullivan and Cuppy of the Clevelands use a glove on the left hand while pitching so as to handle hot grounders with safety" (*St. Louis Post-Dispatch*, September 4, 1894). But by 1896 the practice had become so common that Tim Murnane criticized pitchers like Jack Stivetts who were too stubborn to wear gloves (*Boston Globe*, April 27, 1896). And in the following year, Amos Rusie was described as being one of the few pitchers who didn't wear a glove (*Chicago Inter-Ocean*, August 22, 1897).

9.3.5   Last Gloveless Player.

The last player to take the field in a major league game without a glove was almost certainly a pitcher. Dan Gutman cited Gus Weyhing in 1901. But the following year *Sporting Life* reported, "Pitcher [Joe] Yeager's split hand is due to the fact that he refuses to wear a fielding glove" (*Sporting Life*, August 9, 1902).

The last prominent nonpitchers to reject gloves were Bid McPhee and Jerry Denny. Denny's career ended in 1894, and Bill James described him as the "last position player who did not wear a glove" (Bill James, *The New Bill James Historical Baseball Abstract*, 68). This, however, can't be true since, as James himself noted, Bid McPhee didn't start wearing a glove until 1896 (Bill James, *The New Bill James Historical Baseball Abstract*, 503). Perhaps James meant that Denny was the last player to retire without ever wearing a glove. But this too is incorrect since Pat Flaherty succeeded Denny as Louisville's third baseman and also played without a glove (*St. Louis Post-Dispatch*, July 30, 1894). Flaherty's major league career lasted less than two months, but a 1910 article also remembered him as the last gloveless infielder ("Modern Ball Hard for Defense," *Bellingham Sunday Herald*, February 27, 1910, 8).

Apparently there were gloveless players in the minor leagues well into the twentieth century. A 1909 article implied that there were still some "small leaguers" who didn't wear gloves ("The Great National Game in Dollars and Cents," *Washington Post*, May 9, 1909).

9.3.6   Pockets.

The pocket in gloves developed gradually as a result of numerous modifications. As early as 1898 outfielder Billy Hamilton was advised to "wear a larger mit and one with a pocket in it. Billy is fast, but has a poor grip after a sharp run" (*Boston Globe*, October 1, 1898). But as is shown by the description in entry 9.3.3 of how Lave Cross "raised a laugh" when he "caught a high foul and then turned the palm of the glove down without dropping the leather," pockets of this era were still negligible in size and effectiveness. Pitcher Bill Doak made the big breakthrough in 1919 when he devised the idea of a glove with a pocket between the thumb and index finger that could be adjusted by manipulating the leather laces. Doak sold the idea to Rawlings Sporting Goods, and it became the basis of today's fielder's glove. But, as discussed under "One-handed Catches" (4.4.1), it was still many years before the glove was able to secure the ball reliably without help from the bare hand.

9.3.7   Flexible Heels.

As described in the entry on "One-handed Catches" (4.4.1), the introduction of the flexible heel in 1959 further eased the fielder's task and brought gloves closer to the snaring nets that Frank Frisch derided.

9.3.8   Slot for Index Finger.

William Curran gives this account of the origin of the small slot for the index finger in the back of gloves: "Sometime in the 1950s, Yankees catcher Yogi Berra injured the index finger on his left hand. To spare the tender digit some of the pounding it would take inside the catcher's mitt, Yogi slipped it outside and continued to catch. The finger felt so good out there in the air and sunshine that Yogi did not bother to put it back into the mitt after it had healed. Other American League catchers, sensing that the perennial MVP winner had discovered some arcane method for eliminating passed balls, quickly pulled their fingers from the mitt in imitation." Naturally this created a demand, and it eventually also became standard for fielders' gloves to be made with a special slot for the index finger (William Curran, *Mitts*, 82–83).

9.3.9   Breaking In.

The technique of breaking in a glove must be almost as old as gloves themselves, as the *Milwaukee Journal* reported in 1901: "Jimmie Burke is mourning the loss of his fielding glove. Someone stole it while at the Springs, and Jimmie sort of suspects that it left with the Chicago team. 'I would not care so much,' said Jimmie, 'only I had just got it broke in'" (*Milwaukee Journal*, April 15, 1901).

9.3.10   Six-fingered Gloves.

The six-fingered glove was invented by glovemaker Harry Latina for Ken Boyer. Its best-known user was Ozzie Smith (Vince Staten, *Why Is the Foul Pole Fair?*, 99).

9.3.11 Oversized Catchers' Mitts. Frustrated by his catchers' inability to control Hoyt Wilhelm's knuckleball, on May 27, 1960, Baltimore manager Paul Richards introduced an enormous catcher's mitt. Such mitts were banned after the 1964 season by a rule restricting catchers' mitts to no more than thirty-eight inches in circumference and a maximum distance from top to bottom of fifteen and a half inches.

9.3.12 Gloves Being Left on the Field. Until the 1954 season it was common practice for fielders to leave their gloves on the field while their team batted. The outcome of one pennant race was affected by this custom. On September 28, 1905, the Athletics beat the White Sox 3-2, with Topsy Hartsel scoring the winning run after Harry Davis's line drive deflected off Hartsel's own glove. The Athletics ended up beating Chicago for the pennant by two games (Robert L. Tiemann, "Hartsel Scores on Hit Off Hartsel's Glove," *Baseball Research Journal* 17 [1988], 33).

Researcher Frank Vaccaro noted that the impetus for banning the practice may have been provided by a game between the White Sox and Senators on July 12, 1952. The hometown Senators were behind 1-0 in the fifth when Chicago shortstop Sam Dente tripped over the glove of opposing number Pete Runnells on what would have been the third out. Washington then rallied for two runs and hung on for a 2-1 victory.

In spite of the apparent need to end this practice, researcher Wayne McElreavy reports that news of the ban in November 1953 was not received warmly. American League president Will Harridge threatened to ignore the rule after seven of the league's eight clubs voiced opposition. Casey Stengel complained: "There is no sensible reason for the rule which forces the players to carry their gloves off the field after each half inning. . . . We are trying every which way to speed up games. Now we have a rule which makes for delays. I don't get it. I would like to see the rule repealed" (Dan Daniel, "A. L. Balks Over Rule on Bringing Gloves Off Field," *Sporting News*, March 24, 1954).

The Eastern League notified its clubs not to observe the rule. Other minor leagues discussed following suit, with one even threatening to fine players if they carried their gloves off the field (*Sporting News*, March 24, April 14, 1954). But Commissioner Ford Frick and National Association President George Trautman stood by the new rule, and eventually the uproar died.

(iv) Protective Equipment

The introduction of almost every piece of protective equipment in the nineteenth century was met with resistance. The first and foremost objection was that the new piece of equipment conflicted with the ideal of manliness. A secondary consideration, but a far from trivial one, was the reality that players had to pay for their own garb.

Once a piece of equipment passed these tests, however, the "tipping point" occurred, and generally in little time its usage became universal. Obviously this was first and foremost the result of the natural instinct for self-preservation. It also reflected the enormous incentive that clubs and players had to avoid serious injuries. A club was unlikely to have an adequate replacement available, while the injured player himself was even worse off, as his contract could be terminated with ten days' notice.

9.4.1 Rubber Mouthpieces. The first form of protective equipment was the rubber mouth plate. Before the mask became popular in 1877, the catcher used "to hold in his teeth a large piece of solid rubber for the purpose of protecting them" (*Williamsport Sunday Grit*, June 7, 1891). The device also "covered the lips and provided protection for the teeth. It proved so efficient that all the leading catchers adopted it" ("When Ball Players Wore Neither Gloves Nor Mask," *Miami Herald*, June 3, 1912).

Not everyone agreed with that assessment. Cap Anson later claimed, "This piece of rubber was invented by a chap in Boston. The inventor thought it would resist the force of the blow in case the ball hit the catcher in the mouth." He added, "The rubber was an awkward thing and not a success. Shortly after it was placed on the market I read in the Chicago papers of a lad catching in an amateur team who was almost choked to death with one of those rubbers. A foul caught him full on the rubber and rammed it down his throat" (*Sporting News*, January 23, 1897, 2). James Tyng was just as unimpressed, calling it "a small piece of rubber held between the teeth, and which, if struck by the ball, it was popularly supposed would prevent the disagreeable contingency of being forced to swallow one's teeth" (*Philadelphia Press*, reprinted in the *Cleveland Plain Dealer*, May 12, 1888). According to an 1883 article, the rubber "did not come into general use" (*Grand Rapids* [Mich.] *Morning Democrat*, September 4, 1883).

Nonetheless, with no alternatives quite a few catchers are known to have used the rubber mouthpiece during the mid-1870s (*Jackson Citizen*, August 16, 1875; *Chicago Tribune*, July 26, 1877; *Atlanta Constitution*, February 12, 1893; Jonathan Fraser Light, *The Cultural Encyclopedia of Baseball*, 142). The advent of the mask made the rubber obsolete, and the game's first piece of protective equipment passed out of baseball without fanfare.

9.4.2 Catchers' Masks. The first catcher's mask was designed by Harvard baseball captain Fred Thayer in the mid-1870s. But the identity of the first catcher to don a mask was the subject of lively controversy in the nineteenth century and may never be definitively resolved. The two main claimants both caught for the Harvard nine, only a year apart.

Henry K. Thatcher, a Maine physician, staked his claim in 1896. He explained that the development of the curve led to the protective device: "I used to wear a rubber band over my mouth, but I decided that this was not enough protection for me. When we played our first game in the Spring of 1876, I put on a mask which I had made from heavy wire. The edges were wound with leather, and I had a strap on the chin and another at the forehead. My chum, Fred Thayer, helped me to make it, and I confess it was a queer-looking thing. It was ridiculed the first time I wore the mask, partly because it was a new thing, and partly because the people considered that a catcher did not need any protection for his face. I threw the mask away" (reprinted in A. H. Spink, *The National Game*, 384, who misidentified him as "Howard Thatcher").

James A. Tyng, Thatcher's successor as Harvard's catcher, responded angrily and termed Thatcher a "prevaricator." He gave this version: "The first public appearance of the mask was in the Spring of 1877, not 1876, as he places it. I was at the time a member of the Harvard nine, and Thayer, who was then captain of the nine, wanted me to fill the position of catcher. To this my family were opposed, on account of the danger, and I suggested to him the idea of having a mask made that would protect my face. He followed my suggestion and a wiremaker in Boston made me a mask, which, although heavy and clumsy, compared to the one now in use, answered the purpose for which it was intended, and this mask was worn by me in the three remaining years that I played and caught

on the nine" (reprinted in A. H. Spink, *The National Game*, 385).

Two eyewitnesses give equally contradictory accounts. Warren R. Briggs, a contemporary and acquaintance of both men, favored Thatcher's claim. He wrote that in the early summer of 1875 he was catching for an amateur nine in Boston when he heard rumors "of a face protector or mask that Fred Thayer, captain and third baseman of the Harvard nine, was getting up, and which Thatcher, who was catching for Harvard at that time was to use. Naturally I was interested in the new-fangled protector and went to Thayer's room some time during the Summer or Fall of '75, saw a working model of the device, and, if I remember rightly, made some suggestions concerning it. Soon after this, either in the Fall of 1875 or in the Spring of 1876, I procured one of these masks, of whom I cannot remember, but I think through Thayer, and used it a little during the early games of 1876. I left Boston on the 5th of July, 1876, and came to this city, where I have resided ever since. I brought with me at that time the mask to which I have referred, and have it in my possession today, a relic of the past and, I believe, one of the first things of its kind ever used. Later I saw Tyng using the same thing, but as I left Boston a year before the date he mentions, and as I saw a model of the device some months before in Thayer's room, I do not think there can be any doubt about the accuracy of my statements" (reprinted in A. H. Spink, *The National Game*, 384).

A. G. Spalding addressed the topic in 1911, claiming, "That Dr. Thatcher was *not*, and that James Tyng *was*, the first catcher to wear the mask in a regular game it is quite possible to demonstrate by competent witnesses" (A. G. Spalding, *America's National Game*, 478). As with so many of Spalding's claims, however, his rhetoric outpaced the facts. He offered two pieces of support for his claim. One of these is a letter from George Wright, who indicated that Tyng was the first man whom he saw wearing a mask. Obviously this does not mean that Thatcher did not wear one earlier.

The more substantive piece of evidence is a 1911 letter from Fred Thayer himself. Thayer indicated that Thatcher was the Harvard catcher in 1876 but left school at the year's end. Thayer thought Tyng would be the best man to play the position, but Tyng proved "timid." Accordingly, Thayer designed a mask based upon the fencing mask, and he said that Tyng first wore it against the Live Oaks of Lynn in April 1877 (the entire letter is reprinted in A. G. Spalding, *America's National Game*, 478–479).

There is no way to reconcile such contradictory accounts, making it impossible to be certain whether Thatcher or Tyng first wore the catcher's mask. Nonetheless it seems easier to imagine that Thayer had forgotten and that Tyng had never known about Thatcher's brief experiment with the mask than it is that both Thatcher and Briggs made up or fantasized their accounts.

What is beyond question is that Tyng's use of the mask caused it to become popular, and this happened surprisingly quickly. Reports about the mask were circulating by the end of January, when Henry Chadwick remarked: "The baseball players used to laugh at the idea of cricketers wearing batting pads and gloves, until they faced swift bowling themselves; then they thought better of the idea. Recently defensive articles have been introduced in baseball, Mr. Thayer of the Harvard College Club having invented a steel mask for protecting the face of the catcher of the nine. It is constructed of upright bars about an inch apart, and stands out from the face 3 or 4 inches, being fastened at the top of bottom. It has proved a valuable protection to the face, and is in daily use at the gymnasium" (*New York Clipper*, January 27, 1877). Word spread rapidly, and by March accounts were springing up in far-flung places of the catcher from Harvard who had "invented a brass wire mask for the face" (*Woodstock* [Ont.] *Review*, March 9, 1877).

Reactions were mixed. Tyng recalled that when the mask "made its first appearance on the field it was a subject of ridicule to the 'bleaching board' element, and all such guys as 'mad dog' and 'muzzle 'em' were very frequent whenever I went up behind the bat; while on the part of the opposing players I was subjected to good natured though somewhat derisive pity. For the first year, if I remember rightly, hardly anyone beside myself used the mask, but broken noses and damaged eyes soon brought conviction that catching behind steel bars was preferable to unnecessarily exposing one's features as a target for erratic foul tips, and the general adoption of the mask was the consequence" (*Philadelphia Press*, reprinted in the *Cleveland Plain Dealer*, May 12, 1888). The *Providence Dispatch* sneered at Tyng's mask: "The near future may bring about many other improvements in the equipments of a base ball player, and we shall probably soon behold the spectacle of a player

sculling around the bases with stove funnels on his legs, and boiler irons across his stomach" (*Providence Dispatch*, reprinted in *Boston Globe*, May 19, 1877). Another newspaper added, "There is a great deal of beastly humbug in contrivances to protect men from things which do not happen. There is about as much sense in putting a lightning rod on a catcher as there is a mask" (quoted in Dan Gutman, *Banana Bats and Ding-Dong Balls*, 186).

Henry Chadwick took the opposite position: "Thayer's invention to protect the catcher from dangerous hits in the face when playing close up behind the bat attracted considerable attention. In fact the wire mask is something all catchers who face swift pitching should have. It is light, simple and a sure protection, not in the way in any respect" (*Brooklyn Eagle*, May 19, 1877).

He reiterated this theme in succeeding months, with increasing conviction (*Brooklyn Eagle*, June 15 and August 13, 1877). Even so, in July Louisville's Charley Snyder was reported to have "bought himself a catcher's mask while in Boston, but he hasn't mustered up a sufficient amount of heart of cheek, whichever it may be, to introduce it to a Louisville audience yet" (*Louisville Courier-Journal*, July 6, 1877). Frustrated, Chadwick remarked, "The amateur catchers have wisely adopted this valuable invention, and why the professional catchers do not use it, is a puzzle." He suggested that the solution was that professional catchers "have not, as a class, the moral courage to face the music of the fire of chaff and raillery from the crowd, which the wearing of the mask frequently elicits. Plucky enough to face the dangerous fire of balls from the swift pitcher, they tremble before the remarks of the small boys of the crowd of spectators, and prefer to run the risk of broken cheek bones, dislocated jaws, a smashed nose or blackened eyes, than stand the chaff of the fools in the assemblage" (*Brooklyn Eagle*, August 16, 1877).

The poor catcher of 1877 was in the unenviable position of being accused of not being "plucky or manly" if he wore a mask, but equally likely to be insulted if he shunned the protective device (*New York Clipper*, August 25, 1877). Given those alternatives, it is not surprising that the professionals soon donned masks to avoid adding injury to the inevitable insults.

The first professional to wear the mask may have been Pete Hotaling of the Syracuse Stars, who was still recovering from the effects of being struck in the eye with a foul tip. He acquired his mask by a circuitous route, according to sportswriter P. S. Ryder: "Hotaling was the first player to don a mask. A graduate of Harvard invented the mask and sent it to Homer Ostrander. Homer showed me the new article and I gave it to Hotaling. Peter donned it and afterwards brought it with him to Chicago. He loaned it one day to Cal McVey, the Chicago backstop. When President [William] Hulbert saw the mask he gave orders to McVey to take it off and never wear it again. 'Don't you ever let me see you with that trap on in a game,' was Hulbert's order to McVey" (*Sporting News*, October 30, 1897).

Hotaling began wearing the mask in July 1877. When he wore it during a game in Chicago, bemused reports indicated that it "had never before been seen on the Chicago grounds. The crowd variously named it 'the rat-trap' and 'the bird-cage'" (*Chicago Tribune*, July 20, 1877). On August 8, 1877, Mike Dorgan became the first National League catcher to wear one. Like Hotaling, Dorgan was recovering from an injury and does not appear to have continued wearing the mask.

Scott Hastings was yet another catcher who experimented with the mask after being hit in the face with a foul, but he was uncomfortable with it: "The use of the wire mask he finds bothers his playing, and it has been discarded for the teeth rubber" (*Chicago Tribune*, July 26, 1877). This was not the only complaint about the new device. The *New York Clipper* reported: "This 'mask' is composed of brass wires, and fastened around the head by a strap. It works fairly well, but needs a powerful thrower to use it, as it is apt to jar the head, thereby upsetting the aim of the thrower" (*New York Clipper*, April 14, 1877). In addition, several catchers discovered that a hard foul ball could drive the wires into their face and cut them (Fred W. Lange, *History of Baseball in California and Pacific Coast Leagues, 1847-1938*, 11).

Nonetheless most catchers found these drawbacks preferable to the alternative, and interest in the new invention continued to spread. Soon after designing the mask, Fred Thayer "visited the club room of the Boston nine, then at 39 Eliot street, and spoke to Harry and George Wright and others of the players present about the new invention. Most of them laughed at the idea of a man going around with a cage on his head. Harry, however, always ready and curious enough to look at anything new in base ball, asked Thayer to bring in the affair. The young man accordingly did so, and

stood at one end of the room with it on, allowing the players to throw balls at it, which he easily butted off" (*Grand Rapids* [Mich.] *Morning Democrat*, September 4, 1883).

Thayer received a patent for the mask in 1878 and he arranged to have George Wright's sporting goods firm of Wright & Ditson manufacture it. By the early 1880s the mask had become a standard piece of the catcher's gear and Thayer was using his law degree to defend his patent. Among his successful lawsuits was one against A. G. Spalding and Brothers in 1886 for patent infringement.

Even after the mask became commonplace in the East, it continued to encounter resistance when it made its first appearance in new areas. For example, when Rooney Sweeney introduced the mask to California while playing for Oakland in 1883, he "was 'booed' until he took it off in disgust. Later the fans began to see the benefits of the wire covering and it gradually became popular" (*San Francisco Chronicle*, December 19, 1909, 54).

9.4.3 Billy Goats. In 1976, Dodgers catcher Steve Yeager was standing in the on-deck circle when his teammate's bat shattered and splinters lodged in Yeager's neck. When he returned to action, he introduced the "billy goat" neck guard, which hangs down from the mask to protect the catcher's throat. It soon became popular with major league catchers.

This was not an entirely new concept. Researcher Reed Howard alerted me to an 1887 description of National League umpire Herman Doscher wearing a mask that had "a protection attachment for the throat" (*Sporting Life*, August 31, 1887). In the 1888 *Spalding's Official Base Ball Guide*, A. G. Spalding & Brothers advertised a newly patented neck-protecting mask with a "peculiar shaped extension at the bottom which affords the same protection to the neck as the mask does to the face." The ad claimed that the neck protector "does not interfere in the slightest degree with the free movement of the head." But the fact that it took so long to catch on in the major leagues suggests that the catchers who tried it may have felt otherwise.

9.4.4 Hockey-style Masks. Catchers' masks have of course changed considerably in the years since Thayer modeled one on the fencer's mask. Those alterations have primarily been evolutionary in nature.

Arguably the most radical change to the mask came in 1996 when Blue Jays catcher

Charlie O'Brien donned a hockey-style mask. After attending a Toronto Maple Leafs hockey game, O'Brien became convinced that a goalie's mask would be more effective for catchers. He helped design a prototype based upon the goalie's mask, but designed to offer greater vision and protection. He first wore the hockey-style mask in a major league game on September 13, 1996. The new design caught on quickly, and its greater protection allowed catchers to shed the "billy goat" neck guards.

9.4.5 Chest Protectors. Sportswriter William Rankin wrote in 1910, "During the summer of 1876 Denny Clare, now a Brooklyn politician and known as one of the cleverest domino players in the country, wore a padded vest, from which, I believe, the chest protector had its origin" (*Sporting News*, February 3, 1910).

The description suggests that Clare probably wore his vest under his uniform, as was the case with one worn by Charley Bennett of Detroit in 1883. Bennett later explained that his wife was concerned about his health, so with his help she created a "crude but very substantial shield . . . by sewing strips of cork of a good thickness in between heavy bedticking material." When Bennett tried it out, it proved so effective that he allowed pitches to hit him square in the chest and "rebound back almost to the pitcher" without experiencing "the slightest jar" (Maclean Kennedy, "Greatest Backstop of Them All Was the Detroit Boy, Charley Bennett," *Detroit Free Press*, March 30, 1913; Maclean Kennedy, "Charley Bennett, Former Detroit Catcher, Inventor of Chest Pad," *Detroit Free Press*, August 2, 1914; *Leslie's Illustrated Weekly* printed a similar article on October 15, 1914, which is quoted in Vince Staten, *Why Is the Foul Pole Fair?*, 263).

Lee Allen reported in 1968 finding an article crediting Bennett with pioneering the chest protector but wisely cautioned that "the exact year was not given, so it is impossible to say that Bennett's contribution was a 'first,' a very dangerous word to employ in writing baseball history" (*Sporting News*, April 6, 1968; reprinted in Lee Allen, *Cooperstown Corner*). Fortunately the increased availability of microfilm now makes it possible to date Bennett's contribution with greater precision. At the start of the 1883 season, the *Detroit Free Press* commented: "A heavy cork pad protects Bennett's chest from foul tips this season" (*Detroit Free Press*, May 1, 1883). A couple of weeks later another Michigan newspaper remarked on the

"heavy cork chest-protectors" being worn by catchers (*Lapeer Democrat*, May 16, 1883). Catcher Phil Baker was also reported to have used a chest protector in 1883 (*Cincinnati Enquirer*, June 8, 1884).

Use of such devices became far more widespread during the following season with the introduction of the first commercially marketed chest protector. A product of the fertile mind of Hartford inventor William Gray, who would later invent the pay phone, the Gray's Patent Body Protector used the same principle as the pneumatic bicycle tire to shield the catcher's entire chest and groin area with an inflatable pad (*Hartford Courant*, January 26, 1903). The protector passed every test, including one in which Jim O'Rourke of Buffalo "donned the shield and allowed himself to be pounded with fists and clubs, players also jumped on him, and the test was completed by [Jim] White standing ten feet away and throwing the ball against the chest-protector with all his force, and O'Rourke did not feel the slightest shock" (*National Police Gazette*, April 19, 1884).

Gray's chest protectors also attracted comment for their unusual appearance: "[Ed] McKenna, the catcher of the Nationals, wore in yesterday's game the first body-protector ever used in a championship game in this city. It is made of rubber cloth and inflated with air. He looked like a knight of old equipped in armor for a battle when he donned his mask and other trappings" (*Cincinnati Enquirer*, May 29, 1884). Rudolph Kemmler was said to look "like a back-stop when he wears the body protector," which may be how the catcher came to be referred to as the backstop (*Columbus* [Ohio] *Dispatch*, May 21, 1884). Another game account noted, "[Harry] Decker appeared yesterday with a contrivance that likened him to a muffin-maker. (Not that he did any muffing, however.) It is a breast protector of the latest improvement and saves a catcher many hard knocks" (*Evansville Journal*, August 3, 1884).

While these descriptions suggest bemusement, there seems to have been little of the resistance that usually met new kinds of protective equipment. By June, *Sporting Life* reported that many catchers were now using chest protectors (*Sporting Life*, June 10, 1884). The following month a correspondent commented, "The chest protector is coming into general use. It is as necessary as the mask" (*Sporting Life*, July 23, 1884).

As with the catcher's mask, the *Brooklyn Eagle* offered a staunch defense of the chest protector: "the catcher who refuses to wear such a protector from severe injuries simply because 'it looks so queer,' or because a lot of fools in the crowd laugh at him, is no better than the idiots who quiz him" (*Brooklyn Eagle*, June 1, 1884). The support was echoed by *Sporting Life*: "The usefulness of the Rubber Body Protector was fully illustrated in a recent game in Hartford. . . . The usefulness of the Body Protectors have [sic] become an established fact, and the sooner all catchers adopt them the sooner we shall see more confidence displayed in them" (*Sporting Life*, July 30, 1884).

By the end of the 1884 season it was catchers who *didn't* wear the new gear who were being mocked. One game account reported that rookie New York catcher Henry Oxley must have arrived from the "Green Mountains" because he wore neither a mask nor a chest protector. Oxley saw "the catcher of the other club strapping on a chest protector, so he asked him what he was doing that for." He then put it on, but wore it without blowing it up until another player took pity on him and explained that it had to be inflated to offer protection (*St. Louis Post-Dispatch*, August 23, 1884).

It wasn't long before other possible uses were noticed. A want ad after the season read: "Wanted, a base ball catcher's body protector till April 1, '85 for polo playing. If any damage is done will fully repay" (*Sporting Life*, February 4, 1885). This was no small consideration in the days when players paid for their own equipment.

Curiously, an 1890 article gave this account: "The catcher's breast-protector, or the 'sheepskin,' as it is often contemptuously referred to, is neither neat nor gaudy, but, like a trick mule in a kicking match, it gets there just the same. This most useful piece of the base-ball paraphernalia had a hard time getting a foothold. The catchers were slow in adopting it, and the spectators at first guyed as baby-play. [Jack] Clements, the great catcher of the Philadelphia League team, was the first to wear a catcher's protector in a game before a Cincinnati crowd. He was then back-stopping Jersey Bakely with the Keystone Unions, at Philadelphia, in 1884. Considerable fun was made of the protector, and the writer distinctly remembers that it was made the subject of adverse newspaper comment by one of the best base-ball authorities in America. Now it is different" (*Sporting News*, November 1, 1890).

This description sounds credible, yet contemporary articles give little indication of such ridicule. Perhaps the truth lies somewhere in between. It should also be noted that this article's claim that Jack Clements was the first to wear a chest protector in Cincinnati is contradicted by the *Cincinnati Enquirer* of May 29, 1884, which gave the distinction to Ed McKenna.

In any event, by 1890 the chest protector had become established. In succeeding years the inflatable rubber vests gave way to leather and canvas protectors filled first with cotton felt, then with kapok, and eventually with foam. Each of these changes was designed to improve the catcher's range of motion. They were also redesigned in the early twentieth century to provide greater protection for the shoulders and collarbone ("Baseball Inventions," *Boston Globe*, April 24, 1904, 24).

9.4.6   Shin Guards. New York Giants catcher Roger Bresnahan is generally credited with introducing them to baseball in 1907. As with so many claimed firsts, a closer look reveals a somewhat different picture, though Bresnahan unquestionably played a major role.

Shin pads began being used by cricket batsmen in the 1830s as a direct result of the introduction of over-the-top bowling deliveries. They were more necessary in that sport because of the batsman's need to protect the wicket, whereas "in base ball there is no need of leg guards or pads for the batsmen, as they can jump aside and avoid balls likely to hit them" (*Brooklyn Eagle*, August 16, 1877). By 1893 shin pads were being worn by hockey players and soon became common in that sport (Michael McKinley, *Putting a Roof on Winter*, 33). At least some football players were also using shin guards in the nineteenth century (Robert W. Peterson, *Pigskin*, 19).

Their use in nineteenth-century baseball, however, was sporadic. Tim Murnane claimed that in 1871 the King Philip club of East Abington, Massachusetts, had a young pitcher "named 'Ferd' Thompson, who wore high-legged boots with his trousers tucked inside, and I believe was the first man to wear any protection on his shins" (*Boston Globe*, January 17, 1915). Frederick K. Stearns later claimed that in the 1870s Frank Bliss always caught "with his trousers tucked in long boots" (*Michigan Alumnus*, November 2, 1922). It seems likely that these boots were intended to act as shin guards. Researcher David Arcidiacono discovered an intriguing 1888 ad that advised, "They can't spike you if you use Rawlings' Leg Guards . . . Prevents Spiking, Prevents Bruising, Prevents

Breaking. To be worn under or over the stocking" (*Sporting News*, June 16, 1888, 8). It is said that nineteenth-century black pioneers Frank Grant and Bud Fowler wore primitive shin guards because they were spiked so often by vindictive white players. (See Ned Williamson's comments under "Feet-first Slides" [5.2.2] for details.) A 1930s newspaper article stated that Morgan Murphy briefly wore shin guards in the early 1890s. He was catching for Cincinnati at the time and "was spiked, but he was needed so badly that a light temporary shin guard was arranged to wear under the stocking of his left leg" (Harry A. Williams, *Los Angeles Times*, February 28, 1932).

Infielder Harry Steinfeldt, who went on to fame as the fourth member of the Chicago Cubs' Tinker-to-Evers-to-Chance infield, began wearing shin guards in 1897 (*Cleveland Plain Dealer*, August 6, 1897). By the time of his major league debut the following spring, he was already being "advertised as a hard thrower, who stopped the ball with his shins, which were covered with pads, and then relied upon his strong arm to do the rest. But this was a dainty notion. He is a clean fielder and does not wear the pads for the purpose stated, but as a protection against the sharp spikes of that class of player who delight in cutting up a rival's shins, and he has suffered that unfortunate experience. After his recovery he secured whalebone shin pads that cannot be penetrated by spikes" (Arthur Titcomb, syndicated column, *North Adams Transcript*, May 2, 1898). Another sportswriter described Steinfeldt's shin pads as being "of the regulation cricket variety. They extend from just above the shoe tops to the knee, and in no way interfere with the movements of the legs. They are worn under the stockings and are not noticeable unless special attention is drawn to them. Besides being a protection against hard hit balls that manage to elude the hands, they afford excellent protection from spikes" (Unidentified clipping, Chadwick Scrapbooks).

As is suggested by the statement that the shin guards did not obstruct Steinfeldt's movements, a major problem was that such devices typically impeded running. John B. Foster recalled many years later that the catcher on his amateur team in the 1880s wore rubber boots with cotton batten in them, but found that he could barely move (*Sporting News*, January 31, 1935).

By the early twentieth century new types of shin guards were earning trials. According to researcher Dan Hotaling, early-twentieth-century catcher Mike Kahoe told his family he had been the first player to wear shin guards. Kahoe's obituary in *Sporting News* stated: "Roger Bresnahan's claim that he was the first catcher in the majors to wear shinguards was always disputed by Kahoe. It was asserted that Kahoe, while with the Cubs in 1902, donned the protection when struck on the leg by a pitched ball. A British cricket player and sporting goods salesman suggested the catcher try on a pair of shinguards used in cricket, which he did. However, he did not use them regularly until later. Bresnahan is credited with having introduced the shinguards to the majors in 1907" (Frederick Ivor-Campbell, "When Was the First? [Continued]," *Nineteenth Century Notes* 95:1, [Winter 1995], 1; *Sporting News*, May 25, 1949). But no contemporary documentation of Kahoe's contention has been found. Instead, when shin guards began to catch on in 1907, Kahoe was quoted at length on the new equipment and made no mention that he had ever worn them before (*Washington Post*, June 17, 1907).

There is clear evidence that shin guards were being used in the major leagues by 1904. Columnist A. R. Cratty wrote in that year that Boston catcher Tom Needham "earned fame over the circuit for getting his man at the rubber. He stood right there and defied spikes. As a result, the youth was laid up a number of times. The Reds gave it to him once in their tour. The sore had to be scraped day after day for two weeks. Then Needham was forced to go to Philadelphia, where a metal shin guard was made for him. George Wright, the veteran, made the protection and declared that this was the first time he had produced anything of that kind for a base ball player" (*Sporting Life*, October 15, 1904).

Other similar experiments followed. In 1905 Billy Sullivan was "considering adopting shin guards as a protection from the eels [spit balls]. He got two nasty blows on the shin, the second one making him dance merrily for a time" (*Chicago Tribune*, May 1, 1905). Nig Clarke later claimed that "in 1905, while with Cleveland, he took to wearing the brand of shin guards which are used in football. However, these did not seem to cover enough territory, and late that season he switched to the cricket shin guards, which provide protection for the knees as well as the front of the lower leg." Clarke showed sportswriter Harry A. Williams a photo to support his contention (*Los Angeles Times*, May 10, 1915).

Lee Allen noted that Red Dooin made this claim to having inspired Bresnahan: "I had a special type made, substituting papier-mâché for rattan to make them lighter. One day Bresnahan crashed into me at the plate and somehow came in contact with my legs. 'What have you got on under your stockings?' he asked. I told him they were shinguards." Dooin kept these shin guards on while batting (Lee Allen, *The Hot Stove League*, 96).

Obviously Roger Bresnahan did not invent shin guards, nor was he the first to wear them in a major league game. But neither did he claim to have invented this form of protective equipment. What Bresnahan did was to play a crucial role in popularizing them by showing that it was practical to run while wearing them.

He did so when he strapped shin guards over his pants in the Giants' opening day game on April 11, 1907. The *New York Times* remarked: "Bresnahan created somewhat of a sensation when he appeared behind the bat for the start of play, by donning cricket leg guards. . . . The white shields were rather picturesque, in spite of their clumsiness, and the spectators rather fancied the innovation. They howled with delight when a foul tip in the fourth inning rapped the protectors sharply" (*New York Times*, April 12, 1907).

The reception around the league was mixed. The *New York Sun* sniffed, "The latest protection for catchers looks rather clumsy, besides delaying a game while the guards are strapped above the knee and around the ankle, and it is doubtful if the fad will ever become popular" (quoted in Paul Dickson, *Baseball's Greatest Quotations*, 20). Pittsburgh owner Barney Dreyfuss campaigned to have them banned but garnered little support. The general feeling seems to have been that the day had passed when manliness could be deemed more important than safety. One reporter commented that there was now "no chance for any such interference with a player's right to wear what protection he pleases, provided it is not injurious to other players" (*Washington Post*, May 16, 1907).

Giants manager John McGraw had to overcome his initial misgivings, as Bresnahan explained: "McGraw thought they would interfere with my running, and looked askance at them at the beginning of the year, but he has changed his mind. . . . Last year my legs were bruised from the knees down, and part of the time it was all that I could do to walk after a game. That interfered with my running a great

deal more than the shin guards possibly can interfere" (*Washington Post*, May 12, 1907).

The reaction of rival catchers was aptly summarized by Cubs receiver Johnny Kling, who said he would follow Bresnahan's lead "as soon as I can muster up nerve enough." He explained, "The roasting the rooters gave Bresnahan during the New York series here has taken away my nerve and I cannot muster up courage enough to wear them at home. I guess I will try them away from home first and then it won't be too bad" (*Washington Post*, June 17, 1907). Bresnahan confirmed that at first he got an "awful razzing. . . . Fans called me everything from 'Sissie' to 'Cream Puff.' But it wasn't long before all catchers were using them" (*Sporting News*, May 9, 1936).

As shin guards became common, descriptions of them usually included references to Bresnahan. William J. Hennessey, writing about the Connecticut League in 1909, observed, "Shinguards, a-la-Bresnahan, is [sic] the vogue this season. Last year Beaumont was the only backstop to don the leg armor and the idea was looked upon as a novelty, but the value of them is becoming more apparent each season" (*Sporting News*, April 29, 1909).

As acceptance of the use of shin guards by catchers grew, a number of variants were attempted. Cleveland catcher Nig Clarke, for instance, wore thin pads that "do not interfere with his running, so he does not have to discard them when he is not behind the bat" (*Washington Post*, August 9, 1907). Detroit's Charley Schmidt donned "an elaborate suit of armor on his left leg . . . concealed under his uniform. Its sole purpose is to protect him from the spikes of runners whom he is blocking off, and it does him no good in case of wild pitches or foul tips. Some of the third basemen follow the Schmidt system to greater or less extent" (*Detroit Free Press*, April 30, 1910).

As this last comment suggests, other fielders were also experimenting with shin guards. At the outset of the 1908 season it was reported that "shin guards are to be worn by [second baseman Harry] Niles and [shortstop Kid] Elberfeld, according to the latest edict of the Yankee commander. The kind selected are not as bulky as those worn by Roger Bresnahan" (*Sporting Life*, April 4, 1908). For greater mobility, each player wore only one shin guard: "Elberfeld and Niles, of the Highlanders, wear shin guards to protect their legs from the base runners' spikes. Elberfeld wears his on the right leg and Niles has his on the left" (*Sporting Life*,

May 2, 1908). Unfortunately Elberfeld was injured later that week when a runner slid into his unprotected left leg, and the experiment was discontinued.

A few pitchers even joined the trend. In 1910 a Houston pitcher named Merrill "trotted out to the slab wearing one guard on his right leg. It was one of the short guards, such as were made popular by Nig Clarke, with no loose extensions to come above and to protect the knee cap" (*Detroit Free Press*, April 30, 1910). Tim Murnane reported in 1915 that several pitchers were sporting shin guards (*Boston Globe*, January 17, 1915).

9.4.7 Knee Caps.
Knee caps began to appear at about the same time as shin guards and appear to have been a direct borrowing from football. A 1906 note observed: "Catcher [Howard] Wakefield, of Cleveland, has purchased a pair of foot ball knee caps and will wear them this coming season. He claims they will protect his knees when catching" (*Sporting Life*, March 24, 1906).

9.4.8 Knee Savers.
The Knee Saver is the name of the foam pads that today's catchers strap on behind their shin guards. The device was introduced by AliMed in 1997 to support the knees and reduce strain while crouching.

9.4.9 Batting Helmets.
Many years after the fact, a man named C. Wickliffe Throckmorton claimed that in the late 1880s "a player from the New York A. C. was hit in the head by a pitched ball. Shortly afterward he appeared on the field wearing a helmet. He was laughed at and gave up the idea" (letter to the *New York Times*, August 28, 1937). This would be one of the earliest instances of what would become an extraordinarily fierce resistance to head protectors.

In the same season that Roger Bresnahan introduced shin guards, he was hit in the head with a pitch in a game on June 18, 1907. While hospitalized he decided to use a primitive helmet known as the Head Protector, invented in 1905 by Frank Mogridge and marketed by the A. J. Reach Company (Dan Gutman, *Banana Bats and Ding-Dong Balls*, 211). Sportswriter J. Ed Grillo commented, "If Bresnahan continues his policy of protecting himself against injury with all sorts of devices, it will require a small express wagon to drag his pharphernalia [sic] to and from the grounds before and after each game" (*Washington Post*, July 11, 1907).

Bresnahan's experiment was short-lived as were several others in succeeding years. Freddy Parent donned a pneumatic head protector after two 1907 beanings, but he stopped wearing it the following spring (Dan Desrochers, "Alfred L. 'Freddy' Parent," in David Jones, ed., *Deadball Stars of the American League*, 416; *Sporting Life*, April 25, 1908). Frank Chance donned protective headgear in 1913, but it was little more than a sponge wrapped in a bandage (Gerard S. Petrone, *When Baseball Was Young*, 84). In 1914 Utica pitcher Joe Bosk was wearing "a headgear with a pad on one side as a protection while he is batting. Bosk was a victim of a bean-ball in 1911, and he doesn't want to run any chances of having the same thing happen again" (*Toronto Globe*, April 27, 1914). Three years later Phillies manager Pat Moran "adopted the new cork-cushioned caps for his ball players, believing them a fine thing to minimize injuries from bean balls. If they prove satisfactory it is likely other clubs will take the idea" (*Sporting Life*, April 7, 1917).

The fatal beaning of Cleveland's Ray Chapman in 1920 brought calls for protective headgear. During spring training the following season, the Indians experimented with leather helmets similar to the ones then being used by football players. But the players found them uncomfortable, and the effort was abandoned.

At some point Negro Leaguer Willie Wells wore a modified construction worker's hard hat following a beaning. John Holway reported that this happened in 1925 (John Holway, "Willie Wells," *Baseball Research Journal* 17 [1988], 52). Other sources, however, list the date as July 4, 1940, or as sometime in 1942. Researcher Larry Lester appears to have pinpointed the events as actually occurring in 1937 and cites an August 26, 1937, account in the *New York Age*. Lester reports that Wells was expected to miss the rest of the season after being beaned by Ray Brown, but instead he made an amazing recovery and soon returned to the field with the hard hat.

The subject gained additional attention from the near-fatal beaning that same year of Mickey Cochrane of the Detroit Tigers. Clark Griffith tried to convince his Washington players to wear helmets but "the players, after taking a look at the lop-sided caps, vowed they wouldn't wear the dizzy-looking things. They'd rather get hit in the heads, they said" (Shirley Povich, *Washington Post*, August 1, 1937). Modifications to the helmet did nothing to lessen their opposition: "Most players argue against the helmets that have been suggested for them. They say such headgear would be too heavy or cumbersome, might make it more difficult for them to see or would not really protect all the vital spots. The real reason is that baseball resists a change and the old Oriole tradition that a player should show no fear, just as he should try to conceal an injury, still holds on" (Hugh Bradley, *New York Evening Post*, reprinted in *Sporting News*, May 2, 1938).

Several serious beanings in 1940, especially one suffered by Brooklyn's Joe Medwick, brought renewed attention to the issue. An advertisement for a batting helmet with earflaps appeared in *Sporting News* on July 4, 1940 (page 8). Larry MacPhail began to look into the issue and he insisted that all players in the Brooklyn organization wear some kind of head protection in 1941, though he gave them a choice about what type of headgear they wore.

Ford Frick had designed a full-fledged helmet, but the Dodgers' players found it uncomfortable. Instead they chose a design created by two Johns Hopkins surgeons, Dr. George E. Bennett and Dr. Walter Dandy. Their creation, which became known as the "Brooklyn safety cap," was described as follows: "Zippered pockets are cut in each side of a regulation baseball cap. Into one of these pockets on the side he faces the pitcher, the batter will slip a plastic plate which is about a quarter of an inch thick and little more than an ounce in weight. The plate, about the width and length of a man's hand, covers the vulnerable area from the temple to about an inch behind the ear" (*Chicago Tribune*, March 9, 1941).

The Washington Senators also required players to wear protective headgear, and the press hailed the clubs for breaking "a stubborn Big League stand against this sensible protection" (Bob Considine, *Washington Post*, May 15, 1941). By this time several minor leagues were starting to mandate that players wear helmets as well. Nonetheless major leaguers continued to resist such headgear, and they again fell into disuse.

Branch Rickey brought helmets back with the Pirates in 1952, and required his players to wear them in 1953. The plastic caps, made by Rickey's own company, elicited the usual backlash from fans and players. Joe Garagiola recalled, "It was awful. You see, we wore them all the time, not just at bat. And in the bullpen, the kids would be bouncing marbles off our helmets all day long. The fans called us coalminers, and the things were really heavy to wear" (quoted in Mike Sowell, *The Pitch That Killed*, 289). Meanwhile "rival players thought those helmets were really funny and made such knee-slapping remarks as: 'Where's the polo match?'" (Bob Addie, *Washington Post*, May 5, 1960).

This time the batting helmets finally gained acceptance, though the Pirates soon began wearing them only while batting. By 1958 both major leagues required players to wear either helmets or plastic liners inside their caps. As Fred Hatfield later recalled, "Some of us used to kid guys in helmets by saying they looked ready to play football. If you played before the rule came in, you didn't have to wear one. I never wore one. I had to have something, so all the time I had this little plastic liner inside my baseball cap, on the sides of my head" (quoted in Danny Peary, *We Played the Game*, 278).

Hatfield and his peers gradually gave way to a generation of players who had grown up wearing helmets and had no such qualms. By 1971 all batters were required to wear one.

9.4.10   Earflaps.

Helmets with earflaps began in Little League and, as with regular helmets, encountered considerable resistance when first worn by adults. Sportswriter Bob Addie reported in 1960, "The 'earmuff' or Little League helmet made its major league debut last night when Jim Lemon became the first major leaguer to wear the new type protective helmet." The sight of a major leaguer wearing a Little Leaguer's equipment provoked "much merriment." Other players bolstered their opposition to the innovation by contending that "the new helmet doesn't give complete vision" (Bob Addie, *Washington Post*, May 3 and 5, 1960). But the new helmets steadily gained popularity and in 1974 were made mandatory in the major leagues.

9.4.11   Batters' Shin Guards and Shields.

A. G. Spalding's sporting goods firm was offering shoe plates and pitcher's toe plates in the 1880s, but the intention was to protect the shoe rather than the wearer (Dan Gutman, *Banana Bats and Ding-Dong Balls*, 224–225). As noted in the entry on shin guards (see **9.4.6**), turn-of-the-century catchers Red Dooin and Nig Clarke wore light shin guards that they did not have to take off between innings. The custom of batters trying to protect themselves from fouling balls off their shins is of much later vintage.

The first batter regularly to wear a shin guard to protect himself against foul balls appears to have been Vic Wertz, who reportedly began wearing "a fiber shin guard when batting" in 1952 (Louis Effrat, *New York Times*, September 30, 1954). Wertz is best remembered for hitting the ball in the first game of the 1954 World Series on which Willie Mays made a spectacular running catch. What is forgotten is that Wertz's shin guard also played a key role in the game, and that afterward he was more frustrated about that than by Mays's catch.

Wertz led off the sixth with a single, one of his four hits in the game. An outfielder's throw behind him got away and Wertz could have advanced to third except for his shin guard: "When he returned to first and kicked the bag, he inadvertently opened the clasp of the guard. This flapping fiber, which weighs approximately a pound, hampered his running and he elected to remain at second" (Louis Effrat, *New York Times*, September 30, 1954). He was stranded there, setting the stage for the Giants to win in extra innings on Dusty Rhodes's home run. After the game Wertz complained, "I've worn that thing all season and I have my first trouble with it in the World Series" (AP: *Los Angeles Times*, September 30, 1954).

These protective devices played a more positive role in the following year's World Series when the Yankees' Joe Collins hit two home runs in the opening game while wearing a shin guard (Red Smith, September 29, 1955, reprinted in *Red Smith on Baseball*). Collins had begun wearing a "leather and sponge-rubber covered metal guard" after fouling a ball off his ankle in June that led to phlebitis. Sportswriter Joseph M. Sheehan explained, "Self-inflicted foul injuries are not uncommon in baseball. But, except to a few unfortunate players, like Collins and Cleveland's Vic Wertz, they happen only once in a blue moon. Wertz . . . has worn a guard on his right leg for several years. Collins joined Vic in this practice a couple of weeks ago. If Joe has anything to say about it, the guard will be standard equipment for him from now on" (Joseph M. Sheehan, *New York Times*, September 10, 1955).

Since shin guards could pose an obstacle while running, by the 1960s some batters were opting for guards that protected only the feet. *Sporting News* reported in 1965 that Al Kaline was wearing a specially designed shoe with a toe guard on his left foot to protect him against foul balls (*Sporting News*, March 13, 1965).

9.4.12 Sliding Pads. Henry Fabian claimed many years later that he had introduced the

sliding pad while playing for New Orleans in 1883. His sister had made it for him, which caused his teammates to tease him that he had simply borrowed her bustle (*Sporting News*, February 15, 1934).

In 1886, Sam Morton took out a patent on a sliding pad that protected the side and hip. The *St. Louis Post-Dispatch* observed, "Those players of the Browns who have sliding proclivities will have the danger of an injury averted the coming season by the use of the Morton patent sliding pad" (*St. Louis Post-Dispatch*, March 13, 1886). The device encouraged more daring slides, and hook-slide popularizer Mike Kelly (see **5.2.3**) gave "Sam Morton's sliding-pad his hearty indorsement. This little invention is to enable runners to steal bases without injury to their cuticle" (*Sporting News*, March 17, 1886).

In 1899, Fred Clarke introduced a "new style of sliding pads. The new pads are adjustable affairs, and are separate from the pants. The old style, which were sewed to the pants, were not suitable because they became stiff and hard from usage and washing" (*Sporting Life*, April 21, 1899). He continued to modify it and finally patented it in 1912 (Dan Gutman, *Banana Bats and Ding-Dong Balls*, 230).

Despite improvements, many felt that sliding pads were more of a liability than an asset. Old-time ballplayer Dasher Troy explained in 1915, "A player does not have to slide often, but if he wears pads he has to carry them around all through the game. They interfere with free motion and are a hindrance to him in every way. With practice he can do without pads quite as well and with little risk" (John [Dasher] Troy, "Reminiscences of an Old-Timer," *Baseball Magazine*, June 1915, 94).

9.4.13 Sliding Gloves. At about the same time, a few base runners began wearing gloves while running the bases. When Ed Andrews and Jim Fogarty of Philadelphia reached base during the 1886 season, they would don "a huge pair of buckskin gloves" to protect them during their headlong "air dives" that became known as the "Philadelphia patent" slide (*St. Louis Post-Dispatch*, May 31, 1886).

9.4.14 Jockstraps. Jockstraps were being advertised by the sporting goods stores by the 1880s (Dan Gutman, *Banana Bats and Ding-Dong Balls*, 227). The identity of the first baseball player to wear one is unknown, and perhaps that's just as well.

(v) Miscellaneous Equipment

9.5.1 Bat Bags. Bat bags have been a part of baseball since at least 1875, when one was mentioned in a game account (*Cincinnati Enquirer*, September 8, 1875).

9.5.2 Doughnuts. Elston Howard was responsible for pioneering the use of the weighted doughnut on bats, which was originally known as "Elston Howard's On-Deck Bat Weight." According to Howard's widow, the device was invented by a New Jersey construction worker named Frank Hamilton, who showed up at Howard's door around 1967 looking for someone inside baseball to help him market them. Howard became an enthusiastic proponent of the doughnut, explaining, "Instead of swinging two or three assorted bats like warclubs, you swing your own bat with the added weight. It slips right off when you go up to the plate and then your own bat feels as light as a toothpick" (Arlene Howard with Ralph Wimbish, *Elston and Me*, 153–154).

9.5.3 Batting Gloves. In 1901 sportswriter John B. Foster described Hugh Jennings's proclivity for being hit by pitches. Foster observed, "Hughey Jennings had lots of fun flirting that big glove of his into the ball, and many and many a time he was made a present to first when he was no more entitled to it than the Kohinoor [a very valuable diamond]" (*Sporting Life*, April 6, 1901). This certainly seems to indicate that Jennings wore some form of glove while batting, but I have found no other confirmation of this.

Batting gloves can next be documented to have appeared on a major league baseball diamond in 1932, when *Sporting News*'s Brooklyn correspondent informed readers that local players "Johnny Frederick and Lefty O'Doul have introduced something new in the way of shock absorbers for their hands when at bat. When Frederick is about to take his turn at the plate, he bandages his left thumb with the same sort of material that is used to stuff shoulder pads worn by football players. O'Doul wears an ordinary street glove when he's facing the pitcher. Injuries led the two Brooklyn players to introduce the new-fangled devices and they contend their methods are better than the ordinary sponge usually held onto the handle of the bat with strips of adhesive tape. Frederick . . . injured his thumb late in the season of 1930 . . . and as the injury seems a permanent one, Johnny probably will employ the shock absorber all the time. O'Doul, however, will discard the glove as soon as his right wrist, injured when struck by a pitched ball in the training campaign, entirely mends" (*Sporting News*, May 12, 1932).

That year Frederick hit six pinch-hit home runs, doubling the previous best and establishing a major league record that still stands. Nonetheless batting gloves disappeared from baseball for many years. Bobby Thomson was given one by a golf pro in 1949, and they were occasionally used in batting practice and spring training during the 1950s (Jonathan Fraser Light, *The Cultural Encyclopedia of Baseball*, 85). Ken Harrelson is credited with reintroducing them in the 1960s and Rusty Staub with helping popularize them.

9.5.4 Spikes. Spiked shoes go all the way back to the Knickerbockers, who in turn borrowed them from cricket. Researcher John Husman reported that the Knickerbocker records show they were using metal spikes with canvas shoes in 1849. In 1859 the *New York Herald* explained, "In both games [baseball and cricket] the players wear a peculiar kind of buckskin shoes with a long spike in the sole, to prevent them from slipping" (*New York Herald*, October 16, 1859). The following year Henry Chadwick counseled: "The bases should be made of the best heavy canvas, and of double thickness, as there will be much jumping on them with spiked shoes" (*Beadle's Dime Base-Ball Player*, 18). The *Brooklyn Eagle* added in 1865, "Every ball player should wear shoes with good spikes, that he can break up at short notice, and stop short, without slipping down" (*Brooklyn Eagle*, June 19, 1865).

A more difficult question to answer is how sharp these spikes were. It is safe to say they varied widely, since those who could afford baseball shoes wore ones of "homespun pattern, with spikes made by the village blacksmith and set in the soles of ordinary shoes by the local cobbler" (Clarence Deming, "Old Days in Baseball," *Outing*, June 1902, 358). Several photographs on the website of the Vintage Base Ball Association (http://www.vbba.org) confirm that quite a few base runners of this era wore footgear that would have been very dangerous to any fielders who got in their path.

At first this wasn't a great concern since sliding was rare in early baseball and was usually headfirst (see **5.2.2**). Yet even without sliding, a sharp spike poses a considerable risk. An

1867 match in Rockford, Illinois, saw two players be "frightfully lacerated by being spiked," which prompted a reporter to suggest that ballplayers "discard the use of spikes" (*Chicago Tribune*, July 6, 1867). Henry Chadwick advised the following year that baseball shoes "should be made with stout soles, having four short spikes instead of three long ones; the injuries from large spikes being very severe at times when running the bases" (Henry Chadwick, *The American Game of Base Ball*, 23). One approach that was tried was shoes with removable spikes (Chadwick Scrapbooks, unspecified 1887 article).

When sliding became commonplace in the 1880s, the dangers of spikes became increasingly evident. At first, fielders bore the brunt of the damage, but soon they began to retaliate; Jimmy McAleer later recalled that Jack Glasscock positioned himself so that "if you slid into the base it was right into his spikes, blocking off the bag like a barb-wire fence" (quoted in the *Los Angeles Times*, February 7, 1904).

The result was that spikes were banned for a couple of years (Harold Seymour, *Baseball: The Early Years*, 187). The prohibition proved ineffective as the club most associated with sliding, the St. Louis Brown Stockings, began to "wear gigantic shoe plates made of fine steel, and sharp enough to whittle a stick of wood. So it's the same as if they had the biggest kind of spike" (*Philadelphia Herald*; quoted in the *Cleveland Leader and Herald*, May 3, 1886).

Moreover they were greatly missed since, as Topsy Hartsel explained in 1904, "the spikes now used by all players seem to be the only thing now devised which will keep a man from slipping and falling as he runs down the base line." Hartsel reported that no other footwear suited the peculiar needs of baseball: "Various trials of rubber soles and leather cleats, like those of football players, have been made, but nothing except the spikes proved satisfactory" (*Washington Post*, September 11, 1904).

In consequence, spikes were brought back, apparently with an informal understanding that forbade the razor-sharp spikes used by track stars and golfers. Nonetheless it took some time for a consensus on the ethics of sliding with spiked shoes. Base runners such as Ty Cobb felt that flashing the spikes was "a case of beating the other fellow to the punch" since otherwise they were liable to be blocked by an infielder (Ty Cobb, *Memoirs of Twenty Years in Baseball*, 43).

According to the 1928 *Babe Ruth's Own Book of Baseball*, deliberate spiking had gone from being common in the 1890s to being virtually unheard of by the 1920s (Babe Ruth, *Babe Ruth's Own Book of Baseball*, 235–239). His reputation notwithstanding, Cobb's contemporaries were adamant that he did not make a practice of deliberately spiking fielders (Richard Bak, *Peach*, 63–64).

9.5.5 Sunglasses. Looking into a blinding sun was one of the greatest torments faced by early ballplayers. They would have been very grateful to be able to leap forward in time and purchase a pair of sunglasses.

By the late 1880s players were experimenting with smoked or tinted glasses. A number of sources report that Paul Hines wore sunglasses as early as 1882 (for example, David Pietrusza, "Famous Firsts," *Total Baseball VI*, 2507). But researcher Rick Stattler has found no evidence that Hines began doing so before 1888. The fact that his sunglasses drew considerable attention at that time suggests that they were still very unusual then (*Indianapolis News*, April 12, 1888; *Providence Journal*, April 22, 1888; *Boston Globe*, April 17, 1888). If Hines indeed first wore sunglasses in 1888, he was preceded by Tom Poorman, who in 1886 began wearing "blue goggles to keep the sun out of his eyes" (*Boston Globe*, June 9, 1886). Three years later St. Louis owner Chris Von der Ahe complained that the Kansas City grounds were "the worst I ever saw. They are laid out so that the sun shines in all the players' eyes. Why the right fielder has to wear smoked glasses. That is a fact. [Tommy] McCarthy had to buy himself a pair with which to play" (*St. Louis Post-Dispatch*, May 7, 1889).

Von der Ahe's remark makes clear that such devices were still uncommon at the end of the 1880s, but the next few years saw them begin to catch on. A clear indication of this occurred when Cleveland outfielder Jesse Burkett was criticized for not wearing a pair in an 1893 game (*Washington Post*, August 13, 1893). Soon fans expected them, and in 1897 a Chicago sportswriter quipped, "There are grave fears that the Chicago public will rise in its might and create a demand for caskets if [George] Decker plays in left field and declines to wear smoked glasses this year" (*Chicago Inter-Ocean*, February 28, 1897). Nonetheless the inconvenience of taking them on and off and the glare created by the metal dissuaded some outfielders from wearing them. In the early twentieth century some opted for eye black (see **26.1.3**) instead. Thus the innovation described in the next entry was a godsend for outfielders.

9.5.6 Snap-down Sunglasses.

In 1912 Pittsburgh player-manager Fred Clarke devised an "improved 'sun-cap' for outfielders. This idea is an improvement over the cap worn by the boss last season, in that it permits of the wearer snapping the glasses into place with a flick of the finger, and at the same time doing away with the glare of metal which formerly was found obnoxious. The glasses are now fastened in an aluminum sheath, which is fitted above the peak. There is a small lever which releases the spring and this allows the glasses to drop down into position before the wearer's eyes. Fred showed the idea to several of the St. Louis outfielders and all were loud in their praise for it" (*Sporting Life*, April 6, 1912). Clarke filed a patent for the device in 1915 and received it the following year (Dan Gutman, *Banana Bats and Ding-Dong Balls*, 216).

9.5.7 Rosin Bags.

Of all the items in the baseball firmament, the innocuous rosin bag would seem one of the least likely to prompt a heated debate. And yet the rosin bag was at the center of one of baseball's most singular controversies.

Rosin (also spelled resin) is a natural substance derived from sap that retains some of its stickiness even in powdered form. Its value in helping the pitcher grip the ball may have been recognized as early as 1878, when Cincinnati pitcher Will White "rubbed some rosin on his hands" during a game (*Cincinnati Commercial*, August 23, 1878; quoted in Howard W. Rosenberg, *Cap Anson 3*, 360). By 1893 an article noted: "About a half dozen times last year the ball got pretty greased in the outfield, and it was pretty hard to hit. In using a greased ball our pitchers always had a lot of powdered rosin in their pockets, and it wasn't very hard to keep control of the ball" (*Sporting News*, January 21, 1893).

But it seems to have been several years before rosin became a more regular feature of baseball. Christy Mathewson claimed in 1912 that this came about in an unusual way: "An old and favorite trick used to be to soap the soil around the pitcher's box, so that when a man was searching for some place to dry his perspiring hands and grabbed up this soaped earth, it made his palm slippery and he was unable to control the ball.

"Of course, the home talent knew where the good ground lay and used it or else carried some unadulterated earth in their trousers' pockets, as a sort of private stock. But our old friend [pitcher Arthur "Bugs"] Raymond hit on a scheme to spoil this idea and make the trick useless. Arthur always perspired profusely when he pitched, and several managers, perceiving this, had made it a habit to soap the dirt liberally whenever it was his turn to work. While he was pitching for St. Louis, he went into the box against the Pirates one day in Pittsburg. His hands were naturally slippery, and several times he had complained that he could not dry them in the dirt, especially in Pittsburg soil.

"As Raymond worked in the game in question, he was noticed, particularly by the Pittsburg batters and spectators, to get better as he went along. Frequently his hands slipped into his back pocket, and then his control was wonderful. Sometimes he would reach down and apparently pick up a handful of earth, but it did no damage. After the game, he walked over to Fred Clarke, and reached into his back pocket. His face broke into a grin.

"'Ever see any of that stuff, Fred?' he asked innocently, showing the Pittsburg manager a handful of a dark brown substance. 'That's rosin. It's great—lots better than soaped ground. Wish you'd keep a supply out there in the box for me when I'm going to work instead of that slippery stuff you've got out there now. Will you, as a favor to me?'

"Thereafter, all the pitchers got to carrying rosin or pumice stone in their pockets, for the story quickly went round the circuit, and it is useless to soap the soil in the box any more" (Christy Mathewson, *Pitching in a Pinch*, 294–295).

Umpire Billy Evans observed in 1914: "The use of rosin carried in the hip pocket has been for many years a practice resorted to by many pitchers. By placing rosin on the hands, a pitcher is enabled to get a much better grip on the ball, and in the use of the curve, is able to produce a much better break. This practice has also been much discussed, but nothing has been done relative to its abolition" (Billy Evans, syndicated column, *Atlanta Constitution*, November 8, 1914).

After the 1919 season a wide variety of "foreign substances" were banned in an effort to eliminate trick pitching and rosin was construed as falling under this heading. John McGraw complained that "the rule which prevents the pitchers from using resin on their fingers in order to remove the gloss from the cover of the ball is largely responsible for the fact that they are not getting much stuff on it" (*Lima* [Ohio] *News*, June 17, 1920). Pitcher Slim Sallee was ejected from a 1920 game for using resin and suspended for ten games (Paul Sallee and Eric Sallee, "Harry Franklin 'Slim' Sallee," Tom Simon, ed., *Deadball Stars of the National League*, 347).

As a rule, however, the prohibition appears to have proved unenforceable. Since resin left no discernable mark on the ball and pitchers needed only a few grains to dry their fingers, the rule was easy to get around. As columnist Westbrook Pegler explained, some pitchers "would sprinkle the powder on their handkerchiefs, which they kept in their hip pockets, and between throws they would finger the handkerchief, ostensibly to wipe off the perspiration. Or if a pitcher was not addicted to any such refined apparatus as the hankie he would dab his fingers in a bag of resin on the bench. Every well equipped bench had its resin bag, concealed in the trainer's satchel, and one good dab was sufficient to last almost for a full inning" (*Chicago Tribune*, February 14, 1926).

Another ruse that pitchers employed was "using resin as batsmen. It was not against the rules for a pitcher or any other player to rub a little resin on his hands to keep his bat from slipping. And as there are no wash basins on the average playing field, of course, the pitchers have not been able to get the proscribed stuff off before they went back to the pitcher's box. Some pitchers are alleged to have developed an idea that they had to bat every inning, judging from the frequency with which they prepared to grapple with the slippery willow" (John B. Foster, *Detroit News*, February 4, 1926).

As a result, the use of resin seems to have continued unabated. This caused very little consternation until the notion of legalizing the substance was raised. Most people in baseball seem to have assumed that pitchers derived little or no benefit from resin and given it even less thought. And yet there was just enough doubt to ignite into a firestorm of controversy.

At a 1925 mid-season meeting to discuss the explosion of offense, National League owners concluded that the ball was not livelier. They decided, however, to toss pitchers a bone by authorizing league president John Heydler

"to confer with Ban Johnson, President of the American League, as to the advisability of the umpire bringing a bag of resin to each game and placing it behind the pitcher's box for the pitcher's use in drying his perspiring hands and enabling him to get a better grip on the ball, which now is being done in the Southern Association" (*New York Times*, July 16, 1925).

The joint rules committee followed up that winter by passing a rule instructing umpires to prepare a rosin bag that pitchers "may" request to use. The choice of the word "may" would prove fateful. In February, American League owners voted not to approve the rule, citing the possibility that it would lead to the return of freak deliveries. They contended that the word "may" gave them the choice of whether to adopt the new rule (*Los Angeles Times*, February 10, 1926). Commissioner Kenesaw Mountain Landis told reporters that the option belonged to the pitcher rather than the league, but he made no immediate formal response.

Members of the press were as usual eager for any whiff of controversy to enliven the clichés of spring training. They were therefore delighted by the opportunity to portray the rosin bag as "another test of strength" between Landis and his longtime nemesis, Ban Johnson (Frank Young, "Landis Wants Uniform Code," *Washington Post*, April 11, 1926). Westbrook Pegler used a particularly fanciful analogy: "The law was being flouted, so the major leagues, unable to abolish the evil practice, got around the trouble by abolishing the law that made it an evil practice. . . . The same idea might be helpful elsewhere. If homicide were legalized there would be no murder" (*Chicago Tribune*, February 14, 1926).

Reporters also tried to draw pitchers into the maelstrom, but most did not seem terribly excited. When a reporter polled the Cubs' pitchers, youngsters like Fred Blake and Tony Kaufmann expressed interest, but the great Grover Cleveland Alexander begged to differ. Alexander explained, "Why, a lot of fellows have been fooling around with the stuff under cover for three or four years, and it hasn't helped many of them. I don't like it because I can't handle it. I tried it some years ago, but my hand became so sticky that I was helpless" (Irving Vaughan, "Alex's Off Resin Ball, He Says as Cubs Roll West," *Chicago Tribune*, February 12, 1926). Another veteran pitcher, Jimmy Ring, was even more emphatic: "All this talk about the resin bag bringing back trick pitching is simply hysterical talk. . . . By the time the resin is sifted through a silk bag, as provided by the rules, it will be of no aid to trick pitching" (quoted in *New York Times*, February 20, 1926).

By this time seven minor leagues had joined the American League's insurrection, forcing Commissioner Landis to issue a carefully worded edict. He observed that "Allowing the pitcher to dry his hands by the use of powdered resin, as specifically limited by the hereinafter rule, does not affect the prohibition against the resin ball, any more than allowing him to dry his hands with dirt (which is universally permitted, despite the absence of any rule allowing it) affects the prohibition against the mud ball, or dirt ball" (letter to John H. Farrell, president of the minor leagues, *Los Angeles Times*, April 2, 1926). He accordingly ordered all leagues, including the American League, to ensure that its umpires had a rosin bag on hand for any pitcher who requested one.

This still left the American League with a loophole, and Ban Johnson was quick to take it. He announced that the junior circuit would comply with the letter of Landis's order by requiring umpires to prepare rosin bags for each game. At the same time he instructed managers not to allow their pitchers to request to use one!

And so the regular season began with the issue still unresolved. By this time the whole escapade had begun to resemble nothing so much as the story of the Emperor's New Clothes. As obvious as it seemed that there was nothing to be seen, there was still the lurking suspicion that someone else might really be seeing something. In the intensely competitive world of sports, the smallest suspicion that an advantage is being gained can easily develop into rampant paranoia.

The atmosphere that resulted is nicely captured in this bizarre account: "[Cubs pitcher] Bob Osborn was guilty of a terrible crime when he started to pitch in the fifth. He picked up the resin bag and dusted it on the ball. Umpire [Charlie] Moran called time and threw the pill out of play. The rule says you must put the resin on the hand and then on the ball. The effect is the same" (*Chicago Tribune*, April 29, 1926).

The 1926 season proceeded with neither side flinching. National League pitchers used the resin bag when needed, though there were no obvious signs that it helped much. American League umpires prepared resin bags for every game, and the league's pitchers obediently refrained from using them, with apparently only one minor breach. On a rainy August day, Yankee pitcher Dutch Reuther asked the home-plate umpire for resin while batting so that he could get a better grip on his bat (James R. Harrison, "40,000 See Yankees Divide Homecoming," *New York Times*, August 15, 1926).

That year's World Series brought renewed attention to the year-long standoff between Landis and Johnson. It was one thing for all teams in the league to comply with Johnson's instructions, but quite another for the American League champion Yankees to concede any potential advantage to their National League opponents, the Cardinals. At least one New York pitcher did succumb to temptation, and it was the same moundsman who had earlier experimented with resin.

The *Chicago Tribune* recounted in mock horror after the third game: "Dutch Reuther was detected in a horrible blunder in the first inning. He picked up the resin bag and dusted his fingers, though it is restricted for use only by National League pitchers. President B. B. Johnson of the American League was looking the other way" (*Chicago Tribune*, October 5, 1926). The *New York Times* reported that Reuther also used the rosin bag in the second inning. But the controversy that had made for such lively press during spring training seemed tepid in the midst of a dramatic World Series, and the issue soon died.

The following spring a *New York Times* reporter tried to revive the controversy when rookie Yankee pitcher George Pipgras used the rosin bag during an exhibition game against the Boston Braves. The reporter observed mischievously that Pipgras "had better look out or the Goblins will get him. This constitutes a high crime and misdemeanor in the American League. There is no rule against it, but the managers have requested the pitchers to refrain, and sometimes a request is as good as an order" (*New York Times*, March 20, 1927).

But it was no longer possible to generate much interest in "the resin bag, which was supposed to work such miracles but which in reality is nothing more than a joke" (Irving Vaughan, *Chicago Tribune*, May 16, 1927). Paradoxically, as it became generally accepted that the resin bag was of relatively little help, this only strengthened the American League's resolve since a competitive advantage was not at stake. Johnson was succeeded as American League president by E. S. Barnard, but both sides remained firmly entrenched in their positions. American League umpires continued to prepare rosin bags for each and every game, American League pitchers continued to refrain from asking for them, and the press and public paid no attention.

That was how matters still stood in 1931 when Barnard and Johnson died, their passings separated by a single day. Newly elected league president Will Harridge announced that the rosin bag would be allowed in the American League, but the resolution of the once contentious issue barely warranted mention in the sports pages (*Chicago Tribune*, May 28, 1931). Three days later American League pitchers were finally at liberty to use the resin bag in a game in the nation's capital. In a fittingly anticlimactic resolution, neither pitcher used it until the fourth inning (*Washington Post*, May 31, 1931).

Chapter 10

UNIFORMS

JERRY SEINFELD has observed that, as a result of free agency, longtime fans of a club are rooting for little more than laundry. The quip is apt, but it must be noted that baseball uniforms have always held a deep significance for fans. As early as 1869, Henry Chadwick recognized that "one of the last things a club should find occasion to do is to change the colors or form of its uniform" (*National Chronicle*, March 20, 1869). By the 1880s it was already recognized that the color of a club's "hosiery . . . has, in some sense, become its trade-mark" (*Detroit Free Press*, December 11, 1881). This tradition is maintained by such current nicknames as the Red Sox and White Sox.

The earliest baseball uniforms borrowed touches from military attire and from firefighter's uniforms (most notably the bib, which was intended to protect the shirt from cinders and other debris). These highly respected associations helped convey a sense that the game was worthy of adult attention. Clubs that took pride in their uniforms have always been viewed as commanding respect while derision has been accorded those who neglected their garments.

Those wishing to visualize the development of the uniform are directed to this fine website, created by Tom Shieber of the Baseball Hall of Fame: http://baseballhalloffame.org/exhibits/online_exhibits/dressed_to_the_nines/

10.1 Uniformity. Uniforms of a team were not required to be identical "in color and style" until 1899. Uniformity had been the custom long before then, though, but occasionally a player did not conform. The most notable example came in the wake of the Great Chicago Fire of 1871,

which destroyed the ballpark and possessions of that city's entry in the National Association. The club mustered on in pursuit of the pennant, wearing a piebald mix of uniforms borrowed from other clubs: "[Ed] Pinkham wore a Mutual shirt, Mutual pants and red stockings. Bannock [Michael Brannock], a player picked up for this eastern trip, wore a complete Mutual uniform, except the belt which was an Eckford. [Tom] Foley was attired in a complete Eckford suit. [George] Zettlein, 'he of the big feet,' wore a huge shirt with a mammoth 'A' on the bosom. [Ed] Duffy appeared as a Fly Awayer. Some wore black hats, a few regular ball hats, others were bare-headed" (Preston D. Orem, *Baseball [1845–1881] from the Newspaper Accounts*, 140).

10.2 Caps. The first uniform adopted by the Knickerbockers in 1849 included straw hats to shield the players' eyes from the sun. It wasn't long before the need for headwear that stayed on the head while running became apparent. Around 1851 the Knickerbockers and other early clubs adopted baseball caps, which were already being used in cricket.

10.3 Cap Backward. The sporting of a backward baseball cap (by players other than the catcher) is a recent fashion trend that is sometimes viewed as disrespectful to baseball traditions. Not surprisingly, however, it is not unprecedented. Bryan Di Salvatore observed that 1880s outfielder George Gore would sometimes "play the clown by turning his cap brim backward" (Bryan Di Salvatore, *A Clever Base-Ballist*, 207).

10.4 Knickerbockers.

While the Knickerbocker club of New York was responsible for many firsts, knickerbockers (or knickers) weren't one of them. Early uniforms generally consisted of "white duck trousers, full length, a white flannel shirt, and a white flannel jockey cap" (*Williamsport Sunday Grit*, June 7, 1891). To prevent tripping over the long pants, early "ball tossers either strapped their trousers around their shoes, as Uncle Sam does in pictures, or wore them clamped about their ankles like the bicycle riders with trouser guards" (*St. Louis Post-Dispatch*, April 4, 1898). George Wright, for example, recalled that he tied up the bottom of his trousers with slate straps (*New York Sun*, November 14, 1915).

By the late 1860s baseball was borrowing the use of shorter pants from cricket. The trend-setter may have been Charley Walker of the Actives of New York, whose 1881 obituary described him as "one of the first to adopt the now prevalent custom of wearing knee-pants and stockings as part of the uniform" (*New York Clipper*, June 11, 1881). The article does not specify when Walker first wore knickerbockers, but the heyday of Walker and his club came between 1864 and 1866.

Although Walker probably preceded them, the Red Stockings of Cincinnati were the first entire club known to have worn knickerbockers and undoubtedly were responsible for popularizing them. As early as 1867 they were described as "the Cincinnatians in white flannel suits, with knee breeches and red stockings, a la Young America Cricket Club" (*The Ball Player's Chronicle*, July 25, 1867). By the club's historic 1869 season, this fashion statement was identified with the Red Stockings (Henry Chadwick, *National Chronicle*, March 20, 1869).

Harry Wright is often credited with bringing knickerbockers to the Red Stockings, and indeed he was quoted in 1875 as stating that the club's cricket-style uniform "originated with me" (*Cincinnati Enquirer*, August 20, 1875). But researcher Mark Alvarez suggested that George Ellard, who brought Wright to Cincinnati, may have been responsible (Mark Alvarez, "William Henry Wright," in Frederick Ivor-Campbell, Robert L. Tiemann, and Mark Rucker, eds., *Baseball's First Stars*, 177). This contention was supported by Ellard's son, who reported that his father arranged for a tailor named Bertha Bertram to make the Red Stockings' uniforms from 1867 to 1870. While knickerbockers were not specified, the younger Ellard wrote that the style introduced by Mrs. Bertram "has been

changed but very little up to the present day" (Harry Ellard, *Base Ball in Cincinnati*, 54).

The fashion statement was taken note of by many, including the Chicago businessmen who resented the baseball supremacy of Cincinnati and formed the White Stockings in 1870. Partway through that same season the Mutuals of New York adopted "corduroy knee-breeches" (*New York World*, June 7, 1870). With the country's top clubs wearing knickerbockers, it was not long before they were a standard part of the baseball uniform.

They also became part of the identity of baseball. The shorter pants drew attention to the socks and led to nicknames like Red Stockings and White Stockings. The names of no fewer than three current major league teams—the Boston Red Sox, Cincinnati Reds, and Chicago White Sox—reflect this influence.

10.5 Uniform Colors.

Early baseball clubs had one uniform; it would have seemed extravagant to have another for changing. If they had a spare uniform, it was generally for other purposes. The *Fort Wayne Daily News* reported in 1883, "The Fort Wayne nine will have two suits, one to play ball in and the other to wear when they call on their girls" (*Fort Wayne Daily News*, April 3, 1883).

Moreover most clubs used white as the base color and were distinguished only by the color of such accessories as their stockings, belts, and armbands. This meant it was never easy for spectators, umpires and fellow players to distinguish the players. If two clubs happened to use similar secondary colors, it became virtually impossible to tell the fielders from the base runners.

As noted in the next entry, at least one club appears to have experimented with separate road and home uniforms in the early 1870s, but this was an expense that most clubs were unwilling to assume. Consequently, before the idea of separate home and road uniforms was permanently adopted, efforts to make it easier to distinguish the players were regularly made and were just as regularly greeted with ridicule.

In 1872 the Lord Baltimores donned yellow silk shirts and black pantaloons. The enterprising club hoped to remind observers of the state bird of Maryland, the oriole, but instead they were dubbed the Canaries.

The White Stockings of Chicago hit upon a new scheme in 1876 so that "spectators can easily and certainly tell the players apart as they are in the field. Capt. Spalding's idea is to furnish each player with a different colored cap, and then put the names of the colors against those of the players on the score cards. There will, however, be some opposition to this idea, and it is not at all certain to win. A collection of heads under the proposed plan would look like a Dutch bed of tulips. It is, however, certain that the plan, if adopted, would be a useful one, if not ornamental" (*St. Louis Globe-Democrat*, March 19, 1876, 2).

The Spalding who was behind this scheme was Albert G. Spalding, who just so happened that same year to have opened a baseball emporium that would grow into a sporting goods giant, in large part because of his ability to secure exclusive National League contracts. It would not be the last convergence between the National League's choice in uniforms and the fortunes of Spalding's firm (Peter Levine, *A. G. Spalding and the Rise of Baseball*, 71–76). The White Stockings did indeed adopt the experiment and initial reports were favorable, but after some mocking comments were made, it was abandoned (*Chicago Tribune*, April 21 and 23, 1876; Neil W. Macdonald, *The League That Lasted*, 90–91; Susie McCarthy in Bill James, *The New Bill James Historical Baseball Abstract*, 23).

A similar scheme was tried in 1879 when plans were made for the White Stockings to wear a "queer uniform" that "will consist of a white shirt and white knee-breeches as in former years, but each player will have different colored cap, belt, necktie, and stripe around stocking at calf of leg" (*Chicago Tribune*, March 16, 1879). The *Boston Globe* noted the convenience of this scheme for spectators, who would "be able to follow a man wherever he may go around the field, either in base running or change of position. The colors will be placed opposite the player's name on the score sheets furnished at the gate" (*Boston Globe*, March 21, 1879).

Another prominent professional club, the Worcesters, also decided to have each player to wear "a band of his color an inch wide on his cap" and to have the name of the color "printed against the player's name on the scorecard" (*Boston Globe*, April 8, 1879). Not everyone greeted the new scheme enthusiastically, with the *Syracuse Courier* dubbing the White Stockings "the Chicago Rainbows" (quoted in the *Chicago Tribune*, March 30, 1879).

The experiment proved short-lived, but in 1882 the National League made a more ambitious effort along the same lines. It is of-

ten reported that only the Detroit Wolverines implemented the innovation, but the following account leaves no doubt that it was a league-wide endeavor: "The new system uniforms by position. All the catchers in the league will be dressed precisely alike with the exception of their hose, which will be of their club color, and so of all the pitchers, first basemen, and so on through the list. The report fixes the color of each article of dress for each player. The shirts, belts, and caps for the various positions are to be as follows: Catcher, scarlet; pitcher, light blue; first base, scarlet and white; second base, orange and black; third base, blue and white; short-stop, maroon; right field, gray; center field, red and black; left field, white; first substitute, green; second substitute, brown. The trousers and neck-ties of all players are to be white, and the shoes leather. In the matter of the colors of stockings, the committee, as far as possible, allowed each club to retain the hosiery which has, in some sense, become its trade-mark. The stockings to be worn by the members of the different nines are as follows: Boston, red; Chicago, white; Detroit, old gold; Troy, green; Buffalo, gray; Cleveland, navy blue; Providence, light blue; Worcester, brown.

"This will give a rainbow hue to the diamond and make the spectators wish they were color blind. Picture [Detroit catcher Charley] Bennett in leather gaiters, golden stockings, white trousers and red belt, red shirt and white tie, a red cap crowning the whole! With the addition of mutton-chop whiskers, he could easily be mistaken for a Canada milkman, while [first baseman Martin] Powell will look as if his uniform was made of the pieces that were left over after Bennett's and [outfielder George] Wood's had been constructed. The umpires seem to have been entirely overlooked. Serpentine pantaloons, in imitation of a barber's pole, harlequin jacket and a circus clown's wool hat, would give them a neat and not particularly gaudy suit, and afford a kaleidoscopic effect as they skipped up to first base along with a batsman. A log cabin bed quilt, worn as a toga, would highten [sic] the effect and add dignity to the office. A revived interest in the national game may reasonably be expected all over the country" (*Detroit Free Press*, December 11, 1881).

So why was the scheme tried? Mike Roer and Peter Levine suggest that A. G. Spalding was again behind the idea and that it proved to be another windfall for his sporting goods company (Mike Roer, *Orator O'Rourke*, 99;

Peter Levine, *A. G. Spalding and the Rise of Baseball*, 78).

The sarcasm proved justified. Spectators ridiculed the uniforms, which became known as "monkey suits," "zebra uniforms," and "clown suits." If the batting team's first baseman reached first, the pitcher could not tell the two men apart and was liable to throw to the wrong one on a pickoff attempt (William D. Perrin, *Days of Greatness*, 15). Early in the season the *Boston Post* remarked, "Every time a league team appears on the ball field in uniform, the absurd legislation of the League relative to the colors and style of the uniform is universally commented upon and condemned. None feel more sensitive over the situation than the players themselves. The sentiment will be overwhelmingly in favor of the repeal of the rule at the next meeting of the League" (reprinted in *Cleveland Leader*, May 4, 1882). Jim O'Rourke declared, "It is an insult to all of us to make a professional baseball player dress like a clown. If we are unfortunate enough to play near a lunatic asylum, we are likely to wind up inside looking out." Even Oscar Wilde commented unfavorably on the experiment (both cited in Mike Roer, *Orator O'Rourke*, 99).

The only positive comments came from the *Chicago Herald*, which was developing a cozy relationship with the club and claimed to have earlier been the first paper to break the news about the uniform scheme. Even its reporter filed a mixed account that predicted the uniforms would "become favorites," then added, "The league managers must make some other portions of the uniform beside the stocking to distinguish between clubs, as the breeches of the players are continually slipping down, hiding those from view. The caps should be of the same color as the stockings, leaving the spectator to know the positions by the shirts and the club of the player by the caps" (*Chicago Herald*, April 16, 1882). Nobody else believed the bizarre scheme could be salvaged, and the league soon brought the "kaleidoscopic mess" to a merciful end (William D. Perrin, *Days of Greatness*, 15). Of course the repeal of the rule enabled Spalding to sell more new uniforms and reap additional profits.

At least one American Association club, the Cincinnatis, also adopted this scheme in 1882 (*Cincinnati Commercial Tribune*, April 15, 1882). David Nemec claimed that the National League was following the lead of the American Association (David Nemec, *The Beer and Whisky League*, 37). But since the National League had adopted the new uniforms by December 1881, when the Association was still in the planning stages, this seems unlikely.

10.6 Road Uniforms. After the unsuccessful experiments described in the preceding entry, an older idea was revived. The St. Louis (Union Association) club of 1884 unveiled a dark blue traveling suit. When this was described as a first, however, a *St. Louis Post-Dispatch* reporter claimed that Troy had unsuccessfully tried the same idea in 1871 (*St. Louis Post-Dispatch*, February 21, 1884).

Baseball was still not quite ready to embrace the added expense of separate road and home uniforms. But the game's growing prosperity and the continued need to distinguish players made the idea's eventual acceptance inevitable. In 1883 Cleveland adopted white uniforms for National League games and grey ones for exhibition contests (*National Police Gazette*, April 28, 1883). A Cleveland fan suggested in 1887 that clubs should wear blue on the road and white at home (*Cleveland Leader and Herald*, May 29, 1887).

Researcher David Ball discovered evidence suggesting that a practical consideration helped white to become customary for the home team. In 1889, John Morrill became captain and manager of the Washington team and expressed a preference for "having two uniforms entirely distinct, and yet not so different in color and style as to prevent the team being known by its regular uniform. In all probability the two uniforms will be two shades of gray, with blue stockings for both. The darker uniform will be best adapted for traveling purposes and the lighter for use at home, where laundries are more convenient" (*Washington Star*, April 13, 1889).

It gradually became customary for the home side to wear white and the visitors colored uniforms (George L. Moreland, *Balldom*, 20). This practice was finally mandated by the rulebook in 1904 and thereafter was strictly enforced. In the opening game of the 1907 World Series, the host Chicago Cubs wore spiffy new gray uniforms with slight pinstripes. But National Commission chairman Garry Herrmann was disturbed by "the fact that it was difficult to distinguish the players of the two teams, and an order was issued that the Cubs must wear their white uniforms to-morrow, while the Tigers will have to wear theirs in Detroit" (*Washington Post*, October 9, 1907). The Cubs reverted to "their soiled and worn white home uniforms" for their remaining home games (AP: *New York Times*, October 10, 1907). Sportswriter Joe S. Jackson noted in 1911 that the Giants and Phillies had had to get permission to sport a black pinstripe on their home uniforms (*Washington Post*, February 17, 1911).

10.7   Shorts. Short skirts were a feature of the All-American Girls' Professional Base Ball League, which lasted from 1943 to 1954. The intention, however, was to emphasize the players' femininity, and the strawberries that resulted when they slid made it clear that the uniforms were not designed with function in mind.

The Hollywood Stars of the Pacific Coast League had a very different motivation for taking the field on April 1, 1950, wearing "T-type rayon shirts and white pin-striped flannel shorts with hose rolled below the knee." Manager Fred Haney denied that the experiment was an April Fool's Day gag or a sign that the club was "going Hollywood." He said his club would wear the shorts on warm days and even nights and predicted they would become "standard equipment."

Haney explained that he came up with the idea after reading an article about how record-breaking performances in other sports were being attributed to improvements in equipment. He began to think about the baseball uniform and concluded that it was not built for speed. Haney elaborated: "It stands to reason that players should be faster wearing them—and that half step going down to first alone wins or loses many a game. These outfits weigh only a third as much as the old monkey suits and when both are soaked in perspiration the difference is greater yet. And if a couple of pounds makes so much difference in a horse race, think what shedding them should do in baseball." He also felt the shorts would provide a "greater freedom of motion in fielding and throwing."

Haney was aware of concerns about sliding, but he was convinced this would not prove a problem. He explained that he and Stars second baseman Gene Handley had "spent over an hour trying slides in them and we never got a scratch. The boys still wear sliding pads under their shorts and the roll of the sox protects their knees. There may be a little reluctance at first to hit the dirt, but I think they'll soon get over that" (Al Wolf, "Hollywood Stars Blossom Out in Shorts (for Speed)," *Los Angeles Times*, April 2, 1950). The Stars wore the shorts frequently in 1950 but only occasionally after that, finally abandoning them for good after the 1953 season (Stephen M. Daniels, "The Hollywood Stars," *Baseball Research Journal* 1980, 161).

Several other clubs in warm-weather climates experimented with shorts. Branch Rickey liked Haney's idea and ordered a similar set for the Dodgers' farm club in Fort Worth. Pueblo of the Western League announced on May 29, 1950, that they would also wear shorts that summer. Abilene of the West Texas–New Mexico League tried shorts for two games later that season but went back to regular uniforms due to mosquitoes. Spokane also tried shorts in 1951 but, like the other clubs, soon abandoned them (Mark Armour, ed., *Rain Check*, 90).

Maverick owner Bill Veeck's White Sox became the first major league team to experiment with shorts when they donned Bermuda shorts for a game against the Royals on August 8, 1976. Veeck explained, "We had to wait until this late in the summer to wear them because we had to get the right pads under the socks to protect the knees." The team stole five bases in the game and manager Paul Richards reported "no skinned knees" (*Chicago Tribune*, August 9, 1976).

10.8   Short Sleeves. As with pants, early uniform shirts were quite formal and gradually became more casual. Many shirts of the 1860s featured bibs and neckties, a fashion statement borrowed from the fire companies with which they were often closely connected. They gradually became more casual in the 1870s, and the first club to wear short-sleeve shirts may have been a Harvard club (Susie McCarthy in Bill James, *The New Bill James Historical Baseball Abstract*, 23). Researcher Tom Shieber reports that the Chicago Cubs were the first club to wear sleeveless uniforms in 1940.

10.9   Fabrics. Henry Chadwick declared in 1869, "Flannel is, of course, the only suitable article for pants and shirt" (*National Chronicle*, March 20, 1869). Most early clubs followed this guideline, but not all. Harry Ellard, for example, reported that the Louisville Base Ball Club of 1865 sported blue jeans (Harry Ellard, *Base Ball in Cincinnati*, 54).

According to Marc Okkonen, until well into the twentieth century baseball uniforms remained either 100 percent wool flannel or a blend of wool and cotton. Okkonen observed that the "weight of these wool and cotton flannels was gradually reduced in half by the 1940s but the problems of durability and shrinkage had not improved much. The advent of synthetic fibers in the post-WWII era (NYLON, DACRON, ORLON) paved the way for improved blends." The 1960s saw a blend of Orlon and wool gain popularity. Double knits were introduced in 1970, and their superiority in comfort and durability soon made them standard (Marc Okkonen, *Baseball Uniforms of the Twentieth Century*, 1).

10.10 Team Names and Logos on Uniform Fronts.
In the 1860s it was uncommon for clubs to spend money to place lettering on their uniforms. Those that did generally economized by placing only the initial letter (see, for example, Mark Rucker, *Base Ball Cartes*, and the special pictorial issue of the *National Pastime*, issue 3, 1984). Clubs instead often wore monogrammed belts or armbands (see *The Barry Halper Collection of Baseball Memorabilia: The Early Years*, 88, 95).

By the 1870s club names on uniforms were becoming more common, and a few began to add a logo. One of the pioneers was the Maple Leaf Club of Guelph, Ontario, whose natty uniform was "made of gray cloth, with tasteful trimmings of green silk. The breast is ornamented with a maple leaf of fine green silk, which shows the natural 'ribbing' of the leaf, and is artistically done. The belt is made of a dark shade of green. The stockings were imported from Hawick, Scotland. The cap is of a gray material, with a green edge" (*St. Louis Globe-Democrat*, May 6, 1877, 7). A picture of the uniforms of the Maple Leaf Club appeared in *Harper's Weekly* on September 12, 1874, which probably influenced other teams. In 1875 it was announced that "a small 'red stocking' and the words 'St. Louis' will be worked on the shirts" of the new uniforms of the St. Louis Reds (*Chicago Tribune*, April 4, 1875). Susie McCarthy noted that by 1876 the members of the amateur Skull and Bones club of Massachusetts also bore logos on their shirts (Susie McCarthy in Bill James, *The New Bill James Historical Baseball Abstract*, 23).

During the 1880s logos became more common and often quite elaborate. In 1883 New York's National League entry began sporting the "coat of arms of City of New York on the breasts of their shirts" (*St. Louis Globe-Democrat*, March 28, 1883).

Researcher Tom Shieber discovered that the Buffalo entry in the Federal League in 1914 was the first major league club to spell out its name in script lettering rather than block lettering. The Cardinals experimented with script lettering in 1918 and 1919 but soon abandoned it. Marc Okkonen reported that the Detroit Tigers brought the feature back in 1930 and popularized it (Marc Okkonen, *Baseball Uniforms of the Twentieth Century*, 4).

10.11 Sanitary Hose.
Nap Lajoie was spiked severely in 1905, and the dye in his stockings was blamed when blood poisoning resulted (*Sporting Life*, January 6, 1906). Three years later Fred Merkle suffered a case of blood poisoning that caused his foot to swell to the size of a pumpkin, prompting fears that it would have to be amputated and necessitating two operations (David W. Anderson, *More Than Merkle*, 142; *Sporting Life*, July 19, 1908; *New York Evening Journal*, July 11, 1908, quoted in G. H. Fleming, *The Unforgettable Season*, 120).

Some clubs gave up colored socks as a result of incidents like these, but others instead started to wear white sanitary hose under the colored socks to guard against infection. This produced a dramatic result in Boston, where the National League club had originally been known as the Red Stockings and still sported that distinctive look. But when the team chose to give up their red socks, the look was appropriated by the crosstown American League team, which became known as the Red Sox (Troy Soos, *Before the Curse*, 110).

A 1912 article observed: "These days up-to-date basemen not only wear an asbestos or leather pad around each foot and ankle, but have white stockings under their colored ones, if their uniforms call for colored stockings. White stockings prevent blood poisoning if a man is spiked" (*Indianapolis Star*, March 3, 1912). I'll leave it to readers to decide whether the use of asbestos as a protective device represented progress.

Marc Okkonen pointed out that another practical consideration undoubtedly was a major factor: white socks were much easier to wash every day, especially while a team was on the road.

10.12 Jackets.
The idea of wearing some form of jacket over the uniform goes back to at least 1869, when Henry Chadwick noted, "It is advisable to have a flannel jacket to wear in case of a sudden change of weather, or to throw over the shoulders when in a perspiration and resting after play" (*National Chronicle*, March 20, 1869).

The earliest jackets were designed for appearance rather than functionality, however, as the *Chicago Tribune* explained: "The White Stockings players are hereby served with notice that the audience have seen and admired their new white coats, and generally approve them. They are no part of a player's field uniform, however, and look wonderfully out of place buttoned around a player as he goes to bat or takes his position in the field" (*Chicago Tribune*, May 11, 1877, 5). The *Indianapolis Journal* was similarly critical of the local team when they wore their jackets during an exhibition game on a cold day (quoted by the *Louisville Courier-Journal*, May 13, 1877). Henry Lucas's St. Louis entry in the Union Association was even reported to have jackets made of the "finest silk" (*Sporting Life*, April 30, 1884).

By the turn of the century the standard garb was a double-breasted coat "with large pearl buttons and two-tone trimmings on the sleeve ends, pocket flaps and collar" (Marc Okkonen, *Baseball Uniforms of the Twentieth Century*, 8). In 1906 the New York Giants began wearing a new garment over their uniforms as they made their way to the ballpark and back. It was described as a cross between a bathrobe and an ulster (Sporting Life, April 21, 1906).

About the same time clubs started to wear team sweaters over their uniforms on cold days, and the concept of warm-up jackets that were more suited to the exigencies of baseball soon followed. In 1909, as the result of a suggestion by pitcher Ed Killian, the Tigers ordered "jackets, in addition to the sweaters, to fit over the latter, for the pitchers" (*Detroit Free Press*, March 2, 1909). A 1913 article noted, "Ollie Chapman, a Cincinnati ball player, has invented a protective sleeve for pitchers and catchers to prevent their arms from cooling off between innings" (*Sporting News*, January 30, 1913). By the 1920s the windbreaker style of jacket had begun to appear (Marc Okkonen, *Baseball Uniforms of the Twentieth Century*, 8).

10.13   Numbers on Uniforms. As discussed in entry **10.5**, early experiments with uniform colors were designed to give each player a distinguishing look. Over the next half-century the idea of having numbers on players' uniforms was regularly proposed but was met with surprisingly stout resistance. Cincinnati apparently discussed the idea in 1883, and it was proposed again in 1894. Players, however, appear to have believed that the numbers would make them look like prisoners, and the plans were shelved.

Researcher Tom Shieber discovered that in 1907 innovative minor league manager Al Lawson ordered numbers for his Reading club. Whether the numbers were actually worn is unknown (*Sporting Life*, April 27, 1907). Shieber also reports that the Cuban Stars, one of the greatest African-American clubs of the era, wore numbers on their sleeves in 1909.

Hockey teams began wearing numbers on their jerseys in 1912, prompting renewed talk of bringing the feature to baseball (Michael McKinley, *Putting a Roof on Winter*, 85). The Cleveland Indians wore numbers on their sleeves in a game on June 26, 1916, but the numbers proved too small to read.

The St. Louis Cardinals announced before the 1923 season that their players would wear six-inch high numbers on both sleeves that corresponded to their place in the batting order. Manager Branch Rickey explained, "I think we owe it to the patrons. . . . The fans do not know all the players. Even I, a manager in the same league, when away from home, must often call an usher aside and ask him who this or that player is. And, if I do not know the players, how is any ordinary person to figure it out" (*St. Louis Post-Dispatch*, March 6, 1923). The plans were delayed, but the Cardinals wore small numbers on their sleeves on April 15, 1924. The experiment ended after the 1925 season.

The two St. Louis teams then found a surprising alternative to numbers on uniforms. As Gene Karst explained, each player was assigned a "scoreboard number" that "appeared on the hand-operated scoreboard as the player took his turn at bat. Only then, if you didn't already know him by his appearance . . . could you be sure of who the batter was." While this system was not ideal for fans, it had a major benefit to the Cardinals and Browns. Karst noted that sales of the official scorecards were often damaged by competition from unauthorized rivals. In response, the two teams would periodically foil the independent vendors by changing all of the players' numbers. These switcheroos also crossed up fans who brought scorecards from previous games to the ballpark (Gene Karst, "The Great Days, The Great Stars," *National Pastime* 2 [Fall 1982], 49). So it is easy to see why teams were in no hurry to put permanent numbers on uniforms.

On January 22, 1929, the Yankees announced that their players would wear numbers on the backs of both their home and road uniforms. The numbers corresponded to their spot in the batting order, which is why Babe

Ruth wore number 3 and Lou Gehrig number 4. The Cleveland Indians joined them in part by adding numbers to their home uniforms. The Yankees' opening day game was rained out, giving the Indians' players the distinction of being the first major leaguers to play a regular season game with numbers on their backs. The Indians won the historic April 6 game in eleven innings over the visiting Tigers.

This time the innovation finally caught on in the American League. The National League actually banned uniform numbers for several years afterward, but by 1933 all teams in the major leagues were wearing numbers.

Even after numbers became part of the uniforms, the St. Louis teams continued their efforts to prevent the sale of unauthorized scorecards. Karst explained, "For a time, the Cardinals and Browns used two sets of numbers for their players. One was the new uniform number. The other was the old scorecard number—a different number entirely—that popped up on the scoreboard when the player took his turn at bat. Confusing . . . but anything to sell more scorecards!" (Gene Karst, "The Great Days, The Great Stars," *National Pastime* 2 [Fall 1982], 49).

10.14   Player Names on Uniforms. White Sox owner Bill Veeck pioneered the use of players' names on road uniforms in 1960 during spring training. As with numbers, the new addition was met with resistance. Sportswriter Bob Addie noted that it was a scheme that would "delight fans and disturb concessionaires" (*Washington Post*, March 3, 1960). The vendors who sold programs were not the only ones to express hostility. When the uniforms were unveiled, opposing players dubbed them the "silent scoreboard" uniforms. Addie reported a few weeks later that the names had "been cause for much hilarity among the brothers in arms. A ballplayer beats a joke to death. There are the same old cracks with few variations. The White Sox must be getting a trifle nauseated at the constant ribbing" (*Washington Post*, March 31, 1960).

The kidding must have grown old very quickly. A few weeks later the innovation was reported to have "met with such favor that it will be continued throughout the regular season." White Sox manager Al Lopez commented, "What difference does it make? After a while you don't even think about it. I can remember when I first came up in the late twenties, the players weren't even wearing numbers" (*New York Times*, April 10, 1960).

10.15   Pinstripes. The Yankees first wore their signature pinstripes in 1912 but were far from the originators of this fashion trend. Researcher Tom Shieber discovered that three major league clubs experimented with pinstripes in 1888—Washington and Detroit of the National League and Brooklyn of the American Association. Marc Okkonen reported that around 1907 pinstriping returned in the form of "a fine, narrowly spaced line on the road grays that was barely visible from a distance. The Chicago Cubs were probably the first to use this pattern, but the Boston Nationals went a step further with a discernable green pin stripe on their 1907 road suits. The Brooklyn club was yet more daring with a fine blue 'cross-hatch' pattern on their '07 road grays" (Marc Okkonen, *Baseball Uniforms of the Twentieth Century*, 1).

Within a few years the pinstripes became much more conspicuous. Before the 1911 season Giants manager John McGraw came up with "a new idea, a white uniform with black perpendicular stripes" (*Sporting News*, February 16, 1911). Over the next two seasons the Phillies and several other clubs adopted visible pinstriping on their home uniforms. By the time the Yankees permanently joined the trend in 1915, about half of all major league teams sported distinct pinstripes on their home uniforms (Marc Okkonen, *Baseball Uniforms of the Twentieth Century*, 1).

10.16   Patches. Clarence Deming reported that in the early days of baseball it was "the habit of the better class of clubs [to exchange], just before each match, silk badges imprinted with the club name. The players wore these accumulated trophies pinned upon the breast, sometimes with startling color effects; and the baseball man was proud, indeed, who could pin on the outside of his deep strata of badges a ribbon from the mighty Atlantics, Mutuals, or Eckfords, attesting his worth for meeting giants, if not mastering them" (Clarence Deming, "Old Days in Baseball," *Outing*, June 1902, 359).

Marc Okkonen believes that the Chicago White Sox ushered in the custom of sporting shoulder patches in 1907. While the wording on the small patch cannot be read clearly, it seems likely that it proclaimed the club's status as world champions. American flags and other patriotic emblems became a familiar sight during World War I, and commemorative patches have made regular appearances on baseball uniforms ever since (Marc Okkonen, *Baseball Uniforms of the Twentieth Century*, 5).

10.17   Armbands. It was not uncommon for early baseball clubs to wear some form of mourning when appropriate. When Tommy Miller died in 1876, each of his St. Louis teammates wore "a badge of mourning" for thirty days (*New York Clipper*, June 10, 1876). An 1884 account noted: "The Fort Waynes will wear white and black rosettes in memory of their late captain, John McDonough" (*Sporting Life*, August 13, 1884). There were many other instances; Tom Shieber has compiled a list on the Hall of Fame website.

10.18   Retired Numbers. Lou Gehrig, in 1939, was the first player to have his uniform number retired. Retired uniform numbers remained uncommon until the 1960s.

10.19   Rally Cap. A "rally cap" can be seen when all the players on one team's bench wear their caps in an unusual fashion, such as inside out, in hopes of stimulating a comeback. *The Dickson Baseball Dictionary* indicated that rally caps were introduced by the Texas Rangers in 1977 (Paul Dickson, *The Dickson Baseball Dictionary*). It seems more likely that it was actually the University of Texas.

The world champion 1986 Mets seem to have ensured the popularity of the rally cap on the major league level. Its originator, Howard Johnson, acknowledged that he had borrowed it from collegians: "All the colleges have them. One day [after a loss] . . . I was sitting on the bench thinking: 'Why not us?'" (Joseph Durso, "Mets Wear Their Own Style," *New York Times*, July 14, 1986).

Chapter 11

SKULLDUGGERY

"In the scrub games tricks were often resorted to for advantage. . . . These antics prevented the exercise for which the game was instituted and had no good effect."—*Boston Journal*, March 6, 1905

"A winning team is made up of men who will 'turn tricks' when they have a chance—men who study points, and work every advantage to win. All is fair in love and war, and the same may be said of baseball."—Charles Comiskey, quoted in *Chicago Tribune*, April 28, 1889

MANY ENTRIES in this book concern players who sought to bend, reinvent, or subvert the game's rules, practices, or customs to their own advantage. Some went further, perhaps crossing the imaginary line between stretching and flouting the rules. To outsiders that line often seems to be drawn in an incomprehensible manner, yet ballplayers have little trouble understanding it. Consider, for example, the comments of Christy Mathewson and Ty Cobb, two all-time greats with very different reputations for ethics.

Mathewson explained, "Even though the Athletics are charged with stealing the signs whether they did or not, it is no smirch on the character of the club, for they stole honestly—which sounds like a paradox." He then modified Charles Comiskey's dictum slightly by adding: ". . . All is fair in love, war, and baseball except stealing signs dishonestly, which listens like another paradox" (Christy Mathewson, *Pitching in a Pinch*, 143–144).

Ty Cobb had virtually the same viewpoint: "In the minds of the public there seems to be

an impression that sign stealing is illegal—at any rate, unsportsmanlike." He explained that sign stealing "is not so regarded by ballplayers" as long as it was done on the field. But as soon as mechanical devices were introduced, Cobb described the practice as "reprehensible" (Ty Cobb, *Memoirs of Twenty Years in Baseball*, 83).

(i) Garden Variety Trickery

11.1.1 Fixed Games. The Mutual club of New York was beaten 23-11 by the Eckford club of Brooklyn on September 28, 1865. The uncharacteristically poor play of Mutual catcher William Wansley attracted considerable attention and he was moved to the outfield after committing his sixth passed ball. After the game a committee of players accused Wansley, who admitted having received $100 from a gambler named Kane McLoughlin to throw the game. He had split the money with two teammates, Edward Duffy and Tom Devyr, in order to ensure the success of the plot. The three players were barred from baseball, but all were eventually reinstated (Dean A. Sullivan, ed., *Early Innings*, 49–53).

The extent of game fixing in early baseball is difficult to establish, since suspicions and accusations were far more common than actual proof. The best-of-three and best-of-five formats were particularly vulnerable to manipulation and led to direct charges of "hippodroming." In 1871 a Chicago sportswriter wrote in disgust: "According to previous arrangement, the Chicago base ball club was yesterday beaten again—the Olympics of Washington making

13 to their 8. The horse-racing program was as follows: These two clubs were to play each other for 'the best three in five games.' The Olympics had beaten once and the Chicagos twice, and if the latter had made yesterday's game they would have won the best three out of five, and the two clubs could have played together no more this season. So to secure the gate money of another game it was agreed that yesterday's contest should result in a tie [in the series], and thus another game would be necessary" (*Chicago Evening Mail*, July 1, 1871; reprinted in *Baseball in Old Chicago*, 25).

When the National League was formed in 1876, it went to great lengths to depict its product as clean baseball. How much this was reality and how much propaganda is debatable. The 1877 National League pennant race was tainted by a game-fixing scandal while the 1876 race was affected by the "Double-ball Racket" (see **11.1.12**). What is beyond dispute is that professional baseball was greatly damaged in the late 1860s and early 1870s by the public perception that games were often not on the level. The message that the National League had ended such practices, whether true or not, was enormously important to the future of the game.

11.1.2   Double Fix. Baseball's troubles with gambling reached a nadir in a game between Chicago and the Philadelphia White Stockings on October 14, 1875, when "It was openly charged on the field that it was a 'hippodroming' affair or 'double-cross,' players on both sides endeavoring to 'throw' the game" (*New York Clipper*, October 23, 1875).

11.1.3   Umpire Implicated in a Fix. National League umpire Dick Higham was accused of involvement in fixing games in 1882 and was fired. Higham's behavior was suspicious, but his descendant Harold Higham and Larry Gerlach have researched his case extensively and shown that his guilt is not entirely clear (Larry R. Gerlach and Harold V. Higham, "Dick Higham," *National Pastime* 20 [2000], 20–32). Higham is the only major league umpire to be fired for game fixing.

In the years before Higham there were sporadic attempts to bribe umpires, and accusations of crooked umpires were made from time to time. There is, of course, no way to prove or disprove such allegations now. But it seems safe to assume that the majority were simply sour grapes.

Since the Higham case there have been no serious accusations of umpire corruption. That is, of course, first and foremost a tribute to the integrity of the men in blue. In fairness, however, it should be noted that the presence of four umpires would make it very difficult for gamblers to be confident that a single umpire could decide the outcome of a game.

11.1.4   Doing It with Mirrors. A manager who wins games without much apparent talent is said to be "doing it with mirrors." The metaphor corresponds to an actual practice that was occasionally attempted in early baseball. In 1886 a rumor was "afloat that they have a new scheme in Kansas City to disable batters. A small boy perches on a roof outside the grounds, and with a piece of looking-glass reflects the sun's rays into the batter's eyes" (*Boston Globe*, May 18, 1886). In an 1897 National League game in Chicago: "A strange episode came up in the eighth. [Pirates right fielder] 'Patsy' Donovan made a sudden run toward Umpire [Jack] Sheridan and a moment later four small boys were chased off the field. The youngsters, under the leadership of 'Rusie,' the youth who attends to the park, were holding pieces of looking glass in the sun, and throwing the reflections into the eyes of the Pittsburg batters" (*Chicago Tribune*, July 31, 1897, 4). A 1905 article reported: "A Toledo bleacherite used a mirror to blind the Columbus players when at bat. Manager Clymer was backed up by the other occupants of the bleachers in having the disreputable and dirty practice abated" (*Sporting Life*, June 10, 1905). Bill Veeck reported that in 1935 the Cubs sold "Smile-with-Stan-Hack" mirrors and added that it was "rather strange how often the makeup of female bleacherites seemed to need attention when the opposition was hitting" (Bill Veeck with Ed Linn, *Veeck—As in Wreck*, 160).

11.1.5   Skip Play. The skip play, by which a runner took advantage of the single umpire to cut inside of a base, was associated with Mike Kelly in the 1880s (*Detroit Free Press*, May 10, 1886; *Boston Globe*, June 8, 1889). Kelly biographer Marty Appel has demonstrated that Kelly had a reputation for using this tactic, but he was far from alone (Marty Appel, *Slide, Kelly, Slide*, 48–49). It was a fairly regular practice in the 1870s and almost certainly originated not long after the rules specified that runners had to touch each base.

11.1.6   Electronic Sign Stealing. Throughout the 1900 season the Philadelphia Phillies were very successful at home. Two men who turned out to have a great deal to do with this were a seldom-used reserve player named Pearce "Petey" Chiles, who usually coached third base, and an even more infrequently used catcher named Morgan Murphy. There was widespread suspicion that the two were stealing signs. Indeed, when Murphy had signed his contract, the *Boston Herald* remarked, "Hereafter it will be the proper thing for a club to carry with it a sign discoverer" (*Boston Herald*, reprinted in *Brooklyn Eagle*, February 4, 1900).

But it was not until Cincinnati visited Philadelphia for a game on September 17, 1900, that the secret was revealed. The *Philadelphia Inquirer* described the bizarre scene that interrupted the game: "In the third inning of the first game Tommy Corcoran, the captain of the Cincinnati team, walked over to the coachers' box at third base and began to scratch gravel in a way that made Petey Chiles look like a blacksmith. But there was an apparent purpose in Tommy's scratching. In fact, his actions caused consternation on the bench which is held down by the genial [Bill] Shettsline, for, while Corcoran was in the midst of his energetic endeavors, Groundkeeper [Joe] Schroeder, accompanied by a sergeant of police, swooped down upon the Cincinnati generalissimo, but not before he had lifted a board, disclosing a nicely prepared hole, in which was snugly fitted an electric apparatus.

"Of course, there was considerable commotion among the players and the spectators, the latter of whom had no idea what was coming off. [Cincinnati coach] Arlie Latham was among the first to get a peep in the little vault.

"'Ha! Ha!' he said. 'What's this? An infernal machine to disrupt the noble National League, or is it a dastardly attempt on the life of my distinguished friend, Col. John I. Rogers?' . . .

"Cleverly concealed in the cache was a little telegraphic instrument, by which Morgan Murphy, chief of the signal service, tipped off to the coacher the kind of ball that the pitcher was about to deliver. The coacher in turn tipped off the batsman and there you are.

"Before he arrived in this city, Manager Bob Allen, of the Cincinnati Club, was told that the Phillies were using some sort of electric signals on the pitchers. Allen started an investigation, with the disclosure stated above.

"This may be honest base ball, but the general public has nothing but contempt for people who play with marked cards" (*Philadelphia Inquirer*, September 18, 1900).

Arlie Latham later explained that he concluded there must be something buried under the third-base coaching box because Chiles was standing with one foot in a puddle (Christy Mathewson, *Pitching in a Pinch*, 145–148—though there are many errors in this account). The fact that Chiles's leg often seemed to twitch while he was coaching likely also contributed to the discovery (Joe Dittmar, "A Shocking Discovery," *Baseball Research Journal* 20 [1991], 52).

The buzzer scheme sent—ahem—shockwaves through the baseball world. Two days later Petey Chiles got a bit of revenge on the Reds. He spent the game coaching from first base while standing in the position and regularly twitching. The Reds came out again and began digging furiously but found only a piece of wood that Chiles had buried there. Ten days later the Reds uncovered a more conventional sign-stealing ring in Pittsburgh. It transpired that Pittsburgh and Philadelphia had been aware of each other's systems but had agreed not to reveal the other club's secret (Joe Dittmar, "A Shocking Discovery," *Baseball Research Journal* 20 [1991], 53).

Christy Mathewson contended that Philadelphia gained an important residual benefit from their buzzer. He claimed that the team's batters had convinced pitchers that they could hit high fastballs during the 1900 season, and as a result got a steady diet of curves in the years that followed (Christy Mathewson, *Pitching in a Pinch*, 48).

The Phillies' buzzer scheme was many years ahead of its time. Nothing as sophisticated is known to have been used again, though clubs have of course used binoculars and the like. George Will noted that in recent years clubs have used satellite dishes and telecasts to learn their opponents' signals (George F. Will, *Men at Work*, 53–54).

11.1.7   Jewelry. According to Patsy Donovan, 1880s pitching star John Clarkson wore "a big belt buckle in such fashion that it flashed light into the batters' eyes" (*Washington Post*, August 9, 1903). The issue of batters being distracted by pitchers' apparel has resurfaced in a number of different guises over the years, as reflected in a series of rules changes to eliminate items that might distract batters.

In 1931 the major leagues banned pitchers from having glass buttons or polished metal on their uniforms. Eight years later it was mandated that the pitcher's glove could be only one color. In 1950 pitchers' gloves were further restricted from being either white or gray. The pitcher was also prohibited from having ragged sleeves or attaching items of different colors to his uniform.

Nonetheless it is safe to assume that rule makers in 1950 could not have anticipated several recent instances. Arthur Rhodes, for example, was ordered to remove an earring that was said to be distracting hitters. Trever Miller was told that he would have to wear long sleeves to obscure the tattoos that cover his arms.

11.1.8   Jumping Jacks.

In a game on August 9, 1950, Boston Braves batter Bob Elliott asked the second-base umpire to move out of his line of vision. This gave Giants second baseman Eddie Stanky an idea, and he stationed himself exactly where the umpire had been standing and moved around to distract Elliott. His tactic attracted little attention, so Stanky refined it. When the Giants played the Phillies two days later, Stanky "drove Andy Seminick, Philadelphia's catcher, all but crazy with his annoying habit of planting himself behind second and waving his arms to distract a batter as the pitcher delivers."

The umpires could find no rule to prevent it, so after the game they attempted to contact National League president Ford Frick for a ruling. Unable to track him down by the opening of the next day's game, they asked Giants manager Leo Durocher not to repeat the tactic until Frick could render a decision. Durocher agreed, but during the game Seminick precipitated a brawl with a hard slide into third base. Durocher then told Stanky to do as he pleased, so he recommended his jumping jacks and the umpires ejected him.

A heated debate ensued. Phillies manager Eddie Sawyer called it "unsportsmanlike and strictly bush league stuff." Durocher, however, maintained: "Smart ball players have been pulling stuff like that for all the twenty-five years I've been in baseball and it's perfectly legal as far as I'm concerned. . . . After all, this is not Chinese checkers we're playing" (Joseph M. Sheehan, *New York Times*, August 12, 13, and 14, 1950).

Additional arguments were advanced on both sides. Some wondered how Stanky's tactic was any different from a base runner who jockeys off a base to disconcert the pitcher. But others felt that distracted batters would be unable to avoid pitched balls and noted that

Seminick had been hit by a pitch while Stanky was distracting him (*Washington Post*, August 14, 1950).

Ford Frick ended the debate by instructing umpires to eject fielders for "antics on the field designed or intended to annoy or disturb the opposing batsman" (*Chicago Tribune*, August 14, 1950).

11.1.9   Corked Bats.

The art of corking bats is an ancient one. Henry Chadwick complained in 1867 about the recent practice of using bats illegally "made with insertions of rubber or whalebone" (Henry Chadwick, *Haney's Base Ball Player's Book of Reference for 1867*, 119). In 1888, George Wright claimed that around 1860 "a hollow ash bat, loaded with a movable ball of lignum vitae, was used as an experiment by some players. A hole was bored some distance into the larger end of the bat, the lignum vitae ball inserted, and the hole stopped up. This ball played freely back and forth in the hollow, and whenever the batsman brought forward the bat for the stroke the ball rolled toward the end away from the handle and the ball sent in by the pitcher struck the bat at a point opposite the lignum vitae ball. There was little advantage gained by this, however, as the rolling and snapping of the ball inside of the bat often sounded like the 'tick' of a foul ball, and occasioned considerable trouble."

Later in the same article, Wright added, "A laughable thing happened in connection with another 'crank' bat once while I was testing it. . . . Some person had taken a bat, bored a hole in the larger end for about six inches, inserted several small rubber balls about two inches in diameter and plugged up the end with cork, so as to give the bat no additional weight. The idea was to have a springy bat that would not crack.

"I was striking, and neither the pitcher nor catcher knew any thing at the time about the 'crank' bat. A ball was pitched and I struck at it, but unfortunately the stopper in the end of the bat came out, and three or four of the rubber balls flew out in all directions. . . . I was put out on a 'foul,' one 'liner,' one 'pop fly,' and two 'sky-scrapers' all at once. This was certainly discouraging for a batsman, and I need hardly say that this unfortunate episode brought its career to a timely close" (*Boston Herald*, reprinted in *Cincinnati Enquirer*, April 29, 1888).

An 1883 article recalled that during the post–Civil War boom, "One country nine, famous for its prowess in hitting, had its bats made of huge square pickets 'whittled' down at one end. Another team bore vast round beams of bass-wood as large as a man's thigh, bored out and charged with cork to make them light" (*New York Evening Post*, reprinted in the *Detroit Free Press*, May 23, 1883).

Undeterred by the failure of his earlier experiment, in 1874 George Wright unveiled a four-dollar bat with "a cane fitted through the whole length of the bat, which makes it proof against breaking from hitting a ball with it, and the cane imparts an elasticity to the bat, which is a great aid in batting" (unidentified clipping, 1874 Scrapbook, Baseball Hall of Fame). In 1875 Joe Blong of the Covington Stars was caught using a "spring bat" that "was made a little too heavy and bored at the end to lighten it" (*Cincinnati Enquirer*, August 23, 1875; *Lexington Press*, quoted in *Cincinnati Enquirer*, August 28, 1875). John Gruber noted that bats of the 1870s were subject to "desecration by having holes bored into them, in which metal, particularly lead, was poured." As a result, the National League approved a rule change in 1876 that added the word "wholly" to the requirement that bats be made of wood (John H. Gruber, *Sporting News*, November 11, 1915).

The new wording did not of course eliminate the practice of tampering with bats. A game between the Blue Sox of Owosso and the Brown Stockings of Flint prompted charges of doctored balls and "corked bats" (*Owosso* [Mich.] *Press*, August 8, 1877). Howard Rosenberg cites several additional examples of illegal bats (Howard W. Rosenberg, *Cap Anson 3*, 374–377). A St. Louis man named Charles Held even patented a corked bat in 1903 (Dan Gutman, *Banana Bats and Ding-Dong Balls*, 24–25).

Dan Gutman noted that it is safe to assume there was very little bat-corking from the 1920s to the 1950s. This wasn't the result of a change in ethics but rather a change in batting philosophy (Dan Gutman, *It Ain't Cheatin' If You Don't Get Caught*, 77). As discussed under "Weights" (9.2.3), Babe Ruth's success with massive bats led to these becoming the weapons of choice among sluggers. Since cork makes a bat lighter, the hitters who did doctor their bats during this era usually did so by adding heavier substances such as nails (Dan Gutman, *It Ain't Cheatin' If You Don't Get Caught*, 72–73). Even so, St. Louis Browns slugger Ken Williams used a bat in 1923 that was bored out and had a wooden plug inserted in its base. When Washington filed a complaint, American League president Ban Johnson ruled that bats were legal only if made of a single solid piece of wood (Al Kermisch, "Ruth's Laminated Bat Banned in 1923," *Baseball Research Journal* 1983, 49). When batters began to realize that bat speed generates more force than bat weight, corking again made sense.

11.1.10   Ejection Scoffing. It is common knowledge that ejected managers continue to make decisions from the tunnel or the clubhouse. A few have attempted to be more blatant.

Browns manager George Stovall was indefinitely suspended by American League president Ban Johnson following a run-in with umpire Charley Ferguson on May 4, 1913. But the *Washington Post* observed, "Although George Stovall is supposed to be an exile from baseball, he sits near the St. Louis bench and directs his team through a hole. Looks like a case of making a farce of Ban Johnson's sentence" (*Washington Post*, May 12, 1913).

Venice manager Hap Hogan was ejected from a Pacific Coast League game the following season. When he tried sitting in the stands in his uniform and signaling to his players, the umpire again tossed him out. Hogan responded by putting a Panama hat and frock coat over his uniform and continuing to pass instruction along to his players (*Los Angeles Times*, April 18, 1914).

On June 29, 1989, Boise manager Mal Fichman was ejected from a game but returned to the field disguised as team mascot Humphrey the Hawk. He received a one-game suspension.

In a June 9, 1999 game, Mets manager Bobby Valentine was ejected but "reappeared on the bench in a disguise: black Mets t-shirt, baseball-type cap, sunglasses and a fake moustache" (Murray Chass, "Mets Woes Are Hard to Conceal," *New York Times*, June 11, 1999). Valentine initially denied that it was him but eventually owned up and was suspended for two games. He maintained that his action was not that singular: "I've heard of managers coming back as part of the ground crew, or sitting in a front-row seat and giving signs. Or sitting in the bleachers with binoculars, or standing behind a photographer or a TV cameraman" (Dave Anderson, "Manager Issued a Foolish Challenge," *New York Times*, June 12, 1999).

11.1.11   Fake Foul Tips. As described under "Foul Ground" (1.20), most of the bat-and-ball games that preceded the Knickerbockers did not include the concept of foul territory. This meant that, as noted under "Bunts" (2.2.1), it was considered good play in some versions for the batter to deliberately tip the ball over the catcher's head. It therefore seemed only fair to credit a catcher with an out if he thwarted this tactic, and this continued to be the rule under the Knickerbockers' rules. That remained the case until enterprising catchers began to find ways to exploit this rule.

Tim Murnane reported that Bill Craver, who was banned from baseball after the 1877 season, "had a way of snapping his fingers, claiming the ball tipped the bat, and often making outs in this way" (*Boston Globe*, January 17, 1915). *Sporting News* noted in 1886, "Ball players in Pittsburg are talking about the smart young catcher of an amateur club, who was remarkable for catching many batsmen out on foul tips, even when the bat didn't seem to strike within three or four inches of the ball. An investigation revealed that the catcher had a gum band attached to his glove, and when he desired to foul out a man he would raise the band with one finger, and when the ball passed under the bat release it. The band would snap against the glove and all within hearing would hear a supposed foul tip" (*Sporting News*, June 21, 1886).

Connie Mack was particularly associated with this tactic, and he later explained how it was eliminated: "Probably a little trick which I introduced and worked repeatedly under the old 'foul tip' rule was responsible for the change in this rule. When the batter was declared out on a 'foul tip' caught directly off the bat, and after the introduction of the big mitt for catchers in 1885 or 1886, as a batter would swing at a ball and miss it cleanly I would frequently clip the tip of my big mitt with the finger tips of my right hand, making a sound exactly as though the batter had tipped the ball with his bat and, as I caught the ball, the umpire invariably called the batter out on a caught 'foul tip.' In fact, in the majority of cases the batter himself was fooled and actually thought he was legitimately retired. Subsequently the rule was changed so that a foul ball had to go at least ten feet in the air or be caught ten feet away from the plate for the batter to be declared out, so this trick was no longer possible" (Connie Mack, "Memories of When the Game Was Young," *Sporting Life* [monthly], June 1924).

An 1891 article observed, "Several seasons ago, when foul tips were out, it used to be an easy play for catchers to snap their fingers, making a noise resembling a foul tip and securing a put-out whenever necessary. Mike de Panger [DePangher] used to work this dodge in a more artistic fashion than any other catcher" (*Williamsport Sunday Grit*, June 7, 1891). Charles "Pop" Snyder was also said to have been a master of snapping his finger to simulate a tip (R. M. Larner, "Old-Time Baseball in the White Lot," *Washington Post*, June 26, 1904).

The issue was resolved after the 1888 season with the rule change noted by Mack. The tactics of catchers such as Craver and Mack were an important reason for the rule change, but another major factor was the introduction of catchers' mitts (see 9.3.2). For the next six seasons, a foul tip was a nonplay even if caught. After the 1894 season the rule was adjusted so that a caught foul tip counted as a strike.

11.1.12 Double-ball Rackets. The fact that only one ball was used in early baseball left considerable room for shenanigans. The St. Louis club of 1876 was later accused of using the "double-ball racket." Whenever St. Louis went to bat a lively ball was used, but when their opponents were at bat a dead one would be substituted. The ploy was said to have been used in a three-game series against Hartford from July 11 to 15 (*Sporting News*, March 10, 1888). Hartford entered the series in a tight race with Chicago for the pennant, but after three straight shutout losses the race was essentially over.

This posed a huge threat to the game's integrity, and steps were immediately taken to address it. The *Chicago Tribune*, which had become the league's unofficial mouthpiece, declared, "The obvious and feasible way out of the unpleasantness of having different kinds of balls is for the League to settle upon specifications for a contract with some good maker for a perfectly uniform ball for all games for the championship, and then make the Secretary their agent to take the balls from the maker, stamp them, and sell them to the clubs" (*Chicago Tribune*, November 19, 1876, 10). Soon the league did follow that course, entering into a contract with Louis Mahn of Boston to make the official league ball with the understanding "that he should submit all balls for league use to the Secretary's inspection, and that after being approved each one should be packed in paper and in foil to exclude the atmosphere, and then sealed in a box so as not to be opened until delivered to the umpire just before the game" (*Chicago Tribune*, December 10, 1876, 7).

An 1878 game account reported: ". . . Early in Tuesday's game the ball all of a sudden became soft and mushy. No one could account for it, but the general impression was strong among the players that a soft ball had been run in between innings by the visitors. To prevent the repetition of the 'same old game,' the Umpire took possession of the ball just so soon as an inning was finished and held it till the pitcher was in his position ready to deliver it" (*Cincinnati Enquirer*, May 31, 1878).

Following the 1879 season the National League took additional steps in the form of "a rule requiring the contractor to furnish all League balls to the League secretary and subject to his inspection, and the seal of that officer is the final evidence of the legality of each ball" (*Chicago Tribune*, October 26, 1879, 7). While not a foolproof solution, the National League did have comparatively few complaints in later years.

By contrast, rival leagues lacked the central organization necessary to take such precautions and continued to be plagued by the issue. Near the end of the 1878 season, the *Tribune* boasted, "The League has been using a uniform and excellent ball, which has given general satisfaction. The International Association advertised that they would use the same kind and quality, and entered into some sort of contract to that effect; but they missed a trick when they neglected to have the balls used by them inspected by some one in the same way that the League balls have all been inspected by Secretary [Nick] Young. In the first part of the season all went well, but after a while a difference began to be seen, and it was rumored and asserted that the maker was filling orders with fast or slow balls to suit the people to whom he sold them. . . . When the Chicagos went to New Bedford on their last trip they played with a ball marked 'International Association,' according to the rule in such case made; but they had hardly finished two innings before it began to act like one of the old soft balls that Bradley used to be so successful with in St. Louis, and long before the game was over it became a physical impossibility to hit this mush ball outside the diamond. So strange did this appear to the Whites that they cut open the ball after the game and found just what they expected—a lump of mud rubber, which bears no resemblance to the ounce of rubber which should be there" (*Chicago Tribune*, September 1, 1878).

Since the precious status of baseballs (**1.26** "New Balls") made it impossible to eliminate such tricks, alert clubs began to take their own precautions. An unspecified player explained in 1893, ". . . Whenever a new ball was thrown out last season and we were in the field it was tossed to the pitcher, who put his private mark on the same, so the visitors could not change the ball. With our pitchers it was the custom to put two marks with a long finger nail on the ball across one of the seams which would remain there as long as the ball was in play" (*Sporting News*, January 21, 1893).

Nevertheless, new variations continued to emerge, and Howard Rosenberg found multiple examples during the 1894 season (Howard W. Rosenberg, *Cap Anson 3*, 361). In 1899, Arthur Irwin singled out Minneapolis manager John S. Barnes for waiting until his team was ahead and bringing out "a stack of springy balls on tap in his ice chest. The refrigerator warped the rubber in the sphere and when it met the bat, it sputtered feebly into the hands of an infielder like the last dying kick of a Fourth of July skyrocket." Irwin reported that another team's captain "dropped half a dozen balls into a flour sack and pounded them with an ax" (quoted in Gerard S. Petrone, *When Baseball Was Young*, 118).

According to Irwin, New Orleans manager Charlie Frank took such shenanigans to a new level in the early twentieth century. Frank brought to each game a valise that contained "four rows of baseballs. The first row consisted of new, good baseballs; the second row, new punk balls. Those in the third row were balls that had an abnormal amount of rubber in them. The fourth row also held dirty balls, but they were as dead as Caesar. And accordingly, as Charlie's team was in the lead or behind, he would throw out those balls.

"The scheme Charlie worked was this. He'd break the seal of the box, of course, take out the balls, tie a piece of cord around them, and hang them up in a dry refrigerator for a few days. At the end of that time, you could slam them on the ground with all your might but they wouldn't bounce half an inch. The fourth row of balls he had in his valise were of the same sort."

Thus prepared, Frank was able to supply whatever type of baseball would be most advantageous to his team. Irwin added: "Of course, it is customary for the umpire to examine the cover of the new balls to see that the seal is not broken. But Frank had a way of getting around that too. Instead of handing the ball to the umpire, he'd take it out of his valise and slam it on the ground. The box would burst open, the ball would roll out, and the ump, suspecting nothing, would hand it to the pitcher" (quoted in Gerard S. Petrone, *When Baseball Was Young*, 119).

As a result, by the early twentieth century, umpires were taking responsibility for the supply of balls before the game started, which made it virtually impossible for the home team to change to dead balls after grabbing the lead. Even this did not entirely eliminate such chicanery. Dan Gutman reported that in the 1960s light-hitting clubs were still freezing balls before games to handicap the opposing team's sluggers (Dan Gutman, *It Ain't Cheatin' If You Don't Get Caught*, 83–84).

11.1.13 Hidden-potato Tricks. Minor league catcher Dave Bresnahan of Williamsport pulled the hidden-potato trick on August 31, 1987. He threw a peeled potato wildly to third base and then tagged the runner out when he trotted home. The umpire ruled the runner safe and fined Bresnahan, who was released by the Indians the next day. While the play received enormous publicity, there was nothing new about it.

In 1889 a member of the Staten Island Athletic Club pulled a similar play in a game against Yale. The umpire ruled the runner safe, and the player was asked to resign from the club (H. Allen Smith and Ira L. Smith, *Low and Inside*, 116). According to an 1895 article, "A Lock Haven (Pa.) player named Dunkle has invented a new trick. A game was in progress at Williamsport on Thursday and had proceeded to the ninth inning. Lock Haven was one score ahead. Williamsport was at the bat. One of the runners was on first and the Lock Haven pitcher pretended to throw the ball to the first baseman to catch the runner, but it (not the ball, the potato) went over the baseman's head, and the runner started for second. Before he arrived there, however, the pitcher tossed the real ball to the second baseman and the umpire called the runner out. The Williamsporters refused to call it a square deal and the game ended" (*Dallas Morning News*, November 12, 1895).

Legendary umpire Bill Klem observed in 1908: "An old gag they used to spring was that of pelting some object high over a base-runner's head and then nailing him with the ball in play. Of course that sort of thing was not covered in the rules. But the trick was never tolerated. Umpires invariably sent the man back. Some half dozen narrowly escaped lynching, however, on the stand" (quoted in *Sporting Life*, May 16, 1908).

A player named Marshall Mauldin recalled a Lafayette teammate attempting the play in a 1934 Evangeline League game. With runners on second and third, the catcher "threw wild into left field and the man on third and the man from second came legging it home. Imagine their embarrassment when our catcher stood right in front of the plate and tagged each one out with the ball. While the boys, out yonder, were chasing an iced potato, whitewashed. He brought it along from home for an emergency. The umpire, of course, was standing behind the pitcher with men on the bases and a big beef went up, naturally. Our catcher claimed he just happened to see the potato lying there and was throwing it off the ballfield, but I guess the umpire didn't believe him 'cause he just put the men back on base" (quoted in Dennis Snelling, *A Glimpse of Fame*, 169).

Harold Seymour cited a couple of additional instances of the hidden-potato play being used in nonprofessional games (Harold Seymour, *Baseball: The People's Game*, 127, 588). So Bresnahan's tactic just revived a seemingly forgotten ploy from an earlier era.

11.1.14 Chalk Erasing. It is a curious paradox that the pitcher's area was being delineated by permanent markings in the 1880s (see 14.3.8) while batters continue to be confined by chalked lines. As early as 1906 umpire Hank O'Day suggested that white rubber strips be used to mark the batter's box so that batters could not obliterate the lines. But batters continue to stand between chalk lines that they can and do erase.

11.1.15 Obstruction. In spite of rules to the contrary, many clubs of the 1880s and 1890s took advantage of the single umpire to obstruct base runners. The ploy is usually associated with the Baltimore Orioles of the 1890s, but they were not the first to use it.

An 1888 note explained: "The St. Louis Browns are playing as tricky ball as ever, and have added this new wrinkle: Whenever an opposing base-runner is on third, as soon as the ball is hit the entire infield, except the man to whom the ball is batted, will start for home, ostensibly to back up the catcher, but really to block the runner, as each one after the other will cross the base path in front of him and thus retard his progress. They do not injure him, but simply block him adroitly" (*Toledo Blade*, May 26, 1888).

Once it became common to have more than one umpire (see **8.1.3**), it became much harder for fielders to obstruct a base runner without being detected. But as discussed under "Catchers Blocking the Plate" (**4.4.11**), an unwritten exception seems to have been made for the catcher.

11.1.16   Who's on Second (and Third)? Fred Clarke tried a novel tactic in 1897: "In Sunday's game at Chicago Captain Clarke of the colonels quietly detached the second base from its moorings, ran down to third and, when caught, showed the base to [umpire Hank] O'Day and claimed that he had stolen it and was safe as long as his hands were on the bag. It was a new point in baseball and the crowd laughed weirdly through the misty rain. O'Day called him out, and the joke was on little Freddie. Clarke was sorry a moment later, when [Hans] Wagner hit sharply into center—a hit that would have tied the score" (*Nebraska* [Lincoln] *State Journal*, August 4, 1897).

(ii) Gardening Variety Trickery

The phrase a "level playing field" is now largely used as a metaphor, but that wasn't always the case. In early baseball, clubs often derived obvious advantages from a groundskeeper who could tailor the ballpark to their strengths. Christy Mathewson noted, "For a long time it was considered fair to arrange the home field to the best advantage of the team which owned it, for otherwise what was the use in being home?" (Christy Mathewson, *Pitching in a Pinch*, 291).

As described in my biography of two renowned early groundskeepers, brothers Tom and John Murphy, during the 1890s these efforts created the largest home-road differentials in won-lost percentages in baseball history (Peter Morris, *Level Playing Fields*, 117). The situation prompted Washington manager Tom Loftus to declare in 1903 that he had won "a signal victory in the meeting of the rules committee last week. He was bitterly opposed to the action of some club managers building a mountain out of the pitcher's box and making the base lines from the plate to first and third bases mere gutters for the convenience of the players who could dump the ball into the diamond and have it stay there. Teams which contain several good bunters made troughs of these base lines, so that when a ball rolled to them it would not go into foul territory unless there was force enough behind it to carry

it out of the trough. There certainly was a great advantage in that scheme to a team of bunt hitters. The practice of raising the pitcher's box to a dizzy height was another abuse that aided some clubs and pitchers. A twirler like Cy Young, who depends upon wonderful speed, found a great advantage in the high box, for he would shoot the ball down to the batter, and in descending to the plate it was given added force. It was a trick more than an innovation" (*Washington Post*, March 1, 1903, 32).

Nowadays major league baseball goes to considerable lengths to ensure that ground conditions are standard at all major league parks. Groundskeepers at grass parks still find ways to help the home club, but they do so in comparatively subtle ways. George F. Will explained that a good groundskeeper can greatly increase the chance of a bunt staying fair or rolling foul: "A determined groundskeeper for a bunting team should be able to build an inward slope on the foul lines, a decline of as much as two inches in the two feet from the foul line to the infield grass. Such a slope radically improves the odds on a bunt staying fair" (George F. Will, *Men at Work*, 267). Similarly, groundskeepers can still aid the home club by keeping the grass longer or shorter and the ground harder or softer, depending on the makeup of their club. But these methods are a far cry from the brazen tactics of earlier years.

11.2.1   Unplayable Grounds. The *St. Louis Post-Dispatch* reported in 1884 that Cleveland had had several injuries at once during the previous season. So when a slight rain fell, manager Frank Bancroft attached a hose to a hydrant and flooded the grounds. Providence manager Harry Wright had to agree to a postponement (*St. Louis Post-Dispatch*, August 25, 1884).

11.2.2   Slow Base Paths. When Abner Dalrymple reached the National League in 1878, he found that "Sliding to bases was a hazardous performance. . . . [Boston second baseman Jack] Burdock proposed to stop base stealing. He carried in his pocket gravel that was like broken stone. If a dangerous base stealer made first base Burdock scattered this treacherous gravel around second base. Many a man, before he was familiar with Burdock's defense, came up with injured leg, face, arm, or hand. After a while few men would undertake to steal Burdock's base" (*Chicago Tribune*, September 23, 1928, A7). In 1882 Chicago player-manager Cap Anson accused the Buffalo club of having "erected a sandhill just inside of first base for the purpose of making it uphill work for the Chicagos to steal down to second. There being no base-runners in the Buffalo team, of course the mound makes no difference to them" (*Chicago Tribune*, May 14, 1882). An 1886 series in Philadelphia saw the home club put pebbles on the base paths to deter St. Louis's base stealers. The Browns brought out brooms and swept them away. Charley Comiskey claimed there was fully a foot of sand around the bases to impede them (*Sporting News*, June 7 and 14, 1886).

Such tactics have remained part of the arsenal of groundskeepers ever since. The most notable instance occurred in 1962 when San Francisco Giants groundskeeper Matty Schwab, Jr., flooded the infield to slow down Maury Wills. The resulting mess was known as "Lake Candlestick." The Giants rewarded Schwab by voting him a full World Series share.

11.2.3 Mound Building. Until 1950 the rules specified that pitchers' mounds could be no more than fifteen inches high, but did not require a standard height. The early history of the mound is discussed in a later entry (see **14.3.9**).

Altering the height of the mound gradually developed into an art form. Researcher Steve Steinberg alerted me to this explanation by Arthur Daley: ". . . Home teams build them high or low in order to take advantage of whatever special deliveries their star hurlers possess. As a means of utilizing to the full the blinding side-arm speed of Walter Johnson, Washington leveled off the 'mound' so completely that it almost was a depression instead of an elevation. Usually it was so scuffed that finding the rubber was not easy. Hence Senator pitchers acquired the understandable habit—shame on them!—of edging up a few inches before each pitch" (Arthur Daley, *Inside Baseball*, 61).

Bill Veeck described the mound as one of the prime concerns of the man whom he referred to as "the Michelangelo of grounds keepers," Emil Bossard. Veeck explained, "Our mound at Cleveland always changed according to the pitcher of the day. Bob Feller always liked to pitch from a mountaintop so that he could come down with that great leverage of his and stuff the ball down the batter's throat. Ed Lopat of the Yankees liked a wide, flat mound. When

Lopat was pitching against Feller, we'd make it so high that if he had fallen off he'd have broken a leg. An artist like Bossard takes both pitchers into consideration and keeps sculpting and shaping the mound daily to give the greatest possible advantage to the home team" (Bill Veeck with Ed Linn, *Veeck—As in Wreck*, 161).

Until 1950 there was nothing illegal about such tactics. In that year a standard mound height of fifteen inches was finally written into the rulebook. Groundskeepers continued to tailor the slopes to the preference of the home pitchers, but the growing prominence of relievers limited the effectiveness of these shenanigans. Yankees reliever Ryne Duren explained, "Bob Turley wanted the mound at Yankee Stadium to be flat and since he was the top gun of the staff in 1958, the groundskeepers kept it that way. I preferred it to be sloped. . . . One day, I threw my first pitch and my foot hit the ground and I thought my knee was going to hit me in the chin" (quoted in Danny Peary, *We Played the Game*, 420).

In 1969, after the most dominant season for pitchers in recent history, the mound was lowered to its current height of ten inches. Major league baseball now regularly measures mounds to ensure compliance.

11.2.4 Dimensions. On April 25, 1981, Seattle manager Maury Wills had the grounds crew enlarge the batter's box because Oakland had been complaining that Seattle player Tom Paciorek was stepping out of the box. Wills was suspended for two games.

11.2.5 Soaping the Soil. Another trick of early groundskeepers was adding soap to the soil around the pitching area. Christy Mathewson explained the purpose: when an opposing pitcher "was searching for some place to dry his perspiring hands and grabbed up this soaped earth, it made his palm slippery and he was unable to control the ball" (Christy Mathewson, *Pitching in a Pinch*, 294).

Groundskeepers who used this technique, such as Tom Murphy, tipped off the home pitchers as to where they could find reliable soil (Burt Solomon, *Where They Ain't*, 71). The entry on rosin bags (**9.5.7**) explains how pitchers eventually discovered an effective remedy to soaping the soil.

Chapter 12

TIMEOUTS

Reader: "Why does a batter get out of the box when a foul ball is knocked and there is a man on base?" Answer: "For the same reason that a hen crosses a dusty road. There is no known reason for either."—(*Washington Post*, October 11, 1908)

IF A nineteenth-century ballplayer could view baseball as it is played in the early twenty-first century, he would undoubtedly be amazed at how the game has grown and shocked at how it has changed. Of all the changes, perhaps none would surprise him more than the frequency with which the action halts. In nineteenth-century baseball something was always happening and players and fans were always kept on their toes, as the examples in this chapter will show.

This was not merely a feature of the game—for many it was baseball's distinguishing characteristic. When American baseball players toured England in 1874, a London sporting paper remarked, "In the cricket field there is at times a wearisome monotony that is entirely unknown to baseball. To watch it played is most interesting, as the attention is concentrated but for a short time and not allowed to succumb to undue pressure of prolonged suspense . . . it is a fast game, full of change and excitement and not in the least wearisome" (*London Field*, quoted in Adrian C. Anson, *A Ball Player's Career*, 73–74). Another British reporter marveled, "In base ball, action is continuous and rapid" (*Saturday Review*, August 15, 1874; reprinted in *Sporting News*, February 25, 1909). An 1889 tour of Australia yielded similar praise of baseball's

brisk pace (Mark Lamster, *Spalding's World Tour*, 139).

Such statements would certainly not be made about baseball today. Fans accustomed to nine-inning games that often last well over three hours will be startled to learn of sportswriter Charles Peverelly's 1866 pronouncement that "An American assemblage cannot be kept in one locality for the period of two or three hours, without being offered something above the ordinary run of excitement and attraction. They are too mercurial and impulsive a race not to get too drowsy and dissatisfied with anything which permits their natural ardor to droop even for a brief space of time" (Charles Peverelly, *The Book of American Pastimes*, 338).

The change in the pace of the game reflects a more dramatic revolution in the way Americans view time. There is a simple explanation for why baseball is the only major team sport played without a clock: baseball came of age as a professional sport in the 1860s and 1870s while sports like football and basketball did not reach a similar stage until three or four decades later. In the interim, Americans' attitudes toward time had been changed forever by the 1883 introduction of standard time at the behest of the railroads.

Historian Michael O'Malley portrayed this event as a fundamental break: "Once individuals experienced time as a relationship between God and nature. Henceforth, under the railroad standards, men and women would measure themselves in relation to a publicly defined time based on synchronized clocks." The result was that the final decades of the nineteenth century saw "a constant process of negotiation and redefinition of time's role and meaning in daily life" (Michael O'Malley, *Keeping Watch*, 145, 148).

This chapter assesses the impact of this society-wide redefinition of time on the game of baseball—how the pace of action on the diamond went from rapid and continuous to leisurely and disjointed, and how other aspects of baseball were affected by that change.

12.1 Calling Time. While they may not be happy about it, today's fans are accustomed to "time" being called on countless occasions in the course of a game. Although players can only request that an umpire call a timeout, these requests are routinely granted unless action is under way. But it wasn't always this way.

The game's early rules specified only that the action began when the umpire called "Play" and continued until he called "Time." The expectation was that a timeout would be called only when absolutely necessary, such as when the ball was lost. After the 1876 season the *Chicago Tribune* complained, "So much unnecessary and annoying delay has frequently been caused by calls for 'time' from the players, for no more valid reason than that they wanted to tie a shoe or tighten a belt, that it seems well to add to Sec. 7, of Rule 3, some such phrase as this: 'The umpire shall suspend play only for a valid reason, and is not empowered to do so for trivial causes, or only because a player may request it'" (*Chicago Tribune*, November 19, 1876, 10).

Those exact words were added to the National League rulebook in 1877. Early that season a batter named John Remsen asked for time in the middle of an at bat. The umpire who granted the request was lambasted by the *Tribune*: "It can hardly be said to come within this rule to stop play to throw the other side off their balance, or to give time to a rattled player to collect his thoughts. It is doubtful whether any excuse can be found for Remsen's conduct in standing astride of the plate so as to stop the game until he got ready to have it go on again" (*Chicago Tribune*, May 20, 1877).

At season's end umpires were again instructed to be stingy about granting stoppages. The *Brooklyn Eagle* explained that the umpire "can now only call 'time' when a player has been actually injured or taken ill. Before, the rule was that a player could call time to dispute the umpire's decision even" (*Brooklyn Eagle*, January 27, 1878). The *Chicago Tribune*'s baseball reporter expressed satisfaction that

the power to call time, which had "always been vested in, and generally abused by, an umpire, is now restricted to cases 'of illness or injury to himself or a player'" (*Chicago Tribune*, December 9, 1877).

Umpires, already filling a most unenviable position, cannot have been happy about having to enforce this dictate. How does one tell a batter that he doesn't have something in his eye?

The result was that the game started down a slippery slope. While the rule makers did their utmost to keep the ball continuously in play, the need for exceptions became clear. A new rule in 1887, for instance, specifically gave the umpire the right to call time "in case of annoyance from spectators."

Rain also had to be added to the list of reasons for stopping the action, though every effort was made to keep such interruptions as rare as possible. Henry Chadwick counseled umpires not to "suspend play on account of rain, unless it rains so heavily that spectators are obliged to seek shelter from 'the severity of the storm.' An ordinary drizzle or gentle shower does not produce this effect as a rule" (*Spalding's Official Base Ball Guide*, 1890, 179).

Another issue was blocked balls (see **12.6**)—balls that were touched by spectators. Everything possible was done to keep the ball live under such circumstances, but this only encouraged onlookers to try to help one side by interfering. The rule makers reluctantly had to add a provision that stopped play if a spectator ran off with the ball or deliberately knocked it out of reach.

With each additional new reason for stopping the action, umpires felt more inclined to be lenient about granting discretionary requests for timeouts. In turn, such requests gradually became more common and the resultant timeouts more lengthy. Sometimes this was simply stalling, but there were also practical considerations.

Substitutions became legal in the 1890s (see **1.32** and **6.2.1**), which further slowed the pace of the game. Another factor was the increasing amount of equipment; a reporter complained in 1898 that "the spectacle of a batsman selecting a bat, fumbling over a pile of sticks like an old lady gathering huckleberries, breeds a tired feeling among spectators" (quoted in Gerard S. Petrone, *When Baseball Was Young*, 63). As coaching and sign stealing (see **6.5.2**) became important parts of the game, signals increased in complexity, and the time needed to send and receive them created additional delays.

Pitchers eventually began to step off to receive signs and thereby put the ball out of play, a practice described as early as 1913 (*Washington Post*, July 13, 1913).

In addition, it had been customary for nineteenth-century baseball games to be played with a single ball. At one time a rule on the books required the game to be stopped for five minutes so that everyone could search for a lost ball. Even after this quaint rule was abandoned, a new ball was generally put in play only when the original one was lost. Only in the early twentieth century did it become customary to replace balls that had become worn or damaged (see **1.26**).

This created yet another reason for "time" to be called on a regular basis as well as an additional pause in the action while the pitcher rubbed the new ball until it met his satisfaction. After the hullabaloo over the emery ball (**3.2.13**), there were still more interruptions when batters asked the umpire to inspect the ball. If the requests led to a change of baseballs, the entire ritual started anew.

By the early twentieth century the game had assumed a more leisurely pace, and a new generation found the rules on timeouts archaic and perplexing. In 1907 a fan who inquired, "Has a batter any right to step out of the box after commencing his time of bat until it is finished?" was told that no such privilege was recognized in the rule book, but that most umpires permitted such interruptions (*Chicago Tribune*, August 11, 1907, A4).

A 1915 article added: "For a good many years you probably have wondered why a batsman always steps out of his box and carefully remains out of it while baserunners return to their bases after a foul ball has been batted. If the batsman forgets to do so he is almost sure to be ordered by the manager or coach to get out of the box in such cases. This applies, of course, to fouls that are not caught . . . ignorance of the playing rules is usually responsible for this practice.

"Ninety-nine out of every 100 average players will tell you if you ask them, that if a batsman stands in his box after hitting a foul ball, the pitcher can deliver the sphere as soon as he gets it again. But if the batsman gets out of his box, that stops play until the runner gets back. They will tell you that if the batsman remained in his position and the pitcher delivers the ball before the runner touches his base after a foul, the runner will have to go back anyway, before he can advance on a base hit. This isn't true.

"It doesn't make a bit of difference whether or not the batsman gets out of his box after a foul. It doesn't make a bit of difference whether the pitcher waits for the runner to go back before delivering the ball, and if the batsman should whale a pitched ball over the fence while a base runner was on the way back to his base after a foul hit. It would not make a bit of difference either.

"The reason is that the ball is automatically put out of play when a foul is made and not caught. It is just the same as if the umpire called 'time' for an injury or change of players. Nothing can happen legally until the ball is put in play again by the umpire. According to the rules, the umpire is supposed to call 'play' after every foul that is not caught. If you don't believe it read rule 36 in any guide or rule book.

"That the umpire doesn't call this after [every] foul is due to habit. That formality has been neglected so long that it has come to be understood that play shall be suspended until the runner gets back. Legitimately, the umpire is required to call 'play' at the start of a game or an inning before the pitcher delivers the ball, but only a few of them do it nowadays. Perhaps this disregard of a minor formality is responsible for growth of the misapprehension that the batsmen must get out of position after a foul to keep the ball out of play" (*Detroit Free Press*, September 26, 1915).

What's more, as is discussed under "Quick Pitches" (see **12.9**), the unfairness of allowing pitchers to hold the ball without pitching while giving batters no recourse was becoming increasingly apparent. The cumulative effect of these factors was for umpires to gradually become still more lenient about granting requests for time—but not without a fight.

When Ernie Stewart began umpiring in the American League in the early 1940s, supervisor Tom Connolly urged umpires to "Keep the ball in play" and "not to call time unless there was an injury or something of that nature." Stewart even boasted about denying players' requests for timeout (Larry R. Gerlach, *The Men in Blue*, 122–123). Bill James confirmed that before World War II, umpires "were very much in the habit of enforcing a certain degree of attention to time." Ones who were lax about this "were subject to criticism from the press, and were sometimes fined by the league, simply for failing to 'move the games along'" (Bill James, *The New Bill James Historical Baseball Abstract*, 320).

The fight seems to have gone out of umpires for a very simple reason: night games (see **14.1.3**). James perceptively observed, "Baseball's poetic and lyrical celebrants are fond of pointing out that baseball is the only major team sport without a clock. What these people don't understand is that, until about 1945, baseball *did* have a clock. It was called the sun" (Bill James, *The New Bill James Historical Baseball Abstract*, 319–320). When most stadiums suddenly acquired lights, there was no longer a sense of urgency about moving games along. The effect was dramatic.

By the time Larry Gerlach interviewed Ernie Stewart in the 1970s, Stewart complained, "One thing I detest about the umpire today is that they call time too often. They'll call time twenty times in a ball game" (Larry R. Gerlach, *The Men in Blue*, 122–123). Nowadays twenty stoppages in a game would be a remarkably small number, and too much has changed for it to be likely that this trend will ever be reversed.

But it is worth noting that frequent timeouts not only slow the pace of the game but have also reduced its spontaneity. Early ball games regularly featured plays that relied on alertness—stealing bases while a fielder was busy arguing with the umpire or otherwise distracted, quick pitches (**12.9**), hidden-ball tricks (**4.4.10**), and other plays defying categorization that will be described in the next few entries. All these have been rendered more difficult to execute, if not obsolete.

While the increased length of ball games has spawned many complaints, there has been less attention to the specific issue of timeouts. Yet it is important to recognize that the shift from a game in which time was rarely out and in which the action was virtually continuous to one in which timeouts are frequent has removed one of the features that initially distinguished baseball. This has occurred as the result of a series of accommodations to new conditions rather than as a conscious decision.

It is striking to compare baseball to the other major sports in this regard. In early basketball, for example, every basket was followed by a tip-off at center court. In hockey's early days, play stopped every time the puck went behind the goal line (Michael McKinley, *Putting a Roof on Winter*, 29). In football, the offensive side's option to begin play at any point is often exploited by means of no-huddle and two-minute attacks. Meanwhile baseball has moved steadily toward discontinuous action.

12.2 Pay Attention! The rules that were devised to ensure nonstop action led to many plays that seem absolutely bizarre to current sensibilities. In many instances the rule makers recognized that their intentions were being subverted and modified the rule in question. Yet each of these examples stays true to the basic principle that players—as well as spectators and umpires—had to be constantly paying attention at early baseball games because action was likely to break out when least expected.

A perfect example is an 1888 account of a game between the Mutuals of New York and the Eurekas of Newark in 1862. In the bottom of the tenth inning, Ed Brown of the Mutuals reached first with two out, took second on a passed ball, and stole third on a close play. He then loudly offered to fight any of the Eureka players. As soon as they had gathered around him, he ran home with the winning run (*New York Mail and Express*, reprinted in the *Chicago Inter-Ocean*, March 11, 1888; the Mutuals did indeed beat the Eurekas 14-13 in ten innings in a game on August 21, 1862).

Another instance was described in 1905: "At the Lowell-Harvard game on the Common May 15, 1867, a new rule was nicely demonstrated; the pitcher must be at his plate after 'called balls' before he could play, but the pitcher had followed the ball too near the striker and Mr. [George A.] Flagg, who was on third base, made a dash home and got there before the pitcher could resume play" (*Boston Journal*, March 6, 1905).

Part of the appeal of such plays was the risk on both sides. A perfect example is a rule that specified that a runner could not advance after a foul ball until the pitcher had possessed the ball. A few heady clubs realized that this presented a golden opportunity for the defense, as is shown by this 1861 account of a match between the Enterprise of Brooklyn and the Gotham of New York: "Ibbotson [of the Enterprise] was the fourth striker, and began with a high foul ball over the catcher's head. Cohen the catcher returned the ball to McKeever the pitcher, who purposely allowed it to slip through his hands towards right field, seeing which, [Enterprise base runner] Smith forgetting that it was a returned foul ball, and that he could not make his base until the ball had been settled in the hands of the pitcher, ran for his third base, when McKeever immediately picked up the ball and stood on second base, thus putting out Smith, it not being requisite to touch the player in such cases" (*New York Clipper*, August 31, 1861).

12.3 Hat Catches. As the preceding entry showed, the emphasis on keeping the action going sometimes led to imaginative efforts to take advantage of loopholes in the rules. Another instance was based upon Section 22 of the 1857 rules, which stated, "If any adversary stops the ball with his hat or cap, or takes it from the hands of a party not engaged in the game, no player can be put out unless the ball shall first have been settled in the hands of the pitcher."

This rule was obviously intended to penalize a player who used his cap, but the Red Stockings of Boston saw it as an opportunity. They tested their interpretation in a game on September 14, 1872. The opposing team had loaded the bases with no one out when pitcher A. G. Spalding induced an easy pop-up to shortstop George Wright. Spalding later recalled that Wright removed his cap and "deftly captured the ball therein. He then quickly passed it to me, standing in the pitcher's box. Under the rule, the ball was now in play. I threw it home, from whence it was passed to third, second and first, and judgment demanded of the umpire on the play." After deliberation, the umpire decided that, the rules notwithstanding, the play would not count at all (A. G. Spalding, *America's National Game*, 165–166).

A new, clearer rule was enacted in 1873 and modified in 1874. The revised wording awarded base runners a base if a fielder used his cap.

12.4 Broom Makers' Trots. Another example of the difficulty of designing rules to ensure a lively pace was an 1882 controversy over a rewording of the rule allowing a base runner to return to his base after a foul ball. As a sportswriter explained, the amended rule stated "that the runner will be allowed to return without being put out, provided he returns on the run; but the penalty is not expressly defined, and one result is that under a definition of the existing rule a runner failing to run back to a base can only be decided out when he is touched off a base when walking back" (*St. Louis Globe-Democrat*, June 17, 1882, 12). That was exactly what happened in a game on May 5, 1882, and the umpire's decision that Cap Anson was out because he *walked* back to his base after a foul caused a storm of protest (David Fleitz, *Cap Anson*, 150). In response, "runners evaded the law generally by adopting the 'broom maker's trot,' a mere leisurely jog" (John H. Gruber, "The Baserunner—Part Two," *Sporting News*, March 9, 1916). At the end of the season, Bid McPhee observed that the rule was aimed at "expediting

the game, though a few of the umpires were technical about it and put the base-runner out when he had only a few steps to go, if he failed to make them on a trot. The umpires have exercised their discretion all season as to whether or no a man should go out for not running back" (*Rocky Mountain News*, December 18, 1882, 2). The wording was revised that winter, and the controversy died.

12.5 The Litmus Test. Tim Murnane offered this description of a play that took place in a game on June 27, 1911: "[Stuffy] McInnis of the Athletics went to the plate as the first man up in the eighth. [Ed] Karger, pitching for Boston, had hurried to the box and Nonnemacher [catcher Les Nunamaker] was back of the plate, without his mask on. Karger found the players still walking on and off the field and tossed the ball to the catcher. McInnis reached out and tapped the ball to center, the Athletic players yelled 'Run!' and away went McInnis around the bases for a 'home run,' as no Boston player went after the ball.

"When the ball was hit, [Philadelphia outfielder Bris] Lord was crossing the field to the visitors' bench, and even [Philadelphia second baseman Eddie] Collins, who had stopped to talk to [Boston's Tris] Speaker, was still on the infield. Umpire [Rip] Egan allowed the run. The Boston spectators, the best posted fans in the world, lost their respect for Connie Mack's boys then and there" (*Sporting News*, July 6, 1911).

This play is as good a litmus test of two mutually incompatible outlooks as can be imagined. To the sensibility that dominated nineteenth-century baseball, McInnis's tactic is a heady one that exemplifies the principles of continuous action and of constant vigilance. But to a new generation that accepted frequent interruptions in the action as the price to pay for a game that rewarded planning and preparation, this was nothing but a cheap trick. The fact that this play occurred in 1911 is appropriate because, as will be clear throughout this chapter, the second decade of the twentieth century saw baseball make major strides away from continuous action and toward disjointed action.

12.6 Blocked Balls. A major obstacle to keeping the action nonstop was the fact that spectators often stood very near the field of play. At an 1860 game the field was so closely surrounded by onlookers that "players on the second base are frequently at a loss to know whether the third base is occupied or not" (*Philadelphia Morning Philadelphian*, August 27, 1860; quoted in George B. Kirsch, *The Creation of American Team Sports*, 192). Occasionally spectators were actually in fair territory.

In response, the blocked-ball rule was instituted to keep the action going when the ball was touched by a spectator. Since it was generally the fielding team that benefited if the ball was stopped by a spectator, the rule required the fielders to return the ball to the pitcher in his box before they could retire a base runner. Thus the blocked-ball rule essentially gave the runner a risk-free opportunity to take extra bases.

Play was supposed to be stopped if a spectator actually ran off with the ball or deliberately knocked it out of reach. But since the intention was to keep the action going, play generally continued if at all possible. For example, in an 1882 game, "the ball went into the crowd and became a block ball. Connolley went to field it, and as a small boy tossed it to him, [Joe] Weiss of the Cass struck it with his bat, allowing [Tommy] Shaughnessy to reach third base before the ball could be sent to center. This was not exactly right, but as there is no rule covering such work, it was passed by" (*Grand Rapids* [Mich.] *Democrat*, August 18, 1882).

The rule was also designed to limit the ability of partisan fans to help the home nine. This was illustrated by a crucial 1883 game in Boston in which Providence shortstop Jack Farrell threw wildly to first base on a ground ball hit by Boston's Jim Whitney. Whitney continued to round the bases while the fielders chased the ball. Then an unthinking spectator picked up the ball and tossed it to a Providence fielder. His intervention may well have prevented the run, but it was a mixed blessing for Providence as the ball now had to be relayed to pitcher Charley Radbourn before a play could be made on Whitney. Since Radbourn had "held his head and stuck to the box," Providence did profit from the spectator's interference, but at least it required alertness by the fielders for this to occur (William D. Perrin, *Days of Greatness*, 31).

The blocked-ball rule created scenarios for which there are no contemporary equivalents. This 1894 account is a prime example: "[Second baseman] Joe Quinn was the only one of the Browns equal to an emergency which arose in the second game at Sportsman's Park Sunday afternoon. [Ollie] Smith, the Louisville left fielder, hit down to short stop. [Shortstop

William] Ely made a great stop, but his quick throw went ten feet over [first baseman Roger] Connor's head. One of the spectators, who was inside the ground, picked up the ball. This made it a blocked ball, and it had to be held by the pitcher while standing in his position before it was in play. [Pitcher "Pink"] Hawley had run over to back up Connor. The Louisville players yelled 'Blocked ball' to Smith, who was sprinting around the bases, while Hawley started for the box on the run."

It was obvious that Hawley could not get back to his position in time, and the quick-thinking Quinn realized that only a decoy could save the day. He "ran to the pitcher's box and called to Connor to throw the ball. When Joe caught it, he made a bluff of throwing it to cut off Smith, who was ready to turn third base." If Smith had recognized that it was Quinn rather than Hawley in the box, he could have run home with impunity. But he didn't, and hustled back to third base. When Smith realized that he had been deceived, "it was too late for him to make another effort to score, as Hawley had reached the box and the ball was in play" (*St. Louis Post-Dispatch*, July 31, 1894).

This account also suggests one of the reasons why teams were reluctant to use pitchers to back up throws from the outfield (see **4.3.2**).

By this time few understood the rule and all its implications. Sportswriter John H. Gruber had to offer this explanation after another sequence that confused most onlookers: "A block ball is a batted or thrown ball that is stopped or handled by any person not engaged in the game. Whenever a block occurs the base runners may run the bases without being put out until the ball has been returned and held by the pitcher standing in his position. In spite of the fact that the entire rule, 35, including three sections, treats of the block ball, yet every time one occurs on the home grounds some player slips up on it. In the opening game last Thursday [St. Louis's Heinie] Peitz knocked the ball into the crowd against right field fence and scampered around the bases. When he reached third base some of the St. Louis coachers yelled for him to hold the bag, while others shouted for him to go home. In the meantime [Pittsburgh right fielder Patsy] Donovan secured the ball from the hands of a spectator and threw it to [first baseman Jake] Beckley, who wheeled around and let it fly to [catcher Connie] Mack at home base with the evident intention of heading off any attempt to score by Peitz. [Pitcher Ad]

Gumbert stood in his position and yelled without avail. But the moment Mack got the ball he shot it to Gumbert. Only then did the dull heads of both nines tumble to the racket. Had Peitz used his brain he would have scored during all the fuss and turmoil and Beckley would have had a sickly sensation for the balance of the afternoon" (John H. Gruber, *Pittsburgh Post*, May 6, 1894).

The blocked-ball rule was still on the books in 1916 and, as far as I can tell, for many years after that (*Washington Post*, July 30, 1916). But long before it was eliminated the rule had been rendered obsolete by several developments. The first was that the building of permanent stadiums made fan interference a rare occurrence. When overflow crowds did occur, it became increasingly common to institute special ground rules and, as the *Chicago Tribune* explained in 1909, "when ground rules are made that disposes of the blocked ball rule" (*Chicago Tribune*, July 11, 1909). Finally, as we have seen throughout this chapter, changing times meant that there was no longer an expectation of nonstop action.

12.7 Throw Me the Ball. During an 1889 game, while Chicago's Cap Anson was arguing with the umpire, "[Chicago pitcher Ad] Gumbert, who held the ball, turned around and faced [Pittsburgh base runner Al] Maul. The latter invited him to 'throw it here,' and he accommodatingly made the throw. Maul let the ball pass him and bolted for home, which he reached before [Chicago outfielder Jimmy] Ryan could field the ball and get it to the plate. Anson did not realize what was going on until the run was scored. Then he began to inquire how the ball got to centerfield. Gumbert answered: 'I thought the umpire had called time, and threw the ball to Maul when he asked me to.' The spectators became hysterical over the performance" (*Chicago Tribune*, April 26, 1889).

The same trick was used in at least three other professional games that season, prompting Henry Chadwick to scold: "It is bad enough in players to stoop to such contemptible tricks, but a line should be drawn when managers take a hand in any such work" (*Spalding's Official Base Ball Guide, 1890*, 132–133). Yet its use continued. Anson himself pulled the trick while coaching in a game against the Giants on June 8, 1895 (David Fleitz, *Cap Anson*, 236). In 1896, while coaching at third base, Pittsburgh's Denny Lyons fooled future Ivy League profes-

sor and university president Ted Lewis with what was even then described as "one of the moldiest chestnuts known to baseball." Lyons "called to Lewis to let him see the ball, and the youngster, never dreaming of a trick, tossed it toward Denny. Of course the latter stepped aside, and then broke for the plate, which he reached in safety, while [base runner Connie] Mack went to second. It was the old, old trick, and [umpire William] Betts refused to send Lyons back to third" (*Boston Globe*, July 15, 1896). And the great African-American pitcher Rube Foster pulled the trick at a key moment of a close 1907 game against the Indianapolis ABCs (Robert Cottrell, *The Best Pitcher in Baseball*, 35).

In 1908 umpire Bill Klem referred to this tactic as if it were a part of the past: ". . . The coacher used to tell the pitcher the ball was ripped or something like that, asking him to throw it to him that he might examine it. Then the coacher would side-step the throw and let the base-runner advance. According to the rules, this ruse is permissible to this day. But what umpire would stand for it, even if a big league pitcher were foolish enough to be hoodwinked?" (quoted in *Sporting Life*, May 16, 1908).

Klem was wrong, however. A 1915 syndicated column by Honus Wagner included pitcher Al Mamaux's description of how he fell for this trick in one of his first major league appearances: "It was in Chicago, and I obligingly tossed a ball to Roger Bresnahan, of the Cubs, and darned near lost the ball game then and there. There were two men out and Chicago players on first and second bases. Roger was coaching at third base. He was talking to me— not trying to kid me or get me up in the air, but chatting in a friendly sort of way. Finally, there was some sort of an argument at the plate. The ball had been returned to me by our catcher, and I was standing near the pitching mound trying to steady myself and looking at the ball.

"'Say, Al, toss that ball here so I can take a look at it,' Bresnahan yelled to me.

"I didn't give the thing a second thought. I just tossed it to him, and darned if he didn't step to one side and yell to the runners to 'Come on.' They came, all right. Each advanced a base, and they would have gone farther if [Pittsburgh infielder] Jimmy Viox hadn't run like an Indian and retrieved that ball in a hurry.

"Well, maybe our gang didn't ride me. I heard nothing else for a month or more. But it cured me. I wouldn't toss a baseball to an opposing coacher now if the umpire told me to do it. I'd hand the onion to the ump and let him do what he wanted with it" (*Detroit Free Press*, July 25, 1915).

Mamaux debuted in 1913, but he pitched only one game that season and was not charged with an error. So most likely this took place in 1914.

Wagner's column describing Mamaux's blunder appeared in late July 1915, and perhaps it inspired St. Louis manager Miller Huggins to revive the "moldy chestnut" two weeks later. On August 7, 1915, while coaching at third, Huggins took advantage of Brooklyn pitcher Ed Appleton: "In the seventh inning of the Saturday game, with the score a tie and three Cardinals on bases, Miller Huggins was coaching at third base. Youngster Appleton was pitching and was more or less befuddled by the situation he was facing. Huggins, an alert student of things psychological, suddenly called to Appleton to throw him the ball; he wished to see if it had John K's [National League president John K. Tener's] signature on it, perhaps. The innocent boob on the pitching box accommodatingly tossed the ball to Huggins; the Cardinals' manager sidestepped, the ball went to the grandstand and the runner on third scampered home with the run that was enough to win" (*Sporting Life*, August 12, 1915).

The reception to the play was lukewarm. *Sporting Life* wrote: "It was a smart trick, at least a sharp one, and it is not the intention to criticize Huggins for his part, since such tricks are permitted, but we do protest that such a thing makes a farce of the game, stirs ill feeling and bring [sic] down ridicule upon the hapless wight who is made the victim." Noting President Tener's efforts to eliminate the hidden-ball trick, the article suggested that it was only right to "place the 'Throw me the ball' trick in the same category as the hidden ball trick. If there is no room for one in the game there certainly can be no room for the other" (*Sporting Life*, August 12, 1915).

It does not appear that a specific rule was passed to forbid this tactic, but it seems to have died out at this point, yet another casualty to baseball action becoming discontinuous.

12.8   Team Stalling. Early ballparks did not have lights, which meant that a club with a small lead could stall in order to preserve a victory. This practice had already begun to emerge before the Civil War, causing Henry Chadwick

to write in 1860, "There has been one or two instances where this contemptible conduct has been resorted to" (*Beadle's Dime Base-Ball Player*, 30). Stalling became increasingly prevalent as competitiveness began to transform the game. In a typical example, an 1866 article noted: "the Resolutes began to play a 'waiting' game, by which they succeeded in prolonging the contest till it began to grow dark and the Umpire called the game" (*Brooklyn Eagle*, September 3, 1866). Meanwhile clubs that were ahead might make deliberate outs to hasten the conclusion.

Eventually "the unmanly and disreputable style of play known as 'playing a game into the dark'" was made far less common by rule changes that designated five innings as an official game and introduced the concept of suspended games (Henry Chadwick, *Haney's Base Ball Player's Book of Reference for 1867*, 55). But even today clubs occasionally stall if rain is on the way and they think they may be able to avert defeat by preventing the game from becoming official. Such tactics also date back to the nineteenth century. An 1880 article, for instance, noted that, "[Cap] Anson's sharp practice in getting the Umpire to call 'Time' twice on account of a slight fall of rain let the Chicagos out of what promised to be a defeat at the hands of the Cincinnatis on May 8, and finally prevented the playing of five full innings" (*New York Clipper*, May 22, 1880).

12.9   Quick Pitches. The changing perception of the quick pitch is one of the best indicators of the shift in the pace of baseball. In the twentieth century the quick pitch came to be viewed as a dubious tactic and in time was effectively eliminated. There was no such stigma attached to it in the nineteenth century. Once called strikes were introduced, the batter was expected to be ready at all times for the pitcher to deliver the ball.

This precept couldn't be strictly enforced in the 1860s because batters were allowed to be very specific about the pitches they requested. But when the strike zone became larger in the 1870s, pitchers were able to exploit inattentive batters with quick pitches. Henry Chadwick counseled in 1873: "From the moment the batsman takes his stand at the bat, to the time he strikes a fair ball, he should stand in proper form for hitting at every ball, or he will be sure to be caught napping by a skillful pitcher" (*New York Clipper*, April 12, 1873). As this suggests, pitchers and catchers who combined on a quick pitch were not viewed as behaving unethically but as forcing the batter to remain alert.

By the mid-1870s quick pitches had become a big part of the confrontation between pitchers and hitters. Henry Chadwick gave this description of a September 8, 1876, game between the White Stockings of Chicago and the Mutuals of New York: "[A. G.] Spalding's rapid style of sending in ball after ball as quickly as returned to him, together with his frequent change of pace, bothered the Mutuals strikers exceedingly. After striking at a ball, they would take things leisurely, instead of always being ready to strike, and the result was a fair ball would come to them before they were prepared to hit it, and a strike would necessarily be called" (*New York Clipper*, November 4, 1876).

Other pitchers began to imitate Spalding, and they received help from catchers who fired the ball back to them. After the 1876 season Henry Chadwick commented, "This point was played by [St. Louis pitcher George] Bradley last season almost as frequently as Spalding, and its success was mainly due to [catcher John] Clapp's quick returns" (*New York Clipper*, December 30, 1876). In 1877 St. Louis's new pitcher, Fred "Tricky" Nichols, was commended for "having improved greatly since last season, and the rapidity with which the ball was transferred backwards and forwards between [catcher John] Clapp and himself proved very puzzling to several of the Louisville batsmen" (*Louisville Courier-Journal*, May 30, 1877). At the season's end Henry Chadwick reported: "A feature of the season's catching was the general introduction among the best catchers of the leading nines of the rule of a prompt return of the ball to the pitcher . . . [which] enables the pitcher to take advantage of a batsman's being off his guard" (*New York Clipper*, December 1, 1877).

Hitters gradually learned to keep their guard up. The frequency of successful quick pitches declined, but the tactic remained part of every savvy pitcher's repertoire. Some pitchers devised new variations on the old theme. In 1878 pitcher Gid Gardner of the Clinton Club combined with catcher Barney Gilligan on an effective ruse. Gilligan "would turn around as if to walk toward the fence, the batter would wait for him to get in position. Gardner would shoot the ball over the plate. Gilly would turn around and meet it and 'one strike' would send a shiver down the spinal cord of the batsman" (Frank H. Pope, *Boston Globe*, March 24,

1889). Charlie Sweeney of Providence devised this new way to catch "the batsman napping" in 1884: "The catcher trundles the ball slowly to him; he picks it up, and before he has fairly straightened himself in his position the ball is driven over the plate for a strike" (*Sporting Life*, May 28, 1884).

Some pitchers turned the screws still further by deliberately keeping the batter waiting for the pitch. When complemented by the threat of the quick pitch, such stalling was a very effective way of keeping batters off balance. In considering these descriptions, bear in mind that the impression of never-ending delay is largely a result of the contrast to the usual rapid-fire pace of the game.

One of the earliest masters of the art of purposeful stalling was A. G. Spalding, whose routine inspired this 1870 description: "On receiving the ball, he raises it in both hands until it is on a level with his left eye. Striking an attitude, he gazes at it two or three minutes in a contemplative way, and then turns it around once or twice to be sure that it is not an orange or a cocoanut. . . . Assured that he has the genuine article, he then winks once at the first baseman, twice at the second baseman, and three times at the third baseman, and after a scowl at the short stop and a glance at the home-plate, finally delivers the ball with the precision and rapidity of a cannon shot" (*New York Star*, reprinted in *Chicago Tribune*, June 2, 1870).

Jim "Pud" Galvin likewise was described as follows: "Galvin turns the ball round in his hands six times, mops his forehead with his right hand, pulls a kink out of the seat of his pants, pulls out his handkerchief and wipes the sweat off his eyes, turns to [second baseman Chick] Fulmer and asks what o'clock it is, lays the ball between his feet, pats both hands in the dust, wipes the dust off on his trousers, licks the end of his fingers, pitches the ball over his left shoulder, absorbs a little more dust with his palms, tells the boys to look out and—pitches the ball. James is death to weak-nerved people" (*Cincinnati Enquirer*, reprinted in the *Buffalo Republic*, August 2, 1879).

Another reporter nominated 1890s star pitcher George Cuppy as "the 'slowest ever' and then some," but explained that, as with Spalding and Galvin, "There was method in his intolerable loitering. While the hungry spectators were looking at their watches and swearing, the impatient batter was sweating from nervousness and that was what Cuppy wanted" (*Sporting News*, September 22, 1906).

An exasperated sportswriter wrote in 1884, "Much of the real beauty of the game was spoiled by the style in which [Bob] Barr and ["Daisy"] Davis manipulated the sphere. They are worse than two old women over a cup of tea. A man can take a nap and get awake again while either one of these snails are getting ready to pitch. They are like many other idiotic asses who occupy the same position and imagine they are impressing the spectators and the club officials with their importance by delaying the game in this manner" (*National Police Gazette*, September 20, 1884).

An 1885 piece nicely described the effects of "the tedious slowness of some pitchers in handling the ball. When a pitcher, after getting it into his hands, invariably goes through a large variety of twistings and turnings, changes his position, rubs his arm and his spine and feels if all the bones are in proper position for a great (?) effort before delivering the ball, and repeats the same manoeuvers each time, the spectators get restless and lose interest. The query is often heard 'Is ――― going to pitch to-day?' And if answered in the affirmative, 'Well, I guess I won't go, he's too slow. Life is too brief and the benches too hard'" (*Sporting Life*, August 19, 1885).

George Nicol was said to be "the most energetic young man, perhaps, in his line of business that ever worked here. It is estimated that he walked 10 miles yesterday between the pitcher's box and home. Every time he pitches a ball he walks up so that the catcher can hand it to him. This delays the game somewhat and gives the spectators a tired feeling, but it affords Nicol exercise" (*San Francisco Examiner*, April 15, 1893). And St. Louis pitcher Silver King took "as much time to deliver each ball as [deliberative] Senator [William M.] Evarts does to write a sentence" (*Cincinnati Times-Star*, May 4, 1892).

Worcester's Lee Richmond, before delivering a pitch, "work[ed] his feet like a chicken cock getting ready for a dirt-bath. After this he goes through the boa-constrictor performance of sliming the ball, spitting on his hands, rubbing them on the ball, and then rubbing off the ball. All this time the other eight 'Wooster' men play statue business—Cain and Abel, Ajax, etc. He then turns his right side to the batter, looks all around at the statues, at the surrounding housetops, then up at the heavens, and then commences a painful working of the shoulders, as though something was biting him between the blades. After this is kept up for some time,

and the batter's arms are reasonably supposed to be limp from holding up the bat, the pitcher apparently says to himself, says he: 'Well, I guess I'll send one in,' and in it goes—a swift curve, hard to hit if sent in without so much delay, and rendered more so by the delay" (Chadwick Scrapbooks; also *The Capital*, reprinted in *New York Clipper*, March 20, 1880). As the description notes, batters squirmed during such routines, but they could not afford to relax or a quick pitch might suddenly whistle past them.

The great early-twentieth-century African-American pitcher Rube Foster was another master of disrupting batters' rhythm. He liked to swing his arms "like the pendulum of a clock" and then spring into his windup when least expected (*Philadelphia Item*, March 5, 1905, 11; quoted in Robert Cottrell, *The Best Pitcher in Baseball*, 20). Inattentive batters also found to their dismay that Foster possessed "the faculty of whipping the ball across the plate with or without the preliminary winding up . . . and he can do it underhand, with a side-wheel motion, overhand, or apparently snap it with his wrist" (Frederick North Shorey, "A Historical Account of a Great Game of Ball," *Indianapolis Freeman*, September 7, 1907, 7; quoted in Robert Cottrell, *The Best Pitcher in Baseball*, 35). That skill, combined with Foster's willingness to stall interminably, put the batter in a helpless dilemma (Robert Cottrell, *The Best Pitcher in Baseball*, 27).

By the early twentieth century the legitimacy of such tactics began to be questioned, since all the risk was on one side. In 1910 sportswriter J. Ed Grillo criticized Eddie Plank for causing "a lot of delay by his antics on the rubber. His great scheme is to pretend that he does not see the catcher's sign, thus making the batsman wait until he is nervous" (*Washington Post*, April 15, 1910).

Batters who were put in this situation understandably began to ask for time. In 1917 sportswriter I. E. Sanborn denounced umpires for having "allowed the batsman to stop plays by stepping out of the batsman's box while the pitcher was ready to deliver the ball, or even after he had started his windup. You have seen it. With a pitcher stalling for time on the slab, the batsman often gets nervous, steps out of his box, and feigns to have something in his eye or to need more dirt on his hands. In such case the umpires have let him get away with it, calling time illegally in many cases" (*Sporting Life*, June 2, 1917). While Sanborn's interpretation of the rules was indisputably correct, he ignored a more basic point. Allowing the pitcher to stall indefinitely while providing the batter with no recourse did not satisfy most people's idea of fair play, with the result that umpires became more willing to grant requests for timeouts.

Toward that end, American League umpires were instructed around 1913 not to recognize the quick pitch (Eugene Murdock, *Baseball Between the Wars*, 21). The quick pitch remained legal in the National League and, according to Fred Snodgrass, who played in the National League from 1908 to 1916, it was a constant threat for batters. Snodgrass recalled: "You didn't dare step into the batter's box without being ready, because somebody with a quick delivery would have that ball by you before you knew what happened. That was part of the game. The instant you stepped into that batter's box you had to be ready. If you were looking at your feet or something, the way they do today to get just the right position and all, well by that time the ball would already be in the catcher's mitt" (Lawrence S. Ritter, *The Glory of Their Times*, 99–100).

This meant that the World Series became the main battleground for the issue. After the 1913 Series a fan inquired about an incident in the fourth game of the World's Series in which Philadelphia's Rube Oldring "stepped out of batter's box to smear his hands with dirt and took an unreasonably long time to do it. [New York pitcher Rube] Marquard shot one over and Giants claimed a strike, which [umpire "Rip"] Egan refused to allow; was Egan correct; where does Oldring get his authority to suspend play at will?" The paper responded, "It is up to the umpire to keep the game going without unreasonable delays; evidently Egan did not think Oldring was unnecessarily delaying the game; it's all up to his judgment" (*Sporting News*, October 30, 1913).

In the ensuing years, umpires became increasingly lenient about granting time to batters and thereby rendered the quick pitch obsolete. Its swan song may have occurred in the final game of the 1928 World Series. With the score tied in the seventh inning, Cardinals pitcher Willie Sherdel apparently struck Babe Ruth out on a quick pitch. But Commissioner Landis had ruled before the Series that quick pitches would not be allowed. Granted another swing, Ruth homered and the Yankees went on to complete the four-game sweep (Marshall Smelser, *The Life That Ruth Built*, 384).

While the demise of the quick pitch was largely unlamented, its passing removed another tie to the days when baseball was a game associated with spontaneity.

12.10   Human Rain Delays. In the 1970s and '80s, Mike Hargrove became known as the "Human Rain Delay" for his painstaking preparations while batting. Deliberate batsmen such as Hargrove and Nomar Garciaparra often take the brunt of the frustration that many fans feel over the slow pace of today's game. But they were far from the first to attract such criticisms.

As noted in the preceding entry, in the early days of baseball batters could not afford to stall lest they fall victim to a quick pitch. Moreover they weren't even supposed to take their time coming to the plate, with an 1880 article declaring: "It should be the duty of each Captain and his assistant to see that every player who is next at bat has his bat in hand, and that he runs to the plate and gets ready for striking. A good way to secure this would be to fine a few of the laggards who keep the spectators waiting for their laziness" (*Chicago Tribune*, May 7, 1880). This precept was reinforced by an 1882 rule that counseled the next two batters to be waiting for their turn with bats in hand.

When umpires began to grant discretionary timeouts, stalling by batters began to be part of the game. Thayer Torreyson was described in 1898 as "a study. He takes a crouching position, lunges fiercely at the first high one pitched; if he misses connection, down goes the bat, he expectorates in both hands, grabs up two hands full of earth, drops it, rubs his hands on his new uniform, snatches up the stick and resumes his crouching posture" (*Youngstown Vindicator*, April 26, 1898).

Hugh S. Fullerton enumerated several other slowpokes: "Did you ever watch Frank Chance come to bat? He steps up, grasps his bat, taps the plate, holds his bat in his right hand, while he pulls up his belt with his left, places his bat between his legs, pulls his cap on tighter, pulls up his trousers, grabs the bat again, taps the plate, and is ready. He goes through these same motions every time he faces a pitcher, and it is a cinch he wouldn't hit .200 if forced to leave them out.

"Kip Selbach was another who had a pantomime he had to perform before hitting. He adjusts belt, cap, trousers, then raps his left foot with the bat, holds up his right foot and raps that, knocking all the dirt out of his spikes, and then, after another pull at his cap, is ready for business. He is a nervous hitter, and pitchers like Clark Griffith used to take advantage of his nervousness and keep him fretting by delaying the pitch until he couldn't hit much of anything. Dad Clarke vowed that Selbach couldn't take the ball in his hands and make a hit if the pitcher was slow, and it is notorious that Selbach never could hit those slow ball pitchers—especially the infamous Nig Cuppy.

"Another pantomimist was Pete Browning, who went through all sorts of antics before settling down to hit. He rearranged most of his clothing before he stepped up" (*Chicago Tribune*, April 29, 1906).

Hughey Jennings recalled that "every time ['Socks' Seybold] went to the plate he felt obliged to go through a whole rigmarole of stunts which would take him a full minute or more to perform" (quoted in F. C. Lane, *Batting*, 208). Walter McCreedie was described as going "through the tactics in preparing to bat that made Al. Selbach famous. He knocks the dirt off the soles of his shoes, gives his trousers a hitch, pulls down the peak of his cap, gives his trousers another hitch, and pulls down the back of his cap. Then he is ready for action" (*Sporting Life*, May 2, 1903).

Presumably most of these early "pantomimists" did not go through these rituals be-

tween every pitch. But Sy Sutcliffe was described in 1885 as "very anxious to hit the ball, and looks as though he can hardly wait to have it pitched to him. He gives his shoulders a rock, hitches up his pants nervously, spits on his hands, rocks again, taps the plate hurriedly and shifts about restlessly until he strikes. Then, if he misses, he hurriedly taps the plate again and goes over the previous performance" (*Sporting Life*, September 23, 1885).

12.11   Commercial Breaks. When baseball games first began to be televised, the assumption was that any commercials would be worked around the action, rather than the other way around. In 1965 columnist Bucky Summers observed of an ABC telecast: "There was a commercial at the end of each half inning, but this was expected. Much to the credit of baseball was the fact that the game was not held up in order to complete the speel before play was resumed. . . . This in itself was refreshing after suffering through football season when the paying customers are forced to wait until the commercial is over before anything happens" (Bucky Summers, "Still Baseball on TV," *Frederick* [Md.] *Post*, April 20, 1965). It would not be long before baseball would go the way of football.

Chapter 13

BUILDING A TEAM

IF YOUR favorite major league team doesn't have much talent, at least it has a sizable group of people—the general manager and his assistants, the farm system director, a staff of scouts—who are exploring a variety of means of acquiring and developing new talent. In contrast, nineteenth-century clubs generally had one lone man who wore all these hats and many more. If this overworked individual found himself short a player in the National League's debut year of 1876, none of the methods of acquiring talent available to today's general manager were available. Not only were cell phones far in the future, but so were trades, player purchases, farm teams, drafts, scouts, and tryout camps. As a result, more often than not he would sign the first decent candidate at hand. It is small wonder that these men became known as "hustlers" (see **6.1.3**). This chapter describes the origins of all of the tools now available to general managers, with the exception of cell phones.

As important as the role of general manager is, there is no authoritative way to single out one man as the first to have this role. Early managers handled many of the functions of today's general manager, but the position has expanded enormously since then. As a result, it is not possible to pinpoint the first general manager.

Even determining the first man to hold this title is tricky. Bill James claimed that Billy Evans was the first man to hold the title of general manager, in 1927 (Bill James, *The New Bill James Historical Baseball Abstract*, 128). In fact a 1916 article reported, "Branch Rickey's official title with the St. Louis Browns is 'vice president and general manager'" (*Sporting News*, February 10, 1916). Moreover the title is a sufficiently generic one that it had been used earlier for different responsibilities. In 1879, for example, reports had Jim White bringing in his brother-in-law to act as "General Financial Manager and Official Scorer" of the Cincinnati club, while Philadelphia's Al Reach was referred to in 1883 as "General Manager A. J. Reach" (*Chicago Tribune*, May 11, 1879; *Philadelphia Times*, reprinted in the *St. Louis Globe-Democrat*, March 26, 1883). Of course neither man's duties corresponded to those of today's general managers.

(i) Minor Leagues

Probably the most common recourse for plugging a hole is to call someone up from the minors. Baseball's farm system has a complex history, and it is noteworthy that other major sports such as football and basketball still have no equivalent. In order to understand how the farm system developed, it is necessary to review the origins of the minor leagues and the early attempts to forge a workable relationship between the minor and major leagues.

13.1.1 Minor League. Many sources list the International Association, which started play in 1877, as the first minor league. This is the ultimate example of the revisionism that can result when the victors write history. The International Association was a competitor to the National League that did very respectably in head-to-head competition. It had none of the characteristics of a minor league (see **18.4.1**).

The League Alliance was also formed in 1877 and had the important characteristic that its contracts were honored by the National League. But competition between the clubs was quite disorganized: "there was no rule to prescribe how many games League Alliance clubs should play to make a series, and therefore, although Indianapolis made the best record, the St. Paul Red Caps were credited with winning the championship" (*Reach's Official Base Ball Guide, 1884*, 25). This makes it hard to argue that it was a league in any meaningful sense; David Ball characterizes it as more of a trade group. A New England League was operating in this same year, but its organization was even looser (Charlie Bevis, *The New England League*, 14–29).

The Northwestern League of 1879 appears to have been the first circuit to function unquestionably as a league while also subordinating itself to the National League. Ted Sullivan, who had more firsthand knowledge of nineteenth-century minor leagues than anyone else, wrote in 1905 that this was the first minor league (*Sporting News*, February 4, 1905).

The Northwestern League went defunct after one season, and the next three seasons saw only a few modest attempts at a minor league. The Eastern Championship Association was formed in 1881 by five clubs, but only three completed their schedules. The League Alliance was reconstituted in 1882 but with only two clubs (*Reach's Official Base Ball Guide, 1884*, 25–26).

In March 1883 the Northwestern League was revived and took the historic step of joining with the National League and American Association to sign the Tri-Partite Agreement. This accord bound the three leagues to honor one another's contracts, with the Northwestern League paying its players lower salaries. For the 1883 campaign the Northwestern League was joined by the Inter-State Association. By one way of looking at the matter, this makes those two circuits the first minor leagues.

Even then, David Ball makes a strong argument that these leagues were not truly minor leagues. He contends that no league was contractually defined as such until 1885, noting that the Tri-Partite Agreement provided the Northwestern League with the same voice in the governance of the agreement as the National League and American Association. It also had the same ability to reserve its players, who were not subject to being drafted by the higher-

paying leagues. Only in matters of salaries was it subordinate.

In subsequent years the National League and American Association were joined to leagues throughout the country by the series of pacts that became known as the National Agreements (see **18.2.3**). By 1885 the National Agreement gave these clubs a lower place in the hierarchy in exchange for protection from player raids. Thus the minor leagues have existed continuously since at least 1885, if not earlier.

13.1.2   Climbing the Ladder. As soon as there were acknowledged "minor leagues," the major leagues became covetous of those leagues' best players. Moreover it seemed only fair to give the players in these circuits the opportunity to advance in their profession. Finding a satisfactory way of accomplishing this end would, however, prove extremely difficult.

In the 1885 National Agreement, minor league clubs were denied the right to reserve players. Presumably the expectation was that this would drive down the price of these players, but that didn't happen. Instead it gave the minor league clubs every incentive to dispose of their best players at season's end. The result was that the best minor leaguers acquired extravagant reputations, and by season's end it was acknowledged that "competition will be great, the price run up and clubs with deep purses will bag the game" (*Sporting Life*, September 9, 1885).

Less affluent clubs began to scout around for alternative methods of player acquisition. Louisville manager Jim Hart, for instance, was described as being "one of the wide-awake kind. Instead of waiting until the end of the season . . . he quietly slips off, pays as much for a release as it would cost him anyhow in the fall through bidding by different clubs, and captures the acknowledged best pitcher in the South" (*Sporting Life*, September 9, 1885). Other clubs experimented with rudimentary forms of the farm system.

All these efforts convinced players of the value of their services. According to Ted Sullivan, by the end of the 1880s "the Northwest was the ball players' Klondike. There was where the boys picked up golden nuggets from rich moguls' pockets. It was before the era of minor league reservations, and after the last day of September players were eligible to sign with league clubs. In the fall of '87 a great aggregation of management talent waited for the hour to arrive when the game of grab could commence." New York's Jim Mutrie supposedly became so desperate that he threw a player "into a hack, drove him fourteen miles into the country and actually pressed $1,000 into his hands for his autograph" (*Oklahoma City Daily Oklahoman*, April 22, 1898). The natural result was that player costs continued to escalate.

In 1889 the owners attempted to implement caps on player salaries, but this move led to the formation of the Players' League in 1890 and a costly war. When the Players' League folded after one season, and the American Association followed suit one year later, the National League owners were finally in position to adopt a more efficient system.

The owners did not take long to create and begin refining a concept that had been proposed in Francis Richter's Millenium [sic] Plan. The idea was the draft system (described in the next entry), which was ostensibly designed to allow players to advance up the ladder. But it didn't escape notice that the new system would also mean savings for the major league owners: "The draft system under the new national agreement is going to knock chunks off base ball salaries once it gets into operation and the fight is over. This is sure, because it will stop the competition between clubs which has driven prices up. Under it correspondence will show priority. First come will be first served" (*Williamsport Sunday Grit*, March 29, 1891).

13.1.3 Drafts. The first player draft was instituted in 1891, not 1892 as stated in the first edition of this book. Early that year the newly created Board of Control met in Chicago and announced "laws governing the transfer and the reservation of players. . . . In case a higher League desires to draw on a lower League in a certain class for a player and comes to terms with the player, he can be drawn, and the Board guarantees an indemnity to the club drawn upon" (*Cincinnati Enquirer*, February 15, 1891; thanks to David Ball). The price that the minor league club received for a drafted player was based upon a class system. The minor league team also had the right to apply to the Board of Control to block the draft if it would create a hardship. While this seemed fair, it proved a major problem since most clubs considered it a hardship to lose one of their best players in mid-season. The first appeal occurred in late May when Chicago drafted Albany catcher Marshall Brown. The appeal process dragged

on and showed the system to be seriously flawed (*Chicago Tribune*, May 27, 1891, 6).

By 1892 the National League had absorbed the American Association. As the only major league, it worked in tandem with selected minor leagues to create a more workable system by which players could reach the pinnacle of their profession. The 1892 National Agreement established the first minor league classification system, under which each minor league was classified as either A or B. During the offseason, which ran from October 1 to February 1, a National League club could draft a minor leaguer and would pay the minor league club $1,000 for a Class A player or $500 for a Class B player. If more than one club selected the same player, the winner was drawn out of a hat. Class A clubs could also draft players from the B circuits.

The system led to the promotion of many players. For example, a note after the 1892 season indicated: "Baltimore has notified the Atlanta management that [it] has drafted [Jack] Wadsworth, and that he will play in that city this coming season" (*Atlanta Constitution*, February 19, 1893). The classification system was extended in the years that followed, and by 1896 it reached as low as Class F.

By then, however, problems with the system were becoming apparent. Johnny Evers and Hugh Fullerton reported that all too often major league clubs drafted "players from lower class leagues, not for themselves but for other clubs of lower rank with which secret agreements have been made" (John J. Evers and Hugh S. Fullerton, *Touching Second*, 50). As is discussed in the next entry, there was a price for such favors.

Eventually efforts were made to protect minor league clubs from losing an excessive number of players in the draft, but this rule too had unanticipated consequences. It soon became apparent that a major league club could help a minor league club by drafting a player the big club didn't want—effectively protecting a better player on the minor league team. These favors, naturally, were also done with the expectation of receiving something in return.

In addition, the lure of new talent often led to chicanery. Under the initial rules, minor leaguers were available to the first team that presented a paid claim to National League president Nick Young on or after October 1. As a result, it became "the practice for the managers of certain clubs, or their duly authorized agents, to surround 'Uncle Nick's' home at midnight on September 30, and as soon as the clock strikes twelve, to rush in and lay claim to such players as they desire for the coming season" (*Cleveland Leader*, September 21, 1897).

Such loopholes meant that the draft never functioned smoothly and was always susceptible to manipulation. Nonetheless it remained the basic mechanism for player advancement until the farm system became prevalent.

Although this draft lost much of its importance with the advent of the farm system, it continues to this day and is now known as the Rule 5 draft. Blue Jays general manager Pat Gillick brought renewed attention to the Rule 5 draft in the 1980s by using it to acquire budding stars like George Bell. Clubs still use this draft and occasionally manage to pluck a gem from a rival's farm system.

13.1.4 Pick of the Club. As described in the preceding entry, the most commonly exploited flaw in the draft system was the opportunity it provided a major league club to place a minor league club in its debt. Naturally a major league club that did such a favor expected something in return, and the resulting arrangement became known as the "Pick of the Club."

For example, an 1895 note reported, "[Marty] Hogan has been farmed out to Indianapolis on satisfactory conditions. It was agreed between the two clubs that Hogan is to remain with the Hoosiers all season. Should he prove a success he can be reclaimed for the St. Louis team next season. Should there be another outfielder more valuable than Hogan, St. Louis will have first claim to him next season" (*Sporting Life*, May 18, 1895). And the following year: "Charley Reilly has been released to Syracuse by the Philadelphia Club under agreement that the Philadelphia Club have the right to draft any one Syracuse player, including Reilly himself, gratis, for the season of 1897. Nor will the Syracuse Club release any player to an outside club without first consulting the Philadelphia Club officials" (*Sporting Life*, March 7, 1896).

This ploy was extended in the ensuing years, and new variants were added. The *Chicago Tribune* offered several examples in 1906: "Sometimes a club owner is compelled to 'cover up' players in order to secure favorable training grounds, sometimes it is done to create friendly relations with a minor club and secure reliable tips on good material in other clubs of the same league suitable for future purchase or draft" (quoted in *Sporting Life*, March 24, 1906).

It proved exceedingly difficult to prevent these kinds of shady dealings. In 1905 Charley Comiskey was reported to have "drafted a number of gentlemen from his faithful friend, [Milwaukee manager] Joe Cantillon. . . . Usually Commy drafts Joe's best men every fall, and then returns them back to him, but this time he says if the men make good they will stick" (*Sporting Life*, September 9, 1905). But with no definitive way to determine whether such promises were sincere, the abuses continued.

One such deal could have changed baseball history. In 1908 Cantillon, now managing Washington, agreed to let Kansas City have pitcher Clyde Goodwin for $1,000, "providing, however, that there was no cash to be paid down, but an option given the Washington club on the pick of the Kansas City pitchers for $2,500, and if such selection was made Goodwin was to figure in the deal at the price agreed upon." Kansas City tried desperately to get out of the deal when Boston offered them far more for one of their pitchers, and Cantillon finally agreed to rework the deal. By doing so he lost out on the opportunity to have Smoky Joe Wood join Walter Johnson on his pitching staff (*Washington Post*, June 2, 1908).

One of the masters of this tactic was Branch Rickey. Sportswriter John B. Sheridan observed in 1920: "Rickey did not devise the 'pick of the club' scheme of trading between major and minor league teams. But he worked it to its finest development." As Sheridan explained, Rickey's chief scout Charley Barrett would sign more prospects than the Cardinals could possibly use. He would then offer a minor league club several of the players in exchange for the "pick of the club" at season's end (*Sporting News*, February 5, 1920). In some ways this was the ultimate embodiment of Rickey's "quality out of quantity" philosophy of player development.

Rickey was far from alone, however. The Giants used the scheme to get a Hall of Famer, as Travis Jackson explained: "The New York Giants sent an outfielder named Joe Connolly to Little Rock with the understanding that he could stay there and play center field all season if the Giants could have first pick of the Little Rock players at the end of the year. It turned out I was the first pick and at the end of the '22 season they told me to report to the Giants" (Walter M. Langford, *Legends of Baseball*, 92).

As is seen in the next entry, the "Pick of the Club" scheme overlapped with and often complemented early versions of the farm system.

13.1.5   Farm Clubs and Farm Systems. Most sources credit Branch Rickey with inventing the practice of farming, but this is at best an oversimplification. Rickey was unquestionably the first man to put together what we now call a farm system, in which a player can advance from the lowest rung of the minor leagues to the major leagues while remaining the property of the same organization. But the system of major league clubs using minor league clubs as farm clubs had a lengthy, well-publicized, and controversial history before Rickey's entry into the field.

It could be argued that the use of farm clubs dates all the way back to the very earliest baseball clubs. These clubs were represented in matches by their "first nine," but they also had second and third nines and often junior nines. These extra nines provided reserves when a member of the first nine was injured or unavailable and also helped develop new players. The junior nine in particular became a fertile source of new talent. In 1868, for instance, a Washington paper remarked: "The Junior Nationals include among their number several promising young players, and the Washington Clubs could not do better than to organize a junior nine for each club to form a corp de reserve to replace retired stagers who may become played out" (French Scrapbooks, unidentified clipping, May 1868). Henry Chadwick even advocated making these informal relationships more systematic by hinting that senior clubs should sponsor junior clubs by providing them with equipment (*Brooklyn Eagle*, August 23, 1864; cited in William J. Ryczek, *Baseball's First Inning*, 59).

The League Alliance, formed in 1877 and revived in 1882, was another very rudimentary prototype of the farm club. In 1883 Providence manager Harry Wright "decided to put two teams on the field, one to be composed of the regulars and the other of young players of more than local renown, of which Providence in that year boasted a plenty. . . . [Wright] started . . . to comb the local sandlots for players for the Reserves, and gathered some promising material. . . . All the reserves were signed to regular contracts . . . [for] about what they could earn at their regular employments. . . . It was Manager Wright's idea to have the Grays play a match every day, putting the reserves against the regulars when there was no game with outside teams" (William D. Perrin, *Days of Greatness*, 22).

Wright's scheme was greeted with widespread criticism. Chicago president A. G. Spalding used a publication called *American Sports* to make "a grand boo-hoo over Harry Wright having from 20 to 22 professional players signed with Providence." In the article, Wright's reserves were referred to as a "plug team" that "will surfeit the Providence public with baseball and detract from the interest heretofore taken in the contests between the giants of the diamond field (meaning, of course, the Chicagos)" (quoted in *National Police Gazette*, May 12, 1883). Others resorted to mockery, such as the sportswriter who wrote: "Manager Wright has the idea that the larger the number of players the greater the chance of winning the championship. . . . This makes about the sixteen hundred and eightieth player that Wright has signed this season. As only nine can play at any one time, however, Wright contemplates using the spare force in lending them to the state to break stone" (*National Police Gazette*, May 5, 1883).

Wright's reserves disbanded within a few months, leading some to assume that the critics were correct. But Providence sportswriter William Perrin believed that Wright's plan had "worked beautifully," and Troy Soos likewise argued that the reserve squad had played its intended function by supplying Providence with replacements for injured regulars and by preparing several promising young players for professional careers (William D. Perrin, *Days of Greatness*, 22; Troy Soos, *Before the Curse*, 67).

The perception of such clubs changed that winter when the Union Association mounted a challenge to the existing major leagues and the reserve rule. The National League and American Association fought back by forming reserve clubs with the aim of keeping players away from the upstart league. The idea of a "Base Ball Academy" caught on quickly, and A. G. Spalding now became a chief proponent, announcing in October that his Chicago club "has decided to engage for next season an auxiliary team of ten or twelve young players from semi-professional and amateur ranks, put them on salary and keep them in training under the direct supervision of Captain Anson with the view of developing base ball talent to supply players in emergencies, and with a view of increasing the supply of available men in the country. The rules by which each club can reserve eleven men will tend to make good unengaged players scarce" (*Wheeling Register*, October 20, 1883).

As one reporter noted, "Harry Wright was ridiculed last season for thinking of such an idea as a reserve team. Now the Boston, Chicago, Cleveland, New York, St. Louis, Allegheny and Cincinnati have followed the example of the old man" (*Brooklyn Eagle*, April 13, 1884). Even minor league clubs such as Evansville and Milwaukee made plans for reserve nines.

The reserve teams were characterized as "virtually a training school for professional base-ball players, and is a move that should have been started before" (*Chicago Inter-Ocean*, March 18, 1884). The Union Association lasted only one year, and its demise removed the most obvious reason to sign extra players to contract. By then all of the reserve nines had disbanded, a development that led one sportswriter to dub them an "an expensive fizzle" (*National Police Gazette*, June 28, 1884).

But most observers had come to recognize the advantages of having additional players available. *Sporting Life* concluded, "The reserve plan has served to develop some strong young players, a number of whom are now playing on the regular nines. This was the main object of the reserve nines." Several clubs loaned players to short-handed rivals, prompting a reporter to comment, "This thing of one club lending players to another is a new wrinkle, and it strikes us that it is in violation to the National Agreement, else what is to prevent the New Yorks from borrowing [Tim] Keefe and [Billy] Holbert from the Metropolitans? The Buffalos, however, are letting [Arthur] Hagan play with the Minneapolis club on condition that he shall be on hand when the Buffalos want him. If this is regular it will be of invaluable benefit to the Metropolitan Exhibition Company" (*National Police Gazette*, July 5, 1884). And indeed, as discussed in entry **13.2.3**, Keefe was transferred to the New Yorks after the season.

With the need and the potential benefits so great, owners soon found new ways to keep players in reserve. In January 1887 the Emporia, Kansas, club offered to keep and pay the salaries of two Cincinnati players for the season, then return them at season's end. While the arrangement fell through, other major league clubs took heed. Detroit president Frederick K. Stearns was paying particularly close attention.

As the regular season opened, word leaked out that Stearns "had been frying a kettle of fish that will open the eyes of [A. G.] Spalding and the other league moguls when the operation is concluded" (*Detroit Free Press*, May 2, 1887). Detroit had three players—Jimmy Manning,

Bill Shindle, and George Knowlton—who had been with the team during training camp but had not made the team.

Rather than having to release them, Stearns now had the means to have his cake and eat it too: "Manning, Shindle and Knowlton will be loaned out, not released, to a crack club not in the National League [which turned out to be Kansas City of the Western League], which will pay them the same salaries they now receive. That this is a ten strike must be admitted. Manning, Shindle and Knowlton will not sever their connection with the Detroits, neither will the club have to pay their salaries. If by sickness or accident any of the others of the club should be laid up, the team will not be weakened perceptibly, as a dispatch will bring either or all of the loaned players into the breach as fast as the cars can carry them" (*Detroit Free Press*, May 2, 1887).

Stearns's tactic soon prompted both imitators and controversy. When Cincinnati loaned pitcher Henry Kappel to Nashville, Brooklyn manager Charles Byrne commented "that the system of loaning ball players under contract by American Association clubs to clubs in minor leagues is clearly illegal" (*Detroit Free Press*, May 14, 1887). Vociferous protests were also lodged by the New Orleans and Cleveland clubs, and by Southern League president John Morrow and National League president Nick Young. Kappel was speedily recalled by Cincinnati, and Memphis agreed to forfeit the games it had won while he was in the lineup (*Sporting Life*, May 18, 1887; *Detroit Free Press*, May 18, 1887). Similar protests met Indianapolis's attempt to loan Joe Quinn to Duluth, and instead Quinn's contract was sold to the Northwest League team (*Indianapolis Sentinel and News*, June 7, 1887).

With that tactic meeting so much resistance, the 1888 season instead saw several major league clubs purchase minor league teams and operate them as farm clubs. In contrast to the season before, this practice was conducted openly and created relatively little controversy.

For example, within months of the end of the 1887 campaign, Washington president Walter Hewett revealed that "he is largely interested in the Troy Club, and proposes to make it a training-school or feeder for the Washingtons" (*Washington Post*, December 4, 1887). Washington manager Ted Sullivan "organized and managed the Troy team, which was a member of the International Association, while at the same time he acted as a business agent for the Washington Club, who also controlled the Troy

Club" (*New York Clipper*, January 12, 1889). *Sporting News* later characterized the Troy club as "the first base ball farm" and noted, "Once a week Sullivan would run over to Troy to see how his farm was getting along and to give some orders to his manager. So it may fairly be said that he was the first manager to run two clubs in one season—a major and a minor" (*Sporting News*, December 30, 1909). While the arrangement attracted little attention, there is no indication it was a secret, with the *Washington Post* remarking at mid-season: "Perhaps few of the Washington baseball public are aware that situated in Troy is an annex to the club here" (*Washington Post*, June 24, 1888).

Researcher David Ball discovered several other major league clubs that operated farm clubs during the 1888 season. New York Giants president John B. Day had previously owned both of New York's major league franchises and had taken advantage of this situation to make a number of dubious transactions (see **22.5.2** and **13.2.3**). After the 1887 season Day announced plans to take over the Jersey City club in the Central League and "run it as a reserve for the New-York Club. He thinks that the only way to secure good players is to secure a club in a minor league and develop young men" (*New York Times*, November 5, 1887).

Day reportedly assured Jersey City manager Patrick T. Powers that he would not "take any of the Jersey City players out of the club before the end of the season" (*Chicago Herald*, April 22, 1888). But dual ownership allowed him to sign "a small army" of players during the offseason and then assign them as he saw fit—a precursor to Branch Rickey's "quality out of quantity" philosophy (*Sporting Life*, November 9, 1887). And some contracts were transferred during the season (*New York Times*, July 18, 1888).

St. Louis Brown Stockings owner Chris Von der Ahe operated the St. Louis Whites of the Western Association as a farm club, signing no fewer than twenty-nine players to 1888 contracts by December 1887. Chicago White Stockings president A. G. Spalding appears to have pursued a similar course with another Western Association club, the Chicago Maroons. Although Sam Morton was the nominal president of the Maroons, the club had close connections with the local major league franchise (*Sporting Life*, December 10 and 31, 1887; *Philadelphia Record*, quoted in *Cincinnati Enquirer*, December 29, 1887).

There were hints of several other alliances between major league and minor league clubs that amounted to farming, most notably one involving Philadelphia and Allentown of the Central League (*Philadelphia Record*, quoted in *Cincinnati Enquirer*, December 29, 1887; *Sporting Life*, January 18, 1888). A particularly ominous portent was the grumbling of a *Sporting Life* correspondent from Columbus, Ohio, that Lima had captured the Tristate pennant in large part because of players farmed out by Chicago. In September he intimated: "Lima, for her peculiar, yet fortunate personal relations with Spalding, Anson & Co., has been enabled to receive many inside tips, as well as players, from the Chicago contingency" (*Sporting Life*, September 19, 1888). He went further the following month, complaining that Lima "had a clear advantage over other League cities because of Manager [William] Harrington's intimate relations with Spalding, Anson & Co., of Chicago, who kept him well supplied with good material" (*Sporting Life*, October 31, 1888).

Like so many nineteenth-century minor league clubs, the farm clubs were not financial successes. The St. Louis Whites folded in June 1888, and while the other clubs made it through the season, none seem to have been in the black. The Maroons disbanded at season's end, while the Washington club quietly disposed of its Troy farm club (*Washington Post*, November 14, 1888). Ownership of the Jersey City club in 1888 was reported to have resulted in a $17,500 loss, and although it returned as "an annex to the New York League Club" in 1889, Day apparently sold out in June (*Cincinnati Enquirer*, June 14, 1889; *Sporting Life*, June 19, 1889). Not surprisingly, a consensus emerged that such ventures were too expensive to be maintained.

That perception was one of several factors that led to the multiple experiments with farm clubs in 1888 being followed by six lean years for farming. A second was the concern voiced by *Sporting Life*'s Columbus correspondent that farming could destroy a minor league's competitive balance. Another important reason was that the attention of the established leagues was focused on the player revolt that led to the creation of the Players' League in 1890. In addition, as is discussed under "Trades" (see **13.2.3**), any exchange of contracts during this period meant releasing the players with the risk of losing them altogether.

By the mid-1890s the latter two problems had been eliminated. The National League was firmly established as the only major league while the rules and practices had changed so that its clubs could move players from minors to majors more easily. As a result the farm issue returned with a vengeance in 1895 when John T. Brush began to take advantage of his dual ownership of Cincinnati (National League) and Indianapolis (Western League).

The frequent transfers of players between Brush's two clubs prompted criticisms of a system that "permits the big league to pull back farmed-out players whenever their services are needed" (*Sporting Life*, May 18, 1895). A particular concern was that the major leagues reaped benefits from the system at the expense of the minor leagues.

One of the first men to appreciate this was Patrick T. Powers, who had managed the Giants' Jersey City farm club in 1888. Now president of the Eastern League, he understood the damage that could result from farming. Powers declared, "Each club should stand on its own bottom and each player should be signed regularly and not allowed to be taken away in mid-season just when the man is a drawing card and a favorite, developed at the expense of the local people. . . . No player's services should be accepted by any minor league club without a distinct understanding that the man shall not be recalled before the close of the playing season" (*Sporting Life*, December 7, 1895).

Yet others, such as sportswriter F. E. Godwin, defended farming: "President Brush has been severely criticized for transferring players to and from the Indianapolis Club, but he puts up the money to maintain a club in the Hoosier town, and if he develops a youngster or wants to strengthen his smaller club when he has too many men on his Cincinnati list I see no harm in making the exchange. The idea of having a 'farm' for the development of players is bound to become popular. In the near future I look for a number of magnates to pay for clubs in minor leagues for the benefits that will accrue from the polishing process" (*Sporting Life*, October 12, 1895).

One thing was clear: as long as the practice was legal, it would continue and expand. In mid-season 1895 a Chicago sportswriter observed: "Rockford is our supply depot" (*Sporting Life*, August 24, 1895). By season's end the *Columbus* (Ohio) *Dispatch* was claiming direly that the Western League clubs were all farms now, without individuality or independence (quoted in *Sporting Life*, December 7, 1895). The offseason brought new reports: "It

is understood that Youngstown is to be another Cincinnati farm" (*Sporting Life*, February 22, 1896).

By 1896 the players were beginning to grumble: "Within a few weeks [Bill Hassamaer] was farmed out, recalled and released by Louisville. 'Roaring Bill' is of the opinion that it is not a string which a club has on a player. 'It's a rope, and it's around a fellow's neck,' is his explanation" (*Brooklyn Eagle*, July 18, 1896). The opportunity for advancement had become so illusory that one sportswriter maintained, "Minor league players dislike being drafted by the big league clubs, and especially by clubs that have a pretty good string of experiments on hand. Under the latter circumstances it gives them little chance to demonstrate what they can do, and if they show any speed the prospects are that they will be placed on the farm team 'to develop' and there they may remain for a season or two seasons—perhaps forever—shut off from all possibility of catching on with another league team and passing a base ball life in comparative seclusion. Eventually their salaries become smaller than what they really would draw as first-class 'unfarmed' minor league players. But the club that has drafted them has them by the throat and they must play at the orders of this club or get out of the business entirely." As confirmation, recent draftee George Nicol was quoted as saying, "It isn't a pleasant thing, being drafted, especially when you have a large-sized idea in your mind that you will soon be given a ticket calling for a berth way down upon the farm. . . . I would rather be playing in my old stamping ground, but I guess it can't be helped." After concluding that the system was broken beyond repair, the sportswriter wryly added, "The farming system by the way is slated to make its appearance at the coming league meeting, and, as usual, nothing will be done with it" (*Sporting News*, November 7, 1896, 2).

There was indeed no effort made to address the issue, and by the following year the newspapers had joined the chorus. A Hartford sportswriter noted, "The local newspapers have begun a sort of a mild war on the teams in the Atlantic League who have 'farmed' players in their ranks, and there is likely to be some trouble over the awarding of the pennant should any of the teams using farmed players win the flag" (*Sporting Life*, July 24, 1897). The *Detroit Free Press* advocated "getting rid of the 'farming' evil as was practiced on behalf of Cincinnati at Indianapolis this year" (*Detroit Free*

Press, October 24, 1897). The *Cincinnati Times-Star* complained: "The present arrangement is that the minor leagues are deuces in the deck. Their magnates put out their good money for franchises, develop players who put the clubs on a paying basis and then are compelled to give up their star players for a paltry $500 or less, without any appeal or recourse" (reprinted in *Sporting Life*, November 6, 1897).

Clubs were also beginning to combine farming with the "Pick of the Club" scheme (described in the preceding entry). The *Cincinnati Times-Star* explained: "According to many reports, a scheme has come up that beats this farming idea all hollow, only in this new practice major league clubs are deprived of the privilege of securing men that they need and who should be accessible to them. The scheme works as follows: A minor league manager who has several players he would like to keep goes to his friend, the major league manager, who does not need the men, and requests him to draft these men or purchase them outright before the drafting season opens—as 'some other manager wants them,' the arrangement between the minor league manager and his friend being that the players are returned to the minor league after the drafting season ends. In this way the minor league manager holds his players and can sell them if he chooses. Of course, he furnishes the money used in 'drafting' or 'buying' the players." Numerous instances were then cited (reprinted in *Sporting Life*, November 6, 1897).

A minor league manager explained the ins and outs: "The secret of Cleveland's purchase of half a dozen players from the Toledo Interstate team last fall is out. Manager [Charles] Strobel tells it himself. He says: 'I sold pitcher [George] Kelb, [Bert Myers], [Erve] Beck, pitcher John Blue and Captain Bob Gilks to Cleveland. I had an understanding with [Cleveland owners] the Robisons that they would buy these players, put them on the reserve list, so they could not be drafted, and put a price on their releases high enough to prevent any club buying them. Now if none of them is bought at the prices fixed between us all of them but Kelb will be turned back to me by April 10. For this accommodation pitcher Kelb is given to Cleveland outright—not farming—it is really protection. If he suits Cleveland they will buy Beck; if not fast enough I get him back'" (*Sporting Life*, February 5, 1898).

Strobel's account makes it easier to understand why minor league clubs would agree to such arrangements. Hunting for new talent could be costly and time-consuming, and it must have been especially frustrating to know that any good player would soon be lost through the draft. So minor league clubs were naturally tempted by the prospect of a cheap, regular supply of talent.

By 1898 an exasperated Ned Hanlon contended that it would be entirely possible, under the existing rules, for him to farm out stars like Hughey Jennings and Willie Keeler if he desired. He added: "I know of National league players whom other clubs would like to have who will be sent to 'farms' and paid small salaries, simply because the prices put upon their releases are out of all reason. It is simply an outrage—nothing less—and ought to be stopped" (*Sporting Life*, February 5, 1898).

John T. Brush's dual ownership of the Indianapolis and Cincinnati franchises continued to fan the controversy. Sportswriter James Andrew denounced the hypocrisy of claiming that transfers between these two clubs represented legitimate opportunities to advance: "Does any one believe that the Cincinnati Club in drafting all the players of the Indianapolis team which everybody knows it cannot and does not desire to use has had in view even in the slightest degree the welfare of the players or to enable them to advance in their profession?" (*Sporting News*, October 30, 1897).

Brush offered this defense: "As to 'farming' as the transfer of players to a club of an inferior league for development is called, I can't see where it is wrong in theory or practice. If the Cincinnati Club buys a player it acquires an interest in him just as it would if it bought real estate. If the Cincinnati Club is unable to use that player it certainly has the right to dispose of him outright or to send him to another club temporarily until he becomes skillful enough to be used by it. There is no reason why the Cincinnati Club should lose the money it has invested in a player any more than it should sacrifice a real estate investment which did not turn out as well at first as was anticipated. The loan of players by the Cincinnati Club to the Indianapolis Club was beneficial to both parties. It assisted us in the development of our surplus players and built up that city in a base ball sense" (*Sporting News*, May 7, 1898).

But few were buying his version. A *Sporting News* correspondent responded: "From Mr. Brush's standpoint, there is nothing unfair or unsportsmanlike in making minor league teams play against National League talent. That is exactly the condition that has obtained in the Western League every season since Indianapolis became a farm for Cincinnati" (*Sporting News*, June 4, 1898). Another sportswriter pointed out: "Although the rules plainly state that no farmed player shall be recalled . . . before the end of the season, John T. [Brush] goes right ahead and switches players where he can use them to best advantage. Less than two weeks ago, he sent Damman [Billy Dammann] to the Hoosier capital, presumably to help the Indians out during their series with the Blues, for immediately after the completion of the series, he recalled Damman. He then sent Marvin Hawley to the farm club and called it a trade, but has since recalled Hawley" (*Sporting Life*, June 11, 1898).

Instances of the unfairness of Brush's farming practices continued to surface. This example was cited at the start of the 1898 season: "It seems to be rather a hard matter for a 'farmed' player to keep track of himself. Word comes from Washington that Mike Kahoe, who supposed that he belonged to the Cincinnati Club, was released to Indianapolis some time in February. When he joined the Hoosiers last season Kahoe was signed to a Cincinnati contract. When the season closed he was on the reserve list of the Cincinnati Club. As the Cincinnati Club did not tender him a contract before the first of March Kahoe—who was ignorant of the fact that he had been released to the Indianapolis Club—thought that he was free to sign where he pleased. Now comes the information that the Cincinnati Club gave up its claim to him in February and as the Indianapolis Club offered him a contract within the limited time he must go to the Hoosier capital. It seems strange that this transfer should be made without the consent of the other clubs and without being mentioned in President Young's official bulletins. Still the information from headquarters says that all this did happen, so there was nothing for Kahoe to do but to sign an Indianapolis contract. And next fall, when the drafting season opens, it will be found that the Cincinnati Club has drafted Kahoe before any league that may want him. And thus will his prospects of breaking into fast company be killed. Verily, the farming and drafting systems are the pride of the magnates—or should be" (*Cincinnati Times-Star*, reprinted in *Sporting Life*, April 9, 1898, 2).

A particularly flagrant example of the "injustice of the farming rule" was "the case of outfielder [Charles] Frisbee, of the Bostons.

Frisbee was turned over to Tom Loftus, of the Grand Rapids team in the Western League, along with $1000, in the deal for backstop Sullivan. This exchange of dollars and one human being for a likely player gave Frisbee a right to file a large and vociferous wail, and he is backed in his grievance by some National League managers, who are desirous of signing so promising a player as the athlete who was relegated to the Grand Rapids farm. In other words, the Boston Club handicaps the future of one good player for the sake of experimenting with another. In the obscurity of a minor league Frisbee may run to seed and his hopes of a future be blasted by the selfishness of grasping magnates. And this is called advancing players in their profession, in the very words of the National Agreement! Out upon such perversion of law and justice" (*New York Telegram*, reprinted in *Sporting News*, December 2, 1899). Frisbee, who had batted .329 in his rookie season of 1899, would have only thirteen more major league at bats.

In 1900, National League players formed the Players' Protective Association, a modest form of a union. One of this body's goals was putting an end to farming, a practice that it contended was thwarting players from rising in their profession. The National Association of Professional Base Ball Leagues, formed in 1901, also took an anti-farming stand (Mike Roer, *Orator O'Rourke*, 222–224). The American League tried to lure players that same year by promising not to farm them. Before the season began, however, there were reports that Detroit was using Montreal as a farm club.

The 1903 National Agreement finally made some effort to limit farming by banning multiple ownership. The agreement also included this provision: "The practice of 'farming' is prohibited. All right or claim of a major league club to a player shall cease when such player becomes a member of a minor league club, and no arrangement between the clubs for the loan or return of a player shall be binding between the parties to it or recognized by other clubs" (*New York Times*, August 30, 1903, 3; quoted in Mike Roer, *Orator O'Rourke*, 228). Robert Burk, however, noted an important loophole: "In its place the pact created an 'optional assignment' procedure in which a major leaguer could be sold to a minor league club, with his former employer retaining the option to repurchase" (Robert Burk, *Never Just a Game*, 164).

The result was that it remained easy for a major league club to collude with a minor league club. In 1904 Chicago (National League) made a test case by openly selling George Moriarty to a minor league club with the proviso that they could buy him back before the drafting season for the same price. They asked the National Commission to rule on the case, and it was approved (*Chicago Tribune*, June 26, 1904).

With no check on open arrangements, illicit agreements were rampant. The *Washington Post* explained, "One of the tricks of baseball is for major league clubs to 'buy' stars of the minor organizations before the drafting season opens, and hold the players until the following spring, when they are turned back to their original owners. [Charles] Comiskey last year secured Jakey Atz and others from New Orleans and turned them back without even a trial. He has just 'purchased' Jakey again with some others, and it is suspected that New Orleans is being protected in the same old way" (*Washington Post*, August 25, 1904).

The *Detroit News-Tribune* observed that the National Agreement had helped preserve the integrity of minor league pennant races: "The really raw character of the plan, as exemplified by John T. Brush, the originator, in its operation between the old Cincinnati and Indianapolis teams, has disappeared, and it is very seldom that a player, when once sent to the minors, emerges until the end of the season." But players continued to be denied the opportunity of advancement: "Modern farming is carried on through fake sales of players to a major league team at the close of a season, the players being returned to the little team when the time comes for the beginning of another season. The cases of [Jake] Gettman and [Frank] Laporte, of Buffalo, 'purchased' by Detroit at the close of 1903, were deals of this character exposed for the failure of the players to report even for trials in the spring" (reprinted in the *Washington Post*, September 18, 1904).

In 1906 the National Commission modified its rules in an effort to eliminate farming: "It is specifically stated in the rule that the club which purchases a player from another club and sells him back to that club without giving him a trial on the field will be considered guilty by that act of purchasing the player merely to cover him up for the benefit of the club which first sold him. Hitherto there has been no definition by which guilt or innocence could be determined. The new provision it is expected will result in a practical abolition of the evil system which has grown to such proportions that few clubs in either major league have not engaged in it

more or less. It still will be possible, of course, for clubs to cover up some players by taking them on the spring training trips and making at least a pretense of giving them a trial, but that will be an expensive process" (*Chicago Tribune*, March 4, 1906).

The new rules had teeth in the form of fines of up to $1,000 for offenders, and fines were indeed levied regularly (*Chicago Tribune*, March 28, 1906; April 10, 1906). Nevertheless the fines did little to stem the tide. One sportswriter calculated that "Of the 68 players alleged to have been purchased by the minor leagues last fall, waivers have been asked on all but 18. This is a nice testimonial to the practice of 'covering up'" (*Washington Post*, March 3, 1906).

Washington manager Joe Cantillon was particularly flagrant about subverting the intentions of the draft: "Cantillon has drafted about 20 players from the minor leagues. . . . Of the entire squad, it is not likely that one will ever wear a Washington uniform. Cantillon, however, has holes to plug up in other clubs which have given him material, and he will do it by the draft route" (*Washington Post*, September 1, 1907).

By 1909, *Sporting Life* reported that "the 'farming' evil under the species 'optional agreement' guise has spread into all leagues" (*Sporting Life*, January 2, 1909). The *Chicago Tribune* went further, pronouncing the rules to be "absolutely a dead letter so far as current practice is concerned. There are hundreds of farmed players in the minor leagues today. They are not called that by name and they are not actually loaned to minor league clubs with the understanding they may be recalled on demand. A subterfuge in the form of an 'option' agreement has been sanctioned by the national commission which bears the same relation to farming that a time loan does to a call loan in banking. The players are 'sold' to minor league clubs with a written agreement that they can be repurchased in August at a fixed price and that no other club shall have a right to purchase or draft them if the original loaning club cares to exercise its 'option.' Yet the foundation of organized baseball says specifically, 'All right or claim of a major league club to a player shall cease when such player becomes a member of a minor club.' And the national commission expects respect for itself and the laws it is supposed to enforce!" (*Chicago Tribune*, July 11, 1909).

Sportswriter Joe S. Jackson wrote in 1911 that with the exception of Washington "there seems to be no ownership in the country that is not engaged in a wholesale juggling of players to evade the rules made for the protection of the sport" (*Washington Post*, September 26, 1911).

When Chicago Cubs owner Charles Webb Murphy was sanctioned in 1913 for having a secret agreement with the Louisville club, *Sporting News* pointed out the hypocrisy of singling Murphy out: "'Farming' is forbidden by the National Agreement, and is practiced by every club owner in the two big leagues. It has been done so openly by some of the moguls that the example made by Murphy is all the more deplorable" (*Sporting News*, August 28, 1913). A follow-up piece added, ". . . It is likely that 'side agreements' enter into almost every big deal made between a major and a minor league club. It is an indisputable fact that every major league club has minor league affiliations, which enable them to place surplus talent much more advantageously than would otherwise be the case. These affiliations also result in the 'covering up' of valuable players to protect them from the draft by other clubs which might use them" (*Sporting News*, September 4, 1913).

With the farming laws regarded as a "dead letter," major league owners now dropped the restriction on owning minor league clubs. Cleveland became particularly active in this regard. A 1912 article reported that "the Cleveland American League Club is figuring on taking Marion's franchise in the Ohio State League and using this city as a farm" (*Sporting Life*, March 16, 1912). By 1916, Charles Somers of Cleveland owned Waterbury of the Eastern League, New Orleans of the Southern League, and Toledo of the American Association (Robert Burk, *Much More Than a Game*, 35). In 1921 Chicago Cubs owner William Wrigley purchased the Los Angeles Angels of the Pacific Coast League.

Moreover the intent of these arrangements was unmistakable. In 1911 sportswriter I. E. Sanborn pronounced it an open secret that White Sox owner Charles Comiskey was one of the purchasers of the Des Moines club and that "the purpose of the new arrangement [is] to put Hugh Duffy in charge of Comiskey's interests in the Iowa club and let him train and develop young players for the White Sox. Instead of loaning out his promising youngsters here and there to clubs whose managers are subject to change and who often know less about the science of baseball than the young players themselves, Comiskey, under the plan evolved, can plant young players in Des Moines and be sure that Duffy will teach them something, for there is no question about the former Sox manager knowing inside baseball. In that way young players obtained from the minor leagues, who give evidence of becoming good players, can be polished off and given experience in actual games under Duffy's generalship instead of being kept on the bench at the south side with small chance of getting into actual contests" (I. E. Sanborn, "Jimmy Callahan New Sox Manager," *Chicago Tribune*, October 23, 1911, 12).

It should be clear by this point that the farm system the Cardinals developed in the 1920s and 1930s was not something that Branch Rickey in any meaningful sense "invented." What Rickey did was to tinker with, and then reinvent and expand, an existing idea that had previously been prohibited or deemed too costly.

While other major league clubs had owned minor league clubs, this practice was widely considered to be an almost certain moneyloser. This conclusion was founded upon the perception that a minor league club could not produce enough talent suited to the needs of the major league squad to justify the expense. Rickey saw matters otherwise, however, and began to purchase minor league clubs.

Rickey's decision was driven by two important factors. The first was that minor league owners such as Jack Dunn of Baltimore were demanding exorbitant amounts for stars like Jack Bentley and Lefty Grove, and keeping the players if their price wasn't met. This not only drove up the price of talent but also meant that low-budget teams like Rickey's Cardinals would never be able to acquire such players.

This in turn led Rickey to realize that ownership of an entire network of farm clubs could become profitable if, in addition to producing talent for his club, it also yielded excess talent that he could sell to his rivals. Thus Robert Burk has suggested that Branch Rickey was not an inventor but a man with a genius for organizational tinkering: "What set Rickey's approach apart from that of his predecessors was his early grasp of the importance of integrating within the same parent club office the signing of entry-level talent, management of the player promotion process at all levels, and maintenance of a deliberate surplus of young talent to leverage down the major league payroll and make additional profits through sales of surplus players" (Robert Burk, *Much More Than a Game*, 35).

Rickey also recognized that this approach to player development allowed him to make more effective use of his scouts. Previously, major league scouts had been on the lookout for major league–ready talent, but the ownership of multiple minor league clubs allowed the Cardinals to stockpile promising but raw players. Rickey began to evolve his "quality out of quantity" philosophy and instructed chief scout Charley Barrett to sign players who still needed seasoning. As early as 1921, columnist John Sheridan observed that "Barrett's activities are more in the line of finding young players for trading and training purposes than for picking up big league stars" (*Sporting News*, August 4, 1921).

Playing no small part in this scheme was Rickey's self-interest. Beginning with his first Cardinal contract in 1918, Rickey received a share of the club's profits. He would ultimately realize a significant part of his income from the sale of the excess talent produced by the Cardinals' farm system (Murray Polner, *Branch Rickey*, 112; Lee Lowenfish, *Branch Rickey*, 140, 181).

By the middle of the decade Rickey's efforts were attracting attention that was bolstered by the success of his team. After the Cardinals won the 1926 World Series, sportswriter John B. Sheridan described "the Cardinal system of replacement, that is ownership of a 'vertical trust,' a number of minor league clubs of varying classifications, D, C, B, A, and AA, through which the Cardinal replacements are moved for educational purposes" (John B. Sheridan, *Sporting News*, December 23, 1926).

The success of the Cardinals naturally prompted other clubs to imitate Rickey's methods. On December 15, 1932, major league owners approved the idea of "chain store" baseball in spite of the objections of Commissioner Kenesaw Mountain Landis. Landis would continue to throw wrenches in the works for the remainder of his life by periodically ordering the release of covered-up players. But even the mighty Landis was not able to undermine a system now firmly in place.

Lee Lowenfish notes that by 1938 almost every major league club had begun to imitate Rickey's system. Influential opponents like John McGraw were dead, and even Commissioner Landis, according to a 1937 *Sporting News* editorial, might be "pained, but scarcely surprised to note a baseball world that has been completely 'Rickeyized'" (Lee Lowenfish, *Branch Rickey*, 279). Another *Sporting News* editorial observed that farm systems were not merely expanding but fundamentally changing

in nature: "Unless all signs fail, 1934 promises to become known as the 'year of the farms.' Formerly, the fountain head of the system was the major league club. Now a number of the minor league clubs are going in for the farm stuff and the end is not yet in sight" (*Sporting News*, March 15, 1934). By 1940 even Landis had essentially abandoned his war on the farm systems (Lee Lowenfish, *Branch Rickey*, 308).

13.1.6   Player Development Plan. For several decades after the permanent establishment of chain-store baseball, minor league owners continued to exercise considerable autonomy. Their freedom to make player personnel decisions allowed them to retain local players who had no hope of making the majors, and these "career minor leaguers" often became fan favorites.

But the future of the minor leagues was jeopardized in the 1950s by a precipitous decline in attendance. As a result, on May 18, 1962, major league baseball adopted the Player Development Plan. The majors increased funding of the minors, in exchange for authority over personnel issues. The plan also abolished Classes B, C, and D and replaced them with the Rookie Leagues. This effectively rendered the minors the developers of talent for the majors that they have been ever since. In the process, the "career minor leaguer" became effectively extinct, yielding his place to younger prospects.

(ii) Trades and Sales

Trades and sales are such an accepted part of baseball today that it is easy to forget how strange they must have once seemed. Just imagine opening the business section of a newspaper and reading that Charles Schwab had sent a money manager to Merrill Lynch for an investment adviser and a bond specialist to be named later. Or that your local hardware store had swapped employees with one of its competitors. The earliest baseball trades understandably struck observers as being equally peculiar. *Sporting Life* observed in 1884, "There is a great deal of nonsensical twaddle uttered by ill-informed base ball reporters about players being bought and sold. If these gentlemen would trouble themselves to examine the rules bearing on the subject they would discover that no player can be transferred, no matter what the consideration, without his own free will and consent. Buying a release from contract is a legitimate transaction and of frequent occurrence in theatrical and business affairs" (*Sporting Life*, August 13, 1884).

13.2.1 Sales. In 1887, John Ward wrote, "The 'buying and selling' of players was unheard of three years ago" (quoted in Bryan Di Salvatore, *A Clever Base-Ballist*, 195). This was not quite true since, as *Sporting Life* noted in the above passage, buying a release was always a possibility.

The first player sale probably occurred in 1875 when the Athletic Club of Philadelphia purchased the release of Bill Craver and George Bechtel from the cross-town Centennial Club. Francis Richter claimed: "The Centennials played but few games, and their brief existence is only noteworthy for the fact that with them began the sale of players, a custom that has grown to tremendous proportions since. The Centennial Club contained but two first-class players—Craver and Bechtel. The rival Athletic club, of Philadelphia, wanted these two, and two wealthy members of the club paid an official of the Centennial Club $1500 to have the two players released and transferred to the Athletic Club. This was done and shortly after the Centennial Club disbanded. It was a peculiar fact that the first sale of players brought retribution with it, as Craver turned out to be crooked, and Bechtel took [Cap] Anson's place so often that the latter became dissatisfied and later seceded to the Chicago Club" (Francis C. Richter, *Richter's History and Records of Base Ball*, 47). David Ball analyzed the historic deal in considerable detail, noting among other things that the recent end of slavery was another factor that made player sales a touchy subject (David Ball, "The Bechtel-Craver Trade and the Origins of Baseball's Sales System," *Base Ball* 1:1 [Spring 2007], 36–55).

Henry Chadwick reported after the 1878 season that the "system of releasing players" had led to considerable abuse. He explained that a club could put together a strong lineup, only to have a rival try in mid-season to induce its "players to 'get a release' and then join them, offering tempting baits for secession. As the rule admits of releases and new engagements, of course it does not take long for tempted players to work things to suit them so as to obtain the required release" (*New York Clipper*, January 4, 1879).

There was, however, no viable way to eliminate this possibility. As a result, any time a player went into a slump, there began to be whispers that he was "playing for his release." This state of affairs was harmful both to individual players and to the integrity of the game itself, and it paved the way for open sales of players.

In 1882, John Corkhill was sold for $300 (James A. Williams, quoted in *Sporting Life*, April 25, 1891). By 1884 it was becoming more common for clubs and players to mutually agree to terminate a contract. During that season it was reported that Lew Simmons of the Athletics "gave the Lynn Club $250 for the release of [Henry] Oxley, their catcher," though the deal seems to have fallen through (*New York Clipper*, June 21, 1884). After the 1884 season Tom Deasley learned that New York's National League entry placed more value on his services than did his current employers. So "he paid the St. Louis Club $400 for his release. He then came to [New York], and was at once engaged at a salary of $3,000" (*New York Sun*, April 4, 1886).

Player sales grew after that, in large part because they were much easier to implement than trades. But they remained odious to the players. In his 1887 article "Is the Base Ball Player a Chattel?," John M. Ward reasoned, ". . . When the Chicago club sells [Mike] Kelly for $10,000, it simply makes that sum out of Kelly. . . . Kelly received his salary from Chicago and earned every dollar of it several times over, and yet the Chicago club takes ten thousand dollars for releasing Kelly from a claim for which it never paid a dollar" (John M. Ward, "Is the Base Ball Player a Chattel?," *Lippincott's* 40 [August 1887], 310–319; quoted in *Baseball in Old Chicago*, 50). As Mark Lamster observes, the Kelly sale occurred at a time when labor unrest, spurred by recent events like the Haymarket Affair, were once more making player sales a highly charged issue (Mark Lamster, *Spalding's World Tour*, 37). The 1889 public statement by the players' union, the Brotherhood (see **18.3.1**), similarly denounced the fact that "Players have been bought, sold and exchanged, as though they were sheep, instead of American citizens" ("Brotherhood Manifesto," November 4, 1889; reprinted in Dean Sullivan, ed., *Early Innings*, 188–189). Deacon White was more succinct, famously saying, "No man is going to sell my carcass unless I get half" (quoted in Lee Lowenfish, *The Imperfect Diamond*, 34).

With the threat of the Players' League looming, the National League finally offered to compromise. The league first promised to give players a quarter of their own purchase price and then even offered to let players negotiate their own sales. A. G. Spalding maintained that these concessions would "[do] away with the systems of sales, over which there has been such an outcry by the seceding players and their organs" (*Spalding Guide, 1890*, 26; Mike Roer, *Orator O'Rourke*, 153).

The players had less leverage after the Players' League folded, but they still tried to obtain a part of their purchase prices. William "Kid" Gleason boasted in 1894 about having been "after a $500 slice of the $2,400 [Ned] Hanlon paid Chris [Von der Ahe] for me, and I am not violating any confidence in assuring you that I got it. When Willie figures in a deal he makes it a point to see that his interests are not neglected" (*St. Louis Post-Dispatch*, September 22, 1894).

13.2.2 Going-out-of-business Sales, Garage Sales, and Shopping Sprees.

By 1883 the reserve rule (see **18.2.1**) had been expanded to the point where owners could essentially retain their entire team. Of course, being able to reserve all these players didn't mean that the club had to sign all of them—or even try to do so. Predictably, some owners began selling off their reserved players to balance their budgets while other owners took advantage of the situation by going on shopping sprees.

As noted in the preceding entry, sales of any sort still created controversy. For example, the sale of Fred Lewis in the midst of the 1883 season elicited this comment: "The Philadelphias, when they found all hope was lost of their winning the league championship, adopted a new scheme, and are now selling their players in order to get their money back. Lewis was sold to St. Louis for $800, which shows the market for flesh and blood is as good as it was in the days of slavery" (*National Police Gazette*, August 4, 1883).

Researcher David Ball believes that the Fort Wayne club of the Northwestern League may have initiated the mass sale of players by selling most of its reserved players after the 1883 season. The *Cincinnati Enquirer* observed with alarm, "From present appearance it looks as though the managers of the Fort Wayne club had entered the field this season with no other object in view than that of speculating in human beings under the provisions of the reserve rule. . . . Already they have sold three players at figures that will come pretty near paying all the preliminary expenses of the club for next season" (*Cincinnati Enquirer*, reprinted in the *Washington Post*, February 3, 1884). The Fort Wayne club, however, defended its actions by pointing out that the players could have jumped to the Union Association and arguing that it was merely making sure it received something in return (*Fort Wayne Gazette*, January 29, 1884).

The sensitivity of the issue was shown when the *Terre Haute Courier* claimed in June 1884, "The Evansville managers are pursuing the plan adopted by the Fort Waynes last year, that of selling off their players like so many cattle." The *Evansville Journal* issued an angry denial, and a war of words ensued (*Evansville Journal*, June 13, 1884).

David Nemec reported that the Washington entry in the American Association held a fire sale in July 1884 and disbanded shortly thereafter (David Nemec, *The Beer and Whisky League*, 67). It appears that they succeeded in selling only one player, Frank Fennelly, but the proceeds helped the club pay the delinquent salaries of other players. Three Ohio clubs—Columbus, Toledo, and Cleveland—followed this example at season's end by selling most of their players to Pittsburgh, St. Louis, and Brooklyn, respectively, and giving up their major league franchises.

The 1885 season saw Detroit president Frederick K. Stearns make two major purchases to upgrade his talent. In June he purchased most of the players of Indianapolis's Western Association franchise, including future Hall of Famer Sam Thompson. This transaction, however, illustrated the difficulty of player sales—in order to prevent interference, the Indianapolis players were shipped by train to Cleveland where a little steamer was chartered "from the Detroit and Cleveland Navigation Company and the former Indianapolis players were loaded on board with instructions to the captain to cruise completely out of sight for the next ten days and then steam for Detroit Harbor. . . . On the morning of the 26th the little craft steamed into Detroit River and a sea-weary crowd of ball players landed at the Detroit docks, several of them getting into action against Providence next day" (Guy M. Smith, "He Could Catch Anything," Typescript in Jim McGuire Hall of Fame file). On September 17 Stearns added Buffalo's entire infield, the so-called Big Four of Dan Brouthers, Hardie Richardson, Jack Rowe, and Deacon White. The new acquisitions turned a woeful team into a pennant contender in 1886 and a world champion in 1887. But then his fellow owners modified the system for compensating visiting clubs and made it impossible for Detroit to afford such a payroll, causing Stearns to step down. His successors sold off the high-priced players after the 1888 season and then folded the team.

In the intervening three years, such block-buster sales had become commonplace, with Chicago selling Mike Kelly and John Clarkson for the shocking prices of $10,000 apiece and St. Louis auctioning off stars like Dave Foutz, "Doc" Bushong, and Bob Caruthers. As described in the preceding entry, there was strong resistance to sales at first, but the opposition lost ground after the failure of the Players' League.

By the end of the century, the buying and selling of players was sufficiently accepted for a precursor of today's hierarchical farm system to begin to emerge. "Developing base-ball players is quite a profitable undertaking these days," observed Cincinnati sportswriter Charles Zuber in 1899. "The crop of good players always is short, and the manager who can bring to light a bonafide phenom is certain to make money out of him. Take the Cincin-nati club as a buyer for instance. In the last three years it has paid out cash money to se-cure [Ted] Breitenstein, [Heinie] Peitz, [Red] Ehret, [Bill] Hill, [Tommy] Corcoran, [Jack] Taylor and [Kip] Selbach from major league clubs, and has paid extra money—above the drafting price—for [Algie] McBride, [Harry] Steinfeldt and [Noodles] Hahn. It is safe to say that the club has expended between $15,000 and $20,000 for players in the last three years. Other clubs also have invested much money in purchasing players outright, although none of them has spent as much money as Cincinnati." Zuber then explained that "Using players as merchandise is of comparatively recent origin." He summarized the history of such transactions and then quoted Frank Bancroft's description of how at one time, "If a club had an extra man that it had no real use for and some other club wanted him, he was given away—not sold. In consequence teams were more evenly matched than they are now." Zuber closed by remarking, "However those days are gone. Players change teams now only through sale, trade or when their usefulness is gone" (reprinted in the *Daily Iowa State Press* [Iowa City], March 6, 1899).

13.2.3 Trades. Even the idea of a trade was pretty much unheard of until 1883, and it was several more years before it was practical to consummate one. The most obvious reason for this was that exchanges of human beings raised the basic human rights issue noted in the rhe-torical title of John Ward's 1887 essay, "Is the Base Ball Player a Chattel?" Trades also brought into question the principle of the mutuality of a contract, an especially prickly topic in the 1880s because of the recent implementation of the reserve rule. The result was that in order for two clubs to complete such a transaction, they first had to agree on the players to be exchanged, then convince all those players to cooperate.

This meant that talk about trades was more common than actual swaps. During the 1883 season Ted Sullivan, manager of the St. Louis (American Association) club, "made a proposi-tion to the Buffalo league club, asking the man-agers whether they would release [Jim] Lilly or Schaeffer [George Shafer] for Tom Sullivan" (*St. Louis Post-Dispatch*, June 26, 1883). Even if Buffalo had agreed in principle to this ar-rangement, it would have been another matter to orchestrate it—once players were released, another owner might swoop in and sign them.

This possibility haunted every prospec-tive transaction. One of the most notorious examples occurred after the 1884 season, when pitcher Tony Mullane attested in a notarized statement that he would sign with St. Louis if released by Toledo. Instead Mullane inked a contract with Cincinnati and was blacklisted for the 1885 season (Jon David Cash, *Before They Were Cardinals*, 96–97).

While owners were chastened by such inci-dents, the more determined ones were willing to go to considerable lengths to complete a deal. According to Harold Seymour, "*Sporting Life* reported that in one instance 'wine and women' were used" (Harold Seymour, *Baseball: The Early Years*, 168). A different diversionary approach was employed by the ownership that controlled the New York franchises in both major leagues. After the 1884 season star play-ers Tim Keefe and Dude Esterbrook were sent from the Metropolitans to the New Yorks in exchange for two lesser players, Frank Hankin-son and Ed Begley. Reportedly Jim Mutrie took Keefe and Esterbrook on a cruise during the period they were released to ensure that neither signed with another club (David Nemec, *The Beer and Whisky League*, 92). As noted under "Waivers" (**13.3.2**), Seymour traced the origins of baseball's waiver rules to this dubious ar-rangement.

Obviously, owners who wanted to make a deal badly enough were usually able to find a way to surmount the formidable obstacles. The ones that proved easiest to consummate were between a major league club and a minor league club, since such trades offered advancement to the player(s) going to the majors and greater security to those headed to the minors.

Late in the 1885 season Louisville manager Jim Hart acquired highly regarded pitcher Toad Ramsey from Chattanooga, "giving in exchange for him, beside the cash bonus, [John] Connor, the young pitcher he secured from the Buffalos, who is scarcely strong enough for the American, but should do exceedingly well in the Southern League. If Ramsey proportionately pitches for Louisville anything like the ball he pitched for Chattanooga he will prove a treasure for his new club. The bonus paid for the transfer is $750. Chattanooga wanted $1,000 and Manager Hart offered $500. After considerable dickering the difference was split at $750, Hart agreeing, in addition, to give Chattanooga Connor. Ramsey, who has been anxious to get away from Chattanooga, gladly entered into the deal and signed with Louisville for $200 per month" (*Sporting Life*, September 9, 1885).

Researcher David Ball found evidence of a similar deal and a near miss the following summer. He cited a note in *Sporting News* that "it is said" that the Athletics had obtained Macon's star pitcher Cyclone Miller in exchange for cash and their reserve battery of Charles Gessner and Bill Dugan. Late in the 1886 season the Athletics reportedly offered Al Atkinson and cash to St. Joseph for Silver King, though the deal fell through. Ball noted that since minor league teams lacked reserve rights, it was in their best interests to dispose of their best players during the season rather than lose them without compensation. The minor league club also needed to get at least one player in return, since few capable replacements were available. This explains why the pattern of all three deals was a potential star going to the major league club in exchange for cash and a lesser player or players.

The 1886 season saw increasingly common rumors of trades between major league clubs. The *New York Sun* reported, "There is much talk of trading players by several of the Western clubs" (*New York Sun*, July 4, 1886). The most sensational rumor was of a blockbuster deal in which St. Louis would send Fred Dunlap, Jack Glasscock, and Emmett Seery to Boston in exchange for Sam Wise, Tom Poorman, Joe Hornung, and either Charlie Parsons or Billy

Nash (*Boston Globe*, June 4, 1886). David Ball has discovered at least a dozen other rumored trades between major league clubs during the 1886 campaign. But only in November did the first such trade occur when the Browns sent Hugh Nicol to Cincinnati in return for Jack Boyle and $350.

The complications involved in completing even that trade make it easy to understand why nothing had come of the earlier rumored deals. Cincinnati manager Gus Schmelz explained that he gave St. Louis owner Chris Von der Ahe a document reading, "I hereby agree to pay $350 and Catcher Boyle for the release of Hugh Nicol, conditional on Nicol's signing with the Cincinnati B.B. Club." Von der Ahe gave him a similar document, and both were then presented to league president Wheeler C. Wikoff, who agreed not to approve the two players' releases until they had been signed by their new clubs. Schmelz then instructed Cincinnati president Aaron Stern not to mention the arrangement until he had secured Nicol's signature, before rushing to the player's hometown of Rockford to sign him (Gus Schmelz to Aaron Stern, November 12, 1886, Cincinnati Reds collection, Cincinnati Historical Society, box 2, file 35).

All of these machinations make it easy to see why trades remained uncommon for several more years. They gradually increased in frequency as owners gained the upper hand and inserted clauses in contracts that required players to go wherever their contracts were assigned. David Ball reports that an April 17, 1896, bulletin by National League president Nick Young included the following items: "Released—by Chicago to Cincinnati—Asa Stewart; by Baltimore to Syracuse—George Carey." He believes that this is the earliest official reference to a player's contract being directly transferred from one club to another without the formality of a release.

Even then not all players meekly acquiesced to being shuffled about like pieces of property. As with purchases, many players demanded compensation before agreeing to a trade, and some went further. Brooklyn outfielder Mike Griffin was traded after the 1898 season and found that his new club would not honor his old contract. He successfully sued for damages, but as a result his fine career ended prematurely.

Clark Griffith's career could have met a similar fate. An 1899 article reported that he and Chicago teammate Jimmy Callahan were "up in arms against proposed trades involving them. Griffith says he will quit the game before he allows himself to be traded to some club for which he does not care to play. Callahan, who has been mentioned as likely to be traded to Boston, says he wants to remain in Chicago if he cannot go to the New York Club. In speaking about the evils of the trading system, Callahan said: 'They have put many a good man out of the business. . . . If we are the attraction which draws the money into the box office, we certainly ought to have something to say about our location on the base ball map. . . . I, for one, do not intend to figure in any trade unless I can better myself by so doing'" (*Sporting News*, December 30, 1899).

As a result of such complications, David Ball reports that it became a fairly common practice during the late 1880s to agree upon a cash equivalent for each player in a trade. Thus if one of the players did not sign with the team he was supposed to go to, the releasing club would pay the money instead. These agreements eroded the bargaining power of a traded player and gradually helped make trades more routine.

Of course players never became entirely reconciled to trades. In 1969 Curt Flood reacted to being traded to the Phillies with words that echoed the title of the essay written by John Ward eighty-two years earlier: "I do not, however, consider myself to be a piece of property to be sold regardless of my desire" (quoted in Charles P. Korr, *The End of Baseball as We Knew It*, 84). Flood lost his subsequent court challenge to the reserve clause, but the support he won from his fellow players helped lead to the ten-and-five rule (see **13.2.7**) and to free agency (see **18.4.5**).

13.2.4   Three-way Trades. Following the 1908 season the Giants traded Roger Bresnahan to St. Louis in a three-team deal. Cincinnati sent George Schlei to New York; St. Louis shipped Ed Karger and Art Fromme to Cincinnati; and St. Louis sent Red Murray and Bugs Raymond to New York (*Sporting News*, December 31, 1908).

13.2.5   Players to Be Named Later. *Sporting Life* reported in 1915, "The Baltimore Club has traded Bill Bailey, the southpaw pitcher, to Chicago for pitcher Dave Black and a pitcher yet to be named" (*Sporting Life*, September 25, 1915).

13.2.6   Throw-ins. There is of course no way to determine a highly subjective category like the first throw-in. Willie Keeler, however, was one of the earliest throw-ins and was likely the first afterthought in a trade to unexpectedly develop into a superstar. He may also have been the first player referred to by this term, as *Sporting Life* claimed in 1895 that Keeler was "the man who was 'thrown in' to fill out" a deal in which Baltimore manager Ned Hanlon secured Keeler and Dan Brouthers in exchange for Bill Shindle and George Treadway (*Sporting Life*, July 13, 1895). According to Burt Solomon, the trade was originally going to be a straight-up swap of Brouthers for Treadway. When Brooklyn asked for Shindle as well, Hanlon requested Keeler. Since Brooklyn intended to release Keeler, they acquiesced (Burt Solomon, *Where They Ain't*, 57–58).

13.2.7   Vetoed Trades. On February 25, 1973, a new Basic Agreement gave the right to veto a trade to players with ten years of major league service and at least the last five with the same team. The "ten and five rule" was often referred to as "the Curt Flood Provision" because it addressed one of the main concerns that prompted Flood's challenge to the reserve clause (Charles P. Korr, *The End of Baseball as We Knew It*, 128). Ten-and-five player Jim Perry of Minnesota was traded to Detroit the following month and consented to the deal (*Sporting News, Baseball: A Doubleheader Collection of Facts, Feats and Firsts*, 454).

Ron Santo became the first player to exercise the ten-and-five rule on December 5, 1973, when he turned down a trade that would have sent him from the Cubs to the Angels. After vetoing the trade, Santo realized that he had put himself in a unique position: "I was concerned. It really didn't hit me until a couple of days later. I realized the Cubs didn't want me and I couldn't possibly play for them again" (quoted by Joe Mooshil, AP wire service story, December 12, 1973). Fortunately for Santo, the Cubs soon arranged a new trade that sent him to the crosstown White Sox.

(iii) Roster Restrictions

13.3.1   Roster Sizes. Roster sizes and efforts to get around them in one way or another affect almost all the basic strategies used by general managers to accumulate and retain talent.

Until 1889 substitutions were allowed only in the case of severe injury. As a result, as noted under "Insertion of Substitutes" (**6.2.1**), most major league clubs carried ten or eleven players. Some went with only nine, hiring managers or even groundskeepers with the expectation they would serve as emergency substitutes. There was staunch resistance to adding any more players. The *Boston Sunday Herald*, for instance, scoffed at the idea that Boston might try a thirteen-man roster in 1877, pointing out that this would mean that four players were "lying idle all the time. It need hardly be said that this is too large a number to carry" (reprinted in the *Chicago Tribune*, December 3, 1876). And a few months later the *Chicago Tribune* stated that even an eleventh man was generally regarded as a "luxury" (*Chicago Tribune*, March 4, 1877, 7).

In the years since, roster sizes have more than doubled, but rarely has an increase come without resistance from some quarters. This was particularly true in the 1890s when the legalization of substitutes led to rapid increases in roster sizes. For example, in 1892 the *Brooklyn Eagle* contended that the local club's decision to carry seventeen or eighteen players that year was too many (*Brooklyn Eagle*, June 8, 1892). The *Washington Post* argued that on a club that "burdened itself with too many players," a starter was liable to become "disturbed and made nervous by thinking there is another on the team waiting to take his place." It added that a large bench was unnecessary because there was "time enough to look around for a man to fill a position when the one who has it has failed" (*Washington Post*, February 16, 1890).

As of 1899, clubs were carrying 17 to 20 players (*Philadelphia Evening Bulletin*, April 17, 1899). In response, *Sporting News* observed: "The costly experience of the National League clubs in carrying players for whom they can not find a regular position and who are not even needed as substitutes, may lead to a much-needed reform. It is said that there is a movement under way to limit each National League club's right of reservation to 16 players" (*Sporting News*, August 4, 1900).

The 16-player limit was indeed passed that winter (*Chicago Tribune*, March 29, 1901, 9). But such initiatives became impossible during the challenge of the American League, since teams in both leagues were anxious to stash extra players on their rosters. Sportswriter J. Ed Grillo noted that the richer clubs benefited: "As many as 38 [players] have been carried through a season by some club which could afford it,

while one of the weaklings was scouring the country in search of material not as good as that which the strong club was paying to remain idle" (*Washington Post*, December 24, 1909).

Once a permanent peace between the two leagues had been reached, they were quick to reinstitute a firm limit on roster sizes. It took a little longer to settle on the perfect number. Today's size of twenty-five was proposed before the 1909 season and was widely reported as having been adopted (for example, *Chicago Tribune*, February 18, 1909). But other accounts described the limit only as a proposal that was likely to be adopted (*Washington Post*, February 14, 1909). Implementation of the restriction must indeed have been delayed, because after the 1909 season many newspapers carried word of a "new" rule limiting rosters to twenty-five players between May 1 and August 20 (*Washington Post*, December 16, 1909; *New York Times*, December 16, 1909; *Detroit Free Press*, April 10, 1910).

At the same time the prototype of the forty-man roster was created to prevent clubs from bringing enormous aggregations to training camp. In 1910 sportswriter A. J. Flanner explained the ramifications of a new rule that clubs could only bring thirty-five players to spring training: "In recruiting for 1911, the big league manager must consider the quantity and quality of members of his team during the present race, as well as the number and ability, present and prospective, of players on whom he has option, before he can intelligently start to secure minor league stars either by purchase or draft" (*Sporting News*, July 21, 1910).

Minor league roster sizes remained smaller but were beginning to succumb to similar pressures. Early in the 1916 Eastern League campaign the clubs voted to expand rosters from thirteen to fourteen when they realized that "the teams would be unable to get along with only four pitchers during the hot weather when they are playing doubleheaders" (Will Anderson, *Was Baseball Really Invented in Maine?*, 31).

Major league roster sizes were reduced during World War I, but they returned to twenty-five following the war's end and have stayed there ever since, with a few short-lived exceptions. After the 1931 season, rosters were cut from twenty-five to twenty-three because of the depression. The twenty-five-player limit was temporarily waived at the end of World War II to accommodate homecoming veterans and again in 1949 when Mexican League jumpers were reinstated ("Player Limit Suspended, Easing Way for Reinstatement of Exiles," *New York Times*, June 7, 1949, 35). In the early 1990s owners briefly cut back to twenty-four-man rosters in another cost-saving measure.

One thing that has never changed is the intimate connection between roster sizes and player development stratagems. In 1915, when the National League restricted roster sizes to twenty-one, John McGraw complained that he was paying scout "Dick Kinsella $5,000 a year to select the pick of the minors and it is pretty tough now that it develops that most of Dick's work has been for the benefit of other teams" (*Sporting News*, February 25, 1915).

13.3.2   Waivers. Major league baseball has had waiver rules since 1885, but they have undergone many alterations over the years as the problems they were intended to address have changed.

The earliest waiver rules were created in an apparent effort to stem the growing threat of clubs selling off their best players to teams in a rival league (see **13.2.2**). Harold Seymour suggested that an infamous deal in which John B. Day essentially transferred star players Tim Keefe and Dude Esterbrook from his American Association franchise to his National League club was the spur (Harold Seymour, *Baseball: The Early Years*, 169). As befits this modest aim, the rules were simple and essentially required that a player had to be offered to every other team in the league for a period of ten days before his contract could be sold to a club outside the league. The early waiver rules involved no payment for a claim and had plenty of loopholes.

In theory, even a trade could not be completed without the players clearing waivers, but in practice owners routinely passed if they knew a trade was being made. For example, researcher David Ball found an 1889 article explaining that the Washington management had "made arrangements for the exchange of [Jim] Whitney for ["Egyptian"] Healy [of Indianapolis] and the league clubs have been requested to waive claims for both men." To get the process started, Indianapolis sent a telegram to National League president Nick Young that read: "Whenever League clubs waive claim to Whitney and Healy and Washington releases Whitney Indianapolis will accept his services. At the same time Indianapolis will release Healy" (*Washington Post*, March 24, 1889).

Once farm clubs (see **13.1.5**) became a common way for major league clubs to stockpile players, the waiver rules were modified to try to prevent this practice. As the waiver system and its goals became more complex, the earlier spirit of cooperation disappeared, which made it necessary to clarify or amend the procedures. For example, it was made explicit that a club could revoke its waivers if the player was claimed. A claiming fee was also added to deter frivolous claims. In addition, fairer rules were created for situations when more than one team claimed the same player (originally the player had been allowed to choose).

Despite such amendments, the waiver system proved an imperfect means of preventing farming. For one thing, as is discussed under "Gentlemen's Agreements" (see **13.3.5**), clubs could easily conspire to evade the rules. A related problem was caused by the original club's prerogative to revoke the waivers after a claim. Sportswriter Jack Ryder wrote in 1915, "Usually at this time of the year a raft of requests for waivers is coming in, so that, if obtained, deals for the players may be made with minor league clubs" (*Cincinnati Enquirer*; quoted in *Sporting News*, December 2, 1915). Clubs that put in claims would likely end up only with unwanted players, so it usually made more sense to pass and let a few capable players slip to the minors. Other abuses of the system were discussed in the entry on farm clubs.

In spite of its many problems, the waiver system was retained and expanded in hopes of remedying a widening range of problems. In the process the waiver rules have greatly increased in complexity. It would now be difficult if not impossible to make a succinct summary of what they accomplish.

It can safely be said, however, that one major goal was improving competitive balance. At the 1921 winter meetings a rule giving the first shot at waived players to the weakest teams was instituted. As is discussed in the next two entries, a similar desire to achieve greater parity motivated restrictions on late-season trades between contenders and also-rans, especially when the players were passing from one league to the other.

13.3.3   Interleague Trading. As noted in the preceding entry, the waiver system was created in 1885 in part to prevent deals between the National League and the American Association. The same principle applied for much of the twentieth century to transactions between the American and National leagues.

The first such trade took place in 1903, during a brief truce between the warring leagues. *Sporting Life* gave this account of the historic event: "Cincinnati has secured second baseman Tom Daly and outfielder [Cozy] Dolan from the Chicago American League Club in exchange for infielder George Magoon. This is the first inter-league deal as yet consummated" (*Sporting Life*, June 20, 1903).

After a permanent peace had been reached, the two leagues made a concerted and highly effective effort to prevent such trades because of fears that a tail-ender in one league could sabotage the other league's pennant race by selling their best players to a contender. It thus came as a great shock to the baseball world when star Yankee pitcher Hank Borowy, despite a 10-5 record, cleared waivers on July 27, 1945, and was sold to the Cubs for a figure close to $100,000. Borowy went on to complete a twenty-win season and lead his new team to the National League pennant.

The transaction raised the hackles and suspicions of many owners. According to sportswriter Warren Brown, however, the explanation was more plebeian: "There were no 'angles' to the deal and no skullduggery as many charged. It was the age-old exemplification of the utter silliness of the waiver rule. Periodically each major league club asks waivers on ballplayers on its reserve list, possibly to establish whether there is any demand for them, possibly just to keep in practice. Most clubs have become committed to the theory that it is useless to refuse to waive on any player who is known to have two arms and two legs, since most of the time the waivers will be withdrawn anyhow. So clubs are apt to be careless in perusing the waiver lists, and even more careless in making an immediate note of someone who must be claimed at once. In the instance of Borowy such American League clubs as said (afterwards) that they could have used Borowy, quite forgot to make a claim for him until it was too late" (Warren Brown, *The Chicago Cubs*, 220).

Red Smith explained in 1952 that teams were continuing to exploit the flaws in the waiver system either by colluding or by loading the waiver wires until someone got through. He elaborated: "Each summer for several years now, the fans have seen the Yankees reach out when the struggle got hot and pluck out of the National League a Johnny Mize or Johnny Hopp or John Sain or Ewell Blackwell. . . . In recent years, National League clubs have contrived to get waivers on players whom the Yankees wanted so the players could be sold to the Yankees at prices far above the waiver figure. On the surface this is entirely legal. [Dan] Topping is telling the truth when he says that the Yankees have not violated the letter of the rule in these deals. He is mistaken when he says there has been no violation of the spirit of the rule" (Red Smith, September 3, 1952, reprinted in *Red Smith on Baseball*).

After the 1952 season the major leagues addressed the issue by requiring two-league waivers on interleague trades after the June 15 trading deadline. An AP report explained that the new rule "will not permit the kind of deals the New York Yankees have been making with National League clubs in recent years. Some even called it a 'Stop the Yankees' move. Last August the Yanks acquired lanky Ewell Blackwell from Cincinnati for $30,000 and 3 players, about 2 months after the trading deadline. They did it under the old waiver rule by which all National League clubs passed up a chance to get Blackwell for the $10,000 waiver price. Once out of the National, he could be sold for whatever the Reds could get. In the future, a player from the league—like Blackwell—would have to be waived out of the National and by all the other American League clubs through the normal waiver channels" (AP: *Washington Post*, December 8, 1952). Of course the rule did not entirely eliminate such deals, but the added restriction did address the widespread perception of unfairness.

Following the 1958 season the owners approved the concept of a brief window for interleague trading without any waivers after each season. The first one lasted from November 21 to December 15, 1959, and nine trades involving thirty players were made during that period. The first trade occurred on November 21 and saw the Red Sox send Dick Gernert to the Cubs for Dave Hillman and Jim Marshall. The most significant was probably a trade in which the White Sox sent Johnny Callison to the Phillies in exchange for Gene Freese (*Sporting News, Baseball: A Doubleheader Collection of Facts, Feats and Firsts*, 441).

The first true blockbuster interleague trade did not come until December 9, 1965, when Cincinnati sent Frank Robinson to Baltimore for Milt Pappas, Jack Baldschun, and Dick Simpson.

13.3.4 Trade Deadlines. The other effort to ensure that late-season trades could not undermine pennant races was the creation of a deadline on trades within a league. As has been the case with many rules, the general principle was established before all the details were ironed out.

According to researcher Cliff Blau, the first trade deadline was established in the National League before the 1917 season. The new rule dictated that a sale or trade could not take place after August 20 unless the players had cleared waivers within the league. *Sporting Life* observed that this was "aimed at the practice of strengthening pennant factors at the expense of second division clubs." It cited a number of trades from recent seasons that had prompted the rule and pointed out that the Giants had been involved in every one of the trades (*Sporting Life*, March 24, 1917).

The junior circuit established a similar rule in 1920, with a deadline of July 1. In 1921 both leagues agreed on a trade deadline of August 1.

The longtime deadline of June 15 had an intriguing origin. At the end of July 1922 the city of St. Louis was abuzz. The Browns were atop the American League standings while in the senior circuit the Cardinals were hot on the heels of the Giants. Was an all–St. Louis World Series possible?

In a few short days these hopes were dealt two severe blows. The Yankees beat the August 1 trade deadline by acquiring Joe Dugan from the cash-strapped Red Sox, then the Braves shipped star pitcher Hugh McQuillan to the Giants. When the dust settled, that year's World Series featured two New York clubs again while the city of St. Louis fumed.

At Branch Rickey's urging, the city's Chamber of Commerce and Rotary Clubs wrote letters of protest to Commissioner Kenesaw Mountain Landis. Landis couldn't move the World Series to St. Louis, but he did share their concern. The rule was modified that winter so that thereafter a deal could not occur after June 15 unless the players cleared waivers (Frederick Lieb, *The St. Louis Cardinals*, 96; David Pietrusza, *Judge and Jury*, 246–247). The compromise seemed to satisfy all parties, and June 15 remained a significant date on the baseball calendar until it was changed in 1986 to July 31.

Nevertheless, with the vagaries of the waiver system it has always been possible to make trades after the deadline, even ones including star players. This has become still easier in recent years. Some of the reasons for this trend are discussed in the next two entries.

13.3.5 Gentlemen's Agreements. Further complicating efforts to understand the waiver rules is the fact that their theory and practice have often been quite different. The earliest waiver rules were intended to prevent players being sold out of the league, so it appears that fellow owners routinely passed when a trade *within* the league was being made.

Such "gentlemen's agreements" continued after the waiver rules were expanded, and frequently subverted the intentions of those rules. Sportswriter Joe S. Jackson explained in 1911, "Magnates are only like other men, and it is possible to induce one to waive on some one he really wants when it is intimated to him that his own requests for waivers, if he has a deal on later, will be blocked just as a comeback" (*Washington Post*, January 11, 1911).

Understandings like these are very difficult to prevent, and they had become so common by 1926 that Edgar Wolfe, a Philadelphia sportswriter who used the penname "Jim Nasium," observed, "For every law that has ever been written there is an 'unwritten law' to nullify it, and the 'unwritten law' that has been worked till the cows come home in baseball is the much-discussed 'gentleman's agreement.' The 'gentleman's agreement' or 'unwritten law' as applied to the waiver rule, if put into words, would read: 'If you waive claim on my players I'll waive claim on yours.' And through the application of this unspoken word, which is an invisible club that each big league team holds over every other big league team, the waiver rule is rendered inoperative and each year big league teams send back to the minor leagues many players who would strengthen a lot of other teams in the big leagues" (*Sporting News*, December 30, 1926).

13.3.6 Waiver Blocking. The fact that most waivers are revocable enables clubs to ask waivers on large numbers of players, only to revoke those that are claimed. Nothing is lost if the waivers are revoked; on the other hand, a player might slip through and allow a trade well after the trade deadline.

A general manager of a contending team looks very foolish if one of his rivals acquires a player when he could have prevented the deal just by making a claim. As a result, sportswriter Mike Berardino noted in 2003, "Waiver blocking became something of a sport unto itself for a while there in recent years."

This, however, is a dangerous game. As Berardino pointed out, the claiming club sometimes gets stuck with the player and his large salary as the result of their claim, if the waiver is not revoked. Examples include Randy Myers, whose enormous contract the 1998 Padres were saddled with when they tried to block a National League rival from acquiring him; and Jose Canseco, who became an inadvertent member of the 2000 Yankees. As a result, general managers must think long and hard before engaging in waiver blocking (Mike Berardino, "Economic Climate Could Snuff Out Waiver Blocking," *Baseball America*, September 1–14, 2003).

13.3.7   Damn Yankees. The Yankees cruised to four straight American League pennants and World Series titles from 1936 to 1939. After the fourth championship, Washington owner Clark Griffith proposed a new rule prohibiting teams from making trades with or selling players to the previous season's pennant winner unless the players cleared waivers. The rule was passed unanimously by the American League but rejected by the National League, so it applied only to the Yankees.

According to sportswriter John Drebinger, the intention was "preventing a repetition of a deal such as the Yankees engineered last Winter when they obtained [pitcher] Oral Hildebrand" (John Drebinger, *New York Times*, December 8, 1939). Baseball historian Talmage Boston suggested that other clubs feared the Yankees would pursue bigger fish: "With the unlimited Yankees bank account during depression times, and a vast supply of talent in the New York farm system, the other teams foresaw the Bronx Bombers going into the marketplace to get even better by trading for the likes of Hank Greenberg" (Talmage Boston, *1939, Baseball's Pivotal Year*, 128–129).

In 1940 the Yankees were dethroned by Greenberg and Detroit. It was assumed that the rule—which was generally regarded as "an effort to hamstring the New York Yankees"—would be dropped at that point (Irving Vaughan, *Chicago Tribune*, December 11, 1940). Instead, American League owners voted 5-3 to retain the rule (John Drebinger, *New York Times*, December 11, 1940).

The decision was widely criticized, and at a mid-season meeting American League owners voted to repeal the rule, effective at season's end. A *New York Times* reporter saw the reversal as proof that anti-Yankees sentiment had been behind the rule: "This restriction unquestionably prevented a fifth straight pennant for the Yankees last year. . . . It was not, however, until the ruling hit the Tigers a severe blow this year that this opposition gained the upper hand" (James P. Dawson, "American League Lifts Trading Ban," *New York Times*, July 8, 1941).

(iv) Scouting and Player Development

13.4.1   Scouts. In the early days of baseball the acquisition of new players was an ad hoc process. The "hustlers" (see **6.1.3**) who managed clubs were too busy for scouting trips and, while club directors sometimes tried to help out, they did not necessarily have a keen eye for talent.

"Call us, we won't call you" was thus the mantra. As often as not, new players were signed sight unseen as a result of recommendations or when the players themselves sought out the manager. Some ambitious ballplayers took out newspaper ads, such as the 1866 ad that read: "WANTED—By a base ball pitcher, a 'sit' as a compositor on a weekly paper" (*Kalamazoo Telegraph*, September 5, 1866). While the amateur era prevented him from being more explicit, the gratuitous mention of his ballplaying skill suggests a belief that it would make his services more attractive.

Ads by players became common in the 1880s when sporting papers proliferated, and continued into the 1950s. In 1978, Earl Williams revived this tradition by taking out an advertisement—"1971 National League Rookie of the Year . . . No Police Record, HAVE BAT—WILL TRAVEL—WILL HUSTLE"—to publicize his availability (*New York Times*, June 12, 1978; Robert Cole, "Ball, Bat and Ad," *Baseball Research Journal* 8 [1979], 77).

The glaring "lack of some convenient means of communication between ball-players who want engagements and ball clubs wanting players" led the *Chicago Tribune* in 1878 to offer "its services, so far as they may serve, to bring the employer and employe into communication. From this time until the opening of the playing season . . . each issue of *The Sunday Tribune* will contain in its Base-Ball Department a register of players who desire engagements for 1878, and also of clubs, or associations, which have needs of players" (*Chicago Tribune*, January 13, 1878, 7). But this addressed only the communication issue; there was still no reliable way for ball clubs to determine if an applicant had the necessary skills. The result was that players got tryouts on the basis of persistence—one extreme example saw pitcher John Greenig, a Civil War veteran in his late thirties, receive tryouts from numerous professional clubs and even make one disastrous major league appearance because he wrote so many letters that exaggerated his credentials. It was a terrible system, but baseball could not afford a better one.

There was at least a growing realization that teams needed to initiate the search process, as is demonstrated by the reaction to a couple of exceptions. In 1876 the *Chicago Tribune* chided, "A curious idea is manifested in the *Clipper* by an advertisement of the Louisville Club for players. Generally a club has only to pick out from applications" (*Chicago Tribune*, December 10, 1876, 7). There was a similar reaction when the secretary of Milwaukee (Northwestern League) placed an ad for a first baseman, a second baseman, and a shortstop in a Chicago sporting periodical in the midst of the 1884 season. A Milwaukee journalist observed, "This is another of the stupid moves that have been the cause of so much dissension in the club. It is not very probable that the players at present filling the positions mentioned will be fired with zeal at the sight of the advertisement. The fact of advertising for players is generally considered the exclusive right of country clubs, the pride of towns like Mukwonago, as the men in charge of a metropolitan team are supposed to know when a valuable player is on the market. At present the veriest tyro in baseball matters knows that the equal of Milwaukee's shortstop cannot be secured for love or money, as they are all playing for big salaries. It is also extremely doubtful if advertising will bring replies from players as good as either the present second baseman or first baseman" (*Milwaukee Sentinel*, June 22, 1884, 3).

But while this way of doing business became the norm, it remained difficult to determine whether a valuable man was on the market. Budget concerns instead forced teams to rely on informal scouting networks. An 1891 article observed that Chicago manager Cap Anson "has agents in all parts of the country who are instructed to keep their eyes open for promising base ball material. Whenever one of these agents thinks he has discovered something in Anson's line he writes to him, and if the answer is favorable, perhaps he sends the 'find' on for a trial" (*Williamsport Sunday Grit*, August 23, 1891).

As difficult as it was to justify the cost of talent hunts, neither could clubs afford to stand pat as losses mounted and attendance dwindled. And the ad hoc methods of player acquisition meant that there was often a better player out there—if only the team could find him. So more organized forms of scouting began to emerge. The first prominent scout was T. P. "Ted" Sullivan, who was a ubiquitous figure in the baseball world in the nineteenth and early twentieth centuries and has been unjustly forgotten. Sullivan was born in Ireland around 1850 and raised in Milwaukee. After playing baseball at college, he organized a minor league team in Dubuque in 1879 and began an enduring relationship with one of his players, Charles Comiskey.

During the 1880s, Ted Sullivan managed major and minor league clubs throughout the country. His energy, charisma, and salesmanship became bywords though, like many of the "hustlers" (see **6.1.3**), he was less proficient at following through on what he started. Among his many accomplishments was the creation of one of the first farm teams in 1888 (see **13.1.5**).

By the 1890s, he had turned his skills primarily to the discovery of new talent. Having the field largely to himself, Sullivan worked for any club that would hire him. While he was especially associated with some clubs, he remained independent enough to be billed as "a broker in base ball players" (*St. Louis Post-Dispatch*, July 20, 1897).

For example, late in the 1891 season, *Sporting News* reported that Sullivan had outmaneuvered Jim Mutrie of the Giants to sign two players for St. Louis and remarked: "Ted Sullivan has captured many a good man for the St. Louis Browns. Indeed, he has signed more good men for that club than any other man we know of and in choosing players he very seldom makes a mistake" (*Sporting News*, September 12, 1891). But within a couple of months, the same journal observed: "Ted Sullivan, the base ball scout, is in Chicago in the interests of the Baltimore Club after Jack Pickett and has offered him $3,000 with $400 advance, for next season" (*Sporting News*, November 21, 1891).

During the 1890s it became the conventional wisdom that Ted Sullivan's "abilities as a base ball hustler and judge of a player's merits are well known throughout the country"

(*Sporting News*, March 5, 1892). Edgar Wolfe, the Philadelphia sportswriter writing as "Jim Nasium," later aptly noted that Sullivan "put into successful operation the first scouting system and 'discovered' and helped to develop many of the game's greatest stars of other days" (Jim Nasium, "'Ted' Sullivan, Baseball Pioneer," *Sporting Life* [monthly], January 1923).

By the turn of the century the scouting field was becoming increasingly competitive. Sullivan still had the clout and reputation to remain autonomous, as is shown by references to "the many youngsters he has signed this summer for clubs which he represents as scout," and "The veteran Ted Sullivan, who has been scouring the country for three months as player-hunter for the major leagues" (*Washington Post*, September 9, 1904; *Sporting Life*, March 25, 1905).

A few others achieved similar independence. Jimmy Callahan, for example, was reported in 1908 to have been "in the employ of several major league clubs last season as a scout, and he was paid for his work" (*Washington Post*, April 26, 1908). But scouting was becoming a big business, with Garry Herrmann of Cincinnati reportedly spending $100,000 on scouting in the first decade of the twentieth century (unspecified 1911 article by sportswriter Ren Mulford, Jr., reprinted in *Baseball Research Journal* 28 [1999], 89).

In exchange for writing such sizable checks, club owners expected loyalty. By the end of the first decade of the twentieth century, the system of scouts who work exclusively for one club was emerging. Prominent early full-time scouts included Larry Sutton of the Dodgers and Charley Barrett of the Cardinals. As discussed in previous entries (see **13.1.4** and **13.1.5**), Barrett was a pivotal figure in the transition of scouts from hunters of major league–ready talent to searchers for talented but raw players. The tireless pursuit of the "arm behind the barn" remained the essence of the profession for another four decades until it was again revolutionized by the introduction of the amateur draft (see **13.5.3**) in 1965.

13.4.2 Cross-checkers. Cross-checkers are now an integral part of scouting. A cross-checker reviews all the players recommended by regional scouts. This serves both to double-check the original advice and to prioritize the thousands of draft-eligible players.

While the logic of having cross-checkers is obvious, the expense involved means that they did not become commonplace until the amateur draft era. It can be argued that Ted Sullivan was not only the first scout but the first cross-checker as well. In 1905, *Sporting Life* reported that Cliff Blankenship "is on the coast acting as a scout for Cincinnati" (*Sporting Life*, August 19, 1905). A follow-up note a month later observed: "Ted Sullivan is checking the players recommended by Blankenship and has signed pitcher [Carl] Druhot" (*Sporting Life*, September 9, 1905).

In the years that followed, clubs undoubtedly had players double- and even triple-checked, especially when a significant signing bonus was involved. This was particularly true because so many clubs received tips from bird dogs. The discovery of Hall of Famer Gabby Hartnett was a perfect example, according to this account: "The 1921 season wasn't half over before Kitty Bransfield, former big leaguer, who was umpiring in the league and who was an ivory outpost for the Cubs, became convinced the young catcher was a worthy major league prospect. Kitty passed the word along and eventually came old Jack Doyle, Cubs scout, to whom was intrusted the final say. Doyle thought Bransfield's hunch was justified, so the deal was closed" (Irving Vaughan, "Hartnett's Dad Inspired 'Gabby' to Become Catcher," *Chicago Tribune*, May 10, 1925, A2). But no systematic approach to cross-checking was used for the simple reason that the players signed by regional scouts represented little or no investment to the clubs.

Branch Rickey of the Cardinals was notorious for signing players to "desk contracts," which he would simply discard if the prospect didn't make good. A player named Don Bollman recalled going to a Cardinals tryout camp during the depression and being thrilled at being signed to a contract. He reported to spring training thinking of himself as "the owner of a baseball contract . . . to me it meant a job, as it did to others. The fact of the matter was, it meant nothing. When I finally arrived at the ball park, I found EIGHTY other guys with the same folded paper, and only *four* positions available" (Don Bollman, *Run for the Roses*, 59). Although Rickey was extreme in his adherence to a "quality out of quantity approach," almost every club sought ways to allow regional scouts to sign players without making a sizable investment.

Baltimore Orioles scouting director Jim McLaughlin introduced a more systematic approach to cross-checking in the mid-1950s (Kevin Kerrane, *Dollar Sign on the Muscle*, 141).

The inauguration of the amateur draft in 1964 (see **13.5.3**) meant that every draft pick represented a twofold investment by the club—not merely the bonus to be paid that player, but forgoing the opportunity to sign other players. The use of cross-checkers accordingly became standard.

13.4.3 Central Scouting Bureau. Not long after teams began to employ their own scouts, it became apparent that scouting represented a considerable expense. They began looking for ways to reduce their costs and soon recognized the duplication of labor in having several teams send scouts to look at the same player and pronounce him no good.

They thus began to kick around the idea of having a talent hunter who would file initial reports to more than one club. The one concern was whether such a scout could be trusted to be candid with all the teams.

Fortunately the ideal man was at hand. Cincinnati scout Louis Heilbroner had experience in managing, scouting, and front office work and was known for keeping a dope book on every ballplayer in the country. Just as important, he had a reputation for scrupulous honesty and as "the first scout in the country to throw off the rubber shoes and mysterious air that formerly marked big league searches for available material."

As a result, on the recommendation of major league presidents Ban Johnson and Tom Lynch, Heilbroner was hired to work as a "special agent for several American and National league clubs. He will furnish dope for these clubs on promising players and will line them up for contracts and in other ways help recruit pennant-winning aggregations" (*Fort Wayne News*, January 30, 1910).

This idea was revived many years later with the advent of the major leagues' Central Scouting Bureau.

13.4.4 Scouting Other Teams' Rosters. Early scouts like Ted Sullivan concentrated on minor leaguers, semipros, and amateurs in hopes of discovering what later became known as "the arm behind the barn." Once it became common for scouts to work exclusively for one organization, a new direction in scouting emerged.

At the onset of 1912 spring training, *Sporting Life*'s Pittsburgh correspondent gave this description of the "delicate job" that scout (and former Phillies manager) William Murray had been given: "He isn't there to criticise players

or offer any suggestions to Cap. [Fred] Clarke. He has a distinct and separate duty. Murray's aim is to observe carefully and consistently the workouts of [various clubs'] recruits, paying attention in detail to their quantities and defects. This estimate is to guide Murray and mates in their search campaign for the summer. Colonel Dreyfuss [Pittsburgh owner Barney Dreyfuss] suggested the idea. Every Autumn clubs pick up numerous young players mainly on scout suggestions. They are taken on training pilgrimages and tested. Most every one has more or less talent. They drift back to the minors. Unquestionably some are pretty good. If kept they might become league artists in a season or two. The major portion of this type, however, has been turned back. Next season the same state of affairs is shown.

"Colonel Dreyfuss and business associates have realized that some folly was attached to this method. Was it business acumen to send back this class of youngsters and immediately start scouts out in search of new players, then to pick up boys, pay high prices and go on repeating the process season in and out? Murray will see the tests, observe virtues and defects of players and then give decision as to the likelihood of finding youngsters with more talent than the ones on hand. If he thinks that there is yet hope of digging up boys better balanced, then his decree will banish one or two ball tossers back to the minors and the secret service department will start a quest for the objects devoutly wished for. Sounds like a fine plan, and is to be given a thorough trial by the Pittsburg Club" (*Sporting Life*, March 30, 1912).

In the following week's issue, Cincinnati correspondent Ren Mulford, Jr., added: "Picking stars out of the bushes is not quite as easy a task as it was in the long-ago. During the season there are relatively as many scouts on the trail as you'll find hunters in the Adirondacks during the open season for big game. Scouts are so thick now they are in each other's way. Did you observe that [New York Highlanders scout] Arthur Irwin spent the Spring in friendly visits to the training camps? He was with the Red bunch long enough to get his eyes on most of the material in action. Then he hiked it for other fields. Why the expeditions? Say, just watch Col. Irwin. When the strings are cut on the hopefuls or by any hook or crook some promising youngster is allowed to get away, the chances are that a New York American tag will be quickly affixed. Billy Hamilton, of the Boston Nationals, is another of the scouts who has been looking the Reds over on Southern fields. The idea is not a half-bad one. Many a star-in-embryo has been eclipsed by early managerial action only to break out with more brilliancy in other company" (*Sporting Life*, April 6, 1912).

The new system cannot have entirely caught on, since sportswriter James Crusinberry reported after the 1919 campaign: "When a manager sends a scout out to spy on the training camps of his rivals he's stepping a bit farther than any one ever has before." He explained that Cubs manager Fred Mitchell had assigned newly hired scout Patsy Donovan "to get the 'dope' on dozens and dozens of the live looking youngsters, and then when the rival big league managers ask for waivers, as they always do, the Cubs will know which ones might be worth claiming" ("Cubs to Scout for Talent in Enemies' Own Back Yards," *Chicago Tribune*, December 18, 1919).

13.4.5   Advance Scouts. Tony Kubek reportedly claimed that advance scouting was originated by Casey Stengel in 1957 (quoted in George Will, *Men at Work*, 16). Perhaps what Kubek meant was that Stengel started the practice of having a scout whose specific job was advance scouting, because Bill James correctly responded, ". . . The idea that advance scouting began in 1957 is so misguided as to be comical," and cited many earlier examples of advance scouting (Bill James, *The Bill James Guide to Baseball Managers*, 206).

The practice was most common at the World Series, for the obvious reason that it featured opponents who were unfamiliar with each other's tendencies. Connie Mack sent Athletics pitcher Chief Bender to scout the Cubs before the 1910 World Series (*Sporting Life*, March 25, 1911). Christy Mathewson reported that Mack did likewise the following year, sending "spies" to track "the Giants for weeks previous to the [1911] series" (Christy Mathewson, *Pitching in a Pinch*, 278). In 1913, with the Giants and Athletics again about to meet in the World Series, Mack sent at least three players to watch Rube Marquard pitch a September 26 game (Larry Mansch, *Rube Marquard*, 136).

Bill James cited a number of other examples from the 1920s, '30s, and '40s, the most notable being Mack's sending Howard Ehmke to watch the Cubs in the weeks before Ehmke's surprise start in the 1929 World Series (Bill James, *The Bill James Guide to Baseball Managers*, 206). So it seems clear that the idea of advance scouting has been around for a long time, its use limited

only by the usual consideration of whether the benefits outweighed the expenses.

Today there are signs that the traditional advance scout may be a dying breed. Sportswriter Mike Klis observed in 2003 that the "advance-scouting era" appears to be giving way to the "era of advanced technology," in which a videotape package is put together from televised games of a team's next opponent. Klis suggested that the Indians pioneered this practice in 1994, though it appears that they used videotape only to complement their advance scouting. Since then, such clubs as the Cardinals, Tigers, Rockies, Twins, and Padres have at least experimented with eliminating advance scouts altogether (*Baseball America*, August 4–17, 2003).

13.4.6   Tryout Camps. Tryout camps are associated with Branch Rickey, but they also date back to the nineteenth century. For example, an 1891 article reported that Chicago manager Cap Anson "Frequently . . . will appoint a special day for examining candidates for his team. He is constantly besieged with applications from all parts of the country. He will marshal 30 or 40 of these applicants at the ball grounds and put them through their paces. From his long experience on the ball field he is able to 'size up' a player almost at sight" (*Williamsport Sunday Grit*, August 23, 1891).

Branch Rickey began using tryout camps in St. Louis in 1919, and they enabled him to sign talented players like Ray Blades and Jim Bottomley. As the value of the camps became apparent, Rickey began to hold them in a variety of Midwestern towns. Some believed that he needed these camps to supply players to his ever-expanding farm system, but he maintained that it was the other way around—that all the talent discovered at the camps made it necessary to create additional farm clubs (Lee Lowenfish, *Branch Rickey*, 118, 156, 338).

13.4.7   Baseball Schools. Baseball schools have had a sporadic history. As early as 1883, A. G. Spalding announced plans to open a "Base Ball Academy" where Cap Anson would serve as lead instructor (*Sporting Life*, November 21, 1883). Spalding's goal appears to have been to keep players from signing with the upstart Union Association, and the school did not last long.

Periodic efforts to start baseball schools occurred in succeeding years. Chicago infielder Fred Pfeffer, for example, ran an instructional camp of some sort (Jonathan Fraser Light, *The Cultural Encyclopedia of Baseball*, 373). An 1889 note indicated, "Billy Holbert, of the Metropolitan Club, proposes to start training classes for young base ball players, with the idea of bringing out new material. It is his purpose to organize three classes—one in New York, one in Jersey and one in Connecticut—and to give one or two morning lessons a week at each place. In this way he could continue to play ball and teach as well" (*Sporting Life*, April 17, 1889).

After the 1913 season, former major leaguer Charley Carr brought a new level of planning to the baseball school. Sportswriter Stanley T. Milliken noted: "At last the idea of a regular baseball school has passed from a possibility to a reality. Next Friday Charley Carr will formally open the doors of his baseball university at San Antonio, Tex., for the matriculation of those ambitious youngsters who would enter the big leagues via a route which they hope will entirely eliminate the bush circuit. For several years such a baseball school has been talked over, and many of the leading big club managers have advocated the plan, provided experienced men were put in charge of the project. Carr appears to have entered the field thoroughly equipped, for, according to his prospectus, Owen Bush, Lou Criger, Otto Williams and other well-known baseball players will compose the faculty. The field at Hot Sulphur Wells, San Antonio, will include twenty diamonds, shower, locker rooms, and all other equipment and paraphernalia necessary to teach the novice how to play like Wagner, Collins, and Mathewson" (*Washington Post*, December 29, 1913). The school closed within eight months (*Washington Post*, August 16, 1914).

Bobby Gilks opened a school in Pensacola, Florida, the following year and tried to benefit from the failure of Carr's enterprise. Gilks "made several important changes in the preamble and methods. His school is not to be for every pupil that sees fit to enroll including amateurs. He will make a specialty of recruit pitchers and catchers of major and big minor league teams, taking pay for their development from the clubs that own them rather than the players themselves" (*Lincoln* [Nebr.] *Daily News*, February 13, 1915).

It was not until the late 1920s that enough parents were willing to pay for instruction for their sons to make the idea a permanent part of baseball. Tubby Walton formed a particularly successful school in 1928, and rivals sprang up

during the 1930s (Furman Bisher, *Atlanta Journal*, February 2, 1961).

The best-known baseball school was the academy operated by the Kansas City Royals, which yielded one star in Frank White and another ten-year major leaguer in Ron Washington. Since then, however, clubs have been reluctant to operate such schools, since the amateur draft makes it difficult for them to retain the talent they produce. Clubs do continue to operate academies in Latin American countries, where the amateur draft is not in effect.

13.4.8 Radar Guns. The primary "tool of the trade" for scouts is the radar gun. While accurate handheld radar guns are a recent innovation, the concept of measuring the speed of pitchers is an ancient one.

An 1884 article noted that Longine's chronographs had been used to measure the speed of several major league pitchers. The results were not very meaningful, however, as the reported times that it took for pitches to reach the plate varied from one-fifth of a second to three-fifths of a second (*Sporting Life*, April 23, 1884).

On October 6, 1912, the speeds of Walter Johnson and Nap Rucker were tested at the Remington Arms Plant in Bridgeport, Connecticut. The pitchers' speeds were measured by the time it took for their pitches to reach a steel plate five yards away. Johnson's speed was estimated at 83 miles per hour and Rucker's at 77, but several factors contributed to the low speeds. Most notably, the pitchers had to alter their natural arm motion so that the ball could pass through a two-foot square and be measured (*Syracuse Herald*, October 20, 1912; Eric Enders, "George Napoleon Rucker," Tom Simon, ed., *Deadball Stars of the National League*, 284).

Researcher Dick Thompson discovered an account of an interesting attempt at measurement that occurred in 1939: "The new meter, which gives an immediate reading which engineers said compared with standard laboratory meter accuracy, is built in a trailer. You throw into a hole two feet square. Just inside is a set of photo-electric tubes, and five feet back is another set. The device measures the ball's speed between the two points and flashes it on a scale facing the pitcher" (AP: *Richmond Times-Dispatch*, June 6, 1939).

Several creative but not very precise methods were used to try to measure the speed of Bob Feller's fastball. After that, the practice was pretty much abandoned for a generation.

The handheld radar gun made its way into baseball in an interesting manner. In the fall of 1974, Michigan State University head baseball coach Danny Litwhiler read in the school newspaper that campus police were using radar guns to catch speeders (Steve Orr, "MSU Police Get Radar Gun," *State News*, October 10, 1974). The potential of such a device for baseball scouts struck Litwhiler, and he convinced a campus policeman to try it out while one of his pitchers threw the ball.

While the police cruiser had to be on the field in order to gauge the speed, the experiment was otherwise successful. Litwhiler believed that all teams should have equal access to this new tool, so he wrote an open letter to Commissioner Bowie Kuhn describing his discovery. Radar guns began to be used at spring training the following spring and have since become an essential scouting tool (Dan Gutman, *Banana Bats and Ding-Dong Balls*, 70–72).

During the preparation of this book, Danny Litwhiler returned to the Michigan State campus to have his uniform number retired. I made a copy of the original article and presented it to him. He recognized it immediately and exclaimed, "That's the article!"

13.4.9   Baseball Ages. If the radar gun has become the scout's greatest ally, "baseball age" may be the scout's most persistent nemesis.

Because age is considered an important indicator of a prospect's potential for development and of a player's likely decline, fictitious ages have been adopted by players and are known as "baseball ages." As Jim Bouton noted, "Most baseball people have two ages, real and baseball. The older they get the greater the discrepancy between their numbers" (Jim Bouton, *Ball Four*, 117).

The practice is far from new. In 1880 a reader sent an inquiry to the *Chicago Tribune* and was informed, "We don't know how old [Larry] Corcoran is, nor who is the youngest player in the league. The age of a ball-player, like that of a lady, is a delicate question; and, out of consideration for juveniles of the tender years of [veterans] Joe Start and Bob Ferguson, we hesitate to open up the subject" (*Chicago Tribune*, July 11, 1880).

In recent years some players in Latin American countries, where documentation of birth records can be very difficult to come by, have devised a new version of the baseball age by claiming a greater age than their real one in order to sign a professional contract. The most celebrated case involved Adrian Beltre, whose agent, Scott Boras, attempted to get his player declared a free agent because the Dodgers had been complicit in the deceit.

This is not entirely new either, however, as Dizzy Dean once tried to get out of a contract by claiming he had been under twenty-one when he signed it. When the Cardinals produced his birth certificate to prove that he had indeed been of legal age, the dizzy one blithely issued a press release stating: "I find that I am past 21 years of age." Dean acknowledged to reporters, "I'm 22 all right. I musta been thinkin' of my brother Paul's birthday. He'll be 22 one of these days. Or is it 20? Or 19? I reckon I'll have to ask him" (Robert Gregory, *Diz*, 86, 88).

(v) Miscellaneous

13.5.1   Central Pool of Players. In 1892 the Western League found a novel way to address the tendency of competitive pressure to drive up costs—it signed players to league contracts. League president James Williams of Columbus then selected eight teams of twelve players apiece with the intention of creating parity. In conjunction with these steps, a salary cap was instituted, all salaries were guaranteed, and player sales were banned.

Unfortunately, success of the scheme relied upon attaining competitive balance, and that proved elusive. Worse, Columbus proved to have by far the most talented roster, prompting whispers of favoritism. By July the novel league had degenerated into "a ragged and disorganized mob of otherwise good ball players," and it disbanded (Dennis Pajot, "1892 Western 'Lottery' League," unpublished paper).

A similar method was used by the All-American Girls Baseball League.

13.5.2   Expansion Drafts. The first specific expansion draft occurred on December 14, 1961, when the newly franchised Angels and Senators each selected twenty-eight players from other American League teams. There had, however, been several earlier instances of using similar procedures to redistribute talent to a new or weak entry. When Detroit entered the National League in 1881, the seven existing clubs each protected the five players allowed by the reserve rule (see **18.2.1**), which enabled the Wolverines to sign a strong contingent from the leftovers. In December 1939, under pressure from league president Will Harridge, every American League team agreed to offer one player off their roster for sale to the woeful Browns (William Mead, *Even the Browns*, 65).

13.5.3   Amateur Drafts.

The amateur draft was adopted on December 4, 1964, with the aim of eliminating bidding wars on unproven talent. The first draft took place on June 8 and 9, 1965, at the Hotel Commodore in New York City, and Rick Monday was the first player selected. The draft marked a sea change for player development in general and scouting in particular, since scouts had to convince the general manager to choose their player. Kevin Kerrane's wonderful *Dollar Sign on the Muscle* offers an especially insightful look at the changed nature of scouting.

13.5.4   Free-agent Reentry Draft.

Baseball's first free agent draft took place on November 4, 1976, with twenty-four major leaguers who had played the 1976 season without a contract being eligible for the draft. By drafting a player, the team obtained only the nonexclusive right to negotiate with that player.

13.5.5   Tampering.

The free agency era has put a renewed emphasis on tampering. The concept is far from new, however. Efforts to sign other clubs' players were a constant problem in the 1870s and helped lead to the adoption of the reserve rule. That rule forbade tampering but didn't entirely eliminate it. For example, sportswriter John B. Sheridan wrote in 1920, "Connie Mack's rule to penalize any club magnate or manager convicted of tampering with another club's player went through and was made strong. It provided no magnate, manager, player or agent of a club could get away with even a hint to a player of another team that it would be to such a player's advantage if he could get a transfer" (*Sporting News*, February 19, 1920).

Chapter 14

BALLPARKS

(i) The Parks

14.1.1 Enclosed Baseball Stadiums. The fences at a baseball stadium now denote home runs. Fans enjoy a special thrill when a ball flies over the wall or when an outfielder leaps high to capture a ball that seemed destined to leave the playing field. But such walls were originally constructed with the very different purpose of keeping people out, and thereby making professional baseball possible.

As early as the 1850s the idea of professional baseball was being actively considered. The largest obstacle was the impracticality of collecting admission to an open field. The first professional match was accordingly played at a horse racing track in Long Island on July 20, 1858, and there were other occasional efforts. In 1857 the Massapoags of Sharon visited Boston and "obtained permission from the city to make an enclosure on the Commons" (*New York Clipper*, November 7, 1857). Many years later the *Washington Post* reprinted a September 10, 1858, account from an unnamed Boston paper of a game the day before, which noted, "A space was inclosed so as to allow the game to proceed without hindrance" (*Washington Post*, September 25, 1909). An enclosed cricket stadium was sometimes used for baseball games in Philadelphia.

In 1862 the Union Grounds in Brooklyn became the first enclosed stadium primarily used for baseball. William Cammeyer bought an abandoned lot at the corner of Marcy Avenue and Rutledge Street in Brooklyn's Williamsburgh section in 1861. Having successfully used the facility as an ice skating rink in the winter of 1861–1862, he began to consider ways to use it for summer activities. In February 1862 he announced construction plans that would enable the Union Grounds to offer such activities as gymnasium instruction and riding lessons. Cammeyer also listed baseball as a possible use for the grounds, but it seems to have been little more than an afterthought since he estimated that rent charged to baseball clubs would represent only 2 percent of the total revenues.

By the time the Union Grounds opened in May 1862, however, Cammeyer had gained an appreciation of baseball's promise as a revenue sport. The first baseball match was played there on May 15, 1862, in front of 3,000 spectators who paid no admission fee. Thereafter fees were collected, and this proved so successful that Cammeyer decided on a share of the gate receipts instead of charging rent to the clubs. Baseball soon became the principal attraction of the Union Grounds, causing competitors to scramble to construct rival diamonds (William J. Ryczek, *When Johnny Came Sliding Home*, 29–31).

Enclosed stadiums were thus inextricably tied to the collection of admission fees, a relationship explored further in entry **18.1.2**. The principle of economic exclusiveness that fences brought to baseball was soon reframed as a moral issue. The *Brooklyn Eagle* observed in 1864, "Admission to the grounds is only secured on condition of proper conduct, and this is one great advantage of enclosed ball grounds" (*Brooklyn Eagle*, June 29, 1864). While the writer of these words was not identified, it certainly sounds like Henry Chadwick.

Not everyone was persuaded that it was a moral issue, such as the Milwaukee journalist who in 1879 sarcastically described baseball as "a game played by eighteen persons wearing shirts and drawers. They scatter around the field and try to catch a cannon-ball covered with rawhide. The game is to get people to pay 25 cents to come inside the fence" (*Milwaukee Sun*, reprinted in the *Detroit Post and Tribune*, August 2, 1879).

The baseball fence would prove a particular nemesis to young boys, who would try almost anything to get past or see over them (see **15.1.2**). The 1887 World's Series was a movable feast with games all over the country. A day before one game played at Boston's Union Park, a group of boys burned down the left-field fence so they could watch the World's Series (Jerry Lansche, *Glory Fades Away*, 110).

Yet the exclusiveness inherent in enclosed stadiums came to be recognized as conferring special status on those who paid admission. In 1886 Harry Wright said, "The Chicago grounds come nearer to my idea of a base ball inclosure than any other in this country. Surrounded by a high brick wall, which does not mar and disfigure adjoining property like the unsightly board fences, it gives the game a privacy which cannot be had where mobs and crowds hang around for a peep through the knotholes and cracks" (*Brooklyn Eagle*, February 7, 1886).

The walls originally intended to keep things out eventually came to keep in a special sense of belonging and community. And so F. Scott Fitzgerald aptly described baseball as a game "bounded by walls which kept out novelty or danger, change or adventure" (F. Scott Fitzgerald, "Ring Lardner," *New Republic*, October 11, 1933, 254). The related topic of "Spite Fences" is discussed in the chapter on marketing (see **16.2.3**).

14.1.2 Fireproof Stadiums. Nineteenth-century ballparks were made primarily of wood, and they burned down with disheartening regularity.

In 1887 Philadelphia Phillies owner Al Reach built the first ballpark that was not wholly constructed of wood. The Philadelphia Base Ball Park, also known as the Huntington Street Grounds, had a brick exterior, but its interior was made of wood. In 1894 the interior burned down, so Reach replaced it that offseason with one made of steel. The brick-and-steel facility, which later became known as the Baker Bowl, remained the home of the Phillies until

1938 (John Shiffert, *Base Ball in Philadelphia*, 121–122, 166–167).

In 1894 Cincinnati owner John T. Brush took advantage of new engineering trends in making major renovations to League Park. The park reopened with a new grandstand that was a hybrid of iron and wood. But the new grandstand burned down on May 28, 1900, while the old wooden stands survived. Fire again destroyed the grandstand on May 4, 1901, causing Brush to vow to build a main grandstand of steel and stone. He followed through on this pledge, but the rest of the seating area remained wood (Greg Rhodes and John Snyder, *Redleg Journal*, 110, 137, 139).

In 1905 the Columbus Senators of the American Association tore down the grandstand and replaced it with a double-decked concrete-and-steel grandstand. The bleachers were made from the wood of the old grandstand. The new stadium drew huge crowds and prompted major league owners to consider similar renovations (Marshall D. Wright, *The American Association*, 22).

The first true major league concrete-and-steel ballpark was probably Philadelphia's Shibe Park, which opened in 1909. It was followed by eight more fireproof stadiums in the next fifteen years.

14.1.3 Night Games. A book could be written about the history of night baseball, and indeed one has: David Pietrusza's *Lights On!* In a nutshell, the idea of playing under the lights intrigued many people long before it became practical from either a technological or financial standpoint. But what makes this such a compelling story is that once the numerous technological and financial obstacles had been overcome, there turned out to be a deep-seated underlying objection to night baseball.

The first preliminary effort took place on September 2, 1880, when teams from two Boston department stores played at Nantasket Beach, Massachusetts, under thirty-six carbon-arc electric lights. Three hundred onlookers watched from the balconies of the nearby Sea Foam House, and differing accounts emerged (Preston D. Orem, *Baseball [1845–1881] from the Newspaper Accounts*, 342). The *Boston Post* claimed that "A clear, pure, bright light was produced, very strong and yet very pleasant to the sight" (*Boston Post*, September 3, 1880; quoted in Oscar Eddleton, "Under the Lights," *Baseball Research Journal* 1980, 37–42). The *New York Clipper* was less optimistic: "It cannot be said that baseball is likely to be played extensively at night, for the players had to bat and throw with some caution, and the errors due to an imperfect light were innumerable. Fly-balls descending perpendicularly could be caught easily, but when batted a long distance it was easier and safer to get the ball by chasing it after it struck the ground. To the spectators the game proved of little interest, since in general only the players' movements could be discerned, while the course of the ball eluded their sight" (*New York Clipper*, October 2, 1880).

On May 16, 1883, two semipro teams played in Chambersburg, Pennsylvania, by the light of a portable dynamo resting on a flat car. Few details of that game survive, but a much-better-documented night game was played a couple of weeks later, on June 2, in Fort Wayne, Indiana. (Some sources suggest that a second game was also played.)

The *Fort Wayne Daily News* previewed the game, which featured the Methodist-Episcopal College and a local amateur nine: "Apropos of the proposed games of base ball by electric light, it has been suggested that high flies would penetrate a region of outer darkness which the electric light would not reach, and it would be impossible to judge where the balls would come down. 'Why not coat the ball with luminous paint?' suggests a friend" (*Fort Wayne Daily News*, May 28, 1883).

The *Daily News* gave this account of the game in its June 4 issue: "The grounds were illuminated by 17 Jenny [sic] electric lamps suspended, three from the grand stand and the rest from poles placed about the limits of the enclosure. The light was found sufficient to permit of sharp infield play and precise throwing and catching. It was noticed that as the heavens grew darker the apparent illumination of the grounds correspondingly increased. . . . There were no mishaps of any kind save a rather noticeable irregularity of the illumination on two occasions."

Sporting Life added: "The inclosure, which is four hundred by four hundred and fifty feet, was lighted by seventeen of the lamps of the Jenney Electric Light Company, of Fort Wayne. They were suspended as masts, except three that were attached to the front of the grand stand. One of the lights was behind the pitcher, which seemed to light up the diamond splendidly, while the light at the corner made it light enough to see the ball plainly in the center field. The atmosphere was heavy at times, which caused a very noticeable and favorable effect on throwing the light down on the field. All the lights had a powerful reflector behind them. The only thing to mar the exhibition was the light going out entirely twice, caused by defective brushes at the power-house. It was found necessary to change the ball quite often. When a ball became dirty, it could not be seen. With between twenty-five and thirty lights there is no question but what electric light ball playing is an assured success" (*Sporting Life*, June 10, 1883).

The *Fort Wayne Daily Gazette* claimed the game would "make Fort Wayne historic and cause her name to be mentioned wherever civilization extends" (*Fort Wayne Daily Gazette*, June 3, 1883; reprinted in Don Warfield, *The Roaring Redhead*, 57). Not everyone agreed, with one sportswriter offering this sarcastic evaluation: "it is something that Manager [James] Mutrie of the polo grounds should by all mean go into, as there are thousands of people in New York who would gladly visit the polo grounds to see the Metropolitans and the New Yorks swooping around over the grounds with lanterns in their hands, looking for the ball" (*National Police Gazette*, June 23, 1883). Even so, the boast of the Fort Wayne paper was not entirely unfounded. In 1960 an obituary appeared in *Sporting News* for Sam Wolf, one of the pitchers in the game (*Sporting News*, May 18, 1960).

Experiments with night baseball continued. In 1887 plans were announced to play night ball at St. George Grounds in Staten Island. A Mr. Johnson of the Edison Electric Light Company of New York had concluded that lights placed above the field would not work. After consulting with Thomas Edison himself, however, Johnson planned to "line the *outside* of the diamond, foul lines and extremes of the outfields with electric lights placed *beneath the ground* and projecting, by means of powerful reflectors, the rays upward through covering-plates of corrugated glass" (*Sporting Life*, March 30, 1887).

John T. Brush experimented with installing a lighting system at Indianapolis's Tinker Park in 1888, and initial reports were encouraging. The lights were "located along the centre field fence about thirty yards apart, being between thirty and forty feet high, have a cross-bar at the top like that on a telegraph pole and about the same length. The cross-piece had burners on the upper side, about six inches apart, and when the gas was turned on it makes a solid flame, say about four feet long. The two burners alone make the park perfectly light, and the ball could be seen as well as daytime" (*Sporting Life*, August 29, 1888; quoted in Larry G. Bowman, *Before the World Series*, 145). But a second test on September 6 was less successful, and the idea foundered (*Sporting Life*, September 12, 1888; quoted in Larry G. Bowman, *Before the World Series*, 145).

The problem this time wasn't a lack of light—in fact, there was too much in Brush's estimation. Rather, the issue was that the light didn't quite reach the surface of the playing field, with the result that pitches and fly balls were easily visible but that ground balls could not "be seen with any satisfaction." There was talk of repositioning the lights, but nothing happened (*Indianapolis Sentinel*, September 7, 1888; quoted in Al Kermisch, "Indianapolis Experimented with Baseball by Gaslight," *Baseball Research Journal* 1982, 66–67).

Galveston and Houston played under the lights on July 22, 1892. Los Angeles and Stockton of the California League played two games under electric lights in July 1893. But *Sporting Life* reported in 1895, "The Chattanooga Club contemplates baseball by electric light. The scheme has been tried many times—always a failure" (*Sporting Life*, July 6, 1895).

Another exhibition game under electric lights was played in San Antonio, Texas, on July 16, 1897. On the evening of May 14, 1902, Scranton and Lancaster played under electric light at Scranton's Athletic Park, "in the presence of one of the biggest crowds that ever saw a game in that city. Arc lights set on twenty foot poles at short intervals made it easily possible for the players to handle and the spectators to follow the ball. Scranton won by a score of 8 to 6. There were only five errors on both sides" (*Sporting Life*, May 24, 1902). An experimental game was played at Athletic Park in Battle Creek, Michigan, on September 4, 1904. The field was illuminated by twenty-five arc lights strung around the field (Marc Okkonen, *Minor League Baseball Towns of Michigan*, 8).

The first serious effort to bring night baseball to the major leagues was initiated in 1908. Cincinnati Reds president August "Garry" Herrmann teamed up with inventor George Cahill and a group of Cincinnati businessmen to form the Night Baseball Development Company. On June 18, 1909, their product was demonstrated for the first time when two Elks teams played an experimental game at Cincinnati's home park. Five temporary 100-foot towers of arc lights

powered by a 250-horsepower dynamo were installed for the game.

Reviews were mixed. The number of strikeouts was inordinately high, and the outfielders' adventures with fly balls caused sportswriter Ren Mulford, Jr., to write that "the game was a novelty and at times took on the elements of a diamond comedy." But Reds manager Clark Griffith said he was "surprised at the ease with which the game was played," and Herrmann announced that "Night baseball has come to stay" (all quotes from David Pietrusza, "The Cahill Brothers' Night Baseball Experiments," *Baseball Research Journal* 23 [1994], 62–66).

Cahill's next attempt came in Grand Rapids, Michigan, on July 7. After a regular game, Grand Rapids and Zanesville played an exhibition game under the lights. Cahill received assistance from the Grand Rapids-Muskegon Power Company in powering his lighting system. Still, the results were disappointing, as it was reportedly "impossible to follow a fly ball" (*Chicago Tribune*, July 9, 1909).

The following season Cahill persuaded Charles Comiskey to let him stage a night game at White Sox Park. On August 27, 1910, two local clubs played under 137,000 watts of candlepower. More than 20,000 fans attended the exhibition, and accounts were quite favorable. The *Electrical Review and Western Electrician* reported that "the ball was clearly observed at all times. . . . The Players did not complain of glare from the lamps, some contending that it was not as troublesome as facing the sun" (quoted in David Pietrusza, "The Cahill Brothers' Night Baseball Experiments," *Baseball Research Journal* 23 [1994], 62–66). The *Chicago Tribune* claimed that "The ball could be followed as readily as if thrown under natural light, and the players declared that nothing interfered with their vision." It added that even better results could be expected when the voltage was increased and the lamp operators gained experience (*Chicago Tribune*, August 28, 1910). For reasons that are not entirely clear, however, this was Cahill's last effort to light a baseball game.

Toward the end of the 1915 season, Robert B. Ward, one of the owners of the Brooklyn Federal League team, announced plans to install light towers and play a night game (*Sporting Life*, September 11, 1915). Delays brought the regular season to a close before the game could be played, but the lighting system was tested and deemed a success. Then the sudden death of the sixty-three-year-old Ward from heart failure derailed the idea. According to *Sporting Life*, "just before Robert B. Ward died he spent something like $18,000 to install a newly-patented lighting system that he believed would make night base ball practical" (*Sporting Life*, December 25, 1915). Ward's passing meant the end of his pet scheme and contributed to the demise of the Federal League.

As Stuart Shea points out, the first major league night game took place on July 1, 1918, when the Boston Braves hosted Brooklyn in a 6 p.m. start. Since Braves Field did not have lights, every effort was made to expedite play, and the game lasted only seventy-two minutes. Only fifteen hundred showed up for the contest, even though soldiers and sailors were admitted free. The *Boston Globe* succinctly forecasted, "Twilight games are not likely to become a fixture" (Stuart Shea, *Wrigley Field*, 86–87; *Boston Globe*, July 2, 1918, 5).

Of course evening games had no chance to become regular occurrences until a major league stadium had lights. With no major league owner ready to carry on Ward's legacy, no progress was made toward night baseball in the 1920s. One reason for this was the legitimate concern that the frequency with which fly balls were lofted above the lights would make evening baseball forever impracticable. But in a decade that saw streetlamps proliferate, the readiness with which night baseball was abandoned is striking.

George Cahill moved on to sports like boxing and football, and the latter sport's progress was in stark contrast to that of baseball. Football had been a relative latecomer to night action, with the first such professional game having been played in Elmira, New York, in 1902: "The *Elmira Daily Advertiser* did not explain how the field was illuminated, beyond saying that electric lights were used. Tradition has it, though, that huge searchlights were placed at opposite ends of the field, so that the players must have spent most of their time squinting into the glare" (Robert W. Peterson, *Pigskin*, 35).

But by the late 1920s, professional, college, and even high school football stadiums were beginning to install permanent lighting structures. Wellington High in Wellington, Kansas, played under twenty two-thousand-watt lights on September 20, 1929, using a white football (Duane Frazier, "Wellington Celebrates the Evening It Lit Up High School Football," *Wichita Eagle*, September 10, 2004). On November 6, 1929, in Providence, the first National Foot-

ball League night game was played, with the ball again painted white for visibility.

The decade thus ended with professional baseball lagging behind even high school football, but the impetus for renewed efforts at night baseball was provided by the stock market crash of 1929. Shocked owners of Negro Leagues and minor league clubs realized that this would devastate their core market, and a few of these owners had the foresight to immediately reach out to a new clientele of workingmen by offering evening games. Negro Leagues teams were swift to capitalize on the new opportunity in part because they already had a tradition of working into the evening. As Donn Rogosin explained, many Negro Leagues teams of the 1920s played "twilight games," which began when day-shift workers got off for the day and ended when the sun set (Donn Rogosin, *Invisible Men*, 23).

J. L. Wilkinson, owner of the Negro National League's Kansas City Monarchs, took out a $50,000 loan that winter and purchased a portable 100-kilowatt generator with a 250-horsepower, six-cylinder engine. Mounted on the beds of Ford trucks, the lighting system generated nearly 200,000 watts, and the Monarchs hit the road. The portable lighting system was unveiled in Enid, Oklahoma, on April 28, 1930, and was an immediate success. Chet Brewer, who played in the first game, marveled, "people would come from miles around to see that baseball could be played at night! In Enid, Oklahoma, you never saw so many people" (Donn Rogosin, *Invisible Men*, 128). The excitement continued as the team moved to other towns, causing the *Kansas City Star* to rave that night baseball "will revolutionize the old game, restoring small town baseball on a paying basis" (reprinted in Larry Lester, "Only the Stars Come Out at Night!," *Unions to Royals*, 8–10).

That same offseason, minor league teams in Des Moines, Iowa, and Independence, Kansas, announced plans to install lighting systems. Independence played the historic first regular-season night game against Muskogee on April 30, 1930, and Des Moines followed suit two days later. There were a few glitches, and fans had some trouble picking up the ball, but the players reported that the adjustments were relatively minor (Bob Rives, "Good Night," *National Pastime* 18 [1998], 21–24).

More important, night baseball drew enough fans for these owners to recoup their investments quickly. The success of the two minor league pioneers attracted considerable attention, but even more important was the example of the touring Monarchs, who brought night baseball to the doorsteps of skeptics. While the noisy engine of the Monarchs' generator drew some complaints, the game they were playing was recognizable as baseball. Other minor league owners raced to jump on the bandwagon, and by the end of the year no fewer than thirty-eight minor league teams had lighting systems in place (Larry G. Bowman, "The Monarchs and Night Baseball," *National Pastime* 16 [1996], 80–84).

As so often happens, once the momentum shifted it was those who resisted change who came under pressure. Four of the six teams in the Piedmont League added lights in 1930, and soon the other two were struggling to stay competitive. But rather than expressing sympathy, the four clubs with lights told the holdouts to install lights or leave the league. Nonetheless major league owners remained steadfast—Sam Breadon of the Cardinals was the only one who favored night ball, and he was powerless to act because his team was playing in a stadium owned by Browns' owner Phil Ball (William B. Mead, *Two Spectacular Seasons*, 31).

The success of night baseball in the teeth of the Great Depression was striking and made the major leagues' resistance to the idea all the more conspicuous. And, as G. Edward White pointed out, their reasons sounded increasingly hollow. Giants owner Charles Stoneham, for example, continued to maintain in 1934 that batters would become tentative from playing at night (G. Edward White, *Creating the National Pastime*, Chapter 5 passim, especially 173).

White noted that once the specific concerns about night baseball had been allayed, those with reservations began to describe it as "unnatural." He suggested that such concerns could have hidden an underlying fear—that night baseball would bring more members of the working classes to the ballpark. Washington owner Clark Griffith went so far as to characterize night baseball as "just a step above dog racing" (quoted in Don Warfield, *The Roaring Redhead*, 59). The message seemed to be that night play might be very well for football, but baseball wanted to attract a more affluent class of fans.

On December 11, 1934, Cincinnati president Larry MacPhail brought the issue to the National League's winter meeting. According to MacPhail, Commissioner Kenesaw Moun-

tain Landis told him before the meeting: "Not in my lifetime or yours will you ever see a baseball game played at night in the majors." But MacPhail's three-hour presentation was so convincing that he got the necessary votes to allow any team to schedule a maximum of seven night games per season (Don Warfield, *The Roaring Redhead*, 57–58).

MacPhail's Reds were the only club to take advantage of the opportunity in 1935. General Electric installed 632 lights in Crosley Field, and the first night game took place against the Philadelphia Phillies on May 24, 1935. More than 29,000 fans turned out, including George Cahill, the inventor who had tried to interest major league owners in night baseball a quarter-century earlier. Franklin Delano Roosevelt threw the switch from the White House to turn on the lights for the historic game.

Two long fly balls were dropped (and scored as base hits), but otherwise things ran smoothly. But the success of the venture did little to dispel the widespread reluctance of the owners. The American League denied requests by Cleveland owner Alva Bradley to stage evening games, then banned night baseball entirely. No other major league team duplicated the experiment until MacPhail was hired by the Brooklyn Dodgers in 1938.

Eventually the continuing financial struggles of major league clubs forced them to reconsider. In 1939 the American League reversed its position and three clubs added lights, with the circuit's first night game taking place at Shibe Park in Philadelphia on May 16, 1939. More than 55,000 fans thronged to a June 27 game in Cleveland. By 1941 twelve of the sixteen major league franchises had staged at least one night game. But even when these experiments proved a financial success, evening baseball continued to be looked upon as a novelty that would lose its appeal if overused.

The turning point was President Franklin Roosevelt's famous "green light" letter of January 15, 1942. Major league owners had asked the president's advice as to whether baseball should continue in spite of the war. Roosevelt advised them to go ahead because the game was good for the country's morale and added, "incidentally, I hope that night games can be extended because it gives an opportunity to the day shift to see a game occasionally" (*Washington Post*, January 17, 1942; quoted in Dean A. Sullivan, ed., *Middle Innings*, 182). As a result, the allotment of seven night games per team was doubled to fourteen, and the attendance at these games was so large that unlimited night baseball was approved in July 1944.

By 1948 every major league club except the Chicago Cubs had lights, and night baseball was well on its way. The first night World Series game took place in Pittsburgh on October 13, 1971, between the Pirates and Orioles, and it would soon become common for World Series games to be played under the lights. Even the Cubs finally began playing a limited schedule of evening encounters in 1988.

In many ways the history of night baseball parallels the emergence of competitiveness (see **1.29**) eighty years earlier. Opposition to the idea was much stronger than the reasons being given for that resistance, suggesting underlying concerns about class issues. Resistance was swept away by the coming of a major war, with the reminders that a war always brings of the fundamental ties that bind mankind.

14.1.4   Twinight Games. As described in the preceding entry, the first major league night game was a Boston-Brooklyn contest on July 1, 1918, which started at 6 p.m. and was completed in a mere seventy-two minutes. Such start times were also a prominent part of Negro Leagues baseball, but obviously they could not become regular occurrences in the white major leagues until their stadiums had lights.

The U.S. government mandated dimouts during World War II due to fears that the Germans could use city lights to sink boats near New York City and other coastal cities. One consequence was that the Giants and Dodgers were allowed only one hour of artificial light per evening. They switched their game times to what were initially called "twights," but soon became known as "twilight" or "twinight" games.

14.1.5   Domes. No doubt the game's earliest players and spectators wished they could have a roof over their heads on rainy days. But they also must have believed that such a thing was impossible. Indeed a forward-thinking inquirer was informed in 1868 that "Such a thing as a covered ball ground is out of the question" (*New York Clipper*, May 30, 1868; reprinted in William J. Ryczek, *When Johnny Came Sliding Home*, 272).

There were at least a couple of nineteenth-century facilities large enough for contemplating indoor baseball. An 1884 article reported,

"The managers of the Institute Building, Boston, are quite enthusiastic over the prospect of indoor base ball games. The inclosure is about 100 yards long by 30 wide, amply enough for an indoor foot ball field. The ball will be manufactured especially for this occasion, and will be smaller than the regulation size, and the base lines will be shortened" (*Sporting Life*, December 3, 1884). And, as noted in the entry on "Batting Cages" (**14.4.10**), college clubs of the 1890s were practicing in increasingly large and sophisticated edifices.

But the obstacles to truly playing baseball indoors continued to appear insuperable. Even if the enormous engineering and architectural issues could be resolved, there was the equally daunting challenge of creating a suitable field surface indoors. As early as 1911, legendary groundskeeper John Murphy built indoor diamonds of real grass and sod for a couple of college nines so that they would be able to practice during the winter. There was talk that major league clubs would follow suit, but John McGraw scoffed at the idea: "It may be all right for the colleges, but it will never do for a ball club that has to go through an entire season of 154 games" (*Coshocton* [Ohio] *Morning Tribune*, November 19, 1911).

In 1939 the New York Cubans of the Negro National League played on a field flanked by East Fifty-ninth, East Sixtieth, First Avenue, and the East River, and quite a bit of the playing area was covered by Manhattan's Queensboro Bridge. Phil Lowry claimed that this was the first covered ballpark, and Donald Dewey and Nicholas Acocella erroneously termed this the first indoor stadium (Phil Lowry, *Green Cathedrals*, 203; Donald Dewey and Nicholas Acocella, *The Ball Clubs*, 259). But this is not really indoor baseball.

By the 1950s architecture had progressed far enough to make indoor baseball seem conceivable. In 1952 Norman Bel Geddes, who designed the Dodgers' spring training complex, responded to a request from Walter O'Malley and submitted a design for a domed stadium in Brooklyn with artificial turf. Bel Geddes' futuristic plans included "a retractable roof; foam rubber seats, heated in cold weather; a 7,000-car garage from which fans proceed directly into the ball park; automatic hot dog vending machines everywhere, including mustard; a new lighting system minus the present steel towers, and a synthetic substance to replace grass on the entire field and which can be painted any color" (*New York Times*, March 6, 1952).

When O'Malley moved the Dodgers to Los Angeles, he again discussed the possibility of a retractable domed stadium (*Los Angeles Times*, May 30, 1957). Back in New York, the city jilted by the Dodgers and Giants announced plans on November 17, 1959, for a New York team in the Continental League that would play in a retractable dome at Flushing Meadows. William A. Shea, the chairman of Mayor Robert Wagner's Special Committee on Baseball, concluded that a transparent retractable roof could be built for $1.75 million and recommended its construction (Edmond J. Bartnett, "Shea Wants Roof on Baseball Park," *New York Times*, November 18, 1959).

Instead it was Houston voters who approved a domed stadium on January 31, 1961, assuring that the city would receive an expansion team. Another vote on December 22, 1962, completed the stadium's financing. With President Lyndon B. Johnson in attendance, the stadium opened on April 9, 1965, for an exhibition game against the New York Yankees. While the game was played at night and went relatively smoothly, it was already apparent that the dome's skylights would make it impossible to see fly balls during daylight hours. As columnist Red Smith quipped: "They have licked every problem except good weather" (Red Smith, April 12, 1965, reprinted in *Red Smith on Baseball*).

The Houston Colt 45s experimented with yellow, red, orange, and cerise balls but eventually realized that a new roof covering was needed. On April 19 the ceiling was painted to eliminate glare from the sun. This in turn caused the grass to die, leading to another first—artificial turf (see **14.2.6**).

The first fully retractable roof was Toronto's SkyDome, which opened on June 5, 1989. The word "fully" is used in deference to Olympic Stadium in Montreal. After years of technical problems, it had finally become possible to open or close most of the Olympic Stadium roof in 1988, but it took too long to make the switch during a game.

(ii) The Dirt

14.2.1   Level Playing Fields. When Houston's current ballpark was built in 2000, a conscious effort was made to reproduce some of the eccentricities of old-time stadiums. One such feature was a slope leading up to the outfield wall, which was inspired by a similar one at Crosley Field in Cincinnati. This nod to the

past became known as Tal's Hill in honor of club executive Tal Smith, who was responsible for many of the ideas. Smith remarked, "The one feature I'm surprised I got included was the hill in center. I always figured someone would come along and take it out of the plans" (Leigh Montville, "Field of Screams," *Sports Illustrated*, May 22, 2000).

We now take level playing fields so much for granted that it is difficult to appreciate that the diamonds Tal Smith was recalling had already been stripped of most of their eccentricities. If Smith had tried instead to recreate one of the earliest baseball diamonds, he would have added many more hills and valleys to the blueprints and thrown in a few stray trees for good measure.

The etymology of the terms infield and outfield is suggestive and remains pertinent. Both were common Scottish farming terms: "infield" referred to the land near the farmhouse that was kept fertilized and tilled; "outfield" was arable land farther from the farmhouse that was cropped but not tilled or fertilized. The usage of these terms came to baseball by way of cricket, and their origins were reflected in the practice of early baseball clubs, which put considerable time into grading and sodding the infield, and much less into caring for the outfield.

As a result, while the phrase "level playing field" is a metaphor today, it had a very literal meaning in early baseball. In 1863 a Philadelphia newspaper described a game played at Princeton: "No one but a topographical engineer could describe that ground. To get to first base you ran up a hill, ran down to second base, up to third base and home base. The right field played at the top of a hill, the center field at the bottom and the left field in a gully. To the Nassau players, who had been accustomed to and had overcome the difficulties of fielding on such a ground, the irregularities were of no account, but the effect was terrible on the Philadelphians, while the weakening feeling of playing on empty stomachs also told heavily against them. The Athletics, however, always play a good uphill game, and this was decidedly up hill and down hill too" (James M. DiClerico and Barry J. Pavelec, *The Jersey Game*, 175). Journalist Clarence Deming claimed that one local sportswriter sarcastically attributed a defeat to the fact that "the visiting club labored under the difficulty of playing on a level field" (Clarence Deming, "Old Days in Baseball," *Outing*, June 1902, 360).

The newspapers of opposing towns were not hesitant about pointing out such deficiencies. In 1875 an Ionia, Michigan, newspaper wrote sarcastically about the home field of the Medley Club of Portland: "With the exception of a few trifling defects, such as a circus ring in the center of the diamond, carelessly left there by Van Amburgh a few days ago; a series of hills and valleys, in the midst of which the ground is laid out, and a score or two of stumps and stone heaps in the out field, separated here and there by rail and board fences, the Medley's ground is probably one of the finest to be found in the whole State" (*Ionia Sentinel*, June 25, 1875). A ballpark in Lincoln, Nebraska, was "so undulating that a man who is tall can, if he is at the home plate, just see the outfielders' caps, and the outfield is notified of a hit over the infielders' heads by the blowing of a horn on the players' bench" (*Sporting News*, June 14, 1886).

As described in "Outfield Placement" (see 4.2.8), one of the consequences of such playing conditions was that outfielders were assigned to left, right, or center field based on how good they were at running up and down hills.

14.2.2   Ground Rules. The phrase "ground rule" is now heard most frequently when a batted ball bounces over the fence, a play that many announcers incorrectly refer to as a "ground rule double." It is in fact no such thing—ground rules are rules that are specific to a stadium's idiosyncrasies, whereas this play is a double because of a universal major league rule. The mistake is, however, a perfect illustration of how the concept of the ground rule has gone from being a major part of baseball to an obscurity understood by few.

The Knickerbockers' original rules specified: "But one base allowed when a ball bounds out of the field when struck." When this rule started to be modified to suit the contours of the field, ground rules entered baseball. Section 32 of the 1857 rules stated: "Clubs may adopt such rules respecting balls knocked beyond or outside the bounds of the field as the circumstances of the ground may demand, and these rules shall govern all matches played upon the grounds, provided that they are distinctly made known to every player and umpire and the referee previous to the commencement of the game."

The haphazard condition of many early playing fields led to some curious ground rules. An 1870 account of a game in Calumet, in Michigan's Upper Peninsula, noted: "Before

the game a rule was made that balls batted into a certain potato patch in the right field should only count as one base" (*Portage Lake* [Houghton, Mich.] *Mining Gazette*, August 25, 1870). For an 1871 game in Tecumseh, Michigan, "balls batted into an adjacent corn field" were designated as singles (*Adrian Times and Expositor*, July 6, 1871). In 1867 Henry Chadwick offered suggestions on how to deal with balls that struck obstacles like trees, houses, and fences, stressing that all such "special rules" needed to be "mutually agreed to" before the game began (Henry Chadwick, *Haney's Base Ball Player's Book of Reference for 1867*, 16).

As is explained in the entry on "Blocked Balls" (see 12.6), balls that went among the spectators were generally kept in play in early baseball, but by the twentieth century these too were increasingly being covered by ground rules. Ground rules continued to be a major part of baseball in the early twentieth century when overflow crowds were often allowed to stand in roped-off areas of the outfield, necessitating custom-made rules for balls hit into those sections. Today, however, ground rules rarely affect play, and when they do it is on a strange event like a towering fly ball that strikes a speaker attached to the roof of a domed stadium. Accordingly, it is not surprising that so few announcers understand the distinction.

14.2.3   Tailoring a Park to a Team or Player. The often odd configurations of early ballparks occasionally made it possible for a home team to gain a substantial advantage by manipulating the ground rules. The most notable example was the very short right-field fence at Chicago's Lake Front Park. For years balls hit over it counted as doubles, but in 1884 they became home runs. The gerrymandering enabled four White Stockings players to hit more than twenty home runs. But early groundskeepers had their hands full just making a field playable, without worrying about trying to help the home team. Only in the 1890s did the groundskeeper's art and the tools of the trade progress to the point that clubs began thinking of ways to give themselves a home-field advantage.

The battling Baltimore Orioles of the mid-1890s were most associated with this tactic. Groundskeeper Thomas J. Murphy worked closely with the players on what park factors to include. Hugh Fullerton described the results: "The most unfair grounds ever constructed were those of Baltimore. . . . The team that won three championships there was composed of small, fast men, bunters and clever base runners. The ground was sloping toward right field, where [Willie] Keeler played, and right field always was ragged and full of weeds, rough spots, hollows, and hills. Besides, the base lines were filled in with a cementlike substance, which was wetted down and tamped hard. The edges of the base lines were banked up like billiard cushions to keep bunts from rolling foul. The pitcher's box was a foot higher than the plate. The runways were down hill to first base, down hill to second, up a steep grade to third, and down hill to home. In right field Keeler had a lot of runways, like rabbit paths, that no one except himself knew, and he knew the angles of a throw when the ball rolled down the hill, out into foul ground, and into the deep gulley [sic] against the stand. . . . The grounds, adapted perfectly to the home team's style of play, did more to win pennants than anything else" (*Chicago Tribune*, August 5, 1906).

Although Baltimore led the way, other clubs tried hard to keep pace. At Cleveland's League Park, according to sportswriter Harry Weldon, "The base path from third base to the home plate is 'banked up' like the turn of a race track. It is at least six inches higher on the outer edge than it is on the inner. Any slow ball hit down the third-base line on the Cleveland diamond will stay on fair ground; to go foul it will have to 'run up hill.' The slow taps dumped by players rarely have 'the legs' to climb an incline. Base runners coming from third to home on the Cleveland ground have to lean over like a trotting horse making a turn on a race track" (*Cincinnati Post*, quoted in *Chicago Post*, May 7, 1897).

In 1895 Charles Comiskey had seven left-handed hitters in his St. Paul lineup and "adjusted his diamond so that the right foul line crosses the fence just a little beyond first base, nearly twenty-five feet nearer even than the close fence at the grounds back of the West. In order to make this arrangement some strange work had to be done in the rest of the field, the third base being almost within a traveling distance of the front of the bleacher, and the left foul line running almost parallel with the long fence. One-half of the grand stand, too, has to face the sun in order to accommodate Charley's eccentric batsmen" (*Sporting Life*, May 4, 1895).

Similar ploys have been attempted by many twentieth-century clubs. Perhaps the most notable example came when the Pirates acquired Hank Greenberg in 1947 and immediately reduced the distance to the left-field fence by thirty feet. The new area beyond the fence became known as Greenberg Gardens. Sportswriter Larry Marthey cited a number of earlier examples involving such sluggers as Al Simmons and Ted Williams (Larry Marthey, "Park Tampering Is Old Custom," *Detroit News*, April 7, 1959, T-15).

Frank Lane took the practice to another level in 1949 by moving the fences at Comiskey Park in or out when specific opponents were in town. A rule had to be passed to prevent such shenanigans (Michael Gershman, *Diamonds*, 94–95). Kansas City Athletics owner Charles O. Finley had a similar battle with Commissioner Ford Frick in the mid-1960s over his "Pennant Porch."

The computer age brought a new twist in the 1980s. White Sox employee Dan Evans operated a computerized tracking system in 1982 and noticed that his club had hit far more balls to the Comiskey Park warning track than had their opponents. In response the club shortened the distances to the fences in 1983 and saw positive results (Alan Schwarz, *The Numbers Game*, 143). Even in this instance, however, it was only the tool that was new. In 1937 Brooklyn manager Burleigh Grimes announced his intention to "count the number of drives his boys bounce off the [right field screen in Ebbets Field] in comparison to the enemies' totals," then decide how many bases such hits be allowed by the ground rule (Richard McCann, NEA wire service: *Frederick* [Md.] *Post*, May 13, 1937).

Perhaps the most unique home-field advantage in baseball history was one inadvertently gained by the American League's Philadelphia Athletics in 1902. John I. Rogers, owner of the Philadelphia Phillies, had Pennsylvania Supreme Court injunctions against a number of top American League players for breaking their contracts with him. As a result, when their teams visited Philadelphia, such stars as Nap Lajoie, Ed Delahanty, and Elmer Flick did not accompany them. This helped the Athletics compile a 56-17 home record and win the American League pennant.

Chapter 11, part two, has several examples of dubious ways in which a groundskeeper gave his team an advantage against a specific rival.

14.2.4 Dragging the Infield. According to baseball historian William B. Mead, Cincinnati Reds manager Luke Sewell introduced the practice of having the grounds crew drag the infield in mid-game. This took place during Sewell's tenure as manager of the Reds, from 1949 to 1952. Mead stated that this was done both to keep the infield surface smooth and to increase concession sales (William B. Mead, *Even the Browns*, 68).

But Pacific Coast League player Chuck Stevens told Andy McCue in 1997 that the Hollywood Stars started the practice at about the same time. From 1949 to 1951 the Stars had a quick-working pitcher named Jack Salveson. According to Stevens, concessionaire Danny Goodman came up with the idea of dragging the infield so that he would have more time to sell refreshments when Salveson was pitching (May 17, 1997 interview, cited in Andy McCue, "The King of Coolie Hats," *National Pastime* 19 [1999], 24–27).

Whichever one came first, the custom soon caught on. Jonathan Fraser Light noted that an April 24, 1968, game between the Astros and Mets ended in the twenty-fourth inning on a bad-hop grounder. As a result of this play, Mets general manager Johnny Murphy successfully pushed for a rule that the infield be dragged every five innings during an extra-inning game (Jonathan Fraser Light, *The Cultural Encyclopedia of Baseball*, 308).

14.2.5 Tarpaulins. Abner Powell is often credited with inventing the tarpaulin, based upon his 1943 claim to have done so while running the New Orleans club (Val J. Flanagan, "Rain-Check Evolved to Check Flood of Fence-Climbers, Says Originator, Now 83," *Sporting News*, April 8, 1943). While Powell did not specify a year, he did not become involved with the New Orleans club until 1887, and the tarpaulin was in use several years earlier.

Henry Chadwick commended St. Louis "ground-keeper" August Solari for having "introduced an improvement which might be copied to advantage. It is the placing of tarpaulins over the four base positions to protect them from wet weather" (reprinted in the *St. Louis Post-Dispatch*, March 15, 1884). The fact that Solari had been the owner of one of the first important St. Louis baseball fields may have contributed to his farsighted approach.

Within two weeks the pitcher's box was also being covered with a tarpaulin (*Sporting Life*, March 26, 1884). By May the tarpaulin was being hailed as a great success and an additional one had been added to cover the base paths (*St. Louis Post-Dispatch*, May 5, 1884; *Cincinnati Enquirer*, May 12, 1884, discovered by David Ball and cited in Frederick Ivor-Campbell,

"When Was the First? [Part 4]," *Nineteenth Century Notes* 95:3, 4, Summer/Fall 1995, 12).

An 1893 note made clear that by then it had also become routine for the area around home plate to be covered: "After every game the pitcher's and batter's boxes [in Pittsburgh] are covered over with large tarpaulins, in case it should rain before the next game, and to keep the ground from dew" (*Sporting News*, December 9, 1893). One club tried to expand the protected areas; an 1887 note reported that the Philadelphia Athletics "will try the plan of spreading tarpaulin over the entire diamond during threatening weather and light rain. It is thought this will obviate the necessity of postponing a good many games because of short, heavy showers" (*Milwaukee Sentinel*, February 28, 1887, 8). But it was not until the twentieth century that clubs began to cover their entire infields with a single tarpaulin.

In 1906 it was reported that "Protection for the diamond during rain varies at different parks. Some clubowners protect only the pitcher's slab or the home plate, others cover the bases as well, and one clubowner, [George] Tebeau of Louisville, is said to have a circus tent with which he covers the whole infield when it rains" (*Chicago Tribune*, September 30, 1906).

Others wondered if there wasn't a more efficient way to cover the infield. Washington inventor Lee Lamat announced plans in 1907 to "build a truck on very wide wheels, which will be placed in the center of the diamond. The canvas is rolled up on it and will be run out in all directions covering the entire infield by means of small trucks, which carry the canvas to the extremes of the infield. In this way the infield can be covered and protected from the rain in less than ten minutes, and it can be cleared and ready for play in about the same time" (*Washington Post*, June 15, 1907).

Sporting Life reported at the start of the 1908 season: "Pittsburg, always in the lead, will spring a novelty at the base ball grounds this season. The Pittsburg Base Ball Club proposes to solve the 'wet grounds' problem. A contract was signed yesterday by [owner Barney] Dreyfuss with the Pittsburg Waterproof Company for a tarpaulin to cover the entire playing field at the ball park. The tarpaulin will contain 1,800 yards of brown paraffined duck and will cost $2,000. It will be 120 × 120 feet square. The center of the tarpaulin will be attached to a truck 10 × 15 feet. The truck will be three feet high and the wheels will have a tire six inches wide. The tarpaulin and transportation truck were designed by the Pittsburg Waterproof Company, which will make application for a patent. Before and after a game, particularly in threatening weather, the truck will be run out and the playing ground covered with the tarpaulin. Should there be a shower within half an hour of the time for beginning the game, or should there be a heavy rain at night, the tarpaulin will protect the playing field, and there should be no more deferred games on account of wet grounds, unless the rain should fall during the progress of a game. It is calculated that the cover can be spread in 15 or 20 minutes and removed within the same length of time. When not in use it will be folded on top of the truck and the latter trundled to a remote part of the field" (*Sporting Life*, May 2, 1908). The "canvas tent" was unveiled for the first time on May 6 (*Chicago Tribune*, May 7, 1908).

Other clubs were quick to adopt Barney Dreyfuss's idea. Within two weeks of the Pirates' announcement, Chicago owner Charles Webb Murphy followed suit (*Sporting Life*, May 16, 1908). In 1910 revered Giants groundskeeper John Murphy ordered one for the Polo Grounds and traveled to Pittsburgh for "lessons on the way they spread their canvas" (*Sporting Life*, June 4, 1910, 9). By 1912 most other clubs had adopted the technique, as sportswriter Joe S. Jackson explained: "These covers cost about $3,000 exclusive of apparatus for handling the same. But one of the covers will pay for itself out in a season, and may do so on a single holiday. In baseball you never have a chance to make up the losses sustained by postponement of an opening day or a national holiday contest" (*Washington Post*, January 7, 1912). In 1915 the National League required clubs to have the covers (Jonathan Fraser Light, *The Cultural Encyclopedia of Baseball*, 720).

14.2.6 Artificial Turf. When Walter O'Malley asked architect Norman Bel Geddes in 1952 to submit plans for a domed stadium to replace Ebbets Field, the resulting blueprints included "a synthetic substance to replace grass on the entire field and which can be painted any color" (*New York Times*, March 6, 1952). The idea seemed inconceivable to many, but little more than a decade later it became reality.

In the early 1960s a company called Chemstrand created a product called "ChemGrass." When the grass in the Houston Astrodome began to die after the ceiling had been painted, team owner Judge Roy Hofheinz had Chem-Grass installed in the Astrodome, first in the infield and then in the outfield. The company reportedly installed its product for free in exchange for the right to use the name Astro-Turf.

The first major league game played with AstroTurf covering both the infield and the outfield occurred on July 19, 1966. An AP report indicated that the novel surface "caused no flagrant bad hops or handicaps for outfielders. In fact, the players went about their actions just as if it was on grass" (AP: *Los Angeles Times*, July 20, 1966).

The only serious objection was raised by the irascible Cubs manager Leo Durocher, who protested that turf was not "a true surface for baseball" and threatened to have his outfielders wear sneakers during the team's next visit to Houston. The Astros responded by sending Durocher one of the last divots of natural grass and suggesting that the balding manager use it "to cover his dome" (UPI: *Washington Post*, July 22, 1966).

It is less clear why non-dome clubs began to install artificial turf, a trend started by the White Sox in 1969 and followed the next year at Busch and Riverfront stadiums. Al Lopez believed that, "management likes it because it reduces the number of rainouts" (quoted in Walter M. Langford, *Legends of Baseball*, 223). Reduced maintenance costs undoubtedly played a role as well.

(iii) The Basics

14.3.1 Bases. Robin Carver wrote in 1834 that the game of "Base, or goal ball" used "four stones or stakes" as bases (Robin Carver, *The Boy's and Girl's Book of Sports*, 37). William Wheaton, one of the original members of the Knickerbockers, later recalled that the club's predecessor began in 1837 and used "no regular bases, but only such permanent agents as a bedded boulder or old stump" (*San Francisco Examiner*, November 27, 1887).

Frank G. Menke contended that a change over the next few years had important consequences. He indicated that between 1835 and 1840, "Because so many players were injured by collision with them, the four-foot high stakes were discarded and flat stones were substituted at the stations. [The] expression 'run to your stake' was abandoned for 'run to your base.' Stones soon were found impracticable for bases because many boys stumbled over them, and this brought sacks filled with sand into existence. These were referred to as 'bases,' and the game came to be known, for the first time, as 'baseball'" (Frank G. Menke, *The Encyclopedia of Sports*, 26). This version appears to be over-simplified, and yet there is probably at least a grain of truth in it. It also receives some support from an old-time Boston ballplayer's recollections of an 1855 game: "The word base was not used at that time, the infield being shown by bounds, or byes: it was probably introduced to designate the game from other games of ball and on account of the bounds being changed to a firmer base" (*Boston Journal*, February 22, 1905). In addition, the 1858 Dedham rules for the Massachusetts Game specified the use of "wooden stakes, projecting four feet from the ground." In any event, it remained common in very early baseball to use posts or whatever was handy for bases.

The 1857 rules were the first to be more specific, requiring that the bases be "canvas bags, painted white, and filled with sand or saw-dust." Complying with these guidelines proved problematic. Two injuries in an 1858 game between the Niagaras of Buffalo and the Flour Citys of Rochester led to the use of sand in bases being condemned as "a dangerous practice" (Priscilla Astifan, "Baseball in the Nineteenth Century," *Rochester History* LII, No. 3 [Summer 1990], 9).

Another practical consideration doomed the use of sand. Henry Chadwick observed in 1860 that sand made it difficult to carry the bases to the field, with the result that bases filled with hair were being given a try (*Beadle's Dime Base-Ball Player*, 18). The demise of one of St. Louis's earliest baseball clubs, the Excelsiors, was in part attributed to the tiring ordeal of "carrying the old style sand bag bases back and forth the long distance to the grounds" (E. H. Tobias, *Sporting News*, November 16, 1895).

As a result, requirements became less rigid. An 1864 book suggested that the bases be "made of canvas, or some heavy stuff, and filled with cotton or hair" (*American Boy's Book of Sports and Games*, 84). The 1866 rules required only that the bases be "filled with some soft material." Clubs continued to improvise and, in an 1871 game in Kalamazoo the bases were denoted by "stakes driven in the ground or bits of board" (*Kalamazoo Daily Telegraph*, June 3, 1871).

14.3.2 Home Plate. A child who finds it confusing that a five-sided rubber object is referred to as a plate has a good point. Home plate was originally a round iron plate, with the name apparently referring to the metal rather than the shape. Both the shape and substance of home plate changed frequently in the nineteenth century.

There was no strike zone (see **1.11**) in early baseball; the pitcher was required only to pitch "to the striker." Home plate was not mentioned as a target until 1857, when the rules specified a circular iron plate for home base (William J. Ryczek, *Baseball's First Inning*, 182). The *New York Herald* observed in 1859, "The home base is marked by a flat circular iron plate, painted white" (*New York Herald*, October 16, 1859). Of course not all clubs complied with such rules, prompting Henry Chadwick to complain, "Many of our clubs have an iron quoit for the home base that is in direct violation of the rule, which states that the home base must be marked by 'a flat circular iron plate'" (*New York Clipper*, April 23, 1864). Three years later, he counseled, "The home-base quoit should be flat, as the rule requires, and not rising in the centre, as some do; for when a ball touches the latter, instead of rebounding for the catcher, as it would do if the base were flat, it flies off at a tangent, and allows of bases being run on the passed ball" (Henry Chadwick, *Haney's Base Ball Player's Book of Reference for 1867*, 11). Nevertheless many baseball fields continued to feature raised plates that interfered with play and posed a serious hazard to base runners.

A one-foot-square plate was introduced in 1868, and in 1874 it was rotated so that one point was closest to the pitcher. This was a significant change because, without changing the size of the plate, it gave the pitcher seventeen inches of strike-zone width instead of twelve inches.

In 1872 the requirements dictated that home plate be made of white marble or stone. By 1875 it had changed to "either stone or iron" (*St. Louis Democrat*, March 7, 1875). Colored stone was preferred by some clubs, so as to avoid "the dazzling reflection that in iron plates causes trouble to pitcher, catcher and batsman" (*Cincinnati Enquirer*, September 9, 1875).

When slides became common in the 1880s, the hard surface prompted concerns that launching oneself toward a base was "not so dangerous on the bags, but it is a little risky when it comes to the home plate" (*New York Clipper*, March 6, 1880). In 1885 the American Association specified white rubber for the plate while the National League gave clubs the choice of rubber or stone. Two years later, when the leagues consolidated their rule books, they settled on rubber but retained the obsolete name.

Pitcher Robert Keating was the inventor of the rubber plate adopted by the major leagues, and he gave this explanation of its advantages: "A batter can get a better start in running to first base, because as soon as his foot touches the plate it sends him off on a bound which the old plate cannot do. In striking the plate with the bat, it will not jar the batter's hands, and a player running in cannot hurt himself in sliding on it. The plate is twelve inches square, fits into an iron casting which sets in the ground, and can be removed without trouble at any time" (*Base Ball Gazette*, April 23, 1887; see also *Baltimore Daily News*, March 9, 1887, and *Sporting Life*, August 24, 1887. Thanks to researchers Reed Howard and Marty Payne for help in locating sources). Keating invented the plate in 1886 and patented it one year later, then went on to hold more than forty patents for motorcycles, shaving devices, flushing valves, bicycle wheels, and the like (Daniel E. Ginsburg, "Robert M. Keating, Inventor," *Baseball Research Journal* 1982, 135–136).

The five-sided home plate was introduced following the 1899 season. While this did not actually change the size of the strike zone, it made it easier for the umpire to call close pitches. The 1900 *Spalding Guide* explained that the new shape "enables the pitcher to see the *width* of base he has to throw the ball over better than before, and the umpire can judge called balls and strikes with less difficulty" (*Spalding's Official Base Ball Guide, 1900*, 201).

Fred "Crazy" Schmit attempted to take credit for the new shape, writing to the *Sporting News* in 1900 to explain that pitchers were less likely to get strikes on the corner when dirt obscured those corners (Tom Shieber, "The Evolution of the Baseball Diamond," in *Total Baseball IV*, 120). Schmit's nickname and eccentric behavior make it difficult to take his claim seriously.

A much more plausible candidate is Michael T. McMahon, an umpire from Belleville, New Jersey, who was given credit at the time for having "first suggested the change in the home plate. His idea was, though, to put the square front toward the catcher, in order to obviate disputes over batted balls hitting the plate. This idea of McMahon was sent to President [Nick] Young, who acknowledge [sic] receipt and submitted the plan to Chairman [Jim] Hart, of the Playing Rules Committee. The latter thought so well of it that he incorporated it in his amendments submitted to the League, except that he places the square front toward the pitcher instead of the catcher. McMahon still thinks, however, that his original idea was the better one" (*Sporting Life*, September 23, 1899).

Home plate has remained essentially unchanged since the 1900 season, except for the addition of beveled edges after the 1936 season.

14.3.3   Chalk Lines. One of the difficulties of this project is the tendency for a few famous players and clubs to be credited with every conceivable first. Chalk lines are a perfect example. A 1905 obituary of William B. Wing, who was in charge of the home park of the Red Stockings of Cincinnati from 1869 to 1872, stated that he "devised the scheme of whitewashing the foul lines on the baseball diamond, which took the place of the old custom of plowing up the field" (*Sporting Life*, August 19, 1905). Lee Allen, who should have known better, also credited Wing (*Sporting News*, April 12, 1969; reprinted in Lee Allen, *Cooperstown Corner*).

In fact, chalk lines had been required by the rule book much earlier. John H. Gruber explained that until 1860 "the playing ground was a mere waste field, punctuated by white bags on three corners of a square, and by an iron plate (very rusty, no doubt) on the other. The umpire, sitting under an umbrella on one side of the catcher, score book in hand, naturally made more mistakes in deciding fair and foul balls than was comfortable to him or agreeable to the players and spectators" (John H. Gruber, "The Playing Field," *Sporting News*, November 25, 1915). To remedy the situation, a change required "a chalk or white line to be made between home and first base, and home and third base, as lines whereby foul balls can be judged" (*New York Clipper*, June 29, 1861).

In 1870 the rules specified for the first time that chalk also be used to delineate the areas reserved for the pitcher and batter. The following year, according to Gruber, the chalk lines were extended to the foul poles for the first time. The result of all these added lines was that the "mere waste field" of eleven years earlier had been transformed into "a field with a net of charming lines, restful to the eye, forming an attractive frame to the green diamond with its gleaming white corners" (John H. Gruber, "The Playing Field," *Sporting News*, November 25, 1915).

14.3.4 Warning Tracks and Padded Fences.

Early baseball fields sometimes had a slope leading up to the fence to warn outfielders of their peril. Once these began to disappear, collisions with the fence became more common. Pete Reiser of Brooklyn had a frightening series of collisions with outfield fences, including a 1947 crash that was so violent that last rites were administered (but he recovered). The Cleveland Indians had padded their fences before the 1947 season and Reiser's injury impelled other clubs to take action (*Sporting News*, February 23, 1947). The Dodgers added padding to their fences in 1948, and other clubs pioneered warning tracks. On July 12, 1949, owners agreed that all stadiums would have a ten-foot warning track by the start of the 1950 season.

14.3.5 Batters' Boxes.

The positioning of the batter was first addressed in the 1857 rules, when he was required to stand in line with the plate. Since the pitcher was required to throw the ball "to the bat," there is no evidence that this rule was enforced with much vigilance.

Beginning in 1867 a series of rules was enacted to prevent batters from stepping backward before swinging. Tom Shieber explained that this seemingly peculiar tactic was a result of the definition of a foul ball at the time—balls were fair if they initially hit the ground in fair territory, and foul if they first hit in foul ground. This meant that batters could gain a couple of advantages by stepping backward. If they took their best swing at a pitch but dubbed it, it would be a foul ball. And if they got a pitch they couldn't handle, they could deliberately foul it. With fouls not counting as strikes, batters had much to gain by stepping backward and little to lose.

As result, a rule was introduced in 1867 that at least one of the batter's feet had to be in line with the plate when he struck the ball. Henry Chadwick was a strong proponent of the rule, maintaining that it was necessary to prevent the batter "from standing back of the line of his position, thereby increasing the distance between himself and the pitcher and obtaining a better opportunity of judging the ball; besides which, a poorly hit ball which would strike the ground in front of the home base—if the batsman stood on the line of his base—and lead to his being put out, is changed to a foul ball by his standing back of his base, and he thereby escapes the penalty of his poor batting." Chadwick also insisted that it was important to prevent the batter from stepping forward or backward to strike the ball (Henry Chadwick, *Haney's Base Ball Player's Book of Reference for 1867*, 21).

It is not entirely clear whether others agreed with Chadwick about the importance of restricting the batter's movements. What is clear is that the rule failed miserably—umpires interpreted and enforced it in a wide variety of ways, often with unintended consequences. The rule was modified several times in succeeding years (see Tom Shieber, "The Evolution of the Baseball Diamond," in *Total Baseball IV*, 115–116, for more details).

In addition to these batting tactics, hitters were taking advantage of their freedom to roam by using some dubious stratagems that umpires had little power to prevent. Whenever a teammate was attempting to steal, batters would try to hinder the catcher's throw in a variety of ways. Rules were instituted to prevent some of the more flagrant abuses, such as kicking the ball away from the catcher. But umpires were hard-pressed to prevent more subtle approaches, such as trying to stand close enough to the catcher to impede his throw (John H. Gruber, "Out for Interference," *Sporting News*, February 24, 1916).

Accordingly, the batter's box was introduced in 1874, forcing the batter to stand in a clearly delineated area. As Tom Shieber observes, "With this rule change, the line of the home base lost its original purpose and now served only to define the location of the batter's box" (Tom Shieber, "The Evolution of the Baseball Diamond," in *Total Baseball IV*, 116). It was a very significant change, simultaneously making the umpire's life easier and giving the batter full freedom to adopt any type of stance (see **2.1.6**).

The original batter's box measured six feet by three feet and kept the batter one foot from home plate. Although not explicitly stated in the rules, Henry Chadwick's gloss on the rules noted that the batter's box should be "marked out with chalk lines" (*New York Clipper*, April 18, 1874). It was anticipated that the batter's box would "make 'fair foul' hitting doubly difficult" (*Boston Advertiser*, March 3, 1874). But the fair-foul proved resilient, and, as discussed in entry **2.2.2**, it was finally abolished in 1877 by a rule change.

The advent of "Curves" (**3.2.3**) was another factor in the introduction and subsequent increase in the size of the batter's box, since many believed that batters deserved more latitude to chase the elusive pitch. As a sportswriter commented, "the legislation has been one-sided, always in favor of the pitcher and never in favor of the batsman, with the single unimportant exception of giving him (practically) four strikes in certain cases. The rules have penned him up, restricted the size of his bat, and raised all the trouble they could with him. Now, if you want more batting without destroying the characteristics of the game, let the batter loose at curved balls; let him go where they are, and if one of them shoots away from him let him have a chance to go where it is and hit it. If that one thing were done the game would be improved wonderfully" (*Chicago Tribune*, July 28, 1878, 7). The current dimensions (six feet by four feet) and distance from the plate (six inches) were adopted by the National League in 1885 and by the American Association the following season.

14.3.6 Three-foot Line.

The rule requiring a base runner to stay within three feet of the baseline was adopted in 1882. John Gruber explained the reasons for the new rule: "Runners from home to first, after they had hit the ball, acquired the habit of zigzagging their way to the initial sack, and so interfering with the ball thrown there to head them off" (John H. Gruber, "The Playing Field," *Sporting News*, November 25, 1915). Some umpires took the new rule very literally. Al Kermisch noted that in a National League game at Buffalo on May 29, 1882, umpire James L. Hickey called Cleveland's John Richmond out for going outside the line after a base on balls (*Baseball Research Journal* 14 [1985], 18).

14.3.7 Pitcher's Box.

As discussed in the introduction to Chapter 3, the pitcher's box was introduced in 1863 as two parallel lines; the pitcher had to be standing between them to deliver the ball. It was modified repeatedly and finally eliminated after the 1892 season. A *Sporting Life* correspondent remarked in 1893, "The old expression 'The pitcher was knocked out of the box,' must be amended under the new rules. 'He was knocked off the rubber slab,' might do" (*Sporting Life*, June 3, 1893). In the ensuing years the term "pitcher's box" was eliminated from the rulebook, and various writers objected to the use of the outdated phrase. Sportswriter I. E. Sanborn, for example, chided a reader: "The Sox did not knock any pitcher 'out of the box,' as there is no pitcher's box" (*Chicago Tribune*, June 16, 1907). None-

theless, baseball's affection for traditions—even outmoded ones—enabled the term to stubbornly resist all such efforts. Phrases like "back through the box" and "knocked out of the box" endure to this day.

14.3.8 Pitching Rubbers.

The story of the transition from a box to today's rubber is a circuitous and often fascinating one. The outer limits of the pitcher's box were originally marked only with chalk lines that connected the pitcher's points. With the umpire stationed behind the plate, many pitchers took advantage to stray outside the box.

As early as 1860 Henry Chadwick recommended: "The line of the pitcher's position should be marked by the insertion in the ground of a piece of hard wood, six feet long, about two inches wide, and from six to eight deep. It should be inserted so the umpire can see it" (*Beadle's Dime Base-Ball Player*, 18). In 1874 it was announced that "The pitcher's position is hereafter to be marked by four square quoits in the corners, between which white lines shall be drawn, doing away with the pieces of wood which have proved so awkward" (*Boston Globe*, March 3, 1874, 3).

It is not known how commonly such instructions were followed, but if they were, they proved ineffective. Pitchers continued to step over the boundary, with 1880s pitcher Guy Hecker of Louisville being one of the most notorious offenders. Cincinnati's Will White decided to do something about it before an 1884 game in Cincinnati. White "ordered two smooth, flat stones to be set into the ground, one before and behind the box, and wholly outside of the lines. The effort is to keep the pitcher's feet wholly within the box as the rules require. If he steps over the line the spikes in his shoes strike the smooth stone, and he slips as well as leaves a tell-tale mark on the stone that cannot be rubbed out. To say that Hecker was struck when he saw those stones is to draw it mild. Of course he 'kicked' and called upon the umpire to have them removed. The umpire, however, said that the stones were wholly outside of the box, and if he pitched according to the requirements of the rules, he would not touch them. Furthermore, Mr. [Robert] Ross said that he was surprised that the same precaution against illegal pitching had not been taken by other clubs, and said that every diamond should have those stones set. Hecker pitched standing in the box, as the rules require, and was batted hard. Once he stepped out on the stones and his foot slipped, nearly splitting him to the shoulder" (*Sporting Life*, August 6, 1884).

The following week it was Cincinnati's turn to visit Louisville, which meant that payback was in order. Cincinnati pitcher Billy Mountjoy was known to make a sidestep to the right. Accordingly, "Joe Gerhardt had a smooth stone a foot wide laid inside the pitchers' box the whole length of the right side" (*Sporting Life*, August 13, 1884). Mountjoy was unable to adjust, and was shelled.

An account several years later indicated that the Metropolitans tried the same tactic against Hecker later that season, but that he adapted by switching to rubber-soled shoes. The ploy was more effective when the Metropolitans employed it against Richmond pitcher Ed Dugan, who "had a long jump, and until he struck the polished surface of that marble slab was considered a good pitcher. Dugan couldn't understand just what happened to him when he pitched the first ball of the game. He took his usual jump, his right foot struck the slab, the ball went one way and Dugan the other. When he saw the slab he was one of the wildest men ever seen on a ball field and offered to put up a deposit for the privilege of whipping everybody in the lot. But he pitched the game out and has never pitched since" (*Williamsport Sunday Grit*, June 14, 1891).

This novel method of enforcing the rules captured the imagination of many. One account commented that "[Sportswriter O. P.] Caylor's flag-stone patent would be of wonderful service were it used on [Tommy] Lee, of the Baltimore Unions, as he jumps out of the box every time he pitches a ball" (*National Police Gazette*, September 13, 1884). At season's end, a note observed: "Many ways may be devised for detecting any encroachment of the pitcher beyond the front line of the box, such, for instance, as a strip of thin rubber, several inches high, painted white, placed longitudinally along the front line" (*Sporting Life*, November 5, 1884).

The following spring brought this announcement: "It has been decided to recommend all managers to put a marble slab in front of the pitcher's box to keep him from overstepping his bounds in that direction. 'Jumping out of the box' was last season the greatest source of annoyance to umpires, and was the means of causing intense dissatisfaction among audiences" (*Sporting Life*, April 8, 1885). Henry Chadwick added: "The umpires have requested

all American clubs to place a marble or glass slab, a foot wide, on the front outer edge of the pitcher's box" (*New York Clipper*, reprinted in *St. Louis Post-Dispatch*, April 11, 1885).

The practical consequences were again spectacular in 1885. Baltimore manager Billy Barnie placed a marble slab "in front of the pitcher's box at Oriole Park to prevent the 'twirlers' from overstepping the bounds. The new arrangement has worked splendidly, and when the pitchers get over the line they invariably lose their footing and take a drop. [Pitcher Tom] Lovett, of Providence, on Monday fell three times on account of 'this yer'rangement,' as he remarked" (*Williamsport Sunday Grit*, April 26, 1885).

In 1886 a stone slab was officially added to the American Association's rule book. Caylor was likely thinking of this season when he explained in 1891 that the goal of keeping the pitcher "within the bounds of his position resulted in another rule which compelled each club to put a smooth piece of marble in the ground and on a level with the surface, just in front of the forward line of the 'box.' The consequence was that any pitcher who tried to 'overstep the bounds' must step upon this marble with his spiked shoes and would surely slip. The remedy worked well in one way and illy in another. Every offending pitcher fell a victim to the marble slab; but several were so seriously strained by the slip up that a prejudice gradually arose against the slab's use. Then two pitchers began to use shoes with rubber soles instead of spikes, and thus shod they stepped upon the marble with impunity" (O. P. Caylor, "The Theory and Introduction of Curve Pitching," *Outing*, August 1891).

In response to these two pitchers, Caylor noted, the marble slab was replaced with a rubber one. The slab was eliminated from the rules after only one year, for two main reasons. First, an effort was being made to standardize the rules of the two major leagues. Second, a new rule required the pitcher's back foot to remain in contact with the back line of the pitcher's box. The back line thus essentially assumed the role of today's pitching rubber and effectively prevented pitchers from stepping beyond the front line.

When the Players' League was formed in 1890, league secretary Frank Brunell declared that the new circuit intended to "improve the rules of the game as it goes along, and thus lead the procession in more than playing strength." Toward this end, the "flat iron plate or stone" around the pitcher's area was replaced with "wooden pegs" (*Chicago Herald*, March 30, 1890).

In 1893 the pitcher's box was finally eliminated entirely in favor of a single plate with which the pitcher's foot had to remain in contact until the ball left his hand. No doubt it was with a mind to the previous experience with pitchers' footing that this was made of rubber, and became known as the rubber. Although it has been made of rubber ever since, the same quaint urge that keeps "knocked out of the box" current has spawned terms like "slab-man," "on the slab," and "slab artist."

After the 1896 season, Henry Chadwick began to campaign to eliminate the pitching rubber and return to a box. He maintained that the new rule wasn't working because it was commonplace to see a pitcher hedge on the requirement "to have his pivot foot in contact with the rubber plate of his position, and this violation of the rule was occasioned by the pitcher's inability to get as firm a foot hold for his pivot foot on the rubber as he can when standing on hard ground" (*Sporting News*, October 31, 1896). The idea of bringing back the old rule was discussed extensively in the pages of *Sporting News* that winter, but when the rules committee met no change was made (*Sporting News*, February 20, 1897).

14.3.9 Mounds. The pitcher's mound originated sometime in the late 1880s or early 1890s, but there are surprisingly few claimants for the distinction of having created the first mound. John Thorn and John Holway suggested that John Ward may have pioneered the mound in 1893, but Ward biographer Bryan Di Salvatore disputed this (John Thorn and John Holway, *The Pitcher*, 149; Bryan Di Salvatore, *A Clever Base-Ballist*, 433).

In fact the baseball mound does not appear to have been invented by anyone at all, but instead to have had humbler origins. Researcher Tom Shieber explained, "A common theory is that soon after the allowance of overhand pitching, it became apparent that a downward slope over the range of the pitcher's stride increased the speed of a pitched ball. Groundskeepers, in an effort to aid the pitcher's footing after a rain storm, would often add dirt to the pitcher's box area, but soon dirt was requested with or without rain" (Tom Shieber, "The Evolution of the Baseball Diamond," in *Total Baseball IV*, 120).

This hypothesis that the earliest mounds were intended for drainage is supported by references such as this one: "When the Trenton team reached the Hartford ground yesterday they found five men with sponges hard at work on the diamond, and [pitcher Mike] Tiernan was mounted on a pile of sawdust" (*Trenton Times*, April 28, 1885). Researcher Clifford Blau discovered a claim before the 1888 season that the pitcher's box at the St. Louis grounds had "a decided elevation above the batter's box." According to the note's author, St. Louis pitcher Bob Caruthers had gained an advantage from the raised pitching area and would not be as effective now that he had been sold to Brooklyn (*Sporting Life*, February 22, 1888, 5).

Aside from this claim, however, most references to mounds in this period imply that they were perceived as drainage devices rather than as potential competitive advantages. There are two plausible explanations for this. One is that few realized that such an elevation would benefit the pitcher. Another is that some crafty souls did recognize the potential benefit but sought to keep this knowledge to themselves. Since such coyness can never be ruled out, it is impossible to determine precisely when mounds changed from being utilitarian anti-flooding devices to deliberately crafted pitchers' aids. Nonetheless it is worth trying to narrow it down.

A roundup of the usual suspects must begin with the Orioles' innovative duo of manager Ned Hanlon and groundskeeper Thomas J. Murphy. Hugh Fullerton later reported that during the Orioles' heyday in the mid-1890s, "The pitcher's box was a foot higher than the plate" (*Chicago Tribune*, August 5, 1906). Hanlon moved on to manage Brooklyn in 1899 and brought the pitcher's mound with him. At the beginning of the season New York manager Buck Ewing predicted "that Brooklyn will have the best of it this season, as Hanlon has raised his pitcher's box nearly one foot, making it difficult for the visiting players. The home players are able to overcome the handicap by practice." Ewing complained that "Hanlon has no more right to raise his pitchers' box a foot than New York has a right to dig a trench one foot deep from the home plate to the pitcher's box at the Polo Grounds" (*Boston Globe*, reprinted in *Sporting Life*, April 7, 1899).

By this time others were using similar techniques. The pitcher's area at the National League ballpark in Washington was reportedly six inches higher than the rest of the field in 1894, prompting speculation "that a raised box gives the home twirlers an advantage over the visitors" (*Brooklyn Eagle*, June 20, 1894). David

Ball discovered a claim by Dick Harley in 1897 that New York manager Bill Joyce had "worked the old racket at the Polo Grounds. . . . Scrappy [Joyce] has built up the pitcher's box, and the result is a handicap to the visiting pitchers and the visiting batsmen." Harley believed that this gave an advantage to tall New York pitchers like Jouett Meekin and Amos Rusie while handicapping visiting pitchers who were unaccustomed to the raised pitcher's area. "I do not know whether there is any rule against this trick of palming off a 'phony' pitcher's box on a visiting club, but there ought to be. I am told that Scrappy worked the same trick when he was in Washington. It's an old one, and the inventor of it was Mike Kelly. Mike introduced the trick when Larry Cochrane [sic] pitched for Uncle Anson's Chicago Whites, back in the eighties" (*Washington Post*, August 29, 1897). This last claim must be taken with skepticism, since Harley was far too young to have firsthand knowledge of these events, and Corcoran and Kelly were already dead.

By the turn of the century, mounds were becoming a common sight. In 1900 the success of Cleveland in the American League (then still a minor league) was attributed to "the fact that in the different parks the pitcher's box was raised from one to two feet, thus enabling the pitchers to throw down hill, and get not only more speed, but better control as well. This is the case in every city except Cleveland. Here the batters' box has been raised nearly twelve inches above the pitchers' slab, and the boxmen are forced to throw up-hill. The Cleveland pitchers, working at home half the time, have thoroughly mastered the difference in the two positions, and can, by reason of the fact that they work oftener at home than on any other one field, have much greater command of the ball and know exactly how to work the variations in their delivery. The question of relative positions of the plate and pitcher's box with the other parts of the diamond is one which just now is of much interest, and will be discussed at the annual meetings this fall" (*Sporting Life*, September 8, 1900).

As described in the introduction to Chapter 11, part two, at the instigation of Washington manager Tom Loftus a rule was instituted in 1903 that mounds could not exceed fifteen inches in height. While this rule was primarily designed so that home teams could not force visiting pitchers to adapt to life on a hillock, the idea that mounds benefited pitchers was

gaining currency. Before the season a *Sporting Life* correspondent observed, "Last year every ground in the Eastern League had a raised pitcher's box, and it increased the power of the slabmen" (*Sporting Life*, March 21, 1903). A follow-up piece reported: "The Washington Club has protested all games played in Boston on account of an illegal pitcher's box, the allegation being that the box is higher than fifteen inches" (*Sporting Life*, May 16, 1903).

Adoption of a maximum mound height did not prevent clubs from tinkering with its height to suit the preferences of its pitchers and to inconvenience the opposing pitcher. Brooklyn manager Ned Hanlon responded to the new rule by altering the pitcher's area whenever Christy Mathewson was scheduled to pitch there. According to Mathewson, "Every time he thought I was going to pitch there, he would have the diamond doctored for me in the morning. The groundkeeper sank the pitcher's box down so that it was below the level of all the bases instead of slightly elevated as it should be" (Christy Mathewson, *Pitching in a Pinch*, 288). In 1911 a minor league club in Kansas City announced plans to have no mound and instead to elevate the catcher's box in hopes of hampering opposing base stealers (*Sporting News*, March 16, 1911). As is discussed under "Mound Building" (**11.2.3**), such tactics continued until 1950.

In addition, acceptance of the notion that pitchers benefited from a mound was still far from universal. In particular, *Sporting Life* editor Francis Richter attributed the decline in hitting to his pet peeve, the foul strike. But players had begun to recognize a relationship, and when *Sporting News* polled players after the 1904 season on how to increase offense, Jack Holland of Spokane suggested putting hitters above pitchers (*Sporting News*, December 17, 1904).

14.3.10 Pitcher's Paths. Old-time ball fields usually featured a pitcher's path or alley leading from the plate to the mound, a characteristic that has been revived at the home parks of Detroit and Arizona. The origins of the path are somewhat obscure, but researcher Tom Shieber has unearthed what is almost certainly the explanation. He noted that early baseball clubs often played on cricket grounds, where the two wickets were connected by a dirt path to ensure more reliable bounces. He speculates that early baseball clubs found that the path led to fewer passed balls and made it customary.

Shieber cites a description that appeared in the *New York Clipper* in July 1860.

Shieber's theory accounts for how these dirt strips originated, but it doesn't explain why the alleys were retained long after catchers were stationed directly behind the plate. I think the explanation is simple: since it is very difficult to maintain grass in well-trodden areas, the alleys represented the groundskeepers' best effort to keep foot traffic off the grass. They probably had a hard time convincing the players to comply, but at least the groundskeeper and his assistants could do so.

This hypothesis also explains why the alleys gradually disappeared without much notice being taken. Once the sizes and budgets of grounds crews increased and ventilation and irrigation improved, there was less need to keep traffic off the grass. Eventually pitcher's paths began to be eliminated altogether.

(iv) The Amenities

14.4.1 On-deck Circles. It appears that the on-deck circle was created with the same basic aim as the coach's box (see **7.1.1**). In 1886 it was reported that Fred Dunlap of St. Louis had recently objected to Detroit's Dan Brouthers standing close to the plate while Hardy Richardson batted (*Boston Globe*, June 17, 1886, 8). The idea of requiring the next batter to stand well back from the plate was in evidence even in 1878 when a Brooklyn sportswriter observed: "A space of ground has been laid out under the new code within which no player or person other than the batsman, catcher or umpire is allowed to enter during the contest. This space is included in the triangular portion of the field in which the line of the catcher's fence is the base, while the continuation of the foul lines from the home base to the catcher's line form the side lines. This was done for the purpose of preventing players of the batting side from standing behind the umpire and judging the balls sent in over home base. Even the captains are kept from entering this space" (*Brooklyn Eagle*, January 22, 1878, 3).

But baseball had more pressing concerns. An 1897 rule change apparently abolished even an informal on-deck circle by specifying that members of the batting order had to remain on the bench unless called upon to bat or coach (*Chicago Inter-Ocean*, February 8, 1897). As a result, it was decades before the on-deck circle was introduced. Waite Hoyt said that by the time he debuted in the American League in 1919, "two or three batters were allowed to stand up, waiting for their turns to bat. There wasn't any batting circle then and they stood where they wanted to." An opponent took advantage of this in Hoyt's first game to call him "every dirty name he could think of" (Eugene Murdock, *Baseball Between the Wars*, 32). The on-deck circle appears to have debuted soon afterward, but I have not been able to pinpoint the details.

14.4.2 Hitting Backgrounds. Greg Rhodes and John Snyder claimed that a hitter's background was first introduced when Cincinnati's League Park was redesigned in 1894. Batters had been complaining that advertisements in center field were obscuring their vision. As a result, park superintendent John Schwab created a deep green backdrop in center field (Greg Rhodes and John Snyder, *Redleg Journal*, 111; Rhodes and Snyder listed this as John Schwab's son Matty, but he did not succeed his father as the club's groundskeeper until 1903).

When Brooklyn's Washington Park opened in 1898 it was immediately apparent that it had been designed by architects "not versed in the practical ins and outs of base ball. They extended the center-field bleachers across the field from left to right, thus balking the vision of the batsman and backstop. When the Dodgers leave for their Western trip President [Charles Ebbets] will employ a gang of carpenters to lop off 200 feet of bleacher room in center, thus giving the batsmen and wind paddists [catchers] a clear view of the perspective in the deep center garden. The lopped-off seats will be transferred to right field" (*Sporting News*, May 21, 1898).

Christy Mathewson noted in 1912 that clubs were becoming increasingly aware of the importance of hitting backgrounds: "Frequently, backgrounds are tampered with if the home club is notably weak at the bat. The best background for a batter is a dull, solid green. Many clubs have painted backgrounds in several contrasting, broken colors so that the sunlight, shining on them, blinds the batter. The Chicago White Sox are said to have done this, and for many years the figures showed that the batting of both the Chicago players and the visitors at their park was very light. The White Sox's hitting was weak anywhere, so that the poor background was an advantage to them" (Christy Mathewson, *Pitching in a Pinch*, 296).

Johnny Evers and Hugh Fullerton observed in 1910 that many pitchers would "shift from side to side in the slab to make the ball come to the batter on a line with some blinding sign." However, because there were more batters than pitchers on every team, they were able to "insist upon good solid green backgrounds to increase hitting, and overrule the pitchers, who prefer glaring yellow, or white, or a motley of colors" (John J. Evers and Hugh S. Fullerton, *Touching Second*, 117).

Good hitting backgrounds became standard after several serious beanings were attributed to batters' inability to pick up pitches. Players' Fraternity head David Fultz lobbied on the issue, and in 1914 the National Commission passed a rule that every park in the majors and high minors had to have a blank green wall in center field (Robert F. Burk, *Never Just a Game*, 194, 197).

This rule was not always adhered to closely. Luke Sewell recalled that when he came up in the early 1920s, "they had advertising signs out on the wall in center field and the pitchers would throw out of those signs, making it a little hard to see. Connie Mack had a scoreboard out there that his lefthanders would pitch out of" (quoted in Walter M. Langford, *Legends of Baseball*, 132).

14.4.3 Foul Poles. Henry Chadwick advised in 1860: "The foul ball posts are placed on a line with the home and first base, and home and third, and should be at least 100 feet from the bases. As these posts are intended solely to assist the umpire in his decisions in reference to foul balls, they should be high enough from the ground and painted so as to be distinctly seen from the umpire's position" (*Beadle's Dime Base-Ball Player*, 18).

14.4.4 Screen on the Foul Pole. On July 15, 1939, in a game at the Polo Grounds between the Reds and Giants, Harry Craft of Cincinnati hit a ball down the left-field line. The ball went into the stands near the foul line, which was marked only by a white pole. Home plate umpire Lee Ballanfant called it a home run, prompting heated protests from the Giants. Giants shortstop Bill Jurges ended up exchanging punches with umpire George Magerkurth, and both were suspended for ten games. The Giants' loss was magnified the next day when Jurges's replacement, Lou Chiozza, broke his leg. As a result, National League president Ford Frick mandated screens being added to the foul poles to make the call easier for the umpire (for

Ballanfant's version of the incident, see Larry R. Gerlach, *The Men in Blue*, 41).

14.4.5 Backstops. Some form of backstop was in use by 1867, when a Detroit newspaper complained that "The 'stop' bound behind the catcher was too close to this player" (*Detroit Advertiser and Tribune*, September 20, 1867). Most early backstops appear to have been utilitarian affairs which offered limited protection to the spectators while often obstructing their view.

By the end of the 1870s these were beginning to be replaced by screens. When Detroit's Recreation Park opened, plans were made "to put up a wire screen behind the catcher instead of the unsightly boards generally used" (*Detroit Post and Tribune*, April 28, 1879). Cleveland also installed a wire screen "in front of the grand stand . . . to protect its occupants from foul flies, etc." (*Chicago Tribune*, May 11, 1879). David Nemec included in his *Great Encyclopedia of 19th Century Major League Baseball* a photo of Providence's Messer Park in 1879 that appears to include a protective screen (David Nemec, *Great Encyclopedia of 19th Century Major League Baseball*, 125).

The early screens were not terribly popular. Researcher Frank Vaccaro found that a wire screen was installed at Milwaukee's Wright Street grounds on June 25, 1884. Upon its debut, the local paper commented, "The wire screen recently erected in front of the grand stand protects spectators from ugly fouls, and does not interfere in the least with the view of the field" (*Milwaukee Journal*, June 27, 1884). But it was removed only one week later in response to the complaints of spectators (*Milwaukee Journal*, July 3, 1884).

Acceptance of backstops increased after they had been modified to make them less of an impediment to sight lines. An 1890 article, for instance, explained that wire gauze was being used to protect spectators without obstructing their view (W. Harrison Daniel and Scott P. Mayer, *Baseball in Richmond*, 28).

14.4.6 Benches. In the early days of baseball, benches and chairs were not required, and players often had to sprawl on the ground or sit with the spectators. It was not until 1882 that the National League mandated that stadiums have a bench, and—since discretionary substitutions were not allowed (see **1.32**)—only a single bench was obligatory. In 1886 it became a requirement for each club to have its own bench.

14.4.7 Dugouts. Once benches came into vogue, players generally sat on an uncovered bench when not on the field. This could understandably be unpleasant, and occasional efforts were made to afford them protection.

An 1877 account of a game in Cincinnati referred to players sitting "under the awning" (*Cincinnati Enquirer*, July 5, 1877). The *Washington Post* noted in 1884, "The awnings which Mr. [Lloyd] Moxley has had placed over the players' seats are both useful and ornamental" (*Washington Post*, May 11, 1884). The home field of Brooklyn's American Association entry in 1889 had an "awning over the players' bench" (*Sporting Life*, June 26, 1889). An unsourced 1994 article claimed that, following a contentious loss to Rochester on April 15, 1890, New Haven manager Walter Burnham built a long, red-and-white-striped awning to protect his players from the verbal abuse of fans and from the sun (Donovan Shilling, "How the Rochester Nine Helped Create Baseball's Dugout," *Rochesterian*, May, 1994).

Not everyone thought this innovation was a good thing. A Grand Rapids, Michigan, reporter observed in 1898, "They think a great deal of their players down in Dayton or else the men must be a trifle tender. The management has erected little roofs over the players' benches in front of the stand. Of course those roofs will afford protection from sun and rain, likewise explosive peanuts and torpedo-laden cushions" (*Grand Rapids* [Mich.] *Evening Press*, April 20, 1898).

The comment about the players being a "trifle tender" helps explain why these efforts were only sporadic. Nonetheless something had to be done, as the exposed benches made it possible for the home teams to make things quite uncomfortable for their guests. During an 1885 feud with Pittsburgh manager Horace Phillips, St. Louis owner Chris Von der Ahe "got even by placing the visiting players' seats so that the Pittsburg men would have to sit in the sun" (*Boston Globe*, August 14, 1885).

Such shenanigans were likely responsible for an 1899 rule requiring that visiting clubs be provided with benches "covered by a roof and closed at the back and each end" (*Indiana State Journal*, February 22, 1899). Louisville president Harry Pulliam claimed that Ned Hanlon was responsible for the rule change. According to Pulliam, Hanlon "referred to the roastings

visiting players were forced to endure from the Louisville bleachers and declared for covered benches as a means of protection. So the rule was passed and we provided a covered bench."

But Louisville provided them in such a way that they gave Hanlon no satisfaction. The awnings were slanted so that the sun's rays shone directly in the players' faces, and they prevented the air from circulating. The players found them intolerable and tried to leave, but Louisville captain Fred Clarke pointed this out to the umpire and they had to return (*Sporting News*; reprinted in *Brooklyn Eagle*, February 4, 1900).

By this time, steps were finally being made toward creating actual dugouts. A *Sporting Life* correspondent noted in 1895: "The experiment will be tried on the Philadelphia grounds of keeping all ball players except those actually playing or coaching out of sight of the spectators. This result will be attained by having the players' benches under the stand instead of in front of it" (*Sporting Life*, May 4, 1895). In 1899 the National League ruled that players' benches had to be situated at least twenty-five feet from the foul lines. This made it logical to situate them under the stands, and within a few years sunken dugouts had become the norm.

The convenience of air conditioning does not appear to have been added to dugouts until 1956, when this feature was introduced in Cincinnati (*Sporting News*, March 7, 1956).

14.4.8 Bat Racks. In 1882 the National League directed its teams to provide bat racks "sufficient in size to hold twenty bats." The requirement was dropped in 1893, and the racks were replaced by bat bags, presumably because they were easier for traveling. Bat racks do not appear to have again become standard until the 1920s.

14.4.9 Boxes for Balls. In 1912 a box for balls was installed in each National League park. The move was indicative of the new emphasis on replacing balls and on umpires controlling the supply of balls.

14.4.10 Batting Cages. The prototype of the batting cage may have been introduced in Providence in 1879, according to this note: "The Providence Club will have a room arranged under the grand stand of their ground, 110 feet long, 19 feet wide and 16 feet high, intended for baseball practice on rainy and cold days" (*New York Clipper*, April 12, 1879).

Indoor batting cages were popularized during the 1880s by college baseball teams, which were obliged to find a way of practicing indoors while the weather was still inclement (*Boston Globe*, March 8, 1885; *Outing*, April 1890). As an 1887 article put it, "Who has not seen the members of a nine at work in the cage of a gymnasium has missed a royal spectacle. . . . The cage, though it is quite possible that the room for base ball practice is not known by that name everywhere, is so called because the walls are protected from injury by a great netting that, attached to the cornice, hangs clear to the floor at a distance of a foot or more from the wall. The candidates for the position of pitcher stand near one end of the cage and fire away at the batsman at the other end. The catcher, with his mask, sometimes takes his appropriate position back of the batsman, but generally the ball is allowed to go by if he fails to hit it, and, striking the net, it falls sluggishly to the floor and is tossed back to the pitcher. The batting is as vigorous as if the men were in an open field and a game were in progress. Bang! and the ball whizzes past the pitcher's head with force enough to make a three-base hit if no enterprising fielder gathers it in, and whuff! it goes against the net, loses all its energy, and rolls lazily along back to the pitcher. They don't practice base running, but nearly every other feature of the game attracts the attention of the players in the gymnasium" (*New York Sun*, January 9, 1887).

The size of these cages increased rapidly. In 1886 Yale began using a "plainly built shed-like building, about 60 feet in length and not more than one-quarter as wide" (*Yale Daily News*, December 17, 1885; quoted in Mike Roer, *Orator O'Rourke*, 125). But by 1893, Walter C. Bohm reported, "Princeton's cage is a model, and surpasses anything of its kind in the country. It is a substantial brick building nearly two hundred feet long and sixty feet wide. Twenty-four great skylights in the high roof admit an abundance of light and make it easy for the batters and fielders to see the ball as though they were on an out-of-door diamond. The floor is of smooth, hard clay. Big stoves at each end of the structure make exercise comfortable on the coldest days" (Walter C. Bohm, "College Baseball," *Los Angeles Times*, May 21, 1893).

The benefits of these cages to college nines spurred efforts to bring them to other settings. During the 1888–1889 world tour led by A. G. Spalding, George Wright built a cage of sorts on one of the ships to limit the loss of baseballs overboard (Mark Lamster, *Spalding's World Tour*, 117). Soon outdoor batting cages were being created by draping nets around home plate. Sportswriter Tim Murnane noted in 1894 that Boston "manager [Frank] Selee will suggest to the owners of the club the putting up of nets such as they use at the big colleges for batting practice" (*Boston Globe*, May 7, 1894).

The first permanent outdoor batting cage was introduced at the University of Chicago in 1896 by legendary football coach Amos Alonzo Stagg. A newspaper account explained: "The idea is Stagg's own and has never been made use of before by any team. The new cage will be built at the north end of Marshall field, east of the grand stand. It will be of wire netting fastened to upright posts set firmly in the ground; its length will be 70 feet and its width ten feet, so as to give ample room for the battery and the batter to work. A roof of the same material will prevent the ball from soaring too high from terra firma." The cage provided the additional benefits of saving time chasing balls and keeping "the men from tramping over the outfield until the grass, which is about to be sown, has got a start" (*Decatur Review*, April 7, 1896).

Stagg's innovation does not appear to have caught on, probably because most college nines could afford the luxury of indoor batting cages. These cages grew increasingly elaborate, with Yale announcing plans in 1905 for "a one-story large cage nearly as big as any field base ball diamond" at a cost of $35,000 (*Sporting Life*, February 4, 1905). The West Coast's first batting cage was built at the University of Southern California in 1906 and the 20 × 24 × 10-foot enclosure was hailed as a great convenience: "Under ordinary conditions batting practice is attended with much labor and several extra fielders are needed to keep the stick artists busy. The cage takes the place of the fielder and catcher" (*Los Angeles Times*, April 29, 1906).

Professional baseball was very aware of the benefits of these batting cages. Detroit third baseman Doc Casey prepared for the 1901 season by practicing at the cage at Johns Hopkins University (*Detroit Free Press*, February 28, 1901). Three years later it was reported that "Negotiations toward securing the use of the Johns Hopkins University cage for the Baltimore players to practice in are progressing" (*Sporting Life*, March 19, 1904).

But large stationary indoor cages were not practical in the major league stadiums of the era, where space was at a premium. The earliest indication of the use of cages by a professional club that I have found was a 1906 reference to a "batting cage" at Chicago's West Side Park (*Chicago Tribune*, March 23, 1906).

The breakthrough that would lead to their permanent use came later that year when a man named Wellington Stockton Titus applied for a patent for a portable batting cage. Researcher Ken Tillman explained that Titus was helping his cousin, a Princeton baseball player, get some practice when he decided that there had to be an alternative to the constant retrieval of balls (Ken Tillman, "The Portable Batting Cage," *Baseball Research Journal* 28 [1999], 23–26).

So Titus designed a "base ball back stop" on wheels and applied for a patent on December 20, 1906. His patent application explained that his invention allowed a batter to "stand in position to bat with greater certainty to any particular fielder or portion of the field without the danger of any ball pitched or fielded to him being stolen by any onlookers."

Initially chicken wire was used for the screens, but after trial and error it was replaced with twine. Titus may have been influenced by hockey goals, to which netting had begun to be commonly attached in 1900 (Michael McKinley, *Putting a Roof on Winter*, 37, 54). Titus received a patent on April 7, 1907, but before then he had already signed a contract with A. G. Spalding and Brothers to manufacture the portable batting cage.

The earliest indication I have found of the portable batting cage being used came in 1908 when the *Washington Post* informed its readers, "The batting cage on wheels which has been added to the park paraphernalia is a very useful contrivance. It not only prevents delays during batting practice, but it saves balls and lots of time" (*Washington Post*, April 23, 1908).

Nonetheless Titus's invention seems to have been slow to catch on, with many remaining unaware of its existence. *Sporting Life* reported in 1911, "The Washington players, in training at Atlanta, are using a batting cage 70 feet long, 14 feet high and 35 feet wide. Manager [Jimmy] McAleer may be the originator of this scheme as far as professional ball players are concerned, but the cage has been in use at the leading colleges for many years" (*Sporting Life*, March 25, 1911). Three years later *Sporting News* published a photograph of batting cages and described them as a new idea of Branch Rickey's (*Sporting News*, February 26, 1914).

14.4.11 Pitching Machines. The pitching machine is a classic example of an idea whose potential value was recognized long before anyone could figure out how to actually make one suited to the practical requirements of baseball.

Ted Kennedy, a pitcher of the 1880s who had a role in several important inventions, may have been the first to try his hand. In 1910 columnist Eddie Wray described Kennedy's endeavors in the 1880s: "Ted set to work to devise a pitching gun that would serve up any kind of a curve, at any given height, at any rate of speed desired. He could mix a high inshoot with a low drop, a straight fast one with a slow floater—in short, anything. So Ted came around with this gun and the writer induced Manager [Jimmy] McAleer to give him a trial. But after Ted's gun delivered a few curves with a muzzle velocity of 1000 feet a second around the ears of the batters, they said 'Nay, Paulin!' and refused to face machine pitching" (*St. Louis Post-Dispatch*, August 19, 1910).

Pittsburgh players Fred Carroll and Billy Kuehne devised "a very curious yet simple means for training the eye to judge swiftly pitched curved balls. The machine, or whatever it may be called, has been erected in the extensive back yard of an Allegheny residence and the boys expect to do business with it daily. At the upper end of the yard the machine is set up. It is a spring securely fastened to a piece of heavy timber. On the top of the spring is a cup-like arrangement in which the regulation base ball snugly fits. This is pulled down and fastened to an ingeniously made catch, or series of catches rather, for it can be set at any curve or angle to suit the operator. The spring is on a line with a home plate at the lower end of the yard. One of the players manipulates the machine, while the others take turns with the bat. A ball is placed in the cup, and the operator fastens the spring down to any catch he chooses, the combination of curves and straight balls being almost innumerable, while at the same time it is an utter impossibility for the batsman to anticipate how it is going to come. When ready the operator releases the catch and the ball is thrown with the force of a bullet. It requires a mighty quick eye to get on to it, and furnishes not only excellent practice but a great deal of amusement. The balls go over the plate much swifter than it is possible for the strongest pitcher in the country to send them, and by becoming proficient in sizing them up a batsman will have no difficulty in hitting the most skilled twirler, as the hardest pitched ball would look slow and easy in comparison with those thrown by the spring. The inventors will probably apply for a patent" (*Pittsburgh Commercial Gazette*, reprinted in *Columbus* [Ohio] *Press*, March 15, 1890).

More publicity was received by a device that was invented by Princeton mathematics professor Charles H. Hinton in 1896. Initial reports described it as "a machine that will pitch balls automatically, and that will curve them also. The apparatus will deliver a ball every twenty seconds, but the time between balls can be changed. The speed of the balls can be regulated as well as the curves. The balls always go directly over the plate. It is said that the Princeton tigers will use this for batting practice next year" (*Boston Globe*, April 16, 1896).

Professor Hinton referred to his creation as an "automatic pitcher," but it so closely resembled a gun that it soon became known as a pitching gun. A very detailed description explained how an initial "experimental gun" had been transformed into a "perfected gun" that could deliver "a baseball at any speed and give an outcurve and an incurve, a drop, and a rise" ("Gun Used in Baseball," *Chicago Tribune*, December 6, 1896, 29). A demonstration took place in a Princeton gymnasium on December 15, 1896: "The gun, which is a breech-loading cannon, 24 inches in length and placed upon a two-wheeled carriage, was put at one end of the gymnasium. At the other end was a net, at which the professor pitched several balls from his cannon. All were successful and the curves could be seen as distinctly as if sent from the hand of one of Princeton's 'varsity twirlers" (*Nevada State Journal* [Reno], December 26, 1896). Encouraged, the school's baseball club made plans to use it for winter practice (*Newark Daily Advocate*, December 16, 1896; Lee Allen, *The Hot Stove League*, 96).

Hinton gave a more extensive display of the machine at Princeton the following June 10 in front of a large crowd that included Mrs. Grover Cleveland. The machine pitched for both sides in an exhibition game between two Princeton social clubs, allowing four hits and one walk in three innings. This description was given of the machine's workings: "The gun is discharged by the batsman who, when ready for the ball to be delivered, steps upon an electrical intercepting plate which is connected by wires with the trigger of the cannon. The speed with which the ball is thrown is regulated by compressed air, and pronglike projectors from the cannon's mouth impart a rotary motion to the

sphere when it is discharged, producing a curve in any direction according as the position of the projecting prongs is changed" (reprinted in *Delphos* [Ohio] *Daily Herald*, June 11, 1897).

Hinton's machine had fixed the problem that had doomed Kennedy's: "During the first inning, the batsmen were timid about standing near the plate and the big curves caused them to jump back. But, as the big gun continued to throw strikes, they plucked up courage, stood closer to the plate, and succeeded occasionally in making safe hits." The machine did, however, have one serious drawback: "the long time required for reloading" between pitches (reprinted in *Hawaiian Gazette*, July 13, 1897). As a result, it was eventually concluded that the gun was "impractical for regular use" (*North Adams* [Mass.] *Transcript*, June 13, 1898).

Hinton moved on to the University of Minnesota, where he continued to work on the project. He unveiled a retooled version of the gun in Memphis on August 13, 1900. The exhibition impressed onlookers and Hinton was hopeful that his invention would "take the place of pitchers in the preliminary spring batting practice." But this goal was thwarted by the length of time it took to reload the machine, and Hinton died in 1904 without perfecting his gun (Dan Gutman, *Banana Bats and Ding-Dong Balls*, 45–46).

The goal of a pitching machine didn't die with Hinton, but nor did it make much progress in the years that followed. In 1903 the Senators tried practicing against a device invented by a fan named R. Howard Lake that was "capable of throwing the ball with regulated speed and accuracy" and of giving "a curve which will fool expert batsmen. . . . The gun which shoots the ball resembles in appearance a rapid-fire gun, and its propelling force is furnished by compressed air. The ball is placed in a cartridge-like affair, which slides into the breech of the machine. By pressing on the end of the cartridge the compressed air is released into the chamber, and the ball sent on its mission of fooling the batsman. The fast downshoot displayed was excellent, as were the in and outshoots" ("Pneumatic Pitcher Works Like a Charm," *Washington Times*, August 16, 1903, 4). According to another account, Lake's invention was "nothing less than a pneumatic gun that can shoot any kind of a curve at moderate speed. It looks somewhat like a telescope mounted on a frame and contains a tube thirty-six inches long, its diameter slightly longer than a baseball. The rear end is fitted with a breech cap, and by this means any desired curve may be produced at the will of the operator. It is a very ingenious machine and the inventor hopes to get the baseball men interested in it so that the clubs may adopt it for giving the batters practice and saving the pitchers" ("Baseball Inventions," *Boston Globe*, April 24, 1904, 24). George Cahill, pioneer of baseball lighting systems, was reported in 1908 to have invented a pitching machine that employed compressed air (David Pietrusza, "The Cahill Brothers' Night Baseball Experiments," *Baseball Research Journal* 23 [1994], 62–66). Yet no advances appear to have been made toward solving the critical problem of excessive reloading time.

The growing list of unsuccessful efforts caused sports columnist Eddie Wray to sniff in a 1910 column: "Every known gun has either recruited the hospital list or frightened out of the prospective slugger every vestige of desire to increase his batting efficiency. The pitching gun is a beautiful theory. It is also a dead one" (*St. Louis Post-Dispatch*, March 1, 1910). But then, only a few months later, Wray reported, "An Annapolis professor is said to have invented a pitching gun which will do all that [Ted] Kennedy claimed for his" (*St. Louis Post-Dispatch*, August 19, 1910).

In a 1938 issue, *Sporting News* had a photo of a new pitching gun being used in St. Louis. Unfortunately it had the same limitation that had long plagued such efforts: it was capable of throwing only four balls per minute (*Sporting News*, September 8, 1938).

The prototype of today's pitching machines, which utilize spinning wheels to propel the baseball, was patented in 1956 by a Detroit policeman named Eliot Wilson. The patent was then purchased by a man named John Paulson, who created Jugs, Inc., in the early 1970s to sell the device (Dan Gutman, *Banana Bats and Ding-Dong Balls*, 53).

14.4.12 Bullpens. Baseball's earliest "bullpens" were not places for pitchers to warm up but rather discount seating areas. A local paper reported in 1877, "The bull-pen at the Cincinnati Grounds, with its 'three-for-a-quarter' crowd, has lost its usefulness. The bleaching-boards just north of the north pavilion now hold the cheap crowd which comes in at the end of the first inning on a discount" (*Cincinnati Enquirer*, May 9, 1877). On April 4, 1879, the National League's Providence Grays introduced a "bull pen" in center field, which fans could enter after the fifth inning by pay-

ing a reduced fifteen-cent admission fee (James Charlton, ed., *The Baseball Chronology*, 38).

Bullpen was also the name of an early ball game. The *Oxford English Dictionary* notes that it appeared as early as 1857 and meant "A schoolboys' ball game, played by two groups, one group outlining the sides of a square enclosure, called the 'bull-pen,' within which are the opposing players."

The enclosure we now call a bullpen began much later because relief pitchers were highly uncommon in early baseball. The reasons that led to its emergence were described in 1890: "The attention of club officials has been called to the dangerous practice of pitchers exercising in front of the grand stand. Time and again has the ball passed into the stand and hit spectators, who are at the mercy of the ball, as they seldom see it until there is no time for avoiding it. Pitchers can practice just as well in front of the club house where their graceful movements can be admired without any dangerous results from wild pitching. It is to be hoped that the abominable practice will be stopped" (*New York Clipper*, May 3, 1890).

It was a couple more decades before relief pitchers became common enough to make permanent bullpens necessary. Their name primarily reflects the fact that the area was an enclosure, but it may also have been influenced by the Bull Durham signs that were prominent in ballparks from 1911 to 1913 (see **18.6.3**). Supporters of this theory note that the earliest known reference dates to 1913: "Ira Thomas is the skipper of the [Athletics'] pitchers. He corrects the faults of the youthful trajectory hurlers and takes them to the 'bullpen' in the afternoon and keeps them warmed up" (*Washington Post*, August 17, 1913).

14.4.13 Bullpen Phones. Bullpen phones seem to have made their way into baseball with a minimum of publicity. The earliest allusion to one that I could find was a 1930 reference to a bullpen phone at Yankee Stadium (*Sheboygan* [Wis.] *Press*, July 25, 1930).

Eddie Collins reported that Fred Lake devised a forerunner to the bullpen phone during his stint as Red Sox manager, which lasted from 1908 to 1909. According to Collins, "Lake devised a scheme whereby he could keep in touch with his warm-up battery out back by the clubhouse, and at the same time not leave the playing field. He rigged up an electric battery, with the bell in the clubhouse and a push button on the bench. One ring meant 'warm up,' two rings 'work hard,' and three rings 'come in to pitch.'" Unfortunately the electric battery failed one day, and struggling pitcher Frank Arellanes was forced to remain in the game and endure a drubbing (*Washington Post*, February 5, 1911).

14.4.14 Pennants and Bunting Flying. Capturing the pennant was not just a metaphor in early baseball—clubs vied for the right to fly pennants that were expensive and elaborate. As noted under "Trophies" (**22.3.1**), pennants were being awarded as early as 1858, though the one referred to in that entry does not appear to have been flown at a ballpark. James Terry noted that Brooklyn's Union Grounds were decorated with bunting and the whip pennant signifying the national championship when the Eckfords of Brooklyn defended the title against the Mutuals of New York in 1862 (*Brooklyn Eagle*, August 25, 1862; James L. Terry, *Long Before the Dodgers*, 38).

The entry fees in the first major league, the National Association, went to the purchase of a pennant. The tradition continued when the National League debuted in 1876. As an 1877 article explained, "The whip-pennant is a flag of the national colors, emblematic of the League championship. It costs $100, and is inscribed with the motto, 'Champion Baseball Club of the United States,' with the name of the club and the year in which the title was won. The champion club is entitled to fly the pennant until the close of the ensuing season" (*New York Sunday Mercury*, August 25, 1877). Providence won the 1879 pennant, and the *Providence Journal* reported as the start of the next campaign approached: "Workmen were engaged in erecting the staff from which the championship pennant is to wave this season, at Messer park, yesterday afternoon. It will be located in close proximity to the grand stand, on the eastly end, and towers 20 to 30 feet above the roof, being surmounted by a gilt ball and fitted with halliard attachments. The pennant has been manufactured by J. Harry Welch, of this city, and . . . is of burgee design, with white centre, red trimmings and 'Providence Champions, 1879,' in blue letters in the centre. Its dimensions are 28 × 12 feet, and it will be thrown to the breeze on Saturday, May 1, at 2 o'clock, an hour previous to the Providence-Boston game, which inaugurates the League season of 1880" (*Providence Journal*, reprinted in the *New York Sunday Mercury*, May 8, 1880). After a second

title in 1884, the Providence club flew a pennant made "of white silk with black letters and trimmings, and a beautiful piece of work it was of the whip variety and about 30 feet long" (William Perrin, *Days of Greatness*, 54).

Pennants in early baseball were intended to be flown only by clubs that had earned the right to do so. This custom had begun to change by the 1880s and, as with so many innovations, it was greeted with snide remarks. A reporter observed in 1888, "The Pittsburg public will have the satisfaction of seeing a new flag flying over their ball park this season. The management has decided to purchase one, as the team failed to win one" (*Williamsport Sunday Grit*, April 8, 1888).

14.4.15 Clubhouses. Clubhouses for home teams are nearly as old as baseball. The Olympics of Philadelphia, a pioneer town ball club, had a clubhouse; when it was built is unclear, but it was certainly one of the earliest. In 1865 the *Brooklyn Eagle* commented on improvements at the Capitoline Grounds: "The club rooms are completed, and right cosey little spots they are. There is abundant closet room, prettily grained, and the floors are covered with cocoa matting. The Enterprise room has a handsome curtain, containing all the 'working tools' of the game" (*Brooklyn Eagle*, July 6, 1865).

It was much longer before visiting clubs could expect such facilities. According to an 1884 article, "In the club house which the Alleghenys propose building will be two large dressing-rooms for the players—one for each nine. They will be fitted up in good style, and will contain a large closet for each of the men to keep his uniform in. In the center of these rooms a huge shower bath will be constructed, with vulcanite pavement, so that the players, as soon as they get through practice, can get a good shower bath and rub themselves down" (*Milwaukee Sentinel*, February 11, 1884). Nonetheless, well into the twentieth century visiting players dressed in their hotels, a practice that could subject them to harassment en route to the ballpark. On June 19, 1906, the National League passed a resolution that requested clubs to provide dressing rooms for visiting clubs, but for several years afterward most road teams continued to have to dress in their hotels. As the concrete-and-steel stadiums were built, it gradually became standard for them to have clubhouses for the visiting teams.

(v) Items Added for Spectators

14.5.1 Turnstiles. In early baseball the visiting club often received a predetermined "guarantee" instead of a portion of the gate receipts. The reason for this was simple: there was no way for the visitors to be certain of the attendance count, which led to arguments and hard feelings. The guarantee system eliminated the disputes but created an equally serious problem. The visiting club had no direct financial incentive to place a competitive club on the field, an issue that would plague the National Association.

Thus the introduction of turnstiles at the end of the National League's first season in 1876 was one of the new circuit's signature innovations. Henry Chadwick noted that one of the agreements reached at the league's annual meeting was that "each club should use a self-registering apparatus, connected with a turnstile to indicate exactly how many persons go into each ground for each game" (*New York Clipper*, December 23, 1876). This made it viable for the visiting club to receive a portion of the gate receipts and also helped ensure competitive balance.

The turnstiles also eliminated some newspaper puffery. After one of the first home games of the 1878 season, a Cincinnati paper remarked: "Before the days of turn-stiles the crowd would have gone down in newspaper history at about thirty-five hundred, but the turn-stiles counted sixteen hundred, and probably two hundred more came in through the carriage-gate" (*Cincinnati Enquirer*, May 2, 1878).

14.5.2 Luxury Boxes. The concept of luxury seating is as old as ballparks themselves, though its form has changed dramatically over the years. The biggest challenge for owners has been making such locations distinctive enough to make wealthy patrons feel coddled and set apart, without alienating the spectators who paid less to enter.

Efforts to do so date all the way back to Brooklyn's Union Grounds, which became the first enclosed stadium primarily used for baseball in 1862 (see **14.1.1**). The Union Grounds featured a structure for the select few that was actually located on the field of play in deep center field. Nine years later, proprietor William Cammeyer hit upon a new scheme by erecting "a platform in front of and above the dressing rooms of the Mutual Club to which persons who wish to be exclusive can obtain admission by the payment of an extra quarter" (*New York Clipper*, June 3, 1871).

As seating for the general public improved, it became harder to find convincing ways to offer premium accommodations. The *Washington Post* offered a glimpse of the future in 1884 by observing that "A number of clubs also have private boxes" (*Washington Post*, March 16, 1884). Philadelphia introduced "opera seats" in 1883, and some sort of higher-priced seating area was created that year in Chicago, but descriptions were vague and most box seating of this era appears to have entailed little more than placing railings around the regular seats (*National Police Gazette*, April 28, 1883; David Fleitz, *Cap Anson*, 108; *Chicago Inter-Ocean*, April 17, 1887).

One creative way in which clubs tried to make box seating a little more distinctive was by elevating the occupants above the action. In 1887 Detroit owner Frederick K. Stearns and his guests occupied a special director's box that was referred to as "the big sky box" (*Detroit Tribune*, September 29, 1887). On February 2, 1888, the Indianapolis entry in the National League introduced forty-two private boxes on the roof of its new grandstand, to be sold only to season subscribers (Jim Charlton, ed., *The Baseball Chronology*, 73). Some minor league clubs made similar efforts. A San Jose newspaper announced these plans for the local ballpark in 1891: "The grand stand will be two stories in height, and in the upper part of the structure will be located a number of private boxes, similar in construction to those at the Haight-street grounds in San Francisco. A sufficient number of these private apartments will be erected to supply the demand of all who desire the privacy afforded by this arrangement. Access to these boxes will be had from the rear of the grand stand and over the roof of that structure, which will be facing westward" (*San Jose Evening News*, February 17, 1891).

But the temporary nature of most nineteenth-century ballparks limited the ability of owners to offer premium seating to any of their customers. Accordingly, this was an idea that came to fruition only with the advent of the fireproof concrete-and-steel stadiums (see **14.1.2**).

In 1909 Phillies management brought a new sophistication to the marketing of luxury seating. The *Philadelphia Ledger* explained: "Base ball 'fans,' since base ball was born, have been accustomed to a grandstand accommodating an aristocracy of 'rooters.' To enter this precinct was the privilege of any one willing to part with twice the price of a perch on the bleachers, so that there was no hard feeling.

"But private boxes where there was real exclusiveness, where the 'guests' were on an invitation basis and outsiders had no redress, was a new idea to followers of the national game.

"The boxes were filled, evidently the new idea is a success, and the fact that the management rather made this outcome assured by modern methods of securing box-holders did not detract from the obvious enjoyment of the favored who sat in base ball's new 'third heaven.'

"There was just a suggestion of a subpoena, or a call on an office-holder for a campaign contribution, in the method of the management in filling the boxes. Polite—very polite—little notes were forwarded to 40-odd prominent men, known to be able to sign checks up to an [sic] including $350 without any danger of any haggling at the bank. The 'bids' read something like this:

"'Dear Sir: Inclosed please find a ticket for a private box at the Philadelphia Base Ball Park, in return for which please forward your check for $350.'

"While the sum of $350 was not asked for all the boxes, it is probable that the 44 choice box reservations yielded an average amount of $350 per box" (reprinted in *Sporting News*, April 29, 1909).

These aggressive marketing techniques appear to have been successful, as team president Horace Fogel said after the season, "Last season the box feature of the Phillies' grounds was so popular that it has been decided to enlarge upon it" (*Sporting News*, December 9, 1909).

That same year saw Forbes Field open in Pittsburgh with three hundred luxury boxes. To confer a sense of distinction, brass nameplates were affixed to each box (*Sporting Life*, May 29, 1909).

As with any successful idea, the "box feature" was widely borrowed and modified. John B. Sheridan recommended in 1922 that clubs offer: "very commodious boxes, lots of space, rocking or reclining chairs, chairs fit for ladies to sit in. . . . A certain number of these boxes de luxe might be held for rental by the day, week, series, etc. Of course, the rentals of these boxes de luxe must be much higher than that of the average box" (*Sporting News*, February 9, 1922). The Tigers stroked the egos of their "private box holders" in 1923 by publishing their names

in the *Detroit Free Press* (*Detroit Free Press*, April 22, 1923). Larry MacPhail upgraded the Yankees' marketing in 1946 by unveiling the concept of Stadium Club seating.

In the 1960s technological advances led to the birth of a new word for luxury seating. Dale Swearingen explained: "Comfort was indeed the word for these second generation stadia, and that word was spelled L-O-G-E. These modern contrivances accomplished two significant things: First, they helped foster a caste system with respect to spectators and second, they wreaked havoc with upper deck seating geometries. The caste system was created in essence when loges became a necessary evil for funding purposes. Loge goers demanded optimum viewing location, exclusive parking, segregation from other fans, and catered food service. Because optimum viewing was a priority, loges were often hung from beneath the upper deck in one, two, or even as many as three tiers. A simple corollary is that the greater the amount of private funding required for a stadium, the greater the number of loges and the greater the negative impact on the upper deck geometries" (introduction to Philip Lowry, *Green Cathedrals*, xiv–xv).

Perhaps the *ne plus ultra* of the trend to viewing seats as status symbols occurred in 1965 with the opening of the Astrodome. The new stadium featured dugouts 120 feet long, surpassing the size of any previous dugouts. Club owner Judge Roy Hofheinz remarked that the innovation was not made with the convenience of the players in mind. Rather, he explained that fans liked to say that their seats were behind the dugout, so the club was accommodating as many as possible! (Robert Lipsyte, "Johnson Attends Opening of Houston's Astrodome," *New York Times*, April 10, 1965).

Interestingly, a longtime feature of Cuban baseball stadiums bears similarities to the earliest form of luxury seating that appeared in Brooklyn in 1862. The structure is a shaded pavilion known as a glorieta, which Roberto Gonzalez Echevarria described as "a sort of large gazebo from which women and other spectators watched games protected from the sun and in which dances, dinners and literary soirees were held" (Roberto Gonzalez Echevarria, *The Pride of Havana*, 86). The glorieta is not merely a relic of the past. It has developed over the years so as to have kinships both with the earliest form of premium seating and with today's luxury box (Roberto Gonzalez Echevarria, *The Pride of Havana*, 86, 95–96).

14.5.3 Press Boxes. Since the people who write accounts of baseball games inhabit the press box, this locale has always received a considerable amount of newspaper coverage. Just as with spectators' seating, status has often been an underlying concern.

Henry Chadwick noted in 1867 that the Union Grounds in Brooklyn had "a special department erected for the legitimate members of the press whose duty it is to report the contests which take place. In view of the fact, however, that nearly every daily paper sends a competent short-hand reporter, the seats are not quite numerous enough." Later that year he reported that the Capitoline and Irvington grounds had similar accommodations (*The Ball Player's Chronicle*, June 13 and August 8, 1867).

But being close to the action proved to be a mixed blessing. In a game at the Irvington grounds, a fight among the spectators spilled over into the press area and the reporters were toppled (*The Ball Player's Chronicle*, August 8, 1867). Henry Chadwick reported that during an 1867 game against the Mutuals, Athletics pitcher Dick McBride "exercised himself in the foul ball line for twenty minutes, the scorers' stand apparently being his objective point. By one shot he demoralized friend [William] Meeser, who sat next to us, and by another nearly knocked [David] McAuslan out of time, Gill, of the *Clipper*, changing his base during the flying of the shells from McBride's battery. After having considerable fun to himself, Dick hit a hot fair grounder to third" (*The Ball Player's Chronicle*, August 22, 1867).

Nor was this the last time that reporters had reason to suspect that balls were being deliberately directed at their sanctuary. The issue resurfaced when Athletic Park, home of the Washington entry in the American Association, opened in 1884. The reporters' stand was so close to the field that "general interest is about evenly divided between the game and luckless reporters. [Catcher John] Humphries seems to take a fiendish delight in allowing balls to go by him" (*Washington Post*, April 13, 1884).

Reporters understandably began to agitate for seating assignments that offered more protection while still allowing them a good view of the action. Henry Chadwick reported approvingly in 1870 that the Olympic Club of Washington had established new grounds that included "a fine pagoda over the back stop, secluded from the crowd, for the scorers and reporters of the press" (*New York Clipper*, February 19, 1870). The issue was addressed at the Philadelphia grounds by building in 1871 "a reporters' stand . . . sufficiently elevated to be out of the reach of strong foul balls that may chance their way" (quoted in Michael Gershman, *Diamonds*, 19). Others followed suit.

The general establishment of separate areas for the press was not without controversy. For one thing, reporters often had vastly different ideas of suitable accommodations. At Detroit's grand baseball tournament of 1867 they were housed in a huge box constructed around the trunk of a large elm. A Chicago reporter grumbled that "the most splendid arrangements are made for everybody except the reporters of the press" (*Chicago Tribune*, August 16, 1867). A scribe from Rochester, New York, however, went out of his way to praise the special arrangements provided for the press, which he said gave them a splendid view of the whole field (*Rochester Evening Express*, August 21, 1867; quoted in Priscilla Astifan, "Baseball in the Nineteenth Century Part Two," *Rochester History* LXII, No. 2 [Spring 2000], 18).

Another common complaint was voiced by a London (Ontario) reporter in 1877: "so long as the Directors of the Club allow the Press Stand to be used as a 'free and easy' resort, to the annoyance and discomfort of the Press representatives, the latter cannot be expected to do the work assigned them. (This is hint no. 1.)" (*London Free Press*, May 10, 1877). It would be far from the last such hint.

And the stakes were high. As the start of the 1877 season approached, the *Indianapolis Sentinel* gave bountiful coverage to the local club. But then its April 8 issue carried these angry comments: "After all the free advertising the papers have given the base ball club, the reporters are being very scurvily treated by the managers of the park. There is scarcely any accommodation provided for representatives of the press to take reports of the game, and what few there are, are monopolized by the official scorer of the club and his cronies" (*Indianapolis Sentinel*, April 8, 1877). The *Sentinel's* reports on the team diminished rapidly after that, and four weeks later it referred to baseball as the "National Nuisance" (*Indianapolis Sentinel*, May 6, 1877).

By the 1880s, requests for enclosed facilities were becoming common. At some ballparks they were accommodated, though it is often difficult to determine whether a "box" was a genuine enclosure or merely a roped-off area. An account of 1885 renovations to Philadelphia's Recreation Park mentioned that "the reporter's pavilion has been boxed in" (*Sporting Life*, July 15, 1885). Additional amenities were beginning to appear, with Chicago reporters being promised "proscenium boxes, with cushioned chairs and velvet carpets" in 1883 (*National Police Gazette*, April 28, 1883). Other requests were for more practical items, such as "a wider table made on the scorer's stand . . . for those who use books to score" (*Harrisburg Patriot*, May 14, 1890).

Unfortunately, as the facilities for reporters became more appealing, the problem of outsiders trying to take the seats increased. The *Washington Post* noted in 1884 that reporters' names now appeared on the desk in front of their chairs (*Washington Post*, April 6, 1884). Such hints seem to have done little to reduce the problem. A Boston reporter complained in 1886, "The press enclosure at the Boston grounds is made for the use of the directors of the club, the members of the press and such others as the directors and reporters invite to occupy seats there. Many people do not seem to understand this fact, and crowd into the enclosure, to the great discomfort of those for whose special convenience it is set apart" (*Boston Globe*, May 31, 1886).

This problem was naturally most prevalent whenever the enclosure was most needed, such as on rainy days or when a big crowd was on hand. It was especially conspicuous at postseason matches, where both issues often arose. The 1897 Temple Cup prompted bitter complaints about the inadequate facilities for the press at Boston's South End Grounds. The Boston club sold to the public all the seats in the "miserable unscreened press stand," which "offers opportunities to practice lively dodging of foul tips and wild pitches." Sportswriters had to pay for admission and were consigned to "the slanting roof of the stand, accompanied by the telegraph operators, where they perched among the rafters and trusted a kindly Providence to keep the wires clear" (reprinted in Ernest J. Lanigan, *The Baseball Cyclopedia*, 103).

A continued lack of adequate facilities for reporters led to the foundation of the Baseball Writers Association of America in 1908, whose first major demand was permanent press boxes at all ballparks (see **23.1.4**).

14.5.4 Covered Seating. Early baseball matches were sometimes played in structures such as racetracks that already had covered seating. It was not long after the emergence of ballparks designed for baseball that similar ac-

commodations began to be added. In 1864 the Capitoline Grounds in Brooklyn erected "covered seats for lady spectators" (*Brooklyn Eagle*, June 1, 1864).

14.5.5 Reserved Seats (with exact seating specified). The Cincinnati grounds were remodeled in 1880 with the result that "Every seat in the grand stand is numbered and provided with backs that reach to a man's shoulder, making them most comfortable" (*New York Sunday Mercury*, March 6, 1880). The next few years saw a number of experiments with reserved seating. When Detroit got its first major league team in 1881, it was decided that "Every holder of a season ticket [to Recreation Park] will have an opportunity to draw for a choice of seats, and that seat will be reserved for them throughout the season. No other seats will be reserved, but will be open to whoever wishes to pay fifteen cents therefor. When a seat is reserved its number and section will be placed upon the season ticket, so that no mistakes can occur" (*Detroit Free Press*, April 23, 1881).

Such innovations were generally part of an effort to attract upscale spectators. For example, in 1883 Chicago's grandstand was improved so that it was "no longer a mere rude succession of benches, but is laid off into some 2,000 numbered and separated spaces, so that the buyer of a reserved seat actually receives an armed seat and not a chance on a bench" (*Chicago Times*, April 22, 1883). The following year St. Louis's Union Association club added the new feature of folding opera chairs (see **14.5.8**), "each of which is to be numbered so that the patrons of the park can engage their seat before the game, and have just the same assurance of getting a good seat, even if they come late, that they have at the theatre" (*St. Louis Republic*, March 23, 1884).

But the feature proved less popular with punctual spectators. The *New York Sun* reported in 1886 that "The reserved-seat plan at the Polo Grounds has been done away with, and hereafter the early comers will get the best seats" (*New York Sun*, September 5, 1886).

14.5.6 Cheap Seats. Cincinnati sportswriter O. P. Caylor observed in 1877, "The bull-pen at the Cincinnati Grounds, with its 'three-for-a-quarter' crowd, has lost its usefulness. The bleaching-boards just north of the north pavilion now hold the cheap crowd which comes in at the end of the first inning on a discount" (*Cincinnati Enquirer*, May 7, 1877).

14.5.7 Standing Room Accommodations. Standing room tickets were being sold by at least 1886, when the *Detroit Free Press* reported: "After the seats have been all sold a sign 'standing room only,' will be put up" (*Detroit Free Press*, August 17, 1886).

14.5.8 Folding Chairs. In 1884 "folding opera chairs [were] placed in the grand stands of several clubs" (*Washington Post*, March 16, 1884). The experiment obviously was successful as Brooklyn owner Charles Byrne announced before the 1887 season, "Both the old and new grand stands will be fitted up with the Andrews folding chair, which will be found to be a great improvement over the chairs formerly in use, being much more comfortable and convenient and doing entirely away with the dragging of chairs over the floor" (*Brooklyn Eagle*, March 23, 1887).

14.5.9 Seat Cushions. Lee Allen reported in a 1968 column, "Cushions were first rented by grandstand customers at the park in Cincinnati on June 25, 1879" (*Sporting News*, April 20, 1968; reprinted in *Cooperstown Corner*).

14.5.10 Dugout-level Seating. Dodger Stadium has the most famous example of dugout-level seating for fans. Bob Timmermann points out that a press release on the Dodgers website states that the seats came about because "The dugout boxes, which afforded a ground-level view of the game, was an idea that [owner Walter] O'Malley borrowed from Japanese ballparks he saw during the Dodgers' goodwill tour of the country following the 1956 season."

But neither the Dodgers nor the Japanese can claim preeminence. In 1903 *Sporting Life* recorded, "The boxes at the Jersey City grounds are under the grand stands, and the occupants sit below the field level, the ground coming up to their waist, an innovation which makes the play seem prettier" (*Sporting Life*, June 20, 1903).

14.5.11 Upper Deck. *Sporting Life* described improvements to Philadelphia's Recreation Park in its July 15, 1885, issue, one of which was that "immediately adjoining the grand stand double-deck pavilions have been built."

14.5.12 Music. Music was played at early ballparks from time to time, but as part of a special event. For example, in an 1867 match between clubs from Wauseon, Ohio, and Morenci,

Michigan, both towns brought brass bands along to entertain the onlookers (*Adrian Daily Times and Expositor*, August 26, 1867). Around the same time, a composition known as the "Silver Ball March" was played at matches in New England for the silver ball that symbolized regional supremacy (Troy Soos, *Before the Curse*, 23). The city of Philadelphia was represented in the National Association by two franchises from 1873 to 1875, and games between the rivals were accompanied by a brass band from each club (Tim Murnane, *Boston Globe*, January 31, 1915). The Cincinnati Orchestra was "specially engaged" to perform during one 1875 game (*Cincinnati Enquirer*, September 9, 1875). When the Federal League debuted in 1914, Chicago Whales owner Charles Weeghman hired no fewer than ten brass bands for the April 23 opening of the ballpark now known as Wrigley Field (Stuart Shea, *Wrigley Field*, 47).

The popularity of such events caused some to propose that they become regular occurrences. Longtime Chicago president James A. Hart favored "adding music to the games as a regular feature. His idea never proved popular with his associates, and was not adopted. When music does become a regular thing at ball parks it will be another instance in which Mr. Hart proved himself several years ahead of the game" (*Washington Post*, August 3, 1913). St. Louis Cardinals' owner Helene Britton was another believer in music at the ballpark. She turned the team's home field into a "baseball cabaret" by hiring bands and a singer whose daily routine included "parad[ing] in front of the bleachers, singing at the top of his voice into a large megaphone" (Bill Borst, "The Matron Magnate," *Baseball Research Journal* 1977, 28).

But the cost of hiring that many people limited such performances to special occasions. The situation didn't change until public address systems made it possible to amplify music. On April 26, 1941, the Chicago Cubs unveiled an organist named Roy Nelson, who entertained the crowd with "a varied program of classic and soulful compositions" (*Sporting News*, May 1, 1941). Other clubs soon chimed in.

14.5.13 Public Address Systems. As noted in "Ball and Strike Signals" (**8.5.2**), umpires were expected to address crowds during the nineteenth century. Increasing crowd sizes made this impractical, and megaphones began to be used around the turn of the century. The Giants introduced the first electronic public address system on August 25, 1929: "One of the most

interesting features at the Polo Grounds yesterday was the operation of the Giants' newly
installed amplifying set, which not only broadcasts the batteries and substitution of players
but which enables the umpire to call out each
ball and strike so all may hear. This he does by
standing on two plates behind the catcher and
talking into a microphone attached inside his
mask. To [umpire] Charlie Rigler fell the lot
of introducing the innovation to the fans and
even the players had to admit that Charlie had
an excellent voice, though as usual they did
not always agree with his decisions" (*New York
Times*, August 26, 1929). Baseball historian Dan
Krueckeberg offered this description: "[Rigler]
donned a mask equipped with a microphone
connected by wires to metal soles fastened to
his shoes. Behind the batter's box a copper plate
was installed from which a network of hidden
wires led to an amplifier, or what one New York
paper called 'an umplifier.' The moment Cy
stepped on the copper plate his voice could be
heard in all parts of the park. Cy announced the
batteries before the game as well as the strikes,
fouls, and balls which he called throughout the
game" (Dan Krueckeberg, "Take-Charge Cy,"
National Pastime, Spring 1985, 10).

Public address systems, however, do not
appear to have become commonplace until the
1940s. The practice of announcing the lineups
before games may have originated at Yankee
Stadium on Opening Day of the 1943 season,
when the *New York Times* recorded: "Introducing a custom, the entire batting order of the
teams was announced before the game" (James
P. Dawson, *New York Times*, April 23, 1943).

14.5.14   Scoreboards. The limited size of
early baseball crowds ensured that the scoreboard was also a gradual development. Early
spectators could sit close enough to the scorer's
table that there was no need for an enlarged
tote board. As crowd sizes grew, the need for a
board that was distinct from the scorer's table
slowly became evident. For instance, at a game
in Columbus, Ohio, in 1875, mention was made
of the "bulletin-board near the scorers' table"
(*New York Clipper*, July 17, 1875). In Hornellsville, New York, word came in 1878 that "A
black board sixteen feet long and six feet high is
being made, and will be placed against the right
field fence, and the result of each inning will be
placed thereon so that spectators may know the
score through the game" (*Hornellsville Tribune*,
May 14, 1878).

The result was that the evolution of scoreboards into more elaborate affairs occurred not
at ballparks but outside of newspaper offices.
The practice seems to have originated out of
necessity. As historian George B. Kirsch noted,
by the late 1860s, large crowds often "hovered
around the doors" of newspaper and telegraph
offices awaiting the results of baseball matches
(George B. Kirsch, *The Creation of American
Team Sports*, 203–204).

The throngs became such a nuisance that
action was necessary. E. H. Tobias's chronicle
of the history of baseball in St. Louis recorded
that the 1875 season saw the emergence of the
prototype of the sports bar: "Massey's billiard
hall, corner of Fourth and Olive streets . . .
became the gratifying point for base ball news,
arrangements having been made with the Western Union Telegraph Co. for a report of each
half inning, which, on receipt, was displayed on
a black board, thereby rendering the place the
most popular resort in the city. It was a new departure that took from the start and every one
asked: 'Why hadn't it been done before?' Soon
afterward the newspaper offices adopted the
same method to the great delight of all classes,
ages and sex" (E. H. Tobias, *Sporting News*,
February 8, 1896). An important game that
season was followed eagerly throughout the
city: "All the newspaper offices and a number
of prominent saloons exposed bulletins, upon
which was represented the result of each inning
as telegraphed from the baseball park" (*New
York Clipper*, May 22, 1875).

Other St. Louis establishments joined the
fray. In 1884 a local paper remarked: "With
commendable enterprise, Frank H. Ellis, 406
and 408 Locust st., has had a telephone wire
erected between his elegant saloon and Union
Sportsman Park, over which, during the season, every inning will be reported. He will also
be able to furnish particulars of the game, how
the boys are doing, and can furnish his callers
with as much information as if they were on the
grounds. He will also post the games as played
in other cities by innings. The place promises
to be the most popular resort of all lovers of
the National game" (*St. Louis Sunday Sayings*,
May 25, 1884).

Bulletin boards in saloons and in front of
newspaper offices soon became a popular feature in many other towns. The boards attracted
enormous crowds and prompted business for
the saloons and for Western Union while not
interfering with the business of the newspaper

and telegraph offices (Gerard S. Petrone, *When Baseball Was Young*, 59). They also created new enthusiasts for the game of baseball while deepening the allegiance of existing fans—and yet, as we shall see in the entry on "Telegraphs" (see **16.3.2**), not everyone saw it that way.

14.5.15   Out-of-town Scoreboards. In 1880 "improvements" were "made at White Stocking Park during the absence of the Chicago team. A large bulletin-board has been erected upon which will be painted in large figures, legible to all the spectators, giving [sic] the results of innings both here and in the League games played elsewhere" (*Chicago Tribune*, June 20, 1880). The feature caught on, with "Telegraphs" (**16.3.2**) being used to provide up-to-date and accurate results. A Harrisburg paper bragged in 1890, "A telegraph office will be erected and the score by innings will be received and marked as the game progresses on a large score board on the field, from all the national and players' and American association games. A telephone office will connect with the dispatcher's office in the Pennsylvania railroad yard and by this means railroaders will be called and their names marked on a large board near the office to which they will have access. The same telephone will be used by the newspaper offices to bulletin the score by innings" (*Harrisburg Patriot*, April 21, 1890). By 1894 telephones had been installed at the Cincinnati ballpark to keep the board up to date (*Sporting Life*, April 14, 1894).

14.5.16   Electronic Scoreboards. As is common with technological innovations, the electronic scoreboard emerged in fits and starts as America lurched into the electronic age. Nevertheless many of the key elements of today's multi-media extravaganzas were in place earlier than might be expected.

The *New York Sun* reported in 1888: "A new feature was introduced on the Boston grounds on Friday in the shape of a base ball register. A board partition was erected on the centre field fence, a little to one side of the flag pole. By means of electric wires which run from the board along the fence to a position in the pavilion an operator sitting in the latter, by touching a knob registered on the board the decisions of the umpire as to balls and strikes, giving the number of each, and also whether a batter or runner was out, or when the ball hit was a foul. This will prove an advantage to those people who in case of unusual noise can-

not hear the umpire's decision" (*New York Sun*, May 27, 1888).

Sportswriter Ren Mulford, Jr., added this description two years later: "A yellow signboard at the end of the right foul line stares one in the face. The inscription 'Base-ball Register' is seen at the top, and below are four black openings—well, to be expressive, about as large as 'one-eighth.' There are the words 'Strike,' 'Ball,' and 'Out' over the first three spaces—the last is blank, but if the umpire announces a tip behind the bat, 'Foul' mysteriously tumbles into place with magic rapidity. The echo of the umpire's voice in calling balls and strikes scarce reverberates from far in the distance before you see the figures roll into the spaces marked off. The idea is truly Bostonian, and the registering is done by electricity by a young man who touches a series of buttons in the grand stand" (*Chicago Inter-Ocean*, September 4, 1890).

An electrically operated scoreboard was introduced at the grounds of the St. Louis American League franchise in 1902: "The St. Louis grounds are adorned by a score board that will be of considerable value when the electronic apparatus that goes with it is put in working order. There is a place on the board on which is posted the number of the inning, as well as the half, and there is also one usual arrangement for display of score by inning, all of this being attended to in the ordinary manner. The new features are three large dials, one to indicate the number of men that are out, another the number of strikes on a batsman, and a third the number of called balls on the batsman. The figures for these three dials are to be controlled by the club's official scorer, sitting in the press box, keys connected with electrical apparatus being under his hand. The board will be of especial value when there are big crowds, many of the spectators being so far from the umpire that they cannot well hear what he says. The apparatus is already in place, but is waiting a stronger battery than the first one provided" (*Detroit Free Press*, May 1, 1902).

Before the 1907 season, American League President Ban Johnson was quoted as saying: "I shall endeavor for the benefit of the fans to have the club owners adopt the electrical score board. It is an excellent device in that it will make the work of the umpires easier. I am sure it will be appreciated by the public, especially on the days when the crowds are large" (*Detroit Times*, February 25, 1907).

A product called the Rodier Electric Baseball Game Reproducer was introduced in 1909.

Because it was frequently referred to as the electric scoreboard, it is often described as baseball's first electronic scoreboard. But, as is discussed in the entry for "Broadcasts of Baseball" (see **16.3.3**), it was designed for use outside of ballparks.

14.5.17   Messages on Scoreboards. The *New York Times* informed Yankee fans before the 1959 season that an "electronic marvel" would be ready to greet them on Opening Day. The article explained that the club's new scoreboard would include a "changeable message area of seven lines, eight letters to the line, at the bottom of the center tower. Here unusual plays, rulings and pertinent information can be flashed on a moment's notice" (*New York Times*, February 12, 1959). Two months later the *Times*'s coverage of Opening Day included a photo of the "miracle board" bearing the words "THIS IS TURLEYS FIRST OPENING GAME START AS A YANKEE" (*New York Times*, April 13, 1959). It obviously took more than a miracle to produce an apostrophe.

14.5.18   Exploding Scoreboards. The exploding scoreboard was introduced in 1960 by master showman Bill Veeck, who spent $800,000 to be able to generate high-tech pyrotechnics after every White Sox home run. The scoreboard had its first opportunity to explode on May 1, 1960, following an Al Smith homer: "As the ball landed in the 415-foot center field bull pen, the board lighted up like a giant pinball machine and rocket type aerial bombs shot skyward from ten launching towers across the top of the board" (UPI: *Holland* [Mich.] *Evening Sentinel*, May 2, 1960).

Fans loved the scoreboard, but not everyone felt that way. During a May 22 game the scoreboard went haywire and stayed on for a full minute after a Minnie Minoso home run, prompting reporters to dub it "Veeck's Folly." A week later Cleveland Indians outfielder Jimmy Piersall fired a baseball at the scoreboard and called it "baseball's biggest joke."

14.5.19   Computer-generated Scoreboards. Charley Finley's "Fun Board," installed in Oakland in 1969, provided fans with a variety of messages, cartoons, and automatically computed statistics. Its manufacturer claimed that the Fun Board was the first computer-controlled scoreboard used in any sports stadium (UPI: [Reno] *Nevada State Journal*, April 2, 1969). Sportswriter Ron Bergman explained,

"The Astrodome scoreboards in Houston, for instance, operate by projecting films behind them onto photo-electric cells. The Finley Fun Board, however, is totally activated by pressing a button on the computer operated from a booth at press box level" (Ron Bergman, "Computer Calls Shots for Finley Fun Board," *Sporting News*, May 24, 1969).

14.5.20   Replays on Scoreboards. In 1976 the Yankees and Red Sox became the first clubs to have instant replay on their scoreboards. Things went smoothly until a game at Yankee Stadium on August 8, 1976, when a controversial call went against the home side. After the game the Yankees were fined $1,000 by the American League for using the replay board to "produce fan reaction against the umpires." League president Lee MacPhail alleged that the Yankees had shown a replay of the play, then put the names of the umpires on the board, and that a fan had responded to this provocation by throwing a bottle at one of the umpires.

The Yankees' version was rather different. They maintained that the bottle had been thrown before the replay was shown and that the umpire's names had appeared a full inning afterward. A spokesman for George Steinbrenner was defiant: "The board cost us $3 million and we see no reason, with this great innovation, why fans at the ball game should see any less than the fans at home" (*New York Times*, August 11, 1976). The umpires responded by requesting a unilateral ban on scoreboard replays (*Sporting News*, August 28, 1976). They didn't entirely get their way but were assured that close plays would not be shown.

14.5.21   Color Replays on Scoreboards. Color replays were first seen at a major league game at the 1980 All-Star Game in Los Angeles when the new Diamond Vision scoreboard was unveiled.

14.5.22   Parking Facilities. The first baseball fans to fork out extra for parking were the patrons who paid an additional twenty cents to bring their carriages into Brooklyn's Capitoline Grounds in 1864 (James L. Terry, *Long Before the Dodgers*, 45). Other ballparks followed suit; the entry on "Season Tickets" (see **15.1.1**) mentions that the Forest Citys of Cleveland offered a season ticket plan in 1871 that included carriages. A ballpark built in Evansville, Indiana, in 1877 was fifty feet wider and one hundred feet longer than strictly necessary "in order to accommodate those who will attend in carriages, and who would prefer occupying them to taking seats in the amphitheatre" (*Evansville Journal*, April 30, 1877). But it seems safe to assume that spectators at these parks didn't encounter the traffic jams that became common in the twentieth century.

The automobile revolution soon gave rise to parking issues. The new bleachers installed at Boston's Huntington Avenue Baseball Grounds in 1904 were designed to accommodate "automobiles and pleasure carriages" (Jacob Morse, *Sporting Life*, May 21, 1904). When Philadelphia's Shibe Park opened in 1909 it featured "a two-hundred-car public garage equipped with a complete service department" as well as an auxiliary garage for the vehicles of management and ballplayers (Bruce Kuklick, *To Every Thing a Season*, 28). The crosstown Phillies took notice and revamped their own stadium at season's end: "The main reason for the rebuilding of the left field bleachers is to make room beneath for a garage. The Fifteenth Street side of the grounds on the outside has always been crowded and many persons have been kept away from games in the past because they did not care to risk their machines in the street. Under the new plans every machine can be taken care of and will be safe in the garage" (*Sporting News*, December 9, 1909).

Once automobiles became affordable for middle-class Americans, parking became an enormous part of the ballpark experience. Sportswriter John B. Sheridan observed in 1922 that, "The man who drives his car to the baseball park takes on a free-for-all fight" for the few parking spots on the street (*Sporting News*, February 9, 1922).

14.5.23 Drive-in Ballparks. Horseless carriages were allowed to flank the outfield fences at many early ballparks. According to Al Reach, it was a common sight for baseball diamonds to be "two-thirds surrounded by carriages and wagons" (*Sporting Life*, March 13, 1909). In a legendary eighteen-inning 1882 National League game, a potential game-ending home

run was averted when Detroit outfielder Lon Knight retrieved the ball from between the spokes of a carriage and relayed it home to nab Providence batter George Wright at home plate.

Researcher David McDonald reported that between 1912 and 1915 the Ottawa Senators of the Canadian League allowed motorists to drive their cars into Lansdowne Park. Their vehicles were parked down the outfield lines and were supposed to be at least forty feet from fair territory, but the rule was rarely enforced. There were sometimes enough cars to necessitate special ground rules, such as a game on Queen Victoria's Day in 1913 that drew fifty-two cars—about 10 percent of the number of automobiles in the entire city (David McDonald, "The Senators' Diamond Dynasty," *Ottawa Citizen*, March 25, 2003).

The Albuquerque Sports Stadium, which opened in 1969, featured a bluff behind the outfield wall where fans could park and watch the game. Dukes general manager Jim Blaney said that fans who parked in the section "bring campers, school buses, anything. Whenever something happens, they honk horns instead of clapping" (quoted in David Pietrusza, *Minor Miracles*, 69). The Dukes left town after the 2000 season; by the time baseball returned to the stadium in 2003, the drive-in area had been eliminated.

14.5.24 Amusement Rides. After the 1885 season the Metropolitans were sold to the owner of a Staten Island amusement park, and for the next two seasons the ball club was used as little more than another attraction. On May 23, 1897, Brown Stockings owner Chris Von der Ahe opened a "shoot the chutes" waterslide at St. Louis's Sportsman's Park to try to attract—or distract—customers who were not interested in watching his last-place team.

14.5.25 Day Care. In 1903, the Columbus entry in the American Association announced plans to add a nursery (*Sporting Life*, April 18, 1903).

Chapter 15

FANS

THERE IS a very long tradition of fans who take the game too seriously. As early as 1872 a Cleveland newspaper bemoaned, "It pains us to announce the fact that another promising young man, the pride and joy of his parents, has succumbed to that fell destroyer—base ball. Ever since the spring weather opened he has been troubled with the premonitory symptoms of the disease, and a boot poultice applied daily by his father produced no effect save to develop the complaint, while of late he has been comparatively useless to his employers, and spent his time in reading ten cent works on the 'National Game,' and hanging around the boarding places of the members of the Forest City club" (*Cleveland Leader*, May 3, 1872). Four years later a concerned father wrote to the *Rochester (N.Y.) Evening Express* to complain that his son's "foolish infatuation" with baseball was being fed by the paper's lengthy accounts, with the result that he was "scarcely fit for anything else" (*Rochester Evening Express*, May 26, 1876; quoted in Priscilla Astifan, "Rochester's Last Two Seasons of Amateur Baseball," *Rochester History* LXIII, No. 2 [Spring 2001], 8).

In the 1880s two terms emerged to describe devoted baseball followers, neither of which initially had positive connotations. The word "crank" was popularized at the 1881 trial of Charles Guiteau, the assassin of President James Garfield, where it was used to describe a person who becomes deranged by an obsession.

The term "fan" emerged at about the same time and was no more flattering. While usually claimed to be a shortened version of "fanatic," there is strong evidence that it may in fact derive from a perceived similarity to the type of fan that blows wind but produces no substance. This likeness was so striking to one reporter that he observed in 1889: "The 'fan' has a mouth and a tongue. In fact that is about all there is to him. The other members are so small that they are lost in the shuffle. The 'fan' uses his mouth and tongue whenever there is no occasion to use them. People would rather not listen to him but he is irrepressible and will talk whether one likes it or not. . . . The 'fan' always jumps at conclusions; he never stops to investigate. If he was to do a little investigation he would not be a 'fan'" (*Sporting News*, November 2, 1889).

Although it was easy—then as now—to poke fun at the obsessive nature of baseball aficionados, their allegiance was the foundation of the game's development into a profitable and successful enterprise.

(i) Getting Them in the Door

15.1.1 Season Tickets. The sale of season tickets began as soon as clubs started to schedule an extensive number of games. In 1870 the White Stockings had "150 honorary members, who pay ten dollars a year each and get a season ticket" (*Titusville* [Pa.] *Morning Herald*, November 18, 1870). The *Dickson Baseball Dictionary* cited an 1870 example of the term. The following season the Forest Citys of Cleveland announced these plans: "Season tickets are provided in two classes. The first is sold for $10 and admits the possessor with a lady and carriage to all games played this season. . . . The other class of season tickets will be sold for $6 each, and admit the bearer alone to all games played this season" (*Cleveland Leader*, May 9, 1871).

15.1.2   Knothole Gangs. The first organized Knothole Gang was established in St. Louis in 1917 by businessman W. E. Bilheimer. As Lee Lowenfish explains, it was no coincidence that that year also saw the switch of the team to community ownership (Lee Lowenfish, *Branch Rickey*, 89–90). The idea of the Knothole Gang was used to create civic pride and to help sell stock in the team, with each fifty-dollar purchase of stock entitling the investor to one kid's ticket in that special section (Frederick G. Lieb, *The St. Louis Cardinals*, 61). According to Branch Rickey, the section was filled with as many as ten thousand boys and five thousand girls for a single game (Branch Rickey, *Branch Rickey's Little Blue Book*, 75).

The idea was based upon a much older tradition. As early as 1868 spectators were staking out "the prominent 'peek-holes' in the fence" (*New York Clipper*, September 12, 1868; quoted in George B. Kirsch, *The Creation of American Team Sports*, 195).

It was usually children who peered through the knotholes. A reporter observed in 1869: "The gamins in possession of knot holes in the fence and of precarious positions on top of the fence were as numerous as on any previous occasion" (*New York Herald*, June 18, 1869). In 1886 the *New York Times* wrote of a huge crowd: "the hundreds of knotholes in the fence that surround the large grounds were plugged up by youthful eyes whose owners' pockets could not stand the strain that would necessarily have been imposed upon them had they passed through the gates" (*New York Times*, June 1, 1886). Some ballparks were even designed with the hope of eliminating such spectators. When Chicago opened a new ballpark in 1878, it was reported, "The fence around the ground will be of planed and matched boards and painted. It will no doubt have to be hued to prevent the small boy from cutting a peep-hole, as he would be sure to do if left to his own wicked devices" (*Chicago Tribune*, March 24, 1878, 7). In 1890 the directors of the New Haven club concluded that "it does not pay to have all the knots driven out of the fence to give the boys a chance to see games, and they have decided to issue tickets to boys under 12 years for 15 cents" (*Boston Globe*, March 9, 1890).

The experience of watching a ball game through a knothole became such a familiar part of boyhood that is was memorialized in a poem that began: "We could see the pitcher very well,/ But not the man at bat,/ Through the hole we found in the left-field fence,/ But we never minded that./ A part we saw, and a part we heard,/ And as regards the rest,/ We used the imagination heaven/ Has given the boys and guessed" (*Detroit Tribune*, reprinted in the *Chicago Inter-Ocean*, February 14, 1897).

Owners could hardly blame such youngsters for trying to watch the games, but adults were another matter. An 1883 account reported: "Large as the audience has been at many of the games at League Park, a much larger audience has regularly witnessed the contests from positions outside the enclosure. It appears that knives and even hatchets have been mercilessly used in the cracks of the pine fence, and hundreds of peep holes have been made by grown men oftener than by boys, persons who believe a day is well spent in standing without the fence and 'getting a quarters worth the best of them base ball fellows'" (*Fort Wayne Daily News*, June 2, 1883). In 1886 Harry Wright said, "The Chicago grounds come nearer to my idea of a base ball inclosure than any other in this country. Surrounded by a high brick wall, which does not mar and disfigure adjoining property like the unsightly board fences, it gives the game a privacy which cannot be had where mobs and crowds hang around for a peep through the knotholes and cracks" (*Brooklyn Eagle*, February 7, 1886).

Additional precautions continued to be taken, and the issue took on some of the characteristics of the ongoing battle over "Spite Fences" (see **16.2.3**). A 1903 article reported that the Pirates were adding "a new right field fence which, on account of its peculiar construction, will be expensive. The fence will be a double one, and will be nearly three feet thick. The old joke about watching the game through a knothole will have to go out of commission next summer, for if the small boy knocks a hole through the outside lining, all he will see will be the braces which hold the inside boards in place. The fence is similar to the one used in the Chicago National league park" (*Pittsburg[h] Post*, March 22, 1903).

15.1.3   Rain Checks. The origins of the rain check have been complicated by confusion over a couple of issues. The first is the distinction between the concept of a rain check and the means of distributing them. The second is that, as with Ladies' Day (see **16.1.7**), the concept was experimented with many times before owners accepted that it made good business sense. As a result, while it is often reported that rain checks were first used in baseball in the late 1880s, they are actually much older than that.

In fact the National League faced controversy over the subject from its founding in 1876. The home opener in St. Louis was rained out, but none of the gate money was refunded. Fans were outraged, and an editorial in a local paper denounced the club: "Such a policy may be penny wise, but it is pound foolish, as well as dishonest" (*St. Louis Globe-Democrat*, May 5, 1876). The club was forced to do damage control, and within weeks this policy was posted on all league grounds: "After one inning has been played no tickets will be returned. If the game is called tickets will be returned, good for any game played on the grounds, but in no case will the money of admission be returned" (*New York Sunday Mercury*, May 20, 1876).

St. Louis ended up going further than the rest of the league; an 1877 note stated: "The St. Louis club is the only nine in the league which gives its patrons the right to see a full game or no pay. In Chicago and other cities, after the first inning is interrupted by the rain the spectators are supposed to have received their money's worth. In St. Louis 'rain checks' are issued in such cases. Last Saturday rain is said to have cost the St. Louis club $150, the Chicagos demanding pay for everyone thus admitted on checks" (*Chicago Times*, July 8, 1877; thanks to David Ball). In light of the cost, the National League voted to end the practice of giving rain checks on March 8, 1881. The issue remained a contentious one in the ensuing years, with the *St. Louis Post-Dispatch* reporting in 1883: "The crowd insisted that they should get back either money or rain-checks, but President [Chris] Von der Ahe refused to do either" (*St. Louis Post-Dispatch*, June 21, 1883).

Abner Powell is usually credited with inventing the rain check in the late 1880s, but he made no such claim. What Powell actually took credit for was inventing the *detachable* rain check. A 1943 article by a sportswriter who had interviewed Powell made clear that the practice itself was already in vogue: "all ball clubs used a hard rectangular cardboard ticket, which was sold over and over again, day after day. Ticket buyers would turn them in to the gatekeeper, who deposited the pasteboards in a box. . . . If rain halted a game before the fifth inning, the spectators would line up at the gate to receive a

ticket for the next day as they passed out of the park" (Val J. Flanagan, "Rain-Check Evolved to Check Flood of Fence-Climbers, Says Originator, Now 83," *Sporting News*, April 8, 1943).

The spectators were handed the same tickets they had turned in at the gate. But Powell found that the number of tickets refunded would usually exceed the original sale. He attributed this to boys who had scaled walls, slipped through the drainage ditch, or sneaked in the service entrance. Accordingly, he devised detachable tickets, so that rain checks could be issued only to actual ticket purchasers. The article does not specify a year, but Lee Allen indicated that this took place in 1888 (Lee Allen, *The Hot Stove League*, 95).

It seems to have taken many more years before the practice of issuing rain checks became firmly established in the major leagues. In 1906 *Sporting Life* reported, "The Brooklyn Club will start off with the new ticket system which it put into effect late last year. Every purchaser of a ticket will receive a postponed game check" (*Sporting Life*, April 21, 1906).

(ii) Root, Root, Root for the Home Team

15.2.1 Partisanship. Consistent with the game's gentlemanly origins, early baseball fans were censured if they showed partisanship. Henry Chadwick was a leader in this regard, but many newspapers followed his example. For instance, the *Philadelphia Mercury* complained in 1867 that "the behavior of some of the friends of the Harvard [club] was not calculated to exalt them in the estimation of disinterested spectators. Their friendship for the Harvards led them into extremes. . . . If Harvard College inculcates or encourages such conduct, and lets loose upon the world such narrow-minded, selfish and ungentlemanly specimens of unfinished humanity, the fanaticism ascribed to be popular in this vicinity is not likely to decline or die out with the rising generation" (reprinted in *The Ball Player's Chronicle*, July 4, 1867).

When the Red Stockings of Cincinnati completed a big 1870 win over the Athletics of Philadelphia, "cheers went up as enthusiastic as ever distinguished favorable election returns" (*Rocky Mountain News*, June 24, 1870). And the *Detroit Evening News* observed in 1875, "In large cities the spectators of a base ball match applaud good play without reference to the club. But in the rural villages, when the local club is being worsted, they observe an ominous silence when the visiting nine makes good hits or catches, and when the match is over the whole population gets together and groans at the umpire" (*Detroit Evening News*, June 19, 1875).

Historian Allen Guttmann noted that Walter Camp tried to convince football spectators to adopt a similar nonpartisanship. But, Guttmann contended, "This historically unprecedented code of sportsmanship was an anomaly. The history of sports spectatorship shows nothing quite like it prior to the Victorian era" (Allen Guttmann, *Sports Spectators*, 88–89).

The expectation of nonpartisanship gradually faded, but it took a long time for it to disappear entirely. An 1896 writer, for example, lectured: "The members of the [visiting] St. Hyacinthe team were much pleased at the generous treatment they received from the grand stand in the matter of applause when they made a good play. This is only fair to both sides and shows a commendable desire on the part of the audience to appreciate good playing, no matter which side it comes from. We hope that impartial applause will be a feature of every game played on the home grounds this season" (*Malone* [N.Y.] *Gazette*, June 5, 1896).

15.2.2 Tipping the Cap. The custom of players tipping their caps to the fans goes back to the nineteenth century. Indeed, an 1891 editorial complained that there was a need for "a school of cap-tipping among the baseball heroes of our land" because the response to applause on the part of too many ballplayers was to "pick up a supposed pebble, throw it out of harm's way, spit several times against the wind, and finally raise the visor of a cap two inches—just far enough to cause the body of the article to wobble like the waves of a theatrical sea" (*Sporting Times*, September 26, 1891).

15.2.3 Fan Clubs. Boston's Royal Rooters became famous at the turn of the century and attracted many imitators. But an earlier such organization was reported in 1890: "A society of base ball cranks has been formed in Evansville, Ind. A suitable decoration will be worn by the members" (*Columbus* [Ohio] *Press*, February 14, 1890).

15.2.4 Booing. Instances of spectators hissing can be documented as early as 1867 (see **8.2.1** "Verbal Abuse"; also, George B. Kirsch, *The Creation of American Team Sports*, 186).

Predictably, Henry Chadwick was outspoken in his opposition, writing in an account of a heatedly contested June 1, 1867, match between the Lowell Club of Boston and the Harvard nine: "sharp, short huzzas and hisses follow[ed] the plays and decisions made, the former being excusable, but the latter a disgrace" (Henry Chadwick, *The American Game of Base Ball*, 87). In September he expressed outrage at Washington spectators for being "guilty of the low vulgarity of hissing the umpire where the decisions did not suit their partisan prejudices" (*The Ball Player's Chronicle*, September 26, 1867, 6).

An exception is instructive. In an 1867 game in Portland, Maine, between the Cushnocs of Augusta and the Eons of Portland, umpire Henry Dennison ruled so frequently for the home side "as to call forth repeated and almost unanimous demonstrations of disapprobation in storms of indignant hisses from the crowd of spectators in attendance, whose sympathies were naturally with their own townsmen, but whose love of fair play prompted this uncomplimentary expression of their feelings" (*Maine Farmer*, August 8, 1867, 2). Note that the hissing in this instance was made in the spirit of fair play and against the interests of the home side, and therefore justifiable.

Despite such admonitions, hissing had become common enough by the 1870s that the 1876 National League Constitution instructed that "any person hissing or hooting at [the umpire] . . . must be promptly ejected from the grounds." This doesn't seem to have helped much, as an 1884 account noted: "The season is but two-thirds over, and yet it has been marked by cowardly personal assaults on umpires in the field, scenes of disgraceful rows by club 'heelers' hissing and insulting remarks by partisans in grand stand assemblages" (*Brooklyn Eagle*, August 17, 1884).

Umpires were the most frequent targets of this abuse, but players also increasingly came to be on the receiving end. As described in several earlier entries (see **2.2.1** "Bunts," **2.2.2** "Fair-fouls," **5.5.1** "Running into Fielders," and **6.4.1** "Intentional Walks"), players were usually hissed not for inept play but for tactics that were deemed unmanly or unsporting. Yet there were exceptions, as Chadwick noted with dismay later in his account of the Lowell-Harvard match: "The yells of derision, when errors were committed, were only equalled by the jeers of juvenile roughs in New York on similar occasions, and were entirely out of place as emanating from an educated crowd" (Henry Chadwick, *The American Game of Base Ball*, 87).

With expressions of spectator disapproval being uncommon, there was no standard method of showing displeasure. Hissing seems to have been intended as an imitation of a goose. In an 1876 game William Hague dropped an easy fly and "Some ill-mannered spectators undertook to usurp the goose's place and started to hiss the player for his blunder, but they promptly put stoppers on their tongues when told if persisted in, the outside of the gates would be happy to make their acquaintance. This is the first instance in this city, as far as our recollection leads us, where such an attempt has been made to express disapprobation of a player, and we hope never to see it again; a player feels badly enough over a blunder committed by himself, without cutting him still further by jeers and hisses" (*Louisville Courier-Journal*, July 14, 1876). An 1876 game account stated: "The crowd to-day hooted [Dory] Dean and filled the air with quacking in the ninth inning" (*St. Louis Globe-Democrat*, August 4, 1876, 8). Presumably, Dean knew what they meant.

15.2.5 Organized Rooting. As discussed in the chapter on coaches, coaches of the 1880s functioned as combination noisemakers and cheerleaders, with only occasional interruptions to direct base runners. By the twentieth century, fans were beginning to follow their lead, but their efforts weren't always appreciated. *Sporting Life* reported in 1904: "A blow has been struck in Denver at the time-honored privilege of the rooter to howl himself hoarse if the exigencies of the situation demanded it. An order has been issued by the owner of the team that 'rooting' must stop, and policeman are now stationed in front of the various stands to enforce the rule. The fans are indignant, and threaten to stay away from the game unless the order is rescinded" (*Sporting Life*, May 28, 1904).

Four years later the *Philadelphia Record* remarked, "So Ban Johnson is to put a stop to the disgraceful organized 'rooting' by baseball fanatics which marked the close finish in the American League pennant race last season. Decent patrons of the game will be thankful and all fair-minded individuals will laud Johnson on the stand he has taken, for some of the carryings-on last year were very unsportsmanlike.

This organized 'rooting' for the purpose of rattling the players of the opposing team was started last year in Chicago by the followers of the White Sox, and was taken up at Detroit and also in this city. All sorts of noise-making devices were called into use to help along the work of disconcerting the players of the visiting team, and the sounds produced were simply hideous to all save the frenzied base ball 'fans,' who felt that they were helping to win the game. A man who pays to see a base ball match is entitled to shout his lungs out, if he chooses, hooting the players of either team or cheering any play that excites his admiration. But there is no reason why anyone should be allowed to go to a game armed with a megaphone for the express purpose of hurling epithets at the players of either team, or why a number of individuals, all armed with megaphones, should be permitted for day after day to make remarks to the players of the opposing team that angers or disconcerts them so that they cannot play their best ball" (reprinted in *Sporting Life*, April 11, 1908).

15.2.6 Curtain Calls. Writer Bruce Shlain credited Mark "The Bird" Fidrych with being responsible for the first curtain call in 1976 (Bruce Shlain, *Oddballs*, 151). While Fidrych may have helped to revive this tradition, he certainly didn't originate it.

For example, during Detroit's first major league game in 1881, the *Detroit Free Press* reported that Charley Bennett hit a home run that "was loudly applauded, and the crowd would not desist until he bowed in acknowledgment" (*Detroit Free Press*, May 3, 1881). In 1884 *Sporting Life* noted that in Cuba "a home run raises the vast assemblage to its feet as one man and one woman, and the play has to be stopped until the 'home skipper' has passed in front of the grand stand and received not only the congratulations of the beautiful ladies, but many golden tokens of appreciation" (*Sporting Life*, June 10, 1884).

15.2.7 Brooms. The use of brooms to commemorate a sweeping victory or a series sweep is much older than today's fans might expect. Brooms may have been borrowed from competitions between fire engines, where they were used to symbolize having "swept away" all rivals. Their popularity was probably also aided by the fact that they helped identify a small group of spectators who were rooting for the visiting team. In any event, they played a major role in the fun in nineteenth-century baseball grandstands.

After the Atlantic Club of Brooklyn beat the Unions of Morrisania in 1868 to recapture the championship, this account appeared: "In procession came three carriages, and in front of the first one was elevated a broom, the pine handle of which was ornamented with gay colored ribbons; the occupants of the carriages appeared to be enjoying a happy state of feeling. Inquiry was made, and the well-informed were heard to say that it was the Atlantic Club returning from Morrisania, after playing with the Union Club, and that the broom carried in front meant that having whipped the champions, it could now sweep everything out of its way" (*Brooklyn Eagle*, October 7, 1868).

When Boston won a big game at Hartford in 1875, the team was accorded a reception at the Boston train station by a large throng that included fifty men with brooms who led a parade through the streets (*Boston Herald*, reprinted in *St. Louis Globe-Democrat*, May 24, 1875). In 1880, after the White Stockings of Chicago reeled off a historic twenty-one straight victories, Worcester secretary Frank Bancroft presented Chicago captain Anson with a scarf-pin featuring "a broom in miniature, crossed by a bat, a ball and the word 'Chicago' on a scroll,—emblematic of the ball-player who sweeps everything before him, and whose team has 'cleaned out' the cream of the League" (*Chicago Tribune*, June 20, 1880, 7). The symbolism was appreciated by Chicago club president William Hulbert, who presented the players with "gold 'broom' badges, emblematic of their ability to sweep everything before them" (*New York Clipper*, July 31, 1880; "Dalrymple, Old Star, Recalls Baseball in '80s," *Chicago Tribune*, September 23, 1928, A7). When the Providence Grays returned home after clinching the 1884 National League pennant, "a new broom was given each player and during the parade to the Narragansett Hotel that followed they wore the brooms over their shoulders" (William D. Perrin, *Days of Greatness*, 52).

This mode of celebration reached a new level of popularity in 1886. In early May a sizable assemblage of New York partisans accompanied their team to Philadelphia for a series: "Upwards of 9000 persons witnessed the game, including a couple of hundred New Yorkers. The latter brought with them a bunch of new brooms which they tacked to the posts of the grand stand, in which they occupied seats. They meekly but gracefully presented the brooms to the Philadelphia players at the conclusion of the game" (*Boston Globe*, May 4, 1886). A few days later, Columbia students celebrated a win over Harvard with "a pair of crossed brooms" (*Boston Globe*, May 9, 1886).

In late June the second-place and defending champion Chicago White Stockings visited surprise league leaders Detroit for a crucial three-game series. Detroit's Wolverines entered the series with a perfect 18-0 record on their home grounds, and Chicago partisans were willing to try anything to break the skein. As a result, a mascot and nearly two hundred well-wishers equipped with brooms, whistles, duck calls, wooden clappers, and other noisemakers accompanied the Chicago club to Detroit on a special train. Upon disembarking, the throng caused quite a commotion in downtown Detroit by holding aloft large brooms with the inscription "Record breakers" as they were led to their hotel by Chicago stars "Cap" Anson and Mike Kelly (*Boston Globe*, June 20, 1886).

At the first game of the series the next day, the visitors' hex seemed to work as Detroit's star catcher Charley Bennett was injured in the eighth inning, and a passed ball by his replacement allowed the White Stockings to score the winning run. But Chicago's luck turned the next day with Anson sitting out because he had gone fishing and caught a fish that showed him its teeth before it died. He considered this to be such a harbinger of bad luck that he believed it useless for him to play (*Chicago Tribune*, June 22 and 23, 1886). Detroit won the second and third games, leading many of the Chicago supporters to abandon their brooms or meekly surrender them to their hosts.

The next month a crowd of Detroiters accompanied the Wolverines to Chicago sporting miniature brooms on their lapel pins. They proved even less successful, as Chicago swept the three-game series en route to regaining the championship.

While these discouraging results put a damper on the use of brooms, the practice did not entirely vanish. In 1904 Boston's Royal Rooters brought brooms with them to New York for the season's pivotal series. And so when today's fans celebrate a sweep of a series by waving brooms they are merely reviving a very old tradition, which is steeped in the superstitions of the nineteenth century.

15.2.8   Radios at the Ballpark. The Reverend Percy Kendall brought a thirty-inch, seventeen-pound "portable" radio to Cleveland Indians games as early as 1937 (G. Edward White, *Creating the National Pastime*, 221). But the practice naturally did not become prevalent until radios had become significantly smaller. Red Smith, in a 1948 column, mentioned that during that year's furious American League pennant race between the Red Sox and Indians, fans at Fenway were listening to Cleveland's game against Detroit (Red Smith, October 4, 1948, reprinted in *Red Smith on Baseball*).

By 1955 Smith was reporting with dismay that there were sections in Chicago's Wrigley Field and Philadelphia's Connie Mack Stadium where the radio broadcast of the day's game was piped through the amplifiers: "There the customer who has paid for the privilege of watching with his own eyes sits helpless while a disembodied huckster plucks at his sleeve, bludgeons him with advice, burdens him with statistical trivialities, embarrasses him with autobiographical revelations, hectors him to buy beer or cigarettes" (Red Smith, August 22, 1955, reprinted in *Red Smith on Baseball*).

15.2.9 Helping (or Hindering) Players. The blocked-ball rules of early baseball (see **12.6**), though intended to take the fans out of play, sometimes had the opposite effect. The importance of the early umpire's cry of foul gave spectators another way to interfere. As early as 1857 spectators were yelling "foul" on fair hits to trick the opposing club (*Porter's Spirit of the Times*, September 5, 1857; cited in George B. Kirsch, *The Creation of American Team Sports*, 192–193).

Tim McCarver noted that a much more recent spectator found a similar way to involve himself in the game. McCarver described a 1997 game at Cincinnati's Cinergy Field in which a Reds fan waited until Mets catcher Todd Hundley set up and then yelled his location to the batter. According to McCarver, "Hundley had to figure out how to cross up the fan, and his manager, Bobby Valentine, had to resort to shouting gibberish to drown him out" (Tim McCarver with Danny Peary, *Tim McCarver's Baseball for Brain Surgeons and Other Fans*, 69).

(iii) You Can't Beat Fun at the Old Ballpark

For some fans, if the home team doesn't win it's a crying shame, but others are just out to have a little fun.

15.3.1 Beer at the Ballpark. At least some National Association clubs sold alcohol in the stands. But National League founder William Hulbert was opposed to the sale of alcohol, and Cincinnati's expulsion after the 1880 season was at least in part the result of beer sales.

After the American Association was founded a year later, the sale of alcohol at its parks became one of its best-known features. It is said that tavern owner Chris Von der Ahe bought the St. Louis Brown Stockings to assure that he would have the lucrative beer concession.

The last major league team not to sell beer at the ballpark was the expansion Toronto Blue Jays, because the province of Ontario refused to allow the team a liquor license. Many believed this was the result of a promise that Ontario premier William Davis had made to his mother. When she died, the club received permission to sell beer in 1982.

15.3.2 Food. A three-course meal featuring a pasta dish was served at Brooklyn's Union Grounds in 1862 (David Pietrusza, Lloyd Johnson, and Bob Carroll, eds., *Total Baseball Catalog*, 28).

15.3.3 Peanuts. Buffalo's National League club was offering five-cent bags of peanuts at its park in 1885 (*Providence Sunday Dispatch*, June 1, 1885; thanks to Rick Stattler). The *Youngstown Vindicator* reported in 1898, "the man who held the refreshment privileges last year, will have charge again this season. As usual, no intoxicants will be sold and mild peanuts, red, white and yellow pop, etc., will be dispensed" (*Youngstown Vindicator*, April 7, 1898).

15.3.4 Hot Dogs. With its large German population, St. Louis featured a popular "Weiner wurst" stand in the 1880s (*Cleveland Leader and Herald*, March 20, 1886). It is more difficult to be certain of who first thought of packing sausages in buns, but legendary concessions operator Harry M. Stevens claimed to have originated the practice at the Polo Grounds in April 1901. Stevens credited his son Frank with having convinced him that fans would welcome a change from ham and cheese sandwiches (Frederick G. Lieb, "A Man Who Has Made Millions from By-Products of Sport," *Sportlife*, December 1925, 94).

15.3.5 Sushi. Researcher Bob Timmermann noted that sushi undoubtedly made its baseball park debut at a stadium in Japan. It was introduced to the United States by the Hawai'i Islanders of the Pacific Coast League, then brought to the major leagues by the San Diego Padres in 1989. The innovation did not impress San Diego police officer Rick Schnell, who commented, "This sushi stuff is ridiculous. They ought to be selling hot dogs and hamburgers. They've never done those that good to begin with. Sushi makes us the wimp capital of baseball—at least until October, when we'll beat everybody. But in October, when the World Series comes here, selling sushi will be embarrassing. We'll have to be extra good just to cover up the scorn'" (*Los Angeles Times*, April 4, 1989). Other fans seem to have been more accepting. The Angels added sushi the following year, and the Dodgers a few years later.

15.3.6   Seventh-inning Stretch.

The seventh-inning stretch is often erroneously said to have originated in the early twentieth century when President William Howard Taft arose from his seat in the middle of the seventh and fans respectfully did likewise. In fact, stretches were in use as early as the 1860s, though it took many years for the seventh inning to become standard.

After a June 1869 game the *New York Herald* reported, "At the close of the long second inning, the laughable stand up and stretch was indulged in all around the field" (quoted in Jonathan Fraser Light, *The Cultural Encyclopedia of Baseball*, 662). That same year Harry Wright wrote: "The spectators all arise between halves of the seventh, extend their legs and arms, and sometimes walk about. In so doing they enjoy the relief afforded by relaxation from a long posture on the hard benches" (quoted in Greg Rhodes and John Erardi, *The First Boys of Summer*, 70).

An entrepreneurial San Franciscan named W. J. Hatton helped arrange the Red Stockings' 1869 visit to California. To increase revenue, a ten-minute intermission took place after the sixth inning. A Cincinnati reporter called this practice "a dodge to advertise and have the crowd patronize the bar" (*Cincinnati Commercial*; quoted in Greg Rhodes and John Erardi, *The First Boys of Summer*, 70).

This inning also came to be viewed as a lucky one for the club, with an 1875 game account stating: "Here was the famous old seventh inning of the old Reds, an inning in which they were never known to fail to make a run

when they were behind" (*Cincinnati Enquirer*, September 10, 1875). It was this combination of events that seems to have been responsible for the seventh-inning stretch.

Eventually the tradition spread to other cities. Jonathan Fraser Light cited this description in *Sporting News* of a game between the New York Giants of the National League and Brooklyn of the American Association in the 1889 World's Series: "As the seventh opened somebody cried, 'Stretch for Luck!' And instantly the vast throng on the grand stand rose gradually and then settled down, just as long grass bends to the breath of the zephyr" (Jonathan Fraser Light, *The Cultural Encyclopedia of Baseball*, 246).

15.3.7   The Wave.

One might think that at least the wave is a recent addition to baseball. But there is compelling evidence to the contrary.

Tom Shieber reports that a Hall of Fame volunteer discovered a clipping giving this account of an October 15, 1866, match between the Atlantic and Athletic clubs that took place at the Capitoline Grounds in Brooklyn: "Quite an amusing scene was here enacted. One individual, cramped by sitting two or three hours on the low temporary bench at the left of the field, stood up, stretched his body, arms and neck to their fullest tension, and appeared to feel quite refreshed; his next neighbor imitated his example, and one after another almost every one in the crowd stood up, straightened himself and then resumed his seat. The effect was ludicrous to the extreme, and after the straightening process had been indulged in all around the arena the portion of the crowd on the left commenced waving their handkerchiefs to the crowd on the right, and these returned the salute, so that at one time there were at least a thousand cambrics shaking around the field. This episode seemed to put the crowd in extra good humor, and from time to time the process was repeated."

Dean A. Sullivan discovered this 1889 account of a forfeited game between St. Louis and Brooklyn: "The bleacheries were black with people and on the pathways surrounding these seats the people were jammed together in one immovable mass, and the only time they could gather themselves together was when the excitement got the best of them and everybody was forced to throw up their hands and were compelled to sway about like a WAVE on the ocean from the irresistible and frenzied throng" (*Brooklyn Eagle*, September 8, 1889; reprinted in Dean A. Sullivan, ed., *Early Innings*, 183). The description of that fall's World's Series that was cited in the preceding entry is clearly the same idea. Gerard S. Petrone reported that Detroit fans were also using a version of the wave in 1900 (Gerard S. Petrone, *When Baseball Was Young*, 173).

15.3.8 Fireworks. Chris Von der Ahe began luring fans with displays of fireworks at Sportsman's Park shortly after purchasing the St. Louis Brown Stockings in 1882 (*St. Louis Globe-Democrat*, June 30, 1882; thanks to Cliff Blau and Jeff Kittel). He eventually began using pyrotechnics for additional purposes. After capturing the 1885 pennant, the members of the club made a triumphal march through the city accompanied by "a bewildering discharge of fireworks" (*St. Louis Globe-Democrat*, October 8, 1885). Before the 1886 season, Von der Ahe was said to have "a new scheme. He intends to fire off a bomb that can be heard all over St. Louis five minutes before the beginning of each game. His object is to notify people on bad days if there is to be a game" (*Boston Globe*, January 18, 1886). It seems unlikely that this harebrained scheme was ever tried; if it were, Von der Ahe would presumably have quickly learned that there were a lot of St. Louis residents who preferred not to receive such notifications. That same year the Metropolitans were moved to Staten Island in order to pair baseball with "other attractions, such as electric and pyrotechnical displays" (*Sporting News*, May 17, 1886).

15.3.9 Hit/Error Posted on Scoreboard. John B. Foster reported in 1923 that there had been a proposal at the recent American League meetings to post whether a play was scored as a hit or an error on league scoreboards. The proposal was defeated for a surprising reason. Foster explained that there was a significant amount of wagering in the stands on the result of individual plays, and the owners feared that posting scoring decisions would only encourage this practice (*Sporting News*, March 8, 1923).

The scheme does not appear to have reemerged until 1928, when the *New York Times* mentioned: "An innovation at the Polo Grounds is a system of signaling the official scorer's decision on closer plays. A little arm is thrown up on top of the score board, between 'strikes' and

'balls' and shows an 'H' for a hit and an 'E' for an error" (*New York Times*, April 14, 1928).

(iv) Souvenirs

Whether any object is worth keeping or not is in the eye of the beholder, a reality driven home to many youngsters when their prized baseball card collections were thrown out by unappreciative parents. In early baseball matches the losing club presented the winners with a baseball, and these were often regarded as trophies. For example, the Atlantics of Brooklyn preserved more than two hundred such souvenir balls in a glass case (photo in James L. Terry, *Long Before the Dodgers*, 77). But, as is explained in the chapter on marketing (see **16.2.7** "Keeping Balls in the Stands"), it was many years before spectators had the opportunity to keep foul balls.

Early baseball enthusiasts nevertheless accumulated a variety of keepsakes. Obvious candidates such as programs and baseball cards are discussed in the entries that follow, but they were far from the only souvenirs. Newspaper clippings were a popular one, as is shown by an 1886 reference to "the base ball cranks of Boston, such as General Dixwell, who keeps four different base ball scrapbooks, one for each Boston morning paper, and spends all the time he has when not witnessing ball games, in figuring out averages" (*Boston Globe*, May 17, 1886).

In general, collectibles were fairly rare among early baseball fans, and some of the items that were preserved are surprising. Seymour Church, for example, accumulated a large gallery of baseball-related art (*Sporting Life*, November 18, 1905).

15.4.1 Throwing Balls Back onto the Field. The recent practice of Chicago Cubs fans of throwing opposition home run balls back onto the field is new to a certain extent, since it does not appear that fans had ever before done this to show their allegiance to the home team.

But there is nothing new about fans throwing balls back on the field. As noted in the introduction to this section, fans in early baseball were not allowed to keep foul balls, and regularly threw them back onto the field. Even when this began to change, some spectators followed the old practice; Shirley Povich noted in 1931 that fans at Griffith Stadium were given a "crescendo of razz" if they committed a "breach of etiquette" by tossing a ball back onto the field (*Washington Post*, July 6, 1931). During World War II it became customary for fans to throw foul balls back onto the field so they could be donated to military posts (William Mead, *Even the Browns*, 2).

15.4.2 Scorecards/Souvenir Programs.

Scorecards had begun to appear by 1866 and are first known to have been sold at a match that year between the Atlantics of Brooklyn and the Athletics of Philadelphia (Dan Gutman, in *Banana Bats and Ding-Dong Balls*, 108, said the game occurred on October 11, 1866; in the special pictorial issue of the *National Pastime* in 1984, John Thorn gave the date as October 1, 1866; the two clubs actually played on the 15th and 22nd of that month). Researcher Mark Rucker tracked down a copy of "Parker's Improved Score Cards," used at a game played in Hoboken, New Jersey, on October 29, 1866 (Frederick Ivor-Campbell, "When Was the First? [Continued]," *Nineteenth Century Notes* 95:1 [Winter 1995], 2). The word "Improved" implies that they had been used still earlier.

An important step toward turning score-cards into keepsakes occurred in 1871 when Mort Rogers of Boston began selling scorecards with photographs. Another new touch was added in 1879 when it became popular to attach handles so that they could be used as fans (*Detroit Post and Tribune*, August 2, 1879).

By the 1880s scorecards were coming to be viewed as an essential part of the ballpark experience. As discussed in "Submitting Lineups" (6.3.1), an 1881 rule requiring managers to submit their lineups by 9 a.m. was intended to ensure that that day's scorecards were accurate. *Sporting Life* observed in 1884, "one requires a score card at a ball game quite as much as a programme at a theatre. It is wanted for constant reference to identify players, positions, striking order, & c., even if you do not keep the score" (*Sporting Life*, April 23, 1884).

They were also becoming increasingly elaborate. The St. Louis Browns commemorated Ladies' Day in 1883 "by the presentation to every lady attending of a handsome souvenir score card" (*St. Louis Post-Dispatch*, May 23, 1883). Two days later the paper reported: "The 500 souvenir programmes . . . were given away early in the day."

A sure sign they were becoming more popular is the emergence of competition. An 1886 article observed, "Boston management refuses to give out the batteries because somebody is printing and selling a rival score card. In spite of this precaution the outside score-card people get it as right as the inside. In ten games the official score card has been right but two. The public wants to know who the pitchers are to be, and the management loses money by not announcing them" (*Boston Globe*, June 6, 1886).

The demand and the competition inspired some clubs to produce still fancier scorecards, as this 1890 article demonstrates: "The official score book of the Brooklyn Club, of the National League, is not only a novelty in its way, but is neat and handsome. The book contains thirty-two pages, over which are distributed beautifully engraved likenesses, with biographical sketches, of every member of the team. The two middle pages are devoted to the scoring of the game. The frontispiece is the design of Secretary Charley Ebbets, of the Brooklyn Club. The bat contains the name 'Brooklyn.' The homeplate beneath has the words 'at home with,' and then twenty-four balls, arranged in the form of a diamond, has the games to be played at home, and in chronological order. Upon each corner is a base with various inscriptions thereon. Nothing like this score book has ever been published before" (*New York Clipper*, May 3, 1890).

15.4.3 Baseball Cards.

Baseball and photographs began to—ahem—develop at about the same time, and there was a natural desire to combine them. As documented in Mark Rucker's beautiful book *Base Ball Cartes*, one of the earliest manifestations occurred in the 1860s with the carte de visite. As Rucker explained, a carte de visite was a paper photoprint of approximately two-and-a-half by four inches that was glued to a card mount. The carte de visite originated in France in the 1850s and was popular in the United States in the 1860s and 1870s.

These cartes gradually evolved into trade cards, with the photographs of ballplayers being used to promote businesses or commercial products. Cigarette manufacturers began to mass-produce them in the 1880s (David Pietrusza, Lloyd Johnson, and Bob Carroll, eds., *Total Baseball Catalog*, 118).

The first card to depict a bat-and-ball game may predate the Knickerbockers. Researchers Henry Thomas and Frank Ceresi reported that a card depicting a pitcher tossing a ball to a batsman was discovered in a Maine attic a few years ago. While the exact date and provenance of the card cannot be established, there is evidence that it may date to the 1830s and be part of a series of illustrated children's educational cards (http://www.fcassociates.com/ntearlybb.htm).

15.4.4   Tickets.

Lee Allen pointed out that the greatest obstacle to tickets becoming souvenirs was a practical one: "In the earliest days spectators turned in oblong tickets, which the takers deposited in boxes and used again and again for subsequent contests" (Lee Allen, *The Hot Stove League*, 95).

At least one person must have hung on to a ticket from an 1866 game, since sportswriter William Rankin reported in 1909, "I have one of the original tickets used on the old Capitoline Grounds, Brooklyn, in 1866. The size of the ticket—which is red,—and the inscription on it, are as follows:

> Capitoline Grounds
> 25 CENTS
> Weed & Decker, Proprietors" (*Sporting News*, October 7, 1909).

The twentieth century has seen interest in this form of souvenir manifest itself in particularly excessive forms. For example, sportswriter Jerry Crasnick observed: "There were 15,758 people in the Wrigley Field stands on May 6, 1998, when Cubs righthander Kerry Wood struck out 20 Astros in his fifth major league start. A day later, 150 would-be capitalists called the Cubs' box office looking for unsold tickets from the game as collector's items" (Jerry Crasnick, *Baseball America*, October 27–November 9, 2003).

15.4.5   Autographs.

According to Lee Allen, the first recorded autograph request was received by the Cincinnati Reds on May 10, 1890, from a woman who was working on a quilt and wanted to reproduce the players' signatures (Lee Allen, *The Hot Stove League*, 147).

At first pass it would seem unlikely that an 1890 autograph request could be a first. A fascination with autographs that was initially considered a "fad" swept the country in 1883 (*Washington Post*, April 8, 1883). The fad proved to have staying power, and between 1890 and 1910 "a flood of magazine articles defined the 'art' of autograph collecting" (Frank W. Hoffmann and William G. Bailey, *Sports and Recreation Fads*, 19–21).

Rather than targeting athletes, however, early autograph seekers generally sought out intellectuals. Serious hobbyists wrote letters to prominent writers, politicians, scientists, and ministers in hopes of receiving a signed letter in reply. These requests placed considerable demands on the time of recipients, and collectors gradually realized that their chance of success was better if they asked only for a signature.

The fact that ballplayers were not the targets of early autograph collectors reflects the low social status of athletes at the beginning of the twentieth century. Turn-of-the-century outfielder Davy Jones, for example, had to break up with his high school sweetheart: "baseball wasn't a very respectable occupation back then . . . after I became a professional ballplayer her parents refused to let me see her any more. Wouldn't let her have anything more to do with me. In those days a lot of people looked upon ballplayers as bums, too lazy to work for a living" (Lawrence S. Ritter, *The Glory of Their Times*, 38).

The status of baseball players rose rapidly in the first few decades of the twentieth century. In 1925 Ty Cobb observed, "There was a time—twenty years ago—when first-class hotels would not take ball clubs as guests. Now the most refined hotels in the country seek baseball patronage. That is certainly an indication of progress" (Ty Cobb, *Memoirs of Twenty Years in Baseball*, 6). (An indirect beneficiary of this progress was Davy Jones, who ran into his high school sweetheart after both were widowed and finally married her.)

This coincided with autograph seekers beginning to seek signatures instead of highly crafted letters, with the result that it became more and more common to target athletes and movie stars. By 1937 requests to ballplayers for autographs had become common enough that Pepper Martin began using a rubber stamp for autographs.

15.4.6   Stamps.

The first U.S. postage stamp with a baseball theme was issued in 1939 to honor the centenary of the now discredited story of Abner Doubleday's invention of the game. Several foreign countries had earlier featured baseball on stamps, beginning with the Philippines in 1934 (Robert Obojski, *Baseball Memorabilia*, 89).

15.4.7 Bobbleheads, etc. Researcher Andy McCue reported that longtime Los Angeles Dodgers concessionaire Danny Goodman claimed to have introduced bobblehead dolls and plastic bats, both in 1958, as well as souvenir hats, pennants, and other souvenirs (Andy McCue, "The King of Coolie Hats," *National Pastime* 19 [1999], 24–27).

15.4.8 Fantasy Camps. Randy Hundley staged the first fantasy camp for adults in Scottsdale, Arizona, in January 1983. Sixty-three men paid $2,195 each to work out with members of the 1969 Cubs (Roy Blount, Jr., "We All Had a Ball," in John Thorn, ed., *The Armchair Book of Baseball*, 67–82).

Chapter 16

MARKETING AND PROMOTIONS

"What is the use in doing anything to help baseball? Ain't we done everything we could do to kill it? And look at it!" (Pirates owner Barney Dreyfuss, quoted in *Sporting News*, February 9, 1922).

"I don't care what you say about me or my ball club, just so you say something" (onetime Cubs owner Charles Webb Murphy, a former journalist, quoted in *Sporting News*, December 15, 1921).

A CHAPTER on marketing was not in the original plans for this book. The idea gradually forced itself upon me as entry after entry showed that many of baseball's best marketing techniques were not created by design. In fact a long line of the innovations that have helped increase the audience for the game first had to overcome stubborn resistance from ownership.

In most cases the owners have contended that the benefits of exposure were outweighed by the costs of what they viewed as giving away their product. Eventually they have given in and reluctantly embraced new media and concepts that have brought baseball to a wider audience and thereby paved the way for the wealth that the game enjoys today.

An irritated Ted Sullivan once observed that baseball owners were "wise in everything, excepting the art of making the public believe that the time has come to give up the half-a-dollars . . . they do everything on earth except-ing to make arrangements for the pleasing of the public. I cannot understand it. I fail to remember any particular occasion when any

considerable crowd of people went out to a ball park to look at a magnate" (*Sporting Life*, January 5, 1901).

The point is not simply to bash the owners. There are two basic ways to promote a product: by making it scarce and hoping to increase its perceived value, or by giving it away. Needless to say, the two are in direct conflict, meaning that promotional efforts always tiptoe a delicate line between exposure and overexposure.

In many cases, as we shall see, the owners had understandable reservations that would have concerned any good businessperson. But by putting these items together in a chapter, a clear and intriguing pattern emerges in which efforts that were initially deemed to be "giving the product away" have consistently been the ones that produced long-term growth.

That pattern is, I believe, worthy of con-sideration by the people who currently market baseball. They might particularly want to think about it when they reflect upon the shortsighted policy of allowing World Series games to start at times that mean they will conclude after the bedtimes of the next generation of fans.

The first section of this chapter considers planned promotional events, such as days and giveaway items. The second section examines the unplanned promotional concepts that have often overcome the protests of owners to out-strip promotions that were carefully conceived. The third section looks at mass media, as the inception of each new medium has led to an impassioned dispute about whether it will at-tract new fans or cause existing ones to stay at home.

(i) Planned Days and Events

16.1.1   Schedules. Within two years of the first predetermined league schedule (see **22.1.4**), a couple of savvy businesses had begun giving away pocket schedules. At the start of the 1879 season, the *Chicago Tribune* observed: "Clayton and Co., of 83 Madison Street, have issued for gratuitous distribution neat cards giving the dates and places of all League games for the season. They are convenient and popular" (*Chicago Tribune*, April 6, 1879). Another note that same week informed readers, "Wright, Howland & Mahn, dealers in base ball goods, 30 Kneeland Street, Boston, have flooded the country with their business cards, on the reverse side of which is printed the schedule of league games for 1879—a judicious piece of advertising, which will doubtless pay well" (*St. Louis Globe-Democrat*, April 13, 1879, 13).

16.1.2   Advertising Campaigns. Nineteenth-century baseball clubs naturally thought about ways to advertise games, but their efforts remained modest. According to Harold Seymour, most settled for notices in the local papers and such methods as "streetcar billing, sign boards at street corners, handbills, window hangers, posters, and boys parading the streets with banners" (Harold Seymour, *Baseball: The Early Years*, 196). At the start of the 1877 season, an Indianapolis newspaper announced: "W. B. Pettit, of the Occidental hotel, has kindly consented to fly a flag from the staff on his hotel on days when there is a game. Many of the clubs coming here will stop at his house, it being the ball tossers' headquarters" (*Indianapolis Sentinel*, April 1, 1877). Pettit became the team president a year later and plastered the town with large photos of pitcher Ed Nolan and catcher "Silver" Flint that bore the inscriptions "The Only Nolan" and "The Champion Catcher of America." This caused quite a bit of discussion about "the good or bad taste of hanging up such pictures in the windows about town" (*Chicago Tribune*, May 5, 1878).

These pictures also attracted considerable attention, and Nolan's nickname stuck. By and large, however, such advertisements were not terribly effective. Worse, as described in the entry on "Hustlers" (**6.1.3**), such campaigns smacked of the circus and could backfire if not executed properly. The over-the-top publicity for an 1875 tournament in Ionia, Michigan, caused a resident of the nearby town of Lyons to complain, "Posters and bills announcing and giving the programme of the tournament are scattered about town in such profusion as to give one an idea that it is to be the grandest and most important event of the century, and that little villages were made for the sole purpose of proclaiming and making known to the public" (*Ionia Sentinel*, July 23, 1875). An Evansville sportswriter justifiably grumbled in 1884, "The base ball streamers on the street cars are rapidly losing their value as advertisements of the game, because of the neglect of those who should see to having them put on and taken off the cars according to circumstances. Yesterday there was no game, and yet the cars throughout the day advertised a game for the afternoon. To-day there will be a game, and those who were deceived by the streamers yesterday cannot be expected to pay any attention to them to-day or hereafter. Either the streamers should be removed permanently or they should be brought into use only when a game is to be played" (*Evansville Journal*, July 9, 1884).

By the mid-1880s clubs were at least thinking about new ways to attract spectators. As noted under "Fireworks" (see **15.3.8**), Chris Von der Ahe announced before the 1886 season that he would "fire off a bomb that can be heard all over St. Louis five minutes before the beginning of each game" (*Boston Globe*, January 18, 1886). There is no evidence that his scheme was tried, but he did display a golden ball with the words "Game Today" or a flag reading "No Game Today" from the Golden Lion Saloon (Harold Seymour, *Baseball: The Early Years*, 196).

Another club devised a much more ambitious approach. The *Cleveland Leader and Herald* explained: "Detroit believes that advertising is profitable. The base ball games in that city this season will be billed like a circus. Secretary [Bob] Leadley is sending out advertising matter for the opening games in Detroit to all the cities and villages throughout the State, and excursion trains will be run to many of the games" (*Cleveland Leader and Herald*, April 26, 1886).

Most nineteenth-century clubs, however, relied upon less expensive forms of marketing. Until around 1910, major league teams commonly dressed at their hotel so that the players could serve as moving billboards as they walked to the ballpark (Gerard S. Petrone, *When Baseball Was Young*, 17). This practice continued in the minor leagues; a 1917 article observed: "Under a ruling adopted at the [Western League's] meeting visiting teams must 'parade the streets to the parks in uniforms,' for the purpose, it was said, of advertising" (*Sporting Life*, January 27, 1917).

Philip K. Wrigley brought a new sophistication to baseball marketing shortly after he inherited the Chicago Cubs from his father in 1932. J. G. Taylor Spink reported in 1935 that the maverick Wrigley was launching an actual advertising campaign, "somewhat to the amazement of his fellow magnates." Wrigley's bold idea was a series of advertisements in Chicago papers over the winter designed to bolster attendance that summer. No doubt the bleak economic situation contributed to his willingness to try new ways of drawing fans to the ballpark.

Wrigley's assistant, Charles F. Drake, explained that "the theme of the campaign is sunshine, recreation and pleasure. Mr. Wrigley is applying merchandising methods to baseball. It is his belief that, in the past, too much stress has been laid upon the team through newspaper publicity and not enough attention given to selling baseball as a great outdoor game, offering many healthful benefits and hours of pleasure to the fans. It is perhaps unusual to launch a campaign of this character in the winter, with no immediate prospects of a return at the gates. But Mr. Wrigley has found in his chewing gum business that constant repetition of advertising builds in the public's consciousness a desire for a product, so he is applying the same principle to advertising the Cubs."

In addition, Wrigley had hired a young man whose job was "to circulate through the park, learn the wishes of the fans, and try in every way possible to obtain ideas that will make Wrigley Field more enjoyable." He could hardly have found someone better suited for the position: the young man he hired was Bill Veeck (*Sporting News*, January 17, 1935).

16.1.3   Public Relations Director. During the nineteenth century, leagues occasionally had an employee who devoted much of his time to press releases and other public relations matters. When the Players' League was launched in 1890, it was commended for "selecting Frank Brunell its Secretary. He has been in the newspaper business and recognizes the value of advertising. The newspapers all over the country have been 'worked.' It matters not how trivial an item of news may be, Brunell manages to have it sent out by the different press associations, and it appears in every paper of any consequence the following morning" (*Louisville Courier-Journal*, March 9, 1890).

Individual clubs, however, never had such employees. The closest to an exception appears to have been Washington pitcher and medical student James "Doc" McJames. Since he couldn't pitch every day, his education was put to use in 1897 by making him also the "advance agent and press-notice maker for the senators, going on ahead of the nine to arrange for accommodations, etc." (*Chicago Post*, May 20, 1897).

In 1905 the Giants assigned Charles Webb Murphy to head "the club's Bureau of Publicity." Murphy "started off at a rapid pace, and he promises to keep the scribes loaded up with stories. Murphy's engagement is another illustration of the changes that follow when competition becomes keen" (*Sporting Life*, February 18, 1905). But his tenure was brief because later that year Murphy purchased the Cubs, who became the Giants' bitter rivals.

It appears to have been another twenty-five years before the position reemerged. Gene Karst was a Knothole Gang alumnus who had interned at the *St. Louis Globe-Democrat* in 1930 and become frustrated by the poor quality of the publicity material provided by major league teams. Much of the copy was written by the traveling secretary, and Karst often had to rewrite it entirely to make it usable (Bill Borst, *Baseball through a Knothole*, 60–61).

That gave Karst an idea, and he wrote to Branch Rickey, who hired him as "Director of Information" of the St. Louis Cardinals (Gene Karst, "The Great Days, The Great Stars," *National Pastime* 2 [Fall 1982], 50; Lee Lowenfish, *Branch Rickey*, 207–208). Karst summarized his responsibilities: "I offered radio stations and metropolitan and rural newspapers within a 300-mile area baseball material featuring the Cardinals. This resulted in our getting great quantities of space in numerous sports pages and lots of free time on the radio. The game was not so commercialized in those days. Players cooperated, making public appearances on the air and at community-sponsored luncheons and dinners, for free" (Gene Karst, "Ready for the New Asterisk War?," *Baseball Research Journal* 26 [1997], 66–67). All the free exposure thus garnered helped broaden and expand the club's fan base.

16.1.4   Days. A common feature of early baseball was the benefit game, which was staged to raise proceeds for a needy player or someone else associated with the game. It was also customary to admit women free because of their beneficial influence on the male patrons (see **16.1.7** "Ladies' Day"). But today's practice of having fan-oriented days, either to attract a certain type of spectator or to give a free item to fans, does not seem to have appeared until the 1880s. The National League Providence Grays staged a "children's day" on August 25, 1882, during which "more than nine hundred boys and a few girls kept the police busy keeping order" (William D. Perrin, *Days of Greatness*, 18; *Worcester Evening Gazette*, August 25 and 26, 1882). Lee Allen reported that the Phillies held a bootblack day during spring training in 1883, admitting bootblacks, newsboys, and other urchins free (Lee Allen, *Sporting News*, April 20, 1968, reprinted in *Cooperstown Corner*).

In 1914 owner Charles Weeghman of the Chicago entry in the new Federal League courted fans with an array of days that honored specific groups (Stuart Shea, *Wrigley Field*, 53–55). The established major leagues responded in 1915 with such events as Boosters Day, Flag Day, Newsboy Day, and Schoolchildren's Day (Jonathan Fraser Light, *The Cultural Encyclopedia of Baseball*, 593). But this practice fell out of favor after the demise of the Federal League.

It was revived in the 1930s when baseball clubs began to introduce new marketing techniques to lure fans to games. One such entrepreneur was Al Eckert of Springfield, Missouri, whose initiatives prompted *Sporting News* to report in 1933 that "special nights of all sorts have been found highly successful by Eckert. At these 'special nights' he has staged pajama parades, horse shows, given away electric refrigerators, cash, free tickets, honored various ball players, and managers, used the city's famous Boy Scout band for concerts before the games, and countless other little tricks to pep up attendance" (*Sporting News*, January 19, 1933).

Not everyone welcomed this innovation. A 1935 *Sporting News* editorial acknowledged that such events boosted attendance but warned that they had "a tendency to cheapen the game if indulged in too often. Such days may keep the ordinary fan at home waiting for a bargain day. He asks himself why he should pay the regular price for admission when his attendance can be postponed until a 'community day.' He gets the idea that baseball is available with the purchase of a tube of shaving cream or a loaf of bread, or that a quarter will do the same duty at the park gate as will a half-dollar or dollar." The editorial concluded that the "community day" was a good idea on rare occasions, "but harmful if it

becomes a common practice" (*Sporting News*, July 18, 1935).

16.1.5 Fan Appreciation Days. In 1933 Larry MacPhail, then president of the Columbus team, "inaugurated a system of 'appreciation days,' on which thousands of unemployed fans were permitted to witness the games free of charge" (*Sporting News*, February 23, 1933).

16.1.6 Bat Days. The idea of giving a free item to fans may have occurred to some early club owners, but they no doubt concluded that the expenses would outweigh the benefits. Chicago Federal League owner Charles Weeghman gave out thousands of team caps when the club debuted in 1914, but his course was a rare one. By contrast, as Stuart Shea has noted, the Yankees refused for many years to license the sale of team caps, believing that allowing non-players to wear them would cheapen the logo (Stuart Shea, *Wrigley Field*, 50).

In particular, giving away a valuable item like a bat would have seemed madness. Accordingly, it was not until 1952 and under unusual circumstances that Bat Day became part of baseball. Bill Veeck was running the St. Louis Browns "when a guy who dealt in bankrupt firms came around with a shipload of homeless bats. I foisted him off on Rudie Schaffer, and Rudie worked out a deal in which we paid eleven cents for every finished bat, and the guy threw in all the unfinished ones for free. This gave us some indication why the firm had gone bankrupt, since the wood alone was worth more than we were paying. Rudie came back and suggested that we give them away on Father's Day" (Bill Veeck with Ed Linn, *The Hustler's Handbook*, 16).

The giveaway proved very popular, and similar events were successfully tried in other cities. This helped change the idea of a promotional day from one on which certain types of fans got in free to one in which the fans got free stuff.

16.1.7 Ladies' Days. In an important sense there is no such thing as a first Ladies' Day, since the practice of admitting female spectators without charge began almost as soon as admissions were charged at baseball games. This course was initiated in Brooklyn in 1865: "Hereafter ladies will be admitted free of charge, to all matches on the Capitoline grounds. No tickets of admission will be required" (*Brooklyn*

Eagle, September 4, 1865). At one of the first games with paid admission in Michigan, a state championship game on June 8, 1866, between the host Detroit Base Ball Club and the Washington Base Ball Club of Bay City, men were charged ten cents while women were admitted free. Similarly, admission was first charged in St. Louis for a game on July 10, 1867, with men paying twenty-five cents and ladies being admitted gratis (E. H. Tobias, *Sporting News*, November 16, 1895).

The practice remained common for many years to come. Ladies were admitted free when the Red Stockings played at Pittsfield, Massachusetts, on June 3, 1870 (Greg Rhodes and John Erardi, *The First Boys of Summer*, 103). It was reported that the customary free list would be suspended for a much-anticipated 1875 game in Detroit, with the "exception of ladies, who are always free" (*Detroit Evening News*, August 28, 1875). A typical 1876 ad in a Rochester, New York, newspaper read: "ADMISSION TWENTY FIVE CENTS, LADIES FREE" (*Rochester Democrat and Chronicle*, September 1, 1876; reprinted in Priscilla Astifan, "Rochester's Last Two Seasons of Amateur Baseball," *Rochester History* LXIII, No. 2 [Spring 2001], 8). In 1878 the *Washington Post* reported that "admission is fixed at the low figure of ten cents, with no charge for ladies" (*Washington Post*, April 25, 1878). There is documentation of countless other instances.

Special arrangements were often made for women attending early baseball games. At an 1857 match it was reported that "A tent for the female friends of the players had been prepared" (*New York Clipper*, July 18, 1857). Separate seating accommodations for women was also a common practice.

This was not simply a case of generosity or chivalry on the part of owners, since it was generally accepted that the presence of women increased male attendance and ensured better behavior from the men. As Henry Chadwick explained, "The presence of an assemblage of ladies pacifies the moral atmosphere of a base ball gathering, repressing, as it does, all outbursts of intemperate language which the excitement of a contest so frequently induces" (*The Ball Player's Chronicle*, June 13, 1867).

The attentions directed at female spectators sometimes had unexpected results. One newspaper account chided Frank Norton for having "one bad fault, and that is endeavoring to make fancy catches when the ladies are on the ground. Those look pretty but are not safe"

(William Rankin scrapbook, April 17, 1869). And a University of Michigan student managed to get picked off first base while trying to catch the eye of a "pretty Detroit lady in the gallery" (*Detroit Post*, September 30, 1867).

It has often been reported that Ladies' Day originated in the 1880s and was either invented by Abner Powell or popularized by handsome pitcher Tony Mullane. It is true that it became more popular to advertise Ladies' Day as an attraction in the 1880s. But the billing of Ladies' Day as a special event suggests not that this was a new idea but just the opposite—that it had become the norm to charge women for admission. Indeed, in 1882 a Chicago newspaper boasted: "The Chicago Club has no need to have a 'Ladies' Day' to fill its grand stand. Ladies of Chicago are so enthusiastic over base ball that they would pay to see a good game, and would despise an escort who would wait until a 'free' day to take them to the White Stocking Park" (*Chicago Herald*, May 21, 1882). And by the following year there was already a lively debate about who had invented Ladies' Day (*National Police Gazette*, September 15, 1883).

In succeeding years Ladies' Day went in and out of fashion as owners vacillated on whether they could afford to admit women for free, which led to considerable confusion. The National League banned the practice in 1909, and the Cubs tried unsuccessfully to repeal the ban in 1914 (Stuart Shea, *Wrigley Field*, 39–40). Perhaps this is what led Curt Smith to credit the invention of Ladies' Day to William Wrigley, who bought a controlling interest in the Cubs in 1918 (Curt Smith, *Voices of the Game*, 14). Incredibly, *Baseball Magazine* ran an article on Ladies' Day in 1939, asking players' opinions on the idea, which apparently was again being considered new. Jim Bagby, Jr., called Ladies' Day "a truly wonderful institution" and added, "I wonder why they didn't think of it a long time ago" (Harold Winerip, "Opinions on Ladies' Day," *Baseball Magazine*, July 1939; reprinted in Sidney Offit, ed., *The Best of Baseball*, 132–136). Ummmm, they did!

16.1.8 Name-the-team Contest. In the nineteenth century the formal name of a club was usually along the lines of the "Washington Base Ball Club." Many clubs did have nicknames and some of these were long-standing, but others were prone to change without much warning if their popularity waned.

The first name-the-team contest seems to have taken place in 1905, when the new Washington owners decided that they were "tired of the nickname 'Senators,' and want somebody to suggest something better. President [Thomas C.] Noyes has offered a season ticket to the person sending in the best nickname for the club" (*Sporting Life*, February 11, 1905). Over the next month 2,305 suggestions were received, some of which "contained a great deal of originality. One man asks that the club be called the 'Ball-bearers,' because they are so easily worked. Another thinks the 'Weather Prophets' would be a good name, presumably because they are so unreliable. Others want the club called the 'Worms,' because they will turn. Some names in the batch that will probably be considered are Atoners, Waifs and Improvers" (*Washington Post*, March 12, 1905). Some fans included lengthy justifications of their choices. A proponent of the name Hornets who must have had a lot of time on his hands explained: "All the letters in the word 'Hornets,' except 'H,' are found in 'Senators,' with the addition of 'as.' This is significant, as it gives us 'Has.' But the 'Hornet' is a bee without an 'N.' Therefore, we will expect to have lively bees this year instead of 'has beens'" (*Washington Times*, March 2, 1905, 8). Eventually the name "Nationals" was selected because this was the name of successful Washington clubs of old.

Ironically the "new" name did not capture the public imagination, and newspapers again began to refer to the team as the Senators. Nonetheless Nationals remained the club's official nickname until 1956. Another strange coincidence occurred when baseball returned to Washington a century after this contest and once again settled upon the name of Nationals.

16.1.9   Talking to Fans. Perhaps the ultimate example that the people who run baseball have not always promoted their product very well was a short-lived 1932 National League rule that uniformed personnel could not talk to fans. On April 27, Cardinals manager Gabby Street broke the rule in a game in Cincinnati when an uncle whom he had not seen in twenty years hailed him. Street stopped to talk to his long-lost relative and was fined five dollars for doing so (*Sporting News*, May 5, 1932). The bizarre rule was rescinded on May 19.

(ii) Promotional Concepts and Themes

16.2.1   The National Pastime. Arguably baseball's first and most effective marketing

technique was the positioning of baseball as America's national game. This will be discussed in more detail in Chapter 25.

16.2.2   Code of Conduct. Owners have long recognized that squeaky-clean behavior by the players would be beneficial for business. Getting them to behave has been another matter. The *St. Louis Post-Dispatch*, for example, wrote in 1889, "Such language as 'say, yer rotten, yer stinkin',' as Tebeau yelled frequently at Latham yesterday is rather coarse to be used in the presence of ladies and should not be tolerated on the ball field" (*St. Louis Post-Dispatch*, April 27, 1889). But how do you prevent players from hollering "yer rotten, yer stinkin'"?

Clubs of course have always been free to implement and enforce their own team rules, and many have tried to require a high standard of personal conduct. Philadelphia owner John I. Rogers, for example, claimed in 1898 that all his players had signed temperance pledges (*St. Louis Post-Dispatch*, April 10, 1898). But this could obviously lead to double standards for star players.

In 1898 the National League adopted a much more comprehensive player behavior code which had been devised by Cincinnati owner John T. Brush. The Brush Resolution was intended to eliminate cursing and other conduct that was being blamed for declining attendance. But the way the idea was implemented turned off potential supporters. As one unidentified player explained, "We are not refusing to sign because we object to a rule forbidding the use of indecent language on the ball field. The sense of the rule is all right, but its passage and the hullabaloo Brush made about it reflected on every ball player in the League. There was nothing for the public to think but that we were a foul-mouthed lot. There are men of that calibre in base ball as there are in every profession, but they are exceptions to the general run of players, and could have been suppressed if the umpires, managers and League presidents did their plain duty under the old rules. . . . Base ball is a clean, gentlemanly game, and Mr. Brush has done it more harm than good by the hurrah he has excited over his resolution" (*Sporting Life*, April 23, 1898, 1; the ballplayer was identified only as a college man who played for the Browns). Press members also found the measure too harsh, suggesting that the owners "could readily have suppressed single-handed the evils complained of . . .

without publicly pillorying ball players as a class of unclean and obscene ruffians" (*Sporting Life*, April 16, 1898, 4).

The biggest problem was that the proposed penalties were far too harsh. Even Giants' owner Andrew Freedman condemned the draconian punishments, adding, "I do not think that the using of obscene language on the ball field is nearly as bad as it has been pictured" (*Oklahoma City Daily Oklahoman*, February 18, 1898). As a result, before the new season had even opened, the Brush resolution had come to be regarded as "a dead letter" (*Sporting News*, March 25, 1899, 4).

A still more unrealistic approach was to involve law enforcement, such as when catcher John J. Dillon of Albany was arrested for using profane language during a game at Binghamton on June 12, 1905 (*Sporting Life*, July 1, 1905). Such efforts were obviously doomed, and though the standard players' contract continued to forbid certain activities, the owners gradually came to accept that some forms of morality cannot be legislated.

When the All-American Girls Baseball League was formed in 1943, it made a similar effort. The league instituted a strict contract filled with behavioral restrictions based upon the Actors' Equity agreement. Players were forbidden, among other things, from smoking, drinking hard liquor, or appearing "unkempt" in public. Any social engagement had to be approved in advance by the club's chaperone.

Nor were the clauses restricted to "don'ts." In the early years of the league, players were required to attend a charm school at which they were taught etiquette for social occasions, beauty tips, and how to "avoid noisy, rough and raucous talk and actions." One player later remembered how hard it was "to walk in high heels with a book on your head when you had a charley horse" (Lois Browne, *Girls of Summer*, 38–39, 43–45).

16.2.3 Spite Fences. In 2002 the Chicago Cubs draped their wire fences behind the bleachers to prevent the long-standing practice of watching the game from the rooftops of the apartments overlooking Wrigley Field. This was only the latest—and indeed was one of the most civil—skirmishes in a perennial battle. Indeed, it is not too strong to say that no sooner did baseball begin to be played in enclosed stadiums (see **14.1.1**) than people started trying to find sneaky ways to get inside the walls or watch the game by some other means.

This was particularly common in the early days of professional baseball. An 1862 benefit game in Brooklyn for the United States Sanitary Commission prompted complaints about the many "dead heads" who sat on "the surrounding embankment" so as to avoid paying (William J. Ryczek, *Baseball's First Inning*, 190). In 1874 a St. Louis sportswriter wrote sarcastically, "The only show for the dead-heads to see the great game of base ball to be played this afternoon at the Grand Avenue Park is to go up in a balloon and anchor over the park, there being no railroad cars in the neighborhood to climb up on" (*St. Louis Democrat*, July 19, 1874). The following year the Keokuk Westerns of the National Association disbanded shortly after the local paper complained that "Men and boys who would scorn to steal into a circus under the canvas, will sit on an adjacent fence and take in a ball game that other people pay their 25 or 50 cents to see" (quoted in John Liepa, "Not Yet Ready for the Big Leagues," *Iowa Heritage Illustrated*, Spring 2006 (87:1), 21). Boston installed a barbed-wire fence around the South End Grounds one year later and reported that it significantly reduced the number of gate-crashers (Michael Gershman, *Diamonds*, 29). That alone did not prove enough, and three years later the club announced plans to make the fence around the grounds "20 feet higher, much to the grief and disgust of the people on adjacent streets who have been in the habit of letting seats on their roofs at reduced rates" (*New York Clipper*, September 13, 1879).

Similar conflicts were occurring in other cities. Hartford president Morgan Bulkeley erected an addition to his outfield fence that year to stem the practice of parking carriages outside the grounds and charging people to sit on top of them (David Arcidiacono, *Grace, Grit and Growling*, 61). A different tack was taken in Rochester, New York, where the club persuaded the city fire marshal and wooden building commissioner to declare rooftop throngs unsafe (Priscilla Astifan, "Baseball in the Nineteenth Century Part V," *Rochester History* LXIV, No. 4 [Fall 2002], 5).

The *Washington Post* complained in 1878, "unless the lovers of this game relinquish choice positions outside the fence and plunk down their money and come within, the plans of the club for a brilliant series of games will be seriously crippled" (*Washington Post*, April 22, 1878). The *Brooklyn Eagle* observed that same year: "The Centennial Ground is not the most attractive place for spectators. If the covered seats happen to be full—and they only seat about 200 on each stand—and the people have to stand around to watch the game, they immediately become the target of abuse from the fence peepers, who claim the right to drive every man standing inside the enclosure who is in the way of their view out of their view" (*Brooklyn Eagle*, August 22, 1878).

The following year Henry Chadwick urged the Jersey City management "to put up some barrier cutting off the free view of the play on the field obtained from the trestle-work 'grand-stand' outside the inclosure back of the catcher's position" (*New York Clipper*, June 28, 1879). Many clubs did just that, such as Louisville's American Association club, which announced in 1884: "The fence around the Eclipse Park will be built four feet higher to exclude all outside dead-heads" (*Louisville Courier-Journal*, March 23, 1884).

This was clearly about more than just saving money. During the 1880 season, for instance, some Clevelanders "would not pay fifty cents to see the game, but hired a three dollar rig instead, so that they could stand on the buggy seat and look over the fence" (*Cleveland Leader*, April 15, 1881). Moreover some spectators were so anxious to get a free view of the action that they disregarded personal safety. The *Washington Post* observed in 1884, "The building inspector has warned the owners of the building near the National grounds not to allow so many people on the roof of the building. An accident is liable to occur there any game" (*Washington Post*, July 6, 1884). Twice during the 1875 season, spectators in Columbus, Ohio, were injured when the roof of a shack near the park collapsed under the weight of too many people (*New York Clipper*, July 24, 1875).

A paper in Columbus, Ohio, reported in 1883: "The owner of the lot on the west side of Recreation Park not being satisfied with a scaffold, has erected a regular tier of seats over looking the grounds. He will probably make quite a 'spec' tomorrow on this little enterprise, although he is reported as being opposed to Sunday games. As a piece of 'gall' and littleness this takes the premium" (*Columbus Sunday Morning News*, July 8, 1883).

But in fact, if such a premium had been offered, there would have been stiff competition. An 1886 account noted, "The directors of the Bridgeport Club have decided to tar the telegraph poles and the trees that surround their grounds so as to keep people from climbing them to watch the game" (*Detroit Free Press*,

April 7, 1886). At a game in Boston on July 19, 1884, the spectators who climbed poles to witness the game got an even more unpleasant surprise. Someone painted the poles during the game, so the freeloaders had to ruin their clothes in order to get down (*Sporting Life*, July 30, 1884).

In 1886 the National League's Detroit Wolverines unsuccessfully sued a man who had been selling seats overlooking Recreation Park. After losing the case, the club built a fifty-foot fence to settle the matter. The *Detroit Free Press* reported, "The struggle of the tower stand-builders and the fence-builders is still going on at Recreation Park, with the odds in favor of the latter. An enterprising firm is erecting an advertising fence that will shut out the view from outside stands, and the sharks that have lived off the base ball club will have to go to work again" (*Detroit Free Press*, June 4, 1886).

That same season, Boston was involved in a conflict with an entrepreneur named Sullivan who erected a tall tower overlooking right field and began selling admission to it. Boston management erected a screen to block their view, so Mr. Sullivan added another story to his structure, prompting another addition to the screen (*Boston Globe*, May 31 and June 1, 1886).

Sullivan eventually outlasted the ball club, and Sullivan's Tower became one of the Hub's landmarks (*Boston Globe*, July 29, 1888; August 4, 1892; April 19, 1896). The tower inspired one regular to write a poem that included stanzas such as this one: "Packed like sardines in a box / One tier above another / We all look down for miles around / (Enough to make 'em shudder); / Some pays a dollar to see the fun, / But Me and Din McQuade, / We pays a dime to see the nine/ From Sullivan's palisade" (*Boston Globe*, July 10, 1889).

In the 1890s club owners began rigging up giant canvases to "down the 'dead heads' who line the roofs of houses surrounding the ball grounds" (*Sporting Life*, May 5, 1894; *Williamsport Sunday Grit*, May 21, 1893). The multi-tiered stadiums built in the early twentieth century gradually made the issue less common. But the problem continued to plague semipro and barnstorming clubs. Guy Green, who managed a famous touring club of Indians in the first decade of the twentieth century, wrote with dismay about the "deadheads" who sought to watch without paying. He observed that "The number of people who will put forth five dollars' worth of effort in order to see a twenty-five cent ball game without paying the admission price, is surprising" (Guy W. Green, *Fun and Frolic with an Indian Ball Team*, 37–40). Small-town papers like the *Belle Plaine* (Minnesota) *Herald* regularly complained about spectators who "selected the best places to witness the game and then didn't even have a nickel when the hat was passed around" (Tom Melchior, *Belle Plaine Baseball, 1884–1960*, 47; also 50, 53, 69, etc.).

From time to time new moves and counter-moves were introduced. In Adrian, Michigan, in 1910 the home team moved the location of the scoreboard in order to block the view of employees of the Lamb Fence Factory, who had been watching the games with a powerful tele-scope (Marc Okkonen, *Minor League Baseball Towns of Michigan*, 4).

An amusing indication of the persistence of this practice came during World War I when the Bureau of Internal Revenue ruled that "perchers" were subject to a special war tax on baseball tickets. The decision warranted men-tion in the *Wall Street Journal*, which explained, "Enterprising owners and occupants of build-ings who are charging for seats on the roof are expected to collect it." Cited as an example was the case of an African-American woman whose yard adjoined a ballpark and who had been "turning an honest penny by the sale of seats in a tree. The price was five and ten cents depend-ing on how high her patrons had to climb. Since hearing from the Bureau of Internal Revenue the cost of seats has gone up to six and eleven cents, the extra cent being added to the war rev-enues" (*Wall Street Journal*, May 23, 1918, 2).

The most celebrated case of the twentieth century took place at Philadelphia's Shibe Park, home of the Athletics. Soon after the park opened in 1909, residents on North Twentieth Street, across from the ballpark, began charging admission to watch games from their homes and rooftops. By the late 1920s the practice had grown to the point that thousands of spectators were watching from the rooftop stands, and the club felt compelled to act.

The Athletics first attempted to address the problem by using their political contacts to en-force building codes and fire regulations. Then they attempted to compromise by asking ten-ants to agree not to undersell them nor to sell the rooftop seats unless a game was sold out. When neither course was successful, the ball club took a more direct approach. Before the 1935 season the club built a thirty-eight-foot corrugated metal addition to the twelve-foot right-field fence.

The addition was constructed to end the practice of deadheading, but it may have ulti-mately done the club more harm than good. Bruce Kuklick noted that what became known as the "spite fence" engendered fan bitterness against the club that lasted for years and even generations (Bruce Kuklick, *To Every Thing a Season*, 73–76).

16.2.4   Doubleheaders. More than one game was sometimes played on a day in the early days of baseball, but this practice had largely ended before the advent of professional base-ball. There were two good reasons for this. First, owners saw no reason to give away twice as much of their product for the regular price. Second, the absence of lights meant that play would have to begin very early to be certain of completing two games.

Boston did host a planned separate-admis-sion doubleheader on July 4, 1873 (William J. Ryczek, *Blackguards and Red Stockings*, 116). Twinbills were occasionally staged in the en-suing years, usually out of necessity when a canceled game had to be rescheduled. A two-for-one doubleheader was staged in Worcester (then a National League city) on September 25, 1882, but it was a desperate ploy by a franchise that disbanded at the end of the season (Troy Soos, *Before the Curse*, 57).

As Charlie Bevis has reported, the 1880s saw separate-admission doubleheaders become common on holidays. Initially there were only two such holidays during the season—Decora-tion Day (now Memorial Day) and Indepen-dence Day. But in 1888 Labor Day began to be recognized by several states, and it became a national holiday in 1894. All three holidays pro-vided a special opportunity for working-class fans to attend games, which ensured enough demand for a morning game and an afternoon game (Charlie Bevis, "Holiday Doubleheaders," *Baseball Research Journal* 33 [2004], 60–63).

By the turn of the century, holiday twinbills were routinely drawing enormous crowds. Cin-cinnati business manager Frank Bancroft tried to capitalize by introducing the idea of playing two games for a single admission price on non-holidays. He also coined a new term for them, as was explained in an 1898 article: "Bancroft is responsible for 'double header' being used to designate 2 games for 1 price of admission. Bannie advertised his double attraction as a 'double header,' and it was not long until every club in the league was using the term" (*Cincin-nati Enquirer*, July 24, 1898).

The practice was met with considerable resistance. Sportswriter H. G. Merrill, for example, argued that the practice cheapened the game: "I sincerely trust that both the big leagues will refrain from indulging in double-headers, or 'bargain days' to the extent that was the case last season" (*Sporting News*, July 30, 1904).

Despite such naysayers, doubleheaders became a fan favorite. Researcher Charlie Bevis reported that during World War I the separate-admission twinbill began to go out of favor, and the 1920s saw the single-admission double-header become a mainstay on Sundays and holidays (Charlie Bevis, "Holiday Doubleheaders," *Baseball Research Journal* 33 [2004], 60–63).

16.2.5   Pennant Races. A pennant race is one of the most surefire ways to raise the level of interest in baseball, though it is impossible to guarantee one. Indeed, the paradoxical reality is that it is easier for a league's owners to do things to ruin the pennant race of a rival league than to ensure that they have one themselves. It is sometimes claimed, for example, that the American League made a deliberate effort in its early years to sign players from every National League team except Pittsburgh, thereby ensuring that the Pirates would run away with the pennant. While it seems unlikely that there really was a plan by the American League, the National League's dull pennant races did help the American League gain fans.

16.2.6   World Series. The World Series has proved to be a crucial marketing tool for baseball, creating the suspense and anticipation that enliven the dog days of the long season. Like so many of the game's most effective marketing devices, its importance was discovered accidentally.

As noted in chapter 22, baseball postseason championships date back to the early 1880s. These were, however, generally viewed by those inside baseball as just a way of making a little extra money. There was an understandable sentiment that the season-long accomplishment of amassing the best record was a more significant achievement than the results of a short series.

This was particularly the case in the early 1880s when the American Association was perceived as being inferior to the National League. As the decade wore on, the strengths of the two leagues became more balanced, and interest in the series showed a corresponding rise. When the two leagues merged after the 1891 season, the newly formed big league experimented with

a couple of different formats for recapturing fan interest. These showed some promise at first, but anticipation about a series between clubs that had been competing all year soon waned. The lack of interest reflected the fact that the players continued to regard the regular season as the true championship and the Temple Cup as merely a way to make quick cash.

The American League's emergence as a rival major league, followed by the 1903 peace treaty between the leagues, created a potential windfall. Not only was there natural curiosity about which champion club was better, but the interest was further fueled by the well-documented animosity between the two leagues. Baseball cashed in immediately with a World Series that was a financial success, and yet many within baseball viewed the event as little more than an exhibition. Tim Murnane, for instance, pointed out that the concept of such a series was a dubious one and referred to the contests as being "but exhibition games" (*Boston Globe*, August 23 and September 6, 1906).

The 1904 season saw renewed enmity between the two leagues that piqued interest in a postseason series. Instead, as the New York Giants moved toward clinching the 1904 National League pennant, club owner John T. Brush announced that his team would not face the American League champions. He explained that the champion of the National League should not have "to submit its championship honors to a contest with a victorious club of a minor league" (quoted in Benton Stark, *The Year They Called Off the World Series*, 160).

This reasoning was obviously disingenuous, since the American League's representatives had triumphed in the 1903 series. It is equally clear that Brush's decision was greatly influenced by the seething resentment that he and Giants manager John McGraw held for key American League figures, most notably circuit president Ban Johnson.

Nonetheless it must be emphasized that Brush's position is far more reasonable than it appears today. He and McGraw were voicing the sentiment of many by viewing the regular season as the true championship and believing that postseason games could only detract from that accomplishment. Whether this was their true motive or merely a justification, the principle they cited is a legitimate one. McGraw had especially good reason to have felt this way, since he had played in all four Temple Cups in the early 1890s (see **22.2.2** "Intramural Playoffs") and learned how a postseason playoff can undermine the regular season. Moreover, the fact that the Giants were sacrificing the opportunity to make a substantial amount of money suggests that principle played at least some role in their decision.

Whatever their motivation, Brush and Mc-Graw seem to have been genuinely surprised by the extent of the backlash that ensued. The *New York World* typified the response, asking what right Brush had "to deprive the baseball public of an opportunity to see what would undoubtedly be the most interesting baseball series ever played? He gets his money from the sport-loving public of this city and should consider their wishes" (quoted in Benton Stark, *The Year They Called Off the World Series*, 163). The *Chicago Tribune* was even more direct, calling Brush "a businessman, and not in any sense of the word a sportsman" (quoted in Benton Stark, *The Year They Called Off the World Series*, 165). Note the fascinating turn of events: instead of being credited for forsaking a mercenary series, Brush is being accused of denying the public of something they demanded.

Fans joined in the outcry, with one writing: "Public opinion says play! and few there are who have dared to face public opinion and attend its overthrow!" (letter to *New York Herald* by C. Allyn Stephens; quoted in Benton Stark, *The Year They Called Off the World Series*, 164). John Brush stuck to his guns, and the World Series was not played that year. Nonetheless he clearly realized that he had misgauged public sentiment and, as a result, forsaken both a lucrative opportunity and a splendid marketing tool for baseball. That offseason he helped negotiate the Brush Rules, which established the World Series as an annual showcase for baseball.

16.2.7 Keeping Balls in the Stands. Early baseball matches concluded with the ritual of the losers presenting a baseball to the winning side. Some clubs would proudly display the balls thus earned in a special trophy case (see 22.3.1 "Trophies"). While few of today's fans are aware of this long-extinct custom, the mad scrambles for foul balls suggest that fans continue to sense that there is a special status associated with taking a ball home from the game.

In early baseball there was no question of fans keeping balls that went into the stands. As noted in the entry on new baseballs (1.26), the rules referred to the ball in the singular until 1876. The rules also specified that the game be stopped for up to five minutes so that players

could search for a lost ball. As late as the 1880s, legendary manager Harry Wright was keeping a log of every ball owned by his team and its condition.

Nor were balls that were hit out of the grounds abandoned. Small children gathered outside ballparks during games, hoping to retrieve a foul ball and receive the customary reward of free admittance. "Foul balls," declared the *Chicago News* in 1884, "were invented in the interest of the small boy, and one is admitted every time the ball goes over the fence" (reprinted in the *Winnipeg Times*, May 23, 1884). But adherence to the custom was not universal; researcher David McDonald found that a Toronto paper reported in 1887: "Fifteen balls were knocked over the left field fence at Buffalo Monday and were stolen by bad boys" (*Toronto World*, June 1, 1887).

In response, clubs became more systematic in their ball-retrieval methods. Washington hired a fleet-footed groundskeeper named Charlie in 1892 to chase down balls. By 1899 the club had hired a fleet of young boys to fetch baseballs (Gerard S. Petrone, *When Baseball Was Young*, 58). As discussed in the entry on "Deliberate Fouls" (2.3.2), clubs also tried many ways to discourage players from hitting foul balls.

By the turn of the century it was becoming increasingly common for fans to try to retain foul balls. According to a 1902 note, "Baseballs that go into the stands at St. Louis are hopelessly lost, the man who first gets his hands on the flying sphere clinging to it" (*Detroit Free Press*, May 2, 1902).

But baseball management was not willing to surrender the point without a fight, sometimes literally. It is said that when a spectator at a game in New York refused to return a foul ball, John McGraw responded by stealing the man's hat. At least a couple of fans—one in Washington in 1901 and another in New York in 1903—were arrested for trying to keep foul balls (*Washington Post*, May 1, 1901; *New York Sun*, April 22, 1903). In Chicago, sportswriter W. A. Phelon reported that Cubs president James A. Hart "turned policeman the other day . . . the balls hit into the seats are not coming back as they used to and Mr. Hart determined to make an example of somebody. Finally, seeing a well-dressed man in a box hide a ball under his hat Mr. Hart went after him, pulled him out of his box, and after a short but brilliant battle, had him arrested. Harry Pulliam and Willie Shettsline watched the fray with great enthusiasm, and offered many valuable suggestions as to the best way of catching, holding and whacking the prisoner." The fan, Samuel Stott, was a member of the Board of Trade and he "retaliated by getting out warrants charging Mr. Hart with fifty-seven different varieties of offenses" (*Sporting Life*, July 1, 1905; *Chicago Tribune*, June 22, 1905).

The mayhem continued to spread to other cities. Francis Richter reported after a 1905 game in Philadelphia, "At least fifty balls were stolen during Saturday's game. Nearly every ball batted into the crowd was pocketed" (*Sporting Life*, July 15, 1905). *Sporting Life* noted the following year that "sometimes balls knocked into the crowd mysteriously disappear" (*Sporting Life*, March 31, 1906). In 1907 Boston manager Fred Tenney reportedly was offered a bonus if the National League club made a profit, so he tried to secure it by going into the stands to retrieve foul balls (Troy Soos, *Before the Curse*, 122–123).

As this suggests, the considerable expense of baseballs meant that ball clubs did not see the issue as a symbolic one. The *Ottawa Citizen* reported in 1913: "Prosecutions will follow if the deliberate appropriation of baseballs continues at Lansdowne Park. Yesterday no fewer than four which went into the grandstand were pocketed by souvenir-hunting fans or youngsters. The balls cost about $1.50 each, and the supply is one of the biggest items of expenditure which the Ottawa club has to foot. Chief Ross has instructed the men to keep a sharp lookout on the thieves" (*Ottawa Citizen*, August 19, 1913).

As it became harder to rely upon children to retrieve balls hit out of the park, more clubs began to station grown men behind the stands to throw back foul balls (*Boston Globe*; reprinted in *Sporting Life*, September 30, 1905). This began as another cost-saving measure, but before long it was recognized that this lent itself to strategic possibilities. Brooklyn manager Wilbert Robinson began to notice in 1915 that the speed of ball retrieval in Boston seemed to vary. Balls were returned much more rapidly when the visiting club was batting, thus giving the home club more opportunities to hit newer, livelier balls. Accordingly, "Claiming that Jack Coombs had been deprived of a win in Boston by fans keeping balls, [Robinson] urged Dodger fans to be selective, just as they were in Beantown. The locals there, he claimed, kept only balls that had been battered and scuffed when the local team was at bat. This forced the

umpires to put a clean ball into the game to the advantage of Boston's batters. Robbie urged Brooklyn's fans to do the same. 'Throw back the scuffed balls if our team is in the field,' he counseled, 'and give our pitchers an edge.' To Ebbets' chagrin, Brooklyn fans were impartial in their greed. They kept every ball they could get their hands on and battled ushers and park police to keep them" (Jack Kavanagh and Norman Macht, *Uncle Robbie*, 79).

Since fans were no more willing to concede the point than were the denizens of baseball front offices, the conflict raged on. In addition, the nature of baseball meant there would be plenty of foul balls to spark such confrontations. As a result, ushers, policemen, and stadium officials continued to battle fans for stray balls, engendering no end of ill will.

The first man to wave the white flag was former Chicago Federal League franchise owner Charles Weeghman, who purchased the Cubs after the 1915 season and brought a new mentality to the senior circuit. On April 29, 1916, he announced that the team's fans would be allowed to keep balls hit into the stands. It is often assumed that Weeghman's concession was the turning point for the issue, but other owners were reluctant to follow his cue. The Phillies, for instance, requested compensation for eight baseballs hit into the stands during pregame batting practice at Weeghman Park and retained by the fans (*Chicago Tribune*, July 15, 1916).

It accordingly seems more accurate to view Weeghman's decision as the first of several important factors that led to the change. The second one was initiated during World War I when owners donated used balls to servicemen. As Billy Evans explained in 1920, this generosity had unintended consequences:

"The baseball fan for some reason believes any ball he grabs becomes his property. Such a custom was largely developed during the war days. At that time if a ball was fouled off and secured by one of the spectators he tossed it to one of the men in the service—provided an attendant approached to get the ball. If no attendant was in the vicinity the fan often appropriated the ball for himself. Otherwise he looked around for a fellow in the garb of the army or navy and tossed it to him. A patriotic spirit kept the attendant from seeking the ball from a man in the service. Now that the war is over, the custom of tossing the ball around the stand continues. If some one gets a ball, and an attaché of the park spots him, and approaches to get it, he tosses it back or forward a few rows. This practice continues until the attendant gives up in disgust" (*Sporting News*, December 30, 1920).

Another contributing factor was the concerted effort being made to replace used balls with fresh ones. While major league owners still wished to retain used balls, they now only wanted to do so for use in practice. This made the position of those charged with trying to retrieve balls even more difficult. How do you tell a fan who has caught a prize that it needs to be returned so it can be dropped in a ball bag for use in practice?

The trend toward replacing balls is often attributed to the fatal beaning of Ray Chapman in 1920. In fact it had begun more than a decade earlier and had accelerated when fans responded positively to the home run feats of Babe Ruth. But Chapman's tragic death certainly placed renewed emphasis on replacing sodden baseballs, since he had apparently been unable to pick up the discolored ball that killed him.

The final factor was a May 16, 1921, incident in which a fan named Reuben Berman caught a foul ball at the Polo Grounds. When asked to return it, Berman instead followed the practice described by Evans and tossed it to another spectator. He was interrogated by security officers and ejected from the ballpark after being refunded the price of his ticket. Berman sued for $2,000 in damages and won his case, though he was awarded only $100 (Peter Segroie, "Reuben's Ruling Helps You 'Have a Ball,'" *Baseball Research Journal* 20 [1991], 85; David Mandell, "Reuben Berman's Foul Ball," *National Pastime* 25 [2005], 106–107).

The decision in the Berman case applied only to New York, and even there it is far from clear that it would have survived appeal. The recent court case involving two fans who claimed to have ownership of Barry Bonds' seventy-third home run revealed that there is little legal precedence for the voluntary relinquishment of valuable property. So the club could certainly have taken its chances on appeal.

But developments of the preceding five years had changed the climate dramatically. Clubs were beginning to recognize that winning such legal battles would cost the club too much in ill will. Thus the Giants gave in to the inevitable and decided not to appeal.

The issue continued to flare up in other ballparks. Within months of the Berman case, Pittsburgh police arrested three fans for keeping foul balls at Pirates games. The fans threatened legal action and prompted Pittsburgh Director of Public Safety Robert Alderdice to call a halt to such arrests (*New York Times*, July 10, 1921). Park officials, however, could still take action. The next year an eleven-year-old Philadelphia boy named Robert Cotter was arrested and spent a night in jail for keeping a foul ball. He was released by a judge who commented, "Such an act on the part of a boy is merely proof that he is following his most natural impulses. It is a thing I would do myself" (Tim Wiles, "The Joy of Foul Balls," *National Pastime* 25 [2005], 104). A similar incident in Washington in 1924 saw a fan named William E. Drury arrested and charged with petty larceny ("Keeps Foul Ball; Held for Theft," *Washington Post*, August 19, 1924; cited in Reed Browning, *Baseball's Greatest Season, 1924*, 170). In 1930 the Chicago Cubs, no longer owned by Charles Weeghman, had a seventeen-year-old Cubs fan named Arthur Porto arrested after he tried to keep a foul ball. In court the next day, the judge ruled that the boy had a right to the ball, and the charges were dismissed (*New York Times*, June 26, 1930).

These futile endeavors pretty much ended the owners' hopes that the law would side with them—the next notable instance came in 1937 when a spectator at Yankee Stadium tried to remove a ball lodged in the screen behind home plate, was roughed up by ushers, and then sued the Yankees, winning $7,500. During World War II it was customary to donate used balls to soldiers, but after the war the owners finally conceded the issue, and foul balls became souvenirs.

While it may seem in retrospect that the owners' relinquishment of balls hit into the stands was inevitable, that wasn't the case. In many other sports, such as basketball, tennis, soccer, and volleyball, fans still routinely return balls that leave the playing area. The Negro Leagues continued to do everything possible to keep balls in play, including the old tactic of allowing free admission to any child who retrieved a ball hit out of the stadium (Donn Rogosin, *Invisible Men*, 72–73). Negro Leagues owner Abe Manley once even sent a note to one of his players in the middle of an at bat threatening to fine him the cost of the lost baseballs if he fouled off any more pitches (Brad Snyder, *Beyond the Shadow of the Senators*, 158).

16.2.8 All-Star Games. The first major league All-Star Game was announced on May 18, 1933, and took place at Chicago's Comiskey Park on July 6, 1933. The event was the brainchild of *Chicago Tribune* sports editor Arch Ward and was played as part of the World's Fair.

Of course the idea of an All-Star Game was not new, dating all the way back to an 1858 game at the Fashion Race Course, when the best players from Brooklyn and New York had thrilled baseball's first paying spectators (see "Admission Fees," **18.1.2**, for more details). Nor was there anything new about Arch Ward's idea. In 1908 a fan named Arthur H. Koehne wrote to inquire, "In the event of a Field Day, which, in my estimation, appeals to every fan, why not play an inter-league game after the field contests have been decided, provided the sixteen major league teams gather, as no doubt they can when the Eastern teams go west and vice versa. A battery could be chosen from one team and for the remaining seven positions one man could be selected from the other seven teams. A formidable team from each league could then take the field and play a game which every fan in the country would be interested in beyond the question of a doubt" (*Sporting Life*, April 11, 1908).

Baseball Magazine had also lobbied for such an event for many years. Ward's colleague at the *Tribune*, George Strickler, noted that such an event "had been talked about for years. It was thought to be impossible. But Arch had sufficient persuasion and was enough of a politician to put it over" (quoted in Jerome Holtzman, *No Cheering in the Press Box*, 157–158).

According to Strickler, Ward had to use all of the *Tribune*'s clout to make the game a reality: "the National League almost killed it. Arch had to put pressure on the Boston Braves and Judge Fuchs. Arch called Fuchs and said, 'Look, we're going to announce this the day after tomorrow, and either we're going to announce there is a game, or that we almost had one and didn't because of you. Now can you and the National League stand that kind of publicity?'" (quoted in Jerome Holtzman, *No Cheering in the Press Box*, 158).

The first All-Star Game was thus apparently played under coercion and was intended to be a one-time-only event. But the game proved both a popular and aesthetic success. It began with the teams entertaining the fans by playing hand-over-hand on a bat to decide which team would bat first. A Babe Ruth home run provided a fitting climax to an American League victory. Perhaps most important, nearly fifty thousand fans turned out for the game and half a million cast votes to select the participants.

The senior circuit requested a chance to host a return match the following year, and its success caused the All-Star Game to become an annual event and a great showcase for baseball. The Negro Leagues began their own long-running All-Star series one month later, also at Comiskey Park. The crucial big payday that the games provided was a factor in keeping several struggling Negro Leagues teams alive during the ensuing years (Neil Lanctot, *Negro League Baseball*, 188). The success of the concept also prompted Arch Ward to follow it up the next year by inaugurating football's College All-Star Game, which pitted the best college seniors against the NFL champions.

(iii) Mass Media

The fundamental dilemma of marketing is deciding when giving away one's product stimulates interest and when it amounts to no more than giving away for free what one wanted to sell. For baseball owners this issue has always been crystallized when new communications media make it possible for fans to follow the games without going to the ballpark. Not without cause, owners have been apprehensive about the effects of new media on attendance. Will the new medium fire the faithful up about the home club and get them to attend more games? Or will they become complacent and replace the ballpark experience with the vicarious one? These same basic questions have recurred with each new medium of mass communication.

16.3.1 Newspaper Coverage. Newspapers don't seem like a very powerful medium to us today, but they were an extraordinarily potent one in mid-nineteenth-century America. On one hand, they were well established as the country's most important and effective means of mass communication. Yet rather than becoming stodgy, as usually happens to long-established media, newspapers had been infused with a new sense of immediacy by the introduction of the penny paper in the 1830s. This development changed the basic dynamic of the medium by creating a new feeling of interactivity. As Paul Starr observed, newspapers suddenly "anticipated the modern structure of media enterprise" by selling "their readers to advertisers as much as they sold copies to readers" (Paul Starr, *The Creation of the Media*, 131–135).

As a result, when baseball entered the picture the hold of newspapers on the public imagination was profound. Moreover, baseball's great boom from 1865 to 1867 came at a time when the newspapers needed the game to fill the news void that had resulted from the end of the Civil War. Baseball would likewise come to rely deeply on the newspapers, yet the game's relationship with this medium remained uneasy, a development that would prefigure similar discomfort with the more rapid media that later emerged.

Early baseball reporters generally had a very close relationship with the clubs they covered. More than a few, such as William Cauldwell (see **23.1.3** "Baseball Reporters"), were members of the clubs on which they reported. Today that would be viewed as a breach of journalistic ethics, but in the 1860s that whole concept was still in the developmental stage.

By the late 1860s, distance was developing between players and reporters. Part of the problem was that players usually enjoyed coverage only when their club was doing well. But the development of an adversarial relationship often manifested itself in much more tangible forms.

At least one player prefigured Steve Carlton's policy of not speaking to reporters. When early star Jack Burdock died in 1931, his obituary noted that he had been asked to reminisce about his career by New York sportswriter Joe Vila, but had replied: "I never talked to a reporter when I was playing ball, and it is too late to begin now" (*Sporting News*, December 10, 1931).

An 1864 confrontation led Henry Chadwick to invoke the royal "we" in reporting that Charles Bomeisler of the Olympics of Philadelphia had "threatened us with personal chastisement if we ever put his name in the papers again" (*New York Clipper*, August 13, 1864; William J. Ryczek, *Baseball's First Inning*, 124–125). As described in the entry for "Press Boxes" (**14.5.3**), Chadwick seems to have suspected that Dick McBride was deliberately aiming to hit reporters with foul balls during an 1867 game. In 1870 Bob Ferguson "threatened to knock every tooth out of the head" of a *New York Herald* reporter who had questioned his competency as captain of the Atlantics of Brooklyn (*New York Herald*; reprinted in Preston D. Orem, *Baseball [1845–1881] from the Newspaper Accounts*, 105). The *Herald* pre-

dictably responded by dramatically reducing its coverage of the Atlantics—with the result that the paper was scooped when Ferguson's team staged the historic upset that ended the two-year unbeaten streak of the Red Stockings of Cincinnati (George Bulkley, "The Day the Reds Lost," *National Pastime* 2 (Fall 1982), 7).

An 1895 article reported that at least one player had followed through on his threats: "[E. T.] Purcell, the new catcher of the [Norfolk, Virginia] team, thinks the newspapers have only the right to praise and not condemn a player's work. So when Mr. Tanner, of the 'Pilot' staff, 'wrote him up' not to his liking, the said Purcell proceeded to punch Mr. Tanner's head" (*Sporting Life*, May 18, 1895).

Threats of violence were not always one-sided. Early in the 1885 season, Louisville catcher Dan Sullivan was arrested for assault on a *Louisville Commercial* reporter (*St. Louis Post-Dispatch*, May 30, 1885). David Nemec noted that the reporter "swore revenge and had a big family in the Louisville area to help him carry out the threat. Fearing for his life if he went back to 'the dark and bloody ground of Kentucky,' Sullivan gladly accepted a transfer to St. Louis" (David Nemec, *The Beer and Whisky League*, 102).

It was rare, but not unheard of, for such antagonism to go beyond spontaneous outbursts and wind up in court. In 1883 *Harrisburg Sunday Telegram* editor John Moore described Thomas Burns of the local minor league club as a ruffian, and Burns responded by suing for libel (*Sporting Life*, September 24, 1883). In 1878 George Campbell of Syracuse umpired a game between clubs representing Rochester and Buffalo. The *Buffalo Express* accused him of dishonesty, and Campbell sued the paper. He agreed to drop the case two years later when the newspaper printed an apology (*New York Clipper*, May 8, 1880; October 16, 1880). There is at least one more recent instance of this sort. In 1954 *Durham Morning Herald* sports editor Jack Horner wrote a column entitled "Incompetent Umpires Always End Up in Rhubarbs." The subject of the piece, Carolina League umpire Harry "Ike" Reeder, was not rehired the following season. Reeder then sued Horner and his paper and received a substantial settlement (Jim L. Sumner, *Separating the Men from the Boys*, 135).

Some reporters were made to feel unwelcome in slightly subtler ways. Chicago captain Jimmy Wood informed a *Chicago Tribune* reporter in 1875 that "there are thousands of people who buy the papers simply for the reports of the games, and who would not otherwise think of looking at a newspaper" (*Chicago Tribune*, June 18, 1875). Nor were players alone in trying to inconvenience reporters, as in 1877 the National League tried to make reporters pay for admission to the ballpark.

While the friction manifested itself in a variety of ways, the underlying conflict remained the same. The newspapers, having advertised the games, felt obliged to report on the games regardless of the result. The players, in contrast, wanted coverage only of their triumphs.

The result of such incidents was to seriously damage a valuable—*and thus far free*—means of publicity. Historian George B. Kirsch reported that "by the late 1860s many [newspapers] had begun to charge a fee for announcements of club meetings and elections of officers. Some, like the *Philadelphia Press*, refused to cover ball games unless the clubs advertised in their columns" (George B. Kirsch, *The Creation of American Team Sports*, 203).

Other newspapers responded with sarcasm, such as the Michigan newspaper that reported after an 1875 game: "We made inquiries as to the result and received this intelligence: Aughhellwedontwantanypuffonthat" (*Jonesville Weekly Independent*, May 13, 1875). In a similar vein a Grand Rapids, Michigan, newspaper wrote sardonically in 1879: "The Hastings base ball club played a game yesterday. A Grand Rapids nine was present, but it is understood that they took no part in the game, as they refuse to say anything about the score when approached on the subject" (*Grand Rapids Daily Leader*, August 31, 1879). Many papers did the game even more harm by simply dropping their coverage.

The task of journalists who continued to report on baseball was not easy. A Chicago newspaper noted in 1870, "It became customary last season to publish the scores of games played between the less known clubs of this city—clubs with barbaric, comic, stupid or overridiculous names, and whose scorers did write most villainously, and spelt at random. . . . A report of one of these games would be left at the office, stating that the Young Americas had beaten the Hopefuls by a gigantic score. The next day the Captain of the Hopefuls, aged 4 to 9, after climbing our 80 stairs with great difficulty, would appear panting, and claim that his organization had the great score, and the others, the small one. He would frequently argue for half an hour as to the vital impor-

tance of a correction, and would denounce the unscrupulous mendacity of the Young Americas. Repressing a strong inclination to give him five cents to buy marbles with, we promised to correct, and he went downstairs exultant" (*Chicago Times*, November 27, 1870; quoted in Robert Pruter, "Youth Baseball in Chicago, 1868–1890," *Journal of Sport History* 26:1 [Spring 1999], 14–15).

Too few baseball players seem to have realized the consequences of such shortsighted attitudes. One exception appears to have been A. G. Spalding. Anticipating by nearly a century the maxim that "the only bad publicity is no publicity," Spalding claimed in his autobiography that attacks on him by a Chicago journalist were helping his club's attendance. Consequently, when they began to subside, he began sending the reporter additional material (Albert Spalding, *America's National Game*, 527–528; Peter Levine, in *A. G. Spalding and the Rise of Baseball*, 44–45, discussed this claim without reaching a firm conclusion on it).

The twentieth century saw the issue continue to percolate. Sportswriters of the first half of the century were often grouped into either the "gee whiz" or the "aw nuts" school. The "gee whiz" writers, such as Grantland Rice, accepted the public's adulation of athletes and did nothing to challenge that mind-set. The "aw nuts" school, exemplified by such writers as Westbrook Pegler, Ring Lardner, and W. O. McGeehan, took a more cynical, world-weary approach. They sought to demythologize ballplayers, though never to debunk them.

By the second half of the century the "gee whiz" school had lost favor. A new group of sportswriters sprung up who were known as the chipmunks. This new breed saw no reason to write as if they were "grateful to be covering the great New York Yankees" (David Halberstam, *October 1964*, 175–176). Instead they asked tough questions of the players and were willing to debunk when necessary. They were so anxious not to be hero worshipers that, in the view of sportswriter Jimmy Cannon, "they only discuss what they've written. They don't watch the game. They hate baseball. They hate the players" (quoted in Jerome Holtzman, *No Cheering in the Press Box*, 280).

By this time most clubs accepted the basic premise that newspaper coverage was good for business whether it was positive or negative. As a result, even reporters such as the chipmunks who raised the hackles of players and management were viewed as necessary evils.

But a reservoir of antipathy to printed criticisms surfaced when active players began to write books that offered a candid view of the game. When Reds pitcher Jim Brosnan published *The Long Season* in 1960, the club tried to silence him by invoking a clause in the uniform players' contract that forbade players from saying or writing anything without his team's permission.

Bill Veeck noted that that approach demonstrated an extremely shortsighted viewpoint: "Brosnan should have been a gift from heaven. Here is a character no one could possibly make up, a big-league ballplayer who writes a best-selling book. Here you have a character who writes better than most of the writers and knows what he is writing about. If I had him I'd not only permit him to go around making speeches blasting me and baseball, I'd pay him to do it. I'd challenge him to a public debate (wouldn't it be a shame if we swindled some free TV time?) and I'd pen angry broadsides to answer his angry broadsides. (Wouldn't it be a shame if customers came into the park to boo or cheer him—or me—in person?)" (Bill Veeck with Ed Linn, *The Hustler's Handbook*, 132).

Veeck obviously believed in the maxim that there is no such thing as bad publicity, but few in baseball shared this view. When Jim Bouton's *Ball Four*—written with "chipmunk" Leonard Shecter—hit the best-seller list a decade after Brosnan's book, baseball again reacted with outrage and dismay.

16.3.2 Telegraphs. American newspapers, telegraphs, and railroads all came of age during the 1850s and 1860s and made the country seem a much smaller place. The parallel development of baseball was closely tied to each.

Telegraphs began to be used to transmit baseball results back to newspaper offices almost as soon as the technology allowed. The development prompted a reporter for the *Doylestown* (Pennsylvania) *Democrat* to marvel in 1867: "We scarce supposed in our hours of buoyant boyhood . . . that the telegraph, then unknown, would, by woven wire, hasten to inform distant parts of our Union by sunrise next morning how Jim's side had come out first best, but that Joe's side made excellent playing" (quoted in *The Ball Player's Chronicle*, August 8, 1867). Soon results were being relayed not just at the end of a match but often inning by inning. The Red Stockings of Cincinnati relayed home the results of an 1869 game in Troy after each inning, and several cities repeated the experiment in 1870 (Greg Rhodes and John Erardi, *The First Boys of Summer*, 86).

An 1875 article gave this description of how updates were relayed from the Cincinnati ballpark: "During the whole progress of the game, a man sat in the broiling sun on the top of the high center-field fence with a white and red flag in his hand. With these he signaled the score each half inning across the river. The red flag represented Cincinnati, and the white flag Chicago. A whitewash he signaled by waving the white for Chicago, and the red for Cincinnati. Each tally was signaled by raising the flag up and immediately lowering it again. A man on the Ohio side of the river received these signals and telegraphed the result up to Hawley's on Vine street every half inning" (*Cincinnati Enquirer*, August 10, 1875).

As noted in the entry on "Scoreboards" (**14.5.14**), by 1875 saloons were contracting with Western Union to receive updated reports on baseball games. This created several concerns. There was at least one instance of Western Union employees being accused of taking advantage of inside information to wager on baseball games (*St. Louis Globe-Democrat*, August 4, 1876, 8). In addition, with many newspapers posting the telegraphed results on large bulletin boards, club owners became concerned about the erosion of their fan base.

When the practice caught on in Hartford, the *Hartford Courant* noted that this was a cheap form of advertisement (*Hartford Courant*, May 30, 1876; quoted in David Arcidiacono, *Grace, Grit and Growling*, 60). Club president Morgan Bulkeley didn't see it that way and made several efforts to curtail the practice, even trying to prevent the telegraph company from buying a ticket. Bulkeley gave up only when it became clear that he was creating ill will (David Arcidiacono, *Grace, Grit and Growling*, 60–61).

Club managements elsewhere were also casting a wary eye toward such practices: "The manager of the Cincinnati Club has refused to allow the score of games played in the pork-packing city to be telegraphed to the pool-rooms by innings, hoping thereby to secure the attendance at the games of those who generally learn of the play on the outside. The press of that city informs him that it 'won't work'" (*Boston Globe*, May 19, 1877).

This didn't stop clubs from trying. A report soon surfaced from Troy that "An amusing controversy is going on between the Troy Club and the Atlantic and Pacific Telegraph Company. The company having refused a request to frank all messages on club affairs, their operator was refused admission to the ground and accordingly climbed a convenient pole and tapped the wire. The manager was so pleased with the operator's exploit that a seat is to be rigged on the pole. To prevent a successful issue of this device, the Troy directors have ordered a large canvas to obstruct the operator's view" (*New York Clipper*, July 24, 1880).

By this time telephones were being used as well. An 1880 article observed, "Down at Worcester the telephone exchange advertises to furnish the score of all the League games played at the home grounds by innings to the subscribers at the rate of twenty-five cents per game. Rather a novel idea" (*Washington Post*, May 16, 1880).

The controversy was still raging in 1886 when the *St. Louis Post-Dispatch* observed, "The system adopted by [local owners] Messrs. [Henry] Lucas and [Chris] Von der Ahe of withholding the score of the games played at their parks from the bulletins down town has been tried and found wanting. The policy will not gain the good will of the public for either manager. Of course the cranks will continue to go to the parks whether the score is bulletined or not, but it is a question whether it is not better to have their good will as well as their good money" (*St. Louis Post-Dispatch*, April 10, 1886).

That same year Boston sold exclusive rights to telegraphing scores from their ballpark to the Baltimore and Ohio Company, and denied the previous year's company, the Western Union Telegraph Company, access to their grounds. Western Union responded by constructing a perch for their operator, a man named Tobin, on a telegraph pole overlooking the park. The Baltimore and Ohio erected a screen to block his view, but someone poked holes in it. When it was repaired, Western Union put up a new pole, prompting another rejoinder (*Boston Globe*, May 31 and June 1, 1886).

By this time, however, a resolution was at hand, and it came in a form that would become a recurring element in the introduction of new media. Western Union began to pay clubs for broadcast rights around 1886, and the company expanded the practice in the 1890s (Jonathan Fraser Light, *The Cultural Encyclopedia of Baseball*, 223–224).

But the transition was often rocky. A bitter dispute occurred in 1897: "There is war to the death between newspapers formerly served by the United Press and the Western Union Telegraph company. The war has centered upon and is caused by the baseball extras got out in several cities in the league by afternoon newspapers. The Western Union has a contract with the National League whereby it has a practical monopoly of every ground in the circuit. When the season opened the telegraph company notified its operators to handle no stuff for papers belonging to the United Press unless they rescinded entirely their contracts with the Postal company and used only Western Union wires. Threats of arrest on the ground of refusing to carry matter were made, but so far nothing has developed except that the reporters have been put to great trouble to get their matter to their papers. The papers most interested have set up the claim that the telegraph company is a common carrier and subject to a suit for damages" ("See Baseball Through a Telegraph," *Chicago Tribune*, May 11, 1897, 4).

The turmoil continued in 1898 when Western Union was either no longer paying for its privileges or the amount being paid was not enough to satisfy many owners. Washington owner J. Earl Wagner ordered Western Union to remove its wires from his ballpark, explaining that he believed "the company should pay a privilege the same as the score card man and peanut vender" (*Sporting Life*, April 2, 1898). Several other National League owners attempted "to bar the Western Union's 'ticker' wires from their grounds, because they believe that if such a move is made the gate receipts will be increased." But other clubs were beginning to recognize the value of such publicity. The New York club, for instance, "refused to entertain the proposition, for it is believed that the 'ticker' helps to boom base ball" (*New York Sun*, reprinted in *Sporting Life*, January 8, 1898).

When necessary, compromises were reached. A 1906 article noted that the Southern League had renewed an exclusive contract with Western Union for telegraphing within the ballpark "with the condition that no tickers are to be used and no information furnished to matinees at home when the club is at home. When the club is abroad and a matinee is given in the home town, no results on tickers are to be allowed" (*Sporting Life*, March 31, 1906).

As we shall see in succeeding entries, these controversies and their resolution would prefigure later ones involving threats and perceived threats from new media.

16.3.3   Broadcasts of Baseball. The visual appeal of tracking the results of games on blackboards and bulletin boards is limited, which led to some noteworthy efforts to embellish the telegraphed results of the ball games.

In 1884, under the name Messrs. Morgan & Co., three telegraph operators from Nashville, Tennessee—J. U. Rust, E. W. Morgan, and A. H. Stewart—hit upon an innovative way of turning the dots and dashes into a form of performance art. Their dramatization of a game that the local club was playing in Chattanooga proved so popular that they began to expand it.

The next year the Augusta, Georgia, correspondent to *Sporting Life* reported: "We have a blackboard at the Opera House and a diamond on it, with holes punched for each base, with flags showing how each base runner gets his base, with the batting order of each nine. The whole game is sent by telegraph, showing how each player plays. They charge ten cents for each day. We have gotten the games played by our nine in Atlanta, Chattanooga, Memphis and Nashville and will get Columbus and Macon" (*Sporting Life*, May 27, 1885).

A few weeks later his Nashville counterpart added, "We have been able to keep up with every item of each game played by our home team while on our trip, by the introduction on the stage of our Masonic Theatre of a black board picturing the diamond position of players, batteries, etc., with telegraphic reports of complete details of the game, viz., strikes, balls, etc., etc. It is novel and almost as interesting as being on the grounds where the game is progressing, several hundred miles away. It is managed by Messrs. Morgan and Rust, two enterprising telegraphers" (*Sporting Life*, July 8, 1885).

The idea seemed nearly ready to be launched in major league cities. The *Boston Globe* reported, "Ormond H. Butler, ex-umpire and ex-manager, sees millions in a new idea. He is negotiating for a down-town theatre or hall in Chicago to report games by telegraph. The stage is to be set in the form of a miniature ball field, on which every movement of the game will be shown" (*Boston Globe*, August 10, 1885).

By the following spring, additional dramatic elements had been added to the performance: "Several hundred people were present again today at the opera house to witness the game between Atlanta and Charleston. A novel feature of the report was the actual running of the bases by uniformed boys, who obeyed the telegraph instrument in their moves around

the diamond" (*Atlanta Constitution*, April 17, 1886).

The show was next taken to major league cities, where it was warmly received. The *Chicago Tribune* gave a detailed account: "A small but deeply interested crowd of spectators assembled in Central Music Hall yesterday afternoon to witness the game between the Chicago and St. Louis teams by means of the new system introduced by a couple of enterprising young men of Nashville, Tenn., and which last week created no little enthusiasm at Cincinnati in demonstrating the play of the Cincinnati and St. Louis teams at St. Louis.

"Upon the stage was a canvas screen, twenty feet square, and upon it was painted a very realistic view of a ball-field, with the diamond in the centre and the fence, hills, and blue sky beyond. In the centre of the pitcher's and catcher's box, at the home-plate, and at each of the three bases slots had been cut, through which an assistant behind the picture inserted 12 x 4 inch cards bearing the names of the players as they took their positions. A telegraph operator was seated at one corner of the scene, the wire from the instrument before him connecting with one in the grand stand at St. Louis. At fifteen minutes to 4 o'clock the operator announced the batting orders of both teams with [John] Gaffney as umpire. At 4 o'clock the instrument ticked out 'Game,' and a minute after 'Play ball.' Instantly the name of [Emmett] Seery appeared at home plate, and those of [John] Clarkson and ['Silver'] Flint as the Whites' battery. 'One strike,' called the operator, then 'one ball,' 'two, three, four, five, six balls,' and the name of Seery disappeared from the home plate and reappeared at first base, while that of Glasscock showed up at the home plate. 'One strike, two strikes,' called the operator, and the crowd applauded Clarkson. 'Three strikes, and Glasscock knocks the ball to ['Cap'] Anson, who throws to Clarkson at first. Glasscock out, and Seery to second on the play,' called the operator and the crowd applauded and seemed delighted with the novelty of witnessing a game 300 miles distant. [Fred] Dunlap then made a two-bagger through centre, and Seery came home. [Alex] McKinnon hit the ball, and got to second on a bad throw, but was cut off at the home plate from centre, while [Jerry] Denny was left on first.

"Next the Chicagos came to bat, [Abner] Dalrymple reaching first on called balls, and in this and the succeeding half inning each play was promptly telegraphed and promptly announced. To those who knew the players personally, the exhibition was wonderfully realistic, and the many little points in play brought out made it more so. In the third, for instance, Glasscock hit foul and instantly the operator announced, 'Foul ball over the grand-stand. A new ball.' Again in the third [George] Gore was caught while trying to steal second and the operator announced, 'Gore kicking hard, but Anson laughing at him.' In the fifth came the announcement: 'Fine stop by [Tom] Dolan. Hurt his finger. All the players around him. [Charlie] Sweeney very wild. They are now pulling Dolan's finger in place. Game.' And the play went on as before. It was a close game up to the eighth inning, when unfortunately the wire got out of gear somewhere along the line, and a wait of nearly ten minutes occurred. Then the rest of the game was rapidly announced, and the score stood 7 to 3 in favor of the White Stockings. The exhibition, it is thought, will be very popular in Chicago while the home team is absent in the East. Today's game between the Chicago and St. Louis teams will be called at Central Music Hall promptly at 4 o'clock" (*Chicago Tribune*, May 4, 1886).

The unique performance arrived in Detroit on July 8, 1886. Six hundred spectators turned out at the Detroit Opera House to watch an enactment of the home team's game at Chicago. The audience got into the spirit of things, bursting into applause when Detroit did well, and hissing whenever the name of Chicago captain "Cap" Anson was announced.

Morgan and Rust seem to have abandoned the project, but others took it up and added new touches. The *New York Sun* reported in 1890: "On and after April 25, it will be possible to witness two league base ball games, played miles apart, at the same time, in Webster hall, 119 East Eleventh street. The hall will be connected by telegraph wires with every league ball ground in the United States. Reporters will telegraph every play which will be immediately reproduced on one of the improved base ball bulletins in Webster hall. Each of the bulletin boards will be fifteen feet square. The background is white, and the lettering which refers to both of the clubs playing is in black" (reprinted in *Columbus* [Ohio] *Post*, April 24, 1890). In 1895 the *Washington Post* noted: "Manager Eugene Kernan will inaugurate a new system of illustrating baseball games in detail from the stage of the Lyceum this summer, while the Senators are out of the city" (*Washington Post*, April 14, 1895).

By this time technological upgrades were breathing new life into the presentations. An 1895 account from Philadelphia explained: "The new system of electrical reproduction of ball games known as the Crowden system, invented by Mr. Samuel H. Crowden, of Richmond, was produced at the Walnut Street Theatre last week and voted a great success. . . . The feature is the exact reproduction of every move and play of the participants in the game. The field is laid out in an exact representation of the regular diamond. Every player is in his position and constantly in motion, giving the appearance of being living. Each player is equipped with a ball and a bat and when he makes a catch or throws the ball it can be seen in his hands, or when batting, the bat, which is connected by his legs, works automatically and comes into a position for striking.

"After a man has made a catch or a batter has hit the ball the ball is thrown to the base or player and the batsman drops his bat and runs. Slides to bases, running for fouls, caught napping, and the pitcher and catcher in convention are all equally and minutely displayed. The most important feature is that when a ball is hit the audience can see where it goes, by whom it is fielded, and where it is thrown. Every game played away from home will be exactly reproduced at the Walnut Street Theatre by this system, and anyone failing to witness it will miss the greatest thing in this way ever exhibited" (*Sporting Life*, July 6, 1895).

The reliance on new technology enabled these depictions to appeal to a class of fans who were not at home in opera houses but were beginning to discover the appeal of the new genre of motion pictures. *Sporting Life* observed in 1900: "During the playing season, while the Pittsburg team is on the road, the games are reproduced in miniature at the Academy. Betting on the game and on fouls is in full blast, foul balls being recorded by the flashing of a red light. It is said that frequently the telegraph operators miss the foul balls, or at times there is a lull in the games, and to keep interest alive a few extra fouls are added to make the betting more keen" (*Sporting Life*, November 3, 1900).

Large crowds watched the two spectacular pennant races of 1908 from afar on lighted electric diamonds (David W. Anderson, *More Than Merkle*, 157, 171). The 1909 campaign saw the introduction of the Rodier Electric Board Game Reproducer, which kept a running tally of outs, innings, and score and used electric lights to simulate the action. The Rodier machine was unveiled on July 16, 1909 in Washington, D.C., and more than two thousand fans stood in the street and "watched" a game that was being played in Detroit (Gerard S. Petrone, *When Baseball Was Young*, 59–60). Excitement about the new board was so great that during the 1909 World Series between Pittsburgh and Detroit, the device was installed at Washington's Columbia Theater and fans paid twenty-five cents to watch the progress of the Series "be vividly reproduced" in the comfort of theater seating (*Washington Post*, October 5, 1909).

Yet another new version, the Star Baseball Player, was unveiled in 1913. An Auburn, New York, reporter found it "all that was advertised. Each movement of the baseball was shown minutely play by play and instead of an audience interested in the mechanical marvel it was just as if a real ball game was in progress on the stage with the rooters right out in front. As the various plays were shown the audience rooted, cheered, threw hats in the air, and pandemonium reigned as some of the fine plays were presented. The bleachers at Norwood Park in the old days didn't have anything on the actions at the Auditorium yesterday afternoon" (*Auburn Citizen*, October 8, 1913, 5).

The novelty of paying admission to theaters for such reproductions wore off, presumably a victim of competition from the far more captivating images that could be viewed at nickelodeons. But monitoring the results of important ballgames on electric telegraph boards remained a popular custom for another decade. Thousands gathered annually in New York's Times Square to monitor the results of the World Series in the era's closest equivalent to "real time." The practice began to dwindle in 1921, the year radio broadcasts were initiated (Dan Gutman, *Banana Bats and Ding-Dong Balls*, 116–117).

16.3.4   Radio Broadcasts. In *Middle Innings*, Dean Sullivan reprinted an article published during the 1920 World Series that described what might have been a radio broadcast. The article recounted a "wireless party" hosted by the *Cleveland Press* during the fifth game of the World Series. It explained that hundreds of wireless men within a 750-mile radius were able to receive and "listen" to play-by-play reports sent by U.S. Naval Station electrician A. A. Penland. The article always placed the word "listen" in quotation marks, leaving doubt as to the nature of the broadcast ("Wireless Fans Fan at Press Series Party," *Cleveland Press*, Oc-

tober 12, 1920; reprinted in Dean Sullivan, ed., *Middle Innings*).

What is generally considered to be the first radio broadcast of a major league game took place on August 5, 1921, when Harold Arlin announced a game between Pittsburgh and Philadelphia for KDKA in Pittsburgh. Arlin said later that the broadcast of baseball was viewed by the station as "sort of a one-shot project" (Curt Smith, *Voices of the Game*, 7).

That perception reflected the fact that, once again, baseball had gotten in at the outset of a new medium to which its fortunes would become closely tied. KDKA is credited with initiating the heyday of radio's popularity with its November 2, 1920, broadcast of the results of the presidential election. At that point there were only a handful of radio stations in the whole country; it took a full year for a significant number to emerge and a radio craze to ensue (Paul Starr, *The Creation of the Media*, 330–331).

By that time the enduring link between radio and the national pastime had begun. Listeners of at least three stations were able to hear some coverage of the 1921 World Series. KDKA listeners heard Grantland Rice give periodic updates of the action. Meanwhile Tommy Cowan did studio recreations of the entire Series based upon reports from the ballpark that were broadcast on WJZ in Newark and WBZ in Springfield, Massachusetts (Curt Smith, *Voices of the Game*, 8).

At the following season's World Series, radio announcers "sent play by play a talked off story of the big games" (*Sporting News*, October 12, 1922). The 1923 World Series was the first to be broadcast nationally, with Graham McNamee providing the play-by-play.

Beginning in 1924 the Cubs became the first team to allow regular radio broadcasts of their games. Cubs' owner William Wrigley had made effective use of advertising to sell chewing gum and believed that more exposure could only help. In keeping with this philosophy, instead of giving one radio station an exclusive license to broadcast the team's games, he allowed any station to do so. Soon as many as five stations were sending their own announcers to call the games, and all the exposure helped attendance (Stuart Shea, *Wrigley Field*, 116–117).

But other owners were less sure that this approach would work, and it is hard to blame them. The confusion of baseball owners mirrored American society's deep confusion about the new medium. As Paul Starr has noted, radio had an amalgam of the characteristics of the media that preceded it, making it difficult to know how to treat it.

Was radio part of the press and worthy of the First Amendment privileges accorded newspapers? Was it merely a form of entertainment like the movies? Or was it a common carrier like the telephone or telegraph that ought to provide equal access to all? And what would be the respective roles of private enterprise and government? Which governmental department should set policies for radio broadcasts—the Navy, the Post Office, Commerce, or a new one? While the resolution of these issues may seem inevitable in retrospect, Starr observed that "before 1927 it was far from obvious what the outcome would be" and that other countries took very different courses from the one pursued in the United States (Paul Starr, *The Creation of the Media*, 329–330).

The dilemma was especially immediate in the case of baseball since radio stations did not have to pay for broadcast rights, which made baseball a very appealing programming option. But most major league clubs were reluctant or unwilling to allow radio broadcasts, fearful they would hurt attendance. This concern was apparently belied by the fact that Cubs attendance was booming, but most owners saw no reason to take the chance that this trend would continue. Their anxiety was undoubtedly increased when radio was blamed for a sharp decline in the sale of sheet music and records (Paul Starr, *The Creation of the Media*, 339).

It would seem that there was no possibility for compromise: a team had to either prohibit broadcasts or allow them and have faith that they were expanding the fan base. The two St. Louis teams, however, did find an imaginative middle ground by permitting play-by-play accounts as long as they were dull and included no commentary. The *Sporting News* predicted that this compromise would prove "mutually satisfactory to both the fans and the magnates, for there are some announcers prone to wander far from the actual occurrence on the field" (quoted in William B. Mead, *Two Spectacular Seasons*, 24).

The first major league team to allow play-by-play broadcast of all their games was the Cincinnati Reds in 1929, with announcer Harry Hartman calling the games for WFBE in Cincinnati. But that same year saw the backlash against radio broadcasts begin to gain momentum, especially in the minor leagues. Club officials in San Francisco did a study and concluded that

attendance dropped by 12 percent when games were broadcast. The Southern League took action and banned radio altogether (*Sporting News*, May 16, 1929).

Baseball owners continued to have a skittish attitude toward radio during the 1920s and 1930s. Any dip in attendance during the period led to talk of prohibiting radio broadcasts and often to actual bans. After the 1932 season, with the country in the throes of the Great Depression, these concerns were particularly widespread. With many expecting major league owners to announce a ban on radio broadcasts at their winter meetings, Cincinnati Reds broadcaster Harry Hartman made the case that "radio is the best advertiser that baseball could want."

Hartman argued that ticket prices "would strain any man's pocket book these days. Citing this situation of the man who can't afford this, it is better to at least keep his interest in the game alive, and radio will do that. If he is given a broadcast account of the game, he will remain sport conscious, and let me say here, that the desire in any rabid, dyed-in-the-wool baseball fan is much too strong to be satisfied with just the mere broadcasting of a game. He must go out there to his park and see it for himself. Take radio away from the man who can't afford the price of attending games regularly and you take away a customer who would occasionally attend the game if he has the money." Hartman further contended that radio broadcasts were essential to bringing the game to new fans and to shut-ins and the handicapped (*Sporting News*, November 17, 1932).

By then, however, the commercial tenor of American radio was becoming established, which brought a solution to the thorny issue. Rights to broadcast the World Series were sold for the first time in 1934 to the Ford Motor Company for four years at $100,000 per year. The problem was not resolved overnight, as the three New York clubs maintained a non-radio pact until 1939. But once big-money sponsorships entered the picture, it was inevitable that baseball would overcome its resistance to radio broadcasts.

16.3.5 Television. The first televised baseball game may have occurred in Japan. Researcher Bob Timmermann brought my attention to the fact that the Japanese were experimenting with prototypes of television by the early 1930s. One of the sites was Waseda University in Tokyo, and on February 17, 1931, an attempt was made there to televise a baseball game. If the game was indeed visible, it was seen only in a laboratory.

The first U.S. telecast of a baseball game was of a collegiate game between Princeton and Columbia on May 17, 1939. The game was shown on w2xbs, an experimental NBC station in New York City. NBC program manager Thomas H. Hutchinson said presciently, "outdoor sports will furnish much of the most interesting material we could televise." Announcer Bill Stern was assigned "to identify players and interpret the play," and it turned out that that was exactly what he had to do (*New York Times*, May 18, 1939).

The *Times* reported the next day that "Those who watched the game at Radio City agreed that the commentator 'saved the day,' otherwise there would be no way to follow the play or to tell where the ball went except to see the players run in its direction. The announcer revealed whether it was a foul ball or hit" (*New York Times*, May 19, 1939).

The single camera that was used proved incapable of keeping up with the action. At the start of the game the position of the sun caused the entire screen to be "blurred, with the reproduced faces dark. But as the game progressed the sun moved around out of the camera's 'eye' and the diamond became clear and the skyline of apartment buildings sharply defined in the background."

Unfortunately the greater ease of viewing the apartment buildings did not make it much easier to follow play: "Seldom were more than three players visible on the screen at one time, and until the picture was clarified after the fourth inning the outfielders were 'forgotten men.' The ball was seldom seen, except on bunts and infield plays comparatively close to the camera, stationed between third base and home plate" (*New York Times*, May 19, 1939). Stern later admitted, "We actually prayed that all the batters would strike out because that was the one thing that the camera could record" (Leonard Koppett, "A Little Game That Turned TV Loose on Sports," *Sports Illustrated*, May 10, 1965).

Despite the inauspicious debut, at least one commentator recognized the potential of the new medium. *New York Times* columnist Orrin E. Dunlap, Jr., observed, "It's no easy trick to put a baseball acreage and its scattered action on a 9 by 12 inch screen." He explained that the newness of the technology and the expense of cameras meant that it was too soon "to 'paint'

electronically such a panoramic view," but he expressed confidence that "the future will bring the complete picture." Dunlap predicted that baseball telecasts would eventually blend the angles of multiple cameras trained on home plate, the infield, the outfield, and even one atop the grandstand for a bird's-eye view and another with "a roving assignment" of the dugout and bleachers (Orrin E. Dunlap, Jr., "Batter Up!," *New York Times*, May 21, 1939).

The first telecast of major league baseball was a Reds-Dodgers game on August 26, 1939. The game was broadcast by Red Barber and again appeared on w2xbs. In return for allowing the game to be televised, Larry MacPhail asked only that NBC install a set in the Dodgers' press box. The *New York Times* reported that "considerable progress" had been made since the Columbia-Princeton game (*New York Times*, August 27, 1939). Two cameras were used in this game, both on the third base line, but one by the visitors' dugout and the other behind the right-handed batters' box. In addition, a truck was set up outside the ballpark.

Seeing the ball remained a major problem for viewers. Sportswriter Harold Parrott reported, "The players were clearly distinguishable, but it was not possible to pick out the ball." Another account was slightly more optimistic: "At times, despite the great speed of play, the baseball was visible in the television image, particularly when Pitchers Luke Hamlin and 'Bucky' Walters resorted to slower delivery, or when the batter drove out a hit directly away from the iconoscope camera" (both quoted in Lawrence S. Katz, *Baseball in 1939*, 115).

16.3.6   Sale of Television Rights. The Yankees sold telecast rights for $75,000 in 1946 (Jonathan Fraser Light, *The Cultural Encyclopedia of Baseball*, 725). It was a decision that would have far-reaching repercussions.

Baseball was noticeably less cautious in its approach to television broadcasts than had been the case with radio. There are several apparent reasons for this tendency. One is that the fears about radio hurting attendance had proved largely unfounded. Another is that some of baseball's efforts to restrict broadcasts fell afoul of antitrust laws and had to be dropped (Dean Sullivan, ed., *Late Innings*, 42–45).

Perhaps the biggest reason was that baseball began to accept television money at a time when the technology of the medium was still quite primitive. By the 1940s the ball itself had become visible to viewers, but not much else was.

The quality of the telecasts of this era is illustrated by a humorous set of "Unofficial Rules and Regulations of TV Baseball" created by columnist Weare Holbrook in 1951. Holbrook observed that the players all appeared to be wearing uniforms of "a pale gray, shaggy material which occasionally sprouts feathers" and could only be "distinguished by the numerals on their backs—with the exception of numbers three, five, six and eight, which can't be distinguished at all." This difficulty was compounded by the fact that only one to three players were visible at a time, who: "may be (a) pitcher, batter, and catcher, or (b) base runner and infielder, or (c) outfielder. This count does not include fractional players. A double play, for example, may include the base runner, the second baseman, and the legs of the shortstop; and a pop fly may include an outfielder and the truncated torso of the third baseman."

At least the ball was now "a white fuzzy object about the size and shape of a half-dissolved aspirin tablet." Batters swung at it with a bat that seemed to "be constructed of some flexible, rubbery substance which enables it to grow longer when held horizontally, and thicker when held vertically" (Weare Holbrook, "TV Scrambles a Ball Game," syndicated column, *Washington Post*, August 5, 1951).

Such features meant that when owners first began to sell telecast rights in 1946, they did not anticipate that television would become much of a substitute for attending a game. Baseball came to rely on television revenues, and when the technology began to advance dramatically it was difficult to go back. As a result, money has been a driving force in the relationship between baseball and television to an even greater extent than was the case between baseball and radio.

There was, of course, some resistance. For example, Branch Rickey protested in the early 1950s: "Radio created a desire to see something. Television is giving it to them. Once a television set has broken them of the ball-park habit, a great many fans will never reacquire it. And if television makes new baseball customers, as some are claiming, why don't Broadway productions televise their shows? The only way you can see a Broadway production is to buy a ticket—and I cannot concede that baseball has, under the oft-used heading of the 'public interest,' any obligation to give away continuously at only a fraction of its real worth the only thing

it has to sell" (*Newsweek* interview, quoted in Robert W. Peterson, *Pigskin*, 200).

But money rather than arguments would carry the day. Within a year of the first sale of baseball television broadcasting rights, those revenues played a key role in the funding of the first major league pension fund. While a pension fund is certainly unobjectionable, other consequences of baseball's reliance on television money raise much more serious concerns.

Leonard Koppett, for instance, wrote in 1964 that "The trouble with television is that it exists. . . . A baseball game on television remains a television show: it may make some baseball addicts, but it certainly makes more television addicts. Thus, one more distinguishing feature of baseball is removed and it becomes 'just another entertainment'" (Leonard Koppett, "The Ex-National Sports Looks to Its Image," *New York Times*, December 20, 1964).

Such developments as the broadcast of World Series games at hours far too late for youngsters to watch cause understandable concern that baseball is allowing itself to become "just another entertainment."

16.3.7   Real-time Broadcasts. The most recent dispute over whether broadcasts promote or give the product away is the still ongoing controversy over real-time broadcasts and webcasts. In 1996 the NBA sued Motorola and STATS, Inc., on the grounds that a real-time data service being offered by those companies was an unlicensed broadcast. The defendants ultimately won the case by successfully arguing that the essence of their product was gathering and transmitting facts (Alan Schwarz, *The Numbers Game*, 188–192). The issue, however, has not gone away, and the increasing sophistication of webcasts has brought it back to the fore.

In spite of the precedent of the Motorola and STATS, Inc., case, the position of major league baseball continues to be that "pitch-by-pitch is an exhibition of a baseball game" (Bob Bowman, chief executive of Major League Baseball Advanced Media, quoted in Alan Schwarz, "Real-time Broadcasts Lead to Copyright Questions," *Baseball America*, September 15–28, 2003). As a result, Alan Schwarz predicted that "when a site starts streaming the trajectory of the ball, and has lifelike, animated men throwing it to first, you can bet a clarification of 'news' will be in order" (Alan Schwarz, "Real-time Broadcasts Lead to Copyright Questions," *Baseball America*, September 15–28, 2003).

Chapter 17

STATISTICS

BASEBALL EMERGED as a prominent part of the American experience in the mid-nineteenth century, at about the same time that statistics were also becoming a staple of American life. Historian of science Thomas Kuhn characterized the mid-century as the scene of a second scientific revolution that revolved around quantification (Thomas S. Kuhn, "The Function of Measurement in Modern Physical Science," *Isis*, Vol. 52, Issue 2 [1961], 161–193; quoted in Jay Bennett and Aryn Martin, "The Numbers Game: What Fans Should Know About the Stats They Love," Eric Bronson, ed., *Baseball and Philosophy*, 234).

As baseball sought to appeal to adults instead of children, it made use of this emphasis on measurement and quantification. Early baseball statistics were based largely on those of cricket, but it would not take long for that to change. By the 1870s a reporter wrote that "the present system of scoring seems rather a pretext for practicing book-keeping by double, treble or quadruple entry in the open air" (unnamed Western paper, reprinted in *St. Louis Globe-Democrat*, April 9, 1876). The game was well on its way to amassing the formidable and often baffling array of statistics that it now features.

All these numbers were an effective way of demonstrating that what had once been a child's game could now be taken seriously. Before long, another discernible theme to all the measurements emerged: baseball as a democratic institution. Slowly but surely, baseball statistics came to embody the notion that every player's contributions counted and were being measured. As sportswriter Jim Murray later quipped, "A king may be a king because his father was, but a ballplayer is a major leaguer only so long as his average shows he is" (quoted in Jonathan Fraser Light, *The Cultural Encyclopedia of Baseball*, 626).

This reality caused Grantland Rice to observe, "I have often wondered how the populace at large would feel if the daily records of every one were exposed to public inspection—the politicians, bankers, lawyers, doctors, union labor and industrial leaders, writers, radio artists, grocers, butchers, clerks and all others who make up the motley mass of humanity. . . . The ball player has no such soft break. The box score soon proves whether he is a Williams, DiMaggio, Feller, Marion or a Class B product headed for the bush again" (Grantland Rice, *New York Sun*, April 16, 1946).

A final theme that recurs throughout this chapter is that baseball statistics have been very conservative entities, often intended not so much to measure the accomplishments that win games but to encourage acts that embody desirable moral traits. There was widespread sentiment in the nineteenth century that pitchers had usurped too great a role and that walks and strikeouts were bad baseball. Beliefs such as these were reflected in early baseball statistics, which is why, for example, batting average has always been one of the game's magic numbers while on-base percentage didn't emerge for another century. The latter statistic is a better measurement of the value of a player's contribution, but the former is a better embodiment of an accepted nineteenth-century principle that taking a base on balls was "something no good batsman likes to do" (*Brooklyn Eagle*, May 9, 1871).

More than with the topic of any other chapter in this book, the history of baseball statistics is a work in progress, in need of continual rewriting and reexamination. Bill James is most responsible for this process because of his persistence in empirically testing assumptions about baseball statistics that had long been taken for granted. His approaches and ideas have inspired an entire generation of analysts, many of whom have made their way into baseball front offices. While I follow the results closely, especially James's ongoing work and that of the *Baseball Prospectus* team, I have primarily confined myself in this chapter to tracing the origins of traditional measures. More recent approaches and statistics are too new to evaluate fairly, too technical to summarize aptly, and simply too abundant to do justice to them in this work. Fortunately Michael Lewis's *Moneyball* and Alan Schwarz's *The Numbers Game* have begun the process of telling that story in the depth it deserves. Still more fortunately, most of the pioneers are still active in the field and are more than capable of telling their own stories.

17.1 Box Scores. The earliest known box score appeared in the *New York Herald* on October 25, 1845, after a game between the New York Base Ball Club and a club from Brooklyn. The box score (which is reproduced in Melvin L. Adelman's "The First Baseball Game, the First Newspaper References to Baseball, and the New York Club," *Journal of Sport History* 7:3 [Winter 1980], 134) includes only the names of the eight players on each side, along with the number of runs scored and outs made by each.

A 1925 article by a writer named H. H. Westlake contended that the box score was invented by Henry Chadwick in 1859. Westlake reprinted a box score that appeared in the *New York Clipper* in 1859. He acknowledged that there were earlier box scores but pointed out that the 1859 box score was expanded to include five categories: runs, hits, putouts, assists, and errors.

Westlake did not explain why these categories are essential to a box score. Instead he brought out all the rhetorical whistles and bells to state as a "fact" that "the real simon-pure discoverer and inventor of the now invaluable box score was none other than Henry Chadwick, now passed to the great beyond and remembered as the famed 'Father of Baseball'" (H. H. Westlake, "The First Box Score Ever Published," *Baseball Magazine*, March 1925;

reprinted in Sidney Offit, ed., *The Best of Baseball*, 68–73).

This article was highly influential, and *Baseball Magazine* received more requests to reprint it than any other article in its fifty-year history (Sidney Offit, ed., *The Best of Baseball*, 68). As a result, Chadwick is generally credited with being the inventor of the box score. But the facts seem to suggest that, at most, Chadwick deserves credit for adding a few categories to it.

Chadwick's 1859 creation was not the end of the expansion of the box score. On August 7, 1860, the *Detroit Free Press* published an astonishingly detailed box score of the first defeat ever suffered by the Detroit Base Ball Club. It began with a basic table listing hands left (outs) and runs for each batter. A second table broke down the outs created by each batter into five different categories. A third table delineated the number and type of outs recorded by each fielder. The fourth and final table enumerated each inning's totals of pitches thrown by the pitcher, foul balls hit, and passed balls (reprinted in Peter Morris, *Baseball Fever*, 59).

As if this weren't enough, additional notes pointed out details for which there was not sufficient room, including the one batter who had the misfortune to strike out. In short, it had almost everything that today's most demanding baseball fan could ask for—with the glaring exception of the base hit. This omission will be discussed in entry **17.3**.

17.2 Line Scores. A line score would have been a printer's nightmare in the very early days of baseball, when nine innings was not standard (see **1.6**) and dozens of innings might have to be played to reach a conclusion. Accordingly, it was not until 1855 that line scores began to emerge, and they became common after nine innings became the norm in 1857.

17.3 Base Hits. As noted in the entry on "Box Scores" (**17.1**), base hits were almost always missing from early box scores. Their absence seems shocking at first, but on reflection it becomes more understandable. Much of baseball's scoring system was borrowed from cricket, where a hit almost always meant at least one run. As a result, cricket scorekeepers understandably kept track only of runs. The early developers of baseball scorekeeping saw no reason to keep track of base hits in a sport where runs determined the victor.

The Westlake article cited in entry **17.1** suggests that Henry Chadwick included base hits in an 1859 box score, but if so that was not customary. At some point Chadwick became convinced that this statistic was needed. He wrote in the 1864 *Beadle's*, "Many a dashing general player, who carries off a great deal of eclat in prominent matches, has all 'the gilt taken off the gingerbread,' as the saying is, by these matter-of-fact figures, given at the close of the season; and we are frequently surprised to find that the modest but efficient worker, who has played earnestly and steadily through the season, apparently unnoticed, has come in, at the close of the race, the real victor."

After reflecting on this for a few years, Chadwick decided on an appropriate course. He initiated the recording of base hits in *The Ball Player's Chronicle* during the 1867 season, and stressed before the 1868 season that "there is but one true criterion of skill at the bat, and that is the number of *times* bases are made on clean hits" (*The Ball Player's Chronicle*, September 19, 1867, 6; Henry Chadwick, *The American Game of Base Ball*, 64, 68). At a game between the Eckfords of Brooklyn and the Mutuals of New York on August 14, 1868, he went further by offering a bat to the player who made the most safe hits. Nearly half a century later, Jimmy Wood claimed with pride that he had earned the prize by making four hits, and "that bat, suitably engraved, is my most treasured possession today" (James Wood as told to Frank G. Menke, "Baseball in By-Gone Days," syndicated column, *Marion* [Ohio] *Star*, August 15, 1916).

Chadwick then began to campaign for the new statistic. He repeatedly pointed out that run-scoring depended on teammates while there could "be no mistake as to the feat of a batsman making his first base by a good hit or by an error of a fielder. This therefore becomes the only criterion of batting, and therefore in judging a batsman's skill we should first look to his score of the number of times he makes his first base on a good hit or by an error of a fielder" (*National Chronicle*, January 9, 1868). Before long he was proclaiming, "the fraternity in general now recognize that style of batting which secures the first base by 'clean' hits the greatest number of times as the only true criterion of skillful and scientific play at the bat" (*Brooklyn Eagle*, March 25, 1872). Chadwick had a tendency to present his own views as being those of "the fraternity in general," but in

this case base hits did indeed become a standard baseball measure.

Contemporary statistical analysts point out that a shortcoming of statistics like hits and batting average is that they make no distinction between a single and a home run. That was not an oversight on Chadwick's part. While he initially advocated tracking both the number of base hits and the total bases from those hits, he always believed that the former was more important (Henry Chadwick, *The American Game of Base Ball*, 62–68). As the years went by, he became increasingly critical of using total bases and even tried to convince his readers that in most cases a single was preferable to a home run. He explained that the object of the batter is "to secure [a run] with the least fatigue. If the batsman hits the ball over the heads of the outfielders he gets his run at once, but at what cost? Why at the expense of running one hundred and twenty yards at his utmost speed, the result being that he arrives home out of breath, and entirely unfit for further play without rest" (*New York Clipper*, April 12, 1873).

Ironically, Chadwick eventually came to feel that by popularizing hits he had helped to create a monster. In 1880 he complained, "Until a system of averages is adopted which will do justice to the class of batsmen who sacrifice their individual record in order to play for the side, the season's averages, as now made out, will continue to be erroneous data" (*New York Clipper*, December 11, 1880). Five years later, he added: "What with the scoring rules of the League and American associations which not only give such prominence to batsmen who make 'two and three baggers' and 'home runs,' and the system of publishing the batsmen's average every month, every encouragement is given to players to play ball not for the side, but for their individual records." The man who had once presented averages as the only way to ensure the accurate measurement of every player's contributions now complained that averages neglected clutch hitting (*Brooklyn Eagle*, August 4, 1885).

Others shared this outlook. According to an 1876 article, there was "a strong probability that a different mode of scoring will be adopted by the League. The individual base-hit score will be abandoned, and the result announced in the summary like earned runs, i.e.: 'Base hits—Cincinnatis, 8, Chicagos, 9.' Instead of the base-hit column will be the first base column, in which will be credited the times a player reached first base in each game whether by error, called balls or a safe hit. The intention is to thereby encourage not only safe hitting, but also good first base running, which has of late sadly declined. Players are too apt, under the present system of averages, to work only for base hits, and if they see they have not made one, they show an indifference about reaching first base in advance of the ball. The new system will make each member of a club play for the club, and not for his individual average" (*New York Sunday Mercury*, September 2, 1876).

17.4 Batting Averages. The idea of attempting to measure the frequency with which a batter made a base hit is almost as old as the base hit. Henry Chadwick published a table of hits divided by games played in his *National Chronicle* on January 16, 1869. Two of the publications for which Chadwick wrote, *Beadle's Dime Base-Ball Player* and the *New York Clipper*, were soon publishing averages that were computed by using games played rather than at bats as the denominator.

This method was less precise than a batting average, but there were two good reasons for the choice. First, the average reflected the influence of cricket, where batters generally got to hit until they were retired, so that opportunities were equal. Second, counting the number of at bats represented considerable extra work and didn't seem worth the bother.

As these averages began to be taken more seriously, their inequities became more apparent. The season-ending statistics of two 1870 clubs, the White Stockings of Chicago and the Stars of Brooklyn, included hits, at bats, and the percentage thereof (Marshall Wright, *The National Association of Base Ball Players, 1857–1870*, 287). Most, however, were slower to adapt.

When the National Association was formed in 1871, league secretary Nick Young continued to divide hits by games played. H. A. Dobson of the *New York Clipper* wrote to Young to point out two problems with this method: "In the first place, it is wrong from the fact that members of the same nine do not have the same or equal chance to run up a good score. In the second place it is wrong when comparing averages of players of different nines" (*New York Clipper*, March 11, 1871).

Dobson proposed a fairer method of compiling the new league's averages: "According to a man's chances, so should his record be. Every time he goes to bat he either has an out, a run,

or is left on his base. If he does not go out he makes his base, either by his own merit or by an error of some fielder. Now his merit column is found in 'times first base on clean hits,' and his average is found by dividing his total 'times first base on clean hits' by his total number of times he went to the bat. Then what is true of one player is true of all, no matter what the striking order" (*New York Clipper*, March 11, 1871). The Boston and Cleveland clubs issued statistics in which batting average was computed on the basis of hits per at bats in 1871 (Ralph E. LinWeber, "Baseball Guides Galore," *Baseball Research Journal* 1982, 61).

Nick Young, however, resisted the calls for change. As late as 1875 the *Brooklyn Eagle* was still presenting "batting averages" that were calculated by dividing hits by games played (*Brooklyn Eagle*, February 4 and March 29, 1875). Accordingly, John Thorn and Pete Palmer have concluded that batting average was "first introduced in its current form" in 1874 (John Thorn and Pete Palmer, *The Hidden Game of Baseball*, 17). It was the *Boston Globe* that did the legwork and was able to inform its readers: "Prior to the departure for England, the batting average of the Boston Club was made out, by which George Wright takes the lead, having made 54 base hits in 139 times at bat in 27 games, or a percentage of .388; Spalding was second, with 75 first base hits in 198 times at bat in 38 games, a percentage of .378" (*Boston Globe*, August 10, 1874).

The *Globe*'s enterprise was probably the result of the reporter's greatest bugaboo: the slow news day. In the middle of the 1874 season, the Boston and Philadelphia clubs made a month-long tour of England in an effort to increase overseas interest in America's national pastime. So this initial offering of the current version of batting average was most likely a reporter's desperate effort to give his readers fresh news about a team that was an ocean away. At any rate, when the home club was again stateside, the *Globe* seems to have returned to more standard forms of coverage.

In 1875 college averages were computed by using at bats, but these involved far fewer games. It was not until 1876 that anyone was again willing to undertake the spadework necessary to compute major league batting averages based upon at bats.

At the end of that season the *Chicago Tribune* presented a complete table of games played, at bats, hits, and batting averages, and commented: "It has been a matter of no little difficulty to obtain the record of times at bat with sufficient accuracy to base a table on it, but by dint of much corresponding the necessary figures have been obtained, and a table is made on the correct basis. It is the first time that anything of the kind has been attempted in the United States, and it would be fair for such other papers as prefer to use these figures to making out lists of their own (for which many of them may very likely not have the data) to remember where they found them" (*Chicago Tribune*, October 23, 1876).

Henry Chadwick commended *Tribune* reporter Lewis Meacham for averages "very promptly made out on the bases of times at the bat" (*New York Clipper*, November 11, 1876). Otherwise the *Tribune*'s plaintive cry for some credit for all its hard work seems to have fallen upon deaf ears, as the figures were widely reprinted without attribution.

Even some *Tribune* readers did not appreciate the new statistic. "I would like to know," asked one, "whether several of the men have improved since last year, or whether they have fallen off, and the only record I have of last year is in the shape of the *Tribune*'s list, which gave only the average of base-hits to a game. I cannot compare that with the table you published last Sunday, and I therefore respectfully ask you to give an old-fashioned list. . . . I am sure it would oblige many persons, who, like myself, can hardly keep up with the improvements of scoring the game." It was an understandable request, and Meacham provided the requested information, though perhaps with gritted teeth (*Chicago Tribune*, November 5, 1876, 10).

The following year the *Tribune* indulged in some justifiable boasting for having published batting averages based on at bats on the day after the last game of the season (*Chicago Tribune*, October 7, 1877). In 1878 the National League began to use at bats to calculate their official batting averages, and the public soon came to expect and even demand a new standard of speed and accuracy in their averages (John H. Gruber, "Order of Batting," *Sporting News*, February 10, 1916).

As noted in the preceding entry, Henry Chadwick eventually had a change of heart about base hits and batting average. In 1902 he commented, "A batsman's effectiveness is shown by the number of base hits he makes which forward runners, not by the figures of his base hit percentage" (*Spalding's Official Base Ball Guide, 1902*, 70).

17.5   Earned Run Averages. It is not surprising that the concept of the "earned" run, with its strong moral undertones, was championed and likely invented by Henry Chadwick. As Jules Tygiel has observed, the term "earned" originally reflected the batter's perspective rather than the pitcher's. Accordingly, earned runs were designed to isolate runs garnered by safe hits from those resulting from "skillful base running and the fielding errors such running involves" (*Spalding's Official Base Ball Guide, 1894*, quoted in Jules Tygiel, *Past Time*, 25).

While most observers shared this general outlook, not everyone agreed with how Chadwick categorized baserunning. Sportswriter O. P. Caylor, for example, maintained that "an earned run was a run made purely by batting or clean base stealing. . . . The player must earn it by reason of his own or his team's merits, not by reason of a failure of his opponents" (*Base Ball Gazette*, April 22, 1887).

By the 1870s the role of pitchers—so long a subject of controversy (see Chapter 3, especially the introduction)—was being grudgingly accepted as a permanent part of the game. At the end of the 1876 season the *Chicago Tribune* published a list of pitchers in order of earned runs allowed per game (*Chicago Tribune*, November 5, 1876, 10). Henry Chadwick wrote with his usual conviction in 1879 that "the only correct basis of a pitcher's skill is that of earned runs" (*New York Clipper*, November 29, 1879). In 1888 the National League and American Association began officially to track the statistic.

But using a hitter's statistic as a yardstick for pitchers was not ideal. The inconsistency of giving a pitcher a free ride for walks and stolen bases did not escape notice. A *Sporting Life* correspondent grumbled that "many pitchers save their records by deliberately giving bases on balls, knowing that earned runs cannot be secured, and thus they save their records" (*Sporting Life*, October 24, 1891). The additional complication of scorekeeping inconsistencies from park to park meant that the statistic was not the most accurate measure of a pitcher's performance.

Even Henry Chadwick, rarely one to reverse his course, became a harsh critic of the statistic he had once championed: "The absurd system of scoring earned runs which governs the code of scoring rules and which mixes up runs earned off the *fielding* as well as the pitching, entirely precludes the use of such earned runs as the basis of estimate. We have therefore ranked the pitchers of 1889 in the order of best percentage of victories" (*Spalding's Official Base Ball Guide, 1890*, 45–46).

Earned runs accordingly fell into disrepute. *Sporting News* explained in 1910: "There is no such thing now, officially, as an earned run. When earned runs were recognized, their specifications changed frequently. There were times when reaching first on four balls, a steal of second and a home run would have meant two earned runs. In 1897, however, the last year they were recognized, an earned run was only credited when scored by the aid of base hits alone" (*Sporting News*, September 1, 1910).

The next few years, however, saw increasing sentiment to rework the statistic. By 1912 there was "a move to bring back this feature of the box score, and it is probable that if it is revived a run starting with a base on balls will be counted as one earned, there being no legitimate reason why the pitcher should be favored" (*Washington Post*, May 12, 1912).

That was precisely what happened in the National League that season, with league secretary John Heydler advising "official scorers this year to include bases on balls in earned runs, but not to include stolen bases" (*Chicago Tribune*, June 16, 1912). At season's end, Heydler decided to rank pitchers on this basis in the official statistics (I. E. Sanborn, "Rates Pitchers by New Method," *Chicago Tribune*, December 9, 1912).

Most observers recognized that the resulting statistic was fairer to pitchers on weaker teams, and it was adopted for 1913 by the American League and many minor leagues, with a few modifications. The *Washington Post* applauded the decision to scrap the "archaic system" of ranking pitchers by their won-lost records. It noted that pitchers would henceforth be ranked "according to their efficiency. The new rating will be based on a modification of the old 'earned run,' the difference being that the modern 'earned run' will include all tallies for which a pitcher is responsible, either by being hit safely or by giving base on balls or wild pitches. Stolen bases also will figure in 'earned runs' on the theory that a considerable percentage of steals are due to the pitcher's inability to hold the runners to their bases, thereby making it practically impossible for catchers to throw them out" (*Washington Post*, June 22, 1913).

The paper went still further a couple of months later, noting how preferable this revised calculation of earned run average was to "the absurd system, left over from the dark ages of baseball, of rating pitchers by the number of games their teams won or lost for them" (*Washington Post*, August 31, 1913). And yet, more than ninety years later, pitchers continue to be given an inordinate amount of credit for the "number of games their teams won or lost for them."

17.6 Won-Lost Percentages. The *Chicago Tribune* observed in 1877, "the *St. Louis Republican* offers a column of 'percentage of games won to games played,' and adds that it is 'something never before published.' The truth is that Little Walker, of the *Chicago Times*, invented, applied and kept up that system through 1870" (*Chicago Tribune*, October 3, 1877). It is not clear whether this comment refers to the records of teams or pitchers, but at least it shows that the concept of using percentages to measure records dates back to very early baseball.

17.7 Runs Batted In. According to Ernest Lanigan, an unspecified Buffalo paper introduced RBIs in 1879 (Ernest J. Lanigan, *The Baseball Cyclopedia*, 56). The following year the new yardstick was picked up by the *Chicago Tribune*. After explaining the method of computing runs batted in, the *Tribune* informed readers: "These figures may, we think, be taken on the whole as a fair criterion of the value a batsman is to his team; for surely the man who hits safely when men are on bases, or who hits so hard as to compel fielding errors on the other side, is of far more value to his club than the man who earns a base for himself twice as often, and makes a weak hit or fouls or strikes out when the bases are loaded."

The *Tribune* noted that Chicago first baseman Cap Anson led the team in the category and claimed that he "undoubtedly leads the league." It further added: "If the record had been kept since the organization of the League it would unquestionably be found that no man ever played ball who batted home so many runs as Anson has done. He seems to have in a wonderful degree the genius of hitting at the right time—an accomplishment which all batsmen will do well to cultivate to the best of their ability" (*Chicago Tribune*, July 11, 1880).

Perhaps the *Tribune* thought that having a local player on top in the category would lead to its ready acceptance. If so, they were mistaken. According to Preston D. Orem, "Readers were unimpressed. Objections were that the men who led off, [Abner] Dalrymple and [George] Gore, did not have the same opportunities to knock in runs" (Preston D. Orem, *Baseball [1845–1881] from the Newspaper Accounts*, 336).

Henry Chadwick, however, liked the statistic and crusaded for it. In 1891 the National League's official scorers were instructed to keep track of runs batted in, causing the onetime advocate of hits and batting averages to write exultantly that the change was "one of the most important amendments made to the scoring rules for several years past. . . . Hitherto, the so-called 'best batting average' of the season has been that of the batsman who had the best percentage of base hits, entirely irrespective of whether the base hits had either forwarded runners around the bases, or had sent runs in. The new rule does away with the old and unjust method of deciding a batsman's ability . . . [and] substitutes data which really affords a true criterion of skill" (*Sporting Times*, April 4, 1891).

Alas for Chadwick, few shared his enthusiasm, and less than two months into the season the statistic that had become known as "Papa Chadwick's Runs Batted In" was "thrown down and dragged out by the Joint Committee on Rules." Chadwick took the news very hard, blaming "the clamor of certain scribes of New York and Philadelphia" and adding with uncharacteristic sarcasm, "To be consistent, the Board should at once do away with sacrifice hits, readopt foul bound catches and introduce a livelier ball so as to make record batting the feature of the game and encourage slugging for home runs." But others saw it differently, with an editorial in *Sporting Times* describing the RBI as a "useless detail" that served no "practical purpose" because it gave all the credit to the man "who is lucky enough to make a hit when the bases are occupied" and none to the teammates whose hits had started the rally. Sportswriter Hugh MacDougall went further, implying that Chadwick had "sprung" the new statistic "upon an unsuspecting public in the guide books of 1891" without the approval of the league's committee on rules (*Sporting Times*, May 16, 1891).

Ernest Lanigan reported that the statistic was popularized again by the *New York Press* when he became its sports editor in 1907. The RBI finally became an official statistic in 1920.

17.8   Runs Batted In Opportunities. The same basic problem with runs batted in that

was pointed out by *Tribune* readers in 1880 has been a recurring theme of recent sabermetricians. Their mutual complaint is that the statistic is misleading because it takes no account of the number of opportunities. John Thorn and Pete Palmer reported that runs batted in opportunities were an official statistic for the first three weeks of the 1918 American League season. It proved to be too much work and was dropped (John Thorn and Pete Palmer, *The Hidden Game of Baseball*, 25). Elias Sports Bureau began to track the statistic again in 1975, but it has attracted little attention (Dennis Bingham and Thomas R. Heitz, "Rules and Scoring," *Total Baseball IV*, 2549).

17.9   Strikeouts. Tallies of strikeouts were rare in early baseball, for several reasons. First, as John Thorn and Pete Palmer noted, Henry Chadwick "saw them as a sign of poor batting rather than good pitching," and convinced many others to view them that way (John Thorn and Pete Palmer, *The Hidden Game of Baseball*, 25). Chadwick rarely passed up an opportunity to counsel: "Great speed with an inaccurate delivery may yield outs on strikes, but that is no criterion of a pitcher's skill, though many entertain that erroneous idea" (*New York Clipper*, November 4, 1876).

Second, strikeouts were viewed as making for dull baseball, increasing the sense that they should not be encouraged in any way. As one reporter put it, "Those who attend the games enjoy a good fielding game much better than one won by the crooked and deceiving balls thrown by a pitcher, which causes the umpire to call 'three strikes, and out'" (*Grand Rapids* [Mich.] *Daily Democrat*, August 16, 1883). Finally, since an out is an out, there is no obvious reason to track strikeouts any more than, say, foul outs.

Nonetheless the advent of overhand pitching in the early 1880s led to dramatically higher strikeout totals and greater attention being paid to the statistic. In 1887 pitchers' strikeouts began to be tabulated. Batters' strikeouts began to be reported by former major leaguer Clarence Dow of the *Boston Globe* in 1891 but did not become an official National League statistic until 1909. Bill James noted, however, that the New England League, a minor league, tallied batter's strikeouts in 1890, nearly two decades before the major leagues began to do so (Bill James, *The New Bill James Historical Baseball Abstract*, 64).

17.10 Walks. Even more than strikeouts, walks were viewed as failures rather than successes in early baseball. The schizophrenic treatment they received reflects the fact that their origins (see **1.10** "Balls and Strikes") led them to be regarded as, at best, a necessary evil. Henry Chadwick classed them with wild pitches and passed balls as "battery errors." In 1876 they were grouped with outs (John Thorn and Pete Palmer, *The Hidden Game of Baseball*, 36). Nick Young informed scorers before the 1877 season that "Bases on balls should be charged as an error against the pitcher" (*Chicago Tribune*, April 26, 1877).

A controversial one-year experiment in 1887 saw walks counted as hits. This attracted widespread opposition, and walks were the subject of many derisive references. At the end of the campaign the *New York Times* wrote, "It is true that patience and good judgment on [the batter's] part may help to earn a base under such circumstances, but it is mainly due to the pitcher's error, and the phrase 'phantom hits' shows the popular estimation of such additions to batting records" (*New York Times*, October 9, 1887). Others referred to them as nominal hits or bloodless hits.

Bases on balls by batters were tabulated by Clarence Dow of the *Boston Globe* in 1891 and occasionally tracked by the National League in subsequent years. In 1899 Washington co-owner J. Earl Wagner expressed the opinion that "a record should be kept of the number of bases on balls worked by each player. I suppose [John] McGraw of Baltimore has walked oftener than any batsman in the league to date. Working pitchers for free passes is one of the nerviest and brainiest devices in team work at the bat, and these achievements in securing dead-head passages to the base should be featured in the records" (*Denver Evening Post*, July 28, 1899). They finally became an official National League statistic in 1910, and the American League adopted them three years later.

17.11 Total Bases Run. Total bases run was a statistic kept during the 1880 season, which credited players for each base advanced. The statistic was the brainchild of onetime cricket player Harry Wright, who suggested "that the score-sheet shall be changed so as to place to the credit of each player the total number of bases run during the game, with the exception where he reaches first base as the result of the putting out of another player" (*New York Clipper*, February 21, 1880).

It took only one season to make it abundantly clear that a figure that was a basic unit in cricket was essentially meaningless in baseball. Not only was it a lot of work to compile, it measured neither team success—since the team derived no benefit from advancing a runner to third—nor individual accomplishment. Puzzled fans "besieged" club directors with questions about the significance of the new statistic. Meanwhile a correspondent for the *New York Sunday Mercury* called on editors not to "disfigure the columns of their papers with any T. B. R. or C. O. . . . only print scores that can be read by a person with a common school education" (*New York Sunday Mercury*, April 3, 1880). Pete Palmer and John Thorn understandably called it a "wonderfully silly figure which signified nothing about either an individual's ability in isolation or his value to his team" (John Thorn and Pete Palmer, *The Hidden Game of Baseball*, 19).

Nonetheless it seems worth remembering because it is indicative of the great difficulty of adapting statistics from the apparently similar game of cricket to baseball. Oh, and since Abner Dalrymple was crowned as the only champion, it means that at least one Abner D. had a significant baseball accomplishment.

17.12 Catcher's ERA. Craig Wright, a pioneer of sabermetrics who helped popularize the catcher's ERA, credited the Japanese with introducing this measurement to him: "In 1982 I read a very interesting article contrasting the attitudes found in Japanese baseball and in American baseball. The central point was that in Japan they emphasize the idea that a team is more than the sum of its parts. Players are evaluated not just on their individual accomplishments, but also by their impact on their teammates and, ultimately, the team itself. The strongest example of this principle is their attitude toward catchers. When a pitcher is struggling in a game, the Japanese manager will sometimes change the whole battery, or perhaps leave the pitcher in and change catchers. And in their statistical records, many teams keep track of the number of runs allowed per nine innings caught for each of their catchers—a catcher ERA, or CERA" (Craig Wright and Tom House, *The Diamond Appraised*, 22).

17.13 Fielding Percentages. The basic concept of the fielding percentage, in which the number of chances successfully handled by a fielder is divided by his total opportunities, was in place by the 1870s, and the term came into use a few years later. Indeed, John Thorn and Pete Palmer note that there were six standard fielding categories in 1876 and the same number a century later (John Thorn and Pete Palmer, *The Hidden Game of Baseball*, 19). That stands in stark contrast to the proliferation of statistics used to measure the performance of pitchers and hitters.

17.14   Range Factor. Bill James is rightly credited with giving attention to range factor as the best measure of defensive prowess. In doing so he was not creating a new measure so much as reviving a very old one.

John Thorn and Pete Palmer noted that journalist Al Wright devised a statistic called "fielding average" in 1875 that was calculated by dividing putouts plus assists by games played: "Does Wright's 'fielding average' look familiar? You may have recognized it as Bill James's Range Factor! Everything old is new again" (John Thorn and Pete Palmer, *The Hidden Game of Baseball*, 19).

The idea has continued to resurface periodically. Sportswriter Thomas S. Rice argued in 1922, "To our mind the element of fielding averages which tells the most, and as a rule, is the only element of real weight, is the number of assists, especially in the case of infielders. You can't get assists unless you go after the ball or have the brains to station yourself where the ball is likely to go. The percentage of assists per game for an infielder will come pretty near to demonstrating his effectiveness and his general helpfulness. Further, as the more desperate the chances at which the player stabs the greater will be his number of errors, as a rule, errors for a man who excells in assists are a sort of tribute to the winning spirit" (*Sporting News*, January 13, 1922).

Forty-five years later, Lee Allen observed, "fielding cannot be measured to the same fine degree that batting is. Fielding percentage is almost meaningless, and lifetime fielding is almost never published. . . . There is one way in which fielding ability can be demonstrated to some extent, and that is to rate players by the chances they accept per game" (*Sporting News*, July 15, 1967).

17.15   Sacrifice Hits. The idea that a batter deserves credit for giving himself up to advance a runner seemed to originate in the late 1870s as a linguistic idea, with the invention of the com-

mendatory term "sacrifice hit." The earliest use of the term that I have found appeared in the *Detroit Post and Tribune* on April 20, 1878.

The following year the *New York Clipper* claimed that Ross Barnes "was among the first to practically introduce the now well-known 'sacrifice hits,' which were written up in baseball books of 1869–70" (*New York Clipper*, May 3, 1879). I believe this statement confuses two different concepts. The bunt (see **2.2.1**) had begun to emerge by the late 1860s, but the term "sacrifice hit" does not appear to have been in use that early.

Additionally, the idea of expending an out to advance another runner is the product of a later era. In the 1860s, when the bunt originated, the offensive side was so dominant that it would have been foolish to deliberately give up an out. Thus a player who bunted was doing so with the intention of getting a base hit. During the 1870s, however, run scoring dropped so precipitously (see **1.30**) that a sacrifice hit became a much more reasonable strategy. Since the bunt was out of favor by then, I assume that the "sacrifice hits" referred to above were grounders or fly balls (such as the "right field base hit" discussed in the next entry) that advanced a base runner.

It was not until bunts returned to prominence that batters were given any statistical credit for a "sacrifice hit." In 1889 the statistic began to be officially compiled, but batters were still charged with a time at bat. It took about five more years before the batter's "sacrifice" was recognized by not charging him with an at bat.

17.16   Sacrifice Flies. The sacrifice fly has an extraordinarily schizophrenic history which reflects controversy over whether it should be regarded as a deliberate and successful attempt to drive in a runner or an unsuccessful bid for a hit. John H. Gruber stated that, before scoring rules began to be standardized in 1880, a few scorers advocated the "right field base hit," in which a batter would be credited with a hit for deliberately hitting a fly ball that advanced a runner (John H. Gruber, "Base Hits," *Sporting News*, April 6, 1916). Sacrifice flies were included with sacrifice hits in 1889, but five years later the scoring practice was changed so that a sacrifice could only be credited on a bunt. The sacrifice fly was introduced as an official statistic in 1908, but the rule was repealed or modified several times before finally coming back for good in 1954.

17.17 Saves. Wouldn't it be great to invent a statistic to prove that you were right about something and everyone else was wrong? And then have everyone else not only accept your premise but make it one of the game's fundamental measures? According to sportswriter Deron Snyder, that's exactly what happened to Chicago scribe Jerome Holtzman.

Snyder explained that Holtzman invented the save because he believed that Cubs relief pitchers Don Elston and Bill Henry had had better years than Pirates reliever Elroy Face in 1959. Nobody took his argument seriously because the Cubs relievers had no statistics as glitzy as Face's 18-1 won-lost record. So Holtzman invented the save to prove his point (Deron Snyder, "A Stat Worth Saving," *USA Today Baseball Weekly*, July 21–27, 1999).

As with the sacrifice hit, acceptance of this statistic was eased by the fact that it measured a concept that was already part of the language of baseball. Negro National League founder Rube Foster wrote in 1907 that when a young pitcher is used in relief, "it is natural that he should want to save the game, and so is likely to forget to get into the pitching gradually" (Jerry Malloy, ed., *Sol White's History of Colored Base Ball*, 99). Johnny Evers and Hugh Fullerton referred in 1910 to Ed Walsh having "saved" two late-season games (John J. Evers and Hugh S. Fullerton, *Touching Second*, 256). In a 1911 game account, sportswriter I. E. "Sy" Sanborn described how Mordecai Brown "had to rush to the rescue" of starter "King" Cole in the sixth inning, prompting manager Frank Chance gave Brown fifty dollars from his own pocket as a reward for the "feat of life saving" (*Chicago Tribune*, May 21, 1911).

Thus, as with many other statistics, the save originated as a linguistic means of expressing a principle that was deemed important—in this case, that pitchers should finish what they start. The acceptance of this term paved the way for an actual measurement to be devised and become popular.

17.18 Stolen Bases. Stolen bases were a big part of nineteenth-century baseball but were not tracked at all until 1886. Even then official scorers had such different ideas of what constituted a stolen base that the *Providence Journal* concluded that the new rule was "not observed with sufficient uniformity to be of any benefit" (quoted in *Cleveland Leader and Herald*, May 16, 1886). Reaching a consensus on the matter proved very difficult, with the unfortunate re-

sult that the statistic was not valid for comparison purposes until 1898. Even more regrettable is that many have used this dispute as an excuse to disregard all nineteenth-century statistics.

17.19 Caught Stealing. Ernest Lanigan says that totals for caught stealing began to be tracked in 1912 at the request of catcher Charles Schmidt (Ernest J. Lanigan, *The Baseball Cyclopedia*, 56). Schmidt presumably was primarily interested in this statistic from the catcher's perspective, but Lanigan compiled it both ways. His totals for caught stealing by both catchers and base runners appeared in December of 1913 in both *Sporting Life* and *Sporting News*.

17.20 On-base Percentages. On-base percentage, which measures how frequently a batter reaches base by hit, walk, or being hit by a pitch, was one of the formulas used by statistician Allan Roth in the early 1950s at the behest of Branch Rickey (Branch Rickey, "Goodby to Some Old Baseball Ideas," *Life*, August 2, 1954, 78–87; cited in Alan Schwarz, *The Numbers Game*, 58–59). Pete Palmer was the first to isolate on-base percentage, and he added it to the American League averages book in 1979. It finally became an official statistic in 1984 (John Thorn and Pete Palmer, *The Hidden Game of Baseball*, 25).

17.21 Slugging Averages. Henry Chadwick published a table of total bases divided by games played in his *National Chronicle* column of February 13, 1869. But as discussed in entry **17.3**, Chadwick was not fond of extra-base hits, and the statistic was not permanently adopted until 1923 (John Thorn and Pete Palmer, *The Hidden Game of Baseball*, 21).

17.22 Quality Starts. Author Glenn Guzzo reported that around 1985 *Philadelphia Inquirer* sportswriter John Lowe introduced the quality start, which is defined as any start in which the pitcher lasts at least six innings and allows no more than three earned runs. Lowe saw two primary benefits to the statistic: (1) it was an accurate reflection of what managers expected of their starting pitchers, and (2) fans could easily calculate the statistic by glancing at a box score.

17.23 GWRBI. The game-winning RBI was added to the roll of official statistics in 1980 and dropped nine years later.

17.24 Individual Statistics Emphasized.
There have long been divergent viewpoints as
to whether keeping track of individual statistics encourages or discourages team play. As
noted in the entry on base hits (17.3), Henry
Chadwick initially depicted them as a way of
ensuring that each player did his part, but later
had doubts.

Individual statistics were being widely disseminated by the 1870s, and it did not take
long before awareness of them began to have an
effect on the game. By 1878 there were calls to
abolish the base hit and error columns from the
box score because they caused players to "play
for themselves and their records, rather than for
their clubs" (*New York Sunday Mercury*, August
3, 1878). The term "record player" became
common in the 1880s to refer to a player who
would not jeopardize his own numbers to try
to help the team.

This was most conspicuous with fielders,
who could usually avoid being charged with an
error by not quite getting to a hard-hit ball. In
1877 a fan wrote to ask if a player could "stand
still and let the ball pass in order to keep an
error from being marked against him." He was
told: "It is not beyond the bounds of possibility
for a player to do as you say, but he would be
exercising very poor judgment. In the first place
the scorers would justly scratch down against
him the largest error recognized by the fraternity, and, last of all, the directors of the club
would take him out and 'jayhawk' him" (*Louisville Courier-Journal*, July 14, 1877). Pitchers
similarly were accused of deliberately walking
dangerous batters, since bases on balls did not
count toward earned runs. An 1891 article observed, "The record playing fielder is frowned
upon alike by player and public, but the record
playing pitcher has in many instances been getting away with it in good style and drawing big
incomes" (*Sporting Life*, October 24, 1891).

Batting statistics were less prone to manipulation, but they certainly did attract the attention of players. In 1885 George "Orator" Shafer
complained to his team owner that the official
scorer was short-changing him (*St. Louis Post-
Dispatch*, July 9, 1885). A 1900 article observed
that hitters kept close tabs on their batting
averages and that, "According to several ex-
Indianapolis players, [George Hogriever] sends
his base hit record home to his wife every night
and has her figure out his percentage at the end
of every week" (*Sporting Life*, November 17,
1900). Washington co-owner J. Earl Wagner
likewise maintained that he knew of a National
League player who "keeps double entry books
on his batting, and doesn't care whether his
team wins or loses just so long as he manages
to squeeze in a hit or two each game" (*Denver
Evening Post*, July 28, 1899).

17.25 Career Milestones Emphasized. When
the countdown to Carl Yastrzemski's three
thousandth hit in 1979 became a media circus,
Red Smith wrote: "When Cap Anson reached
3,000 hits in 1897, there was no congratulatory
phone call from President McKinley, who was
preoccupied getting a protective tariff through
Congress. When Ty Cobb made it in 1921, news
accounts of the game mentioned his achievement in the 12th or 14th paragraph. When Sam
Rice retired in 1934 with 2,987 hits, it didn't occur to him that maybe he should stick around
for 13 more" (Red Smith, September 14, 1979,
reprinted in *Red Smith on Baseball*).

I presume that Smith's point is that earlier
generations made less of a fuss about career
milestones. This is a valid point, but it is important to emphasize that it reflects in large
part the unavailability of reliable counts. In
addition, there are problems with many of his
assertions.

When Cap Anson reached the three-thousand-hit mark, it can be safely assumed that no
one had an accurate total. Indeed, Anson's total
has been changed several times since then. If
his National Association hits are included, he
would actually have reached three thousand
in 1894.

According to Marc Okkonen, when Cobb
reached three thousand hits on August 19,
1921, there was no coverage at all in the local newspapers (Marc Okkonen, *The Ty Cobb
Scrapbook*, 157). Again, it is possible that journalists had a slightly different count. Walter
Miller, a teammate of Tris Speaker, recalled that
when Tris Speaker got his three thousandth hit,
"I don't remember a person saying a darn word
about it" (Eugene Murdock, *Baseball Between
the Wars*, 247). Once more, it is hard to be sure
whether this meant that no one thought it significant or that no one had an accurate count.
The latter seems more likely, since when Babe
Ruth hit his five hundredth home run in 1929,
he "dispatched a courier in quest of the price-
less ball" and exchanged it with the passerby
who had retrieved it for twenty dollars and
two autographed baseballs (*New York Times*,
August 12, 1929).

We can be surer in the case of Sam Rice,
who later recalled, "At that time not much at-

tention was paid to records. The truth of the matter is I did not even know how many hits I had. A couple of years after I quit, Clark Griffith told me about it, and asked me if I'd care to have a comeback with the Senators and pick up those thirteen hits. But I was out of shape, and didn't want to go through all that would have been necessary to make the effort. Nowadays, with radio and television announcers spouting records every time a player comes to bat, I would have known about my hits and probably would have stayed to make 3,000 of them" (Lee Allen, *Kings of the Diamond*; quoted in Jonathan Fraser Light, *The Cultural Encyclopedia of Baseball*, 736).

Yet Rice's profession of being unaware of the milestone stands in very stark contrast with the case of Sam Crawford. Early in his career, Crawford was told that Cap Anson alone had collected 3,000 hits. "It seemed a staggering total," Crawford recalled in 1917. "I was fairly swamped by it. But then and there the idea crystallized in my mind that some day in the far off future I, too, would like to register my three thousandth hit . . . it has been my chief ambition for a good many years to make three thousand hits." When the 1915 season ended, Crawford was only 35 and was within 150 hits of the magic number. He thus imagined that reaching his goal would be "a rather simple matter. . . . But the spring brought a different story. They told me I had slowed up, that I would have to begin to take my turn on the bench." The slugging outfielder was still 57 hits shy of 3,000 when the 1917 season started, but he remained confident that "I can still get those three thousand hits if only I have the chance" (Sam Crawford, "My Three Thousandth Hit," *Baseball Magazine*, August 1917, 420, 457). Alas, he played sparingly in 1917 and struggled when he did. After collecting only 18 hits all season, he announced his retirement. That winter there were rumors he would sign with Cleveland or the St. Louis Cardinals and continue his pursuit of 3,000 hits. In the end, however, he chose to play for Los Angeles in the Pacific Coast League in 1918. Sam Crawford averaged nearly 200 hits per season in four years in Los Angeles but never returned to the major leagues, thus falling a mere 39 hits shy of attaining his "chief ambition."

Rice's intriguing contention that radio and television announcers were responsible for the heightened awareness of career milestones is difficult to prove or disprove. What is indisputable is that the three-thousand-hit barrier

assumed a new prominence as baseball was making the transition to new forms of media coverage. In 1942 Paul Waner became the first major leaguer in seventeen years to reach the milestone and was conscious enough of the event that he asked the official scorer not to credit him with a questionable hit. By the time Stan Musial became the next player to join the three-thousand-hit club in 1958, its significance was assumed.

It is also worth noting that there is no particularly good reason for the inordinate publicity given to the three-thousand-hit plateau in recent years. Baseball has so many statistical categories that not all of them can receive the same attention. Sportswriters have simply chosen to emphasize three thousand hits, five hundred home runs, and three hundred pitcher wins while downplaying equally impressive accomplishments, such as one thousand stolen bases, two thousand runs scored, or two thousand RBIs.

Thus the lack of attention to the milestones cited by Red Smith is a complicated phenomenon that cannot be entirely attributed to a lack of interest in statistical accomplishments. Instead a particular milestone comes to be viewed as important based on a number of factors, such as context, attainability, and assorted imponderables.

Due to the vagaries of early record-keeping, it is hard to be sure what was the first milestone to attract widespread attention. The most likely candidate is Cy Young's five hundredth win, which *Sporting Life* hailed as "a unique feat requiring 21 years of continuous effort, which has no parallel in baseball annals, and may never be repeated by any pitcher now before the public, with the possible exception of the illustrious Mathewson" (*Sporting Life*, July 30, 1910; reprinted in Reed Browning, *Cy Young*, 188).

17.26   Streaks. Tracking the length of any particular streak does not require an enormous amount of work. Determining where a streak ranks in comparison with every other player in the history of the game is an extremely daunting task. Thus, as with career milestones, the emphasis on streaks in recent years has been made meaningful by a great deal of hard work by baseball record-keepers.

That does not of course mean that it is only a recent phenomenon for streaks to capture the public's imagination. Around 1910 performance streaks began to attract attention, but there was no accurate tally of the record for such streaks. Rube Marquard's nineteen straight victories in 1912, for example, attracted enormous attention, but there was no consensus as to whose record he was pursuing (Larry Mansch, *Rube Marquard*, 106; Francis C. Richter, *Richter's History and Records of Base Ball*, 247). Walter Johnson was closing in on the record for consecutive scoreless innings in 1913 when it was disclosed that he was actually chasing Jack Coombs and not "Doc" White, as had been supposed (Dick Jemison, "Jack Coombs, Not Doc White, Scoreless Innings Champion," *Atlanta Constitution*, May 14, 1913; George L. Moreland, *Balldom*, 218–219). In 1914 George L. Moreland reported that the longest hitting streak was twenty-five games by Otis Clymer. Later research discovered some much longer streaks, including a forty-four-gamer by Wee Willie Keeler (George L. Moreland, *Balldom*, 271).

Even earlier than that, there had been fascination with consecutive-games-played streaks. This seems to have begun in the 1890s when several catchers, most notably minor leaguer Henry Cote and National Leaguers Deacon McGuire and Chief Zimmer, attracted considerable attention for their hardiness by long skeins of playing in every game (George L. Moreland, *Balldom*, 208; *Syracuse Herald*, August 17, 1890).

This interest gradually transferred to players at other positions. In 1909 it was reported that James "Lil" Sager of Evansville had played in 506 consecutive games, which was claimed to be the longest such streak "since the introduction of the national game" (*Sporting News*, July 29, 1909). Sager's streak was finally snapped on May 6, 1911, after 895 games in which he had not missed an inning (*Sporting Life*, June 17, 1911).

Someone soon concluded that the major league record for consecutive games played was 525. During the 1919 season, Fred Luderus of the Phillies had a streak of more than 400 games, but it looked like it would end when he was replaced in the starting lineup. Statistician Al Munro Elias pleaded with the Philadelphia manager to get Luderus in the game, and he was eventually used as a pinch hitter. Luderus ran his streak to 533 games and was hailed as the new record-holder (Joe Dittmar, "Fred Luderus," Tom Simon, ed., *Deadball Stars of the National League*, 206). But Luderus lost his record to a long-retired player when "baseball historians dug into the musty archives of the sport to find that George Pinckney, shortstop of

the Brooklyn club of 1885–90, had taken part in 578 games without a break" (*Atlanta Constitution*, June 16, 1920).

Thereafter the interest in streaks was assured. During spring training of 1923 a great deal of attention was paid to the fact that Everett Scott had played in more than one thousand consecutive games. One writer crowed that "The odds against beating Scott's record in the future are anything you choose to name" (*Sporting News*, March 22, 1923). A few months later a youngster named Lou Gehrig made his major league debut.

17.27 Record Bureaus. Erratic record-keeping persisted well into the twentieth century, but, as shown by the burgeoning interest in streaks, it was not the result of a lack of interest. A 1910 *Sporting News* editorial observed that "Scores of fans over the country daily already ask questions pertaining to base ball records no one can answer with assurance for the simple reason that in the past no authentic record has been made of the hundreds of things in base ball calling for emulation."

It accordingly suggested: "The next important evolution of base ball should be a bureau of records, the possibilities of which are as alluring as they are broad. Established under the auspices of the National Commission . . . its first duty should be to receive the official scores direct from official scorers throughout all organized base ball. . . . Such a system would not only relieve the various league presidents and secretaries of laborious routine labor, but would insure the preservation of base ball records in full—which is at present left to private enterprise and is therefore on a more or less haphazard basis. The second prominent advantage to accrue from such a bureau would be the preservation of acknowledged specific records, without which base ball has already been too long" (*Sporting News*, August 18, 1910). Unfortunately, nothing came of this suggestion.

17.28 Single-season Records. As with career totals, seasonal records often got little attention in early years due to the difficulty of keeping track of them. Seasonal totals were not official until tallied at season's end, making it very difficult to honor record breakers. Alan Schwarz cited a 1910 article that observed, "By striking out ten of the White Sox yesterday Walter Johnson established a new strikeout record—it will take the official count to decide whether he has fanned 307 or 308 to date" (*Washington*

Evening Star, September 29, 1910; quoted in Alan Schwarz, *The Numbers Game*, 39).

An extreme example happened when Owen Wilson hit thirty-six triples in 1912, a record that still stands. It was not until the following spring that Ernest Lanigan pointed out that Wilson had established a record. The reason it had taken so long to figure this out was that a typographical error had led to Napoleon Lajoie being listed with forty-three triples in 1903 instead of thirteen (the figure has since been corrected to eleven). Lanigan noted that the same typo had also deprived Joe Jackson of credit for having established a new American League record for triples (*Sporting News*, March 13, 1913).

17.29   Detailed Breakdowns. The Dodgers' 1954 yearbook included "a section entitled individual batting breakdowns. It gives each Dodger regular's games played, at bats, hits, home runs, runs batted in and percentage at home and on the road, in day and night games, for each month of the season, before and after the All-Star game, at home against each club, on the road against each club, against right-handed and left-handed pitching, with nobody on base (NOB), with runners on base (ROB) and as a pinch-hitter.... There are similar gory details about pitching, fielding, opposing players, life-time records, all-time Dodger marks and so on" (INS wire service: *Syracuse Herald Journal*, April 18, 1954).

17.30   Asterisks. When Roger Maris hit sixty-one home runs in 1961, the asterisk suddenly became the most notorious symbol in baseball. As has frequently been pointed out, Commissioner Ford Frick did not actually specify that an asterisk be used to denote that Maris's feat had occurred during a season eight games longer than the one played by Babe Ruth (Ford Frick, *Games, Asterisks and People*, 154–155). But in any event there was nothing new about having an asterisk in a baseball record book. Gene Karst explains that he wrote to *Who's Who in Baseball* editor F. C. Lane in the early 1930s to suggest that league leaders be denoted with an asterisk. Lane began to do so in the 1933 edition (Gene Karst, "Ready for the New Asterisk War?," *Baseball Research Journal* 26 [1997], 66–67).

17.31   Tape-measure Home Runs. The idea of estimating the length of home runs surfaced in baseball's early days. In 1865, Lip Pike's

brother Boaz "struck the longest ball yet batted on the field, not less, perhaps, than 600 feet straight ahead" (*Brooklyn Eagle*, July 11, 1865). As with many baseball statistics, it was some years before the need was felt for more precise measurement. Moreover the accomplishment was highly dependent upon the elasticity of the ball being used.

As a result, far more attention was given to the measurement of long throws. Throwing contests were common in early baseball, and records were kept with great care. When Ed Crane apparently broke John Hatfield's long-standing record in 1884 with a throw of 135 yards, 1 foot, and ½ inch, the exact distance was verified by a team of civil engineers (*Cincinnati Enquirer*, October 14, 1884). Nonetheless the throw was not generally accepted (George L. Moreland, *Balldom*, 265).

The 1880s saw the concept of measuring long home runs come into vogue. Lee Allen reported that a fungo hit by C. R. Partridge of Dartmouth College in 1880 was measured at 354 feet, 10 inches (*Sporting News*, April 20, 1968; reprinted in *Cooperstown Corner*). It was topped two years later: "Oscar Walker yesterday at the suggestion of several friends ascertained the exact place where his long hit on Sunday landed. The measurement was carefully made and the tape line told a story of 427 feet, or 142 yards 1 foot, which will do to start a record of long hits against" (*St. Louis Post-Dispatch*, April 11, 1882). According to Sam Crane, in 1890 Buck Ewing made "the longest hit ever made on the present Polo Grounds. It was a wallop over the left-field fence away down where the old open fifty-cent seats and the bleachers joined. There have been many balls hit over the same fence since, but none so near to Eighth avenue. . . . The spot where it went over the fence was long marked by a small flag, as was Mike Tiernan's smash over the right-field fence, on what is now Manhattan Field" (Sam Crane, "Buck Ewing" [Fifty greatest series], *New York Journal*, January 20, 1912).

17.32   Simulation Games. The national pastime has long inspired efforts to recreate its pleasures in the form of parlor games. As statistics have become a larger part of the baseball experience, their role in these endeavors has seen a corresponding increase.

"Parlor Base-Ball" was invented by Francis Sebring, a pitcher for the Empire Base Ball Club in the mid-1860s. Sebring's game was depicted in the December 8, 1866, issue of *Frank Leslie's*

Illustrated Newspaper and was advertised in the November 17 issue and in other sporting papers. The game used springs to propel a coin from the pitcher to the batter and then out into the field (David Pietrusza, Lloyd Johnson, and Bob Carroll, eds., *Total Baseball Catalog*, 322).

In 1885 pitcher Jacob Aydelott moved closer to simulation when he patented a game that was also called "Parlor Base Ball." Aydelott's game involved drawing from a deck of 125 cards that represented specific events (*Sporting Life*, February 25, 1885).

Dice soon began to be used to create randomness. In 1886 the McLoughlin Brothers of New York City unveiled a dice-based game known simply as the "Game of Base Ball." The following year Philadelphians Edward K. McGill and George W. Delany devised "a new 'game of base ball,' played by means of the chances of dice, each throw constituting a different point of play. Two dice and nine counters, with the board in question, form the materials of the new game and it is played by from 2 persons to 18. It is an excellent parlor game, especially for boys familiar with the points of play in base ball" (*Brooklyn Eagle*, January 9, 1887).

The first commercially marketed game to try to replicate actual player performance was Clifford Van Beek's "The National Pastime," which he started working on in 1923, patented in 1925, and began to distribute in 1931. It was followed by the more widely marketed Ethan Allen's "All-Star Baseball" in 1941. Van Beek's game used cards while Allen's used a spinner and individualized game pieces for each batter. The new features meant that hitters would produce results that resembled their real-life records, but there was no such allowance for pitchers. These games might be viewed as yet another reflection of the mind-set that pitchers had usurped a role in baseball to which they were not entitled. (Perhaps it is no coincidence that Allen was a major league outfielder.)

It was another generation before simulation games took the next step and incorporated the performance of pitchers and fielders. Richard Seitz introduced "APBA" in 1951, and Hal Richman followed with "Strat-O-Matic," a game he developed during the 1950s and began to mass-market in 1961. Although based upon different principles, both games yielded a degree of statistical realism previously unknown. APBA and Strat-O-Matic attracted loyal bands of followers and dominated the market until the computer revolution, which brought a bevy of new, still more statistically sophisticated games.

17.33 Rotisserie Leagues. So-called rotisserie baseball has brought fascination with baseball statistics to an implausibly wide audience. Daniel Okrent sketched out the basic rules for rotisserie baseball on November 17, 1979, on a flight to Austin, Texas. He presented them to a group of friends at a restaurant called The Pit, but they were uninterested. Two weeks later he explained them to another group of friends at La Rotisserie Francaise in New York, and the game was born.

While the specifics of rotisserie baseball were new, others had previously arrived at similar concepts. Frank W. Hoffmann and William G. Bailey reported that a man named Joe Morgan of Middletown, Ohio, began running a similar league in 1964 and wrote a book about it in 1975 (Frank W. Hoffmann and William G. Bailey, *Sports and Recreation Fads*, 121–123). The writer Jack Kerouac also created a game that operated along the same general lines. And my editor, Ivan Dee, was a founder of the Chicago Baseball League, which started in 1978 and continues to this day. Even Okrent had been inspired by a game designed by Bob Sklar, one of his professors at the University of Michigan (Sam Walker, *Fantasyland*, 64–65).

Chapter 18

MONEY

"Just why the nines are called amateurs is a hard question to answer, as all the resident professionals in both cities will play with the clubs."—*St. Louis Post-Dispatch*, May 29, 1886

"Johnny Leber . . . will not report. He says he can make more money playing 'amateur' ball in Cleveland."—*Sporting Life, April* 14, 1917

THE PARADOX embodied in these epigraphs reflects a deep ambivalence that has always characterized the relationship between baseball and money. That relationship has attracted increasing attention in recent years, for the obvious reason that baseball players have become extraordinarily well paid, but there is nothing new about it, as the following entries will demonstrate.

(i) The Transition from Amateurism to Professionalism

During the 1860s and early 1870s, despite vociferous protests from many quarters, baseball was transformed from an amateur activity to one in which money played a pivotal role. The basis of professionalism varied from club to club, with cooperatives and stock corporations the most common forms. The stock corporations made it possible for nonplayers to profit from baseball for the first time, and some did. But the precarious financial situation of the clubs meant that for the most part professionalism enriched only the ballplayers themselves, and most of them were struggling to make enough to live on.

18.1.1 **Organization.** Although the Knickerbocker Club was opposed to professionalism, the club's members sowed the seeds for professional baseball. At a club meeting on December 6, 1856, a resolution was passed calling for a convention of the various clubs playing baseball so as to make possible the "getting up of grand matches on a scale not hitherto attempted" (*Spirit of the Times*, January 3, 1857). The convention was held at Smith's Hall, 426 Broome Street, New York City, on January 22, 1857, and was attended by sixteen clubs, all of them from the New York City area. It led directly to the founding of the National Association of Base Ball Players (NABBP) and to the adoption of a code of standardized playing rules.

While baseball clubs had previously collected membership fees, the convention may have marked the first exchange of money between clubs. A man named W. W. Armfield, representing the Eagle Club, moved that each club remit two dollars to cover incidental expenses. The motion passed, prompting treasurer E. H. Brown of the Harlem Club to inform the assemblage, "I don't take Spanish quarters." Brown then collected two dollars from each club, and baseball began a long and relentless march toward professionalism (*Spirit of the Times*, January 31, 1857; reprinted in Dean Sullivan, ed., *Early Innings*, 22–24).

Although the NABBP maintained a rule against professionalism until the 1869 season, it became increasingly evident that it lacked the ability to enforce the rule. Moreover baseball's new level of organization soon ensured that the influence of money would be felt.

18.1.2   Admission Fees.

A fifty-cent admission charge—a significant amount of money for the time—was collected for a series of 1858 games between all-star squads of players from Brooklyn and New York City. The games were played at the Fashion Race Course, in what is now Corona, with the proceeds going to a fund for widows and orphans (James L. Terry, *Long Before the Dodgers*, 23).

Some fifteen hundred people attended the first game on July 20, in spite of the cost and the inaccessibility of the grounds. The game was umpired by E. H. Brown of the Metropolitans—presumably the same man who had declined to take Spanish quarters at the previous year's meeting.

Because early parks were not enclosed, it was several years before admission fees became common. The first enclosed stadium to host baseball regularly was Brooklyn's Union Grounds in 1862. Many spectators initially balked at the prospect of paying admission to watch a baseball game, but most of them "gradually became used to the idea" (James Wood as told to Frank G. Menke, "Baseball in By-Gone Days," Part 3, syndicated column, *Indiana* [Pa.] *Evening Gazette*, August 17, 1916).

One of the things that helped ease the transition to collecting admission fees were exhibition "benefit" games, which were staged to raise money for a worthy cause. For example, a ten-cent admission was charged at an 1862 game between the Atlantics and Eckfords of Brooklyn to raise funds for the Sanitary Commission (*Brooklyn Eagle*, November 5 and 7, 1862). Often, however, benefit games were thinly veiled methods of getting around the NABBP's rules and paying the players. An 1861 account stated: "a complimentary arrangement for the benefit of Messrs. Pearce and Creighton, of the Atlantic and Excelsior clubs, took place on Thursday, Nov. 7th . . . from the comparatively slim attendance of spectators, we should judge that these benefit matches do not find favor in the ball playing community, free contests being the order of the day among them" (*New York Clipper*, November 16, 1861).

When a worthy cause was involved, such games gradually gained acceptance. The 1864 announcement that benefit games would be played for soldiers in Brooklyn was warmly received: "Such a class of matches, while they would commend themselves to the patronage of every admirer of the game, if only for the charitable objects in view, would be entirely devoid of the objectionable features of the championship contests, which experience has taught us to be prolific of ill feelings between rival organizations, and productive of scenes at ball matches likely to bring discredit upon the same" (*Brooklyn Eagle*, June 1, 1864). Philadelphia's new ball grounds at Twenty-fifth and Jefferson Streets were inaugurated on May 25, 1864, with a benefit game for the Sanitary Fair that raised five hundred dollars (*New York Clipper*, November 6, 1880).

The new Philadelphia grounds were unenclosed, which presented a daunting problem for anyone hoping to collect an admission fee. This didn't stop Athletics president Colonel Thomas Fitzgerald from trying to do so at a match later that year: "At the various entrances . . . the Colonel posted his doorkeepers. It may be asked (as this was a kind of historic occasion) who these doorkeepers were. But those who know the Colonel do not need to be told. The doorkeepers were the Colonel's sons—not all of them, but those who were, at the time being, the smaller of the series. The receipts of the afternoon were $14. This was not a heavy return, considering especially that the crowd was greater than had ever up to that time attended a match in that city. But the entrance charge was considered more or less as a joke by nearly everybody" (*New York Clipper*, November 1, 1879). Experiments like this made it clear that an enclosed stadium was a prerequisite for collecting admission fees and, as was noted in the entry on "Spite Fences" (**16.2.3**), even that was far from foolproof.

18.1.3   Professional Players.

The identity of the first professional player will always be clouded by the rules of the National Association of Base Ball Players, which meant that he received the money under the table and therefore had good reason not to advertise the fact. When Al Reach died, it was reported that he had been the first player to be regularly paid, receiving twenty-five dollars a week before 1860. But Reach's playing career doesn't seem to have begun in earnest until 1861, and the amount cited probably refers to what Reach received for joining the Athletics in 1865.

A much more likely candidate is Jim Creighton, who was almost certainly receiving under-the-table payments for several years before his premature death in 1862. In 1873 the *Brooklyn Eagle* referred to "the noted Excelsiors, who in 1859 practically inaugurated the professional system by their engagement of Creighton, the first pitcher to introduce the disguised underhand throw of the ball to the bat" (*Brooklyn Eagle*, July 16, 1873). If Creighton wasn't the first, he was certainly one of the earliest. Historian John Thorn notes that George Flanley moved from the Stars to the Excelsiors along with Creighton and may well have also been paid. Thorn has also identified a couple of earlier players whose change of clubs suggests the possibility of some sort of compensation: Lewis Wadsworth (who switched from the Gothams to the Knickerbockers in 1854) and a man named Pinckney (who briefly left the Union Club of Morrisania to join the Gothams in 1856) (Protoball website). There is, of course, no way to be certain that any of these players received financial inducements.

18.1.4 Professional Player to Change Cities.
As with the first professional, Al Reach's name is frequently cited. A. H. Spink indicated that "Reach had been playing with the Eckfords of Brooklyn, when Philadelphia enthusiasts, who wanted to get a great team together for the Athletics of that city, offered him a salary which he accepted and it was the first ever paid a professional player. Subsequently [Patsy] Dockney and [Lip] Pike of the Atlantics of Brooklyn were also offered salaries to join the same team" (A. H. Spink, *The National Game*, 190).

But even if Reach did receive a salary to move to Philadelphia, he likely wasn't the first. Spink claimed that this happened in 1864, while Melvin Adelman gave the year as 1863 (Melvin Adelman, *A Sporting Time*, 151). In fact Reach didn't begin to play with the Athletics until 1865. Two seasons earlier, pitcher Tom Pratt of the Athletics had joined the Atlantics in mid-season and led them to an undefeated season in 1864.

In 1891 an old player wrote to the *Philadelphia Times*: "I distinctly remember, after the Rebellion, the start of the professional business. William [sic] Pratt was taken over to Brooklyn to play with the Atlantics, under salary. The Mutual Club, of New York, was the great rival of the champions across the river, and Pratt's pitching ability was needed by the Brooklyn club. Dick McBride about the same time was put into the City Treasurer's office, with a $1200 salary and nothing to do. There were no contracts in those days, but the Athletics, just the same, captured Al Reach from the Eckford, of Brooklyn, and set him up in a cigar store on the south side of Chestnut street, above Fourth. Then followed [Patsy] Dockney, from New York, who used to play ball every afternoon

and fight and drink every night. He was a tough of the toughs. Next came Lip Pike and Fergy Malone, and so on until the nine was composed of players for cash, although an attempt was made to keep it from the public" (reprinted in *Sporting Life*, October 24, 1891).

While the nature of the question makes it impossible to prove, it seems most likely that Tom Pratt was the first player to be lured from one city to another by money. Incidentally, the importing of paid professionals bore an intriguing relationship to the Civil War. The *Brooklyn Eagle* reported on August 25, 1863, that Pratt had been discharged from his regiment and joined the Atlantics.

18.1.5 Players Lured West by Money.
Detroit may not seem like the West today, but in the 1860s that was how it was considered. For the 1865 season, Henry S. Burroughs of the Eurekas of Newark moved to Detroit and became the captain of the Detroit Base Ball Club. Burroughs also served as a "professor" of gymnastics at the Detroit Gymnasium, where he did offer instruction. But the newspapers of other cities stated that he received some inducements to move to Detroit, and there is evidence to support this claim (see Peter Morris, *Baseball Fever*, 91).

18.1.6 Revolving.
By the end of the 1850s, baseball clubs were actively recruiting the best players of other nines, and those who accepted such offers were known as "revolvers." An 1859 note, for instance, stated that the Jefferson Club's "former catcher, McKeever, has been enticed away from them by the Gothams" (*New York Atlas*, June 19, 1859). The 1860s saw revolving develop into one of baseball's most intractable problems. It may surprise many to learn that the source of this practice was cricket.

As early as 1857, American cricketers were complaining about "the unfair custom of cricketers, who belonged to different clubs, for the purpose of playing in matches" (*Porter's Spirit of the Times*, May 9, 1857; quoted in George B. Kirsch, *The Creation of American Team Sports*, 30). In 1861 the *New York Clipper* observed: "the 'revolver' system not only deprives the contest played in that way of all interest, as a test of strength and skill between the two clubs, but as it is a system of taking unfair advantages over opponents, it in all cases leads to ill feelings on both sides" (*New York Clipper*, July 13,

1861). Once again, the sport being described was not baseball but cricket.

And while baseball may have borrowed revolving from cricket, the practice is much older than either sport. Astylos of Kroton won two sprints apiece in the ancient Olympiads of 488, 484, and 480 B.C. In the latter two he announced himself as being from Syracuse to win favor from the king of Syracuse. The citizens of Kroton responded by pulling down his statue and converting his house into a prison. A century later Sotades of Crete won the same long-distance race in two successive Olympiads. In the second he accepted a bribe from the Ephesians and proclaimed himself to be from Ephesos, which led to his being exiled from Crete (Pausanias, ca. A.D. 170, quoted in Stephen G. Miller, *Arete*, 183–184).

18.1.7 Player Banned for Accepting Money.
According to A. H. Spink, a player named James E. Roder was expelled from the Empire Club of New York in 1865 for accepting money to play (Alfred H. Spink, *The National Game*, 5). The NABBP's rule against professionalism was essentially unenforceable, so it would have been up to an individual club to take such action. With help from researcher Brian McKenna, I have determined that Spink's version of events was incorrect in several details. The man in question was named James E. Ryder, and he was expelled on October 9, 1865, after being charged with collecting purported expense money for an out-of-town game and then pocketing it (*New York Clipper*, December 22, 1866, 290).

18.1.8 All-professional Clubs.
All questions involving early professionals are made problematic by the National Association of Base Ball Players' ban on professionalism, since players could not be candid about receiving payments. The question of the first all-professional club is even thornier, because it is still harder to determine how many players on a club were being paid.

Additionally, many early clubs played on a co-op basis, by which players would recoup their expenses by sharing gate receipts. Sometimes such clubs were described as professionals, other times as amateurs. It is therefore likely that all the members of some clubs were receiving payments by the early 1860s, though they may have been meager amounts.

A still more common practice was to recruit players with the promise of a well-paying do-nothing job. One of the most prominent examples was the famous National Club of Washington, many of whose stars were lured to the capital from New York by offers of positions in the Treasury Department. As Ted Sullivan later remarked coyly, "They were nearly all clerks in the Government Departments at Washington, but I cannot gainsay that they did not get their jobs in Uncle Sam's service for being the possessors of par excellent baseball skill" (*Washington Post*, February 11, 1906).

By the mid-1860s salaries were common enough that there may have been some all-salaried clubs. A. H. Spink claimed the Forest City Club of Rockford, Illinois, was the first club to pay regular salaries to its players, though this seems unlikely (A. H. Spink, *The National Game*, 5). In an 1895 interview, Joe Start said of the early Atlantics: "We didn't get any salaries, I remember very well, for three or four years . . . [they were introduced] about 1866, as near as I remember" (*Sporting Life*, November 16, 1895). Wes Fisler, an early member of the Athletics, recalled many years later that the players collected 60 percent of the gate receipts for one year and then were put on salary, but he did not specify the exact years (*Philadelphia Press Sunday Magazine*, September 26, 1920).

In 1869 the NABBP finally changed its policy and let clubs designate themselves as either amateur or professional. The Red Stockings of Cincinnati were one of the clubs that chose the latter course by openly announcing that its players would receive salaries. It is difficult to overestimate the importance of the club's demonstration that season that professional baseball did not have to be sordid. But the oft-repeated statement that the Red Stockings were the first all-professional club is simply untrue.

Even the contention that they were the first all-salaried nine is open to dispute, as at least one other club announced plans to pay a salary to each of its players. Before the season began, the *National Chronicle* reported: "The [Mutual] Club will adopt a new system this coming year in dealing with their professional members. A stated sum per season is to be given each professional, in lieu of the gate money dividend heretofore awarded" (*National Chronicle*, February 20, 1869). The following week it added, "The Mutuals have organized for the campaign in tip-top style, and are in a flourishing condition. They have $15,000 in their club treasury, have twelve picked professional players from which to select their nine, each of whom will not only receive a regular salary to be paid whether games are played or not. . . . Premiums will be paid to those who excel in the special departments of the game as shown by regular statistics at the close of the season" (*National Chronicle*, February 27, 1869).

A number of other clubs chose open professionalism in 1869, but as far as is known all of them adopted the cooperative method. The 1870 season saw eighteen clubs play as professionals, with five of them joining the Mutuals and Red Stockings in paying salaries (*New York Times*, April 7, 1870; reprinted in William J. Ryczek, *When Johnny Came Sliding Home*, 263). The National Association included a number of cooperative clubs, but most of them were unsuccessful and salaries have been a standard feature of major league baseball since the advent of the National League in 1876.

(ii) Owners Grab the Reins

With the advent of the National League in 1876, the control of clubs by outside parties seeking to make a profit became a permanent part of baseball. The owners, or magnates as they were usually called in the nineteenth century, instituted the new features that will be discussed in this section.

In the owners' view, these provisions were necessary to reinvent baseball as a stable business. The players, however, soon began to suspect that the owners' primary consideration was actually their own profits.

18.2.1   Reserve Rule/Clause. Before the adoption of the reserve rule in 1879, players had essentially been free agents at the end of their contracts. That didn't stop clubs from trying to hang on to their players. The rules of the National Association of Base Ball Players dictated that clubs had to honor each other's expulsions. When Lipman Pike resigned from the Irvington Club in 1867 in order to play for another club, the Irvingtons voted instead to expel him. As William J. Ryczek points out, if other clubs had honored this vote, it would have amounted to an early version of the reserve rule (William J. Ryczek, *When Johnny Came Sliding Home*, 145).

Within a few years of the organization of the National League in 1876, the circuit had begun to compile a blacklist (see **18.2.2**) which it used for similar purposes. Before then, however, the league's owners were also laying the groundwork for a more comprehensive restriction on players' leverage. At their annual meeting following the 1877 season, all six owners pledged not to begin discussing 1879 contracts with players until September 1, 1878 (*Brooklyn Eagle*, January 27, 1878, 3).

Two years later they went much further. At a meeting in Buffalo on September 29, 1879, the six returning National League clubs agreed to recognize each other's rights to retain the rights to five players. The new rule is often reported to have been the brainchild of Boston owner Arthur H. Soden (see, for example, Francis C. Richter, *Richter's History and Records of Base Ball*, 280). According to researcher David Ball, however, the evidence is far from clear-cut. A year later the *New York Clipper* referred to Soden as the man who "originated" the rule that was initially known as the five-men rule (*New York Clipper*, October 16, 1880). Yet only a few years later the *Chicago Herald* declared: "The fact is Mr. [William] Hulbert was the author of the reserve rule, and at the recent league meeting in Buffalo the fact was unanimously conceded" (*Chicago Herald*, March 7, 1884). So it seems more likely that the rule was a joint effort rather than the idea of any one owner.

Albert G. Spalding, who was Chicago club secretary when the reserve rule was instituted, later made this response to its critics: "The fact is the reserve rule was aimed squarely at the Chicago management. It was adopted more as a curb to Chicago than for any other reason. I can make this as plain as A B C. At the time the reserve rule went into effect the Chicago club was about the only one in the country that was self-supporting, and for a number of years the attendance on games in Chicago had practically supported the League, as the clubs in Syracuse, Troy and Worcester could not begin to draw like the attendance we did there. The men who put up money for clubs in smaller cities became discouraged. They said: 'It's no use for us to get together a good team, for as soon as we develop some good crack players Chicago comes and gets them away from us by offering a bigger salary than we can afford to pay.' The complaint against us was a natural one, and so I repeat what I know to be a fact when I declare that the reserve rule was aimed against Chicago. The sale of the release of players is the natural outgrowth of the reserve rule, and that the reserve rule is absolutely necessary is a fact recognized by both players and managers" (*Base Ball Gazette*, April 22, 1887). As with most of Spalding's commentary, however, these remarks are self-serving and must be taken with a large dose of salt. The less wealthy clubs did support the reserve rule in hopes of limiting costs and achieving greater competitive balance, but it seems unlikely that they originated it. And his claim of universal recognition of the need for the rule is simply untrue.

The enactment of the reserve rule was not officially announced, but it seems to have been an open secret. Henry Chadwick commented perceptively, "The plan said to be adopted by the League to prevent competition between the several clubs for the others' players is open to criticism, as by it a League club could force a player who had been with it the past season to either play at a reduced salary or play with no League club the coming year" (*New York Clipper*, October 18, 1879).

Immediate controversy ensued when Chicago signed Troy's Fred Goldsmith two days later. The Troy club naturally objected that this was "a violation of the arrangement entered into at the recent Buffalo meeting, and will protest against the action of the Chicagos in the matter" (*New York Clipper*, October 11, 1879). A couple of months later, Buffalo complained that Cincinnati had signed one of its reserved players, John Clapp (*New York Clipper*, December 6, 1879). The reserve rule thus began on a fittingly contentious note.

The new rule essentially ended the career of one of the greatest players of the era. George Wright had led Providence to the National League pennant in 1879 but wanted no part of the new rule: "There appears to be no prospect of settling the difference between George Wright and the Providence management. Being still held by the 'five men' rule, Wright cannot sign elsewhere, although he would like to go to Boston" (*Chicago Tribune*, January 18, 1880).

Wright turned down the club's offer and told a reporter that the "so-called 'five-man agreement' was outrageous, with no particle of justice in it" (quoted in the *New York Clipper*, September 4, 1880). He refused to report to Providence and played in one game for Boston on May 29. The game was protested, and he then sat out the remainder of the 1880 season amid accusations that a superstar had been "driven from the League by the selfish and arbitrary action of one of its members" (*Boston Herald*, reprinted in *Worcester Gazette*, April 5, 1880). Providence relinquished the pennant to Chicago while Wright turned his attention to business.

A motion was made to repeal the rule at the next year's meeting, but it survived and was strengthened in subsequent years (*New York Clipper*, October 16, 1880). The number of players who could be reserved was steadily increased, and from 1883 onward it encompassed enough players that owners could essentially retain their entire team. The rule was incorporated into a standard clause in player contracts that asserted the club's right to retain the player if it so desired, thereby becoming known as the reserve clause. Moreover the owners considered the clause to be perpetually renewable—that unilaterally renewing it one year gave them the right to do so again the next year.

After winning fifty-nine games in 1884, Charley Radbourn observed, "The only difference between the league and slavery is that the managers can't lick you. They have you down so fine that you have no say in the matter at all. I sign a contract with a club, and they can hold me forever, if they see fit, or so long as I want to play ball." The noose was tied still more tightly by the various contracts known as the National Agreements (see **18.2.3**). These accords ensured that leagues would respect each other's reserves. Thus even a superstar like Radbourn thus had only the most limited of options: "I can jump a contract with the league and join the association, but I can never get back into the league. If I was offered $1,000 a year more by another club I couldn't go, unless I got a release; and there is a combination among the managers to not make any such offer as it might be possible to buy yourself off" (*Williamsport Sunday Grit*, October 19, 1884).

The reserve clause seemed rather obviously to lack "mutuality," a fundamental principle of contract law. Owners did their best to avoid legal challenges because they suspected "that their contracts will not stand a test. There is no mutuality, the club having the right to reserve from year to year, and to release at any time, while the player cannot change his employment of his own accord" (*Washington Post*, June 4, 1910). In the 1912 National Agreement, owners tried to address the concern by specifying that 75 percent of a player's salary was for that year's service and the balance was for the right of reservation.

Somehow the owners managed to forestall or deflect legal challenges to the reserve clause for nearly a hundred years. Courts often seemed to be swayed less by legal principles than by the owners' claims that baseball could not survive without the reserve clause. As the *New York Clipper* snidely put it, "they say it is the reserve rule that has elevated baseball and made it what it is. No doubt. Turkey for the clubs and buzzard for the players" (*New York Clipper*, May 3, 1890).

The reserve clause stood until pitchers Andy Messersmith and Dave McNally did not sign contracts for the 1975 season and then brought a grievance to a three-man arbitration panel. Curiously, like baseball's early umpiring system (see **1.13** "Judgment Calls"), it consisted of two highly partisan representatives—Marvin Miller of the players' union and owners' negotiator John Gaherin—and a neutral third party, Peter Seitz. Seitz, in casting the deciding vote, wrote that the owners' position was "incompatible with the doctrine or policy of freedom in the economic and political society in which we live," and declared both players free agents. After two unsuccessful appeals of the ruling, the owners negotiated the issue with the players' union and a limited form of free agency was incorporated into the 1976 Basic Agreement.

18.2.2 Blacklists. In its first two seasons the National League agreed on most of the essentials of what became the blacklist. From the league's debut in 1876, a player who had been let go by one club was required to show that he had received an "honorable release" before being eligible to play with or against any other teams.

The league continued to fine-tune and expand this powerful tool as owners became more aware of the benefits of collective action. At its annual meeting following the 1877 season, all the clubs agreed to charge each player thirty dollars for his uniform and fifty cents per day for transportation while on the road. The agreement was sealed with this clause: "And we further agree that we will not engage or play any player that may be released by any club subscribing hereto on account of disagreement between such player and his club growing out of any stipulation of this agreement" (*Chicago Tribune*, December 9, 1877, 7). According to Worcester president Freeman Brown, at the league meeting following the 1879 season, league president William Hulbert proposed that "eight or ten of the high priced men, who are known to be grumblers, be shelved by the clubs signing an agreement not to hire such players. The proposition met with the hearty endorsement of six clubs, and would have been adopted, had not the two remaining clubs requested that the matter be left over until next fall, when they agreed to join in the agreement. In the meantime President Hulbert is to perfect

a plan of arranging salaries, and it is safe to say that it will take definite shape next fall" (*Cleveland Leader*, March 16, 1880).

On September 29, 1881, the National League adopted a formal blacklist, thereby supplying muscle to the reserve rule by ensuring that no other team could negotiate with a player who had refused to sign with the team that had reserved him. The players on the first blacklist were Sadie Houck, Lipman Pike, Lou Dickerson, Mike Dorgan, Bill Crowley, John Fox, Lew Brown, Edward Nolan, Emil Gross, and Ed Caskin. There were no specific criteria for inclusion, so players could be added for arbitrary reasons.

After the National Agreement (see **18.2.3**) had been expanded to include most professional leagues, a blacklisted player was left with few if any options for making a living in baseball. The blacklist thus proved a powerful device that the owners could hold over the heads of players. The unpopularity of the blacklists was one of the reasons for the founding of the Players' League in 1890.

The Players' League folded after one season, and the owners thereafter ceased to publicize the blacklist. But while it received less publicity, the list continued to be an effective method of discipline. Many "outlaw leagues" thrived in the early twentieth century, but players who joined them knew that they might not be able to return to organized baseball.

The teens and twenties saw a significant number of players banned from organized baseball for life. Most were players such as the Black Sox who had been involved in gambling, but others, such as Ray Fisher, were blacklisted at the whims of capricious owners.

The blacklist returned to prominence in 1946 with the challenge of the Mexican League. Jumpers were threatened with bans from organized baseball for up to five years, which helped dissuade many potential defectors.

18.2.3 National Agreement. The first National Agreement, often referred to as the Tri-Partite Agreement, was signed by the National League, the American Association, and one minor league, the Northwestern League, on February 17, 1883. The three circuits agreed to expand the reserve rule and to respect one another's contracts, territorial rights, and blacklists. Subsequent National Agreements followed, expanding the number of leagues involved and forming the basis of organized baseball. The leagues that signed the National

Agreement became collectively known as organized baseball, while nonsignatory leagues were referred to as outlaws.

18.2.4   Territorial Rights. Territorial rights, by which a league grants each club an exclusive franchise for its city and the immediate vicinity, have played an important role in the history of professional baseball in general and the National League in particular.

The high expense of travel was probably the most important obstacle faced by the early clubs that made tentative steps toward professionalism. It was therefore a windfall to have a strong rival in close proximity—indeed a virtual necessity for survival. That was changing by the late 1860s as cheap railroad travel began to make professional baseball viable. Clubs no longer necessarily appreciated having a rival nearby since this cut into the attendance of both clubs.

The National Association, which operated from 1871 to 1875, allowed any club to join by paying the small membership fee. As a result, more than one club could, and often did, share the same town. On one hand, this was convenient for visiting clubs and could create rivalries. On the other, one of the clubs would usually overshadow the others. By the end of the National Association's existence, most felt that the benefits of such an arrangement were outweighed by the disadvantages.

When the National League succeeded the National Association in 1876, it restricted membership to large cities and gave each of its members a guarantee of territorial exclusivity. The league's initial plan granted clubs a modest five-mile territorial right, an apparently arbitrary choice that took on importance when Albany sought to join in 1879 and the Troy club did not want so close a rival. The actual distance between the city centers was about eight miles, but the Troy city engineer used the closest city limits and gave a sworn statement that the two cities were four and three-quarter miles apart (*Chicago Tribune*, April 27, 1879). A year later the Troy owners decided it would be advantageous to have such a rivalry. Accordingly, the critical distance specified by the league's constitution was modified to four miles. But Albany chose not to enter the National League.

Territorial rights have remained a foundation of the National League ever since and were expanded to include rival leagues by the various National Agreements (see **18.2.3**). While a number of cities have been and continue to be simultaneously represented in the American and National leagues, only the Brooklyn Dodgers and New York Giants have ever competed in the same league and municipal region.

In spite of the storied rivalry between those clubs and the recent success of interleague play, there seems to be no thought of repeating that endeavor. Indeed, there has recently been talk of whether Baltimore's franchise has been damaged by the relocation of the Montreal Expos to Washington, D.C. That is an interesting development, considering that Washington had an American League club at the time that Baltimore moved from St. Louis.

In 1947, when the signing of Jackie Robinson and other stars by white teams threatened the future of the Negro American and National leagues, both leagues applied to become part of organized baseball. They were turned down, however, with George Trautman, president of the National Association of Professional Baseball Leagues (NAPBL), citing territorial rights (Neil Lanctot, *Negro League Baseball*, 326–327).

The territorial rights of minor league clubs has again been a hot-button issue in recent years. Minor league owner Joe Buzas was fined more than $2 million for violating the rights of the Salt Lake City Trappers of the Pioneer League by moving his Triple A Portland, Oregon, franchise to Salt Lake City in 1994. In 1999 the Yankees and Mets waived their territorial rights, enabling the New York–Penn League to place franchises in Staten Island and Brooklyn.

(iii) Players Seek a Bigger Share

Once baseball was established as a profitable industry, players began to raise concerns about the practices of owners. As we shall see in these entries, it took many years before the players were able to organize themselves effectively and thereby create the adversarial system that is the basis of today's collective bargaining arrangement.

18.3.1   Unions. Players' unions have a long but intermittent history and have generally sprung up in response to the introduction of new tactics by owners, such as the reserve rule or salary caps.

Ballplayer-turned-sportswriter Tim Murnane claimed that an early attempt at unionization was made by several Boston players, among them A. G. Spalding: "About 1872 or 1873, in the old gymnasium on Elliott street, with George Wright, Ross Barnes, Harry Schaffer and Jim White, Albert and his fellow-players went so far as to draw up an agreement for the players' signatures." Murnane indicated that "The objects of that proposed brotherhood were commendable, and, like most organizations of the kind, it was intended as a hold back to the men who were running the business at a pressure too high for the equal benefit of all" (*Chicago Tribune*, January 12 and 19, 1890; *Sporting Life*, October 5, 1887).

The idea again surfaced at the end of the National League's first season when the *Chicago Journal* reported that there was talk of forming "a protective society by which ball-players are to protect themselves against untrustworthy clubs and managers." The item led the *Chicago Tribune* to reply, "The best organization of that kind possible is the National League, which provides, as the *Journal* evidently does not know, that a club may, and must, be expelled for not paying its players. Can the *Journal* suggest any society which would have the same power?" (*Chicago Tribune*, December 2, 1876, 7). As should be evident from these comments, the *Tribune* was the house organ for National League founder William Hulbert and his fellow owners during the league's early years. The possibility of some such association was also mentioned by the *New York Sunday Mercury*, where it was described as a "means of self-defense" against the recent decision of the owners to charge players for their uniforms (see **18.5.3**, "Contract Perks") (*New York Sunday Mercury*, January 6 and 20, 1877).

In 1883 the *Cleveland Leader* reported, "In order to get square with the eleven men agreement [i.e., the reserve rule] entered into by the professional associations, the players are agitating a project for organizing a protective association, which every professional player will join" (*Cleveland Leader*, March 30, 1883).

These plans apparently foundered, causing a reporter to comment the next year: "Baseball players appear to be driven like a flock of sheep. There is nothing like a protective organization among them, and until they band together for mutual protection and benefit, they must expect to get the worst of it" (*Washington Post*, March 16, 1884).

One year later, journalist and minor league manager Billy Voltz attempted with little success to form a protective association. Instead John Montgomery Ward and several New York teammates secretly formed baseball's first such organization, the Brotherhood of Professional Base Ball Players, in October 1885 (Robert F. Burk, in *Never Just a Game*, p. 96, placed the date of the Brotherhood's formation on October 22, 1885, five days after the owners had made their plans for a salary cap public. Bryan Di Salvatore, however, stated in *A Clever Base-Ballist*, p. 176, that the meeting took place three days before the owners' announcement).

As Bryan Di Salvatore has noted, the Brotherhood tried to avoid the appearance of being a union. Its constitution was "vague, formal, and highminded," with an emphasis on such unthreatening principles as aiding "a brother in distress" and promoting "a high standard of professional conduct" and "the interests of the game of base ball" (Bryan Di Salvatore, *A Clever Base-Ballist*, 175–177). During the 1886 season players from other teams were covertly recruited, until its membership included 90 percent of National League players (Bryan Di Salvatore, *A Clever Base-Ballist*, 178). The Brotherhood went public on November 11, 1886.

The defining moment of the Brotherhood was the formation of the Players' League, which competed with the two existing major leagues in 1890. This would also prove to be the union's swan song, as the upstart league folded after one year. The National League took full advantage of the players' defeat. After merging with the American Association and thereby reducing the players' leverage, it slashed salaries and moved the game dangerously close to becoming a trust (see **22.5.3**).

By the late 1890s the players were sufficiently fed up to again consider organizing (*Cincinnati Commercial-Tribune*, reprinted in the *Chicago Inter-Ocean*, April 19, 1897). The spring of 1898 brought rumors of a players' union that would demand higher salaries, pay for spring training, and the abolition of the compulsory farming system (*St. Louis Post-Dispatch*, April 6, 1898). Clark Griffith kept the idea alive in 1899, and it gained additional impetus after the season when the elimination of four National League clubs threw many players out of work (*Washington Post*, April 3, 1900).

As the opening of the 1900 season approached, American Federation of Labor president Samuel Gompers explained why he believed the time was right for a movement that could succeed where the Players' League had failed: "The Brotherhood was practically a fight of capital against capital; the present movement has simply in mind the formation of an organization of a self-protecting and benevolent character." Gompers indicated that he was willing for a union of baseball players to operate under the AFL's auspices but expressed a preference that they go it alone: "Personally I would like to see the players organize, with officers from their own ranks, and I know there are some bright, level heads among them" (quoted in the *Washington Post*, April 3, 1900).

On June 9, 1900, the Players' Protective Association was organized in New York. The association decided not to join the AFL, and veteran player Chief Zimmer was elected as president. The Protective Association pursued an aggressive agenda of reform, with one hundred players gathering in New York on July 29 to demand an end to the unpopular practice of farming (see **13.1.5**) and a share of the purchase price when sold. Rumor also had the association reaching out to minor leaguers so that "before the season closes there will not be a ball player in the country unassociated with the organization" (*Washington Post*, June 28, 1900).

The association initially won some important concessions from the owners, but its claim to moral high ground was weakened that offseason when players began to jump their contracts to join the American League. With the players no longer unified, the association faltered, and by 1903 it was dead (Francis C. Richter, *Richter's History and Records of Base Ball*, 161–165). Its demise prompted the *Washington Post* to remark, "The apathy of the players in allowing their union to blow up would indicate they have little fear of a deep cut in salaries. Fancy stipends may be chopped some, but the normal pay will not shrink, the wise ones say" (*Washington Post*, August 9, 1903). That mind-set remained in ascendance for another decade.

The Players' Fraternity was formed during the 1912 season and made permanent on October 20. Headed by lawyer and former major leaguer Dave Fultz, the fraternity made some initial progress but failed to establish a working relationship with the owners (Francis C. Richter, *Richter's History and Records of Base Ball*, 165–172). The fraternity was one of the casualties of the demise of the Federal League; three more decades would pass before there was another serious attempt to unionize.

On April 17, 1946, labor relations lawyer Robert Murphy formed the American Baseball Guild and began trying to convince major league players to join. Ralph Kiner later recalled that Murphy cannily "was careful not to call it [the Guild] a 'union'; he always had a euphe-

mism" (quoted in Charles P. Korr, *The End of Baseball as We Knew It*, 16). Even so, the idea created considerable anxiety. Jack Norworth, author of "Take Me Out to the Ball Game," was quoted in *Sporting News* as saying that if the Guild were successful, it might inspire him to write a new song in which "ticket line" would rhyme with "picket line" (*Sporting News*, June 5, 1946).

The idea made major league owners even more anxious, and they swiftly announced plans to offer several concessions to the players. These included a minimum salary, spring training expenses (which is still known as "Murphy money"), and the first pension fund for players. This conciliated a sufficient number of players, and the Guild did not win the necessary votes. Murphy abandoned his efforts, but not before telling a reporter, "The players have been offered an apple, but they could have had an orchard" (quoted in Lee Lowenfish, *The Imperfect Diamond*, 151).

On August 21, 1953, player reps Ralph Kiner and Allie Reynolds hired labor leader John Norman Lewis to give them legal advice during negotiations with the owners. Lewis's goals were limited and his accomplishments still more modest, but his hiring established the Players Association as a permanent entity. Lewis was succeeded in 1959 by the equally innocuous Judge Robert Cannon, who continued to focus on gaining improvements to the players' pension fund while stressing that he "was not there to fight ownership" and had no desire to "jeopardize the fine relationship existing between the players and club owners" (quoted in Charles P. Korr, *The End of Baseball as We Knew It*, 27, 23).

Under Cannon's leadership, the Players Association remained, in the words of longtime director Frank Scott, a "House Union" (quoted in Charles P. Korr, *The End of Baseball as We Knew It*, 2). Charles P. Korr noted that during these years, "Even the word 'union' did not come easily to the vocabulary of the players; 'association' and 'players' group' were the preferred terms" (Charles P. Korr, *The End of Baseball as We Knew It*, 1).

In 1966, when Marvin Miller replaced Cannon, the Players Association quickly assumed the traditional functions of a union. Although some player reps continued to be uncomfortable with "the word 'union,'" Miller distanced the organization from such euphemisms (Bob Barton, quoted in Charles P. Korr, *The End of Baseball as We Knew It*, 108). He declared in 1972, "I don't know why there is confusion about this, but the Major League Baseball Players Association is a union in structure, in purpose, in its functioning, it is a union under the law, and it has all the rights, duties, and obligations of any other bona fide union" (quoted in Charles P. Korr, *The End of Baseball as We Knew It*, 66).

18.3.2 Player Strikes.

Baseball has been blighted by a series of strikes and lockouts over the past thirty years. While shutting down the entire game is a new development, the threat of such disruptions by individual teams has a much longer history than most fans realize.

According to Jimmy Wood, labor unrest was part of baseball as early as 1865. Owners of ball fields had been keeping all the admission fees in exchange for allowing players to play and practice rent-free. But when players became aware of the profits that could be made, they demanded: "Give us part of the gate receipts or we won't play!" They were eventually allotted 25 percent of the gate receipts, but soon they decided that wasn't enough. They next demanded 35 percent—"again threatening a strike"—and got it. Within two years "the players, by use of threats of quitting the diamond, had forced the club owners [sic] to pay them 75 per cent of the gross receipts of each game, that sum being divided equally among the players" (James Wood, as told to Frank G. Menke, "Baseball in By-Gone Days," Part 3, syndicated column, *Indiana* [Pa.] *Evening Gazette*, August 17, 1916).

Once leagues were developed, club owners signed players to contracts that minimized their leverage. It was not, however, long before the threat of strikes again surfaced. Milwaukee entered the National League in 1878, but the club was plagued by financial woes. With a few weeks left in the season, the club had fallen behind in paying its payroll, and before a home game against Indianapolis on August 31 the players "refused to put on their uniforms until satisfaction was given." After a half-hour delay, all except pitcher Sam Weaver were talked into playing. In an odd coincidence, Milwaukee lost 9-0—the same score as would have resulted from the forfeit. To nobody's surprise, the club disbanded at season's end (*Milwaukee Sentinel*, September 2, 1878; cited in Dennis Pajot, "1878—Milwaukee a National League City" [unpublished paper]).

The 1889 season witnessed two more incidents. On May 2 the St. Louis Browns nearly went on strike after owner Chris Von der Ahe fined "Yank" Robinson. Robinson refused to play again until the fine was withdrawn, and his teammates planned to join his strike. The other Browns finally agreed to play their next series but lost three straight to lowly Kansas City by lopsided margins, prompting suspicions that they had deliberately thrown the games (Al Kermisch, "Yank Robinson's One-Man Strike in 1889," *Baseball Research Journal* 1981, 66–67). A month later, Louisville was in the midst of a major league record twenty-six-game losing streak when team owner Mordecai Davidson threatened to fine his players if they lost their next game. Since Davidson was behind in paying the team their salaries, the players were understandably outraged, and only six of them showed up for the team's game on June 15. The team used three local recruits and was beaten 4-2. The regulars returned the next day.

Both disputes were fueled by a contentious relationship between players and owners which led to the formation of the Players' League in 1890. With three major leagues, everyone lost money in 1890. The Philadelphia franchise in the American Association was especially hard-hit and fell far behind in paying its players. By the end of the season most of the players had abandoned the club, and it relied more and more on picking up local amateurs.

When Cleveland star Addie Joss died suddenly in 1911, American League president Ban Johnson initially refused to cancel Cleveland's scheduled game with Detroit on April 17, the day of the funeral. But with Cleveland on the verge of revolt and Detroit rumored to be likely to join them, Johnson backed down and canceled the game.

The following year the Tigers did hold a one-day strike on May 18, 1912, in protest of Johnson's suspension of Ty Cobb. Detroit manager Hugh Jennings penciled two coaches and seven sandlot players into the lineup and was beaten 24-2. The regular Tigers returned the next day at Cobb's urging.

Another crisis occurred in 1914 when pitcher Clarence Kraft was ordered by the National Commission to report to Nashville in the Southern League. Kraft understandably balked when he learned that he would receive $150 less a month in Nashville than he had been earning for Newark of the International League. Players' Fraternity leader David Fultz saw the case as the epitome of the need for reform. After a number of threats, he prepared "a letter which is generally termed in baseball circles an ultimatum from the fraternity to organized baseball" (*Washington Post*, July 21, 1914). A strike was averted when Charles Ebbets purchased Kraft's contract and assigned him to Newark with back pay.

Midway through the 1918 World Series, the players on both sides threatened to strike over the paltry shares they were to receive. The start of the fifth game had to be delayed when the players refused to take the field. The owners refused to budge, however, and were successful in convincing the players that they would appear greedy if they went on strike while the country was at war.

On July 10, 1943, Brooklyn's players skipped batting practice, and there was talk of a strike to protest manager Leo Durocher's suspension of pitcher Bobo Newsom. Only the last-minute intervention of Branch Rickey enabled the Dodgers to field a team. Brooklyn took out their frustrations on the Pirates instead, with ten-run outbursts in both the first and fourth innings (Lee Lowenfish, *Branch Rickey*, 332–334).

A few weeks later, on July 28, 1943, the Phillies nearly struck to protest the firing of manager Bucky Harris. On June 7, 1946, the Pirates voted 20 to 16 to walk out for that day's game—but a two-thirds vote was necessary to strike, so the game went on.

Strike action at the minor league level has been different in nature because of the comparative ease of replacing the players. But strikes did occur when conditions became intolerable. Historian William Akin, for example, describes strikes by West Virginia minor league clubs in 1897, 1907, and 1909 after the players had experienced lengthy waits for paychecks (William Akin, *West Virginia Baseball*, 45, 61–62, 65). In 1950 the Waterbury team of the Colonial League fired all its players on July 14 after they refused to board the team bus because of several issues, including the safety of the vehicle. The issue became moot when the Colonial League disbanded the next day.

The first collective strike took place in 1972 when the major league season was delayed by a strike that wiped out 36 games. Since then labor disputes have plagued major league baseball. The 1981 major league season was interrupted by a two-month strike that led to the cancellation of 706 games. Another strike began on August 6, 1985, but was settled after one day.

A lockout interrupted spring training in 1990 and delayed the start of the season by a week. In 1994 the last two months of the season and the World Series were canceled due to baseball's longest and most harmful strike. The 1995 season was also shortened by eighteen games because the previous season's strike was not resolved until the eve of the season.

18.3.3 Player Reps.

With the threat of Robert Murphy's Guild looming, baseball owners invited player representatives to attend several of their meetings in 1946 and 1947. Commissioner Ford Frick maintained that the invitation was not a preemptive move; he claimed that he had been planning to do so since 1936, "but inertia got hold of me" (William Marshall, *Baseball's Pivotal Era, 1945–1951*, 74–75). Each league was represented by three players—Johnny Murphy, Mel Harder, and Joe Kuhel from the American League, and Dixie Walker, Marty Marion, and Billy Herman from the National League. Murphy and Walker acted as spokesmen for their respective leagues and were the only players invited to most of the meetings. As is noted in the next entry, they were accorded significant concessions on such issues as pensions. The success of Murphy and Walker at gaining ground on these fronts was made easier by their willingness to accept the reserve clause, which both men defended as being "essential for the players' protection as well as the owners'" (AP: *Washington Post*, January 21, 1948).

18.3.4 Pension Fund.

There is no better symbol of the deep enmity between players and owners than the problems that have plagued the seemingly innocuous issue of pensions. Umpires actually had a pension plan several years before players did (Herbert Simons, "Life of an Ump," *Baseball Magazine*, April 1942; reprinted in Sidney Offit, ed., *The Best of Baseball*, 156–162). Hall of Fame umpire Jocko Conlan even chose to end his playing career and become an umpire in large part because of the pension (Jocko Conlan and Robert W. Creamer, *Jocko*, 19).

With Robert Murphy attempting to form a players' guild, major league owners finally agreed to a pension plan for players on July 8, 1946. The details were ironed out by a committee that included player representatives Johnny Murphy of the Yankees and Dixie Walker of the Dodgers, and were approved by the owners on February 1, 1947. The plan guaranteed any player with five years' service an income of at least fifty dollars a month beginning at age fifty. The moneys were drawn from contributions by both players and owners, along with All-Star Game revenues and World Series broadcast revenues (John Drebinger, "Pension Program for Players Voted by Major Leagues," *New York Times*, February 2, 1947). The plan went into effect on April 1, 1947, and the first pension recipient was the widow of Ernie Bonham, who died in 1949 while still an active player.

Lee Lowenfish noted that "Because the pension was established by the owners as a sop to forestall player unionization, it would regularly become an area of great controversy every five years when it came up for renewal" (Lee Lowenfish, *The Imperfect Diamond*, 149). That was not an overstatement.

By the early 1950s owners were refusing to give the players an accounting of the pension fund. In fact there was no pension fund. More recent requirements that pension money be held in trust did not yet apply, so pension revenues and payments were being made from the commissioner's central fund (Charles W. Bevis, "A Home Run by Any Measure," *Baseball Research Journal* 21 [1992], 67).

Ongoing concerns about the pension led the players to hire their first paid representative, John Norman Lewis, in 1953. Pensions still topped their agenda in 1966 when Marvin Miller was hired to head the Players Association. A near-strike in 1969 and baseball's first in-season strike in 1972 both revolved around pension issues. In 1994 the already contentious negotiations were further damaged when the owners withheld a scheduled payment to the players' pension fund (Charles P. Korr, *The End of Baseball as We Knew It*, 75–76, 103–115, 259).

18.3.5 Player Agents. Player agents as we now know them did not exist in the nineteenth century, though there were some attempts along that line. Researcher Bryan Di Salvatore found an ad in the *New York Clipper* of February 16, 1884, for a Baseball Employment Bureau operated by S. G. Morton of Chicago, secretary of the Northwestern League. Clubs paid ten dollars or players five dollars to use Morton's services. Di Salvatore also found a note in the *New York Clipper* of November 6, 1886, describing an agency started in Philadelphia by O. P. Caylor. This note indicated that there had been a similar agency in Philadelphia sixteen years earlier but that its unidentified founders "speedily found that there existed no field for such an agency" (cited in Frederick Ivor-Campbell, "When Was the First? [Part 4],"

Nineteenth Century Notes 95:3, 4 [Summer/Fall 1995], 10–11).

Researcher David Arcidiacono discovered this 1891 advertisement in *Sporting News*: "'Base Ball Agency—For Ball Players and Managers wanting engagements and players. Will handle business for players who wish a transfer from one club to another. Would like to hear from all disengaged players.' W. R. Harrington—Chicago" (*Sporting News*, January 10, 1891, 5). Minor league executive Jesse Frysinger set up a player agency in Chester, Pennsylvania, in 1901 to capitalize on his extensive connections: "it is safe to say there are few clubs or players within a radius of 300 miles he doesn't know personally. Last season he secured positions for several hundred players and aided over 50 clubs to get good men" (*Chester Times*, reprinted in *Sporting News*, May 11, 1901). In 1905 sportswriter Tim Murnane recorded the formation of another such agency: "The International Base Ball Bureau of Syracuse, N.Y., with George Geer and Jay Faatz as managers, is now open for business. The idea is to furnish jobs for ball players and umpires taking as a fee one half of the first month's salary" (*Sporting News*, January 7, 1905).

Player agents in their current form seem to have first entered the game in the 1920s. A *Sporting News* correspondent reported in 1922: "Officials of clubs in the Coast League say it's hard to find a good looking prospect these days who isn't being 'managed' by somebody. If the ball player is asked to sign a contract his answer is that his 'manager' will have to be consulted about the terms. . . . Sometimes a busher demands a bonus as high as $1,000 or $1,500 before he signs, and the manager-agent also gets a cut out of that" (*Sporting News*, February 9, 1922). Syd Pollock, later the owner of the barnstorming Indianapolis Clowns, also ran a player placement agency in Westchester County, New York, that year (Alan Pollock, *Barnstorming to Heaven*, 72).

Another *Sporting News* correspondent noted five years later, "Branch Rickey, acting as field agent for Sam Breadon, discovered that [Tommy Thevenow] had an adviser, manager, or something. Great horrors, multiplied! When this intelligence was transmitted to Breadon, the even-mannered chief executive of the Cardinals fairly exploded. With each spoken word rolled clouds of blue smoke. Private managers. They're the bane of Sam's life.

"It will be recalled that Rogers Hornsby had a manager, or two, to advise him in his late lamented affair with the Cardinals, so it takes no stretch of the imagination to appraise the feelings of the club president—Rickey's too, for that matter—when Tommy bobbed up with his 'adviser.'

"Forthwith came an ultimatum from Breadon. Tommy was advised to rid himself of 'his friend' before he could expect further consideration from the club in re his contract. Therein, the Cardinals are holding out, with no telling when the matter will be adjusted if both sides hold their ground.

"'I am sick and tired of this "third party" business when it comes to dealing with ball players,' said Breadon. 'I offered Thevenow a more substantial salary than ordinarily is given a second year man. But it's not a question of salary now, but a question of 'third party' advice that is holding the player back" (*Sporting News*, March 10, 1927).

Management continued to fight the use of agents tooth and nail. Joe Medwick and Johnny Mize antagonized Rickey by trying to use agents to negotiate their contracts, and he subsequently traded away both future Hall of Famers (Lee Lowenfish, *Branch Rickey*, 302, 314). Players won the right to hire representatives in 1946, but only for financial planning rather than negotiating. In the 1960s pitcher Earl Wilson brought agent Bob Woolf with him to help negotiate his contract, but Woolf was asked to leave by Tigers general manager Jim Campbell. Woolf sat out in the car, and Wilson periodically asked for bathroom breaks so he could get advice (John Helyar, *Lords of the Realm*, 94).

Only in the 1970 Basic Agreement were agents granted the right to take an active role in contract negotiations.

18.3.6   Basic Agreement.

The first Basic Agreement between the players and owners was signed on February 19, 1968. As Charles P. Korr has noted, the very idea of a collective-bargaining agreement "ran counter to the norms of professional sports" (Charles P. Korr, *The End of Baseball as We Knew It*, 69). Thus members of management such as Braves general manager Paul Richards viewed the development as "the end of baseball, as we knew it." The assessment proved so apt that it became the title of Korr's outstanding history of the Players Association (quoted in *Atlanta Journal*, December 1, 1967; reprinted in Charles P. Korr, *The End of Baseball as We Knew It*, 1). Most of baseball's labor

wars in the years since have concerned the renewal of the Basic Agreement.

(iv) Negotiations

Players and owners have sought to strengthen their bargaining positions in a number of creative ways, but as a rule the same few basic factors have always been most important.

18.4.1   Rival Major Leagues.

Challenges to the National League date back to its beginning in 1876. Some of these stimulated competition and brought new life to the game while others created a warlike atmosphere that damaged and impoverished both sides. The consequences have been less equivocal for players, invariably providing them with leverage that has led to material improvements in their lot.

The rival leagues that have earned official recognition as "major" are the American Association (1882–1891), the Union Association (1884), the Players' League (1890), the American League (1901–present), and the Federal League (1914–1915).

It is important to understand, however, that the decision to categorize a rival league as "major" is not always cut and dried. There are those who contend that some of the above leagues were not of sufficient quality to warrant major league status. On the other hand, there have been numerous other threats to the recognized major leagues that were taken very seriously at the time, whether or not they ever played a game.

In 1894 Fred Pfeffer, Billy Barnie, and Al Buckenberger were behind an abortive effort to revive the American Association (David Q. Voigt, *The League That Failed*, 212–213). The effort was detected by the National League, whose board blacklisted all three men and wrote sanctimoniously: "To-day the future of base ball is confronted by a new condition, a condition which in every particular is as harmful and in many respects far more dangerous than open dishonesty or flagrant dissipation. That is, treachery within the lines. To-day, and for months past, we have had men identified with professional base ball who for years have been the beneficiaries of the game, have received liberal compensation for the work they have done, earned their livelihood entirely and absolutely from the opportunities afforded them by clubs and organizations operating under the national agreement, and we find and now know that these men, during this time, have persistently been identifying themselves with schemes and combinations the sole purposes of which are to weaken and perhaps destroy the splendid fabric of our national game" (*Spalding's Official Base Ball Guide*, 1895, 5). The blacklist was lifted, but the initiative had been crushed.

A more protracted effort to revive the American Association occurred in 1900. Such prominent baseball men as Cap Anson, Al Spink, and John McGraw were involved in the venture, but the league never got off the ground. It did, however, pave the way for the success of the American League (Adrian C. Anson, *A Ball Player's Career*, 329–336).

The American and National leagues were at peace by 1905, but it was not long before other leagues were challenging them for supremacy. According to Francis Richter, there was an abortive scheme to merge the Eastern League and American Association into a third major league in 1907 (Francis C. Richter, *Richter's History and Records of Base Ball*, 156). Eccentric genius and former professional ballplayer Al Lawson formed a rival known as the Union League that began the 1908 season but lasted only a few weeks (*Sporting Life*, December 21, 1907, 2; Lyell D. Henry, Jr., *Zig-Zag and Swirl*, 32–33; Jerry Kuntz, "Tramping Through the Baseball Subculture: The Career of Alfred W. Lawson," *Base Ball* 1:2 [Fall, 2007], 93–103).

In 1910 a promoter named Dan Fletcher began work on a novel rival league that he called the All-Star League, but which was generally referred to as the Option League. Fletcher had little money of his own but nonetheless was the front man for a very ambitious scheme (*Frederick* [Md.] *News*, November 2, 1910). He began signing major leaguers to optional contracts, which guaranteed them a $10,000 bonus to sign a subsequent contract with a league *if Fletcher was able to organize one*. If the league did not materialize, they received nothing (*Nebraska State* [Lincoln] *Journal*, October 23, 1910).

Exactly how many major leaguers Fletcher signed up is a matter of debate. Fletcher himself claimed to have the signatures of eighty star players, and sportswriter William A. Phelon estimated that he signed "some 70 well-known players" (William A. Phelon, "Shall We Have a Third Big League?," *Baseball Magazine*, March 1912, 10). Others believed the figure to be lower, but even detractors of the scheme acknowledged that "a great many players did

sign these conditional contracts" (Francis C. Richter, *Richter's History and Records of Base Ball*, 157).

By December it was clear that the league would not be able to make a go of it (*Wisconsin Daily Northwestern*, December 10, 1910). Nonetheless the effort "demonstrated that the big baseball asset is easily acquired" and that "players are simply crazy for something to break loose," which doubtless encouraged other rival leagues (*Indianapolis Star*, November 13, 1910). Fletcher's league had another intriguing legacy. His league acquired a plot of land in Chicago that was bordered by Sheffield, Addison, Seminary, and Waveland, and began grading it (*Washington Post*, December 30, 1910). The Federal League subsequently acquired the land and built the stadium that is now called Wrigley Field.

Sportswriter W. A. Phelon believed that while Fletcher showed the potential for a rival big league, he also damaged the cause: "Fletcher spoiled the players. One and all of them, they are now as suspicious of new league promoters as a tomcat is suspicious of three bulldogs." To characterize the response of star players to talk of new leagues, Phelon used a phrase that would be featured in a much more recent movie: "No more Fletcher stuff in mine. Show me the money, right here in my hand, and I'll talk to you" (William A. Phelon, "Shall We Have a Third Big League?," *Baseball Magazine*, March 1912, 11).

As a result of this suspicion, the next few seasons saw a number of efforts that were modest in scope and produced still less impressive results. In 1912 John T. Powers of Chicago outlined plans for a Columbian Baseball League, which was to be centered in the Midwest with franchises in Kansas City, Chicago, St. Louis, Louisville, Indianapolis, Detroit, Cleveland, and Milwaukee. Cap Anson was reportedly also a principal in the endeavor, but interest proved tepid and the circuit never played a game (*New York Times*, January 14, 1912; February 13, 1912; *Chicago Tribune*, March 6, 1912; Francis C. Richter, *Richter's History and Records of Base Ball*, 158).

The United States League got a little further that same year. This rival was the brainchild of William Abbott Witman, Sr., of Reading, Pennsylvania, and fielded clubs in Chicago, Cleveland, Cincinnati, Pittsburgh, New York, Reading, Richmond, and Washington. The effort was plagued from the start by indecision as to whether it was challenging the existing major leagues. Witman made brave talk about the antitrust activities of the existing major leagues and about omitting the reserve clause from contracts. Yet at the same time he emphasized that his league would respect the contracts of organized baseball and had no intention of starting a war (*Atlanta Constitution*, December 22, 1911; *Washington Post*, January 30, 1912). The result was the perception of the new league as "meek" (*Los Angeles Times*, March 10, 1912). Worse, it meant that the league was made up of castoffs from organized baseball. A few well-known names such as Jack O'Connor and Deacon Phillippe signed on as managers, but the only noted player to sign was Bugs Raymond, a notorious drinker. The league began play on May 1 but was on shaky financial footing from the start and folded after five weeks (Francis C. Richter, *Richter's History and Records of Base Ball*, 158).

Witman revived the United States League for the 1913 season, limiting his scope this time to the East Coast by awarding franchises to Baltimore, Brooklyn, Lynchburg, Newark, New York, Philadelphia, Reading, and Washington. The league commenced play on May 10 but folded only three days later, leaving many players stranded (*Chicago Tribune*, May 15, 1913; Francis C. Richter, *Richter's History and Records of Base Ball*, 158–159).

The apparently fruitless efforts of 1912 and 1913 did yield one highly significant outcome. In 1913 John T. Powers formed another independent league along the same lines as the Columbian and United States leagues. The new Federal League operated for one season as an independent minor league and was not perceived as a threat by organized baseball. After one year it reinvented itself as a rival major league and became the most serious challenger of the twentieth century.

The collapse of the Federal League after two seasons, along with the entry of the United States into World War I, left the field free of challengers for several years. By the 1920s it had become clear that there was a large group of players of major league caliber who were being denied access based solely on their skin color. At least one promoter, George Herman "Andy" Lawson, considered a rival major league that would be based on these talented players. Lawson, whose brother Al's 1908 Union League was discussed earlier in this entry, announced plans for his own Continental League

in 1921 and hinted that he would use African-American players (David Pietrusza, "The Continental League of 1921," *National Pastime* 13 [1993], 76–78). Neither the plan nor the league came to fruition, so many of the era's best players never played in the recognized major leagues and instead competed in the leagues now collectively known as the Negro Leagues.

In 1946 the Mexican League lured a number of well-known players from the major leagues. The circuit's promising start was quickly thwarted by financial and logistical problems. It survived until 1948 but by then had ceased to be a threat to the National and American leagues (Lee Lowenfish, *The Imperfect Diamond*, 158–159).

In the late 1940s and early 1950s the Pacific Coast League featured many Western players of major league caliber who preferred playing closer to home. There was serious talk that the PCL deserved to be considered a major league. The league's unique status was acknowledged with an unprecedented "open" classification. But any chance of major league recognition ended when the Giants and Dodgers moved west.

That same move prompted New York City mayor Robert Wagner to announce plans to start a Continental League after the 1958 season. The prospective new league gained credibility when Branch Rickey signed on as one of its leaders. The new circuit was scuttled by the National League's decision to grant New York an expansion franchise, but it demonstrated that a rival league didn't even have to play a game in order to improve the lot of ballplayers. Expansion naturally provided major leaguers with much greater job security. Charles P. Korr suggested that this paved the way for the increased militancy of the Players Association in the 1960s, which in turn allowed player salaries and benefits to soar (Charles P. Korr, *The End of Baseball as We Knew It*, 80).

There have been a few scattered efforts in the last thirty years to form a rival major league. A World Baseball Association was proposed in 1974. Donald Trump at one point made plans to launch The Baseball League. The United Baseball League was formed in 1994 with intentions of beginning play in 1996. None of these enterprises made it past the drawing board.

The National League's first major rival was actually none of the above. The International Association, formed in 1877, was the logical successor to the loosely organized National Association. This league has been denied "major league" status due to its loose organization and lack of a fixed schedule.

That decision is, to be blunt, an example of the fact that history is usually written from the perspective of the victors, if not actually by them. The idea that a fixed schedule is a litmus test of major league status is very difficult to justify, especially since the National League didn't have one in 1876. Loose organization is an even more nebulous claim.

When more important criteria are considered, little doubt is left of the league's status. The International Association competed with the National League for players and featured players of comparable quality. It proved its strength with competitive results in head-to-head games against the National League.

The International Association lasted for four years, though it changed its name midway through. On February 19, 1879, the league became known as the National Association because it no longer had any Canadian entries. Whether it is officially recognized or not, the International Association was the first rival of the National League.

18.4.2 Leverage. The basic economic principle of supply and demand has always exerted a powerful influence on player salaries. The presence of a rival major league, in particular, has invariably driven up salaries and related forms of compensation. The threat of jumping to an "outlaw" minor league has also afforded valuable leverage to a discontented ballplayer.

Until the 1879 adoption of the reserve rule (see **18.2.1**), the players had the ultimate form of leverage. Since they were all free agents at the end of each season, players could get market value for their services by threatening to jump to a rival club. Some found ways to artificially inflate the demand; according to Tim Murnane, after pitching a no-hitter in 1875 Joe Borden was "cute enough to lay up for the rest of the season" and thereby secured a three-year contract for much more than his value (*Boston Globe*, February 19, 1900).

The reserve rule changed everything, because owners could take advantage of their exclusive rights to use a "take it or leave it" approach. Suddenly the only leverage players had was to threaten a change of profession. Player salaries were low enough in the 1880s to make such threats plausible, but even then most baseball players were relatively well paid and were

unlikely to be able to make similar amounts in another line of work.

But some at least did have legitimate alternatives. In particular, management found that a "take it or leave it" approach would not work with collegians of the era. Yale star Bill Hutchison received his diploma in 1881 but turned down all baseball offers to pursue business. Only financial reversals prompted him finally to return to baseball in 1886. Columbia Law School graduate John Montgomery Ward was said in 1893 to be "making the customary midwinter bluff of the ball player of retiring from the diamond. As usual in such cases, it will not amount to anything" (*Sporting News*, January 21, 1893). But Ward did indeed retire after the 1894 season to practice law.

Others realized there was no harm in bluffing, a tactic that became especially associated with Deacon White. White's threats to retire had begun in the 1870s and became annual events after the adoption of the reserve rule. The *Cincinnati Enquirer* observed before the 1885 season, with only slight exaggeration: "Deacon Jim White is working his annual racket of coquetry with the management of the Buffalo Club. He says that it is not likely that he will play ball the coming season, as his farm near Corning, N.Y., needs his undivided attention. Jim has made this same little speech every winter for the past thirteen years, and about the time the salary is raised to a figure that meets his views he concludes that the cows, watermelons, turnips and such can take care of themselves another year anyhow and signs a contract" (reprinted in *Sporting Life*, January 7, 1885).

Less educated players had more limited options, but they still tried to cultivate them. Some of these efforts were quite transparent; in 1894 it was reported that "Silver King has decided that after all ball playing is preferable to 'laying brick'" (*Sporting Life*, March 31, 1894). But others were more successful. For example, John McGraw and Wilbert Robinson operated a profitable tavern in Baltimore that enabled the pair to hold out in 1900 and eventually gain generous contracts.

The spiraling salaries of recent years have largely rendered leverage obsolete. Most players could not say with a straight face that they were thinking of pursuing a more lucrative career. There is still one exception that is even built into major league bonus rules: if a player is a legitimate prospect in another sport, usually football, a major league team is allowed to offer him bonus payments that are spread out over several years.

18.4.3 Salary Caps.

Some sort of salary cap was a regular topic of discussion among owners during the early years of the National League. An 1878 note warned that National League owners had suffered from the national depression and that, "under the present system the loss must fall upon the association from whom the players get the money received and much more. The League declines to continue business on this principle, and takes this time to announce to players that for the season of 1879 the aggregate salaries paid by each club must not exceed the sum which the expenses of this year has shown can be earned. It was not, however, after discussion, deemed wise at this time to attempt to restrict any association as to what it shall pay any or all of the men in its employ" (*California Spirit of the Times*, August 31, 1878). As mentioned in entry **18.2.2**, the following year's postseason meetings saw league president William Hulbert assigned to "perfect a plan of arranging salaries." The idea of a salary cap was again proposed after both the 1882 and 1884 seasons but was not implemented (*Sporting Life*, December 3, 1884, 5; Mike Roer, *Orator O'Rourke*, 148).

On October 17, 1885, the National League and the American Association jointly announced a $2,000 maximum player salary to begin the following season. Most major league owners found ways around the rule, rendering it largely ineffective. Nonetheless the announcement had an enduring influence, since baseball's first union (see **18.3.1**), the Brotherhood, was formed within days. The threat of salary caps and labor unrest have gone hand in hand ever since.

Salary caps were widely attempted in minor leagues of the era, where it seemed that they might have a greater chance of success. After all, minor leaguers had virtually no leverage, so the caps could be announced openly: "The New England League . . . has fixed a salary limit" (*Boston Globe*, June 6, 1886). Yet these were invariably scuttled when one owner broke the rules to give himself a better chance of winning, which forced others to follow suit. It became proverbial that "no salary limit rule can be devised so air tight that any manager can't blow through it any time he really tries" (*Sporting News*, January 2, 1913).

On November 21, 1888, the National League passed the Brush Classification Plan. This plan, proposed by Indianapolis owner John T. Brush, classified all players as A, B, C, D, or E, with prescribed salaries for each grouping. The maximum player salary for the top group was $2,500, far lower than what many players were then making. (As will be discussed under "Performance Bonuses" [**18.5.12**], an exception was made for captains.) To add insult to injury, players in the lower ranks could be assigned to sell tickets or sweep the ballpark (Troy Soos, *Before the Curse*, 86). The rule was announced three days after Johnny Ward, head of the Brotherhood, had left for Australia as part of an around-the-world tour. The touring players did not learn of the plan until February and were outraged when finally informed (Mark Lamster, *Spalding's World Tour*, 168–169). The extremely unpopular rule was one of the main causes of the formation of the Players' League.

The idea of a salary cap has continued to emerge sporadically. Before the 1919 season, National League owners voted "in a heated moment" to adopt a salary cap of $60,000. But "after being ridiculed for two days as 'minor leaguers,' the action of the 'heated moment' was rescinded" (James Crusinberry, "Salaries of Cubs and Giants Prove Limit Rule Impossible," *Chicago Tribune*, January 20, 1919, 13). During World War II the government imposed salary and price controls. Major league teams were instructed that a player's 1943 salary could not be lower than the lowest-paid member of the team had received in 1942, nor higher than the top salary paid by the team in 1942. Recent years have seen the owners push for some form of salary cap, with the players staunchly opposing any such restrictions.

18.4.4 Minimum Salaries.

Minimum salaries entered baseball with the National Agreement (see **18.2.3**). In the Tri-Partite Agreement of 1883, the fifth clause guaranteed minimums of $1,000 per year to players reserved by the National League and American Association, and $750 to those reserved by the Northwestern League. The same minimums were retained by the 1884 National Agreement, with the Eastern League subsequently being added with an $800 minimum.

Even the efforts of owners to limit player salaries in ensuing years retained this feature. The 1885 attempt to institute a salary cap (see **18.4.3**) continued the $1,000 minimum. The

Brush Classification Plan, introduced in 1889, guaranteed a minimum salary of $1,500. Experience eventually taught owners that ceilings were more easily evaded than were minimum salaries. Accordingly, wage controls of all sorts dropped out of baseball for many years.

This feature was permanently reintroduced in 1946, when a $5,500 minimum salary was established as part of the owners' efforts to avert the formation of a player's guild.

18.4.5   Free Agency. Baseball entered the free-agency era in 1975, but the concept of free agency is a much older one. Before the introduction of the reserve rule (see **18.2.1**) in 1879, all baseball players had access to free agency, since they had the same freedom enjoyed by workers in any industry—the prerogative to sign with another club at the expiration of their contracts. The reserve rule/clause removed this right by enabling clubs to continue to hold exclusive rights to players after the expiration of their contracts. It remained a bone of contention between owners and players for almost a century.

As discussed in the entry on "Leverage" (see **18.4.2**), most players expressed their discontent by holding out or threatening to retire. There have always been a few, however, who made more direct challenges, and some of these players have succeeded in attaining free agency. Typically owners have been willing to compromise on an individual case if it helped preserve their ability to reserve most players.

Hall of Famer Jim O'Rourke, who was a law student on the side, appears to have been the first such player. A 1910 review of his career, apparently told by O'Rourke, gave this account:

"When Harry Wright asked him to sign with Boston [for 1880], O'Rourke said, 'Sure, I'll go, if you promise not to reserve me.' Wright had to promise, and he stood by smiling at O'Rourke's sharpness as the boy signed the contract. Each year thereafter, before he signed, both in Boston and Buffalo, O'Rourke forced his employers to waive the reserve clause.

"O'Rourke was the only player in base ball smart enough to succeed in doing this, and he got away with it for seven years. He even played in or [sic] the famous John B. Day, owner of the New York Nationals. It was in 1884 that Day went to the farm home of O'Rourke to sign him.

"'Name your figure,' said Day, 'and it will be paid, because I've got to have you.'. . .

"'I will sign for $4,500 a year for three years,' said O'Rourke, 'if you waive the right to reserve me at the end of that time.' Day promised, and from 1885 to 1887 young O'Rourke was the pet of base balldom.

"'But when my three-year contract expired in 1887,' said O'Rourke, 'I noticed none of the managers were bidding for me, even though I was unreserved.

"'I knew then there was a deal on whereby I would have to go back to Day, even if he had not reserved me, so I went to him and said, 'Well, John, you fellows have caught up to me at last, and nobody seems to want me. I would like to play for you.'

"'Delighted to have you,' said Day, and he doubled O'Rourke's salary" ("Forty Two Years of Base Ball," *Kalamazoo Evening Telegraph*, February 26, 1910). O'Rourke biographer Mike Roer confirms this version of events (Mike Roer, *Orator O'Rourke*, 85, 117).

The Union Association was founded on September 12, 1883, as a direct challenge to the reserve rule. One of its initial resolutions was the bold statement that "we cannot recognize any agreement whereby any number of ballplayers may be reserved for any club for any time beyond the terms of their contract with such club." The "outlaw" circuit lasted only one year.

Joe Gerhardt signed a one-year contract with Louisville in 1884 with the reserve clause removed. He signed to play with New York the next season (Ralph L. Horton, "Joe Gerhardt," in Frederick Ivor-Campbell, Robert L. Tiemann, and Mark Rucker, eds., *Baseball's First Stars*, 67).

In 1885 the Brotherhood of Professional Base-Ball Players was formed with star player and law student John Ward as its leader. The Brotherhood enabled the players collectively to voice their opposition to the owners' strong-arm measures, including the reserve clause. In 1890 the players formed their own league, which was explicitly based upon free agency. Cap Anson claimed, "Any player who was dissatisfied with his location could apply to the board to be transferred without the payment of anything to the club losing his services" (Adrian Anson, *A Ball Player's Career*, 291). But the Players' League folded after one year, and the subsequent merger of the National League and the American Association left the owners with more power than ever.

Players did not, however, entirely abandon their desire for free agency. John Ward retired following the 1894 season, but New York continued to reserve him. Ward appealed for free agency, though he had no intention of returning to the playing field. The owners may have suspected that he was setting the stage for a lawsuit, and they headed him off by finally granting him his release in February 1896.

Giants pitcher Amos Rusie sat out the 1896 season and then sued Giants owner Andrew Freedman for $5,000 and his release. The other league owners were worried that the suit might bring down the reserve clause, and paid the $5,000 to Rusie. Rusie thereby made $2,000 more for not pitching that season than he would have done by pitching.

Although entirely forgotten today, Mike Griffin was the Curt Flood of the 1890s. Brooklyn's captain and a veteran star center fielder, Griffin became involved in a prolonged dispute after the 1898 season when the club tried to alter the contract that had already been signed. Griffin retired and successfully sued Brooklyn, but his career was over at age thirty-three.

After a long holdout, John McGraw and Wilbert Robinson signed contracts with St. Louis on May 8, 1900. According to McGraw, "Both Robbie and myself refused to sign a contract which would hold us over another year, regardless of our wishes. . . . The reserve clause was stricken from our contracts. This made us free agents at the end of the season, giving us the right to go to another club or anywhere we pleased" (John McGraw, *My Thirty Years in Baseball*, 123–124). McGraw accordingly claimed that he and Robinson were not contract jumpers when they signed with the American League.

Johnny Evers and Hugh Fullerton indicated that the National League responded to such threats by passing a new rule that stated: "Where the contract does not contain a reservation clause, every club, nevertheless, has a right to reserve a player unless the contract itself contains a written stipulation that the player is not to be reserved" (John J. Evers and Hugh S. Fullerton, *Touching Second*, 51–52).

The issue receded into the background for a decade and a half but resurfaced in 1914 with the emergence of the Federal League. A limited form of free agency was granted by the National Commission on January 6, 1914, in an attempt to avert the challenge of the Federal League. Robert Burk explained, "Ten-year major league veterans, in a change dubbed the 'Brown rule' in honor of the veteran pitcher [Mordecai 'Three-Finger' Brown], received the right of

unconditional release" (Robert Burk, *Never Just a Game*, 197).

After the Federal League folded, the National Commission was quick to remove this exception. The Commission took an ad in the *Sporting News* to emphasize that "A non-reserve clause in the contract of a major league player without the approval of the Commission shall not be valid" ("Ball Players," *Sporting News*, February 17, 1916). In a November 1916 memo, clubs were informed: "The Commission has reason to believe that some major league players, whose expired contracts did not contain a renewal clause, will decline to concede further claim of their respective clubs to their services on the ground that at the expiration of their contracts they become free agents. . . . With full realization that the reserve rule is not only a bulwark of professional base ball, and of inestimable benefit to the players, in assuring them as a class, regular employment at salaries adequate to their expertness, the Commission will hold in all such cases that the major league club, to which a player was under contract at the close of last season is entitled to retain him for 1917, if it so desires, and will not countenance the claim of any other club to such player that is not predicated on his purchase or release from his 1916 Club. The Commission will not approve or recognize any contract not in the new form and without change or modification of any of its provisions in any particular" (quoted in *Outside the Lines*, Fall 1999). This return to the previous way of doing business was included in the new player contract, which was made public on December 2 (I. E. Sanborn, "New Contract of Majors Has Ten Day Clause," *Chicago Tribune*, December 3, 1916).

The reserve clause was finally brought to the Supreme Court in 1922, where Justice Oliver Wendell Holmes, Jr., wrote a ruling that held that baseball was not interstate commerce and was therefore exempt from antitrust laws. While the legal basis of this finding struck many as dubious, baseball players had no choice but to accept it. With the courts against them and no rival league to turn to, most players came to view the reserve clause as a necessary evil, with some even defending it against periodic challenges.

Nonetheless Commissioner Kenesaw Mountain Landis, in his crusade against farm systems, declared many players free agents. Most were minor leaguers, but there were some major leaguers, such as Benny McCoy. When he was declared a free agent after the 1939 season, ten teams bid for his services. Hall of Famer Rick Ferrell was declared a free agent by Landis shortly before his rookie season of 1929, and signed a lucrative contract with the Browns that included a $25,000 bonus (Bob Matherne, "Free Agents Profiting by Landis Action," NEA wire service story, *Frederick* [Md.] *Post*, April 3, 1929).

By the 1940s the concept of free agency had passed out of baseball. Yankee star Tommy Henrich actually claimed to have been the first free agent, yet another indication that baseball firsts remain a confusing topic and that ballplayers are rarely aware of the history of the game (Tommy Henrich, *Five O'Clock Lightning*, 2).

The tide began to turn when Curt Flood was traded from the Cardinals to the Phillies in October 1969 but chose instead to challenge the reserve clause. His case went all the way to the Supreme Court, where he lost in a 5 to 3 ruling. In writing the majority opinion, Justice Harry Blackmun offered tepid support for the reserve clause by acknowledging: "If there is an inconsistency and illogic in all this, it is an inconsistency and illogic of long standing that is to be remedied by the Congress and not by this Court."

Players Association executive director Marvin Miller became convinced that the rule would finally fall if he had a test case to take to grievance arbitration (see **18.4.10**). But he needed a player to complete an entire season without signing a contract, and the owners did their best to preclude this from happening. Ted Simmons played much of the 1972 season without signing his contract, but in August he received an offer that he couldn't refuse. Five players began the 1973 campaign without contracts and seven more in 1974, but each eventually got an offer that was too tempting, so Miller still did not have his test case (John Helyar, *Lords of the Realm*, 131–135).

Catfish Hunter was awarded free agency on December 13, 1974. The issue, however, was the nonfulfillment of his contract by Oakland owner Charles O. Finley. As a result, it didn't set a precedent regarding the reserve clause.

The following season, Andy Messersmith and Dave McNally finally gave Marvin Miller his test cases by completing the season without signing contracts. Their grievance led to them being declared free agents by a three-man arbitration panel on December 23, 1975. The owners immediately fired arbitrator Peter Seitz, but

they were too late to prevent the free-agency era from beginning.

18.4.6 Collusion. This point overlaps with a number of other entries in this section, but it bears repetition. Between 1986 and 1988 major league owners conspired to devastate the free-agent market by agreeing not to make offers. In 1990 they were found guilty of collusion and agreed to pay $280 million in damages.

What needs to be emphasized is that there is nothing new, or necessarily illegal, about collusion among owners. Indeed it can be argued that the unique nature of baseball's reliance upon the success of competitors has always made collusion essential. Simply honoring the reserve clauses of competitors can be construed as collusion. As described in the entry on the "Reserve Rule/Clause" (see **18.2.1**), an important preliminary step was an agreement by National League owners to limit advance signings. The blacklists went much further, since they placed restrictions on players who were not under contract at all. There were also informal blacklists or "gentlemen's agreements" that were imposed on players for a variety of reasons.

Jim O'Rourke claimed to have been a victim of the same practice for which the owners paid so heavily a century later. In the passage that appeared in the preceding entry, he indicated that he was free to sign with any club after the 1887 season but "noticed none of the managers were bidding for me, even though I was unreserved. I knew then there was a deal on" ("Forty Two Years of Base Ball," *Kalamazoo Evening Telegraph*, February 26, 1910).

The Brush Classification Plan of 1888 extended such restrictions to the entire league. The *Chicago Tribune* noted, "The general settlement appears to be that the classification scheme is illegal. It places a limit on the value of every classified player's services, which is opposed to the rulings of the United States Supreme Court. Some lawyers say it is a clear case of conspiracy, nothing more or less" (*Chicago Tribune*, April 29, 1889).

But it didn't really matter whether it was conspiracy or not. As long as representatives of baseball's owners—first the National Commission and then the commissioner—determined baseball law, there was nothing illegal about conspiracy. As Johnny Evers and Hugh Fullerton observed, "Only the bitter rivalry between club owners, and the desire to satisfy players and keep them satisfied in order that they will do their best work, prevents wholesale horizontal decreases of salaries in the major leagues, where the combination is most powerful" (John J. Evers and Hugh S. Fullerton, *Touching Second*, 53–54).

Likewise, when Jim Brosnan's diary of the 1960 campaign, *The Long Season*, was published, Gabe Paul expressed concern that Brosnan's description of agreeing with former teammate Ernie Broglio to pitch high fastballs to each other might be considered collusion. "Collusion?" Brosnan later asked rhetorically. "Nobody even knew what that was back then" (John Skipper, *Inside Pitch*, 59).

The situation changed only when the owners agreed to characterize certain collusive activities as illegal. A clause added to the 1976 Basic Agreement specified, "Players shall not act in concert with other Players and Clubs shall not act in concert with other Clubs." Lee Lowenfish noted: "Ironically, it was the owners in 1976 who insisted on this language because they were worried that a players' agent might get his clients to act in concert" (Lee Lowenfish, *The Imperfect Diamond*, 263). Charles P. Korr suggested that memories of the Koufax-Drysdale joint holdout of 1966 (see **18.4.9**) impelled the owners to take this course (Charles P. Korr, *The End of Baseball as We Knew It*, 63).

It was under this provision that the Players Association filed a "collusion" grievance. The word "collusion" thereby entered the language of baseball and continues to exert its influence. John Helyar quoted an unnamed baseball man as saying, regretfully, "There was no collusion like old-style collusion" (John Helyar, *Lords of the Realm*, 95).

It is also worth noting in this regard that there is still a very fine line between legal and illegal forms of collusion. A perfect example is the current practice of "slotting," by which the major leagues have driven down the market value of draft choices by recommending bonus amounts for each slot in the amateur draft. While this seems to smack of collusion, Alan Schwarz explained, "Some people have mentioned the word 'collusion' in both the [Landon] Powell case and in referring to [Major League Baseball Executive Vice President of Baseball Operations Sandy] Alderson's predraft pep talk, but baseball's collusion rules apply only to major league free agents. Clubs are free to set a common strategy with respect to the draft" (*Baseball America*, October 2–15, 2000).

18.4.7 Big Market / Small Market Disparities. A familiar contention of ownership in recent years is that escalating salaries have created disparities between large- and small-market clubs. The idea that there is something new about such disparities is laughable. In fact, despite frequent protestations to the contrary, the evidence suggests that parity has steadily increased over time.

Take for example this complaint: "Chicago and New York are now able to handicap all other cities by paying men salaries of such magnitude as to make it impossible for their smaller-quartered competitors to get them." That was written in 1883! (*Cleveland Herald*, reprinted in *Perry* [Iowa] *Pilot*, July 11, 1883).

An 1884 article noted the complaint of the Cleveland owner that salaries were "clean out of sight." As a result, it claimed that "the richer, and naturally the larger cities, have gradually strengthened their teams, while the poorer, and, just as naturally, the smaller cities, have not only lost ground by the loss of old men by various means, but have been unable to pay the ruinous prices demanded by the new men" (*Sporting Life*, December 3, 1884). The article indicated that the rich clubs were Chicago, New York, Boston, and Providence, while the poor ones were Cleveland, Detroit, Philadelphia, and Buffalo.

Longtime baseball man James A. Williams wrote in 1891, "When professional base ball was young and its managers new the system of small percentages to visiting clubs and meagre guarantees, barely sufficient to pay traveling expenses, were adopted. This soon developed the fact that certain clubs were bound to make big money under the system, while others either made no money at all or lost. Then the latter demanded a great percentage in order that they, too, might reasonably expect some return for their investment and labors, but that spirit of cupidity and selfishness that has been the bane of the business almost since its inception came to the front and was able for years—13 in the league and 8 in the Association I think—and by skillful legislation was able to prevent any change to a fair division of receipts. In the meantime the smaller cities in each organization put up their money, labored hard to keep up with the procession, but dropped by the wayside" (*Sporting Life*, October 31, 1891).

In 1913 the president of the St. Louis Browns said, "Under the present system in the major leagues it's extremely hard for tailend clubs to edge into the first division. The winning clubs make big money, and for that reason they pay big money for talent. They sometimes pay fabulous and senseless prices for promising men. The owner of a losing club would go bankrupt trying to compete against the winners, figuring that a few of the high priced individuals would fail to deliver" (*New York Sun*, September 14, 1913).

In recent years Commissioner Bud Selig has advanced the idea that clubs now, for the first time in baseball history, go to spring training without any reasonable hope of winning. The commissioner might find it interesting to read an article that appeared before the 1913 season. In it, Boston Braves captain Bill Sweeney predicted that his Braves would fight it out for fifth with the Cubs that year (*Sporting News*, March 27, 1913).

18.4.8 Holdouts. It is usually reported that the first holdout was Charles Sweasy of the 1870 Red Stockings, who demanded a raise from $800 to $1,000 and ultimately received it. But it is debatable whether Sweasy was really a holdout since he could have signed with another club.

The first post-reserve-rule holdouts were George Wright and Deacon White. Wright's case was discussed under the entry on the reserve rule (**18.2.1**). Deacon White also held out at the beginning of the 1880 season but eventually came to terms. Thereafter White voiced his opposition to the reserve rule by threatening retirement so many times that the *Cincinnati Enquirer* observed in 1888, "Deacon Jim White has just succeeded in making his forty-second annual retirement and is about ready to go to work again. The 'Deacon,' in his great act of 'How Not to Retire,' can knock [opera singer Adelina] Patti, [actress Sarah] Bernhardt et al., with their 'stolen diamond' stories all into a cocked hat when it comes to getting a big lot of advertising without putting up a cent for it. White has sprung the chestnut about going to work on his Corning farm in New York State once too often. It doesn't go with people who know him" (*Cincinnati Enquirer*, March 25, 1888).

Holdouts remained a major part of baseball for close to a century. Since the implementation of salary arbitration in 1973, they have become very rare.

18.4.9 Joint Holdouts. Sandy Koufax and Don Drysdale held the most famous and most influential (see **18.4.6** "Collusion") joint holdout before the 1966 season. Dodgers owner Walter O'Malley expressed his displeasure: "Baseball is an old-fashioned game with old-fashioned traditions" (quoted in John Helyar, *Lords of the Realm*, 23). But Koufax and Drysdale's tactic was far from new.

After the 1870 season, Bob Ferguson negotiated with Chicago and offered his services and those of a teammate in 1871 for $4,500. The proposal was accepted, but the deal fell through, perhaps because the two sides had different understandings about the identity of the second player (*Chicago Tribune*, January 22, 1871, 4). Jim O'Rourke and his brother John negotiated as a pair before the 1880 season, a tactic that enabled them to avoid the then-new reserve rule (Mike Roer, *Orator O'Rourke*, 83–85). John McGraw and Wilbert Robinson achieved a similar result. When the Orioles franchise folded in 1900, their contracts were transferred to St. Louis. But since the two men were co-owners of a profitable tavern in Baltimore, they jointly held out until the season had begun and they received an offer they couldn't refuse. McGraw claimed that not only did they get astronomical salaries, but that the reserve clause was removed from their contracts (John McGraw, *My Thirty Years in Baseball*, 123–124).

Ed Delahanty and Napoleon Lajoie held a joint holdout in Philadelphia that same year (Mike Sowell, *July 2, 1903*, 27–28; Jerrold Casway, *Ed Delahanty and the Emerald Age of Baseball*, 178–179). Batterymates Bill Killefer and Grover Cleveland Alexander used a similar tactic in 1917, with the great pitcher agreeing to "a compact with Killefer whereby the two are to stand together in their dealings with the Philadelphia Club" (*Sporting Life*, February 3, 1917).

18.4.10 Arbitration. For much of baseball history, the absence of impartial arbitration meant that owners could issue ultimatums during negotiations, while holdouts were the only means by which players could draw their own line in the sand. There are two basic forms of neutral arbitration that have been added by the Basic Agreement: grievance and salary arbitration. Each was introduced in the early years of Marvin Miller's tenure as executive director of the Players Association, and each has had a dramatic impact on the game. Neither, however, was remotely a new concept.

The Tri-Partite Agreement of 1883 created an Arbitration Committee, which consisted of three representatives of each of the three leagues that signed it (*Reach's Official Base Ball Guide, 1883,* 52). The Arbitration Committee was retained in the National Agreement that succeeded it, as was its partisan makeup (*Reach's Official Base Ball Guide, 1884,* 39). This provided players with a forum for grievances but not one that was as impartial as they would have liked. It appears that few players brought appeals to it, and the ones that did were either turned down or saw the matters referred back to the league in question.

When the Players' Protective Association was founded in 1900, its initial list of grievances included a request for a Committee of Arbitration that would consist of one representative from each side and a neutral third member. The idea proved to be well ahead of its time, with *Sporting Life* editor Francis Richter later commenting that "if adopted the game would become demoralized by endless appointments of and squabbles with arbitration committees" (Francis C. Richter, *Richter's History and Records of Base Ball,* 162–164). Association president Chief Zimmer eventually agreed to drop the idea.

Once the American and National leagues reached a peace agreement, players were granted a form of arbitration. The three-man National Commission began to hear grievances regularly, and the details of these cases were usually published in the sporting press, which gave wronged players some hope for redress in cases of rank injustice. But since all three members of the National Commission represented ownership, it was in no way an impartial system.

In 1910 Johnny Evers and Hugh Fullerton modestly suggested that allowing players to present a defense and holding public hearings would improve the system. With a touch reminiscent of *Alice in Wonderland,* they questioned the fairness of instances where "the Commission, or one member of it, states weeks in advance of a hearing what the decision will be" (John J. Evers and Hugh S. Fullerton, *Touching Second,* 55).

Accordingly they presented these demands: "an impartial court of three or five men not vitally interested in baseball, men who have no baseball connections, especially no financial ones. The players desire that this court shall codify and print all existing laws, and submit them to all members of the agreement for ratification. Finally, they demand that the court shall

sit openly at stated intervals to hear causes, and take the evidence on both sides" (John J. Evers and Hugh S. Fullerton, *Touching Second,* 55).

It is hard to find anything unreasonable in these requests, yet owners continued to resist impartial hearings. They did replace the National Commission with a single commissioner after the 1920 season, but the commissioner remained an employee of the owners. As a result, one of the planks of Robert Murphy's unsuccessful 1946 effort to form a guild was "Arbitration in the event player and management cannot agree on salary" (*Sporting News,* June 5, 1946).

Once Marvin Miller became head of the players' union in 1965, he pushed hard for grievance arbitration, a staple of other industries. The owners were at first adamantly opposed to this concept but gradually yielded ground. The 1968 Basic Agreement included a grievance procedure that represented a compromise between the two positions. The fact that spelling out the procedure took up five pages of the twenty-four-page document indicates how painstakingly this middle ground was mapped out. The owners felt reassured by the role retained for the commissioner while the players took heart from knowing they now had a viable recourse when they felt wronged (Charles P. Korr, *The End of Baseball as We Knew It,* 71–73).

In 1970 the players pressed for eliminating the commissioner from the process altogether, and ownership again conceded ground. John Helyar indicated that Commissioner Bowie Kuhn was finally won over by the arguments of his adviser Lou Hoynes and owners' negotiator John Gaherin. Kuhn's basic objection was that the powers of his office should not be diminished. Hoynes and Gaherin contended that arbitrators would handle "nuts and bolts" issues, such as inspecting a hotel to decide if it was first-class. They persuaded the commissioner that getting involved in such disputes only diminished his prestige, and that he could retain control of issues that involved the "integrity of the game" and "public confidence" while ceding lesser matters to the arbitrator (John Helyar, *Lords of the Realm,* 113–114).

Kuhn later commented, "While I thought the change was neither necessary nor beneficial, and though it could not have been made without my consent, I reluctantly went along. There had never been a commissioner whose fairness in disputes between clubs and players could be questioned, and if anything they had probably been more sympathetic to the players' side of disputes. But provisions of this kind were commonplace in American collective bargaining agreements and could not realistically be resisted by sports managements—nor have they been. So the clubs and I concurred" (Bowie Kuhn, *Hardball*, 141).

As a result, impartial grievance arbitration—with the one important exception that the commissioner could intervene if the "integrity of the game" was involved—was incorporated into the 1970 Basic Agreement. The first case to be arbitrated involved whether Alex Johnson could be placed on the disabled list for psychological problems (Jonathan Fraser Light, *The Cultural Encyclopedia of Baseball*, 32).

Three years later the players received the right to salary arbitration. The owners' negotiators sold the plan to the owners as a minor concession that would cost relatively little money and would have the additional benefit of ending holdouts. More important, it would give an appearance of fairness that would lessen the effectiveness of Marvin Miller's calls for free agency. The owners approved "final offer arbitration" by a 22 to 2 vote, and it was added to the new Basic Agreement on February 25, 1973 (John Helyar, *Lords of the Realm*, 160–161).

The first player to go to salary arbitration was Minnesota pitcher Dick Woodson, whose case was heard on February 11, 1974. Woodson won his case and, while the amounts were not officially released, it was generally reported that he received $29,000 instead of the $23,000 being offered by the Twins. This seemed a small price to pay.

Within a few years both forms of arbitration would have extraordinary consequences. The grievance arbitration process made free agents first of Catfish Hunter, then of Andy Messersmith and Dave McNally, and, finally, of any player who played out his option. The salary arbitration process had initially led to modest increases because it compared players to others with similarly limited options. After the advent of free agency, the salaries commanded by free agents began to set the standard for arbitration cases.

This in turn pushed the value of free agents still higher. From the owners' perspective it was a vicious cycle that led to skyrocketing salaries. The players instead saw it as proof that their salaries had been artificially limited all along.

(v) Contracts

As we shall see in this entry, the provisions in players' contracts have always been closely tied to the threat of rival leagues.

18.5.1 Contracts. Although professionalism was not acknowledged until 1869, researcher Greg Rhodes reports that at least a few members of the Red Stockings of Cincinnati had signed contracts in 1868 (*New York Clipper*, March 13, 1869). Once the game entered the era of open professionalism, contracts quickly became part of the game. John Thorn tracked down a 650-word contract for the 1871 season by which Cap Anson committed himself, among other things, "to conduct himself, both off and on the Ball Ground, in all things like a gentleman . . . to abstain from profane language, scuffling and light conduct, and to discourage the same in others . . . to practise at least two and a half hours per day . . . to use his best endeavours to perfect himself in play. Always bearing in mind that the Object in view in every game is to win."

18.5.2 Player Threats to Sue over a Contract. Researcher Richard Hershberger found that Dave Eggler sued the Philadelphia Club for his unpaid 1874 salary and was awarded $337.57 (*New York Clipper*, October 7, 1876). The club's unsuccessful defense was that the stock organization that backed the 1876 ball club was different from the one that had not paid Eggler two years earlier (*New York Sunday Mercury*, October 21, 1876). Philadelphia ball clubs of that era suffered constant financial woes and were able to use this argument regularly. After the 1877 season, Ezra Sutton won a lawsuit against his 1876 club, the Athletics, but was unable to collect because the club was no longer in existence (*New York Sunday Mercury*, January 19, 1878).

18.5.3 Contract Perks. After the completion of the National League's first season in 1876, the owners addressed the issues of the expenses incurred by players while on the road. But if the players were expecting generous per diems, they were sadly mistaken. The owners instead decided that a thirty-dollar charge would be assessed for the cost of the player's uniform. Another fifty cents a day would be *deducted* from his contract for traveling expenses for each day the club was away from home (*New York*

Clipper, December 23, 1876). These were far from trivial amounts, and players were similarly expected to pay to clean their uniforms and to purchase any equipment they would need (John Glasscock, quoted by John E. Wray in the *St. Louis Post-Dispatch*, reprinted in *Sporting News*, November 8, 1917; *New York Clipper*, January 10, 1880).

Needless to say, players were disgruntled about these duns, especially in Boston where penny-pinching owner Arthur Soden was already charging players for game tickets for their wives. When Soden added yet another fee—a twenty-dollar deduction to clean players' uniforms—Jim O'Rourke rebelled. O'Rourke prided himself on keeping his uniform immaculate and therefore found the policy both unfair and insulting (Mike Roer, *Orator O'Rourke*, 71). He declined to re-sign with Boston in 1879 in part as a protest of the assessment (Bernard J. Crowley, "James Henry O'Rourke," in Frederick Ivor-Campbell, Robert L. Tiemann, and Mark Rucker, eds., *Baseball's First Stars*, 125).

O'Rourke returned to Boston a season later, but he and his brother John threatened not to sign their 1880 contracts unless the offensive clauses were removed. Boston refused to do so, and an impasse was averted only when club supporters volunteered to pay for the expenses (*New York Clipper*, January 10, 1880).

Owners continued steadfastly to resist the concept of reimbursing players for even direct out-of-pocket expenses. In 1900 the Players' Protective Association requested the owners pay the doctor bills of a player who was injured during play. The idea was rejected by the owners (Francis C. Richter, *Richter's History and Records of Base Ball*, 162–163). The cost of players' travel and lodgings on road trips was also deducted from their paychecks ("The Great National Game in Dollars and Cents," *Washington Post*, May 9, 1909).

It was the formation of the Players' Fraternity in 1912 that finally brought relief. While the owners rejected the Fraternity's more far-reaching demands, they did make some concessions. Two of these points were the reimbursement of some preseason travel expenses and finally the dropping of the $30 charge for uniforms (though players continued to pay for their own shoes) (Francis C. Richter, *Richter's History and Records of Base Ball*, 168–171). By 1917 players received $1 to $1.50 in meal money per day while on the road, which was a reasonable approximation of the typical cost (Jack Glasscock, quoted by John E. Wray in the *St. Louis Post-Dispatch*, reprinted in *Sporting News*, November 8, 1917).

More generous per diems originated in 1946 for a similar reason—Robert Murphy's attempt to form the Players' Guild. In order to prevent the formation of anything resembling a union, the owners gave ground on a lot of minor issues, including this one. The per diems accordingly became known as "Murphy money," a term still in use.

18.5.4   Multi-year Contracts. With almost all issues involving contracts, the terms that owners were willing to grant varied with the amount of competition for the players' services. This is particularly true with long-term contracts.

Harry Wright seems to have pioneered the multi-year contract in the mid-1870s. In 1875 he offered George Latham a three-year contract if he played well (Harry Wright correspondence; quoted in William J. Ryczek, *Blackguards and Red Stockings*, 201). Pitcher Joseph Borden signed a three-year contract with Boston that called for $1,900 in 1876, $2,000 in 1877, and $2,100 in 1878 (*New York Sunday Mercury*, October 21, 1876). That was followed by reports of "a sort of regular army enlistment made by Lewis J. Brown for four years in Harry Wright's corps" (*Chicago Tribune*, December 3, 1876). Wright also extended a four-year contract to John Morrill and appears to have given a three-year deal to Jack Manning (*Chicago Tribune*, August 27, 1876). None of the five was an established performer, and only Morrill would go on to stardom, although Brown was a standout catcher when sober.

Signing so many unproven players to long-term contracts seems a foolhardy move on the part of the usually canny Wright. One possibility is that he overreacted to having lost four of his stars to Chicago after the 1875 season, since all but the Latham contract came in the wake of this calamity. There is evidence that the Latham contract was not entirely guaranteed, with Boston retaining the right to release him at any time (William J. Ryczek, *Blackguards and Red Stockings*, 200–201). But that Borden's contract was guaranteed is confirmed by multiple sources, including Tim Murnane, who was signed on the same day as Borden (*Boston Globe*, September 6, 1875; Tim Murnane, *Boston Globe*, February 19, 1900; *Washington Post*, March 16, 1884). The signing proved fateful.

Borden had a disappointing first season with Boston and made his final appearance in mid-July. But the club was still obligated for the two-plus years remaining on his contract, so after two months club management "hit upon a plan for utilizing 'Josephs,' or Borden, their useless whilom pitcher. Failing to induce him to throw up his contract, they have now given him a daily round of duties to perform, such as overseeing the ground, keeping the grass neatly trimmed, etc.; also compelling him to practice daily, mornings and afternoon, and, in short, keeping him much busier than he would be if on the nine. 'Joe' doesn't relish this kind of work much, but he is bound to stick" (*Boston Herald*, September 15, 1876). Borden continued to "cheerfully" report for work twice a day and tend the grounds, meanwhile getting legal advice that the contract was binding (*Hartford Times*, September 20, 1876, quoted in David Arcidiacono, *Grace, Grit and Growling*, 58; Tim Murnane, *Boston Globe*, February 19, 1900; *New York Sunday Mercury*, January 20, 1877). Eventually club president Arthur Soden negotiated a buyout (*New York Sunday Mercury*, February 11, 1877; *Cincinnati Enquirer*, February 15, 1877).

Frank Flint and John Ward both had two-year contracts covering the 1880 and 1881 seasons (*New York Clipper*, October 16, 1880; Bryan Di Salvatore, *A Clever Base-Ballist*, 136). The fact that two of the thirty original reserved players chose that moment to sign two-year contracts is puzzling. Ward, at least, was far too astute to sign a contract that benefited only his employer. And yet it also seems unlikely that clubs would have guaranteed two years of a contract when the standard contract guaranteed only ten days. My guess is that their respective clubs offered them some financial inducement to sign up for an extra year.

The owners were in the ascendancy for most of the 1880s. The lone exception was the chaos initiated by the Union Association in 1884, which enabled Fred Dunlap to sign a record-breaking two-year contract calling for $3,200 in 1884 and $4,000 in 1885 (*Philadelphia Item*, quoted in *Washington Post*, March 16, 1884). But the upstart league didn't even last as long as Dunlap's contract, with the result that there were few if any long-term contracts for the remainder of the decade. Jim O'Rourke, as described in the entry on free agency (see **18.4.5**), claimed to have had a three-year contract that began in 1885. But if he did, he had relatively little company. By 1885 the National Agreement prohibited multi-year contracts, though a few star players were still demanding and receiving them.

The advent of the Players' League in 1890 brought short-lived hope to the players. All its players signed three-year contracts, but that turned out to be three times as long as the league lasted. The National League and the American Association fought back by offering three-year contracts that year. By the time these had expired, the National League had eliminated both its rivals and embarked upon a decade-long austerity movement (Robert F. Burk, *Never Just a Game*, 108, 124).

The pendulum swung again when the American League was formed in 1901. Soon there were regular reports of multi-year contracts, led by the five-year contract that induced Bobby Wallace to jump from the Cardinals to their crosstown American League rivals (Scott E. Schul, "Rhoderick John 'Bobby' Wallace," in David Jones, ed., *Deadball Stars of the American League*, 777). A 1903 report observed: "Fred Parent is the only player who is bound to the Boston Club for more than one season. He has two years to run. Criger, Young and Ferris are the only [other] players signed for another season" (*Sporting Life*, October 24, 1903). Fred Clarke signed a three-year, $22,500 contract in 1904 (*Sporting Life*, February 3, 1906). By 1907 the Chicago Cubs had Three-Finger Brown, Jimmy Sheckard, and Carl Lundgren signed to three-year contracts and Johnny Evers to a two-year contract (*Sporting Life*, April 20, 1907).

When the Federal League emerged as a rival to the National and American leagues following the 1913 season, many players used the sudden demand for their services to demand multi-year contracts that would lock in the higher salaries. For the two years of the Federal League's existence, the players remained in the driver's seat. But by the end of the 1915 season it was clear that would change.

Sportswriter H. T. McDaniel observed: "Signs of the coming of economical measures have not been lacking, but it has remained for the bosses of the Chicago Cubs to come out with the flat-footed announcement that hereafter they'll give no player a long contract. Hereafter no player will be tendered a contract for longer than two years, and that will be only in exceptional cases. The rank and the file must be satisfied with one-year contracts.

"Ostensibly the reason for this switch back to old principles is that long agreements give players ample opportunity to shirk. That's one reason, and undoubtedly a good one, but there is another cause, and that is when a player loses form and slides in ability there is no protection for the owner who has given a long contract.

"The Federal League's greatest trouble right now is that it is tied up with three and five-year contracts to players who have seen their best days. National and American League owners are also up against the same proposition, though to a lesser degree than the outlaws.

"With one-year contracts in vogue there'll be no hesitancy in slicing salaries or in attaching the tinware [i.e., releasing him] when a player slips. With long-time agreements this protection for the owners is impossible" (H. T. McDaniel, *Cleveland Leader*, reprinted in *Sporting News*, December 2, 1915).

The Federal League signed a peace treaty with the other major leagues a few weeks later. With the players' bargaining power thus curtailed, long-term contracts soon became very rare. *Sporting Life* observed, "The long term contracts have been abolished for all time. The club owners were forced to give such contracts three years ago because of the fight with the Federal League. But the behavior of some of the star players who tied up their employers for three consecutive seasons has put an end to the custom. . . . Feeling sure of their salaries they did not extend themselves. They regarded base ball as a secondary consideration and thought more about automobile driving and tango teas than their duties on the field" (*Sporting Life*, February 3, 1917).

The last poignant reminder of the Federal League's penchant for multi-year contracts was a player named Rupert Mills, who had signed a two-year contract before the 1915 season. When the league folded a year later, Mills, who had studied law at Notre Dame, saw no reason why his contract should not be honored. Club owner Pat Powers thought he could deter Mills by suggesting sarcastically that he ought to perform in order to be paid. This tactic proved no more effective than had the attempt nearly four decades earlier to discourage Joe Borden. Mills began showing up for work at the empty park each morning and practicing baseball drills. He explained to the press, "I report every morning at 9:30 o'clock for morning practice and work out until 11 o'clock. I do mostly pitching in the morning to get wise to my curves for the afternoon game and when the umpire—that's me too—calls 'Play' I just go out and bang the ball around the lot." Eventually, Powers gave in and bought out his contract (Cappy Gagnon, *Notre Dame Baseball Greats*, 73; Irwin Chusid, "The

Short, Happy Life of the Newark Peppers," *Baseball Research Journal* 20 [1991], 44–45).

In the aftermath of the Federal League's demise, it was several years before long-term contracts came back into vogue. Appropriately, Babe Ruth led the way, signing a three-year contract in 1919 and a five-year deal in 1922. The prosperity of the 1920s enabled a few other stars to land multi-year pacts, such as Edd Roush, who signed three-year contracts in both 1924 and 1927 (Eugene Murdock, *Baseball Between the Wars*, 140, 153).

During the Great Depression multi-year contracts again became rare. Marty Marion signed a four-year contract in 1936 and claimed that this was one of the first long-term contracts (William Mead, *Even the Browns*, 43). In fact it was just the latest revival of a sporadic tradition that was sixty years old, though Marion's case was unusual in that Branch Rickey signed Marion and high school teammate Johnny Echols to four-year contracts straight out of high school (Lee Lowenfish, *Branch Rickey*, 304). Bill Werber offered a surprising explanation for the disappearance of multi-year contracts, maintaining that players of the era didn't want them: "ballplayers in those days, they would not sign a contract for two or three years and you know why they wouldn't? Because they felt they were going to have a great year and they'd ask for more money the next year. I played thirteen years and I never had more than a one-year contract—never wanted more than one year. I felt like I was going to have a hell of a year and next year I'd stick 'em" (quoted in Brent Kelley, *In the Shadow of the Babe*, 117).

The dawn of the free-agency era in 1976 placed a renewed emphasis on multi-year contracts. Many clubs, led by the Kansas City Royals, sought to lock up their best players and avoid the threat of losing a star to free agency. But the tactic proved a double-edged sword, often locking a club into a contract that lasted much longer than the player's effectiveness.

Whether to sign a player to a long-term contract remains a crucial dilemma for general managers. At least, however, they no longer have to worry whether the players will be distracted by tango teas.

18.5.5   Guaranteed Contracts. In the nineteenth century, player contracts were guaranteed only for ten days unless specified otherwise. The 1879 adoption of the reserve rule (see **18.2.1**) accordingly meant that players were committed to the ball clubs in perpetuity while being assured only of payment for ten days if they were ill, injured, or playing poorly. This naturally struck the players as unjust, but it reflected the reality of baseball's shaky financial status, which dictated that no one in the game had much assurance of what the future would bring. Minor league clubs routinely went belly-up in midseason and left their players without an income, so there was limited sympathy when a similar fate befell an unproductive player.

St. Louis outfielder Henry Oberbeck was released in 1883 for alleged "inefficiency" and sued to receive his salary for the full length of the contract. The case was "regarded as a test case, and was fought very earnestly," with Oberbeck winning (*Louisville Courier-Journal,* March 4, 1884). But it was soon forgotten.

The early twentieth century saw baseball make great strides toward financial stability, which made the persistence of the ten-day clause all the more irksome to players. After the 1902 season Ed Delahanty signed a contract with New York that called for him to be paid even if he were injured or enjoined by the courts from playing for New York. But Delahanty was a star with the leverage of a rival league; most players continued to enjoy no such security.

As discussed under "Pay for Injured Players" (**18.5.6**), by the early twentieth century there was an unwritten understanding that clubs should not release a player who was injured in the course of play. In 1916 the National Commission finally guaranteed the right of injured players to be paid for the balance of their contracts. But this still left players vulnerable to being released, traded, or sent to the minors with payment at the prior rate continuing only for ten days. In addition, the National Commission's apparent generosity was further undercut by its simultaneous efforts to eliminate long-term contracts.

The inequity of the ten-day clause was one of the themes of Robert Murphy's 1946 attempt to form a player's guild. In order to thwart Murphy, the owners agreed to extend the period to thirty days (Robert F. Burk, *Much More Than a Game,* 93; *Chicago Tribune,* September 17, 1946). Player representative Dixie Walker commented that the increase was "not too important. The owners would have changed that to sixty days—even a year—if we wanted it. We didn't asked [sic] for any more than thirty days for a very good reason. Old ball players would have been hurt more than anyone else. The veteran released outright would never be given

a chance to make a comeback if the club had to guarantee him a year's pay—even two months' pay for signing a contract. But a club like the Yankees will gamble 30 days' pay on George McQuinn being able to help them. Who can tell but maybe he'll have several more years of baseball because of this new chance?" (Michael Gaven, "Big League Blues," unidentified clipping in Max Lanier Hall of Fame File, apparently from February 26, 1947).

In the free-agent era, increased player leverage has brought a new level of security to contracts. They are still not entirely guaranteed, however, and players like Ron Gant and Aaron Boone have been released for being injured in the course of prohibited activities.

18.5.6   Pay for Injured Players. Early baseball had such razor-thin profit margins that early contracts were guaranteed only for ten days. Players with serious injuries were routinely released, and this did not offend the sensibilities of the period. An 1876 note stated, "The Athletics have only $847.21 in the treasury. [Ezra] Sutton has been refused his pay on account of his inability to play third base. He said that his arm was bad and he could not play there, but he was willing, while disabled, to take half pay" (*Boston Daily Advertiser,* June 16, 1876). In 1880 the *New York Clipper* commended William Hague, who "had the misfortune to lame his arm, and, finding that he could not throw with his usual precision, he honorably asked to be released" (*New York Clipper,* October 23, 1880).

An exception occurred in 1879: "The Stars of Cincinnati at a recent meeting passed a resolution to allow both Miller and Houtz (two of their players who are disabled, and likely to be for some months) their full salary, and furnish men to play in their positions" (*New York Clipper,* July 5, 1879). But it is hard to know whether this club acted out of magnanimity or to ensure that it did not lose these players to rival teams.

Moreover such generosity was far from universal. Ross Barnes was the National League's leading hitter in 1876 but missed most of the following year due to illness. Chicago withheld his salary, and Barnes sued but lost his case. In reporting the result, Henry Chadwick argued for a middle ground in such cases: "If illness is induced by the work of his services on the ballfield, then a player's salary should not be stopped on that account. But, if it arises from ordinary causes, it is rather hard upon a club to demand pay for the time lost" (*New York Clipper*, December 7, 1878).

This position will seem harsh to today's ears, but it is not unreasonable in the context of the era. Concepts such as worker's compensation and sick pay were still emerging or in the future, and baseball was not in a position to be more generous than other American employers.

When Cap Anson suffered a serious liver ailment in 1879, it revived the issue: "A nice point is likely to arise out of Anson's retirement. It will be remembered that Ross Barnes was in 1877 a member of the Chicago team, but became afflicted almost in the same way as Anson is, so that he was unable to play for the remainder of that season. He was denied his salary, and had to sue for it. The courts decided against him. Now Barnes wants to know whether the Chicagos will pay Anson in full this season, so as to keep him next year. Barnes says if they do they must also pay him. He will have a voice in the matter, being still a stockholder of the Chicago Club" (*New York Clipper*, September 13, 1879).

Similarly, at an emergency meeting in the midst of a disappointing 1881 campaign, some Providence stockholders "demanded to know why the salaries of players out of the game because of illness or injury was not taken from their pay. One mentioned the fact that [Paul] Hines had been out of the line-up for several days because of an injured finger, and declared Hines owed the club $100" (William D. Perrin, *Days of Greatness*, 13).

By the 1880s players had begun to take precautions. When Detroit's Jimmy Manning broke his arm in 1886, the *Detroit Free Press* reported, "Every member of the Detroit team carries an accident policy. The boys also have a mutual benefit association. A portion of his salary will be paid by the club and, all in all, Manning will receive about $75 a week" (*Detroit Free Press*, June 5, 1886).

An infielder named John Pickett was released by Baltimore in the middle of the 1892 season. Since his contract did not include the usual ten-day clause, Pickett sued for the balance of his 1892 salary. Baltimore contended that they should not have to pay because the ballplayer "was slow in his movement, and had a sore arm which incapacitated him from being of service to the club." Pickett won his case but never played in the major leagues again (Robert Burk, *Never Just a Game*, 124; Jim Charlton, ed., *The Baseball Chronology*, 96).

A few years later Baltimore took a different tack with John McGraw by continuing to pay his salary while he recovered from typhoid. The ostensible reason was that "Baltimore always appreciates the services of faithful, hustling players like McGraw" (*Boston Globe*, July 2, 1896). It seems more likely, however, that the real difference was that McGraw was a star, and the Orioles were unwilling to risk losing his services to a rival. Unproven rookies were not so fortunate, with Chicago's Josh Reilly having his pay stopped that same season when he contracted typhoid fever (*Cincinnati Enquirer*, July 12, 1896; reprinted in Howard W. Rosenberg, *Cap Anson 1*, 146–147).

In 1900 Philadelphia tried to have it both ways by suspending injured Harry Wolverton (*Sporting Life*, August 22, 1900). Fortunately the advent of the American League gave players some leverage. The players came to expect fairer treatment in the ensuing years, though there were still exceptions. In 1904, for example, "The news of the release of Pat Carney, the Boston Nationals' outfielder and emergency left-handed pitcher, came as a great surprise to Boston fans. . . . As Carney was injured in the middle of the season, while actually playing for the Boston management, his release is entirely against the ethics of the National League. Players generally are not released when laid up in service" (*Washington Post*, September 9, 1904). Both Pittsburgh and Chicago offered contracts to Carney, but he indicated a preference for making "the Boston magnates 'come across' with the balance of his salary" (*Washington Post*, September 24, 1904).

In 1908 Ty Cobb demanded a clause that would guarantee his contract in the case of injury. National Commission chairman Garry Herrmann responded: "That's a very peculiar demand Cobb makes. Our base ball contracts protect a player for a reasonable period if he is injured while playing. But such a clause is hardly necessary. Every club will protect its players. I have never heard of one that would not." After citing several examples of injured players who had been retained by their club, he concluded, "Of course, a club reserves the right to release a player when he becomes absolutely useless. But you look back over base ball, and you will find that mighty few deserving men have ever been treated shabbily. . . . It is patent that no club is going to run the risk of losing a player by cutting off his salary because he is injured" (*Sporting News*, February 6, 1908).

On December 2, 1916, the National Commission approved a new wording for player contracts that made explicit an injured player's right to be paid for the remainder of his contract. The owners maintained that this merely ratified what was already customary, while the players felt there were still exceptions (I. E. Sanborn, "New Contract of Majors Has Ten Day Clause," *Chicago Tribune*, December 3, 1916).

Around this time, in July 1915, the National League created the first Disabled List. But the rule was scrapped after the 1916 season and wasn't revived until 1941, when both leagues adopted a rule allowing clubs to place up to two players on the disabled list for a minimum of sixty days (thanks to Cliff Blau). The rules have changed frequently since then.

As was always the case with financial matters, the Negro Leagues lagged far behind their white counterparts. In 1940 Newark Eagles pitcher Daltie Cooper broke his foot during a game and was promptly released by team owners Abe and Effa Manley. Cooper appealed to the New Jersey Workmen's Compensation Board, and an arbitrator found the team liable and forced the Manleys to admit they were violating the law by failing to provide disability insurance (Neil Lanctot, *Negro League Baseball*, 183–184).

18.5.7   Pay for Spring Training. The general sentiment in the nineteenth century was that players ought to report for the start of the season in condition. Ownership felt that if the players required time to get into shape, they had no right to be paid for that time.

By the twentieth century, spring training had become customary (see **24.2.2** and **24.2.3**) and the issue of payment for this period began to be controversial. Johnny Evers and Hugh Fullerton wrote in 1910, "One constant source of friction is the rule governing reporting for spring training. Many players have other business interests and object to spending six weeks training, without pay, when the time might be profitably occupied" (John J. Evers and Hugh S. Fullerton, *Touching Second*, 54). In 1912 the new baseball Fraternity requested that the players' salaries include spring training. Tigers owner Frank Navin indignantly responded that he had no intention of paying players to get in shape (*Sporting Life*, November 30, 1912).

In the face of mounting pressure from the players, the owners pled poverty. In 1915, in order to cut costs, the National League mandated that training camps could open no earlier than March 1. The *Sporting News* showed why it was becoming known as the owners' mouthpiece by writing: "Base ball is the only business where a highly paid employe is prepared for his work at the expense of the employer and the club owners are beginning to acknowledge the sense of the argument that it is a burden that they should not be expected to shoulder. Within the next few years, and a pin may be stuck in this prediction, players will be ordered to report to their managers a week or ten days previous to the opening of the season for instruction in team drills and signals. It will be required of each player that he shall be in physical condition to do his best, and if he is not, suspension without pay will follow until he is in that condition" (*Sporting News*, March 4, 1915).

A seemingly inevitable showdown was averted by the willingness of large crowds to pay to watch spring training games. It slowly became clear that neither the owners nor the players needed to bear the costs when the fans were more than happy to do so. By 1923 the *Sporting News* had changed its tune and now editorialized that it was unfair for owners to make money off spring training exhibition games without paying players (*Sporting News*, March 1, 1923).

My understanding, however, is that the owners never did concede the point. The players instead settled for higher salaries, an earlier start to paydays, and spring training expense money.

18.5.8   Year-round Pay. Early contracts usually ran for six months, which meant that the owners' financial obligations to their players began on Opening Day and ended as soon as the season ended. As players took advantage of this to engage in lucrative barnstorming tours, owners began to reconsider. Chris Von der Ahe, in particular, was concerned that his players were getting injured during these games.

Jonathan Fraser Light explained that matters came to a head in 1899 when a player named George Wrigley tried to join a major league club after his minor league club's season ended. As a result, language that became known as the Cincinnati Agreement was added to the standard playing contract. It read: "The Club's right of reservation of the Player, and renewal of this contract as aforesaid, and the promise of the Player not to play otherwise than with the Club or an assignee thereof, have been taken into consideration in determining the salary specified herein and the undertaking by the Club to pay said salary is the consideration for both said reservation, renewal, option and promise, and the Player's service" (Jonathan Fraser Light, *The Cultural Encyclopedia of Baseball*, 612; see also *Sporting News*, January 13, 1900).

This prevented players from joining other clubs, but it did not stop barnstorming. Some clubs tried twelve-month contracts in 1910 (Robert Burk, *Never Just a Game*, 183). S. E. McCarty noted after the 1915 season that owners were again considering twelve-month contracts to eliminate barnstorming (*Pittsburgh Leader*, reprinted in *Sporting News*, November 4, 1915).

18.5.9   Pay for Performance.

The idea of paying players based upon performance is a very old one. As early as 1878 it was reported that Indianapolis president William Pettit "proposed at a recent meeting of that club a scheme for grading the salaries of professional players in 1879, which is decidedly unique" (*New York Clipper*, April 20, 1878). Pettit's idea involved having the league secretary divide the players into first and second class based on their statistical performance, and paying them accordingly (*New York Sunday Mercury*, April 13, 1878).

A 1911 article reported, "Chief Bender of the Athletics has had a peculiar contract to sign for the last several seasons." It explained that, beginning in 1908, "Connie Mack, instead of giving the Indian a big salary, as he deserves, has him sign a blank contract, and at the end of the season he puts in a bonus which he thinks pays for the Indian's work" (*Mansfield* [Ohio] *News*, September 23, 1911).

While such a system would appear to have many advantages, it is easy to see how it could lead to hard feelings, especially if tried on a large scale.

18.5.10   Signing Bonuses.

The entry on "Climbing the Ladder" (18.2.3) includes a Ted Sullivan anecdote about an under-the-table signing bonus. Although Sullivan was noted for his exaggerations, no doubt some such payments were made. Giving an "advance" to a player who signed a contract was also a common practice in nineteenth-century baseball. As the word implies, the advance was supposed to be repaid, but that didn't always happen.

The National League did its best to discourage the advance system. By 1884 Chicago was charging players 8 percent interest on advances

(*Chicago Tribune*, March 23, 1884, 3). A rule prohibiting advances entirely was adopted at the same 1879 meeting at which the reserve rule (see 18.2.1) was introduced (*New York Clipper*, October 11, 1879). But this proved impractical because players were not paid during the offseason, and many of them needed the advances to report. Players also had another reason for insisting on advances. "There was a time," explained Tim Murnane, "when all players were looking for at least one month's salary in advance, not that they were in actual need of the money, but they wanted to be on the safe side should the club prove slow in meeting their obligations. Years ago a ball player would consider the advance money the only indication of a club's soundness, and would name the price they would work for along that basis" (*Boston Globe*, January 20, 1907, 52).

Thus advances had some similarity to signing bonuses, yet owners resisted the concept of overtly paying a player for his signature. Jack Barry, for example, demanded a $500 signing bonus to sign with the Athletics in 1907. Connie Mack acquiesced but requested that Barry keep the bonus a secret, since it was his policy not to pay signing bonuses (Norman Macht, "John Joseph Barry," in David Jones, ed., *Deadball Stars of the American League*, 625).

As noted in the entry on rival major leagues (18.4.1), Dan Fletcher's 1910 attempt to compete with the existing major leagues was based entirely on signing bonuses. The established leagues remained reluctant to adopt this practice but eventually did so.

In 1927, for example, St. Louis Browns owner Phil Ball offered Ty Cobb a $40,000 contract plus a $10,000 signing bonus (*Sporting News*, February 17, 1927). Cobb turned it down and signed with the Athletics instead. It is not clear who was the first player to accept a signing bonus, but it couldn't have been long past Cobb's refusal since the "bonus baby" era is generally considered to have started with the $20,000 premium paid to Charley Devens in 1932.

18.5.11   Incentive Clauses.

Before the 1869 season the Mutuals of New York announced they would take advantage of the National Association of Base Ball Players' recognition of professional ball and begin to pay salaries. The club added: "Premiums will be paid to those who excel in the special departments of the game as shown by regular statistics at the close of the season" (*National Chronicle*, February 27, 1869).

While incentives were thus part of professional baseball from its outset, they remained rare in early contracts. Early players could be fined for a wide variety of offenses, but rarely were they rewarded. This is nicely illustrated by a story that, even if apocryphal, is highly symbolic. Cincinnati catcher Larry McLean had a clause in his 1910 contract stipulating a fine for drinking liquor. In 1911 it is said that he requested the team pay him a bonus for each time he turned down a drink (H. Allen Smith and Ira L. Smith, *Low and Inside*, 72–73).

Ironically, several nineteenth-century players did have such a clause. In 1884 John Fox of the Alleghenys was to receive a $500 bonus if he did not drink all season, with one account claiming that it applied to his teammates as well (*Washington Post*, April 13, 1884; *Brooklyn Eagle*, April 13, 1884). Ed Williamson reportedly had two separate incentive clauses in his 1888 contract. One called for an $800 bonus if he abstained from drinking, and the second provided for another $200 if he kept his weight below 190 pounds (*Boston Globe*, April 7, 1888). Boston catcher Marty Bergen became so notorious for erratic behavior that in both 1898 and 1899 his "contract called for a stated sum and a bonus to be paid in case his work was satisfactory" (Jacob Morse, *Sporting Life*, January 27, 1900, 9).

18.5.12   Performance Bonuses. Performance bonuses were relatively uncommon in the nineteenth century, though there were notable exceptions. In 1884 the *Brooklyn Eagle* reported, "Should the Louisvilles win the championship, the players of the team are each to receive a handsome cash bonus, and [Guy] Hecker will be given a house and a lot" (*Brooklyn Eagle*, August 10, 1884). A. G. Spalding gave every Chicago player a $100 bonus after the 1885 season "for having abstained from intoxicating drinks and orgies and for winning the pennant" (*Washington Post*, October 7, 1885; quoted in David Fleitz, *Cap Anson*, 129).

The next few years saw bonuses emerge as a way for owners to get around their own efforts to keep salaries low. Most often this was done by appointing a star player as team captain and increasing his salary accordingly. Such bonuses became common enough that the effort to adopt a firm salary cap after the 1888 season (see **18.4.3**) was accompanied by a clause explicitly permitting "the payment of extra compensation for the services of one person to each club as field captain or team manager" (*Chicago Tribune*, November 23, 1888, 5).

While there were real duties associated with these positions, it was generally understood that the extra pay was a way to avoid salary caps. After Jack Glasscock resigned as Indianapolis captain, he complained about a $500 pay cut and had to be reminded that that amount had been his captain's pay (*Chicago Inter-Ocean*, March 11, 1888, 12). Indeed, if the captaincy was already occupied, other approaches were likely to be used. Onetime college star Jim Tyng, for example, was lured out of retirement by a unique contract offer that called for him to receive the maximum "$2000 a year as a player and $1000 a year as director of athletic sports" (*Philadelphia Inquirer*, July 7, 1888).

Bonuses became rarer in the penurious nineties. Captains continued to receive bonuses for fulfilling their duties, but by and large owners took advantage of the single major league to economize.

A 1907 article in the *Detroit Times* showed that the use of performance bonuses had begun to reemerge: "In 1906 Cleveland originated the [bonus] system by offering its pitchers added money to the amount of $500 for the ones that won 20 games or over. Cleveland had a winning ball club that season, led the league for a good share of the time, made a lot of money and finished well up in the race. In 1907 the bonus system was discarded and Cleveland couldn't quite reach the top all season, in spite of her great team. Also her finish, considering her opportunities, was far from being a brilliant one.

"In 1907 the Detroit Tigers furnished the material for the bonus experiment. The team went ahead with a wonderful burst of speed, won the pennant and improved its position from a bonusless sixth in 1906 to the honor of a championship when the twirlers were working for that extra money" (reprinted in *Sporting News*, December 5, 1907).

In spite of these impressive results, the article noted that Tigers owner Frank Navin was mulling over whether to continue the bonuses in 1908. For one thing, American League president Ban Johnson was opposed to the whole concept. In addition, it did not seem fair to give bonuses to pitchers but not to hitters. Yet extending the bonuses to all players would be difficult to do fairly and would amount to a general salary increase.

As owners continued to experiment with bonuses, they learned how difficult it is to unring a bell—once the precedent had been established, players came to expect bonuses. The issue was a contentious one at the owners' meeting following the 1908 season, with National Commission chairman Garry Herrmann blaming Detroit owner William Yawkey for creating a precedent by giving his players a $15,000 bonus after the 1907 World Series. But the *Detroit Free Press* maintained that White Sox owner Charles Comiskey had in fact begun the practice by giving his players a similar bonus after the 1906 World Series (*Detroit Free Press*, February 19, 1909).

The difficulty of eliminating such bonuses was further illustrated by a 1917 article that observed: "Club owners in the major leagues are beginning to feel that they have been making mistakes in offering players bonuses and making them presents at the end of the season for exceptionally good work. Those who have done it have had more trouble signing their players to new contracts than any others. From the *Philadelphia Ledger*, we learn that the Philadelphia National League Club furnishes one instance of how much the players appreciate these gifts. Last season Al Demaree was promised a bonus for winning a certain number of games. On the day he won a double-header he was presented with a $100 bill for his work, and as he accepted it, the cartoonist [Demaree] reminded President [William] Baker not to forget there was a bonus coming to him." After providing additional examples, the writer concluded, "It would be a good thing if a rule were passed prohibiting gifts and bonuses in the future, as there would be less haggling over salaries each year" (*Sporting Life*, March 10, 1917).

In American professional baseball, performance bonuses are now awarded only on a contractual basis. Matters are very different in Japan, where there is a long-standing concept of "kantoku shou" or "fight money"—a cash reward that managers give to players after they play a key role in a victory (David Picker, "More Than a Handshake Deal for Japanese Baseball Players," *New York Times*, April 17, 2007).

18.5.13 No-trade Clauses. NFL players were obtaining no-trade clauses by 1965, but baseball players had a harder time gaining similar guarantees (*New York Times*, January 28, 1965). According to Scott Schul, Bobby Wallace signed a five-year contract with a no-trade clause when he jumped to the American League in 1902 (Scott E. Schul, "Rhoderick John 'Bobby' Wallace," in David Jones, ed., *Deadball Stars of the American League*, 777). On January 9, 1915,

Eddie Collins signed a contract with the White Sox that included the wording: "Player is not to be released to any other club without his consent" (Collins Hall of Fame file; thanks to Rick Huhn). But such clauses were very rare. Requests for such clauses by Frank Howard and Rusty Staub in the early 1970s were refused (*Sporting News*, April 17, 1970, and March 18, 1972). Thus baseball's first no-trade clauses of the unionized era may have been the ones in the ten-and-five rule (see **13.2.7** "Vetoed Trades"), which was included in all contracts as part of the Basic Agreement of February 25, 1973.

Owners continued to oppose extending no-trade clauses to players with less tenure, a course that had unintended consequences. The Dodgers' refusal to grant Andy Messersmith's no-trade request in 1974 led Messersmith to play out his option and bring the grievance that toppled the reserve clause (see **18.4.5** "Free Agency") (Charles P. Korr, *The End of Baseball as We Knew It*, 148). No-trade clauses gradually became common during the free-agent era.

(vi) Commercialization

The incursion of commercialization into the national pastime is not nearly as recent a phenomenon as might be imagined.

18.6.1 Commercialization. Determining when baseball became commercialized is not possible, since elements of commercialism began to creep in very early. In particular, early clubs were not shy about asking local businessmen for financial support.

In 1866, for instance, the *Kalamazoo Telegraph* gave readers this little nudge: "the ball-players of this place have never received assistance or encouragement from the citizens, in the way of defraying expenses on match days or providing them an [sic] uniform, as almost every town is doing or has done" (*Kalamazoo Weekly Telegraph*, October 3, 1866).

Two years later an Omaha, Nebraska, player was more direct: "Our late defeat by the Marshalltown Base Ball Club, Aug. 6th, has called forth a good deal of comment by our citizens generally, and it is hoped that the defeat will be the means of giving a renewed life, vitality and interest in this community to the game, to make this club a success. It will require the good will and pecuniary indorsement of our people. We are all laboring young men. We believe the game in Omaha is beneficial to all young men whom we can interest therein. We know it to

be an honorable game—of national reputation—encouraged by all, disparaged by none,
except it be Omaha, whose citizens, excepting
a few, have ever given us the cold shoulder,
and from them have received no word or act of
encouragement. When the Marshalltown club,
the champions of Iowa, determined to play us,
we endeavored to collect sufficient funds from
our citizens to entertain them while here; we
found it impossible to raise the sum of $100.
No subscription exceeded five dollars, and only
four that amount, a few of two dollars, and the
balance of one dollar donations; and this in a
flourishing city of 17,000 inhabitants. Compare
this with the little city of Marshalltown toward
its club—a city of 3,000 inhabitants. They donated $500 to the club, furnished its members
with uniforms, sent their Mayor with them to
this city, and many of their most wealthy and
influential citizens with their wives, daughters
and friends of the members, accompanied them
here and out of the grounds, to cheer and encourage them.

"We were beaten, yet there is not a member
of the Marshalltown club but acknowledged
that our boys are superior players, *individu-
ally*. But a want of funds has, until the present,
prevented a substantial organization. This was
the cause, and the only one, of our late defeat"
(*New England Base Ballist*, August 20, 1868).

While the Omaha club no doubt wanted
both "the good will and pecuniary indorsement
of our people," there can be little doubt from
this account that financial support was a higher
priority. This new reality caused efforts to so-
licit funds to become more organized during
the 1870s. A newspaper in Marshall, Michigan,
hinted in 1872 that "a committee from the
Pastime will be calling on businessmen this
week to enlist honorary members" (*Marshall
Statesman*, June 5, 1872). A Muskegon paper
went straight to the point: "business men of
our city are invited to give the club a helping
hand. In Grand Rapids the clubs are largely
aided by those interested in the game, and our
citizens are probably aware that the Muskegons
are deserving of their support. The Club desire
to return thanks to Messrs. Hackley & Co., &
C. Davis & Co., for lumber, and to Dr. Marvin,
Harry Pillsbury, and others, for substantial
donations" (*Muskegon News and Reporter*, July
28, 1877).

Plaintive pleas to not "let this nine go to
pieces for want of patronage" became common,
and they began to be accompanied by new ways
of recognizing businessmen who responded to

these appeals (*Kalamazoo Telegraph*, June 24,
1879). Researcher David Arcidiacono discovered an 1875 article noting that the officers
and stockholders of the Elm City Club of New
Haven were open to the possible leasing of the
ballpark fence for advertisements: "The subject
of allowing the fence to be used for advertising
purposes was discussed, and steps will be taken
to lease the fence" (*New Haven Evening Register*,
March 4, 1875).

By the mid-1880s the idea had come to
fruition. An 1886 note stated: "An enterprising Washingtonian business firm has hired a
section of the ball park fence for advertising
purposes, and will give $25 to the first player on
the home team who strikes it with a batted ball"
(*Detroit Free Press*, April 24, 1886). John Thorn
reports that the Polo Grounds had advertising by Opening Day that year. An advertising
fence was also erected at Detroit's Recreation
Park that year in order to prevent spectators
from watching the game from outside the park
(*Detroit Free Press*, June 4, 1886). There may
have been still earlier fence ads—a note in the
Hartford Courant at the start of the 1884 season
stated, "Signs on the base ball fence are to be
let this season for advertisements" (*Hartford
Courant*, March 24, 1884, 1).

A few early clubs went much further, with
some of them starting down the road toward
the much more recent trend of selling naming
rights to stadiums. The 1877 Hop Bitters of
Rochester of the International Association bore
the name of an alcohol-based patent medicine.
It just so happened that team owner Asa T.
Soule was also the president of the Hop Bitters
Manufacturing Company. Henry Chadwick
was appalled by the concept. Much as some
current broadcasters try to avoid using commercialized stadium names, Chadwick referred
to the club as "the nine organized and run by
a firm in Rochester, N.Y., for advertising purposes" (*New York Clipper*, November 15, 1879).
When the Hop Bitters disbanded in 1879, he
remarked acidly, "The Hop Bitters team experiment has simply been a mere advertising dodge,
and now that the manager has accomplished all
the advertising benefit from them he can expect, he comes out in his true colors, disbands
one team, and announces the other as a mere
gate money exhibition team" (*Brooklyn Eagle*,
July 22, 1879).

They were not the last such club, as the
St. Louis Post-Dispatch felt obliged to remind
its readers in 1889, "Clubs having names of
an advertising nature will not be advertised

in this column" (*St. Louis Post-Dispatch*, April 13, 1889). The Page Fence Giants, a top African-American barnstorming club, found time during games to promote the Monarch Bicycle Company and the club's namesake, the Page Fence Wire Company (Jerry Malloy, ed., *Sol White's History of Colored Base Ball*, xxxii; Michael E. Lomax, *Black Baseball Entrepreneurs, 1860–1901*, 136–137). A nine in Jacksonville, Florida, agreed to wear uniforms bearing the name of a bookstore in exchange for a suit of clothes for each player. Their decision prompted a local paper to lament: "that young persons, growing up in a community where shortly they expect to take the honorable places of their fathers and elders, should so compromise their gentlemanly dignity is certainly matter for profound regret. It hurts the pride of every other amateur who hears of it; it matters not who or what the thing advertised may be, whether a great patriarchal trades house or a petty tenement shop; the loved name of amateur, which touches the better part of man, his pride of physical and mental excellence, his love of art for art's sake; of science, for its benefits to man; of skill, for the beauty which displays itself in deft movements, is outraged and abused when it is made merchandise for gain and greed, or betrayed to the common uses of the advertiser" (quoted in Kevin M. McCarthy, *Baseball in Florida*, 10. McCarthy's footnote cites the *Florida Times-Union*, a Jacksonville paper, of May 19, 1883. But his in-text reference gives the year as 1893).

Other manifestations of commercialism in baseball also evoked outraged protests. In 1877 the International Association's booklet of constitution and rules was denounced as "not a creditable publication, because it is defaced on every page with the cards of some uniform-manufacturers. It has almost lost its proper character as a book of rules, and become a mere manufacturers' circular" (*Chicago Tribune*, May 13, 1877).

The most bizarre advertisement of the era—maybe in the history of baseball—was one that appeared in Kansas City in 1888 when that city had entries in both the American Association and the Western Association. The latter club "paid $300 for the privilege of printing a sign on the inside fence of the American association club. The sign, in immense letters, read as follows: 'If you want to see a lively game of base ball go to the grounds of the western association club'" (*Cleveland Plain Dealer*, April 29, 1888).

Thus it is clear that the process of commercialization was beginning to manifest itself in a number of forms by the end of the nineteenth century. It is equally evident that it was continuing to be met with stout resistance.

18.6.2 Endorsements. The earliest commercial endorsement by a ballplayer that I'm aware of appeared in the *Davenport Gazette* on March 26, 1877, with John Dolan, catcher of the Red Stockings of St. Louis, offering a testimonial for the ability of Vordick's Rheumatic Liniment to relieve "a very sore hand, sprained while catching a fly ball." A month later, on April 30, an ad in the *Chicago Evening Journal* read, "The Chicago Base Ball Club delight in drinking mead at Gunther's." The mead being referred to was moxie mead, a soft drink of the time (quoted in *Baseball in Old Chicago*, 38).

18.6.3 Hit Sign, Win Suit. The most famous of all the "Hit Sign" fence advertisements was the "Hit Sign, Win Suit" sign at Brooklyn's Ebbets Field. Brooklyn clothier Abe Stark sponsored this advertisement from the early 1930s until the Dodgers' move to Los Angeles.

Gimmicks of this type date back to the nineteenth century, with an 1886 example at Washington's Swampoodle Grounds being cited in the entry on "Commercialization" (**18.6.1**). Gerard S. Petrone suggested that they gradually evolved from generous offers by local businessmen into more sophisticated advertising ploys (Gerard S. Petrone, *When Baseball Was Young*, 43).

The most famous campaign was the "Hit the Bull" ads sponsored by the American Tobacco Company from 1911 to 1913. The firm erected large wooden bulls to advertise their Bull Durham brand and placed them deep in the outfields—but within the field of play—of stadiums all over the country. A fifty-dollar prize went to any batter who hit one, but the promotion does not appear to have been very costly to the tobacco company. Four Kitty League clubs had the signs but in 1911 only one batter managed to hit one, and in 1912 "all attempts by the players to drive the ball into some part of Mr. Bull's anatomy proved fruitless" (John T. Ross, *Sporting News*, December 12, 1912).

They also proved a menace to outfielders, and Joe Jackson was knocked unconscious when he ran into the bull in a game on September 12, 1913. The injury cost Cleveland its slim chance in the pennant race (Gerard S. Petrone, *When Baseball Was Young*, 43–44). As noted earlier (see 14.4.12 "Bullpens"), the bulls on the outfield grass may have also been responsible for the term "bullpen" becoming the name of the area where pitchers warm up.

18.6.4 Publicly Owned Ballpark.

In 1913 the *Sporting News* reported, "So successful has been the plan of the city owning the ball park in Dubuque, where the Three-I League team plays, that a similar scheme is suggested in Rock Island and the city authorities seem favorable. It is the idea that they shall buy the Rock Island ball park, one of the best equipped in the minor leagues, and lease it for a nominal sum to a club which will secure a franchise either in the Western League, the Three-I or the Central Association" (*Sporting News*, August 28, 1913).

The following month *Sporting Life* reported the results: "Rock Island voted, by a comfortable majority, to indorse the project to purchase a ball park and put the city back on the base ball map with a league team, a canvass of returns from the election showed on Saturday. Five hundred women, voting for the first time under the new Illinois suffrage law, were nearly unanimous in favor of base ball for Rock Island and swelled the majority. The fact that the $20,000 bond issue approved provides for the purchase of six acres outside the park for a municipal athletic field made the proposition specially attractive to women voters. With the ball park privately owned by the Rock Island Base Ball Association, league base ball was not a paying venture in Rock Island" (*Sporting Life*, September 20, 1913). *Sporting News* reported that Rock Island was the first city to have held a special election for such a purpose (*Sporting News*, September 25, 1913).

The first major league park to be publicly owned was Cleveland Municipal Stadium in 1932. Two years later the city of Syracuse found a new angle by making use of Federal Emergency Relief Association (FERA) funds to build a ballpark (*Sporting News*, December 20, 1934).

18.6.5 Corporate Ownership.

When Anheuser Busch purchased the St. Louis Cardinals in 1953, it was the first time the major leagues had had a corporate owner, and this development disturbed many observers. Many of their concerns involved the commercialization of the game.

Columnist Ira Seebacher noted that this new phenomenon was causing speculation as to "whether the club will be run strictly as a sporting proposition with no idea of enhancing the new owners' product." He wondered if the brewery would permit opponents to sell broadcast time on games involving the Cardinals to rival beer companies. He even speculated that the Budweiser eagle might replace the traditional Redbird as the team's logo. He suggested that "the best thing that could happen would be for Ford Frick to step in right from the start and rule that it is undignified to connect too closely any commercial product with baseball. Baseball has dignity and its dignity must not be too brazenly trampled even by such wealthy men as now own the Cards" (*New York Morning Telegraph*, reprinted in *Sporting News*, March 4, 1953).

18.6.6 Naming Rights.

At least one nineteenth-century ball club did something akin to today's practice of selling naming rights. In 1883 a ballpark in Vincennes, Indiana, was "called Peabody park in honor of Captain W. W. Peabody, who gives the ground rent free, and who has otherwise encouraged the enterprise" (*Evansville Journal*, June 15, 1883).

Shortly after Anheuser-Busch bought the Cardinals in 1953 and became the major league's first corporate owners, president August Busch announced plans to rechristen Sportsman's Park as "Budweiser Stadium." After a public outcry, the name Busch Stadium was selected instead. *Sporting News* editorialized that Busch "is to be congratulated on having quickly abandoned his intention to rename Sportsman's Park Budweiser Stadium in favor of Busch Stadium" (*Sporting News*, April 22, 1953). The next year the crafty Busch unveiled Busch Bavarian beer.

There was renewed controversy in 1964 when CBS purchased the New York Yankees. Sportswriter Leonard Koppett noted, "There was talk of conflict of interest; antitrust action seemed possible; for weeks the papers were full of stories about why the deal might be a bad thing" (Leonard Koppett, "The Ex-National Sport Looks to Its Image," *New York Times*, December 20, 1964). Eventually the sale went through, and the concept of corporate ownership came to be taken for granted. In the process, however, onlookers such as Koppett maintained that baseball lost its special status with many fans.

Chapter 19

VARIANTS

BASEBALL AS PLAYED by the Knickerbockers borrowed elements from several bat-and-ball games and established a single way of playing. Thus there were actually variants of baseball before there was regulation baseball, in the form of games known by such names as trapball, rounders, one o' cat, stoolball, roundball, and town ball.

The Knickerbockers' version initially tended to drive out its competitors, most notably the Massachusetts game, also known as roundball. Eventually, however, variant methods of playing the game reemerged. While none have seriously threatened baseball as a spectator sport, some have long and interesting histories. Others sounded like good ideas at first, only to quickly prove otherwise.

Selecting the entries for this chapter was not easy. I have tried to mention any version that became very popular or seemed historically significant. Other games were included because they were revived elements of the earliest days of baseball, or even harkened back to the bat-and-ball games that preceded the Knickerbockers. These criteria are admittedly arbitrary, and many other variants could just as easily have been selected.

19.1 Indoor Baseball. In 1897 an unnamed Chicagoan gave this account of the origins of indoor baseball:

"Indoor baseball originated in Chicago in the old Farragut Club, formerly the greatest aquatic club in the country, but now a matter of history, and came about through a frolic among the members of the club on Thanksgiving Day in 1887.

"The fellows were throwing an ordinary boxing glove around the room, which was struck at by one of the boys with a broom. George W. Hancock suddenly called out: 'Boys, let's play baseball!'

"The boys divided into two teams and took their positions. The boxing glove was used for a ball and the broomstick for a bat. They commenced their sport, using no rules farther than the kind small boys follow on the prairie, but there was great fun. When the afternoon had closed Hancock gathered the members around him and said: 'I believe this affair can be worked into a regular game of baseball, which can be played indoors, and if you all come down Saturday night I'll make up some rules and have a ball and bat which will suit the purpose of the sport and do no damage to the surroundings.'

"And it was thus that Hancock gained the title of 'Father of Indoor Baseball.' He went home and thought out some rules that would equalize the different points of the game. A large, soft ball and a small bat were made, that being the central idea evolved from the boxing glove and broomstick and the material distinction between the new game and its prototype. From this the rest of the scheme was elaborated smoothly enough" (*Detroit Free Press*, December 17, 1897). As Paul Dickson notes, Hancock's claim to be the game's inventor has never been challenged or disputed (Paul Dickson, *The Worth Book of Softball*, 48).

Indoor baseball presented some new hazards, and its inventor did his best to solve them. An 1891 article noted, "George Hancock has invented a bat with a pneumatic tip, which will prevent it slipping from the hand, thus avoiding the liability of accident to spectators" (*Chicago Tribune*, October 25, 1891).

Hancock also published his rules, which—as had been the case with baseball (see 1.3)—helped the new game to spread rapidly. By that winter the game was being enjoyed in lodge halls, gymnasiums, and even dance halls all over Chicago (Paul Dickson, *The Worth Book of Softball*, 48). Indoor baseball had caught on in St. Louis by 1891 and soon become popular in other cities (*Sporting News*, January 24, 1891). Growth continued throughout the 1890s, but then the game moved back outdoors and evolved into softball. By 1915 the indoor version had become rare enough that Jake Stahl invented a new version of indoor baseball using outdoor bats and balls in which the ball was hit into a canvas (*Chicago Tribune*, February 9, 1915).

Although George Hancock's version of indoor baseball was the one that gained popularity and eventually became softball, he wasn't the first to conceive the idea of playing baseball indoors. An 1884 article noted, "The managers of the Institute Building, Boston, are quite enthusiastic over the prospect of indoor base ball games. The inclosure is about 100 yard long by 30 wide, amply enough for an indoor foot ball field. The ball will be manufactured especially for this occasion, and will be smaller than the regulation size, and the base lines will be shortened" (*Sporting Life*, December 3, 1884). The scarcity of indoor facilities of this size naturally restricted this game's growth potential.

19.2 Softball. Softball was derived directly from indoor baseball. It was not long after indoor baseball caught on before the game was brought back outdoors. In 1895 Lewis Rober of Minneapolis was one of the leaders in convincing others of its suitability for outdoor play. Since Rober played for a team named the Kittens, the game was initially known as kitten ball. It was rechristened softball in 1926 by Walter Hakanson of Denver. Paul Dickson has observed that this was a peculiar choice of a name, since it was coined at a time when the ball used was "large and light, but not at all soft" (Paul Dickson, *The Worth Book of Softball*, 48).

19.3 Slow Pitch. Softball was originally played with fast pitching. Slow pitch first emerged around 1933 but did not become the dominant form until the 1950s. This change exemplified the curious tendency of softball to retrace baseball's history in reverse. Another notable case

in point is the Chicago style of softball, which, like early baseball, is played without gloves and with a twelve-inch (rather than a ten-inch) ball that becomes mushy as the game progresses. Columnist Mike Royko was so passionate about these features that he sued to prevent the use of gloves (Paul Dickson, *The Worth Book of Softball*, 122–123).

19.4 Over the Line. Over the Line is one of the many variants of softball, which is distinguished by being played on beaches and usually without baserunning. Like so many offshoots of softball, it has also brought back one of the features of the very early days of baseball by having pitches gently tossed to the batter (Paul Dickson, *The Worth Book of Softball*, 124–125).

19.5 Muffin Baseball. Muffin baseball might not sound like a variant because it was not played by any particular rules. But its disdain for rules was the whole point of it.

By the early 1860s, clubs were being divided up into first nines, second nines, third nines, and so on. The latter groups were often referred to as "muffin" nines, because instead of fielding the ball cleanly they usually muffed it. Rather than taking this name as an insult, the players adopted it as a badge of honor.

With baseball being taken increasingly seriously, muffin games were a way of restoring the fun. They did so by reviving the spontaneity and some of the customs of the earlier, looser way of playing baseball. At the same time they specifically parodied the excesses of professional baseball, such as arguing with umpires and importing outside players.

In their heyday during the 1860s and 1870s, muffin games attracted crowds and newspaper coverage that rivaled or surpassed professional matches. The players were often made up of prominent members of the community, such as politicians, doctors, and policemen, and if they were unfamiliar with the rules, it only added to the merriment. As was noted in one of the earliest accounts of a muffin game, "a more mirth-provoking or enjoyable game of ball is seldom seen. . . . Of course, there is no good playing, but lots of fun" (*Brooklyn Times*, July 7, 1860).

The phenomenon of muffin baseball is described at much greater length in "'Breaking Fingers and the Third Commandment': How Muffin Games Helped Renew a Sense of Belonging," a chapter in my book *Baseball Fever*, and in the final chapter of my book *But Didn't We Have Fun?*

19.6   Baseball on Ice. With baseball and ice-skating both enjoying popularity in the early 1860s, it was inevitable that someone would try to combine them. The success of the experiment was mixed.

The earliest game thus far documented was discovered by researcher Priscilla Astifan. The game occurred on Irondequoit Bay in Rochester, New York, on January 1, 1861, and featured two local clubs, the Live Oaks and Lone Stars. A crowd of more than two thousand witnessed "spirited play" and the added bonus of a triple play (*Rochester Evening Express*, January 2, 1861, also *Rochester Union and Advertiser*, January 2, 1861; cited in Priscilla Astifan, "Baseball in the Nineteenth Century," *Rochester History* LII, No. 3 [Summer 1990], 19).

On February 4, 1861, the Atlantics of Brooklyn beat the Charter Oaks 36-27 in front of a large crowd. The *Brooklyn Eagle* reported, "It will be readily understood that the game when played upon ice with skates is altogether a different sort of affair from that which the Clubs are familiar with. The most scientific player upon the play ground finds himself out of his reckoning when he has got the runaway skates to depend on, and the best skater is the best player" (*Brooklyn Eagle*, February 5, 1861). Atlantics shortstop Dickey Pearce, however, was said to excel on ice, just as he did on land (*New York Clipper*, February 14, 1861; reprinted in James L. Terry, *Long Before the Dodgers*, 94).

A similar game was almost immediately played in Detroit, eliciting this response: "A very interesting game of base ball on skates was played at the park, day before yesterday morning. Quite a large number of spectators were present to witness the sport, it being the first game of the kind ever played, in this city, on the ice. The playing was somewhat mixed on account of some of the best players being the poorest skaters and some of the poorest players the best skaters. The ice was in prime condition, but a pretty sharp breeze which blew all the morning somewhat impeded the game" (*Detroit Free Press*, February 23, 1861).

The novelty of baseball on ice seems to have worn off fairly quickly. Skaters resented the games because of the damage done to the ice (William J. Ryczek, *Baseball's First Inning*, 95). By 1865 the *Brooklyn Eagle* wrote, "We hope we shall have no more ball games on ice. . . . If any of the ball clubs want to make fools of themselves, let them go down to Coney Island and play a game on stilts" (*Brooklyn Eagle*, December 18, 1865; reprinted in James L. Terry, *Long Before the Dodgers*, 94).

While the crowds dwindled, the game continued to attract participants well into the 1880s. Over time, certain modifications to the rules were made when the game was played on ice: "A game on ice is played under rules which admit of five innings as a complete game, though more can be played if there is time. Then, too, only the square pitch or toss of the ball to the bat is allowable, no throwing the ball to the bat by the pitcher being admissable [sic]. The bound catch of a fair ball, too, counts; and each base runner makes every base simply by overrunning the line of the base, he being exempted from being put out in returning by turning to the right after crossing the line of the base. A very dead ball is used. The best skaters are required for the in fielders, and fast skaters for the out fielders. Ten players on each side make a game, there being right short stops as well as the regular short stops" (*Brooklyn Eagle*, January 9, 1887).

The rule changes were not the only element of baseball on ice that evoked early versions of baseball. Similar to muffin baseball, there were regular reminders that the activity could not be taken too seriously. One article assured readers that "it is safe to let loose one's laughter on such an occasion, for even the most enthusiastic of professionals—even he whose daily bread depends upon the game—feels that he is in a position in which he can trifle with the game because of the abnormal conditions under which it is being played" (*Harper's Weekly*, January 26, 1884; reprinted in James L. Terry, *Long Before the Dodgers*, 95).

Baseball on ice became very rare, or at least was attracting far less attention by the 1890s, but it did not entirely vanish. In 1912 it became so popular in Cleveland that plans were announced to form a league if Lake Erie froze over (*Washington Post*, January 1, 1912). *Baseball Magazine* included a photo of the game in its April 1916 issue.

As noted under "Overrunning Bases" (1.8), Jimmy Wood believed that baseball on ice was responsible for the rule change that allowed base runners to overrun first base.

19.7   Roller Skates. Baseball on roller skates was also tried during the 1880s, though with disappointing results: "The experiment of playing base ball on roller skates was tried at the Knickerbockers Roller Skating Rink at the

American Institute, New York, last week, but it was not very successful. A network is required to protect spectators who sit forward of the home base line, and a soft three ounce ball is another requirement. No bases are needed, as a three foot line—as in playing the game on ice—is all that is necessary. The ball can be delivered in any way. Small bats not over two inches in diameter, and not over thirty inches in length, should be used. The batsman should stand so as to have one foot on each side of the home base line, the home base being a painted square on the floor, with a four-foot line drawn through it. A skater in running bases has only to cross the line of each base and then turn to the right and return to the base. Fair balls caught on the bound count" (*Sporting Life*, January 7, 1885).

19.8   Freight-train Baseball. A freight-train brakeman told the *Chicago Herald* in 1886 of a new craze for freight-train baseball. He explained, "We don't do any batting, but we're great on fielding. The head brakeman stands on the front car, the rear brakeman in the middle of the train, and the conductor gets aboard the caboose. Then we play pitch, with the fireman for referee. There ain't many errors, now let me tell you. An error means a lost ball, and the man that lets it get away from him has to buy a new one. The feller that makes a wild throw, or the one that fails to stop a fair-thrown ball is the victim. The craze has run so high that I'll bet there ain't a dozen cars running out of Chicago that don't carry a stack of base balls along in their caboose. They would all say they didn't if you asked 'em, 'cause they don't want the bosses to get onto 'em, but just wait till they get out into the country, and if you're where you can see, you will see how freight-train base ball is played. Fellows that play ball on the ground may think they're having great sport, but if you want fun, and want to have the blood run pretty lively in your veins, just take a hand in a game on top of a freight train going twenty to twenty-five miles an hour" (reprinted in the *Boston Globe*, June 7, 1886).

The incentive of the men to deny this game's existence makes it difficult to know how long it lasted, and it was probably short-lived. But it may be the most bizarre setting in which baseball was ever played.

19.9   Punchball. Bill Mazer described punchball as having "amounted to 'The Official Sport of Brooklyn'" during the 1930s. The game had several advantages that made it well suited to the city streets. Most important, it could be played with minimal equipment—not even a bat—and with little chance of breaking a window or losing the ball. Many of the improvisations were reminiscent of the earliest days of baseball.

To begin with, the game was played with a soft ball: usually a beat-up tennis ball, a "pimple ball," or a "spaldeen," a bouncy rubber ball made by the Spalding Company. Catchers, pitchers, and bats were dispensed with entirely; instead the batter bounced the ball and punched it with his fist to begin the action. In addition, the number of players was flexible: "What also made the game so good was the fact that all you needed for a good game of punchball was four guys: two on each side. Invariably more kids would soon appear on the scene and you could change the team size at will."

Another touch that evoked the early days of baseball was the adaptability of the game to the terrain. Mazer explained: "The punchball 'court' consisted of home plate and three bases. Home plate was an iron sewer cover sitting in the middle of the street. First base would be off to the right, chalked into the pavement alongside the curb about 20 yards or so from home. Second base would either be another sewer top or, if they were too far apart, another chalked base. Third was chalked alongside the left curb opposite first." As described in the entry on "Home Plate" (**14.3.2**), the use of the iron sewer cover for home plate was particularly reminiscent of the early days of baseball.

The unique terrain meant that the game had a language of its own: "'Hitting a sewer,' for example, was the highest praise you could achieve on the block. Hitting a sewer meant that you were able to stroke the ball all the way past second base and on to the next sewer cover and to hell and gone down the street. Since the distance between sewer covers wasn't uniform throughout Brooklyn, there were legends about punchball players who were able to hit two sewers!"

Yet another feature similar to baseball's early days was regional variations in the rules: "Brooklyn featured two versions of punchball. In the Williamsburgh game, a chalked line was drawn across the street from first to third. Any ball that fell in front of the line was considered an out, just as any ball that landed on the sidewalk was ruled out. The Crown Heights version eliminated the 'out line' and allowed for the batter to hit grounders" (Bill Mazer, *Bill Mazer's Amazin' Baseball Book*, 104–106).

19.10 Stickball. Stickball was preferred to punchball by those for whom the greater resemblance to baseball compensated for the risk of lost balls and broken windows. The earliest reference I have found to the game occurred in 1934, when George Daley observed, "Stick ball is a new name to me. . . . [It] is a third cousin to baseball, played with a soft ball and a broomstick on the streets of New York. It is one of the most popular pastimes of boys gathered in various settlement houses. With sand lots getting scarcer and scarcer the youth still find a way to emulate Babe Ruth and get their start in baseball" (*New York Herald-Tribune*, April 19, 1934). Stickball would later become famous as Willie Mays's other favorite game.

19.11 Water Baseball. During the nineteenth century there were several attempts to combine baseball and water. According to an 1879 account in the *Albany* (New York) *Argus*, "A number of young men who are fond of aquatic sports have formed two baseball nines for the purpose of playing a match on the river. They are all good swimmers, of course, that being of more importance than skill, so far as the game is concerned, though they all understand how to play ball very well—this first practice game resulting successfully and creating considerable interest and fun. The game will be played off Boston and Albany Islands. The pitcher, catcher and batsman stand in water up to their waists—the fielders having to take water as they get it, and in the majority of cases will have to do some pretty tall swimming. This is to be the favorite pastime on the Harlem River" (reprinted in the *New York Sunday Mercury*, August 16, 1879). George L. Moreland reported that a game of baseball was played in the surf at Nantasket, Massachusetts, in 1881: "The contestants were clad in bathing costumes and the water was just deep enough to impede the progress of attempts at lively base running. The pitching and batting were quite creditable, but when a run was attempted the result was decidedly ludicrous" (George L. Moreland, *Balldom*, 278). The *National Police Gazette* of August 4, 1883, mentioned a game of baseball in water being played in Baltimore, but didn't provide details.

Early in the twentieth century the efforts resumed. A 1905 account noted that the game had originated the previous summer at schoolboy's camps and was usually played with five players a side: a pitcher, a catcher, and three basemen. It explained: "Each player stands on a square float and a rubber ball is used. When the batter makes a hit he swims for first base and advances as in the regulation game" (*Sporting Life*, April 1, 1905).

An April 3, 1907, article in the *Detroit Free Press* indicated that water baseball had originated in Atlantic City and had been brought to Michigan in 1905, drawing crowds of up to a thousand at St. Clair Flats that year. After limited activity in 1906, the game was again proving popular that spring. It provided this description: "Water baseball is played in a way similar to baseball, bases being used in the shape of floats set out in the same fashion as seen on the diamond, there being first, second and third. There are but two outfielders and no shortstop. The runner must be touched at each base."

Another effort was made in the 1930s when James Reilly, the swimming coach at Rutgers University, "invented a water game based on the diamond sport, but with six players on each team. Instead of batting the ball, players throw it from the diving board and the batter paddles 45 yards to first base. If he gets there before he is tagged or the base touched, he waits for the next man to bring him around by the same method. A catcher, two basemen and three fielders complete the line-up" (*Sporting News*, April 19, 1934).

19.12 Ten-man Baseball. As a result of the gaping holes that resulted when the fair-foul forced the first and third basemen to play close to their respective bases, the idea of adding a tenth fielder in the form of a right shortstop often arose. Researcher Richard Hershberger discovered this idea being proposed at the 1866 Pennsylvania state convention (*Philadelphia Inquirer*, September 28, 1866). This was often combined with the idea of adding a tenth inning, for symmetry. A letter writer to Henry Chadwick's *The Ball Player's Chronicle* asked in 1867 if it was necessary to play ten innings if a tenth fielder were used, and the response was "Certainly not" (*The Ball Player's Chronicle*, June 27, 1867).

Chadwick apparently rethought his position. Before the 1874 season he confidently announced in his annual guides and weekly columns that baseball would henceforth be played with ten players and ten innings. A later account stated that players "rebelled" against having another player "to clutter up the scenery and get in the way of other ball players . . . the game was for nine men and they were darned if they wanted any cricket notions foisted on it by a man who had played cricket all his life and whose head was full of tea and family reunions" (John B. Foster, "When Baseball Was Young," *Watertown* [N.Y.] *Times*, February 14, 1927). This description sounds exaggerated, but in any event the proposed rule change was "defeated by an almost unanimous vote" by the National Association (*Boston Daily Advertiser*, March 3, 1874).

The ten-man game was not adopted by any major clubs, but some clubs in isolated areas assumed that it had become standard and continued to use it for several years afterward. In Ypsilanti, Michigan, for instance, ten-man baseball was the version almost invariably played between 1874 and 1879, though it was very rare elsewhere in the state (Peter Morris, *Baseball Fever*, 313). The ten-man game was also the norm in Cuba for much of the nineteenth century, though it is not known how and why the extra player was added (Roberto Gonzalez Echevarria, *The Pride of Havana*, 104).

Henry Chadwick remained convinced that the ten-man version was the future of baseball and wrote after the 1874 season: "That this rule will ultimately prevail, we have not the least doubt. It took us over five years to teach the fraternity the value of the 'fly games' over that of the old rule of the bound catch, and probably it will be nearly as difficult to remove the prejudice against this later proposed improvement in the game" (undated clipping, Chadwick Scrapbooks).

In succeeding years he continued to advocate ten-man baseball, but after the fair-foul was eliminated in 1877 his calls increasingly fell upon deaf ears. Before the 1878 season the *Chicago Tribune* wrote sarcastically, "It must be getting pretty near the time when the *Clipper* annually brings out its 'ten runs and ten innings' plan. It would be a glorious scheme to rope that new Association into adopting this 'improvement'" (*Chicago Tribune*, February 3, 1878). Undeterred, Chadwick was still advocating ten-man baseball in the early 1880s (see, for example, *New York Clipper*, January 29, 1881).

19.13 No Man Left Behind. After the close of the 1878 season, the Chicago club tried to attract spectators to an exhibition game against Milwaukee by using "the new-fangled scheme

of playing the men back on the bases on which they were left in the previous inning." The game was not an artistic success, as base runners had little incentive to take risks. Nor did it create excitement as Chicago won by a lopsided 26-3 margin. Most important, it was a commercial failure, and "the few people on the ground were at a loss to know how to score this new wrinkle" (*Chicago Tribune*, October 4, 1878).

19.14 Wiffle Ball. In 1953 Dave Mullany, Sr., wished there were a way for his son to throw a curve ball without hurting his arm. He also wanted it to be possible for his son to play baseball in the backyard without breaking windows. So he glued together two plastic cosmetic cases and sliced holes in them to create air resistance. He called the result the Wiffle Ball, because its curving action caused batters to whiff. The Mullany family still manufactures Wiffle Balls.

A somewhat similar idea had been put forward half a century earlier. A 1902 account reported that "Ted Kennedy, the once noted ex-pitcher, has, he claims, invented a special curving base ball which enables a pitcher to mechanically produce an inshoot, out-curve, jump and drop ball" (*Sporting Life*, February 8, 1902).

19.15 Two Swings. Roger Kahn recalled playing a version of baseball called "two swings." When no one was available whom both sides trusted to call balls and strikes, the batter would instead be allowed two swings (Roger Kahn, *The Head Game*, 42). This was therefore a throwback to the days when umpires did not call balls and strikes.

19.16 Donkey Baseball. The original incarnation of donkey baseball occurred in 1861 and did not use actual donkeys. Instead its name was derived from "donkey races," a silly type of contest.

The *Brooklyn Eagle* gave this description of donkey baseball: "Yesterday afternoon a very amusing, and perhaps the most novel match ever played, took place upon the grounds of the Star Club, South Brooklyn. It being on the plan of a 'Donkey Race,' and but for the cold and chilly weather, the affair passed off pleasantly. The conditions of the game were, the nine making the LEAST runs should gain the victory and the player scoring the MOST runs to get the ball" (*Brooklyn Eagle*, November 16, 1861). Although Henry Chadwick noted the following spring that a "series of the 'Donkey Matches'" were planned, interest in these exhibitions does not appear to have been sustained.

The surprising thing is that donkey baseball was revived many decades later as an equally lighthearted game, but this time using actual donkeys. The *St. Louis Post-Dispatch* offered this description on June 8, 1934: "all participants, excepting the catcher, the pitcher and the batsman are astride donkeys. After hitting the ball it is necessary for the hitter to get on the back of a donkey and make his way to first base before the fielders, also on donkeys, retrieve the ball."

19.17   Old-fashion. Colin Howell has documented a fascinating game called "old-fashion" that was played by the Mi'kmaq Indians of Atlantic Canada as recently as the 1940s. Old-fashion preserved an intriguing number of remnants of ball games of the pre-Knickerbockers era, including no foul ground, one out per inning, soaking (see **1.22**), and soft, homemade balls. Based on the accounts gathered by Howell, another resemblance to early baseball was the flexibility of the rules (Colin Howell, *Northern Sandlots*, 186–189).

Chapter 20

INCLUSION

THE FITFUL and still unfinished story of the acceptance of minorities and women into baseball admits of no brief summary. It has produced moments of triumph where baseball has symbolized the broader struggle for equality and set an example for society. But it has also yielded moments of shame where baseball has lagged even behind the rest of the country in the recognition of the universality of human rights, dreams, and ambitions.

It is tempting to say that the one thing this story has never been is dull. But the entry on African-American umpires (**20.1.16**) suggests that even that generalization may be false. It is accordingly wisest to let the entries speak for themselves.

(i) African Americans

20.1.1 African-American Clubs. The Unknown Club of Weeksville, New York, was playing as early as 1859. The New York Anglo-African published an account on December 10, 1859, of a match the Unknowns had played on November 15. Their opponents were the Henson Base Ball Club of Jamaica, New York, who won by a score of 54-43. The racial makeup of the Hensons was not specified in this article, but other references to the club make clear that they were African Americans (Michael E. Lomax, *Black Baseball Entrepreneurs, 1860–1901*, 1, 11). An account of the match and a box score are reprinted on page 35 of Dean Sullivan's *Early Innings*.

The involvement of African Americans in baseball during the game's first great expan-

sion in the 1860s is difficult to measure. The number of documented African-American and integrated clubs during the decade is small, but there could be more that are lost to history. Early box scores and game accounts almost always referred to players by their surnames only, making identification difficult or impossible. In addition, it cannot necessarily be assumed that the presence of African-American and white players on the same club would have drawn attention.

The factors that restricted African-American participation in the 1860s are also tricky to assess. Racial prejudice may have played a role, but it seems more likely that practical considerations were paramount. Most notably, baseball was slow to spread to the South while the African-American population had not yet begun to move north in great numbers. Additionally, baseball was a sport that relied upon leisure time during daylight hours and ready access to an appropriate piece of land, both of which were in short supply for African Americans of the era.

20.1.2 Match Between African-American Clubs. The 1859 match mentioned in the preceding entry was one of the earliest between African-American clubs. But it is unlikely that it was the first, since the game account referred to it as "another victory for the Henson."

Matches among African-American clubs appear to have remained rare for the next few years. In 1862 the *Brooklyn Eagle* printed an account of a game between the Unknowns of Weeksville and the Monitor Club of Brooklyn and observed, "This is the first match to our knowledge that has been played in this city by players of African descent" (*Brooklyn Eagle*, October 17, 1862; reprinted in Dean Sullivan, ed., *Early Innings*, 35–36).

20.1.3 Integrated Matches. Dean Sullivan reported that some sort of baseball game involving players of both races took place on July 4, 1859. An account in the *New York Anglo-African* indicated that Joshua R. Giddings, an abolitionist white congressman, participated in the game. Since Giddings was sixty-four at the time, it can safely be assumed that the competition was not heated (*New York Anglo-African*, July 30, 1859; Dean Sullivan, ed., *Early Innings*, 34).

20.1.4 Integrated Clubs. The 1859 match mentioned in the preceding entry appears to have been a special event, with the two sides being improvised. The difficulties of identifying the race of individual players make it especially hard to pinpoint the first club to include both African-American and white players. That distinction most likely belongs to one of the clubs mentioned in earlier entries, or one of their contemporaries.

It can be said with certainty that an integrated club existed in Northampton, Massachusetts, in 1865. Brian Turner and John S. Bowman, in their excellent history of baseball in that town, demonstrated that Luther B. Askin, first baseman of the Florence Eagles in 1865 and 1866, was of African-American descent. While Askin was light-skinned, Turner and Bowman cited an account by the club's captain to show that he was aware of Askin's race.

What makes this particularly noteworthy is that Turner and Bowman had to unearth the fact. They explained that Askin was known as "Old Bushel Basket" for his catching skills and "was also cited on at least one occasion for 'heavy' hitting. Left unmentioned, however, was the extraordinary fact that he was an African American on a white team" (Brian Turner and John S. Bowman, *Baseball in Northampton, 1823–1953*, 14–15).

The Northampton club was probably not the first integrated club, but it does prove that this first occurred no later than 1865. Moreover the lack of attention paid to this "extraordinary fact" suggests that contemporaries did not view it as all that extraordinary, which means that there could easily have been earlier integrated clubs.

20.1.5 African Americans in Collegiate Baseball. College play would prove an important means of access for African Americans to baseball and many other areas, since it was more difficult to apply racial stereotypes and prejudices to a highly educated man. Intervarsity baseball competition did not become organized until the late 1870s, but baseball clubs were thriving on campuses in the 1860s and 1870s. Some of these clubs competed solely against one another, but many colleges had nines that played outside competition.

Ohio's Oberlin College featured a club called the Resolutes in the late 1860s that included two African Americans, Simpson Younger and J. T. Settle. The Resolutes played several matches each year against semipro and professional clubs. Phil Dixon and Patrick J. Hannigan reported that the club won ten of their thirteen matches while Younger was on the club. All three losses came at the hands of the Forest City Club of Cleveland, a top professional club that was a charter member of the National Association (Phil Dixon and Patrick J. Hannigan, *The Negro Baseball Leagues*, 41).

20.1.6 African Americans in Organized Baseball. Bud Fowler (born John Jackson) played in both the International Association and the New England League in 1878. While there were periods when he played outside of organized ball due to racism, Fowler was still playing in the minor leagues as late as 1895.

In the 1880s Fowler had a good deal of company in organized baseball. (Bob Davids compiled a list of African Americans in organized baseball in the nineteenth century that appears as an appendix in Jerry Malloy, ed., *Sol White's History of Colored Base Ball*, and in Phil Dixon and Patrick J. Hannigan, *The Negro Baseball Leagues*.) By the 1890s the insidious color barrier (see **20.1.9**) was beginning to take its toll. It is often reported that Bill Galloway, who played for Woodstock of the Canadian League in 1899, was the last African American in organized baseball before Jackie Robinson in 1946 (see, for example, Phil Dixon and Patrick J. Hannigan, *The Negro Baseball Leagues*, 80).

In fact there were a few scattered exceptions during those years. Some African Americans were able to pass as white. Dick Brookins, who appears to have been a light-skinned man of mixed race, was able to play in various Class D leagues between 1906 and 1910 (Bill Kirwin, "The Mysterious Case of Dick Brookins," *National Pastime* 19 [1999], 38–43). Jimmy Claxton, who was born in Canada to a white mother and a father of French, African-American, and Indian heritage, played briefly in the Pacific Coast League in 1916 after being introduced as an Indian. His release corresponded to the surfacing of rumors that he was actually an African American (William J. Weiss, "The First Negro in Twentieth Century O. B.," *Baseball Research Journal* 8 [1979], 31–35).

Others, however, attempted to play openly. William Clarence Matthews, an African American who starred for Harvard, played briefly for Burlington of the Vermont League. An African American named Bill Thompson played in the Twin State League of Vermont and New Hampshire throughout the 1911 season. Although his race was no secret, researcher Seamus Kearney reported that Thompson encountered no resistance (Seamus Kearney, "Bill Thompson, Pioneer," *National Pastime* 16 [1996], 67–68). Unfortunately, as noted under "Color Line" (**20.1.9**), within two years the mood in the Twin State League had changed.

20.1.7 African-American Major Leaguers.

Jackie Robinson broke baseball's long-standing color barrier in 1947, yet he was far from the first African American to play major league baseball.

During the research for this book, with help from SABR colleagues Stefan Fatsis, Bruce Allardice, and Richard Malatzky, I was able to confirm that the first man of African-American heritage to play in the major leagues was William Edward White, the son of a white Confederate soldier and one of his slaves. White was a student at Brown University in 1879 and helped his school earn recognition as collegiate champions. When Providence first baseman Joe Start was injured that summer, White filled in for the next game, handling twelve chances flawlessly and getting one hit. Nonetheless it was White's only major league game (Stefan Fatsis, "Mystery of Baseball: Was William White Game's First Black?," *Wall Street Journal*, January 30, 2004, 1).

The next was Moses Fleetwood "Fleet" Walker, who debuted with Toledo of the American Association on May 1, 1884. His brother Welday became the third African-American major leaguer when he joined Toledo in July. The Walker brothers had both attended Oberlin College and the University of Michigan, meaning that the only three African Americans known to have played major league baseball

in the nineteenth century had attended prestigious colleges.

There is compelling evidence that at least one more nineteenth-century player, pitcher Charles Leander "Bumpus" Jones, was an African American who passed as a white. Jones pitched a no-hitter in his major league debut on October 15, 1892, yet would win only one more major league game despite three twenty-win seasons in the minors (Chris Rainey, "A Cincy Legend," Dick Miller and Mark Stang, eds., *Baseball in the Buckeye State*, 7).

In 1901 John McGraw attempted to pass an African-American man named Charley Grant off as an Indian named Chief Tokahoma. His ruse was not successful, and the accepted version of history has it that there were no more serious attempts to break the major league's color barrier until the signing of Jackie Robinson in 1946.

The reality is more complex, due to the influx of Latin players in the intervening years. According to Roberto Gonzalez Echevarria, "Roberto (El Tarzan) Estalella and Tomas de la Cruz, both of African descent, had already played in the majors in the thirties and forties, protected by the American confusion over race, color and nationality" (Roberto Gonzalez Echevarria, *The Pride of Havana*, 45).

Symbolic of that confusion, at least three other Cubans—Pedro Dibut, Oscar Estrada, and Ramon Herrera—played in both the white major leagues and the Negro National League. Quite a few other Cuban-born major leaguers played for clubs like the Long Branch Cubans, which barnstormed with African-American clubs (Dick Clark and Larry Lester, eds., *The Negro Leagues Book*, 255–257).

Peter Bjarkman cited several other Cubans and Puerto Rican Hi Bithorn as other major leaguers who may have been of African descent. He suggested that their omission from the traditional version means that "the full story of baseball's gradual and fitful racial integration has never been accurately told or popularly accepted" (Peter Bjarkman, "Cuban Blacks in the Majors Before Jackie Robinson," *National Pastime* 12 [1992], 58–63).

When Jackie Robinson finally became the first acknowledged African American to play in the white major leagues in more than six decades, it was no accident that he too was a collegian. Negro Leagues great Buck Leonard, for example, was initially dismayed that Robinson had been selected for the role because he believed that other African Americans were better ballplayers. But Leonard came to realize that Robinson's college background was a great asset, making him better prepared for a hostile environment while also making it harder for racists to dismiss him with stereotypes (Brad Snyder, *Beyond the Shadow of the Senators*, 231; John Holway, *Voices from the Great Black Baseball Leagues*, 267).

20.1.8 African-American Tours. The first extensive trip by an African-American baseball club may have occurred when the Bachelor Club of Albany, New York, traveled to Philadelphia to play two Philadelphia clubs in 1867. That same year saw the Pythians of Philadelphia travel to Washington, D.C., for a couple of matches. The first multi-city tour seems to have taken place in 1870 when the *New York Tribune* reported: "The Mutuals, a colored Club of Washington, are on a tour and are now in Western New York" (*New York Tribune*, August 26, 1870). The club played matches in Lockport, Niagara Falls, Buffalo, Rochester, Utica, Canajoharie, and Troy (*New York Clipper*, September 3, 1870; quoted in Michael E. Lomax, *Black Baseball Entrepreneurs, 1860–1901*, 28).

In the mid-1890s the Page Fence Giants of Adrian, Michigan, bought their own railroad car. Researcher Jerry Malloy reported that "the sixty-foot-long, gilt ornamented car was fitted with a lavatory, private manager's office, a state room, kitchen, and a combined dining-setting-sleeping room. Capable of sleeping 20, the car sported leather seats and a Belgian carpet. The coach was staffed with a cook (who pitched in one game) and a porter-barber" (Jerry Malloy, ed., *Sol White's History of Colored Base Ball*, xxxiv). Not only did this innovation make touring cheaper and easier, it spared the club many of the indignities of segregation. Phil Dixon and Patrick J. Hannigan point out that Negro Leagues clubs are strongly associated with endless bus trips, when in fact the clubs traveled almost exclusively by train until the mid-1920s (Phil Dixon and Patrick J. Hannigan, *The Negro Baseball Leagues*, 26).

20.1.9 Color Line. The color barrier that kept most African Americans out of organized baseball until the appearance of Jackie Robinson generally took the form of an unwritten "gentlemen's agreement." When the issue was pushed, however, the prohibition was expressed more openly.

After the 1867 season the African-American Pythian Club of Philadelphia applied for membership in the Pennsylvania Association of Amateur Base Ball Players; the response was ominous. Pythians representative Raymond Burr was advised "to withdraw [rather] than to have it on record that [the Pythians] were blackballed." He declined at first but eventually did so when defeat was inevitable. In a scene that would become all too familiar, Burr found that all the delegates "expressed sympathy for our club" but that only a handful were willing to cast votes in favor of the club. The others claimed that they would "in justice to the opinion of the clubs they represented be compelled, against their personal feelings, to vote against [the Pythians'] admission" (Michael E. Lomax, *Black Baseball Entrepreneurs, 1860–1901*, 22–24).

Two months later the Pythians applied for membership in the National Association of Base Ball Players. That body's nominating committee unanimously recommended that clubs not be admitted if they were "composed of one or more colored persons" (*The Ball Player's Chronicle*, December 19, 1867; reprinted in Dean Sullivan, ed., *Early Innings*, 68–69). The Pythians withdrew their nomination.

An article in Henry Chadwick's *Ball Player's Chronicle* commented that the nominating committee pursued that course in order "to keep out of the Convention the discussion of any subject having a political bearing, as this undoubtedly had" (*The Ball Player's Chronicle*, December 19, 1867; reprinted in Dean Sullivan, ed., *Early Innings*, 68–69). That insidious reasoning—effectively creating a ban without having to take responsibility for having done so—presaged an ugly pattern that would become all too familiar in the 1880s.

As shown in the preceding entries, as baseball developed in the late 1860s and throughout the 1870s African Americans made their way into collegiate, semipro, and professional baseball. In 1875 the Mutual Base Ball Club of Washington, D.C., became the first African-American club admitted to the National Amateur Association of Base Ball Players (*St. Louis Globe-Democrat*, April 12, 1875). While African-American ballplayers of this period undoubtedly encountered some hostility, there do not appear to have been any outright bans on interracial play before the mid-1880s.

There are several plausible interpretations for why the 1870s' apparent progress toward racial harmony was succeeded by a backlash.

The one that seems most compelling to me is that white ballplayers felt threatened not so much by the prospect of playing against African Americans as by the fear of losing to them. The improved level of African-American baseball made this an increasingly likely occurrence in the mid-1880s. For example, when the Cuban Giants' application to join the Eastern League was rejected, the *Meriden Journal* admitted that "the dread of being beaten by the Africans had something to do with the rejection of the application of the Cuban Giants" (*Meriden Journal*, quoted in *Trenton Times*, July 23, 1886; reprinted in Michael E. Lomax, *Black Baseball Entrepreneurs, 1860–1901*, 58).

Whether it was this specific fear or the decade's general deterioration of interracial relationships, the 1880s saw the specter of a color bar begin to loom over baseball. When Fleet Walker signed to play for Toledo of the Northwestern League in 1883, one delegate offered a resolution that would ban African Americans from the league. After a spirited debate the resolution was withdrawn, and the delegate took the curious course of asking that references to his resolution be removed from the minutes (*Grand Rapids* [Mich.] *Times*, March 16, 1883).

The two major leagues were able to avoid confronting the issue directly by having no acknowledged African Americans under contract after 1884. Their absence was generally ignored by the press, but occasionally a candid journalist raised the issue. Rumors in 1886 that New York's National League club was about to sign African-American pitcher George Stovey prompted one scribe to wonder, "would the League permit his appearance in League championship games?" (*Sporting Life*, September 8, 1886; quoted in Mike Roer, *Orator O'Rourke*, 138). Nine years later, John B. Foster added, "Many National League managers sigh because they could not sign [Fleet Walker]. There is no rule against the signing of colored players by National League clubs, but personalities are apt to arise if the experiment is tried, and managers are loth to tempt trouble" (John B. Foster, "Buckeye Boys," *Sporting News*, December 28, 1895).

The International League became their refuge, and the presence of eight African-American players in the league by 1887 made it impossible to pursue the familiar course of a gentlemen's agreement. Several ugly incidents occurred, the most notorious when Chicago's Adrian "Cap" Anson refused to play an exhi-

bition game against Newark if George Stovey pitched (David Zang, *Fleet Walker's Divided Heart*, 54–55). The International League felt obliged to address the issue but, like earlier leagues, chose to do so as coyly as possible. The *Newark Journal* reported that the league's board of directors had held a "secret meeting" and instructed the league secretary "to approve of no more contracts with colored men" (quoted in Jerry Malloy, "Out at Home," in John Thorn, ed., *The National Pastime*, 235).

Obviously a meeting that was reported in the next day's papers could not have been much of a secret. The results that ensued from the meeting are also somewhat curious. The next year the league had only three African-American players, and in 1889 only Fleet Walker. When he left at the end of the season, the circuit remained lily-white until Jackie Robinson joined Montreal in 1946. So it appears that the course taken by the International League was not overtly to ban the entire race but instead to grandfather the current players and sign no new ones.

Not all whites were reticent about expressing racist views. The players on the St. Louis Brown Stockings refused to play an exhibition game against an African-American club because "they drew the color line strongly" (*Philadelphia Sunday News*, quoted in *St. Louis Post-Dispatch*, September 13, 1887). The *Detroit Free Press* observed that there were several African-American players who "would prove a boon to some of the weak clubs of the league and association, but if there is one thing the white ball player insists on doing it is drawing the color line very rigidly" (*Detroit Free Press*, December 4, 1887). Two Syracuse players refused to pose for a team picture because of the presence of an African American (quoted in Jerry Malloy, "Out at Home," in John Thorn, ed., *The National Pastime*, 228–229).

The following year Welday Walker read that the Tri-State League planned to ban African Americans. He wrote an open letter to the league president, arguing that such a rule "casts derision at the laws of Ohio—the voice of the people—that say all men are equal" (*Sporting Life*, March 14, 1888; reprinted in Dean Sullivan, ed., *Early Innings*, 69–70). Walker's reasoning is so straightforward and compelling that a logical rebuttal would be impossible, which helps explain why an indirect course was again pursued.

Apparently the Tri-State League had no intentions of actually passing a color bar. But the number of African Americans in the league fell from four to one that year, and to none the following year. Once again a tacit color line had been created without having to deal with the controversy that would have ensued from an explicit prohibition. The same pattern occurred in other leagues, with the result that the number of opportunities for African Americans in the minor leagues fell dramatically. By the end of the nineteenth century, organized baseball was able to have it both ways—it had made the game lily-white without the appearance of any conscious effort to attain that end.

For nearly fifty years organized baseball clung with equal stubbornness to the color bar and to the myth that it didn't have one. One can find a few rare admissions that such a prohibition did in fact exist. Brian Turner and John S. Bowman have documented a fascinating instance in the Twin State League in 1913.

It is important to stress that the Twin State League had not signed the National Agreement and was technically outside of organized baseball. But the league maintained a good working relationship with organized baseball (Brian Turner and John S. Bowman, *Baseball in Northampton, 1823–1953*, 42).

The Twin State League would have appeared to be the perfect place for an African American to play. Two years earlier an African American named Bill Thompson had spent the entire season in the league without encountering opposition. Nonetheless when the Bellows Falls club attempted to use African-American pitcher Frank Wickware in an August 26, 1913, game against the Northampton Meadowlarks, the Larks refused to take the field.

The controversy that ensued produced some unusually forthright admissions of prejudice. The *Northampton Gazette* wrote: "The color line is drawn in organized baseball. The Twin State league recognizes orders from that commission, refuses to play a ball player when ordered not to, [so] why not in drawing the color line." At a September meeting the directors voted to bar African Americans from the league by a 5 to 1 vote.

As we have seen, such candid acknowledgments of the existence of a color line were rare, which enabled a few African Americans to play in the minor leagues in the early twentieth century. But this decision by a league in which African Americans had been accepted two years earlier made it clear that the color barrier was very real and increasingly inflexible.

In the 1930s professional football attempted to follow baseball's example. While there had been African Americans in the National Football League from its inception, their numbers began to dwindle in the 1930s. By 1933 only Joe Lillard of the Chicago Cardinals remained, and he was let go at season's end. His coach, Paul Schissler, explained that opposing players "took it out on" Lillard and his teammates; accordingly, "We had to let him go, for our own sake, and for his, too" (Thomas G. Smith, "Outside the Pale: The Exclusion of Blacks from the National Football League, 1934–46," *Journal of Sport History* 15:3 [Winter 1988], 255–281; quoted in Robert W. Peterson, *Pigskin*, 179).

From 1934 to 1945 there were no African Americans in the NFL—but the league followed baseball's evasive path and never passed a ban. The extent of the denial is suggested when Chicago Bears' owner George Halas claimed in the late 1960s: "Probably it was due to the fact that no great black players were in colleges then. That could be the reason. But I've never given this a thought until you mentioned it. At no time has it ever been brought up. Isn't that strange?" (quoted in Myron Cope, *The Game That Was*; reprinted in Robert W. Peterson, *Pigskin*, 169).

By the 1930s the myth that there was no color line in baseball was becoming increasingly difficult to sustain. This was not for want of trying; White Sox President J. Louis Comiskey seemed to be reading from the same script as Halas when he maintained "the question . . . has never crossed my mind. Had some good player come along and my manager refused to sign him because he was a Negro I am sure I would have taken action or attempted to do so, although it is not up to me to change what might be the rule. I cannot say that I would have insisted on hiring the player over the protest of my manager, but at least I would have taken some steps—just which steps I cannot say for the simple reason the question has never confronted me" (*Philadelphia Tribune*, March 9, 1933; quoted in Neil Lanctot, *Negro League Baseball*, 223–224).

Yet no matter how adamantly the owners stuck to their story, the success that barnstorming Negro Leagues clubs had against white clubs could not be explained away. Even after efforts were made to reduce such games, the questions persisted. When reporters pressed the question, a few Negro Leagues stars were given sham tryouts (Jules Tygiel, *Baseball's Great Experiment*,

30–46). But no strategy could continue to obscure the increasingly obvious fact that baseball had a color line.

Longtime Commissioner Kenesaw Mountain Landis was still claiming in 1942, "There is no rule, formal or informal, or any understanding—unwritten, subterranean, or sub-anything—against the hiring of Negro players by the teams of organized baseball" (Brad Snyder, *Beyond the Shadow of the Senators*, 188-189; Jules Tygiel, *Baseball's Great Experiment*, 30). Yet there were more and more cracks in this façade as, under pressure, baseball people came out as either opposed to or in favor of a color barrier that supposedly didn't exist (Jules Tygiel, *Baseball's Great Experiment*, 38–42; Neil Lanctot, *Negro League Baseball*, 223-224).

In fact it probably didn't make much difference which side an individual was on; it was the tacit concession that there *was* such a prohibition that mattered. The acknowledgment of overt racial prejudice—at the same time African Americans were fighting in a world war to preserve the freedoms they shared in so unequally—was enough. Once it was generally admitted that baseball actually had a color barrier, it was not long before that barrier fell. That, I believe, is no coincidence.

20.1.10 All African-American / Latin Lineup in the White Major Leagues.

On September 1, 1971, with Philadelphia in town, Pittsburgh manager Danny Murtaugh handed in this starting lineup: Rennie Stennett, 2b; Gene Clines, cf; Roberto Clemente, rf; Willie Stargell, lf; Manny Sanguillen, c; Dave Cash, 3b; Al Oliver, 1b; Jackie Hernandez, ss; Dock Ellis, p. The Pirates won by a score of 10-7, but what was more significant was that not one of their nine starters would have been able to play in the major leagues twenty-five years earlier.

Even after baseball began to integrate, there continued to be rumors that quotas were the latest manifestation of the "gentlemen's agreement." Roger Kahn, for example, observed, "There existed in 1953 what John Lardner called the 50 percent color line; that is, it was permissible for a major league team to play only four black men out of nine. The ratio, five whites to four blacks, substantiated white supremacy. But to have five blacks playing with four whites supposedly threatened the old order" (Roger Kahn, *The Boys of Summer*, 166–167). It was not until July 17, 1954, that the Dodgers fielded a starting lineup with a majority of African Americans

(Jonathan Fraser Light, *The Cultural Encyclopedia of Baseball*, 96).

Thus the symbolic importance of the Pirates lineup on September 1, 1971, was considerable.

20.1.11 African-American Managers.

The first African American to manage in the minor leagues was Stanislaus Kostka "S.K." Govern, a native of the Virgin Islands who had been involved with the Cuban Giants since the club's inception. In 1889 the Cuban Giants were members of the Middle States League, earning Govern the distinction. In late June a second African-American club, the Gorhams of New York, managed by Benjamin Butler, briefly joined the Middle States League (Michael E. Lomax, *Black Baseball Entrepreneurs, 1860–1901*, 89–90, 98–102).

Frank Robinson was the first African American to manage a major league team, being named player-manager of the Cleveland Indians on October 3, 1974. His historic managerial debut took place on April 8, 1975, and he homered to lead Cleveland to a 5-3 victory.

Bill Deane noted that at least a couple of African Americans had filled in on a one-game basis before then. Willie Horton was named "manager for a day" by Detroit pilot Mayo Smith on September 19, 1968, and the Tigers beat the Yankees 6-2. On May 8, 1973, Ernie Banks served as acting manager of the Chicago Cubs after Whitey Lockman was ejected (Bill Deane, "How 'Bout That," *Baseball Research Journal* 20 [1991], 90).

20.1.12 African-American Coaches.

Buck O'Neil was the first African American to serve as a major league coach, holding that position for the Chicago Cubs in 1962. The promotion came after O'Neil had spent seven years in the Cubs organization as a scout and spring training instructor. Although the announcement came during the period when the Cubs were using a rotating head coaching system, O'Neil was not included in the rotation (Richard Dozer, "Cubs Sign Negro Coach," *Chicago Tribune*, May 30, 1962). It is sometimes contended that Rube Foster informally served as a pitching coach for the New York Giants in the early twentieth century, but there is little evidence to support that contention.

20.1.13 African-American General Managers.

Bill Lucas was named director of player

personnel for the Atlanta Braves on September 19, 1976. He held the position until his premature death on May 5, 1979, and fulfilled the functions normally associated with a general manager. Braves owner Ted Turner was nominally the club's general manager, but star outfielder Dale Murphy later commented, "I always thought of [Lucas] as the general manager. I'm surprised to hear that he wasn't the general manager." Lucas's untimely death prevented him from seeing the fruits of his labor when the team whose nucleus he had built captured the 1982 National League West division title (Mark Bowman, "Lucas Left Impression on Braves," article on mlb.com website, February 4, 2003).

Bob Watson became the first African American to hold the title of general manager of a major league club when he was hired by the Houston Astros following the 1993 season. His tenure proved ill-omened; Watson was diagnosed with cancer, and the 1994 season was ended prematurely by a strike. Watson later became general manager of the Yankees and helped the club capture the 1996 World Series, but he resigned in 1998 citing burnout.

20.1.14 African-American Professional Teams.

After the 1875 season the Blue Stockings of St. Louis formed a joint stock company in hopes of raising $1,000 to fund the club for the 1876 season. They quickly raised half the amount, but it is not known what happened after that (*St. Louis Globe-Democrat*, November 16, 1875). In 1882 the *Cincinnati Enquirer* noted that "Philadelphia has a nine of colored professionals," which may have been a club known as the Orions. Several other African-American clubs appear to have operated as professionals over the next couple of seasons (Robert W. Peterson, *Only the Ball Was White*, 34).

The first successful African-American professional team was one formed by Frank P. Thompson in 1885. The club soon became known as the Cuban Giants and became one of the most famous African-American clubs of the nineteenth century, but its exact origins are much less clear.

Baseball researcher Jerry Malloy concluded that Sol White, the first important historian of African-American baseball, was responsible for the confusion. White played on the team and later recalled that when Thompson was head waiter at the Argyle Hotel in Babylon, New York, he "chose the best ball players from among his waiters, and organized a base ball

club to play as an attraction for the guests of the hotel." The players proved very talented, and Thompson took them on the road when the hotel season ended in September (Jerry Malloy, ed., *Sol White's History of Colored Base Ball*, 8).

Sol White was also the source of the most usually cited story of the origin of the inappropriate Cuban Giants name. In a 1938 interview he explained that "the version which came to him is that when that first team began playing away from home, they passed as foreigners—Cubans, as they finally decided—hoping to conceal the fact that they were just American Negro hotel waiters, and talked a gibberish to each other on the field which, they hoped, sounded like Spanish" (*Esquire*, September 1938; reprinted in Jerry Malloy, ed., *Sol White's History of Colored Base Ball*, lix–lx).

Malloy argued that these picturesque tales are of dubious authenticity. He observed that there is no contemporary documentation of pseudo-Spanish being spoken and questioned the likelihood that such a ploy would fool anyone. Malloy also uncovered a very different account of the club's origins that appeared in the *New York Age* in 1887.

This article, written by J. Gordon Street but likely emanating from an interview with Frank P. Thompson himself, indicated that Thompson organized the club as the Keystone Athletics in Philadelphia in May 1885. The club spent most of the summer in Babylon, Long Island. In August they merged with clubs from Washington and Philadelphia and assumed the name of the Cuban Giants (J. Gordon Street, "The Cuban Giants," *New York Age*, October 15, 1887; reprinted in Jerry Malloy, ed., *Sol White's History of Colored Base Ball*, 134–135).

Malloy pointed out several elements of Street's account that make it more credible than White's. First, it appeared in 1887 while the club was still in its prime, while White did not join the club until several years later. Second, the account implies that the players' primary obligation during the summer in Babylon was to entertain guests with their ball-playing. This seems far more plausible than White's version in which a large number of talented ballplayers happened to be working at the same hotel.

Finally, Malloy pointed out that Street's version accounts for manager S. K. Govern becoming involved with the Cuban Giants. Govern had been managing the Manhattans of Washington, one of the three clubs that was involved in the merger. Malloy also uncovered evidence that the Manhattans had previously toured Cuba, which may account for the name assumed by the club (Jerry Malloy, ed., *Sol White's History of Colored Base Ball*, lx–lxi).

20.1.15 Leagues of African-American Teams.

In 1884 there was talk of a "league of colored baseball clubs" that would include teams in Washington, Baltimore, and Pittsburgh. Nothing appears to have materialized (*Washington Post*, February 24, 1884).

The Southern League of Colored Base Ballists was organized in 1886 with three clubs in Jacksonville, two clubs in Memphis, two clubs in Savannah, and one club each in Atlanta, Charleston, and New Orleans. The season was scheduled to run from June 7 to August 25, but details of the league's activities remain very sketchy. No standings are known to have been published, and only the *New Orleans Times-Picayune* ran box scores. Researcher Bill Plott noted that the *Jacksonville Leader* was designated as the league's official organ and suggested that further research into that newspaper's files might be productive (Bill Plott, "The Southern League of Colored Base Ballists," *Baseball Research Journal* 3 [1974]; reprinted in *Baseball Historical Review* 1981, 75–78).

That fall, Walter S. Brown of Pittsburgh announced plans for the National Colored Base Ball League with teams in Philadelphia, Baltimore, Pittsburgh, Washington, Louisville, and Cincinnati. Franchises in New York and Boston were later added while Washington and Cincinnati were dropped. The league was granted protection under the National Agreement and opened play on May 5, 1887, but disbanded before the end of the month (Michael E. Lomax, *Black Baseball Entrepreneurs, 1860–1901*, 63–70; Jerry Malloy, "Out at Home," in John Thorn, ed., *The National Pastime*, 220–222).

Over the next thirty-three years, barnstorming African-American players built the popularity of their game. The potential for remunerative tours left the best clubs with limited incentive to pin themselves down to a league. This did not change until 1920 when the Negro National League, the first of the leagues now collectively referred to as the Negro Leagues, was formed. The league was organized at a meeting at the YMCA in Kansas City, Missouri, on February 13, 1920.

20.1.16 African-American Umpires.

In 1882 the *Grand Rapids* (Michigan) *Democrat* re-ported matter-of-factly that "a Mr. Pierson, colored, of Port Huron," had umpired the previous day's game between clubs representing Grand Rapids and Port Huron (*Grand Rapids Democrat*, September 9, 1882). No additional comment on his race or umpiring was made, which raises the intriguing possibility that there were other African-American umpires at this time. An African-American ballplayer named Harry Herbert umpired one game in the Connecticut State League in 1898 (Mike Roer, *Orator O'Rourke*, 217). If there were others, however, their names are lost to history.

Emmett Ashford became the first African American who is known to have umpired in the minors when he was hired by the Southwestern International League in 1951. It took Ashford fifteen long years before he was hired by the American League on February 20, 1966, and thereby became the first African-American umpire in major league history. The long delay before Ashford's promotion caused considerable press commentary, and this pressure likely had a lot to do with his belated ascension to the American League (Mark Armour, "Emmett Ashford," *National Pastime* 27 [2007], 55–56).

When Wayne Beasley was hired by the Carolina League in 1972, he became the first African-American umpire in a Southern league. There were still only four African-American umpires in professional baseball at the time, and combining the position's onerous duties with becoming a racial pioneer was a volatile mix. It therefore came as no great surprise when Beasley resigned in June.

What did raise eyebrows was the reason cited by Beasley: boredom. He said that racial incidents had been few but explained, "I am despondent. I can't find enough to do during the days. I have read all the books I can and I still can't find enough to keep me busy." Supporting Beasley's contention, another African American was hired to replace him (Jim L. Sumner, *Separating the Men from the Boys*, 133).

20.1.17 African-American Announcers.

In 1965 Jackie Robinson was unveiled by Roone Arledge as one of three "interpretive" commentators who would work the regional telecasts of ABC's Game of the Week (*Sporting News*, March 27, 1965).

20.1.18 African-American Pension Recipients.

William Buckner served as the trainer of

the Chicago White Sox from 1908 until shortly before the start of the 1918 season. Among the obstacles he had to overcome was that during spring training tours of the South "he was not able to get around to see much of the boys in the hotels" (*Chicago Tribune*, March 31, 1908). After Buckner was dismissed in 1918, it was sometimes reported that team captain Eddie Collins asked for his firing, but this makes little sense as Collins was still captain when Buckner returned in 1922. Sportswriter I. E. Sanborn attributed Buckner's dismissal to pitcher Dave Danforth, a Southerner (*Chicago Tribune*, September 19, 1923).

After Buckner returned to the White Sox he remained the club's trainer until 1933 (*Chicago Tribune*, January 29, 1922; *Mexia Evening News*, March 23, 1922; *Washington Post*, April 21, 1933). He continued to work for the club for several more years and became the first African American to collect a pension from a major league ball club (Phil Dixon and Patrick J. Hannigan, *The Negro Baseball Leagues*, 65).

20.1.19   White in Negro Leagues. Eddie Klep pitched for the Cleveland Buckeyes of the Negro American League in 1946. His story was told in great detail by historian Larry Gerlach, whose account corrects many of the inaccuracies about Klep that have appeared in other sources (Larry Gerlach, "Baseball's Other 'Great Experiment': Eddie Klep and the Integration of the Negro Leagues," *Journal of Sport History* 25:3 [Fall 1998], 453–481). Four years later, two more white players, Louis Clarizio and Louis Chirban, played for the Chicago American Giants (Neil Lanctot, *Negro League Baseball*, 354).

(ii) Women

20.2.1   Women Spectators. As noted in the entry on "Ladies' Days" (**16.1.7**), during the early days of baseball the presence of women was believed to ensure a higher class of spectators and better behavior. As a result the presence of women spectators at early baseball games was actively sought, and newspaper accounts almost invariably mentioned their presence. Clubs went to great trouble to make them feel welcome, arranging special seating sections for their convenience and usually admitting them without charge.

The amount of attention lavished on this theme reflected the pedestal upon which women of the era were placed. Being so honored may be flattering at first, but it soon becomes uncomfortable. In addition, the flattery was often mixed with a large dollop of condescension. By the 1870s and 1880s the sporting press was regularly running items that recounted the ill-informed comments of female spectators. For example, the *Milwaukee Journal* remarked in 1884, "The attendance of ladies at the ball park yesterday was large, although less than a dozen understood the game. However, they applauded heartily at each play, not waiting to discriminate between good and bad work" (*Milwaukee Daily Journal*, June 27, 1884).

Nonetheless the presence of women spectators at baseball games has always been strongly encouraged.

20.2.2   Women Players. Women who sought to *play* baseball received a very different response. The dominant theme of the treatment of women in the Victorian era was to restrict them to a narrow, well-defined sphere. As long as they remained within that sphere—as for example by being spectators at baseball matches—they were praised. But actually playing baseball brought attention to women's bodies in ways that were deemed inappropriate, and their participation in the sport was therefore discouraged.

The response to women who tried to play baseball can best be compared to how parents treat children who want to experiment with something beyond their years. Plan A is to watch indulgently and hope the child will tire of it. If that doesn't work, Plan B is executed, which is to suppress the activity with increasing forcefulness.

In my history of early baseball in Michigan I reported on five baseball clubs formed in the state by women between 1867 and 1878. None was treated with outright hostility, but none lasted long. There is thus no way to be certain how often, if at all, Plan B had to be implemented (Peter Morris, *Baseball Fever*, 195–198).

Baseball fared somewhat better at women's colleges, whose isolation undoubtedly made the prospect of athletic women less threatening. In 1866 two baseball clubs were formed at Vassar. The sport was revived there in 1876, and the school's clubs competed against nines from Smith College, Mount Holyoke, Wellesley, and Barnard. Amy Ellis Nutt observed: "Played inside the confines of those campuses, women's baseball was allowed to flourish" (Amy Ellis

Nutt, "Swinging for the Fences," in Lissa Smith, ed., *Nike Is a Goddess*, 35).

As Nutt's formulation implies, there was more resistance at coeducational colleges. A female team named the Dianas was formed at Northwestern in 1869. The Dianas were even challenged by a male team, though they declined (*Chicago Times*, October 22, 1869; quoted in Robert Pruter, "Youth Baseball in Chicago, 1868–1890," *Journal of Sport History* 26:1 [Spring 1999], 6).

Unfortunately this was a rare exception. In 1904 the participation of five women in a pick-up baseball game at the University of Pennsylvania prompted campus officials to ban women from playing baseball (Amy Ellis Nutt, "Swinging for the Fences," in Lissa Smith, ed., *Nike Is a Goddess*, 36).

The response to women who tried to play baseball professionally was much harsher. Two touring clubs of women known as the Blondes and the Brunettes played several games in 1875, beginning with a match at Springfield, Illinois, on September 11. The Blondes won 42-38, and a contemporary newspaper described it as the first game "ever played in public for gate money between feminine ball-tossers" (quoted in Lois Browne, *Girls of Summer*, 15).

But if the clubs expected a supportive attitude to continue, they were sadly mistaken. When they met again in St. Louis the following week, a local paper sniffed: "There were bases, a ball, a bat, and an umpire, but otherwise the game more resembled 'puss-in-the-corner' than base ball. . . . The whole affair was a revolting exhibition of impropriety, possessing no merit save that of novelty, and gotten up to make money out of a public that rushes to see any species of semi-immorality" (*St. Louis Republican*, September 19, 1875).

In 1879 another tour was mounted by two clubs of professional women baseball players billing themselves as the Blondes and the Brunettes. They were presumably not the same players, but the response they evoked was similar.

They were initially met with fairly gentle but unmistakable mockery. According to the *Washington Post*, "the audience roared itself hoarse" at a game in New York. The account made clear that the activity could not be taken seriously: "The players wore small jockey caps atop of their top knots and plaits, and whenever the hats came off, which they always did, all thoughts of ball were, pro tempore, dismissed till the disaster was repaired."

The descriptions of the action were similarly insistent on stressing the appearance of the players: "The blue catcher wore her hair down, and when the umpire had called three strikes on her, she dashed off in a nebulous state, pursued by the ball and generally made her base, since the ball was thrown wide in fear of hitting somebody. The hitting was unique. The bat was held above the head as nearly perpendicular as might be, and brought down with the grace and force that adorn an act of domestic discipline administered with a broom. Naturally almost every ball hit was grounded" (*Washington Post*, May 12, 1879).

Instead of discouraging the women, such accounts stimulated a larger attendance. More than five thousand spectators turned out for a July 4 game in Philadelphia. The newspapers responded by emphasizing that it was not the skill of the players that provided the attraction. It was reported that when the tour passed through New England, "The spectators tease them unmercifully, sometimes trip them up as they run, and even seize and kiss them" (*Muskegon News and Reporter*, August 13, 1879). Another newspaper crowed, "let's have the women here . . . it's better than a circus" (*Adrian Times and Expositor*, August 18, 1879).

As the tour continued, the ridicule became increasingly mean-spirited. The *Detroit Post and Tribune* wrote: "It is a remarkable comment upon the popular taste that the largest crowd assembled at Recreation park since this beautiful resort was thrown open to the public was that attracted Saturday afternoon by the announcement of a base ball match between two female nines, who are making a professional tour through the country. It was the worst burlesque upon the national game imaginable, and not even funny. The females were neither comely, shapely nor graceful, and their awkward antics demonstrated that while there are many things a woman can accomplish playing base ball is not one of them. It is not her great specialty. It does not enable her to do justice to herself. The women of America may do a great many things with impunity, but when she essays base ball she should be kindly but firmly suppressed. It may be mentioned incidentally that after the trouble was all over it was discovered that the young women with red stockings had vanquished the maidens in blue hose by a score of 20 to 19" (*Detroit Post and Tribune*, August 18, 1879). Things grew still worse at a stop in Louisville on August 25: "The spectators were very noisy and boisterous, and when the women left the ground they were stoned" (*New York Clipper*, September 6, 1879).

In succeeding years, accounts of women's professional baseball players grew even more hostile. The *New York Clipper* wrote that winter: "There are some things that women can't do. The teachings of centuries have established the fact that a woman can't play baseball . . . though a woman may rule the universe, she can't play baseball" (*New York Clipper*, March 20, 1880). In 1884 a *Sporting Life* correspondent chimed in: "Females can't play base ball even a little bit, and all attempts to organize and run such clubs must end in disaster. Let us hear no more of female base ball clubs. The public wants none of it" (*Sporting Life*, May 28, 1884). Lest there be any doubt, another correspondent was even more blunt two years later: "The only decent public connection women can have with the game is as spectators" (*Sporting Life*, September 18, 1886; quoted in Jean Hastings Ardell, *Breaking into Baseball*, 104).

Whenever possible, newspapers reinforced this message with condescending accounts that emphasized the players' appearances and attire rather than their play. An 1880 article about two clubs of young women in Cambridge, Massachusetts, for example, centered upon the "common walking dress" worn by the players (*New York Clipper*, March 6, 1880). Three years later this description was included in a game account: "During the initial game in New York between the Blondes and Brunettes, Miss Lyle tried to scoop up a ball on the short bound. She was slightly off in her calculations, and the ball slipped up under her skirt. She squirmed around like an eel in her frantic efforts to dislodge it, to the great amusement of the spectators. Seeing that she could not shake it out she squatted on her cushion and fished it out with her hand, while the crowd were convulsed with laughter" (*National Police Gazette*, October 13, 1883).

If these not-too-subtle hints still didn't work, the press resorted to the ultimate form of suppression by linking female baseball players to sexual improprieties. An Associated Press account of a female club that played in Albany, Georgia, alleged: "The girls are from 15 to 19 years of age, jaunty in style, brazen in manner, and peculiar in dress. When they reached this place their agent obtained room for them at the Artesian Hotel. It was not long before the proprietor discovered that the character of his house was suffering. All the swells of the city were around the place like a swarm of bees. The

proprietor promptly ejected the ball players, and they had to amuse themselves for several hours at the depot until the train arrived. . . . Their conduct was of such a character that respectable ladies got off the cars and waited for the next train" (*Sporting Life*, December 24, 1884).

In 1891 a *Sporting Life* correspondent wrote: "The sentence of Sylvester Wilson, or Franklin, to five years in Sing Sing at hard labor for abducting a sixteen-year-old girl and inducing her to travel with his ladies' base ball team, will likely put an end to all female base ball clubs. For this relief much thanks" (*Sporting Life*, October 31, 1891).

Such comments reflected the views of *Sporting Life* editor Francis Richter, who wrote in 1890: "Woman has no place in base-ball except as patron and enthusiast and female base-ball teams should not be patronized by the public nor encouraged and noticed by the press except in terms of condemnation. No reputable base-ball club should degrade itself and the game by renting these female ball-players and their manager their ball park to play in. Instead, all should imitate the example of President [Charles] Byrne of the Brooklyn club, who refused to lease his ground for such a disgusting exhibition at any price whatever" (*Sporting Life*, August 30, 1890, 8). The endless repetition of this hostile message eventually had the desired effect: professional play by women became scarce in the late nineteenth century. One team that did attempt a tour was met with the headline: "Chase Them: Another Female Troupe to Disgrace Base Ball" (*Sporting Life*, May 5, 1894). In the early twentieth century, with women making strides toward equality, women's professional baseball was revived in the form of the Bloomer Girls and other successful touring teams. A few women even endeavored to break into organized baseball.

20.2.3 Women in Organized Baseball. No woman has ever played in the major leagues, and the few appearances by women in the minor leagues have been very brief.

Lizzie Stroud pitched an inning for Reading of the Atlantic League against Allentown on July 5, 1898, under the name Lizzie Arlington. She allowed two hits but no runs. A game account in the *Reading Eagle* gave a lengthy description of her appearance, noting her "gray uniform with skirt coming to the knees, black stockings and a jaunty cap. Her hair was not cropped short, but was done up in the latest fashion."

The *Eagle* reporter was far less impressed with her pitching, commenting: "She, of course, hasn't the strength to get much speed on and has poor control. But, for a woman, she is a success." On September 7, 1936, Frances "Sonny" Dunlap played right field for the Fayetteville Bears of the Arkansas-Missouri League, going hitless in three at bats ("Women Players in Organized Baseball," *Baseball Research Journal* 1983, 157–161).

Other women did not even make it onto the field. Pitcher Jackie Mitchell was signed by the Chattanooga Lookouts in 1931, but Commissioner Kenesaw Mountain Landis voided the contract. In 1950 Fort Lauderdale of the Florida International League tried to sign All-American Girls Baseball League star Dorothy Kamenshek. She declined, apparently fearing it was a gimmick. Harrisburg of the Inter-State League signed a woman named Eleanor Engle on June 21, 1952, but her contract was disallowed and a ban on women players announced. Near the end of the 1971 season, Raleigh-Durham general manager Walter Brock announced plans to sign Jackie Jackson. The league office talked him out of the idea (Jim L. Sumner, *Separating the Men from the Boys*, 131).

In recent years a few women have broken into professional baseball, all in the independent leagues. Ila Borders pitched in the Northern League and Western Baseball League for four seasons, beginning in 1997. She was followed by Kendra Haynes, an outfielder who played in the Frontier League. Kendall Burnham played very briefly in the Central League in 2003, where she was a teammate of her husband Jake.

20.2.4   Women in Exhibitions Versus Major Leaguers.

Lizzie Murphy, one of the best women professionals of the day, played first base for a major league all-star team in an exhibition game at Fenway Park on August 14, 1922.

Jackie Mitchell, a seventeen-year-old female who had attended Kid Elberfeld's baseball school, pitched in an exhibition game against the New York Yankees on April 2, 1931. She pitched only two-thirds of an inning but made headlines by striking out Babe Ruth and Lou Gehrig consecutively.

It is often contended that the Yankee stars were just playing along with a publicity stunt. But Amy Ellis Nutt noted that "Mitchell, until her death in 1987 at the age of seventy-three, maintained that her fanning of Ruth and Geh-

rig was not a stunt on their part. She claimed that the only instruction given to the Yankee hitters about how to handle her pitches was not to hit the ball directly back at the young girl" (Amy Ellis Nutt, "Swinging for the Fences," in Lissa Smith, ed., *Nike Is a Goddess*, 44).

The great multi-sport athlete Babe Didrikson pitched a scoreless inning for the Philadelphia Athletics against the Brooklyn Dodgers in a spring training game on March 20, 1934. Two days later she pitched for the Cardinals against the Red Sox but allowed three runs in the first inning.

20.2.5   Women Touring Overseas.

The Philadelphia Bobbies, a successful barnstorming club of the 1920s, toured Japan at the end of the 1925 season. The club played games against men's teams in Tokyo, Osaka, Kyoto, and Kobe before a shortage of funds prevented them from continuing on to Formosa (Jean Hastings Ardell, *Breaking into Baseball*, 106–108).

20.2.6   Women on Men's Collegiate Baseball Teams.

At least five women have played for a men's collegiate baseball team. According to Gai Ingham Berlage, a young woman named Margaret Dobson played second base for Vanport College in Portland, Oregon, in a 1951 game against Clark Junior College (*South Bend Tribune*, April 14, 1951; quoted in Gai Ingham Berlage, *Women in Baseball*, 110). Susan Perabo played a single game for Division III Webster College in Missouri in 1985. Julie Croteau played first base for St. Mary's College in Maryland, another Division III school, in 1989. She met with harassment and eventually dropped out of school (Amy Ellis Nutt, "Swinging for the Fences," in Lissa Smith, ed., *Nike Is a Goddess*, 44). Jodi Haller pitched for NAIA St. Vincent's College in Pennsylvania in 1990. Ila Borders broke new ground by becoming the first woman ever to earn a baseball scholarship in 1994. She pitched for NAIA Southern California College for three seasons and then went on to a professional career (see **20.2.3** "Women in Organized Baseball") (Jean Hastings Ardell, *Breaking into Baseball*, 92–95).

20.2.7   Women Drafted by the Major Leagues.

The White Sox selected Carey Schueler, the daughter of team general manager Ron Schueler, in the forty-third round of the 1993 amateur draft. She never played professionally.

20.2.8 Women Coaches. In 1995 Julie Croteau became the first woman to coach for a Division I college baseball program when she was hired by the University of Massachusetts–Amherst.

20.2.9 League of Women. *Sporting Life* reported that a league of female players had been formed in Los Angeles on July 26, 1905 (*Sporting Life*, August 5, 1905).

On February 20, 1943, Philip K. Wrigley announced plans for the All-American Girls Softball League. Wrigley's intention was to have a backup in case the war necessitated the shutdown of major league baseball. Although that did not happen, the women's circuit went ahead and soon gained a life of its own. The league eventually switched to a smaller ball and overhand pitching and lasted for twelve years as the All-American Girls Baseball League.

The players' short skirts were a far cry from the uniforms of earlier women ballplayers. What hadn't changed was the tendency for the players to be judged on their appearance rather than their performance. Lois Browne cited the following example of the press coverage the league was apt to receive: "[Chicago Colleens manager Dave Bancroft] had to consult the chaperon of his charges to find out if his charges felt fit (after a rather long afternoon visit to the beauty parlor) to take the mound against the Muskegon Lassies. Fortunately, the pitcher was ready and willing and looking cute, with long, fluffy hair billowing from under her green cap" (quoted in Lois Browne, *Girls of Summer*, 147).

The All-American Girls Baseball League disbanded after the 1954 season and soon faded into obscurity. It was brought back to the public's attention in the early 1990s by the film *A League of Their Own*, which brought deserved recognition to these pioneers. Curiously, when interest in the league revived it came to be known as the All-American Girls Professional Baseball League.

20.2.10 Women Owners. George Van derbeck's wife briefly became owner of the Detroit franchise in the Western League during the couple's divorce proceedings in the mid-1890s.

The first woman to own a major league team was Helene Hathaway Robison Britton. She was thirty-two when she inherited the St. Louis Cardinals on March 24, 1911, upon the death of her uncle, Matthew Stanley Robison.

In 1916 she and her husband separated, and she assumed his role as team president. In 1912 Milwaukee Brewers owner Charles Havenor died, leaving control of the American Association team to his widow Agnes (*Sporting News*, May 23, 1912). The Brewers won the American Association pennant in 1913. Two female owners, Effa Manley and Olivia Taylor, played prominent roles in the Negro Leagues.

On January 4, 1931, Lucille Thomas purchased the Tulsa franchise in the Western League from St. Louis Browns owner Phil Ball. She became the first woman actually to buy a professional baseball team as opposed to inheriting one, and the development attracted considerable interest. Mrs. Thomas was a former schoolteacher who had studied the organ at the American Conservatory of Music in Chicago before marrying wealthy oil operator C. R. Thomas and establishing herself as a successful businesswoman in her own right.

She faced a formidable task: the Tulsa franchise had no stadium and accordingly had played its home games in Topeka, Kansas, in 1930. The depression was at its height, and Lucille Thomas had barely three months to raise the funds necessary to build a suitable home for the club. She immediately announced plans for a new stadium that would allow night ball, and energetically began the difficult task of finding investors.

Media interest focused on her gender, and she fielded plenty of impertinent, stereotypical questions. She responded as patiently as possible because she realized that the attention might make it easier to raise funds: "If this business of being a woman owner is so novel that I can capitalize on the publicity, I'll do it." She indicated, for example, that she intended to have an immaculately clean ballpark and would like to hire female ushers, but she denied rumors that her players would be required to study etiquette (*Sporting News*, January 22, 1931).

Unfortunately her fund-raising efforts were unsuccessful. Jittery investors were reluctant to back the new stadium, and as Opening Day approached it became clear that one would not be built. Eventually Lucille Thomas conceded the inevitable and surrendered the franchise (*Sporting News*, April 16, 1931).

20.2.11 Women Umpires. Researcher Mark Alvarez discovered that a Mrs. Doolittle signed the Knickerbockers' scorecard as the umpire of a game on June 8, 1847. Little is known about her (Jean Hastings Ardell, *Breaking into Base-*

ball, 138). *Sporting Life* reported in 1905 that Mrs. M. G. Turner of Cleveland had recently umpired a Lower Peninsula Lake League game at Lake Orion, Michigan (*Sporting Life*, February 25, 1905). (The fact that this note ran in February makes me skeptical.)

That same season saw seventeen-year-old Amanda Clement of Hudson, South Dakota, begin to umpire semiprofessional games in Iowa and South Dakota. By 1911 she had earned enough money to attend Yankton College in South Dakota. She went on to a career as a physical education instructor and coach.

During her six years of umpiring, she gained renown across the country. In 1905 *Sporting Life* described Amanda Clement as "probably the only girl in the country who is an umpire of professional base ball games. . . . She has received pay for her services. The ball players, though gallant toward women, frequently criticised her decisions quite as emphatically as they would those of a man. On such occasions she has had no hesitancy in talking back, and on half a dozen occasions has ordered players from games" (*Sporting Life*, October 7, 1905).

Clement herself told a somewhat different story in 1906: "Do you suppose any ball player in the country would step up to a good-looking girl and say to her, 'You color-blind, pickle-brained, cross-eyed idiot, if you don't stop throwing the soup into me I'll distribute your features all over your countenance!' Of course he wouldn't" (*Cincinnati Enquirer*, no date given; reprinted in Amy Ellis Nutt, "Swinging for the Fences," in Lissa Smith, ed., *Nike Is a Goddess*, 40).

In spite of these differing versions, there is no dispute that Clement did earn the respect of the men whose games she umpired. She received frequent commendations for her competence and impartiality (Gai Ingham Berlage, "Women Umpires as Mirrors of Gender Roles," *National Pastime* 14 [1994], 36–37). Nonetheless it was more than fifty years before another woman followed in her footsteps, and her experience was much less pleasant.

Bernice Gera graduated from an umpiring school in Florida in 1967 and began a long struggle to become a professional umpire. After years of litigation she finally became the first woman umpire in organized baseball history when she officiated a New York–Penn League game on June 24, 1972. Several disputes occurred, and she resigned between games of the doubleheader.

Christine Wren umpired in the Northwest League in 1975 and 1976 and in the Midwest League in 1977. She was considered a good umpire by the Midwest League president, but took a leave of absence at season's end and was able to find a better-paying job (Tom Gorman, *Three and Two!*, 167–168). Perry Barber officiated in the independent Atlantic League and also served as the league's director of umpiring (Jean Hastings Ardell, *Breaking into Baseball*, 150). Pam Postema umpired in the minors for thirteen years before being released after the 1989 season. She later filed suit against major league baseball for discrimination and received an out-of-court settlement.

Theresa Cox umpired in the Southern League periodically from 1988 to 1992 and in the Arizona Fall League in 1989 and 1990. Ria Cortesio Papageorgiou umpired in the minor leagues for nine years before being released in 2007. Shanna Kook umpired in the minor leagues in 2003 and 2004.

20.2.12   Women Sportswriters. The paradox that women were welcomed by baseball as spectators but not accepted in other capacities applied even to writing about the game, a sad reality that was thoughtfully explored by Jean Hastings Ardell in a chapter of her recent book (Jean Hastings Ardell, *Breaking into Baseball*, 190–213). Ardell noted that a woman named Ella Black served as a correspondent for *Sporting Life* in 1890, and her work attracted favorable comment. Nonetheless, for the next century women who tried to break into sportswriting were all too often patronized or met with outright hostility.

Polite condescension was the preferred method until the 1970s. Women who attempted to write about baseball found that they themselves were the story, which effectively prevented them from having their work judged on its merits. Nowhere was this more evident than in the headlines affixed to their submissions, which it seems safe to assume were the handiwork of male headline writers. Ella Black's work appeared under such headlines as "Only a Woman: But She Has Some Ideas about the Make-Up of the Pittsburg Clubs" and "The First Game: As Viewed by One of the Weaker Sex"; early-twentieth-century sportswriter Ina Eloise Young's writing ran beneath such titles as "Eying Dresses and Hats as Well as Worlds' [sic] Series Games: Characteristic of Her Sex, Miss Young Notes How Wives of Champion

Ball Players Dress" and "Petticoats and the Press Box"; and during World War II, Jeane Hoffman's byline appeared beneath the likes of "No 'End' to Jokes, Girl Finds, in Yankee Stadium Press Box" (*Sporting Life*, April 12, 1890; April 26, 1890; *Trinidad* [Colo.] *Chronicle-News*, October 15, 1908; *Baseball Magazine*, May 1908; *New York Journal-American*, December 3, 1942; all quoted in Jean Hastings Ardell, *Breaking into Baseball*, 192, 195, 256). Obviously such headlines would have made it difficult to take the accompanying articles seriously.

The second half of the twentieth century saw more women pursuing careers as sportswriters, and their presence was met with increasingly vehement resistance, much of which concentrated on the appropriateness of allowing women in the locker room. Yet the fact that accredited female journalists also had a hard time being allowed to sit in the press box with their fully clothed male colleagues suggests that there were underlying issues (Jean Hastings Ardell, *Breaking into Baseball*, 190–191, 200–201, 206–208). Pioneering sportswriter Anita Martini reported that she was initially not allowed to eat in the press dining room at the Astrodome (Melvin Durslag, *Sporting News*, November 11, 1978). In the past decade or two, this resistance has finally begun to disappear.

20.2.13 Women Broadcasters. In 1938 golfer Helen Dettweiler was hired by the General Mills Company to act as a sort of goodwill ambassador by touring the country and broadcasting local games ("Helen Dettweiler to Become Woman Baseball Announcer," *Washington Post*, June 19, 1938). An article in *Sporting News* later that summer reported that she had already visited twenty cities and that her play-by-play accounts "are authoritative and have gained her much commendation." It added, "Until she entered the field, play-by-play accounts of games had been confined to men, but Miss Dettweiler has succeeded in breaking down that barrier, under the auspices of General Mills, and with the aid of a charming personality and thorough knowledge of the game has brought sample broadcasts from a woman's point of view to thousands of listeners" (*Sporting News*, August 25, 1938).

In the early 1950s actress Laraine Day hosted a fifteen-minute pregame television show entitled "Day with the Giants" while the Giants were managed by her husband, Leo Durocher (*Washington Post*, May 21, 1950). At the tailend of the 1964 season, Charles O.

Finley assigned Betty Caywood to broadcasts of Kansas City Athletics games. Finley made no bones about his intention to exploit her for ratings: "The idea is that by putting a woman on staff we'll appeal to the dolls" (*New York Times*, September 17, 1964).

In 1971 Wendie Regalia began broadcasting Giants pregame shows. She conducted interviews all season long but quit at season's end to break ground in another endeavor—as an agent representing five prominent members of the San Francisco 49ers (AP: *Lima* [Ohio] *News*, December 12, 1971). Five years later Houston sportswriter Anita Martini earned the distinction of being the first woman to broadcast a National League game (Jean Hastings Ardell, *Breaking into Baseball*, 202).

After the 1976 season the White Sox engaged Mary Shane as the first regular female play-by-play announcer (*Chicago Tribune*, December 22, 1976). According to fellow broadcaster Jimmy Piersall, even pioneer club owner Bill Veeck was lukewarm toward the novel concept. As one of four White Sox broadcasters, it was easy to reduce Shane's role. After brief appearances on thirty-five home games, mostly on the radio, she was phased out. Piersall recollected: "She never had a chance. Even a bad baseball player gets at least one full season to see if he'll come around. But because of all the in-bred prejudice against a woman covering a baseball team, Mary didn't even get that. It was a real shame because I think she had what it takes to make it, and some day the idea of a woman bringing a woman's perspective to baseball broadcasting will be a tremendous innovation somewhere." Shane went on to success as an NBA beat reporter (Jim O'Donnell, "Death Stirs Memories of Broadcast Pioneer," *Chicago Herald*, November 5, 1987).

20.2.14 Women Public Address Announcers. Sherry Davis was hired as the public address announcer of the San Francisco Giants in 1992, becoming the first female to hold such a post for any major American professional team. She described her job in considerable detail to George Gmelch and J. J. Weiner in their book *In the Ballpark*. Since 2000 the Giants have employed Renel Brooks-Moon in that capacity.

20.2.15 Women Scouts. The husband-and-wife team of Roy and Bessie Largent scouted the South for the Chicago White Sox in the 1930s, finding such players as Zeke Bonura, Smead Jolley, and Hall of Famer Luke Appling. Researcher Rod Nelson of the SABR Scouts Committee reported that both of their names appear on many, though not all, of the contracts and other official club documents.

An article in *Sporting News* noted, "Mrs. Largent is as much a scout as Roy and it is often her judgment that determines whether a prospect should be obtained or rejected. . . . Mrs. Largent made all the trips with Roy until last year, when her health failed, but she has since fully recovered and again is shouldering her half of the work. He gives her much credit for his success and claims she knows more ball players than any woman in the world" (*Sporting News*, January 10, 1935).

Edith Houghton, who had toured Japan with the Philadelphia Bobbies as a thirteen-year-old in 1925 (see **20.2.5** "Women Touring Overseas"), was hired as a Phillies scout in 1946. According to Phillies owner Bob Carpenter, "She just kept pestering me, and I've always had a weakness for anyone with drive and initiative. She said, 'Just give me a chance.' So I did . . . she went out and signed some players for us. None of 'em made the big leagues, but they were okay. She knew a ballplayer when she saw one" (Kevin Kerrane, *Dollar Sign on the Muscle*, 77). Houghton scouted in Pennsylvania and Ohio for about five years (Jean Hastings Ardell, *Breaking into Baseball*, 108).

The recent trend away from traditional scouting and toward a greater reliance on video clips has provided more opportunities for women to break into the profession. Major league baseball's Scouting Bureau now employs a number of women.

20.2.16 Bloomer Girls. Researcher Barbara Gregorich indicated that the first club to be known as Bloomer Girls originated around 1892 (Barbara Gregorich, "Jackie and the Juniors vs. Margaret and the Bloomers," *National Pastime* 13 [1993], 9). Bloomer Girls became a generic name used by many touring teams of the early twentieth century and often included one or two men disguised by wigs.

20.2.17 African-American Women. The All-American Girls Baseball League never integrated, though two African-American players tried out with South Bend in 1951. But at least three African-American women—Toni Stone, Connie Morgan, and Mamie "Peanut" Johnson—played in the Negro Leagues in the 1950s, with Stone having the most distinguished ca-

reer. While these women were talented athletes, they were hired because of being terrific gate attractions rather than strictly on merit (Alan Pollock, *Barnstorming to Heaven*, especially pages 112 and 244; Neil Lanctot, *Negro League Baseball*, 382–383). Twenty years earlier, Isabel Baxter had become the first woman to play in the Negro Leagues when she played a single game for the Cleveland Giants in 1933 (Jean Hastings Ardell, *Breaking into Baseball*, 110).

(iii) Other Minorities

20.3.1 Jewish Major Leaguers. Lipman Pike starred for numerous clubs in the 1860s and '70s and had a reputation as one of the era's most powerful hitters. He is also credited with being the first Jewish manager, serving as playing captain for Hartford in 1874 and briefly having that role for Troy in 1871 and for Cincinnati in 1877. As was the custom of the day, his heritage was frequently remarked upon. I have found no evidence that he faced the prejudice encountered by later Jewish players such as Hank Greenberg. For whatever reason, Jewish major leaguers remained rare in the nineteenth century. In 1897 O. P. Caylor wrote, "When [Danny] Friend made his appearance with the Chicagos in 1895, it was generally believed and so understood that he was a Hebrew. I took occasion then to call attention to the fact that the Jew in professional baseball playing, in spite of the remunerative returns, had never been an element of competition with the Irish and Germans. Friend promptly denied that he was a Hebrew, and that reduced the case to one in which no member of the Jewish race ever attained prominence as a ball player. Why it is so none has ever tried to explain. It may be that the indolent life of the diamond is not in accord with the constantly active ways of the true Hebrew" (*Philadelphia North American*, March 25, 1897).

20.3.2 Hispanic Major Leaguers. Cuban-born Esteban Bellan played for Troy in 1871, the first year of the National Association.

The first Hispanic to play in the National League was Vincent Nava, a prominent catcher in the early 1880s. Nava's dark skin attracted a great deal of comment, much of it ill-informed. He was often referred to as being either Cuban or African American. In fact, as Joel S. Franks has shown and my research has confirmed, Nava was born in California to a Mexican mother (Joel S. Franks, *Whose Baseball?*, 46).

At some point, Nava's mother married an Englishman named Irwin, and that was the name he used while playing ball in his native San Francisco. When he first came east in 1882 he was initially referred to as Vincent Irwin, but that was soon replaced by Nava (*Cleveland Leader*, March 25, April 12, and April 14, 1882). He became known as Nava in baseball circles, but Californians still clung to the earlier name, referring to him as "Vincent Nava, known on this coast as 'Sandy' Irwin" (*San Francisco Examiner*, January 10, 1887).

The reasons for his name change are not known. Franks speculated that Nava may have been motivated by pride in his heritage but also noted that he could have been trying to make clear that he was not of African-American descent.

When Nava first came east in 1882 to play for Providence, he was accompanied by another young Californian named Mike DePangher. As with Nava, he was described in news accounts as a Cuban, but the 1860 census listed him as "Miguel DePanghere," with a father born in Italy and a mother in Chile. According to Providence sportswriter William Perrin, when the signings were announced at a stockholders' meeting, "There was some opposition to the signing of the players because of their nationality." In the end, however, "the idea went through and the men reported," though only Nava had a significant major league career (William D. Perrin, *Days of Greatness*, 16).

The color line also restricted the access of Hispanics to major league baseball, but its application was very uneven. Cuban-born Chick Pedroes was a longtime Chicago semipro who played two games for the Cubs in 1902. Cincinnati signed two Cubans in 1911, and they were reported to be "two of the purest bars of Castilian soap ever floated to these shores" (quoted in Mark Rucker and Peter C. Bjarkman, *Smoke*, 43). Light-skinned Cubans regularly gained admission to the white major leagues in the ensuing years, but this was not the case for ballplayers from other regions of Latin America.

A rare exception was Louis Castro, a native of Colombia who had a brief major league career and a long minor league career. Castro learned to his chagrin just how seriously race is taken in the United States—while managing the Portsmouth team in the Virginia League he jokingly "told Southern scribes that former president [Cipriano] Castro of Venezuela was his uncle. Then when he learned that President Castro has negro blood in his veins he wished

he could recall the joke" (*Sporting News*, February 20, 1913).

Once the color line was abolished, major league scouts began to hunt for talent in Latin America. Ever since the 1950s, the region has produced a disproportionate amount of talent, including such superstars as Luis Aparicio, Roberto Clemente, Juan Marichal, Rod Carew, Roberto Alomar, Pedro Martinez, and Sammy Sosa.

Lou Castro managed in the minors, and Mike Gonzalez was a longtime major league coach. But the first major league manager of Hispanic origin was Preston Gomez with the San Diego Padres in 1969.

20.3.3   Native American Major Leaguers.
The first Native American to play major league baseball was Tom Oran, who played for one of the two St. Louis entries in the National Association in 1875. Joe Visner, a Chippewa, played for five major league teams between 1885 and 1891. Jim Toy reached the major leagues in 1887, and his nephew later reported that Toy's father was a Sioux. But Toy's father either died or left the family when he was very young, so there is no corroboration of the nephew's claim (Ed Rice, *Baseball's First Indian*, 26–30). Louis Sockalexis became the first prominent Native American major leaguer for Cleveland in 1897, and there is controversy about whether the nickname of the Indians was a tribute to him. Sockalexis's debut prompted sportswriter O. P. Caylor to maintain, "There is no prejudice against the Indian such as has always existed against the negro" (*Philadelphia North American*, March 25, 1897). Chief Bender was the first Native American elected to the Hall of Fame.

20.3.4   Japanese Major Leaguers.
In 1964 Masanori Murakami became the first Japanese player to make the jump to this country's major leagues. He pitched effectively for the San Francisco Giants for two seasons and then returned to his homeland, where there had been some disapproval of his decision to play in the United States.

There had been earlier Japanese ballplayers who were apparently denied the opportunity to play major league baseball by racial prejudice. Sportswriter William F. H. Koelsch reported in 1905: "Shumza Sugimoto, the Japanese ball player, who is now at Hot Springs, and may be taken by [Giants' manager John] McGraw, does not like the drawing of the color line in his case, and says he will remain a semi-professional with the Creole Stars of New Orleans if his engagement with the Giants will be resented by the players of other clubs" (*Sporting Life,* February 25, 1905). Before the 1911 season, McGraw attempted to sign another Japanese star named Togo Hammanoto (Larry Mansch, *Rube Marquard,* 73).

20.3.5 Deaf Major Leaguers. The distinction of being the first deaf major leaguer most likely belongs to Paul Hines, who starred in the majors from 1872 to 1891 despite a severe loss of hearing. Hines was not deaf from birth, and his hearing loss was not total. But it did plague him for much of his career, with the *New York Clipper* stating in 1879 that he was "as deaf as a post" (*New York Clipper,* October 18, 1879). Hines was able to "overcome his infirmity in a measure by means of an acoustic cane" (*St. Louis Globe-Democrat,* March 25, 1883). Even so, he was described by another reporter as "almost totally deaf" and as being unable to hear his teammates yelling (William D. Perrin, *Days of Greatness,* 16; see also *Sporting Life,* July 22, 1883).

Another candidate is Doug Allison, who was the catcher of the famed Red Stockings of Cincinnati and who played in the major leagues from 1871 to 1883. Researcher David Arcidiacono discovered a couple of references to Allison's being partially deaf, including an 1876 article that his deafness resulted from his Civil War service: "Allison was a gunner in Fort Sumpter [sic] during the late war, and is the only survivor of three batches of gunners of six men in each batch. His service during the war accounts for his impaired hearing" (*Boston Globe,* March 24, 1876). Allison was in fact a Civil War veteran, but he enlisted in 1864 and his regiment saw no combat duty, so this account must be taken with a grain of salt. But it seems clear that he was deaf, with an 1879 note also describing him as having "grown deaf and infirm" (*St. Louis Globe-Democrat,* July 27, 1879, 3).

A third candidate was William Craver, another Civil War veteran who caught in the major leagues from 1871 until being banned for life in 1877. In 1892 he filed a pension application and reported that he was "almost wholly unable to earn a support by manual labor by reason of left hand crippled—deafness proceeding from yellow fever" (William Craver Hall of Fame file, Craver's invalid pension, dated June 28, 1892).

These men were succeeded in professional baseball by several products of the Ohio School for the Deaf in Columbus. The school had a prominent baseball team in the 1870s and 1880s, and went on a tour of the state in 1879. Several of its players made the leap to professional baseball. When the school reopened for the 1883–1884 academic year, the school newspaper noted matter-of-factly that students John Ryn and Ed Dundon had spent their summer vacations playing baseball (*Mutes Chronicle,* September 6, 1883).

Dundon had in fact played in the major leagues that summer. His stay in the majors was undistinguished, as was that of Gallaudet student Tom Lynch, who pitched a single game for Chicago in 1884 (see entry **1.32,** "Substitutions" for a description of that game's unusual and controversial outcome). But 1888 saw the debut of Ohio School for the Deaf alumnus Billy Hoy, who collected more than two thousand major league hits while playing for such woeful teams that a reporter quipped that "a pitcher and catcher and Mr. Hoy constitute the Washington Baseball Club. The other six men who accompany them are put in the field for the purpose of making errors" (*Washington Post,* May 11, 1888).

Hoy modestly downplayed the handicaps he had to overcome: "While at school I played catcher and third base as well as outfielder, but in the professional game I have always been in center field, because my deafness is less of a handicap there than it would be as an infielder." He added that there was even less disadvantage when batting: "I can see the ball as well as others and my team mates tell me whether a ball or strike is called by using the left fingers for balls and the right fingers for strikes. In base running the signals of the hit and run game and other stratagems are mostly silent, and the same as for the other players. By a further system of sign [sic] my team mates keep me posted on how many are out and what is going on around me. . . . So it may be seen the handicaps of a deaf ball player are minimized" (*Grand Valley* [Moab, Utah] *Times,* July 12, 1901).

Nor did Hoy's handicap earn him any concessions from opponents. During his second season the Cleveland Spiders recognized that a deaf man would be peculiarly vulnerable to the hidden ball trick and began to scheme. With Hoy on second base, three Cleveland players handled the ball until second baseman "[Cub] Stricker got hold of it and crept up behind

Hoy, hoping that the latter would step off his base. The mute was onto the little game, and when Stricker stood beside him he smacked the hand that held the ball, and the dogskin rolled several feet away. Before Stricker realized what had happened Hoy was safe on third base. Captain [Jay] Faatz made a vigorous kick, but Umpire [Lon] Knight held that there was no rule to cover such a play. It was simply a case of dog eat dog. [Patsy] Tebeau captured the ball during the dispute and concealed it under his arm with the intention of getting even with the mute. The latter was wide awake as usual, and deliberately squatted down on the base and would not move until he saw the ball returned to [Henry] Gruber, who was pitching" (*Sporting Life*, September 11, 1889).

Hoy's success paved the way to the major leagues for R. C. Stephenson, George M. Leitner, William Deegan, Luther Taylor, Dick Sipek, and Curtis Pride. Major leaguers with substantial hearing impairment have included Hines, Allison, Pete Browning, Frank Chance, and Bobby Jones.

Chapter 21

PARTICIPANTS

A LARGE PART of the appeal of the pre-1850 prototypes of baseball was that they were flexible enough to include any number of participants. If twelve children were playing and three more showed up, they could be included. Melville McGee, for instance, offered these recollections about how baseball was played in the 1830s: "It seems to me now as I look back and recall those early days that the young people enjoyed their sports and games and entered into them with far more zest then young people do at the present day. There was no feeling of envy or superiority, or the feeling that you don't belong to my set. All were on a level, and everyone was just as good as any other" (Melville McGee, "The Early Days of Concord, Jackson County, Michigan," *Michigan Pioneer and Historical Collections* 21 [1892], 430).

Of all the elements that the Knickerbockers added to baseball, perhaps the most fundamental was exclusion. Once their rules had been fine-tuned, a baseball match included eighteen players and no more. A game lasted nine innings, and once started, latecomers were excluded. Nonparticipants were excluded from the playing field. Then enclosed fields were adopted, meaning that nonparticipants couldn't even watch without paying admission. The game had changed from an inclusive activity to an exclusive one.

As baseball prospered, the pendulum began to swing back the other way. Clubs discovered a variety of roles for nonplayers, and the ranks of those involved in baseball again started to swell. Not all these people were immediately paid for their work, and many of them wore multiple hats; yet each addition increased the sense that the game was again trying to include a cross-section of Americans.

In 1883 *Harper's Weekly* reported that one stadium had a game-day staff of forty-one people: seven ushers, six policemen, four ticket sellers, four gatekeepers, three fieldmen, three cushion renters, six refreshment boys, and eight musicians (*Harper's Weekly*, May 12, 1883). While I have not tried to ascertain the identity of the first cushion renter, I have tried to explain how and when several new types of baseball people were added.

21.1 Security Personnel. A security force was on hand for an 1858 game at the Fashion Race Course in New York. Coincidentally—or maybe not—this was also the first game at which an admission fee was charged.

21.2 Ticket Takers. In the 1860s and 1870s it was not uncommon for spectators to find their tickets being taken by the home club's extra player. This practice originated for two reasons, one obvious and the other less so.

The obvious reason was that budgets were tight and everyone was expected to help out wherever possible. The more subtle reason dated back to the mid-1860s, when players were successful with their unprecedented demand for a share of the gate proceeds. In order to ensure that they weren't being gypped by the owners of the parks, "the players then appointed one of their number—the extra man—to count tickets" (James Wood as told to Frank G. Menke, "Baseball in By-Gone Days, Part 3," syndicated column, *Indiana* [Pa.] *Evening Gazette*, August 17, 1916).

Alan Pollock noted that the Indianapolis Clowns, the legendary mid-twentieth-century African-American barnstorming team, sometimes revived this practice—especially when they suspected they were not getting their fair share of the gate receipts (Alan Pollock, *Barnstorming to Heaven*, 62).

21.3 Ushers.

The usher had begun to make the lives of spectators easier as early as 1872, when a Cleveland newspaper reported: "The grounds have been 'fixed up' in capital style, having been made quite level and thoroughly rolled. Joe Murch is superintendent. He will have some great improvements made and is making several arrangements for the convenience of those who go to see matched games. Among other changes, ice water will be furnished free to spectators, an usher will be employed to seat ladies, no intoxicating liquors will be sold, lemonade, confectionery, ice cream and fruits may be obtained at the grand stand" (*Cleveland Plain Dealer*, April 20, 1872). Richard Bak claims that it was only after Ty Cobb went into the stands during a 1912 game to attack a heckler that it became standard for all major league parks to employ ushers (Richard Bak, *Peach*, 93–94).

21.4 Vendors.

Vendors seem to attract notice only when they are the subject of a complaint. An Adrian, Michigan, newspaper grumbled in 1879, "Hereafter the vending of peanuts, lemonade, etc., in the grand stand at Blissfield, should be prohibited. People purchase seats there to see the game and not to gaze on the oft-appearing form of the peddler, who is sure to stand just in front of you when a fine play is being made. An indignant public will gratefully remember the manager who will ban these bores from all grand stands forever" (*Adrian Daily Times and Expositor*, August 23, 1879).

An Ohio newspaper echoed the theme in 1898: "Fakirs climbing across the stands during the play are also another unpleasant thing. Of course 'butchers' must hustle and people get thirsty, but when the score is a tie or one run to the good a kid asking if you wish lemonade, gum or pop is a nuisance" (*Youngstown Vindicator*, April 4, 1898). And one year later another sportswriter commented, "The Philadelphia Club has made a change which will be appreciated by its patrons. Venders [sic] of score cards, etc., will only be allowed to call out their wares between innings and before games" (*Philadelphia Evening Bulletin*, April 13, 1899).

In 1952 owner Paul Fagan of the San Francisco Seals tried to ban peanuts because he concluded that it cost the club more to clean them up than they made by selling them. Fans were outraged and promised to bring peanuts into the stadium and make more of a mess than ever. An ambassador from a South American peanut-producing country even called the owner to voice his concerns. Fagan had to concede the point (Dick Dobbins and Jon Twichell, *Nuggets on the Diamond*, 246; Red Smith, March 23, 1952, reprinted in *Red Smith on Baseball*).

21.5 Official Scorers.

In early baseball each club had its own scorer. The position was deemed highly important, and scorers had their own seating area. Nonetheless, until statistics began to develop, their main function was to keep track of the score, and even on this they sometimes disagreed.

As statistics became an important part of baseball, a single person assumed the function of official scorer. It was not long before onlookers were second-guessing his decisions. The *Cincinnati Enquirer* noted in 1878, "The Cincinnati 'official scorer' gets more and more demoralized every day. His score of Wednesday's League game is full of errors" (*Cincinnati Enquirer*, May 3, 1878).

Soon players began to complain as well. In 1885, George "Orator" Shafer reportedly told his team's owner, Henry Lucas, that he wanted to play elsewhere because his base hits were being incorrectly ruled as errors. Lucas asked, "Am I to blame because a reporter makes a mistake?" Shafer replied, "You employ the official scorer that's downing me" (*St. Louis Post-Dispatch*, July 9, 1885).

Shafer's concern reflected his awareness that players were being judged—and being paid—on the basis of their statistical record. Indeed by 1880 Chicago president William Hulbert was employing a special scorer to track such things as "chances to advance men, chances succeeded, total bases, runs batted home" in the hope that he could arrive at "a correct analysis of the batting, and demonstrate a player['s] strength" (*Troy Whig*, June 12, 1880 and *Chicago Inter-Ocean*, May 15, 1880; both quoted in Howard W. Rosenberg, *Cap Anson 1*, 41).

All the attention devoted to the official scorer during the nineteenth century often seems wildly disproportionate. For example, National League owners had countless important issues to discuss following the completion of the league's first season in 1876. At their annual meetings they faced such crucial issues as whether to expel the New York and Philadelphia entries, whether to replace those franchises, devising the first schedule, and fixing the problems caused by hometown umpires. And yet press accounts of the meeting made it sound as though standardized scoring was one of the owners' greatest concerns (*Chicago Tribune*, December 10, 1876, 7).

While this preoccupation seems remarkably shortsighted, perhaps it wasn't. After all, baseball's unparalleled statistical record is the direct result of this early emphasis on standard practices—and it may even be argued that taking this issue so seriously is responsible for the allegiance of all the fans who delight in baseball statistics. In any event, baseball continued to make the official scorer a priority, and in 1897 National League president Nick Young began appointing all official scorers, a move that was hailed as a "change [that] will give the players some sort of justice" (*Chicago Tribune*, March 10, 1897, 8).

21.6 Batboys. The earliest mention of batboys I have encountered is an 1880 reference to "Al. Pierce, the colored youth who used to officiate as bat carrier of the St. Louis Browns" (*New York Clipper*, August 14, 1880). In 1884 the American Association passed a rule permitting the use of a batboy or batgirl. Henry Lucas also used a batboy at St. Louis's Union Grounds that season: "A colored boy in uniform takes the bat from each sticker, and hands it to him when his time to go to the bat comes" (*Cincinnati News-Journal*, May 13, 1884).

21.7 Groundskeepers. The very tight budgets of early baseball meant that the groundskeeping was often done by someone with other responsibilities. August Solari owned and operated St. Louis's Grand Avenue diamond in the 1860s and later became the full-time groundskeeper for several St. Louis teams. When the pitching arm of Joe Borden went dead in 1876, he became the Boston groundskeeper (see **18.5.4** "Multi-Year Contracts"). In the early 1880s Detroit hired groundskeeper John Piggott who could be used as an extra player in case of injury (*Detroit Post and Tribune*, March 30, 1882).

The *St. Louis Post-Dispatch* reported in 1883: "The games played [in New Orleans] now don't draw much more than enough people to pay the salary of the ground-keeper" (*St. Louis Post-Dispatch*, December 24, 1883). The note is significant because it simultaneously demonstrates that groundskeeping was becoming a full-time position and that it remained touch and go whether clubs could afford this added salary.

By the late 1880s the position was so involved that there was no alternative to having a full-time groundskeeper. An 1887 article described Detroit groundskeeper "Uncle" Billy Houston as "without doubt the best base ball ground keeper in the country" and provided a fascinating look at his routine: "Almost anybody can roll and mow a lawn, but the putting of a diamond into the proper condition is an entirely different matter. Uncle Billy has a mysterious method of procedure which he refuses to divulge to anybody. This much he tells of his modus operandi. He uses three or four different kinds of earth, the top layer being black. He sifts all the earth he puts on the runways in order that nothing may be left there that would injure a man in sliding to a base. Mixed in with the top layer of earth is a sort of fluffy weed, which Billy says imparts a springy quality to the runway. As a result of the work he has so far done the runways and spots where the infielders stand are as near perfection as possible, being so level a ball will roll on them like a billiard table. By sprinkling the earth is kept at the proper consistency and the runways are kept so smooth and springy it seems possible for anybody to steal a base.... He watches closely during a game, and if a ball takes an erratic shoot after striking the ground Billy notes the spot, and remedies the defect at the earliest opportunity" (*Detroit Free Press*, May 16, 1887).

And in 1893 this description was offered of the daily routine of Pittsburgh groundskeeper James Pridie: "Every day the club is home the ground is rolled with five ton rollers, and the field is thoroughly sprinkled with water; then the ground-keeper goes over the entire infield with a rake and levels the ground, fills up all the ground, and every little defect is looked after. Then the ground is rolled again. After the work has all been attended to the pitcher and batter's box is chalked, then the base lines, the coachers' and the outside boundary lines are all lined with chalk. After every game the pitcher's and batter's boxes are covered over with large tarpaulins, in case it should rain before the next game, and to keep the ground from dew" (*Sporting News*, December 9, 1893).

In addition to these arduous duties, groundskeepers often wore extra hats. Their responsibilities were apt to include security, crowd control, fire and safety inspections, and other miscellaneous chores. A St. Louis groundskeeper even spied on team owner Chris Von der Ahe and testified at one of his divorce trials (*Sporting Life*, April 6, 1895).

21.8 Batting Practice Pitchers. In early baseball, batting practice was usually just fungo hitting, despite the regular protests of Henry Chadwick (see **2.4.3**). Even once it became a little more organized, it was usually pitched by anyone available who could get the ball over the plate.

The position began to gain a little more prestige when clubs started seeking batting practice pitchers who could simulate a type of pitching that was likely to give the club trouble. In the late 1880s the Detroit Wolverines had a lot of left-handed hitters who tended to struggle against southpaws. In response they often used a left-handed pitcher named Howard Lawrence to pitch batting practice (*Boston Globe*, May 21, 1886).

For many years batting practice was thrown by a member of the staff who was between starts. This was changed in the late 1920s by Cubs pitcher Henry Grampp. Sportswriter Edward Burns observed, "All other major league clubs rotate the job of pitching in batting practice among pitchers several days away from any possible turn to pitch. Not so the Cubs—that's Hank's job 154 days of the season" (Edward Burns, "Henry Grampp's in Town, So All Cubs Feel Fine," *Chicago Tribune*, January 31, 1929).

It was Grampp's "talent for impersonation" that made him so valuable (Edward Burns, "Henry Grampp's in Town, So All Cubs Feel Fine," *Chicago Tribune*, January 31, 1929). Sportswriter James S. Collins explained, "If the Cubs are to face Carl Mays, for instance, Mr. Grampp goes out there and throws up a few underhand balls to the Cub sluggers. If [Grover Cleveland] Alexander is expected to be the opposing pitcher, we are told, he gives an imitation of Alexander's style." Grampp was with the Cubs from 1927 until 1929, yet appeared in only three major league games during these years. Collins observed dryly that the umpire's cry of "Play Ball" was "Grampp's cue to call it a day and hie himself to the showers. Next to managing the Phillies, Mr. Grampp's seems the most unattractive job baseball has offered since an unsung hero filled a line on the Giants'

pay roll as keeper of the late 'Bugs' Raymond" (James S. Collins, "Almost the Naked Truth," *Washington Post*, March 21, 1929). In 1930 Grampp returned to the minor leagues.

Eric Nadel and Craig R. Wright claimed that Grampp was ambidextrous, but the evidence belies this claim (Eric Nadel and Craig R. Wright, *The Man Who Stole First Base*, 14). Burns stated that Grampp "works a half shift when a left hander is slated by the opposition," which doesn't seem to suggest that he threw left-handed (Edward Burns, "Henry Grampp's in Town, So All Cubs Feel Fine," *Chicago Tribune*, January 31, 1929).

Eventually teams began to have left-handed pitchers on hand specifically for this role. Tony Gwynn noted that when he wanted to practice a specific hitting approach in 1988, "I came out early and had our left-handed batting practice pitcher throw to me" (George F. Will, *Men at Work*, 220).

21.9 Ticket Scalpers. Ticket scalpers were plying their trade at baseball games as early as 1886, when the *Boston Globe* reported, "Ticket fakirs made a harvest at yesterday's game. Ten cents was the advance asked on the regular price" (*Boston Globe*, June 1, 1886).

21.10 Trainers. The use of trainers had become common in many sports by the 1890s, including boxing, horse racing, cycling, and track and field. By the late 1880s college baseball nines were beginning to hire professional trainers (*Chicago Inter-Ocean*, February 12, 1888, 12). Major league baseball clubs, however, showed more resistance to the idea.

A few did take the plunge during the latter half of the 1880s. Brooklyn president Charles Byrne referred in 1887 to "our experienced trainer, Mr. McMasters" (*Brooklyn Eagle*, March 23, 1887). Jack McMasters was one of the earliest baseball trainers and may well have been the first man to fill that position full time. A 1900 article reported, "It is not generally known that Jack McMasters, the well-known trainer at Harvard, is the first man who regularly trained a professional baseball team. He was engaged by the late Charles H. Byrne of the Brooklyn club to look after the players of that organization from 1886 to 1890. Previous to that time McMasters had been the trainer for the Williamsburg Athletic club" (*Milwaukee Journal*, April 3, 1900). Lee Allen reported that McMasters had also previously worked with boxers (Lee Allen, *The Hot Stove League*, 114).

Some other clubs were also using trainers. According to Larry Lupo, the Metropolitans had a trainer in 1886 (Larry Lupo, *When the Mets Played Baseball on Staten Island*, 86). Chris Von der Ahe appears to have hired one to work on his St. Louis players in 1885, but only during spring training (*Rocky Mountain News*, April 13, 1887, 10). In 1887 the Phillies hired a man named Tom Taylor who was described as "the attendant, or, as he calls himself, the 'trainer,' of the Philadelphia players. He looks after their wants on and off the field, rubs them down, and evidently considers himself an indispensable part of the club's equipment. He sits on the players' bench during all the games and watches every point with the absorbed attention of a devotee. He is usually accompanied by a big kit of bottles, surgical instruments, and other articles of more or less utility, and the players apparently have implicit confidence in Tom's judgment, or perhaps it is that they regard their enthusiastic admirer as a mascot" (*St. Louis Globe-Democrat*, May 15, 1887, 8). By 1889 the Phillies were employing both a trainer and a team physician (Jerrold Casway, *Ed Delahanty and the Emerald Age of Baseball*, 35). But as the description of Taylor suggests, major league clubs did not accord trainers much professional respect. After the costly 1890 war between the players and the owners, the practice of employing trainers appears to have pretty much died out.

In 1898, with trainers an increasingly prominent feature of other sports, a *Sporting News* correspondent lambasted baseball for falling behind the times: "It is an accepted axiom among athletes of the higher order that no man can train himself. They know nothing of a trainer around base ball teams." He offered a scathing comparison between cyclists and ballplayers: "From the first day the racer goes into training until the last day of the season he is never out of the trainer's sight. The trainer eats, walks, drinks and sleeps with his man. He says at what hour he shall arise and at what minute he shall retire. . . . Now for your base ball player. Every spring he is taken from the North to the South with from 25 to 40 other men of all classes. He has no one to control or direct him. He is free to train himself. I fancy that when Byron wrote that sarcastic line, 'Lord of himself, that heritage of woe,' he had in mind a base ball player in training." The correspondent continued: "I wager that if [New York pitchers Amos] Rusie and [Jouett] Meekin were put in the hands of a competent trainer . . . those great pitchers would be fit as a fiddle on April 1. But the New York club has not got any trainers and it will pay Rusie and Meekin for a month's sitting on the bench. Their combined salaries for that month would pay a good trainer for the season" ("Dan Irish," "System Is Bad," *Sporting News*, February 19, 1898, 2).

Cincinnati owner John T. Brush seemed unimpressed by this reasoning, commenting: "I have often heard the writers confound training with practice. They should make some distinction. A prize fighter trains and a ball player practices" (*Sporting News*, February 26, 1898). Yet within weeks he reversed his course and hired a graduate of a Stockholm medical school: "President Brush has engaged Dr. M. A. Frey, a Swedish massage professor, to look well to the arms and legs of the player. . . . Not only in training, but through the entire season he will be with the team, treating their sore muscles at home and when traveling" (*Sporting Life*, March 5, 1898). Frey, who weighed a mere ninety pounds, quit the position after two years to become a jockey (Lee Allen, *The Hot Stove League*, 114).

In spite of Frey's defection, the use of trainers was recognized as an idea whose time had come. The *Cincinnati Enquirer* confirmed that the expense of a trainer was more than offset by the savings that resulted: "There can be no doubt that the scheme as tried by Cincinnati last year was productive of much good. When 'Buck' Ewing came to Chicago with his victorious Porkopolis players, he emphatically declared that it was the constant care and supervision exercised by Dr. Frey that kept his men in good condition. The doctor, he said, was worth all he cost and many times more. Some of the Orphans last year were in the habit of visiting a Turkish bath establishment to be attended by a skillful masseur and doctor. Their bills were invariably quite steep, and the club paid them without much of a protest. It is thought that the services of a doctor to follow the men would cost little in proportion to what he might save the Chicago Club. 'A rub or two in time might keep some player in the game who might otherwise be out of service for several weeks,' said Jimmy Callahan" (*Cincinnati Enquirer*, January 15, 1899).

Within the space of two years, the perception of the trainer changed from an expensive luxury to a virtual necessity. Tim Murnane observed in 1900, "The need of a trainer, or a rubber, is now keenly felt by [Boston] manager [Frank] Selee. . . . Few up-to-date clubs dream of starting to train for a season's hard work without a skilled trainer. In this respect the Boston club has not advanced one inch, sticking still to the methods in vogue in 1876, when every man was his own trainer and rubber. As players are valuable assets for the big clubs it seems only reasonable that they would take every precaution to keep the boys in the pink of condition by having a man over them who has made the game a life study. This is what Selee believes and would like to see come about as soon as possible" (*Boston Globe*, April 2, 1900).

In 1907 the *Detroit News* reported, "Each year, in the game of base ball, the need of an expert trainer grows more apparent. Foot ball would be thought impossible without the trainer, track athletics would be a joke, but base-ball has grown and prospered with never a thought of a trainer until a few years ago when 'rubbers' were secured to rub down the men. Detroit has taken the first step toward the proper training of the players [by hiring trainer Tom McMahon]. The Tigers will not have a 'rubber' this year. They will have a trainer in every sense of the word" (*Detroit News*, March 13, 1907).

Even after trainers became common, respect for their professional status was slow in coming. Reportedly, early-twentieth-century trainers were expected to look after the team's baggage on road trips (Gerard S. Petrone, *When Baseball Was Young*, 28). Harrison "Doc" Weaver, trainer for the Gashouse Gang Cardinals, signed autograph requests for the players. At least in that instance it could be argued that the task was related to Weaver's job duties since it reduced the arm strain on his players (Gene Karst, "The Great Days, The Great Stars," *National Pastime* 2 [Fall 1982], 50).

21.11 Team Doctors. The idea of referring all the players on a baseball team to one doctor seems to have originated very early. The team rules of the 1872 Forest Citys of Cleveland included one that stated, "No member of the club will be excused from practice or play unless upon a written certificate from Dr. N. B. Prentice, and said certificate must state the cause" (*Cleveland Leader*, March 11, 1872). It is less clear when doctors began to be added to clubs' payrolls. As noted in the preceding entry, the Phillies had a team physician in 1889. Notes in 1888 and 1892 mentioned that Brooklyn was employing a physician named either McLane or McLean (*Brooklyn Eagle*, June 25, 1888, and June 8, 1892; thanks to Cliff Blau for the first

citation). But the extent of their duties would be difficult to determine.

21.12 Public Address Announcers. In early baseball, umpires called out the day's batteries. Of course their cries were inaudible to much of the audience unless the umpire was particularly leather-lunged.

Famed concessionaire Harry Stevens began to extend the practice at the Polo Grounds during the 1890s: "Hustling Harry's innovation of announcing the batteries before the game starts and also calling out the names of players substituted in the middle of a contest has caught the crowd" (*Sporting Life*, May 5, 1894).

When Washington's American League Park opened in 1901, the scorecard concession was awarded to a man named E. Lawrence Phillips who decided that letting fans know the batteries and substitutions would help his business. Megaphones had just been popularized as a result of the prominent role they played in the Spanish-American War. Phillips bought one, and umpires soon allowed him to take over the duty of calling out names (Mike Sowell, *July 2, 1903*, 140).

These early announcers with megaphones stood on the field to address the crowd. Chicago Cubs announcer Pat Pieper was the last practitioner of this tradition. Pieper was seventeen when he started working for the Cubs in 1904 as a popcorn vendor. He had worked his way up to selling peanuts in 1916 when, having heard that the team's announcer had quit, he stopped owner Charles Weeghman and asked for a trial. Weeghman was bemused, but he obliged and was impressed enough to give Pieper the job. For the next six years he used a three-pound megaphone to keep Cubs' fans up-to-date on what was going on. It was not easy work and Pieper later recalled, "I used to have to run up and down the foul lines with my megaphone to make any kind of announcement. On some of those hot Wrigley Field days, I'd lose six or eight pounds" (*Chicago Tribune*, February 18, 1971, E4). In 1922 he switched to a more powerful but less portable fourteen-pound megaphone, and in 1932 he began using a p.a. system (*Chicago Tribune*, September 18, 1940, 23; *Chicago Tribune*, August 30, 1953, D7).

21.13 Clubhouse Attendants. After winning the 1913 city series over the crosstown Cubs, the White Sox voted a full share to "'Billy,' the boy who takes care of their uniforms and has charge of the clubhouse" (*Chicago Tribune*, October 14, 1913).

21.14   Commissioners.
Baseball's first commissioner, Judge Kenesaw Mountain Landis, was appointed on November 12, 1920, and commenced his term on January 12, 1921. The creation of the office is often characterized as being simply a reaction to the Black Sox scandal, but there were other factors involved.

Since 1903 baseball had been governed by a three-man National Commission made up of the two league presidents and one owner. This worked quite well for a while, but by the late 1910s this body's decisions were becoming increasingly controversial. In 1918 Connie Mack refused to accept one of its rulings and obtained a court injunction. Early in 1920 Chairman Garry Herrmann, the only owner to have ever served on the commission, resigned. Herrmann angrily suggested that no club owner was impartial enough to serve on the governing board.

Throughout the year the owners tossed about ideas for replacing the commission. After the Black Sox scandal came to light in September, these ideas began to focus around a three-man board of nonbaseball men known for their impeccable integrity. One of the names that emerged was Judge Landis, best known for his later-reversed decision fining Standard Oil $29 million. The owners no doubt considered the fact that Landis had heard the Federal League's antitrust lawsuits and had delayed his ruling until the Federal League was forced to settle.

The owners went back and forth about whether they wanted a three-man commission or a single commissioner, but eventually decided to offer sole authority to Landis. On November 12, 1920, a party of eleven owners and their representatives traveled to Landis's courtroom to offer him the position. David Pietrusza has observed that the owners probably expected him immediately to recess court in order to hear their offer. Instead he continued his session, and when the restless baseball men made too much noise, the no-nonsense judge threatened to clear the courtroom.

When the case concluded, Landis was offered the position of commissioner. After being assured that he would not have to resign his federal judgeship, he accepted (David Pietrusza, *Judge and Jury*, 161–172).

21.15   Team Psychologists.
Sports psychologist Coleman Robert Griffith was hired by Philip K. Wrigley in 1938 to work with the Cubs and lasted two seasons. In 1950 Wrigley protégé Bill Veeck hired David F. Tracy, a psychologist and hypnotist, to help improve the St. Louis Browns' self-image. The team got off to an 8-25 start and Tracy was let go on May 31. It was not until the 1980s that the role was permanently revived. Dr. James McGee was hired as the Orioles team psychologist around 1982 and counseled players on a variety of issues, including stress and substance abuse. A 1986 article reported that he was still the major league's only psychologist but that other organizations were looking into creating similar positions (AP: *Frederick* [Md.] *Post*, March 13, 1986).

21.16   Traffic Spotters.
When the Houston Astrodome opened in 1965, one of its novel features was a weather station some two hundred feet above the field, from which the air conditioning was controlled. Owner Judge Roy Hofheinz took advantage of this perch to add a novel type of employee—"a traffic spotter, who will radio warnings of potential tie-ups to police stations as far as five miles away" (Robert Lipsyte, "Johnson Attends Opening of Houston's Astrodome," *New York Times*, April 10, 1965). The hope was that this would ease fans' commutes to the ballpark.

Chapter 22

COMPETITION

THE SEARCH for a viable and durable mode of competition has played a major role in the history of baseball. Its importance is easily forgotten because the format used by the major leagues to determine a champion remained essentially unchanged from the introduction of the Brush Rules in 1905 until 1969. The controversy caused by more recent changes, particularly the addition of wild card teams to the playoffs, makes it especially important to understand that the system introduced in 1905 was the result of a long process of trial and error.

(i) Determining a Champion

The earliest popular mode of competition was the challenge system, by which an aspirant challenged the champions to a two-out-of-three series. This worked well if the champions sportingly accepted the gauntlet that had been thrown down. If they didn't, there were, well, problems.

In 1870 two Nevada clubs, the champion Silver Stars of Carson and the challenging Striped Stockings of Elko, were unable to agree upon a basis for a series. So they wrote to Henry Chadwick, who replied that "there is no rule governing the question of sending or receiving challenges. . . . The customary rule here in vogue is for the challenged club to name a day and ground, but it is, of course, optional with the challenging club to accept or not" (reprinted in Robert A. Nylen, "Frontier Baseball," *Nevada* 50:2 [March/April 1990], 56). Others were more categorical, such as Fred Delano of the Brother Jonathans of Detroit, who as-

serted: "A challenge to a game of base ball, as to anything else, gives the challenged party choice of time and place" (*Detroit Free Press*, June 14, 1863).

Such rules naturally made it easy for a champion club to avoid defending its title. The two Nevada clubs never did meet, and many other championships were retained by default.

Tournaments proved a popular alternative to the challenge system, and they often generated tremendous interest and excitement. But, as noted in this chapter's first entry, they too were plagued by problems.

Disputes about the mode of competition often masked a still more troubling underlying issue. Anyone who sought to make money by operating a baseball club looked to the model of capitalism, but unchecked capitalism creates the kind of disparities that ruin a competitive sport. Gross disparities in talent eliminated what was referred to in the nineteenth century as the "glorious uncertainty of base ball," and when the outcome was a foregone conclusion, opposing clubs became "demoralized" and spectators found better things to do.

22.1.1 Tournaments. Noting plans to hold a baseball tournament at the 1865 Michigan State Fair, the *New York Clipper* wrote, "We have had almost every other kind of tournament but base ball, but this exception, it appears, is not to be for long" (*New York Clipper*, August 8, 1865).

That tournament was held in Adrian on September 20–21, and while it generated considerable interest it also showed the limitation of the format. Detroit, then as now, was far and away the state's biggest city and sent a club that included two eastern players, at least one of whom was almost certainly a professional (see **18.1.5** "Players Lured West by Money"). Clubs from small towns like Salem withdrew, and Detroit easily won the four-team tournament (Peter Morris, *Baseball Fever*, 96–101).

Tournaments remained an important part of baseball for the next few years, but the difficulty of adapting them to baseball became increasingly evident. Their intention was to include every club that wished to participate, but it seldom worked out that way. The number of entrants almost never corresponded to the number of clubs that appeared. If the number of entrants was not a power of 2 (2, 4, 8, 16, etc.), byes were necessary, which was intrinsically unfair. Limited daylight made it difficult to play more than two games a day; rain could ruin things entirely.

Moreover, even if everything miraculously ran smoothly, only one club could emerge victorious. All the other clubs were thus inclined to grumble, whether they had a legitimate cause or not. Consequently while tournaments invariably began with great enthusiasm, they often ended with general dissatisfaction. Worse, the grievances were often aired in the newspapers for weeks afterward, leaving a bitter taste in everyone's mouth.

Thus John B. Foster, in an 1895 account of the history of baseball in northern Ohio, remarked: "In years gone by base ball tournaments were quite numerous and popular. Now and then such a tournament is held in this part of the State, but they are not as common as they once were" (John B. Foster, "Buckeye Boys," *Sporting News*, December 28, 1895).

22.1.2 Handicaps.

One way to address competitive imbalance is to devise some sort of handicap or tiered system. Baseball certainly tried this approach.

Tournaments soon began to offer multiple brackets in order to stimulate competition. Sometimes these worked well, but it was impossible to ensure that clubs entered the appropriate division. Far too often a lower tier was won by a club that should have been in a higher division, which only exacerbated hard feelings.

Efforts were made to address these problems. One of the most popular methods was to have separate brackets for junior clubs, which usually featured players eighteen and under. Unfortunately this led to early versions of overage Little Leaguer Danny Almonte and endless tedious complaints by junior clubs that they

had faced allegedly junior opponents who were "bearded like the pard" (*Jackson* [Mich.] *Citizen*, September 18, 1874).

Other clubs advertised for opponents whose average weight was below a certain figure. Still other efforts focused on dividing clubs into arbitrary classes. Obviously these were even more open to chicanery.

Another approach was for a weaker club to be allowed to use extra players and/or have five or six outs per inning when the sides seemed particularly uneven. Cap Anson reported that when his Marshalltown club appeared at a tournament in the late 1860s, opposing clubs refused to play them unless they were allowed six outs per inning (Adrian C. Anson, *A Ball Player's Career*, 38).

A ballplayer named Frank A. Deans recalled many years later that the Actives of Wellsboro, Pennsylvania, were desperate for competition in 1871 but had no worthy rivals. Eventually they convinced a local junior nine called the Red Hots to play them by "conditioning that the Red Hots should put but one Active out for each inning, while the Actives should put out of the Red Hots the usual three at an inning." Two games were played in this fashion, but the results were still so lopsided in favor of the Actives that another game was played "on the same conditions, and Actives playing with but six men (no outfielders—didn't need any)" (*Wellsboro Agitator*, August 14, 1901).

When professional clubs were involved the need for such handicaps was all the more evident, but an 1874 game in Jackson, Michigan, demonstrated why they were doomed to failure. Harry Wright's Red Stockings of Boston won four straight National Association pennants from 1872 to 1875 by increasingly lopsided margins. The game's still shaky economics meant that the club relied heavily upon filling in the gaps in their schedule with matches against semipro and amateur clubs. But with the Red Stockings dominating the National Association, there was no hope that these games would be competitive.

In 1873 the Red Stockings played fourteen games against semipro and amateur opponents and won by a cumulative margin of 524-48. While these contests still drew large crowds, it seemed unlikely that they would continue to do so year after year. Moreover locals resented any sign that the Red Stockings were not putting forth their best effort. After a game in Jackson in 1873, one onlooker complained that the visitors were "simply toying" with their hosts

(*Adrian Daily Press*, August 22, 1873; quoted in Peter Morris, *Baseball Fever*, 298).

Accordingly, in 1874 Harry Wright determined to allow all amateur clubs five outs per inning. This didn't prevent the Red Stockings from winning easily, but it kept the scores a little more respectable. When Boston returned to Jackson, Wright explained these terms, and the home captain reluctantly conceded the point. But the club's first baseman, Hugh Ernst, flatly declared that he would not agree to accept any handicap. The game was finally played on even terms, and the home team was proud of the 19-4 loss (*Jackson Citizen*, July 8, 1874).

This margin was indeed impressive by comparison with the scores by which the Red Stockings were beating their National Association opponents. Unfortunately it also underscored the fact that handicap systems were not a solution to the problems caused by competitive imbalance.

22.1.3 Leagues. A league is a lot of things, but its essence is a group of teams that have agreed on a method of selecting a champion. Developing the first baseball league was a process of trial and error that benefited from earlier failed efforts.

During the 1860s the challenge system was considered the basis of determining the country's best club. For the first half of the decade, the club so designated was usually deserving. In the second half of the decade, the competition became increasingly contrived.

In 1866 the Atlantics of Brooklyn retained the championship because their best-of-three series with the Athletics of Philadelphia was not completed. In 1867 and 1868 the New York clubs froze out outside clubs by scheduling matches in such a way that a challenger could never complete a series in time to claim the title. Matters got downright silly when the Red Stockings of Cincinnati went undefeated in 1869, beating every top club along the way, and yet were still not officially recognized as the national champions.

The challenge system was further undermined by accusations of "hippodroming," a term that meant that the outcomes were predetermined. After the first gambling scandal rocked baseball in 1865, one of the guilty players, Thomas Devyr, explained that co-conspirator William Wansley told him, "We can lose this game without doing the club any harm, and win the home and home game" (quoted in

Dean Sullivan, ed., *Early Innings*, 51). The unfortunate result was that whenever the first two games in a series were split, there were rumors that the clubs had deliberately set up a lucrative deciding game.

By the end of the 1860s, as James L. Terry noted, the system was so obviously broken that newspapers "would refer to various teams as the 'nominal' championship club" (James L. Terry, *Long Before the Dodgers*, 73). As a result, when every major club had at least four losses in 1870, there were numerous claimants to the national championship and no fair way to sort them out.

It was against this backdrop that the National Association of Professional Base Ball Players was formed on March 17, 1871. The historic meeting took place at Collier's Rooms, a saloon located at the corner of Broadway and Thirteenth in New York City. It is sometimes said that the meeting was called by Henry Chadwick. But Chadwick specifically noted, "The origin of this convention should be placed on record, viz., Mr. N. E. ["Nick"] Young, the efficient Secretary of the Olympic Club of Washington" (*New York Clipper*, March 25, 1871; William J. Ryczek, *Blackguards and Red Stockings*, 11–14).

The ten clubs that attended the meeting agreed on a fairly simple format. Every club wishing to compete for the championship was to play a five-game series with every other club, thus determining the champion by head-to-head play. Clubs were responsible for their own scheduling. Each entrant was to submit a ten-dollar entry fee, and the money would be used to purchase a pennant that the champion would fly.

The new league debuted on May 4, 1871, and its historic first game was scheduled to feature Boston and Washington in the nation's capital. Instead that game was rained out, and the first game took place in Fort Wayne, Indiana. It was a symbolic beginning for a league in which things would rarely go as anticipated (David Nemec, *Great Encyclopedia of Nineteenth Century Major League Baseball*, 8).

This was especially true with the format for determining the champion. By mid-season, there were differing opinions as to whether the champion was determined on the basis of series won or games won. This was compounded by disputes over player eligibility and unplayed games. To top it all off, the Great Chicago Fire destroyed the home park and all the possessions of one of the main contenders, the White Stockings of Chicago (William J. Ryczek, *Blackguards and Red Stockings*, 55–63).

The deciding game of the season saw the White Stockings face the Athletics of Philadelphia under bizarre circumstances. The game had to be played at a neutral site in Brooklyn, so only five hundred people attended. The White Stockings wore piebald uniforms borrowed from other clubs, and were without two players who had left the club after the fire.

Adding to the sense of anticlimax, it was generally agreed that a Philadelphia win would make them champions but that if Chicago won the champion might end up being Chicago, Boston, or Philadelphia, depending on the resolution of several claimed forfeits. That was avoided when Philadelphia won the game, but it was clear there was a lot of room for improvement in determining a champion (William J. Ryczek, *Blackguards and Red Stockings*, 55–63).

The National Association lasted five years and never again had a dispute over its champion. This wasn't a good thing—the Red Stockings of Boston captured the pennant by increasingly large margins, finally going 71-8 in 1875, in the circuit's final season. Its open-entry policy accentuated the competitive imbalance as each season began with co-op entries that were soundly thrashed and then withdrew.

In 1876 Chicago president William Hulbert led a coup that created the National League. When almost all the National Association's viable franchises jumped to the new entity, baseball's first major league quietly passed into history. As implied by the word "league," the new circuit was based far more upon the centralized leadership of the club owners.

A number of new policies introduced by the National League were important in ensuring baseball's financial well-being. These included entry criteria and territorial rights (see **18.2.4**), a predetermined league-wide schedule (see **22.1.4**), the turnstile (see **14.5.1**), and the reserve rule (see **18.2.1**). Unfortunately these undeniably significant innovations were later used by major league baseball's Special Records Committee to make the self-serving decision that the National League was the first "major league."

22.1.4   Schedules. The first league-wide schedule was adopted by the National League on March 22, 1877. Before then, clubs arranged the dates and locations of matches by themselves. While this method had obvious disadvantages, it also provided much-needed flexibility when injuries or illnesses made it impossible to field a healthy nine.

22.1.5   Playing Out the Schedule. Until 1908 it was not deemed essential to make up rainouts and other canceled games if there was not a convenient date on which to do so. That season the Tigers finished with a 90-63 mark, and the Indians compiled a 90-64 record. It hardly seemed fair that a rainout had helped determine the pennant, so the American League mandated the following year that clubs had to complete their schedule if the pennant hung in the balance.

(ii) Postseason Championships

In the nineteenth century, what we now call the regular season was often referred to as the championship series. As is often the case, the choice of words was indicative of an essential truth: that having labored long and hard to arrive at a satisfactory way to determine a champion, there was no thought of undermining the outcome with additional games. When viewed from that perspective, what is peculiar is the current tendency of almost all sports to have a long season and then have the same clubs compete again in the playoffs.

Consequently baseball's earliest postseason series came about because of the unique circumstance of having two major leagues that were willing to play each other.

22.2.1   World Series. Despite the rivalry of the International Association and the National League in the late 1870s, there is no evidence of any effort to match the leagues' champions.

The idea did emerge as soon as the American Association was formed in 1882. Even though the two leagues were at war, National League champion Chicago and American Association pennant winners Cincinnati began a series on October 6, 1882. Researcher Frederick Ivor-Campbell concluded that "no one in 1882 saw them as more than exhibition games" (Frederick Ivor-Campbell, "Postseason Play," *Total Baseball IV*, 281). In a telltale sign, for the first game Chicago's Cap Anson left Mike Kelly behind in New York and stationed pitcher Larry Corcoran at shortstop, a position Corcoran had not played all year. But when Cincinnati won the first game, Corcoran returned to the pitcher's box for the second game (David Fleitz, *Cap Anson*, 104–105). In addition, as discussed in the next entry, more attention was attached to the series between Chicago and the National League runners-up, the Providence Grays.

Nonetheless the games did attract attention. After the teams had split two games, the series was abruptly abandoned. Many histories state that the series ended because the American Association threatened to expel Cincinnati. But David Nemec argued that scheduling conflicts were more likely the reason (David Nemec, *The Beer and Whisky League*, 38).

Before the next season the two leagues signed a peace treaty known as the Tri-Partite Agreement (see **18.2.3** "National Agreement"). Preliminary efforts were made to organize a postseason series between the American Association champion Athletics of Philadelphia and the National League champions from Boston. But interest in such a match waned when the Athletics lost several postseason exhibition games against other National League teams (David Nemec, *The Beer and Whisky League*, 54).

The first completed series between the two league champions took place in 1884, with Providence representing the National League and New York the American Association. According to John J. O'Malley, the series was the brainchild of New York manager James Mutrie, who issued the initial challenge (John J. O'Malley, "Mutrie's Mets of 1884," *National Pastime* Spring 1985, 41). The series had no official status, but Providence manager Frank Bancroft boldly declared that the series was for "the championship of America" and that the winner would "fly a pennant next year as champions of America" (*Providence Evening Telegram*, October 17, 1884; reprinted in Frederick Ivor-Campbell, "Extraordinary 1884," *National Pastime* 13 [1993], 19).

Providence earned that right by winning the first two games of the three-game series. The third game was played nonetheless, and Providence won that one too. *Sporting Life* commented: "the result clearly proclaims the Providence Club 'Champions of the World'" (quoted in Frederick Ivor-Campbell, "Extraordinary 1884," *National Pastime* 13 [1993], 22).

The series became an annual event and was held every year through 1890. The annual Spalding and Reach guides began referring to the event as the "world's championship series" and the "world's series." When the two leagues merged in 1892 to form a twelve-team league, several efforts were made to create a valid post-season series. These are discussed in the next entry.

After the American League declared itself a major league in 1901, it spent two years at war with the National League. When peace came in 1903, the idea of a world's series was revived, and Boston of the junior circuit upended the National League's representatives, the Pittsburgh Pirates. It is important to emphasize, however, that the series had no official sanction.

In 1904 the New York Giants won the National League pennant, but Giants manager John McGraw and owner John T. Brush declined to play the American League champions from Boston. Their refusal was widely denounced by the press and the public. McGraw and Brush were portrayed as being motivated either by cowardice or by the well-publicized feuds that both men had waged with American League president Ban Johnson.

As discussed in the other entry for "World Series" (see **16.2.6**), McGraw and Brush also had a legitimate basis for their stance. But they were so clearly in the minority that John Brush rethought his position over the offseason and helped put together the Brush Rules, which would thereafter form the basis of the World Series.

22.2.2 Intramural Playoffs. As noted earlier, a postseason series between the champions of rival leagues has a natural and obvious appeal. A postseason series between clubs that have competed all season, though unquestioningly accepted today, is a much more dubious concept. It has the inherent risk of diluting what is now called the "regular season" and fan interest in those contests.

The idea finally came to fruition in 1882 when controversy about the potential withdrawal of Worcester threw the National League pennant race into chaos. There was an initial announcement that a nine-game series would be played between the two contenders, Boston and Providence, to decide the pennant. In the end, Worcester did not withdraw, but the postseason series was held nonetheless. Despite rumors of game-fixing, the contests attracted large crowds and swelled the treasuries of both clubs. Even so, there is no indication that any thought was given to making such series a regular occurrence.

In 1891 the Eastern League made the novel decision to "divide up each season into two championship seasons and let the winner of the two seasons play off for the championship honors in October." A summary at season's end concluded that this scheme had worked very well, but added that it, "of course, would only be adopted by minor leagues and associations. It is a well-established fact that in nearly every minor association race some of the clubs are always hopeless stragglers in the race before July 4 and often the discouragement is so great both of the club and of its patrons that the only resource is to disband for the remainder of the season and wait for the next year." By contrast, the split-season format would mean that every team "would get 'another chance for its white alley,'" and there would be a new interest in the beginning of the second series of which every club and its friends would loyally partake. Of course, the same club might win both series, but the chances would be against such a result and a third interest would center in the final series. . . . The plan is worth serious consideration by minor leagues" (*Sporting Times*, September 26, 1891).

The concept was brought to the major leagues in 1892, the first season after the National League and American Association had merged into a twelve-club entity. At the end of the first season of the new league, the first-half winner met the second-half champion in the first intramural postseason series. Cleveland and Boston played a classic first game that ended in an eleven-inning scoreless tie. The remainder of the series was less dramatic as Boston swept the next five games. The format was abandoned at season's end.

Two years later a postseason series was revived when Pittsburgh businessman William Temple offered the Temple Cup to the winner of a best-of-seven series between the league's first- and second-place finishers. The Temple Cup was contested for four years and always featured the tempestuous Baltimore Orioles.

But the series were all lopsided, with none requiring more than five games. Additionally, the second-place finisher won three of the four matchups, leaving it debatable which club was the true champion. It appears that the fans cast the deciding vote on the fate of the Temple Cup, for dwindling attendance in 1897 led to the demise of the series.

In 1900 the concept was revived for one year when the *Pittsburgh Chronicle-Telegraph* sponsored a series between runner-up Pittsburgh and first-place Brooklyn, which was won by Brooklyn. The birth of the American League

again made possible a postseason series between clubs that had not faced each other that year. It was accordingly not until 1969 that the championship format again featured rematches of in-season contests.

22.2.3   Neutral Sites.

Many athletic competitions, including the Super Bowl and most NCAA tournaments, are deliberately held at neutral sites. It has been a long time since this was done in baseball, but it was attempted. In 1885 the final three games of the World's Series between Chicago and St. Louis were played in Pittsburgh and Cincinnati. The 1887 Series between Detroit and St. Louis was a fifteen-game extravaganza that included ten neutral-site games in eight different cities. In 1888 games in the series between New York and St. Louis were played in Brooklyn and Philadelphia. Attendance at neutral sites was generally lower, and the experiment has never been repeated.

22.2.4   Best-of Series.

In most early postseason series, the number of games was predetermined and all were played even if one side amassed an insurmountable lead. This was based on the same reasoning that led to the bottom of the ninth being played in baseball games even if the team that batted last was ahead—that baseball was a spectacle, not a competition (see **1.25** "'Walkoff' Hits"). But by doing so, a basic reality was being disregarded. Baseball was a competition, whether that fact was acknowledged or not, which meant that players and spectators lost interest in games that were played after the champion was determined.

There was a more insidious problem associated with playing out meaningless games. As noted under "Fixed Games" (**11.1.1**), there was a strong tendency to assume that a game was fixed when one club staved off elimination. The best way to fend off such rumors was to offer prize money to the winners (see **22.3.5**) and announce beforehand that the series would end when one club had clinched the championship. The 1889 World's Series was the first to do the latter, with a best-of-eleven format that was scheduled to end as soon as one club won six games (Jerry Lansche, *Glory Fades Away*, 157).

The number of games in these series varied in early years. Although a best-of-seven format was used as early as 1885, it was not permanently adopted until 1922.

22.2.5   City Series.

It may seem surprising today, but postseason series between clubs representing the same city in rival leagues once competed with and sometimes even outstripped the series between the champions of the respective leagues.

In 1882 Cleveland of the National League beat Cincinnati of the American Association in a postseason series to determine the top club in Ohio. Peace was made between the two leagues the following year, which led to similar series that capitalized upon natural rivalries in Philadelphia and New York (Frederick Ivor-Campbell, "Postseason Play," *Total Baseball IV*, 281).

This concept was revived in 1903 when the war between the National and American leagues ended. Over the next fifteen years, intracity series in Philadelphia, St. Louis, and Chicago capitalized on deep-seated local interest and became fan favorites. As is evident throughout Ring Lardner's Jack Keefe stories, the event that Keefe called the "city serious" was especially popular in Chicago.

Although canceled when one of the clubs was in the World Series as well as for the First World War and occasional other reasons, the Chicago city series was contested twenty-six times between 1903 and 1942. Researcher Emil Rothe reported that "The dominance of the White Sox in these autumn affairs defies logic," as the Sox won nineteen series while the Cubs won six times, with one tie (Emil H. Rothe, "History of the Chicago City Series," *Baseball Research Journal* 8 [1979], 16).

22.2.6   Shaughnessy Playoffs.

The Shaughnessy Playoffs were a simple and highly effective solution to the complex problems faced by minor league baseball during the Great Depression. Montreal president Frank Shaughnessy proposed that the only way to keep fans interested in the regular season was a postseason playoff among the top four teams. The top team would face the fourth-place team, while the second- and third-place finishers would square off, with the winners meeting for the league championship.

Montreal Herald sportswriter Al Parsley reported that Shaughnessy had borrowed the idea from hockey: "Frank Shaughnessy of the Montreal Royals had to beat down stiff opposition in selling the play-off idea to the International League and American Association magnates. But, as he insisted at the meetings early in the year and as he still maintains, 'something had to be done to protect our baseball investment. Under the old system baseball, from the standpoint of this city's experience, must be considered a poor investment. I am supported in this statement by practically every owner of a Double A club. Here in Montreal we have $1,800,000 sunk into a stadium and club and have been losing money steadily because of waning interest by the 1st of August. With the play-offs, it is confidently believed that we can keep up interest just as they do in hockey. Hockey's success is enough proof that the thing will do in baseball'" (*Montreal Herald*, reprinted in *Sporting News*, February 16, 1933).

There was concerted resistance to the idea because of the obvious fact that the Shaughnessy Playoffs watered down the regular season. Nonetheless there was a dire need to sustain fan interest, and it was hard to dismiss an idea with the potential to increase revenues. In spite of efforts by minor league "czar" William G. Bramham to halt the Shaughnessy Playoffs, they were implemented in the International League and Texas League in 1933.

Fans thronged to the games, and other leagues rushed to adopt them. Their success was such that baseball historian Robert Obojski concluded that it is "generally acknowledged to have saved the minors from total financial ruin in the depression-ridden 1930s" (Robert Obojski, *Bush League*, 46–48). That being the case, even purists reluctantly accepted the Shaughnessy Playoffs.

Major league baseball added intramural playoffs in 1969 and a wild-card team in 1995. (The wild card would have debuted in 1994 if not for the strike.) Like them or hate them, the wild cards and multi-tier playoffs now used by the major leagues are the logical culmination of the Shaughnessy Playoffs.

(iii) Bling Bling

Quick Quiz:

(1) What is the name of the trophy awarded to the champions of the National Hockey League playoffs?
(2) What is the name of the trophy awarded to the winners of baseball's World Series?

If you correctly answered the Stanley Cup to the first question, it doesn't necessarily mean that you're a diehard hockey fan. On the other hand, even a very knowledgeable baseball fan is likely to struggle with the second question. The Commissioner's Trophy simply hasn't captured the public's imagination. That paradox is all the more puzzling because, as this section will show, tangible rewards for championships have played a major role in baseball history.

22.3.1 Trophies. The earliest baseball trophy was the game ball presented by the losers to the winners of each challenge match, as specified by the 1857 rules. The Spalding Collection of the New York Public Library includes a photograph of the trophy case in which the Atlantics of Brooklyn proudly collected and displayed the baseballs they had captured (James L. Terry, *Long Before the Dodgers*, 77). A 1909 article reported that two inscribed baseballs from 1858 were then in the possession of Charles DeBost, whose father had played for the Knickerbockers. The two balls were inscribed with scores from the 1858 Brooklyn–New York City Fashion Course series ("Oldest Baseballs Bear Date of 1858," *New York Times*, January 21, 1909, 7).

Less famous clubs preserved these symbols of their triumphs with equal care. Catcher William Stirling of the Red Herrings of Eaton Rapids, Michigan, a successful club of the 1870s, collected a boxful of souvenir balls, "but went even further than that. He was very handy with the old quill and pen, and after the game the ball was cleaned thoroughly—the name of both teams, the score, place and date were printed on it in a very neat and attractive manner. After the ink dried the ball was given a coat of light-colored varnish to preserve it" (W. Scott Munn, *The Only Eaton Rapids on Earth*, 250–251).

Similarly, a member of an 1864 amateur club in Albany, New York, wrote to a friend after a victory: "The ball is a very nice Hardwood. We shall have it varnished and lettered in the following manner: Won by 1st Nine Hiawatha B. B. C. from 1st Nine Alpine B. B. C. Sept 24th 1864. Score 34 to 25" (quoted in Scott S. Taylor, "Pure Passion for the Game," *Manuscripts* LIV, No. 1 [Winter 2002], 7). E. H. Tobias, who chronicled the earliest days of St. Louis baseball, confirmed that these trophies were "afterwards gilded and the date and the score of the game painted thereon in black letters" (E. H. Tobias, *Sporting News*, November 2, 1895).

This custom was usually enacted at the end of a match with a great display of sportsmanship in which both sides gave three cheers and a tiger to their opponents. But disputes became common enough that the National Association of Amateur Base Ball Players issued specific instructions for "Furnishing the Ball" (*Bay City* [Mich.] *Journal*, July 30, 1872).

Although this ritual is generally recalled as a quaint feature of antebellum baseball, it persisted much longer than that. John H. Gruber noted that once it became customary to use multiple balls during the game, "the winning club demanded and got every ball that had been in play. This led to much wrangling as the players of the losing team were unwilling to give up balls that could be used in practice." Accordingly, the rules were changed in 1887 so that the winners kept only the final ball. Gruber claimed that the custom of awarding the ball at game's end was still in effect in 1915, but by then it was being overshadowed by gaudier trophies (John H. Gruber, "The Ball and the Bat," *Sporting News*, November 11, 1915).

While the game ball was the earliest trophy, it was not long before other forms of recognition were being added. When the Live Oaks of Rochester, New York, were triumphant at the Monroe County Agricultural Society Fair on September 16, 1858, they were invited to have tea with the society's managers and to help in the judging process. The club also received a pennant that was later described as "nothing more or less than an American flag" with the club's name inscribed and its emblem, a wreath of green oak, embroidered upon the stripes (Priscilla Astifan, "Baseball in the Nineteenth Century," *Rochester History* LII, No. 3 [Summer 1990], 7, 17).

By the 1860s jewelers were sculpting elaborate trophies for the winners of prestigious championships. A silver ball was offered to the club recognized as the national champion by the Continental Club of Brooklyn in 1861 and 1862. Frank Queen, the editor of the *New York Clipper*, attempted to revive this tradition in 1868 (James L. Terry, *Long Before the Dodgers*, 35, 37, 73).

Similar rewards were soon being offered at local competitions. In 1862 the proprietors of the Walton House in Rochester, New York, donated a silver ball to go to the winner of a baseball game on ice (*Rochester Evening Express*, January 10, 1862; quoted in Priscilla Astifan, "Baseball in the Nineteenth Century," *Rochester History* LII, No. 3 [Summer 1990], 7). In 1864 John A. Lowell offered a silver ball to the champion team of New England. The trophy was first awarded on September 27, 1864, and remained the subject of heated competition for several years (*New England Base Ballist*, August 13, November 5, 1868). Indeed the competition became so intense that it was decided to melt the ball in a crucible.

Beginning in 1865 a goblet was offered to the champions of the state of Michigan, consisting of "a silver cup, mounted on three miniature bats. The lid of the cup is of oval shape, and in a depression carries a silver ball, the emblem of success. Between the bats, constituting the standard, are also placed fac similes of the square and circular bases. The prize is thus very appropriate, in addition to being of a novel model" (*Detroit Advertiser and Tribune*, September 13, 1865).

That same year saw clubs in Connecticut begin to compete for a miniature bat made from the state's famous Charter Oak. The bat was engraved with a picture of the celebrated tree and was kept in a rosewood case (David Arcidiacono, *Grace, Grit and Growling*, 5). A similar prize was offered by the New England Association two years later in the form of a bat that was reportedly "composed of pieces of wood from the John Hancock house on Benson street, the Lincoln cabin, the old Boston elm, the apple tree under which Gen. Lee surrendered at Appomattox and the battleships Kearsarge and Alabama" (*Boston Journal*, February 22, 1905).

At an 1866 tournament in Rockford, Illinois, clubs vied for the championship of the Northwest and a ball "of full regulation size, two and three-quarters inches in diameter, of eighteen carat gold, and put up in a satin-lined Morocco case," and a bat "of solid rosewood, elaborately mounted with the same quality of gold, and cased the same as the ball" (*Detroit Advertiser and Tribune*, June 21, 1866; reprinted in Peter Morris, *Baseball Fever*, 110). Many similar trophies are described in my history of early baseball in Michigan.

Colorado ballplayers also had an impressive piece of jewelry to aim for by 1867: "The silver ball which is to be presented by Mr. Anker to the champion base ball club of Colorado, may now be seen at his store, on F street. It is a very beautiful piece of workmanship, being the same size and weight of the regulation ball, and ornamented with crossed bats on either side. It bears the following inscriptions: 'Champion Base Ball of Colorado' 'Presented to Champion Base Ball Club of Colorado by M. Anker'" (*Rocky Mountain News*, June 4, 1867).

Other trophies being competed for by 1868 included a gold ball for the champions of Western and Central New York, a silver ball awarded to the best club in Maryland, a gold ball denoting the championship of Wisconsin, and another silver ball for the top club in Maine

(James L. Terry, *Long Before the Dodgers*, 73–74; Will M. Anderson, *Was Baseball Really Invented in Maine?*, 2–3). Canadian clubs were following suit by 1880, commissioning "A model base ball bat in silver" from Peck & Snyder of New York to symbolize the national championship (*Woodstock* [Ont.] *Sentinel Review*, June 4, 1880).

The earliest trophy for a league championship that I am aware of was a parian vase offered to the National League champion in 1881. (Parian is a type of china known for its ivory tint.) This vase was almost certainly one of a pair created by Trenton, New Jersey, pottery makers for the 1876 U.S. Centennial celebrations. The pair was described as follows: "Round the foot of each vase, and standing on the supporting pedestal, are arranged three figures of base-ball players, modelled after a thoroughly American ideal of physical beauty, embodying muscular activity rather than ponderous strength. . . . A series of clubs belted round with a strap ornaments the stem of the vases, and some exquisitely wrought leaves and berries are woven round the top. The orifice is covered by a cupola or dome, composed of a segment of a base-ball, upon which stands an eagle" (Jenny J. Young, *The Ceramic Art: A Compendium of the History and Manufacturing of Pottery and Porcelain* [New York, 1878]; quoted in James M. DiClerico and Barry J. Pavelec, *The Jersey Game*, 200).

The two vases were eventually separated, and one was given to the National League to be used as a symbol of the league championship. According to James M. DiClerico and Barry J. Pavelec, this occurred in 1887, and an article that October reported that the vase had just been received from Messrs. Ott and Brewer of Trenton and was "as delicate and artistic as $500 could make it" (James M. DiClerico and Barry J. Pavelec, *The Jersey Game*, 200; *Boston Globe*, October 3, 1887). But the vase was first mentioned in 1881 (*Detroit Free Press*, July 31, 1881; Chadwick Scrapbooks). So it appears that the vase was offered for several years.

In 1988 art historian Ellen Paul Denker found one of the pair in the Detroit Historical Museum and the other in the New Jersey State Museum. She was able to reunite them for an exhibition at the Metropolitan Museum of Art (James M. DiClerico and Barry J. Pavelec, *The Jersey Game*, 200).

The first postseason trophy seems to have been a silver trophy presented by Metropolitans president Erastus Wiman to the St. Louis

Brown Stockings following the 1886 World's Series. In 1887 actress Helen Dauvray offered the first permanent trophy for the world champions. Manufactured by Tiffany's, the Dauvray Cup was awarded until 1893, when it was succeeded by the Temple Cup.

22.3.2 Individual Awards. At early baseball tournaments it was common to award medals or other jewelry to individual players for a wide variety of accomplishments. Usually these were for Field Day–type events like running and throwing contests. Sometimes other categories were added, such as best captain, most home runs, and best catcher. On one occasion an award was given to the best umpire (Peter Morris, *Baseball Fever*, 296).

To mark the opening of Brooklyn's Union Grounds, a handsome bat and ball were offered to the player scoring the most runs (*Brooklyn Eagle*, May 12, 1862). In later years, individual awards became a popular way to bring attention to a new or unappreciated statistical measurement. As noted earlier, Henry Chadwick offered an engraved bat in 1868 to publicize the category of base hits (see **17.3**).

In 1879 the McKay Medal attracted considerable attention. The *Buffalo Courier* explained that a local man named James W. McKay was offering "a medal to the League player who makes the best combined average in batting and fielding during the season of 1879.... He thinks this will induce the heavy batters to look more to their fielding averages, and the fine fielders to do something in the way of hitting. It will be called the McKay Medal, and any player who wins it this year shall own it. The medal will be of solid gold, five inches high and two broad, and will weigh twenty-five pennyweights. On the top bar will be the words 'McKay Medal'" (reprinted in *Chicago Tribune*, April 6, 1879).

It was pointed out to McKay that this format would give a significant advantage to first basemen, so he eliminated fielding and decided to give it to the player with the highest batting average in seventy or more games. At season's end there was a dispute as to whether Cap Anson or Paul Hines had the highest average, but since only Hines had played in the requisite seventy games, he was awarded the medal (*New York Clipper*, November 22, 1879).

22.3.3 Most Valuable Player Awards. Bill Deane noted that in 1875 Jim "Deacon" White received a silver trophy donated by a wealthy spectator that was engraved with the words "Won by Jim White as most valuable player to Boston team, 1875" (Bill Deane, *Award Voting*, 5–6).

Before the 1878 season, General Thomas S. Dakin, a star pitcher for the Putnam Club of Brooklyn in the 1850s, offered a "splendid gold mounted willow bat" to the best player on the championship-winning team. A committee of three was to make the decision (*New York Clipper*, January 5, 1878). Unfortunately, Dakin died suddenly a few months later, and the idea did not resurface for another thirty years.

When it did, it was once again under rather bizarre circumstances. In 1910 the Chalmers Automobile Company had offered a car to the American League's batting champion. On the last day of the season the St. Louis Browns' third baseman played far too deep, allowing Nap Lajoie to beat out a series of bunt hits in his attempt to catch Ty Cobb and win the automobile. To preclude such shenanigans, it was decided that a vehicle would in the future be given to the player in each league voted "the most important and useful player to his club and to the league at large in point of deportment and value of services rendered" (Bill Deane, *Award Voting*, 6).

The award was withdrawn after the 1914 season, but most valuable player awards returned in 1922 and have been a feature of major league baseball ever since.

22.3.4 World Series Rings and Other Jewelry. When Providence won the 1879 National League pennant, each player was given a badge made up of "a gold keeper, upon which the name of the man and his position will be placed, and suspended from it are two bats crossed, and between them a round plate of pure burnished gold, surrounded half way with a laurel wreath. A half ball will be hung from the keeper, just above the bats, the flat sides toward the ribbons back of the badge. The ribbons will be blue, and on the centre plate will be the words, 'Providence Grays, Champions, 1879,' in blue enamel" (*New York Sunday Mercury*, October 4, 1879). Johnny Ward was one of the recipients, and after his 1887 marriage to actress Helen Dauvray, she began presenting gold medallions to each member of the world champion team.

When the World Series was made a permanent institution in 1905, the agreement between the two leagues called for all of the winning players to receive an "appropriate memento, in the form of a button." Within a few years it appears to have become customary for a small piece of jewelry to be given to World Series champions. According to Jonathan Fraser Light, these were initially stickpins (Jonathan Fraser Light, *The Cultural Encyclopedia of Baseball*, 390).

In 1918 the Red Sox and Cubs delayed the start of the fifth game of the World Series because of a dispute about the purse. As a result, the winning Red Sox received a letter from National Commission member John Heydler informing them that "each member of the team is fined the Series emblems and none would be given" (quoted in Ty Waterman and Mel Springer, *The Year the Red Sox Won the Series*, 271).

Harry Hooper of the Red Sox was particularly upset about this decision and unsuccessfully brought the matter to the attention of every baseball commissioner until his death in 1974. Finally in 1993 the Red Sox held a ceremony for the seventy-fifth anniversary of the championship and gave emblems to descendants of the players (Ty Waterman and Mel Springer, *The Year the Red Sox Won the Series*, 271–273).

As far as I can determine, the custom of awarding World Series rings began in the 1920s.

22.3.5 Cash. By the late 1860s match games for cash purses were becoming fairly common. The first such game in Michigan took place on July 4, 1866, for a $100 purse, and undoubtedly there were earlier such games in other states.

Players also sometimes received bonuses for special accomplishments. The Hartford players, for example, were offered bonuses if they won the 1875 pennant (David Arcidiacono, *Grace, Grit and Growling*, 28).

Formal monetary rewards for the World's Series winners were introduced in 1884, when $1,000 was donated by Al Wright of the *New York Clipper* (Jerry Lansche, *Glory Fades Away*, 37). The tradition continued the following year when St. Louis owner Chris Von der Ahe and Chicago owner A. G. Spalding put up $500 each to be split among the winning side. But when the series was officially declared a tie, the money was returned to the owners.

World's Series shares were thus actually awarded for the first time the following year, when the same two clubs met in a winner-take-all format. Curt Welch scored the series-clinching run on what became known as the "$15,000 slide" (though there is no evidence that he

slid, and the total revenues were a little under $14,000).

In 1887 the American Association inaugurated prize money for the regular-season winner. Chris Von der Ahe had lobbied for such a purse, and his Browns claimed it. The National League had no corresponding prize, but Lady Baldwin reported that Detroit owner Frederick K. Stearns bought each player a new suit of clothes for winning the pennant and added a $500 bonus when the club won that fall's World's Series (*Indiana* [Pa.] *Gazette*, September 27, 1935).

Jim "Deacon" McGuire played for Brooklyn when the club won back-to-back National League pennants in 1899 and 1900. He later reminisced, "President [Charles] Ebbets and the directors voted $4,000 to be divided equally between the players winning the first pennant, each man getting $160, but we didn't do so well on the second one. When we went into the lead the boys began to size up the cash customers from day to day and we were drawing bigger crowds than the season before so naturally we thought we would draw a bigger stake than we received for copping the first one; but when we finished, instead of a cash donation, each player received a pair of gold cuff links" (Guy M. Smith, "He Could Catch Anything," Typescript in McGuire Hall of Fame file).

(iv) Youth

Junior clubs were an important part of early baseball, fostering tournaments and other forms of competition. There was even an active national organization of junior clubs in the 1860s. Gradually, however, organized competition between youngsters faded, with the use of overage players being one of the prime reasons.

By the 1920s interest in major league baseball had reached unprecedented levels. In contrast, youth participation was dropping sharply, with a 1924 survey by the National Amateur Athletic Foundation showing a 50 percent decline. This prompted serious concerns about the future of the game, not unlike the ones that are often expressed today. Newspapers offered dire predictions that the game was dying as a participation sport, and the *New York Times* wrote with dark irony that baseball "continues to hold its supremacy as the game Americans most like to see others play" (quoted in Harold Seymour, *Baseball: The People's Game*, 84).

Into that void stepped a series of youth leagues in the succeeding years.

22.4.1 American Legion Baseball. Major John L. Griffith was executive vice president of the National Amateur Athletic Foundation in 1924 when that organization's survey showed a 50 percent decline in baseball participation among boys. Griffith was also a member of the American Legion and urged his fellow members to address the problem. The result was the first American Legion tournament, staged in 1926.

22.4.2 Little League. Little League baseball was started by Carl Stotz in Williamsport, Pennsylvania, in 1939 to address a couple of wrongs. Stotz's nephews and their friends were having a hard time finding a diamond on which to play. In addition, some elements of the game were ill-suited for boys. Stotz explained: "Nothing was geared to children. The pitcher was too far away to throw hard enough to be effective, so he simply aimed the ball over the plate. The catcher, without a mask, chest protector, or shin guards, stooped over near the backstop, when there was one. The ball usually came to him on a bounce, making him more of a retriever than a catcher" (Carl Stotz and Kenneth D. Loss, *A Promise Kept*, quoted in Talmage Boston, *1939, Baseball's Pivotal Year*, 239–240). So Stotz formed a three-team league for boys twelve and under with sixty-foot baselines and a forty-foot pitching distance that became the first Little League.

The concept spread rapidly and in 1947 Stotz convinced U.S. Rubber (now Uniroyal) to become the corporate sponsor of Little League. Representatives of U.S. Rubber eventually gained control of the Little League board of directors, and Stotz was ousted in 1955. He remained bitter for the rest of his life.

22.4.3 Little League World Series. The first Little League World Series was held in Williamsport on August 21, 1947, with the hometown Maynard Midgets winning.

22.4.4 Babe Ruth Baseball. Babe Ruth Baseball began in Hamilton Township, New Jersey, in 1951 with a single ten-team league for players aged thirteen to fifteen. In the years since, the scope and age range have grown enormously.

22.4.5 PONY Baseball. PONY Baseball, an acronym for "Protect Our Nation's Youth," began in Washington, Pennsylvania, in 1951. Originally for thirteen- and fourteen-year-old boys, it experienced rapid growth and now features seven age groups.

22.4.6 Travel Teams. Following the lead of basketball, many of the best eleven- and twelve-year-old baseball players have forsaken traditional forms of regional competition. Instead these promising youngsters join travel teams and compete in their own tournaments. The national championship of travel baseball is held in Cooperstown, New York, in late August, at the same time as the Little League World Series. The idea was conceived by Lou Presutti on a visit to Cooperstown with his father in 1975.

Allan Simpson explained, "Youth baseball is essentially divided into two levels of competition: recreation leagues and travel leagues. Little League represents the former, and other longstanding organizations like Babe Ruth and PONY Baseball fall on that side of the fence. Membership is structured, with strict eligibility guidelines and rules governing where teams can draw players from, field dimensions and length of season. The competition may be purer, but rec leagues focus more on age than ability. . . . High-powered travel teams, who often play 120 games a year, can load up on players from all over the country" (*Baseball America*, October 27–November 9, 2003).

(v) Is Competition Necessary at All?

While capitalism was the model on which early professional clubs and leagues were based, it seemed most ill-suited to promoting the game. Whenever one club became dominant, it forced its competitors out of business and thereby hurt its own economics. Accordingly, some asked whether competition was necessary or at least sought to restrain competition.

As noted under "Leagues" (see **22.1.3**), clubs that were playing best two-out-of-three series were among the first to show an awareness of this reality. It became proverbial that the first two games of such a series would be split so that the clubs could make more money and the fans would have added excitement. In time, more ambitious schemes were proposed to move baseball away from being a competition and toward being a spectacle.

22.5.1 Socialism in Baseball. Notwithstanding its status as the American national pastime, baseball has a long tradition of socialistic practices. As much as it goes against the instincts of the successful capitalists who own baseball clubs to consider revenue sharing, professional sports as a business uniquely depends upon the success of one's rivals. Even George Will has allowed that "the great American game needs something un-American: socialism" (George F. Will, "Baseball and Socialism," June 18, 1981, reprinted in George F. Will, *Bunts*).

In the first major league, the National Association (1871–1875), many of the clubs were cooperative ventures in which the players split the revenues in lieu of collecting a salary. The co-ops competed against clubs run as stock companies, which were backed by local citizens who had each put forth a modest sum in return for a season ticket. The capital thus generated allowed these clubs to pay their players fixed salaries and thereby to corral better players. They thrashed the co-op clubs, most of which disbanded quickly, sometimes without ever playing a road game.

The advent of the National League brought a system more akin to capitalism to the fore. Although undermined by collusive practices (see **18.4.6**), competition between adversarial magnates remained the league's basic manner of conducting business until the 1890 season.

In that year, with three leagues fighting for survival, major league baseball drifted far from traditional capitalistic practices. This was most obvious in the Players' League where the players owned stock, but there were examples in the other leagues as well. In the American Association the other seven teams agreed to supply the new Brooklyn team with at least one quality player, though only two complied (David Nemec, *The Beer and Whisky League*, 188–189). Meanwhile several National League owners loaned John B. Day money to save the New York Giants from bankruptcy (the ramifications of this event are discussed in the next entry) (A. G. Spalding, quoted in *New York Clipper*, February 5, 1895; reprinted in *Spalding's Official Base Ball Guide, 1895*, 123).

The twentieth century also saw occasional examples of socialistic practices in baseball. When John McGraw and Andrew Freedman stripped the Baltimore Orioles in the middle of the 1902 campaign, other American League owners donated players to keep the league intact. After the 1939 season, after receiving pressure from league president Will Harridge, every American League team offered one player off their roster for sale to the sad-sack Browns (William Mead, *Even the Browns*, 65). The basis of the All-American Girls Baseball League was socialistic, with players being drawn from a single pool and often shifted to help a weak franchise. After airplane travel became extensive in 1958, both major leagues adopted a disaster plan that called for a redistribution of talent if a team were to suffer a catastrophic accident.

In recent years, major league owners have agreed to revenue sharing of income from certain sources, yet have staunchly resisted such tendencies in other areas.

22.5.2 Syndicate Ownership. In 1883 and 1884 the Metropolitan Exhibition Company, of which John B. Day was president, owned the New York franchises in both the National League and the American Association. Day orchestrated at least one highly dubious transfer of players when the Association Metropolitans released Tim Keefe and Dude Esterbrook, and the two players then signed to play for the National League team.

David Nemec suggested that Columbus and Pittsburgh of the American Association may have been under the same ownership in 1884. He also noted that Brooklyn owner Charles Byrne bought the Cleveland club in 1885 and transferred its best players to Brooklyn. Two years later Byrne bought the Metropolitans and again pillaged the club's best players for his Brooklyn squad (David Nemec, *The Beer and Whisky League*, 72).

This destructive practice accelerated in the 1890s. In July 1890 New York Giants owner Day told his fellow National League magnates that he had to have $80,000 or he would be forced to sell his franchise to the Players' League. A. G. Spalding, John T. Brush, and other owners chipped in to keep him afloat (A. G. Spalding, quoted in *New York Clipper*, February 5, 1895; reprinted in *Spalding's Official Base Ball Guide, 1895*, 123). The precarious financial position of the National League after the threat from the Players' League led to several owners having at least a share of more than one franchise. In the American Association, St. Louis Brown Stockings owner Chris Von der Ahe acquired a controlling interest in the Cincinnati franchise.

The potential for conflicts of interest raised by these situations was obvious. By 1898 it was Von der Ahe who was in dire financial straits, and rumors had Cincinnati owner John T. Brush purchasing his team. Baltimore manager and minority owner Ned Hanlon commented, "I do not think that Brush bought the St. Louis team on his own account. It seems to me more probable that he bought it for other parties. I do not know of any rule in the national agreement that prohibits the ownership by one man of more than one major league team, and yet I do not believe that the [league] would permit such a thing. Should Brush continue to own both teams I have no doubt the games between the two clubs would be honestly played, but public opinion would look askance at a series between the two teams, if that series had any bearing on the championship contest. Mr. Brush has been conspicuous in his work for the good of the game, and I do not believe he would be a party to any transactions that would have any tendency to cast public doubt on its honesty. I believe that the national game should be above reproach, and that no two teams in the major league should be controlled by the same personal influence" (*Oklahoma City Daily Oklahoman*, March 11, 1898).

Yet that was exactly what happened in 1899 as the season saw two different dual-ownership situations in the twelve-team National League. Hanlon and Baltimore majority owner Harry von der Horst purchased the Brooklyn franchise, then dispatched many key players and Hanlon himself to the latter club. That situation did not degenerate into a travesty because John McGraw remained in Baltimore, and his canny maneuvers enabled the Orioles to remain very competitive. But a fiasco did occur in Cleveland, where the club's owners, the Robison brothers, purchased Von der Ahe's St. Louis franchise and transferred Cleveland's best players. The remnants of the Cleveland team compiled a 20-134 record and spent the second half of the season on the road because the home fans wanted no part of the sorry spectacle. Several other owners had interests in rival clubs, and the public understandably became deeply cynical about the game's integrity.

Three years later another equally farcical situation occurred. John McGraw was managing Baltimore's American League entry but had a running feud with league president Ban Johnson. Eventually he helped New York Giants owner Andrew Freedman to buy a controlling interest in the Orioles. Freedman promptly released most of Baltimore's players and then signed many of them and McGraw for the Giants.

The potential for conflict of interest led to a 1927 rule banning ownership of more than one major league club. That rule was disregarded in the series of dubious transactions that led to the purchase of the Montreal Expos by the other twenty-nine club owners in 2001.

22.5.3 National Baseball Trust. The *reductio ad absurdum* of the era of syndicate ownership was a proposal made in 1901 by New

York Giants owner Andrew Freedman. Under Freedman's plan the National League would be transformed into a holding company for the league's eight franchises. Each owner would receive a specified share of the whole league, thus jeopardizing the concept of competition.

Freedman and three other owners, John T. Brush, Frank Robison, and Arthur Soden, concocted the plan at a secret meeting at Freedman's estate at Red Bank, New Jersey, in July. It was leaked to the *New York Sun*, which broke the story on December 10 and 11, 1901, and inaugurated a heated controversy. With four owners on each side, a bitter deadlock ensued that was characterized by bizarre machinations.

Eventually the trust was defeated, but not before it had damaged the National League and helped the American League become established as a major league. One element that helped doom the plan was that Freedman assigned himself 30 percent of the stock, more than twice as much as any other owner.

(vi) Other Modes and Types of Competition

22.6.1 Interleague Play. While interleague play debuted in 1997, the idea had been around much earlier. Cubs president William Veeck (father of the innovative owner Bill Veeck) proposed interleague play in the major leagues on August 22, 1933. Veeck died suddenly six weeks later, and the idea was shelved. The younger Veeck later claimed that his father's last words were, "Push inter-league play, and beware of [sportswriter] Westbrook Pegler" (Lee Lowenfish, *Branch Rickey*, 410).

Beginning in the 1950s the idea of interleague play was raised on a regular basis, usually coinciding with a scheme for expansion. The American League suggested interleague play on November 22, 1960, as part of a scheme to allow each league to add one expansion team. On July 31, 1962, the National League rejected Commissioner Ford Frick's proposal for interleague play in 1963. Red Smith wrote in 1973 that the idea had never succeeded because one league or the other was opposed, but that it was again gaining support (Red Smith, May 28, 1973; reprinted in *Red Smith on Baseball*). Several other instances were enumerated in the Spring 1997 issue of *Outside the Lines*, the newsletter of the SABR Business of Baseball committee.

The two Triple A minor leagues, the American Association and the International League, experimented with interleague play between

1988 and 1991. In the end it was decided that the added expense of travel outweighed the benefits.

22.6.2 Tripleheader. There have been three tripleheaders played in the major leagues, all in the National League: Pittsburgh at Brooklyn on September 1, 1890; Louisville at Baltimore on September 7, 1896; Cincinnati at Pittsburgh on October 2, 1920. The first two tripleheaders occurred on the Labor Day holiday, so one game was played in the morning followed by an afternoon doubleheader. In the 1920 tripleheader, play started at noon and continued until darkness ended the third game after six innings (A. D. Suehsdorf, "The Last Tripleheader," *Baseball Research Journal* 1980, 30–32).

Quite a few tripleheaders were played in the minor leagues between 1878 and 1910, for a variety of reasons. The first took place on July 4, 1878, when New Bedford and Hartford sought to capitalize on the traditionally large Independence Day crowd by playing three games in three different cities—New Bedford, Taunton, and Providence. The Saginaw–Bay City Hyphens, perhaps the only team named in honor of a punctuation mark, hosted Montreal for three games on July 4, 1890, one in Bay City and two in Saginaw.

Making up postponed games was a more common reason for such exhibitions. A list of such games appears in George L. Moreland's *Balldom* (George L. Moreland, *Balldom*, 258–259; the list has a number of errors). At least two quadrupleheaders were played for this reason, both of which were sweeps. Researcher Mike Welsh reported that Sioux City beat St. Joseph 6-1, 15-7, 12-5, and 7-4 on September 15, 1889, while researcher Bill Deane found that Hudson topped Poughkeepsie by scores of 2-1, 6-4, 3-1, and 4-2 on September 20, 1903.

Manchester and Portland of the New England League played six games on September 4, 1899, for a different reason. It was the last day of the season, and Manchester was trying to catch Newport for the second-half title. Manchester did indeed win all six games, but the league office threw out all but one of them.

Regardless of the motive, such events had the obvious potential to make a farce of the game. George L. Moreland brought up the issue at the 1910 meeting of the National Association of Baseball Clubs, and a resolution was passed that banned clubs from playing more than two games in a day (George L. Moreland, *Balldom*, 259).

22.6.3 Day-Night Doubleheader. Major league baseball's first day-night doubleheader was played on September 27, 1939, when the Chicago White Sox hosted Cleveland. Separate admissions were charged.

22.6.4 Triangular Doubleheader. Providence and Boston hosted two clubs apiece on Decoration Day in both 1883 and 1884 and on Independence Day in 1884 (thanks to Rick Stattler). Greg Rhodes and John Snyder observed that the Reds scheduled four doubleheaders in 1899 where they hosted two different teams: Louisville and Cleveland on June 11 and September 10; Louisville and St. Louis on August 6 and September 3. Since then there have been only two such doubleheaders played in the white major leagues—the first on September 9, 1913, in St. Louis, and the second on September 25, 2000, in Cleveland (Greg Rhodes and John Snyder, *Redleg Journal*, 129). Doubleheaders featuring three or four teams became a regular feature of the Negro Leagues (Neil Lanctot, *Negro League Baseball*, 185–186).

22.6.5 Intercollegiate Match. Amherst College defeated Williams College 73-32 on July 1, 1859, in a match played by the looser rules of the "Massachusetts game." On the previous day the two schools had squared off in a chess match. The Williams students were let out of classes to watch the match, and nearly the entire student body was in attendance. Dean Sullivan's *Early Innings* includes a newspaper account of the match. Four months later, what may have been the first intercollegiate game played by the New York rules featured Xavier College and Fordham (William J. Ryczek, *Baseball's First Inning*, 130).

Clubs formed at colleges were a major part of the expansion of baseball during the 1860s, though intercollegiate competition was slowed by summer breaks. On April 22, 1876, the "College Base Ball Association of the Northwest" was formed by three schools at a meeting in Waukegan, Illinois. The delegates from the University of Chicago missed their train, which meant that only Racine College and Northwestern University were represented. Nonetheless, ambitious plans were made to welcome "all regularly incorporated colleges." To address the problem of summer vacation, "It was agreed that the championship season should commence May 1st and end the 15th of November, and that no games were to be played in vacation" (*Northwestern University: A History,*

1855–1905, 173). Formal competition between the big Eastern colleges began when the Intercollegiate Base Ball Association was organized in December 1879 (Troy Soos, *Before the Curse*, 58). Varsity baseball clubs began to proliferate in the 1880s.

22.6.6 College World Series.
The University of California defeated Yale 8-7 to win the first College World Series in 1947.

22.6.7 Olympics.
Baseball and the Olympics might seem a perfect match, but that hasn't proven to be the case, despite numerous efforts.

Two exhibition games were played at the 1912 Olympics in Stockholm. One featured a Swedish team against a team of American Olympians from other sports, and the other featured two squads of Americans (Pete Cava, "Baseball in the Olympics," *National Pastime* 12 [1992], 2–8).

Another exhibition game was staged at the 1936 Olympics in Berlin. The contestants were two American amateur teams, and they played in front of a crowd that was estimated at close to 100,000. The German spectators did not understand baseball very well, and the loudest applause was accorded to pop flies. By the end of the game the crowd had thinned considerably (M. E. Travaglini, "Olympic Baseball 1936," *National Pastime* 5 [1985], 46).

A Finnish game named Pesapello was demonstrated at the 1952 Olympics in Helsinki. The game was derived from baseball, but Red Smith was not impressed: "It was invented by Lauri Pihkala, a professor who wears a hearing aid and believes his game was modeled on baseball. Somebody must have described baseball to him when his battery was dead" (Red Smith, August 2, 1952, reprinted in *Red Smith on Baseball*).

The 1956 Games in Melbourne featured an exhibition game between an American and an Australian team. As the game progressed, the stadium began to fill up to its capacity of 114,000 as spectators arrived for the track and field events that were to follow the game. Thus the game may have been witnessed by the largest crowd in baseball history.

After another exhibition at the 1964 Olympic Games in Tokyo, baseball finally became a demonstration sport at the 1984 Games. The first medals in baseball were awarded at the 1992 Olympics in Barcelona.

22.6.8 Old-timers Games / Senior Professional Baseball Association.
Obviously it took a few years before old-timers games could be played, but it was sooner than might be expected. Researcher John Thorn noted that in 1869 the Excelsiors of Brooklyn played a game against their 1859 first nine (cited in Eric Nadel and Craig R. Wright, *The Man Who Stole First Base*, 145).

Such games soon became a popular feature of nineteenth-century baseball. On April 13, 1896, old-timers games were played all over the country for Harry Wright Day, an event that commemorated the first anniversary of Wright's death.

The first attempt to transform the interest that such games generated into an ongoing venture was made in 1935. *Sporting News* reported that "A traveling baseball school, made up of old-time stars who will play games in connection with their instruction classes, has been announced for the coming summer by Walter J. Foley of Framingham, Mass" (*Sporting News*, January 10, 1935). A nineteen-game tour was planned that would feature such stars of the past as Cy Young, Rube Marquard, and Harry Hooper. The tour proved to be a fiasco, and Young had to dip into his own pocket to pay for the food and lodging of his fellow players (Reed Browning, *Cy Young*, 199–200).

A similar plan was inaugurated on May 31, 1989, when the Senior League was founded for players thirty-five and over. The league lasted one full season and part of a second one.

22.6.9 Winter Baseball.
As noted in the entry on "Baseball on Ice" (**19.6**), it was quite common in the 1860s for the game to be played on ice during the winter months. John Thorn informs me that Hick Carpenter and Jimmy Macullar of the 1879 Syracuse Stars were the first active major leaguers to play winter ball in the Caribbean when both men played for the Colon Club of Cuba in the winter following the 1879 season. California was also a popular locale for winter baseball.

For many years the most prominent form of professional baseball played over the fall and winter was barnstorming. Winter baseball thrived in California from the 1920s through the 1940s. The now popular fall instructional leagues began in 1957 when the Cardinals, Phillies, Tigers, and Yankees sent teams to Tampa (Kevin M. McCarthy, *Baseball in Florida*, 126).

Chapter 23

SPREADING
THE WORD

(i) The Writer's Game

As discussed under "Mass-circulated Rules" (1.3), the connection between early baseball and the written word was so intimate that Tom Melville concluded that "baseball was the first game Americans learned principally from print." Melville noted that town ball was "handed down from generation to generation orally" while baseball was learned by reading "printed regulations" (Tom Melville, *Early Baseball and the Rise of the National League*, 18).

This connection was symbolized most prominently in the custom of maintaining a written scorebook of a club's activities and matches. Previously the score, if kept at all, was maintained by someone making notches on a stick. Frank Pidgeon recalled that the Eckfords of Brooklyn were so excited when they scored their first run in their first match game against the Unions of Morrisania that some of their players "ran to the Umpire's book, to see how it looked on paper" (*Porter's Spirit of the Times*, January 10, 1857; quoted in George B. Kirsch, *The Creation of American Team Sports*, 111).

The years that followed would expand and deepen the connection between baseball and the written word.

23.1.1 Newspaper Account of a Game. Researcher George A. Thompson, Jr., discovered brief articles published in New York newspapers on April 25, 1823, that made mention of a recent game of "base ball." The one in the *National Advocate* reported "a company of active young men playing the manly and athletic game of 'base ball' at the Retreat in Broadway (Jones')." Neither this article nor the one in the *New-York Gazette and General Advertiser* mentioned a score or described the play in any detail (George A. Thompson Jr., "New York Baseball, 1823," *National Pastime* 21 [2001], 6–8).

The first known lengthy account of a baseball game appeared in the *New York Morning News* on October 22, 1845, and is reprinted in Dean Sullivan's *Early Innings*, pages 11–13.

23.1.2 Baseball Poem. John Thorn discovered a poem published in 1887 that was said to have first been published some fifty years earlier (*Base Ball Gazette*, April 20, 1887). The poem was sent in by a man named Walter Colton Abbott, of Reading, Michigan, who said that it had originally appeared in the *New York News and Courier* around 1838. It read:

> Then dress, the dress, brave gallants all,
> Don uniforms amain;
> Remember fame and honor call
> Us to the field again.
> No shrewish tears shall fill our eye
> When the ball club's in our hand,
> If we do lose we will not sigh,
> Nor plead a butter hand.
> Let piping swain and craven jay
> Thus weep and puling cry,
> Our business is like men to play,
> Or know the reason why.

A note pointed out that "butter hand" was a precursor to butterfingers.

If Abbott's dating of the poem is accurate, it is likely the earliest baseball poem. It was subsequently noted that the poem was not original but an adaptation of an earlier poem, "The Cavalier's Song" by Scottish poet William Motherwell (1797–1835) (*Base Ball Gazette,* April 22, 1887).

23.1.3   Baseball Reporters. Henry Chadwick is often considered to be the first reporter to write regularly about baseball, but he did not start doing so until 1856. William Rankin accordingly maintained that the first baseball reporter was William Cauldwell, who was secretary of the Unions of Morrisania and one of the proprietors of the *New York Sunday Mercury*. During 1853 he published periodic accounts of the club's activities (*Sporting News,* January 14, 1905). In addition, John Thorn pointed out that William Bray preceded Chadwick as the baseball and cricket reporter of the *New York Clipper*.

23.1.4   Writers' Association. According to Francis C. Richter, the first baseball writers' association was a local group formed in Philadelphia in 1885 (Francis C. Richter, *Richter's History and Records of Base Ball,* 422). The first such organization of national scope, the Base Ball Reporters' Association of America, was formed in Cincinnati on December 9, 1887, with George Munson of the *Sporting News* as president and Henry Chadwick as vice president. Its objectives were to "promote the welfare of the National Game, and to bring about a thorough and regular system of base ball scoring" (*Spalding's Official Base Ball Guide, 1888,* 97–98). The organization lasted three years.

The Baseball Writers Association of America was organized during the 1908 World Series with the less ambitious aim of ending "the overcrowding of the press box" by nonwriters that often occurred at big games (William G. Weart, writing in A. H. Spink, *The National Game,* 350). The organization survives to this day.

23.1.5   Interviews. Historian Paul Starr reported that the interview genre was developed in the 1860s by American newspapermen. He noted that it did not catch on in England and France for another two decades. He suggested that "America's more egalitarian, less deferential culture fostered the invention of a mode

of journalistic inquiry that subjected important people to questioning by mere reporters." Even in the United States, many businessmen and politicians regarded an interview as "an impertinence" (Paul Starr, *The Creation of the Media,* 148).

Interviews of baseball players began to appear in the 1870s, but some of the subjects took an equally dim view of their interrogators. The earliest published interview I have found was conducted with Chicago captain Jimmy Wood in 1875. In it Wood bluntly informed the *Chicago Tribune* reporter that "there are thousands of people who buy the papers simply for the reports of the games, and who would not otherwise think of looking at a newspaper" (*Chicago Tribune,* June 18, 1875).

23.1.6   Baseball Guide. The first baseball guide was the *Beadle's Dime Base-Ball Player,* an annual edited by Henry Chadwick. It first appeared in 1860.

23.1.7   Baseball Periodical. The first American periodical devoted entirely to ball sports was Henry Chadwick's *The Ball Player's Chronicle*. The premier issue proclaimed, "for the first time in the annals of the game, the fraternity can now boast of an 'organ' of their own" and hailed the development as a sign that "base ball is a permanently established institution" (*The Ball Player's Chronicle,* June 6, 1867). The end of the playing season represented a major challenge to the fledgling periodical. On January 2, 1868, it changed its name to the *American Chronicle of Sports and Pastimes,* but the apparent effort to attract a larger readership was unsuccessful, and it folded in June.

23.1.8   Hardcover Book. In 1868 Henry Chadwick published a book that, depending on whether one believes the title page or the page headers, was entitled either *The Game of Base Ball* or *The American Game of Base Ball.* As late as 1888 the scarcity of books about baseball was attracting notice: "Universal as has been the baseball mania, it is an astonishing fact how little literature has sprung up in connection with the game" (*Outing,* November 1888). That would change.

23.1.9   Dictionary of Baseball Jargon. Henry Chadwick compiled a list of baseball terms and definitions for the 1868 book mentioned in the preceding entry. He put together a more comprehensive glossary of terms for the British during an 1874 tour of England by top American baseball players. These last four entries should give some indication of the extent to which Chadwick single-handedly framed the early experience of baseball.

23.1.10 Baseball Novels. Jonathan Fraser Light suggested that the first work of fiction with a baseball theme may have been an 1868 novel entitled *Changing Base* by William Everett (Jonathan Fraser Light, *The Cultural Encyclopedia of Baseball*, 101). As late as 1890 a publisher remarked: "It's a wonder to me that nobody has yet written a baseball novel. I should think that such a venture would meet with a large and ready sale, if it did not become a craze with the horde of admirers of the game" ("A Baseball Novel Wanted," *New York Tribune*, July 20, 1890; reprinted in the *National Pastime* 25 [2005], 126). The oversight was soon addressed, and novels about baseball rapidly became popular.

23.1.11 Books by Ballplayers. In 1884 John F. Morrill wrote an instructional book called *Batting and Pitching, with Fine Illustrations of Attitudes* (Jonathan Fraser Light, *The Cultural Encyclopedia of Baseball*, 102). John Montgomery Ward's *Base Ball: How to Become a Player* followed in 1888.

23.1.12 Autobiographies by Ballplayers. The first autobiography of a baseball player was Mike Kelly's 1888 *Play Ball*, which like many subsequent ones was ghostwritten. The subtitle of the work was either *Stories of the Ball Field* or *Stories of the Diamond Field*, depending on whether the cover or the title page is to be believed (Marty Appel, *Slide, Kelly, Slide*, 129).

23.1.13 Baseball Encyclopedia. George L. Moreland's 1914 *Balldom* and Ernest J. Lanigan's 1922 *The Baseball Cyclopedia* were incomplete but important early attempts to compile historical records of baseball clubs and players. S. C. Thompson and Hy Turkin came out with the first attempt at a comprehensive book of this sort in 1951. Macmillan entered the fray in 1969 with *The Baseball Encyclopedia*, which was also the first book of any kind to be typeset by computer. Pete Palmer and John Thorn brought out the first edition of their monumental *Total Baseball* in 1989.

(ii) Baseball in Other Media

Baseball enthusiasts have attempted to bring their favorite game into a surprising number of media, with mixed results.

23.2.1 Photographs. Connie Mack claimed that a photograph of boys playing baseball on Boston Commons appeared in Robin Carver's 1834 *The Book of Sports* (Connie Mack, *My Sixty-Six Years in the Big Leagues*, 213). This was, in fact, just a woodcut (David Block, *Baseball Before We Knew It*, 197).

Baseball and photography both began to develop in earnest in the 1840s. But early photographs were ruined by any sort of movement, and only a few images of baseball before 1860 are known to exist. Mark Rucker noted that only "a daguerreotype, a few ambrotypes, and some salt prints" have been discovered. By the early 1860s, however, photographs of baseball players became much more common due to the popularity of "cartes de visite." Rucker's wonderful book, *Base Ball Cartes*, offers many stunning examples.

Tom Shieber attempted to pinpoint the earliest baseball photograph. While he acknowledged that dating photos from the mid-nineteenth century is an inexact science, he settled upon one that featured the 1855 Atlantic Base Ball Club of Brooklyn (Tom Shieber, "The Earliest Baseball Photography," *National Pastime* 17 [1997], 101–104).

Researcher John Thorn reports that the earliest halftone reproduction of a photograph to appear in a newspaper was printed in an issue of the *New York Graphic* in 1880. The first photographs of baseball players in action to appear in a newspaper are believed to have been the ones in a set that was published in the *New York World* on April 29, 1886. It was not until the 1890s that it became common for newspapers to print photographs of baseball players.

23.2.2 Songs. In early baseball it was quite common for clubs to walk to the ballpark singing the team song. The Knickerbocker club was joined by the Gotham and Eagle clubs at a dinner on December 15, 1854, at Fijux's restaurant in New York. James Whyte Davis of the Knickerbocker club composed a song for the occasion called "Ball Days," which was so well received that it was printed. In 1858, J. Randolph Blodgett, a player for the Niagaras of Buffalo, published the sheet music for a piece called "The Base Ball Polka." The first published pieces with words appear to have been "The Bat and Ball" and "Base Ball Fever," both in 1867. The All-American Girls Baseball League revived this tradition by having a victory song.

Baseball's informal anthem, "Take Me Out to the Ball Game," was written in 1908 by Jack Norworth and set to music by Albert Von Tilzer. The song's chorus has long been a seventh-inning staple, but many fans are unaware that the song also has two verses that tell the story of the baseball-obsessed Katie Casey. To commemorate the song's centennial in 2008, Andy Strasberg, Bob Thompson, and Tim Wiles wrote a definitive history, *Baseball's Greatest Hit: The Story of "Take Me Out to the Ball Game."*

23.2.3 Records.

"Slide Kelly Slide," a popular song about Mike Kelly, was recorded as early as 1893 but not widely distributed. "Jimmy and Maggie at a Baseball Game" became the first baseball recording to receive extensive distribution in 1906.

23.2.4 Symphonies.

No baseball team seems better suited for epic treatment than the Brooklyn Dodgers. Perhaps that is what inspired composer Robert Russell Bennett, even though he was a Giants fan, to write a 1941 composition entitled *Symphony in D for the Dodgers*.

The symphony was first played on WOR in New York City on May 16, 1941, and was then staged at Lewisohn Stadium on August 3. It was conducted by Hans Wilhelm Steinberg and consisted of four movements. The joyful opening sonata sought to depict "the bedlam and wonderful nonsense exuded by the citizens of Brooklyn when the beloved bums win one." This was succeeded by a dirge that conveyed the city's gloom following a Dodger defeat.

The third movement portrayed the efforts of energetic Brooklyn president Larry MacPhail to acquire Bob Feller. Sportswriter Bob Considine commented that MacPhail was "typically in brass. He is in the form of a scherzo, threaded with hunting horn tootles. Seems the guy is out looking for talent to buy. Beneath the hunting horn ta-ra'ing can be heard a scraping sound which could either have been a carpenter working on the foundation of [Hans] Steinberg's podium or the symbolic sound of the Brooklyn stockholders walking the floor at night, worrying about the way MacPhail is treating O. P. M., which, of course, means other people's money. MacPhail gets into the dag-dangest session

with Alva Bradley, owner of Bobby Feller, that you ever heard emanate from a tuba. But even though MacPhail pleads for Feller through the good offices of 17 clarinets, 14 oboes, 83 bull fiddles and a boat load of refugee French horns, Bradley, the louse, turns him down. 'No,' Bradley answers with 64 saxophones, a mouth organ and comb wrapped in tissue paper" (Bob Considine, "Symphony in D for the Dodgers," *Washington Post*, August 6, 1941, 18).

Despite this disappointment, the symphony ended on a high note. Dodgers broadcaster Red Barber strode from the wings for the final movement and, backed by orchestral music, described Dolph Camilli beating the Giants with a dramatic home run.

The symphony was not a critical success, with the *New York Times*'s Noel Straus observing: "Much was expected of this work with its rich opportunities for wit and excitement. But in reality it fell rather flat on the ears of the moderate-sized audience present. One rather anticipated that the woodwinds would go in for a lot of wild pitching, that there would be barrages of hits by the kettle-drums, and that the brasses would smack at least a few homers over the distant bleachers . . . but nothing of the sort materialized" (Noel Straus, "Stadium Premiere for Baseball Epic," *New York Times*, August 4, 1941).

23.2.5 Operas.

In 1888 John Philip Sousa wrote the score for a comic opera entitled *Angela, or The Umpire's Revenge*. The plot revolved around a pitcher whose complaints about an umpire's calls prompt the latter to retaliate by interfering with the pitcher's romance (H. Allen Smith and Ira L. Smith, *Low and Inside*, 221).

23.2.6 Motion Picture.

Jonathan Fraser Light reported that Thomas Edison released a fragmentary series of baseball images in 1898. Eight years later Edison created the first movie about baseball with a story line, entitled *How the Office Boy Saw the Ball Game*. In 1911 the National Commission negotiated to sell rights to film the World Series, but there are conflicting reports as to whether a movie was made (Jonathan Fraser Light, *The Cultural Encyclopedia of Baseball*, 466). The first footage from an actual baseball game was taken in 1903 during a postseason game between Cleveland and Cincinnati (Lonnie Wheeler and John Baskin, *The Cincinnati Game*, 50). The first ballplayer to appear in a film was Hal Chase in 1911.

(iii) Broadcasting Refinements

Chapter 16 on marketing told of how new methods of broadcasting had to overcome initial resistance. In this section we note some significant advances in radio and television broadcasting.

23.3.1 Pregame Shows. Red Barber called his first Brooklyn Dodger game on Opening Day of the 1939 season, bringing to an end a pact between the three New York teams that prohibited radio broadcasts. For the historic event, Barber was able to convince radio station WOR to give him extra time beforehand to interview managers Bill Terry and Leo Durocher (Bob Edwards, *Fridays with Red*, 61).

23.3.2 Taboos Against Mentioning a No-hitter. Long before radio was invented, it was traditional for teammates not to mention a potential no-hitter in the dugout. Ernest Lanigan explained in 1913, "One sure way to spoil a no-hit game for a pitcher is to remark, particularly in the ninth inning, 'Well, they haven't made a hit thus far.' That almost invariably brings forth one or more bingles" (*Sporting Life*, August 7, 1913).

Red Barber explained how this superstition was transferred to announcers: "This hoodoo business started in the dugouts with a fairly reasonable premise—a teammate would not mention a possible no-hitter for fear of putting undue pressure on his pitcher, who just might be pitching away blissfully unaware of what he was doing. Then, before radio came along, this hoodoo, or jinx, got up to the press box, and the writers turned silent whenever the occasion presented itself. When radio got going, the hoodoo spread into the broadcasting booths. Not mine" (quoted in Bob Edwards, *Fridays with Red*, 76).

Indeed, in the first major league game that Barber broadcast, Lon Warneke had a no-hitter broken up with one out in the ninth inning. Barber mentioned that no-hitter during the game because he was unaware of the taboo, but he continued to defy the convention throughout his career (Red Barber, *1947: When All Hell Broke Loose*, 224–226).

23.3.3 Athletes-turned-broadcasters. The first ballplayer to become a broadcaster was Jack Graney, who called Indians games from 1932 to 1954. Not everyone was receptive to the idea. When Graney was invited to announce

the 1934 World Series, Commissioner Kenesaw Mountain Landis forbade him from doing so on the grounds that the former American Leaguer would be partisan to the junior circuit. Graney wrote tersely to Landis, "my playing days are over. I am now a sportscaster and should be regarded as such." He was allowed to call the 1935 Series (Ted Patterson, "Jack Graney, The First Player-Broadcaster," *Baseball Research Journal* 2 [1973], reprinted in *Baseball Historical Review* 1981, 52–57). Graney's smooth transition to the airwaves paved the way for others, including Harry Heilmann, Waite Hoyt, and Gabby Street, and eventually for broadcasting to become a popular second career for ballplayers.

23.3.4 TV Commercials. Red Barber delivered three commercial messages during the first telecast of a major league game. Red later recounted, "In the middle of the agreed inning, I held up a bar of Ivory Soap and said something about it being a great soap . . . a few innings later I put on a Mobil Gas service-station cap, held up a can of oil, and said what a great oil it was . . . and for Wheaties? This was a big production number. Right on the camera, right among the fans, I opened a box of Wheaties, shook out a bowlful, sliced a banana, added a spoon of sugar, poured on some milk—and said, 'That's a Breakfast of Champions'" (Red Barber, *The Broadcasters*, 134).

23.3.5 Color Television. The first major league game to be telecast in color aired in New York City on CBS Channel 2 on August 11, 1951, and featured the Brooklyn Dodgers and the Boston Braves. Although viewers had to have a homemade converter in order to see the action in color, a CBS spokesman estimated that some one thousand sets were tuned to the game, with ten thousand fans watching the historic event. Special guests at Gimbel's Department Store and at CBS headquarters also watched the telecast (*New York Times*, August 12, 1951).

Red Smith wrote favorably of the experiment the next day but noted: "There was some slight running of colors. When Charley Dressen, the Dodgers' resident djinn, stood on the bare base path to chat with one of his runners, his white uniform was as immaculate as a prom queen's gown. But the camera followed him as he returned to the coach's box beside third, and against this background of turf he turned green, like cheap jewelry."

"Light blues ran a good deal, too, washing across the picture. The Braves' gray traveling uniforms took on an unnatural bluish cast, and when the camera swept the shirtsleeved crowd one had the impression that all the customers had been laundered together with too much bluing in the water. The dark blue of the Dodgers' caps, however, remained fast and true" (Red Smith, August 12, 1951, reprinted in *Red Smith on Baseball*).

Thus for all Tommy Lasorda's claims to have bled Dodger blue, he was not the first Dodger manager to do so.

23.3.6 Instant Replays. According to Jonathan Fraser Light, the first use of instant replay in a baseball game took place on WPIX-TV in New York on July 17, 1959 (Jonathan Fraser Light, *The Cultural Encyclopedia of Baseball*, 372). But it was not until the 1965 season that major league baseball agreed to let ABC use instant replays as a regular feature of baseball telecasts.

Many doubted that the innovation would be good for the game. On the eve of the 1965 season an AP wire service piece noted: "The television people have promised to train the isolated camera on any and all dramatic, close and controversial plays, thereby enabling the viewer to ascertain immediately whether his first impression of the umpire was correct— that he was nothing but a blind Tom." Players like Jim Gentile expressed concern that umpires would respond to this scrutiny by becoming "overcautious" (AP: *Frederick* [Md.] *Post*, March 30, 1965).

Others felt that the effects on umpires would be worse than that. Columnist Ed Nichols suggested that the men in blue would no longer get the benefit of the doubt on close plays: "Everyone in the country will be in position to second guess them . . . there are sure to be a lot of humiliating moments for the umpires" (Ed Nichols, "Isolated Camera Tough on Umps," *Salisbury Times*, December 23, 1964).

The new technology was first used in an ABC broadcast on April 17, 1965 (Bucky Summers, "Still Baseball on TV," *Frederick* [Md.] *Post*, April 20, 1965). Before long it became clear that the initial fears were unjustified. Umpire Joe Paparella later explained, "CBS [sic] had been televising the [American League] games and then wanted permission to use the replays. [American League president] Mr. [Will] Harridge, [umpire] Cal Hubbard, and I talked about it. CBS showed us some slides of

what they would use. They said they were not going to try to embarrass an umpire but just show a close play and let the viewers decide. I'm tickled to death that we approved it for the simple reason that it has shown that umpires are right 99 percent of the time. It has been a shot in the arm to umpires because the public now realizes what a good job umpires do" (quoted in Larry R. Gerlach, *The Men in Blue*, 145).

Sportswriter Arthur Daley reached a similar conclusion: "When television came up with an invention called 'instant replay,' most officials—baseball as well as football—regarded it fearfully as a device of the devil. It would expose their every mistake to the second guessers. They need not have worried. Only with the rarest exceptions does instant replay do anything but confirm the astonishing accuracy of every call" (Arthur Daley, "The Human Factor," *New York Times*, December 20, 1968).

The prominence of instant replays in the 1965 season does appear to have had one notable effect on the umpiring profession. Sportswriter Joseph Durso suggested that the men in blue, fearful of being made to look bad, were becoming more willing to consult with colleagues and reverse a call if necessary. Umpire Tom Gorman commented: "Maybe umpires are consulting each other more. If they are that's good umpiring. You know, if a man can't see a play clearly, he ought to ask somebody's advice, but never on a judgment play or for any reason related to cameras" (Joseph Durso, "The Magic Eye," *New York Times*, August 3, 1965).

23.3.7 Slow-motion Replays. Slow-motion replay was first used during an Army-Navy football game on December 31, 1964 (Jonathan Fraser Light, *The Cultural Encyclopedia of Baseball*, 727). Two months later ABC president Tom Moore announced plans to bring the technique to baseball along with instant replay: "We don't feel baseball has been adequately covered on TV in the past. We propose to use multi cameras, including the instant replay, stop action and slow motion. We intend to apply some of the techniques that have been used so effectively in football. And there are many more opportunities to do it in baseball. For example, while the manager is on the mound we might analyze the situation that confronts him" (Sid Ziff, "TV and Baseball," *Los Angeles Times*, February 28, 1965).

At the initial telecast on April 17, 1965, the slow-motion feature was deemed a disappointment: "The slow motion sequences that were used were taken by the same camera which originally shot the play so that the audience was still the same distance from it and the distance was fuzzy." This was blamed on the fact that it was more difficult for a baseball producer to predict where the action would occur than was the case in football (Bucky Summers, "Still Baseball on TV," *Frederick* [Md.] *Post*, April 20, 1965). The technique was refined and reintroduced by NBC for the 1966 World Series (*Zanesville Times Recorder*, October 6, 1966).

23.3.8   Split Screen. Red Smith said that split screens were introduced because of Jackie Robinson's daring baserunning, so that television viewers could see both the pitcher and Robinson poised to take off from first base (Red Smith, October 25, 1972, reprinted in *Red Smith on Baseball*). If so, the practice did not become common for many years. A 1967 *New York Times* article reported that split screens had occasionally been used in baseball but that

ABC was now introducing split-screen instant replay to football (Jack Gould, "TV: A.B.C. Football, Coverage Scores," *New York Times*, December 4, 1967).

23.3.9   Game of the Week. National telecasts of a featured game began when ABC's *Game of the Week* debuted on June 6, 1953.

23.3.10   Satellite Broadcasts. Baseball was first broadcast overseas on July 23, 1962, as part of a groundbreaking experiment with the Telstar satellite. Viewers in Europe were able to watch twenty minutes of live clips from all over the United States, including ninety seconds of action from a game at Wrigley Field between the Cubs and Phillies. The innovation caused *Chicago Tribune* reporter Edward Prell to wonder whether the Europeans who interrupted their dinner to watch the game had become the first witnesses of night baseball at Wrigley Field (*Chicago Tribune*, July 24, 1962).

Chapter 24

TRAVELING MEN

.

THE LINK between baseball and traveling is profound. Early visiting clubs often had to overcome considerable hardship just to get to the game. For example, a 36-0 loss by the Blue Belts of Leland, Michigan, to the White Stars of Traverse City in an 1876 game was mitigated by the fact that the Blue Belts "walked six miles and came the rest of the way in a rough wagon" (*Grand Traverse* [Mich.] *Herald*, September 7, 1876). Needless to say, visiting clubs were no-shows for a wide variety of reasons, including "choppy seas" (*South Haven Sentinel*, August 11, 1877). It is no coincidence that professional baseball and the building of a national network of railroads in the 1860s and 1870s were near-simultaneous developments. Indeed there is good reason to believe that the railroads saved baseball.

(i) Getting from Game to Game

24.1.1 Tour. The Excelsior club of Brooklyn left on June 30, 1860, for a twelve-day, thousand-mile tour of New York State that saw them beat clubs in Albany, Troy, Buffalo, Rochester, and Newburgh-on-the-Hudson. The point of the excursion was not so much the competition as providing a showcase for the game, by allowing spectators outside the New York City area to see baseball played with a new degree of skill and finesse. One account noted: "no such ball playing was ever before witnessed in Buffalo. The manner in which the Excelsiors handled the ball, the ease with which they caught it, under all circumstances, the precision with which they threw it to the

bases, and the tremendous hits they gave into the long field made the optics of the Buffalo players glisten with admiration and protrude" (*Brooklyn Eagle*, July 9, 1860; quoted in James L. Terry, *Long Before the Dodgers*, 31).

Later that summer the Excelsiors accepted an invitation from a Baltimore club of the same name to travel to Maryland for a game. The emphasis was again on ceremony rather than competition: "It was not thought that the Baltimore Club had *the least show to win*, it was to be a game of instructions" (William Ridgely Griffith, *The Early History of Amateur Base Ball in the State of Maryland*, 6).

The importance of these tours was nicely captured in these reminiscences by a Phila-delphian: "Another Brooklyn club that I recall is the old Excelsior, to which base ball in this country owes more for its establishment on a broad and firm foundation as a national sport than to any of the clubs that were contempo-rary with it or that have followed it. It was the Excelsior Club of Brooklyn that began those base ball tours through the country that did so much to advance the popularity of the game. I speak here more particularly of the New York and Brooklyn clubs of the later sixties because fate dumped me in 'them diggins' after the war, but there are many old Philadelphians whose memories, like my own, will go back to the visit of the Excelsiors to this city in 1860. Unfortu-nately the seed sown by the Excelsiors in those early tours was cast in stony places, for the war intervened and consequently the years between 1861 and 1865 shone with less brilliancy than was to be expected from the furor created all over the country by the Brooklyn boys in those ante-bellum years" ("By an Ex-Editor," *Philadelphia Inquirer*, July 16, 1893).

After the Civil War the rapid expansion of the railway system made far more ambitious tours possible. The Nationals of Washington became the first Eastern team to venture west of the Allegheny in 1867 when they made a three-thousand-mile excursion that included stops in Columbus, Cincinnati, Louisville, Indianapolis, St. Louis, and Chicago. The 1868 Red Stockings of Cincinnati were the first club from what was then known as the West to make an extensive tour of the East. The following year the Red Stockings again crisscrossed the country and took advantage of the newly completed transcontinental railroad to become the first club to venture out to California.

In 1874 Albert Goodwill Spalding organized the first international tour, taking the Athletics of Philadelphia and the Red Stockings of Boston to England and Ireland for a tour (see A. G. Spalding, *America's National Game*, Chapter 13, and Adrian C. Anson, *A Ball Player's Career*, Chapter 9, for the descriptions of two participants. Peter Levine's *A. G. Spalding and the Rise of Baseball*, 17–20, provides a more objective account). Frank Bancroft took the first team of Americans to Cuba in 1879. The first around-the-world tour took place following the 1888 season, when Spalding escorted the Chicago team and an all-star team on a trip to Australia, with stops in Egypt and Europe on the way home (see A. G. Spalding, *America's National Game*, Chapter 18, and Adrian C. Anson, *A Ball Player's Career*, Chapters 18–31, for descriptions by two participants. See Mark Lamster's outstanding *Spalding's World Tour* for a more objective account). Pacific Coast League magnate Mike Fisher took a team on a three-month tour of Japan, China, and the Philippines beginning on November 3, 1908. Another around-the-world tour took place following the 1913 season (see James E. Elfers's *The Tour to End All Tours* for a first-rate chronicle of this expedition).

24.1.2 Eating on the Run. Even today, eating appropriately while traveling can be difficult. For early ball clubs the challenge of arranging meals in a way that would allow them to play their best was daunting. This was compounded by the temptation to indulge in the feasts that host clubs often provided for their guests.

In time, clubs learned the benefits of moderation. When the Nationals stopped in Columbus, Ohio, during their 1867 tour, the local paper observed: "At the close of the game the players partook of a cold lunch, which had been spread in a tent on the grounds. The [host] Capitals, in this respect, followed the recommendation of the Nationals, and we think this plan is better than to get an elaborate meal at a hotel" (*Ohio State Journal*, August 9, 1867).

Cincinnati manager Harry Wright "had a regular diet for [the Red Stockings] while traveling, and the strongest stimulant they were permitted to imbibe was a very delicious drink commonly known as egg lemonade, which the veteran Henry christened the 'Red Stocking punch'" (R. M. Larner, "Beginning of Professional Baseball in Washington," *Washington Post*, July 3, 1904).

When Deacon White captained the Forest City club of Cleveland in 1872, teammate Al Pratt later recalled: "we were never allowed anything but a cold snack at noon. We always went to lunch right at 12 o'clock and then ate but a little cold meat. Some warm meat was imbibed, but everything else cold. White would as soon let us have eat poison as a heavy, warm meal at noon. Some young players of today may laugh at White's methods. I never did. I thought they were all right. I think so yet. That cold, light lunch kept our stomachs from being overworked, our head clear and our eyesight good. The best effect was on the eyes. White always claimed that a man who persisted in eating heavy and warm food at lunch would not have as clear an eye or as good a head for hours after as the man who took his food cold" (*Sporting Life*, April 15, 1905).

24.1.3 Trains. The popular image of early travel by baseball clubs, especially in the Negro Leagues and minor leagues, is of endless trips on the team bus. In fact trains were the virtually exclusive method of transportation for baseball players—regardless of race—from the dawn of professional baseball until the 1920s.

The railroads offered discounts to baseball clubs, though there was talk before the 1887 season that these would be discontinued due to interstate commerce laws (*Cleveland Leader and Herald*, March 13, 1887). But the reality was that there was no affordable alternative for transporting an entire team. Thus the only exceptions were for individual players who chose to travel on their own: "Some of the minor leaguers ride bicycles, or get the old man to take them to the next town in the buggy" ("The

Great National Game in Dollars and Cents," *Washington Post*, May 9, 1909).

Rail travel remained a staple of baseball for more than half a century, and the comfort associated with train rides improved considerably over that period. As noted under "African-American Tours" (see **20.1.8**), some touring African-American clubs traveled in spacious touring cars in which they could sleep in comparative luxury. A 1916 article remarked that major leaguers now all had lower berths, as sleeping in an upper berth was "very 'bush league'" (Willis E. Johnson, "The Player's Life in the Major Leagues," *Sporting Life*, March 4, 1916). This led to the usual grumbling by old-timers. Early sportswriter T. Z. Cowles wrote in 1918: "Ball players of the long ago period were not like their fellows of 1918, born with gold spoons in their mouths. The epoch of princely salaries had not yet dawned. They traveled in ordinary sleeping cars at night, when they could get them. If not, they sat up. No special Pullmans for them" (T. Z. Cowles, *Chicago Tribune*, June 16, 1918).

24.1.4 Team Buses. Once buses were invented in the mid-1920s, owners soon found them to be cheaper and began to switch to them. The development brought great hardship to the Negro Leagues players who began to rely upon them to crisscross the country. As Donn Rogosin explained, early buses were basically big cars with benches for seating, which made sleeping extremely difficult. While they gradually became more comfortable, sleeping during overnight trips remained a challenge. Veteran stars like Dave Malarcher and Judy Johnson, accustomed to the comparative luxury of Pullman travel, could not make the adjustment and retired (Donn Rogosin, *Invisible Men*, 77–78).

The new form of transportation had many other drawbacks. Clubs began to put together grueling schedules and to travel unceasingly. Buses broke down frequently, and the potential for accidents always loomed (Neil Lanctot, *Negro League Baseball*, 154–155). Storage room was also in short supply on early buses. According to his son, in 1948 Syd Pollock bought one of the first buses with enough storage to carry all the team's equipment (Alan J. Pollock, *Barnstorming to Heaven*, 57).

Despite these drawbacks, two basic realities ensured that buses would hitherto be an essential part of the experience of African-American ballclubs. The first was the tremendous savings they represented over train travel. The second

was that discrimination in the South meant that it could be difficult to find lodging for African Americans, and sleeping on the bus was too often the only option available. Even when it wasn't, sleeping on the bus enabled clubs in dire straits to economize.

By World War II, buses had become so integral to the Negro Leagues that the prospect of wartime restrictions on bus travel in 1943 posed a grave threat. Officials of the Negro American and National leagues lobbied long and hard for an exemption, maintaining that their survival was at stake. They pointed out that their arduous travel schedules and the difficulty of finding lodging in the South made buses a necessity. Cum Posey went further, implying that a denial of their request for an exemption would cause some to conclude, "They don't allow Negros in white Organized Baseball, now they make it impossible for them to play Baseball."

Initially the Office of Defense Transportation (ODT) denied their pleas, and the 1943 season started with both leagues again traveling by trains. But soon the policy was reversed, with the Negro American League receiving an exemption in June and the Negro National League obtaining one for the 1944 season. Similar requests by white minor leagues, however, were never granted—ODT officials recognized that segregation made buses a necessity for the Negro Leagues (Neil Lanctot, *Negro League Baseball*, 128–134).

24.1.5 Automobiles. Car travel has never been a major part of baseball because of the need for multiple automobiles to transport a team. One of the rare exceptions left the players involved in little mood to repeat the experiment. Benton Stark noted that the New York Giants and Brooklyn Dodgers traveled to their 1904 season opener in a procession of automobiles, which were still a novelty. One of the vehicles collided with a horse-drawn wagon on the Brooklyn Bridge, and the players decided to continue the trip by train (Benton Stark, *The Year They Called Off the World Series*, 105–106). The development of station wagons did, however, make cars a more practical means of transportation, and the Philadelphia Stars of the Negro American League responded by traveling in two station wagons (Neil Lanctot, *Negro League Baseball*, 378).

24.1.6 Airplanes. On March 6, 1919, the New York Giants announced that they would fly to their season opener in Philadelphia. The

New York World reported that since taking his first flight, Giants manager John McGraw "has never ceased to talk about the birdman stuff." Accordingly, the Curtiss Aeroplane & Motor Company offered to provide a plane to transport the entire team (*New York World,* March 16, 1919). They eventually took the train instead.

The Hollywood club of the Pacific Coast League flew to a game on July 15, 1928. Hollywood owner Bill Lane was convinced "that airplane travel for ball clubs will soon be the rule and not the exception in a few years and decided that he'd be the first club owner to give it a try" (*Los Angeles Times,* July 17, 1928).

The first major league team to fly to a game was the Cincinnati Reds, who flew from St. Louis to Chicago on June 8, 1934, in two Ford Tri-Motors chartered from American Airlines. The innovative Larry MacPhail authorized the flight because of a heat wave, but six Reds players chose a sweltering train ride instead.

There were a few more plane trips in the ensuing years. The Red Sox flew from St. Louis to Chicago on July 30, 1936, and Brooklyn flew the same route on May 7, 1940. But it was not until after World War II that plane travel became common.

On April 16, 1946, the Yankees announced plans to become the first club to travel exclusively by air (Cliff Trumpold, *Now Pitching: Bill Zuber from Amana,* 97). The first team to own its own plane was the Brooklyn Dodgers, who purchased a forty-four-passenger twin-engine plane on January 4, 1957.

24.1.7 Cross-country Trips.
The Red Stockings traveled to California in 1869, but the trip west took nine days and the return trip eleven days, making such trips impractical on any kind of regular basis (Greg Rhodes and John Erardi, *The First Boys of Summer,* 66–69, 72).

The Los Angeles Bulldogs of the American Football League became in 1937 "the first West Coast professional team to host eastern rivals on a regular basis" (Robert W. Peterson, *Pigskin,* 123). Baseball owners were not unmindful of the westward shift of the population, but baseball's daily schedule made it far more difficult to accommodate games in California.

After the 1941 season, a deal to move the St. Louis Browns to Los Angeles was almost consummated. Ratification of the arrangement was scheduled to take place on December 8, 1941 (*Sporting News,* August 4, 1962). Fatefully, the attack on Pearl Harbor occurred on the day

before. The ensuing wartime restrictions on travel eliminated any talk of major league play in California.

After the war the idea continued to percolate, but the general consensus was that it wouldn't be financially viable unless two clubs in the same league were located on the West Coast. Finally the Dodgers and Giants made the historic decision to move to California in 1957. Major league baseball was played on the West Coast for the first time when the Dodgers and Giants faced off at San Francisco's Seals Stadium on April 15, 1958.

24.1.8 International Travel.
The first major league game played outside the United States took place on April 14, 1969, when the Montreal Expos hosted the St. Louis Cardinals.

24.1.9 Accidents.
It was proverbial in the nineteenth century that "a ball team on board a train amounts to a sort of mascotte for a safe journey, so seldom have serious accidents occurred to baseball travelers" (Henry Chadwick, *Sporting Times,* April 4, 1891). In 1876 an accident in which Jack Kent, third baseman of the Pastime Club of St. Joseph, Missouri, fell while boarding a train and had to have his leg amputated was described as baseball's first serious travel accident (*New York Sunday Mercury,* October 28, 1876).

In the years since, baseball clubs have used a wide variety of methods of transportation. While there have been accidents on all of them, the number has continued to be remarkably low considering the millions of miles traveled by baseball clubs. In particular, while individual players have perished in travel-related accidents, teams have been extraordinarily fortunate.

For example, in July 1911 the location of the St. Louis Cardinals' car was changed before a train trip from Philadelphia to Boston. Twelve passengers were killed and many more injured, but the St. Louis players escaped unscathed.

There have been a few tragic exceptions. Raymond Owens and Buster Brown of the Negro American League's Cincinnati Buckeyes were killed in a 1942 accident while returning from a game in Buffalo. On June 23, 1946, the team bus of the Spokane Indians went over a three-hundred-foot cliff in the Cascade Mountains, killing nine players. The team bus of the Duluth, Minnesota, team of the Northern League collided with a truck on July 24, 1948, killing four players and the manager. A 1901 trolley car accident injured six members of the

Syracuse team, with future major leaguer Lee DeMontreville suffering a broken leg (*Sporting News*, June 8, 1901). One of the California Angels' team buses overturned on the New Jersey turnpike on May 21, 1992, with manager Buck Rodgers suffering serious injuries.

24.1.10 Beat Reporters. Henry Chadwick, who was then writing for *The Ball Player's Chronicle*, was one of the first reporters to travel with a ball club when he accompanied the Nationals of Washington on their historic 1867 tour.

24.1.11 Broadcasters. Radio announcers began traveling with teams around 1948. Before that year it was customary for announcers to recreate road games for their listeners based upon accounts of the game they received via telegraph.

24.1.12 Driven to Mound. In 1959 Milwaukee Braves general manager John McHale decided to speed up games by having relief pitchers driven from the bullpen to the mound. He selected a Harley-Davidson "Topper" motor scooter with a special sidecar because its light weight and large tires meant that "pitchers can be driven directly across the outfield turf to the mound. Heavier vehicles would have to take the longer route on the cinder path bordering the fences to the first-base dugout, where the pitcher would still have to walk to the center of the diamond" (*Virgin Island Daily News*, July 14, 1960). The motor scooter was first used on June 23, 1959, when relief pitcher Hal Jeffcoat was brought in from the bullpen by uniformed chauffeur John "Freckles" Bonneau (*Sporting News*, July 1, 1959).

(ii) Spring Training

There are many claims as to which club initiated the custom of spring training. It is not a case of conflicting accounts so much as the fact that anything resembling today's spring training would have been prohibitively expensive for early baseball clubs. If you had asked the captain of an early team if he planned to take his players south for a month to get in condition, he probably would have had a hearty laugh and told you that it sounded like a wonderful idea if you'd like to foot the bill.

As a result, while there was an awareness of all the elements of spring training from the early days of baseball, these components emerged in fits and starts. It was many years before formal training camps became customary, which means that the various elements of spring training are best considered separately.

24.2.1 Preliminary Workouts. It has of course always been appreciated that players in peak condition will play best.

As noted in the entry on "Muscle Building" (**2.4.1**), the Red Stockings of Boston conducted extensive workouts at a local gymnasium before the 1872 season. Tim Murnane reported that these endeavors began each year on March 15 and lasted until the weather allowed them to move outdoors (Tim Murnane, *Boston Globe*, April 19, 1896; February 19, 1900). Before the 1875 season, the New Haven club engaged in a serious workout: "First, each man runs a quarter of a mile, then gentle exercise upon the horizontal bar is taken, after which a trial at vaulting on the vaulting horse is indulged; then a series of Indian Club swinging, followed by the whole team pulling about one mile on the whole apparatus. After all this, the club retires to a bowling alley where they pass and strike balls" (*New York Sunday Mercury*, April 11, 1875; reprinted in Jim Charlton, ed., *The Baseball Chronology*, 27).

In 1877 the Indianapolis management "leased a splendid hall for the use of their players. It is 120 feet long, and divided into a gymnasium, reading and billiard-room." Five of the players were training there by January, with the remainder expected to report in early February (*New York Sunday Mercury*, February 10, 1877).

Undoubtedly every captain in the country would have liked to have had similar resources. Developments such as "Batting Cages" (**14.4.10**) were also intended to make this more practical, but in most cases the reality was that clubs could not afford to pay players for such training drills while players could not afford to quit their offseason jobs to exercise. As a result, preseason training generally remained voluntary and unsupervised. Curry Foley explained in 1891 that any player "who knew what was good for him" began light gymnasium exercise in January to prepare for the season. But he added that there were always some who ended up being "laid up with lame backs and sore arms" because of having sat "around a stove all winter, telling funny stories" and reporting twenty-five pounds overweight (*Sporting Times*, May 2, 1891).

As discussed under "Trainers" (see 21.10), that did not start to change until around 1898 when trainers began to assume control.

24.2.2 Southern Tours. Early clubs were equally aware that a trip through the South would be a wonderful way to prepare for the season. Yet again, the problem was finding an affordable way of doing so.

In 1868 the Atlantics of Brooklyn announced plans for an ambitious Southern tour that would take them to New Orleans, Mobile, Savannah, and other cities (*American Chronicle of Sports and Pastimes*, January 2, 1868). Cold weather postponed their departure several times, and the tour was eventually canceled due to the weather and what was tactfully described as an inability to "come to terms as to the share of receipts" (*American Chronicle of Sports and Pastimes*, February 13, 1868; February 27, 1868; March 5, 1868).

The Red Stockings of Cincinnati and the White Stockings of Chicago both traveled to New Orleans in April 1870 to play exhibition games and round into shape. The Mutuals of New York went to Savannah, Georgia, in 1871 to put the club in condition (*New York Globe*, reprinted in *Sporting Life*, March 31, 1906). In 1877 the Indianapolis entry in the League Alliance conducted a preseason tour that started in Texas and continued on to New Orleans, Memphis, and St. Louis. Providence traveled to Baltimore and Washington to prepare for the 1880 season (William D. Perrin, *Days of Greatness*, 10). But such tours demanded great planning, and there were any number of obstacles.

One of the most daunting was that baseball enthusiasm in the South often lagged far behind the rest of the country. When Frank Bancroft tried to arrange a stop in Montgomery, Alabama, in 1880, he received a firm "no" and this discouraging explanation: "Several reasons might be assigned for this opinion of mine, but the first one is likely to be conclusive: *we have no local club*. For that matter we have *no ball ground,* and a personal experience justifies me in saying that our people have never shown the slightest enthusiasm over baseball as a fine art. You might get your work in quite profitably selling corn solvents or worm medicines; tame Indians, dressed simply in scalping knives and brass band, have been successful lately as advertising mediums, but shows requiring tickets are not looked upon with favor" (*New York Clipper*, January 24, 1880). Moreover, with the Civil War still a recent and bitter

memory, Southerners in communities with baseball teams would not necessarily go out of their way to invite such tours. Consequently many clubs that would have liked to begin the season with a Southern tour ended up staying closer to home.

As the 1880s wore on, baseball interest in the South increased dramatically. Blondie Purcell organized barnstorming tours of the South by major leaguers after the 1881 and 1882 seasons (*National Police Gazette*, October 7, 1882). Undeterred by the situation in Montgomery, Frank Bancroft took another Southern tour while managing Providence in 1884 (William D. Perrin, *Days of Greatness*, 39, 41). The Southern League debuted in 1885 and was an immediate success. Major league teams were quick to capitalize with preseason trips that proved lucrative. Cincinnati made an especially successful tour before the 1888 season—reportedly the entire trip cost the team $2,000 while revenues in New Orleans alone amounted to $1,700 (*Cleveland Plain Dealer*, April 1, 1888).

The new interest made preseason tours a natural, and by the mid-1890s the idea of a Southern tour had gained widespread acceptance. Jack Rowe contended in 1895 that a club that went South gained a significant edge: "the managers who take their men into a warm climate are doing a sensible act . . . the experiments can be tried out, and the men will gradually learn to play together, which means much to a club" (*Spalding's Official Base Ball Guide, 1895*, 125). The *Brooklyn Eagle* solicited opinions on a number of topics from members of the local team before the 1896 season and published the responses. A Southern spring training trip was perceived as a competitive requirement. Pitcher Ed Stein's comments were typical: "I think a Southern trip is almost necessary on account of the warm weather. In the North it remains quite cold during the whole of March and outside practice would be almost impossible. The season starts so early that the players could hardly get in shape in time for practicing here" (*Brooklyn Eagle*, March 11, 1896).

Minor league manager Charles Faatz maintained in 1898 that work in the South was essential for pitchers: "During the winter months the muscles in the arm contract and become stiff and the following spring are in a state that renders them almost useless. Nothing will bring them around except long and steady practice in fairly warm weather. That is one of the principal benefits of the spring trips made by nearly all of the major league teams every year. Gymnasium practice would accomplish the same thing for a pitcher, except that there is danger of the cold settling in the arm when the first outdoor work is attempted" (*Oklahoma City Daily Oklahoman*, February 18, 1898).

Even so, resistance to the entire concept persisted. In a 1903 *Sporting Life* editorial, Francis Richter noted that "President Ban Johnson, of the American League, does not think well of sending teams on long Southern trips for spring practice. In this matter Mr. Johnson is not alone. Many magnates share his convictions on this subject, though they send their teams South. They do this simply because some pro-Southern managers set the pace; the rest follow unwillingly partly not to give the roving teams any possible advantage and partly to avoid possible local charges of needless economy." Richter predicted that such trips would eventually end (*Sporting Life*, April 11, 1903).

24.2.3 Training Camps.

In the mid-1880s the training camp as we know it today came into existence. As discussed in the previous entries, the desirability of collective spring workouts was already recognized. But it was only the growing prosperity of the game and specifically the owners' tightening contractual grip on the players that made formal training camps possible.

An 1887 article in the *Cincinnati Enquirer* noted: "Not over three years ago the idea of training ball players to get them in condition for the season's work was unheard of. Not a club in the country put the men through the preliminary paces in the gymnasium, and a ball-player was not required to report to duty until the team began actual work upon the field." The piece credited Gus Schmelz with helping popularize the practice while managing Columbus in 1884. It observed that in three short years, "what a difference is noticeable. The comparison is striking. There is not a single club in either one of the leading base-ball organizations that does not require the members of its team to go through some form of training for from two to three weeks' time before the regular opening of the season. They are either taken on a Southern trip, where the weather is mild and will admit of outdoor practice, or are put in a gymnasium under the care and direction of a competent instructor" (*Cincinnati Enquirer*, April 3, 1887).

St. Louis Brown Stockings' owner Chris Von der Ahe was one of the first converts. Before the 1885 season he took "a lesson by the Columbus Club" and "put his men to work in a gymnasium, and the result was that when the season opened a team of ball players stepped upon the field to represent St. Louis who were in as good condition as any nine men that ever played on a diamond, and never once during the season was the team crippled. From fourth place in 1884, they won the championship" (*St. Louis Globe-Democrat*, February 21, 1886, 8).

The inaugural issue of the *Sporting News* in 1886 editorialized, "The preparatory work now being done by two or three prominent clubs in the country marks one of the most sensible departures from the old rut in baseball that has ever been made." The publication asked rhetorically: "What has caused this important feature of training to be so long neglected? In the early days of the game no doubt the poverty of the club had something to do with it. But the main reason has been the protest of the players themselves to pull off the 'beef' and harden the muscles" (*Sporting News*, March 17, 1886).

Appreciation of the wisdom of these comments began to spread. In June 1891 Athletics owner J. Earl Wagner declared, "Our men are just beginning to get in condition. Two or three of them have not yet got their extra flesh off. The Bostons took a preparatory southern trip, and when the season opened felt like a lot of two-year-olds" (quoted in *Williamsport Sunday Grit*, June 7, 1891). Once it was perceived that holding spring training gave a club a large competitive advantage, and could even make the difference in winning a pennant, it naturally became standard for every club to conduct one. Preseason training became more systematic and more beneficial in the next few years, when, as noted under "Preliminary Workouts" (**24.2.1**), trainers began to assume control.

It became clear that these benefits were being noticed when minor league clubs began to follow suit. A 1909 article reported that "the southern training camp is no longer the privilege of the rich major leagues. The more important of the minors have taken up the spring practice tours" (*Detroit Free Press*, March 7, 1909).

24.2.4 Spring Training in Florida and Arizona.

While major league clubs today all hold their spring training camps in either Florida or Arizona, those weren't the earliest sites. Both states were still sparsely populated, with swamps and deserts respectively limiting their appeal.

The first major league team to try Florida was Ted Sullivan's Washington club, which prepared for the 1888 season in Jacksonville. One report claimed that the state did not exactly open its arms to baseball, as "the hotel clerk insisted that the ballplayers not eat in the same dining room with the other guests, not mingle with them, and not even mention their profession to the guests" (Kevin M. McCarthy, *Baseball in Florida*, 141). That, however, sounds suspiciously like one of Ted Sullivan's exaggerated stories. One of the players on that club, backup catcher Connie Mack, seems to have had positive memories as his Athletics often trained in Jacksonville.

Bryan Di Salvatore suggested that John Ward began the practice of getting towns to pay to host teams for spring training in 1892 when he convinced Ocala, Florida, to give Brooklyn free use of its field and to pay for some of the team's travel (Bryan Di Salvatore, *A Clever Base-Ballist*, 344). The practice began to expand in the early twentieth century. In 1913 Cubs' president Charley Murphy did "his colleagues one better in commercializing the advertising value of his ball club. Murphy has persuaded the business men of Tampa, Fla., to put up $4,700 in good cold cash to cover the expenses of the Cubs' spring training. The Tampa merchants want the Cubs to go there and have put up the money. . . . Mr. Murphy has generously consented to let the Tampa business men have the receipts of the games to partly reimburse them for handing out the $4,700" (*New York Times*, January 12, 1913).

By the end of the nineteenth century it was pretty much standard for clubs to train in the warmer climes. Few clubs went farther west than Hot Springs, Arkansas, until 1899, when Chicago ventured out to New Mexico, an experiment that was "watched with the closest attention by the [other] club owners" (*Sporting Life*, March 25, 1899).

Texas became a popular spring training spot in the early twentieth century, but it was several decades before Arizona was tried. The first major league club to hold spring training there was the Detroit Tigers in 1929; it was not until 1947 that the Cleveland Indians became the first major league club to establish a permanent training base in Arizona.

24.2.5 Spas. The Chicago White Stockings were holding training camp at Hot Springs, Arkansas, in the mid-1880s. By the turn of the century this resort town had become the place

to train and was hosting several other clubs. Pat Tebeau observed, "Rheumatics throw away their crutches after bathing two weeks at Hot Springs, and if there is another resort in the country where tired limbs can be restored, I want to know about it" (*Sporting News*, February 19, 1896). By that time, however, as noted in the next entry, clubs had begun to discover that many of the benefits of natural spring water could be reproduced elsewhere. This reality, coupled with complaints about poor grounds, overcrowding, and the consequent distractions, eventually led clubs to abandon Hot Springs and move farther south for spring training.

24.2.6 Steam Boxes. Arthur Irwin appears to have introduced steam boxes to baseball before the 1894 season. After being named manager of the Philadelphia Phillies, he unveiled "a scheme to reduce weight in ball players, which he proposes to try on the members of the team. He is going to put sweat boxes at the grounds. The boxes will be heated by steam, and will be low enough to allow a man's head to project when in a sitting position, thus avoiding the injurious effect of breathing the foul air of the sweat box. A man to rub the players down after their sweat will be engaged, and in this way it is hoped to get the heavy-weight members of the team into something like condition by the opening of the season. These vapor baths are highly commended by trainer Will Bryan, of the Pennsylvania University, who introduced them at the University with markedly beneficial effects upon the foot ball candidates" (*Sporting Life*, January 13, 1894).

Two years later Irwin was hired to manage the New York Giants, leading to speculation that he would "introduce his little joker—the sweat box—to the Giants. Amos Rusie will be kept in it a week and 'Sir Artie' will see that the fat boy is fed regularly during the revived inquisition" (*Sporting News*, December 14, 1895). According to a 1900 article, Irwin's players were very skeptical of the contraption, but eventually pitcher Dad Clarke agreed to try the new device. Unfortunately the attendant didn't fully understand the box's workings and turned on all the steam at once. Clarke came running out, screaming, "Turn the hose on me, I'm stewed." He apparently wasn't exaggerating much, as his skin was said to have come off in patches over the next month.

In spite of this less-than-auspicious debut, the concept caught on. The article continued, "The 'lobster pots,' as the players of the New

York team persist in calling the steam boxes, have proved a most valuable adjunct to the training outfit being used daily at the Polo grounds. A player shuts himself in the box stripped to the buff. He seats himself on a shelf prepared for the purpose, shoves his head through the hole in the lid and shouts to an attendant 'Let 'er go.' There is a hissing of steam, a wild shriek from the player and then a gasp of contentment as the searching vapor gets in its parboiling work and locates the stiffness and soreness. Soon the perspiration begins to ooze from every pore and the winter kinks are gradually dissipated and the rusty knee and arm joints work on their hinges with rejuvenated vigor. A half hour's steaming and the player emerges from the box as rosy red as a Baldwin apple. An instant under the shower bath, a dash upstairs into the hands of the rubbers, who work the massage treatment as long as the victim will stand the punching and mauling, and the player is a new man, with all signs of soreness gone and a few pounds of superfluous weight left behind him" (*New York Journal*, reprinted in *Grand Valley* [Moab, Utah] *Times*, June 29, 1900).

As described in memorable fashion in Laura Hillenbrand's *Seabiscuit*, such quick weight-reduction methods became especially popular among jockeys, whose livelihoods directly depended on them (Laura Hillenbrand, *Seabiscuit*, 66–70).

24.2.7   Permanent Spring Training Homes.

As late as 1899 a *Sporting Life* correspondent remarked, "Considering the number of years base ball teams have gone South, it seems strange that no club has yet selected a permanent place for spring practice. They wander around from one place to another down South like the Ponce de Leon looking for the fountain of eternal youth. . . . It is a rare occurrence for a team to train two successive seasons at the same place" (*Sporting Life*, March 25, 1899).

It was several more years before the Giants established the first long-term spring training base, returning to Marlin Springs, Texas, each year from 1908 to 1918. The club's decision to put down roots was facilitated by the skill of groundskeeper John Murphy, who was able to create a grass infield instead of the skin diamonds that had been the norm in arid climates (Peter Morris, *Level Playing Fields*, 101–106).

Gradually other clubs began to follow the Giants' lead. Sid Mercer noted in 1910, "The

establishment of permanent base ball training camps in the South by the New York and Pittsburg clubs of the National League and the advantages of holding preliminary practices on fields laid out to conform to big league standards is paving the way for a system of splendidly equipped base ball plants in Dixie" (*New York Globe*, reprinted in *Sporting News*, December 8, 1910).

Johnny Evers and Hugh S. Fullerton observed in 1912 that there was a movement "more and more toward permanent training camps, and against exhibition tours." They commented that this allowed clubs to use the winter to train and evaluate draftees (John J. Evers and Hugh S. Fullerton, *Touching Second*, 223–224).

Nevertheless a 1912 article noted, "Base ball teams have been traveling South for Spring practice for a great many years, but from the way they shift each season from one place to another it seems as though no club had yet found the ideal training spot." The piece quoted Connie Mack as explaining, "I can't say that I have ever found a place where everything is perfect. I guess our record will show that we have never gone to the same place two years in succession" (*Philadelphia Record*, reprinted in *Sporting Life*, March 9, 1912).

24.2.8   Pitchers and Catchers First.

In February 1903 Connie Mack took a limited squad of players, primarily pitchers, to Jacksonville, Florida. It was explained that "The object of the early visit to the south is to try out the pitchers and get them in good condition for the preliminary games in April with the Phillies" (*Fort Wayne News*, February 25, 1903).

Nap Lajoie sent the Cleveland pitchers and catchers to Hot Springs two weeks before the squad of players in 1905. His reasoning was that the team's pitchers habitually got off to slow starts and he wanted them to be ready for the start of the season (Gerard S. Petrone, *When Baseball Was Young*, 22). This of course forced the catchers to report early as well since, as Casey Stengel famously observed, without a catcher the ball will just roll to the backstop.

Over the next few years this practice gradually went from being the exception to the rule. Sportswriter Joe S. Jackson noted in 1911 that Frank Chance planned to take his young battery members "South two weeks in advance of the team itself, so that he can start them as early as possible. This is a general custom" (*Washington Post*, January 21, 1911).

Chapter 25

AS AMERICAN AS APPLE PIE

AS EARLY AS 1855, baseball was referred to by the Knickerbockers club secretary as "the national game of Base Ball" (minutes of the Knickerbocker Base Ball Club for August 22, 1855; quoted by Frederick Ivor-Campbell, *Nineteenth Century Notes* 92:1 [April 1992], 5–6). It is possible that he simply meant that the game was being played nationally, but the *New York Clipper* left no room for doubt when it announced the following year that "the game of Base Ball is generally considered the National game amongst Americans" (*New York Clipper*, December 13, 1856). That was an extraordinarily bold statement considering that the Knickerbockers' version of the game had yet to travel beyond the New York City area. While baseball was unquestionably being played in many regions, it was still being played in so many different ways that it was not always recognizable as the same game.

Porter's Spirit of the Times was far more accurate when it stated that same year: "We feel a degree of old Knickerbocker pride at the continued prevalence of Base Ball as the National game in the region of the Manhattanese" (quoted in James M. DiClerico and Barry J. Pavelec, *The Jersey Game*, 25). But "the National game in the region of the Manhattanese" doesn't have quite the same ring as "the national game."

Other sources were similarly more precise in describing baseball as "a national game." A description of the first meeting of the National Association of Base Ball Players in 1857 noted that "Base ball has been known in the Northern States as far back as the memory of the oldest inhabitant reacheth, and must be regarded as a national pastime, the same as cricket is by the English" (*Spirit of the Times*, January 31, 1857; reprinted in Dean Sullivan, ed., *Early Innings*, 22–24). There is a big difference between describing baseball as a national game and as *the* national game, but it is a distinction that is easily blurred.

That is exactly what many were willing to do in the late 1850s. Historian George B. Kirsch reported that "references to 'the national game of baseball' appeared frequently in the daily and sporting press throughout the late 1850s," and that "All of the New York City sporting weeklies regularly proclaimed baseball to be 'the national game of ball' before the Civil War" (George B. Kirsch, *The Creation of American Team Sports*, 92, 68).

There were many reasons for this insistence on nationalism. One of the most important was that Americans were quite conscious that cricket was the English national game, and anxious to have a game they could call their own. Walter Bagehot argued persuasively that the "principal thought of the American constitution-makers" was to avoid the shortcomings of the British constitution, specifically the tyranny of King George III (Walter Bagehot, *The English Constitution*, 199). Similarly, a recurring theme in early baseball was to ensure the game's distinctiveness from cricket.

And, while it might be argued that baseball has long since overcome the defensive urge to define itself by its differences from cricket, the issue occasionally resurfaces. A curious example occurred in 1946 when Leo Durocher was asked by Commissioner Happy Chandler to comply with a "good conduct" rule. Durocher responded with a sarcastic reference to a cricket custom: "When shall I serve tea, in the fourth inning, or the sixth?" (*Sporting News*, April 11, 1946).

The decision to style baseball as the national game created an impetus for the game as it spread across the country in the 1860s and 1870s. Instead of just being another newfangled New York fad, an activity billed as the national game had prestige and had to be taken seriously.

In the years to come, baseball's connection to the national identity would manifest itself in an impressive number of different ways. In the process, baseball's right to bill itself by the once extraordinary title of "the national game" would be strengthened and deepened.

(i) Wrapping the Game in the Flag

25.1.1   Flags. Historian George B. Kirsch reported that a group of ladies in Danvers Centre, Massachusetts, presented the local ball club with the Stars and Stripes in 1859 (*New York Clipper*, August 20, 1859; cited in George B. Kirsch, *The Creation of American Team Sports*, 93). The first stadium to fly the American flag appears to have been the Carrol Park Grounds in Brooklyn, home of the Star and Excelsior clubs in 1862 (*Brooklyn Eagle*, March 27, 1862). The flag was also featured two months later at the opening of the first enclosed baseball stadium, the Union Grounds in Brooklyn, and it soon became a familiar sight at baseball diamonds (James L. Terry, *Long Before the Dodgers*, 36).

25.1.2   National Anthem. A band performed "The Star-Spangled Banner" at the opening of Brooklyn's Union Grounds on May 15, 1862. The song, however, was not yet the national anthem, and other patriotic songs were sometimes substituted in the early years of baseball. When the Nationals of Washington visited Chicago on their historic 1867 tour (see **24.1.7** "Cross-country Trips"), a band tried to spur on the home nine by playing "Rally Round the Flags, Boys" (Henry Chadwick, *The American Game of Base Ball*, 96). In the ensuing years, "The Star-Spangled Banner" came to be regarded as the song of choice for patriotic occasions, though it did not officially become the U.S. national anthem until 1931.

A more imposing obstacle was that, in the days before public address systems, it was necessary to hire a band to perform music (see

14.5.12 and **14.5.13**). Despite the expense, "The Star-Spangled Banner" continued to be played on special occasions, especially Opening Day (*San Francisco Examiner*, March 27, 1892; *New York Sun*, April 22, 1903; Benton Stark, *The Year They Called Off the World Series*, 102; Jonathan Fraser Light, *The Cultural Encyclopedia of Baseball*, 474; *Washington Post*, April 23, 1920). At the opening game of the 1918 World Series, with the nation's entry into the world war on every mind, "The Star-Spangled Banner" was played during the seventh-inning stretch. It received a heartfelt reception: "the ball players turned quickly about and faced the music. First the song was taken up by a few, then others joined, and when the final notes came, a great volume of melody rolled across the field. It was at the very end that the onlookers exploded into thunderous applause and rent the air with a cheer" (*New York Times*, September 6, 1918). The display was repeated at the remaining games of the Series, and in subsequent years it became customary to have it performed at the Fall Classic.

The advent of public address systems made it feasible to play recorded music at the ballpark. But it was not until World War II that it became customary for the national anthem to be played before every game.

After the tragic events of September 11, 2001, the seventh inning of baseball games began to be marked by the singing of "God Bless America." This continued a pattern: "The Star-Spangled Banner" was first played at a baseball game during the Civil War; became a World Series tradition during World War I; and became a part of every game during World War II. "God Bless America" was added after 9/11.

25.1.3   Patriotic Club Names. Historian George B. Kirsch noted that many of the names of early baseball clubs had patriotic connotations, such as "Young America, Columbia, Union, Independent, Eagle, American, Continental, Empire, National, Liberty, and Pioneer. Others honored such heroes as George Washington, Alexander Hamilton, James Madison, Thomas Jefferson, Andrew Jackson, and Benjamin Franklin" (George B. Kirsch, *The Creation of American Team Sports*, 93).

25.1.4   President Throwing Out the First Ball. William Howard Taft began this tradition before Washington's Opening Day game against Philadelphia on April 14, 1910. Partisanship appears to have entered into the assessments of Taft's throw. The *Washington Post* rhapsodized that Taft "had done his part so nobly" and showed "faultless delivery" in opening "the season with a true presidential flourish" (*Washington Post*, April 15, 1910). An Associated Press account, however, was not quite as warm: "The president took the ball in his gloved hand as if he were at a loss what to do with it until [umpire Billy] Evans told him he was expected to throw it over the plate when he gave the signal. . . . Catcher [Gabby] Street stood at the home plate ready to receive the ball, but the president knew the pitcher was the man who usually began business operations with it, so he threw it straight to Pitcher Walter Johnson. The throw was a little low, but the pitcher stuck out his long arm and grabbed the ball before it hit the ground, while the insurgents in the bleachers cheered wildly" (AP: *Chicago Tribune*, April 15, 1910).

25.1.5   President to Attend a Major League Game. Benjamin Harrison attended a game on June 6, 1892, between Cincinnati and Washington.

(ii) Talking the Talk

The characterization of baseball as the national game has been justified by a wide variety of different arguments. They have not always been terribly persuasive.

Some have substituted rhetoric for fact. A notable example was A. G. Spalding, who drew support from the discredited notion that Abner Doubleday invented baseball and the questionable idea that the Civil War helped to spread the game: "A National Game? Why, no country on the face of the earth ever had a form of sport with so clear a title to that distinction. Base Ball had been born in the brain of an American soldier [i.e., Doubleday]. It received its baptism in bloody days of our nation's direst danger. It had its early evolution when soldiers, North and South, were striving to forget their foes by cultivating, through this grand game, fraternal friendships with comrades in arms. It had its best development at the time when soldiers, disheartened by distressing defeat, were seeking the solace of something safe and sane; at a time when Northern soldiers, flushed with victory, were yet willing to turn from fighting with bombs and bullets to playing with bat and ball" (A. G. Spalding, *America's National Game*, 92–93).

Others have used politics as the basis of imaginative analogies. A journalist wrote in 1859, "In the American game the ins and outs alternate by quick rotation, like our officials" (*New York Herald*, October 16, 1859). During World War I a British journalist was amazed by the way players argued with the umpire and reasoned: "If the Yanks are not bothered by the overwhelming dignity and autocratic authority of the umpire, they would have no trouble with the Germans" (quoted in Jonathan Fraser Light, *The Cultural Encyclopedia of Baseball*, 626).

Still others contradict each other. The *New York Herald* noted in 1859 that "the English game [of cricket] is so slow and tame, and the American [game of baseball] so full of life" (*New York Herald*, October 16, 1859). Jacob Morse added, "the American would not sacrifice a morning for a cricket game. He is quick and active, nervous and energetic, and he wants his sport to answer the requirements of his temperament. Base ball has suited his purpose admirably" (Jacob Morse, *Sphere and Ash*; reprinted in Dean Sullivan, ed., *Early Innings*, 157). William Wheaton of the Knickerbockers maintained that "The difference between cricket and baseball illustrates the difference between our lively people and the phlegmatic English" (quoted in *San Francisco Examiner*, November 27, 1887). Yet Roger Kahn suggested that "baseball's inherent rhythm, minutes and minutes of passivity erupting into seconds of frenzied action, matches an attribute of the American character" (Roger Kahn, *A Season in the Sun*, 8–9).

These both sound like plausible arguments, and they reflect the dramatic alteration in baseball's tempo that was discussed in Chapter 12. But it can't be true that the American temperament is ideally suited to both paces.

Henry Chadwick also had a rather peculiar take on the matter. He later claimed that while watching a baseball game in 1856 he had been "struck with the idea that base ball was just the game for a national sport for America" (*Brooklyn Eagle*, May 11, 1888). When the Red Stockings and Athletics toured England in 1874 he wrote that "the visit in question has resulted in setting at rest forever the much debated question as to whether we had a National Game or not, the English press with rare unanimity candidly acknowledging that the 'new game of base-ball' is unquestionably the American National Game" (quoted in Adrian C. Anson, *A Ball Player's Career*, 74–75). This raises the obvious question of how the English press would be in any position to determine America's national game.

Perhaps it is better just to feel that baseball is the national game and not to reason why.

25.2.1 National Association of Base Ball Players.

Although writers have not always made convincing cases for why baseball is the national game, they have been much more effective in deflating grandiose claims of national significance. For example, when the National Association of Base Ball Players was formed in 1858, the *New York Clipper* wrote: "This document proposes to call the organization 'The National Association of Base Ball Players'—a misnomer, in our opinion, for the convention seems to be rather sectional and selfish in its proceedings, than otherwise, there having been no invitations sent to clubs in other States. . . . National, indeed! Why the association is a mere local organization, bearing no State existence even—to say nothing of a National one. The truth of the matter is—that a few individuals have wormed themselves into this convention, who have been, and are endeavoring to mould men and things to suit their own views. If the real lovers of the beautiful and health-provoking game of base ball wish to see the sport diffuse itself all over the country—as Cricket is fast doing—they must cut loose from those parties who wish to arrogate to themselves the right to act for, and dictate to all who participate in the game. These few dictators wish to ape the New York Yacht Club in their feelings of exclusiveness—we presume. Let the

discontented, therefore, come out from among this party, and organize an association which shall be National—not only in name—but in reality. Let invitations be extended to base ball players everywhere to compete with them, and endeavor to make the game what it should be—a truly National one" (*New York Clipper,* April 3, 1858).

25.2.2 National League.

The formation of the National League in 1876 evoked similar skepticism about the accuracy of the word "national." A *Brooklyn Eagle* reporter observed, "The League championship rules open with an error, inasmuch as they refer to their code as that of the championship of the 'United States.' It is nothing of the kind; it is simply for the championship of the League Stock Company Association. Suppose the New Haven Club should win a majority of the games played with the Association clubs, would that club not practically win the championship? It reminds me of the three Tailors of Tooley street, proclaiming themselves as 'We, the people of England'" (*Brooklyn Eagle,* March 27, 1876).

25.2.3 We Are the World.

Not content to make debatable assertions of a national scope, some early aficionados of baseball went still further. As early as 1865, claims like this one were being made: "Game 40 to 28, Atlantic ahead, and still the champions of the world" (*Brooklyn Eagle,* August 15, 1865). As noted earlier (see **22.2.1**), by the 1880s the term "World's Series" had been coined.

Chapter 26

MISCELLANY

(i) Keeping Up Appearances

26.1.1 Beards and Mustaches. Facial hair on early ballplayers was not an unusual sight. A reporter wrote in 1891 that twenty years earlier, "The players usually sported chin whiskers, muttonchops or heavy military moustaches" (*Williamsport Sunday Grit*, June 7, 1891). *Sporting Life* confirmed in 1910: "It was no uncommon thing, however, in the old days, to see bearded men playing ball" (*Sporting Life*, October 8, 1910).

By the time the National League was formed, beards were rare, with one sported by 1870s outfielder John Remsen often cited as a novelty. It was claimed that Remsen wore the beard to protest the disputed 1876 presidential election, having "registered an oath not to let a hair-cutter lay hands on him until Tilden takes his seat" (*Louisville Courier-Journal*; reprinted in *Chicago Tribune*, June 3, 1877).

Beards had practically vanished by the 1880s. An 1888 article reported: "It is worthy of remark that the [American] Association since its organization never had a player in its employ who wore P. Rooney Galways or mutton chops, except one [Wesley] Blogg, who caught about two games for the Pittsburgs in 1883. He was short-lived, and when the wind from a few sharp foul tips dallied with his lilacs he threw up the job and quit" (*Williamsport Sunday Grit*, March 18, 1888).

In 1891, piqued at continued references to his advancing years, Cap Anson appeared for a game in Boston on September 4 wearing fake white whiskers and long white hair. He continued to wear the whiskers for the entire game

and, in typically contentious fashion, told the umpire he intended to take his base if a pitched ball touched his whiskers (H. Allen Smith and Ira L. Smith, *Low and Inside*, 19). The following year, Boston repaid the favor. At the suggestion of former White Stocking Mike Kelly, most of the Boston players donned fake whiskers and amusing costumes for their July 11, 1892, game against Chicago ("King Kelly's Costume Caper," *Baseball Research Journal* 1977, 143–144).

Mustaches had also vanished by the early twentieth century. In 1904 outfielder John Titus of the Phillies was reported to be the only National League player to wear a mustache (*Washington Post*, October 2, 1904). In 1908 *Sporting Life* remarked that "For several years Titus has been the only player to wear a 'soup strainer'" (*Sporting Life*, March 28, 1908). These accounts overlook Jake Beckley, who wore a mustache from time to time. In the middle of the 1906 season, Beckley "joined the ranks of the clean-shaven. John Titus is the only National leaguer wearing a mustache today" (*Grand Rapids* [Wisc.] *Tribune*, August 1, 1906). Beckley apparently regrew the mustache and then shaved it off again before the start of the 1907 season, prompting the observation that he no longer "shared with Titus of the Phillies the distinction of being the only major league players daring enough to wear coffee strainers in public" (*Chicago Tribune*, April 12, 1907). Baseball historian David Fleitz reported that Beckley was one of three players to sport facial hair in 1907 but does not specify who the third man was (David Fleitz, "Jacob Peter Beckley," Tom Simon, ed., *Deadball Stars of the National League*, 231).

Titus finally shaved his distinctive red mustache before the 1908 season, prompting one Philadelphia writer to wax eloquent about the breaking of a "link that bound the past to the present." He elaborated: "Philadelphia had for many years the companion piece to the Titus mustache. Monte Cross held on to his till 1904, but when it began to take on a gray tinge at the ends Monte thought it about time to change his disguise. Jake Beckley clung to the old-fashioned imperial for a long time, but even the German was forced to bow to modern customs. Once no big leaguer was complete without upper lip adornment. His mustache was only second in importance to his hat or glove. Photographs of the old-timers, Anson, Kelly, [Dan] Brouthers, all show a fine piratical adornment. Some time in the early '90s the fashion changed. Some baseball modiste of that period decided that the mustache was no longer de rigueur. The edict was promptly obeyed and enough hair was shorn from the faces of ball tossers to stuff a mattress. To the younger generation of fans the Titus mustache was a survival of a remote period—a curiosity. Now even that is gone" (reprinted in the *Syracuse Herald*, April 1, 1908).

In the ensuing years, hirsute players became extremely rare. Players would occasionally sport facial hair during spring training, but the kidding that resulted would usually lead them to part with it before the regular season began. Senators catcher John Henry wore a mustache during spring training in 1917 but shaved before Opening Day (*Washington Post*, May 28, 1917). The Athletics' Wally Schang grew one after the start of the regular season, but his teammates considered it a jinx and he finally removed it (*Atlanta Constitution*, June 18, 1917).

Before the 1918 season, Washington catcher Ed Gharrity's mustache prompted sports columnist Jack Keene to comment, "Bets are now in order as to how long Gharrity will be able to wear it and when he will crack under the strain. He will have to take a line of hoots from the fans that will make him bite his nails a bit. Somehow the fans can't abide a ball player in any sort of whiskers. The feeblest and least offensive of mustaches will have them screaming in fury. Wally Schang almost got stoned last season when he came forth with an embellished upper lip and then [sic] John Henry of the Senators tried to get by with the same idea. Neither went very far with it. The fans won't have it and there you are. It somehow doesn't seem natural" (*Lima* [Ohio] *News*, March 13, 1918). The issue became moot when Gharrity was drafted.

The uniformity of clean-shaven players during the 1920s made the beards worn by the barnstorming House of David ball club all the more distinctive. The next major leaguer to wear facial hair during the regular season appears to have been Allen Benson, a House of David pitcher who was signed by the Senators in 1934. Bill Deane noted that Benson was described as possessing the "novelty of being the first bearded pitcher to appear in the majors for years." It was reported that Benson had "vowed when he was signed by Washington that if he didn't win he would cut off his beard and try it with a mustache alone" (*Sporting News*, August 30, 1934). But Benson didn't get the chance as he was released after two unsuccessful starts.

Benson was followed two years later by Frenchy Bordagaray of the Dodgers. Deane found that Benson reported to training camp in 1936 sporting a mustache and even added a goatee at some point (*New York World-Telegram*, May 19, 1936). Bordagaray hinted that he intended to continue to wear it during the regular season, and Dodgers manager Casey Stengel voiced no objection (*New York World-Telegram*, March 6, 1936). He wore the mustache until late April, then shaved it off but regrew it. Bordagaray recalled that, part of the way through the season, "Stengel called me into his office and told me to get rid of it. He said, 'Frenchy, if there's gonna be any clown on this club, it's gonna be me'" (*New York Daily News*, April 25, 1971; thanks to Bill Deane for providing all these citations).

Bordagaray's experiment was followed by another long gap. Bill Deane has found evidence that Satchel Paige was wearing a mustache when he was signed by the Indians in 1948. But the 1950s saw the ascendance of the "organization man" in American society, and baseball players embodied that conformism. Throughout the turbulent 1960s, major leaguers remained clean-shaven to a man, and it became increasingly clear that this was much more than a grooming decision.

In 1966 Marvin Miller became the first executive director of the Players Association and brought the winds of change with him, in more ways than one. Charles P. Korr has noted that Miller's mustache was mentioned in a disproportionate number of articles about the union (Charles P. Korr, *The End of Baseball as We Knew It*, 272).

By the early 1970s Reggie Jackson and several other members of the Oakland A's brought facial hair back to major league baseball, with the encouragement of owner Charles O. Finley. Not every club was as supportive. Bobby Tolan filed a grievance against the Reds, with one of the issues being his refusal to shave his mustache when told to do so by manager Sparky Anderson (Charles P. Korr, *The End of Baseball as We Knew It*, 138). Tolan won the grievance on narrow grounds, but the Reds continued to enforce the team rule against facial hair for many years. The Yankees still have such a policy, which forced Johnny Damon to shave his trademark beard after signing with the club.

26.1.2 Glasses. Pitcher Will White, a star of the 1870s and 1880s, was the first bespectacled major leaguer. His success did not erase the stigma associated with wearing glasses.

Sportswriter Oliver Abel told this story about early-twentieth-century pitcher Ed Reulbach: "Reulbach was known as the wildest man out of captivity. There were times when his wildness made him the joke of the business. No one could understand his peculiar actions. He was charged with being 'yellow,' and every possible explanation excepting the true one was advanced.

"The truth was that Reulbach had one bad eye, an eye so bad that at times its weakness affected the other, and he lost sight of the plate entirely. When, in the heat and sweat of a hard game, his good eye failed him, he pitched at where he thought the plate was.

"Reulbach never was seen reading a newspaper, or even a score card, or the bill of fare at a table. One night Johnny Kling, who was rooming with him, entered the room and found Reulbach wearing a pair of glasses, reading a newspaper. Caught in the act, he confided in Kling the secret of his eye, and Kling never revealed the fact that the big pitcher's eye was defective. He got away with it for years. [Cubs manager Frank] Chance never knew why his star pitcher had those famous fits of wildness, and the other players never could understand it.

"Years afterward, Reulbach told the joke. But the fact is, the 'joke' was on him. In his effort to keep the others from suspecting that his eyesight was faulty, he over-strained the eye, and it was a long time after he quit the game before the weak eye yielded to treatment and regained part of its strength. Glasses would, perhaps, have made Reulbach the great-est pitcher baseball has ever known" (*Sporting News*, March 15, 1923).

Bespectacled pitcher Lee Meadows had a successful major league career that lasted from 1915 to 1929, but he was convinced that a position player with glasses could not be successful. He explained: "I have worn glasses while pitching for several years and know no reason why they should prove a handicap to any youngster who wants to pitch. There is no chance for him, though, in any other position on the team in my opinion. A spectacled youth cannot play the outfield because it is impossible for him to accurately judge a fly ball while running at full speed. He may not aspire to be a catcher because he cannot wear a mask and spectacles. He will be handicapped in the infield because of the ground he must cover for it is difficult to judge a line drive or a grounder if running at top speed while wearing glasses" (quoted in *Fort Wayne Sentinel*, July 27, 1916).

There was a real basis for these conclusions. Early eyeglasses were not well suited to strenuous activity of any kind and were likely to shatter if they fell off. Pittsburgh pitcher Carmen Hill broke his glasses during a game on September 27, 1927, and had to be replaced (Stuart Shea, *Wrigley Field*, 120).

Nevertheless Meadows was proved wrong halfway through his career, when infielder "Specs" Toporcer reached the major leagues on April 13, 1921. Another landmark event occurred in 1931 when bespectacled Chick Hafey won the National League batting title. Sportswriter Grantland Rice wrote: "It will be interesting to observe whether the success of Chick Hafey in winning the batting championship of the National League last year breaks down the fear of 'four-eyes.' A lot of good ball players, and plenty of umpires, so they will tell you, would have been far better if they had had the nerve to wear glasses during business hours. Ball players have feared that the wearing of specs would give the hint that they were going back" (Grantland Rice, "The Sportlight," syndicated column, March 10, 1932).

26.1.3 Eye Black. It is sometimes said that baseball borrowed the use of eye black from football. But the first football player who is known to have used eye black was Andy Farkas, a Washington Redskins fullback who used it in a game against the Philadelphia Eagles in 1942. Baseball players were in fact doing it much earlier, most notably outfielder Patsy Dougherty.

A 1904 note observed, "Pat Dougherty rubs mud or charcoal under his eyes, after the practice of many minor league ball players, who assert that it lessens the glare of the sun on a bright day" (*Sporting Life*, July 9, 1904). Sportswriter L. W. Herzog confirmed, "Some time ago I noticed an article stating that Ty Cobb always plastered mud under his eyes and that it was an old Indian trick. It's an old Irish trick, too, for Captain M'que Doherty [sic] has done it for years" (*Sporting News*, November 14, 1907). Sportswriter W. A. Phelon wrote in 1905, "Sandow Mertes tried that new sun field wrinkle here [Chicago] the other day—that trick of painting black circles round the eyes instead of wearing smoked glasses. It made Sandow look like an Apache on the warpath, and the only perceptible result was, that Sandow misjudged a long fly and let in the winning run" (*Sporting Life*, June 24, 1905).

(ii) Rituals

26.2.1 Married / Single. Games between teams of married and single men were common in early baseball. The earliest instances I have found occurred in the fall of 1855, when games were played between members of the Bedford Club of Long Island, the Atlantics of Brooklyn, and the Pioneer Club of New Jersey (*Spirit of the Times*, September 29, 1855; *New York Atlas*, September 16, 1855). The concept spread quickly to the rest of the country and became a common way for early clubs to divide into two squads; the *Detroit Free Press* of May 16, 1860, described such a game, as did the *Kalamazoo Gazette* of July 27, 1860. A game between married and single women was played in Rockford, Illinois, in 1870 (*New York Tribune*, August 26, 1870).

26.2.2 Fraternizing. There was no league rule against fraternizing in the early days of baseball, but individual clubs had rules against it. The rules of the Chicago White Stockings in 1883 included one that read: "After coming upon the field in uniform, players must not converse with reporters, scorers, acquaintances, or others in the audience" (*Fort Wayne Daily News*, April 10, 1883).

Joe Cantillon claimed in 1914 that there had been no need for such rules in the early days. He explained: "The players of 25 years ago . . . had far more interest in their play than the athletes of today. Formerly one never saw the members of the teams that were to play a

series standing around together chatting and laughing and visiting before the game started. Every player in those days hated every man on the club to be played that day, and when the two captains came together to consult with the umpire it was like two bull-terriers turned loose from the benches, and once the game started it was for blood and not for averages" (*Minneapolis Journal*, reprinted in *Sporting News*, May 28, 1914).

26.2.3 Pregame Warmups. Pregame rituals were already taking a highly organized form in early baseball, with Cap Anson's Chicago White Stockings following a particularly regimented schedule when at home. The preliminary practice was controlled by a series of gongs.

The home team took the field first to warm up and toss the ball around. When the first gong sounded, the audience entered and the home team left the field and went to their clubhouse. The next gong went off twenty-five minutes before the game and was a signal for the visitors to take the field for their preliminaries.

The third sounding of the gong took place ten minutes before the start of the game, and Chicago retook the field. The fourth gong came eight minutes later and ended all warm-ups. The captains then flipped for choice of innings, and a fifth gong was sounded, at which time the members of the fielding team took their positions (*Fort Wayne Daily News*, April 10, 1883).

26.2.4 Weddings at Home Plate. Cincinnati business manager Frank Bancroft arranged the first wedding at home plate on September 18, 1893. When he heard that assistant groundskeeper Louis Rapp was planning to get married, Bancroft suggested that the ceremony take place at home plate at League Park. The newlyweds received gifts from the Reds, the visiting Orioles, and the fans (*Sporting Life*, September 23, 1893; Harry Ellard, *Base Ball in Cincinnati*, 192–195).

26.2.5 High Fives. Glenn Burke is believed to have invented the high five while playing for the Dodgers in the late 1970s.

(iii) Customs, Traditions, and Taboos

26.3.1 Nostalgia for the Good Old Days. In an 1868 article, old-time player Pete O'Brien (writing as "Old Peto Brine") cited the waiting game (see **2.3.1** "Waiting Out the Pitcher") as a prime example of how "they don't play ball nowadays as they used to" (*The American Chronicle of Sports and Pastimes*, January 9, 1868, 10). There is also nothing new about nostalgia for the days when the only numbers mentioned on the baseball pages were the players' statistics. Sportswriter Bill Hanna observed, "I, for one, pine for the good old days when items about the knobby fingers and eagle batting eye of some diamond favorite filled the public prints, rather than contracts, commissions, injunctions and a hundred and one other matters tiresomely material and not base ball at all." Hanna was writing in 1915 (Bill Hanna, *New York Sun*; reprinted in *Sporting News*, March 4, 1915).

26.3.2   Reports That Baseball Is Dead. When baseball experienced its first great rush of popularity between 1865 and 1867, there was a widespread feeling that "baseball fever" was simply a fad that would soon abate. Accordingly, when the game struggled in 1868 and 1869, many journalists prematurely pronounced the game dead. It was far from the last time.

26.3.3   Custom That the Club That Leads on July 4 Will Win the Pennant. Sportswriter Frank Getty wrote in 1929: "Old Mr. McGillicuddy's diligent young men are in the spot customarily occupied by pennant winners on Independence Day" (*Washington Post*, July 5, 1929).

26.3.4   Sunday Baseball. The issue of Sunday baseball was a contentious and divisive one from the earliest days of baseball until well into the twentieth century.

As early as 1862 the police were becoming involved: "Officer Haslam yesterday espied in Greenpoint some half dozen boys who were engaged in a game of base ball. But the officer although an admirer of the noble game is also opposed to its practice on the Sabbath, so he arrested both the ins and outs and locked them up for the night. This morning Justice Colahan dismissed them with a warning to have their practice days changed" (*Brooklyn Daily Times*, April 28, 1862; reprinted in James L. Terry, *Long Before the Dodgers*, 19).

For the remainder of the nineteenth century, arrests for playing ball on the Sabbath continued to be a regular occurrence. It became proverbial that it took ten men to play on Sunday—nine to play and one to watch for the police (*Grand Rapids* [Mich.] *Times*, May 3, 1871).

Sunday baseball was illegal in the early days of the National League, though a few clubs disregarded the rule. The American Association became the first major league to regularly schedule Sunday baseball games during its initial season of 1882.

Sunday baseball is usually thought of as a moral issue, but, as with night baseball (see 14.1.3), class also played a major role. Since working-class men had six-day work weeks and usually finished work too late for afternoon games, they had few opportunities to visit National League stadiums. This allowed the National League to try to cater to an upscale audience by charging higher admissions. In contrast, the American Association openly courted the working class by offering lower ticket prices, Sunday baseball, and alcoholic beverages.

The National League did not allow Sunday baseball until its merger with the American Association in 1892. Even then, local laws prevented most National League teams from playing Sunday games, and it was decades before some of them did. The state of Pennsylvania was the last holdout, with Pittsburgh and Philadelphia clubs not playing Sunday games in their own parks until 1934.

The major league's first Sunday night game did not take place until June 9, 1963, and only then because of the oppressive daytime heat in Houston. Charlie Bevis's *Sunday Baseball* gives a detailed history of the issue.

26.3.5   Sunday Ballparks. The first major league club to play Sunday games at a different park from their regular park was Syracuse, a National League club that defied the league's prohibition in 1879 and played Sunday games at Lakeside Park to avoid the Blue Laws in their home county. By the late 1880s, having a separate Sunday ballpark was a common practice (Michael Gershman, *Diamonds*, 34).

26.3.6   Numbering System for Scoring. The idea of assigning a number to each defensive position was suggested almost as soon as scorekeeping became part of baseball. But Henry Chadwick objected in 1861 that "if each player retained his position in the field throughout the game, this mode of record would do, clumsy as it is; but when scarcely a game is played wherein changes are not made, it of course becomes entirely unreliable, as it does not designate the fielder who put the striker out, but simply records the position on the field" (*Beadle's Dime Base-Ball Player*, 1861).

Since position in the batting order was the only constant, scorers had to use this number to designate a player. Unfortunately this meant that a scorer could not record the result of a play until he had checked the position in the lineup of each defensive player who had handled the ball. The resulting system was so cumbersome that it took Henry Chadwick some six pages to explain all its intricacies (Henry Chadwick, *The American Game of Base Ball*, 62–68). But there was little alternative.

By 1889 changes in position had become much less common and this prompted a writer in the *New York Mail and Express* to suggest that a single number be used for each defensive position. Chadwick explained the proposal: "The pitcher is numbered 1 in all cases, catcher 2, first baseman 3, second baseman 4, short stop 5, third baseman 6, right fielder 7, centre fielder 8, and left fielder 9. For example, if a ball is hit to third base and the runner is thrown out at first base, without looking at the score card it is known that the numbers to be recorded are 6-3, the former getting the assist, and the first baseman the put-out. If from short-stop to first, it is 5-3. If from the second baseman, it is 4-3. If a dropped third strike, and the runner is thrown out at first, it is K 1-2-3-K, indicating the strike out."

Chadwick believed this idea was "in no respect an improvement on the plan which has been in vogue since the National League was organized," citing a familiar objection: "if you name the players by their positions, and these happen to be changed in a game, then you are all in a fog on how to change them" (*Sporting Life*, May 29, 1889). Yet what Chadwick did not anticipate was that the legalization of substitutions, a gradual process that had begun that season (see **1.32** and **6.2.1**), would mean that the entry of new players into the game would become more common than swaps of position.

This eliminated the main benefit of the system that Chadwick had been using for so long. Moreover, it cannot have taken long for scorekeepers who experimented with the new method to see that it was much simpler to write 4-3 on a grounder to the second baseman than to have to check the position in the batting order of both defensive players.

The new idea appears to have caught on quickly, as researcher Keith Olbermann reports that an 1891 Giants scorecard included "Hints on Scoring" that are a word-for-word reprint of the instructions that had appeared in the *Mail and Express*. It is probably no coincidence

that that was the same year in which unlimited substitutions became legal.

Readers may have noticed that the scoring system introduced around 1889 designated the shortstop as 5, the third baseman as 6, the right fielder as 7, and the left fielder as 9. As Keith Olbermann has explained, the change to today's numbering system occurred during the next twenty years, but what prompted the switches remains mysterious. Olbermann, however, recounts an intriguing explanation for the reversal of the third baseman and short-stop's numbers that has been handed down by credible sportswriters who believe it to be true.

This version pinpoints the early-twentieth-century World Series, for which *Sporting Life* editor Francis Richter and *Sporting News* editor Joseph Flanner were often named official scorers. The two men soon discovered they were using different numbering systems, and quarreled. Richter maintained that the shortstop was the infielder who played between the second and third basemen, so it was only logical to assign him the number between them. But Flanner thought it more appropriate to select a number that reflected the shortstop's traditional role (see **1.15** and **4.2.6**). Richter conceded the point, and Flanner's system has prevailed ever since, even though few fans today are aware that the shortstop was ever considered anything but an infielder (Keith Olbermann, "Why Is the Shortstop '6'?," *Baseball Research Journal* 34 [2005], 16–18).

26.3.7   K for Strikeout. Henry Chadwick did have more influence in shaping the abbreviations used in box scores. He pioneered the use of the letter K to denote a strikeout because "the letter K in struck is easier to remember in connection with the word than S" (*Outing*, July 1888, "Scoring Rules for College Clubs"; also *National Chronicle*, January 30, 1869). Chadwick could never have anticipated how his somewhat arbitrary decision would affect the lives of Roger Clemens's four children, Kody, Kory, Koby, and Kacy.

(iv) Legends and Shrines

26.4.1   Tinker to Evers to Chance. Franklin P. Adams's famous poem first appeared in his *New York Evening Mail* column, "Always in Good Humor," in 1910. According to researcher Cliff Blau, on July 11, 1910, Art Devlin of the Giants grounded into a 6-4-3 double play that saved a Cubs victory and inspired the verse. The next day Adams's column featured the eight-line poem under the heading "That Double Play Again." It was an immediate hit, with parodies appearing almost daily in the *Evening Mail* for the next week, and the *Chicago Tribune* also publishing responses. On July 18 the *Evening Mail* reprinted the poem under the more familiar title "Baseball's Sad Lexicon."

26.4.2 Casey at the Bat. Ernest L. Thayer's poem originally appeared in the *San Francisco Examiner* on June 3, 1888. DeWolf Hopper gave his first of some ten thousand public recitals of the poem the following year.

26.4.3 John Anderson Play. In the early twentieth century the phrase "John Anderson play" was widely used to describe a player who attempted to steal an already occupied base. A typical article explained, "The most famous species of 'bones,' no doubt, are the John Andersons. To be entitled to a place in the John Anderson Order, you must steal second with the bases full. A lesser degree is awarded if you steal third with a man occupying that bag" (*Sporting News*, November 16, 1916).

As Hugh Jennings observed, there was nothing fair about the term: "John Anderson has for years been held up as the leading example of dumb play in base ball because he tried to steal second with the bases filled, but many other players have made the same mistake and escaped criticism. A few years ago even Ty Cobb, admittedly best of all base runners, tried to steal third while Bobby Jones was on the bag" (Hugh Jennings, *Rounding Third*, Chapter 72).

John Anderson played in the major leagues from 1894 to 1908, and the term was already being used toward the end of his playing days. Nonetheless the origins of the term proved difficult to pin down. Rob Neyer's pursuit of the elusive game was described in the *1990 Bill James Baseball Book* (Bill James, *1990 Bill James Baseball Book*, 241).

I was finally able to find it as a result of an article that appeared in *Sporting News* on February 25, 1923. The piece reported that the play took place while Anderson was playing for the St. Louis Browns, and gave enough details that, with the help of the Retrosheet website, I was able to locate a game that seemed to match. The game in question was the first game of a doubleheader on September 24, 1903, with the Browns playing in New York.

The *New York Sun*'s account confirmed that "[Jack] Chesbro was in fine form, except

for a short spell in the eighth inning, when the Browns had him on the grill. They made four hits in a row and would have done more damage but for a stupid play by Anderson. With all the bases occupied and only one out Anderson ran for second on a third strike and was doubled up unceremoniously" (*New York Sun*, September 25, 1903).

26.4.4 Norman Rockwell Painting. Norman Rockwell's famous painting of three umpires checking the sky appeared on the cover of the *Saturday Evening Post* on April 23, 1949.

26.4.5 Called Shot. Baseball has had many claims of "called" home runs over the years, with varying levels of documentation. The earliest such claim may have been made in 1873 about a called shot alleged to have taken place in the first of three 1858 games between the best players from Brooklyn and New York City. According to the reporter, "John Holder, just before going to the bat, bet $75 that he would make a home run, and hitting the ball to centre field, he actually did score the coveted run and won the bet" (*Brooklyn Eagle*, July 16, 1873).

26.4.6 Hall of Fame. The first vote for the Baseball Hall of Fame in Cooperstown, New York, took place on February 2, 1936, with Ty Cobb, Babe Ruth, Honus Wagner, Christy Mathewson, and Walter Johnson being elected. The museum was opened on June 12, 1939.

The concept of a Hall of Fame had currency in baseball long before then, however. A 1903 article noted that "[National League] President [Harry] Pulliam proposes to establish a base ball 'Hall of Fame' at League quarters in New York" (*Sporting Life*, March 21, 1903). But Pulliam's "Hall of Fame" was little more than a photo gallery. He began it with a life-sized photo that was presented to him by 1902 batting champion Ginger Beaumont (*Pittsburg[h] Press*, March 29, 1903). The collection soon included "a large group picture of the Pittsburg Champions, a likeness of President Dreyfuss and all the other magnates of the organization, a large photograph of Rube Waddell, whom Pulliam 'brought out,' a picture of the Harvard baseball team, and one of the Yale football champions (*Pittsburg[h] Press*, May 2, 1903).

Pulliam intended to add a photo of each subsequent batting champion. But the next winner, Honus Wagner, declined the honor because of his disappointment with his poor World Series (*Sporting Life*, April 2, 1904).

Moreover, since Wagner captured six of the next seven National League batting titles, it would have been a rather monotonous display even had Wagner agreed to pose.

After this abortive effort, the term "Hall of Fame" became a figurative way of referring to anyone who achieved a great accomplishment. No-hitters were a prominent example; *Sporting News* reported in 1910, "[Chester Carmichael] earned a niche in the base ball hall of fame the other day by not allowing a single player to reach first base in an East League championship game" (*Sporting News*, August 18, 1910). Diverse other accomplishments prompted this description. For example, a sporting correspondent observed in 1913: "[Thomas] Sindler got himself into the 'hall of fame' last week by pitching a double-header against Kingston" (*Sporting Life*, August 30, 1913). Sportswriter Joe S. Jackson referred in 1911 to batters who collected two hundred hits in a season as members of "the batting hall of fame" (*Washington Post*, September 10, 1911). Bill James noted that "Hall of Fame" was also used as a metaphor for a sportswriter's all-time team (Bill James, *The Politics of Glory*, 5).

In 1922 the U.S. Commission of Fine Arts, an independent agency established by Congress twelve years earlier to offer advice on the architectural and artistic appearance of the nation's capital, recommended the building of a baseball monument in East Potomac Park. The American League liked the idea and budgeted $100,000 for it (*Sporting News*, August 10, 1922). The plan for a monument was pursued for a couple of years, with the intention of commemorating the winners of the most valuable player award, but eventually was abandoned.

26.4.7   The Doubleday Myth. The Doubleday Myth was initiated on December 30, 1907, by a group that has become known as the Mills Commission. This body was charged by A. G. Spalding with determining the origins of baseball and came to the preposterous conclusion that the game was invented by Abner Doubleday.

Robert Henderson is often credited with being the first to debunk the Doubleday Myth in the 1930s, as for example by Leonard Koppett in his introduction to the 2001 reprint of Henderson's *Ball, Bat and Bishop*. While Henderson did an especially thorough job, the gaping holes in the commission's conclusions were documented almost immediately. Sportswriter William Rankin repeatedly used his *Sporting*

News column to point out the flaws (*Sporting News*, April 2, 1908; *Sporting News*, September 9, 1909; A. H. Spink, *The National Game*, 54). Henry Chadwick also joined in the howl of protests. A writer named Will Irwin also addressed the issue in a 1909 *Collier's* article entitled "Baseball: Before the Professional Game."

26.4.8   Washington Monument. Even before the Washington Monument had been dedicated in February 1885, the first attempt had been made to catch a baseball dropped from the top of it.

Sporting Life reported in January, "Paul Hines, [Charley] Snyder, [Phil] Baker and [Ed] Yewell are persevering, and have made several attempts to catch a base ball thrown from the Washington monument. In one instance a ball was thrown off for Snyder to catch, but he was unable to judge it correctly. Hines, who happened to be several yards distant, saw the ball coming his way, put up his gloved hand, but the sphere went through them like a flash, and made a deep indentation in the frozen ground. Phil. Baker captured the ball once unexpectedly, but he held it only momentarily. There seems to be no rule by which the ball falling from such a great distance can be judged" (*Sporting Life*, January 14, 1885).

An account the following week observed: "The impression among the resident ball players is that Baker and Ewell [sic] will catch it if they get under the ball; that Hines is now afraid to make the attempt since he has seen the velocity of the ball. Snyder insists and offers to back up his opinion that the ball will not be caught between this and the 1st of April. . . . Everybody is discussing the subject, and therefore everybody is anxiously awaiting results" (*Washington Herald*, reprinted in *Sporting Life*, January 21, 1885).

Paul Hines gave a somewhat different version in 1906: "A New York man engaged in the business of selling sporting goods made me an offer of $200 for the ball if I succeeded in catching it. The monument at that time was not finished, and the scaffolding built around the top to be used in placing the capstone rose some feet higher than the monument itself. I offered to pay Charley Snyder and some other players to go to the top and toss the ball to me, but none would venture, and I finally employed one of the workmen engaged there. I gave him three balls. The first one he tossed landed on top of a shed. The second dropped into a lake. The third was thrown some distance from where I stood, but I made a run for it, and the ball just tipped the ends of my fingers. Though I had no glove on (we didn't wear 'em then), the ball did not sting my hand as much as many I had caught in center field" (quoted in Gerard S. Petrone, *When Baseball Was Young*, 64).

It was another nine years before the first successful catch was made by Pop Schriver on August 24, 1894. Schriver was followed by Gabby Street on August 21, 1908, and Billy Sullivan on August 24, 1910 (Lee Allen, *The Hot Stove League*, 99; Jack Kavanagh, *The Heights of Ridiculousness*, 1–24; Peter Morris, *Catcher*, 174–175, 227–228).

(v) Injuries and Deaths

26.5.1 X-rays. Pete Cassidy of Louisville was the first ballplayer to receive the then-new x-ray technique on April 7, 1896. Cassidy had suffered a wrist injury, but doctors had been unable to pinpoint the exact problem. The x-rays revealed a loose piece of bone, which was then removed by surgery.

26.5.2 Knee Surgery. For many years ballplayers believed that any type of surgery would be career-ending, so they either played through injuries or gave up the game. In a 1909 article, sportswriter Paul H. Bruske observed that the Detroit Tigers were the exception to the rule that "no man is ever himself again after an operation." He noted the then-remarkable fact that four of the team's players had undergone some sort of surgical procedure and returned to baseball— "Germany" Schaefer for hemorrhoids and Wade Killefer for tonsillitis (both in 1907), Davy Jones in 1906 for "a serious rupture of the abdominal wall," and Ty Cobb in 1906 for an unspecified strain that required "a very delicate operation" (*Detroit Times*, March 29, 1909).

Knee surgery continued to be viewed in this way. New York Giants shortstop Travis Jackson suffered a serious knee injury in 1932, when he was only twenty-eight and later recalled, "I went on the retired list and thought that was it." After a few months, he received a phone call from Giants manager Bill Terry who "wanted to know whether I would have my knees operated on if the Giants would pay for it. I told him, 'That's a silly question, Bill. I can't walk now and I'd do anything to get fixed up.'" Jackson missed an entire year but then returned to form and was eventually elected to the Hall of Fame (Walter M. Langford, *Legends of Baseball*, 101).

26.5.3 Tommy John Surgery. Braves pitcher Harry Hulihan had a tendon grafted from his thigh into his pitching shoulder in 1923. The surgery cured his pain, but he lost his velocity and his career ended (John Bennett, "Harry Hulihan," in Tom Simon, ed., *Green Mountain Boys of Summer*, 116). On July 17, 1974, surgeons transplanted a tendon from Tommy John's right forearm into the left-handed pitcher's throwing elbow. The success of the operation has given new hope to countless sore-armed pitchers since. Indeed, Tommy John surgery has become so common and effective that orthopedic surgeons report that many pitchers and their parents mistakenly view it as a way to improve performance. Some have being asked to perform the procedures on pitchers with minor injuries or even with perfectly healthy arms (Jeré Longman, "Fit Young Pitchers See Elbow Repair as Cure-All," *New York Times*, July 20, 2007).

26.5.4 Ice on Pitching Arm. George F. Will claimed that the now common practice of icing the pitching arm after a start was originated in the 1960s by Sandy Koufax and Don Drysdale (George F. Will, *Men at Work*, 143). It's a difficult claim to substantiate because ice had been used for injuries for many years before then. Exactly who was the first to use ice as a precautionary measure rather than to treat a specific injury is probably impossible to determine, but Drysdale and Koufax do seem to have helped popularize the routine use of ice after a start.

26.5.5 Death Resulting from a Professional Game. Atlanta's Lou Henke died on August 15, 1885, from the effects of an injury he had sustained in a Southern League game the preceding day.

Ray Chapman of Cleveland is the only major league player to die as an immediate result of an on-the-field incident. On August 16, 1920, Chapman was hit in the head by a pitch from Carl Mays of the New York Yankees, and he died the next morning. While the Chapman tragedy is still remembered, the much more recent death of umpire Cal Drummond has been virtually forgotten. Drummond was struck in the mask by a foul tip while acting as plate umpire in a June 10, 1969, game between the Baltimore Orioles and California Angels. He completed the game, but his condition worsened and he spent a week in unconsciousness in a Baltimore hospital. The following spring he was one day away from returning to the major leagues when he collapsed while umpiring a minor league game in Des Moines and died four hours later. An autopsy attributed the death to the foul tip eleven months earlier (Larry R. Gerlach, "Death on the Diamond," *National Pastime* 24 [2004], 14–16). Fatal on-field heart attacks during games were suffered by Negro Leagues player Clyde Nelson on July 25, 1949, and by National League umpire John McSherry on April 1, 1996.

In addition, there have been a number of players whose deaths were attributed to accidents that occurred during major league games. Jimmy Rogers's death on January 27, 1900, was reported to have resulted from his being hit by a pitch while playing for Louisville (*Sporting Life*, January 27, 1900). Athletics pitcher Jim Crabb's major league career was cut short when he was hit in the chest with a line drive. The injury bothered him the rest of his life, and his 1940 death was said to have resulted from complications from the injury (Jerry E. Clark, *Anson to Zuber*, 54). Athletics catcher Mike Powers died in 1909 while he was still an active player, and some linked his death to an injury in a game several weeks earlier. Former Pirates pitcher Jimmy Gardner's death in 1905 was attributed to the effects of a pitched ball that fractured his skull six years earlier (*Sporting Life*, June 24, 1905). Researcher Jack Daugherty discovered a 1912 obituary of former Braves and Giants outfielder Frank Murphy that attributed his death to his having been hit by a pitch during his playing career (*Tarrytown Press-Record*, November 7, 1912).

It is important to remember, however, that many if not all these claims reflect the imprecise medical knowledge of the time, especially regarding physical activity. An 1880 article, for instance, reported that an ex-player named Alexander Trope had died of "a cancer caused by a blow to the stomach by a baseball some five years ago" (*New York Clipper*, September 25, 1880). Another article in the same publication four years later indicated that minor leaguer John McDonough had died from consumption (tuberculosis) contracted from being hit by a foul ball (*New York Clipper*, August 2, 1884).

Many deaths have also resulted from non-professional games, as enumerated by Robert M. Gorman and David Weeks in *Death at the Ballpark: A Comprehensive Study of Game-Related Fatalities, 1862–2007*. Researcher George A. Thompson discovered the earliest known instance. In an 1859 game at Hoboken's Ely-

sian Fields, while chasing a ball that had rolled into a hollow, a player named Thomas Willis slipped and struck his head on a sharp rock, fracturing his skull (*New York Evening Express*, October 22, 1859, 3; *New York Times*, October 22, 1859, 8).

26.5.6 Player to Die of Lou Gehrig's Disease. Former Giants pitcher Claud Elliott, whom John Thorn pegged as the game's first relief specialist (see **6.2.9**), died of amyotrophic lateral sclerosis on June 21, 1923. That same week a young first baseman named Lou Gehrig made his major league debut. Eighteen years later Gehrig died of the same disease, and it was renamed in his memory.

(vi) Hodgepodge

26.6.1 Instant Rules. In theory, new rules may be enacted only at the annual meetings at the season's end. In practice, new interpretations are sometimes added in mid-season if there seems to be no rule covering a situation.

Eddie Onslow reported that Ty Cobb once deliberately kicked a ball that was lying in the base path. According to Onslow, there was no rule against this tactic, so one was made the next day (Eugene Murdock, *Baseball Between the Wars*, 113). Ed Wells claimed that the same thing happened when Joe Sewell made a trench to cause a bunt to roll foul (Eugene Murdock, *Baseball Between the Wars*, 74). Eddie Stanky's attempt to distract batters by jumping up and down was dealt with in the same summary fashion, as were the 1957 efforts to break up double plays (see **11.1.8** and **5.5.3**).

26.6.2 Twins. The Reccius brothers, who played in the 1880s, were long believed to be the first twins to play in the majors—until researcher Bob Bailey established that they weren't actually twins. As a result, the distinction now belongs to George and Bill Hunter, who had brief major league stints—George with Brooklyn in 1909 and 1910, and Bill with Cleveland in 1912.

26.6.3 Teams of Nine Brothers. There were quite a few teams of nine brothers in early baseball, including the Joneses of Indianapolis in 1877; the Maddens in New England in 1878; the Grieshabers of St. Genevieve County, Missouri, in 1884; the Atkins of Mexico, Missouri, in 1888; the Karpens of Chicago in 1890;

the McEntees and Lennons of Joliet, Illinois, in 1890; the Thompsons of Winchester, New Hampshire, in 1898; the Whites of Hammond, Indiana, in 1903; and the Birkenmeyers of Wappingers Falls, New York, in 1904. At least a couple of these teams faced each other; the Lennon brothers beat the Karpens in 1890 and the Whites in 1903 (Charles W. Bevis, "Family Baseball Teams," *Baseball Research Journal* 26 [1997], 8; *Sporting Life*, October 10, 1903).

There continued to be a smattering of such clubs in the 1920s and 1930s, as Charles W. Bevis has documented. The last one may have been the Acerras of Long Branch, New Jersey, who were still playing as late as 1947 (Charles W. Bevis, "Family Baseball Teams," *Baseball Research Journal* 26 [1997], 8–12). Since then, declining family size has spelled the end of such clubs.

26.6.4 Father-Son Major Leaguers.

Herm and Jack Doscher were the first father and son to both play major league baseball. Ken Griffey, Sr., and Ken Griffey, Jr., were the first father and son to be major league teammates.

26.6.5 Baseball-playing Couple.

After the 1883 season, pitcher Bollicky Bill Taylor married one of the players on the "Brunettes," a touring women's team. The couple separated after only two months (Harold Dellinger, "Bill Taylor," in Frederick Ivor-Campbell, Robert L. Tiemann, and Mark Rucker, eds., *Baseball's First Stars*, 163).

26.6.6 Postponed Due to Sun.

A game between Boston and Cincinnati on May 6, 1892, was called in the fourteenth inning because the sun was directly in the batters' eyes. The *Cincinnati Enquirer* reported the next day that both teams agreed with the umpire's decision (Lee Allen, "Called on Account of Sun," *Sporting News*, December 11, 1965; reprinted in *Cooperstown Corner*).

26.6.7 All Nine Positions.

Bert Campaneris was the first to play all nine positions in a single major league game on September 8, 1965. The feat has since been accomplished by Cesar Tovar, Shane Halter, and Scott Sheldon. On August 31, 1974, the Portland Mavericks of the Northwest League rotated after every inning, so that all nine players played all nine positions. Portland won the game 9-8.

26.6.8 Athletes Referring to Themselves in the Third Person.

Billy "Kid" Gleason told a reporter in 1894: "Your uncle [I] was after a $500 slice of the $2,400 [Ned] Hanlon paid Chris [Von der Ahe] for me, and I am not violating any confidence in assuring you that I got it. When Willie figures in a deal he makes it a point to see that his interests are not neglected" (*St. Louis Post-Dispatch*, September 22, 1894).

26.6.9 Extra-inning Games.

It is sometimes claimed that there were extra-inning games played before 1857, but this is a misconception. Nine innings did not become the standard until 1857, and most matches before then were played to a specified score. Such games thus often took more than nine innings, but they were not extra-inning games.

Since early games were high-scoring affairs, extra-inning games were rare. The earliest one listed in Marshall Wright's *The National Association of Base Ball Players, 1857-1870* is a ten-inning game between the Hoboken Club and the Mutuals of New York on August 4, 1859. The extra frame allowed the Mutuals to pull out a 19-15 win. A few months earlier, however, the Senior and Junior clubs of Albany were tied 36-36 after nine innings. The Juniors scored four times in the tenth inning to win (*New York Atlas*, June 19, 1859).

Bibliography

BOOKS

1864 American Boy's Book of Sports and Games (New York, 1864; reprint New York, 2000)

Melvin L. Adelman, *A Sporting Time: New York City and the Rise of Modern Athletics, 1820–70* (Urbana, Ill., 1986)

Aetna Base Ball Association Constitution and By-Laws (unpublished logbook; Burton Collection, Detroit Public Library)

William E. Akin, *West Virginia Baseball: A History, 1865–2000* (Jefferson, N.C., 2006)

Lee Allen, *Cooperstown Corner: Columns from the* Sporting News, *1962–1969* (Cleveland, 1990)

Lee Allen, *The Hot Stove League* (New York, 1955; reprint Kingston, N.Y., 2000)

David W. Anderson, *More Than Merkle* (Lincoln, Nebr., 2000)

Will Anderson, *Was Baseball Really Invented in Maine?* (Portland, Me., 1992)

Roger Angell, *Once More Around the Park: A Baseball Reader* (New York, 1991; reprint Chicago, 2001)

Roger Angell, *A Pitcher's Story: Innings with David Cone* (New York, 2001)

Roger Angell, *The Summer Game* (New York, 1972)

Adrian C. "Cap" Anson, *A Ball Player's Career* (Chicago, 1900; reprint Mattituck, N.Y., n.d.)

Marty Appel, *Slide, Kelly, Slide: The Wild Life and Times of Mike "King" Kelly, Baseball's First Superstar* (Lanham, Md., 1999)

Marty Appel, *Yesterday's Heroes* (New York, 1988)

David Arcidiacono, *Grace, Grit and Growling* (East Hampton, Conn., 2003)

Jean Hastings Ardell, *Breaking into Baseball: Women and the National Pastime* (Carbondale, Ill., 2005)

Mark Armour, ed., *Rain Check: Baseball in the Pacific Northwest* (Cleveland, 2006)

Gustav Axelson, *COMMY: The Life Story of Charles A. Comiskey* (Chicago, 1919)

Walter Bagehot, *The English Constitution* (London, 1867)

Richard Bak, *Peach: Ty Cobb in His Time and Ours* (Ann Arbor, 2005)

Red Barber, *The Broadcasters* (New York, 1970)

Red Barber, *1947: When All Hell Broke Loose in Baseball* (New York, 1984)

The Barry Halper Collection of Baseball Memorabilia (New York, 1999)

Gai Ingham Berlage, *Women in Baseball: The Forgotten History* (Westport, Conn., 1994)

Charlie Bevis, *The New England League: A Baseball History, 1885–1949* (Jefferson, N.C., 2008)

Charlie Bevis, *Sunday Baseball: The Major Leagues' Struggle to Play Baseball on the Lord's Day, 1876–1934* (Jefferson, N.C., 2003)

David Block, *Baseball Before We Knew It* (Lincoln, Nebr., 2005)

Don Bollman, *Run for the Roses: A Fifty Year Memoir* (Mecosta, Mich., 1975)

Bill Borst, *Baseball Through a Knothole: A St. Louis History* (St. Louis, 1980)

Talmage Boston, *1939, Baseball's Pivotal Year: From the Golden Age to the Modern Era* (Fort Worth, Tex., 1994)

Jim Bouton, edited by Leonard Shecter, *Ball Four: My Life and Hard Times Throwing the Knuckleball in the Big Leagues* (New York, 1970)

Larry G. Bowman, *Before the World Series: Pride, Profits and Baseball's First Championships* (De Kalb, Ill., 2003)

James H. Bready, *Baseball in Baltimore* (Baltimore, 1998)

Eric Bronson, ed., *Baseball and Philosophy: Thinking Outside the Batter's Box* (Chicago, 2004)

Jim Brosnan, *The Long Season* (New York, 1960; reprint Chicago, 2002)

Warren Brown, *The Chicago Cubs* (New York, 1946; reprint Carbondale, Ill., 2001)

Lois Browne, *Girls of Summer: The Real Story of the All-American Girls Professional Baseball League* (Toronto, 1992)

Reed Browning, *Baseball's Greatest Season, 1924* (Amherst, Mass., 2003)

Reed Browning, *Cy Young: A Baseball Life* (Amherst, Mass., 2000)

Robert F. Burk, *Much More Than a Game: Players, Owners and American Baseball Since 1921* (Chapel Hill, N.C., 2001)

Robert F. Burk, *Never Just a Game: Players, Owners and American Baseball to 1920* (Chapel Hill, N.C., 1994)

J. P. Caillault, *A Tale of Four Cities* (Jefferson, N.C., 2003)

Bob Carroll, *Baseball Between the Lies* (New York, 1993)

Robin Carver, *The Boy's and Girl's Book of Sports* (Boston, 1834)

Jon David Cash, *Before They Were Cardinals: Major League Baseball in Nineteenth-Century St. Louis* (Columbia, Mo., 2002)

Jerrold Casway, *Ed Delahanty in the Emerald Age of Baseball* (Notre Dame, Ind., 2004)

David Cataneo, *Tony C.: The Triumph and Tragedy of Tony Conigliaro* (Nashville, 1997)

Henry Chadwick, *Chadwick's Base Ball Manual* (London, 1874)

Henry Chadwick, *The American Game of Base Ball* (aka *The Game of Base Ball. How to Learn It, How to Play It, and How to Teach It. With Sketches of Noted Players*) (1868; reprint Columbia, S.C., 1983)

Henry Chadwick, *The Art of Batting* (New York, 1886)

Henry Chadwick, *Beadle's Dime Base-Ball Player* (1860) (reprint: Morgantown, Pa., 1996) (later editions are occasionally cited, but this guide changed little from year to year)

Henry Chadwick, *DeWitt's Base Ball Umpire's Guide* (various years)

Henry Chadwick, *Haney's Base Ball Player's Book of Reference for 1867* (aka *The Base Ball Player's Book of Reference*) (New York, 1867)

James Charlton, ed., *The Baseball Chronology: The Complete History of Significant Events in the Game of Baseball* (New York, 1991)

James Charlton, ed., *Road Trips* (Cleveland, 2004)

Seymour R. Church, *Base Ball: The History, Statistics and Romance of the American National Game from Its Inception to the Present Time* (San Francisco, 1902; reprint Princeton, N.J., 1974)

Dick Clark and Larry Lester, eds., *The Negro Leagues Book* (Cleveland, 1994)

Dave Clark, *The Knucklebook: Everything You Need to Know About Baseball's Strangest Pitch–the Knuckleball* (Chicago, 2006)

Jerry E. Clark, *Anson to Zuber: Iowa Boys in the Major Leagues* (Omaha, 1992)

Ty Cobb, *Bustin' 'Em and Other Big League Stories* (New York, 1914; reprint William R. Cobb, ed., Marietta, Ga., 2003)

Ty Cobb, *Memoirs of Twenty Years in Baseball* (1925; reprint William R. Cobb, ed., Marietta, Ga., 2002)

Mickey Cochrane, *Baseball: The Fans' Game* (New York, 1939; reprint Cleveland, 1992)

Robert Charles Cottrell, *The Best Pitcher in Baseball: The Life of Rube Foster, Negro League Giant* (New York, 2001)

William Curran, *Big Sticks: The Phenomenal Decade of Ruth, Gehrig, Cobb, and Hornsby* (New York, 1990)

William Curran, *Mitts: A Celebration of the Art of Fielding* (New York, 1985)

Arthur Daley, *Inside Baseball: A Half Century of the National Pastime* (New York, 1950)

W. Harrison Daniel and Scott P. Mayer, *Baseball in Richmond: A History of the Professional Game, 1884–2000* (Jefferson, N.C., 2003)

Bill Deane, *Award Voting* (Kansas City, 1988)

Jordan Deutsch, Richard M. Cohen, Roland T. Johnson, and David S. Neft, eds., *The Scrapbook History of Baseball* (Indianapolis, 1975)

Donald Dewey and Nicholas Acocella, *The Ball Clubs: Every Franchise, Past and Present, Officially Recognized by Major League Baseball* (New York, 1996)

Paul Dickson, ed., *Baseball's Greatest Quotations* (New York, 1991)

Paul Dickson, *The Hidden Language of Baseball: How Signs and Sign-Stealing Have Influenced the Course of Our National Pastime* (New York, 2003)

Paul Dickson, ed., *The Dickson Baseball Dictionary*, third edition (New York, 2009)

Paul Dickson, *The Worth Book of Softball: A Celebration of America's True National Pastime* (New York, 1994)

James M. DiClerico and Barry J. Pavelec, *The Jersey Game: The History of Modern Baseball from Its Birth to the Big Leagues in the Garden State* (New Brunswick, N.J., 1991)

Bryan Di Salvatore, *A Clever Base-Ballist: The Life and Times of John Montgomery Ward* (New York, 1999)

Phil Dixon and Patrick J. Hannigan, *The Negro Baseball Leagues: A Photographic History* (Mattituck, N.Y., 1992)

Dick Dobbins and Jon Twichell, *Nuggets on the Diamond* (San Francisco, 1994)

Bert Dunne, *Play Ball!* (Garden City, N.Y., 1947)

Bob Edwards, *Fridays with Red: A Radio Friendship* (New York, 1993)

James M. Egan, *Base Ball on the Western Reserve: The Early Game in Cleveland and Northeast Ohio, Year by Year and Town by Town, 1865–1900* (Jefferson, N.C., 2007)

James E. Elfers, *The Tour to End All Tours* (Lincoln, Nebr., 2003)

Harry Ellard, *Base Ball in Cincinnati: A History* (1907; reprint Jefferson, N.C., 2004)

John J. Evers and Hugh S. Fullerton, *Touching Second: The Science of Baseball* (Chicago, 1910; reprint Mattituck, N.Y., n.d.)

David Falkner, *Nine Sides of the Diamond: Baseball's Great Glove Men on the Fine Art of Defense* (New York, 1990)

Federal Writers' Project, *Baseball in Old Chicago* (Chicago, 1939)

David L. Fleitz, *Cap Anson: The Grand Old Man of Baseball* (Jefferson, N.C., 2005)

G. H. Fleming, *The Unforgettable Season* (New York, 1981)

Stephen Fox, *Big Leagues: Professional Baseball, Football, and Basketball in National Memory* (New York, 1994)

Joel S. Franks, *Whose Baseball? The National Pastime and Cultural Diversity in California, 1859–1941* (Lanham, Md., 2001)

Ford Frick, *Games, Asterisks and People: Memoirs of a Lucky Fan* (New York, 1973)

Cappy Gagnon, *Notre Dame Baseball Greats: From Anson to Yaz* (Charleston, S.C., 2004)

Larry R. Gerlach, *The Men in Blue: Conversations with Umpires* (New York, 1980)

Michael Gershman, *Diamonds: The Evolution of the Ballpark* (Boston, 1993)

A. Bartlett Giamatti, *Take Time for Paradise: Americans and Their Games* (New York, 1989)

Malcolm Gladwell, *The Tipping Point: How Little Things Can Make a Big Difference* (Boston, 2000)

George Gmelch and J. J. Weiner, *In the Ballpark: The Working Lives of Baseball People* (Washington, D.C., 1998)

Warren Goldstein, *Playing for Keeps: A History of Early Baseball* (Ithaca, N.Y., 1989)

Peter Golenbock, *Wrigleyville: A Magical History Tour of the Chicago Cubs* (New York, 1999)

Roberto Gonzalez Echevarria, *The Pride of Havana: A History of Cuban Baseball* (New York, 1999)

Robert M. Gorman and David Weeks, *Death at the Ballpark: A Comprehensive Study of Game-Related Fatalities, 1862–2007* (Jefferson, N.C., 2008)

Tom Gorman, as told to Jerome Holtzman, *Three and Two!* (New York, 1979)

Guy W. Green, *Fun and Frolic with an Indian Ball Team* (1907; reprint Mattituck, N.Y., 1992)

Robert Gregory, *Diz: The History of Dizzy Dean and Baseball During the Great Depression* (New York, 1992)

William Ridgely Griffith, *The Early History of Amateur Base Ball in the State of Maryland* (Baltimore, 1897)

Stephen Guschov, *The Red Stockings of Cincinnati: Base Ball's First All-Professional Team and Its Historic 1869 and 1870 Seasons* (Jefferson, N.C., 1998)

Dan Gutman, *Banana Bats and Ding-Dong Balls: A Century of Unique Baseball Inventions* (New York, 1995)

Dan Gutman, *It Ain't Cheatin' If You Don't Get Caught: Scuffing, Corking, Spitting, Gunking, Razzing, and Other Fundamentals of Our National Pastime* (New York, 1990)

Allen Guttmann, *Sports Spectators* (New York, 1986)

David Halberstam, *October 1964* (New York, 1995)

Brayton Harris, *Blue & Gray in Black & White: Newspapers in the Civil War* (Washington, 2000)

John Helyar, *Lords of the Realm* (New York, 1994)

Robert W. Henderson, *Ball, Bat, and Bishop: The Origin of Ball Games* (New York, 1947; reprint Urbana, Ill., 2001)

J. Thomas Hetrick, *Chris Von der Ahe and the St. Louis Browns* (Lanham, Md., 1999)

Laura Hillenbrand, *Seabiscuit* (New York, 2001)

Frank W. Hoffmann and William G. Bailey, *Sports and Recreation Fads* (Binghamton, N.Y., 1991)

Jerome Holtzman, *No Cheering in the Press Box*, revised edition (New York, 1995)

Arlene Howard, with Ralph Wimbish, *Elston and Me: The Story of the First Black Yankee* (Columbia, Mo., 2001)

Colin Howell, *Northern Sandlots* (Toronto, 1995)

Frederick Ivor-Campbell, Robert L. Tiemann, and Mark Rucker, eds., *Baseball's First Stars* (Cleveland, 1996)

Bill James, *The 1990 Bill James Baseball Book* (New York, 1990)

Bill James, *The Bill James Baseball Abstract* (various years)

Bill James, *The Bill James Guide to Baseball Managers: From 1870 to Today* (New York, 1997)

Bill James, *The New Bill James Historical Baseball Abstract* (New York, 2001)

Bill James, *The Politics of Glory: How Baseball's Hall of Fame Really Works* (New York, 1994)

Bill James and Rob Neyer, *The Neyer/James Guide to Pitchers* (New York, 2004)

Hugh Jennings, *Rounding First* (n.p., 1925)

Harry "Steamboat" Johnson, *Standing the Gaff* (Nashville, Tenn., 1935; reprint Lincoln, Nebr., 1994)

Lloyd Johnson, *Baseball's Book of Firsts* (Philadelphia, 1999)

Lloyd Johnson and Miles Wolff, eds., *The Encyclopedia of Minor League Baseball*, 2nd edition (Durham, N.C., 1997)

David Jones, ed., *Deadball Stars of the American League* (Washington, 2006)

James M. Kahn, *The Umpire Story* (New York, 1953)

Roger Kahn, *The Head Game: Baseball Seen from the Pitcher's Mound* (New York, 2000)

Roger Kahn, *Memories of Summer* (New York, 1997)

Roger Kahn, *A Season in the Sun* (New York, 1977)

Mark Kanter, ed., *The Northern Game and Beyond: Baseball in New England and Eastern Canada* (Cleveland, 2002)

Lawrence S. Katz, *Baseball in 1939: The Watershed Season of the National Pastime* (Jefferson, N.C., 1995)

Jack Kavanagh, *The Heights of Ridiculousness: The Feats of Baseball's Merrymakers* (South Bend, Ind., 1998)

Jack Kavanagh and Norman Macht, *Uncle Robbie* (Cleveland, 1999)

Brent Kelley, *In the Shadow of the Babe* (Jefferson, N.C., 1995)

Kevin Kerrane, *Dollar Sign on the Muscle: The World of Baseball Scouting* (New York, 1984)

George B. Kirsch, *The Creation of American Team Sports: Baseball and Cricket, 1838–72* (Urbana, Ill., 1991)

Charles P. Korr, *The End of Baseball as We Knew It: The Players Union, 1960–81* (Urbana, Ill., 2002)

Bowie Kuhn, *Hardball: The Education of a Baseball Commissioner* (New York, 1988)

Bruce Kuklick, *To Every Thing a Season: Shibe Park and Urban Philadelphia, 1909–1976* (Princeton, N.J., 1991)

Robin Tolmach Lakoff, *The Language War* (Berkeley, Calif., 2000)

Mark Lamster, *Spalding's World Tour: The Epic Adventure That Took Baseball around the Globe* (New York, 2006)

Neil Lanctot, *Negro League Baseball: The Rise and Ruin of a Black Institution* (Philadelphia, 2004)

F. C. Lane, *Batting* (1925; reprint Cleveland, 2001)

Walter M. Langford, *Legends of Baseball* (South Bend, Ind., 1987)

Ernest J. Lanigan, *The Baseball Cyclopedia* (New York, 1922; reprint St. Louis, 1988)

Jerry Lansche, *Glory Fades Away: The Nineteenth-Century World Series Rediscovered* (Dallas, 1991)

Irving A. Leitner, *Baseball: Diamond in the Rough* (New York, 1972)

Peter Levine, *A. G. Spalding and the Rise of Baseball: The Promise of American Sport* (New York, 1985)

Frederick G. Lieb, *The St. Louis Cardinals: The Story of a Great Baseball Club* (New York, 1944; reprint Carbondale, Ill., 2001)

Jonathan Fraser Light, *The Cultural Encyclopedia of Baseball* (Jefferson, N.C., 1997)

Michael E. Lomax, *Black Baseball Entrepreneurs, 1860–1901: Operating by Any Means Necessary* (Syracuse, 2003)

Scott Longert, *Addie Joss: King of the Pitchers* (Cleveland, 1998)

James D'Wolf Lovett, *Old Boston Boys and the Games They Played* (Boston, 1908)

Lee Lowenfish, *Branch Rickey: Baseball's Ferocious Gentleman* (Lincoln, Nebr., 2007)

Lee Lowenfish, *The Imperfect Diamond: A History of Baseball's Labor Wars*, revised edition (New York, 1991)

Philip J. Lowry, *Green Cathedrals: The Ultimate Celebration of All 271 Major League and Negro League Ballparks Past and Present* (Reading, Mass., 1992)

Neil W. Macdonald, *The League That Lasted: 1876 and the Founding of the National League of Professional Base Ball Clubs* (Jefferson, N.C., 2004)

Norman Macht, *Connie Mack and the Early Years of Baseball* (Lincoln, Nebr., 2007)

Connie Mack, *My Sixty-Six Years in the Big Leagues* (Philadelphia, 1950)

Jerry Malloy, ed., *Sol White's History of Colored Base Ball, with Other Documents on the Early Black Game, 1886–1936* (original version 1907; reprint Lincoln, Nebr., 1995)

Larry D. Mansch, *Rube Marquard: The Life and Times of a Baseball Hall of Famer* (Jefferson, N.C., 1998)

William Marshall, *Baseball's Pivotal Era, 1945–1951* (Lexington, Ky., 1999)

Christy Mathewson, *Pitching in a Pinch* (New York, 1912; reprint Mattituck, N.Y., n.d.)

Ronald A. Mayer, *Perfect!* (Jefferson, N.C., 1991)

Bill Mazer, with Stan and Shirley Fischler, *Bill Mazer's Amazin' Baseball Book* (New York, 1990)

Kevin M. McCarthy, *Baseball in Florida* (Sarasota, 1996)

Tim McCarver with Danny Peary, *Tim McCarver's Baseball for Brain Surgeons and Other Fans* (New York, 1998)

John J. McGraw, *My Thirty Years in Baseball* (New York, 1923; reprint Lincoln, Nebr., 1995)

Michael McKinley, *Putting a Roof on Winter: Hockey's Rise from Sport to Spectacle* (Vancouver, 2000)

William B. Mead, *Even the Browns* (Chicago, 1978)

William B. Mead, *Two Spectacular Seasons* (New York, 1990)

Tom Melchior, *Belle Plaine Baseball, 1884–1960* (Belle Plaine, Minn., 2004)

Tom Melville, *Early Baseball and the Rise of the National League* (Jefferson, N.C., 2001)

Frank G. Menke, *The Encyclopedia of Sports* (New York, 1955)

Dick Miller and Mark Stang, eds., *Baseball in the Buckeye State* (Cleveland, 2004)

Stephen G. Miller, *Arete: Greek Sports from Ancient Sources* (Berkeley, Calif., 1991)

Leigh Montville, *Ted Williams: The Biography of an American Hero* (New York, 2004)

George L. Moreland, *Balldom* (Youngstown, Ohio, 1914; reprint St. Louis, 1989)

Peter Morris, *Baseball Fever: Early Baseball in Michigan* (Ann Arbor, Mich., 2003)

Peter Morris, *But Didn't We Have Fun?: An Informal History of Baseball's Pioneer Era, 1843–1870* (Chicago, 2008)

Peter Morris, *Catcher: How the Man Behind the Plate Became an American Folk Hero* (Chicago, 2009)

Peter Morris, *Level Playing Fields: How the Groundskeeping Murphy Brothers Shaped Baseball* (Lincoln, Nebr., 2007)

W. Scott Munn, *The Only Eaton Rapids on Earth* (Eaton Rapids, Mich., 1952)

Eugene Murdock, *Baseball Between the Wars: Memories of the Game by the Men Who Played It* (Westport, Conn., 1992)

Eric Nadel and Craig R. Wright, *The Man Who Stole First Base: Tales from Baseball's Past* (Dallas, 1989)

David Nemec, *The Beer and Whisky League* (New York, 1994)

David Nemec, *Great Baseball Facts, Feats and Firsts*, revised edition (New York, 1999)

David Nemec, *The Great Encyclopedia of 19th Century Major League Baseball* (New York, 1997)

David Nemec, *The Rules of Baseball* (New York, 1994)

William Wells Newell, *Games and Songs of American Children* (New York, 1883)

Rob Neyer, *Rob Neyer's Big Book of Baseball Legends: The Truth, the Lies, and Everything Else* (New York, 2008)

Rob Neyer and Eddie Epstein, *Baseball Dynasties: The Greatest Teams of All Time* (New York, 2000)

Robert Obojski, *Baseball Memorabilia* (New York, 1992)

Robert Obojski, *Bush League: A History of Minor League Baseball* (New York, 1975)

Sidney Offit, ed., *The Best of Baseball* (New York, 1956)

Marc Okkonen, *Baseball Uniforms of the Twentieth Century: The Official Major League Guide* (New York, 1991)

Marc Okkonen, *Minor League Baseball Towns of Michigan* (Grand Rapids, Mich., 1997)

Marc Okkonen, *The Ty Cobb Scrapbook* (New York, 2001)

Michael O'Malley, *Keeping Watch: A History of American Time* (New York, 1991)

Preston D. Orem, *Baseball (1845–1881) from the Newspaper Accounts* (Altadena, Calif., 1961)

Danny Peary, ed., *Cult Baseball Players* (New York, 1990)

Danny Peary, *We Played the Game: 65 Players Remember Baseball's Greatest Era, 1947–1964* (New York, 1994)

William D. Perrin, *Days of Greatness: Providence Baseball 1875–1885* (1928 series of columns in the *Providence Journal* under the title "Line Drives Then and Now," reprint Manhattan, Kans., 1984)

Harold Peterson, *The Man Who Invented Baseball* (New York, 1969)

Robert W. Peterson, *Only the Ball Was White: A History of Legendary Black Players and All-Black Professional Teams* (New York, 1970)

Robert W. Peterson, *Pigskin: The Early Years of Pro Football* (New York, 1997)

Gerard S. Petrone, *When Baseball Was Young* (San Diego, 1994)

Charles Peverelly, *The Book of American Pastimes* (New York, 1866)

David Pietrusza, *Judge and Jury: The Life and Times of Judge Kenesaw Mountain Landis* (South Bend, Ind., 1998)

David Pietrusza, *Lights On! The Wild Century-Long Saga of Night Baseball* (Lanham, Md., 1997)

David Pietrusza, *Minor Miracles: The Legend and Lure of Minor League Baseball* (South Bend, Ind., 1995)

David Pietrusza, Lloyd Johnson, and Bob Carroll, eds., *Total Baseball Catalog: Great Baseball Stuff and How to Buy It* (New York, 1998)

Joseph V. Poilucci, *Baseball in Dutchess County: When It Was a Game* (Danbury, Conn., 2000)

Alan J. Pollock (ed., James A. Riley), *Barnstorming to Heaven: Syd Pollock and His Great Black Teams* (Tuscaloosa, 2006)

Murray Polner, *Branch Rickey* (New York, 1982)

R. E. Prescott, *Historical Tales of the Huron Shore Region* (Alcona County, Mich., 1934)

Richard A. Puff, ed., *Troy's Baseball Heritage* (Troy, N.Y., 1992)

Martin Quigley, *The Crooked Pitch: The Curveball in American Baseball History* (Chapel Hill, N.C., 1988)

Simon Rae, *It's Not Cricket: A History of Skullduggery, Sharp Practice and Downright Cheating in the Noble Game* (London, 2001)

Reach's Official Base Ball Guide, various years

Greg Rhodes and John Erardi, *The First Boys of Summer* (Cincinnati, 1994)

Greg Rhodes and John Snyder, *Redleg Journal* (Cincinnati, 2000)

Ed Rice, *Baseball's First Indian, Louis Sockalexis: Penobscot Legend, Cleveland Indian* (Windsor, Conn., 2003)

Francis C. Richter, *Richter's History and Records of Base Ball* (Philadelphia, 1914; reprint Jefferson, N.C., 2005)

Branch Rickey, *Branch Rickey's Little Blue Book* (New York, 1995)

Lawrence S. Ritter, *The Glory of Their Times* (New York, 1966; reprint New York, 1984)

Mike Roer, *Orator O'Rourke: The Life of a Baseball Radical* (Jefferson, N.C., 2005)

Donn Rogosin, *Invisible Men: Life in Baseball's Negro Leagues* (New York, 1983)

Howard W. Rosenberg, *Cap Anson 1: When Captaining a Team Meant Something: Leadership in Baseball's Early Years* (Arlington, Va., 2003)

Howard W. Rosenberg, *Cap Anson 2: The Theatrical and Kingly Mike Kelly: U.S. Team Sport's First Media Sensation and Baseball's Original Casey at the Bat* (Arlington, Va., 2004)

Howard W. Rosenberg, *Cap Anson 3: Muggsy John McGraw and the Tricksters: Baseball's Fun Age of Rule Bending* (Arlington, Va., 2005)

Howard W. Rosenberg, *Cap Anson 4: Bigger than Babe Ruth: Captain Anson of Chicago* (Arlington, Va., 2006)

Mark Rucker, *Base Ball Cartes: The First Baseball Cards* (Saratoga Springs, N.Y., 1988)

Mark Rucker and Peter C. Bjarkman, *Smoke: The Romance and Lore of Cuban Baseball* (Kingston, N.Y., 1999)

Babe Ruth, *Babe Ruth's Own Book of Baseball* (New York, 1928)

William J. Ryczek, *Baseball's First Inning: A History of the National Pastime Through the Civil War* (Jefferson, N.C., 2009)

William J. Ryczek, *Blackguards and Red Stockings: A History of Baseball's National Association, 1871–1875* (Jefferson, N.C., 1992)

William J. Ryczek, *When Johnny Came Sliding Home: The Post–Civil War Baseball Boom, 1865–1870* (Jefferson, N.C., 1998)

Tony Salin, *Baseball's Forgotten Heroes: One Man's Search for the Game's Most Interesting Overlooked Players* (Indianapolis, 1999)

Alan Schwarz, *The Numbers Game: Baseball's Lifelong Fascination with Statistics* (New York, 2004)

Michael Seidel, *Ted Williams: A Baseball Life* (Lincoln, Nebr., 2000)

Harold Seymour, *Baseball: The Early Years* (New York, 1960)

Harold Seymour, *Baseball: The Golden Age* (New York, 1971)

Harold Seymour, *Baseball: The People's Game* (New York, 1990)

Stuart Shea, *Wrigley Field: The Unauthorized History* (Washington, 2004)

John Shiffert, *Base Ball in Philadelphia: A History of the Early Game, 1831–1900* (Jefferson, N.C., 2006)

Bruce Shlain, *Oddballs: Baseball's Greatest Pranksters, Flakes, Hot Dogs and Hotheads* (New York, 1989)

Tom Simon, ed., *Deadball Stars of the National League* (Washington: 2004)

Tom Simon, ed., *Green Mountain Boys of Summer: Vermonters in the Major Leagues 1882–1993* (Shelburne, Vt., 2000)

George Sisler, *Sisler on Baseball: A Manual for Players and Coaches* (New York, 1954)

John C. Skipper, *Inside Pitch: A Closer Look at Classic Baseball Moments* (Jefferson, N.C., 1996)

Marshall Smelser, *The Life That Ruth Built: A Biography* (New York, 1975 reprint: Lincoln, Nebr., 1993)

Curt Smith, *Voices of the Game*, revised edition (New York, 1992)

H. Allen Smith and Ira L. Smith, *Low and Inside: A Book of Baseball Anecdotes, Oddities, and Curiosities* (Garden City, N.Y., 1949; reprint Halcottsville, N.Y., 2000)

Red Smith, *Red Smith on Baseball* (Chicago, 2000)

Robert Smith, *Baseball* (New York, 1947)

Dennis Snelling, *A Glimpse of Fame: Brilliant but Fleeting Major League Careers* (Jefferson, N.C., 1993)

Brad Snyder, *Beyond the Shadow of the Senators: The Untold History of the Homestead Grays and the Integration of Baseball* (Chicago, 2003)

Brad Snyder, *A Well Paid Slave: Curt Flood's Fight for Free Agency in Professional Sports* (New York, 2006)

John Snyder, *Cubs Journal* (New York, 2006)

Burt Solomon, *Where They Ain't* (New York, 1999)

Troy Soos, *Before the Curse: The Glory Days of New England Baseball, 1858–1918* (revised edition) (Jefferson, N.C., 2007)

Mike Sowell, *July 2, 1903: The Mysterious Death of Hall-of-Famer Big Ed Delahanty* (New York, 1992)

Mike Sowell, *The Pitch That Killed* (New York, 1989; reprint Chicago, 2003)

Albert Goodwill Spalding, *America's National Game: Historic Facts Concerning the Beginning, Evolution, Development, and Popularity of Base Ball, with Personal Reminiscences of Its Vicissitudes, Its Victories, and Its Votaries* (New York, 1911; reprint Lincoln, Nebr., 1992)

Spalding's Official Base Ball Guide, various years

Alfred H. Spink, *The National Game* (St. Louis, 1910; reprint Carbondale, Ill., 2000)

Sporting News *Baseball: A Doubleheader Collection of Facts, Feats and Firsts* (New York, 1992)

Tom Stanton, ed., *The Detroit Tigers Reader* (Ann Arbor, 2005)

Benton Stark, *The Year They Called Off the World Series: A True Story* (Garden City Park, N.Y., 1991)

Paul Starr, *The Creation of the Media* (New York, 2004)

Vince Staten, *Why Is the Foul Pole Fair? (Or, Answers to Baseball Questions Your Dad Hoped You'd Never Ask)* (New York, 2003)

Andy Strasberg, Bob Thompson, and Tim Wiles, *Baseball's Greatest Hit: The Story of Take Me Out to the Ball Game* (New York, 2008)

Dean Sullivan, ed., *Early Innings: A Documentary History of Baseball, 1825–1908* (Lincoln, Nebr., 1995)

Dean Sullivan, ed., *Late Innings: A Documentary History of Baseball, 1945–1972* (Lincoln, Nebr., 2002)

Dean Sullivan, ed., *Middle Innings: A Documentary History of Baseball, 1900–1948* (Lincoln, Nebr., 1998)

Jim L. Sumner, *Separating the Men from the Boys: The First Half-Century of the Carolina League* (Winston-Salem, N.C., 1994)

James L. Terry, *Long Before the Dodgers: Baseball in Brooklyn, 1855–1884* (Jefferson, N.C., 2002)

Cindy Thomson and Scott Brown, *Three Finger: The Mordecai Brown Story* (Lincoln, Nebr., 2006)

John Thorn, ed., *The Armchair Book of Baseball* (New York, 1985)

John Thorn and Pete Palmer, with David Reuther, *The Hidden Game of Baseball* (Garden City, N.Y., 1984)

John Thorn, ed., *The National Pastime* (New York, 1988)

John Thorn and John Holway, *The Pitcher* (New York, 1987)

John Thorn, *The Relief Pitcher* (New York, 1979)

John Thorn and Pete Palmer, et al., *Total Baseball*, various editions

Robert L. Tiemann and Mark Rucker, eds., *Nineteenth Century Stars* (Kansas City, 1989)

Cliff Trumpold, *Now Pitching: Bill Zuber from Amana* (Middle Amana, Iowa, 1992)

Brian Turner and John S. Bowman, *Baseball in Northampton, 1823–1953* (Northampton, Mass., 2002)

Jules Tygiel, *Baseball's Great Experiment* (New York, 1983)

Jules Tygiel, *Past Time: Baseball as History* (New York, 2000)

Bill Veeck, with Ed Linn, *The Hustler's Handbook* (New York, 1965; reprint Durham, N.C., 1996)

Bill Veeck, with Ed Linn, *Veeck—As in Wreck* (New York, 1962)

William R. Vogel, *The History and Manufacture of the Baseball* (unpublished thesis, National Baseball Hall of Fame, 1912)

David Quentin Voigt, *American Baseball, Volume I: From the Gentleman's Sport to the Commissioner's System* (Norman, Okla., 1966)

David Quentin Voigt, *American Baseball, Volume II: From the Commissioners to Continental Expansion* (Norman, Okla., 1970)

David Quentin Voigt, *American Baseball, Volume III: From Postwar Expansion to the Electronic Age* (University Park, Pa., 1983)

David Quentin Voigt, *The League That Failed* (Lanham, Md., 1998)

Paul Votano, *Stand and Deliver: A History of Pinch-Hitting* (Jefferson, N.C., 2003)

Glen Waggoner, Kathleen Moloney, and Hugh Howard, *Spitters, Beanballs, and the Incredible Shrinking Strike Zone: The Stories Behind the Rules of Baseball*, revised edition (Chicago, 2000)

Sam Walker, *Fantasyland: A Season on Baseball's Lunatic Fringe* (New York, 2006)

John Montgomery Ward, *Base-Ball: How to Become a Player* (1888; reprint Cleveland, 1993)

Don Warfield, *The Roaring Redhead* (South Bend, Ind., 1987)

Ty Waterman and Mel Springer, *The Year the Red Sox Won the Series: A Chronicle of the 1918 Championship Season* (Boston, 1999)

Lonnie Wheeler and John Baskin, *The Cincinnati Game* (Wilmington, Ohio, 1988)

G. Edward White, *Creating the National Pastime: Baseball Transforms Itself, 1903–1953* (Princeton, N.J., 1996)

George F. Will, *Bunts* (New York, 1999)

George F. Will, *Men at Work* (New York, 1990)

Pete Williams, ed., *The Joe Williams Baseball Reader* (Chapel Hill, N.C., 1989)

Ted Williams, with John Underwood, *My Turn at Bat: The Story of My Life* (New York, 1969)

Craig R. Wright and Tom House, *The Diamond Appraised* (New York, 1990)

Marshall D. Wright, *The American Association: Year-by-Year Statistics for the Baseball Minor League, 1902–1952* (Jefferson, N.C., 1997)

Marshall D. Wright, *The National Association of Base Ball Players, 1857–1870* (Jefferson, N.C., 2000)

David W. Zang, *Fleet Walker's Divided Heart: The Life of Baseball's First Black Major Leaguer* (Lincoln, Nebr., 1995)

Joel Zoss and John Bowman, *Diamonds in the Rough: The Untold History of Baseball* (New York, 1989)

NEWSPAPERS AND MAGAZINES

This study relies upon an enormous number of articles and notes from newspapers, magazines, and journals, many of them untitled and having no by-lines. In many cases the entire note has already been quoted, which would mean that a researcher would gain little by going back to the original. Rather than trying to list every single article, I have included some of the most valuable ones and those with scopes that go well beyond documenting a particular event or game, since these are the ones a researcher is most likely to benefit by consulting.

Dr. Daniel L. Adams (early Knickerbocker), interview, *Sporting News*, February 29, 1896, 3

Melvin L. Adelman, "The First Baseball Game, the First Newspaper References to Baseball, and the New York Club: A Note on the Early History of Baseball," *Journal of Sport History* 7:3 (Winter 1980), 132–135

William P. Akin, "Bare Hands and Kid Gloves: The Best Fielders, 1880–1899," *Baseball Research Journal* 10 (1981), 60–65

Thomas L. Altherr, "A Place Leavel Enough to Play Ball," reprinted in David Block, *Baseball Before We Knew It* (Lincoln, Nebr., 2005), 229–251

Thomas L. Altherr, "Know Them by Their Autographs," *National Pastime* 18 (1998), 29–31

Priscilla Astifan, "Baseball in the Nineteenth Century," *Rochester History* LII, No. 3 (Summer 1990); "Baseball in the Nineteenth Century, Part Two," *Rochester History* LXII, No. 2 (Spring 2000); "Baseball in the Nineteenth Century, Part Three: The Dawn of Acknowledged Professionalism and Its Impact on Rochester Baseball," *Rochester History* LXIII, No. 1 (Winter 2001); "Rochester's Last Two Seasons of Amateur Baseball: Baseball in the Nineteenth Century, Part Four," *Rochester History* LXIII, No. 2 (Spring 2001); "Baseball in the Nineteenth Century, Part Five: 1877–Rochester's First Year of Professional Baseball," *Rochester History* LXIV, No. 4 (Fall 2002)

Bob Bailey, "Hunting for the First Louisville Slugger," *Baseball Research Journal* 30 (2001), 96–98

David Ball, "The Bechtel-Craver Trade and the Origins of Baseball's Sales System," *Base Ball* 1:1, 36–55

"Baseball Inventions," *Boston Globe*, April 24, 1904, 24

"Bats Used by Leading Hitters," *New York Herald*, reprinted in the *Washington Post*, September 6, 1908, M3

Stan Baumgartner, "Signals," *Baseball Guide and Record Book 1947* (St. Louis, 1947), 124–135

Jay Bennett and Aryn Martin, "The Numbers Game: What Fans Should Know About the Stats They Love," in Eric Bronson, ed., *Baseball and Philosophy: Thinking Outside the Batter's Box*, 233–245

Mike Berardino, "Economic Climate Could Snuff Out Waiver Blocking," *Baseball America*, September 1–14, 2003

Gai Ingham Berlage, "Women Umpires as Mirrors of Gender Roles," *National Pastime* 14 (1994), 34–38

Charles W. Bevis, "Family Baseball Teams," *Baseball Research Journal* 26 (1997), 8–12

Charles W. Bevis, "Holiday Doubleheaders," *Baseball Research Journal* 33 (2004), 60–63

Charles W. Bevis, "A Home Run by Any Measure," *Baseball Research Journal* 21 (1992), 64–70

Dennis Bingham and Thomas R. Heitz, "Rules and Scoring," *Total Baseball*, 4th edition, 2426–2481

Peter Bjarkman, "Cuban Blacks in the Majors Before Jackie Robinson," *National Pastime* 12 (1992), 58–63

Hal Bodley, "Teams Obsess Too Much Over Pitch Counts," *USA Today*, September 17, 2004, 4C

Larry G. Bowman, "The Monarchs and Night Baseball," *National Pastime* 16 (1996), 80–84

Randall Brown, "How Baseball Began," *National Pastime* 24 (2004), 51–54

Bozeman Bulger, "Pitching, Past and Present: The Evolution of the Twirler's Art," *Baseball Magazine*, February 1912, 71–73

George Bulkley, "The Day the Reds Lost," *National Pastime* 2 (Fall 1982), 9

Pete Cava, "Baseball in the Olympics," *National Pastime* 12 (1992), 2–8

O. P. Caylor, "The Theory and Introduction of Curve Pitching," *Outing*, August 1891, 402–405

Henry Chadwick, "The Art of Pitching," *Outing*, May 1889, 119–121

Irwin Chusid, "The Short, Happy Life of the Newark Peppers," *Baseball Research Journal* 20 (1991), 44–45

Eddie Cicotte, "The Secrets of Successful Pitching," *Baseball Magazine*, July 1918, 267–268, 299

Robert Cole, "Ball, Bat and Ad," *Baseball Research Journal* 8 (1979), 77–79

T. Z. Cowles, multi-part series on early Chicago sports history, *Chicago Tribune*, May 26, June 2, June 16, and June 30, 1918

"Cummings Tells Story of Early Days of Curve Ball," *Sporting News*, December 29, 1921, 7

"Curved Balls," *Sporting News*, February 20, 1897, 2

"Dalrymple, Old Star, Recalls Baseball in '80s," *Chicago Tribune*, September 23, 1928, A7

Dan Daniel, "Batters Going Batty from Butterflies," *Sporting News*, June 12, 1946, 3

George S. Davis, "How to Bat," syndicated column, *Warren* (Pa.) *Evening Democrat*, May 26, 1894, 2

Bill Deane, "The Old Hidden Ball Trick: No Longer Banned in Boston," in Mark Kanter, ed., *The Northern Game and Beyond: Baseball in New England and Eastern Canada* (Cleveland, 2002), 69–72

Clarence Deming, "Old Days in Baseball," *Outing*, June 1902, 357–360

Joe Dittmar, "A Shocking Discovery," *Baseball Research Journal* 20 (1991), 52–53, 65

Walter C. Dohm, "College Baseball," *Los Angeles Times*, May 21, 1893, 10

Joseph Durso, "Slider Is the Pitch That Put Falling Batting Averages on the Skids," *New York Times*, September 22, 1968, 198

Oscar Eddleton, "Under the Lights," *Baseball Research Journal* 1984, 37–42

Stefan Fatsis, "Mystery of Baseball: Was William White Game's First Black?," *Wall Street Journal*, January 30, 2004, 1

"The First Detroit Base Ball Club Formed in the *Free Press* Office Twenty-Seven Years Ago," *Detroit Free Press*, April 4, 1884

Val J. Flanagan, "Rain-Check Evolved to Check Flood of Fence-Climbers, Says Originator, Now 83," *Sporting News*, April 8, 1943, 2

Russell Ford (as told to Don E. Basenfelder), "Russell Ford Tells Inside Story of the 'Emery' Ball After Guarding His Secret for Quarter of a Century," *Sporting News*, April 25, 1935, 5

John B. Foster, "Buckeye Boys," *Sporting News*, December 28, 1895, 3

John B. Foster, "The Evolution of Pitching" (part 1), *Sporting News*, November 26, 1931, 5; "The Evolution of Pitching" (part 2), *Sporting News*, December 10, 1931, 6; "The Evolution of Pitching" (part 3), *Sporting News*, December 24, 1931, 6; "The Evolution of Pitching" (part 4), *Sporting News*, January 7, 1932, 6

Duane Frazier, "Wellington Celebrates the Evening It Lit Up High School Football," *Wichita Eagle*, September 10, 2004, 1D, 6D

"George Wright Recalls Triumphs of 'Red Stockings,'" *New York Sun*, November 14, 1915, sec. 6, p. 4

Larry R. Gerlach, "Death on the Diamond: The Cal Drummond Story," *National Pastime* 24 (2004), 14–16

Larry R. Gerlach and Harold V. Higham, "Dick Higham," *National Pastime* 20 (2000), 20–32

"The Great National Game in Dollars and Cents," *Washington Post*, May 9, 1909

Barbara Gregorich, "Jackie and the Juniors vs. Margaret and the Bloomers," *National Pastime* 13 (1993), 8–10

John H. Gruber, multi-part series on baseball rules and customs under a variety of headings, weekly series in *Sporting News*, November 4, 1915–April 6, 1916

Bob Hoie, "The Farm System," *Total Baseball*, 2nd edition, 644–647

John Holway, "Willie Wells: A Devil of a Shortstop," *Baseball Research Journal* 17 (1988), 50–53

"How to Hit a Ball," *New York Sun*, reprinted in *Birmingham* (Ala.) *Evening News*, October 2, 1888

"Dan Irish," "System Is Bad: Ball Players Not Properly Trained," *Sporting News*, February 19, 1898, 2

Frederick Ivor-Campbell, "Extraordinary 1884," *National Pastime* 13 (1993), 16–23

Frederick Ivor-Campbell, "Postseason Play," *Total Baseball IV*, 281–282

Frederick Ivor-Campbell, "When Was the First? (Continued)," *Nineteenth Century Notes* 95:1 (Winter 1995), 1–2

Frederick Ivor-Campbell, "When Was the First? (Part 4)," *Nineteenth Century Notes* 95:3, 4 (Summer/Fall 1995), 10–12

Frederick Ivor-Campbell, "When Was the First Match Game Played by the Knickerbocker Rules?" *Nineteenth Century Notes* 93:4 (Fall 1993), 1–2

Bill James, "A History of the Beanball," *The Bill James Baseball Abstract 1985*, 131–140

Willis E. Johnson, "The Player's Life in the Major Leagues," *Sporting Life*, March 4, 1916

Gene Karst, "The Great Days, The Great Stars," *National Pastime* 2 (Fall 1982), 48–51

Gene Karst, "Ready for the New Asterisk War?," *Baseball Research Journal* 26 (1997), 66–67

Seamus Kearney, "Bill Thompson, Pioneer," *National Pastime* 16 (1996), 67–68

Tim Keefe, "Batting and Pitching," *Kansas City Star*, October 23, 1888

Maclean Kennedy, "Charley Bennett, Former Detroit Catcher, Inventor of Chest Pad," *Detroit Free Press*, August 2, 1914

Al Kermisch, "Umpire Used Hand Signals in 1883," *Baseball Research Journal* 21 (1992), 111

Gene Kessler, "Deacon White, Oldest Living Player, at 92 Recalls Highlights of Historic Career That Started in 1868," *Sporting News*, June 22, 1939, 19

Bill Kirwin, "The Mysterious Case of Dick Brookins," *National Pastime* 19 (1999), 38–43

J. C. Kofoed, "Early History of Curve Pitching," *Baseball Magazine*, August 1915, 55–57

Leonard Koppett, "The Ex-National Sport Looks to Its Image," *New York Times*, December 20, 1964, SM18

Dan Krueckeberg, "Take-Charge Cy," *National Pastime* 4, No. 1 (Spring 1985), 7–11

F. C. Lane, "The Emery Ball Strangest of Freak Deliveries," *Baseball Magazine*, July 1915, 58–72

R. M. Larner, "Old-Time Baseball in the White Lot," *Washington Post*, June 26, 1904, S4

R. M. Larner, "Beginning of Professional Baseball in Washington," *Washington Post*, July 3, 1904, S3

Hal Lebovitz, "Zimmer, Oldest Catcher, Leafs Memory Book," *Sporting News*, January 12, 1949, 11

Larry Lester, "Only the Stars Come Out at Night!: J. L. Wilkinson and His Lighting Machine," Lloyd Johnson, Steve Garlick and Jeff Magalif, eds., *Unions to Royals: The Story of Professional Baseball in Kansas City* (Cleveland, 1996), 8–10

Frederick G. Lieb, "A Man Who Has Made Millions from By-Products of Sport," *Sportlife*, December 1925, 94

"Bob Lively," "Base Ball: How They Play the Game in New England," *Porter's Spirit of the Times*, December 27, 1856, 276–277

Joseph F. Lowry, "Baseball's Magic-Mud Man," *Family Weekly*, September 5, 1965

Connie Mack, "How to Play Ball," multi-part series, *Washington Post*, March 13, March 20, March 27, April 3, April 10, April 17, 1904

Connie Mack, "Memories of When the Game Was Young," *Sporting Life* (monthly), June 1924

Jerry Malloy, "Out at Home," in John Thorn, ed., *The National Pastime* (New York, 1988), 209–244

David Mandell, "Reuben Berman's Foul Ball," *National Pastime* 25 (2005), 106–107

Larry Marthey, "Park Tampering Is Old Custom," *Detroit News*, April 7, 1959, T-15

Beth Martin, "Hey, Blue!," *National Pastime* 18 (1998), 36–46

Andy McCue, "The King of Coolie Hats," *National Pastime* 19 (1999), 24–27

David McDonald, "The Senators' Diamond Dynasty," *Ottawa Citizen*, March 25, 2003

E. L. McDonald, "The National Game of Base Ball Was Born in Fort Wayne," *St. Louis Republican*, reprinted in *Fort Wayne Journal Gazette*, January 26, 1902

P. A. Meaney, "Who Invented the Spit Ball," *Baseball Magazine*, May 1913, 59–60

Leigh Montville, "Field of Screams," *Sports Illustrated*, May 22, 2000

Peter Morris, "'Attaboy!' Originated from the Dynamic Managing Style of Hughie Jennings (Detroit Tigers) in 1907," *Comments on Etymology* 33:1 (October 2003), 2–4

Peter Morris, "Baseball Term 'Bunt' Was Originally Called 'Baby Hit'; Popular 19c. Lullaby 'Bye, Baby Bunting' May Have Produced 'Baby Bunting Hit,' Shortened to 'Bunt,'" *Comments on Etymology* 34:1 (October 2004), 2–4

Edgar Munzel, "Daily Workouts Put Shaw in Pink for Comeback Pitch," *Sporting News*, November 16, 1960, 9

Tim Murnane, "How the Stars Play Combinations," *Boston Globe*, March 10, 1889, 22

"Jim Nasium" [Edgar Wolfe], "'Ted' Sullivan, Baseball Pioneer," *Sporting Life* (monthly), January 1923

Tom Nawrocki, "Captain Anson's Platoon," *National Pastime* 15 (1995), 34–37

Amy Ellis Nutt, "Swinging for the Fences," in Lissa Smith, ed., *Nike Is a Goddess: The History of Women in Sports* (New York, 1998)

Robert A. Nylen, "Frontier Baseball," *Nevada*, Volume 50, Number 2 (March/April 1990), 27–29, 56

"Old Baseball: The Game as the Boys Used to Play it," *Indianapolis Sentinel*, April 3, 1887

James O'Rourke, "Forty Two Years of Base Ball: Wonderful Life Story of Jim O'Rourke" (multipart series), *Kalamazoo Evening Telegraph*, February 24, 25, 26, March 1, 2, 3, 1910

Steve Orr, "MSU Police Get Radar Gun," *State News*, October 10, 1974

Joseph M. Overfield, "The Richards-Jethroe Caper: Fact or Fiction?," *Baseball Research Journal* 16 (1987), 33–35

Joseph M. Overfield, "You Could Look It Up," *National Pastime* 10 (1990), 69–71

Ev Parker, "The Supreme Compliment," *National Pastime* 17 (1997), 138–139

Ted Patterson, "Jack Graney, The First Player-Broadcaster," *Baseball Research Journal* 2 (1973), 80–86, reprinted in *Baseball Historical Review* 1981, 52–57

William A. Phelon, "Shall We Have a Third Big League?," *Baseball Magazine*, March 1912, 10–12, 92

Deacon Phillippe, "Phillippe of Pittsburg Team Discusses Requirements of Successful Pitchers," *Syracuse Post Standard*, March 27, 1904, 10

David Pietrusza, "The Cahill Brothers' Night Baseball Experiments," *Baseball Research Journal* 23 (1994), 62–66

David Pietrusza, "The Continental League of 1921," *National Pastime* 13 (1993), 76–78

David Pietrusza, "Famous Firsts," *Total Baseball VI*, 2507

Bill Plott, "The Southern League of Colored Base Ballists," *Baseball Research Journal* 3 (1974), 91–95, reprinted in *Baseball Historical Review* 1981, 75–78

Barry Popik and Gerald Cohen, "Material on the Origin of the Spitball Pitch," *Comments on Etymology* 32:8 (May 2003), 21–28

Robert Pruter, "Youth Baseball in Chicago, 1868–1890: Not Always Sandlot Ball," *Journal of Sport History* 26:1 (Spring 1999), 1–28

Chris Rainey, "A Cincy Legend: A Narrative of Bumpus Jones' Baseball Career," in Dick Miller and Mark Stang, eds., *Baseball in the Buckeye State* (Cleveland, 2004), 3–7

Bob Rives, "Good Night," *National Pastime* 18 (1998), 21–24

Emil H. Rothe, "History of the Chicago City Series," *Baseball Research Journal* 8 (1979), 15–24

Robert H. Schaefer, "The Lost Art of Fair-Foul Hitting" *National Pastime* 20 (2000), 3–9

John Schwartz, "From One Ump to Two," *Baseball Research Journal* 30 (2001), 85–86

Alan Schwarz, "Real-time Broadcasts Lead to Copyright Questions," *Baseball America*, September 15–28, 2003

Charley Scully, "'Father of the Catching Glove' Admits Split Finger Fifty Years Ago, with Twin Bill Ahead, Was 'Mother,'" *Sporting News*, February 23, 1939, 9

Peter Segroie, "Reuben's Ruling Helps You 'Have a Ball,'" *Baseball Research Journal* 20 (1991), 85

Tom Shieber, "The Earliest Baseball Photography," *National Pastime* 17 (1997), 101–104

Tom Shieber, "The Evolution of the Baseball Diamond," originally printed in the *Baseball Research Journal* 23 (1994), 3–13; reprinted in an expanded version in *Total Baseball IV*, 113–124

Herbert Simons, "Life of an Ump," *Baseball Magazine*, April 1942; reprinted in Sidney Offit, ed., *The Best of Baseball*, 156–162

Duane Smith, "Dickey Pearce: Baseball's First Great Shortstop," *National Pastime* 10 (1990), 38–42

Deron Snyder, "A Stat Worth Saving," *USA Today Baseball Weekly*, July 21–27, 1999

Fred Stein, "Managers and Coaches," *Total Baseball*, 2nd edition, 452–463

A. D. Suehsdorf, "The Last Tripleheader," *Baseball Research Journal* 1984, 30–32

Bucky Summers, "Still Baseball on TV," *Frederick* (Md.) *Post*, April 20, 1965, 9

Scott S. Taylor, "Pure Passion for the Game: Albany Amateur Baseball Box Scores from 1864," *Manuscripts* LIV, No. 1 (Winter 2002), 5–13

Dick Thompson, "Matty and His Fadeaway," *National Pastime* 17 (1997), 93–96

George A. Thompson, Jr., "New York Baseball, 1823," *National Pastime* 21 (2001), 6–8

Ken Tillman, "The Portable Batting Cage," *Baseball Research Journal* 28 (1999), 23–26

E. H. Tobias, sixteen-part history of baseball in St. Louis up to 1876, *Sporting News*, November 2, 1895–February 15, 1896

M. E. Travaglini, "Olympic Baseball 1936: Was Es Das?," *National Pastime* (Winter 1985), 46–55

"Tri-Mountain," three-part series on early baseball in Boston, *Boston Journal*, February 20 and 22, March 6, 1905

John (Dasher) Troy, "Reminiscences of an Old-Timer," *Baseball Magazine*, June 1915, 93–94

Gary Waddingham, "Irish Bob O'Regan: A Bespectacled Ump in the Bush Leagues," *Minor League History Journal* 1:1, 33–36

William J. Weiss, "The First Negro in Twentieth Century O.B.," *Baseball Research Journal* 8 (1979), 31–35

H. H. Westlake, "The First Box Score Ever Published," *Baseball Magazine*, March 1925; reprinted in Sidney Offit, ed., *The Best of Baseball*, 156–162

William Wheaton (early Knickerbocker), interview, *San Francisco Examiner*, November 27, 1887

Tim Wiles, "The Joy of Foul Balls," *National Pastime* 25 (2005), 102–105

Bob Wolf, "Controversy Like Screaming at Danforth 40 Years Ago," *Sporting News*, May 1, 1957, 15

James Leon Wood, Sr. (as told to Frank G. Menke), "Baseball in By-Gone Days," syndicated series, *Indiana* (Pa.) *Evening Gazette*, August 14, 1916; *Marion* (Ohio) *Star*, August 15, 1916; *Indiana* (Pa.) *Evening Gazette*, August 17, 1916

SPECIAL COLLECTIONS AND ARCHIVAL SOURCES

Allen County (Indiana) Public Library; Chadwick Scrapbooks; Bentley Library, University of Michigan; Burton Collection, Detroit Public Library; Cincinnati Reds Collection, Cincinnati Historical Society; Michigan Pioneer and Historical Collections; Michigan State University Library; Library of Michigan; National Baseball Hall of Fame and Museum; Ohio Historical Society; William Rankin Scrapbooks; Peter Tamony Collection, University of Missouri; University of Michigan Library; Wazoo Records, East Lansing

ON-LINE RESOURCES

While on-line resources are always prone to disappearing or changing addresses, a few websites seem well enough established and were valuable enough in my research that it would be inexcusable not to mention them. The Baseball Index (http://www.baseballindex.org), compiled by the Bibliographic Committee of SABR, is an invaluable tool for tracking down sources. The wonderful Retrosheet website (http://www.retrosheet.org) has also been a constant aid in my research. The websites of the Vintage Base Ball Association (http://www.vbba.org) and the National Baseball Hall of Fame (http://www.baseball-halloffame.org) also have considerable relevant material. The early card mentioned in entry 15.4.3 can be viewed at the website of Frank Ceresi and Associates (http://www.fcassociates.com/ntearlybb.htm).

I have also benefited greatly from the free on-line archives of the *Brooklyn Eagle* (http://www.brooklynpubliclibrary.org/eagle/index.htm), the Library of Congress (http://chroniclingamerica.loc.gov/search/pages/), the newspapers of Utah (http://www.lib.utah.edu/digital/unews), Missouri (http://newspapers.umsystem.edu) and Colorado (http://www.cdpheritage.org/newspapers/index.html), and the diverse offerings of the Amateur Athletic Foundation of Los Angeles (http://search.la84foundation.org) and the Old Fulton Post Card site (http://www.fultonhistory.com/Fulton.html). My work has also been made easier by the subscription-based archives of ProQuest, newspaperarchive.com, and genealogybank.com.

Name Index

Topical Index

Topics that cover a whole chapter or section are in bold.

A NOTE ON THE AUTHOR

Peter Morris has established himself as one of the foremost historians of early baseball in America. His *A Game of Inches*, first published in 2006, was the first book ever to win both the coveted Seymour Medal of the Society for American Baseball Research and the Casey Award from *Spitball* magazine as the best baseball book of the year. Mr. Morris has also written *Catcher*, a study of how the man behind the plate became an American folk hero; *But Didn't We Have Fun?*, an informal history of baseball's pioneer era; *Level Playing Fields*, about the early days of groundskeeping; and *Baseball Fever* (also a Seymour Medal winner), the story of early baseball in Michigan. A former national and international Scrabble champion, he lives in Haslett, Michigan. For more information, see his website, www.petermorrisbooks.com.